THESE UNITED STATES

Our nation's geography, history and people

THE READER'S DIGEST FAMILY REFERENCE SERIES

THE READER'S DIGEST ASSOCIATION
Pleasantville, New York

SECOND PRINTING

The credits which appear on page 236 are hereby
made a part of this copyright page.

Library of Congress Catalog Card Number: Map 68-2

Printed in the United States of America

ACKNOWLEDGMENTS

Special Consulting Editor

CHARLES B. HITCHCOCK

M.A., D.SC. (Hon.), Director Emeritus, American Geographical Society, New York, N.Y.

The Reader's Digest expresses its gratitude to the following, who have generously contributed to and advised on the preparation of this book.

James R. Anderson, PH.D., Department of Geography, University of Florida

Peter L. Bernstein, B.S., Department of Economics, New School for Social Research; President, Bernstein-Macaulay, Inc., New York, N.Y.

James A. Bier, M.S., Department of Geography, University of Illinois

Donald Bogue, PH.D., Department of Sociology, University of Chicago

Henry W. Bragdon, M.A., Editor, The New England Social Studies Bulletin

Hilda Cole, Putnam Valley, N.Y.

John Cumberland, PH.D., Bureau of Business and Economic Research, University of Maryland

Frederick J. Dockstader, PH.D., Director, Museum of the American Indian Heye Foundation, New York, N.Y.

Roman Drazniowsky, PH.D., Map Curator, American Geographical Society, New York, N.Y.

Thomas H. Everett, M.S., N.D.H., Director of Horticulture and Senior Curator of Education, The New York Botanical Garden, Bronx, N.Y.

Rhodes W. Fairbridge, D.SC., Department of Geology, Columbia University

Nordis Felland, B.S. in L.S., Chief Librarian, American Geographical Society, New York, N.Y.

William C. FitzGibbon, Pleasantville, N.Y.

Paul C. Franks, PH.D., Department of Geology, New York University

John A. Garraty, PH.D., Department of History, Columbia University

Jean George, Chappaqua, N.Y.

Arch C. Gerlach, PH.D., Chief Geographer, United States Geological Survey, Washington, D.C.

William H. Goetzmann, PH.D., Department of History, University of Texas

Robert Handy, PH.D., Department of Church History, Union Theological Seminary

David Harris, M.D., M.P.H., Assistant Commissioner—Maternal and Child Health Services, New York City Health Department, New York, N.Y.

Hazel Holly, Nieman Fellow, Harvard University; Editorial Consultant, Washington, D.C.

Donald Q. Innis, PH.D., Department of Geography, State University College, Geneseo, N.Y.

Serge A. Korff, President, American Geographical Society, New York, N.Y.

George H. T. Kimble, PH.D., Research Director, United States Geography Project, Twentieth Century Fund, New York, N.Y.

A. W. Küchler, PH.D., Department of Geography-Meteorology, University of Kansas

Hans H. Landsberg, M.A., Resources for the Future, Inc., Washington, D.C.

Shannon McCune, PH.D., LL.D., Director, American Geographical Society, New York, N. Y.

Helene Mandelbaum, Briarcliff Manor, N.Y.

Jonathan Messerli, PH.D., Department of Education, Teachers College, Columbia University

Robert Meyer, Jr., Festival Information Service, New York, N.Y.

Benjamin F. Miller, M.D., School of Medicine, University of Pennsylvania

O. M. Miller, Assistant Director, American Geographical Society, New York, N.Y.

William B. Overstreet, Assistant Chief, National Atlas Project, United States Geological Survey, Washington, D.C.

Ralph S. Palmer, PH.D., New York State Museum, Albany, N.Y.

Nicholas Panagakos, Science Editor, Goddard Institute for Space Studies, National Aeronautics and Space Administration, New York, N.Y.

G. Etzel Pearcy, PH.D., The Geographer, Department of State, Washington, D.C.

Jesse M. Putney, Babson Institute

Ward Randol, Executive Director, The Explorers Club, New York, N.Y.

Burt Salwen, PH.D., Department of Anthropology, New York University

William Shannon, Assistant Public Relations Director, Madison Square Garden, New York, N.Y.

Harold Sprout, PH.D., Department of Politics, Princeton University

William Stiles, Museum of the American Indian Heye Foundation, New York, N.Y.

George Switzer, PH.D., Department of Mineral Sciences, Smithsonian Institution, Washington, D.C.

Anthony E. Tancreto, M.A., Meteorologist in Charge, Weather Bureau Office, New York, N.Y.

William Warntz, PH.D., Professor of Theoretical Geography, Harvard University

Lauris B. Whitman, PH.D., Department of Research, National Council of the Churches of Christ in the U.S.A.

Ernest W. Williams, Jr., PH.D., Graduate School of Business, Columbia University

Evan McLeod Wylie, New York, N.Y.

Wilbur Zelinsky, PH.D., Department of Geography, Pennsylvania State University

Artists: Norman Adams, John Ballantine, Robert Bryant, Liam Dunne, Cecile Duray-Bito, Lowell Hess, John Morris, Maynard Reece, William Sayles, Isidor Steinberg, William Steinel, Joseph Wagner

American Automobile Association, Washington, D.C.

The American Waterways Operators, Inc., Washington, D.C.

Association of American Railroads, Washington, D.C.

Civil Aeronautics Board, Washington, D.C.

Federal Communications Commission, Washington, D.C.

Federal Power Commission, Washington, D.C.

Federal Reserve System, Washington, D.C.

General Drafting Co., Convent Station, N.J.

Goddard Space Flight Center, National Aeronautics and Space Administration, Greenbelt, Md.

Interstate Commerce Commission, Washington, D.C.

Transportation Association of America, Washington, D.C.

U.S. Department of Agriculture, Washington, D.C.

U.S. Department of Commerce, Washington, D.C.

U.S. Department of Health, Education and Welfare, Washington, D.C.

U.S. Department of the Interior, Washington, D.C.

U.S. Department of Labor, Washington, D.C.

U.S. Department of Transportation, Washington, D.C.

U.S. Department of the Treasury, Washington, D.C.

Water Resources Council, Washington, D.C.

We also wish to thank all the others—government officials, geographers, cartographers, designers, editors, researchers, technicians and staff members of the American Geographical Society—who gave valuable assistance in the preparation of this book. See also the Credits on page 236.

Contents

Introduction

No one knows who drew the first map. Possibly it was done on the limestone wall of a cave by early man to show where waterholes lay. As far back as 1335 B.C., the Egyptians compiled maps to establish boundaries. The Babylonians, the Greeks and later the Romans were all accomplished cartographers. But old-time sailors contributed most to the science of map-making: returning from voyages across strange seas, they brought charts and sketches of the coastlines of new lands and continents.

In such a manner the mapping of what is now the United States of America began. The colonists and settlers continued the work, recording rivers and lakes, mountains and valleys as they pushed farther and farther inland.

The Reader's Digest book of *These United States* presents a reconstruction of this changing face of America—from the tracing of the earliest routes of the explorers to the most recent mapping of the nation.

During the last two decades, the changes in many aspects of our country have gone deeper than most people realize, so deep as to be almost revolutionary. These new developments are charted and discussed in this volume in the light of the very latest data. One of them is the vigorous expansion of our present population, exceeded probably only by India and China among the great nations. This in turn has had an overwhelming impact on the educational system, where one of the major accomplishments has been the incredible speed with which public junior colleges have been built to accommodate the ever-increasing numbers of high school graduates. An agricultural revolution, while not quite comparable to the industrial revolution of the last century, has made farming into big business, with corporations moving in to produce food on the assembly line.

As our national wealth has increased, so has the role of government, until it now consumes a surprising one fifth of the goods and services which the country produces. To say that the United States is a "nation on the move" is a description of more than the automobile age. Charts and maps show that 40 million people have been changing residence each year. Others demonstrate that the results of recent progress have not been exclusively beneficial: air and water pollution, shortages of health personnel, urban traffic congestion, erosion of the soil, disappearing native flora and fauna.

Paradoxical as it may seem, even some of our most ancient history is "new." Archaeological discoveries of the last few years have brought to light new evidence of the earliest inhabitants of the present United States and their customs, reaching back many thousands of years.

The past of the continent itself is illustrated in an outline of the geologic upheavals that convulsed this land for upward of 600 million years. In this we discover

THE UNITED STATES AND ITS NEIGHBORS

The boundary between the United States and Canada has been the longest unfortified frontier in the world for more than a century. It extends nearly 4000 miles from Maine to the Pacific, with an additional 1500 miles since the acquisition of Alaska in 1867. To the south, the Rio Grande forms half of the boundary with Mexico, running to the midpoint of the 1900-mile border.

Canada occupies about half of North America—its 3,851,809 square miles exceeding the area of the continental United States, which covers 3,608,787. Mexico accounts for the remainder with 761,000 square miles.

The principal highways connecting the United States with its neighbors are shown here. U.S. citizens and aliens make more than 60 million frontier crossings from Canada each year, while the number from Mexico is close to 125 million.

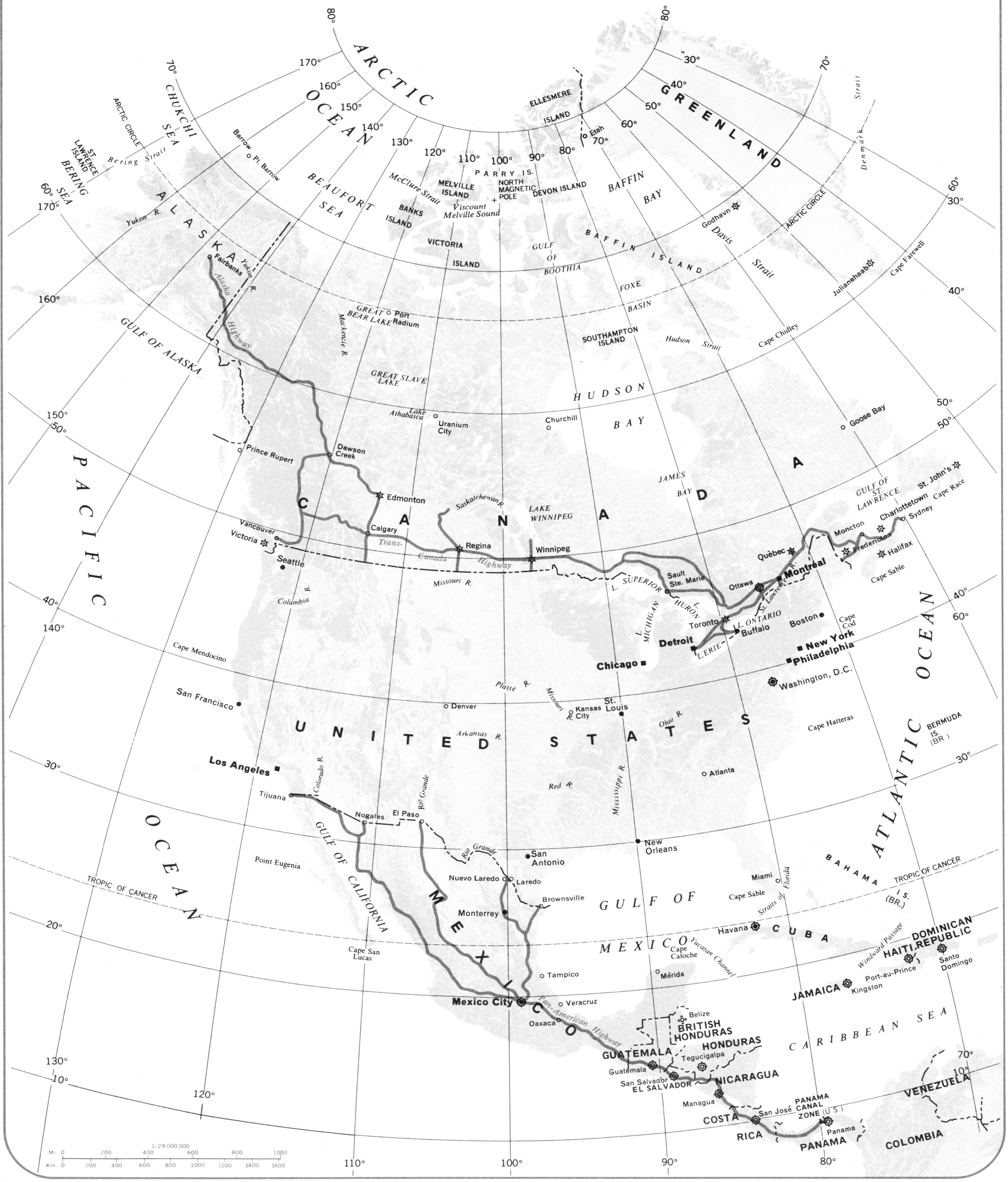

that the equator once traversed what is now the United States from Southern California to the mouth of the St. Lawrence River.

Our history is mapped from those days down to the present, which is represented by a 62-page folio of maps of the United States and its possessions. The clean, uncluttered look of this section has been achieved by eliminating roads and highways and showing them in a separate eight-page folio. This device also permits the cartographers to include the names of far more cities, towns and physical features than are usually found on maps of a similar scale.

From our natural resources, our vigor, our imagination has sprung a way of life unmatched in the history of the world. The United States, with all its imperfections, is the masterful creation of its people, its land and its history. They are all depicted in *These United States.*

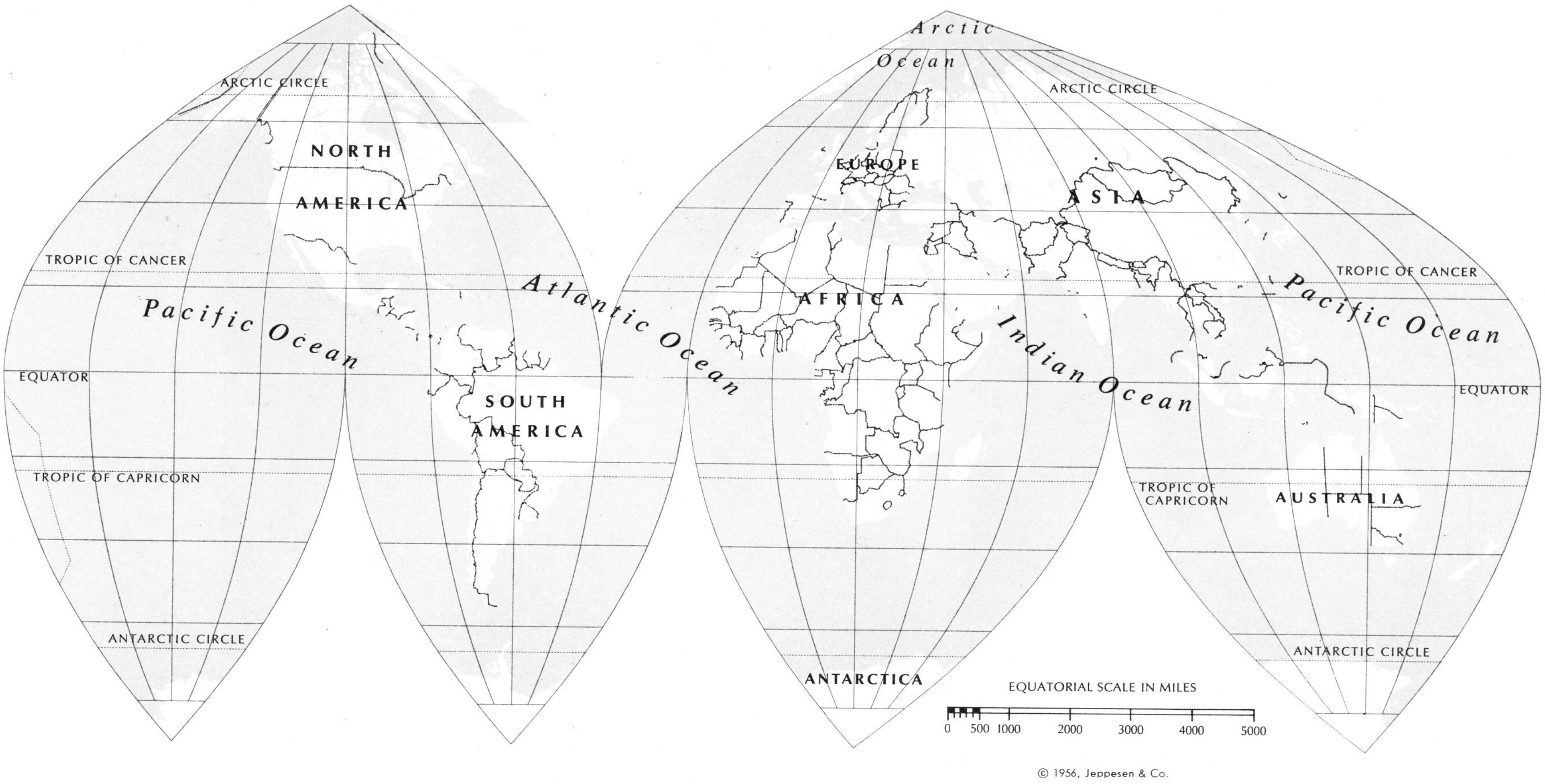

A world map printed as a rectangle presents a distorted picture of the globe because it does not take into account the curvature of the earth. The above map does. Known as a Parabolic Interrupted Equal Area Projection, it shows all the continents in their proper size-relationships. The shape is explained by the small drawings which demonstrate what happens when the surface of a globe is "peeled" and laid out flat on a drawing board.

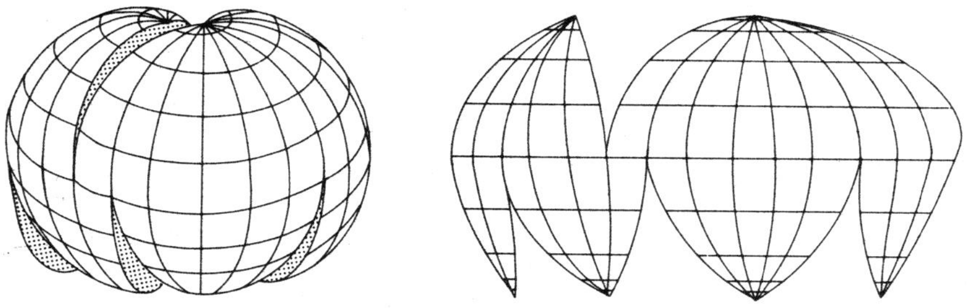

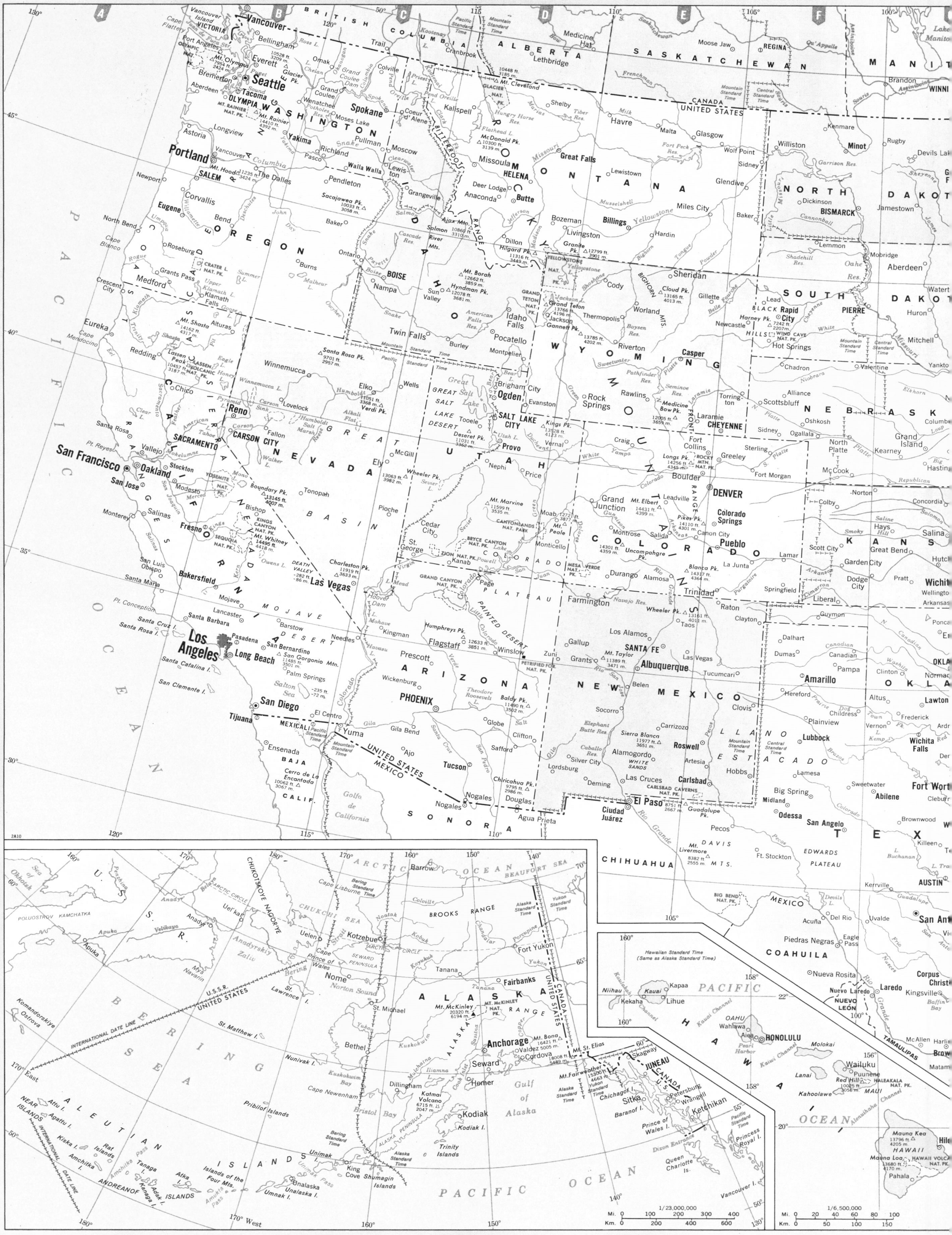

BRITISH COLUMBIA
ALBERTA
SASKATCHEWAN
MANITOBA
CANADA
UNITED STATES
WASHINGTON
OREGON
IDAHO
MONTANA
WYOMING
NORTH DAKOTA
SOUTH DAKOTA
NEBRASKA
KANSAS
NEVADA
UTAH
COLORADO
CALIFORNIA
ARIZONA
NEW MEXICO
OKLA.
TEXAS
MEXICO
BAJA CALIF.
SONORA
CHIHUAHUA
COAHUILA
NUEVO LEÓN
TAMAULIPAS
PACIFIC OCEAN
ROCKY MTS.
GREAT BASIN
MOJAVE DESERT
COLORADO PLATEAU
PAINTED DESERT
GREAT SALT LAKE DESERT
LLANO ESTACADO
EDWARDS PLATEAU
Vancouver
VICTORIA
Seattle
OLYMPIA
Tacoma
Spokane
Portland
SALEM
Eugene
Boise
BOISE
HELENA
Butte
Great Falls
Billings
BISMARCK
PIERRE
Rapid City
CHEYENNE
DENVER
Colorado Springs
Pueblo
SALT LAKE CITY
Ogden
Provo
Reno
CARSON CITY
SACRAMENTO
San Francisco
Oakland
San Jose
Fresno
Bakersfield
Los Angeles
Long Beach
San Diego
Tijuana
Las Vegas
PHOENIX
Tucson
Albuquerque
SANTA FE
El Paso
Ciudad Juárez
Amarillo
Lubbock
Odessa
San Angelo
AUSTIN
San Antonio
Mt. Rainier 14410 ft. 4392 m.
Mt. Whitney 14495 ft. 4418 m.
Mt. Elbert 14431 ft. 4399 m.
DEATH VALLEY -282 ft. -86 m.
ALASKA
ALASKA RANGE
BROOKS RANGE
BERING SEA
ALEUTIAN ISLANDS
ARCTIC OCEAN
BEAUFORT SEA
Gulf of Alaska
Anchorage
Fairbanks
Nome
JUNEAU
Mt. McKinley 20320 ft. 6194 m.
U.S.S.R.
INTERNATIONAL DATE LINE
1/23,000,000
HAWAII
PACIFIC OCEAN
HONOLULU
OAHU
Kauai
Niihau
MAUI
Molokai
Lanai
Kahoolawe
Mauna Kea 13796 ft. 4205 m.
Mauna Loa 13680 ft. 4170 m.
Hawaiian Standard Time (Same as Alaska Standard Time)
1/6,500,000

LIFT OUT

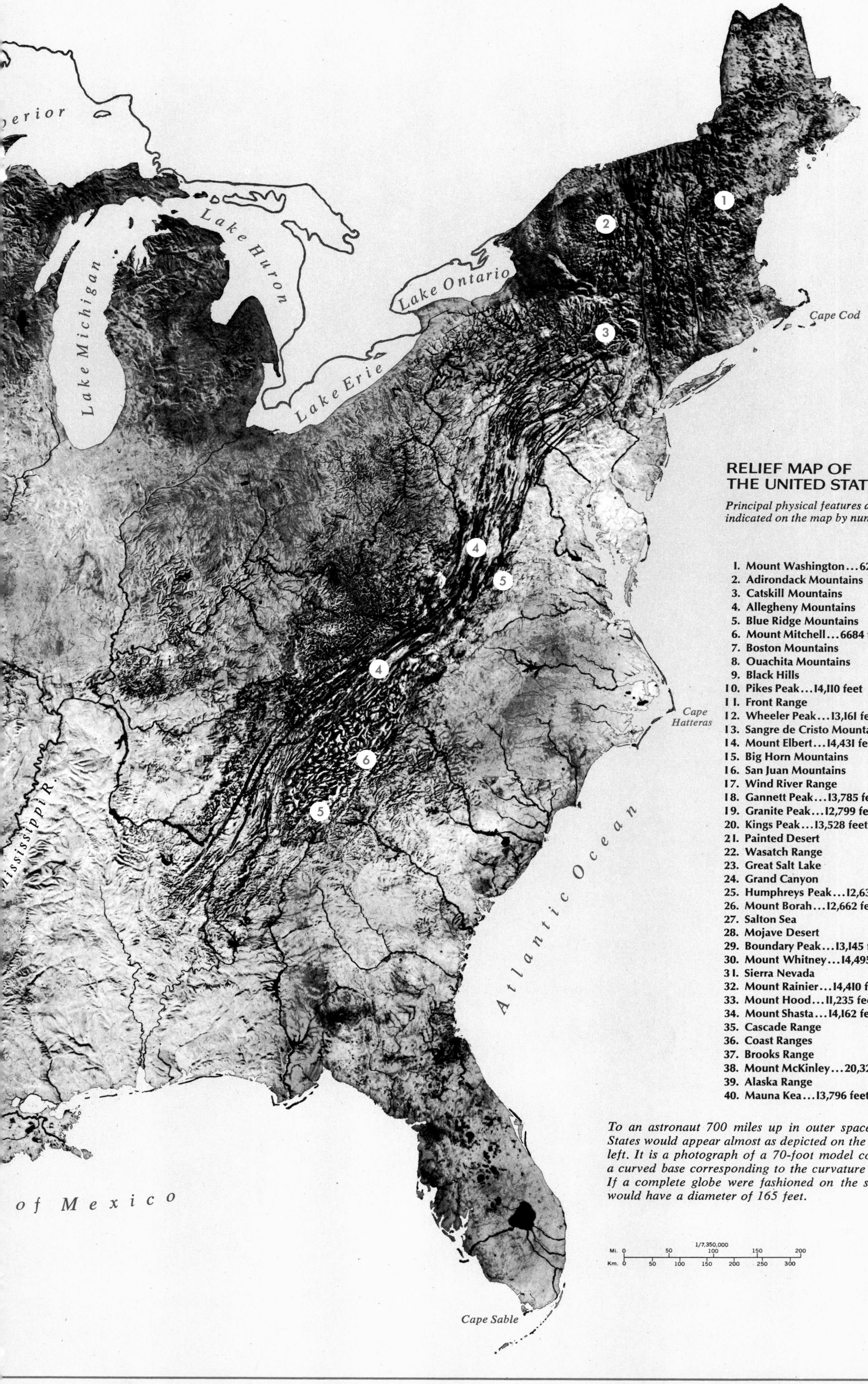

RELIEF MAP OF THE UNITED STATES

Principal physical features are indicated on the map by number

1. Mount Washington . . . 6288 feet
2. Adirondack Mountains
3. Catskill Mountains
4. Allegheny Mountains
5. Blue Ridge Mountains
6. Mount Mitchell . . . 6684 feet
7. Boston Mountains
8. Ouachita Mountains
9. Black Hills
10. Pikes Peak . . . 14,110 feet
11. Front Range
12. Wheeler Peak . . . 13,161 feet (New Mexico)
13. Sangre de Cristo Mountains
14. Mount Elbert . . . 14,431 feet
15. Big Horn Mountains
16. San Juan Mountains
17. Wind River Range
18. Gannett Peak . . . 13,785 feet
19. Granite Peak . . . 12,799 feet
20. Kings Peak . . . 13,528 feet
21. Painted Desert
22. Wasatch Range
23. Great Salt Lake
24. Grand Canyon
25. Humphreys Peak . . . 12,633 feet
26. Mount Borah . . . 12,662 feet
27. Salton Sea
28. Mojave Desert
29. Boundary Peak . . . 13,145 feet
30. Mount Whitney . . . 14,495 feet
31. Sierra Nevada
32. Mount Rainier . . . 14,410 feet
33. Mount Hood . . . 11,235 feet
34. Mount Shasta . . . 14,162 feet
35. Cascade Range
36. Coast Ranges
37. Brooks Range
38. Mount McKinley . . . 20,320 feet
39. Alaska Range
40. Mauna Kea . . . 13,796 feet

To an astronaut 700 miles up in outer space, the United States would appear almost as depicted on the relief map at left. It is a photograph of a 70-foot model constructed on a curved base corresponding to the curvature of the earth. If a complete globe were fashioned on the same scale, it would have a diameter of 165 feet.

1/7,350,000
Mi. 0 50 100 150 200
Km. 0 50 100 150 200 250 300

Lake Su
Yellowstone
Missouri R.
Rio Grande
Rio Grande
Gulf
Pacific Ocean
HAWAII
Ka Lae
1/7,900,000
Mi. 0 50 100 150
Km. 0 50 100 150 200 250
7
8
9
10
11
12
13
13
14
15
16
17
18
19
20
21
22
23
25
26
40
© Babson Institute

ONTARIO
QUÉBEC
MINNESOTA
WISCONSIN
MICHIGAN
IOWA
ILLINOIS
INDIANA
OHIO
PENNSYLVANIA
NEW YORK
MISSOURI
KENTUCKY
TENNESSEE
ARKANSAS
MISSISSIPPI
ALABAMA
GEORGIA
FLORIDA
LOUISIANA
SOUTH CAROLINA
NORTH CAROLINA
VIRGINIA
WEST VIRGINIA
MARYLAND
NEW JERSEY
MAINE
NEW BRUNSWICK
NOVA SCOTIA
LAKE SUPERIOR
LAKE MICHIGAN
LAKE HURON
LAKE ERIE
LAKE ONTARIO
GULF OF MEXICO
ATLANTIC OCEAN
STRAITS OF FLORIDA
BAHAMAS
CUBA
HABANA
Chicago
Detroit
Cleveland
New York
Philadelphia
Baltimore
WASHINGTON D.C.
BOSTON
Montréal
OTTAWA
TORONTO
St. Louis
Memphis
New Orleans
ATLANTA
Miami
Houston
Dallas
Pittsburgh
Milwaukee
Minneapolis
ST. PAUL
Cincinnati
Louisville
1/10,500,000
Mi. 0 50 100 150 200
Km. 0 100 200 300
POPULATION LEGEND
Over 1,000,000
500,000-1,000,000
250,000-500,000
100,000-250,000
25,000-100,000
Under 25,000
CAPITAL CITIES ARE INDICATED BY CAPITAL LETTERS
2A10

PART I

The 50 States

In the Declaration of Independence, the 13 colonies expressed their determination to become "free and independent states," and so they did. Vermont was the first to join the original 13 on March 4, 1791, while Hawaii, the last, became the fiftieth state on August 21, 1959. In this section the maps of the individual states, arranged in alphabetical order for easy reference, have been designed to show 42,000 place-names, almost twice the number usually shown on maps of this size. Important towns within metropolitan areas surrounding major cities are shown on special insets. And an eight-page map tracing the major state and Federal highways begins on page 163.

America's place-names reflect the history of the country, ranging from those bestowed by Indians before the white man arrived (Susquehanna and Michigan) to recent ones derived from scientific achievements (Atomic City, Idaho). The origins of the early settlers are clearly shown along the eastern seaboard by names borrowed from England (Boston and New Jersey), from Holland (Rensselaer and Tappan Zee), from Wales (Bryn Mawr and Bangor), and Germany (Lititz and Hamburg). In Florida, the Southwest and the West, many are Spanish (Boca Raton, Santa Fe and Los Angeles); in Louisiana and the old Northwest Territory, many are French (Baton Rouge and Eau Claire); and in Alaska there are a few remaining Russian names (Pribilof and Baranof, among others).

As memory of the mother tongues and countries in Europe dimmed, the men responsible for naming towns, rivers and mountains turned to domestic sources. One was popular military and political heroes: Washington, Jefferson, Perry, Decatur, Jackson, Houston, Lincoln. The nature of the land, its flora and fauna, suggested descriptive terms: Boiling Springs, High Point, Elk City, Palm Beach, Bald Knob. Others were just made up: Penn Yan because it was settled by families from Pennsylvania and Yankees from New England; Texarkana because it straddles the border of Texas and Arkansas. The gold and silver rushes during the second half

(Continued)

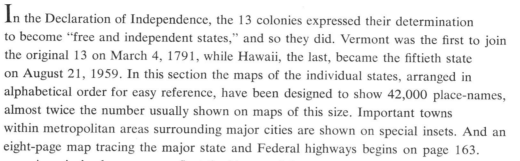

of the nineteenth century resulted in many a Silver City and Silver Springs as well as Gold Stone and Gold Creek. The rough and ready pioneers of the West who did not stand on ceremony were also responsible for such picturesque nomenclature as Tombstone, Last Chance, Deathball Creek, Two Bit Gulch and Chicken Thief Flat. Founders or prominent landowners were honored by cities and towns: Lord Baltimore, Jonathan Dayton, Moses Cleaveland, Nathaniel Rochester.

In the following pages, a brief, fact-filled article gives the essential character, history, economic activities and outstanding traits of each state. The largest cities are also described. Population figures for states are the Census Bureau's provisional estimates of July 1, 1967; those for the cities are the 1960 census totals.

In size, there is an enormous contrast in the range of states: from the 1214 square miles of little Rhode Island to the 586,400 square miles of the vast reaches of Alaska. The United States is huge, fourth on earth after the Soviet Union, Canada and Communist China. Ka Lae, Hawaii, and West Quoddy Head, Maine, the southwesternmost and northeasternmost points in the nation, are some 5200 miles apart. Point Barrow, Alaska, in the north, and Key West, Florida, in the south are separated by about 4400 miles. The country's jurisdiction extends even farther, from Pacific possessions and administered territories such as Okinawa, just south of Japan, to the Virgin Islands in the Caribbean, 9150 miles away.

An average of 29 inches of rain falls on all parts of the United States each year, but Nevada, the driest state, averages only 8.81 inches while Louisiana's mean is 55.11 inches. The wettest place is Mount Waialeale, Kauai, Hawaii with 471 inches of rainfall yearly, and the most parched is Death Valley, California, with 1.35 inches. (Mount Waialeale's annual average is also the world's record, while the Atacama Desert in Chile has so little rainfall it is barely measurable.) The temperature in Death Valley hit a blistering 134° F. in July 1913, only 2° below the global mark set in 1922 at Al'Aziziyah, Libya. Fort Yukon, Alaska, endured the bitter opposite, –78° F. in January 1934, which was still much "warmer" than the –127° F. recorded at Vostok, Antarctica in 1960. Alaska has the highest point in the country, the top of Mount McKinley, 20,320 feet above sea level. Mount Everest in the Himalayas is the tallest in the world at 29,028 feet. The lowest point in the United States is in Death Valley, 282 feet below sea level (the lowest land point on earth is on the shores of the Dead Sea in the Near East, 1004 feet lower).

The Mississippi, the Missouri and the Red Rock form the third largest waterway, 3860 miles (after the Nile at 4132 and the Amazon at 3900). Lake Superior is the largest freshwater lake in the world, at 31,820 square miles, and only one inland saltwater body is larger, the Caspian Sea at 151,123.

As the nation expanded westward beyond the original 13 states, the geographical center of the country shifted. Starting in 1783 from a point in the center of Ohio, it moved to just west of Castle Rock, South Dakota, with the admission of Hawaii and Alaska to the Union in 1959. In 1790 when the first census was taken, the original location of the center of population was east of Baltimore, Maryland. As of 1960 this center point had jumped to a place 6½ miles northeast of Centralia, Illinois, 50 miles from the Mississippi River. The population has grown from 3,929,214 in 1790 to 31,443,321 in 1860 and to an estimated 200,271,000 in January 1968. The state population spread reaches from 273,000 residents of Alaska to 19,163,000 people in California, 70 times greater. New Jersey has almost 894 inhabitants for each of its 7836 square miles, compared with the Netherlands, one of the world's most densely populated countries, whose population per square mile is 969. Alaska, whose forests, mountains and tundra are still largely a frontier country, has only 0.4 persons per square mile.

The place-names of America show the panorama of the American world. Small clusters of homes, blinding white deserts, massed industrial plants, lakes our forefathers knew—there is no end to the contrasts among them. Even to look at these names is to begin a knowledge of the land.

ALABAMA

In the cotton state of Alabama a strange monument stands in the public square of the town of Enterprise, dedicated to that archfoe of cotton, the boll weevil. The insect virtually wiped out the crop of 1910, forcing the farmers to diversify and never again to rely solely on cotton for a livelihood. Many products from the peanut —dyes, flour and insulating boards—had been developed by George Washington Carver, the Negro scientist. This vine was one of the new crops to be cultivated and grew so successfully that the grateful planters put up the unusual tribute to their insect benefactor.

Events of the region now known as Alabama began with the mystery-shrouded activities of the Stone Age people who inhabited Russell Cave in Jackson County more than 9000 years ago. Hernando de Soto, the Spanish explorer, is believed to have been the earliest European visitor, in 1540. The first permanent white settlement was established at Mobile by the French in 1711. French rule gave way in 1763 to British. After the Revolutionary War, England turned most of the territory over to the United States, but ceded the coastal strip to Spain. This area was finally seized by the United States during the War of 1812. Settlers began to arrive in fairly large numbers after the war, and Alabama was admitted to the Union as the twenty-second state on December 14, 1819.

It was in Alabama, shortly after the Revolutionary War, that Alexander McGillivray, the son of a Scotsman, became the leader of the Indians of the powerful Creek Nation in its bitter fight against the United States. It was there, in 1807, that Aaron Burr was arrested for treason and his conspiracy crushed. And it was in this very "Cradle of the Confederacy" that a determined effort was made in 1861 by a small group to set up a pro-Union state called Nickajack.

The Confederacy was organized in Montgomery, which served as its first capital. The principal military engagement in the state was the Battle of Mobile Bay, won by Union forces under Admiral David Farragut in 1864. Economically Alabama suffered more in nine years of Reconstruction than it did in four years of war, and Federal troops were not withdrawn until 1876.

Woodland covers almost two thirds of the state, mainly in pine forests. Lumber production is important, as are forest products such as turpentine, tar and rosin. Traditionally an agricultural region, with cotton still the leading crop, Alabama has forged ahead in manufacturing, with its center at Birmingham, the largest city. Mobile, second in size, is also a flourishing industrial center as well as Alabama's only seaport. The hub of agricultural trade is Montgomery, capital and third largest city.

In the northern part, where the Appalachian Mountains gradually slope down to the plains, lie Alabama's vast deposits of iron ore and coal. Here also the Tennessee River flows through the state. Thanks to the Tennessee Valley Authority (TVA), which operates 32 dams—Guntersville, Wilson and Wheeler are the three in Alabama —the river has been turned into a producer of inexpensive electric power, which has brought prosperity to farms and towns. Alabama now stands sixth in the United States in hydroelectric development.

Stretching across the center of the state is the prairie land known, because of its black clay soil, as the Black Belt. It is in this region, where once cotton was king, that livestock production has become a major industry.

In contrast to Alabama's many antebellum ways and customs are the Redstone Arsenal and George C. Marshall Space Flight Center at Huntsville, in the northern part of the state. Many of the nation's first rockets were developed there, and plans are now being perfected for landing the first man on the moon.

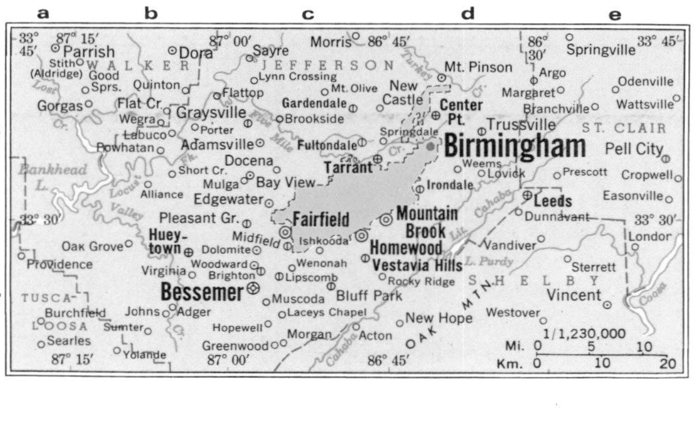

BIRMINGHAM

Steep hills border the narrow valley of the city, supplying the iron, coal and limestone that feed the steel mills of this "Pittsburgh of the South." Red Mountain, now a suburban section, was the source of red iron ore hauled by wagon trains to Selma, where cannons were made during the Civil War. In 1871 Birmingham, named for the English city which was famous for its iron- and cloth-making, was founded by a real-estate company in a cotton field at the junction of two railroads. The first plot in the well-laid-out business district sold for $100. Steel became Birmingham's destiny, and few traces remain of the plantation society of the antebellum South. Production began in 1888, and the furnaces still light up the sky at night. Other important manufactures are cast-iron pipe, cotton goods, cement and coal-mining machinery. Birmingham is known for the beauty of its parks, recreational facilities and residential areas, especially when azaleas, dogwood and roses are in bloom. High above this newest of Southern cities, silhouetted against the sky on the tallest ridge, is an unusual villa. The author Carl Carmer describes it: "the lovely temple of Vesta, in exterior at least an exact replica of that jewel of stone that sleeps . . . in distant Italy." (Pop. 340,887.)

ALASKA

This great, faraway land, most northern of all the United States, is a region of vast distances, spellbinding scenery and fantastic contrasts. Alaska is the largest state in the Union, nearly one-fifth as big as the other 49 lumped together, yet the population is the smallest. It is often thought of as an icy waste, but in some parts of the state the thermometer may top 100° F. and snow rarely falls. The southern panhandle, lying between Canada and the Pacific Ocean, is one of the country's wettest regions. The famous Gold Rush city of Nome lies farther west than Honolulu. Little Diomede Island pops out of the sea only three miles from Russian territory.

Rightly called America's last frontier, Alaska has thousands of miles of unexplored, untamed wilderness and an unparalleled variety of wildlife. This fauna ranges from moose, mountain sheep, caribou, reindeer, grizzly bears, wolves and wolverines on land—and millions of ducks and geese in the swamps and river basins—to whales, polar bears, fur seals and walruses in the sea.

Among the geographic marvels are the nation's 14 tallest mountain peaks, including Mount McKinley, highest (20,320 feet) in North America, and the state's largest glacier, Malaspina. On winter nights, displays of the aurora borealis (northern lights) illuminate the horizon with swaying curtains of iridescent color.

Fishing, mining, lumbering, trading and construction are Alaska's chief industries. The most important commercial fish is salmon; the catch is processed in Ketchikan, which has some of the largest packing plants in the industry. In recent years lumber products have outranked fishing in economic importance. Much of Alaska's great natural resources—gas, oil, mineral deposits—remains to be tapped.

Russians knew of the existence of a "Great Land" to the east as early as 1700. Explorations conducted by Captain Vitus Bering, a Dane, for the Russian navy revealed that Asia and North America were not connected. The strait between the two continents was later given his name. By 1784 Russia had established fur-trading settlements on Kodiak Island, and it continued to dominate the region for nearly 100 years. Sitka became the capital. For decades, while San Francisco remained an obscure Spanish village, Sitka was a thriving city that manufactured bells for California missions and attracted sailing ships bringing traders and adventurers from all parts of the world. Eventually, however, Russia's interest declined to the point where Alaska was offered for sale to the United States in 1867. Secretary of State William H. Seward persuaded a hostile and critical Congress to approve its purchase for $7,200,000. For many years thereafter Alaska was scornfully referred to as "Seward's Folly." Now its natural resources and strategic location make it one of the nation's most valuable possessions. Statehood was finally achieved in 1959.

Mountain ranges and island archipelagos divide Alaska into distinctly different regions. In its moist southern portion the temperature is comparable to Philadelphia's. Here is the state's most magnificent scenery: great forests, massive glaciers, tiny fishing villages set in narrow fjords below towering cliffs. Juneau, the capital, is a seaport ringed by snow-capped mountains.

In the middle section, which extends from Anchorage to Nome to Fairbanks, winters are much longer and colder; the mean temperature is strikingly similar to that of Scandinavia. Summers are so mild that the Matanuska Valley, just north of Anchorage, is the chief agricultural region, devoted to vegetable crops and dairy farms. In this region the sun shines for 20 hours daily in midsummer, while a winter's day may last only four hours.

The coast along the Gulf of Alaska is heavily forested, but toward the interior, big timber gives way to plains and bleak tundra through which the Yukon River, fourth largest in North America, rolls for 1979 miles. Into this area in 1898 poured the first gold seekers on their way to the Canadian Klondike and Yukon territories. Alaskan fields were discovered soon after. In recent years increased operating costs and the government-controlled price of gold have made gold mining on a large scale unprofitable, although many smaller installations continue production. Fort Yukon, 150 miles north of Fairbanks, has recorded the extremes of Alaska's startling climate: —78° F. in the winter and 100° in summer.

Above the Arctic Circle lies Alaska's "top of the world," flat, dry and treeless as a desert, where Eskimo tribes still hunt seal, polar bear and walrus. Barrow, situated on a tip of Alaska extending into the Arctic Ocean, is the world's largest Eskimo village and the nation's northernmost town. Nowadays curious summer tourists fly north to view the Eskimo games and dances, to purchase their furs and handicrafts, and to sample reindeer steaks and chunks of whale meat.

The most forbidding and desolate face of Alaska is found in the Aleutian Island chain that curves southwestward from Anchorage 1200 miles out into the Pacific Ocean. These barren, rocky islands, marked with the plumes of smoking volcanoes, are virtually uninhabited except for a scattering of Aleut tribesmen and the sailors, soldiers and airmen who man outpost bases such as the U.S. Naval Station on Adak Island. Isolation, storms, fogs and williwaws—savage windstorms that strike with sudden, shrieking fury—discourage visitors from lingering long in the Aleutians.

Today many Americans are "pioneering" in Alaska. No other state is attracting so many new settlers in proportion to population. Jet airliners now fly in to all the major cities. Modern ferries for automobiles, cruising the safe, calm waters of the beautiful Inland Passage, link British Columbia's Prince Rupert with the Alaskan cities of Ketchikan, Sitka, Juneau and Skagway. An auto-carrying railroad connects Skagway with the Alaska Highway at Whitehorse in the Canadian Yukon. Built as a military supply line during World War II, the road commences in Dawson Creek, British Columbia, and runs northward 1523 miles to Fairbanks.

Depending on one's personal tastes, life in Alaska can run the gamut from golf courses and trim split-level homes to trading posts in Eskimo villages where some men hunt, women work and children play just as they did 3000 years ago. Despite the hazards of a high cost of living and limited job opportunities, many newcomers find the scenic grandeur and sense of freedom from urban pressures so exhilarating that they consider their new way of life well worth the struggle. The saying, "If you live in Alaska more than two years, your feet will be frozen in it," seems truer than ever.

ANCHORAGE

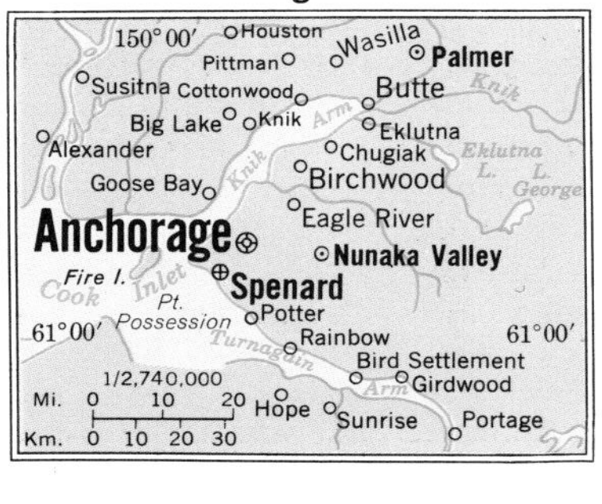

Alaska's largest city, Anchorage lies 1475 air miles north of Seattle. It was built in 1914 on a long bluff overlooking Cook Inlet on the Pacific Ocean. The city began as a ship-supply depot for the construction of the Alaska Railroad. During World War II it played an important role in North American defense. There are television stations, apartment houses, a symphony orchestra and a downtown shopping center where parka-clad Indians shop side by side with stylishly dressed matrons. Its International Airport, handling flights to and from the Orient and Europe (via the polar route), has become one of the world's major airline crossroads. Summers are warm here and days so long that golfers can play almost all night. Winter temperatures average 13° above zero and snow seldom reaches a depth of more than three feet. The rugged Chugach Mountains nearby provide an endless variety of sports, both summer and winter. (Pop. 44,237.)

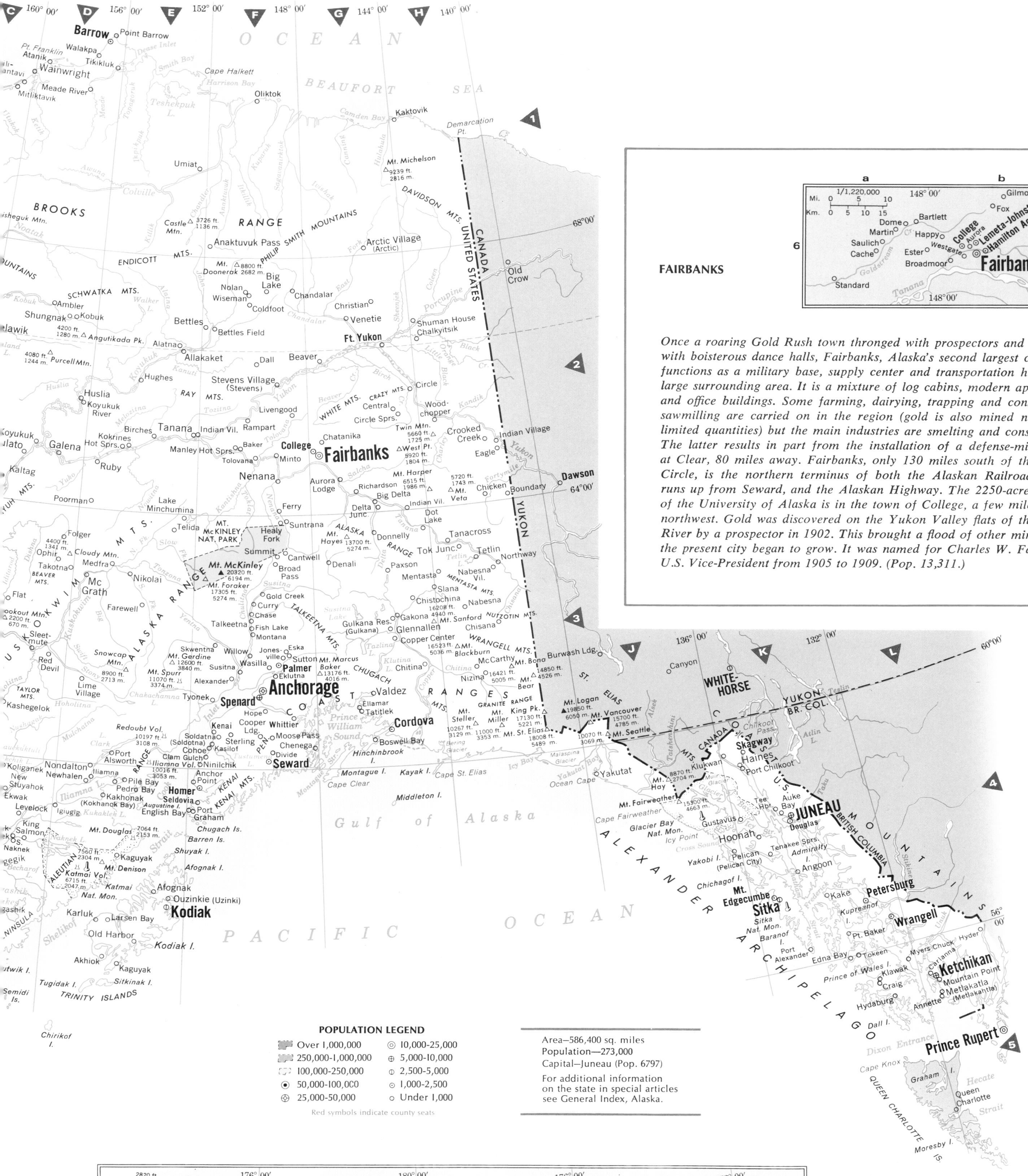

Once a roaring Gold Rush town thronged with prospectors and crowded with boisterous dance halls, Fairbanks, Alaska's second largest city, now functions as a military base, supply center and transportation hub for a large surrounding area. It is a mixture of log cabins, modern apartments and office buildings. Some farming, dairying, trapping and considerable sawmilling are carried on in the region (gold is also mined nearby in limited quantities) but the main industries are smelting and construction. The latter results in part from the installation of a defense-missile site at Clear, 80 miles away. Fairbanks, only 130 miles south of the Arctic Circle, is the northern terminus of both the Alaskan Railroad, which runs up from Seward, and the Alaskan Highway. The 2250-acre campus of the University of Alaska is in the town of College, a few miles to the northwest. Gold was discovered on the Yukon Valley flats of the Chena River by a prospector in 1902. This brought a flood of other miners, and the present city began to grow. It was named for Charles W. Fairbanks, U.S. Vice-President from 1905 to 1909. (Pop. 13,311.)

POPULATION LEGEND

Over 1,000,000	10,000-25,000
250,000-1,000,000	5,000-10,000
100,000-250,000	2,500-5,000
50,000-100,000	1,000-2,500
25,000-50,000	Under 1,000

Red symbols indicate county seats

Area—586,400 sq. miles
Population—273,000
Capital—Juneau (Pop. 6797)

For additional information on the state in special articles see General Index, Alaska.

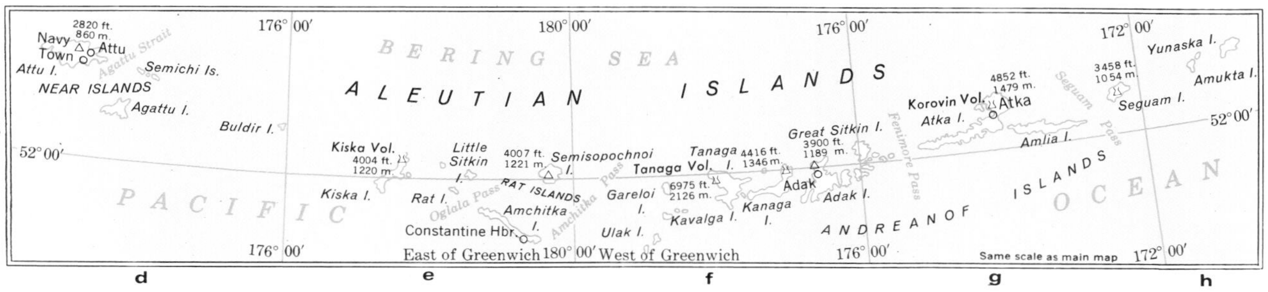

1/7,150,000 — 1 in. = 113 mi. — 1 cm. = 71.5 km.

0 50 100 150 200 250 300 Miles
0 100 200 300 400 500 Kilometers

Polyconic Projection

ARIZONA

Deep down at the bottom of the Grand Canyon, where the turbulent waters of the Colorado River rush and thunder past a sandbar, an Indian glances upward. He sees mile-high striated walls on the layers of which is written the history of the earth. From an airliner a passenger gazes down on the awesome beauty of the great irregular gash in the vast region of mountains, forests and desert that stretches to the southern horizon. Vertically the distance between the two men is no more than eight miles, but it encompasses a span of millions of years. And in only an infinitesimal speck of this time, modern man's technology has transformed a huge prehistoric wilderness into a wealthy and enthralling American state.

Sun and space, once Arizona's most forbidding features, have become its richest possessions. The immense deserts, formerly scorned and dreaded, now yield rich crops. Forests, canyons and far-flung plains draw a host of visitors, recreationists and new residents for its young cities.

The homes of some of the region's pre-Columbian inhabitants have been remarkably well preserved. Near Phoenix stands the Casa Grande, a four-story adobe structure built more than 800 years ago and often called America's first skyscraper. A deep cave at the Navaho National Monument holds an entire village of houses laid out on streets and courts. The cliff dwelling known as Montezuma's Castle, reached by a series of ladders, is five stories high. It was built in a natural recess halfway up a perpendicular 145-foot precipice and was named by explorers who mistakenly believed that the construction was Aztec and that the Mexican emperor had lived there.

Marcos de Niza, a Franciscan priest, led an expedition searching for gold and precious gems into Arizona from Mexico as early as 1539. But savage Indians and scorching deserts proved so formidable that Spain abandoned further efforts to explore and colonize the region. The land languished for more than 300 years as intractable wilderness. By 1850 only one wagon road had crossed the territory. Plodding camel caravans, introduced because of their usefulness in African deserts, carried freight for a brief time in 1857 over what is now U.S. Route 66. Apaches and Navahos fiercely resisted the white settlers and explorers.

Gold and silver strikes of the post-Civil War period touched off a rush to stake claims. U.S. Army Cavalry units finally subdued and rounded up the Indians. (Today Arizona has more Indians—83,387—than any other state, but most of them live on reservations.) Later discoveries of rich deposits of copper drew more men and money into the region. Since 1907 Arizona has been the nation's greatest producer of copper. The mines also yield large quantities of lead, tungsten and other important metals.

Paradoxically it was water, the scarcest resource in this part of the American landscape, that enabled Arizona to become a populous state and provided it with a glowing future. Mormons, in the 1860's, were the first settlers to notice signs that ancient Indian tribes had diverted rivers to irrigate their plantings of corn and cotton. The pioneers quickly discovered that the barren brown soil was astonishingly fertile when given water. The almost constant sunshine made it possible to produce crops all year round; now Arizona ranks third in irrigation farming. In the central and southern parts of the state, evergreen, man-made oases—nourished by dams, reservoirs and more than 4000 miles of canals—deliver bumper crops of cotton, barley, melons, oranges, lemons, lettuce and dates.

Water again provided a great surge of Arizona's growth when wild rivers were harnessed for hydroelectric power. The gigantic Hoover Dam on the Colorado River and a succession of others on the Colorado, Salt, Verde and Gila rivers have supplied enormous quantities of electric power for factories which have made manufacturing the biggest industry in Arizona.

In the 1950's the advent of modern air-conditioning systems for homes, cars, offices and industrial plants gave Arizona a golden opportunity for growth and economic expansion. The major cities, Phoenix and Tucson, once drowsy winter resorts for wealthy Easterners, mushroomed into completely air-cooled metropolitan centers where people live and work in comfort every month of the year. In this migrant-population explosion, Tucson jumped from 45,000 in 1950 to 236,000 in 1965; Phoenix from 106,000 to past the half-million mark.

Each year Arizona plays host to huge numbers of visitors. They gaze at its modern desert cities with a mixture of stunned admiration and disbelief. They explore its canyons, pine forests, cattle ranges and Indian pueblo ruins, and discover its resorts. Many suddenly decide to make this colorful and exciting state, the second fastest-growing in the nation, their new home.

PHOENIX

Because it was built on the ruins of a prehistoric city, Arizona's capital adopted the name of the phoenix, a mythical bird which was consumed by flames every 500 years and then immediately arose again from its own ashes. Irrigation canals have transformed Phoenix into a twentieth-century oasis which looms up out of the vast Southwestern desert. Well-tended lawns in residential areas are shaded by eucalyptus, palm and cottonwood trees. Tourists enjoy the warm, dry climate on dude ranches which are distinctively Western in style. Situated in an oval valley rimmed by majestic mountains, the city originated as a hay camp for the U.S. Army Cavalry in the 1860's. The first building, an adobe general store, also served as the courthouse; the second was a brewery. After 1879, parched residents could buy ice, delivered in a wheelbarrow, at seven cents a pound. One of the early industries was raising ostriches to supply the plumes which fashions of the 1890's demanded. Phoenix has become a shipping point for crops and beef cattle raised in the area and a center for manufacturing cotton, refining minerals and processing food. On the busy downtown sidewalks stolid Indian women display their handmade pottery, waiting for buyers among the visitors clad in ten-gallon hats and high-heeled cowboy boots.

Area—113,909 sq. miles
Population—1,635,000
Capital—Phoenix (Pop. 439,170)

For additional information on the state in special articles see General Index, Arizona.

POPULATION LEGEND

Over 1,000,000	10,000-25,000
250,000-1,000,000	5,000-10,000
100,000-250,000	2,500-5,000
50,000-100,000	1,000-2,500
25,000-50,000	Under 1,000

Red symbols indicate county seats

1/3,660,000 — 1 in. = 57.8 mi. — 0 20 40 60 80 100 120 140 160 Miles
1 cm. = 36.6 km. — 0 20 40 60 80 100 120 140 160 180 200 220 240 Kilometers

Lambert Conformal Conic Projection

ARKANSAS

Tucked away in the lower Mississippi Valley close to the heart of the continent, Arkansas is a state whose fascinating history and diversified economy are little known to most Americans. Few realize that while Michelangelo was creating his masterpieces in Italy, helmeted Spanish conquistadores led by Hernando de Soto spent nearly a year in Arkansas.

Arkansas is one of the two smallest states west of the Mississippi. Its name has nothing to do with Kansas but was derived by early French explorers from the name of an Indian clan called the Arkansea. All who dwell there are fiercely united against attempts to pronounce the word like Kansas, but this is about as far as unanimity reaches in Arkansas.

There is no such thing as a typical "Arkansawyer" because geography separates the state into widely varied regions in which people live distinctly different kinds of lives. In the northwestern corner, where rich soil and a moderate climate are ideal for general farming, orchards and poultry raising, the life is very much like that in neighboring Missouri. Farther south, in the Ozark Mountains, a leisurely pace, quaint manners of speech, love of legends and country music remind one of the mountaineering folk of Tennessee. Lumbering is the chief industry there.

In contrast, the valley of the Arkansas River, which bisects the state, is becoming a bustling industrial center resembling parts of Ohio. To the southwest on the Gulf plain, a region of oil wells and cattle ranches blends in with neighboring Texas and Oklahoma. The economy of eastern Arkansas, whose border follows the winding course of the Mississippi River for 500 miles, is based on extensive cotton and rice plantations similar to those in Mississippi and Louisiana.

The Mississippi River fashioned much of the history and social structure of Arkansas. Nearly 100 years before the American Revolution, when the English and Dutch colonists stayed close to their settlements on the Atlantic Coast, the French had already established the first European outpost in the lower Mississippi Valley at the mouth of the Arkansas River. One of the most bizarre attempts at colonization occurred under their rule. John Law, a Scottish economist, was given control of the entire Louisiana Territory in 1717 and issued banknotes in France which were to be repaid from profits he expected to make in Mississippi Valley trade. The area around the French fort in Arkansas was to be his own duchy. Many Germans responded to his call for settlers and 800 of them were sent to the river outpost. They barely survived one winter before Law's "Mississippi Bubble" burst. The disillusioned pioneers straggled back to New Orleans and eventually settled north of that city. Thomas Jefferson's purchase of the Louisiana Territory from Napoleon in 1803 touched off a wave of exploration and immigration in the Arkansas region. Some Americans from the East hacked their way along Indian trails of western Kentucky and Tennessee. The majority chose the easier water routes, floating down the Ohio and Tennessee.

Progress in taming this vast area was painfully slow until the invention of the steamboat burst the bonds of the wilderness. In 1822 the first stern-wheeler battled 300 miles of snags and sandbars up the Arkansas River to Fort Smith. By the mid-1820's these craft, their decks crowded with Federal troops, homesteading families, traders, trappers and farmers, were thrashing their way upstream into westernmost Arkansas. So shallow was the draft on shoal-water vessels that a joke arose—Arkansas steamboats would run wherever the ground was a little damp.

Huge cotton plantations spread through the lowlands along the Mississippi. Slaves, mules, machinery for cotton gins and lavish furnishings for plantation mansions were now easily transported upriver. So swift were the changes that in 1836, when Arkansas became the twenty-fifth state to enter the Union, the population was estimated at more than 50,000. Cotton continued to dominate politics as well as the economy. Arkansas aligned itself with the other slave states, and its regiments fought with the armies of the Confederacy from Shiloh to Gettysburg and Appomattox. Skirmishes and minor battles occurred within its boundaries until Union forces gained control of the Mississippi in 1863.

The chaos of Reconstruction brought a decade of devastating financial woes, bitter clashes between carpetbaggers and the Ku Klux Klan, the latter allied with die-hard remnants of Confederate political groups. Personal tragedies overshadowed all else as soldiers returned to find their plantations and farms in ruins. The despair of some was so overwhelming that they left Arkansas forever, journeying westward to start new lives in Oregon and California. Others stubbornly stuck it out until the coming of the railroads in the 1870's brought another period of prosperity. Inland regions that had been inaccessible to steamboats were thrown open to farming, lumbering, mining and manufacturing. Discoveries of bauxite (aluminum ore), coal, petroleum and natural gas in southern Arkansas and increased interest in cattle-raising and rice-growing expanded the range of economic activity.

As the railroads brought in immigrants from Germany, Italy and Austria, and as descendants of Negro slaves migrated northward to Chicago and Detroit, the population of Arkansas became considerably more diversified than in other parts of the Cotton Belt. Industrial growth has been faster there than in much of the South; in the last two decades the number of manufacturing jobs has more than doubled. Since 1955 the energetic Arkansas Industrial Development Commission, working with scientific, cultural and educational agencies, has been particularly successful in attracting and establishing new businesses to give the state a broader economic base.

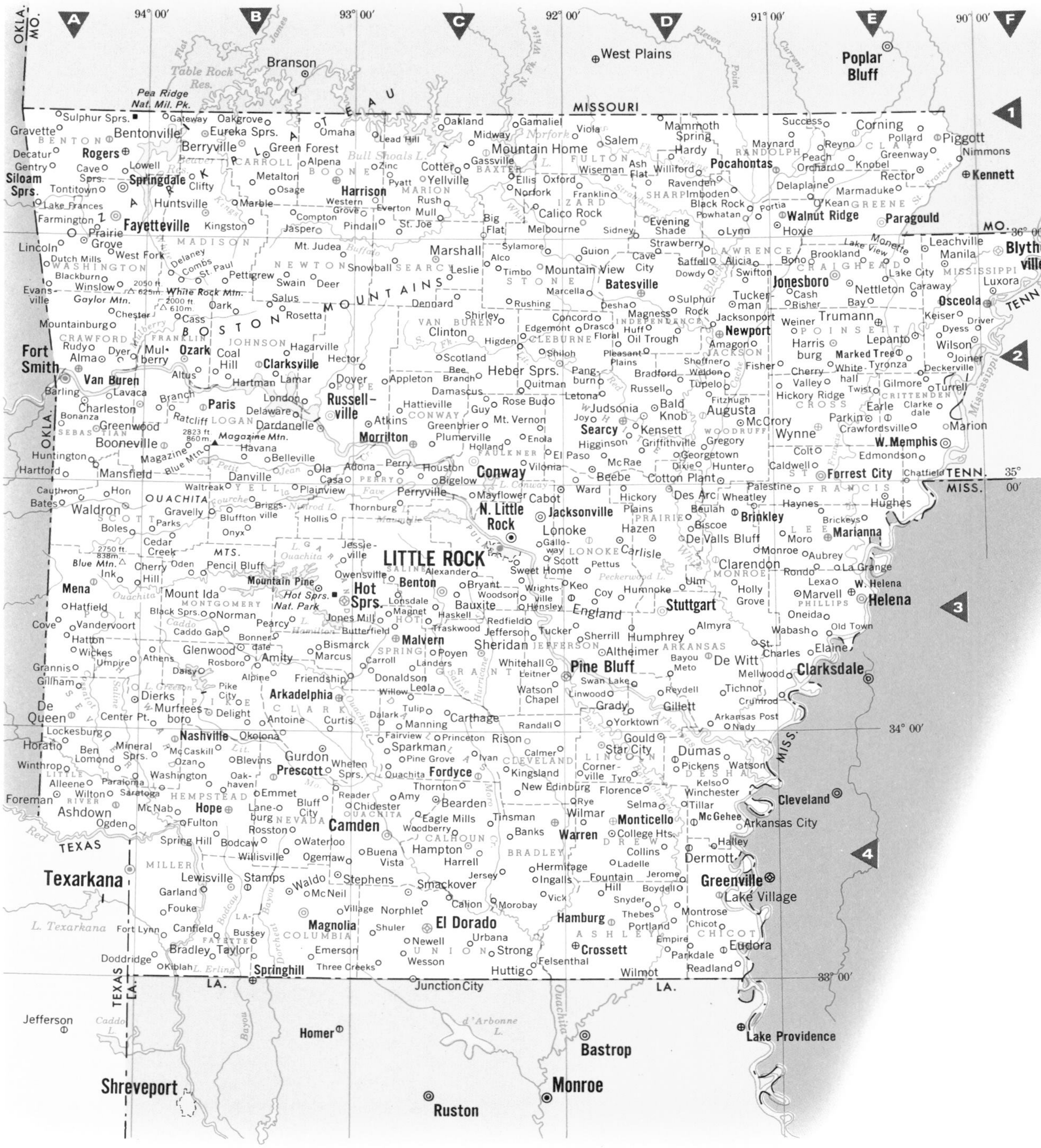

Area—53,104 sq. miles
Population—1,969,000
Capital—Little Rock (Pop. 107,813)
For additional information on the state in special articles see General Index, Arkansas.

POPULATION LEGEND

Over 1,000,000	10,000-25,000
250,000-1,000,000	5,000-10,000
100,000-250,000	2,500-5,000
50,000-100,000	1,000-2,500
25,000-50,000	Under 1,000

Red symbols indicate county seats

1/2,710,000 — 1 in. = 42.8 mi. — 1 cm. = 27.1 km.

0 20 40 60 80 100 Miles
0 20 40 60 80 100 120 140 160 Kilometers

Lambert Conformal Conic Projection

© General Drafting Co., Inc.

LITTLE ROCK

In 1722 a French explorer established a trading post on the banks of the Arkansas River at its junction with the Great Southwest Trail. This natural pathway had been followed for centuries by Indians and then by traders, pioneering scouts and homesteading families. He named the site La Petite Roche (the little rock), to distinguish it from a larger bluff nearby. Laid out in 1821 by a land speculator, Little Rock grew from a boisterous frontier town to a busy steamboat port, state capital (1836) and modern industrial center, surrounded by a rich farm, cotton and dairying area. It is the principal market for the state's agricultural products. More than 300 manufacturing plants turn out chemicals, furniture, prefabricated houses and house trailers, food products, watches, clocks and other items. Little Rock is unique in having three capitol buildings: territorial, old state and new state. Lovely gardens have earned it the nickname of City of Roses.

CALIFORNIA

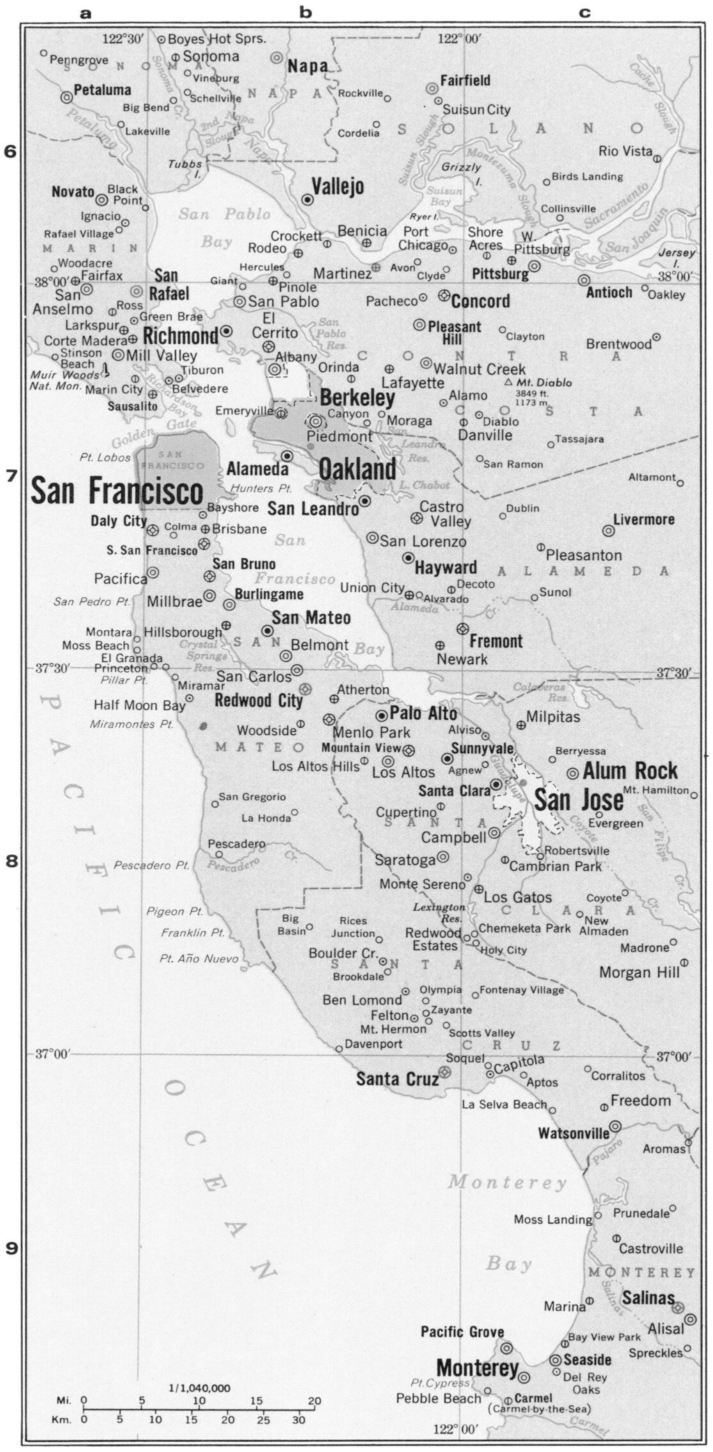

Californians like to boast that their state has the finest of everything—the largest trees, the best climate, the grandest vacationland, the biggest crops, the longest bridges—and in December 1962, they claimed the greatest population of all the 50 states when they outstripped New York with a count of more than 17,000,000 inhabitants and nearly 1000 pouring in every day.

The same attractions that the early Spaniards enjoyed in California in the 1500's, the gold miners in 1849 and the land seekers in 1887 still beckon newcomers. On the coast the climate is mild and stimulating, the mean temperatures ranging from 47° to 60° F. in San Francisco and 54° to 68° F. in San Diego; excellent ports and bays have brought industry and commerce. The hot, dry climate of the irrigated desert and Central Valley, the state's horn of plenty, has made California the nation's biggest producer of 56 crops, among them lettuce and carrots, and grapes for its wine industry. There are hundreds of miles of beaches and, not far away, the snows and trails of the Sierras for skiers and hikers. California's gold today is in its industries—auto plants and shipyards and, more recently, electronics, aircraft and missiles, which came to the state after World War II because of the large working force available there, and now in turn attract new arrivals in a continuing cycle of growth.

Two states in one, California has two poles—San Francisco, the city of hills in the north, and Los Angeles in the south. In the northern interior are the Mother Lode country, its Gold Rush towns almost abandoned; breathtaking Yosemite Valley with mile-high Sierra peaks and 2000-foot waterfalls; blue 22-mile-long Lake Tahoe straddling the Nevada border; and 4000-year-old redwoods, one of them 36 feet in diameter. In the southern interior are the resorts of Palm Springs and Salton Sea; oil fields, cattle ranches and orange groves; and mines that produce more than 200,000,000 dollars' worth of talc, cement and boron a year.

The northern two thirds of the state cradles Central Valley, 400 miles long and 50 miles wide, rimmed almost entirely by mountain ranges. Below the Amargosa Mountains lies Death Valley, the continent's lowest area (282 feet below sea level). Sixty miles away is Mount Whitney, the highest point (14,495 feet) in the United States south of the Canadian border.

Four foreign flags—Spanish, British, Russian and Mexican—have flown over the region, and each country has left its mark. Columbus had heard of a legendary California from Caribbean natives; in 1536, Cortés discovered Lower California, and in 1542 Captain Juan Rodríguez Cabrillo sailed up the coast. Other Spaniards followed during the next 100 years, but no one penetrated inland. Sir Francis Drake sailed into a bay north of San Francisco in 1579 and named the land Nova Albion, or New England. But it was not until 200 years later that Father Junipero Serra led the Spanish Franciscans overland from Mexico. Hoping to civilize and convert the Indians, they eventually founded 21 missions, each a day's ride from the last. They were accompanied by Captain Gaspar de Portolá, who established presidios (garrisoned posts) with small military staffs to protect the missions from hostile Indians.

The settlements received little support from Spain, and when Russian fur traders set up a stockade named Rossiya about 100 miles north of San Francisco in 1812 and hoisted the Russian flag, the Spaniards were too weak to repel them. But after the sea otters—the principal source of revenue—had been virtually exterminated along the coast, the Czarist colony fell upon hard times. Farming and shipbuilding were tried and then given up as unprofitable. The settlement was finally evacuated in 1841, and the whole property, including French cannons abandoned by Napoleon on his retreat from Moscow, was sold for $30,000. John Sutter, the Swiss immigrant who bought it, had founded New Helvetia, later Sacramento, the state capital. The Russian village, now known as Fort Ross, has been restored and is open to visitors.

In 1822 Mexico won independence from Spain; three years later California voluntarily became a Mexican territory. Captain John C. Frémont, an American topographical engineer, established the Bear Flag republic in 1846. Two years later California was annexed by the United States at the conclusion of the Mexican War, and the Californians demanded statehood in 1849. The next year the territory became the thirty-first state.

Settlers were already arriving in prairie schooners from the East. One was James Wilson Marshall, who was hired to build a sawmill for John Sutter in the town of Coloma. Marshall found a gold nugget in January 1848, and the Gold Rush began. Thousands dropped their work to stake out claims; San Francisco was briefly deserted. Gold seekers came overland and by sea around the Horn, and the state's population grew from 15,000 in 1847 to 379,994 in 1860. In 1869 the first transcontinental railroad was completed, largely by imported Chinese laborers, and soon sale of land along the railroad right-of-way brought thousands more in a land rush. Waves of arrivals came again in the 1930's, from the dust bowl of Oklahoma and Arkansas; and following World War II the migrants from the rest of the nation doubled the population in 20 years.

Today California looks to education and industry for growth in the future. The state has a thoroughly democratic public-education system which assures tuition-free schooling from kindergarten through college. More than 80 junior colleges provide for nearly 460,000 students; nine campuses of the University of California carry an enrollment of about 86,000.

California's industrial and agricultural future depends on increasing its supply of available water; four fifths of the state's vast agricultural crop is produced on irrigated land. The $2.6 billion Feather River project will bring mountain water to dry southern areas—creating new arable ground, with more crops—and inevitably, an ever-growing population.

SAN FRANCISCO

California's northern metropolis has a gemlike setting: steep hills adorned with gleaming white buildings command breathtaking views of the bay, the Golden Gate Bridge and the coastal mountain ranges. San Francisco is one of the world's greatest seaports, as well as the leading banking and financial center west of Chicago. Its Chinatown is the largest Chinese settlement outside the Orient. The mixture of European, American and Asian cultures has created a fascinating cosmopolitan city, famous for its gay night life and excellent restaurants. Colorful cable cars that have clanged and crawled up and down steep streets since 1873 are busier than ever. At 5:13 a.m. on April 18, 1906, a violent earthquake followed by fire destroyed 30,000 buildings and virtually wiped out the business district, but the area was rebuilt within nine years. One reason for San Francisco's charm: it is miraculously free of heavy industry, although now surrounded by the sixth largest urban area in the United States. All the steel mills, oil refineries, shipyards and industrial plants lie to the south or across the bay. Ocean breezes and fogs create autumnlike temperatures the year round and the coolest summer climate of any large American city. (Pop. 740,316.)

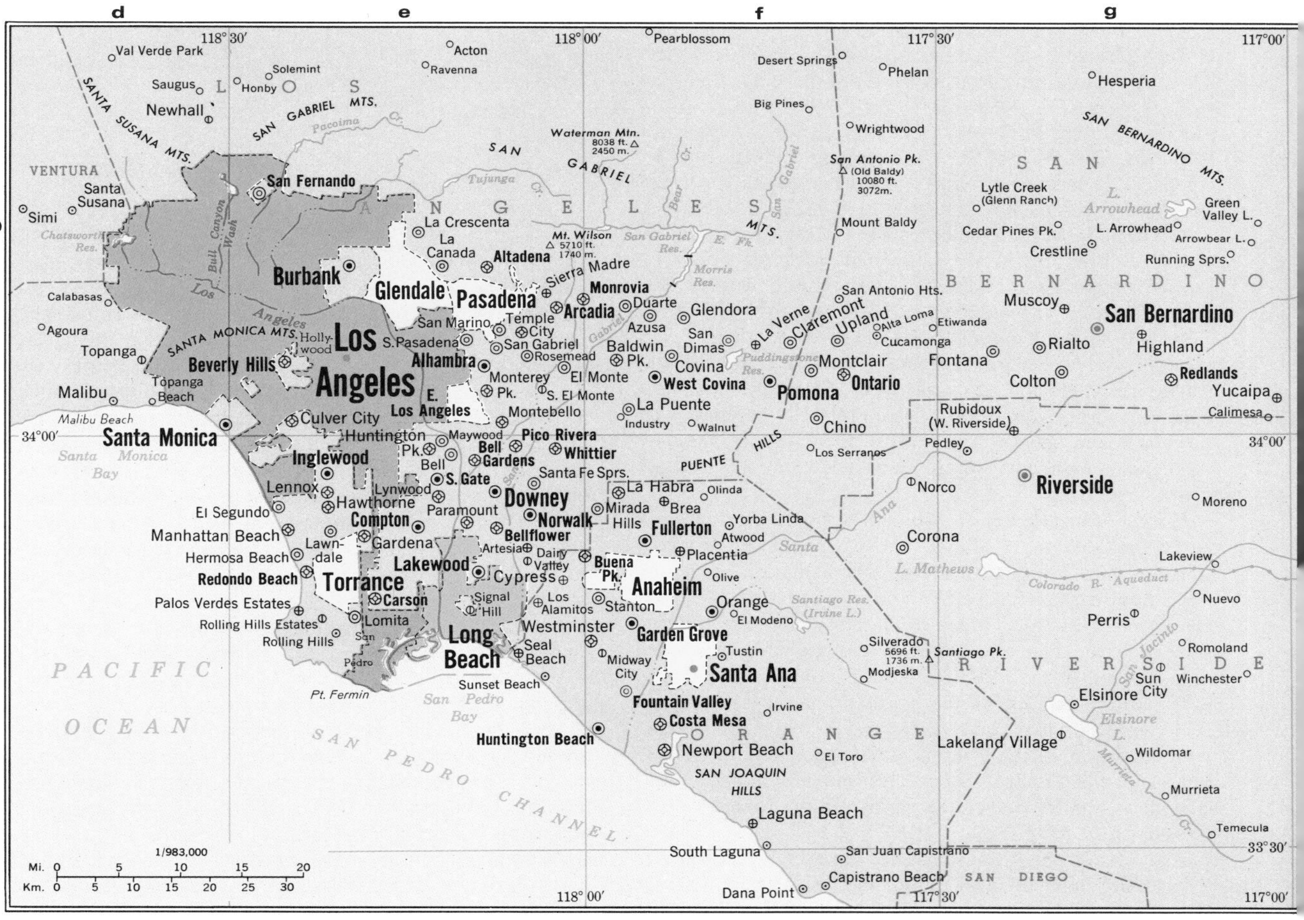

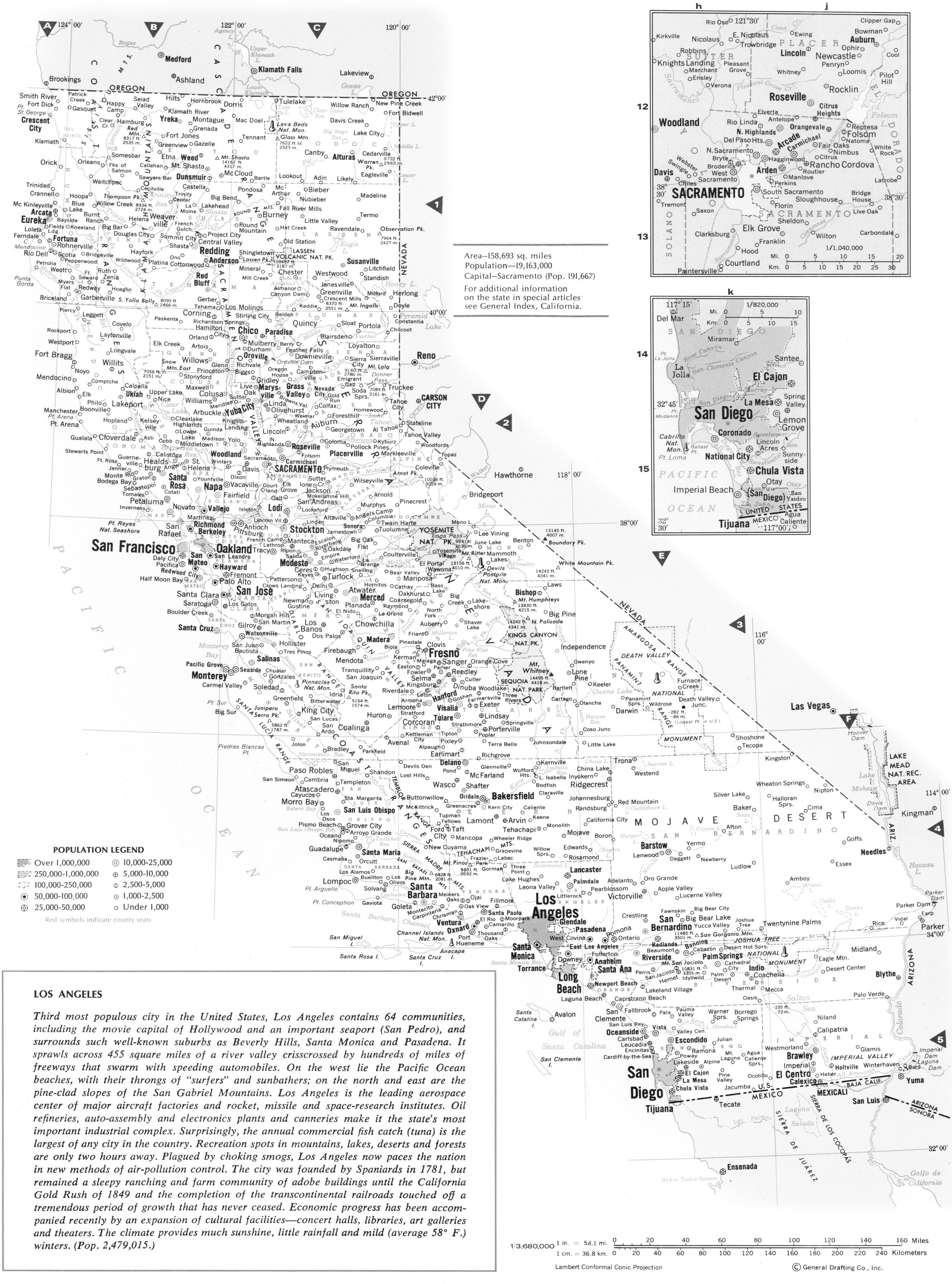

Area—158,693 sq. miles
Population—19,163,000
Capital—Sacramento (Pop. 191,667)

For additional information on the state in special articles see General Index, California.

LOS ANGELES

Third most populous city in the United States, Los Angeles contains 64 communities, including the movie capital of Hollywood and an important seaport (San Pedro), and surrounds such well-known suburbs as Beverly Hills, Santa Monica and Pasadena. It sprawls across 455 square miles of a river valley crisscrossed by hundreds of miles of freeways that swarm with speeding automobiles. On the west lie the Pacific Ocean beaches, with their throngs of "surfers" and sunbathers; on the north and east are the pine-clad slopes of the San Gabriel Mountains. Los Angeles is the leading aerospace center of major aircraft factories and rocket, missile and space-research institutes. Oil refineries, auto-assembly and electronics plants and canneries make it the state's most important industrial complex. Surprisingly, the annual commercial fish catch (tuna) is the largest of any city in the country. Recreation spots in mountains, lakes, deserts and forests are only two hours away. Plagued by choking smogs, Los Angeles now paces the nation in new methods of air-pollution control. The city was founded by Spaniards in 1781, but remained a sleepy ranching and farm community of adobe buildings until the California Gold Rush of 1849 and the completion of the transcontinental railroads touched off a tremendous period of growth that has never ceased. Economic progress has been accompanied recently by an expansion of cultural facilities—concert halls, libraries, art galleries and theaters. The climate provides much sunshine, little rainfall and mild (average 58° F.) winters. (Pop. 2,479,015.)

COLORADO

Heights dominate Colorado, which has the highest average elevation—6800 feet—in the nation. Even the lowest point, at the eastern edge, is 3350 feet. And of North America's 98 mountains reaching 14,000 feet or more, 54 lie in Colorado.

The state forms a tidy rectangle (sharing with adjacent Wyoming the distinction of having four absolutely straight borders) and its people are concentrated in a north-to-south panel. This lies between the arid, wind-eroded plains which stretch toward Kansas, and the towering Rocky Mountains.

Coronado, the first European to enter Colorado, sought gold there in 1540. A few other Spaniards followed during the next 250 years. In 1806 explorer Zebulon Pike gave his name to a snow-capped peak rising 5000 feet above the plains to a total height of 14,110 feet. "Pikes Peak or Bust" became a slogan for the drivers of ox-drawn wagons in the westward migration; today a quarter of a million motorists a year drive around the hairpin turns to the peak's summit. It remains Colorado's best-known mountain, though the state has 31 that soar higher. Mount Elbert, at 14,431 feet, is the tallest in all the Rockies—and Mount Evans, west of Denver, features the nation's highest auto road up to its 14,264-foot peak.

Mountains and forests have brought Colorado a tourist boom greater than the early Gold Rushes. Aspen, Central City, Estes Park and Colorado Springs are among the major playgrounds of the United States. Vacationists also can swim in natural warm-water pools surrounded by snow, roam the two National Parks and 12 National Forests, hunt deer or elk, cast for trout or jog along scenic trails on horseback. For the truly hardy there is mountain climbing.

Colorado's growing travel industry offers its 6,000,000 annual visitors wide variety: rodeos, tours of Indian cliff dwellings, winter-sports carnivals, Sahara-like sand dunes, fairs and fiestas, Buffalo Bill's grave, dude ranches, the rosy-tinted sandstone Garden of the Gods and the awesome Royal Gorge spanned by the world's highest bridge.

The adventurous can shoot the rapids of the shallow streams rushing down from the snowy peaks of the Rockies. More of the country's important rivers have their sources in Colorado than in any other state—among them the Arkansas, the North and South Platte, the Rio Grande. The state was named for the mighty Colorado River, with its vivid red stone gorges; Colorado is Spanish for "colored, red."

Rivers originating here not only water the farmlands of 19 states but also supply Colorado's network of canals and irrigation ditches, augmenting the meager 14- to 16-inch annual rainfall. Coöperative irrigation projects were formed as early as the 1870's. It was one of the sponsors of these, New York newspaperman Horace Greeley, who urged young men to "go west." The 1870's were a time of major expansion. In 1876, a century after the Declaration of Independence, Colorado was admitted to the Union as the thirty-eighth state.

Irrigation of the rich but dry soil has produced bountiful crops of sugar beets, wheat and other grains, fruits and especially potatoes. Cattle, sheep and poultry (particularly turkeys) rank high in economic importance. Meanwhile, industrial Colorado produces steel rails and mining machinery, as well as missile and aircraft parts.

The state's mineral resources include the nation's richest uranium deposits. Grand Junction, the focus of uranium operations on the Colorado plateau, is the western headquarters of the Atomic Energy Commission's raw-materials division. Climax Mine, near Leadville, is the world's largest source of molybdenum, vital for hardening steel. Lead, tungsten, zinc and copper are also important. Although gold, then silver, first brought prospectors flocking to Colorado, today these metals are mined largely as by-products of other ores.

The first Colorado Gold Rush—some 50,000 prospectors strong—came in 1859, one year after the precious metal was found at Cherry Creek, now the site of Denver. Nearby Central City, in the mining area, was once called "the richest square mile on earth." A major silver strike diverted wealth seekers for several years after 1877, until a second gold boom in the Cripple Creek area in 1891.

Colorado's underground wealth is not limited to metals. Coal underlies perhaps one quarter of the state; the oil-shale deposits in the Colorado River Valley are among the world's richest (yielding more than 15 gallons of petroleum per ton of shale rock), and vast reserves of natural gas are being tapped by pipelines.

Wide-open spaces surround a few population clusters. Almost a million of Colorado's 1,977,000 people live in and around Denver. The second city and industrial center, Pueblo, has a population of only some 90,000 and Colorado Springs about 70,000.

Near Colorado Springs is the headquarters of NORAD (North American Air Defense Command), charged with protecting the continent against air attack. It jointly involves the Royal Canadian Air Force and the U.S. Air Force, Army and Navy. The combat operations center lies 1500 feet under Cheyenne Mountain outside of the city. Nearby is the "West Point of the Air," the U.S. Air Force Academy, which was established there in 1958. As further symbols of the times, more than 150 civil and military airports dot the state's rugged terrain.

Once away from these centers, Colorado retains the flavor of its Kit Carson and mining-town past; many communities—such as Bonanza and Mayday, Paradox and Hesperus, Snowmass and Powderhorn—number their inhabitants by the score or sometimes by the handful. And only some hundreds live in Fairplay, Hygiene, Hasty and Manassa—there are more than 200 towns with fewer than 2500 persons. Still common are false-front stores and frame buildings lining an unpaved main street. Yesterday's frontier persists on the state's Rocky Mountain slopes, where black bears and bobcats outnumber men, and on the grassy plateaus and wooded mesas.

DENVER

Nicknamed the Mile High City because of its altitude, Denver has a dramatic western backdrop provided by the Front Range of the Rocky Mountains. Starting as four ramshackle mining towns hurriedly built on the South Platte River during the disappointing gold discoveries of 1858, the city later served as a base camp for miners who struck out west to gold and silver fields. Today tourists are attracted by the sparkling vitality of the dry, sunny climate and by the proximity to mountain scenery rivaling that of the Alps. One hundred parks are included within the city boundaries; a gold-domed capitol looms over an outstanding art museum, the State Historical Museum and the imposing Civic Center. Since World War II many Federal government bureaus have been established here and in nearby Boulder. A huge Titan missile plant and companies specializing in electronics and spacecraft products have spurred the economy and brought a sense of tomorrow to the pioneer city.

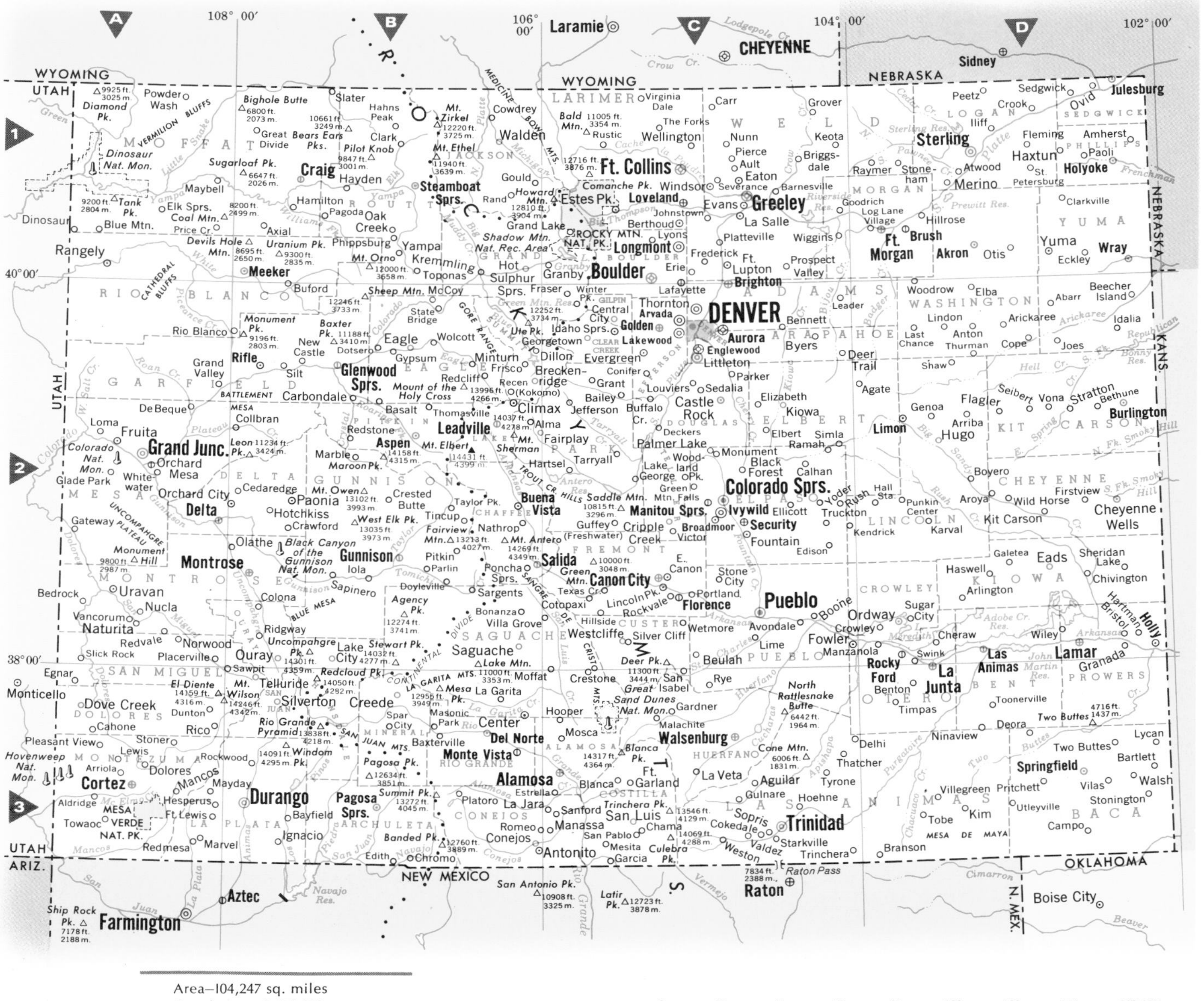

Area—104,247 sq. miles
Population—1,975,000
Capital—Denver (Pop. 493,887)

For additional information on the state in special articles see General Index, Colorado.

13,570,000 1 in. = 56.3 mi. 0 20 40 60 80 100 120 140 160 Miles
1 cm. = 35.7 km. 0 20 40 60 80 100 120 140 160 180 200 220 240 Kilometers

Lambert Conformal Conic Projection

© General Drafting Co., Inc.

POPULATION LEGEND

- Over 1,000,000
- 250,000-1,000,000
- 100,000-250,000
- 50,000-100,000
- 25,000-50,000
- 10,000-25,000
- 5,000-10,000
- 2,500-5,000
- 1,000-2,500
- Under 1,000

Red symbols indicate county seats

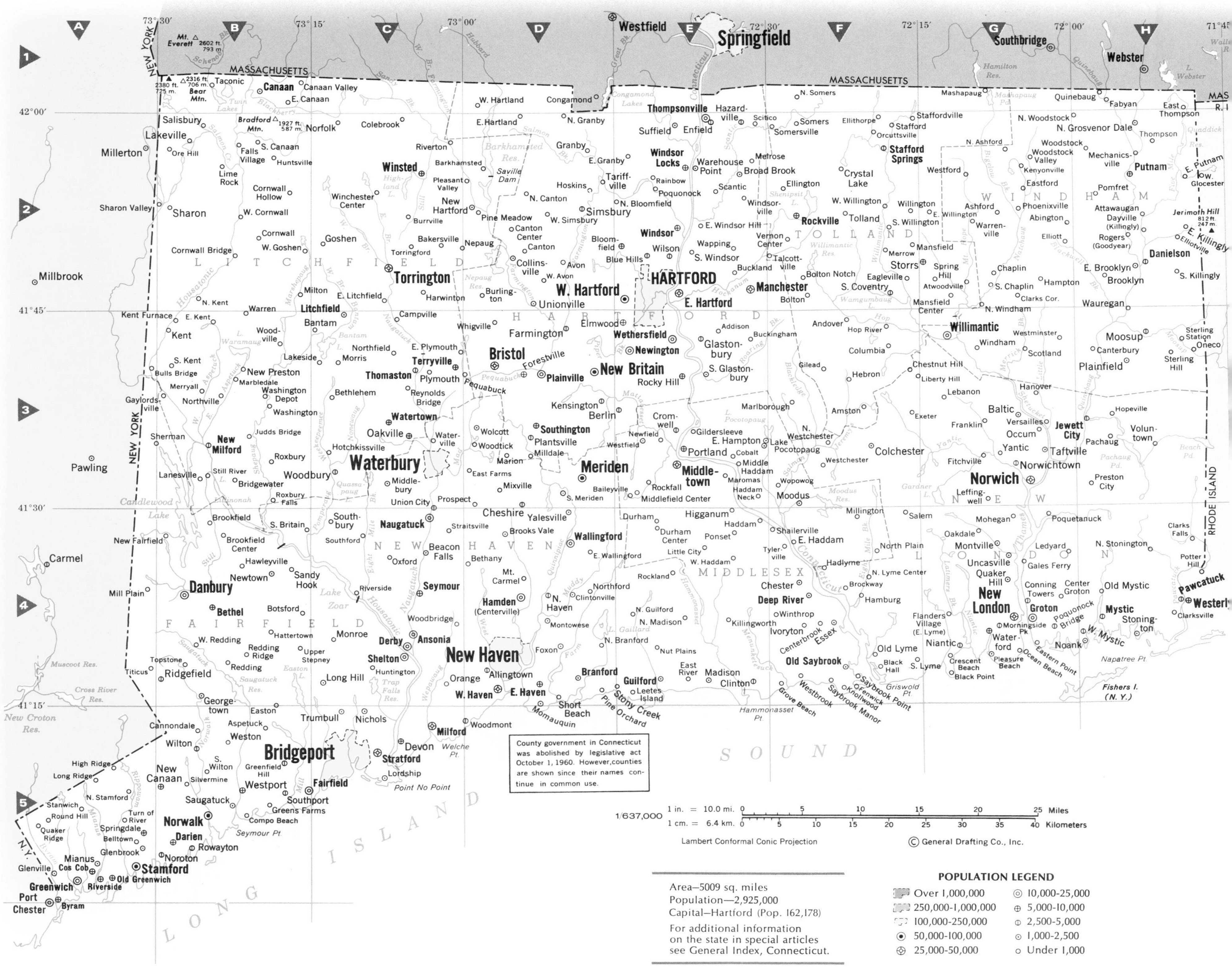

CONNECTICUT

At night the sky around Salisbury glowed as if it were reflecting an eternal inferno; by day the sky was yellowed by the smudge from the furnaces and the enormous charcoal pits; day and night the whole area was haunted by the ominous grunts of the furnace bellows and the unearthly screech of the revolving waterwheels.

—WILLIAM STORRS LEE, The Yankees of Connecticut

• • •

This was the scene in northwestern Connecticut during the American Revolution. Iron furnaces and forges were pouring out cannon barrels, tons of cannonballs and shot and shell for Washington's army and for American fighting ships.

From Connecticut ports and harbors along Long Island Sound, small privateers, even some whaleboats, put out at night to harass, raid and plunder British schooners bound for New York. On dark nights, patriots such as Nathan Hale were landed behind British lines on Long Island. Benedict Arnold, then a daring American officer of untarnished honor, rode a plunging horse through the ranks of Redcoats to avenge a British raid on Danbury. More than 30,000 men from Connecticut joined the Continental Army. So much forage and farm produce were supplied to the quartermaster corps that Washington himself dubbed Connecticut "the Provision State."

Ever since its founding, the third smallest state in the Union has contributed far more than its share to the defense and growth of the United States. Sons of Connecticut, tinkering with all sorts of gadgets and machinery, have come up with inventions that changed the world's way of life and affected the course of its history.

Eli Whitney made cotton the king of the American South with the cotton gin; in his gun factory, he evolved the concept of interchangeable parts, which was to lead to the American brand of mass production. Seth Thomas invented the modern clock. The first practical American steamboat was constructed by a young native named John Fitch. Another, Linus Yale, developed the modern lock, and Charles Goodyear discovered the process that made it possible to vulcanize rubber. Connecticut now leads the nation in the production of nuclear submarines, helicopters and silverware. Yale University, fourth oldest institution of higher learning in the United States, founded in 1701, continues to play a dominant role in education.

The valley of the Connecticut River, navigable as far as the region of Hartford, was first explored in 1614 by the Dutch captain Adriaen Block and attracted English settlers from the Massachusetts Bay Colony between 1630 and 1660. In its rich farmlands they raised fine tobacco leaf and vegetables for the markets of New Haven and New York. The river and deepwater harbors of Long Island Sound soon made Connecticut a dominant force in the American colonies. During the second half of the eighteenth century, when West Indies trade was at its height, New London and Mystic were crowded with white-sailed, square-rigged merchant ships loading and discharging their cargoes. Later, whalers departed frequently on Pacific and South Sea voyages.

For nearly three centuries Long Island Sound, with 253 miles of Connecticut coastline, was the major commercial route linking Boston with New York, and New England with the Middle Atlantic regions. The era of the steamboat introduced the greatest fleet of inland vessels the world has ever known, churning along the Sound and up the Connecticut River to Hartford.

But now the Sound lies gray and woefully deserted all winter, save for an occasional oil barge. With the coming of spring it is transformed into a private ocean for sailing craft and cabin cruisers. Yacht clubs and beaches have made suburban strips of Connecticut's shore some of the most sought-after and expensive real estate on the East Coast. Between New Haven and Greenwich thousands of citizens commute daily by car and train to New York. Thousands more work in the manufacturing centers of Bridgeport, Hartford, Waterbury and New Haven.

Despite its suburbias, more than half of Connecticut is covered by forest. In its hilly northern regions some former pasturelands have become ski centers.

HARTFORD

A handsome, well-planned city on the west bank of the Connecticut River, 50 miles inland from Long Island Sound, Hartford lies in a beautiful valley surrounded by gently rolling woodlands. English colonists from Massachusetts established a permanent settlement in 1635 on the site of a small fort built by Dutch fur traders who had explored the river two years earlier. Once a busy steamboat port, the city has become industrially important, with factories for airplane engines and propellers, firearms, typewriters, brushes and precision machine tools. When the four-day Wall Street fire of December 1835 destroyed 650 buildings in New York, Eliphalet Terry, president of a Hartford insurance company, pledged his personal fortune at his bank and drove to New York in a sleigh to pay off all claims in full. His action was one factor in giving Hartford companies a reputation for reliability, and today the city is known as the insurance capital of the United States, with 30 companies having total assets of almost $21.5 billion.

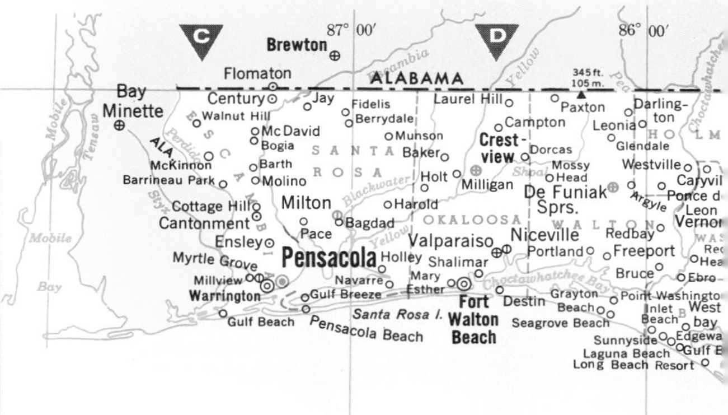

DELAWARE

Diminutive Delaware, smallest state in the Union except Rhode Island, has played a surprisingly large role in revolutionizing not only the American way of life but the lives of peoples around the globe. For decades the du Pont company dominated the world munitions industry, and du Pont nylon has transformed the textile business. There is scarcely a corner of the globe that does not benefit from products manufactured in Delaware.

Although it resembles a tiny wedge on most maps, the contrasts within Delaware's own boundaries are equally startling. Wilmington, the largest city, is one of the most extraordinary manufacturing centers on the Atlantic Coast. In nearby Dover, the capital, are the legal homes of some 50,000 U.S. companies incorporated under Delaware's liberal tax and business laws. Yet less than 50 miles away in the downstate counties are small, neat towns; tranquil, white-mansioned estates adorned with boxwood and rose gardens; tiny fishing villages and farm communities; lonely salt marshes and white sand beaches that appear to be untouched by the rapid tempo of the twentieth century.

Even in its agricultural products, Delaware specializes in the unexpected. Although three fifths of the state is fertile land whose corn, tomatoes and soybeans find a ready market, the Delaware farmer's biggest money-maker is the three-pound spring, or broiler, chicken. One hundred and fifty million of them account annually for 60 percent of the total current farm income.

Delaware's low-lying, lightly forested shores near the Atlantic were among the first to be explored and settled by European colonists. In August 1609, Henry Hudson, the English navigator commissioned by the Dutch East India Company to search for a passage to China and the Indies, discovered both New York's Hudson River and the Delaware Bay and River. The Dutch first named the Hudson the "North River" and the Delaware the "South River," laying claim to all of the 10,000 square miles in between. By 1624 New Netherlands trading posts had been established at Fort Amsterdam (New York City) on the Hudson and at Fort Nassau (Gloucester, New Jersey) on the Delaware.

The Delaware region soon attracted another European power: Sweden. Fort Christina, named after the Queen of Sweden, was founded in 1638 on the present site of Wilmington. The Swedish colonists purchased, from the local Indian tribes, all the land on the western shore of Delaware Bay and upriver as far as Trenton. Cattle, sheep, horses and farming equipment were brought across the Atlantic, and soon Swedish forts, blockhouses and trading posts were sprinkled up and down the river and bay. Friendly relations were established with the Indians. Land was cultivated. Gristmills, houses, wharves and small factories were built. It is not generally known that these Swedish colonists of Delaware built the first log houses on American soil. In contrast to the clapboard homes of New England and the brick and stone structures of the Dutch and the Virginia colonists, these were found so suitable for pioneering life in a forested country that they were adopted in many American settlements.

For ten years Governor Johan Printz, a former cavalry officer whose epic bulk caused the Indians to name him "the Big Tub," battled with enormous determination to maintain Sweden's control over the Delaware region, but the fertile soil, mild climate and strategic waterways proved far too desirable to be held without endless struggles and skirmishes. Control shifted to the Dutch, then to the English, and the area finally became part of William Penn's colony. In 1704 the "lower counties," as Delaware was called, were separated from Pennsylvania with Penn's consent because they wanted self-government under their own elected assembly.

Delaware's regiments fought valiantly in Washington's armies throughout the Revolution, although they were unable to prevent the British from seizing Wilmington and Philadelphia. In 1787 this was the first state to ratify the American Constitution. After the war the new state prospered. By the time the first of the du Ponts, a young French immigrant named Eleuthère Irénée du Pont, had established a small gunpowder mill on Brandywine Creek near Wilmington in 1802, leather tanneries, textile works and factories for manufacturing nails, snuff, paper, carriages and iron were going full blast. A canal connecting Delaware Bay with Chesapeake Bay, originally planned by the Swedes in 1654, was finally completed in 1829, thereby providing a safe inland-waterway route between Philadelphia, Wilmington and Baltimore. After the Civil War, in which Delaware furnished 13,000 Union troops, construction of a main-line railroad through Wilmington tended to industrialize the city and the upper corner of the little state. The bypassed downstate counties remained primarily quiet rural communities devoted to farming, fishing and country living. The building of the Chesapeake Bay Bridge, linking lower Delaware and Maryland's Eastern Shore with Annapolis and Baltimore, and the completion of the tunnel-bridge system across the mouth of the bay have now placed southern Delaware on main routes of north-and-south travel and will undoubtedly bring major changes to this part of the state.

MIAMI

A spectacle of glittering white skyscrapers, exotically landscaped private homes, palm-lined boulevards and spreading suburbs, Miami and its neighboring community, Miami Beach, draw more vacationists than any other resort city in the United States. A year-round playground for sunning and swimming, its attractions also include racetracks, nightclubs, yachting, sports fishing and sightseeing. But besides tourism, Miami also boasts light industries (electronics, boats, wearing apparel), a busy seaport and one of the world's great international airports. It is a major crossroads for trade and transportation between the United States and Latin America and the West Indies. The region consisted of little more than mangrove swamps, sand dunes and palmetto barrens until Florida's famous builder and promoter, Henry Flagler, pushed a railroad line south from West Palm Beach in 1896, built the first resort hotel and financed Miami's development. Smogless, it has the most winter sunshine of any Eastern city. (Pop. 291,688.)

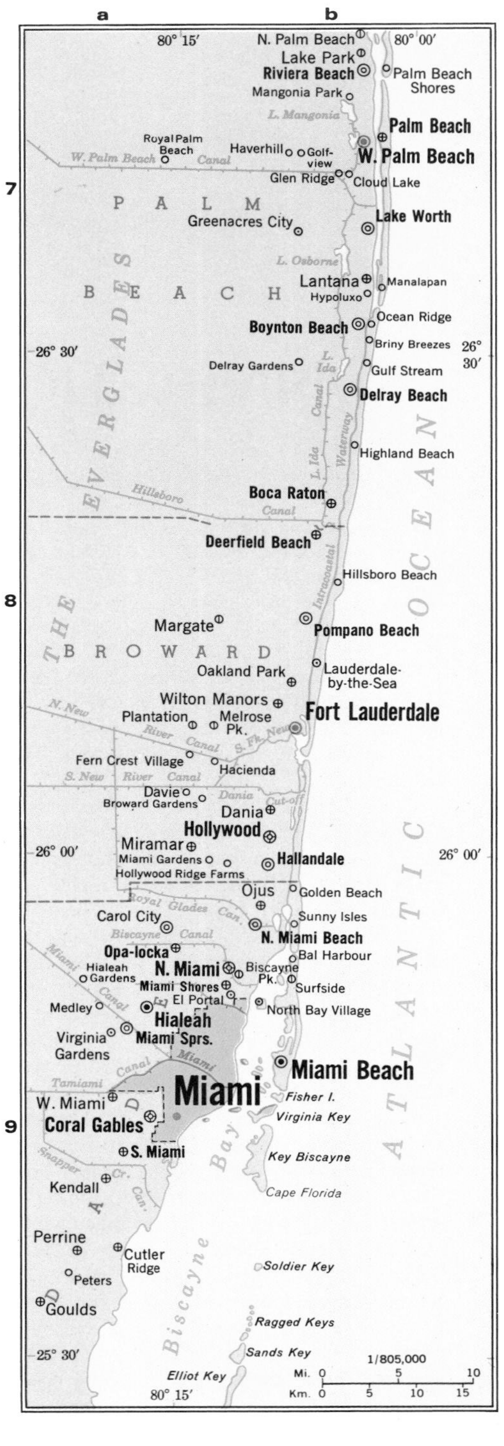

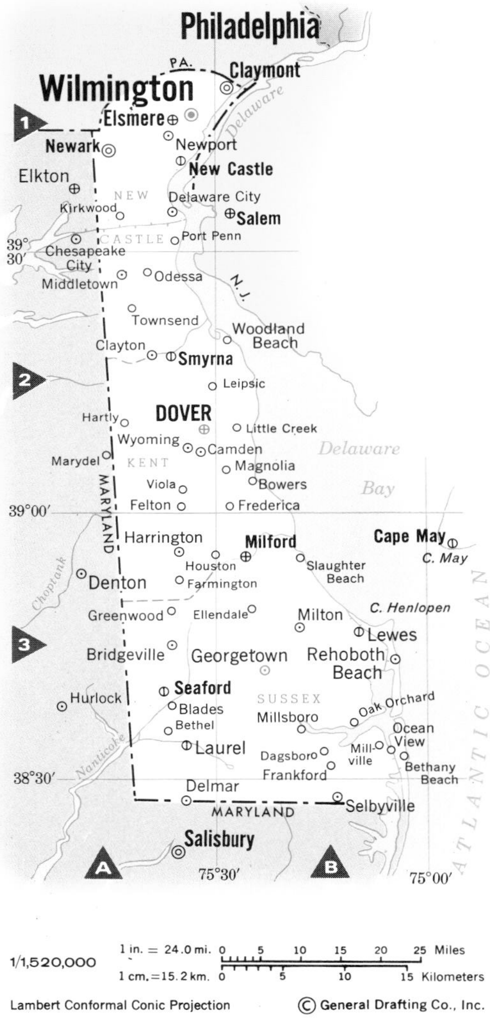

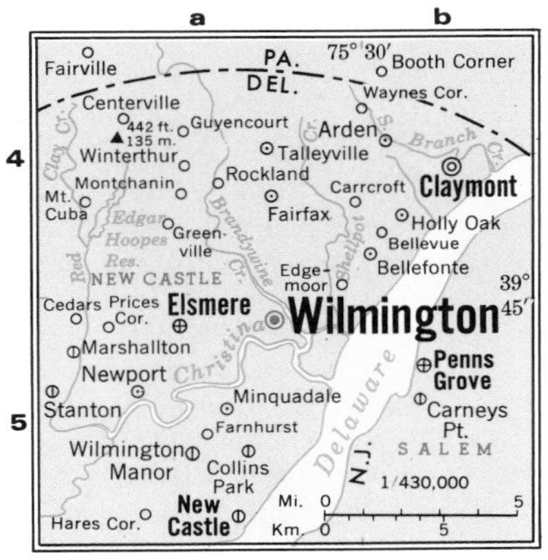

WILMINGTON

Situated on the west bank of the Delaware River in the northern tip of the state, Wilmington is surrounded by a tremendous industrial and commercial complex of docks, shipyards, rail yards and the plants and factories of more than 300 corporations whose products range from matches to computers for spacecraft. Its waterfront handles the cargoes of oceangoing freighters from around the globe. An array of giant chemical installations has earned the city the title of "Chemical Capital of the World." The first iron steamer to be constructed in the United States was launched there in 1836. Before the Civil War, Quakers who took a strong antislavery stand made Wilmington an important stop on the Underground Railway. (Pop. 95,827.)

Area—2057 sq. miles
Population—523,000
Capital—Dover (Pop. 7250)
For additional information on the state in special articles see General Index, Delaware.

POPULATION LEGEND

Over 1,000,000
250,000-1,000,000
100,000-250,000
50,000-100,000
25,000-50,000
10,000-25,000
5,000-10,000
2,500-5,000
1,000-2,500
Under 1,000

Red symbols indicate county seats

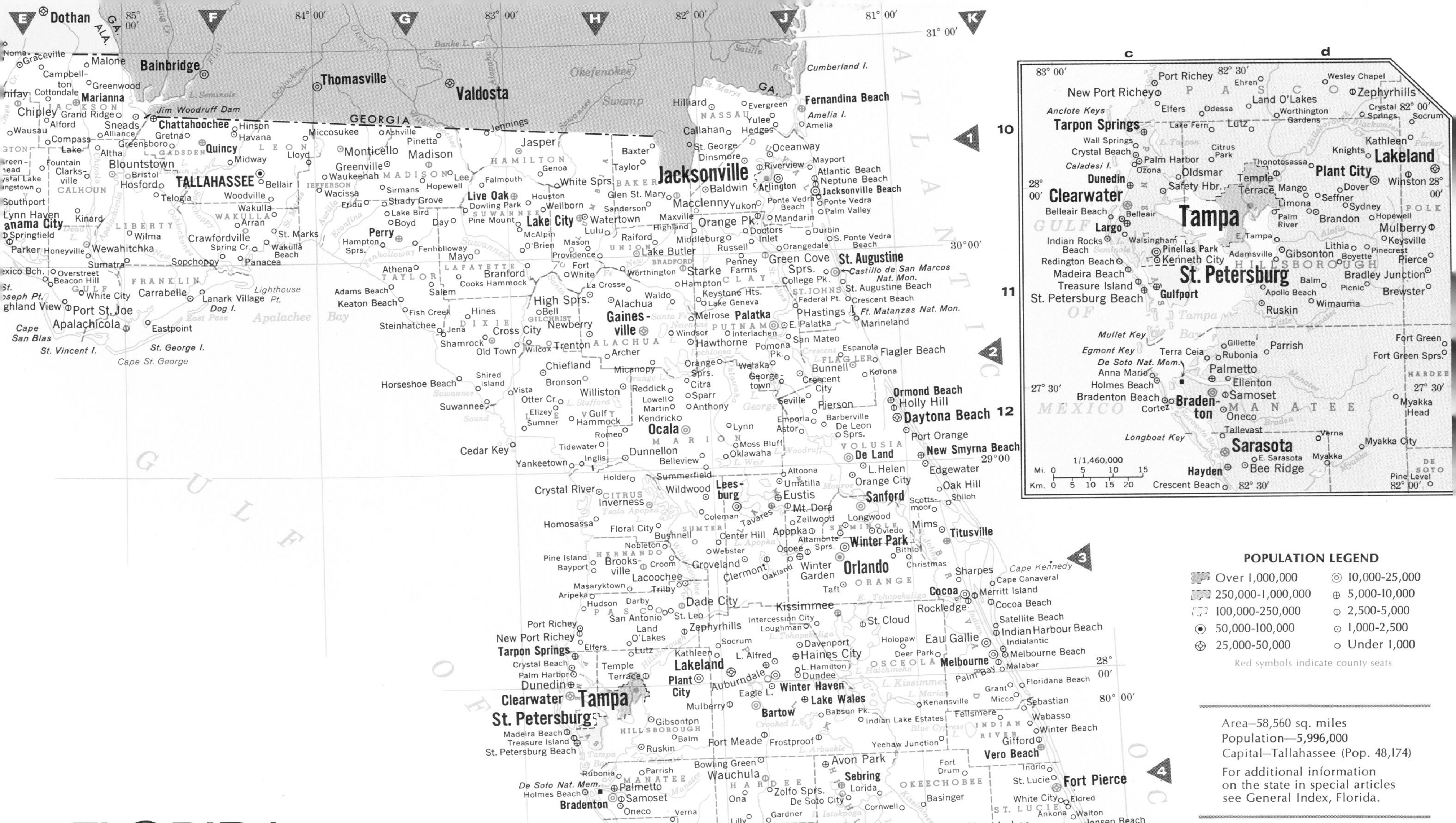

FLORIDA

Who doesn't know all about Florida? Some of the facts are quite surprising. Its northern boundary is 100 miles farther south than the southern boundary of California. The eastern beach on the Atlantic is farther west than Buffalo, New York. Most of the state lies due south of Ohio and Indiana and the extreme western corner reaches a point only a few miles east of Chicago. Florida is also far larger than most people realize: 367 miles across its northern boundary and 500 miles long as it juts southward in a giant peninsula. It is bigger than New York or Pennsylvania. Actually, only one state east of the Mississippi River—Georgia—is greater in size.

Everyone is aware of the space-rocket center at Cape Kennedy where astronauts are launched into orbit. Here, too, "Moonport, U.S.A." will be the takeoff point for the first historic manned flights to the moon. Yet 75 years ago, most of the east coast was an unexplored wilderness of magnificent beaches and jungle glades inhabited by alligators, rattlesnakes, cougars, deer and tropical birds.

It was not until the 1880's that fortune finally smiled on Florida. For nearly four centuries this corner of the North American continent, blessed with a balmy, subtropical climate, fertile soils and a wealth of natural riches, lagged behind the other colonies and states as the tide of migration and expansion moved westward. Ponce de León and his Spaniards discovered the territory (1513), butchered and enslaved the Indian tribes and established the first permanent settlement, St. Augustine (1565). They also introduced horses, oranges and lemons, figs and sugarcane to Florida, and found the prairies ideal for raising cattle. English and French colonists harassed the Spanish, with England finally emerging the dominant power. During the American Revolution, Florida was the only loyal British province south of Canada. After the war Spain returned to Florida, but finally ceded it to the United States in 1819. The Americans devoted the nineteenth century to subduing the Seminole Indians. (Those in the Everglades today were the last American Indians to sign a treaty with the United States.) Negro slave labor cleared the land for cotton and sugarcane plantations and orange groves in the western part of the state.

During the Civil War, Florida served as a major food-supply base for Confederate troops. The bitter turbulence of the postwar Reconstruction period slowed the state's development so that, as late as 1890, Key West with a population of only 18,000 was Florida's largest city. Toward the turn of the century the railroads opened up the beautiful low-lying peninsula with its 30,000 lakes, hundreds of rivers and 1500 miles of beaches. After World War I, the famous Florida real-estate boom brought hundreds of thousands of land speculators and settlers. In one year—1925—as many as 2,500,000 people entered Florida.

Although the land boom collapsed, Florida soon rallied and since 1940 has been one of the fastest-growing states in the Union. It now leads California in

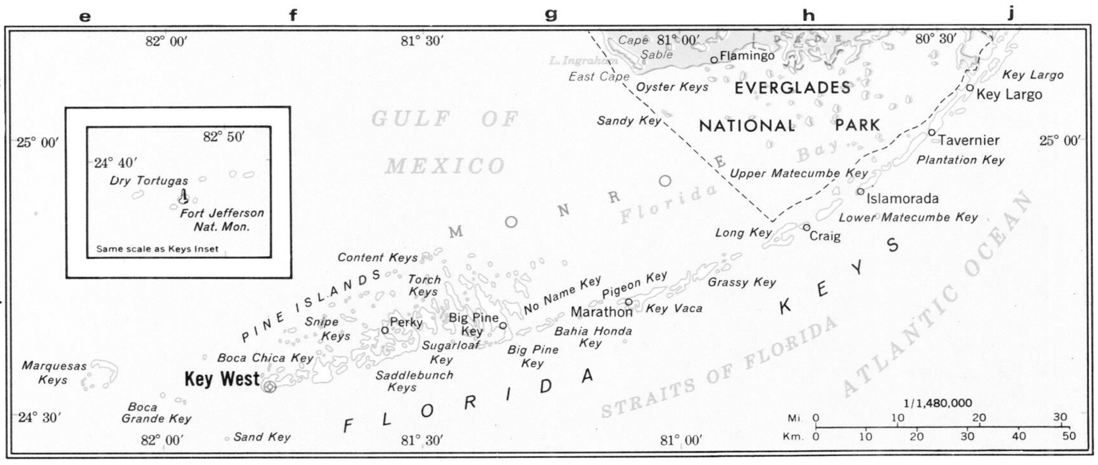

the production of citrus crops and some market vegetables. Surprisingly, it also vies with Western states such as Wyoming in the production of beef cattle on inland ranches and grazing lands. The commercial fisheries and forest-product industries are among the foremost in the nation. Space-age technology and the development of Cape Kennedy have boomed the east-coast region all the way from Jacksonville to Miami. But tourism, worth two and a half billion dollars a year, is the state's largest industry. Jet airliners have made Florida the favorite year-round vacation resort for people dwelling as far away as New England, Canada and Denver. In midwinter Florida is usually sunny and green, with temperatures varying from mild to comfortably warm, when most of the country is blanketed with snow and ice or plagued by dismally gray, rainy days. February is the peak tourist month; another tide sweeps in during the traditional vacation months from June to September.

GEORGIA

In times when progress passes old traditions by—and often loses its way in the process—Georgia provides an example of how to have both. Few states have made more astonishing advances in the last two decades; fewer have more jealously guarded their past and the signposts embedded in it. Though there is mammoth new industry among the magnolias and a Western cattle husbandry thrives on converted cotton fields, antebellum social graces are still practiced. The rose festivals continue. Stately big houses and quiet streets are preserved. And Georgians give the impression that they know where they're going because they know where they've been.

Georgia never comfortably fitted the sleepy Deep South stereotype. The largest state east of the Mississippi, it has long shown the leadership that made it the Empire State of the South. It was first to send a woman to the Senate, to grant women full property rights, to give the vote to 18-year-olds. Since World War II, Georgia has increased the value of its manufactured products by nine times, twice the national average.

The state has been endowed with a rich bequest in the form of many natural resources. The variety of the soil—sandy red clay, sandy loam and limestone—is such that it could produce nearly every crop grown in the temperate zone. Brief, mild winters and long, warm summers with plentiful rainfall provide an equable climate. The land is amply wooded, largely by pine, which grows to a height responsible for the expression "tall as a Georgia pine."

The topography of Georgia ranges from a 150-mile-wide shelf of flatland on the coast to a rolling plateau area, with Appalachian and Blue Ridge peaks in the north. Signs of an old shoreline where the ocean once lapped against the plateau bluffs can still be seen. When the waters receded from the flats—which are only 500 feet above sea level—they left the red soil for which the state is famous. The ocean did not withdraw entirely; some of it stayed in the huge primeval Okefenokee Swamp, a populous wildlife refuge shared with Florida.

De Soto crossed Georgia in 1540. French settlers in 1564 were succeeded by the Spanish and later by the English. James Oglethorpe, their leader, named the land—last of the 13 colonies and later the fourth state—for King George II. Three months after Savannah was founded in February 1733, the first non-English immigrants arrived: Italian Piedmontese to teach the colonists to cultivate silkworms. The venture was not successful. Other Europeans followed, seeking political and religious freedom. Oglethorpe had originally banned slavery, but in 1749 the colony's trustees acceded to pressure from the settlers and reversed his ruling.

During the Revolutionary War, Georgians clashed with the British in small-scale encounters. The first great battle of the Civil War fought in the state was at Chickamauga in September 1863. The following spring General William T. Sherman began an extensive campaign in northern Georgia and occupied Atlanta. His troops set fire to the city and began their march to the sea, cutting a 60-mile swath of destruction. They left a heritage of resentment that has been long in subsiding. The old one-crop economy was intimately linked with the paternalistic attitude toward Negro labor that picked the cotton. Since 1961 Georgia has ceased major resistance to school integration and has more Negro legislators than any other Southern state.

Industrial modernization, which technically began with Eli Whitney's invention of the cotton gin in 1793, accelerated when synthetic-textile plants left New England to settle in Georgia; textiles are now the biggest industry. Aircraft plants have come, and chemical works. Gigantic paper mills, some with pulping machines longer than a city block, moved in to take advantage of the state's easily reforested pines. Half the world's supply of naval stores—turpentine and rosins—come from these trees. Cotton, still the chief cash crop, gave way in large part to forage growth for purebred Herefords and Black Angus cattle from the west. Mockingbirds now sing over "Western" ranches. Tobacco, corn and peanuts were planted to diversify agriculture. Georgia is no longer first in peach-growing (California is), but does lead the nation in raising broiler chickens, peanuts, pecans and pimientos. Other major production ranges from china clays and baseball bats to peppermint sticks and granite.

But Georgia remains rooted in its old customs. Hominy grits, sweet potatoes, corn bread, fried chicken, peaches and turnip greens continue to be favorite foods, and many families eat black-eyed peas and hog jowl on New Year's Day for good luck. In sun-blessed villages, farmers congregate on Saturday afternoons at courthouses where statues of Confederate soldiers stand guard.

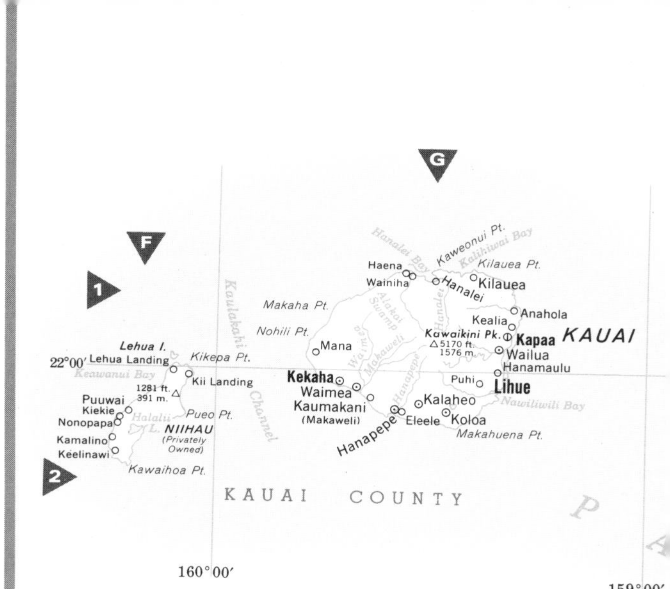

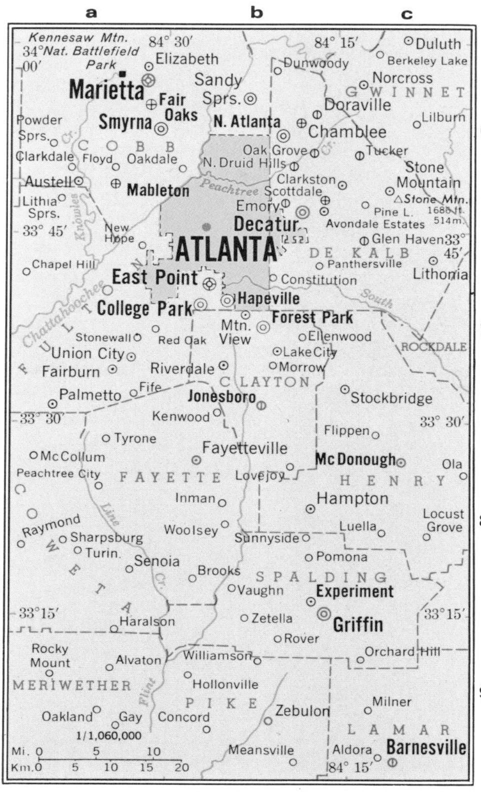

ATLANTA

Named Terminus in 1837 when a young surveyor drove a stake into the moist red earth to mark the end of a projected railroad in northwest Georgia, Atlanta now is served by seven railways and seven airlines. As the commercial and financial heart of the Southeast, it draws business from all over the United States. Some 400 of the nation's 500 leading firms have branch offices in Atlanta. Although burned to the ground during the Civil War, the city and its economy were quickly rebuilt by energetic Atlantans; within five years the population doubled. In 1868 Atlanta became Georgia's capital. Northern investments helped make it the trading center of the New South. Coca-Cola originated in Atlanta in 1886, but the city is also well known for paper, meat products and textiles. Peachtree Street, the city's main thoroughfare, symbolizes progress with one of the highest skyscrapers in the South, the 41-story First National Bank. It stands in the downtown banking area known as Five Points, also called "the Wall Street of the South."

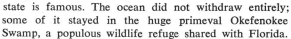

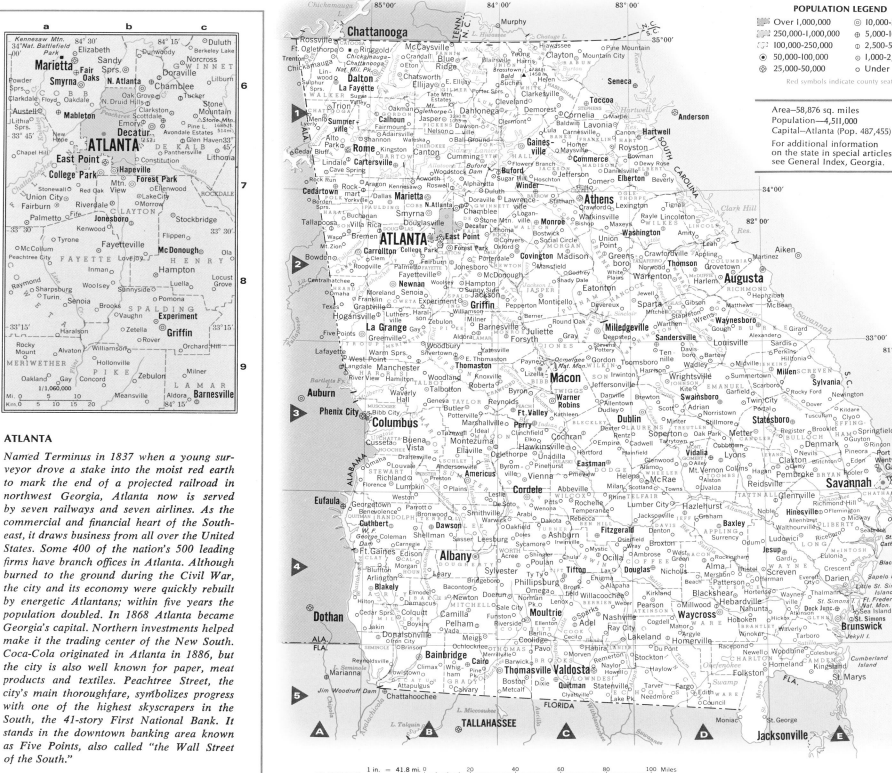

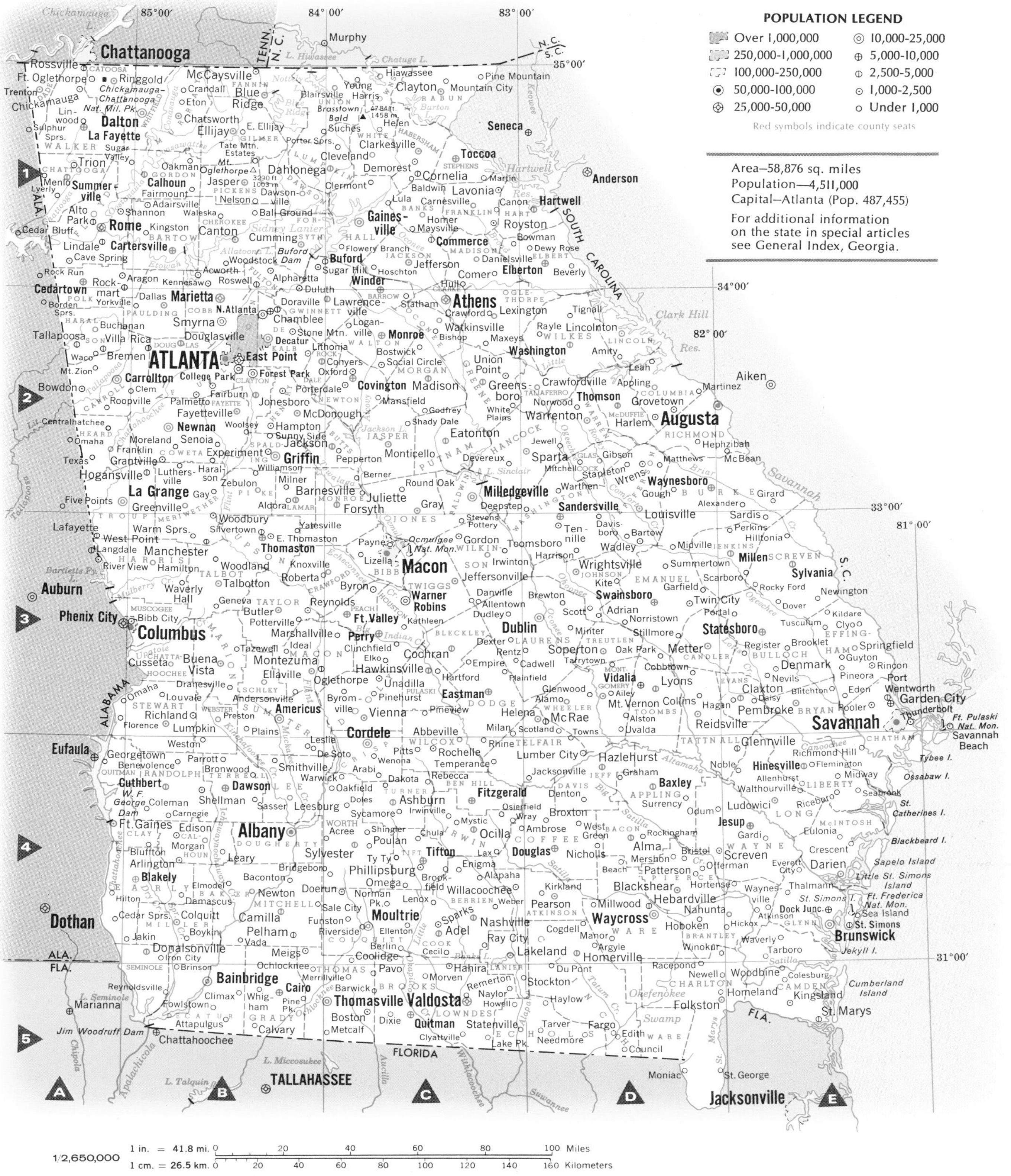

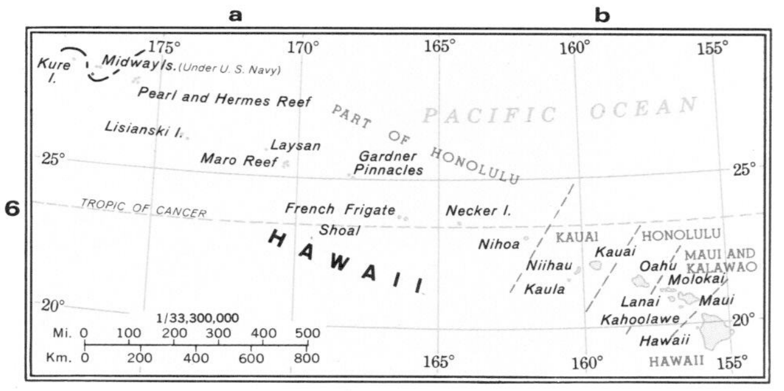

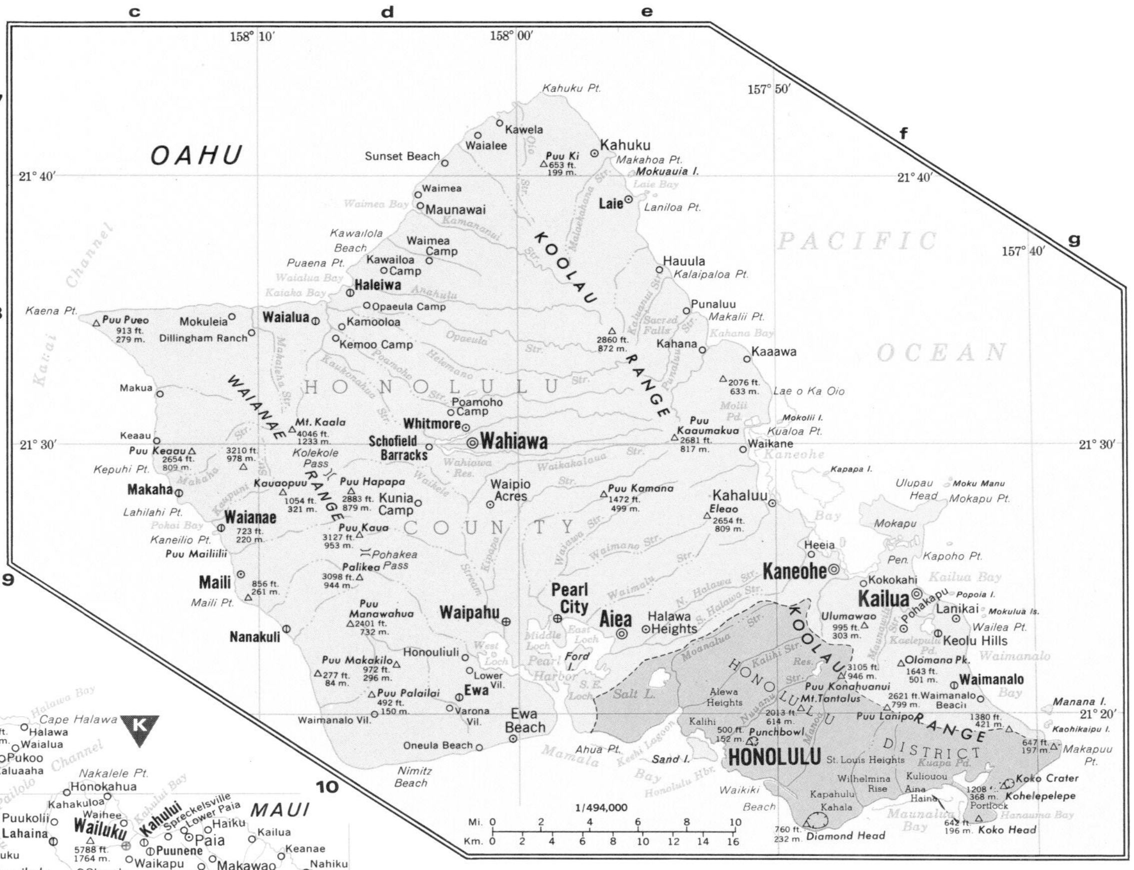

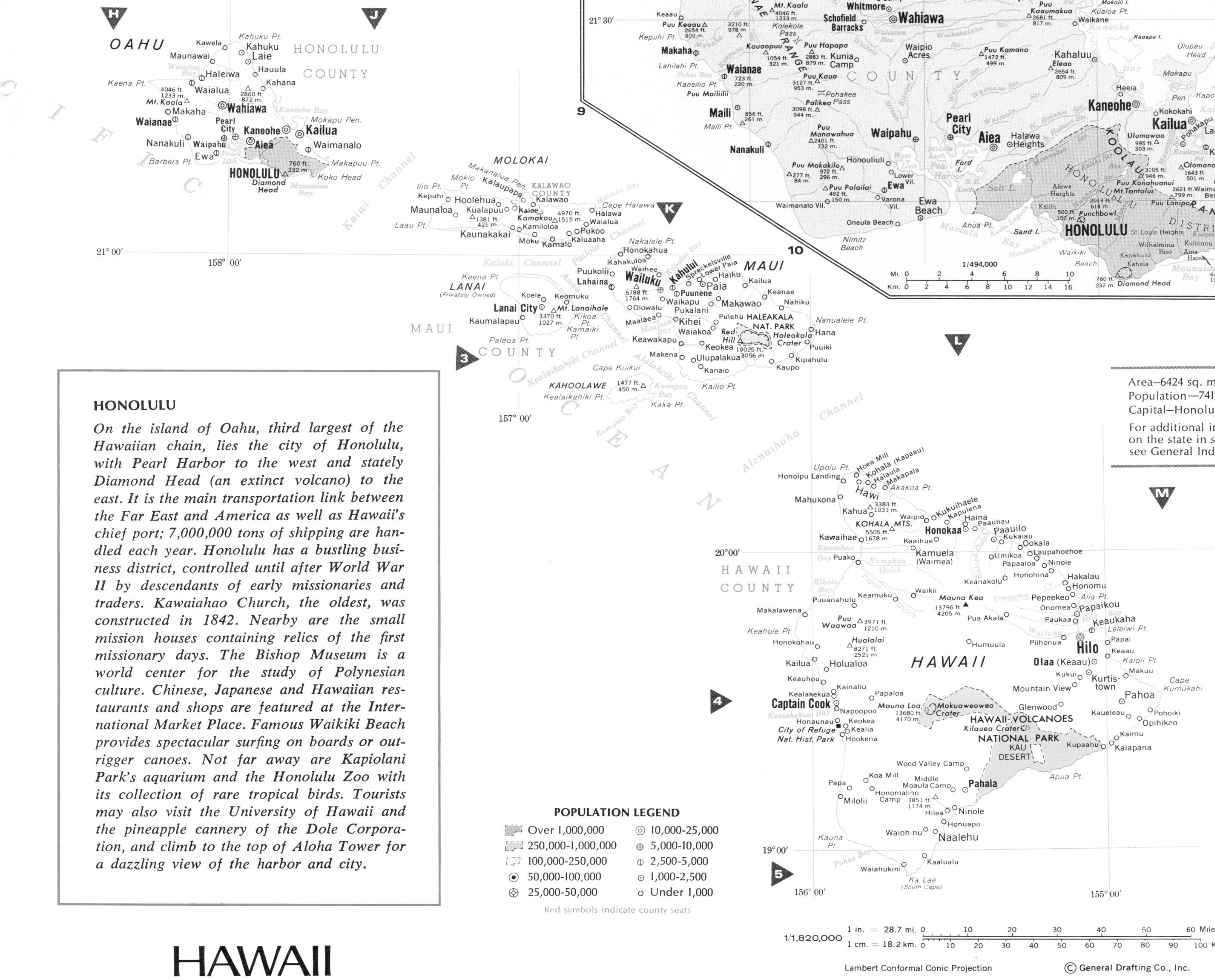

HONOLULU

On the island of Oahu, third largest of the Hawaiian chain, lies the city of Honolulu, with Pearl Harbor to the west and stately Diamond Head (an extinct volcano) to the east. It is the main transportation link between the Far East and America as well as Hawaii's chief port; 7,000,000 tons of shipping are handled each year. Honolulu has a bustling business district, controlled until after World War II by descendants of early missionaries and traders. Kawaiahao Church, the oldest, was constructed in 1842. Nearby are the small mission houses containing relics of the first missionary days. The Bishop Museum is a world center for the study of Polynesian culture. Chinese, Japanese and Hawaiian restaurants and shops are featured at the International Market Place. Famous Waikiki Beach provides spectacular surfing on boards or outrigger canoes. Not far away are Kapiolani Park's aquarium and the Honolulu Zoo with its collection of rare tropical birds. Tourists may also visit the University of Hawaii and the pineapple cannery of the Dole Corporation, and climb to the top of Aloha Tower for a dazzling view of the harbor and city.

Area—6424 sq. miles
Population—741,000
Capital—Honolulu (Pop. 294,194)

For additional information on the state in special articles see General Index, Hawaii.

HAWAII

The fiftieth and newest state, Hawaii is a land of beaches, sunny farmlands, tropical rain forests and smoldering volcanoes. The eight principal islands welcome 600,000 visitors a year and comprise a shipping center and military outpost. Lying roughly on the latitude of Mexico City, they form the southern end of a long chain that stretches across nearly 2000 miles. The capital, Honolulu, where four fifths of the population live, is known as the Crossroads of the Pacific.

Many of the inhabitants were once tourists who stayed to enjoy a land of palm trees and soft breezes. Others are descendants of early Polynesians who have intermarried with later arrivals. Only a few hundred pure-blooded Hawaiians are left; about 15 percent of the population is predominantly Hawaiian or part-Hawaiian, 28 percent is Japanese, 38 percent Caucasian (or haole), 10 percent Filipino and 9 percent of Chinese, Korean and other origin. More than one third of the marriages today are interracial—60 different racial combinations have been found in this amazing melting pot.

The Hawaiian language, a simple tongue with an alphabet of just 12 letters, is still spoken in a few rural villages, and many of its expressive words have been adopted by islanders of all nationalities—words like *pau* for "finished," *kamaaina* for "old-timer," *malihini* for "newcomer" and *aloha,* which can mean "hello" and "good-bye" or "I love you." Nicknamed the Aloha State, Hawaii traditionally greets visitors with flowers garlands, or leis.

For years Hawaii was the country's western military front, unrecognized as such by most mainlanders until the Japanese struck at Pearl Harbor on December 7, 1941. Since then, Federal activities have expanded so that one fifth of the labor force is now on the government payroll, which provides more income than the two major crops—sugar and pineapple—and the chief industry—tourism—combined.

Among the 50 states, Hawaii is unique in several respects. It is separated from the mainland by 2397 miles of Pacific Ocean; it is the southernmost state; and it is the only one that was originally an independent monarchy, with its capitol a former royal palace. When it achieved statehood, it was the wealthiest territory ever to join the Union and had the highest level of education of any to enter.

Hawaii was probably settled by Tahitians who arrived in giant canoes 1000 years ago. Spanish, Dutch and Japanese explorers may have visited the islands as early as the 1500's, but the official discovery by the Western world came in 1778, when Captain James Cook of the British Navy landed and named the chain the Sandwich Islands in honor of the Earl of Sandwich, First Lord of the Admiralty. Cook traded with the islanders, who first believed him a god, but in 1779 was killed by them in a dispute over the theft of a boat.

Until that time Hawaiians (who got their name either from an early leader, Hawaailoa, or the legendary Polynesian homeland, Hawaiki) had lived under tribal chiefs. In 1782 one of them, Kamehameha I, with the help of the white men's firearms, undertook a war of conquest and united the islands, founding a dynasty that endured for a century. His descendants still live in the islands.

The first Protestant missionaries arrived in 1820. They converted the natives and persuaded them to give up their tapa-cloth skirts for the Mother Hubbard, the forerunner of the *muumuu*—a long, colorful dress frequently worn by islanders and tourists. In 1848 King Kamehameha III divided the land, which had been owned by the monarch, among the people. Many Hawaiians sold their shares to white men, and thus began some of the largest estates. With the loss of their lands and exposure to white men's diseases, the native population declined.

White traders and landowners brought in Chinese laborers for the cane fields in 1851, and in the next 50 years immigrants arrived from Polynesia, Japan, Portugal, Puerto Rico, Korea and the Philippines. In 1893 Queen Liliuokalani was deposed in an American-led revolution, and the following year a Republic of Hawaii was formed with Sanford Dole as president. The United States annexed the islands in 1898 and established an incorporated territory, which by then had a population of 154,000, half the number of inhabitants on the islands when Cook discovered them.

Despite repeated pleas from the islanders, Congress for 56 years opposed statehood because of the distance that separated Hawaii from the mainland and because of doubts that people of Oriental descent and culture would be assimilated. But the bravery of the Japanese-Americans in World War II, the lack of a single native act of sabotage and the approval of statehood for Alaska in 1958 countered these arguments, and Hawaii was admitted to the Union in 1959.

The four major islands in the state are the sites of volcanoes whose ash has made fertile farmlands for sugar and pineapple, yet varying amounts of rainfall and the presence or absence of rivers give each island its own distinct character. Oahu, "the gathering place," is the most densely settled. To the north are the Koolau Mountains, from whose windswept precipice, the Nuuanu Pali, one has a fine view of mountains, tropical beaches and eucalyptus forests. Another range, the Waianae Mountains, runs along the southwestern coast, and between the two are cane fields and pineapple plantations.

The largest island is Hawaii, with five volcanoes, including Mauna Loa and its Kilauea crater, which still hisses and flames in occasional spectacular eruptions, and Mauna Kea, the highest volcano at 13,796 feet. There are lush tropical forests inland, and Hilo, a port, is the state's second city. The individually owned 262,000-acre Parker Ranch on Hawaii is second only in size to the King Ranch in Texas. Flower farms raise orchids and other blossoms that are exported throughout the world.

Maui, "the valley island," is made up of two volcanic masses with rich bottomlands running between them. Haleakala, one of the volcanoes, has an enormous inactive crater which is 22 miles around and 3000 feet deep. The island is named after a god who is supposed to have fished the islands out of the sea with a giant fishhook.

Kauai, "the garden island," has the state's only navigable rivers, which have carved rugged scenic canyons from the lava beds. In Hanalei Valley, rainfall is heavy enough for raising rice, which is harvested in primitive style with water buffaloes and horses. Sugar and pineapple plantations nearby use the most modern methods.

The four smaller islands are Lanai, "the pineapple island," owned entirely by the Hawaiian Pineapple Company; Molokai, "the friendly island," site of a leper colony and cattle ranches; Niihau, "the mystery island," owned in feudal style by one family and closed to visitors; and Kahoolawe, a barren, uninhabited dot of land off Maui. The state also includes the string of islands and reefs, with the exception of Midway, as far west as Kure.

Travel from one island to another is mostly by plane, although there are still some interisland vessels. Ships bring tons of freight and thousands of visitors each year, but most people come by air, for this once remote tropical resort is now only four and a half hours from San Francisco by jet airliner.

IDAHO

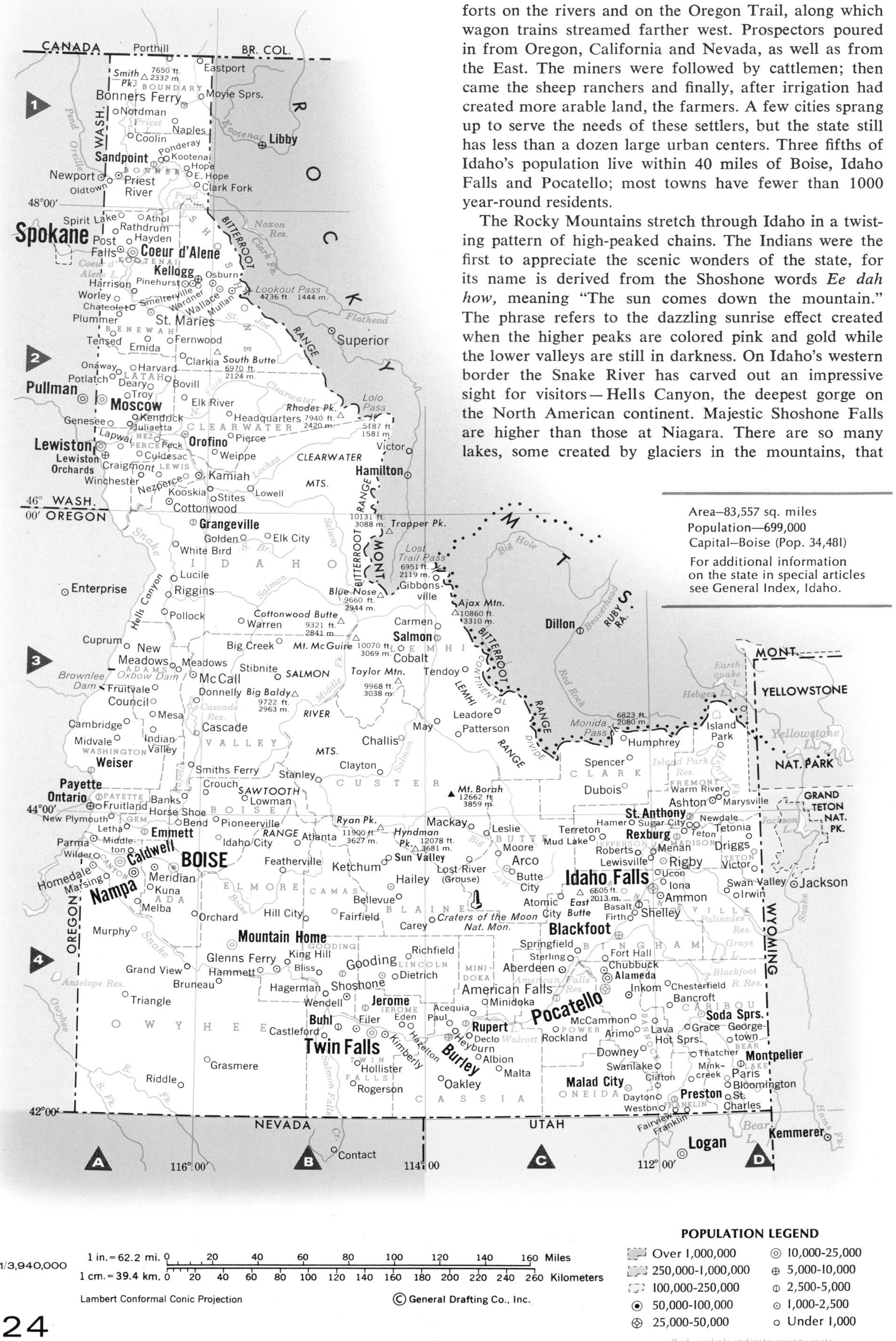

Idaho is unusual among the Rocky Mountain and Pacific states in that its first great influx of settlers came from the West instead of the East. Lewis and Clark had crossed the region in 1805; some Mormons had started farming in eastern Idaho in the mistaken belief that they were on Utah territory, which Brigham Young had chosen for settlement. But until gold was discovered in the 1860's there were only a few fur-trading posts and forts on the rivers and on the Oregon Trail, along which wagon trains streamed farther west. Prospectors poured in from Oregon, California and Nevada, as well as from the East. The miners were followed by cattlemen; then came the sheep ranchers and finally, after irrigation had created more arable land, the farmers. A few cities sprang up to serve the needs of these settlers, but the state still has less than a dozen large urban centers. Three fifths of Idaho's population live within 40 miles of Boise, Idaho Falls and Pocatello; most towns have fewer than 1000 year-round residents.

The Rocky Mountains stretch through Idaho in a twisting pattern of high-peaked chains. The Indians were the first to appreciate the scenic wonders of the state, for its name is derived from the Shoshone words *Ee dah how,* meaning "The sun comes down the mountain." The phrase refers to the dazzling sunrise effect created when the higher peaks are colored pink and gold while the lower valleys are still in darkness. On Idaho's western border the Snake River has carved out an impressive sight for visitors—Hells Canyon, the deepest gorge on the North American continent. Majestic Shoshone Falls are higher than those at Niagara. There are so many lakes, some created by glaciers in the mountains, that no accurate estimate of their number exists. Craters of the Moon National Monument was named because its terrain resembled a telescopic view of the moon's landscape. Man-developed attractions such as Sun Valley, once a ski resort but now a year-round vacation spot, also draw tourists. Many families in the northern part of the state bring wild game to the larder—elk, deer, bear, moose and antelope, along with mountain brook trout, lake bass and pickerel.

Idaho is primarily a rich agricultural region, best known for large baking potatoes. It ranks second to Maine as a potato producer, and is also second as a grower of sugar beets. Cattle and sheep ranches are scattered throughout the plains and valleys of the south and in the mountain valleys of the northwest. The principal industry is food-processing. Lumber is important, and the world's biggest white-pine sawmill is at Lewiston, the state's "seaport" at the junction of the Snake and Clearwater rivers.

With the exception of the Rocky Mountain area, where the winters are severe, Idaho has a milder climate than the Plains states to the east of it. The ranges protect the rest of the state from northern winter winds, yet do not block warmer air currents coming east from the Pacific.

The mountainous northern sliver of the state known as the Panhandle thrusts up between Montana and Washington to make a common frontier with British Columbia. This odd-shaped appendage exists because the boundaries of the other states carved out of the old Oregon Territory were fixed before those of Idaho. Here are some of the world's richest mineral deposits. Idaho leads the nation in silver production, is second in lead and third in zinc. Among the most famous mines are the Sunshine, largest silver mine in the United States; the Bunker Hill, one of the biggest lead mines; and the Morning, where workmen have hollowed out whole mountains and blasted and tunneled their way more than a mile below the surface of the earth.

To protect its natural resources in the future, Idaho is practicing wildlife and soil conservation. Reforestation has provided a second growth of timber for lumbering companies. Mining installations are not allowed to pollute rivers and streams. Every effort is made to maintain the conditions which led A. B. Guthrie, Jr. to write in *American Panorama:* "No state can surpass, if any can equal, its contrasts, its extremes, its huge natural fancies that exist as if to stun wonder."

Area—83,557 sq. miles
Population—699,000
Capital—Boise (Pop. 34,481)
For additional information on the state in special articles see General Index, Idaho.

BOISE

Nestling at the northern end of the great Boise River Valley, the city of Boise is surrounded by a rich farming region which produces hay, grain, vegetables and fruits—particularly prunes. It has few manufacturing plants but an abundance of tree-shaded, landscaped homes. Still standing is the old United States Assay Office, through which more than $75,000,000 in gold and silver bullion is said to have passed during early mining days. Boise is noted for its colony of Basques, one of the largest in the world. They originally came from Spain and drifted into Idaho as sheepherders. The summer festival and Sheepherders' Ball in December attract Basques from neighboring Northwestern states who join in the colorful dancing, feasts and jai-alai games. Beneath Boise are hot (170° F.) springs, which many homeowners have tapped to obtain free heat.

ILLINOIS

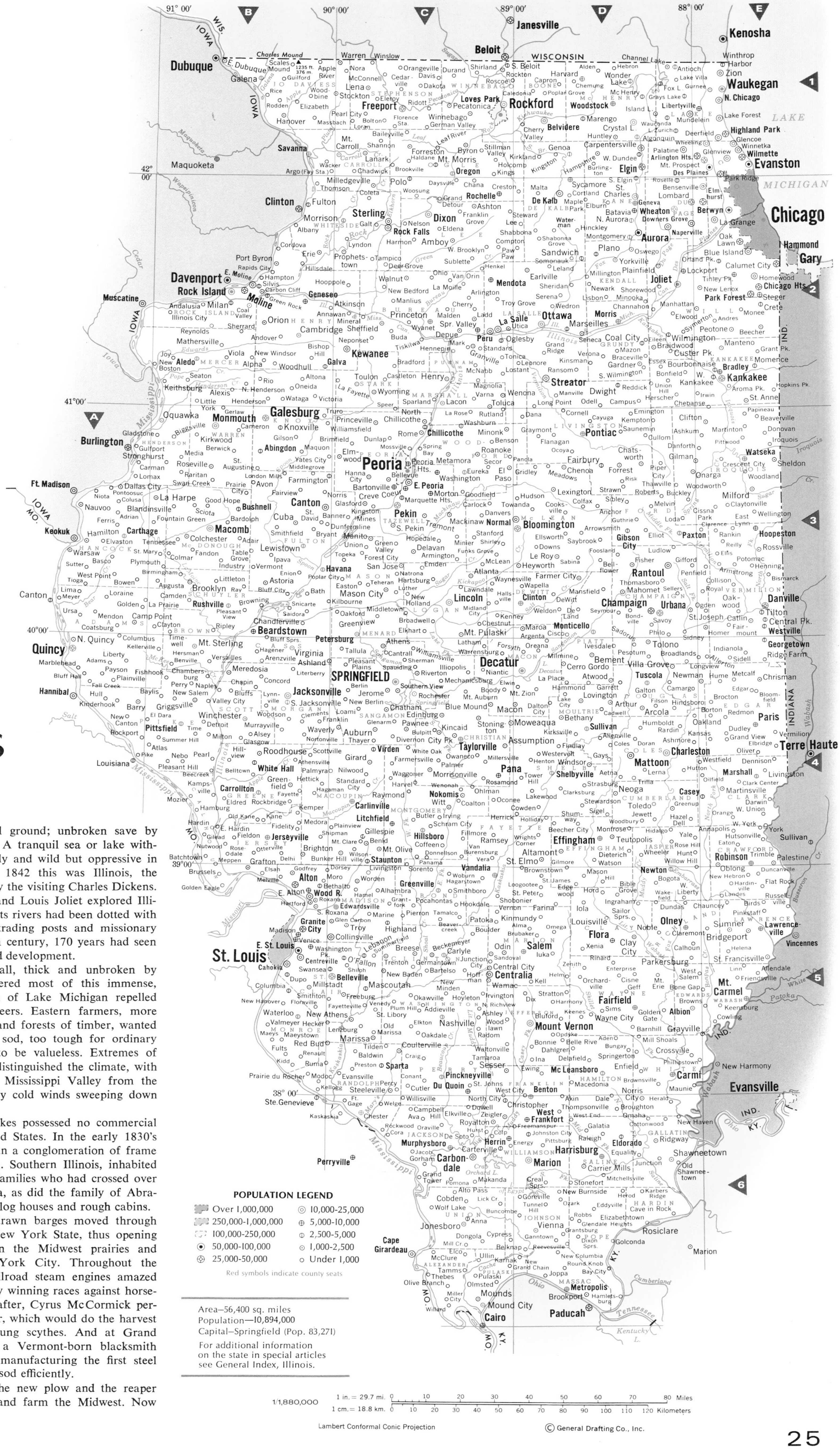

"A vast expanse of level ground; unbroken save by one thin line of trees. . . . A tranquil sea or lake without water. . . . It was lonely and wild but oppressive in its barren monotony." In 1842 this was Illinois, the Prairie State, as described by the visiting Charles Dickens. Father Jacques Marquette and Louis Joliet explored Illinois in 1673, and although its rivers had been dotted with French and British forts, trading posts and missionary camps since the seventeenth century, 170 years had seen little progress in farming and development.

The ocean of grass — tall, thick and unbroken by plow or spade — that covered most of this immense, flat region west and south of Lake Michigan repelled rather than attracted pioneers. Eastern farmers, more familiar with deep valleys and forests of timber, wanted no part of it. The prairie sod, too tough for ordinary plowshares, was assumed to be valueless. Extremes of temperature, then as now, distinguished the climate, with hot winds blowing up the Mississippi Valley from the Gulf of Mexico and bitterly cold winds sweeping down from the Arctic.

Until 1825 the Great Lakes possessed no commercial link with the eastern United States. In the early 1830's Chicago was little more than a conglomeration of frame shacks in a lakeside marsh. Southern Illinois, inhabited mainly by American farm families who had crossed over from Kentucky and Indiana, as did the family of Abraham Lincoln, was a land of log houses and rough cabins.

In 1825 the first mule-drawn barges moved through the new Erie Canal into New York State, thus opening an all-water route between the Midwest prairies and New England and New York City. Throughout the Eastern states, the first railroad steam engines amazed spectators and passengers by winning races against horse-drawn vehicles. Soon thereafter, Cyrus McCormick perfected his mechanical reaper, which would do the harvest work of a dozen hand-swung scythes. And at Grand Detour, Illinois, in 1837, a Vermont-born blacksmith named John Deere began manufacturing the first steel plow that broke the prairie sod efficiently.

Together, the railroad, the new plow and the reaper made it possible to settle and farm the Midwest. Now the people came to the prairies, not by wagon train or oxcart, but by barge, steamboat and train; not by the hundreds but by the tens of thousands and eventually by the hundreds of thousands. In the half century between 1840 and 1890 the population of Illinois zoomed from 476,000 to nearly 4,000,000.

The great European migrations of the nineteenth century were just getting under way. On the heels of the English and Scots came the Irish. Then followed Norwegians, Germans, Poles, Czechs, Russians, Italians, French, Dutch and Belgians. To many the state offered living space for homes, farms and crops such as they had never dreamed of. The immigrants came first as homesteaders—"sodbusters"—to make the Illinois prairies one of the most productive farming regions in the country. Later, as Chicago grew into a city, they came to labor in its stockyards, railroad yards, mills and factories, to be succeeded in turn by great numbers of Negroes migrating from the South. (Today Chicago has a Negro population almost as large as that of Virginia.)

In the 1850's Chicago and Illinois became the heart of a giant new industry. Iron ore was shipped down the Great Lakes from northern Minnesota, while up from southern Illinois, which had been found to have the richest bituminous-coal deposits in the nation, came mile-long freight trains of fuel for the blast furnaces and foundries.

So great a state that it stretches about one third of the distance between Lake Michigan and the Gulf of Mexico, Illinois has ranked first in the production of corn and soybeans, second in hogs, sixth in wheat and oats. Yet scattered through its fertile farmlands are half a dozen large industrial centers, turning out all kinds of goods from locomotives and farm tractors to beer, electrical equipment, liquor and candy bars, which, with Chicago's production, make Illinois the third most important manufacturing state.

CHICAGO

A huge transportation web centers in Chicago, linking the Atlantic and Pacific coasts. Its air, rail, bus and truck terminals daily handle more travelers and freight than those of any other city in North America. Since the St. Lawrence Seaway opened Lake Michigan to oceangoing vessels, Chicago has become the world's largest inland port. A bustling melting-pot city, it echoes the Indian chegagou, *meaning "strong" or "powerful." Blast furnaces and foundries, stockyards and meat-packing plants, flour mills and grain elevators, factories and distilleries all have helped to enrich this industrial giant, and Chicago's self-confident vigor rings in the civic motto: "I Will." Art galleries, museums, universities and concert halls attest to its cultural progress. The downtown commercial center, encircled by elevated train lines, is called The Loop. Chicago was among the first to build skyscrapers—its profile is constantly changed by new towers. Today as always, a lusty, restless, striving spirit keeps the second metropolis in the nation one of America's most exciting cities. (Pop. 3,550,404.)*

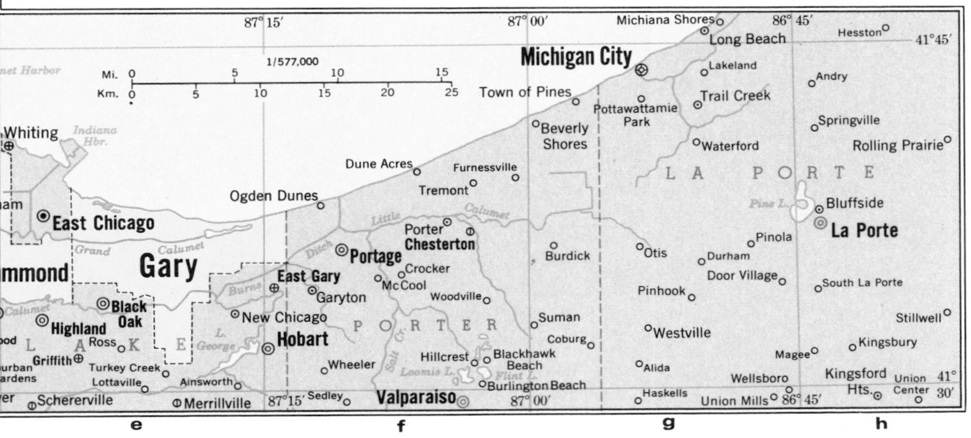

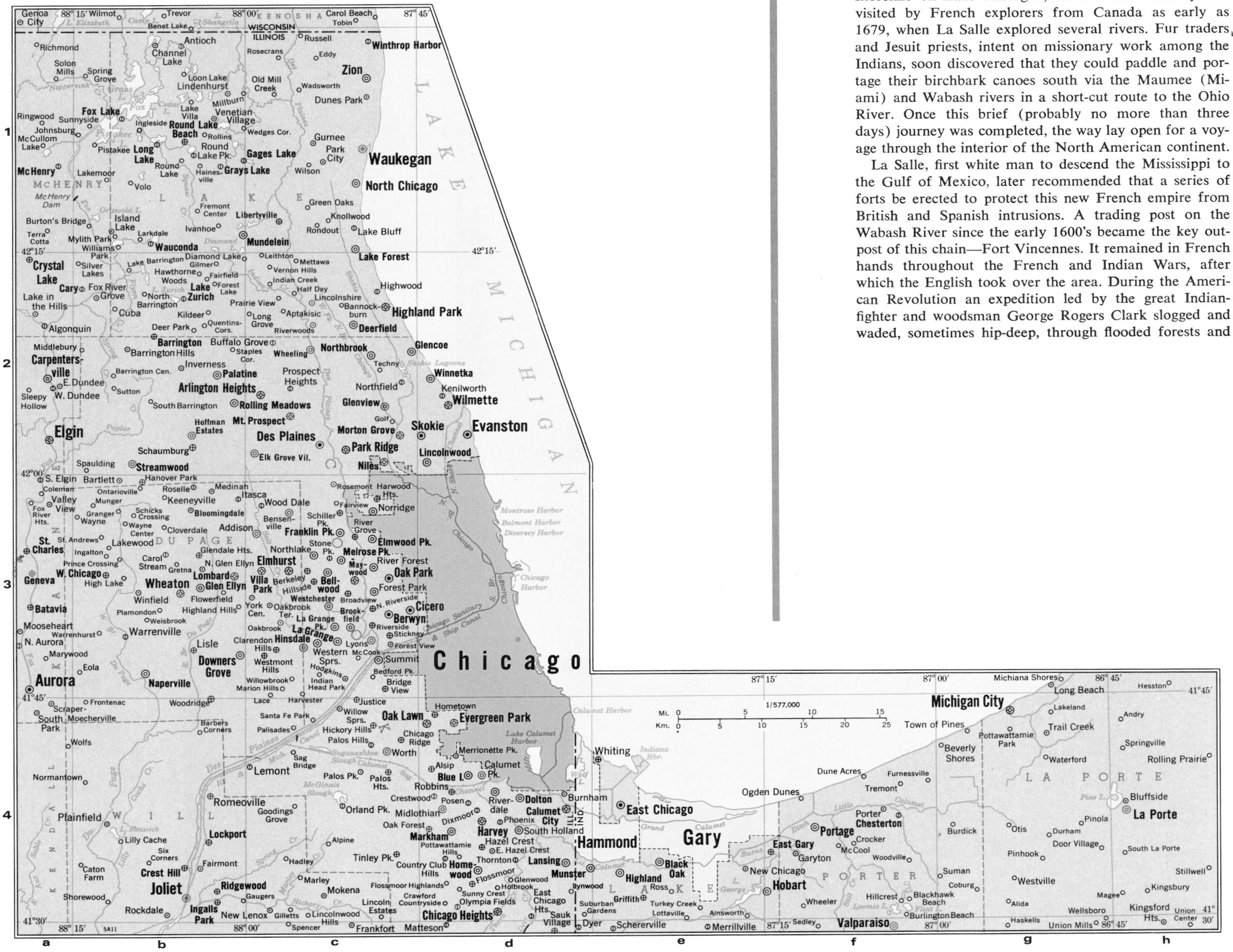

INDIANA

Giant steel mills, pouring white-hot molten metal from noisy blast furnaces, big red barns and prairies green with tall, tasseled corn—these are the contrasting scenes of Indiana. Still an important farm state, with the third largest corn crop in the nation, Indiana now also ranks third in steel and has risen to eighth place in the nation in overall industrial production.

While Indiana's heavy industry is concentrated in an enormous steel-mill complex shared with Illinois in the north, a wide variety of goods is being turned out by factories in such cities as Elkhart (musical instruments and mobile homes), South Bend (machine tools), Fort Wayne (gasoline pumps, trucks and electronic equipment), Kokomo (auto parts and accessories), Terre Haute (plastic film and food products), Lafayette (aluminum), Bloomington (color-television sets), Evansville (refrigerators and air conditioners) and Muncie (bottles, jars and furniture). Industries employ nearly six times as many of Indiana's people as agriculture and bring in almost five times as much income; yet about three quarters of the state's area is farmed, and outside of the cities one is never far from farm tractors, harvesting rigs, hogs and corn.

Easily accessible from the Great Lakes because of a shoreline on Lake Michigan, the Indiana Territory was visited by French explorers from Canada as early as 1679, when La Salle explored several rivers. Fur traders, and Jesuit priests, intent on missionary work among the Indians, soon discovered that they could paddle and portage their birchbark canoes south via the Maumee (Miami) and Wabash rivers in a short-cut route to the Ohio River. Once this brief (probably no more than three days) journey was completed, the way lay open for a voyage through the interior of the North American continent.

La Salle, first white man to descend the Mississippi to the Gulf of Mexico, later recommended that a series of forts be erected to protect this new French empire from British and Spanish intrusions. A trading post on the Wabash River since the early 1600's became the key outpost of this chain—Fort Vincennes. It remained in French hands throughout the French and Indian Wars, after which the English took over the area. During the American Revolution an expedition led by the great Indian-fighter and woodsman George Rogers Clark slogged and waded, sometimes hip-deep, through flooded forests and icy marshes to launch a surprise attack on the British garrison at Fort Vincennes in the winter of 1779. From then on, the region belonged to the United States.

The north side of the Ohio River had long been considered "Indian country," containing in the eighteenth century one of the greatest concentrations of Indians east of the Mississippi. As a territory and later a state it naturally came to be called Indiana.

A land rush occurred shortly after the War of 1812, when war veterans and families who had lost homes, farms and estates during British raids on the Atlantic states sought a new start in the West. Early settlements were concentrated in the river districts of southern Indiana near Vincennes, which was the first capital and has remained its most historic town, as well as the oldest. Later waves of immigrants from Europe arrived to farm the central prairie portions of the state.

The least developed area had long been the Calumet swamps and sandhills along the shore of Lake Michigan in the northwest corner of the state. As late as 1900 it was still almost a wasteland. With the coming of the age of steel, however, ore ships began transporting iron from the great deposits in the Lake Superior region of Minnesota and Canada to Lake Michigan and Lake Erie. When bituminous coal, which existed in large amounts in southern Indiana, was found to be ideal fuel for blast furnaces, the Calumet shore quickly mushroomed as the nation's newest steel center. Swamps were drained. Port facilities were installed. Hammond, Whiting and a new city named Gary became part of a tremendous iron and steel manufacturing area. Gary has grown into the state's second largest city, with a population of 178,320. Many of the nation's biggest oil-refining and chemical companies have also built plants nearby.

Heavy urban and industrial development has brought twentieth-century problems—smog and slums among them—to Indiana. In the southern regions the decline in coal mining as steel furnaces have become less dependent on coal has created economic problems. But industrial and agricultural activities have remained balanced and firmly established. Indiana has kept that aura described by its folk poet James Whitcomb Riley: the blue haze of Indian summer deepening over its fields of shocked corn against woodlands blazing with autumn's brilliant colors.

INDIANAPOLIS

When Indiana entered the Union in 1816, Congress offered it the choice of one of four sections of public land for a capital. The legislature picked a square mile in the middle of the state, and in 1821 Indianapolis was laid out in a design patterned after that of Washington, D.C., with broad main streets and avenues. These features have been retained in subsequent expansions. When the state government moved from Corydon in 1825, Indianapolis was a village of only 600 inhabitants. Without navigable water, it was connected with the east in the 1830's by the National Road and in 1847 by railway. Surrounded by rich farmlands, Indianapolis has become one of the largest and most active corn and livestock markets in the country. The city has grown into a leading Midwestern communications, financial and manufacturing center, whose output includes jet engines, telephones, pharmaceuticals and automobile parts. Cars with four-wheel brakes and six cylinders were first produced there. Few of the world's sports events are as outstanding as the annual 500-mile automobile race on Memorial Day.

1:1,810,000 1 in. = 28.6 mi. 0 10 20 30 40 50 60 70 80 90 100 Miles
1 cm. = 18.1 km. 0 10 20 30 40 50 60 70 80 90 100 110 120 130 140 150 160 Kilometers

Lambert Conformal Conic Projection

Area—36,291 sq. miles
Population—4,999,000
Capital—Indianapolis (Pop. 476,258)

For additional information on the state in special articles see General Index, Indiana.

POPULATION LEGEND

Over 1,000,000	10,000-25,000
250,000-1,000,000	5,000-10,000
100,000-250,000	2,500-5,000
50,000-100,000	1,000-2,500
25,000-50,000	Under 1,000

Red symbols indicate county seats

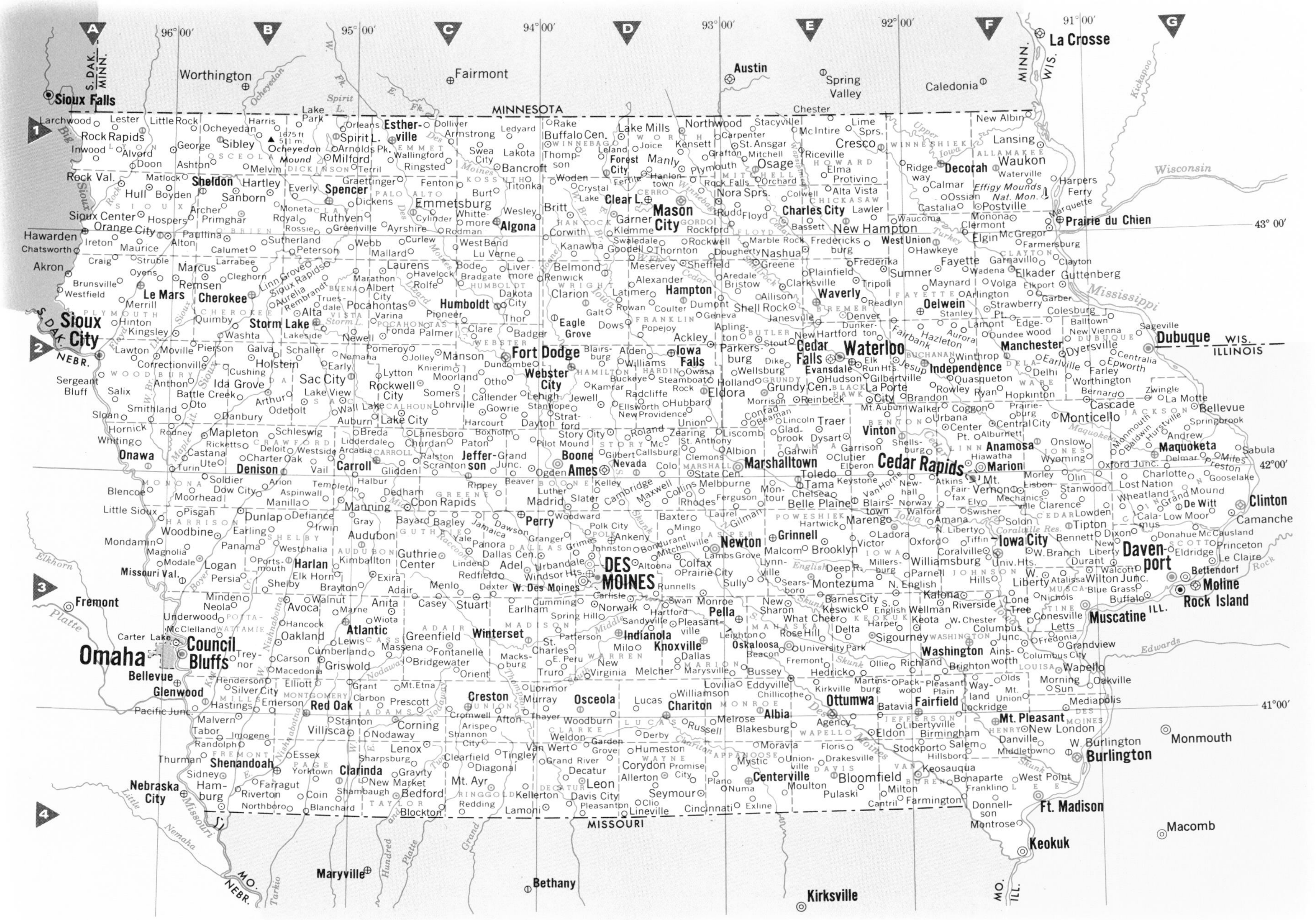

1/2,440,000 — 1 in. = 38.5 mi. 0 20 40 60 80 100 Miles; 1 cm. = 24.4 km. 0 20 40 60 80 100 120 140 160 Kilometers

Lambert Conformal Conic Projection

© General Drafting Co., Inc.

POPULATION LEGEND

Over 1,000,000	10,000-25,000
250,000-1,000,000	5,000-10,000
100,000-250,000	2,500-5,000
50,000-100,000	1,000-2,500
25,000-50,000	Under 1,000

Red symbols indicate county seats

Area—56,290 sq. miles
Population—2,753,000
Capital—Des Moines (Pop. 208,982)

For additional information on the state in special articles see General Index, Iowa.

IOWA

Iowa has become so famous for its agricultural prowess that many Americans think of it as one vast farm. Actually, the state has fewer hired hands than Pennsylvania, and more than half of its people live in large towns and cities. Manufacturing now creates three times as much income as agriculture. Yet Iowa is still one of the richest farming states in the nation; mechanization and automation of equipment make it possible for one man to run a 200-acre, $50,000 unit almost by himself.

The products of the land, from hogs to popcorn and dairy foods, are processed in plants in Iowa's cities, which also manufacture most of the machinery used on the farm. The world's largest wheel-tractor company is at Waterloo. While agricultural plants employ the most workers, electronics, chemicals, drugs and appliance factories are expanding.

Situated near the center of the continental United States, Iowa is also in the middle in other ways: twenty-fifth in size, twenty-fifth in population and twenty-third in manufacturing. Although a genuine prairie state, it is not as flat as its neighbors, Illinois and South Dakota. Iowa raises about ten percent of the nation's food supply, leading all other states in hogs, and is the second largest producer of oats. Indians had grown corn there for centuries before the pioneers came. Hogs arrived in Iowa in the 1840's, herded west by migrant farmers to fatten on the corn. During the depression of 1857, these animals are said to have saved the state from bankruptcy. Now the huge corn crops, frequently largest in the nation, are used primarily for feeding the hogs, which outnumber Iowans about five to one.

Iowa commands a surprising second rank in the raising of cattle, considering that it is only one-fifth the size of Texas, the leading beef state. Rolling pastures in the northern region nourish herds that make Iowa the nation's third producer of dairy commodities.

The biggest week in the state, aside from Christmas, is the one devoted to the fun-and-frolic side of farming. The Iowa State Fair, celebrated in late August, is one of the most famous of its kind in the nation. Prizes are awarded in contests for the best cakes, 4-H Club calves and handsome pigs and to winners of harness races; the bands blare night and day.

French as well as Indian names are common throughout Iowa. Its woodlands and prairies, abundantly watered by rivers and streams flowing east into the Mississippi or west into the Missouri, attracted early French fur traders, who descended from Canada via the Great Lakes and the Mississippi. The two big waterways made Iowa more accessible than some of the other central regions of the continent. By the turn of the eighteenth century, trading posts and forts were scattered up and down both rivers. Settlements were later established on sites nearby; consequently the state's major cities today are situated on these rivers.

Across the prairies of southern Iowa runs the old Mormon Trail worn by the wagons and hand-drawn carts of the thousands of Mormons who fled west in 1846 to escape persecution in Illinois. The route of the "Forty-Niners" bound for California in the Gold Rush days wound west through Des Moines. Council Bluffs attained its first importance as a wagon-train provision station. Iowa was finally transformed from an outpost territory into a state when settled by the European immigrants who streamed westward between 1840 and 1880.

Probably because those early European settlers brought with them such a love for music, Iowa has many of the best and biggest bands in the land. They compete and perform at parades, political rallies, sports events and other public gatherings. Fittingly enough, one of the best cornet players in American musical history, Bix Beiderbecke, was born in Davenport and trained on the Mississippi showboats. The "Missouri Waltz" was written in Iowa, as was "In the Shade of the Old Apple Tree."

DES MOINES

When canoe-borne French voyageurs visited Iowa in the early eighteenth century, they called its prairie waterway La Rivière des Moines (The River of the Monks) for the Trappist missionaries in the area. An Army fort named for the river was established on its banks in 1843, and soon a pioneer settlement grew up. Water-powered gristmills attracted farmers from near and far. Railroads spurred industrial growth that still continues as more Iowans forsake farms for city jobs and suburban living. The products of Des Moines include food and farm machinery, and its business activities involve insurance, banking, printing and publishing. So large is the volume of printed matter (produced by 50 insurance firms and some 60 magazines, farm journals, fraternal and commercial periodicals) that the city ranks among the leading publishing centers in the nation. It was one of the first to adopt the commission form of government. The system developed there, called the Des Moines Plan, has since been copied by many other municipalities. During World War II, the Women's Army Corps (WAC) officers were trained at Fort Des Moines, which became known as the West Point for Women.

KANSAS

For a state where settlement on a large scale did not begin until the second half of the last century, Kansas has had more than its share of hard times and catastrophes. Guerrilla warfare between proslavery and free-state factions during the territorial days of the 1850's attracted a lawless element which, seeking to capitalize on turmoil, was responsible for the epithet "Bleeding Kansas." Once peace was restored, a series of natural disasters began and has continued intermittently. The first severe drought was in 1860; the most recent cycle in 1953–55. Hordes of grasshoppers devoured almost every piece of greenery in 1874; they returned in 1936–37 and 1948. Soil erosion created dust-bowl conditions for a good part of the 1930's, damaging millions of acres. At times the discouraged farmers gave up. In 1889 alone, 50,000 moved to the newly opened Oklahoma Territory.

Yet despite these setbacks, progress has been steady. Droughts and dust have failed to keep Kansas from becoming the largest wheat producer and consequently the most important source of flour in the country. On the treeless western plains, highways stretch straight in unbroken ribbons to the horizon through vast fields of golden grain. This crop is so successful there because it is winter wheat—sown in the fall and harvested in the spring; the variety which ripens in autumn would not survive the blazing summer heat and the relatively small rainfall in this area. German Mennonites who had settled in the Ukraine, and then came to the United States in 1874 to escape compulsory Russian military service, introduced this hardy strain; it had flourished on their semiarid steppes and was named Turkey Red because of the origin and color of the seed.

Climate and soil divide Kansas into two distinct economic regions. The east is lightly forested, has rich alluvial loam and a fairly adequate rainfall; its farms are generally less than 200 acres, and corn is the principal crop. The west has almost no trees, the soil is sandy, annual rainfall is less than half of that in the east; farms are usually more than 200 acres, and wheat is the leading agricultural product. Hogs are raised primarily in the corn-growing areas. Cattle are bred throughout the state, but are concentrated in the east.

Although Kansas is one of the principal food producers in the country, manufacturing has become its biggest source of income. The major industry is transportation equipment, which includes airplanes—both civilian and military—and railroad cars. Food-processing is second. Meat-packing plants were established in the 1860's when Texas ranchers drove their cattle up to the railroads, which then extended as far as Abilene and Salina; the first refrigerator cars for shipping beef from this area pulled out of Salina in 1872.

Surface pools of oil existed in Kansas long before the first well was drilled in 1860; the Indians used it for medicinal purposes, the white drivers on the Santa Fe Trail to lubricate their wagon wheels. The state now ranks sixth in petroleum production, while pipelines carry natural gas as far away as Minneapolis. The first helium gas in the nation was found at Dexter in 1903. Lead and zinc have been mined since the 1870's.

There were few settlers in Kansas until 1854—the country was primarily Indian territory. Francisco Vásquez de Coronado, the Spanish conquistador, came up from Mexico in 1541 seeking the legendary city of Quivira, whose streets were believed to be paved with gold. Nearly two centuries passed before the area was again penetrated by Europeans. This time it was the turn of French fur traders and trappers from Canada, who established scattered trading posts and traveled the shallow rivers in dugout canoes. When American explorers arrived after the Louisiana Purchase, they found buffalo grazing in enormous herds—as many as 500,000 animals in sight at one time. But the leaders of these expeditions considered the plains unfit for human settlement, and for half a century the myth of the "great American desert," which included Kansas, persisted. Yet thousands of pioneers crossed the region on their way west. In 1849–50, 90,000 swept through, attracted by the California Gold Rush.

When Congress finally organized the Kansas Territory in 1854, it gave the inhabitants the right to decide whether to ban or permit slavery once statehood was achieved. This action precipitated a race between two factions. Abolitionists in New England financed the migration of settlers who favored a free state. Slavery proponents by the thousands crossed the boundary from neighboring Missouri. Violence and bloodshed were the result and continued even after Kansas entered the Union under a constitution which prohibited slavery.

The end of the Civil War brought peace, and more than 100,000 veterans arrived to settle on free home-

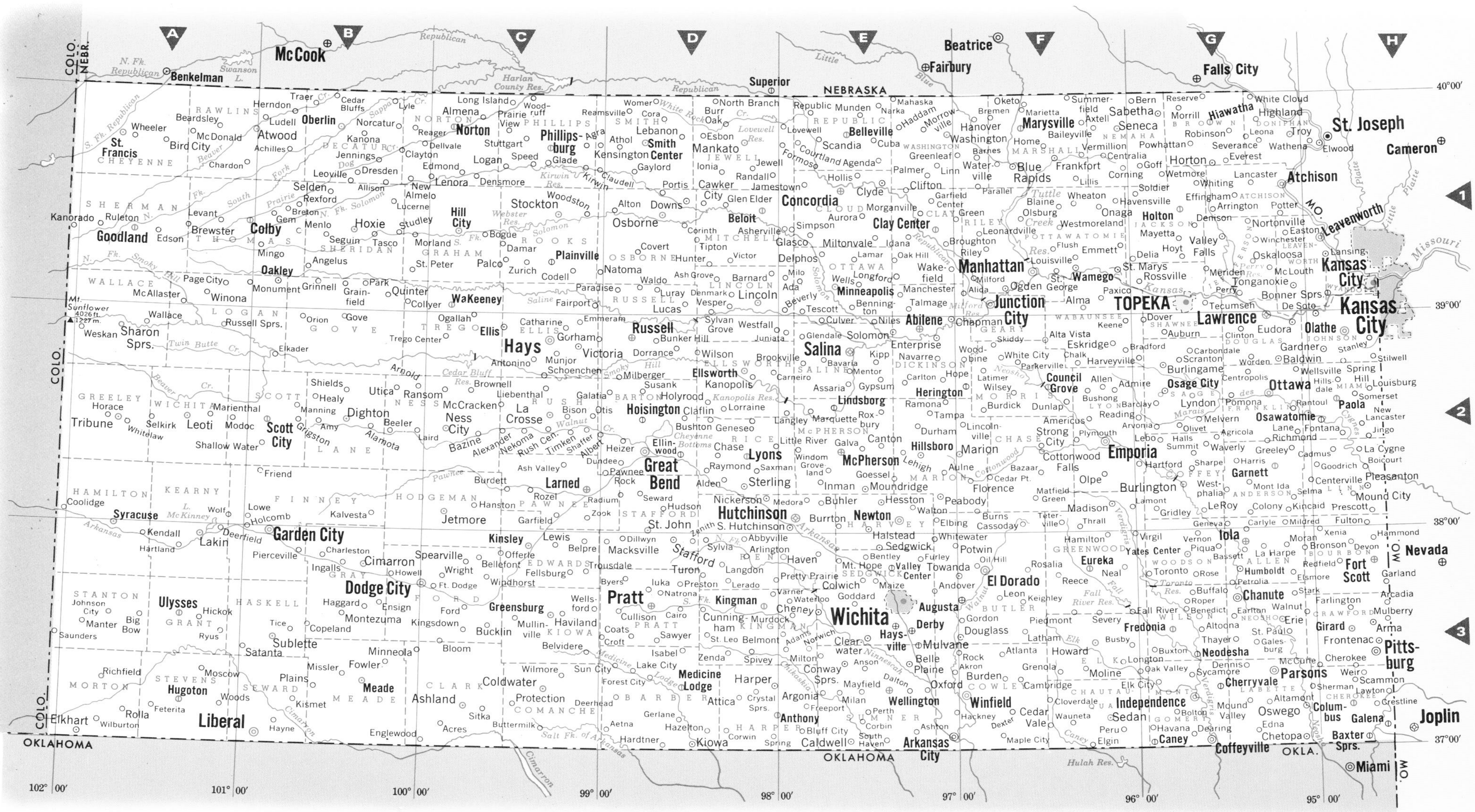

1/2,730,000 1 in. = 43.1 mi. 0 20 40 60 80 Miles
1 cm. = 27.3 km. 0 20 40 60 80 100 120 Kilometers

Lambert Conformal Conic Projection © General Drafting Co., Inc.

POPULATION LEGEND

Over 1,000,000	10,000-25,000
250,000-1,000,000	5,000-10,000
100,000-250,000	2,500-5,000
50,000-100,000	1,000-2,500
25,000-50,000	Under 1,000

Red symbols indicate county seats

Area–82,264 sq. miles
Population–2,275,000
Capital–Topeka (Pop. 119,484)
For additional information on the state in special articles see General Index, Kansas.

WICHITA

Sprawling across the confluence of the Arkansas and Little Arkansas rivers, Wichita's business, residential and industrial districts are connected by numerous bridges across both streams, with the peninsula in between. The city boasts the tallest (18-story) building in Kansas, ranks fourth in milling, third as an inland market for grain, and is the Southwest's center for meat-packing. Once known as the Air Capital of America because 15 factories manufactured a quarter of the nation's commercial airplanes in the late 1920's, Wichita still has the nation's fourth largest concentration of aircraft workers. Its aviation plants have turned out an enormous number of planes, ranging from famous World War II B-29 bombers to smaller private and "executive" planes. The city started as a trading post in 1864 and boomed during the 1870's. Then it was an important point on the Chisholm Trail over which Texas longhorns were driven north to Kansas railroads. Wheat farming with its barbed-wire fencing soon ended the great cattle drives and provided a new economic base for Wichita's prosperity. Oil, discovered in the 1920's, further stimulated the city's growth and added significantly to its wealth. (Pop. 254,698.)

steads offered by the Federal government. Cowboys who came with the cattle drives pioneered the western part of the state, as well as a less welcome group—rustlers and bandits. Their activities were eventually curtailed by such famous men as Wyatt Earp, Bat Masterson, "Wild Bill" Hickok and "Buffalo Bill" Cody. Colorful personalities also emerged from the prohibition and Populist movements in the early 1890's. Carry Nation militantly carried her temperance campaign into saloons, and smashed bars and bottles with a hatchet. Mary Elizabeth Lease campaigned for the Populist ticket, advising the farmers to "raise less corn and more hell." "Sockless Jerry" Simpson, elected three times to Congress on that slate, wore no socks to emphasize the aristocratic background of his banker opponent who wore silk ones.

Conservation is one key to the future welfare of Kansas. Since the 1930's, farmers have been encouraged to practice terracing and contour plowing to prevent soil erosion. The drought of 1955 resulted in the appointment of a water-resources board. Bulldozers have created lakes and ponds as reservoirs, and rows of trees called shelter belts have been planted to cut down the amount of dust in the air. The development of drought-resistant varieties of wheat, hybrid corn and grain sorghums has tended to offset the effect of dry seasons. All these measures have helped restore to useful production the land so widely ravaged by erosion.

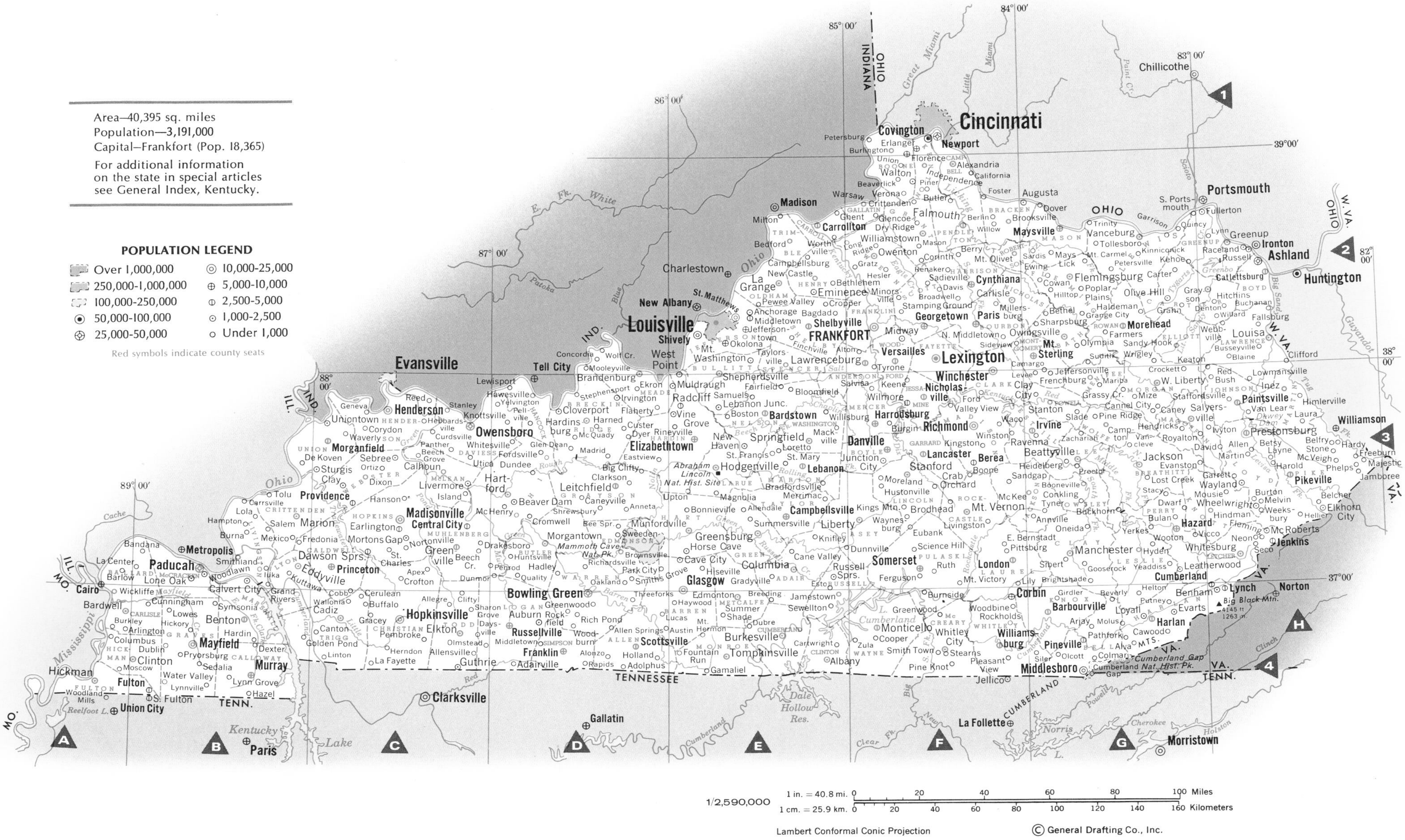

KENTUCKY

The early Kentucky settler is usually pictured as a tall, broad-shouldered, resolute man clad in fringed buckskins and a coonskin cap. In his arms he cradles a long-barreled rifle. Nearby is his log cabin. Television and movies have turned Daniel Boone, America's most celebrated frontiersman, into the legendary prototype of the pioneers who colonized the Bluegrass State.

In 1774 a small group of Pennsylvanians established the first colony in Kentucky. The next year Boone paved the way for the settlement of the area when he opened the Wilderness Road to the West beyond the Appalachians and led a party of North Carolina colonists through the Cumberland Gap into the heart of Kentucky. There he directed the construction of a fort that would become Boonesborough. The Wilderness Road later branched off to reach the Falls of the Ohio River, the site of Louisville.

Kentucky, of course, would have been settled without Daniel Boone. Reports of the green-meadowed, bluegrass valleys that lay beyond the mountains had trickled back east from Indians and from other trappers and woodsmen who had scouted the region. As the pressure for migration westward built up among the colonies of the Atlantic seaboard, land speculators became interested.

Between 1775 and 1800 the Wilderness Road drew thousands of settlers into this region, continuing westward along the latitude of Virginia. After the American Revolution, many restless soldiers, church groups and often even entire villages migrated to Kentucky. They raised tobacco and corn. By 1792 the territory had a population of 73,000 and the first college west of the Alleghenies—Transylvania.

As recently as 1950 two thirds of Kentucky's people dwelt in rural areas but only a quarter of the population was employed in agriculture. The central bluegrass country fulfilled its early promise; here are elegant, white-fenced farms on which are bred some of the finest race-horses in the world. Tobacco is still a major crop, and Kentucky ranks second only to North Carolina in the production of varieties of pipe and cigarette tobacco. Its distilled-spirits industry—noted for bourbon and rye whiskeys—is booming.

After World War II the demand for coal declined and mechanization of mining brought poverty and hardship to the eastern mountain regions. But industry surged ahead. Factories were built along the Ohio River, from Louisville to Paducah, turning out an unusual range of products: iron and steel, bathroom equipment, chemicals, rubber goods, petroleum products, plastics, electrical equipment, baseball bats, paints, varnishes, pickles and shoelaces. At Paducah the Atomic Energy Commission has a uranium-separation plant.

In the western part of the state, where the Tennessee River flows into the Ohio, the Kentucky Dam of the Tennessee Valley Authority (TVA) has created one of the largest man-made lakes, 184 miles long. There water-power has made possible dozens of new industries. Kentucky Lake's beautiful state parks and camping grounds draw thousands of visitors. Another attraction is Mammoth Cave, discovered by a bear hunter in the 1790's, a maze of underground lakes, rivers and at least 150 miles of corridors. Cumberland Gap, through which Daniel Boone led his colonists in 1775, is now a national historical park. Two miles of its old Wilderness Road have been preserved, and it is possible to stand quietly in the forests where the Kentucky statesman and orator Henry Clay once did, saying, ". . . listen to the tread of the coming millions."

LOUISVILLE

One of America's most colorful river cities is Louisville. The French explorer La Salle was probably the first white man to visit its site on a low, level plain surrounded by hills and overlooking the Falls of the Ohio. These spectacular rapids, where the river drops 26 feet in one mile, became familiar to pioneer scouts, trappers and fur traders. In 1778 George Rogers Clark established a permanent American settlement which soon expanded into a busy frontier town. Immigrants from the Eastern states floated down the Ohio on flatboats or made their way overland via the Wilderness Road. River trade extended to New Orleans, and during the steamboat era Louisville burgeoned into an important inland port and later into a large manufacturing center. Bourbon whiskey and tobacco, paints and electrical appliances: the range of products is a broad one. But the city is best known for the Kentucky Derby, now the richest, most famous and most romantic horse race, which every year in May, since 1875, has attracted the world's attention to Churchill Downs. (Pop. 390,639.)

LOUISIANA

This is probably the only state in the Union which is still growing in size. Every year the silt deposited by the Mississippi adds about 1000 acres to the Delta in the Gulf of Mexico. Over the centuries the river has deposited 10,000 square miles of the rich alluvial soil in which cotton and rice grow. The Mississippi has enabled New Orleans to become the second largest port in the United States. But it has been a scourge as well as a boon, inundating thousands of square miles at floodtime; a vast complex of levees, pumping stations and spillways has been constructed in the southern half of the state to protect land and people against the ravaging waters.

The Delta is not the only feature which distinguishes Louisiana. The heritage of France has survived for more than two centuries. French is still spoken as a second language in many places, by citizens of New Orleans as well as by trappers and oystermen in the Delta bayous. The famous cuisine is a felicitous blend of French recipes, strong Spanish seasoning and a dash of American-Indian herbs. In addition to settlers from France, the region welcomed the Acadians, driven from their homes in Nova Scotia by the English during the 1750's. Louisiana's inhabitants were so loyal to France that in 1768 they became the first American colonists to rebel. They ousted a Spanish governor and enjoyed ten months of freedom before a military expedition ended their temporary independence. More refugees arrived in 1801 when French rulers and landowners fled Haiti during the revolt of slaves under Toussaint L'Ouverture. While it is an oversimplification to say that the northern half of the state is American and the southern half French, different customs and cultures do exist in the two sections. Louisiana is the only state where civil law is based largely on the French Code Napoléon, which was established by Napoleon Bonaparte.

La Salle reached the mouth of the Mississippi River from Canada in 1682, when the chief means of travel was by canoe and pirogue (a boat made by hollowing out a cypress log). In later colonial times, men and merchandise moved down the Mississippi on rafts and larger craft, which were broken up and sold for lumber on arrival at New Orleans. The introduction of the steamboat in 1812 made it possible to sail upriver as well as down. So began the glamorous era of packet boats, showboats and floating palaces with gambling casinos. One passenger steamer survives to carry tourists between New Orleans and Cincinnati. Most of the cargo is now floated in barges, marshaled by powerful towboats. The river traffic accounts for the fact that Louisiana's three leading ports—New Orleans, Baton Rouge and Lake Charles—are all inland, not on the coast.

Coffee and bananas come into these ports from Latin America. Bales of cotton and sacks of sugar are shipped out. Hawaii is the only state which grows more sugarcane than Louisiana, which is also second in rice production. In its waters and marshes Louisiana nets the nation's second biggest shrimp catch, traps the most muskrats for fur and markets the most frogs' legs. In the state's southern areas the growing season lasts nearly 310 days, from February into December, and the semitropical climate enables some truck gardens to produce crops every three months.

Fertile soil is not Louisiana's only rich natural resource. Below the ground are large deposits of salt, oil, natural gas and sulfur; the oil fields extend out under the Gulf of Mexico, where drilling rigs are set on platforms atop pilings. Oil has not only created a new industry—petroleum refining—it has also provided inexpensive fuel which, in combination with cheap labor, has attracted other new industries. The state's principal manufactured items are chemicals, food products, pulp and paper. The latter come mainly from its fast-growing pine trees. In contrast with the industrialization and urbanization, there are more than 500,000 acres of wildlife preserves, including the foremost wintering area for wild ducks and geese.

The first permanent settlement in Louisiana, which then reached from Canada to the Gulf of Mexico, was established by the French about 1714 at Natchitoches. Few settlers had been sent by Louis XIV, for whom the territory was named, because the government expected to find vast treasures of gold and silver. There were none, and partly because of the lack of revenue, the territory was secretly ceded to Spain in 1762. Napoleon forced Spain to return it in 1800, and three years later he sold the entire region for $15,000,000 to the United States. During the War of 1812, General Andrew Jackson defeated the British in the Battle of New Orleans after a peace treaty had already been signed. Louisiana joined the Confederacy in the Civil War, and parts of it were occupied by Union forces when Admiral David Farragut captured New Orleans in 1862. During the postwar period, Louisiana suffered economically and politically under carpetbag administrations until Federal troops were withdrawn in 1877. Then its modern era began, with engineering and science helping to eradicate yellow fever and to control the Mississippi.

More than 40 percent of the state's income is now spent on the operation of public schools. This system was late in developing because of the large number of private schools and because proud Creoles felt it was a mark of poverty not to send their children to these institutions. A special feature of the Delta appeared with construction of the Lake Pontchartrain Causeway, which crosses 24 miles of water to connect with highways to the north. Although Louisiana, industrialized, has become an urban rather than a rural state, there are still white-pillared plantation houses whose gardens bloom with azaleas and camellias, country streams bordered by magnolia trees, and the quiet backwaters of the Delta where fishermen and trappers can be as far removed from the hectic pace of the twentieth century as their French and Spanish forefathers were.

NEW ORLEANS

William Makepeace Thackeray described New Orleans as the city "where you can eat and drink the most and suffer the least." It is as well known for its French gaiety and charm, for its famous Mardi Gras carnival, as it is for such specialties as oysters Rockefeller, gumbo, bouillabaisse, pompano and pralines. Bourbon Street, considered the cradle of jazz, numbers among its graduates Louis Armstrong and "Jelly Roll" Morton; the city is celebrated in such classics as "Basin Street Blues" and "Way Down Yonder in New Orleans." The old French quarter, the Vieux Carré, which dates from 1718, is the most picturesque district. Balconies with iron-lace railings overhang the sidewalks; oleander and wisteria adorn patio gardens. Tourism, shipping and manufacturing are the city's most important activities. Much of the Mississippi Valley commerce passes through the port. Shipbuilding, oil refining and the production of such petroleum by-products as chemicals and plastics are among the leading industries, to which a newcomer has only recently been added: the manufacture of space rockets and other equipment for American astronauts. (Pop. 627,525.)

Area—48,523 sq. miles
Population—3,660,000
Capital—Baton Rouge (Pop. 152,419)
For additional information on the state in special articles see General Index, Louisiana.

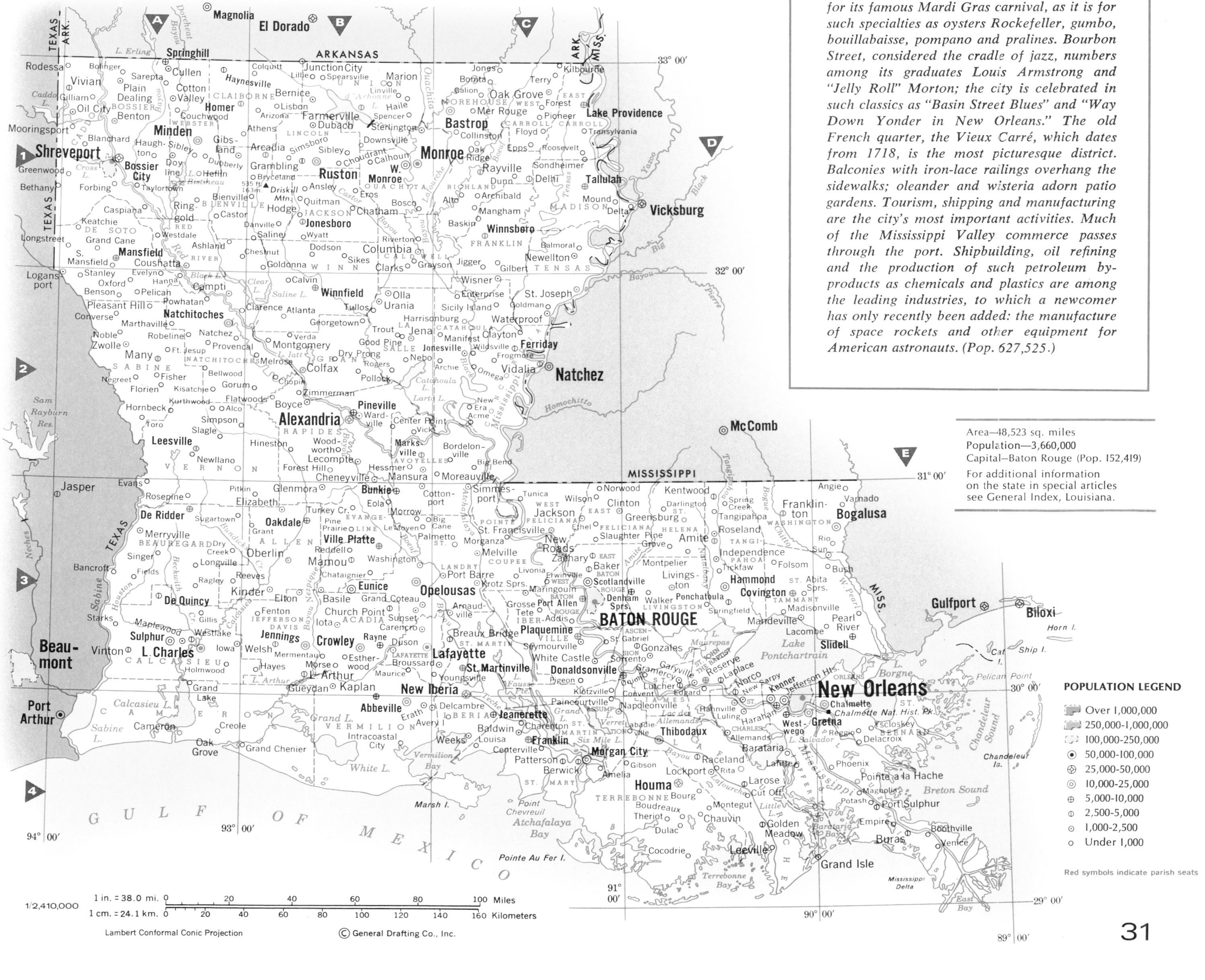

MAINE

Like a powerful magnet, Maine annually attracts more outdoor-loving visitors than any other Eastern state except Florida. Its seacoast, islands and forest wilderness have made vacations, recreation and tourism the second largest industry. More than 2,600,000 people visit the state each year for hunting, fishing, hiking, sailing, cruising, canoeing, mountain climbing and skiing.

Few who come to Maine for the first time are prepared for its size. It is almost as large as all the other New England states combined, and one county, Aroostook, is bigger than Connecticut and Rhode Island together. Within its borders lie 17,000,000 acres of forests, more than 2000 lakes and 5000 rivers. The highly indented coast, if unraveled into a straight line, would stretch from New York to Arizona.

This magnificent seacoast—composed of islands, rocky headlands, whalelike peninsulas and spruce-rimmed harbors—is actually the visible portion of a drowned mountain range. Only the crags and ridges appear above the Atlantic Ocean. Cadillac Mountain, rising straight over Bar Harbor, is the highest point on the Atlantic Coast between Brazil and Labrador. The interior is generally hilly with occasional mountains appearing unexpectedly in the central and western regions. One of them, Mount Katahdin, 5268 feet, is Maine's tallest peak.

Maine is the easternmost state, and its capes and peninsulas have been likened to arms that reach out toward Europe. Consequently some of the white man's earliest contacts with the Western Hemisphere and the North American continent occurred in this vicinity. John Cabot, the Venetian navigator in England's service, came to the area in 1497. Throughout the sixteenth century the coast and rivers were probed by Spanish and Portuguese in search of gold or a Northwest Passage to the Orient.

An English settlement was established at the mouth of the Kennebec River in 1607, but the rigorous Maine winter proved its downfall, and for a time the mainstream of immigration passed to the south—to the colonies of the Massachusetts Bay and the Middle Atlantic region. The Pilgrims who landed at Plymouth Rock set up an outpost in Maine and paid some of the debts owed

POPULATION LEGEND

- Over 1,000,000
- 250,000-1,000,000
- 100,000-250,000
- 50,000-100,000
- 25,000-50,000
- 10,000-25,000
- 5,000-10,000
- 2,500-5,000
- 1,000-2,500
- Under 1,000

Red symbols indicate county seats

Area—33,215 sq. miles
Population—973,000
Capital—Augusta (Pop. 21,680)
For additional information on the state in special articles See General Index, Maine.

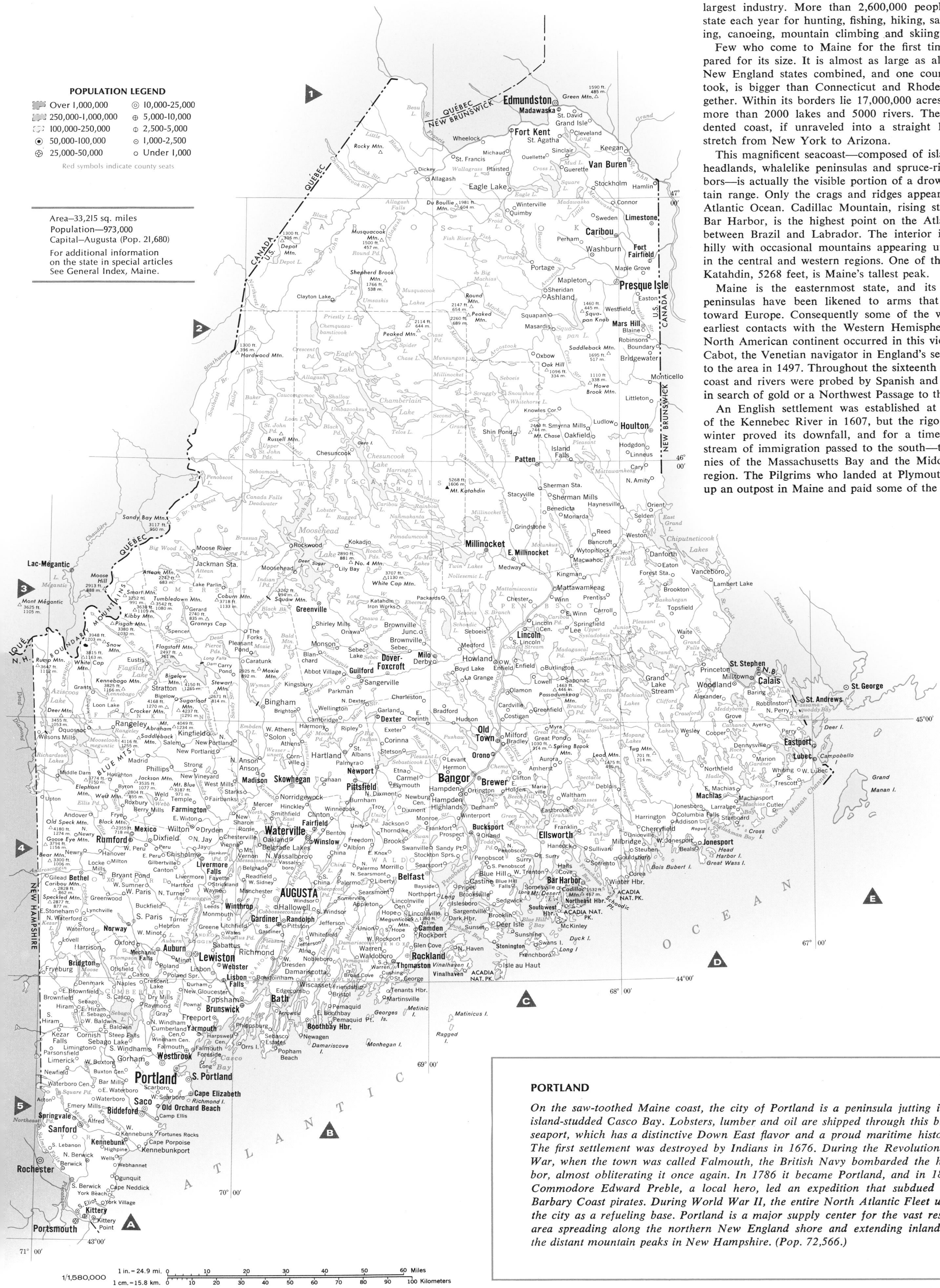

PORTLAND

On the saw-toothed Maine coast, the city of Portland is a peninsula jutting into island-studded Casco Bay. Lobsters, lumber and oil are shipped through this busy seaport, which has a distinctive Down East flavor and a proud maritime history. The first settlement was destroyed by Indians in 1676. During the Revolutionary War, when the town was called Falmouth, the British Navy bombarded the harbor, almost obliterating it once again. In 1786 it became Portland, and in 1803 Commodore Edward Preble, a local hero, led an expedition that subdued the Barbary Coast pirates. During World War II, the entire North Atlantic Fleet used the city as a refueling base. Portland is a major supply center for the vast resort area spreading along the northern New England shore and extending inland to the distant mountain peaks in New Hampshire. (Pop. 72,566.)

on the *Mayflower* with the profits from furs and fishing.

The first settlers built their farms and villages along the rivers which served as transportation routes through the great tracts of virgin forest. In the seventeenth century the valley of the Kennebec provided tall pines for the masts of British navy ships. The first roads over which these timbers were moved to rivers were called "mastways." For many years Maine was part of the colony of, and then the state of, Massachusetts. A party favoring independent statehood gained many adherents during the War of 1812, and Congress separated the two areas in 1820.

Patience, fortitude and flexibility have long been the keys to survival for the people who have chosen to make Maine their home. From colonial days until the present, while other industries have risen, prospered and fallen, the inhabitants have found a livelihood in natural harvests. Maine leads the nation in catching lobsters, canning sardines and picking blueberries. It produces more potatoes than any other state. Lumbering and the manufacture of wood products constitute its principal industry.

In colonial times, the region appeared destined to be an important farm territory. Maine in 1635 had the first water-powered corn-grinding mills in New England. Farmers in the southern part raised sizable crops of corn and hay, and drove cattle and sheep to Massachusetts markets. Then came the opening of the West and the development of large-scale farming in the Ohio and Mississippi valleys. Maine's agriculture declined; quite a few farmers joined the westward migrations. Some never stopped until they got to the other coast in Oregon.

Many of those who remained turned to shipbuilding, and during the nineteenth century Maine led the nation in the construction of large sailing vessels. Even the tiniest coastal towns had shipyards. Their clipper ships and square-riggers held records for the fastest voyages to California and the Orient. The South's cotton crop was transported north to New England's textile mills by Maine's sea captains. Ice from the ponds was carried to tropical ports in the West Indies. Then fortune's wheel turned again. During the Civil War, Confederate privateers captured and sank dozens of Maine's proudest ships. Textile mills began to move south, and eventually refrigeration brought an end to the ice industry. Returning to farming and lumbering, the state developed the potato crop and wood products.

As it became conscious of the value of its scenic and outdoor attractions, Maine began to protect these natural resources. One of the great wilderness regions in the country is Baxter State Park, more than 200,000 acres of woods, mountains and streams near Mt. Katahdin. Although lumber companies control most of the great inland forests, they have banned building developments and made the areas available to fishermen, hunters and campers.

Until recently, Maine was unique in that it held elections for President and Congress in September, two months before the rest of the country. The results so often forecast a national trend that the saying arose, "As Maine goes, so goes the nation." Since 1960 Maine has voted in November.

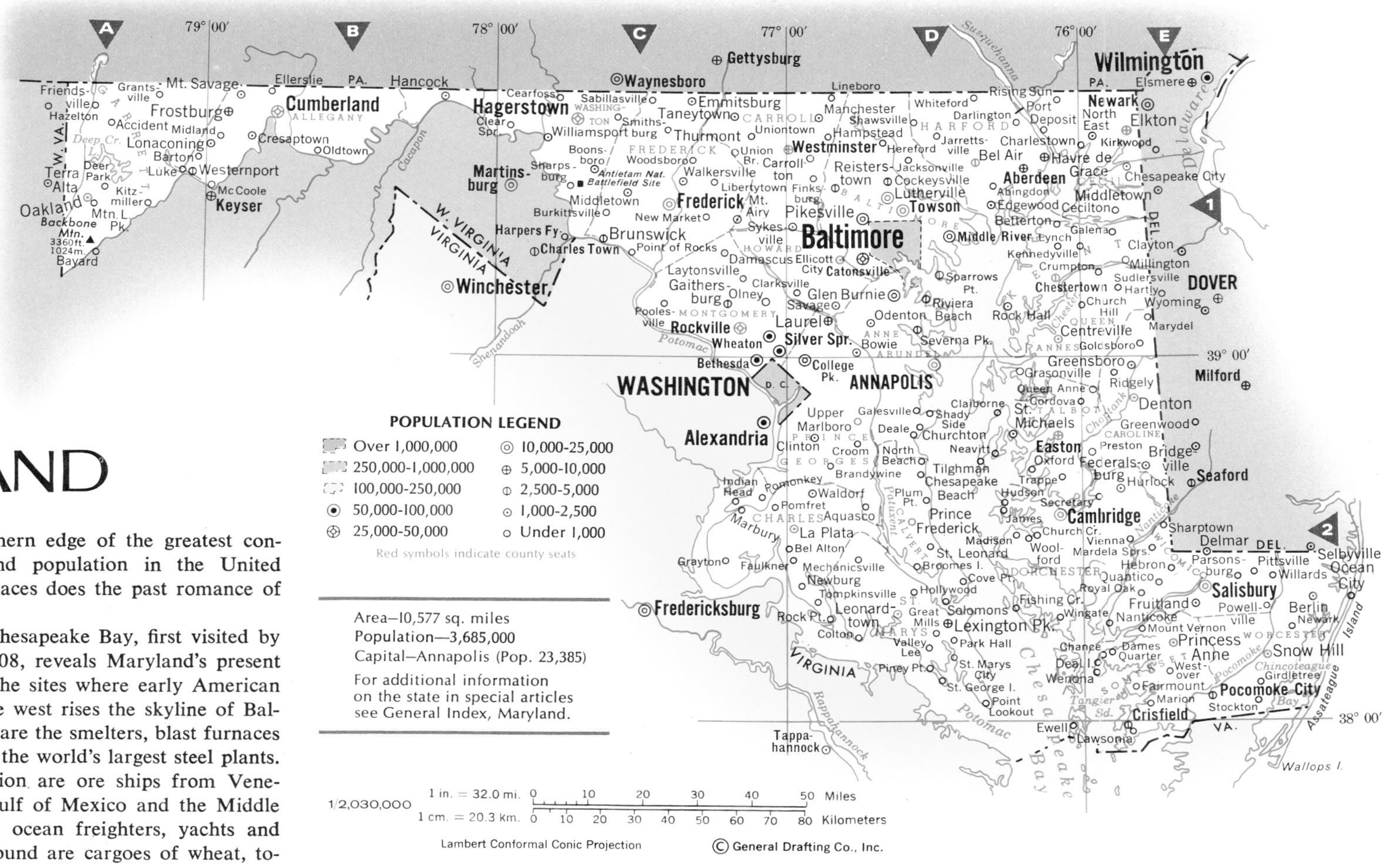

MARYLAND

Maryland is on the southern edge of the greatest concentration of industry and population in the United States. Yet in few other places does the past romance of America lie closer.

A 180-mile sail down Chesapeake Bay, first visited by Captain John Smith in 1608, reveals Maryland's present burgeoning activities and the sites where early American history was written. To the west rises the skyline of Baltimore. At Sparrows Point are the smelters, blast furnaces and rolling mills of one of the world's largest steel plants. Passing in endless procession are ore ships from Venezuela, tankers from the Gulf of Mexico and the Middle East, coastal barges, tugs, ocean freighters, yachts and cabin cruisers. Outward bound are cargoes of wheat, tobacco, locomotives and electrical machinery.

On the edge of Baltimore's harbor lies Fort McHenry, whose unsuccessful bombardment by the British during the War of 1812 inspired Francis Scott Key to write the words to "The Star-Spangled Banner," later the national

WASHINGTON, D. C.

The site of the capital of the United States on the east bank of the Potomac River near its junction with the Anacostia was selected by President George Washington in 1791. The original plan for the city, now the ninth largest in the country, was drawn by a French engineer, Major Pierre Charles L'Enfant. His design included parks and a series of radiating avenues and streets, some as much as 160 feet wide. At first Washington did not grow rapidly, and progress was further retarded in 1814 when the British Army burned its few public buildings. A major influx came during the Civil War. Subsequent massive expansions took place during World Wars I and II. The government clerical force which arrived from Philadelphia, the previous capital, in 1800 numbered 137 persons. Now 28 percent of the working population is on the public payroll. Washington has no heavy industry and even today, although streets are filled with traffic, the city has an air of spaciousness about it. Stately buildings flank beautiful parks, like those which surround the Tidal Basin. Washington has many major educational institutions, museums and fine art galleries. Millions of tourists flock to the city each year to visit the White House and other historic edifices. And towering 555 feet over the 69-square-mile District of Columbia is the imposing Washington Monument. (Pop. 763,956.)

BALTIMORE

Rows of identical attached brick houses, with white marble stoops scrubbed daily by diligent housewives, were the Baltimore trademark for many years. A number of those residences are now disappearing because of the need for new commercial buildings and housing projects, but Baltimore retains a unique cosmopolitan heritage that derives from both North and South. Fourth busiest port of the United States and farther west than any other of the coast, its 46 miles of waterfront offer cheap rates and excellent facilities for handling bulk cargo, such as the raw materials for steel mills and oil refineries. The diversified manufactured products now range from automobiles to textiles; the city is the world's leading source of fertilizers and the second largest supplier of tin cans. In the early decades of the present century, a great fleet of white steamers penetrated all the waterways of Maryland and Virginia. The rivers were the chief means of transportation, and the boats were a spectacular sight when they sailed from Baltimore in the afternoon. (Pop. 939,024.)

anthem. From the great Chesapeake Bay Bridge linking the heart of Maryland with its Eastern Shore, the spires of Annapolis, which is the state capital, can be seen. Here are the same elm-shaded streets once trod by George Washington, Thomas Jefferson, Alexander Hamilton and other members of the Continental Congress. The city is also the home of the U.S. Naval Academy, whose midshipmen have gone on to command America's fighting fleets in every conflict since the Civil War. Colonial and state legislatures have met in the capitol since 1772.

Below the Bay Bridge the Chesapeake fans out to a width of 30 to 40 miles. To the west are the low-lying lands of the Tidewater, where rich Maryland tobacco farms flourished when New England was just a semiwilderness and New York a tiny Netherlands colony. Tobacco still thrives there. In the countryside are some of the most beautiful architectural masterpieces of America—red-brick, high-chimneyed Georgian colonial mansions, elaborately furnished and surrounded by lovely gardens. As in Washington's day, many have private wharves along the Potomac, which forms the western and southern boundary of the state for 285 miles.

Across the bay lies the Eastern Shore, with miles of farms whose harvests of tomatoes, beans and other garden vegetables have made Maryland one of the leaders in canning and freezing vegetables and soups. Cattle and horses are bred in this region, and its broiler chickens make a substantial contribution to the state's economy.

Out on the waters of the lower bay are the shallow-bottom skiffs of oyster "tongers" and the tall masts of the last big fishing fleet under sail in the United States. These "skipjacks" and "bugeyes" belong to the oystermen, who—under conservation laws—must dredge the Chesapeake's celebrated oysters without using motors. The white sails and the offshore duck blinds, screened with marsh grasses and evergreen branches, contrast strongly with the furious modern pace and industrial turbulence of Baltimore. Yet this curious balance has enabled Marylanders to maintain a steady growth during the 300 years in which the region has advanced from an Indian tribal society to an English feudal domain and finally to a democratic state.

Up the Chesapeake in the spring of 1634 sailed the *Ark* and the *Dove,* carrying the first English colonists into a territory inhabited by Indians, whose methods of netting fish had remained the same for over a thousand years. The settlement in the southern part of the state near Leonardtown was the first on land granted under a royal charter to George Calvert, first Lord Baltimore, in 1632. He died before the document was actually signed, and his son Cecilius assumed feudal rulership of a 10,000,000-acre tract of wilderness that stretched from the Susquehanna River to the Potomac. Although Cecilius Calvert, a Roman Catholic, and his colonial assembly enacted a law granting freedom of worship, Protestants twice overthrew his government. In 1691, England intervened, and the colony was ruled by a royal governor appointed by London for the next 24 years until the fifth Lord Baltimore, a Protestant, resumed control of Maryland. It remained in the Calvert family until the Revolution.

The comparatively mild climate permitted long growing seasons, and for the most part the local Indians were friendly. When the clay soil was found to be ideal for tobacco, plantations and large manor estates managed by nobles and worked by commoners and slaves rose along the Potomac and other rivers.

Although ship construction and ironworking became major industries during the eighteenth century, by 1750 Maryland was encountering its first serious economic difficulties. Dependence on tobacco had placed planters in such financial bondage to British merchants that some of Maryland's people described the plant as "also our law, religion and our curse." Extended cultivation of the single crop had exhausted the soil, lowered the quality of the tobacco and diminished the colony's income.

During the Revolutionary War, soldiers from Maryland—regular troops of the line—fought with distinction, particularly at the Battle of Long Island. Their gallantry resulted in the nickname of the Old Line State.

Independence brought great changes. Baltimore was transformed into a major seaport. With the opening of the Western lands, commerce from new settlements in Ohio and Pennsylvania, Indiana and Kentucky flowed directly eastward toward Baltimore. By 1810 it had become the third largest city in America; the harbor was thronged with great merchant ships from the East Indies, Europe and Africa. The Baltimore clippers developed for use on Chesapeake Bay were the forerunners of the famous ocean-going clipper ships. Maryland in 1791 gave the land for the national capital—the District of Columbia.

In 1818 the National Road, the greatest wagon road in the world (on which two six-horse teams could race side by side), was completed from Cumberland as far as the Ohio River, linking Maryland with St. Louis and New Orleans through the steamboat traffic on the Ohio and Mississippi rivers. Begun in the 1830's, the Baltimore & Ohio, first railroad opened for public traffic, was built to compete with New York's Erie Canal. Taking full advantage of the state's geographical location and potential, foresighted leaders had made certain that their people would be able to hold their own with such Eastern giants as New York and Pennsylvania.

Maryland's southern ties to neighboring Virginia and its slave-plantation traditions brought bitter divisions during the Civil War, with the tragedy of brothers and friends arrayed against each other. But the state remained in the Union. The Battle of Antietam, one of the bloodiest of the entire conflict, in which 21,000 men were wounded in a single day, was fought in western Maryland.

Industry, ranging from Baltimore's booming complex to Hagerstown's aircraft plants and pipe-organ factories, now outranks agriculture and fishing in economic importance by five to one, but Chesapeake Bay's seafood is still a multimillion-dollar business. Thanks to the prodigious swarms of marine organisms in the bay's waters, and the many rivers and estuaries that provide natural feeding and spawning grounds, it is one of the nation's richest fishing areas. More than 200 different species of fish are taken by commercial and sports fishermen. The bulk of the Maryland crabs and terrapin are raised in shallow-water "farms" along the Eastern Shore.

While the great bay dominates the eastern half of the state, the central region's rolling Piedmont produces 20,000,000 bushels of corn annually along with hay and wheat. This is also Maryland's "horse country," graced with racehorse breeding stables, steeplechase courses and hunt clubs. Beautiful state forests blanket the western counties. In the Catoctin Mountains is the federally owned retreat used by every President since Franklin D. Roosevelt, known as Shangri-la or—later—Camp David.

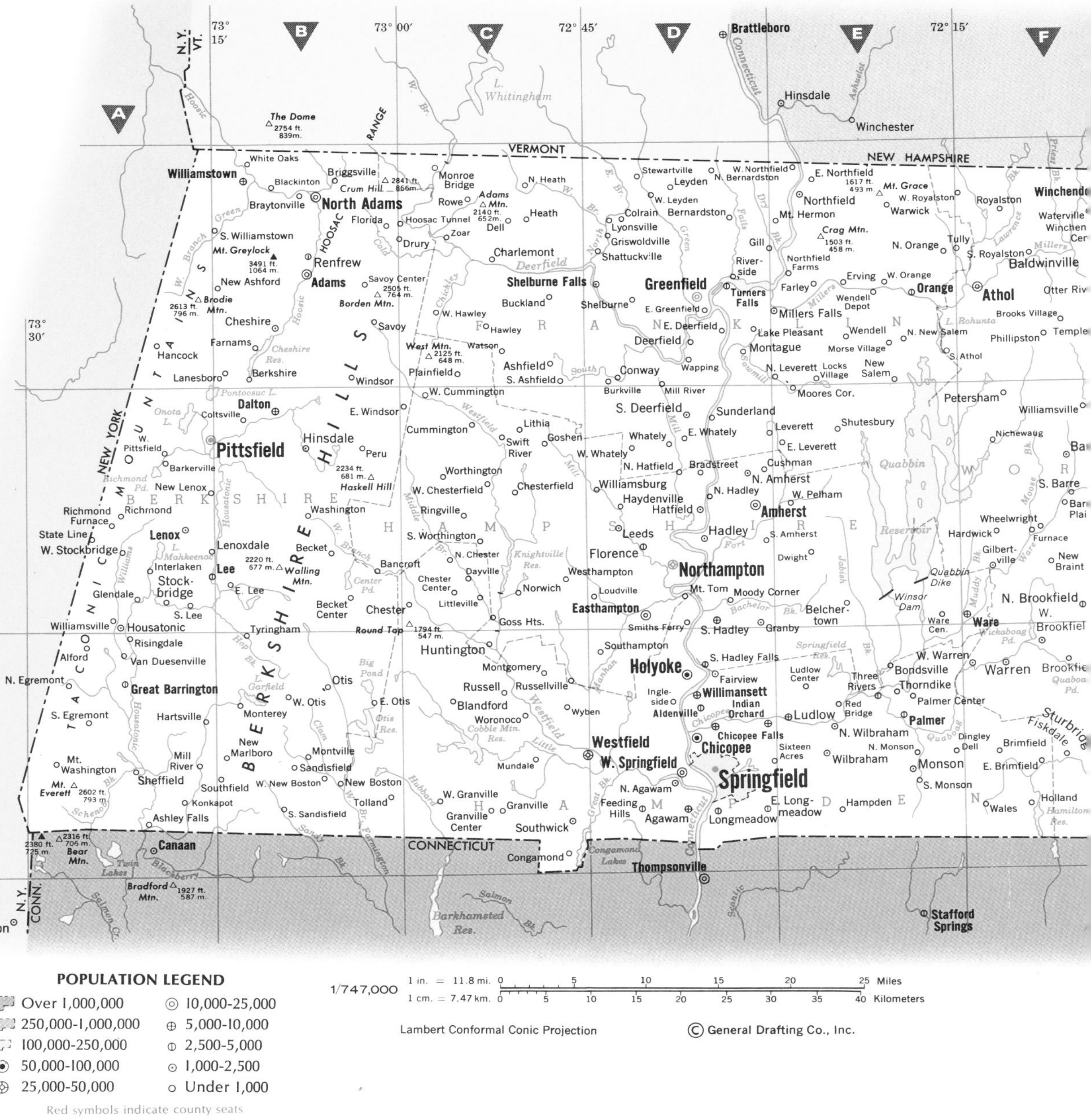

MASSACHUSETTS

From Provincetown, at the outer tip of Cape Cod, to Pittsfield in the western Berkshire Hills, Massachusetts is crowded with museums, monuments, ancient dwellings and restored villages. Everywhere the past is very much a part of the present. At Plymouth women weave wool and dye it with hemlock bark and pokeberry juice; men demonstrate the operation of a saw pit; candles are dipped. At Old Sturbridge Village gristmills grind corn, tinsmiths make lanterns and cookie cutters, while the printer sets broadsides in the eighteenth-century manner. The cradle of Peregrine White, the first Pilgrim child born in America, may be seen at Plymouth; Ralph Waldo Emerson's private study is shown in Concord. "Old Ironsides," as the famous frigate *Constitution* was known, can be toured in Boston, or the visitor may board a model of an 1830 whaler in New Bedford.

For three centuries Massachusetts—a small state, ranking forty-fifth in the Union—has exerted an extraordinary influence on the government, business and mainstreams of thought in the rest of America. It has only one major seaport, a handful of medium-size cities and no giant industrial complexes such as sprawl across the landscape elsewhere. Save for one fairly fertile farm valley (the Connecticut), the land is generally thin-soiled, hilly, rough and rocky or composed of low-lying sand dunes and coastal marshes. But this is one of the leading industrial states and ranks tenth in population.

European explorers and fishermen are believed to have anchored in the bays and harbors of the Massachusetts coast as early as 1500. Some experts believe that the Vikings may have reached Cape Cod shortly after 1000. Not Plymouth with its legendary "rock," but a tiny island in Buzzards Bay, later named Cuttyhunk, was the site of the first known habitation by white men in Massachusetts. In 1602 the English navigator Bartholomew Gosnold established a fort there while visiting Martha's Vineyard. At that time he gave the name Cape Cod—because of the fish offshore—to the long elbow of land that curves out into the Atlantic Ocean.

Then, in the autumn of 1620, the *Mayflower,* carrying the Pilgrims, an English group seeking religious freedom, was driven off course by heavy storms while heading for settlement in Virginia and sought shelter in Cape Cod Bay at Provincetown. It is not necessary to idealize the

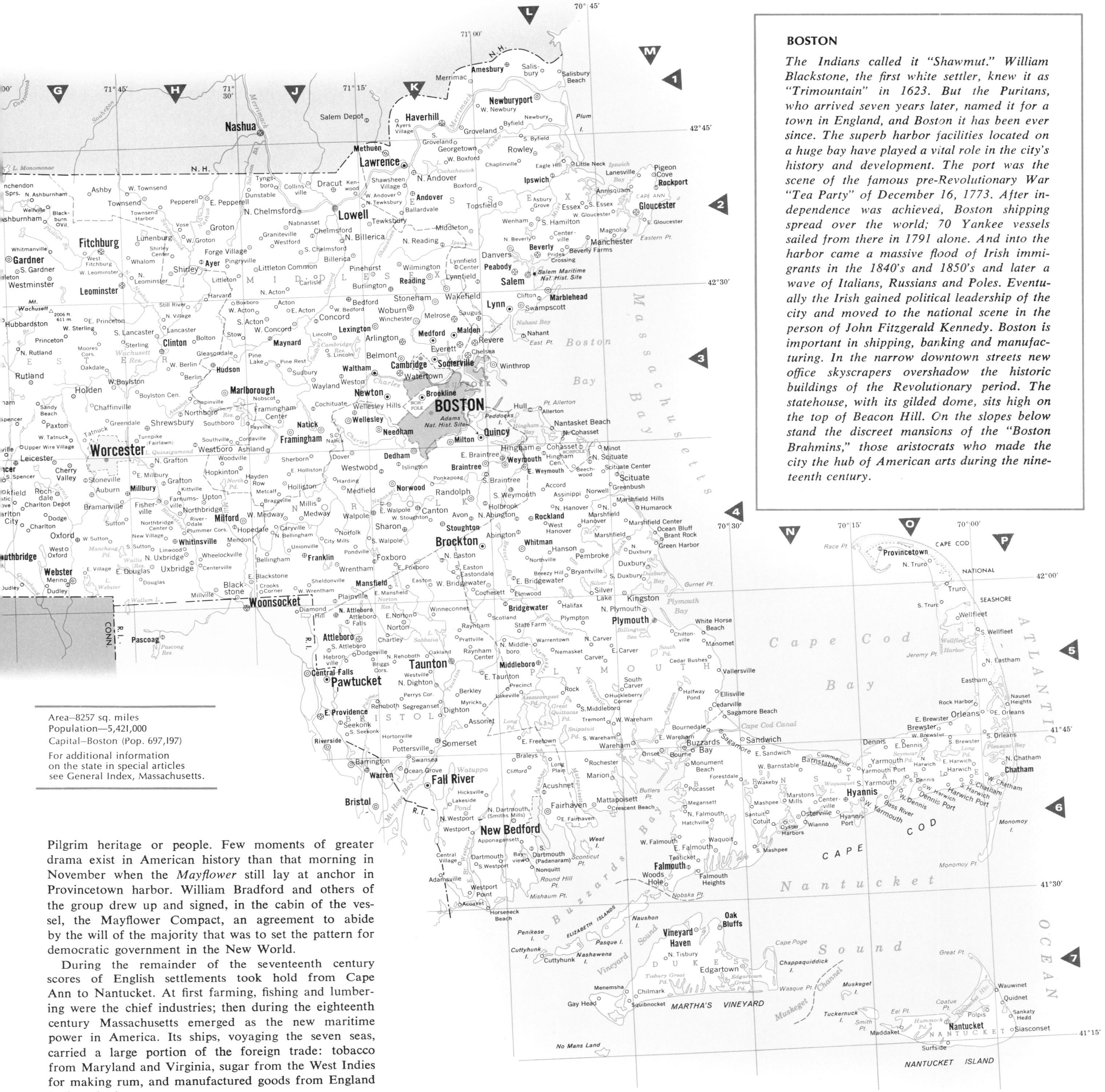

BOSTON

The Indians called it "Shawmut." William Blackstone, the first white settler, knew it as "Trimountain" in 1623. But the Puritans, who arrived seven years later, named it for a town in England, and Boston it has been ever since. The superb harbor facilities located on a huge bay have played a vital role in the city's history and development. The port was the scene of the famous pre-Revolutionary War "Tea Party" of December 16, 1773. After independence was achieved, Boston shipping spread over the world; 70 Yankee vessels sailed from there in 1791 alone. And into the harbor came a massive flood of Irish immigrants in the 1840's and 1850's and later a wave of Italians, Russians and Poles. Eventually the Irish gained political leadership of the city and moved to the national scene in the person of John Fitzgerald Kennedy. Boston is important in shipping, banking and manufacturing. In the narrow downtown streets new office skyscrapers overshadow the historic buildings of the Revolutionary period. The statehouse, with its gilded dome, sits high on the top of Beacon Hill. On the slopes below stand the discreet mansions of the "Boston Brahmins," those aristocrats who made the city the hub of American arts during the nineteenth century.

Area—8257 sq. miles
Population—5,421,000
Capital—Boston (Pop. 697,197)

For additional information on the state in special articles see General Index, Massachusetts.

Pilgrim heritage or people. Few moments of greater drama exist in American history than that morning in November when the *Mayflower* still lay at anchor in Provincetown harbor. William Bradford and others of the group drew up and signed, in the cabin of the vessel, the Mayflower Compact, an agreement to abide by the will of the majority that was to set the pattern for democratic government in the New World.

During the remainder of the seventeenth century scores of English settlements took hold from Cape Ann to Nantucket. At first farming, fishing and lumbering were the chief industries; then during the eighteenth century Massachusetts emerged as the new maritime power in America. Its ships, voyaging the seven seas, carried a large portion of the foreign trade: tobacco from Maryland and Virginia, sugar from the West Indies for making rum, and manufactured goods from England to the colonies.

When the British attempted to regulate this sea commerce with taxes and trade restrictions, Massachusetts reacted with the defiance that led the other 12 colonies to join it in the American Revolution. The conflict actually began just outside of Boston in April 1775 in the famous clashes between American Minutemen and British troops at Lexington and Concord, and gained momentum in 1776 when General George Washington took command of the American forces in Cambridge and drove the British out of Boston.

After the Revolution it appeared that the state's destiny still lay with seafaring. In the first half of the nineteenth century there followed the eras of the clipper trade with the Orient, and the whaling industry focused around Nantucket and New Bedford. Boston and Salem were great international ports. Family fortunes were founded almost overnight. Many a Cape Cod sea captain was as well acquainted with the harbors of Canton, Sydney, San Francisco and St. Petersburg as he was with the India Wharf in Boston.

But the next revolution was at hand. By 1820 water-powered looms were turning in Lowell and Lawrence. The rise of the New England textile industry, its labor force augmented by immigrants from Europe, followed. With the opening of the Erie Canal, Massachusetts farmers found themselves unable to compete with the crops of the rich Middle West and either migrated west themselves or turned to work in mills and factories. In 1900 Massachusetts was making nearly half of the nation's shoes, nearly one third of its woolen goods and a third of its cotton products. Even though the tides of exploration, migration and settlement had flowed steadily westward, the state continued to dominate politics, education and culture. During the nineteenth century some of the greatest names in American literature (Hawthorne, Longfellow, Emerson, Thoreau, Melville, among others) created masterpieces of prose and poetry whose impact on the country has never been equaled by writers of any other region.

In the twentieth century of steam and steel, however, the state's fortunes declined. The textile industry moved south, lured by cheaper labor and lower operating costs. Other states and countries competed for the shoe market. Bitter labor strife paralyzed much of Massachusetts industry. By the time the Depression of the 1930's arrived, the economy had reached a critical level.

During World War II the first stirrings of a new age of science were felt. While Harvard held its place as the greatest of the state's many universities and colleges, Massachusetts Institute of Technology (M.I.T.) emerged as a leading center of science and technology in the United States. Its professors became scientific advisers to the White House and the Pentagon. Research projects led to the development of radar, the enormously complex electronic systems (DEW Line, SAGE and others) which serve as continental air defenses, and some of the first electronic computers. M.I.T. laboratories and classrooms, along with those of Harvard and Tufts, have trained so much scientific talent that a whole new research and electronics industry has been created. Route 128, the highway built around Boston, has become known as Space Highway and Electronics Gulch.

Meanwhile the cities of the interior — Springfield, Worcester and Pittsfield—are again making woolen goods, as well as electrical products, paper and plastics. Tobacco and a large onion crop are grown in the Connecticut Valley.

Tourism is at unprecedented levels. In the western Berkshires skiing, camping and autumn tours follow summer music concerts and dance festivals. The state's Atlantic harbors from Marblehead to Martha's Vineyard are crowded with pleasure boats. Cape Cod's National Seashore, a 40,000-acre area along the outer Cape, attracts a growing number of visitors, while the rest of the peninsula plays host to tens of thousands who come to soak up the sun, surf-bathe, dig clams, fish and enjoy excursion trips to Provincetown's potpourri of painters, Portuguese fishermen and handcraftsmen.

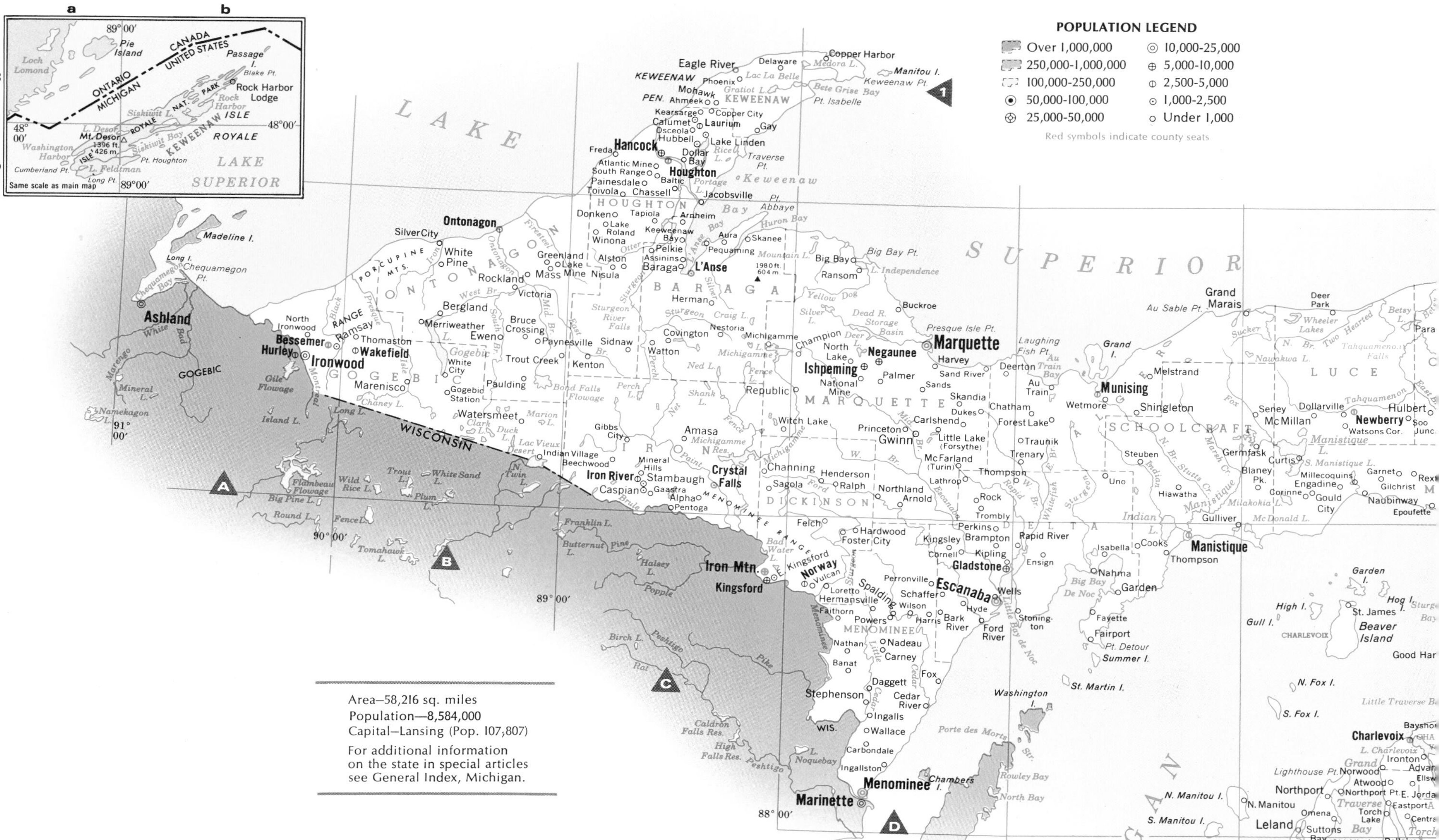

MICHIGAN

Michigan is known as the Wolverine State, but because that animal has not been found there since pioneer days, the automobile might be a more appropriate symbol. The American motor industry began in Michigan; more than 90 percent of the nation's cars are manufactured in the state and the car has, in turn, created the second most important business, the tourist trade.

The first automobile factory was built in Detroit in 1899 by Ransom E. Olds. Borrowing their body designs from existing horse-drawn coaches and carriages, the early manufacturers began production in cities where these vehicles were already being made—Detroit, Flint, Pontiac and Lansing. Then, in 1913, Henry Ford evolved the revolutionary technique of mass production on a moving assembly line, a process which reduced the price of automobiles and brought them within the means of millions of Americans. The history of the industry since that time has been one of continuous growth. In World War II it was converted quickly and entirely to the production of war matériel and turned out an unending stream of airplanes, tanks, ships, artillery and munitions.

The almost unlimited sources of hydroelectric power, the proximity to large markets, the presence of raw materials and the existence of a highly skilled work force have also benefited all industries, and Michigan's inhabitants earn a larger proportion of their income from manufacturing than do the workers of any other state. Furniture, machinery, chemicals, breakfast foods, athletic and sporting goods and bowling-alley equipment are among the important products.

Water Wonderland, the state's other nickname, explains why Michigan attracts more than 15,000,000 vacationists every year. With 3177 miles of shoreline on four of the five Great Lakes and more than 11,000 inland lakes as well as streams and rivers, Michigan has played host to tourists ever since the 1760's. The first summer visitors were friends and relatives of the British soldiers stationed at the fort on Mackinac Island.

Appropriately enough, Michigan was the first state to build a full mile of concrete road in 1908, and today four-lane, limited-access, toll-free highways, many of them following the original Indian trails, speed travelers to their destinations. The completion of the five-mile-long Mackinac Bridge across the Straits of Mackinac in 1957 eliminated a ferry crossing between the two peninsulas and has made the Upper Peninsula more accessible.

Michigan's natural resources were almost disastrously depleted during the 1800's in the mistaken belief that they were inexhaustible. When the white man first came to the region, all but a fraction was covered with forests. The British discouraged settlement to preserve the valuable fur trade. But with the opening of the Erie Canal in 1825, settlers swarmed in from the East. Lumbermen swept across the land like locusts, leaving in their wake cut-over fields, in general unsuitable for agriculture, and destroying the cover for fur-bearing animals. Such game as the passenger pigeon, the wild turkey and the grayling trout disappeared completely.

The state finally inaugurated a conservation program in the 1920's. Lakes and streams were stocked with fish. Reforestation was started on a large scale. Lumber companies now plant more trees each year than they cut. Today about half the state is once again covered by forests. Land acquired for nonpayment of taxes is turned over to the Conservation Department to be used for public purposes, if suitable. Michigan's deer population ranks third in the nation, and the number of licensed hunters is second only to Pennsylvania.

Etienne Brulé, seeking the Northwest Passage to the Orient in 1618, was the first white man to set foot on Michigan soil, at what is now Sault Ste. Marie. It was there that Father Jacques Marquette founded the first permanent settlement in 1668. At the end of the French and Indian Wars in 1763, the British took over Michigan and managed to keep control of it until 1796, 13 years after the peace treaty which ended the Revolutionary War. It was organized as a territory in 1805 under the Northwest Ordinance of 1787 and became the twenty-sixth state on January 26, 1837.

The city of Jackson shares with Ripon, Wisconsin, the claim to being the birthplace of the Republican Party. Antislavery groups, including Free Soilers, radical Whigs and radical Democrats, met in Jackson in 1854 and nominated a slate of Republicans who captured the state legislature that fall. Two years later the Michigan organization evolved into a national party.

The settlers who arrived after the public-land sales began in 1818 were also pioneers in education. Michigan was first to have a state superintendent of public instruction; provide a free high-school education for every child; establish a state agricultural college; and create a teacher-training department at its state university.

The former "happy hunting grounds" of the Indians, Michigan has sources of wealth as diversified as the nationalities of its immigrants. (Detroit is the home of the largest Arabic-speaking community on the continent.) Vacationists camp on what Longfellow called "the shores of Gitchee Gumee" in the Upper Peninsula. Lines of long, low grain and ore carriers, racing to beat the ice in the late months of the year, make the Soo Canal and the Detroit River two of the world's busiest waterways. Railroad passengers entering or leaving Detroit pass mile after mile of specially designed multi-level auto-rack freight cars, some loaded with new automobiles, others awaiting cargo. In the city of Holland, descendants of the Dutch settlers celebrate Tulip Time in May, and the President of the United States receives a cherry pie each July on the occasion of the National Cherry Festival in Traverse City.

1/1,930,000 1 in. = 30.5 mi. 1 cm. = 19.3 km. Miles Kilometers

Lambert Conformal Conic Projection © General Drafting Co., Inc.

DETROIT

The "Motor City" produces more cars and trucks in its industrial expanse than any other city in the world and because of this is the fifth largest in the nation. Even the name of the founder, Antoine de la Mothe Cadillac, who established Fort Pontchartrain there in 1701, has been perpetuated in one of the distinguished makes of cars. But Detroit is not just the city of automobiles. Its 6600 plants turn out a variety of products from steel to salt (which is mined beneath the streets and buildings). As up-to-date as a late-model car, it boasts a magnificent new $100,000,000 Civic Center on a 75-acre river-front site and a unique television traffic-control system that keeps its heavily traveled expressways and highways from being strangled. The mayor-council government is elected on a nonpartisan basis. (Pop. 1,670,144.)

MINNESOTA

(Turn page for state map.)

Of all the legends associated with the green countryside of Minnesota, the most famous are those about the giant lumberjack, Paul Bunyan, and his blue ox, Babe. It was the huge footsteps of Bunyan and Babe, plodding over the prairie land, that formed the more than 11,000 sapphire-tinted lakes strung out across the state. Historically the name Minnesota comes from two Sioux Indian words meaning "sky-blue water"; a more appropriate name would be hard to find for this region.

The Indians were the first to use the lakes and rivers as highways. After them came the fur trappers and lumbermen who floated freshly hewn logs down the streams and rivers to their rudimentary sawmills. Waterpower drove the early flour and lumber mills. Even before the Civil War, summer vacationists from the South were drawn to the cool lakeshores, and today tourism is still a multimillion-dollar business.

Minnesotans are probably among the most enthusiastic sportsmen and nature lovers in the nation, and they have 83 state parks and recreational areas to enjoy. In the thriving big city of Minneapolis are 153 landscaped parks and 22 lakes. The wide variance in seasonal temperature leads to an equally wide variety of sports. During the hot summer days, water skiing, canoeing, sailing, swimming and fishing are all popular pastimes.

Winters are extremely cold, and staunch Minnesotans or hardy visitors get out their skis, skates and iceboats. One most unusual cold-weather sport is ice fishing; determined sportsmen cut holes in the frozen lakes, taking fish from water considerably warmer than the air. Annual snowfall varies, averaging from about 20 inches in the extreme southeast to more than 70 inches in the northeastern corner.

More than 10,000 years ago, glaciers moved across the Minnesota region four times, leveling most of the land. And now, gently rolling plains cover much of the state. As the glaciers slowly edged south, digging pockets of ground that later formed lakes, bogs and swamps, they left behind extraordinarily rich soil. This is Minnesota's most important natural resource, giving it some of the finest farmland in the United States. The best acreage lies in the western and southwestern regions. Minnesota ranks fifth in farm income and is among the top states in growing corn, oats, flax and soybeans. Because of bountiful wheat crops and the importance of dairy products (it leads the country in butter output), Minnesota is sometimes called the Bread and Butter State.

Even so, industry now puts more money into the pockets of Minnesotans than do the farms. The biggest business is food-processing. The state's mills produce about one tenth of the country's flour and many by-products, such as breakfast cereals and cake mixes. Minnesota stands third in meat-packing. In recent years a $700,000,000-a-year electronics industry has been built up. Farm and mining machinery, metal products, abrasives, outboard motors and refrigerators are among the leading manufactures.

For many years mention of Minnesota meant one thing: iron. Three ranges in the northeast provide ore for more than half the iron and steel produced in this country. The Mesabi Range alone produces more than nine tenths of Minnesota's ore. After 80 years of open-pit mining, however, the richest type, hematite, has been dug out. At first experts thought exploitation of the lower-grade reserves would require too expensive a process to be profitable. But an inexpensive method has been developed whereby the ore called taconite is now converted into pellets before shipment, to make it more suitable for use in iron and steel mills.

The state also produces granite, limestone and sandstone, and has the unique distinction of possessing the only large deposit of pipestone in the United States, located in Pipestone County. For centuries, Indians have carved the bowls of their ceremonial pipes from this special rock, and today the National Park Service reserves this stone for the Indians' exclusive use.

Pierre Radisson and Médart Chouart, the first explorers, visited the area before 1660. The French built forts and fur-trading posts. That part of Minnesota east of the Mississippi was lost to England in 1763 but was joined to the territory of the United States after the Revolutionary War. The portion west of the river was acquired from France in the Louisiana Purchase of 1803. Lumbering operations began in the 1830's, and settlers followed in the wake of the timber crews, but Congress did not open the western part to settlement until 1851, when a great wave of migrants swept in. Many thousands came from Norway and Sweden alone in the 1880's and 1890's.

About 45 percent of Minnesota's population is concentrated in the Twin City area – Minneapolis and St. Paul. St. Paul is the center of the printing and publishing business, which ranks third in the state's industries.

People come to Minnesota for many reasons: some to receive topnotch medical care at the world-famous Mayo Clinic and Foundation in Rochester; others to visit the small town of Sauk Centre, home of Nobel Prize winner Sinclair Lewis and the setting for his best-known book, *Main Street*. Still other tourists head for Superior National Forest in the northeast corner of the state. This is an unusual wilderness consisting of forests, rivers, lakes and islands, where the only reconstruction of the landscape is done by busy beavers. There nature lovers can pitch their tents and, as they sit around their campfires at night, listen to the cry of the loons. When morning comes, they can pack provisions in their canoes and plunge even deeper into a land of unspoiled nature—of untamed animals, fish, flowers and sky-blue water.

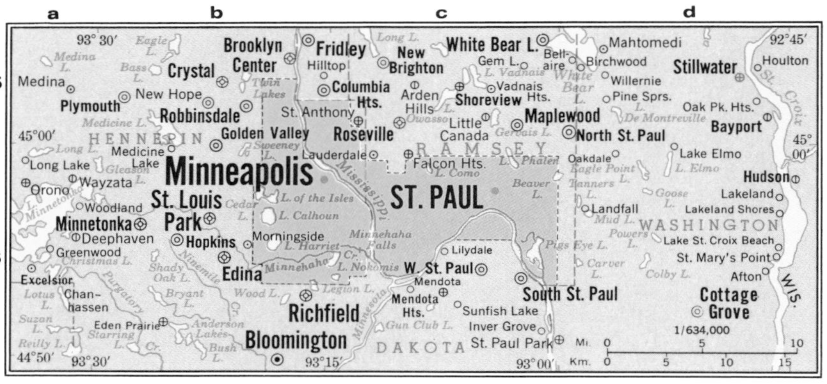

MINNEAPOLIS and ST. PAUL

Straddling the northern reaches of the Mississippi River, the twin cities of Minneapolis and St. Paul make up the major urban center in the northern Midwest. Minneapolis is proud of its size, its industrial diversity and its lakes and parks. In the early years, the mighty Falls of St. Anthony powered lumber and grain mills. When the forests had been denuded, wheat became king, and now stark grain elevators, erupting from the plains, dominate the skyline.

St. Paul is situated on a series of terraces. Railroad yards and factories cover the long riverfront; above them is the business section and on the highest bluff are the handsome residential areas. A friendly rivalry spurs the growth of both cities; one feature they now share is a major-league baseball team, its home park in neutral territory—the nearby city of Bloomington. (Pop. of Minneapolis, 482,872; of St. Paul, 313,411.)

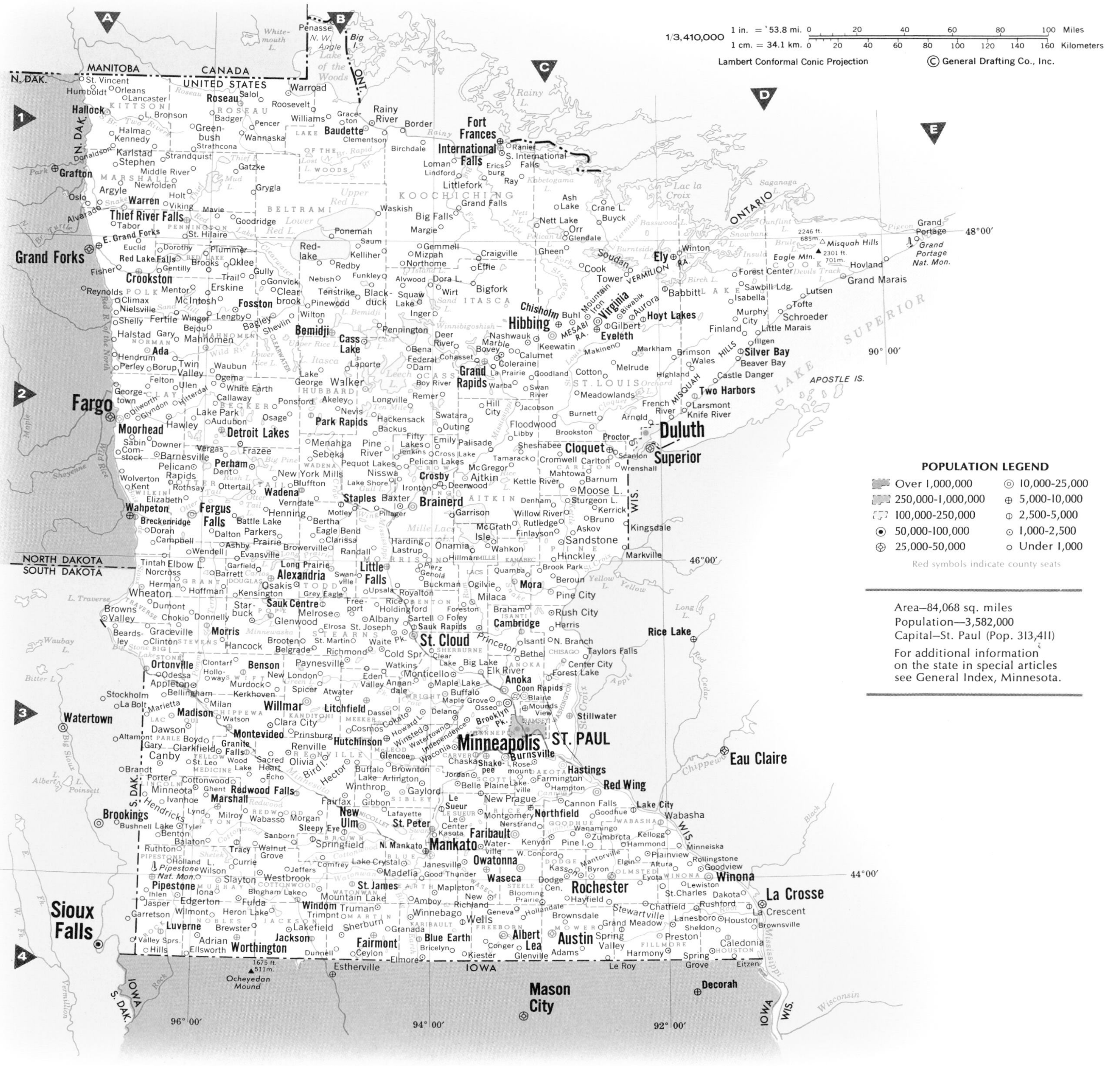

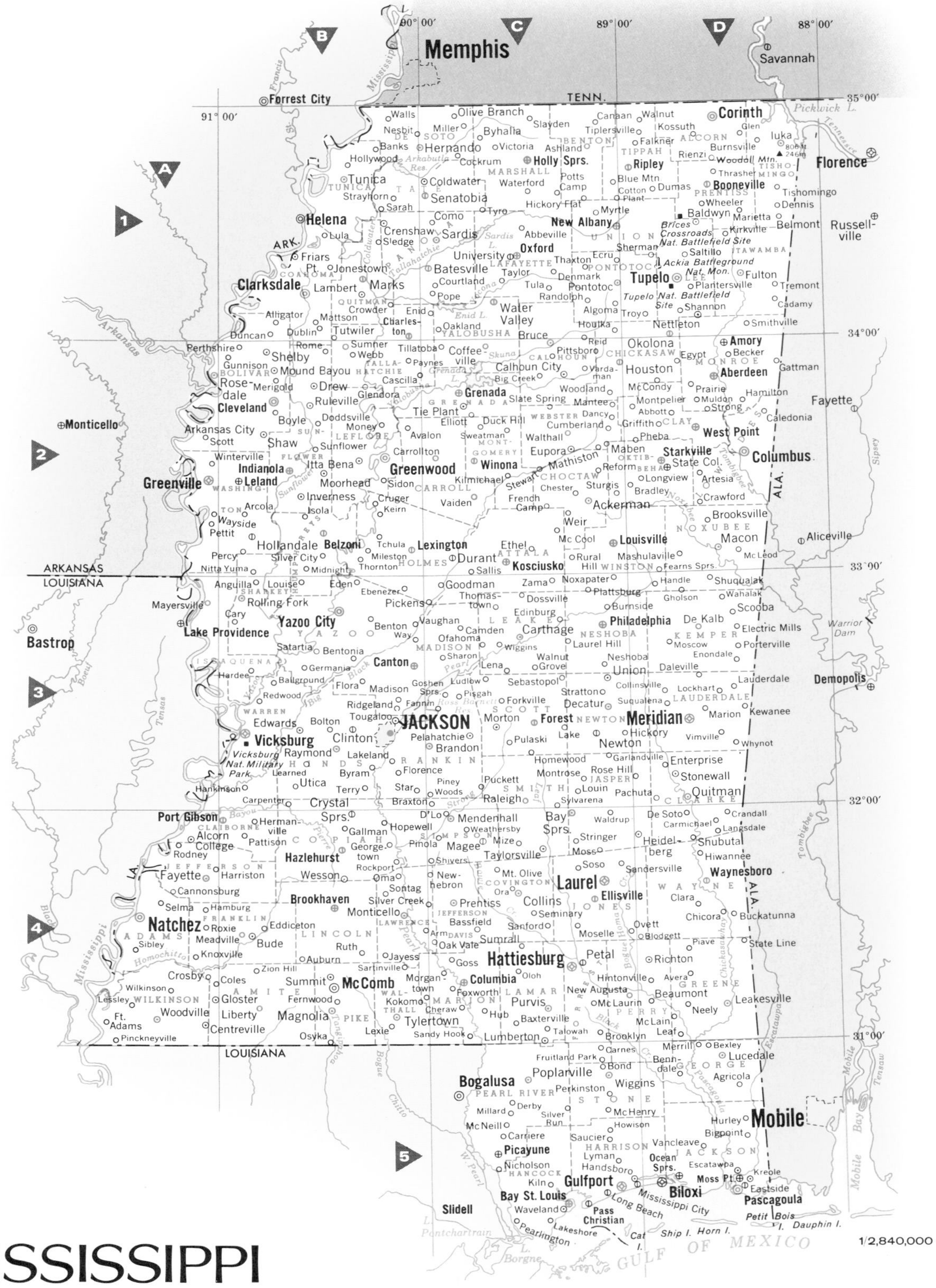

JACKSON

Amid shaded streets, the governor's mansion looks much as it did when it was built in 1842. Twenty years earlier, the legislators of the new state had decided that its capital should be centrally located. They chose the site of La Fleur's Bluff, a trading post on the Pearl River, and renamed it to honor Andrew Jackson. The original plans called for a checkerboard pattern, each square of building alternating with one of green parkland; some of these green squares still exist. During the Civil War several battles took place near the city and it acquired the nickname of Chimneyville because General Sherman burned so many buildings, leaving only the chimneys. Jackson was rebuilt, but it did not really begin to grow until after 1900. In that year the population was only 7816. The once sleepy streets are now busy with the bustle of Federal, state and local government employes, businessmen, conventioneers and industrial workers. A variety of products from textiles to machinery is manufactured there and refineries process petroleum from nearby oil fields. The gracious pace of the past lingers along with reverence for history, but these are fast becoming submerged by the ever-increasing tempo of the twentieth century.

POPULATION LEGEND

Over 1,000,000	10,000-25,000
250,000-1,000,000	5,000-10,000
100,000-250,000	2,500-5,000
50,000-100,000	1,000-2,500
25,000-50,000	Under 1,000

Red symbols indicate county seats

Area—47,716 sq. miles
Population—2,348,000
Capital—Jackson (Pop. 144,422)

For additional information on the state in special articles see General Index, Mississippi.

MISSISSIPPI

Nine different kinds of magnolias grow in the United States, and it is almost certain that a very large percentage of the total is to be found in Mississippi, the Magnolia State. The magnolia is its tree and its blossom is the state flower. Yet a less glamorous plant is far more important to the people who live there. The magnolia may be the symbolic queen of Mississippi, but cotton has been its king since the invention of the cotton gin in 1793.

Almost one half of Mississippi's farm income derives from cotton. The alluvial plain, or the Delta as it is called, which borders the Mississippi River in the western portion of the state, is one of the world's greatest producers of Upland cotton. Consequently the crop and the land on which it is grown have played a large role in the state's development. This region of rich, dark soil attracted settlers from the East in the early 1800's. The warm climate, the long growing season, the formation of large plantations and abundant, cheap slave labor were the ingredients of an early agricultural boom which helped Mississippi become one of the wealthiest states of the new Union. The same factors also shaped the character, attitudes and society of Mississippi's people so firmly that only cataclysmic events have been able to effect considerable changes over the years.

The Civil War ruined the rich agricultural empire founded by the early settlers. On July 4, 1863, Vicksburg, the last Confederate stronghold on the Mississippi River, surrendered to the Union Army. The fall of Vicksburg foredoomed the Confederacy. Bitter strife that has never been completely forgotten marred the postwar Reconstruction period; the state was not readmitted to the Union until 1870. Mississippi is a countryman's state with 65 percent of its population living in a rural environment. Farmers and people who inhabit small towns have, traditionally, been cautious, conservative and generally distrustful of outsiders. And those who suffered through the Reconstruction period, the occupation by Union troops, the carpetbaggers and scalawags, developed an even greater distrust. The land had once given them wealth and comfort; it would do so again when they were left in peace. This attitude, combined with memories of the past, was handed down, generation to generation, and is still very much a force in the life of many Mississippians.

The post-Civil War Mississippians were right about the land. It is the wealth of the state even in the much less fertile central and eastern regions. When the great Spanish explorer Hernando de Soto passed through the area in 1540, he was searching for Indian gold and silver treasure. He found neither, nor did he establish any settlements. De Soto did not recognize that the treasure was the soil. La Salle, who explored the Mississippi River in 1682, may have been more observant. He at least claimed the territory for France. In 1699 the French established a settlement at what is now Ocean Springs on the Gulf of Mexico, and 17 years later a second one at Natchez on the Mississippi. The first Negro slaves were transported from West Africa to Mississippi in 1719. These unfortunates initially worked rice and tobacco estates, and later, cotton fields. Negroes, many of them descendants of the first slaves, constitute 42 percent of the population of Mississippi.

Farms now cover about 60 percent of Mississippi, with cotton still the major crop. The fiber is used for cloth, some of it supplying the textile industry of Meridian and Biloxi, while the seeds are pressed to make cooking oil and the residual hulls are turned into fertilizer and cattle feed. Hay, oats and other field crops are grown in sufficient quantities to support a large livestock and major dairy industry. Mississippi is also a leading producer of peanuts, sweet potatoes and soybeans, and the state's pecans are sold throughout the United States.

Since land and agriculture are so important in the life of Mississippi it is not surprising that one of the forerunners of a famous farm-based movement started here. In 1907 William H. Smith, a superintendent of schools in Holmes County, organized the first demonstration "corn clubs" for boys and girls. The nationwide movement later adopted the name of 4-H Clubs, signifying development of head, heart, hand and health. Mississippi State University has one of the most complete seed-processing laboratories in the world and it has worked with more than 60 nations under the Agency for International Development. It also provides extensive help to a large number of American seed growers.

Much of Mississippi's manufacturing and processing industries is based on land-produced materials. The 2,000,000 cords of pulpwood cut each year are converted into paper products. About a billion board feet of regular lumber are turned out yearly, most of it from the eastern and central pinewoods sections. There are more than 3000 tree farms, all privately owned. In addition, factories in Natchez, Meridian and Greenville extract such wood by-products as pine oil, rosin, tar and turpentine. Food-processing and distribution employ nearly ten percent of the state's working force.

In 1939 petroleum was discovered at the little town of Tinsley (present population 250). This unsuspected natural resource—more than 350,000,000 barrels of oil reserve and an estimated two trillion cubic feet of natural gas—has begun to modify the economic base of the state by attracting new industry, though minerals still account for only nine percent of the state's income.

Mississippi glories in its past, especially treasured recollections of gracious antebellum life and the bravery of its 80,000 men who served the Confederate cause. Magnificent white-columned mansions adorned with marble, candelabra-lit ballrooms, art collections and gardens which were the pride of the South, are preserved in Natchez and other towns. There are more than 1500 historical signs, markers, tablets and monuments around Vicksburg alone. Residents will tell you that Jackson, the capital, was occupied by Union troops four times during the war. They will also remind you that 626 engagements were fought in the state during that great conflict.

Today Mississippi, which has produced such noted men as Jefferson Davis and William Faulkner, faces problems and a bright future. Recent laws enacted by Congress have run head-on into established Mississippi custom and beliefs, and farm mechanization is eliminating agricultural jobs. Yet industry spreads, providing new jobs, and urbanization is slowly modifying some time-worn ideas. At the same time a forward-looking policy of conservation protects the land resources of the state.

MISSOURI

The fertile plains, plateaus and rugged mountains of Missouri were inhabited by the Sioux and Algonquin Indians when the first Frenchmen penetrated the wilderness in 1673. These tribes were hereditary foes constantly at war with each other, but both maintained peaceful relations with the French traders and missionaries who sought only to collect furs and convert the savages to Christianity. French settlements were trading posts and missions, not farms and villages which would encroach on Indian hunting lands.

The Spanish, who took over the area by treaty in 1762, upset this balance by encouraging pioneers from the East. The same policy was continued when the United States acquired Missouri in 1803 as part of the Louisiana Purchase. As the need for land became greater, land agreements with Indians were broken. Bloody Indian raids soon followed the influx of settlers and continued until 1815, when a treaty was signed with 19 of the tribes.

Despite a rapid increase in the number of settlements, the early history of Missouri is one of transient populations. By 1820 the era of steamboats had dawned, and St. Louis on the Mississippi was the western edge of the American frontier. As the tides of fur-trapping, trading, exploration and fortune-seeking swept westward the Missouri River ports were at their peak. Hooting steamboats jammed their waterfronts. Streets were thronged with Indian scouts, trappers, bullwhackers, mule skinners, wagon masters, gunsmiths, gamblers and homesteaders. Armies of immigrants and fortune hunters surrounded the cities in huge tent encampments. Independence, Kansas City and St. Joseph were jumping-off points and supply centers for the Oregon Trail, the Middle Trail to Colorado, the Santa Fe Trail to Mexico, the California and Overland Trails. From these towns, stagecoaches, Pony Express riders and wagon trains set out for the West. Most people came and moved on.

Just before the Civil War the state's role as a way station on the road west began to change rapidly. It continued to be a transportation center, as it is today, but more and more of the thousands who came from the East remained. Large groups of Mormons tried to settle around Independence in the 1830's but were driven away by established settlers. Scotch-Irish Americans came to the farm regions. Germans, fleeing revolutionary troubles in their own country in 1848 and thereafter, settled in the St. Louis area, modifying the aristocratic French-Spanish character of that city. The German influence on parts of Missouri was especially marked. St. Louis contains major shoe factories, legacies of immigrant German cobblers. It is also one of the largest beer-brewing areas in the United States and a major meat-packing center, thanks to German brewers and butchers.

The Civil War brought division to Missouri. It had been admitted to the Union as a slave state and many of its residents, especially those in the "Little Dixie" areas like Howard, Boone and Callaway counties, favored the South. But a convention in March 1861 voted to stay in the Union. Citizens of German origin supplied a good deal of the support for this vote. Bitter guerrilla warfare broke out, and of the 1162 battles and skirmishes which took place in the state (11 percent of those fought in the nation), many pitted brother against brother and father against son. Even after the war guerrillas turned outlaws continued to terrorize the area. One of the most notable of these was the legendary Jesse James.

When peace finally came, business and industry began to prosper once again. In 1904 Missouri's progress received global attention when a World's Fair opened in Forest Park in St. Louis to celebrate the centennial of the Louisiana Purchase. Missouri is now a major industrial and processing state. Twenty-eight percent of its workers are employed in approximately 7000 factories, manufacturing automobiles, railroad cars, trucks, airplanes and buses, plumbing equipment, tinware and farm machinery.

An important part of the processing industry is based on Missouri's agriculture. Meat, corn and dairy products account for a substantial portion of the state's output. One of the world's largest butter and cheese plants is situated in Springfield. Kansas City has a number of flour mills and one of the biggest pancake-flour factories is in St. Joseph. A considerable amount of cotton is ginned in the northern plains sections.

Lead-mining, which was Missouri's first industry, dates to the early 1700's. West and south of St. Louis lies one of the greatest lead deposits in the world. So rich is this lode that Indians and then farmers obtained the ore just by digging near the surface. Herculaneum and Joplin are important lead-smelting centers. The latter also processes zinc, which is present in the same areas in large quantities. Minerals now account for only a small portion of Missouri's income, but the state is still the most important producer of lead in the United States.

Missourians have always had a reputation for skepticism expressed in the saying, "I'm from Missouri, show me." Since the days when it was the starting point for pioneers and gold seekers, however, it has been a land of vision. In 1926, for instance, Charles Lindbergh, an unknown mail pilot, found men there who were willing to finance his dream of flying alone, nonstop, across the Atlantic in a little silver monoplane, *The Spirit of St. Louis.* And in the early 1960's teams of engineers and scientists built the successful Mercury and Gemini spacecraft in St. Louis. All Missourians (including Mark Twain and former President Harry S. Truman) practice the "show-me" philosophy, but none of them has ever been fearful of looking the future in the eye.

ST. LOUIS

Founded by French fur traders, and still an important raw-fur market, St. Louis began as a small post on the Mississippi River in 1764. In the early 1800's it was a principal point of departure for much Western exploration. From there, the journeys of Lewis and Clark and Zebulon M. Pike started. A large waterfront made it an early transportation center. After the Civil War, railroads reached St. Louis in increasing numbers, and now 18 major lines serve the city. With such good location and communications, a leading grain market evolved and large-scale manufacturing developed. But St. Louis is not concerned only with business: Former resident and newspaperman Joseph Pulitzer established the Pulitzer Prizes for great achievements in journalism, letters and music. The City Art Museum contains 7000 works of art. And a new 630-foot stainless-steel arch stands in the city, symbolizing its role as the "Gateway to the West." (Pop. 750,025.)

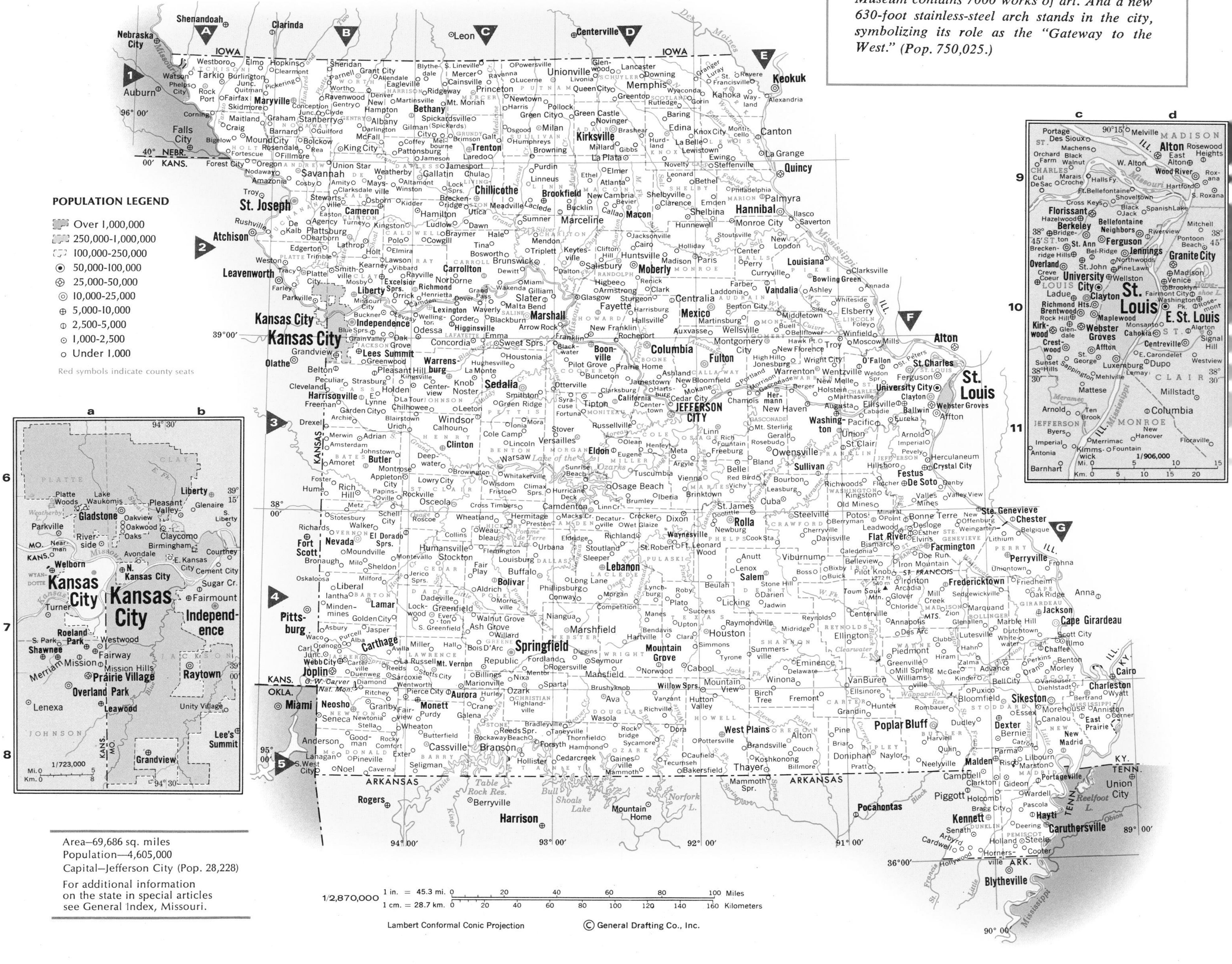

POPULATION LEGEND

- Over 1,000,000
- 250,000-1,000,000
- 100,000-250,000
- 50,000-100,000
- 25,000-50,000
- 10,000-25,000
- 5,000-10,000
- 2,500-5,000
- 1,000-2,500
- Under 1,000

Red symbols indicate county seats

Area—69,686 sq. miles
Population—4,605,000
Capital—Jefferson City (Pop. 28,228)

For additional information on the state in special articles see General Index, Missouri.

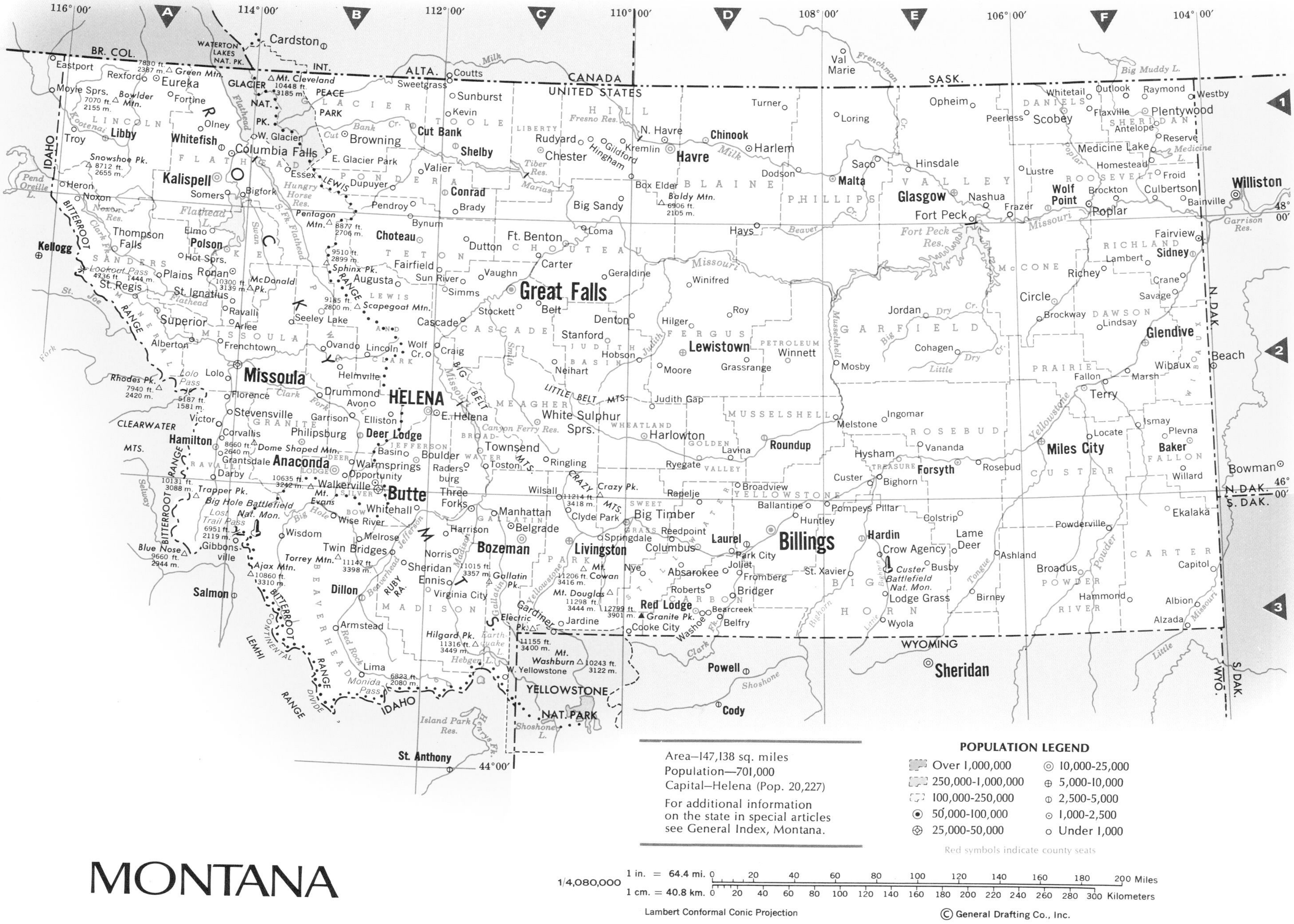

MONTANA

In Butte, hundreds of men a quarter of a mile beneath the city are drilling, dynamiting and bulldozing through solid rock, even while the inhabitants are asleep. Since 1864 a 300-mile honeycomb of tunnels and shafts concentrated in an area of less than six square miles has yielded about three billion dollars' worth of silver, copper, zinc, gold and lead.

Montana calls itself the Treasure State. The deposits beneath Butte are some of the richest in the world. And in the streams nearby, prospectors pick out sapphires, rubies, garnets, agates and other precious and semiprecious stones. Helena, where the state capitol's dome is appropriately sheathed in copper, was established when gold was discovered in Last Chance Gulch, now the city's Main Street.

This is only one of the astonishing aspects of life in Montana. Giant of the Northwest, the fourth largest state is made up of more than 50 mountain ranges, vast expanses of rolling plains, heavily forested wilderness, great cattle and sheep ranches, oil fields, and farms which grow wheat, corn, sugar beets and potatoes. It is also one of the most sparsely populated, with an average of only four persons per square mile.

Within Montana are portions of two of the West's most famous national parks. In the northwest is Glacier National Park with peaks and gorges, 60 glaciers, 260 lakes and huge forests. Here dwell deer, elk, antelope, moose, bear, mountain goats and cougars. In the south is one of the five entrances to Yellowstone National Park, whose canyons, waterfalls and rushing streams provide sportsmen with the finest trout fishing to be found anywhere in the United States.

Eastern Montana is no place for the man or woman who cannot take great extremes of weather. These range from −65° F., registered at Fort Keogh in January 1888, to 117° F., which was recorded twice, at Glendive in July 1893 and at Medicine Lake in July 1937. On the plains, ranchers and wheat farmers bake in summer, and in winter keep a wary eye peeled for blizzards and driving sleet storms. These have caused enormous livestock losses more than once in the state's history. Western Montana, protected from the Arctic winds by the Rocky Mountains, usually has milder winters but lots of snow. Summers in the mountain ranges are delightfully cool.

Local raw materials are the basis of the principal industries—smelting, refining, food-processing and lumbering. Sheep production is important, although it has dropped somewhat since the turn of the century, when the 1900 wool clip was the largest in the nation. Billings is an agricultural trading center and wool-shipping point. Missoula is the home of flour and lumber mills, sugar-refining plants and Montana State University.

The sweet grass that once covered Montana's plains drew huge herds of buffalo into the region, and it was a much-esteemed Indian hunting ground when Pierre de la Vérendrye from Canada first passed through it in 1743. Probably no other state had such an array of colorful tribes which later became famous in American frontier history. Among those with whom the pioneers first traded and then fought were the Sioux, the Crows, the Blackfeet, the Cheyenne, the Flatheads, the Nez Percé, the Assiniboin and the Gros Ventre. Violent skirmishes and battles began in 1805, when the Lewis and Clark expedition crossed the area on its exploration route to the Pacific, and continued until the late 1870's. It was in the Little Bighorn Basin that General George Custer made his famous last stand, where he and his entire attacking column were wiped out to a man. The Indians were finally subdued and the surviving tribes moved to reservations. Native languages, Indian ceremonial dances and meetings are still very much a part of Montana life.

Fur traders were almost the only inhabitants until gold was discovered in 1862, and two years later Congress created Montana Territory, which had successively been part of the Louisiana, Missouri, Nebraska, Dakota, Oregon, Washington and Idaho territories. Mining, ranching and farming drew a wide variety of people. Early gold and silver strikes attracted many deserters from both the Union and Confederate armies. After the war's end Southern veterans left their devastated homes to start new lives in Montana.

Cowboys of Texas, Oklahoma and Kansas, who drove the huge herds of longhorns all the way from Texas to fatten on Montana's buffalo grasses, often remained and became ranchers. The construction of railroads later brought immigrants from Europe—English and Irish to work in the mines, Germans and Scandinavians to farm the land. Many of their descendants keep alive old customs and cultures. Montana was a frontier built by pioneers from many lands.

GREAT FALLS

In 1890 Paris Gibson, a Minneapolis miller, was impressed with the industrial potential of a 75-foot-high waterfall on the Missouri River. He returned three years later to this spot, opposite the Sun River, and laid out town streets, calling his dream city Great Falls. Gibson's vision did not take long to grow into actuality. Within a few years the first of a number of hydroelectric plants was installed. Today five dams on the Missouri supply 230,000 kilowatts of electric power to copper- and zinc-smelting plants. Oil refineries, flour mills and other industrial enterprises have been developed over the years to process resources of the area. The neighboring country is dotted with farms and cattle ranches. The clear air and weather of Great Falls, together with its strategic flight-range in relation to Alaska and the Aleutians, prompted the U.S. military command to build a large air base during World War II. This base has become one of the biggest intercontinental-ballistic-missile (ICBM) complexes, and Air Force personnel and their families make up more than one fifth of the city's population. Great Falls is situated in what used to be the heart of the Blackfeet Indian country, and is surrounded by open spaces and scenic attractions. The Lewis and Clark National Forest is nearby. So is Giant Spring, from which flow 388,000,000 gallons of clear water daily. (Pop. 55,357.)

NEBRASKA

A series of natural and financial catastrophes had to be overcome by its farmers and ranchers before Nebraska achieved the relatively stable economy it has enjoyed in recent decades. Grasshopper invasions, culminating in the disastrous infestation of 1874, drove out many settlers, their wagons bearing signs such as "Eaten out by grasshoppers. Going back East to live with the wife's folks." Whole herds of cattle perished in the blizzard and sleet storms of the 1880-81 winter. Then farm prices collapsed in 1890, and drought conditions lasted for most of the next 11 years. In a single year—1891—thousands of farm families left for the East in prairie schooners.

Prices fell again after the World War I boom. The Depression of the 1930's accelerated the downward trend; corn dropped from 77 to 27 cents a bushel and wheat from 99 to 34 cents. Farmers demonstrated against mortgage foreclosures, sheriffs refused to execute land sales and eventually a mortgage-moratorium bill was enacted. But the state did not fully recover until the early 1940's.

As a result of the natural disasters, Nebraskans take great care in the conservation of their most essential assets, soil and water. Systematic crop rotation, terracing, contour farming and pastureland management are practiced to keep the soil from eroding. Dams have been built for flood control, irrigation and watering livestock. In combination with pumping stations which tap the vast reservoir of groundwater, they now irrigate more than 2,500,000 acres. A pest-control program has reduced the danger of grasshopper plagues.

Nebraskans are as foresighted in government as they are in conservation. The state is on a pay-as-you-go basis, since the constitution bars a public debt of more than $100,000. It has the only unicameral (one-chamber) legislature in the country. Judges, school officials and legislators are elected on a nonpartisan basis. Coöperatives, started in the hard times of the 1890's, play an important role in the economy; nearly 400 associations of this type operate such businesses as oil stations, stores, grain elevators and creameries. Men like William Jennings Bryan and Senator George W. Norris exemplified the progressive spirit.

The state lies midway between the East and West coasts, and is itself divided. The eastern section has fertile farmland like that of Iowa and Kansas. The western region, with half as much rainfall and a lower population density, resembles the cattle ranges of Montana and Wyoming. Native grasslands, where buffalo grazed for centuries, provide valuable feed crops for livestock, and Nebraska is the nation's chief source of dehydrated alfalfa. Beef cattle are the most important product, followed by corn, wheat and hogs.

Coronado first explored the area in 1540, and a few Spanish explorers and French trappers visited Nebraska when it was part of the Louisiana Territory owned alternately by France and Spain. The United States acquired the area as part of the Louisiana Purchase in 1803, and later thousands of pioneers passed through over the Oregon and Mormon trails on their way to homesteads in Oregon and Utah and to gold and silver mines in Colorado and California. Permanent settlement was forbidden until 1854 because the region was maintained as Indian country, and until that year pro- and antislavery groups in Congress could not agree on terms for opening it up. Finally the Kansas-Nebraska Act was passed, creating two new territories instead of one and leaving to the inhabitants the decision of whether or not to allow slavery. Even then, prospective settlers were deterred by false reports of early explorers that the Platte Valley was a great desert unfit for farming. Later, the Homestead Act of 1862 provided free land, and both the end of the Civil War and the start of the Union Pacific Railroad in 1865 encouraged immigration. The railroad, seeing no profit in serving an area with few inhabitants, distributed pamphlets praising Nebraska's farmlands as far away as Europe. Soon war veterans, tenant farmers and German, Czech, Swedish and Danish immigrants were streaming across the Missouri. Lacking timber, those who settled on the grassy plains built sod homes whose walls blossomed with weeds, morning glories and prairie roses during the rainy season. The population grew rapidly, and Nebraska became the thirty-seventh state, in 1867.

Today the buffalo is seen only in game preserves. The nation's only man-made National Forest occupies a site on the formerly treeless plains, in the north-central part of the state. An early sod house still stands near Alliance. In a few places ruts created by the covered wagons which used the Oregon Trail may be seen. The descendants of those tough, determined farmers who stayed in Nebraska to survive the bust-and-boom, drought-and-rain cycles are generally prosperous and, appropriately enough, enjoy the highest life-expectancy rate in the United States.

OMAHA

The ferryboat company which laid out the site of Omaha and gave away free lots to encourage settlement in 1854 was determined that the new city should be the capital of the future state. A $3000 brick capitol was constructed without cost to the territory. Eventually the government moved to Lincoln, but Omaha has been the state's important transportation center since it was founded. The young city was an outfitting and starting point for settlers and miners heading west on the Oregon Trail. One steamboat a day was the average during its peak year as a river port. The eastern terminus of the first railway to the Pacific Coast, it became the nation's fourth largest rail hub. Today, nearby Offutt Air Force Base is headquarters for the Strategic Air Command. Once the principal trading post for buffalo hides, Omaha has grown to be one of the world's largest livestock and grain markets; food-processing is the leading industry. The city is famous for the annual ball staged by the Knights of Ak-Sar-Ben (Nebraska spelled backward), a civic and community promotion organization which also sponsors rodeos and cattle shows. (Pop. 301,598.)

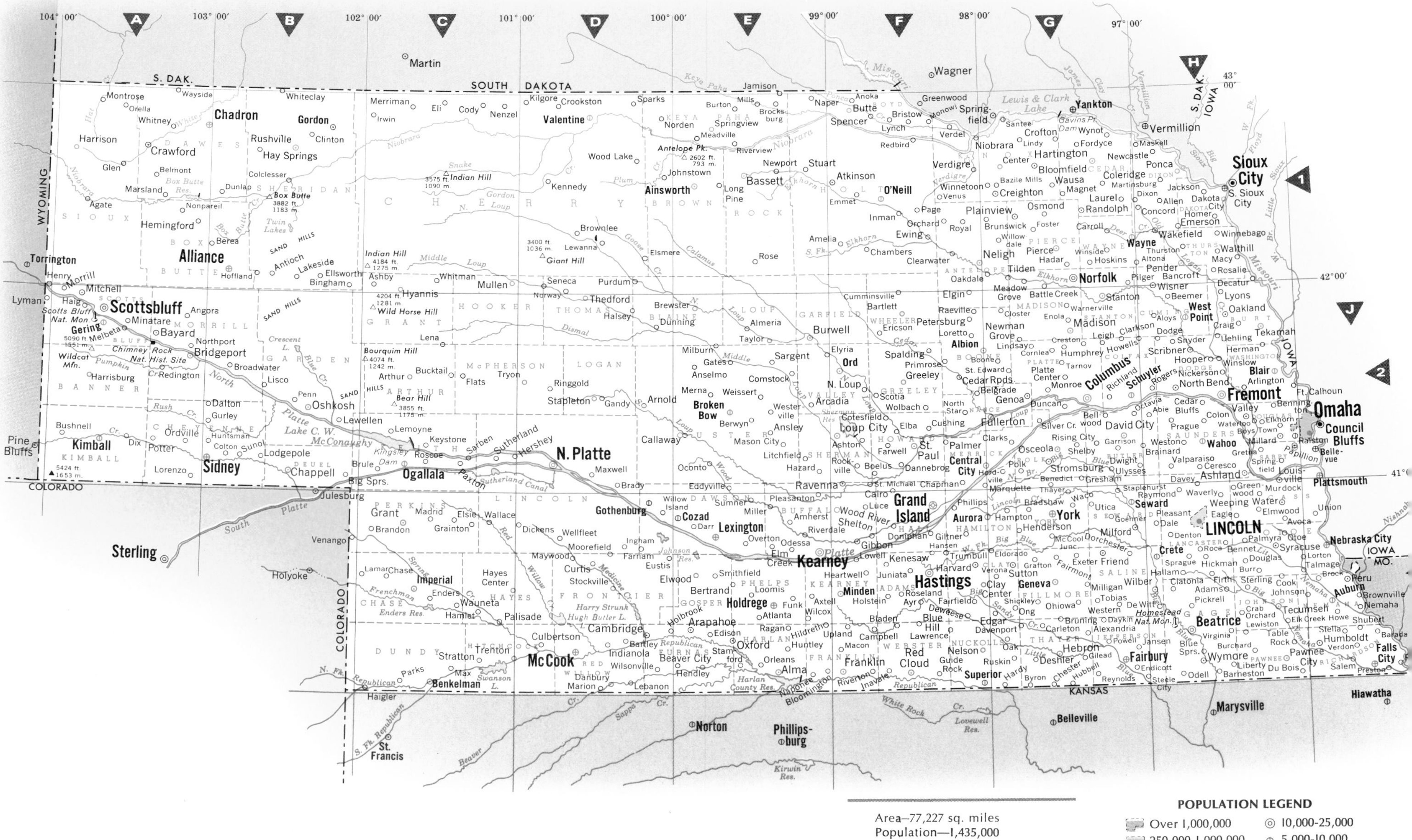

1/2,850,000 1 in. = 45.0 mi. 0 20 40 60 80 100 Miles
1 cm. = 28.5 km. 0 20 40 60 80 100 120 140 160 Kilometers

Lambert Conformal Conic Projection

© General Drafting Co., Inc.

Area—77,227 sq. miles
Population—1,435,000
Capital—Lincoln (Pop. 128,521)

For additional information on the state in special articles see General Index, Nebraska.

POPULATION LEGEND

- Over 1,000,000
- 250,000-1,000,000
- 100,000-250,000
- 50,000-100,000
- 25,000-50,000
- 10,000-25,000
- 5,000-10,000
- 2,500-5,000
- 1,000-2,500
- Under 1,000

Red symbols indicate county seats

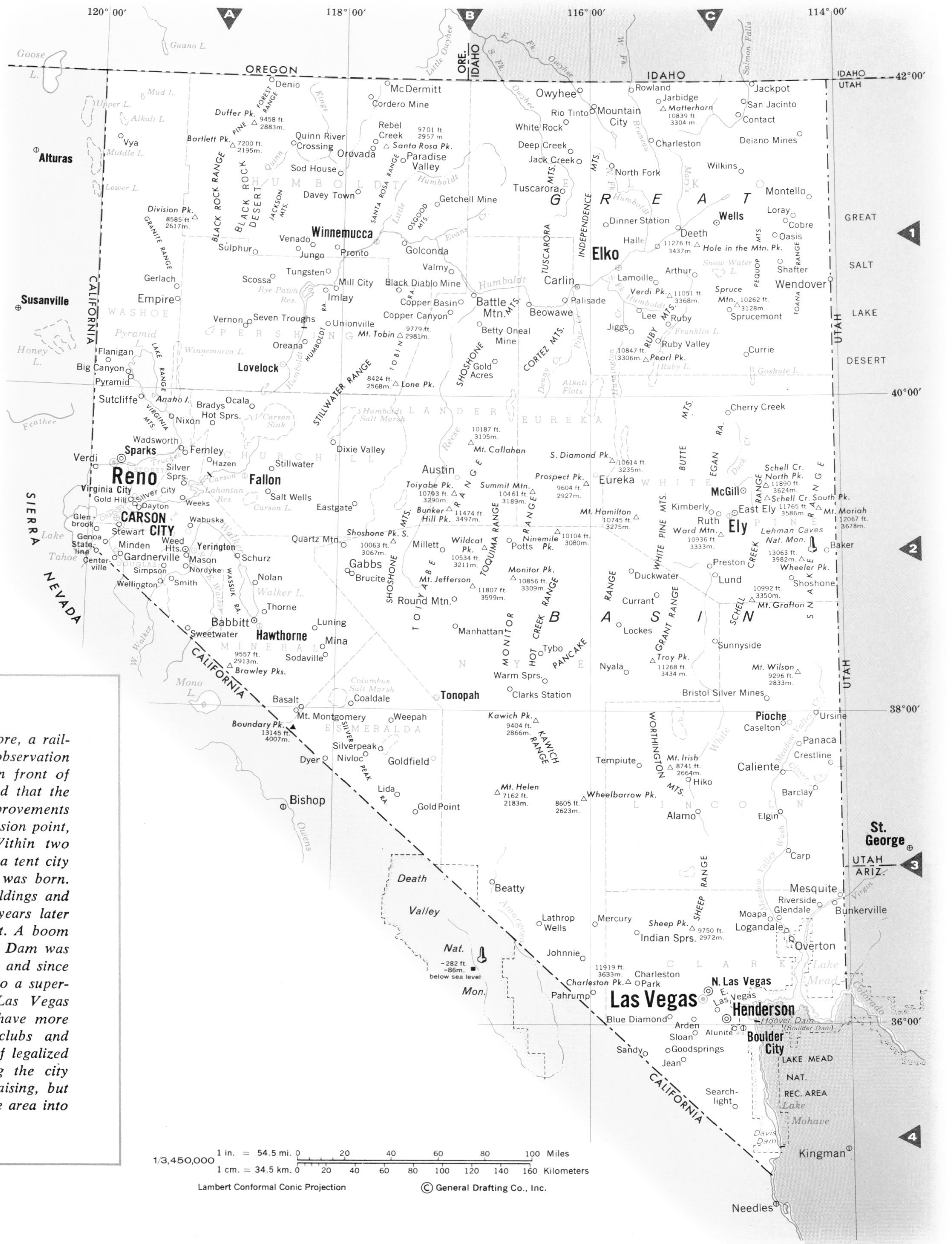

POPULATION LEGEND

Over 1,000,000	10,000-25,000
250,000-1,000,000	5,000-10,000
100,000-250,000	2,500-5,000
50,000-100,000	1,000-2,500
25,000-50,000	Under 1,000

Red symbols indicate county seats

Area—110,540 sq. miles
Population—444,000
Capital—Carson City (Pop. 5163)
For additional information on the state in special articles see General Index, Nevada.

LAS VEGAS

On May 15, 1905, C. O. Wittemore, a railroad executive, stood on a train observation platform in the Nevada desert in front of about 3000 people. He guaranteed that the company would make various improvements on the site it had bought for a division point, if town lots were purchased. Within two days 1200 parcels had been sold, a tent city had been erected and Las Vegas was born. In little more than a month, buildings and streets were taking shape. Four years later Las Vegas became the county seat. A boom hit the city in 1936 when Hoover Dam was built nearby, creating Lake Mead, and since then Las Vegas has developed into a super-luxury resort. Three miles of Las Vegas Boulevard — called The Strip — have more than 300 hotels, casinos, nightclubs and motels thriving on the proceeds of legalized gambling. The lands surrounding the city were always too dry for cattle-raising, but irrigation has now transformed the area into farmland. (Pop. 64,405.)

NEVADA

Nevada was the last of the Western territories to be explored, and it really is not settled yet. Three quarters of its people live in and around Las Vegas and Reno. Aside from cattle and sheep ranches in the north and central sections, and irrigated farmlands in the drier valleys, the rest of this immense state, seventh largest in the nation, sees few people.

In Spanish the word *nevada* means "snow-clad," and the state's name comes from the great range of snowy-peaked mountains—the Sierra Nevadas. They are responsible for making it the most arid state in the country. Moisture-laden rain clouds rolling in from the Pacific Ocean are blocked by the Sierras, which extend north and south along the California border. Without water, most of Nevada remains a barren wilderness of sand, rocks and sagebrush, where summer temperatures may reach 108° F. in the midday sun.

Long after California was settled, when towns were sprinkled all along the west coast of North America from Mexico to Alaska, Nevada remained a forbidding land of mystery. The trapper and explorer Jedediah Smith, who was the first man to make an overland journey from Missouri to California, passed through the region in 1826–27. Smith hoped he might find the legendary Buenaventura River, a great west-flowing tributary rumored to have its headwaters in an inland sea and to be filled with hordes of beaver. But all that Smith encountered was "a country of starvation—sandy plains and rocky hills."

Silver strikes in Nevada's rugged mountains, principally the discovery of the Comstock Lode—which yielded $300,000,000—touched off a great rush of newcomers into the territory between 1859 and 1865. Among the migrants was Mark Twain, who came west by stagecoach, mined silver and stayed to write yarns for the newspaper in Virginia City. None of these settlers dreamed that the territory would ever be good for anything but mining. As late as the 1920's, Reno was a dusty cow town and Las Vegas little more than a scattering of shanties surrounding a rattlesnake-infested railroad junction.

The Depression created such widespread financial distress that Nevada legalized gambling and quick divorces to bring in tourists and travelers from other states. By 1940 these had made Reno a boomtown. After World War II, Las Vegas, closely linked by air and highway with Los Angeles, soon emerged as the greatest gambling show on earth. In one recent year 13,000,000 people arrived to spend $350,000,000.

Contrary to popular belief, Reno, once known as the divorce capital of the world, now records more weddings than divorces. Thousands of Californians come there to be married because of the state's uncomplicated marriage laws. Although gambling is one of its "industries," the city is also Nevada's financial and business center. The dude ranches and the scenery—the Sierra Nevada Mountains and nearby Lake Tahoe—now attract almost as many travelers and vacationists as gamblers, along with a large number of new settlers. For many of these new residents the immense sweep of the Nevada landscape, the arid desert and its invigorating, dry, clean air hold an endless fascination.

Tourism adds most to the state's income, while mining is the leading industry. Manufacturing, in third place, consists primarily of smelting and refining ores. Cattle and sheep, hay, wheat and alfalfa are raised on farms, ranches and government-owned grazing lands. A new industry has been created in the south-central section of the state, where Federal space agencies are developing nuclear reactors for voyages beyond the moon. But more irrigation is believed to be the key to future growth. "The scenery is already here," one oldtimer is fond of saying. "All we have to do is water it."

NEW HAMPSHIRE

From the sky New Hampshire appears to be a magnificent green blanket of forests and farmlands, and a range of lofty mountains. Yet tucked away in its southern river valleys and coastal region are cities such as Manchester, Concord and Nashua, whose mills and factories turn out freight-car loads of shoes, blankets, electrical machinery and paper products. From the state's quarries come the red, white and gray granite used in many public buildings and monuments from Washington, D.C., to Hawaii. Forests provide fir, spruce and other woods which make New Hampshire an important manufacturer of pulp and timber products. Portsmouth, the only seaport, has been renowned as a shipbuilding center since colonial times; it built many great Yankee clippers for the East India trade. Several hundred thousand pounds of lobster are landed by commercial fishermen who sail out of bays and harbors along a sliver (18 miles) of Atlantic coastline.

The largest area of U.S. public lands in the Northeast, the White Mountain National Forest (724,000 acres), is maintained for the production of timber, conservation of wildlife and watershed protection. A highway system developed during the 1950's made much of this region accessible and encouraged a steadily growing influx of year-round visitors. Lake Winnipesaukee, with 136 miles of forested shores and beaches and 365 islands, is a center for water sports. Numerous summer camps for boys and girls are scattered along lakefronts through the forests and mountains.

The White Mountains include six peaks more than a mile high and about 25 that are more than 4000 feet. Mount Washington, 6288 feet, is the highest mountain in northeastern America. In 1869 a cog railway was completed to the summit, carrying as one of its first passengers President Ulysses Grant; today the railway is busier than ever. The Appalachian Mountain Club maintains trails, huts and shelters throughout the region. Those who climb the White Mountains sometimes discover that even in midsummer the peaks above the timberline can be swept by sudden snowstorms, hurricane winds and hail.

Skiing was originally popularized by Norwegians who came to work in the logging camps and lumber mills around Berlin (New Hampshire has one of the oldest ski clubs in the East, founded in 1910). From Cannon Mountain in Franconia Notch, where an aerial tramway runs to the top of a ten-mile ski trail, to Mount Washington are some of the finest winter-sports grounds in eastern North America. Winter carnivals, inaugurated by the students of Dartmouth College in Hanover in the early 1900's, are held in various parts of the state.

Gomez, Verrazano and other early European explorers, probing the New England coast in the 1500's, used the range of mountains 80 miles inland as navigation landmarks. They called them the White Mountains because of the shimmering white outcroppings of mica and granite and the snow-covered peaks. In 1606, King James I of England authorized colonization of the newly discovered American lands from North Carolina to Nova Scotia. Captain John Smith, who had helped establish the first English settlement in the New World at Jamestown, Virginia, scouted the northern Atlantic coast from Maine to Massachusetts in 1614 and anchored in the vicinity of Portsmouth. He presented a map to Prince Charles, later King Charles I, who named the region New England. In 1622 the British Crown granted all of it to a group of English knights and merchants. The slice given to Captain John Mason, a London merchant, became New Hampshire, in honor of the English county in which he had lived.

The French and Indian Wars, together with deep snowfall and impenetrable forest, slowed the new settlement's development. Nevertheless, at the time of the Revolution, New Hampshire was robust enough to rebel strongly

MANCHESTER

Penacook Indians journeyed to the confluence of the Merrimack and Piscataquog rivers because fishing was excellent there. After 1722, when the first white settlers arrived, fishing developed as the major industry. The village was originally named Old Harrytown after a somewhat disreputable local Indian. By 1751 it had become Old Derryfield. In the early 1800's Judge Samuel Blodgett recognized the industrial potential of the rivers and built a canal around the Amoskeag Falls. The town's first cotton mill, built in 1805, was destined to grow into the huge Amoskeag Manufacturing Company, dominating the economy for more than a century. With foresight, the community in 1810 adopted the name of Manchester, the English industrial city. For years Amoskeag was the largest manufacturer of cotton textiles in the world, but it eventually went bankrupt in 1935 due to changes in tastes, mismanagement and Southern competition. The city recovered by diversifying its products, which now number above 100. It has also developed an airpark, where companies using private planes for transportation of executive and sales personnel have built plants around the airport with direct taxiways to their buildings. (Pop. 88,282.)

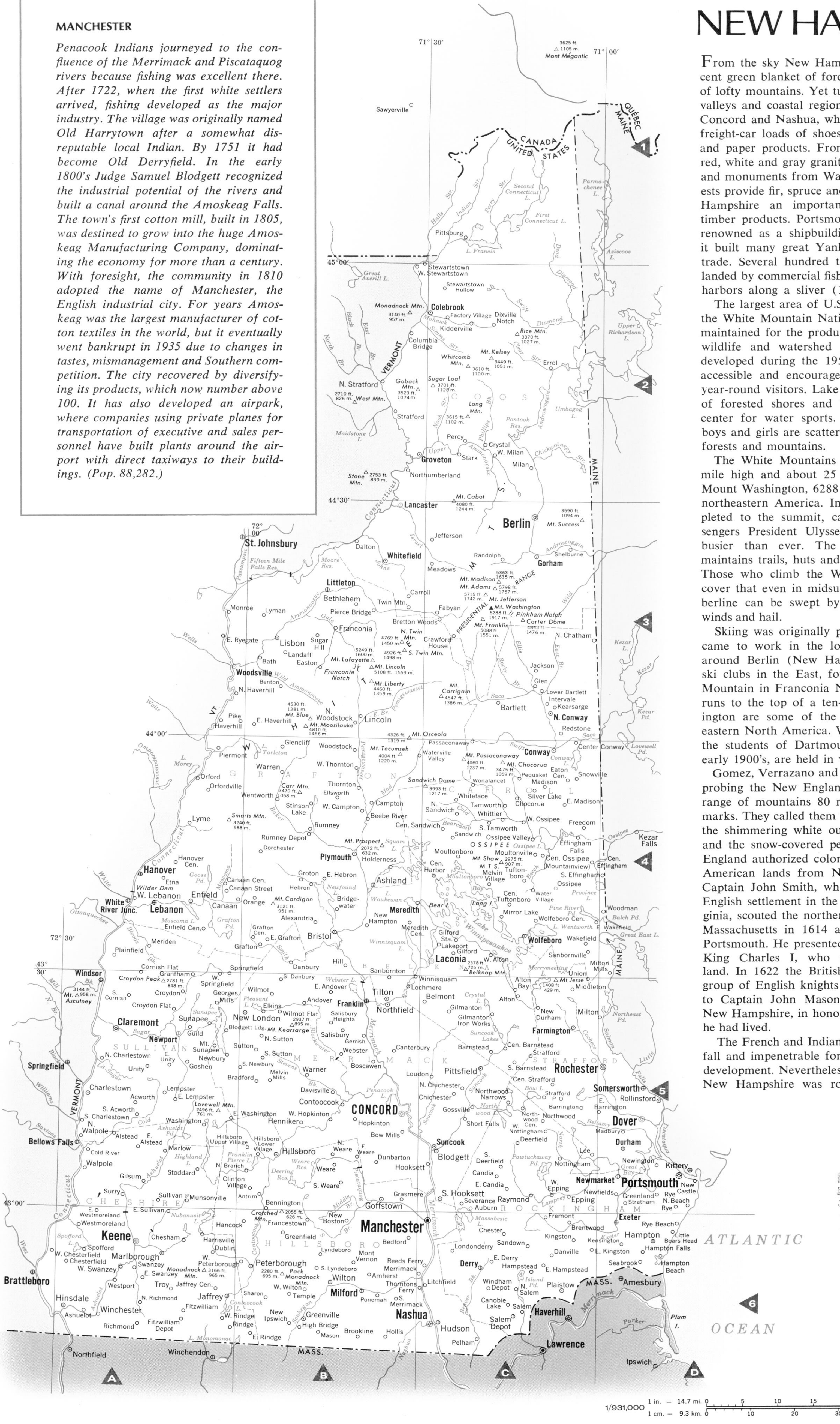

POPULATION LEGEND

Over 1,000,000	10,000-25,000
250,000-1,000,000	5,000-10,000
100,000-250,000	2,500-5,000
50,000-100,000	1,000-2,500
25,000-50,000	Under 1,000

Red symbols indicate county seats

Area—9304 sq. miles
Population—685,000
Capital—Concord (Pop. 28,991)
For additional information on the state in special articles see General Index, New Hampshire.

1/931,000 1 in. = 14.7 mi. 0 5 10 15 20 25 30 35 40 Miles
1 cm. = 9.3 km. 0 10 20 30 40 50 60 Kilometers

Lambert Conformal Conic Projection

against British rule. It was the first of the original 13 colonies to declare war on Great Britain and launched the first warship to fly the Stars and Stripes: the fighting frigate *Ranger* built for Captain John Paul Jones in Portsmouth in 1777. Three New Hampshire regiments played an important role, battling from Bunker Hill to Yorktown, fighting under Washington at Trenton and under Arnold at Saratoga.

Farmers found the thin, rocky soil so discouraging that many abandoned their lands and joined the migrations to the Middle and Far West. Ironically, a number of these families traveled in coaches made in Concord. From 1813 until after the Civil War these sturdily constructed vehicles were a principal means of transportation on the overland routes and a vital factor in the opening of the West.

New Hampshire's first settlers had been primarily of Scotch-Irish descent. As the industrial revolution of the nineteenth century reached New England, waves of mill and factory workers poured in from all over Europe and especially from Canada. Even today about one quarter of the population is of French-Canadian descent. Power looms and shoe factories spread through the river valleys. At the time of the Civil War, cotton-textile manufacturing was the state's key industry. When the textile mills moved south in search of cheaper labor and lower operating costs, New Hampshire's economy was dealt a tremendous blow. But today some of its old mill towns manufacture a wide range of electrical and electronic machinery. Poultry, eggs and dairy products account for most of the farm income.

The great American poet Robert Frost had a special love for New Hampshire. He lived there from his tenth to his forty-fifth year, first taught school there and once noted, "It has been New Hampshire, New Hampshire with me all the way."

NEW JERSEY

The people of New Jersey have long prospered because the state is the well-traveled corridor between New York and Philadelphia. From its earliest days, New Jersey has had a dual orientation, and has been pulled in two directions by the great cities on its front and back doorsteps, both of them natural markets for its agricultural and industrial products.

Verrazano, in 1524, was the first European to see New Jersey's shores. The original settlements across the Hudson River from New York were part of Dutch New Netherlands. To the south, fur trappers and farmers of New Sweden established posts on the Jersey side of the Delaware River. The English, on taking over these lands, gave them to private proprietors, but New Jersey remained divided into two separate provinces, as it had been since 1664.

East Jersey (more accurately, northeast) was noted for its religious tolerance, and was principally inhabited by former New Englanders who resented the rigid restrictions in their own towns—though they brought much of their Puritanism with them. West Jersey, including the southern sections, received an unmistakable Quaker stamp from William Penn's followers, who had settled there before he obtained the grant of Pennsylvania.

After the two Jerseys were united as a Crown Colony in 1702, they shared a governor with New York until 1738. Even then, the old twin capitals of Burlington and Perth Amboy served as alternate seats of the Assembly.

The state's geographic destiny as a corridor was never better fulfilled than during the Revolutionary War when the Continental Army shuttled back and forth. Nearly 100 battles were fought in New Jersey. One which helped to turn the tide was George Washington's victory at Trenton, where he surprised the garrison of Hessians by crossing the Delaware from Pennsylvania on Christmas Night, 1776. American troops were quartered in the state for three winters during the war, and two of its cities, Princeton and Trenton, served as temporary capitals when the fledgling Continental Congress found it dangerous to meet in New York or Philadelphia.

The mixed blessings of the corridor role became evident during the first years of independence. New Jersey suffered economic disaster as its great neighbors erected

NEWARK

For nearly 100 years after its founding in 1666, Newark was almost more puritanical than Puritan New England, original home of the town's first settlers. Resistance to strict church rule came in the 1730's when one member of the congregation harvested his wheat on a Sunday rather than see it spoiled by rain. Several decades passed before there was any appreciable relaxation of the severe ecclesiastical supervision of public and private life. Trade and industry flourished after the Revolution. Some of the earliest important products were beer, jewelry and leather, including patent leather, invented by Seth Boyden, a local resident. Beer and leather goods are still among the major manufactures, which include electronic equipment and chemicals. The city is also the fourth largest insurance center in the nation. The tubes under the Hudson River, connecting Newark with New York City, carry nearly 100,000 commuters each day, and traveling New Yorkers also use Newark Airport. Newark's subway, opened in 1935, was constructed in the bed of the old Morris Canal, which was completed in 1831 to link the city with the Delaware River. (Pop. 405,220.)

high tariff walls. At the Constitutional Convention delegates from New Jersey demanded a national government that would be responsive to the needs of small states and capable of regulating interstate commerce. They came home fully satisfied, and their state was the third to ratify the Constitution. Once again those two colossal urban markets, so easily reached by water, were open to the farmers, iron smelters, leather tanners, brewers and glass-blowers of New Jersey.

Improved transportation and the industrial revolution arrived hand in hand. The Camden and Amboy Railroad was granted a charter in 1830. Tracks were laid from the Delaware River to South Amboy, opposite Staten Island, providing, with ferryboat connections, the first service between New York and Philadelphia. Soon other lines connected inland areas with the city markets. Factories and mills multiplied.

Though three quarters of the land is rural, only 12 percent of its people live in the countryside. Solidly populated industrial areas cling to the major arteries and the transportation terminals. The heaviest concentration—two thirds of the population—is in the thoroughly urbanized northeast. Newark, Jersey City, Elizabeth and Hoboken front on the waters of New York harbor. Bayonne, with its oil refineries blazing, is a unique waterfront sight. Mile after mile of piers and railroad terminals serve a dense manufacturing megalopolis that turns out much of the nation's chemicals, machinery and metal products. These products are some triumphs of New Jersey invention: the electric light bulb and phonograph by Thomas Edison; the magnetic telegraph by Samuel F. B. Morse and Alfred Vail; roller bearings and celluloid by John Wesley Hyatt; smokeless gunpowder by Hudson Maxim; and the revolver by Samuel Colt.

The textile cities of Passaic and Paterson lie just a few miles inland. On the falls of the Passaic River, Alexander Hamilton envisaged, and with others founded, what is now a modern industrial city. Named Paterson, it prospered as a cotton town, and had even greater growth when the dyeing of silk became its chief occupation. It is no longer a one-industry city, but the sprawling mills have left their distinctive mark on the landscape.

The concentrated industrial areas of New Jersey give way to the extensive farmlands that justify the nickname of the Garden State. In the northwest, the valleys between the Appalachian foothills shelter large dairy herds. Throughout the central counties and toward the southwest, the rich soil is ideal for truck farms. The fresh produce of huge, mechanized farming operations is processed or sold in nearby urban markets. New Jersey farmers enjoy the highest gross income per acre in the entire country.

On the sandier coastal plain, orchards yield peaches and apples, and in the marshy bogs closer to the ocean, cranberries thrive. Behind the southeastern coast, the wooded, sparsely settled pine barrens support very few crops, but poultry-raising flourishes to such an extent that, in dollar value, it is the chief agricultural activity of the state.

Cape May was the first of New Jersey's seashore resorts. Presidents Pierce, Buchanan, Lincoln and Grant were among those who summered there. But the pine barrens and adjacent marshlands kept much of the long Atlantic Coast inaccessible for many years. An ambitious railroad man, looking for a place to lay track, found a barely populated ocean island separated from the mainland by narrow inlets. It was named Atlantic City, and a vacation center was born. From Philadelphia and New York for a day, a week or an entire summer, newly prosperous multitudes came to enjoy swimming and sunbathing, boardwalk strolling and amusement piers. Since then the queen of seaside resorts has been joined by a score of others on the Jersey shore, including Asbury Park, Wildwood and Ocean City. The mountain lakes of the northwestern hills provided another vacation-land. Catering to visitors now is New Jersey's largest single source of income. Two major turnpikes which run the length of the state speed both local and inter-state traffic.

New Jersey in the 1790's was the first state to give women the right to vote. But this prerogative was taken away from them in 1807, "for the good order and dignity of the state," because of charges of fraudulent voting. The ballot was not restored to them until the ratification of the Nineteenth Amendment in 1920.

NEW MEXICO

ALBUQUERQUE

Spanish troops of Francisco Vásquez de Coronado passed along the Rio Grande here in 1540, but not until 1706 was a community started, when the Spanish governor moved 30 families from Bernalillo to this spot. The settlement, now known as the Old Town, grew slowly, though it was a trade, religious and cultural center for 200 years. The United States occupied Albuquerque in 1846, and the city began to expand as Americans moved into those territories acquired from Mexico. After the Civil War it became a strategic Army outpost. The Spanish had brought sheep to the area, and today wool and livestock are important to the local economy. Irrigation created a farming boom, which in turn led to the rise of packing plants and canning factories. The city has sawmills, brick and tile works and oil refineries; it also produces precision optical goods and machinery. Modern commercial structures and suburban homes in the newer parts of the city contrast with the flat-roofed colonial buildings of the Old Town. On the crowded downtown streets military personnel from two nearby bases mingle with sightseers, businessmen, cowboys and occasional Indians—the women sometimes in native dress, the men only rarely in blankets. The University of New Mexico, linked to Federal research programs, recently doubled in size and has plans for a one-third increase, to an enrollment of 18,000 students. (Pop. 201,189.)

Some of the nation's most majestic scenery may be glimpsed from a forest trail in the Sangre de Cristo Mountains of New Mexico high above the Indian pueblo village of Taos. To the east, seen through the windswept branches of piñon pines, is a vast expanse of high plains and treeless mesas reaching all the way to Oklahoma. To the north the snow-capped peaks of the southern Rocky Mountains soar through the clouds. In a valley far below to the west, the sparkling rapids of the Rio Grande River rush from a gorge in the Rockies, coursing down through the heart of New Mexico and on into Texas. To the south are immense sun-baked deserts inhabited by prairie dogs, rattlesnakes, coyotes and lizards; green, irrigated farmlands; and air-conditioned cities filled with throngs of people and the hum of modern civilization.

New Mexico is certainly an extraordinary region of the United States. It has known no frenzied Gold Rush or Silver Strike eras. No waves of nineteenth-century European immigrants or land-rush homesteaders ever poured into its territories. Still one of the more sparsely settled American areas south of Canada, the fifth largest state is richly endowed with breathtaking natural beauty, and, while closely linked with the primeval past, it is playing a key role in the new dramas of the Space Age. Its magnificent mountains have impassively witnessed the struggles of mankind since prehistoric times. Stone Age men who first came to the North American continent found their way to New Mexico. Evidences of battles fought thousands of years ago between primitive men and mammoths and giant sloths have been uncovered.

In 1540, the celebrated Spanish conquistador Coronado came up from Mexico in search of the wealth of the legendary Seven Cities—whose streets were said to be paved with gold. After a long march through the valley of the Rio Grande, Coronado found only seven small Indian villages with houses of clay.

The Crown showed little interest in colonization, but during the next 50 years Mexican and Spanish settlements extended north along the Rio Grande as far as Santa Fe. This was founded in the winter of 1609–10 as the capital of the province of New Mexico. Foreigners were banned from the territory until Mexico became independent and

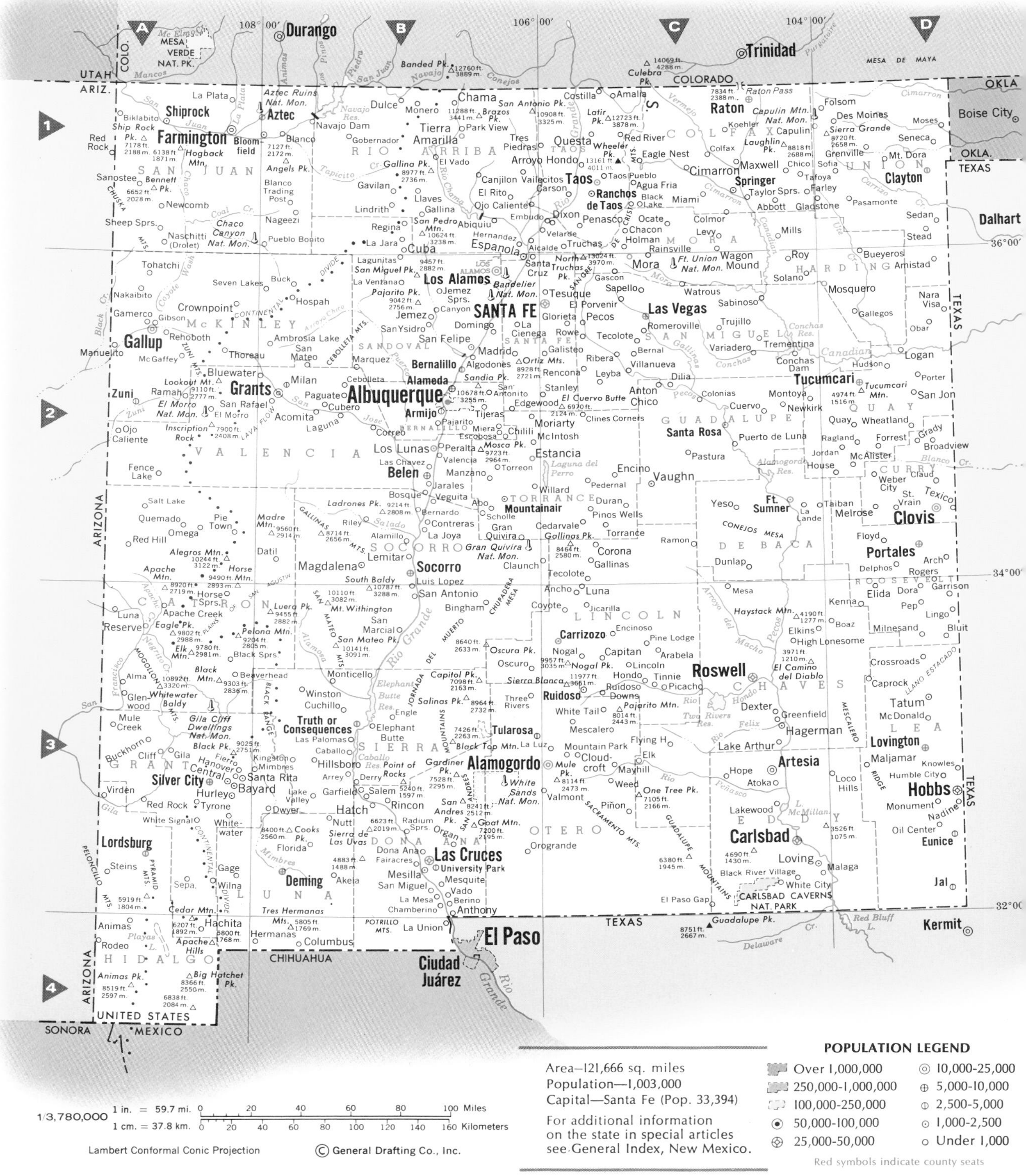

Area—121,666 sq. miles
Population—1,003,000
Capital—Santa Fe (Pop. 33,394)

For additional information on the state in special articles see General Index, New Mexico.

the first Americans arrived. Upon defeating Mexico in 1848, the United States took possession. In 1880, after the construction of railroads to the east and west opened new markets, the territory's expansion began in earnest.

Santa Fe is the oldest seat of government in the nation. Over its adobe churches and ancient buildings have flown the flags of Spain, Mexico, the Confederacy and the United States. Until after the Civil War, Santa Fe flourished as the southern terminus for the ox-drawn wagon trains of the Santa Fe Trail. The deep ruts of the heavy-wheeled carts that made the 1000-mile trek from Independence, Missouri, can still be seen on the vast, open plains in the northeastern corner of the state.

Spanish influences are still strong in New Mexico. There are Spanish newspapers, magazines, films and shops. Restaurants feature Spanish dishes, and Mexican enchiladas (meat or filling in corn pancakes) are staple fare.

Scattered throughout the state are immense deposits of oil, coal, potash, uranium, copper and natural gas, which make mining the most important activity. New Mexico leads the nation in producing uranium and potash. Livestock- and cotton-raising are the principal agricultural pursuits, while the manufacturing output is relatively small. Hobbs, near the Texas border, is a booming oil town. Roswell flourishes as a trading center for the crops of the rich, irrigated farming region in the south and acts as headquarters for the major oil companies operating in that area.

But the Federal government is the largest employer in the state, and jobs connected with national defense have been largely responsible for New Mexico's recent economic progress. Sixty miles northwest of Alamogordo is one of the awesome sites on earth: Trinity, where at 5:30 a.m. on July 16, 1945, mankind exploded its first atomic bomb. Since then the skies have again been lit by the flash of atomic explosions, and deserts and remote canyons reverberate with the thunderous roar of experimental nuclear weapons as well as rockets that will carry men to the moon and beyond. The state's open spaces and dry, sunny climate are ideally suited to space and nuclear research. Alamogordo's population has more than tripled since 1950 as a result of the expanding facilities of Holloman Air Force Base and the White Sands Missile Range where high-altitude weapons are tested. Installations of the Atomic Energy Commission near Albuquerque handle development and production of weapons. Research into the uses of atomic energy is conducted at the Los Alamos Scientific Laboratory.

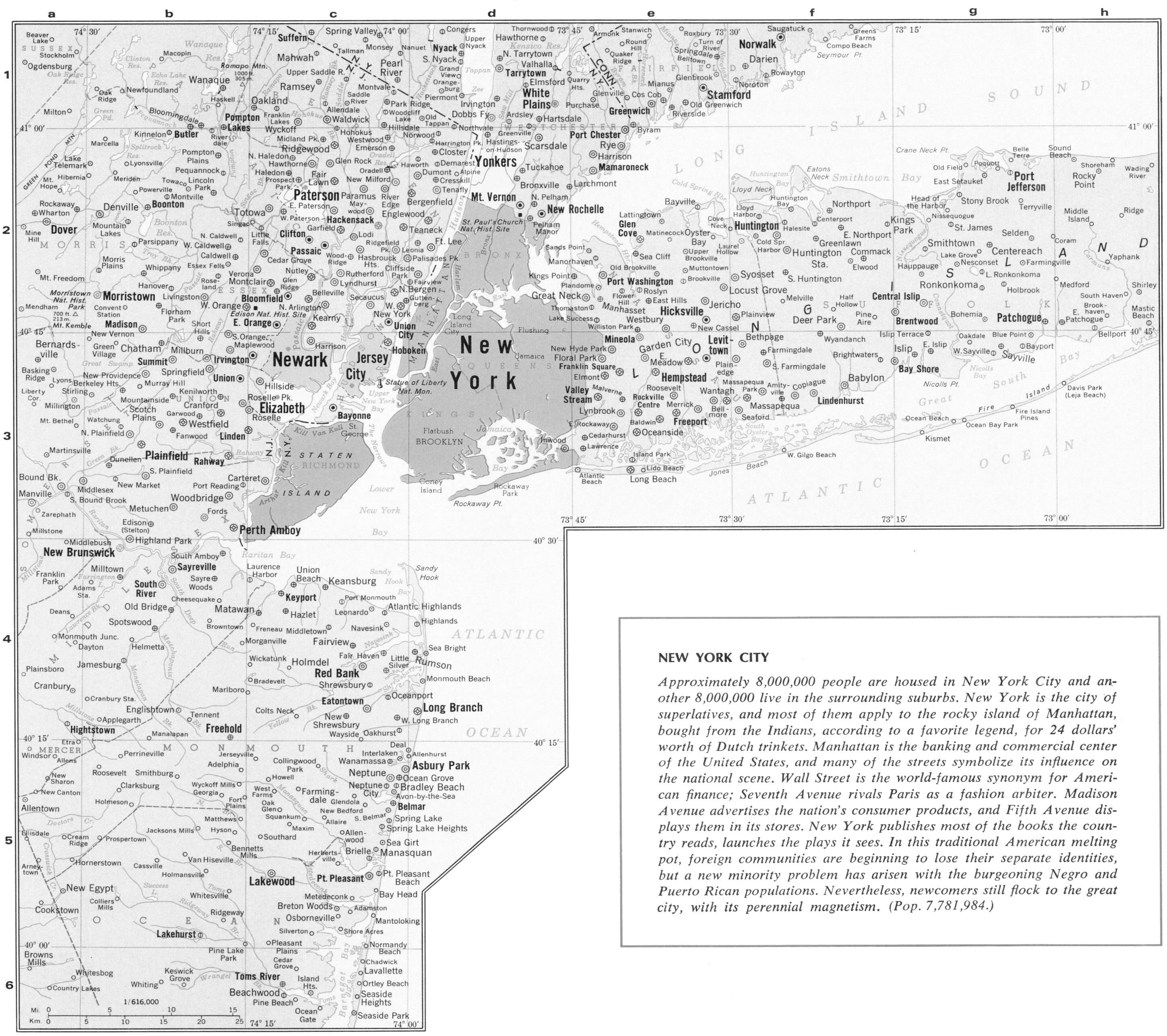

NEW YORK CITY

Approximately 8,000,000 people are housed in New York City and another 8,000,000 live in the surrounding suburbs. New York is the city of superlatives, and most of them apply to the rocky island of Manhattan, bought from the Indians, according to a favorite legend, for 24 dollars' worth of Dutch trinkets. Manhattan is the banking and commercial center of the United States, and many of the streets symbolize its influence on the national scene. Wall Street is the world-famous synonym for American finance; Seventh Avenue rivals Paris as a fashion arbiter. Madison Avenue advertises the nation's consumer products, and Fifth Avenue displays them in its stores. New York publishes most of the books the country reads, launches the plays it sees. In this traditional American melting pot, foreign communities are beginning to lose their separate identities, but a new minority problem has arisen with the burgeoning Negro and Puerto Rican populations. Nevertheless, newcomers still flock to the great city, with its perennial magnetism. (Pop. 7,781,984.)

NEW YORK

(Turn page for state map.)

From the busy ocean harbor of New York City, the inland waterways of the Empire State point north to Canada and west to the Great Lakes and the heart of the country. Enterprising New Yorkers have combined the twin natural blessings of water routes and waterpower, leading the state to its preeminent role in the commerce and industry of the United States.

In an extraordinary historical coincidence, New York's waters were explored from both the north and the south in the same year, 1609. While Henry Hudson sailed up the majestic river that he had found on the Atlantic Coast, Samuel de Champlain, a Frenchman, traveled south from the St. Lawrence River in Canada and discovered the beautiful lake that was eventually to bear his name.

But settlement was sponsored by the Dutch merchants and aristocrats who had backed Hudson's voyage. They divided the fertile riverfront lands into great estates, each under the paternal rule of a patroon who rented individual plots to resident farmers. When the English took control in the late seventeenth century, they confirmed the patroonships and extended the semifeudal system with manorial land grants. Though the absentee lords prospered, the system did not attract the kind of independent pioneering families who would open new frontiers.

North and west of the Hudson, the Iroquois Indians were another formidable barrier to early colonization. Determined to control the lucrative fur trade, the Iroquois Confederacy fought off encroachment by colonists, other Indian tribes and the French filtering down from Canada. The few settlers who dared to penetrate the wilderness lived in the shadow of disaster, such as the 1690 massacre at Schenectady, when 60 colonists were murdered and their homes burned to the ground.

The long struggle between France and England for domination in the New World, and the shifting Indian alliances, kept the interior of New York in turmoil. The

Iroquois tribes were not decisively defeated until after the American Revolution. Those Indians who did not move north to Ontario returned to farming on reservations, where many of their descendants still live.

When the 13 colonies proclaimed their independence, New York was only seventh in population, but a daring idea was soon to increase the population and change that standing. De Witt Clinton, nephew of the state's first governor, campaigned passionately for a canal that would join the Hudson in the east with Lake Erie in the west. He planned a water highway that would follow the river valleys through the Appalachian Mountains, cross the undeveloped interior of the state and reach the rapidly developing territories on the far shores of the Great Lakes. When "Clinton's Ditch," as the 363-mile Erie Canal was called, opened in 1825, he was himself governor and traveled on the inaugural barges that were towed from the lake port of Buffalo eastward across the lowlands to Albany and Troy on the Hudson, then downriver to the Atlantic. Now the state would become the marketplace of the nation, and its great seaport, New York, the gateway to a continent.

Trading posts along the new water route grew into prosperous cities, geared to furnish and supply the westward-bound caravans and to process the raw materials that came from the newly exploited territories. As the frontier receded, the cities turned to the development and manufacture of more sophisticated and specialized products, until New York State was first in value of manufactured goods.

Albany has been the capital since 1797 and was a thriving fur-trading post long before the canal was built. At the crossroads of the waterways, its harbor, 140 miles up the Hudson, has been dredged to accommodate ocean-going vessels. When the state government meets, it faces the monumental task of mediating between the frequently conflicting demands of the great city to the south and the "upstaters"—everyone outside the metropolitan New York City area.

The neighboring settlement of Schenectady was Albany's rival in the colonial fur trade, and later became the center of the locomotive industry. Then Thomas Edison began to manufacture his revolutionary light bulbs in Schenectady and founded the great industry, based on electric products, for which the city is noted.

A short distance to the east, Troy made stagecoaches in its earliest days, then boomed as a steel and iron city. When that industry moved to Pittsburgh, Troy became famous for detachable shirt collars, and later for shirts; the production of clothing is still vital to its economy. Farther west, Utica, a trading and mill town for the Mohawk Valley, grew into another important textile area.

Syracuse, like its namesake in antiquity, was founded on the site of vast salt fields. When the land became too valuable to mine, the city turned to the production of candles, pottery and typewriters. In the mills of Rochester on the Genesee River Falls, much of the young nation's grain was once processed. Then the granaries moved closer to the western wheat fields, and Rochester became the headquarters of optical, photographic and electronic companies.

Niagara Falls, the city and the awesome spectacle, are on the Canadian border. Honeymoon couples and tourists have come from all over the world to stare at the tremendous rush of falling water as the swift-moving Niagara River plunges over a glacially formed cliff. That phenomenon also generates gigantic surges of hydroelectric power that pulse through the entire Northeast.

Buffalo is the state's second largest city and one of the busiest ports in the United States. Grain, iron ore, limestone and other raw materials arrive from the Midwest. Buffalo's mills and factories convert them into food products, pig iron, metal parts, machinery and chemicals.

Water transportation in New York is cheap but slow, and has been supplanted by railroads and superhighways that follow approximately the same route. A notable postwar achievement was the completion of the Thomas E. Dewey Thruway, a 559-mile toll road that speeds automobiles and trucks north and west across the state on a nonstop ribbon of concrete.

Bordered by these land and water highways on the east and north is the extensive Allegheny plateau, a fertile highland of gently rolling hills and wide river valleys. The rich land is particularly suitable for grazing, and much of the state's milk, cheese, eggs and butter comes from this region.

To feed the urban centers, large-scale dairying also takes place on the central plain that slopes north and west toward Lake Ontario; vegetables and fruits from truck farms all over the interior—as well as ducks and potatoes from Long Island—move in a steady stream from well-mechanized rural areas to the crowded cities.

In sharp contrast, the Adirondack Mountains rise in isolated splendor in the northeast. Majestic peaks, their slopes shaded by thick evergreens, tower over a sparsely settled wilderness dotted with mountain lakes. It is a haven for sportsmen and solitude seekers, a vast state park and forest preserve.

A less forbidding range lies farther south and has accommodated summer visitors for more than a century. The Catskills emerge from the wooded west banks of the Hudson where Rip Van Winkle once slept. Here, and in the adjacent Delaware River basin, dairy farmers and vacationing city dwellers share the lush beauty of hills, lakes and forests.

The entire state is sprinkled with areas of startling scenic beauty. Deep in the interior, the slender Finger Lakes sparkle in a setting of woods and rock-walled gorges that were carved by the Ice Age. On the Atlantic, extensive, sandy beaches line the shore of Long Island.

Within its own borders, New York State encompasses much of the astounding diversity of peoples and occupations, of resources and terrain that constitutes a notable American asset.

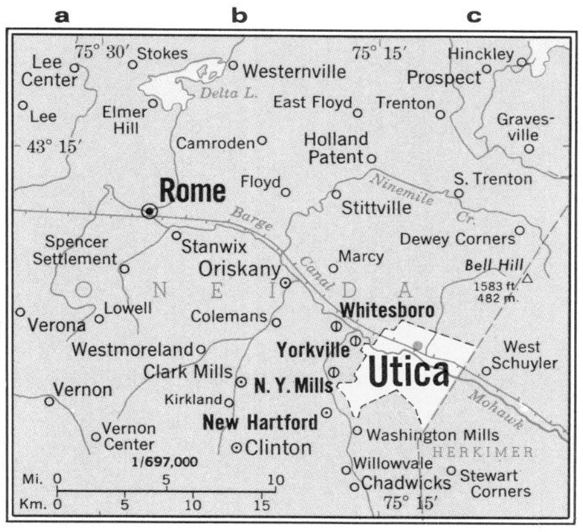

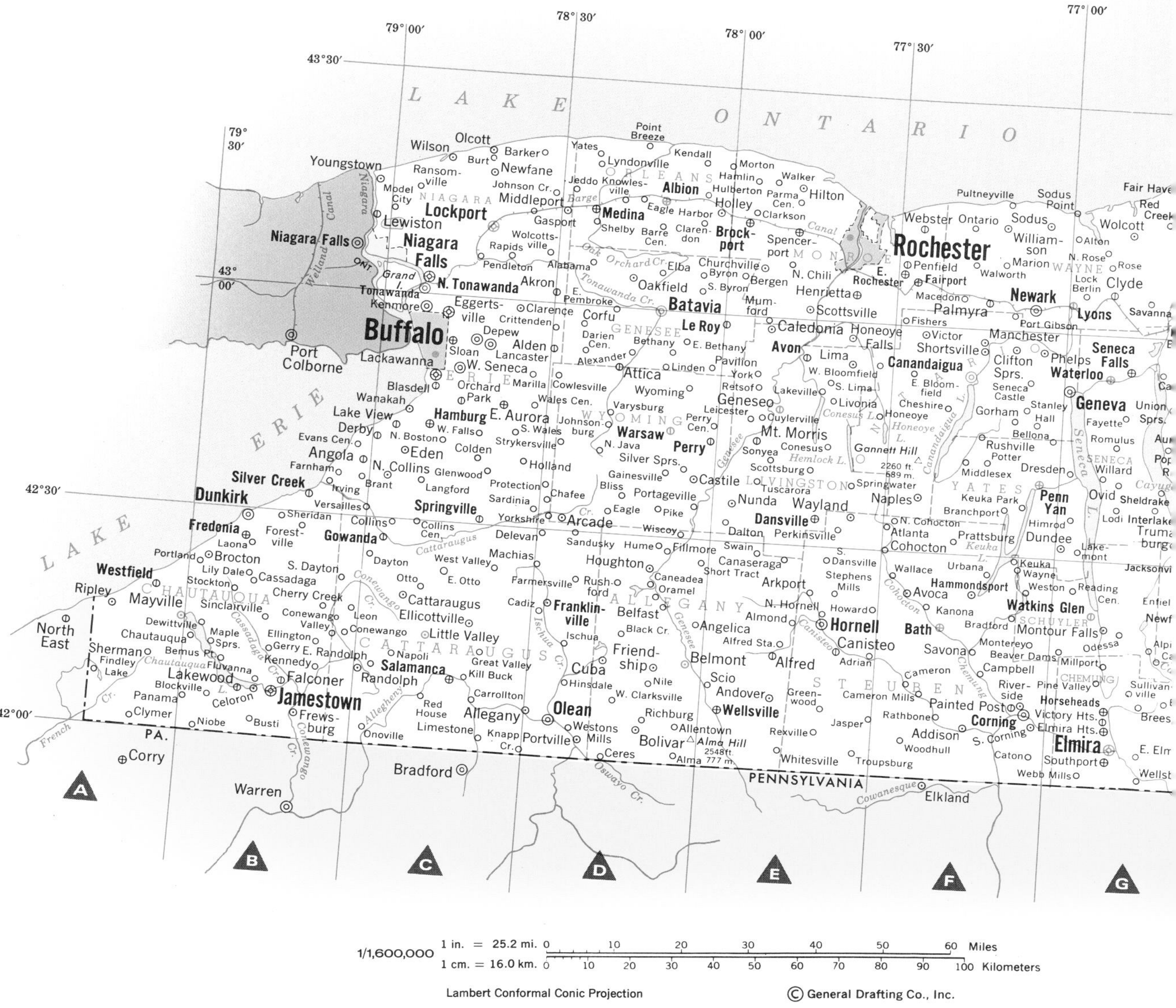

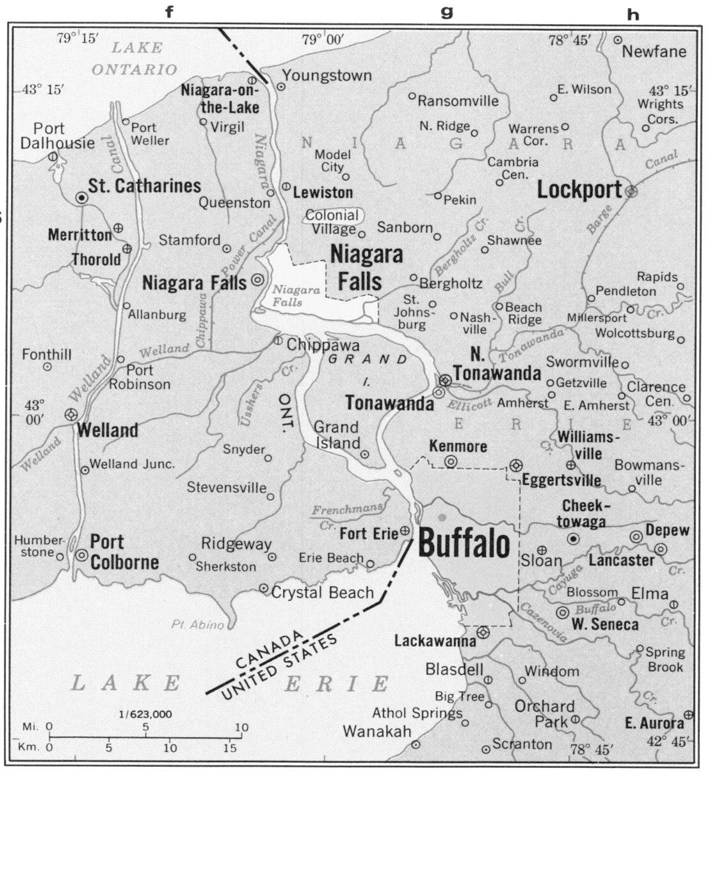

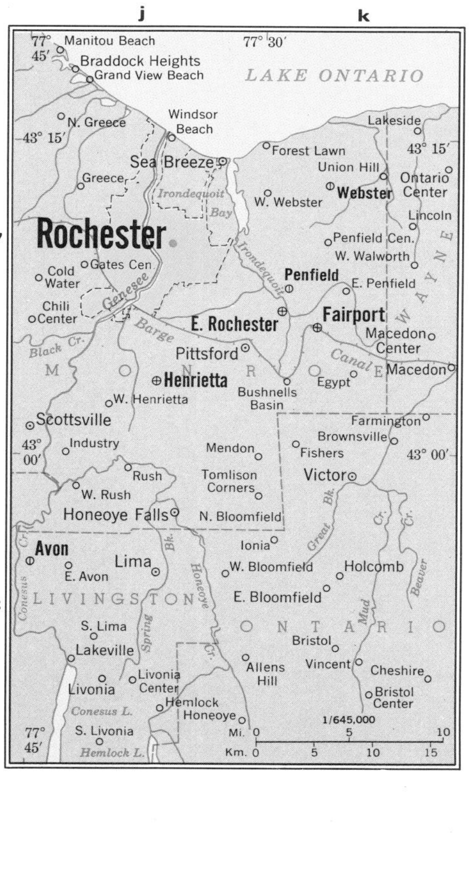

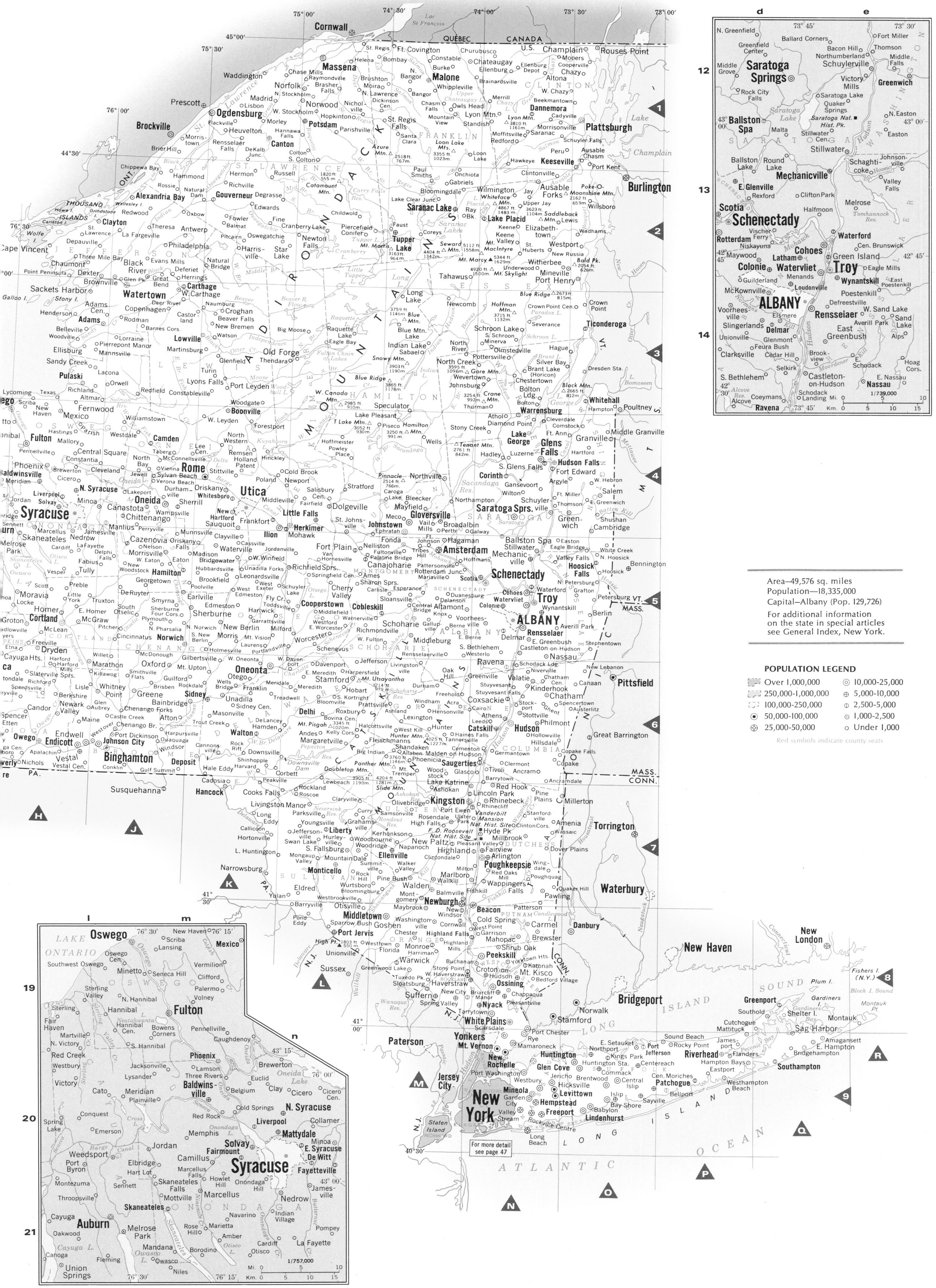

Area—49,576 sq. miles
Population—18,335,000
Capital—Albany (Pop. 129,726)
For additional information on the state in special articles see General Index, New York.

POPULATION LEGEND

Over 1,000,000	10,000-25,000
250,000-1,000,000	5,000-10,000
100,000-250,000	2,500-5,000
50,000-100,000	1,000-2,500
25,000-50,000	Under 1,000

Red symbols indicate county seats

NORTH CAROLINA

Shaped like a menacing bent bow, the Outer Banks of North Carolina form an arc of islands and surf-pounded sand strips that extend south 150 miles from Virginia to Cape Hatteras and Cape Fear. Long, hidden reefs and shifting sandy shoals reach out into the Atlantic another 25 to 30 miles to trap the unwary mariner. Nearby swirl the treacherous currents of the Gulf Stream—the shore is strewn with the skeletons of wrecked ships.

This most dangerous stretch of coast between Canada and Florida, explored by Verrazano in 1524, would seem the place least likely to attract colonists. Yet it was to the Outer Banks' Roanoke Island that Sir Walter Raleigh in 1585 dispatched an expedition of seven ships carrying scientists, physicians, clergymen and soldiers of Queen Elizabeth to establish the first English settlement in North America.

The Raleigh outpost soon vanished. Later, most sea captains who glimpsed the navigational hazards of the Outer Banks hastily crowded on sail and departed. Lacking the readily accessible deepwater harbors of New England and the Middle Atlantic colonies, North Carolina drew its earliest settlers overland from neighboring Virginia in 1653. Ten years later King Charles II rewarded eight court favorites who had helped restore him to the throne with a tremendous land grant, called Carolina. As revised in 1665, it extended from the Virginia border deep into Spanish Florida and from the Atlantic Coast to the "South Seas" (Pacific Ocean). The first colony, established on Albemarle Sound, was called Albemarle and until 1691 had its own governor. After that, the colony was ruled by a deputy of the governor of the entire province of Carolina in Charleston. But the North Carolina pioneers had little in common with the plantation aristocrats to the south, where the lords proprietors had planned to establish three orders of local nobility: barons, caciques and landgraves. There was resentment against the governors, one of whom was jailed during a revolt, and finally in 1712 the two Carolinas were separated. In 1730, one year after the Crown bought out the proprietors, surveyors started to define the boundary between them. The job was not finished until 1815.

Eventually Germans and Swiss, in quest of religious freedom, and Scottish Highlanders, migrating to America after their defeats by the English, braved the shoals of Cape Hatteras and Cape Fear to found New Bern and Wilmington. Others drifted southward from Maryland and Pennsylvania and established backwoods settlements as far west as the Blue Ridge Mountains. During the great waves of European migrations to the United States, few people sought out or reached North Carolina. Consequently, most of North Carolina's white population is Anglo-Saxon. Negroes whose ancestors were brought in as slaves now constitute about one quarter of the state's population.

Without major seaports, canals, railroad lines or large manufacturing centers, North Carolina grew so slowly during the first half of the nineteenth century that it was sometimes called the Rip Van Winkle State. The flourishing urban and plantation life of its sister states, Virginia and South Carolina, passed it by. In the early days, the coastal-plain region, suitable for cotton and rice produced with slave labor, was the most thickly settled and prosperous part. On the forested Piedmont plain and in the foothills of the Appalachian Mountains, the lack of roads and the strenuous exertion required to hew homes and farms out of the wilderness caused many families to leave and join the westward migrations.

The tide finally turned in the twentieth century, and North Carolina is now the most highly industrialized state in the South. First, New England's rich textile industry, lured by cheaper labor costs and an abundance of hydroelectric power, began to move its mills into the central and western sections. Then, during World War I, cigarette smoking became increasingly popular. North Carolina, which had been raising tobacco since the days of Sir Walter Raleigh, was prepared. Nearly half of all the tobacco produced in the United States is grown in the state, and about 60 percent of the nation's cigarettes are manufactured there in the world's largest factories. The household-furniture manufacturing industry has expanded until its output is highest in the country, and production of paper and chemicals is steadily rising. Yet North Carolina has more farms than any other state except Texas, and its crops of peanuts and sweet potatoes are surpassed only by those of Georgia and Louisiana, respectively.

The Great Smoky Mountains National Park, nearly 800 square miles of the wildest highlands in eastern America, lies in western North Carolina and Tennessee. Within its borders are 53 peaks more than a mile high and what is said to be the finest remnant of the great virgin forest that once covered the Atlantic Coast as far as the prairies of the Middle West. The Blue Ridge Parkway, a 469-mile skyline drive from Shenandoah National Park in Virginia to the Great Smoky National Park, is one of the most popular scenic routes for motorists.

The Outer Banks, which played such a large role in shaping North Carolina's history and development, have become part of the Cape Hatteras National Seashore Recreational Area. This region, which had been a graveyard for so many ships, also turned out to be the birthplace of a new form of transportation: at Kill Devil Hills near the village of Kitty Hawk, Wilbur and Orville Wright flew the first power-driven airplane on December 17, 1903.

CHARLOTTE

The area of Mecklenburg County which is now Charlotte was first settled in the 1740's by small groups of colonists. But the townsite itself was not purchased until 15 years later. The price paid for the original 360 acres was only 90 pounds in "lawful money," roughly $450. Charlotte was such a hotbed of Revolutionary War activity that General Cornwallis called it a "hornet's nest." In 1837 a branch of the United States Mint was established and turned out coins until the Civil War. Before the California Gold Rush of 1849, mines in this area were the country's most important source of gold. Rich farmlands surround the city, and these yield big cotton, corn, wheat and truck-farm crops. But it is hydroelectric power, developed from the nearby Catawba River, which has made Charlotte the largest textile-manufacturing city in the United States. (Pop. 201,564.)

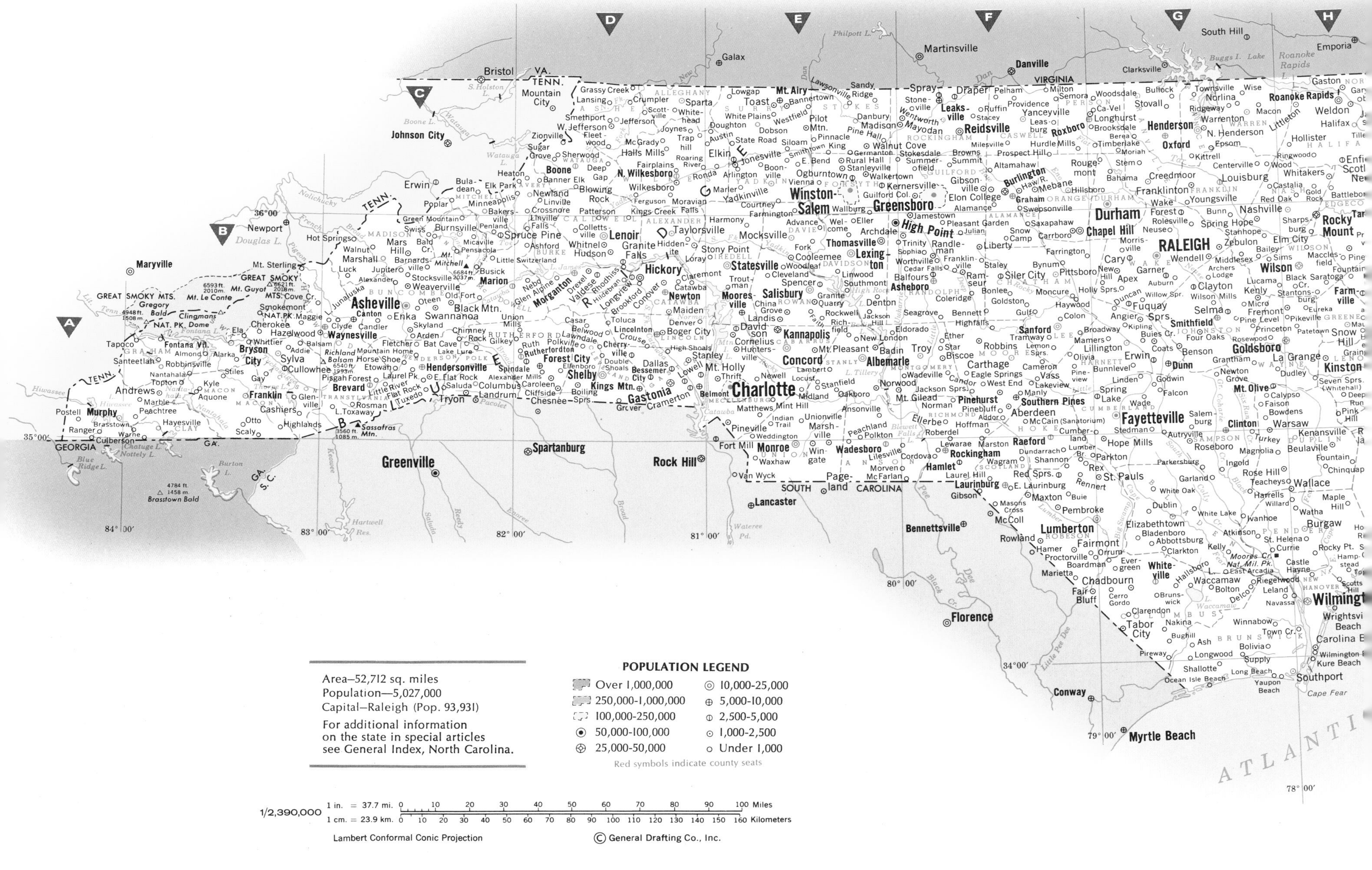

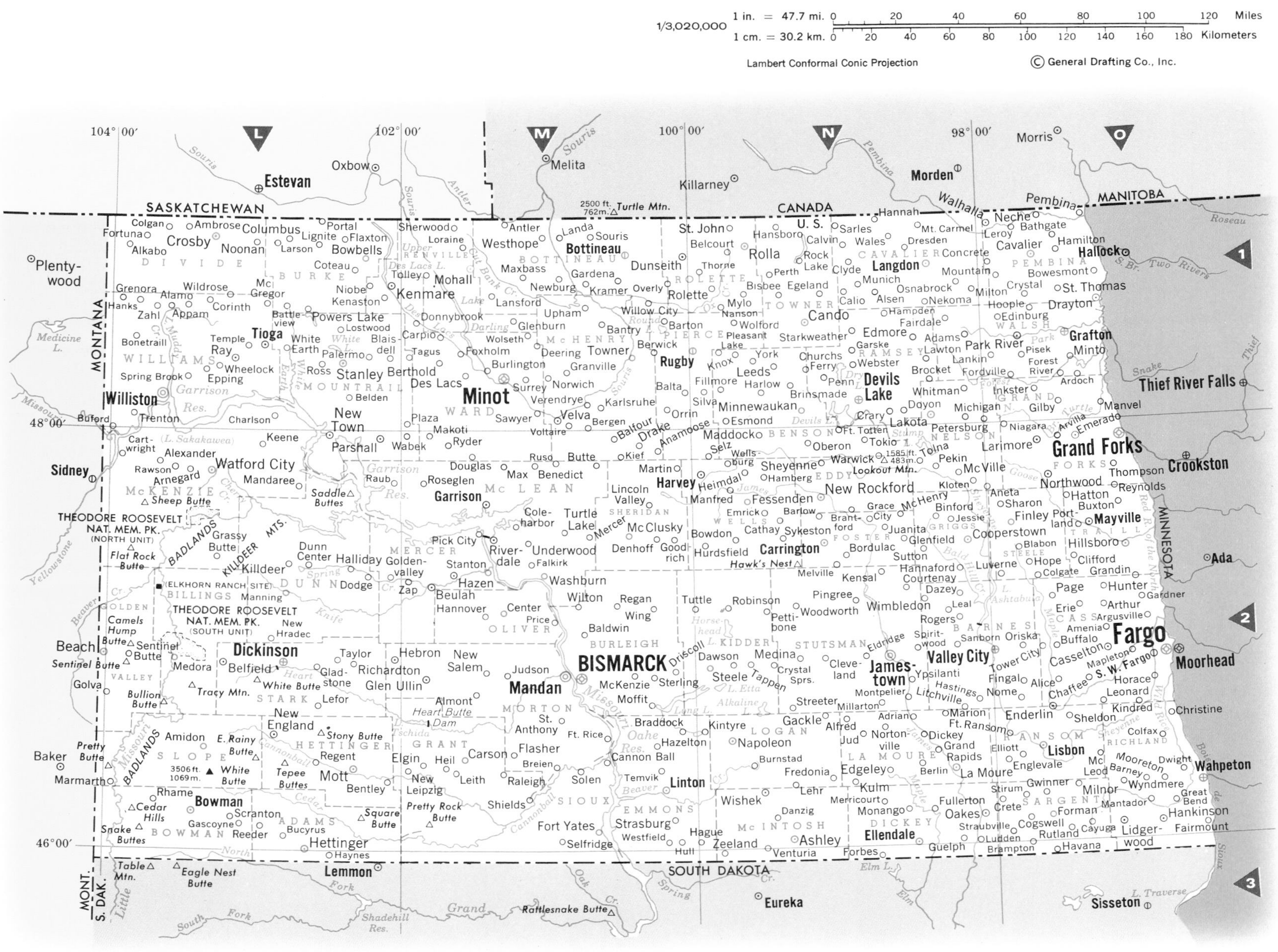

Area—70,665 sq. miles
Population—639,000
Capital—Bismarck (Pop. 27,670)

For additional information on the state in special articles see General Index, North Dakota.

POPULATION LEGEND

Over 1,000,000	10,000-25,000
250,000-1,000,000	5,000-10,000
100,000-250,000	2,500-5,000
50,000-100,000	1,000-2,500
25,000-50,000	Under 1,000

Red symbols indicate county seats

NORTH DAKOTA

FARGO

The selection of a site for a railroad bridge across the Red River in 1871 resulted in the founding of the city of Fargo at the same spot. It was named for William G. Fargo of the Wells Fargo Express Company, a director of the Northern Pacific Railway that was to push across the river at this point. At one time a railroad's land company, in an unsuccessful attempt to gain possession of the area, had all residents of one section arrested on the complaint of selling liquor to the Indians. Like many frontier communities, Fargo had an early history of shooting and carousing. Masses of settlers soon brought pressures for law and order, and the city began to change into a respectable trading center for the wheat-growing region which surrounds it. Fargo is a major farm-equipment distribution point, with food-processing and metal-product industries. The 2063-foot transmitting tower of a local television station is the world's tallest structure. Nearly half the city's residents are of Norwegian origin, and many observe Norway's Independence Day on May 17. (Pop. 46,662.)

No man who came to North Dakota fell more in love with the natural beauty of its wide-open spaces than Theodore Roosevelt. Living there in 1884 as a young Easterner who had turned to ranching to regain his health, he wrote to his family: "The country is growing on me, more and more; it has a curious, fantastic beauty of its own." Years later, when he was immersed in the feverish pace of Washington politics, Roosevelt nostalgically recalled:

We worked [on the cattle ranch] under the scorching midsummer sun, when the wide plains shimmered and wavered in the heat. . . . In the soft springtime the stars were glorious in our eyes each night before we fell asleep; and in the winter we rode through blinding blizzards. . . . Ours was the glory of work and the joy of living.

Roosevelt's words still describe the mood evoked by this vast expanse of prairies, farms and ranches. Few other states are so completely devoted to farming. The typical North Dakota ranch—about 750 acres—is nearly three times larger than the national average, and many run into thousands of acres. From these immense tracts come some of the country's biggest crops of wheat, rye, oats and barley. Only Kansas produces more wheat. From spring plowing until the August harvest, crops and the weather are the chief preoccupations. To a North Dakota wheat farmer or cattle rancher the most fearsome word in the language is drought. A nightmare in the memory of many is the prolonged dry spell which held the Great Plains in its grip during the middle 1930's. Little rainfall, endless high winds and overcultivation created the most devastating and destructive period in the area's history. Out of the suffering and tragedies of this dust-bowl period came new state and Federal conservation programs. These have been so successful that North Dakota has again become one of the world's most productive farming regions.

Discovery of oil and the development of refineries in the northwest corner have started a thriving industry which is bringing in fresh investment capital and adding to the growth and prosperity of cities such as Williston, Minot and Bismarck.

The Frenchman Pierre de la Vérendrye in 1738 was one of the few white men to explore the North Dakota region until 1797, when fur traders established a post there. They did not want permanent settlements to disturb the natural habitat of the valuable beaver, and they succeeded in driving out most of the first colonists who arrived in 1812 from Canada. A trickle of pioneers continued to enter the territory, which was opened to settlement with free land for homesteaders in 1863. The Civil War, insurrections of the Sioux tribes and reports of blizzards, droughts and grasshopper plagues discouraged migration. Many farmers returned East because of the danger of Indian raids. By 1870 North Dakota counted only 2405 inhabitants, and just one homestead claim had been filed. It was the railroads which really filled the plains with people. The Northern Pacific reached Bismarck in 1873, the Montana border in 1881. Then settlers began to stream in. The territory was known by 1885 as "the land of the free and the home of the boomer"—"free" referring to the homesteaders and "boomers" referring to land speculators. Between 1880 and 1890 the population jumped from 37,000 to 191,000.

Most North Dakotans are descendants of immigrants from Norway, Russia, Germany and 39 other countries, who arrived during and after the early period of expansion. They were attracted by the success of the "Bonanza Farms." Most of these had been established by Eastern syndicates which had bought land cheaply from the railroads. These enormous farms ranged in size all the way up to 65,000 acres. They were devoted entirely to wheat, harvested by large crews brought in each fall. So abundant were the crops produced from the rich virgin soil that tales of the wealth to be gained reached all the way to Europe. The railroads slashed their travel rates to make the prospect more tempting, and homesteaders poured in by the thousands. Eventually many families purchased their own smaller tracts from the syndicates.

For many years foreign languages and customs dominated North Dakota cultural life, but the automobile, two World Wars and television have transformed the state into one of the most typically American in the Midwest.

OHIO

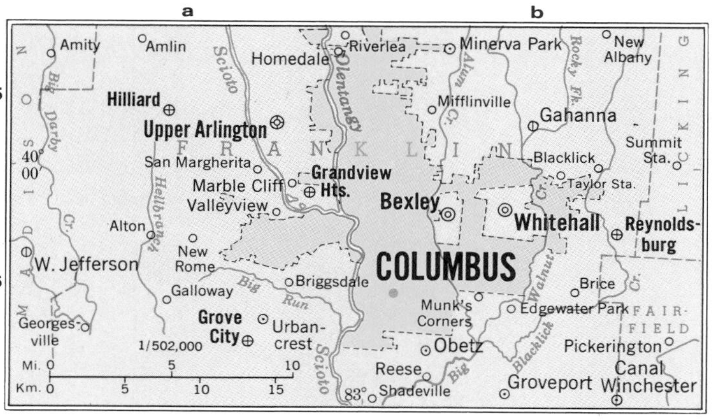

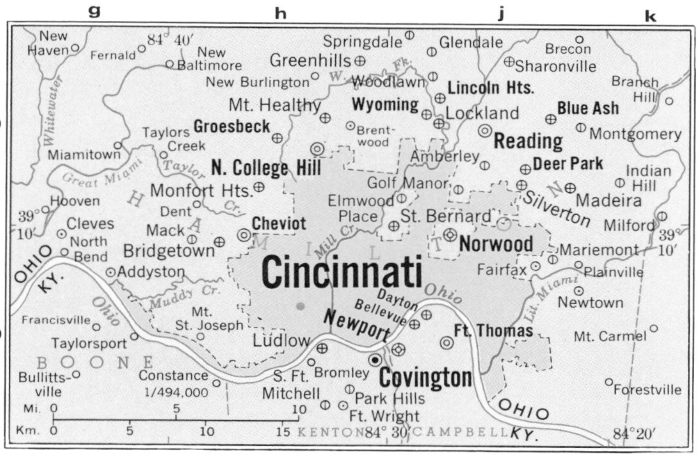

CLEVELAND

Named for its founder, Moses Cleaveland (the spelling was changed by a printer to make the word fit a headline), the Lake Erie port had fewer than 100 inhabitants when incorporated as a village in 1814. The city's growth began when it became the northern terminus of the Erie-Ohio Canal in 1832, and the manufacturing industry on which present prosperity is based dates back to the arrival of the first iron-ore shipment from the Lake Superior region in 1852. The first of many oil refineries was built in 1862 by John D. Rockefeller. Cleveland also pioneered in electric street lighting, installing lamps in 1879. It is now plagued by typical urban problems of slum blight and loss of higher-income groups to the suburbs. A 14,000-acre park system encircles the metropolitan center. The city has planted its streets so thickly with shade trees that it has been nicknamed the Forest City. (Pop. 876,050.)

One afternoon in July 1796, 125 years after La Salle is reported to have visited Ohio, a small party of Connecticut surveyors explored the wilderness that enveloped the south shore of Lake Erie. Camping for the night at the broad mouth of the Cuyahoga River, they decided it formed a natural harbor from which future settlers might ship their produce. In a grove of oak trees, the engineers marked out the borders of a typical New England town square. Seldom has a vision achieved such fulfillment. This same square now lies at the heart of Ohio's largest city, Cleveland, and the unbroken forest of stately timber that swept away to the south became a land of rich farms and cities.

Colonists in the northern regions fought a lonely, bitter struggle for survival, hampered by lack of roads and trade links with the East. Until the War of 1812, British warships dominated Lake Erie. Then the victory of Commodore Perry ended British control of the Great Lakes. The northern Ohio territory was strengthened by the arrival of settlers from Connecticut. These people now accepted the Federal government's offer of free lands in a 120-mile strip along Lake Erie that had long been known as the Western Reserve of Connecticut. Meanwhile Virginia, North Carolina and Kentucky families crossed the Ohio and settled in the central portions of the state.

The completion of the Erie Canal in 1825 at last provided a trade link between Lake Erie and the Atlantic states. Its success touched off a wave of canal-building throughout the East and Middle West, in which Ohio's people joined enthusiastically. Booming cannons, banners, banquets and parades celebrated the opening in 1832 of the first section of a new waterway that was to link Cleveland and the Great Lakes with Portsmouth on the Ohio. Within another year a steady stream of horse-drawn barges began moving up and down its length. Soon more canals were in operation: between Akron and Beaver, Pennsylvania; Lafayette, Indiana, and Toledo; Cincinnati and Dayton; Dayton and Toledo.

Southern Ohio was settled long before the Lake Erie region. When the Louisiana Purchase of 1803 threw open the middle of the continent to exploration and settlement, the Ohio River became the chief route into the new frontier areas. Down the river from Pittsburgh, gateway to the West, floated an endless stream of traders, adventurers and homesteading families carrying with them the provisions, livestock, tools and seeds for crops, gardens and orchards. When they found a suitable spot for a farm, they dismantled their cumbersome craft and used the lumber to build a new home.

Rivermen such as the legendary Mike Fink guided rafts, flatboats and keelboats that could carry as much as 40 tons of freight to St. Louis, Natchez and New Orleans. By 1820 steamboats were operating on the Ohio, quickening the pace of settlement and commerce. Cincinnati soon became one of the busiest inland ports north of New Orleans.

In 1833 a National Road, flung across the center of the state from Wheeling, West Virginia, to Indiana, passed through Columbus, bringing a flood of traffic in which coaches and lumbering freight wagons stretched as far as the eye could see. With a market for its industrial and agricultural products that extended from New Orleans

to New York City, Ohio now underwent a period of prodigious growth. At first, particularly in the north, the New England influence was strongest, manifesting itself in white churches and village greens. Later, both farms and cities attracted new peoples from the Balkans, Germany, France, Poland, Italy and Scandinavia. More than two thirds of the states are larger than Ohio, yet few so successfully combine industry, agriculture and the talents of a polyglot population.

The beginning of the steel era found the state at a strategic point between the huge Mesabi iron-ore deposits of Minnesota and Eastern coal mines. Ohio now manufactures more iron and steel products than any state save Pennsylvania and assembles more automobiles than any other except Michigan. It ranks second in glass, fifth in chemicals and coal. Oil discovered in western Ohio started John D. Rockefeller on his way to wealth.

The cities spawned industrialists and inventors. In a bicycle shop in Dayton, Wilbur and Orville Wright built their first flying machines. Charles Kettering developed the automobile's ignition and self-starter systems in the same city, while James Ritty's "mechanical money drawer" was the beginning of Dayton's cash register industry. In Cleveland, Charles Brush invented the carbon arc light and perfected the first practical storage battery. Toledo's glass factories boomed after Michael Owens developed a machine which turned out bottles by the thousands. A bicycle craze that swept the nation between 1875 and 1900 brought an enormous demand for tires. Akron, where Benjamin F. Goodrich and Harvey Firestone had started small factories, became the rubber-manufacturing center of the continent. Afterwards, with the coming of the automobile, the city continued to dominate the industry.

Residents of Ohio were responsible for innovations in other fields. They established the first interracial, coeducational college (Oberlin, 1833); enacted the first law regulating the working hours of women and children (1852); founded the first professional baseball team (Cincinnati Red Stockings, 1869); and laid the first concrete pavement (Bellefontaine, 1892).

Seven of Ohio's native sons (one less than Virginia, which is the "Mother of Presidents") have gone on to the White House: Ulysses S. Grant, Rutherford B. Hayes, James A. Garfield, Benjamin Harrison, William McKinley, William Howard Taft and Warren G. Harding.

Although 70 percent of its people live in cities, Ohio is a leading farm state. It shears the biggest wool clip east of the Mississippi and grows the sixth largest corn crop. Along the shores of Lake Erie, vineyards yield rich harvests of grapes; southern orchards are laden with tons of apples, pears and peaches. Milk and cream are the biggest cash producers (despite the foreign-sounding name, the world's only factory making Liederkranz cheese is there). The state's farm receipts annually top one billion dollars.

Ohio is unusual in that it was not formally admitted to the Union until its 150th anniversary as a state. After the adoption of a constitution, a state government took office on March 1, 1803, without the usual Congressional legislation. This oversight was remedied in 1953, when President Eisenhower signed a bill retroactive to the original statehood date.

OKLAHOMA

The history of Oklahoma as a settled area is comparatively short because throughout most of the nineteenth century it remained a federally administered Indian territory. Yet progress has been so swift and vigorous that it now ranks fourth in oil production, close behind such giants as Texas, Louisiana and California, and third in natural gas.

There are more than 86,000 wells which tap fields underlying half the state. Cattle graze amid derricks, and grain elevators frequently are found side by side with oil rigs in the farming regions.

Tulsa, the state's second largest city, calls itself the Oil Capital of the World because so many petroleum companies, manufacturers of drilling and refining equipment, and industry publications have headquarters there. The state's largest refinery is within the city limits and many other giant plants are close by. Tulsa originally was an Indian village. Its first, and later wealthiest, residents were Northern Yankees who had learned the oil business in Pennsylvania and hurried out when petroleum was discovered in the territory in the 1890's. Most of the present industry of the state is based primarily on the processing of native raw materials—not only petroleum, but also minerals, meat, wheat and cotton.

Eastern Oklahoma is graced with a plenitude of lowlying mountains, forests and swift-running streams. The rolling prairies to the west are wheat and cattle country. The northern region, settled from the vicinity of Kansas, has more of the flavor of the Middle West, while the southern portion, the state's cotton belt, resembles neigh-

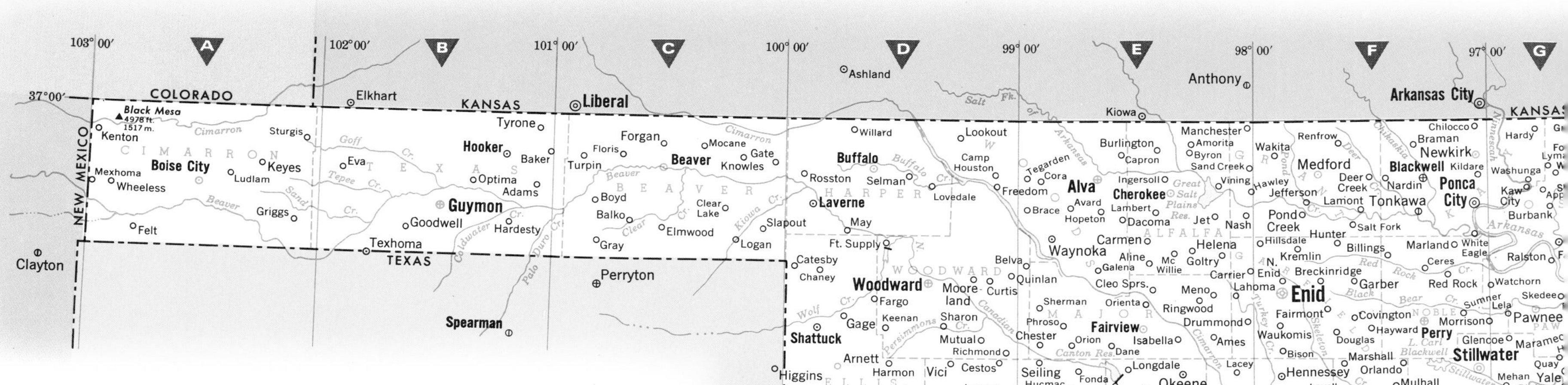

OREGON

The promised land that lay at the end of the historic Oregon Trail for emigrants from the East was sharply divided into two widely contrasting regions by the snow-capped Cascade Mountains. East of the range stretched broad plains and high plateaus. On the western side lush valleys with fertile soil flourished in a mild climate with abundant rainfall. It was the prospect of cheap land in one of these valleys, the Willamette, that attracted the early settlers. Around them lay a great unexplored territory of lofty mountain ranges, tremendous evergreen forests, high plains, desert wastes and, beyond, the rugged Pacific seacoast.

Spanish, British and American ships, in explorations of the Pacific from 1542 to 1800, had glimpsed the shores of Oregon, the Indian name for the Columbia River. Juan Cabrillo was probably the first to sail up the coast from Mexico. Lewis and Clark followed portions of the Oregon Trail on their expedition to the Northwest in 1804–06. Six years later, Astoria, a trading post established by John Jacob Astor's fur company at the mouth of the Columbia, became the first American settlement west of the Rocky Mountains. Trappers and fur traders were followed by missionaries and then by homesteaders. In one of the epic migrations of American history, ox-drawn prairie schooners rumbled 2000 miles to this destination. Many pioneers loaded their covered wagons on rafts and flatboats and floated down the Columbia on the last lap of their trek.

Since 1818 the Oregon region had been occupied jointly by Britain and the United States and open to settlers from both countries. The great influx of American pioneers led to a demand for annexation of the entire area south of 54° 40′. "Fifty-four forty or fight" became a political slogan in the Presidential campaign of 1844. But the issue was settled in a compromise which extended the international boundary along the forty-ninth parallel from the Rocky Mountains to Vancouver Island.

Indian fighting broke out in earnest during the decade after the Civil War, as the tribes saw their hunting grounds increasingly invaded by the white man. Peace was restored in 1878, and the state steadily grew as steamships and railroads formed the links with the rest of the nation. The valleys of western Oregon are now the most developed commercial and industrial regions.

In one caravan of covered wagons that set out for Oregon from Iowa in 1847 were boxes of apple seedlings. Each spring, fruit orchards transform some of the valleys into seas of pink and white blossoms. Through summer and autumn the harvest flows out to all parts of the country and to world markets. Almost every fruit and vegetable that grows in a temperate climate flourishes there. On the eastern side of the Cascades are large farms and ranches where wheat is grown and cattle and sheep are raised. Oregon is a top producer of hops, used in brewing beer and ale.

Pacific salmon return each year to spawn in the rivers; this great catch, together with tuna and albacore from the ocean, makes commercial fishing a major source of income. But tall timber is still king. Vast forests of spruce, western hemlock and Douglas fir blanket half the state. Lumbering is the chief industry, and Oregon leads the nation in turning out lumber and wood products. Some Oregonians are descendants of the lumberjacks who followed timber westward from Maine to the forests of the Great Lakes and then on to the rip-roaring camps made famous in the fiction of Bret Harte.

Waters of the mighty Columbia River, harnessed by hydroelectric dams, supply the power for lumber, pulp and paper mills, canneries and factories. Food-processing—canning, freezing and preserving fish, meat, fruits and vegetables—is the second industry in importance.

Scenically one of the most beautiful states, Oregon includes among its noted attractions Crater Lake, deepest in the United States (1932 feet), and Mount Hood, crowned by snow the year round.

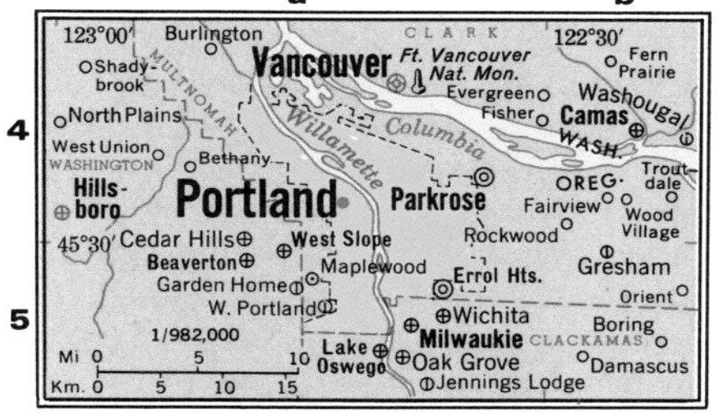

PORTLAND

Amos L. Lovejoy of Massachusetts wanted Boston to be the name of the 640-acre tract on both sides of the Willamette River near its junction with the Columbia, but Francis W. Pettygrove of Maine disagreed. They tossed a coin, Pettygrove won, and Portland has been called by that name ever since 1845. In five years the town had a population of 800 and a steam sawmill. The California Gold Rush attracted half its male residents, slowing the city's growth, but a similar rush in eastern Oregon and the development of salmon fishing brought in many more settlers. A rail line reached the community from the east in 1883, and the first bridge over the Willamette joined its two sections four years later. As a transportation center for Alaska's Gold Rush, the town grew to a city of 200,000. During World War II industry experienced a boom based on wartime production. Portland is an important grain-shipping port and lumbering center and produces textiles, chemicals and electronics components. It is relatively free of smoke because most of its plants are operated by hydroelectric power. The city's unusually pure water comes from a lake at the foot of Mount Hood; drinking fountains on many downtown corners were given by a lumberman who hoped in this way to discourage the consumption of alcohol by his loggers. (Pop. 372,676.)

boring Texas. Oklahoma was part of the dust bowl of the 1930's, and tenant farmers who moved west as migrant laborers became known as Okies.

De Soto and Coronado both explored Oklahoma in 1541, the latter claiming it for Spain, while La Salle included the area in the vast Louisiana Territory he in turn claimed in 1682 for the King of France. A few fur traders from Canada paddled up the Red and Arkansas rivers, but for two centuries no settlements were established. Then in the 1830's the Southeastern states put heavy pressure on the Federal government to move the Indian tribes—Cherokee, Seminole, Choctaw, Creek and Chickasaw—whose homes were in Tennessee, Alabama, Georgia and Mississippi. At that time, the nation's first great westward movement had not yet started, and early explorers considered much of the land west of the Mississippi a barren desert. The Oklahoma region held little appeal for pioneers and settlers bent on getting farther west to Oregon or opening new cotton-lands.

Under treaties signed with the Indian tribes in the 1830's, Oklahoma was set aside for their people as a permanent home for "as long as grass grows and water runs." In what will remain forever a blot on American history, the men, women and children of the "Five Civilized Tribes" were herded west by the U.S. Army. During the march over what became known as the Trail of Tears, 4000 out of 15,000 Indians perished.

The first encroachments on the Indian Territory were for transportation purposes. In 1858 the Butterfield stage line began running its coaches across Oklahoma on the St. Louis-to-San Francisco run. The Missouri-Kansas-Texas Railroad laid down its tracks between 1870 and 1872. Then came the cattle drives up the Chisholm Trail from Texas to Kansas in the 1870's. As the pressure to open more frontier lands for settlement built up in the East, Congress again yielded to groups determined to colonize the Indian Territory.

In 1889, Indian rights to part of the territory were revoked. At noon on April 22, a pistol shot set off a charge of 50,000 homesteaders and land speculators into the so-called Unassigned Lands. By evening almost two million acres had been staked out and claimed. Some groups had secretly crossed the starting line the night before and were called "Sooners," a word which gave Oklahoma its nickname of Sooner State. Later most of the remaining Indian land was taken over by settlers.

Farmers at first had to struggle to make a living. Many rural areas could not support primary schools for more than three months in a year. But gradually the fertile soil and the valuable deposits below it brought prosperity.

Oklahoma's politics in the period after World War I were as freewheeling as its frontier-day activities. Two governors were impeached and removed from office and a third threatened with impeachment; three justices of the Supreme Court were impeached but not removed from office, while a president of the Board of Agriculture was impeached but subsequently acquitted. One of the state's most colorful chief executives was William H. Murray, nicknamed Alfalfa Bill because he was one of the first farmers to grow that crop. He ended the impeachment era by firmly telling a group of senators, "If you've got any impeachment ideas in your heads, hop to it. It'll be like a bunch of jackrabbits tryin' to get a wildcat out of a hole."

OKLAHOMA CITY

This metropolis popped up out of the prairie between noon and sunset on April 22, 1889, when 10,000 settlers arrived after rushing 11 miles from a starting line. There were no Indians to fight, and most of the settlers' energies went into building a city. In less than a year it had a mayor and a council. Mayor Couch didn't hold office long, however, because of a slight argument settled by pistol arbitration. There were some unusual incidents, such as the time a gambler got control of the only town pump and began to sell water; the Army had to be called in to prevent bloodletting. But in a few years flour and cotton mills and packing plants appeared, and Oklahoma City was on its way. Oil found in the late 1920's brought a boom, again not without incidents. In 1930, for example, a well called the Mary Sudik blew its top and sprayed the neighborhood with thousands of barrels of petroleum. There are oil rigs on the lawn of the governor's mansion. Oklahoma City on the banks of the dry North Canadian River is now an industrial, commercial and financial center.

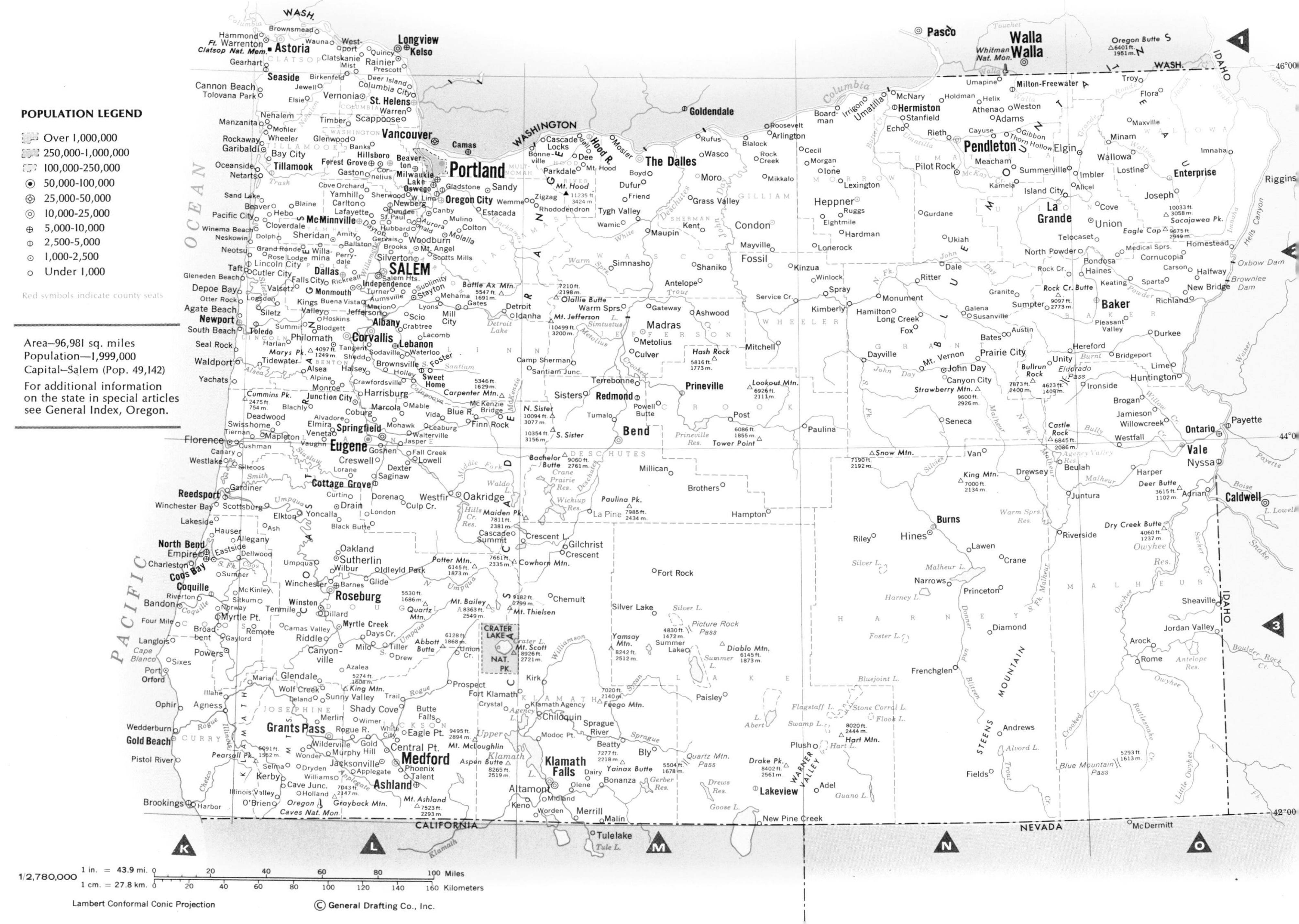

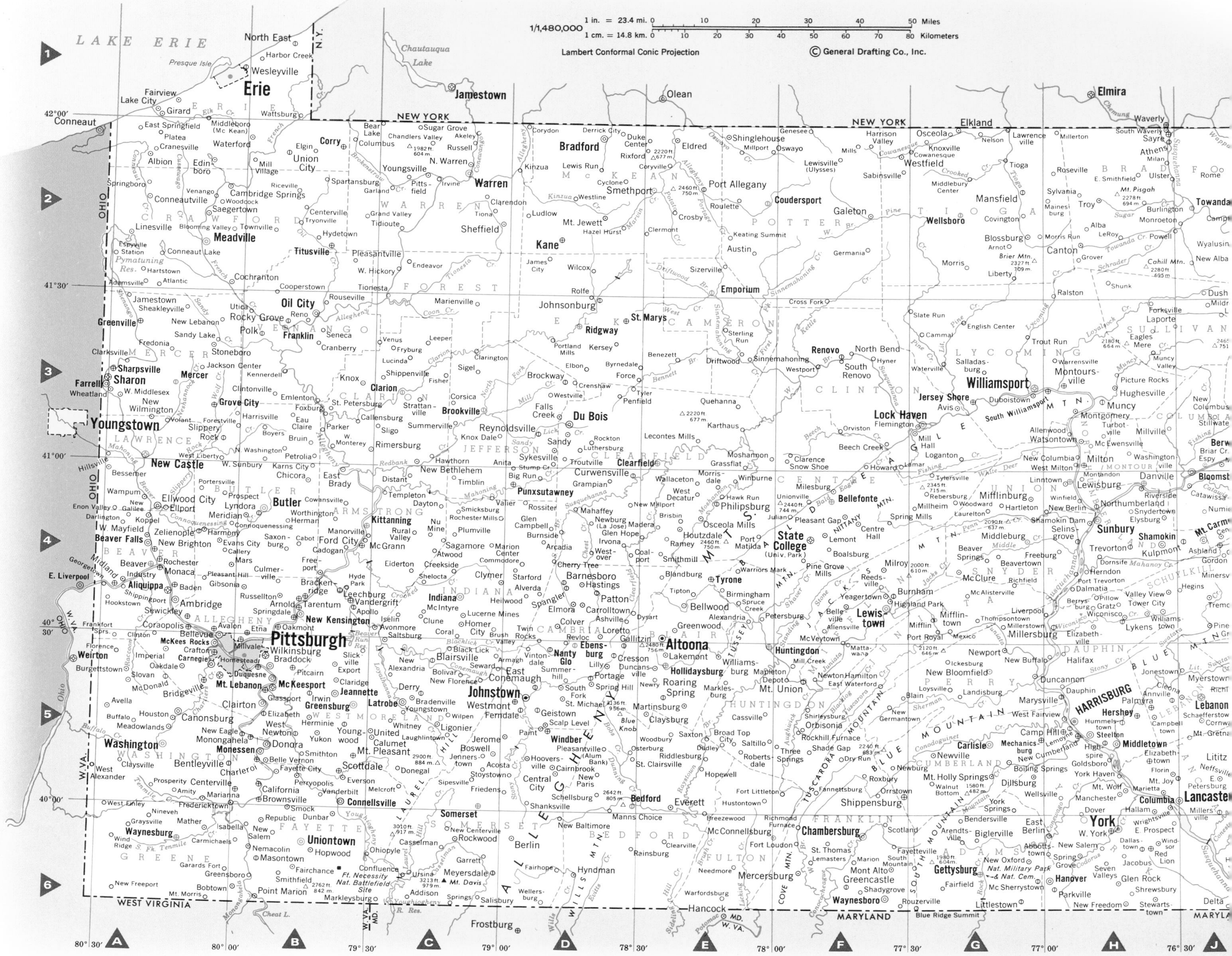

POPULATION LEGEND

- Over 1,000,000
- 250,000-1,000,000
- 100,000-250,000
- 50,000-100,000
- 25,000-50,000
- 10,000-25,000
- 5,000-10,000
- 2,500-5,000
- 1,000-2,500
- Under 1,000

Red symbols indicate county seats

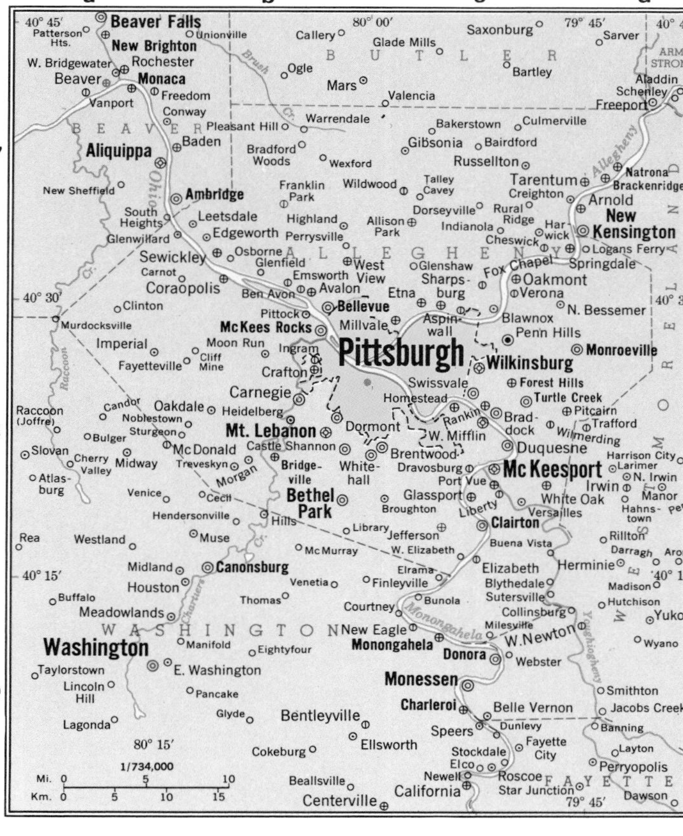

PHILADELPHIA

In the "City of Brotherly Love" (so its founder, William Penn, dreamed), persons of many races and beliefs would live together in harmony. Penn's "greene countrie towne," established in 1682 on the Schuylkill River, quickly attracted the religiously oppressed of Europe. Hard-working artisans, inspired by Penn's vision, built a community whose industry and tolerance gave a direction to the groping new colonies. By the time of the Revolution, Philadelphia was the young country's greatest seaport, market and cultural center. One prominent resident, Benjamin Franklin, campaigned successfully to have the streets paved and lighted. In 1774, the First Continental Congress convened in the city, where the Declaration of Independence was signed two years later. Philadelphia was the capital of the United States from 1790 to 1800. Symbols of its contributions to the nation's beginnings have survived, among them the Liberty Bell, Independence Hall and the homes of historic Americans. The descendants of some Revolutionary heroes, such as General "Mad Anthony" Wayne, are still in residence. Philadelphia hallmarks include row houses, menus featuring scrapple, boaters on the Schuylkill on Sunday afternoons, and vendors offering soft pretzels. While proud of its past, Philadelphia has in the last two decades become increasingly dissatisfied with its present. Business and civic leaders formed the Greater Philadelphia Movement to fight urban decay and to stimulate growth (see pages 102-03). Through a leadership training program, Philadelphians hope to make the modern city as dynamic as the old. (Pop. 2,002,512.)

PITTSBURGH

Squarely in the path of the young nation's westward thrust, Pittsburgh began as a fur-trading post. There the French in the mid-eighteenth century built Fort Duquesne, which later fell to the English and was renamed Fort Pitt. Rich farmlands and timberland surrounded the site, and below—discovered in 1760—was a coal seam extending into four states that was to prove richer in value than any other mineral source ever worked by man. Under industrial and financial leaders such as Andrew Carnegie, Henry Clay Frick, Charles M. Schwab and Andrew Mellon, Pittsburgh burgeoned as a coal, iron and steel producer. Immigrant laborers—Scotch, Irish, German, Italian, Polish, Slavic—poured into this melting pot. Huge fortunes were made in mining, smelting and metal products. One fifth of America's steel-making capacity is concentrated in Pittsburgh. The glow from row upon row of furnaces along the city's three rivers lights up the night sky for miles around. For years, sooty air hung over the area, earning the names "Smoky City" and "three-shirts-a-day town." Today's Pittsburgh has cleaned itself up. Strict smoke ordinances have drastically reduced soot, and the city is among the top ten in America in air purity. Its Golden Triangle, where the Allegheny and Monongahela rivers join to form the Ohio, is the famous business district which has created Pittsburgh's wealth. In this small delta region, sections of the community are connected by about 580 bridges. The city is proud of its natural-science institutes, its spirit of public philanthropy and its good record in race relations. (Pop. 604,332.)

PENNSYLVANIA

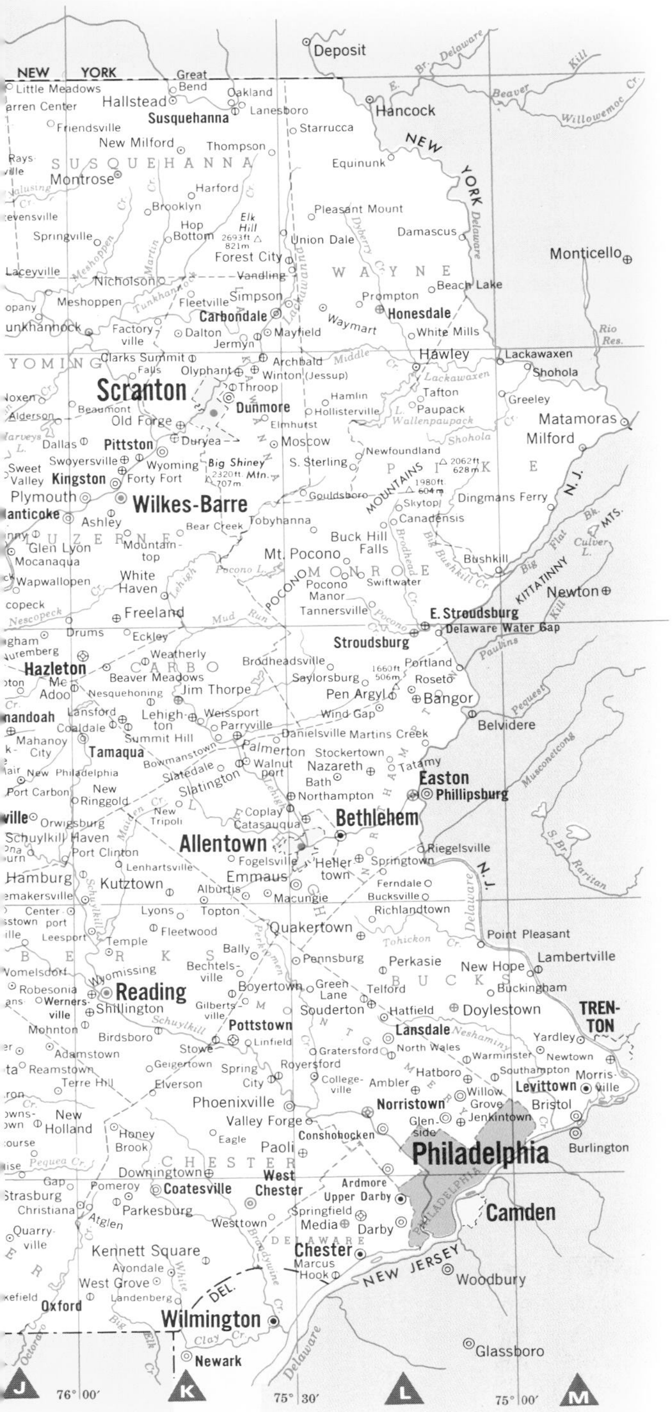

Area—45,333 sq. miles
Population—11,626,000
Capital—Harrisburg (Pop. 79,697)
For additional information on the state in special articles see General Index, Pennsylvania.

Like the United States itself, the Commonwealth of Pennsylvania is a concept as well as a place. It was there that the democratic idea first took deep root in America and spread as the country developed. It was there that Rudyard Kipling, impressed on a visit in the 1890's with both the beauty of the region and the ideals for which it stood, wrote:

They are there, there, there with earth immortal
(Citizens, I give you friendly warning),
The things that truly last, when men and time
have passed.
They are all in Pennsylvania this morning.

The state has so much in common with the nation as a whole that it has been called "a miniature United States." A glance at the map shows that Pennsylvania is remarkably like the United States in its rectangular form. Its river gorges, plains and mountains are reminiscent of the entire country's scenic riches. Both fertile farmlands and mineral resources have, like the nation's, developed a thriving agriculture and a booming industry.

Henry Hudson discovered the Delaware River in 1609 and Etienne Brulé explored the Susquehanna Valley in 1619. Pennsylvania's role as a pilot model of the country began in 1681, when Charles II of England deeded over the region to William Penn as payment of a debt the Crown owed to Penn's father. Penn's goal was to make the new land (Pennsylvania is literally "Penn's Woods") a haven for those Europeans who sought religious freedom. He gave the city he established in 1682 at the junction of the Delaware and Schuylkill rivers the utopian name of Philadelphia—City of Brotherly Love. To it came Quakers, Mennonites, Dunkards, Moravians, Schwenkfelders—and many nonsectarian individuals seeking new hope on earth. Among them, in 1723, was the friendless boy Ben Franklin. English, Welsh, Scotch and Irish settlers, followed by waves of immigrants from continental Europe, pushed through the Cumberland Valley to the mining regions of western Pennsylvania.

Hard workers, inspired by their new freedom and finding the land good, these first Pennsylvanians began to create one of the richest historical chronicles that any region has to its credit. Philadelphia soon became the economic and cultural hub of the colonies. The spirit that brought about national independence from Britain was nurtured there, and in its statehouse (now Independence Hall) the Continental Congress adopted the Declaration of Independence on July 4, 1776. Almost a century later the state which had most helped to forge the Union saw it preserved at Gettysburg in the battle of July 1863.

Pennsylvania's progress was registered with many "firsts"—the first paper mill in America, the first oil well, the first locomotive, the first insurance company, the first savings bank. Its writers and educators founded the first magazine, the first medical school, the first successful daily newspaper, the first subscription library.

Today Pennsylvania is more prosperous and self-sufficient than many a foreign nation. It leads the rest of the states in 50 industrial and agricultural products, including steel and iron. Virtually every bucketful of anthracite coal is mined in Pennsylvania.

"Keystone" state in the geographic arch of the American colonies, Pennsylvania became a great portal through which many pioneers passed en route to the frontier. In the early eighteenth century an unknown Lancaster County artisan built the large, broad-wheeled Conestoga wagon—the prairie schooner that settled the West.

Pennsylvanians became expert road builders. The first paved toll road in the country, between Lancaster and Philadelphia, finished in 1794, was a precursor of the Pennsylvania Turnpike. A half-billion-dollar enterprise, the pike stretches cross-state 470 miles, tunnels deeply through the Allegheny Mountains and has been described as an elongated city with an average population of 112,000 persons a day, all on the move.

Many of the immigrant strains have been absorbed by the state's ethnic melting pot; Eastern European immigrants are predominant around Pittsburgh, as are the English-Scotch-Swedish-German groups in the east. Some of the early religious and philosophical sects that came seeking haven have blended into the larger denominations. But a few have kept their individual identity, mainly the Amish and Mennonites of the Pennsylvania Dutch country in the east-central section. They are the "plain people," seen occasionally driving into town with horse and buggy, and wearing bonnets and broadbrims.

The Pennsylvania Dutch (a corruption of *Deutsch,* meaning German) till the loamy limestone soil of the fertile Great Valley, where gently rolling hills reminded early settlers of the Rhineland. Lancaster ranks among the five richest farming counties of the nation. In some parts, the barns bear "hex signs," colorful decorations mistakenly believed by strangers to be mystical symbols for warding off evil. Market days are a great show—nowhere can one see more magnificent vegetables and fruit, huge washed and even polished specimens. The inhabitants are fond of spiced preserves, home-baked bread, meats at every meal, molasses in pies and cakes. Dumplings and potatoes appear in the same boiled pot dinner. *Schnitz un knepp* (apples and dumplings), chicken corn soup, *lotterwaerich* and *smearcase* (apple butter and rich cottage cheese) have spread the fame of their cookery, as has the noted shoofly pie, served with the bottom layer "wet" or "dry."

The Great Valley is one of two main lowlands in Pennsylvania; the other is the western arm that reaches up to Lake Erie. The land between is largely a succession of forested hills and mountains (one half of the state is covered with groves of oak, maple, pine and hemlock). The narrow valleys are dotted with towns and cities. Valley dwellers go to the cool mountains in summer. The wooded highlands—though tunneled through by road builders, used for recreation by millions, crossed by railroads—are so extensive that some areas are as primitive as they have ever been, with more wild animals than in the time of the Indians.

Many out-of-staters are drawn to the Pennsylvania Dutch countryside, the chasms of the Delaware Water Gap, the Susquehanna River gorges, Pocono Mountains resorts, the Gettysburg battlefield, Valley Forge and Independence-era shrines in Philadelphia. Throughout the state are picture villages glittering in the sun at the elbows of streams, and old countryside houses with stone walls, unchanged in more than two centuries.

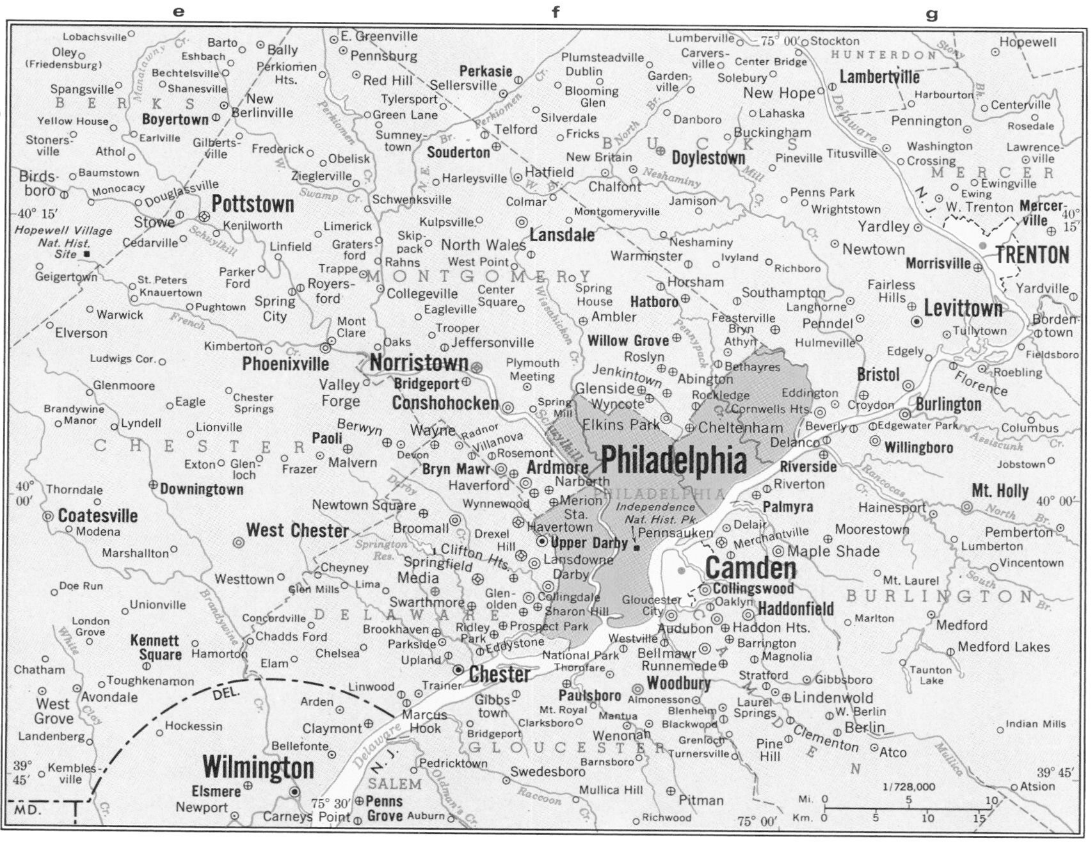

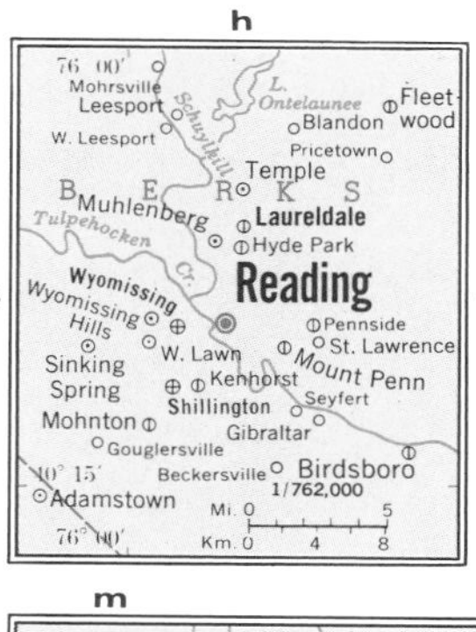

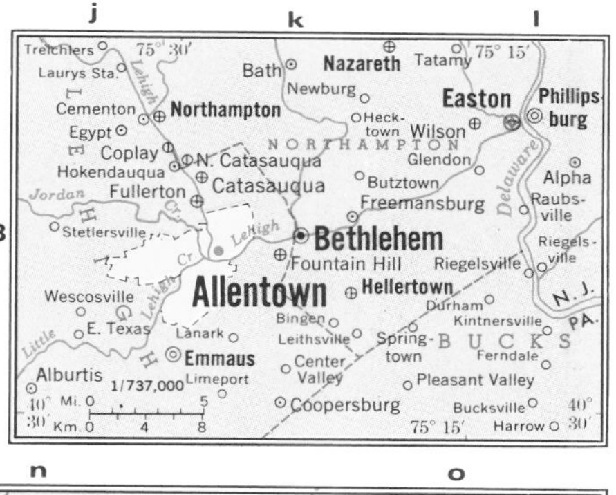

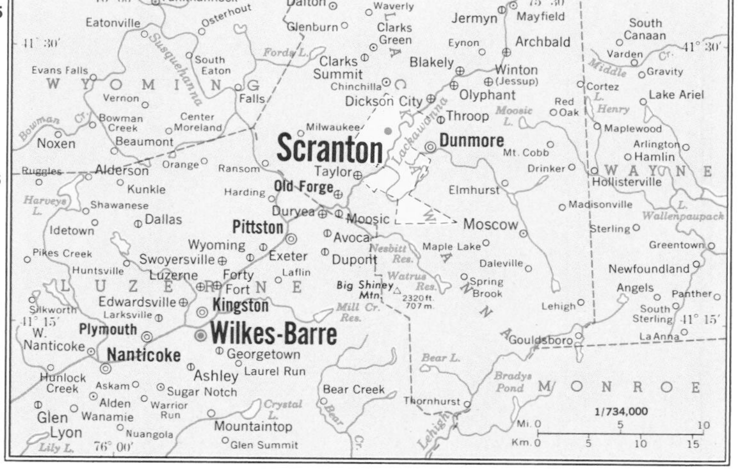

RHODE ISLAND

The smallest state in the Union is roughly 37 miles wide and 48 miles long. It turns its weatherbeaten Yankee face to the sea. Narragansett Bay, explored by Verrazano in 1524, thrusts 28 miles inland from the ocean. Coastal lowlands and the bay islands cover about one third of its territory. From Rhode Island, also called Aquidneck, the state takes its name. Spectacular rocky cliffs tower over many of the island beaches and the shores of the southeastern part. Typical of the rest are sandy beaches, shallow salt marshes, peninsulas and ponds. Forests blanket about two thirds of the state, and many of the rivers, though small, break into sparkling waterfalls as they tumble down from the interior plateau.

The first white settlement in the state was established by Roger Williams, an English pastor who left his home country because he refused to conform to the restrictions of the Anglican Church. Williams spent several years in the Massachusetts Bay Colony but was finally banished because he resisted political influence in religious affairs and declared that the Crown had no right to make grants of land before purchasing it from the Indians. To escape seizure and forcible return to England, he wandered through the wilderness for six months. Finally in 1636 he obtained land from the Indians and founded Providence, today Rhode Island's capital and its biggest city.

Williams spoke the language of the natives and established a firm friendship with them. He and other dissident leaders not only made alliances with the Indians but furnished a haven for minority religious groups.

In May 1776, Rhode Island became the first colony to proclaim its independence from the King of England. Although no major battles were fought there, the area was occupied for almost three years by the British. When the war was over, Rhode Island, true to the individualistic beliefs of Roger Williams, declined to send delegates to the Constitutional Convention in 1787. Its leaders, fearful of Federal regulations and import duties, at first refused to ratify the Constitution. In 1790, faced with loss of all commercial ties, Rhode Island was the last of the original colonies to join the Union.

Many of the early settlers turned to pursuits connected with the sea: fishing, boatbuilding and commerce. From the middle of the 1600's until the late nineteenth century the state's shipyards built hundreds of merchant and whaling vessels.

Some Rhode Islanders joined Massachusetts sea captains in the infamous "Triangle Trade" in rum, slaves and sugar. Ships laden with rum sailed from Newport bound for Africa, where the rum was exchanged for slaves. Then the captains set out for the West Indies, where they traded the slaves for sugar and molasses. Once the ships had returned to Providence and Newport, the molasses was made into rum, and the triangle voyage was repeated. Shipowners also took part in the direct trade between America and ports in the Orient.

A new enterprise begun late in the eighteenth century brought great profits to Rhode Island. In 1789 an Englishman named Samuel Slater built the first power jenny for spinning thread in America, at Pawtucket, which became known as the Cradle of American Industry. Later the first power loom was invented and began operation at Peace Dale. Within a few years, many mills and factories were built along the swift-running streams which provided power for the new machines. Gradually villages grew up around them. The state became famous for weaving textiles, particularly woolens and worsteds. Related industries developed: the finishing and dyeing of cloth and the manufacture of lace and braid. During and after the Civil War the mills began to attract an influx of immigrants, who eventually would make Rhode Island the most densely populated state until the 1960's. It still ranks ninth in the manufacture of textiles, though many mills have moved to the South. Machinery and metal products are now the leading manufactures.

In recent years the entire state has become one of the most popular resort areas on the Eastern seaboard. Block Island, a famous vacation retreat, lies ten miles out in the Atlantic. The warm waters of Narragansett Bay help to make the climate mild; the summers are long and delightful. Rhode Island's seafaring tradition has always attracted yachtsmen and sailors. From May until September the waters off the coast are filled with sailboats and other pleasure craft taking part in regattas, races and cruises.

In the nineteenth century, a town that had been one of the great centers of the slave trade achieved new fame when a notable set of millionaires selected it for their summer playground. Great estates were built along Newport's towering cliffs by men who had made their fortunes in railroads, banking and industry. Society gave lavish parties costing thousands of dollars. Cornelius Vanderbilt, Ogden Goelet, Stuyvesant Fish, John Jacob Astor, Arthur Curtiss James, James Gordon Bennett and Oliver Belmont were among those who deserted their Fifth Avenue mansions in New York to spend the summers on the shore in Newport.

PROVIDENCE

The many historic buildings in Providence have remained undisturbed since the early eighteenth century. A church built in 1775 houses the oldest Baptist congregation in America, founded in 1639. In the steeple of the Unitarian Church hangs the largest bell cast by Paul Revere's foundry. The city began as an agricultural community, became a leading port with shipbuilding yards and finally, in the 1830's, a manufacturing and industrial center. The importance of textile mills led to the founding of the Rhode Island School of Design. A leader in its field, it now also offers courses in fine and graphic arts, interior decorating and jewelry. The making of jewelry was started by the early settlers and still flourishes; one huge plant turns out more sterling silver than any other factory in the world. The city was named by Roger Williams in thanks for "God's merciful providence to him in his distress," and the religious spirit of the first residents is recalled in the names they gave some of the streets—Faith, Hope, Friendship, Peace and Benefit.

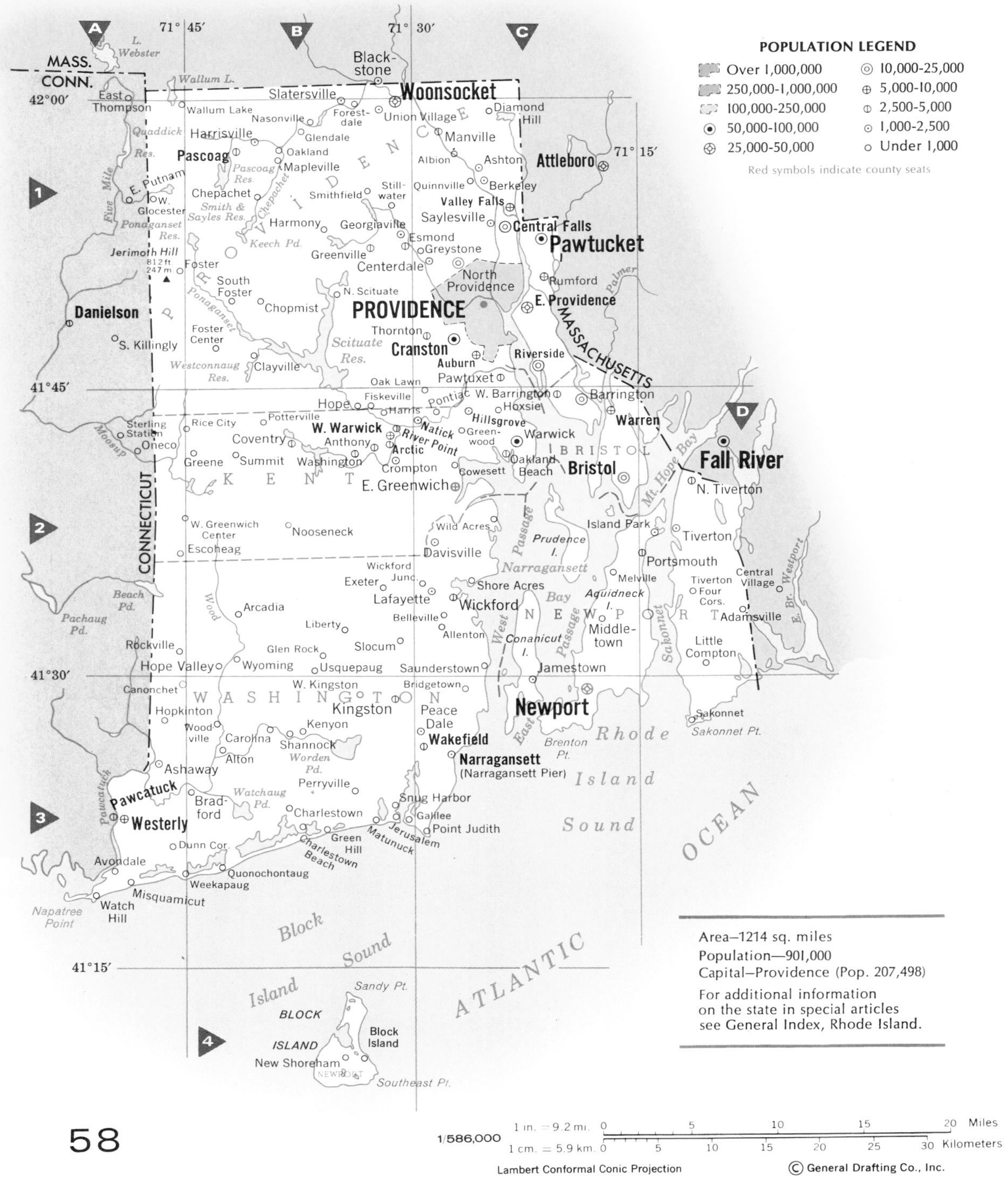

SOUTH CAROLINA

In the early eighteenth century when the vast rice fields of the South Carolina coastal plantations were flooded for the summer months and visited by plagues of malaria, the white planters and their families converged on Charleston. Each spring, one planter's daughter recalled, "my father's entire household migrated to the sea . . . the vehicles, cows, furniture, bedding, trunks, provisions were all put into great flatboats at first dawn and sent ahead. Then the family got into the rowboat (usually captained by a Negro in bright livery) and were rowed down the Pee Dee River."

In Charleston, cooled by sea breezes, the summer was the height of the social season. In white-columned, luxuriously furnished mansions wealthy Carolinians in brocades, powdered wigs and costly jewels gathered for galas, fancy-dress balls, concerts and teas. At the Dock Theater, the first building in America designed for the drama, were presented some of the most brilliant theatrical productions of colonial times.

Such was the life of South Carolina's feudal aristocracy, copied from that existing in England and France. It was based on fortunes made from the slave-labor crops of indigo, rice and cotton. By 1768 South Carolina held one fifth of the total export trade of the English colonies in the New World. Rice was of great economic importance and was used in place of money. In 1820, along with Georgia, the state produced half of the nation's cotton crop and, as late as 1850, more than half of the total rice crop. After the Revolution, a traveling Englishman wrote that "for size and beauty and trade [Charleston] may be considered one of the first cities in British America." By 1791, it had two golf courses.

The division of the state between Upland and Lowland

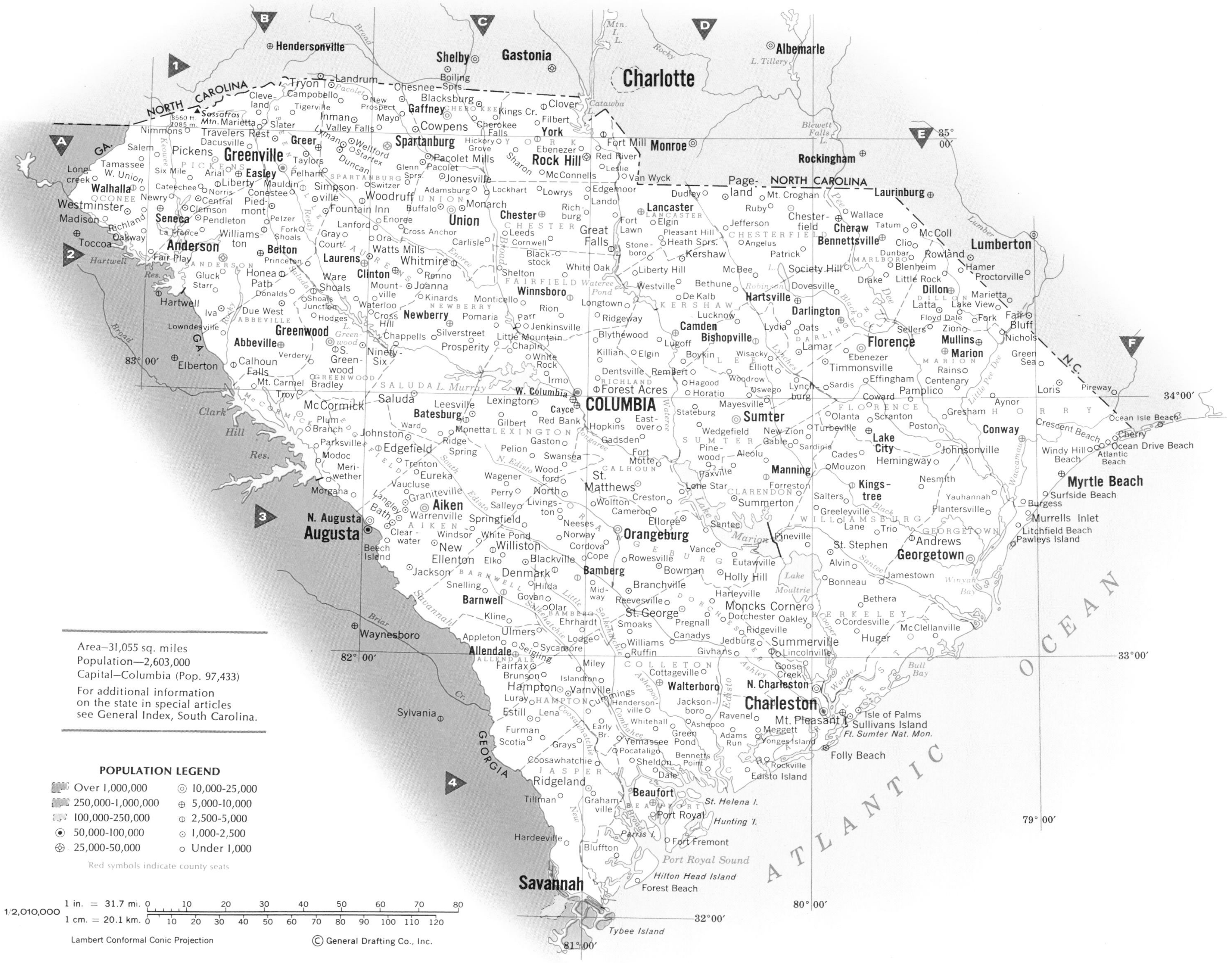

created the greatest industrial asset and the greatest social difference. Twelve large rivers flow from the mountains to the sea. These waters move down the Piedmont plateau with increasing speed, becoming a series of rapids and waterfalls. This abundant source of hydroelectric power is now South Carolina's most important natural resource, turning the wheels of industry and irrigating the fields.

Gordillo and Quexos, who came from Santo Domingo, explored the Carolina coast in 1521, and the Spanish (as early as 1526), the French and the English all attempted colonization for nearly 150 years. Finally, under the royal grant from King Charles II of England to his favorite courtiers in 1663, an English settlement gained a permanent hold on the present site of Charleston. Many colonists were English from Barbados and French Protestants who left their stamp on the culture of the colony. They first dealt in fur trade with the Indians, then in the rapidly expanding plantation crops.

In the Up Country, Indians, thick forests and less fertile soil hindered the development of the region. Gradually it was settled by German and Scotch-Irish immigrants—joined by newcomers drifting down from colonies in the north. These people lived a life typical of American pioneers—dwelling in log cabins, clearing the timbered lands and coping with Indian forays. They had little in common with the planter aristocracy in the Low Country. Despite their strong differences, the two groups united to fight the British in the American Revolution but could not prevent them from seizing control of the state. Small groups of Carolinians under leaders such as Francis Marion ("the Swamp Fox") harassed the British forces, though Charleston was captured. More skirmishes were fought there than in any other state, and the Revolutionary Army prevented the British from joining forces with those in the north.

The first shots of the Civil War were fired when a steamer bringing supplies to the Union forces at Fort Sumter in Charleston harbor was shelled by a South Carolina battery across the bay. Three months later Confederate troops occupied the fort and succeeded in holding it throughout the war despite innumerable Union assaults—one of the longest sieges in modern military history.

But few other states have paid such a heavy price for past riches and glories. The war in which South Carolina fought to preserve slavery cost the lives of 15,000 of its men and millions of dollars' worth of property. The end of slavery destroyed the plantation system; the soil had been so overworked that thousands of farmers migrated to the West. Reconstruction left South Carolina floundering in the depths of an economic depression from which it has only recently emerged. The huge rice crops are gone. Rivers and coastal waterways, once bustling with freight and passenger craft, wind silently through miles of abandoned plantation fields where stark silhouettes of crumbling chimneys mark the sites of former rice mills. Cotton now provides only about one quarter of the state's agricultural income, and much of it is raised on small holdings by white and Negro tenant farmers. Tobacco has become the leading cash crop.

In the 1960's South Carolina has at last begun to regain the vitality it once possessed. Textile mills and factories produce wool, cotton and synthetic fabrics with a market value second only to those of North Carolina. Chemicals have become a major industry. Wood-pulp and timber-products manufacturing centers are spreading through the state. In the Savannah River plant of the Atomic Energy Commission, one of the country's major atomic-energy production and research installations, radioactive materials are turned out for defense and civilian uses. Navy nuclear submarine bases built in Charleston are a symbol of the resurgence of the city as an important seaport.

COLUMBIA

This beautiful, well-planned city of broad avenues, tall, modern office buildings and tree-shaded streets and parks is situated close to the center of South Carolina on a hill overlooking the Congaree River. It is the focus of much of the industrial, commercial and agricultural activity of the state. Chosen as the capital in 1786 in a compromise to end the bitter dissension between the farmers of the Up Country and wealthy planters of the Low Country, it combines the bustle of Up Country communities with the charm and grace characteristic of coastal cities such as Charleston. When Columbia was burned by Union forces under General Sherman in February 1865, the great statehouse of imposing Italian Renaissance design was among the few buildings that survived, and it is still considered one of the most elegant state capitols in the nation.

SOUTH DAKOTA

In the dawn of an April morning in 1743, two fur-garbed French explorers, Louis and François Vérendrye, bade farewell to a tribe of friendly Indians and launched their birch bark canoe into the swift-flowing, icy waters of the Missouri River, which bisects South Dakota. Behind them, on a bluff overlooking the river, buried beneath a pyramid of stones, they left a lead plate inscribed with the date—the earliest record of white men in this trackless, open territory. They had come overland from the west, having given up and turned back from their mission for the French Crown to reach and claim the lands as far as the "western ocean."

Within a fortnight after the Frenchmen departed, an infant was born on the Blue Ridge frontier of Virginia. He was named Thomas Jefferson and was destined as President to acquire the Dakotas and the heart of North America from Napoleon in the Louisiana Purchase.

By the 1820's the first permanent white settlement on the upper Missouri was busily engaged in trading with the Sioux Indians. On the present site of Fort Pierre, it lay within a mile of where the Vérendryes had camped nearly a century before. The first steamboat, the *Yellowstone,* snorted its way over sandbars and snags up from St. Louis to the fort in 1832, reducing to a few weeks a journey that had formerly required months. This development opened up the Dakotas to a period of trapping, Indian wars and gold rushes which would culminate in the settlement of the midcontinent.

When the Dakota Territory was created by Congress in 1861, it included portions of both future Dakotas as well as most of Montana and Wyoming and a chunk of Nebraska. Yet at that time it had only about 2000 white inhabitants. Discovery of gold in the Black Hills in the southwestern corner of the region brought in swarms of prospectors, miners and speculators.

Dakota frontier days rivaled any in the whole West for wild and woolly chapters replete with gold miners, gambling dens, boomtowns, saloons, dance-hall hostesses and gun-blazing battles between sheepherders, cattle ranchers, sheriffs and outlaws. Wild Bill Hickok and Calamity Jane are buried in the cemetery in Deadwood, once a wide-open gold-rush town. As this was Indian land, fights broke out between the U.S. Cavalry and the Sioux. The Indians fled to Montana to hold out, were pursued by Custer and eventually defeated there after Custer's forces were massacred. The coming of the railroads in the 1880's speeded settlement of the eastern farm regions, and homesteaders poured in during the following decade.

What appears to be the small, neat rectangular shape of South Dakota on a map of the entire United States is deceiving. The state covers more territory than most Americans realize: it is bigger than all the New England states put together. To the west of the wide Missouri, where great herds of buffalo once grazed, there are now cattle and sheep ranches. To the east stretches a huge expanse of farmland that produces corn, wheat, hay and oats. Food-processing is the most important industry. South Dakota leads the nation in the production of gold.

The forested Black Hills, with the highest peaks east of the Rockies, are ages older than the Rocky Mountains, the Alps or the Himalayas. Gold miners commonly encounter the skeletal remains of dinosaurs that wallowed in tropical swamps 40,000,000 years ago. In the Badlands—fantastically eroded formations of the landscape—the remains of the saber-toothed tiger and three-toed horse have been found.

The greatest single tourist attraction in the state is Mount Rushmore National Memorial, where the heads of Presidents Washington, Jefferson, Lincoln and Theodore Roosevelt were chiseled from the granite face of one of the Black Hills.

The corroded, encrusted lead plaque buried by the Vérendrye expedition was found by schoolchildren in 1913 and is now in the historical museum of the Memorial Building in nearby Pierre.

SIOUX FALLS

A Canadian explorer's description of the falls on the Big Sioux River so roused the interest of a group of Iowa residents that they went west to establish a settlement in 1856. It lasted for six years before being burned to the ground by Indians. When Fort Dakota was built on the site in 1865, settlers returned, although many of them left again during a grasshopper plague in 1874. Then came the blizzard of 1880, but after that Sioux Falls began to prosper. At the turn of the century, the short time required to establish residence for divorce made it as popular as Reno was to be several decades later. The city is the distribution center for South Dakota trade, with stockyards, meat-packing plants, steel and plastic mills and an atomic-energy plant. The falls, which first powered gristmills, now furnish electricity. Wooded parks, landscaped residential areas and two tree-shaded college campuses cover the slopes and plains above the S-shaped river valley containing the business district. Many buildings are constructed of the pink quartzite which lies beneath the main part of the city. (Pop. 65,466.)

TENNESSEE

Oak Ridge, America's most famous "atomic city," has spread out over 92 square miles in a few short years and calls itself Science City, U.S.A. Yet only a score of miles from where its scientists are probing the secrets of nuclear energy, there are remote hamlets where hardy mountaineers still sing ballads dating back to Elizabethan England. Knoxville is strewn with monuments to the days when it was a frontier town inhabited by the pioneers who opened the West. It is now an industrial city with 500 manufacturing firms which derive much of their power from hydroelectric turbines of the Norris Dam and other dams of the Tennessee Valley Authority (TVA).

Perhaps the greatest contrast of past and present is shown by the wild river, the Tennessee. From the beginning it hindered settlement, was untamable and, in some sections, was virtually unnavigable. Explorers, pioneers and even experienced riverboatmen, accustomed to daily danger, feared the Narrows near Chattanooga and Muscle Shoals, the rapids in Alabama. Now, all is different. The brawling river and all its tributaries are controlled by 32 dams operated by the TVA, which was begun during the Depression. Most of its length is at last navigable.

The purpose of the monumental project was to halt the ravages of floods and to provide hydroelectric power, and so develop new sources of industrial and agricultural wealth for the region. In large part, this aim has been accomplished. While the dams were being constructed, a coördinate program in land salvage began. The soil of the once fertile valley had been worn out by one-crop planting and heavy logging operations, which had gouged deep gullies. Modern methods of contour plowing, fertilization, crop rotation and reforestation revitalized the land and remade it into prosperous farming country.

Actually, the strange, violent course of the Tennessee has set the agricultural pattern of the entire state. The stream is unique. No other big river in America, after heading in one general direction for 350 miles, switches around and flows for 300 miles on an opposite course. The Tennessee forms in the eastern section of the state, loops down into Alabama and then, astonishingly enough, reenters the state, streaming north to join the Ohio River at Paducah, Kentucky.

Thus Tennessee always has been divided into three parts, separated by the eastern and western valleys of the river. The eastern section is dominated by the Appalachian Mountains. The center is a fertile, broad, rolling area which covers about half the state and slopes gradually toward the rich bottomlands in the west.

Cotton, the biggest cash crop, is raised mainly in the western section; Tennessee is among the leading cotton-growers. Farmers in the middle and eastern counties reap large harvests of tobacco as well as corn and hay. The central portion is also important for cattle and for dairy products.

A tremendous postwar boom invigorated established businesses and gave birth to other new industries, such as the production of chemicals, which now ranks first. The state manufactures plastics and many synthetic fibers. Large quantities of aluminum are refined in plants founded many years ago. Food-processing is the second leading industry. One multimillion-dollar business has roots that go deep into Tennessee's past: the recording of country music, with headquarters in Nashville.

Long before the Civil War, men had proved their bravery in skirmishes in the mountains and fields of Tennessee. The state's history is filled with stories of individual courage, of buckskin-clad heroes, and hard-fought encounters. Men like Davy Crockett, David Farragut and Nathan Forrest seem to spring naturally from the region.

De Soto entered the Tennessee Valley in 1540, and for 200 years the territory was scouted by the French

MEMPHIS

Lying along the high bluffs of the Mississippi River in the southwestern corner of Tennessee, Memphis is one of America's great inland ports, the world's largest cotton and hardwood-lumber market and transportation hub of the mid-South. The city's cliffs were well known to explorers, fur traders and flatboatmen as the highest point on the Mississippi between New Orleans and the mouth of the Ohio. A fort on the heights was used successively by the French, Spanish, British and Americans before a town was finally laid out in 1819. Named Memphis because its site was similar to that of the ancient Egyptian capital on the Nile, it grew rapidly during the steamboat era, went bankrupt after occupation by Union troops during the Civil War and was nearly wiped out by epidemics of yellow fever during the 1870's. But Memphis rallied to become a thriving industrial metropolis, equal to its boast, "You can't miss Memphis. It's in the middle of everything and knows it." W. C. Handy, *the famous jazz composer, immortalized the city with his "Memphis Blues" and "Beale Street Blues." (Pop. 497,524.)*

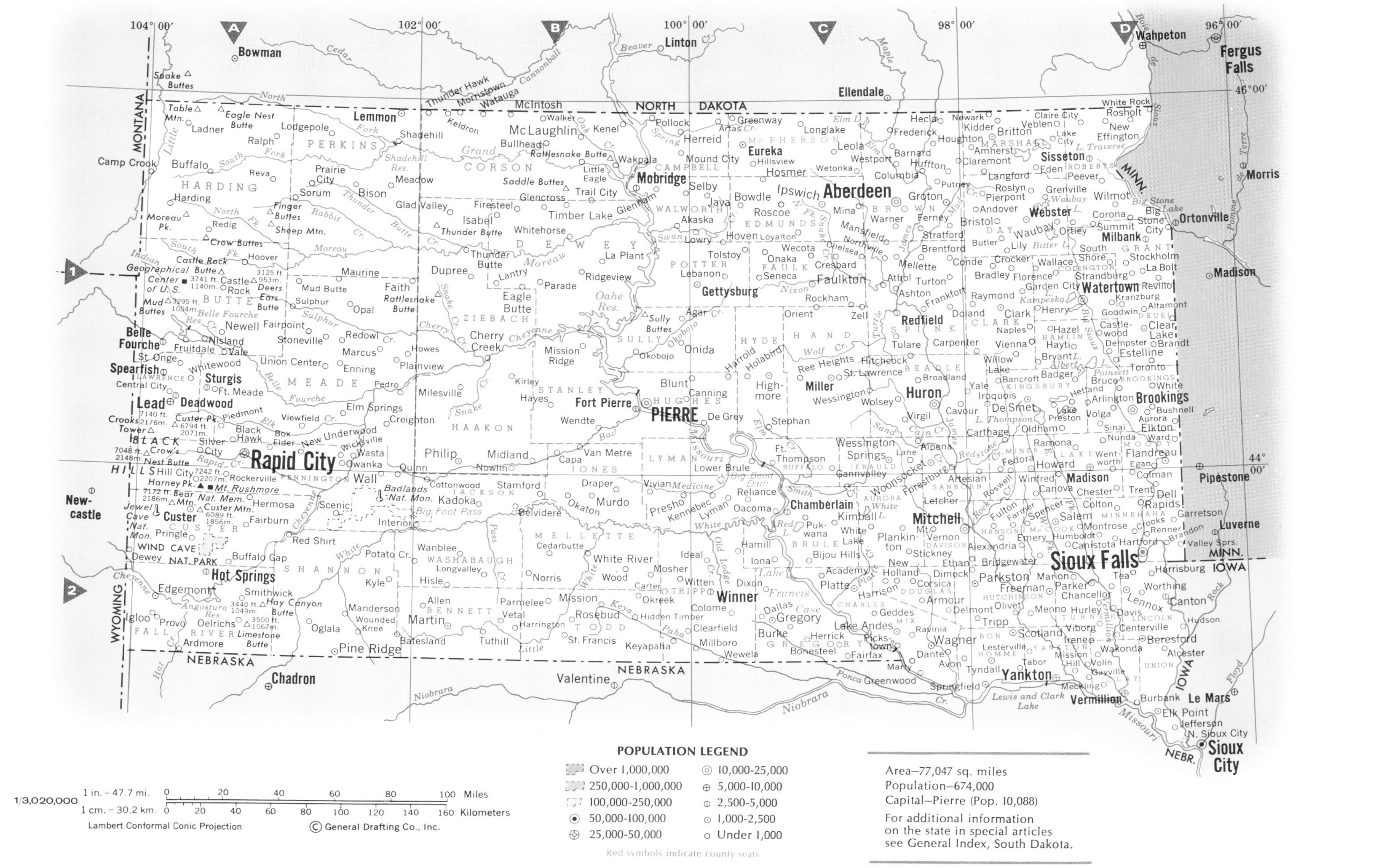

from the west and by English colonists from the east until the British won the French and Indian Wars in the 1760's. Soon after the sound of battle had died away, Daniel Boone rode through the Cumberland Gap looking for good farmland. The men and women who followed Boone settled in Kentucky and Tennessee, wresting a living from the land, fighting and gradually displacing the Indian tribes, the Cherokees of the eastern mountains and the tenacious Chickasaws in the west.

Among those fearless, hardy men one stood out—John Sevier, who was highly skilled in Indian combat. During the Revolutionary War, in a decisive engagement, Sevier and his men, employing Indian tactics, wiped out half of a British force of more than 1000 men and suffered only 28 casualties.

Of Tennessee's various nicknames, the Volunteer State refers to the many soldiers who have served in every war since the Revolution. The combative Andrew Jackson, one of the young nation's fiercest generals, represented the state as a U.S. senator before becoming President. During the Civil War, only Virginia saw more action. Yet Tennessee was divided in its loyalties (the eastern part being strongly Unionist), and was the last to secede.

A visitor can hardly travel throughout the state without noticing reminders of that conflict—battlefield sites, tombstones, markers and military monuments that call to mind engagements such as the Battle of Shiloh, fought in 1862 in southwestern Tennessee. Although General Grant won, the Union's dead and wounded were 13,000, compared with the Confederacy's 10,700.

Sightseers are also drawn to the Great Smoky Mountains National Park with its ample campgrounds, several hundred miles of horse and foot trails and more than 1000 species of trees, shrubs and flowering plants, many of them native to the land. Others are attracted to recreational areas along the lakes created by the TVA dams.

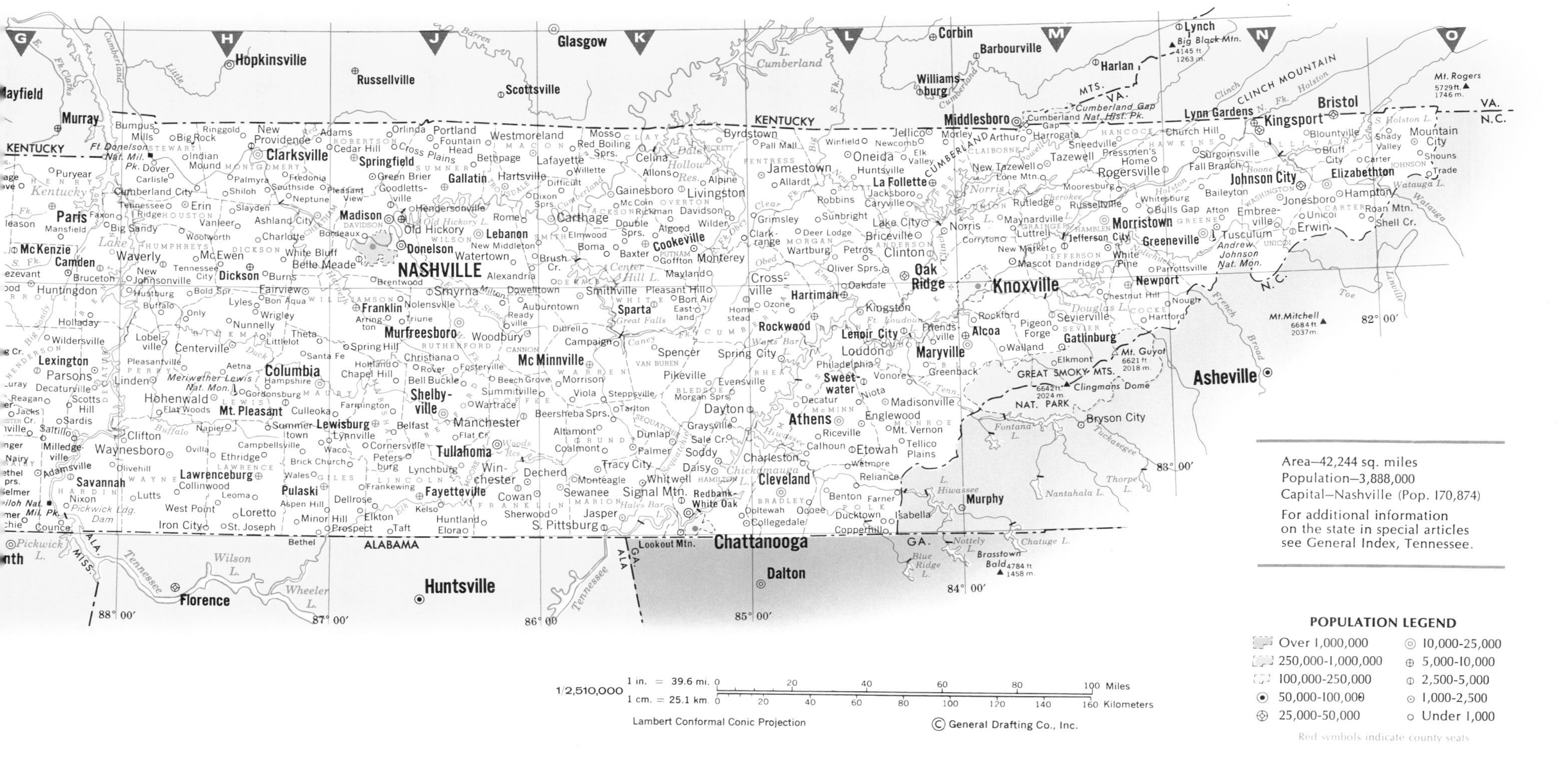

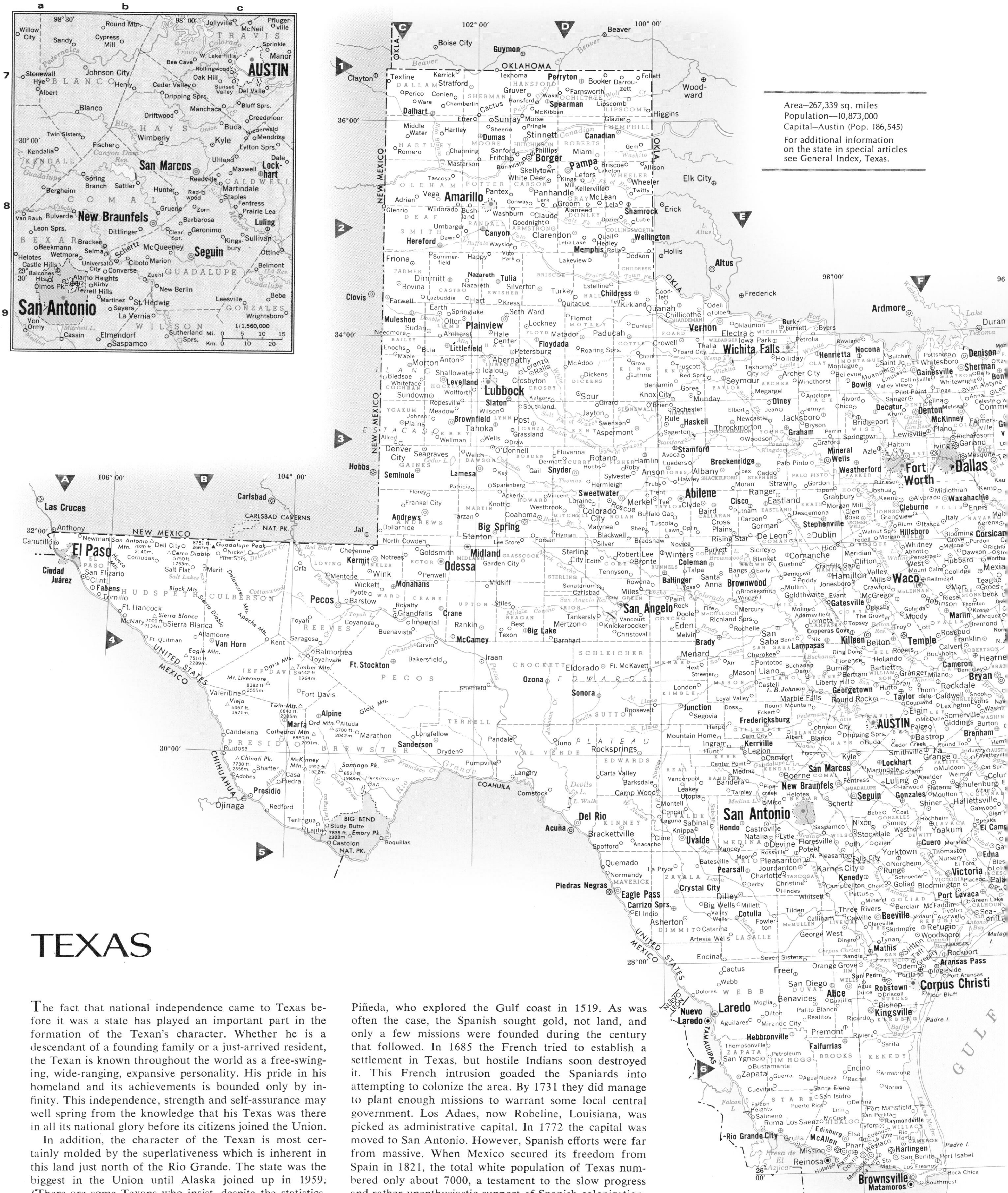

Area–267,339 sq. miles
Population–10,873,000
Capital–Austin (Pop. 186,545)
For additional information on the state in special articles see General Index, Texas.

TEXAS

The fact that national independence came to Texas before it was a state has played an important part in the formation of the Texan's character. Whether he is a descendant of a founding family or a just-arrived resident, the Texan is known throughout the world as a free-swinging, wide-ranging, expansive personality. His pride in his homeland and its achievements is bounded only by infinity. This independence, strength and self-assurance may well spring from the knowledge that his Texas was there in all its national glory before its citizens joined the Union.

In addition, the character of the Texan is most certainly molded by the superlativeness which is inherent in this land just north of the Rio Grande. The state was the biggest in the Union until Alaska joined up in 1959. (There are some Texans who insist, despite the statistics, that it still is.) It has one of the largest ranches in the world within its borders—the fabulous King Ranch, which covers 823,400 acres and is vast enough to be a state all by itself. Texas has the deepest oil well in the world, which plunges 25,340 feet below the surface of Pecos County. Leading the nation in producing carbon black, pure helium, oil and natural gas, Texas also tops all other states in the production of beef cattle, horses, sheep, wool, goats, cotton and rice. Its principal industries are oil-refining, food-processing and the manufacture of chemicals, transportation equipment and machinery.

The first white men to reach the soil of Texas were Spaniards under the command of Alonso Alvarez de Piñeda, who explored the Gulf coast in 1519. As was often the case, the Spanish sought gold, not land, and only a few missions were founded during the century that followed. In 1685 the French tried to establish a settlement in Texas, but hostile Indians soon destroyed it. This French intrusion goaded the Spaniards into attempting to colonize the area. By 1731 they did manage to plant enough missions to warrant some local central government. Los Adaes, now Robeline, Louisiana, was picked as administrative capital. In 1772 the capital was moved to San Antonio. However, Spanish efforts were far from massive. When Mexico secured its freedom from Spain in 1821, the total white population of Texas numbered only about 7000, a testament to the slow progress and rather unenthusiastic support of Spanish colonization.

The same can hardly be said for the growth of Anglo-American villages. Beginning in the early 1820's, people surged over the borders from the North. Stephen F. Austin alone brought some 300 families to found communities at Columbus and Washington-on-the-Brazos. The new republican government of Mexico at first welcomed these Anglo-Americans, many of whom had left the eastern United States as a result of the panic of 1819, in search of new fortunes and new land. For ten years, hordes of newcomers arrived until at last the Mexican government became frightened and, in 1830, banned further immigration. Three years later General Santa Anna became a dictator and soon Texas exploded.

Hostilities had already broken out when Anglo-American leaders met at Washington-on-the-Brazos on March 2, 1836, to issue a declaration of secession from Mexico. Four days later the Alamo mission fortress in San Antonio fell; 187 Texans, fighting like hellions, defended it to the last man—thereby creating a legend which is held in the same reverence in Texas as the story of the Battle of Bunker Hill in Massachusetts. A little more than a month later Colonel William B. Travis' gallant 187 were

HOUSTON

In July of 1824, Richardson Harris of New York led a group of settlers to the meeting point of the Buffalo and Bray bayous about 50 miles from the Gulf of Mexico. The little town prospered, but on April 14, 1836, most of it was burned by its residents during the revolt against Mexico, to keep it from falling into the hands of the Mexican army under Santa Anna. Four months and ten days later, after the defeat of the Mexican dictator, John and Augustus Allen, real-estate promoters, bought the area and named it Houston after the new president of Texas. The Houston Ship Channel, improved over a period of years, is now lined with docks and industrial plants, and the city has become one of the leading ports in the United States. It is the heart of the Texas oil industry and the focus of a huge net of pipelines. But Houston prides itself on being, in addition, an educational and cultural center. It has a large number of colleges and universities, a symphony orchestra and several museums. Some of this booming growth may have been envisioned by the Allens, but their wildest dreams could hardly have included two sights of the metropolitan area. The fabulous manned-spacecraft control center of the National Aeronautics and Space Administration lies about 22 miles from downtown Houston near Clear Lake. An equally imposing structure is the air-conditioned Astrodome baseball and football stadium, which encloses 11 acres. (Pop. 938,219.)

avenged when a small army of Texans took on the much larger force of Santa Anna at San Jacinto, whipped the enemy, captured the dictator and won the war and full independence for the Lone Star State. Sam Houston became its first president, and Texans voted to seek immediate annexation by the United States.

The powers of Europe, who viewed with alarm the rapid increase in size and strength of the United States, would have preferred to see Texas remain a separate country; Northern Abolitionist sentiment in Congress also opposed the annexation of a slave-holding territory. Texas, however, joined the Union on December 29, 1845, as the twenty-eighth state. War between Mexico and the United States followed, ending in the Treaty of Guadalupe-Hidalgo of 1848, which firmly established boundaries between Texas and Mexico. An agreement in 1964 readjusted small parts of that frontier.

Texas has boomed ever since it became a state, and its economy even flourished during the four Civil War years when it was part of the Confederacy. Situated away from the main theater of war, it served as a supply funnel for the military goods and arms that the South purchased in Europe and shipped through Mexico. When the war ended, immigration to Texas began again, with mobs of ex-soldiers rushing into the state to make a new start while land was still available.

The Spanish had early brought cattle to Texas. In 1757, for example, one village on the Rio Grande had a population of 269 persons and 18,000 head of cattle. During the Civil War the herds increased despite tick fever and other natural losses. When communications with the East were cut by the Union naval blockade and the capture of the Mississippi, beef could no longer be shipped to the Confederates. The livestock population became so large and so valueless that some owners never bothered to brand their calves. Many other cattle escaped roundups and ran wild. After the war, Texas was choked with cattle, worthless unless they could be delivered to the railheads in Kansas. The introduction of the Brahman strain from India in the 1870's cut losses due to tick fever, making the situation more acute. The solution to the problem was typically Texan. Between 1870 and 1890 huge drives were organized to herd the cattle over the 1000 to 1500 miles to market. Hell-for-leather cowboys ran them with gusto, and Texas soon became the major beef supplier of the United States. Now aircraft rather than horses are frequently used to round up cattle and locate strays.

The coming of the railroads ended the cattle drives and brought farmers and fences. The open rangeland disappeared as windmills began to pump water from deep wells to the arid soil all over Texas. Cotton had always been one of the biggest crops, but by 1900 wheat was slowly rising in importance. World War I created a tremendous demand for it, and the vast semidesert plains were soon transformed into a massive granary. Peanuts and citrus fruits, in addition to rice, have also become valuable crops as irrigation has spread. Some 100 varieties of cactus, 570 kinds of grasses and more than 5000 different wild flowers grow in Texas, but around the east Texas city of Tyler, a more cultivated crop is raised. Tyler calls itself the Rose Garden of the World because it produces a large percentage of the rosebushes grown in the United States.

To many people the words "Texas" and "oil" are almost synonymous. About 200 of the 254 counties in the state possess oil wells, some of them located in the most unlikely places. A number of the nearly 200,000 Texas wells are in churchyards, farmyards, backyards of suburban homes and even municipal dumps. Oil was first discovered in Texas in 1866, and major production started in the beginning of the twentieth century. The Texas wildcatter, the bet-a-million-to-make-a-billion type, is as much a legend as the cowboy of the cattle drive and, indeed, is considered his direct descendant. Like the trail rider, he struggled against any odds for a big payoff.

Today the wildcatters are mostly gone, and oil exploration is a scientific business for college-trained experts. But their bet-a-million philosophy lives on in the more polished and circumspect, though still expansive, Texan approach to any problem or challenge. The gleaming cities of Dallas, Houston and others are monuments to the industrial and economic achievements of a people who came to Texas from 35 different nations.

UTAH

The beehive on Utah's seal symbolizes industriousness, and that was what early settlers certainly needed to convert a forbidding desert into the thriving state Utah is today. Members of the Church of Jesus Christ of Latter-day Saints, better known as Mormons, had been persecuted in the East and driven from one place to another. They sought a home which nobody else would want, where they could follow their religious and economic beliefs without interference, where they could create a self-sustaining, coöperative agricultural society. So, in July 1847, the Mormons settled in the dry plains around Great Salt Lake. They irrigated the arid but fertile land and soon their religious communities spread into nearby mountain valleys.

Even before the death of their leader, Brigham Young, prospectors and miners began to arrive. The advent of the Union Pacific ended completely the isolation of the Mormons. But because of the colonies so firmly established in the beginning, Mormons even now constitute 60 percent of the population, and their heritage exerts a strong influence on the pattern of life in Utah. Community groups are closely knit. Rare is the town which does not have residents with two or more years' service as Mormon missionaries in foreign countries.

Descendants of pioneers who started the canning industry—with laboriously hand-soldered tins—work in modern meat-packing and other food-processing plants. Where early settlers produced lead bullets from galena ore, their grandchildren manufacture missiles. The church's ban on prospecting for precious metals, in an era when iron and coal were the only mineral necessities, has long since been lifted, and Utah is the nation's second largest producer of gold, copper and molybdenum and third in silver. Economic development since World War II has also been advanced by the discovery of petroleum and uranium.

An irrigation ditch dug in 1847 to divert City Creek in what is now Salt Lake City was the forerunner of a system of 650 dams, reservoirs and mountain tunnels which water the five percent of Utah considered arable. Alfalfa is the biggest crop, but cattle, poultry, eggs and dairy products account for most of the farm income.

In recent years, both the climate and the desert lands have become revenue producers. Motion-picture companies from Hollywood take advantage of the fine weather and colorful scenery to make historical, Biblical and Western films in the southern Kanab region. Millions of people travel to see the fantastic, tinted rock formations of Zion and Bryce Canyon National Parks, the prehistoric cliff dwellings and Rainbow Bridge, the largest and most symmetrical natural arch in the world.

The 13 American colonies had already declared their independence before the first recorded European exploration of Utah was undertaken. Two Franciscan friars, Escalante and Dominguez, led an expedition in 1776 which spent several months (until their guide deserted) looking for a route from Santa Fe, New Mexico, to Monterey, California. The first American visitors were fur trappers and traders who nearly wiped out the beaver population. Brigham Young and his followers in 1850 applied for admission to the Union as the state of Deseret (a word from the *Book of Mormon* meaning "honeybee"). Congress gave them territorial status and changed the name to Utah, from the Ute Indian tribe of the area.

The first transcontinental railroad was completed in 1869 at Promontory, Utah, where the driving of a golden spike celebrated the long-awaited junction of the Union Pacific and Central Pacific lines. But the railroad brought more settlers into the region, and strife began between Mormons and non-Mormons, between the church-governed territory and the Federal government. The church permitted polygamy, a practice viewed with horror in Washington. Requests for statehood frequently resulted only in the passage by Congress of increasingly stricter laws against polygamy. In 1884 alone, 12,000 Mormons lost their citizenship under such laws. The problem was not resolved until 1890, when the church advised its members to abandon polygamy and disband the political party by which it had ruled the territory. A constitution which guaranteed religious freedom and prohibited polygamy was adopted, and on January 4, 1896, Utah became the forty-fifth state of the Union.

SALT LAKE CITY

Deliverance from starvation facing the founders of what was then called Great Salt Lake City is commemorated in a monument to the sea gull. Clouds of crickets were devouring the first-planted crops of the new settlers in 1848 when the gulls arrived—in time to wipe out the crickets and save part of the harvest. Even so, many a settler ate sego-lily bulbs that winter. The state now raises so much food that meat-packing and canning are two important industries in the metropolitan area. Oil is refined, ores are smelted and salt is produced from the brine of Great Salt Lake. An 1847 log house is preserved in Temple Square, where Brigham Young ordered the city laid out "perfectly square," with blocks of ten acres each and streets 132 feet wide. During the summer season, parking on some streets in the center of town is limited to cars with out-of-state license plates. In the Mormon Tabernacle, organ recitals free to the public are held daily, and the famous choir gives concerts on Sunday mornings. Winter tourists come to ski in the nearby mountains. Hogle Zoo boasts of the world's only liger—a cross between a male lion and a tigress.

Area—84,916 sq. miles
Population—1,022,000
Capital—Salt Lake City (Pop. 189,454)

For additional information on the state in special articles see General Index, Utah.

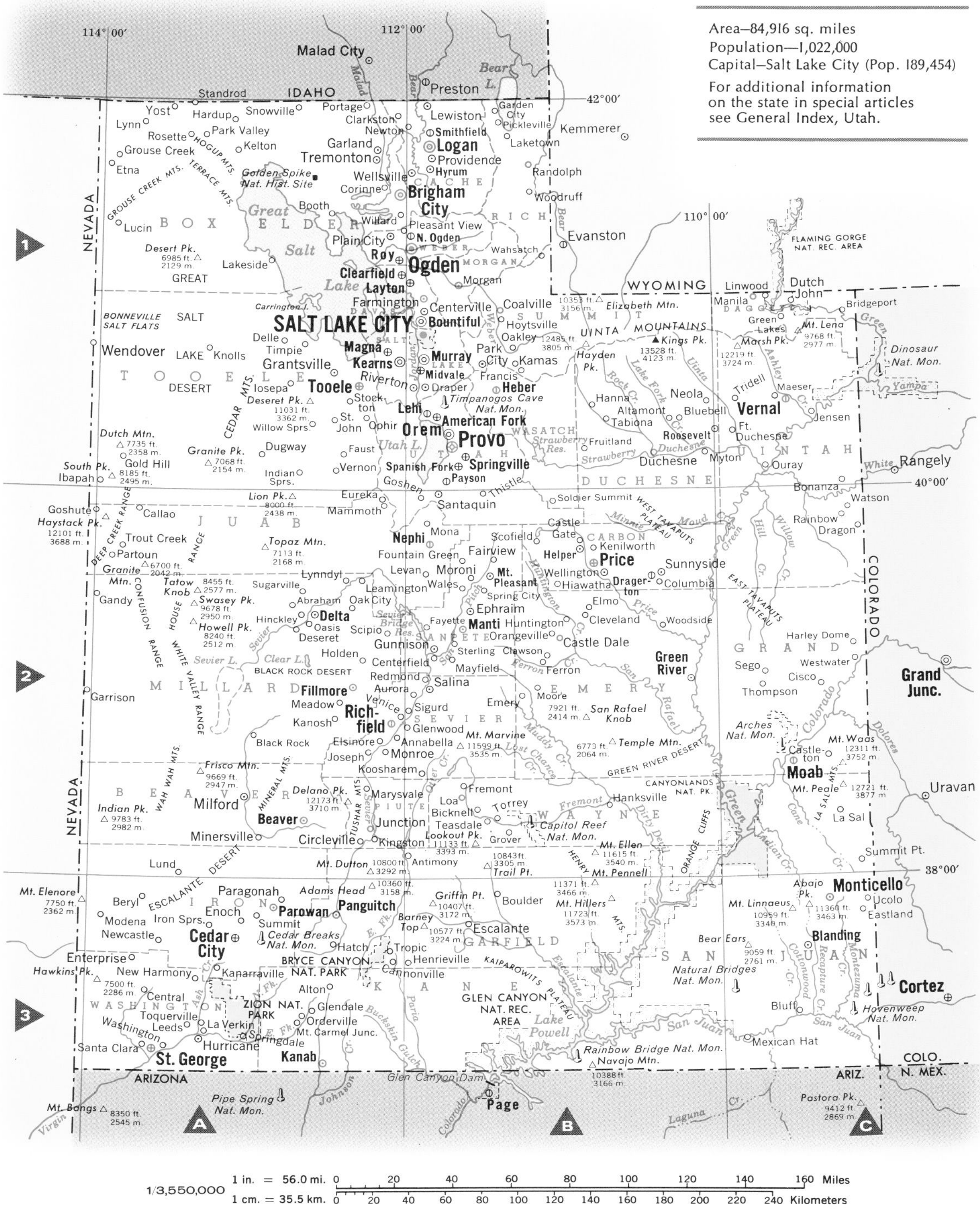

1/3,550,000 1 in. = 56.0 mi. 1 cm. = 35.5 km.

Lambert Conformal Conic Projection

© General Drafting Co., Inc.

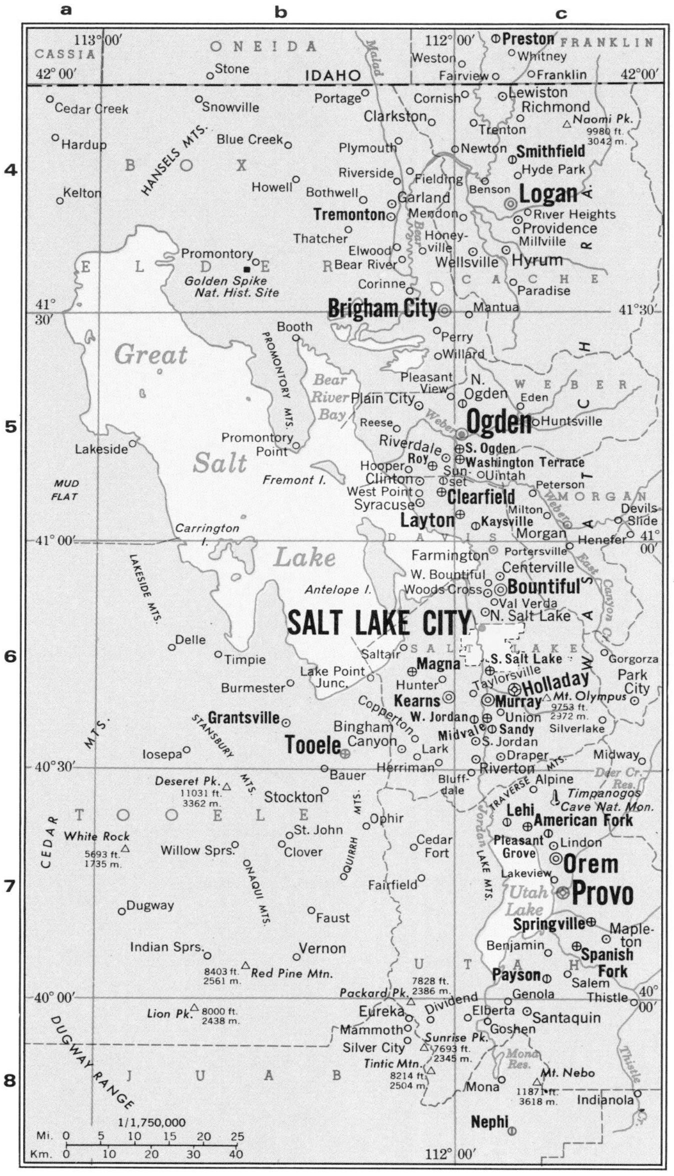

POPULATION LEGEND

Over 1,000,000	10,000-25,000
250,000-1,000,000	5,000-10,000
100,000-250,000	2,500-5,000
50,000-100,000	1,000-2,500
25,000-50,000	Under 1,000

Red symbols indicate county seats

VERMONT

Vermont is one of the smallest states in the Union (forty-third in size, forty-seventh in population), yet it has provided two Presidents—Chester A. Arthur and Calvin Coolidge. And it is widely known for the independence, industriousness, thrift and reserved speech of its inhabitants, traits generally considered to have been epitomized by President Coolidge.

In 1609 Champlain discovered the lake that bears his name and forms about half of Vermont's western border, but the first permanent settlement in the region, Fort Dummer, was established by English colonists from Massachusetts in 1724. From the beginning Vermonters acted on their own. Because of vaguely defined boundaries, the colonies of New Hampshire and New York for some years both claimed lands comprising present Vermont. By 1770 Ethan Allen's famous Green Mountain Boys had organized to protect the early settlers under New Hampshire grants against the "Yorker" intruders from the south. The first military engagement of the Revolutionary War was the sudden and unexpected capture of British-held Fort Ticonderoga in 1775 by this self-constituted army. Another victory—in which these Vermont troops joined with those from two other rebelling colonies—occurred at Bennington in 1777.

In that same year Vermonters, who had not participated in the colonial Declaration of Independence because they had no colonial grant of their own, proclaimed a separate and independent government. So it remained for 13 years, until in 1791 Vermont paid New York $30,000 for its claims and became the first state after the original 13 colonies to be admitted to the Union.

At the Vermonters' constitutional convention in 1777, delegates voted to prohibit slavery. The militant abolitionist policy and verbal attacks on slave-owning states at one point led the legislature of Georgia to adopt a resolution asking the President to hire enough Irishmen to dig a deep ditch around Vermont so that it could be floated out into the Atlantic Ocean and set adrift! In another unique display of political action, Vermont, a hotbed of anti-Masonic sentiment, was the only state to cast its electoral vote in 1832 for William Wirt, the Presidential candidate of the Anti-Masonic Party. The movement, which was encouraged by National Republicans who opposed Jacksonian democracy (President Jackson was also a Freemason), was for a time so influential in Vermont that it elected the governor for four successive years.

Besides prohibiting slavery, the Vermont constitution was the first to allow universal male suffrage with no tax-paying or land-owning requirements and to provide for an educational system from primary schools to a university. A teachers' seminary, opened in 1823, was the first normal school in America, and the country's first pedagogical textbook was written and published there.

The rocky soil and the comparatively short growing season made it difficult for early frontiersmen to earn a living, while the mountain ranges hampered transportation and commerce. In addition to fighting off marauding Indians, the farmers occasionally had to cope with wolves and a type of cougar called catamount. Only after two centuries, when skiing became a popular pastime, were Vermonters able to appreciate the average ten-foot snowfall in the mountain areas.

The opening up of the West created a series of adverse economic repercussions in Vermont. No sooner had its farmers established a prosperous grain and livestock trade than the building of the Erie Canal made accessible the more fertile areas in western New York and Ohio, bringing these products into the Eastern market at lower cost. The farmers then shifted to sheep-raising to supply the New England textile market. After the Civil War, Vermonters found that wool cost less in Montana and Wyoming because of the extension of railroads to the free grazing ranges there. So farmers turned to the manufacture of cheese and butter, products which were in turn displaced by cheaper ones from the dairy regions of the Midwest. The final change was to the sale of fresh milk. Until 1960 there were more cows than people in Vermont, which provides about half the milk consumed in the Boston area.

The mountains, the tree-covered slopes, the lakes and rivers, which impeded the progress of the pioneers, now contribute to Vermont's two largest sources of revenue—manufacturing and recreation. About three fifths of the state is covered by forests, vital to the woodworking, paper and wood-pulp industries. Its maple trees are tapped for the nation's second largest supply of maple syrup and maple sugar. The rivers are sources of hydroelectric power for factories which produce machinery. More than 3,000,000 vacationists—seven times the year-round population—visit Vermont annually. The rocky earth also yields sufficient marble and granite to account for one third of the monuments and statuary in the country besides that used for building purposes. Many inventions were devised by ingenious Vermonters; steel squares, used by carpenters, are still manufactured by the same company which began making them in 1817.

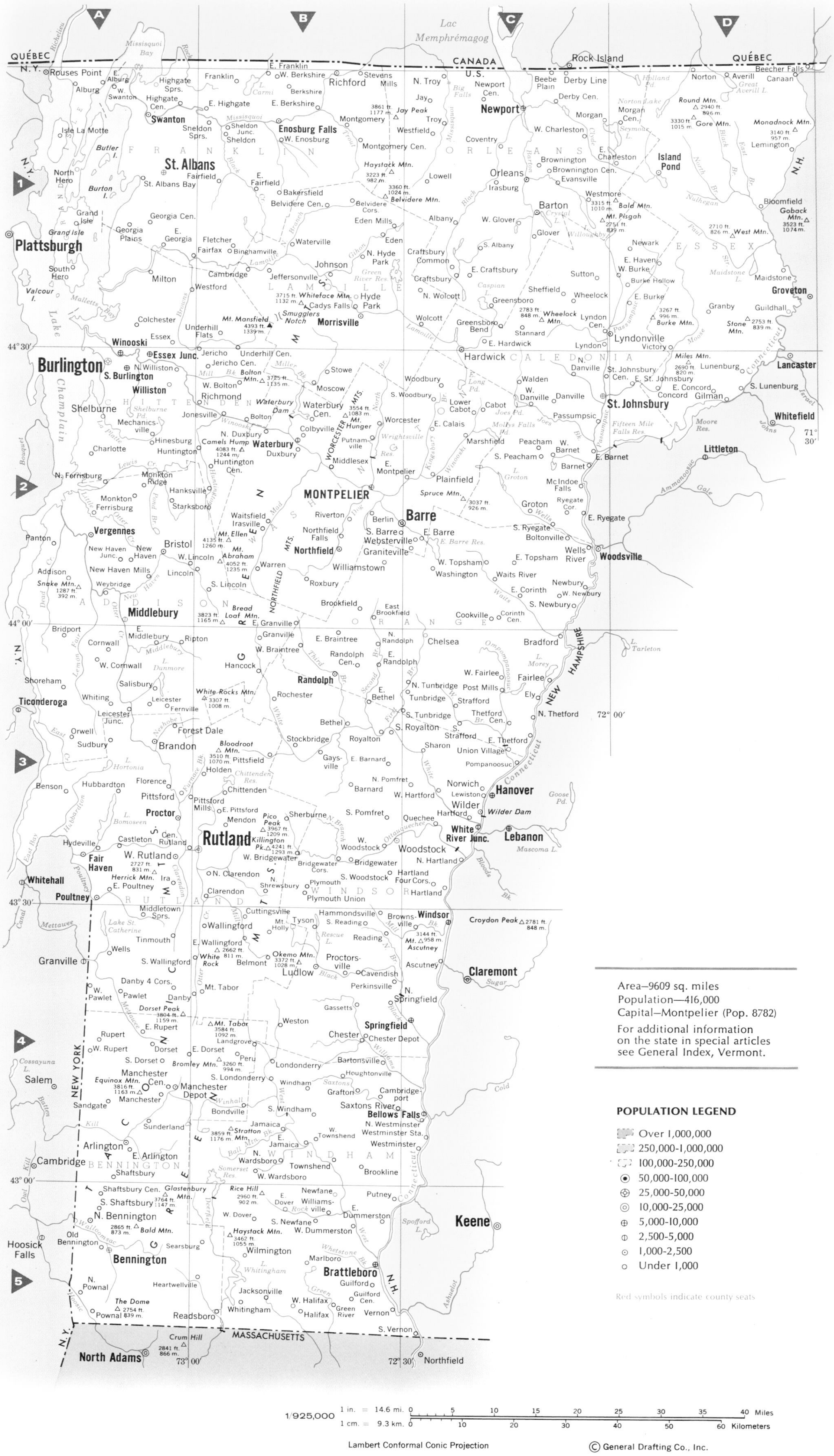

BURLINGTON

The name Burlington comes from the Burling family, which held large tracts of land in the northwestern section of Vermont. The first settlement, established in 1773, hardly had a chance to get started before the Revolution took most of its population off to fight or flee from the enemy. After the war the settlers returned, and this community on Lake Champlain just below the mouth of the Winooski River began to grow again. During the War of 1812 three British ships attacked and were driven off by 13 cannon and some of the 4000 troops stationed there to oppose any possible invasion from Canada. Before 1823 most of Burlington's commerce was with Canada, but the opening of the Champlain Canal to the Hudson that year turned business interest toward New York. By mid-century the timber supply in the area was depleted, and the city then became an important shipping point for Canadian timber destined for American mills to the south. Burlington still deals in timber but it also produces cereals, textiles and aircraft equipment. The population is no longer just New England Yankee; there is also a mixture of French-Canadian, German and Italian. (Pop. 35,531.)

VIRGINIA

A state of rare charm and natural beauty and one of the most fascinating historic corners of America, Virginia, to the eye of the casual visitor, may seem far removed from the swift pace of the twentieth century. A closer look reveals that the Old Dominion is undergoing a rapid change.

Cotton, corn and "taters" still grow, but the songwriter who composed "Carry Me Back to Old Virginny" would never recognize its industrialized cities. More than 300,000 people engage in widely diversified manufacturing enterprises, ranging from the world's largest shipyard to the largest single-unit textile mill on earth. Long freight trains roll out of the coal-mining areas in the Appalachian Mountains. A booming tobacco industry annually produces tons of pipe tobacco and over a billion cigarettes. Some of the leading manufacturers of glass, metals and electrical products have built plants in the state. Chemical and textile factories employ the most people. Food products and transportation equipment are other important manufactures.

Virginia's agriculture is dominated by tobacco, its oldest cash crop. Originally grown on the Tidewater coastal plain, it now is produced chiefly in the south-central section. Orchards in the valleys near Winchester give Virginia a high ranking among apple-growing states. Beef cattle, raised in the southwest, and poultry, eggs and dairy products make strong contributions to the economy. Cotton, once a leading crop, now is a comparatively minor commodity with about 10,000 bales going to market each year. Even peanuts add more to the farm income.

In the sixteenth century all of British North America was called Virginia, in honor of Queen Elizabeth, the "Virgin Queen." While European explorers had been probing the Atlantic Coast since 1500, the first English settlements attempted in what would later become Maine and North Carolina failed or were wiped out.

Then, in the last week of April 1607, three shiploads of colonists, dispatched by the Virginia Company of London, sailed into the mouth of Chesapeake Bay. Passing between two points of land, which they named Cape Charles and Cape Henry in honor of two sons of reigning King James, they established Jamestown, the first permanent English settlement in America, on a peninsula near the mouth of a large river. It, too, nearly foundered because of malaria and fumbling leadership, but was finally saved through the efforts of Captain John Smith, who succeeded in establishing a friendly relationship with the local Indians. From them the Englishmen learned to grow corn and other native crops which would eventually make Virginia one of the strongest and richest of the American colonies. In 1612 John Rolfe cultivated the first tobacco grown by settlers, and the shipment went to England the following year. A Dutch ship landed the first African slaves in North America six years later.

The demand for tobacco in Europe grew so rapidly that during the height of the colonial period it represented between one fourth and one half of the total exports of North America. The English plantation owners prospered. Although the mainstream of the population continued to come directly from the British Isles, German farmers and French Huguenot refugees settled in the central and western mountain regions.

From Virginia's planter aristocracy came many of the leaders of the American Revolution whose energies and philosophy were a prime force in fashioning the greatest democracy in world history. Patrick Henry aroused Virginians and other colonials with his impassioned oratory against the Stamp Act and the famous "Give me liberty or give me death!" speech which he delivered in 1775. Peyton Randolph was made president of the First Continental Congress. Thomas Jefferson had a major role in drafting the Declaration of Independence, and George Washington became commander in chief of the American armies. For his successful efforts in persuading newly formed states to permit a Federal government to regulate trade, raise revenues and protect the rights of individuals, James Madison became known as the Father of the U.S. Constitution. Eight American Presidents, including four of the first five, were native Virginians.

After Virginia joined the rest of the South and seceded in April 1861, Robert E. Lee became commander of the Confederate armies and Richmond the capital of the Confederacy. The state's western counties, whose farmers had long been at odds with the Tidewater aristocracy, remained in the Union and formed West Virginia. As the central theater during most of the Civil War, Virginia was laid to ruin. More battles were fought there than in any other state. The most unusual engagement was at Hampton Roads between the ironclad *Monitor* and *Merrimac,* predecessors of modern warships. Saddled with monumental debts because of the war, Virginia was very slow in recovering.

General Lee's old home overlooks Arlington National Cemetery. Government offices and workers both have crossed the Potomac into the same area: the Pentagon, the world's largest office building; the headquarters of the Central Intelligence Agency; and, in hundreds of developments, the families of Federal employes.

NORFOLK

On the banks of the Elizabeth River where it flows into Chesapeake Bay, Norfolk is one of the leading cities of the New South. Founded in 1682, it soon developed such a thriving sea trade — exporting tobacco, meat, flour and lumber to England and the West Indies, and importing sugar, molasses, slaves and merchant goods—that it became the largest town in colonial Virginia, noted for its elegant brick homes, wealthy maritime traders and throngs of seafarers. Bombarded and burned during the Revolution, nearly wiped out by plagues carried by vessels from the tropics and seized by Union forces in the Civil War, Norfolk always rallied to resume its role as Virginia's principal port of entry. With its neighbors, Newport News and Portsmouth, it lies off Hampton Roads, one of the world's largest anchorages and the Atlantic bastion of the U.S. Navy. Thousands of naval officers and bluejackets and hundreds of ships, from mammoth aircraft carriers to tiny minesweepers, dominate the city's life. Its waters, teeming with naval craft, ocean freighters, tugs, scows and fishing boats, and its waterfront jumble of shipyards, docks and warehouses make Norfolk the most nautical town in the United States. Also an important industrial center, it produces chemicals, cars, plywood, ships and fertilizers. (Pop. 304,869.)

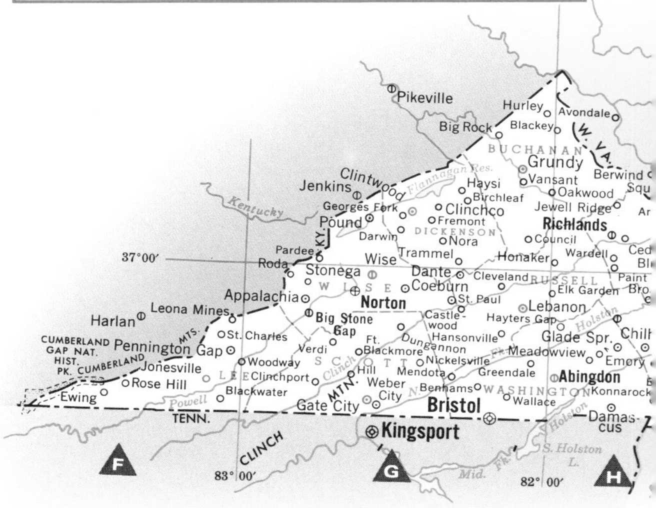

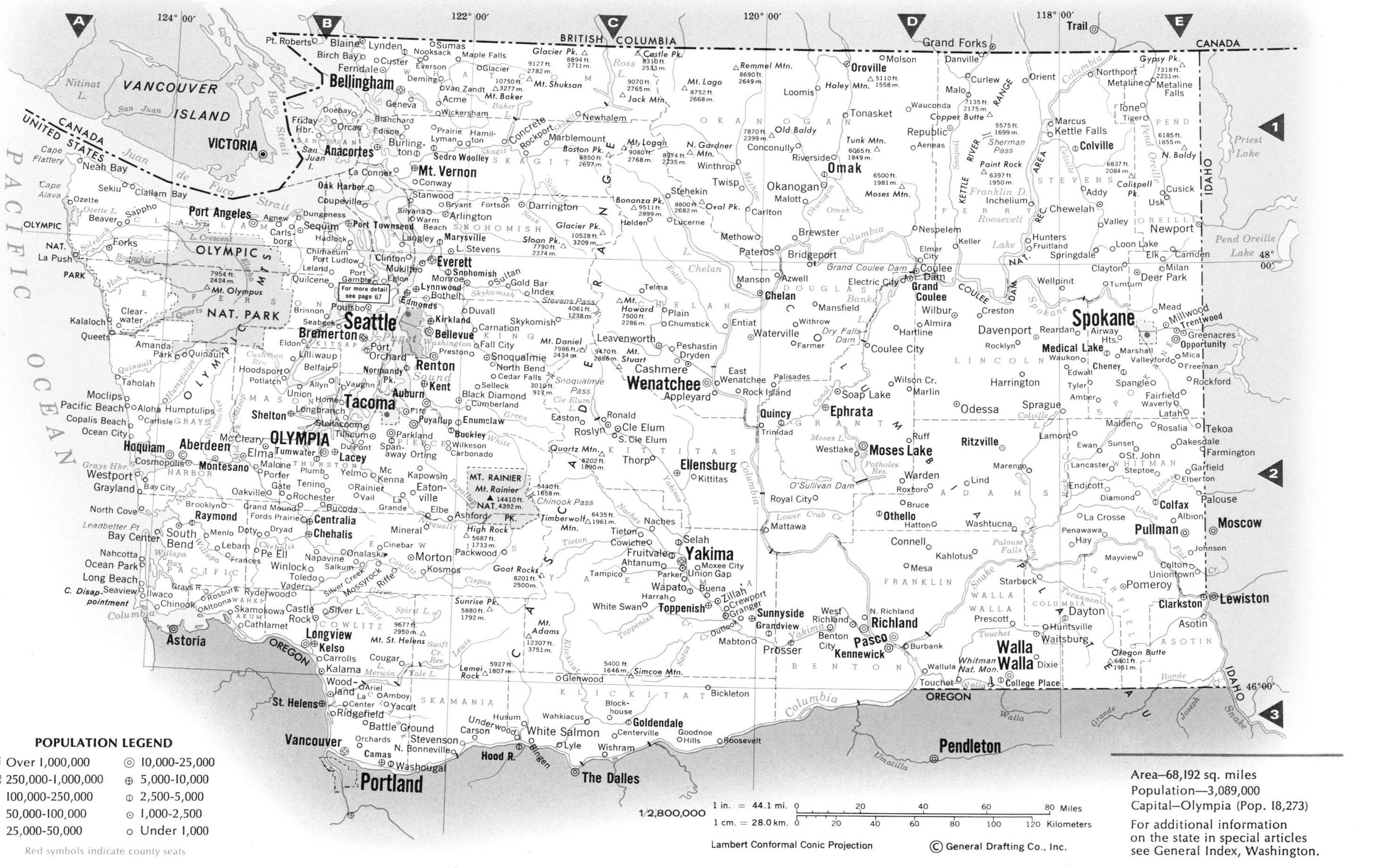

Area—68,192 sq. miles
Population—3,089,000
Capital—Olympia (Pop. 18,273)
For additional information on the state in special articles see General Index, Washington.

Area—40,815 sq. miles
Population—4,533,000
Capital—Richmond (Pop. 219,958)
For additional information on the state in special articles see General Index, Virginia.

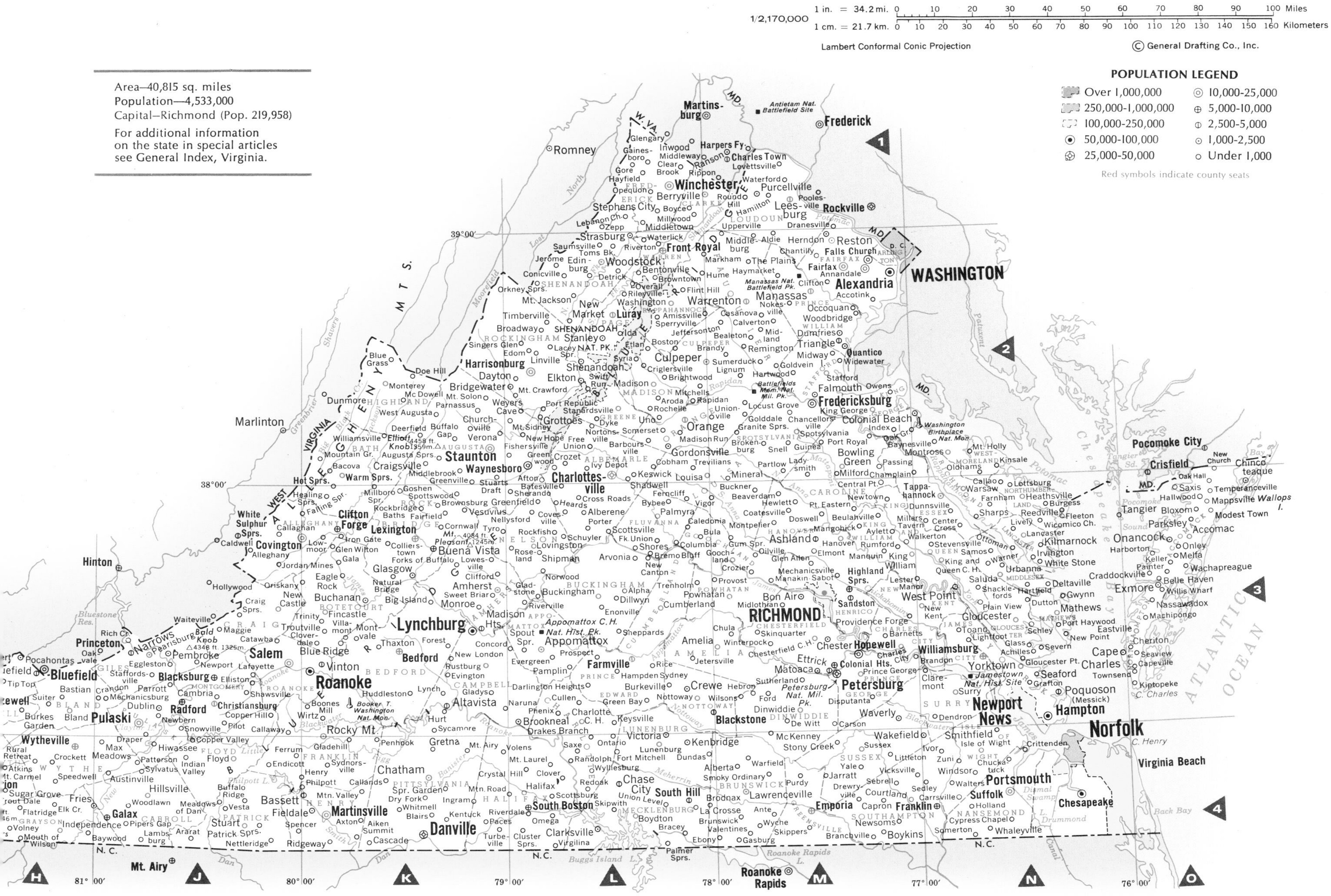

WASHINGTON

On April 29, 1792, as his ship the *Discovery* was beating its way along the coastal waters of a new and strange land, the English explorer Captain George Vancouver made an entry in the logbook: "The most remarkable mountain we had seen now presented itself. Its summit, covered with eternal snow, was divided into a very elegant fork, and rose conspicuously from a base of lofty mountains clothed in the same manner." The mountain was Mount Olympus; the land, which Bruno Heceta and Juan Francisco de la Bodega had claimed for Spain in 1775, was to become the state of Washington.

Like Captain Vancouver and the other navigators and fur traders who first probed the wilderness of the Pacific Northwest, present-day visitors are struck by its scenic beauty and natural wonders. There in incongruous array are glacier-clad volcanic mountains, mossy rain forests dripping with moisture, treeless wastelands of sunbaked lava, an 80-mile-long inland sea (Puget Sound), rushing, power-filled rivers, vast acres of unlogged timberland. Man-made wonders are abundant too—dams the size of super-Niagaras, mountain-piercing tunnels and thriving metropolitan centers.

Vagaries of climate are responsible for many of Washington's physical contrasts and contradictions. The ridge of the Cascade Mountains, extending north and south, not only divides the state into two distinct areas but also influences the weather. Clouds sweeping in from the Pacific are halted by this range so that the western slopes are drenched with an annual fall of 140 or more inches of rain. Packing these slopes are great forests of pine, cedar, western hemlock and giant Douglas fir. On the other side of the Cascades, to the southeast, lies the Columbia plateau, a tableland of bone-dry barrens where the annual rainfall is a scant six inches. Thanks to irrigation, the Yakima and Wenatchee valleys and the Okanogan highlands are exceptionally productive. From these areas come the famous Washington apples. Wheat, the leading crop, and cattle are raised in the eastern section, which is also important for its dairy products.

Named in honor of the first President, the state was originally part of "Oregon Country," as the Columbia River region was called. Both Britain and America claimed ownership to this vast tract because of early ex-

SEATTLE

Five families from Illinois founded Seattle. Their first homes were built on a low point of land, but early in 1852 the settlement moved to the hills above Puget Sound. The history of Seattle is one of alternating economic and population booms and slow periods. Plentiful timber and a fine harbor got the town off to a growing start, with the necessary help of 57 "schoolteachers" imported from the East to become brides of the bachelor population. The gold strikes in the Yukon brought on a shipbuilding boom in the late 1890's. In the first six months of 1897 alone, 74 ships were launched, a record which presaged the even greater production of World Wars I and II. During the latter, aircraft assembly matched shipbuilding as a major occupation. The famous Flying Fortresses and Superforts were turned out in Seattle. The city experienced a postwar slump in the late 1940's but is now expanding, with new shopping centers, office buildings and homes. Prosperity and maturity have polished the rough edges of this lusty town so that it takes pride in growing cultural and educational activities as well as its industrial know-how. (Pop. 557,087.)

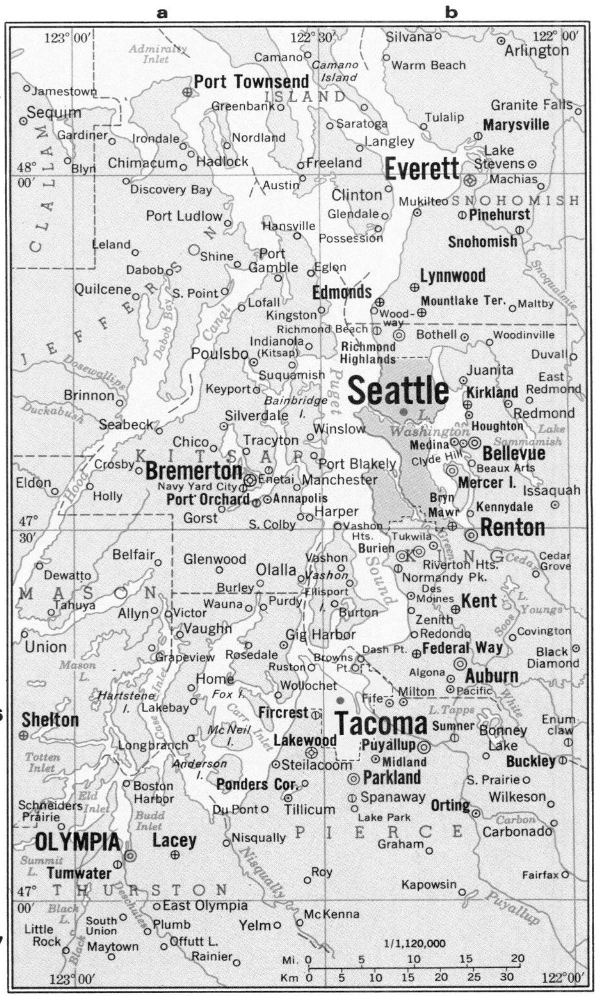

plorations. The United States based its case mainly on the fact that an American sea captain, Robert Gray, in his ship the *Columbia*, first entered and named the Columbia River in 1792. The U.S. position was strengthened by the Lewis and Clark expedition, which reached the mouth of the river in 1805, and by the thousands of settlers who came over the Oregon Trail. In 1846 an agreement between the two countries was finally reached—the land above the 49th parallel went to the British, the land below to the United States, with the exception of Vancouver Island.

Seven years later the Oregon Territory was itself divided, and the area north of the Columbia River became the Washington Territory. In 1863 a great section to the east was carved out to form the Idaho Territory, leaving Washington within its present borders. Settlement was slow until the first railroad connection with the East was made in 1883. After that the population quadrupled in little more than a decade. Irrigation projects, started in the 1890's, opened additional land to cultivation and attracted wheat farmers and fruit growers. World Wars I and II brought influxes of defense-industry workers.

Waterpower—greatest in the nation—is one of the state's foremost natural resources, with the mighty Columbia River the main provider. Pulp, paper and other wood products from nearly 24,000,000 acres of timberland rank high in Washington's swelling assets. Much of the processing of these forest products is done in the Puget Sound area. Thriving along this inland sea with its myriad of islands are the commercial fisheries, shipyards and the plants of the world-leading aircraft industry of Seattle and Tacoma.

Washington made a unique contribution to World War II. At the Hanford Engineering Works, an army of 50,000 workers and their families moved into the hastily constructed tar-paper city of Hanford and began the production of plutonium in sufficient quantity to create atomic bombs.

WEST VIRGINIA

The Mountain State, it is called, and 24,181 square miles could not be better named. With an altitude along the Ohio River less than 600 feet above sea level, it contains almost 500 mountain peaks in its Allegheny ridge, from 2000 to 4860 feet high. Nature formed this land of mountains, high plateaus and valleys over a period of more than 500,000,000 years. The topography, in turn, has influenced every social, economic and political aspect of its inhabitants.

This rugged territory, originally part of Virginia, became the thirty-fifth state of the Union, partly because of its mountainous character. Many pioneers had moved into the area in defiance of a royal proclamation in 1763 which forbade settlement beyond the Appalachians. Within a year of the Declaration of Independence, the Scotch-Irish, Welsh and German farmers tried to achieve statehood as Westsylvania. Ignored by the powerful Tidewater aristocrats, isolated by nature, lacking roads and communications with the East and disinterested in the slave economy of the Eastern majority, West Virginia's highlanders bitterly resented being continuously outvoted. When Virginia seceded in 1861, the mountaineers in less than two months withdrew from Virginia and took the western counties back into the Union as a separate state.

After the Civil War, coal brought new wealth to West Virginia. Although bituminous deposits had been discovered near the Coal River as early as 1742, mining on a large scale did not begin until railroads were built to move it to rapidly growing industrial centers. More than six and a half billion tons of coal have been mined since the 1880's, but geologists estimate there are reserves of 60 billion tons remaining.

Unfortunately coal riches have been a mixed blessing for West Virginia. Strip mining ruined rivers, destroying fish and game, and mechanization of many mines reduced the number of jobs, leaving the unemployed nowhere to turn. But conservation measures are now beginning to reclaim lost land and waters, and scientific research has produced new uses for coal which promise to raise the demand and provide more jobs. The soil is rich in other minerals such as silica, limestone, salt and natural gas.

When a group of European botanists visited West Virginia in the early 1800's, the state was covered with a superb virgin growth of hardwood trees unequaled in Europe or Asia. Most of this forest has been destroyed by lumbering, but controlled reforestation has restored new timber to the state. Nearly 10,000,000 acres contain some of the finest hardwood forests in the nation, and 400 sawmills turn out almost 400,000,000 board feet of prime lumber every year.

Coal and lumber have lost their leading position to manufactures—iron, steel, glass and chemicals. Industry now employs 20 percent of the working population. Though there are nearly 35,000 farms, agriculture has been declining and accounts for only eight percent of the state's income.

In 1748 when George Washington surveyed parts of West Virginia, he stopped at "Ye Fam'd Warm Springs" in Berkeley. Today the springs are still a popular attraction. And those who climb the mountains, breathe the stimulating air, fish the streams or walk the forest trails have little difficulty in feeling the highland spirit which prompted the selection of the state motto: "Mountaineers Are Always Free."

CHARLESTON

Eighty-seven cents was the price paid in 1787 for a claim to a 1040-acre tract at the junction of the Elk and Great Kanawha rivers where Charleston now stands. A military outpost, Fort Lee, was built there the following year. Daniel Boone represented the county of Kanawha in the Virginia Assembly soon after, and the town was established in 1794. Growth was slow until the coming of the Kanawha Turnpike. Then the community became a transfer point for westbound traffic; travelers and merchandise arrived by horse or wagon and continued their journeys by river flatboats to the Ohio and Mississippi. After the Civil War the city began to expand with industries based on nearby coal, natural-gas and oil fields. Charleston itself is crowded into the two narrow river valleys, but the metropolitan area includes 14 contiguous municipalities where most of the factories are situated. The chemical industry, started just before World War I, is important to the city, which has become the nation's leading producer of rayon and also manufactures substantial amounts of a competitive fiber, nylon, and synthetic rubber.

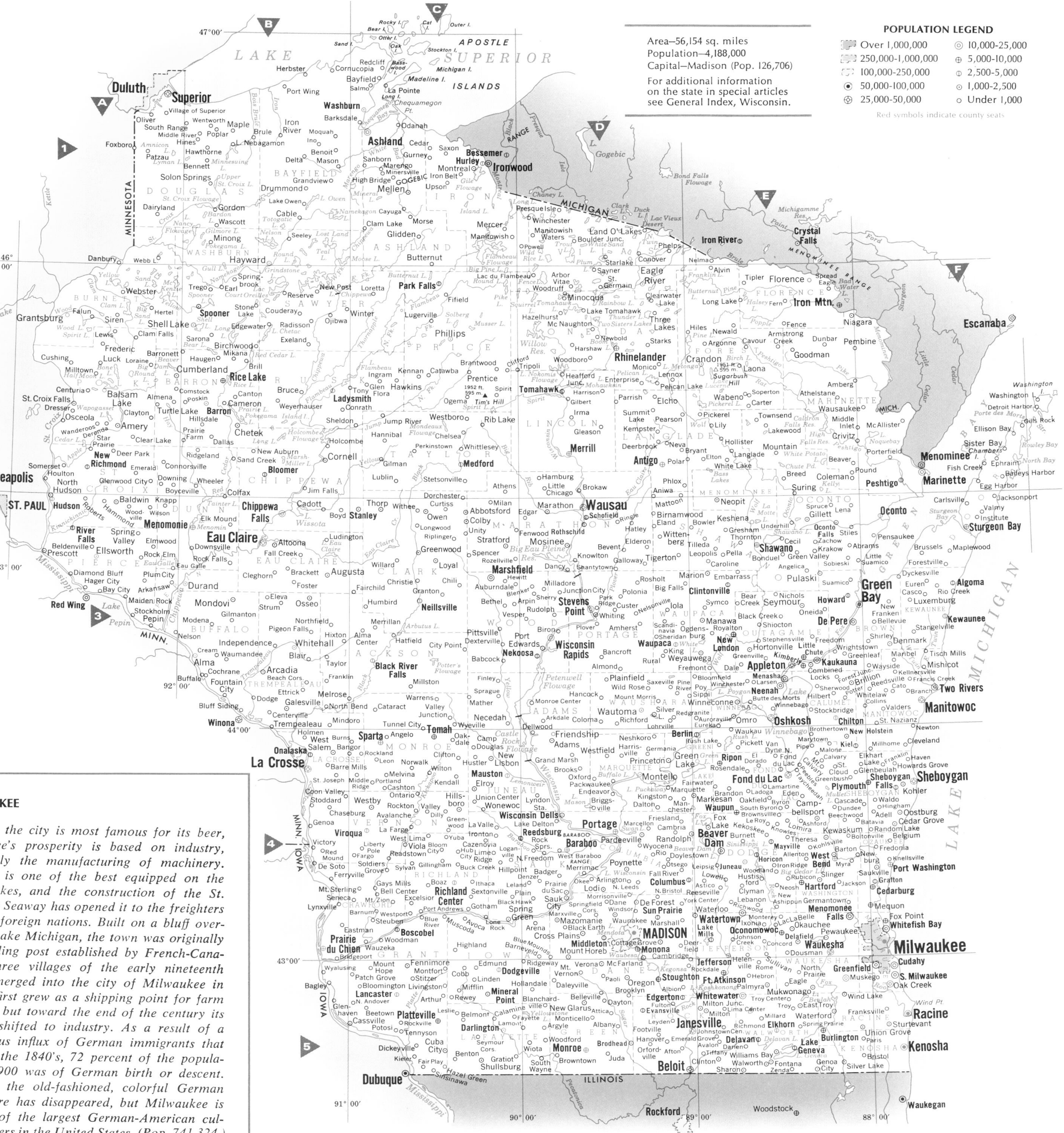

MILWAUKEE

Although the city is most famous for its beer, Milwaukee's prosperity is based on industry, particularly the manufacturing of machinery. The port is one of the best equipped on the Great Lakes, and the construction of the St. Lawrence Seaway has opened it to the freighters of many foreign nations. Built on a bluff overlooking Lake Michigan, the town was originally a fur-trading post established by French-Canadians. Three villages of the early nineteenth century merged into the city of Milwaukee in 1846. It first grew as a shipping point for farm products, but toward the end of the century its fortunes shifted to industry. As a result of a tremendous influx of German immigrants that began in the 1840's, 72 percent of the population in 1900 was of German birth or descent. Much of the old-fashioned, colorful German atmosphere has disappeared, but Milwaukee is still one of the largest German-American cultural centers in the United States. (Pop. 741,324.)

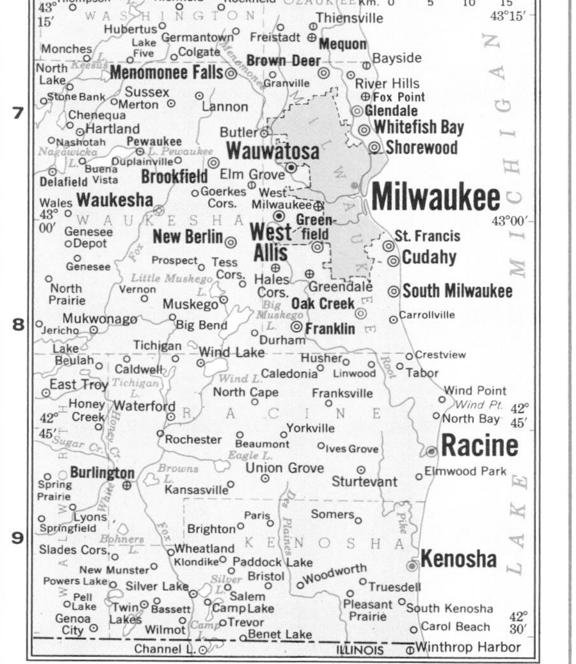

WISCONSIN

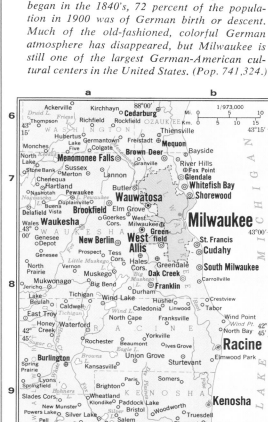

Within America's Dairyland, as the state is deservedly known, lie some 120,000 farms. From white barns and rolling green meadows dotted with grazing cattle an enormous supply of milk is shipped to hundreds of factories large and small scattered widely through the country towns. These account for nearly half of all America's cheeses (Cheddar, Swiss, Limburger, blue and others), about one sixth of the milk for bottling or cartons, more than one fifth of the butter and most of the malted milk.

The name Wisconsin is said to be derived from the Indian word meaning "gathering of the waters," and water has governed much of its development. Its borders are almost entirely of water. With 10,000 miles of waterways, the state lies near the sources of the St. Lawrence and the Mississippi—one the greatest river to the north and the other the greatest to the south.

First traveled by Indians and explored in 1634 by the Frenchman Jean Nicolet, the region soon was active with trading posts and lake and river ports. On an arm of Lake Michigan, a French fur-trading post—the first white settlement—became famous ultimately as the home of a professional football team, the Green Bay Packers. The rivers of Wisconsin provided lumber interests from the East with the means of floating millions of logs from the northern forests to mills and wood-processing plants.

Although Wisconsin has no towering mountains, spectacular deserts, seacoasts or canyons, it draws more than 6,000,000 out-of-state visitors every year—2,000,000 of them from Illinois alone. The northern lakes and forests are speckled with summer camps. Muskellunge, pike, trout and bass attract hordes of fishermen. Washington Island, off the northern tip of Door Peninsula, affords some of the finest fishing grounds in the Great Lakes.

In the northwest corner of the state, the city of Superior shares with Duluth, Minnesota, one of the busiest inland port areas in the world, receiving ships from around the globe via the Great Lakes and St. Lawrence Seaway. As many as 40,000,000 tons of lake and ocean cargoes—iron ore, coal, timber, wheat, farm products and manufactured goods—move in and out of the port annually. Superior has the largest iron-ore docks and the biggest grain elevator in the world.

Wisconsin ranks among the top ten industrial states with its products of iron, steel, aluminum and wood. It leads the nation in the manufacture of small motors for boats and power mowers. The transformation from primeval forest land to a dairy and industrial state came in several stages. The first wave of settlers arrived in 1822, drawn by a lead-mining boom. A second influx followed as land was opened by the defeat of the Indians in the Black Hawk War of 1832. The middle of the century saw the beginnings of migrations from Europe. At that time wheat was the principal crop, and milling the chief industry. Gradually the rural economy shifted toward dairying, though present-day farms still yield more vegetables for canning than half a dozen other agricultural states combined.

The Swiss played a major role in developing the cheese and dairy industries. Green County was selected by Swiss settlers after advance parties had tested other parts of Wisconsin for soil and water conditions most closely resembling those of their native land. Many of its farm villages have a solidly Swiss atmosphere. People of German descent still make up one fourth of the population, having built and staffed breweries that produce more beer and ale than any others in America. After 1900, more Europeans arrived to work in the factories and urban areas. Poles, the second largest foreign group, concentrated in Milwaukee and Stevens Point. Norwegian and Finnish communities grew in the southern portion. Racine became the most Danish city in America.

WYOMING

Although Wyoming has kept pace with modern technology and industry, its heart belongs to the Old West and its heroes. Decorations featuring the cowboy, the Indian and the mountain man are everywhere. In stores, tourist camps and newspapers, the cowboy rides his bucking bronco, the mountain man fights the Indian, the trail boss sits his hardy cayuse while overseeing the herd. Even today, in any town or city there, ten-gallon hats and high-heeled boots are common attire.

Wyoming was in on "the winning of the West" at the beginning. One of the first of the legendary mountain men, John Colter, left the Lewis and Clark expedition on its return trip from the West Coast to trap in the wilderness that is now Yellowstone Park. When he returned to St. Louis after three years, he was full of tales of the great mountains, spouting geysers and teeming wildlife. The fur-trading era began as other traders and mountain men followed: Jim Baker, Jim Bridger, William Sublette, General William Ashley—pioneers who have left their marks in place-names across the state. Ashley revolutionized the fur trade by abandoning fixed trading posts for the rendezvous; the first was held on Wyoming's Green River, where trappers and Indians met in a huge encampment to barter pelts and supplies—ammunition, whiskey, trinkets—and to have fun, gamble and brawl.

As the white man crowded into the Wyoming region, the Indians—the Shoshone, Sioux, Arapaho and Cheyenne—grew resentful. The year 1865 became known as "the bloody year on the Plains." Indians attacked settlers, wagon trains and stagecoach stations. Additional Army forts were built to protect railroad construction crews, but hostilities did not end until 1876 with the defeat of the great chiefs—Dull Knife, Man-Afraid-of-His-Horse, Red Cloud and Crazy Horse.

The cowboy and his business—livestock—have played a major part in the state's frontier heritage. After the Civil War, cattlemen drove as many as 800,000 head a year up the Texas Trail to Wyoming's open ranges for the excellent grazing and for shipment from the Union Pacific Railroad's new terminal at Cheyenne. These men became powerful, fought the homesteaders who fenced in the rangeland, the rustlers who preyed on their herds and the sheepmen whose animals cropped the grass too short. The Johnson County cattle war between the large ranch owners, who imported Texas gunmen, and the "nesters," some of whom were suspected rustlers, had to be stopped by Federal troops. The livestock industry—cattle and sheep—now accounts for $125,000,000 of the state's more than $500,000,000 total product.

Wyoming's biggest economic provider, by far, is the mining industry. Oil, gas and coal produce 55 percent of the state's income. In the early days, oil literally oozed from the ground. Fur traders used it as ointment for muscular pains; Indians traded it to wagon-train immigrants for axle lubrication and harness preservative. In the 1880's oil was discovered in large quantities in the Salt Creek and other fields, but lack of transportation hindered exploitation until 1910. At that time the demand for oil created a boom that attracted thousands of investors and workers. The United States Geological Survey rates Wyoming fifth in oil reserves, with an estimated 1,168,862,000 barrels.

The thin soil, too poor for most farming but ideal for grazing, also covers a variety of minerals—uranium, iron ore, aluminum, asbestos and phosphates. Wyoming stands fourth among the states in coal reserves.

Hundreds of dude ranches do a roaring business; most are near the mountains, where game is plentiful—antelope, elk, moose, deer, mountain sheep and bear, both black and grizzly. There are 14,846 miles of fishing streams. For natural beauty, there are the Yellowstone and Grand Teton National Parks, the Wind River peaks rising to more than 13,000 feet and the Continental Divide, where the mountain waters begin flowing to the east or the west.

Even the winter snows, always a burden to stockmen, have brought added prosperity to dude ranchers and lodge owners. Skiing, introduced by Scandinavian immigrants, had been a working necessity in maintaining telegraph lines and supplying food to snowbound communities. The popular sport draws enthusiasts from the Midwestern states and the Pacific Coast.

Wyoming lives up to its nickname, the Equality State. The women of the Wyoming Territory in 1869 were the first in the world to be granted equal rights. In 1925 Mrs. Nellie Tayloe Ross of Wyoming took office as the first woman in the nation to be elected governor of her state.

Wyoming also lives up to another title, the Frontier State. The man on the horse, the Saturday-night dance hall, the false-front stores with wooden sidewalks, the saloon, the church social with little children bedded down, the gravel roads following old trails to mountain and valley towns: all can still be found. And Wyoming remains the country of the range, where cattle roam, though they are fed hay on the home ranch during the bitter winters.

CHEYENNE

When Major General Grenville M. Dodge was looking for a route for the Union Pacific Railroad through the Laramie Mountains in 1865, he camped at a site on Crow Creek where the Great Plains begin to merge with the steeper slopes. Two years later he selected the spot for the road's division point, and Cheyenne quickly developed into a frontier town with a sizable number of robbers, confidence men and other undesirables. A committee of vigilantes formed in 1868 executed at least 12 men in one year before law and order were restored. Cheyenne is the cattle-shipping point and supply center for the surrounding ranch and grazing area. The city is noted for its Frontier Days festival, held each July since 1897. The celebrators dress in frontier regalia, Indians dance, and cowboys and cowgirls compete in calf-roping, bronco-busting and racing. As many as 200,000 visitors from all over the country swarm through the town. Fort D. A. Russell, an Indian-fighting headquarters in pioneer days, is now the Francis E. Warren Air Force Base, largest intercontinental-ballistic-missile (ICBM) complex in the free world.

Area—97,914 sq. miles
Population—315,000
Capital—Cheyenne (Pop. 43,505)
For additional information on the state in special articles see General Index, Wyoming.

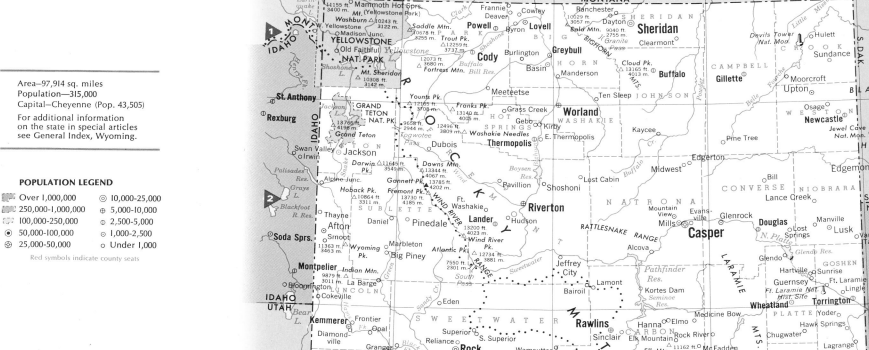

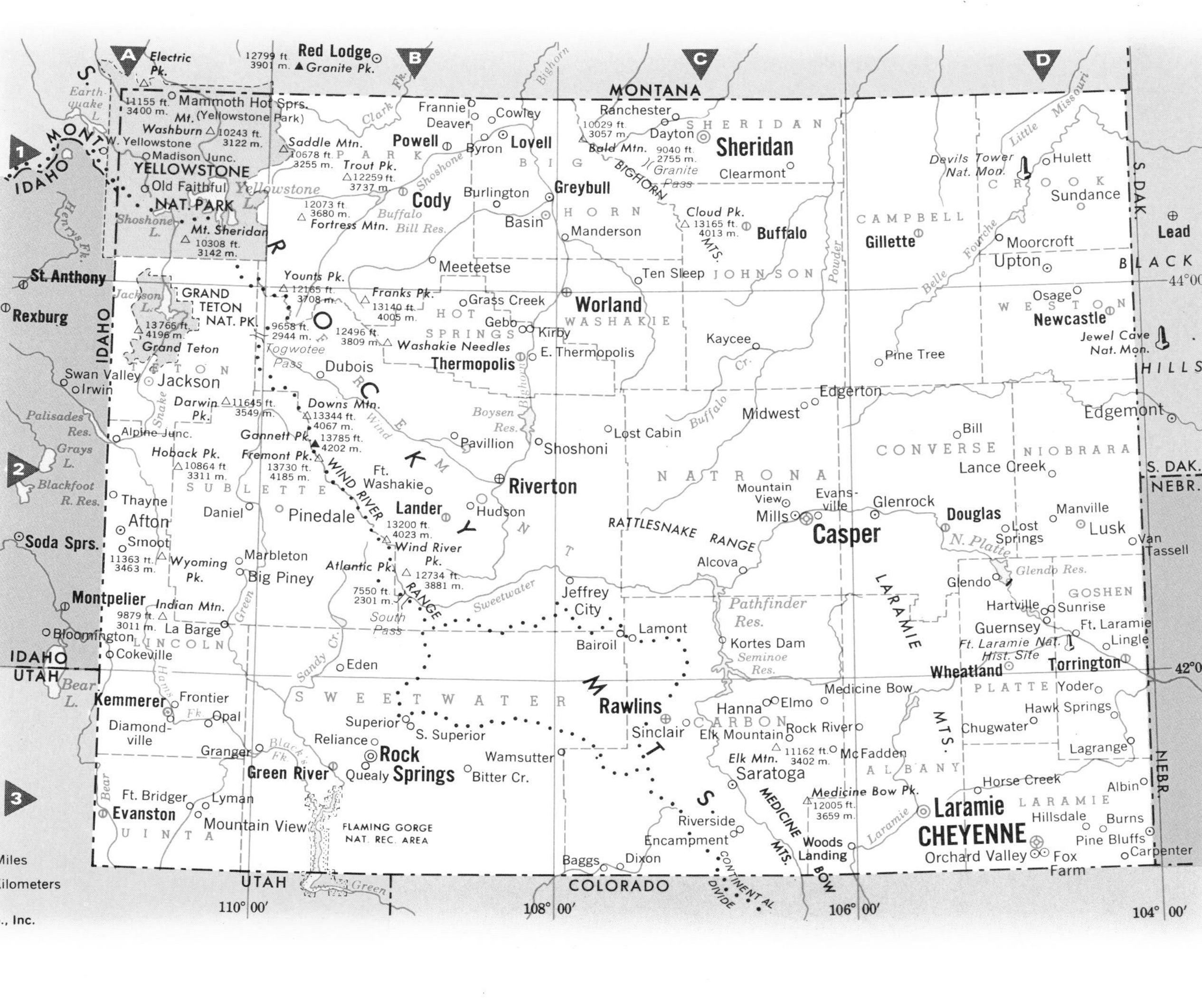

POPULATION LEGEND

- Over 1,000,000
- 250,000-1,000,000
- 100,000-250,000
- 50,000-100,000
- 25,000-50,000
- 10,000-25,000
- 5,000-10,000
- 2,500-5,000
- 1,000-2,500
- Under 1,000

Red symbols indicate county seats

1/3,940,000 — 1 in. = 62.2 mi. 0 20 40 60 80 100 Miles — 1 cm. = 39.4 km. 0 20 40 60 80 100 120 140 160 Kilometers

Lambert Conformal Conic Projection

© General Drafting Co., Inc.

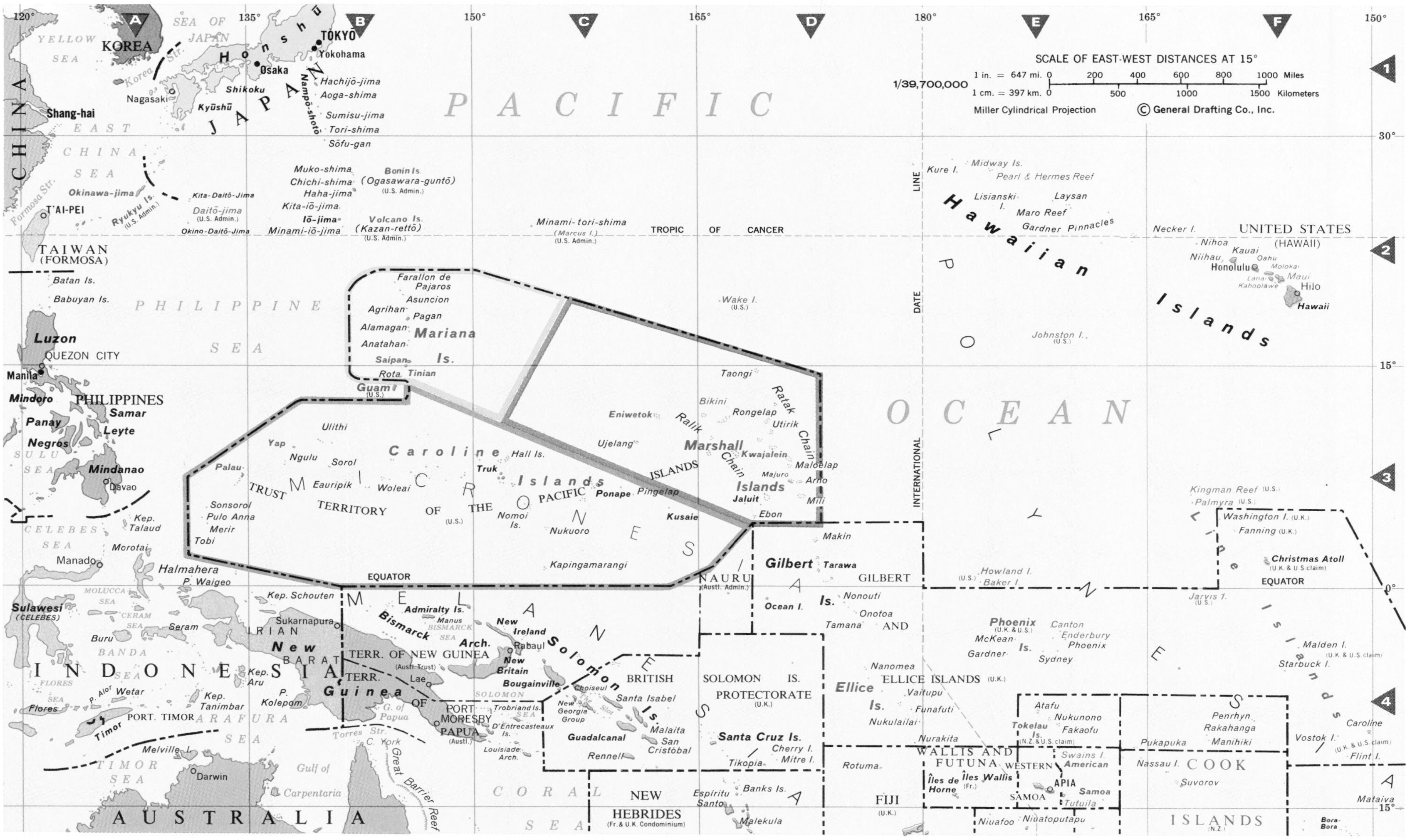

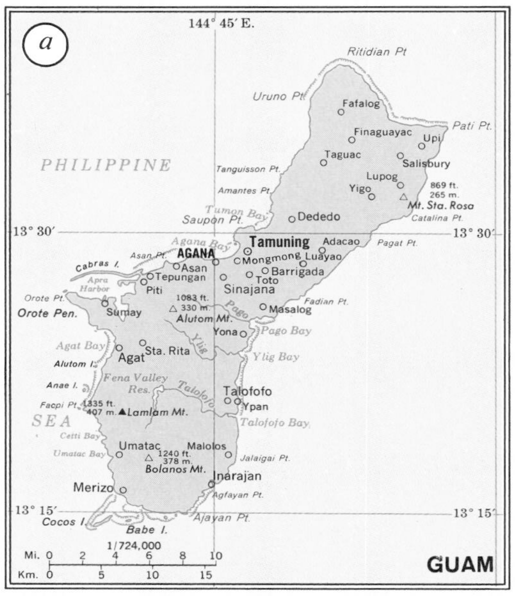

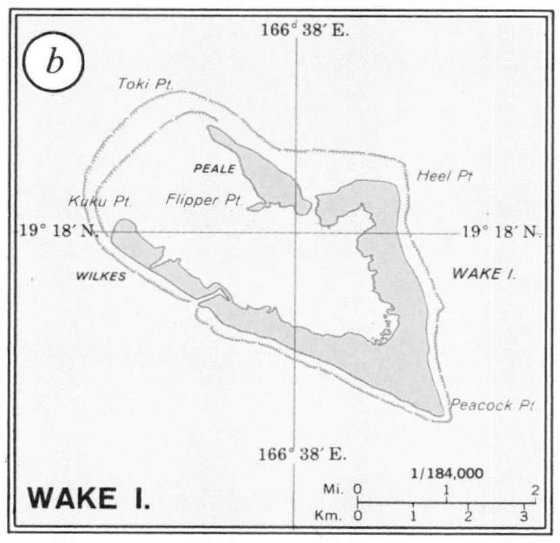

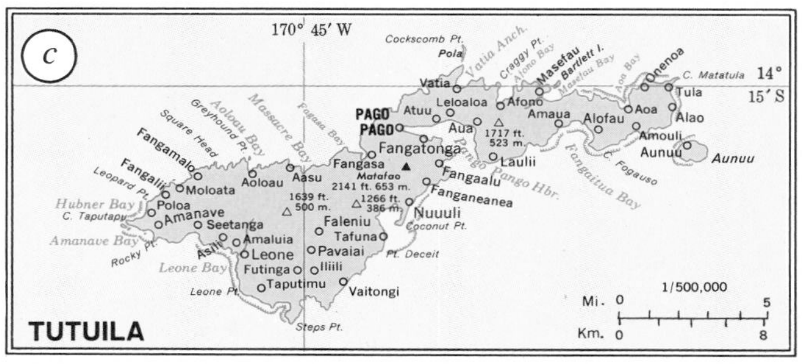

POSSESSIONS AND ADMINISTRATIVE AREAS OF THE UNITED STATES

Johnston Island (E-2) lies 715 miles southwest of Honolulu. Discovered by Charles James Johnston, an Englishman, in 1807, it was annexed by both the United States and the kingdom of Hawaii in 1858. The conflicting claims were resolved when Hawaii became American territory in 1898. *(Area: less than 0.5 square miles; population: 156.)*

Midway Islands (E-2), about 1200 miles northwest of Honolulu, were explored by an American in 1859 and annexed in 1876. The Navy's victory at the Battle of Midway in 1942 marked the turning point in the war against Japan. *(Area: 2 square miles; population: 2356.)*

In 1521 Magellan discovered Guam (B-3; also inset *a*), southernmost of the Mariana Islands which were ruled by Spain for more than three centuries. The United States captured it in 1898 during the Spanish-American War and kept it as a naval base because of its strategic location. Agana is the capital, and the harbor at Apra serves as the principal port. *(Area: 212 square miles; population: 67,044.)*

An American expedition explored Wake Island (D-2; also inset *b*), halfway between Midway and Guam, in 1841. The United States did not formally claim the atoll until 1900, two years after troops had landed there en route to the Philippines. *(Area: 3 square miles; population: 1097.)*

At Pago Pago on Tutuila (E-4; also inset *c*), 2400 miles south of Hawaii, Americans established a coal station in 1872. Britain and Germany in 1899 renounced all claims to the islands east of 171° west longitude, now known as American Samoa, and between 1900 and 1904 various chiefs ceded their territories to the United States. *(Area: 76 square miles; population: 20,051.)*

Palmyra (F-3), an atoll of 50 islands 960 miles south-southwest of Honolulu, is privately owned. The Republic of Hawaii and the United Kingdom both claimed it, and, in 1912, it was annexed by the United States. When Hawaii became a state in 1959, however, this group was not included. *(Area: 4 square miles; uninhabited at the time of the 1960 census.)*

Tiny Kingman Reef (F-3), 35 miles northwest of Palmyra, was visited by Americans in 1853 and annexed by the United States in 1922.

During the nineteenth century American companies worked the guano deposits on Howland and Baker (E-3) and Jarvis (F-4) islands, 1500 to 1600 miles southwest of Honolulu. The United States originally claimed them in 1857, but they were not formally proclaimed U.S. territory until 1935–36. *(Area: 3 square miles; uninhabited at the time of the 1960 census.)*

Scattered across nearly 3000 miles in the Pacific Ocean are some 2100 islands, 97 of them regularly inhabited, which the United States administers as the Trust Territory of the Pacific Islands under supervision of the United Nations. The trusteeship, established in 1947, covers three archipelagoes: the Carolines (A–D-3), Marianas (B–C and 2–3), and Marshalls (C–D and 2–3), discovered by Spanish explorers in the early sixteenth century. The Marianas are also known as Islas de los Ladrones—Islands of Thieves—so named by Magellan in 1521 because of native pilfering of his supplies. Spain ruled them until 1899 when, except for Guam, they were sold to Germany. In 1919 they were mandated to Japan by the League of Nations, to be ruled by her until ready for self-government. Japan withdrew from the League in 1933 and began fortifying the islands in preparation for World War II.

Among the famous battles which took place as American troops began the island-jumping conquest of the Pacific were those at Kwajalein (D-3; also inset *l*), Peleliu, on Palau (A-3; also inset *e*), and Saipan (B-2; also inset *f*). From the airfield at Tinian (B-3; also inset *f*), a B-29 took off at 2:45 a.m. on August 6, 1945, to drop the first atomic bomb on Hiroshima. The second bomb, dispatched three days later, ended the war. Atom- and hydrogen-bomb tests were subsequently carried out in Eniwetok (C-3; also inset *k*) and Bikini (D-3) in the Marshalls. The Yap Island group (B-3; also inset *d*) in the Carolines is noted as the only place in the world which once used circular stone money from six inches to 12 feet in diameter. The territory is administered from the U.S. High Commissioner's office in Saipan. *(Area: 687 square miles; population: 70,724.)*

Under the 1952 peace treaty with Japan, the United States was given the right to occupy and administer a number of island groups which nevertheless remain Japanese possessions. The Amami archipelago was returned to full Japanese control the following year, leaving under American jurisdiction the southern Ryukyus (A-2); Daitō (A-2); the Bonin (B-2), Volcano (B-2) and Marcus islands (C-2). Two nearby islands, Rosario and Parece Vela, are also administered by the United States. A bitter campaign between United States and Japanese forces had been

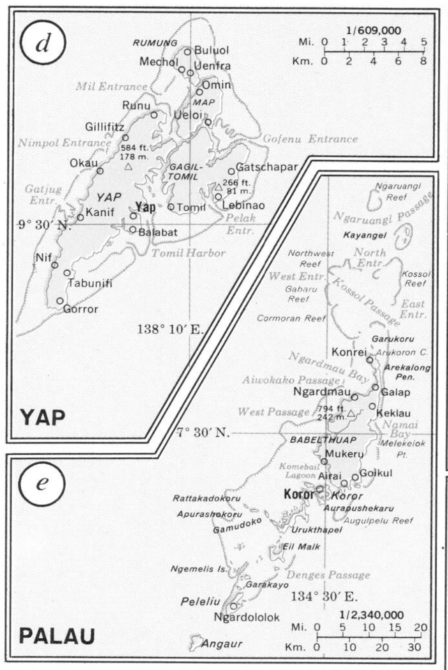

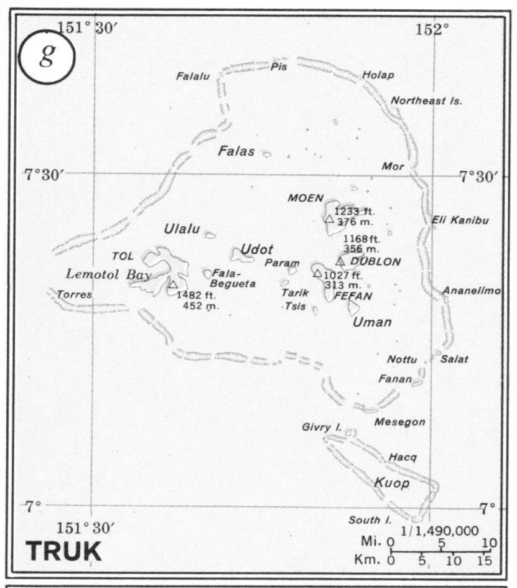

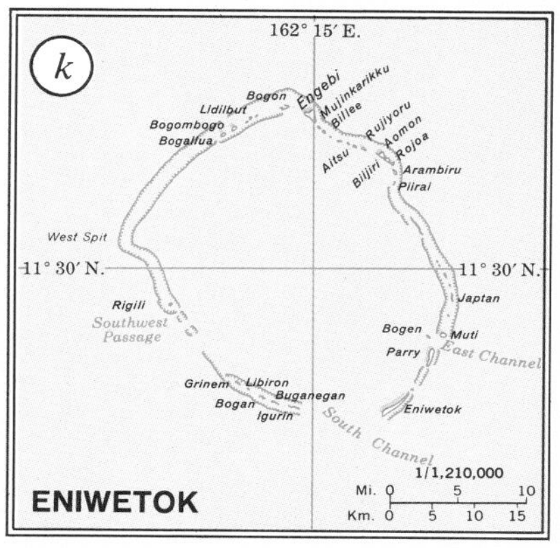

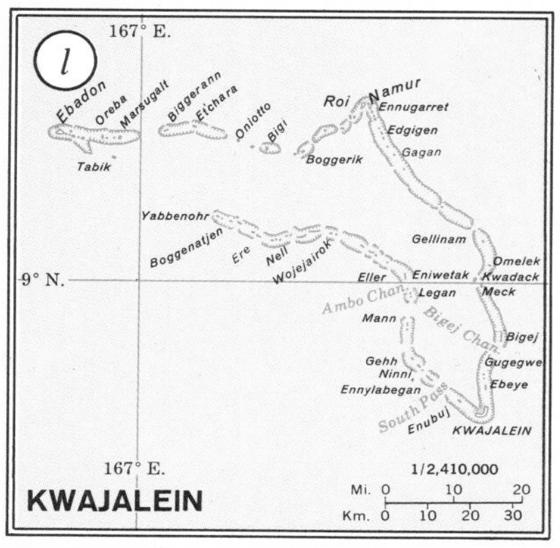

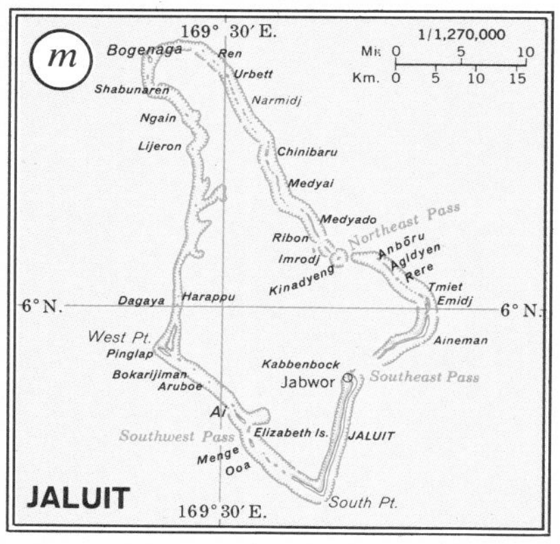

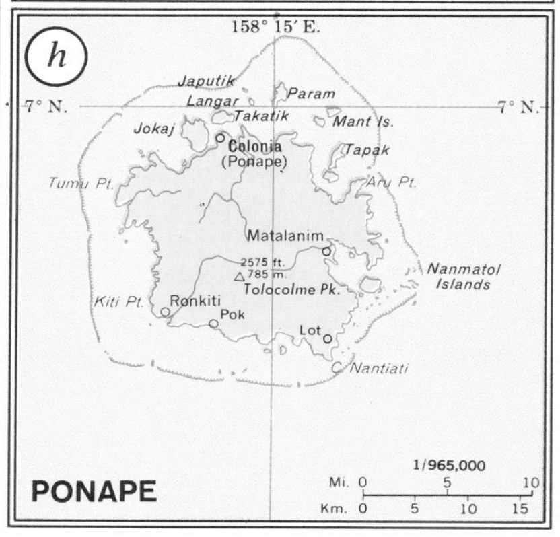

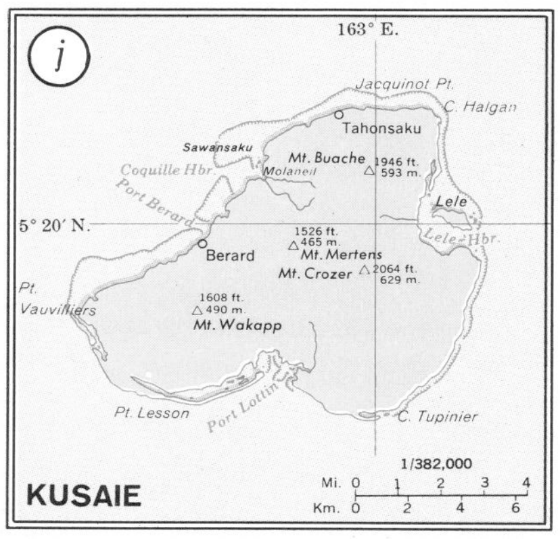

fought on Okinawa (A-2), largest of the Ryukyus. *(Area: 889 square miles; population: 913,215.)*

The United States also claims sovereignty over 25 other islands in the south-central Pacific which, with two exceptions, are actually administered by either New Zealand or the United Kingdom. Discovered in the seventeenth and eighteenth centuries, these small outposts were largely ignored until the middle of the nineteenth century, when their guano deposits were worked by American companies. Later the islands were annexed by Britain. The territory claimed by both the United States and New Zealand consists of the three Tokelau (or Union) Islands (E-4) and the four northern Cook Islands (F-4). The United Kingdom disputes American claims to six Line Islands (F-3–4), five of them uninhabited; four Ellice Islands (D–E-4) and eight Phoenix Islands (E-4). Two of the latter, Canton and Enderbury, have a government in common under which each country has jurisdiction over its own resident nationals. The National Aeronautics and Space Administration exercises the authority for the United States.

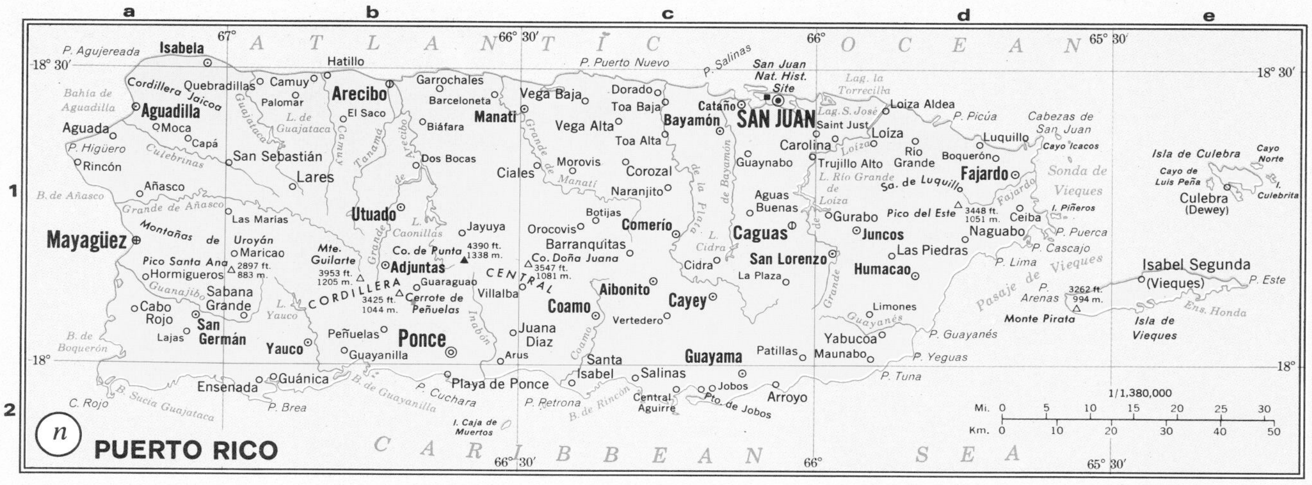

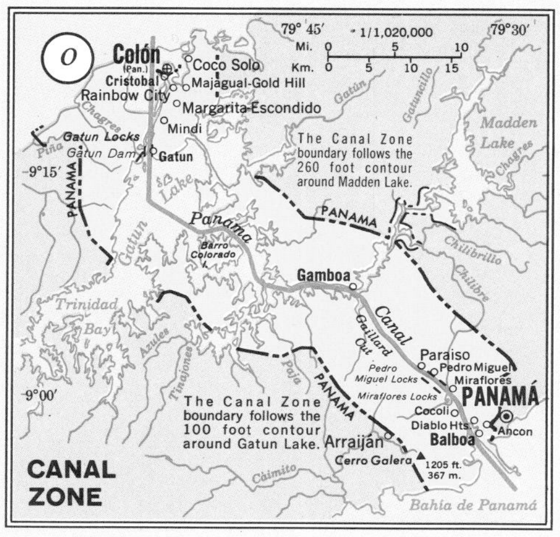

Puerto Rico (E-2, below; also inset *n*) is a self-governing commonwealth associated with the United States, 1000 miles southeast of Miami, Florida. Its inhabitants are American citizens, but do not vote in national elections or pay Federal taxes, and their representative in Congress does not have a vote. Discovered by Columbus in 1493, the island was first settled by the Spanish in 1506. Puerto Rico was ceded to the United States after the Spanish-American War. San Juan is the capital. *(Area: 3435 square miles; population: 2,349,544.)*

Under the terms of a 1903 treaty with Panama (B–C-4), the United States was given permanent control of a 10-mile-wide strip across the isthmus in which to build a canal (inset *o*). An agreement was made with Panama for an annual payment of $250,000, which has since been increased to $1,930,000. *(Area: 553 square miles; population: 42,122.)*

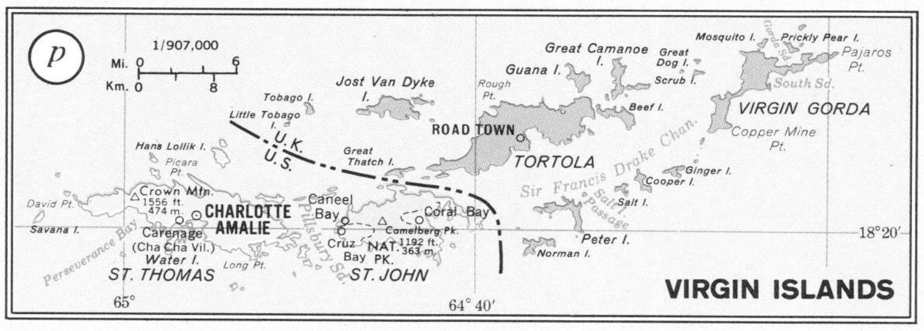

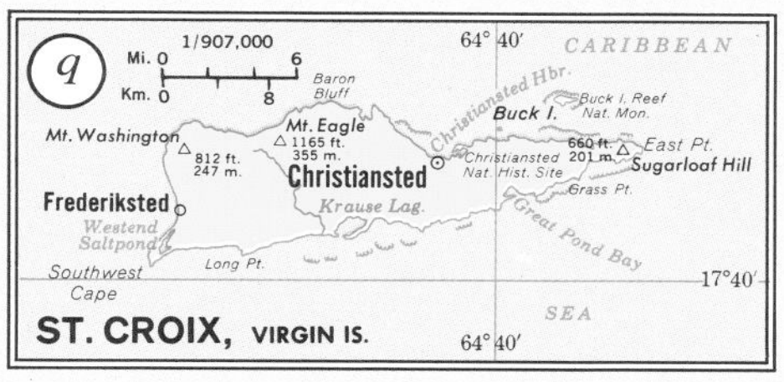

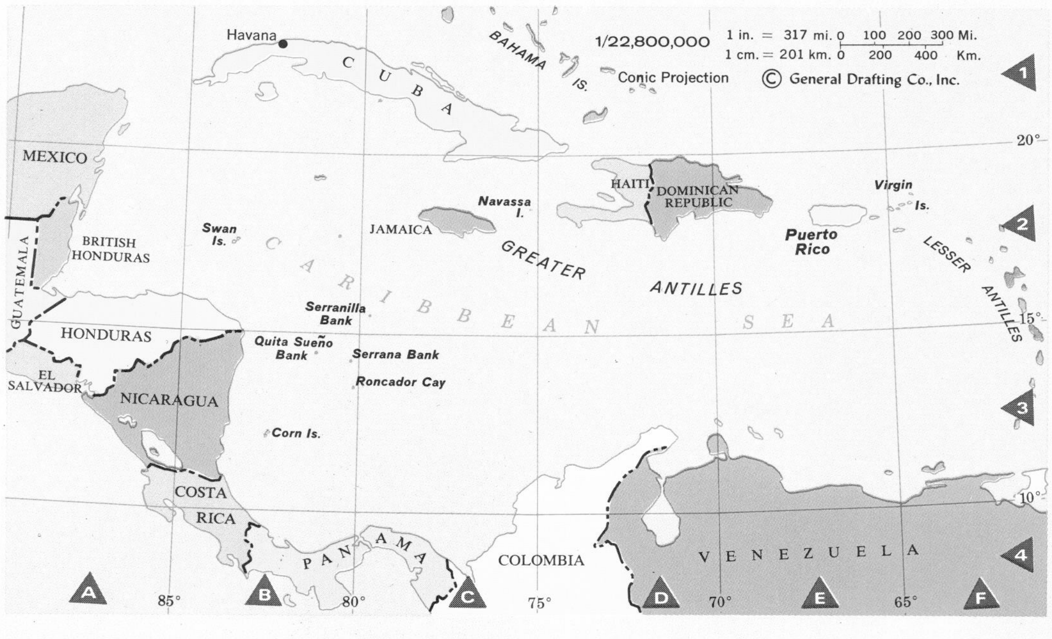

Although Columbus discovered the Virgin Islands (F-2; also insets *p* and *q*), 40 miles east of Puerto Rico, in 1493 and claimed them for Spain, Denmark settled St. Thomas, St. John (inset *p*) and St. Croix (inset *q*). In 1917, the United States bought the islands for $25,000,000. Charlotte Amalie is the capital. *(Area: 133 square miles; population: 32,099.)*

In the Caribbean area the United States also owns Navassa Island (C-2), site of a lighthouse between Haiti and Jamaica, and the Swan Islands (B-2), north of Honduras, where a hurricane reporting station and an aviation navigation beacon are maintained. The Corn Islands (B-3), off the east coast of Nicaragua, were leased from that nation in 1914 for 99 years but the United States has never made any use of them. American ownership of several groups of islets or cays east of Nicaragua is disputed by Colombia. These are Quita Sueño Bank, Roncador Cay, Serrana Bank and Serranilla Bank (B–C and 2–3).

PART II

The People of America

THE FIRST AMERICANS

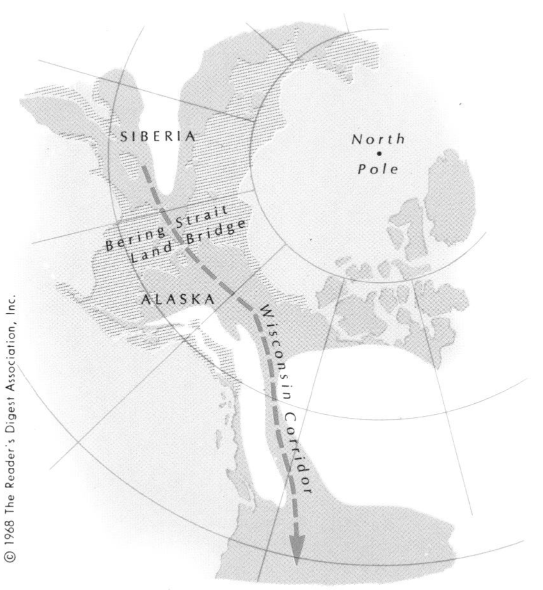

The Bering Strait Land Bridge. *During the Great Ice Age, lasting from 1,000,000 to 10,000 years ago, vast areas of North America were covered by thick fields of ice. As much of the earth's moisture was held in this glacial buildup, water did not return by rivers to the sea. The sea level was at times lowered 200 to 300 feet, creating a land bridge from Siberia to Alaska. Most authorities believe that man first arrived in America across this bridge about 12,000 to 15,000 years ago. Others say 35,000 to 45,000 years ago.*

The Wisconsin Corridor. *The last cycle of the Great Ice Age, known as the Wisconsin, began 65,000 years ago. For the next 50,000 years or more, glaciers covered North America (above). Twice during warm periods there occurred a corridor, over one hundred miles wide, through which early man must have passed southward from Alaska—following the animal herds he hunted. The arrow shows man's pathway. About 11,000 years ago the corridor remained open until the Great Ice Age came to an end. By 9000 B.C., prehistoric man had reached Mexico and, by about 8500 B.C., he had completed the 8000-mile trek to the tip of South America.*

Forty years ago archaeologists had scarcely investigated the American past, though they had been busy for nearly two centuries revealing ancient civilizations and prehistoric man in the Old World. It was assumed that even the most dramatic Indian cultures, such as the Pueblo Builders of the Southwest, were fairly recent. There appeared to be no evidence at all of man's existence in the Western Hemisphere before the first century.

In 1926, at Folsom, New Mexico, an archaeologist unearthed a spearpoint lodged in the ribs of a bison, a species which had been extinct for 10,000 years. From that day, the story of the Stone Age hunters of America has been pieced together and is still being unfolded. In fact, many archaeological sites, including some on these pages, are presently being studied, and scientific findings concerning them have not yet been published. We know that the Paleo (early) Indians, as they are called, arrived across the Bering land bridge (see map at left) over a period of thousands of years. After the land bridge was submerged by melting ice, they probably came by boat across the 56-mile strait. Their chief weapon, sometimes found with the bones of the mammoth, the mastodon, the saber-toothed tiger, the camel, the sloth and with animal subspecies now extinct, was a stone-pointed spear. Distinctively channeled points resembling the one discovered at Folsom have been found in every state except Hawaii.

Strangely enough, only two authenticated skeletons of early man have been found in the United States (and less than 25 in the entire Western Hemisphere). It is thought that these ancient American hunters practiced cremation or exposure of the dead, rather than burial, so that their remains were seldom preserved.

Campfires and spearpoints place the Paleo-Indian hunter in the American West and the Great Plains more than 10,000 years ago. By about 9000 years ago, he had made an important discovery. Elsewhere in the world, except in the eastern Mediterranean, man did not grind grain until he had first learned how to plant it. Here, before the dawn of agriculture, certain cave-dwellers, who were using grinding stones to make red coloring for dyeing hides, began to use the stones to mill wild grains and seeds (sites **19** and **20**).

Early man in the United States also ranks among the world's innovators of agriculture. One of the most ancient examples of domestic grain, ears of cultivated corn dating to 5600 years ago, was found in Bat Cave, New Mexico (site **31**). Primitive forms of potatoes, squash and beans were among the earliest crops.

Evidence of village life is rare in the United States until the first century B.C., when the Stone Age American appears to have taken this important step.

Village Culture After First Century B.C.

The Southwest. In the desert areas of the Southwest, the Hohokam people, probable ancestors of the modern Pimas, were irrigating the land (site **38**). In the plateau areas the Anasazis—in the Basket Maker period of their culture, 1 to 700 A.D.—were building roofed houses in excavated pits (site **39**). Their later stone and adobe dwellings, constructed aboveground (site **42**), became more and more elaborate. Anasazi culture reached its apex in the Great Pueblo period, 900 to 1250 A.D., when they evolved the pueblos—the Spanish word for "villages"—and cliff dwellings familiar to visitors in the Southwest today (sites **44**, **46** and **47**). The Anasazis, with their highly developed priestly class, had no apparent extremes of wealth and status. They were the greatest master builders. Only they grew cotton and wove fabric, and they created some of the finest pottery of the prehistoric people in the United States (see illustration below).

About 1300 A.D., the Anasazis were forced by drought to abandon their most outstanding cliff cities, including Pueblo Bonito and Mesa Verde. Eventually they settled along the banks of the Rio Grande, Pecos and Little Colorado rivers in less impressive pueblos, where their descendants still live. A third group of the Southwest, the Mogollons, dwelling in the higher areas, built smaller pueblos.

The Mound Builders. In the Mississippi Valley, pre-Columbian civilization reached its climax. A high culture (which is being discovered through excavation), it was distinguished by the people's custom of forming burial grounds into mounds of earth. Sometimes in the shapes of animals and birds, they grew more elaborate and numerous over the centuries (see Great Serpent Mound illustration below). Over 100,000 mounds of many kinds have been located. By about 100 B.C. the Hopewell Mound Builders of Ohio reached the most advanced civilization achieved by Indians of the United States (site **37**). Their modeled and carved art objects and their copperware were unsurpassed (see pipe illustration below). A priest-governed people, they buried their dead with trappings comparable to those they possessed on earth. Although the Hopewell Mound Builders disappeared about

Cliff Palace, Mesa Verde National Park, Colorado. Hollowed out of a cliff for protection against enemy raids, this magnificent pueblo, dating from about 1100 A.D., has 200 rooms, 23 kivas (underground chambers).

Stone pipe from Ross County, Ohio (late Hopewell). The Hopewells and other Mound Builders of the eastern United States were the great sculptors of the Indian world, masters of three-dimensional form. This famous stone pipe shows a spoonbill bird perched on a fish. The eyes may have been inlaid, perhaps with shell. Such pipes were probably used in tobacco-smoking religious rituals.

Anasazi jar from Tularosa Canyon, New Mexico (1100–1300 A.D.). The Indians of the Southwest excelled in the art of decorating pottery, fabrics and mosaics. Here a highly developed sense of design, inspired by an animal, is applied to a vessel—one of the best examples of primitive North American art.

Great Serpent Mound near Portsmouth, Ohio. Built about 1000 A.D. and measuring 1330 feet long, 20 feet wide and 2 to 3½ feet high, it is the most outstanding of the mounds shaped like animals or birds. Religious ceremonies were probably performed in the center of the head (upper right).

700 A.D., mound-building continued among the Mississippian Temple Mound Builders (sites **43** and **50** and Cahokia pyramid illustration below), whose mounds served as ceremonial grounds and as bases for temples. De Soto and other explorers of the Southeast encountered the last stages of temple mound-building among the Natchez Indians.

The North Atlantic Region. Known as the Woodland Indians, these tribes were the ancestors of the great Algonquian and other northeastern language groups (see page 80). Less advanced than the Hopewell Mound Builders, they absorbed much of the mound-building civilization: stable agriculture, pottery-making, and trading (site **48**). But they never built large mounds, and their art never rose to so sophisticated a level.

The Great Plains. The horse had evolved in America from a small fox-sized creature over a period of some 50 million years (see page 127). It had crossed the Alaskan land bridge to Asia and Europe but had become extinct in the Americas. The Spaniards brought horses from Europe back to Mexico in 1519, and these escaped to run wild over the American plains.

About 500 A.D., Indians from the nearby eastern woodland area settled in farming villages along the Missouri. By 1700 they began to catch and domesticate horses in great numbers. Abandoning their villages, they reverted to hunting; on horseback they followed the great bison herds that roamed the plains. The nomadic Great Plains Indians in the West also took to horseback, and it was these predators—among them the Sioux, Cheyenne and Comanche—who were some of the most warlike ever encountered by the American settlers on their way west.

The Pacific Northwest and the Great Western Basin. There has been little archaeological investigation of the life that existed in the Pacific Northwest before Europeans arrived. Explorers and traders encountered large villages and a high degree of civilization among the totem-carving Indians of the eighteenth century (see page 80). In the northern part of the Great Basin, rectangular houses, remarkable carvings and fishing equipment, discovered at Wakemap, Oregon (site **41**), indicate that these Stone Age people may have been the ancestors of modern Indians of the Pacific Northwest. In the southern part of the Great Basin, the desert culture of the ancient seed-gathering millers of Arizona (site **19**) and Utah (site **20**) persisted 8000 years almost unchanged, until the coming of the Europeans.

Hawaii. Unlike the continental United States, the islands of Hawaii were very late in being occupied by man. It was not until about 500 to 750 A.D. that the first settlers—Polynesians—came to the islands, probably from Tahiti across 2676 miles of open sea. About the twelfth century additional waves of settlers came in vast fleets of outrigger and double canoes. They established an agricultural and fishing society with feudal kingdoms.

Cahokia Mound, Collinsville, Illinois (replica drawing). This vast earthwork—16 acres at the base, 100 feet high—is one of the greatest building structures of primitive man. Three acres larger in area than the Great Pyramid in Egypt, it was built without use of horses or wheels. The pyramidlike structure was topped by a large temple. It dates from 750 to 1150 A.D.

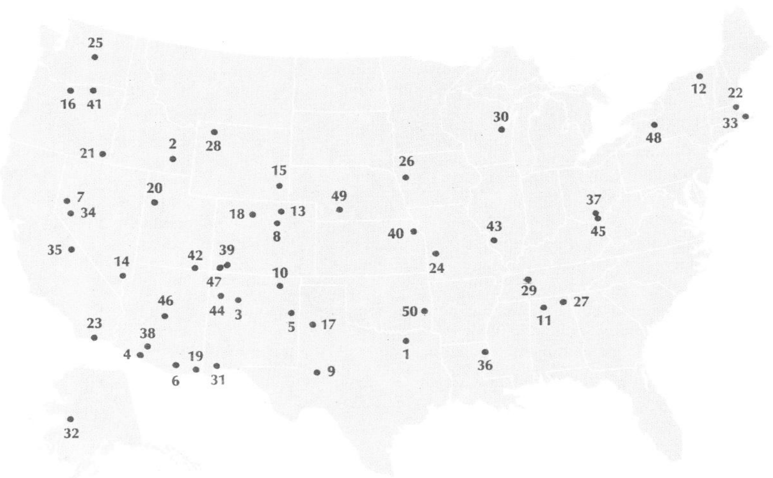

Archaeological sites in the U.S. *Numbers on map correspond to numbers on chart at right.*

50 MAJOR ARCHAEOLOGICAL SITES IN THE UNITED STATES

	Stone Age Sites		Events in the Rest of the World
13,000–8000 B.C.	**1.** *Lewisville, Texas*—Hearths; extinct mammoth, bison, camel and coyote bones; seeds, spearpoint (date in dispute)	30,000–10,000 B.C.	Paleolithic man forced to live in caves around the warm Mediterranean by last Ice Age
12,500 B.C.	**2.** *Wilson Butte Cave, Snake River Plain, Idaho*—Spearpoint, blade		
11,000 B.C.	**3.** *Sandia Cave, Las Huertas Canyon, New Mexico*—Lowest level: spearpoints; mastodon and ground-sloth bones. Higher level: Folsom spearpoints (see below); bones of mammoth, mastodon, extinct subspecies of bison, horse and camel (date in dispute)		
9340 B.C.	**4.** *Ventana Cave, south of Phoenix, Arizona*—Spearpoints; choppers; extinct wolf, jaguar, sloth, tapir and horse bones	10,000 B.C.	Emergence of citylike communities
9200 B.C.	**5.** *Blackwater Draw, Clovis, New Mexico*—Mammoth, camel, extinct horse and bison bones; spearpoints; scrapers; knives. Occupied for thousands of years		
9200 B.C.	**6.** *Lehner Site, Hereford, Arizona*—Mammoth, tapir and extinct bison bones; spearpoints; hearths		
9200 B.C.	**7.** *Fishbone Cave, Winnemucca Lake area, Nevada*—Earliest twined basketry; human and prehistoric horse and camel bones; awls (date in dispute)		
9200 B.C.	**8.** *Dent, Colorado*—Spearpoints; mammoth bones		
9000 B.C.	**9.** *Midland, Texas*—Human remains, including skull (date in dispute)	9000–8000 B.C.	In Near East food gatherers began to move from caves to open-air sites; first huts, storing of wild grain, domestication of dog and goat (later migrants to North America are thought to have brought domesticated dogs with them)
9000–8000 B.C.	**10.** *Folsom, New Mexico*—Spearpoint with extinct bison bones—first proof that man coexisted with extinct mammals in U.S.		
9000 B.C.	**11.** *The Quad Site, Decatur, Alabama*—Spearpoints; drills; choppers		
9000 B.C.	**12.** *Reagen Site, Shawville, Vermont*—Spearpoints; knives; pendants		
8800 B.C.	**13.** *Lindenmeier Site, near Fort Collins, Colorado* (Folsom level)—Extinct bison and camel bones; spearpoints; knives; scrapers		
8500 B.C.	**14.** *Gypsum Cave, Las Vegas, Nevada*—Spearpoints; giant sloth, camel and horse bones; basketry fragments	8000 B.C.	Earliest evidence of agriculture in the Near East; dry conditions caused man to learn irrigation
8000 B.C.	**15.** *Hell Gap Site, Guernsey, Wyoming*—Spearpoints; extinct bison bones; post holes thought to have supported a hide roof		
7800 B.C.	**16.** *Five Mile Rapids, on Columbia River, Oregon*—Elk-antler tools; fish and bird bones. Continually occupied from 8000 B.C. until arrival of Europeans		
7800 B.C.	**17.** *Plainview, Texas*—Spearpoints; extinct bison bones		
7500 B.C.	**18.** *Gordon Creek, Roosevelt National Forest, Colorado*—Human skeleton; hammerstone; scraper	7500 B.C.	Settlement of Jericho, oldest known fortified town
7350–6270 B.C.	**19.** *Sulphur Spring Valley, Arizona*—Hearth fires; bones of extinct mammoth, horse, bison and dire wolf; scraping and cutting tools; earliest grinding and milling tools	7000 B.C.	Man's stone tools becoming more specialized; fewer hunting weapons; various forms of diggers and hoes
7000 B.C.	**20.** *Danger Cave, near Wendover, Utah*—Twined basketry; spearpoints; milling stones; remains of fires; mountain sheep, antelope bones		
7000 B.C.	**21.** *Fort Rock Cave, Fort Rock Valley, Oregon*—Fiber sandals (oldest found); basketry; spearpoints; scrapers; bone awls		
7000 B.C.	**22.** *Bull Brook Site, near Ipswich, Massachusetts*—Spearpoints; scrapers; flaked knives		
7000–1000 B.C.	**23.** *Pinto Basin, Riverside County, California*—Spearpoints; milling stone; extinct camel and horse bones		
7000 B.C.	**24.** *Graham Cave, at junction of Loutre and Missouri rivers, Missouri*—Spearpoints; knives; grinding stones; mortars (date in dispute)		
6700 B.C.	**25.** *Lind Coulee Site, Columbia River Basin, Washington*—Spearpoints; scrapers; knives; bison bones		
6400 B.C.	**26.** *Simonson Site, Quimby, Iowa*—Spearpoints; extinct bison bones	6500 B.C.	Invention of pottery in the Near East
6200 B.C.	**27.** *Russell Cave, Bridgeport, Alabama*—Bones; tools; weapons; pottery; occupied intermittently from 6200 B.C. to 1650 A.D.	6000 B.C.	Lake dwellers of France, Switzerland and Austria: farming, herding; lived in houses
6000 B.C.	**28.** *Horner Site, Cody, Wyoming*—Bison bones; spearpoints; grinding stones; scrapers; choppers; knives; probable storage pits		
5100 B.C.	**29.** *Eva Site, Humphreys County, Tennessee*—Stone and antler spearpoints; antler scrapers; bone needles		
5000–2000 B.C.	**30.** *Oconto, Wisconsin*—Copper spearpoints; knives; harpoon heads; awls; ornaments	5000 B.C.	Spread of metallurgy in the Near East
3600 B.C.	**31.** *Bat Cave, near Magdalena, New Mexico*—Spearpoints; oldest known ears of cultivated corn	4000–3500 B.C.	Sumerians developed cuneiform writing and used wheeled vehicles
3000 B.C.	**32.** *Iyatayet, Cape Denbigh, Alaska*—Spearpoints (date in dispute). (Note: other Alaskan sites discovered thus far are not datable.)	3000 B.C.	First pyramids in Egypt
2300 B.C.	**33.** *Wapanucket, Massachusetts*—Spearpoints; axe; pestles, house floors	2500 B.C.	Earliest South American community life
2000 B.C.	**34.** *Lovelock Cave, Churchill County, Nevada*—Basketry; mats; fur and leather robes; sickles; hunting decoys		
2000–1000 B.C.	**35.** *Stahl, Inyo County, California*—Spearpoints; scrapers; milling stones; evidence of houses (post and holes)	1900 B.C.	First Stonehenge construction in England
	Village-Culture Sites	1225 B.C.	Exodus of the Jews from Egypt
800 B.C.	**36.** *Poverty Point, Louisiana*—Carefully planned and laid-out village about 1250 yards in diameter	500–400 B.C.	Golden Age of Athenian civilization
300 B.C.–700 A.D.	**37.** *Ross County, Ohio* (Hopewell Mound Builders)—Copper tools and breastplates; flint arrow and spearpoints; stone pipes (see illustration); shell, bone, pearl, copper and mica ornaments	500 B.C.	The Mayas probably were living in farming cities in Guatemala
100 B.C.–1200 A.D.	**38.** *Snaketown, Arizona* (Southwest: Hohokam)—Evidence of four-post-roofed pit houses; cooking pits; communal buildings; pottery (largest Hohokam site, 300 acres in area)		
46–330 A.D.	**39.** *Durango, Colorado* (Southwest: Anasazi Middle Basket Maker Period)—Pit storage rooms; remains of houses; basketry	100–200 A.D.	Peak of Roman Empire
200–400 A.D.	**40.** *Kansas City, Kansas area* (Great Plains)—Hopewellian-type burial mounds; evidence of agriculture; pottery	400 A.D.	Rise of Goths, Franks and Gauls in Europe
500 A.D.	**41.** *Wakemap, Columbia River, Oregon* (Great Western Basin)—Remains of rectangular houses; fishing nets and spears; fine carvings		
500–700 A.D.	**42.** *Alkali Ridge, Utah* (Southwest: Anasazi Late Basket Maker and Early Pueblo periods)—Adjoining adobe-covered houses; pottery	600 A.D.	Peak of Byzantine, Persian, Arab civilizations
750–1150 A.D.	**43.** *Cahokia Mound, Collinsville, Illinois* (Temple Mound Builders)—See illustration	700–800 A.D.	Reign of Charlemagne; arrival of Slavs in Europe
919–1300 A.D.	**44.** *Pueblo Bonito, Chaco Canyon, New Mexico* (Southwest: Anasazi)	1000 A.D.	Leif Ericson sighted America; Mayan civilization in Mexico
1000 A.D.	**45.** *Great Serpent Mound, near Portsmouth, Ohio* (Mound Builders)—See illustration		
1100–1300 A.D.	**46.** *Montezuma's Castle, Yavapai County, Arizona* (Southwest: Great Pueblo Era—Five-story cliff dwelling built by Sinaguas	1100 A.D.	Inca civilization in Peru
	47. *Cliff Palace, Mesa Verde Park, Colorado* (Southwest: Anasazi, Great Pueblo Era)—See illustration		
1150 A.D.	**48.** *Sackett Site, Canandaigua, New York* (North Atlantic Village)—Pole prints indicating small wigwams; corn and beans grown	1200 A.D.	Building of Gothic cathedrals
1200–1400 A.D.	**49.** *Medicine Creek, southwest Nebraska* (Great Plains)—Houses	1400 A.D	Invention of printing in Europe
1400 A.D.	**50.** *Spiro Mound, Le Flore County, Oklahoma* (Temple Mound Builders)—Shell ornaments; carved stone and wood		

Oldest known map of America, called Vinland (1) by Leif Ericson, was drawn in 1440. In this detail, Greenland (2) is also shown. The lettering beside Vinland reads, "Island of Vinland, discovered by Bjarni and Leif in company." An Icelandic saga credits Leif Ericson with the discovery, while a Greenlandic saga attributes it to Bjarni Herjolfsson. The map is thought to have been copied by a monk at Basel, Switzerland, from a still earlier one, perhaps Icelandic. There is no indication that Columbus ever saw the map.

FROM SEA TO SEA: EXPLORATION

About the year 1000 A.D. Leif Ericson, on a voyage from Norway to his home in Greenland, made a navigational error or was blown off course. The result: the first sighting of the New World, which he called Vinland. Later a party of Norsemen set sail for Vinland and spent a winter there—probably at Newfoundland or Martha's Vineyard.

Route to the East. Although these voyages were recounted in the Vinland sagas, almost 500 years passed before the official discovery of the New World. During that period a number of developments had been preparing the way for the historic crossing of the Atlantic by Christopher Columbus. From the single-masted, primarily oar-propelled ships of the Norsemen, Europe had progressed to the two- and three-masted sailing vessel. The compass was improved, and those westward stepping-stones, the Azores, were discovered. Equally as important as these physical discoveries, however, was the spur of commerce. The long overland route from the East was costly, and the demand for oriental spices and luxuries had greatly expanded. Columbus and others reasoned that one could reach the East by sailing west. Thinking he had reached the outer islands of the East Indies, Columbus christened the Caribbean natives "Indians." Soon it became certain that a vast land obstacle blocked the water route to the East. In 1507 this obstruction—North and South America—was named after the Italian explorer Amerigo Vespucci.

For the next half century, other explorers from Spain followed Columbus to the New World, venturing onto the mainland: Ponce de León to Florida, Hernando de Soto to the Southeast, Francisco de Coronado and Cabeza de Vaca from Mexico up into the Southwest.

The Atlantic Coast. Only a few explorers from other lands ventured along the North American coast so early, and these men took northern routes in their searches for a pas-

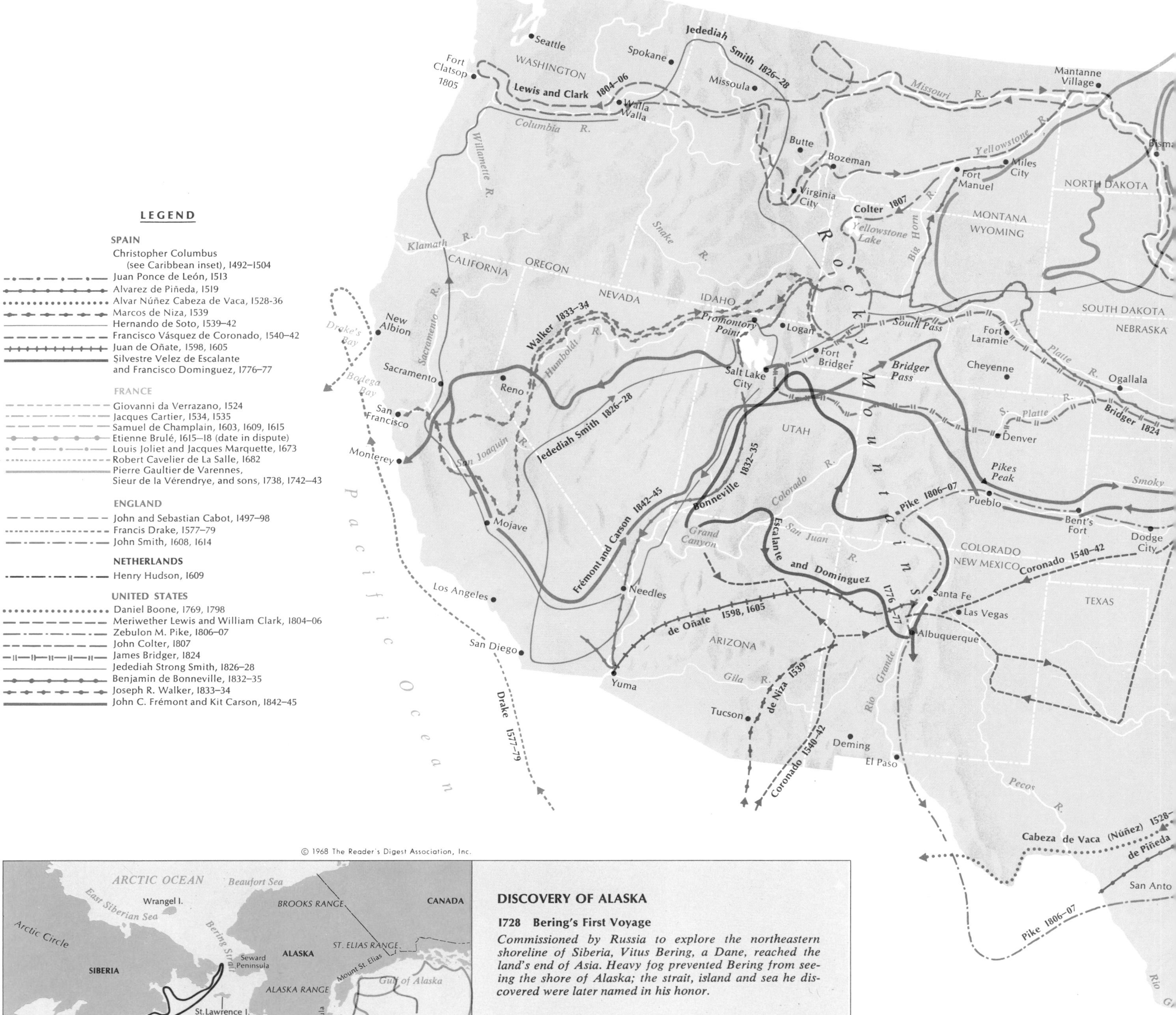

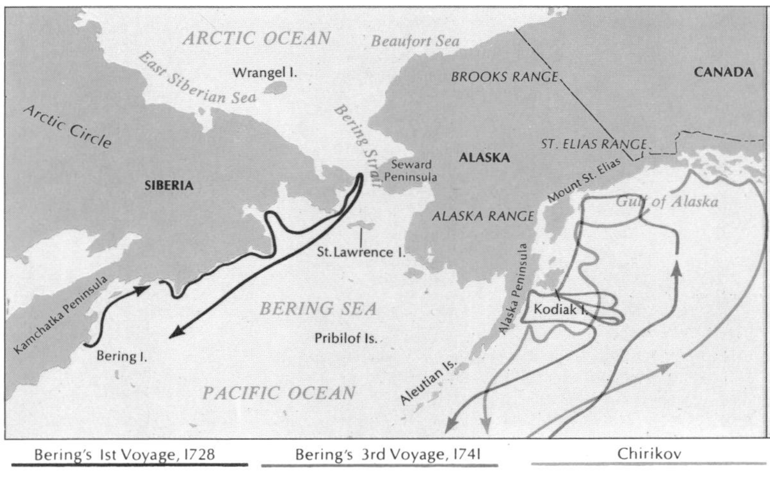

DISCOVERY OF ALASKA

1728 Bering's First Voyage

Commissioned by Russia to explore the northeastern shoreline of Siberia, Vitus Bering, a Dane, reached the land's end of Asia. Heavy fog prevented Bering from seeing the shore of Alaska; the strait, island and sea he discovered were later named in his honor.

1741 Bering's Third Voyage • Voyage of Alexei Chirikov

This two-ship joint expedition, under the overall command of Bering, is officially credited with the discovery of Alaska. Chirikov's ship sighted offshore islands, including the Aleutians. Bering sighted the mainland, namely, the volcano Mount St. Elias. He died on the return trip.

sage to India. The Pope had divided the southern lands between Spain and Portugal—the Portuguese discoveries were confined to eastern Brazil. As early as 1497–98, the Italian John Cabot, sailing under the English flag, explored the coast of North America from Labrador to Chesapeake Bay. Soon, for France, another Italian, Giovanni da Verrazano, entered New York Harbor, and Jacques Cartier sailed down the St. Lawrence River. Late in the sixteenth century, the Englishman Sir Francis Drake took the southern route around the tip of South America, not so much to explore as to pirate Spanish ships sailing through the Straits of Magellan. He sailed up the west coast of the Americas and landed in California.

By 1600, Spanish exploration was for the most part ended (although Juan de Oñate was roving through the Southwest), and the land discoveries by other nations in the North American continent began. For the Dutch East India Company, the Englishman Henry Hudson sailed up the majestic river that bears his name. For France, Samuel de Champlain journeyed to a great lake (later named for him); Etienne Brulé, Robert Cavelier de La Salle, Louis Joliet and Father Jacques Marquette and several others explored much of the midcontinent and down the Great Lakes, the Missouri and the Mississippi rivers all the way to the Gulf of Mexico.

Penetration of the Interior. It was not until the eve of the Revolutionary War that further exploration of the new land took place—by the Spaniards Escalante and Dominguez, the Frenchman La Vérendrye and by the Americans themselves. Farther and farther west they went—a spirited assortment of men: scouts, fur trappers and traders, soldiers, government appointees and prospectors.

First in the hearts of young students of American history is Daniel Boone, the scout who in 1769 led a party through the Cumberland Gap of the Alleghenies into the rich land and hunting grounds of Kentucky. Meriwether Lewis and William Clark were assigned by President Thomas Jefferson to penetrate and explore the 825,000 square miles of the Louisiana Purchase. In 1805 they succeeded in reaching the Pacific Ocean by way of the Columbia River, with the help of the Indian guide Sacajawea (the Bird Woman). Meanwhile Lieutenant Zebulon Pike forayed to the south of Lewis and Clark, his route taking him, in 1806, to the mountain destined to become the most famous in the Rockies—Pikes Peak. That same year, John Colter, the fur trapper and guide, left the Lewis and Clark expedition on its return and, striking off on his own, ventured northward into the Rockies. He became the first white man to see the spectacular geysers and canyons of Yellowstone Park, in 1807.

The Far West. Seventeen years later, trapper James Bridger was the first to gaze upon the Great Salt Lake. In the 1820's, Jedediah Strong Smith explored routes to California, Nevada and Utah, while James Bowie—for whom the bowie knife was named—explored Texas; his exact route is unknown. In the next two decades, the rest of California and much of the Rockies were penetrated. Joseph R. Walker came upon the wonders of the Yosemite Valley waterfalls and rock formations. Benjamin de Bonneville, while not making any outstanding discoveries, wrote an account of his adventures which, edited by Washington Irving, added greatly to the fame of the distant West. Young John Charles Frémont, with his guide Kit Carson, ranged outside of California into Nevada and far northward to the Columbia River.

On horseback, on foot and by boat, these men and others had, by the 1840's, blazed the trails and mapped the routes over which thousands of settlers and fortune-seekers would soon stream westward.

Hawaii. These islands were discovered by the British explorer Captain James Cook on January 18, 1778. He had set sail from England in 1776 and proceeded eastward to New Zealand, then northeast to the Hawaiian Islands. Returning in 1779, Captain Cook was killed by the natives.

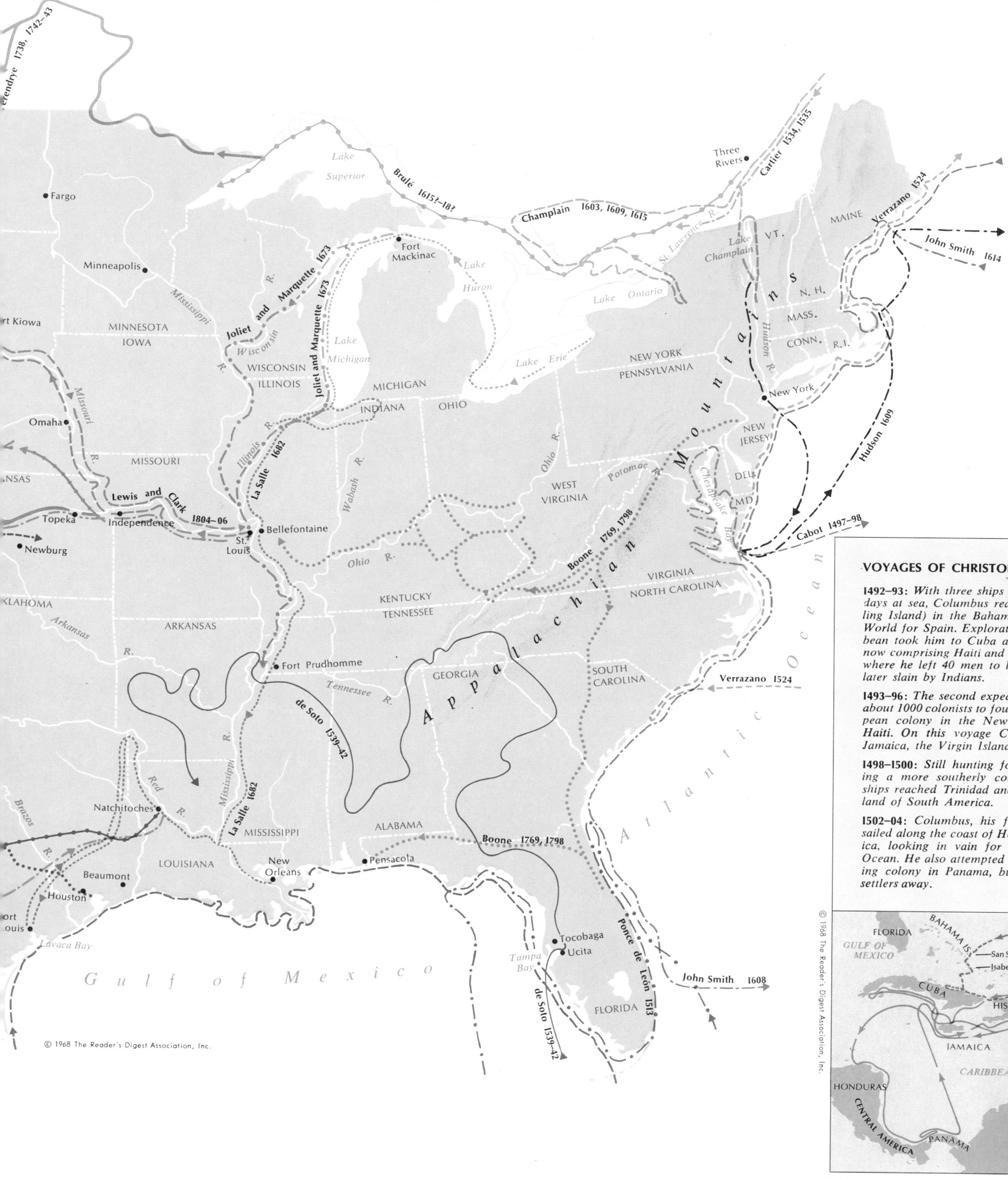

VOYAGES OF CHRISTOPHER COLUMBUS

1492–93: *With three ships and 90 men, and after 70 days at sea, Columbus reached San Salvador (Watling Island) in the Bahamas and claimed the New World for Spain. Exploratory voyages in the Caribbean took him to Cuba and Hispaniola (the island now comprising Haiti and the Dominican Republic), where he left 40 men to look for gold. They were later slain by Indians.*

1493–96: *The second expedition of 17 ships brought about 1000 colonists to found Isabella—the first European colony in the New World—in what is now Haiti. On this voyage Columbus also discovered Jamaica, the Virgin Islands and Puerto Rico.*

1498–1500: *Still hunting for gold, this time following a more southerly course, Columbus with six ships reached Trinidad and Venezuela on the mainland of South America.*

1502–04: *Columbus, his four ships and 150 men, sailed along the coast of Honduras in Central America, looking in vain for a passage to the Indian Ocean. He also attempted to found a gold-prospecting colony in Panama, but the Indians drove the settlers away.*

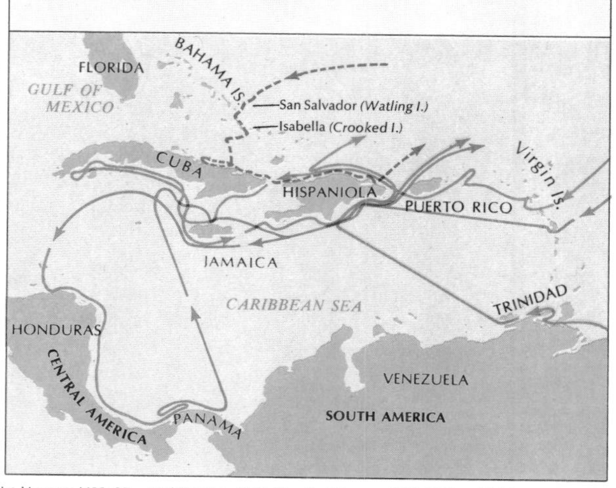

1st Voyage: 1492–93 | 2nd Voyage: 1493–96 | 3rd Voyage: 1498–1500 | 4th Voyage: 1502–04

THE STRUGGLE FOR AMERICA

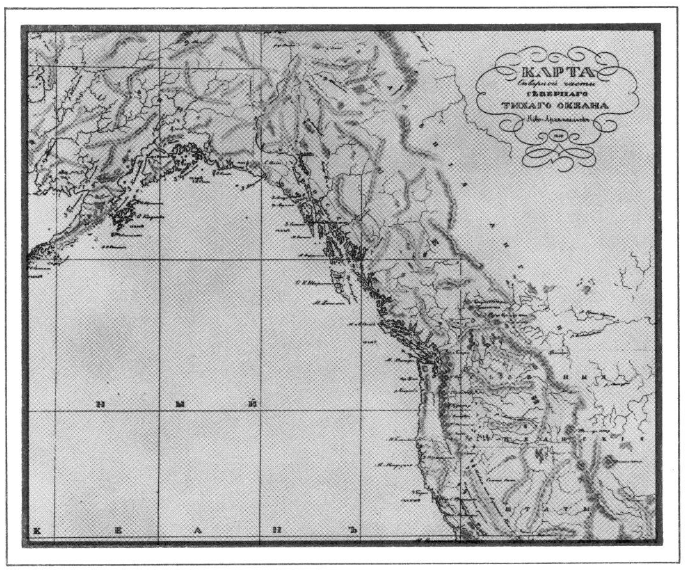

This Russian map, one of a number compiled by Mikhail Teben'kov, was executed in 1849, at New Archangel (Sitka), Alaska, 18 years before the American purchase of the present forty-ninth state. Russian claims, at their height, extended as far south as Fort Ross, near San Francisco.

A famous Dutch map-maker, Jan Jansson, drew the Spanish map (below) in 1623. It portrays the vast territory that the Spaniards of those days considered to be theirs by right of exploration, extending from Florida to "the goodly island" of California.

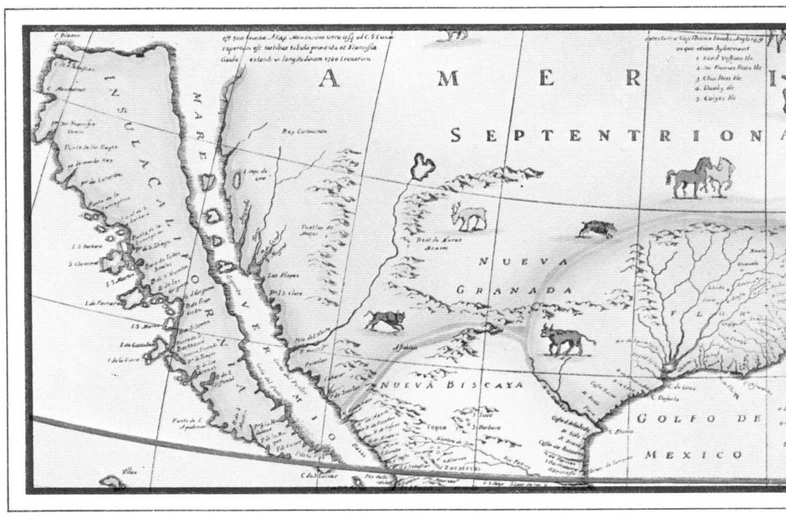

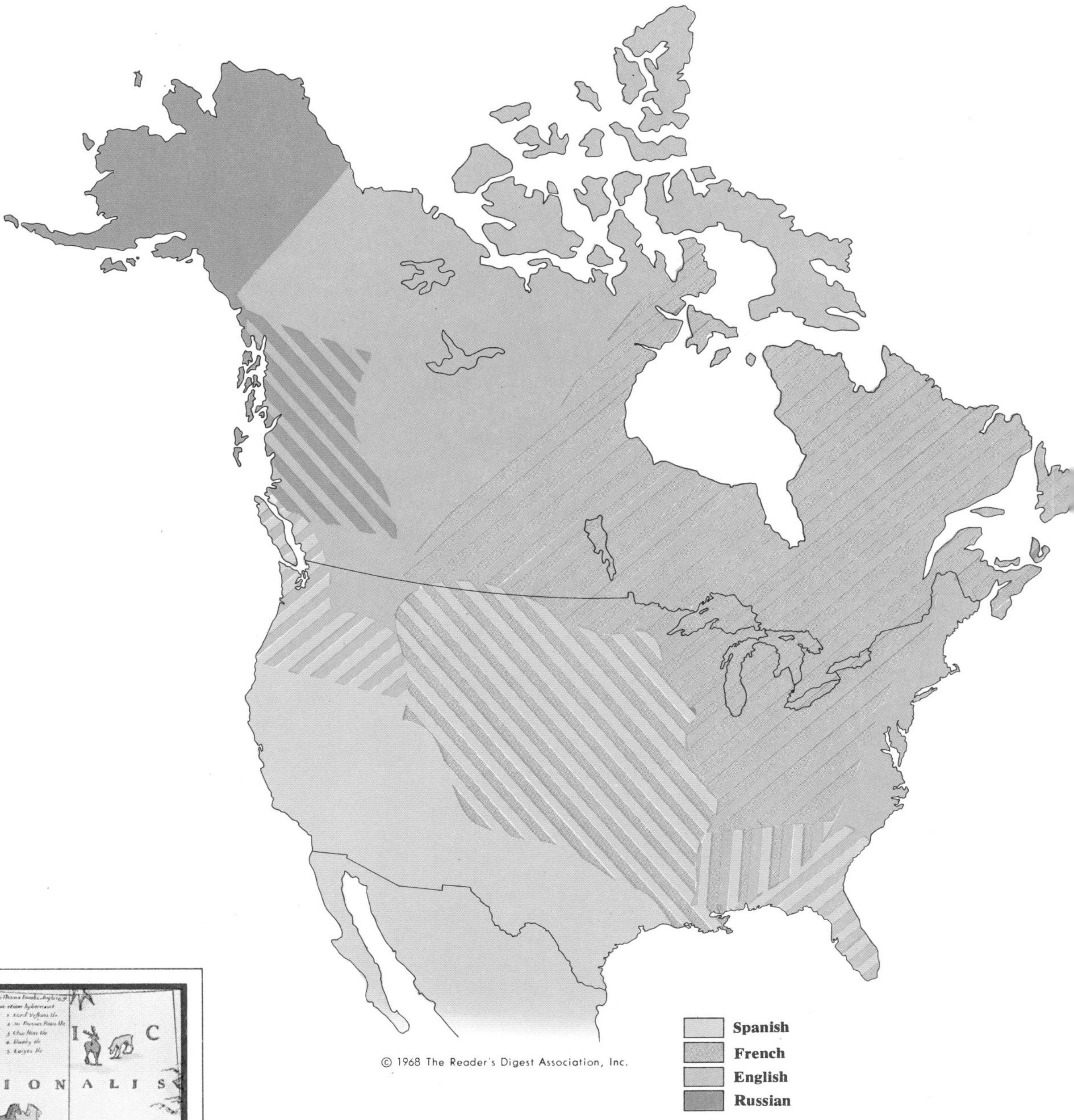

In the dramatic contest between the great European powers for territory on the North American continent, vast sections of land passed from one nation to another as a result of wars and purchases. The diagrammatic map (above) shows the maximum extent of these claims throughout American history. The overlapping of colors demonstrates the loss (or gain) of one country's territory by another. For instance, the original French empire (blue) was finally completely overrun by the claims of other nations. The Swedish and Dutch settlements on the Delaware River and Russia's Fort Ross on the Pacific coast are too small to be shown here.

Spanish Supremacy. The first settlement on the mainland of North America was made by 500 Spanish colonists on the Carolina coast in 1526. It endured for less than a year and its site is unknown. Other short-lived efforts at colonization followed in the mid-1500's, notably in Alabama, on Pensacola Bay in Florida and at Santa Elena, south of Charleston, in South Carolina. The first permanent settlement in the United States was founded by a Spanish naval officer, Pedro Menéndez, at St. Augustine, Florida, in the year 1565.

In their zeal to conquer, colonize and convert, the Spanish built many forts and missions in Florida and along the coast of Georgia and the Carolinas up to the Chesapeake region of Virginia. These missions were established earlier and in greater number than in California.

French Colonies on the Atlantic. The only country bold enough to challenge the might of the Spanish empire was France. In 1562 a group of French Huguenots landed at Port Royal (the former Santa Elena) and erected a fort, Charlesfort, on present-day Parris Island, South Carolina. (The Spanish later built forts also on Parris Island, Fort San Felipe in 1566–67 and Fort San Marcos in 1577–86.) The French colony was beset by trouble and soon abandoned. Another group of Huguenots began a settlement, Fort Caroline, in 1564 near the mouth of the St. Johns River on the east coast of Florida. The following year the Spanish, fearful of French intrusion in the New World, captured Fort Caroline and killed most of its inhabitants. This act was avenged in 1567 when a French expedition descended on San Mateo, as Fort Caroline had been renamed, and wiped out the Spanish garrison. But France's effort to open a southern doorway to the continent was doomed, and it remained for the explorer Samuel de Champlain to launch the vast French empire when he founded Quebec on the St. Lawrence River in 1608.

The English Succeed. England's earliest attempt to gain a foothold in the New World also failed when, in 1585, members of the small settlement established by Sir Walter Raleigh at Roanoke Island, North Carolina, mysteriously vanished. Twenty-two years later, in 1607, another try was made at Jamestown, Virginia. This time the colony of 104 people, after experiencing extreme hardships and difficulties, not only survived but prospered from the growing and curing of tobacco.

Spain had built a flourishing empire in Mexico but had made few efforts to settle the land north of the Rio Grande. In the 1590's the Spanish ventured into what is now New Mexico and established a colony at San Juan, south of Taos (1597). Santa Fe was founded in 1609, the second oldest city in the United States.

The Dutch Venture. One year after Henry Hudson had discovered the Hudson River in 1609, the Dutch introduced a lucrative fur-trading business with the Indians on Manhattan Island (New York City). The colony of New Netherland was officially begun in 1624. It consisted of 30 families as permanent residents and its territory extended from New Amsterdam on Manhattan to Fort Orange (the city of Albany) up the Hudson River.

The immortal band of 102 Pilgrims landed at Plymouth Harbor, Massachusetts (1620). They were followed in 1630 by a large expedition of over 1000 Puritans who arrived in 11 ships and settled on Massachusetts Bay. This was the beginning of the great Puritan migration that brought thousands more to America (1629–40). Another English colony, Maryland, was founded by Lord Baltimore (1634) as a place of refuge from religious intolerance. Other English settlements came to life along the Connecticut River (1635) and in Rhode Island (1636).

Conquest of New Sweden and New Netherland. The Dutch in the meantime had been working to improve and expand their New World holdings. Great feudal land estates called patroonships were granted along the Hudson River to individuals or groups who would bring in 50 persons to settle the land. Extending their interests south to the Delaware River, the Dutch joined with Swedes to build Fort Christiana (now Wilmington, Delaware) in 1638. More small colonies in New Sweden were also established. But friction developed and when the Dutch put up Fort Casimir (New Castle), the Swedes seized it (1654). This action resulted in an armed force of Dutchmen under Peter Stuyvesant of New Amsterdam taking over all of New Sweden in 1655 without a drop of blood being shed.

The same fate soon overcame the Dutch themselves. New Amsterdam in 1664 meekly surrendered to an English naval force. It was renamed New York for Charles II's brother, the Duke of York.

Additional English centers sprang up in North Carolina (1653), New Jersey (1664) and South Carolina (1670). The Quaker William Penn, with a grant from the king,

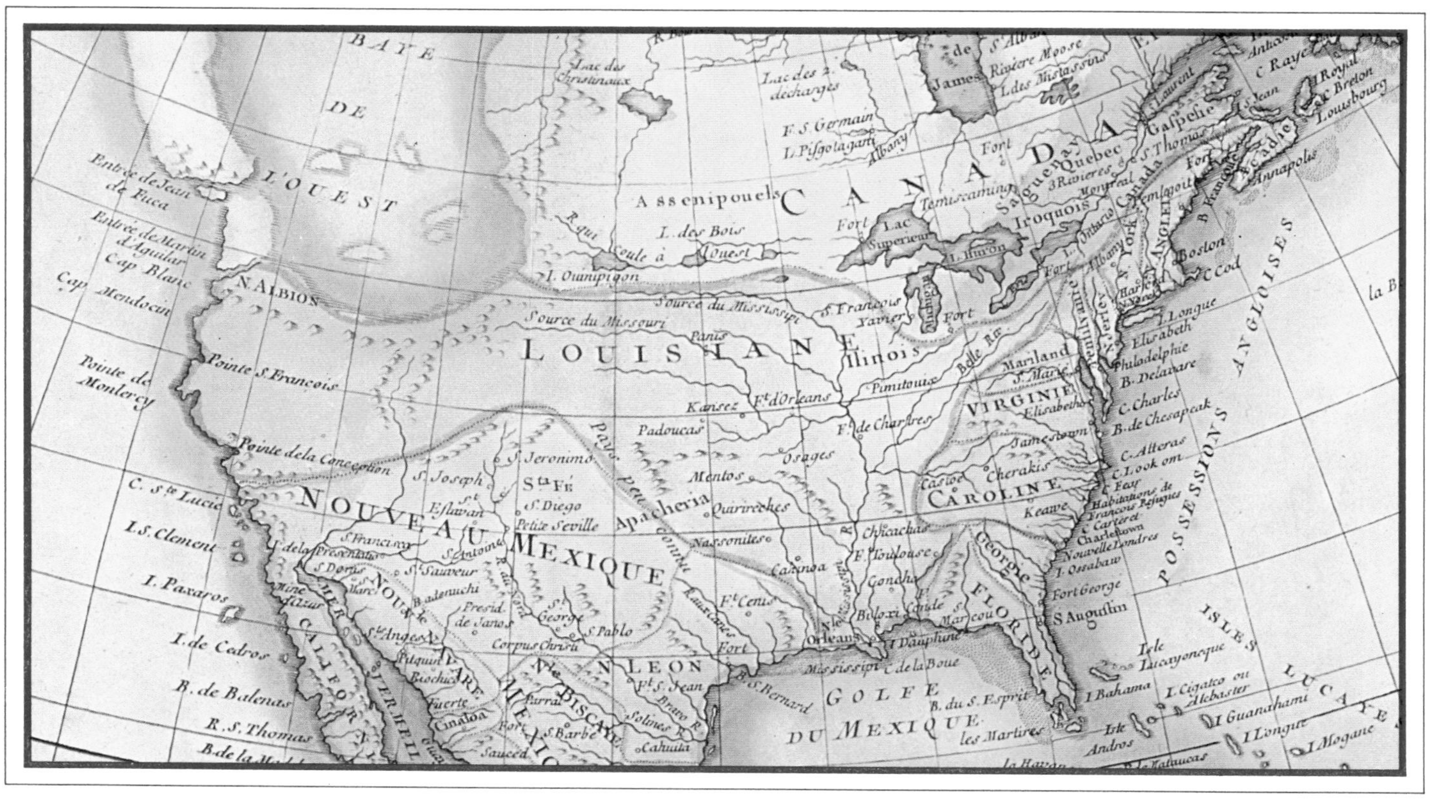

Janvier of Paris gives a false view of French claims in his 1762 map (left) by expanding the Louisiana Territory westward to the Pacific Ocean, which French overland explorers never reached. An interesting area is a mythical "Western Bay" (Baye de l'Ouest).

Drawn by Justin Sanckerts of Amsterdam, the map below shows Dutch-owned New Netherland running from Manhattan to Fort Orange (Albany); and New Sweden occupying a small area on the Delaware River. The inset illustration (lower right) is a scene of New Amsterdam (New York). By 1683, when this map was issued, Dutch and Swedish claims had been absorbed by the English.

Issued in 1763, this official British map (below) marks the new boundaries resulting from the defeat of France and Spain in the Seven Years' War. The area west of the Allegheny Mountains, lettered Lands Reserved for the Indians, *was a controversial section where colonists were prohibited from settling or hunting.*

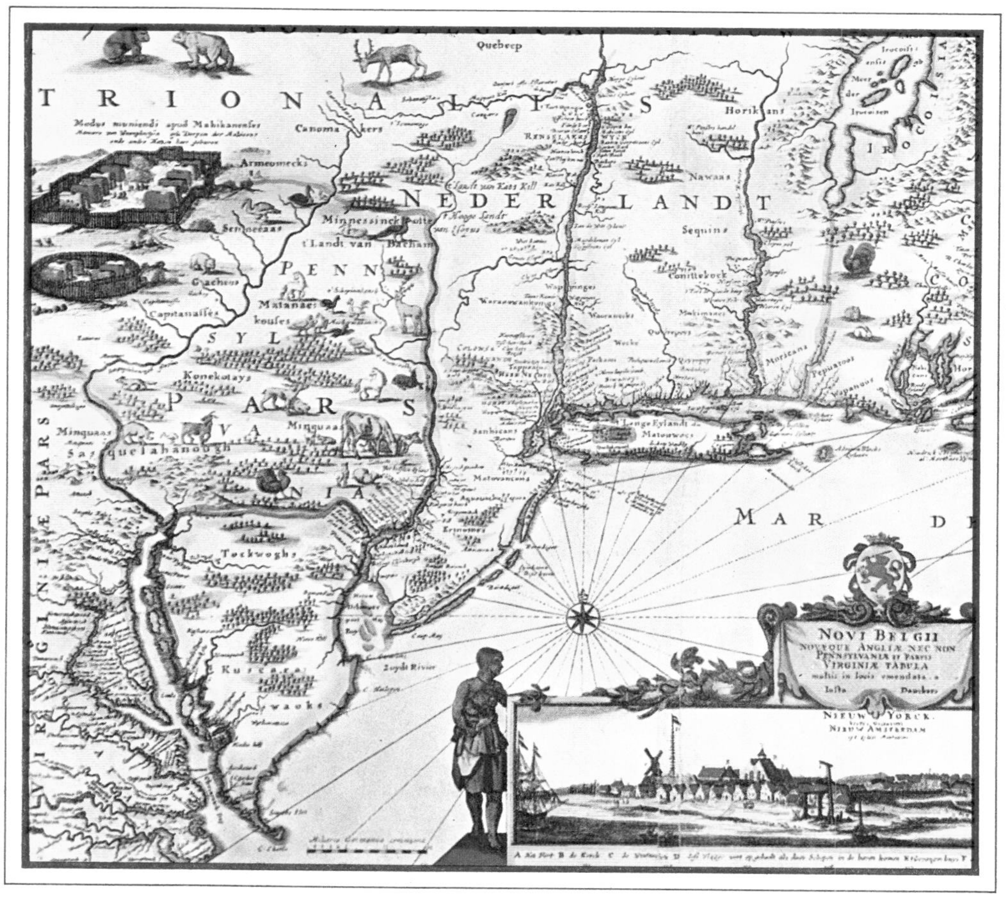

founded a colony on the Delaware in 1681. It became one of the wealthiest and most populated.

The Thirteenth Colony. Trouble broke out between the English and the Spanish in South Carolina when Stuart Town (Port Royal) was wiped out by a Spanish force from St. Augustine in 1686. Militia from South Carolina in turn captured St. Augustine (1702). Charles Town (Charleston) was attacked in 1706 by the French and Spanish fleets during Queen Anne's War. To protect South Carolina, the English established their last colony, Georgia, in 1733.

The 13 English colonies—11 by settlement and two by conquest—stretched from present-day Maine to Georgia. (The total population swelled from 4646 persons in 1630 to 250,888 in 1700.) There was little chance for territorial expansion because of the French, whose great empire took in the entire region of the Great Lakes and the St. Lawrence Valley on the north and extended down the Mississippi River to the Gulf of Mexico on the west with settlements and fortifications at such places as Detroit, Pittsburgh, St. Louis, New Orleans and Biloxi.

Armed skirmishes between the French and English were inevitable and finally a series of bitter wars broke out (1689–1763). By 1750 the population of the English colonies had grown to 1,170,760 while the French had a total of 80,000 people. After a series of reverses, the British launched an invasion of Canada which resulted in the capture of Quebec (1759). This brought about the complete downfall of France's American empire. By the Treaty of Paris (1763), France ceded Canada and all land east of the Mississippi, except New Orleans, to England. Her territory west of the Mississippi and New Orleans went to Spain. The Spanish bartered away Florida to Britain in exchange for Cuba, which the British had held since their capture of Havana in 1762.

Changes were rapidly developing within the English colonies themselves. Their relationship with the mother country, strained as it was over matters of taxes and restrictions, worsened. In 1775, the American Revolution broke out in all its fury, ending with the establishment of the United States as an independent nation.

The decline of Spain's far-flung American empire soon followed. She ceded all the land from the Mississippi River westward to the Rocky Mountains, known as the Louisiana Territory, to Napoleon, Emperor of France. Napoleon, in turn, sold the vast territory to the United States for $14,500,000 in 1803. The United States also succeeded in procuring Florida, which had been returned by England to Spain in 1783.

The Russians Arrive. Still another nation reached out for possessions on the North American continent during the eighteenth century. In 1784, the first Russian settlement was made in Alaska at Three Saints Bay on Kodiak Island, with a second at New Archangel (Sitka) in 1799. Russian fur traders seeking the sea otter had been busy in the region for some time. They now began to push southward down the coast, establishing trading posts as they went.

The Spanish, who believed that they held title to the entire Pacific coastal area of America, became alarmed by the Russian activity. Entrenched in Lower California since 1679, the Spaniards had ignored Upper California, and it was thought to be an island (see Spanish map, opposite page). During the last half of the 1700's and the early 1800's, Spain moved northward, founding San Diego and setting up a chain of missions in Upper California as a bulwark against Russian enroachment. The Russians continued to advance and by 1805 had reached California itself. In 1816 they erected a trading post and fortress named Rossiya (Fort Ross) a hundred miles north of the port of San Francisco. To counter this move, Spain built her last and northernmost mission, San Francisco de Solano at Sonoma, just south of the menacing cannon of the Muscovite Rossiya.

No armed clashes developed, however. The Russian southward drive had reached its high point. With a falling-off of her fur trading and lack of interest on the part of the home government, her California adventure faded. Rossiya was finally given up in 1841 and sold for $30,000 to John Sutter who lived in Mexican California.

Spain, too, began to go into an eclipse. Her western lands were lost first to Mexico in the Revolution of 1821 and by Mexico to the United States in the Mexican War of 1846–47 (see page 88). Then Russia's New World sovereignty vanished completely when, in 1867, Alaska was bought by the United States for less than two cents an acre.

Following Russia's withdrawal, the last episode in the dramatic contest for America took place in faraway Hawaii. Although it had been a constitutional monarchy since 1840, Hawaii became a republic when its queen was deposed in 1893. Seven years later, the tropical land joined the United States as a territory. More than three centuries of struggle had come to an end.

THE INDIAN PEOPLES

An estimated one million Indians were living in what is now the United States (including Alaska) when the first white settlers stepped ashore on the North American continent in the early 1500's. Although these Indians may have all originally belonged to one great race with a common Asian background, they had nothing even faintly resembling a single basic language. More than 200 languages were spoken, each with many dialects.

The various language stocks are shown in different colors on the map below. Of these, the principal families are:

The Algonquians. About the year 1500, the eastern branch of the Algonquians, the Forest Dwellers, were living in bark or thatch-covered huts. A trusting, peace-loving people, the Algonquians were ultimately driven by the Iroquois out of the territory that is central New York. Pocahantas, King Philip, Tecumseh and Pontiac belonged to the Algonquian family.

The western Algonquians, the Plainsmen, were the great buffalo hunters. They followed the herds first on foot, later on horses, frequently stampeding them over cliffs.

The Iroquois. Organized as the Confederation of Five Nations, the Iroquois included the Mohawk, Seneca, Onondaga, Oneida and Cayuga tribes. They not only engaged in devastating war against the Algonquians, but by 1660 they had virtually exterminated three tribes of their own family—the Hurons, the Eries and the Susquehannas. The Iroquois built barrel-roofed dwellings, the famous Long House, which sheltered many families. Each tribe was divided into clans with all children belonging to the mother's branch. In 1722, the Tuscaroras joined the other tribes, forming the Six Nations.

The Caddos. The Pawnees, an outstanding tribe in this family group, were hunters of the buffalo, like the Algonquian Plainsmen. The Pawnees worshiped the sun and the stars with elaborate ritual and ceremonies. Their priests exerted great power, surpassing that of the chiefs. Of all the North American Indian tribes the Pawnees were one of the very few to practice human sacrifice—each year an Indian girl, captured from another tribe, was killed in tribute to the Morning Star. The Wichitas and the Arikaras also belonged to the Caddoan family, as did the Caddo tribe itself.

The Muskhogeans. This group came from the southeast and included the Choctaw, Chickasaw and Creek. Not a warlike people, they proved helpful to the Spanish, French and English explorers because of their interest in farming, but they received deplorable treatment in return.

The Cherokee, although a member politically of this family, were linguistically allied to the Iroquois. In the early 1880's, a Cherokee, Sequoia, created the first North American Indian written language. Earlier the Plains Indians and others used picture-writing as a means of communication.

The Sioux. The life of these proud, marauding people, who made up the largest group of Plains Indians, centered around the buffalo and the horse. Horse-stealing was regarded as one of the manliest of accomplishments. Many tribes belonged to the Sioux family: the Assiniboin; the Crows; the Iowa; the Kansa; the Mandan; the Osage; the Quapaw; the Winnebago, and the Sioux itself. Chiefs Sitting Bull and Crazy Horse were Sioux.

The Na-Dénés. This widely scattered family includes the Tlingits of southern Alaska, the Apaches and the Navahos of the Southwest. People of the waterways, the Tlingits lived primarily on fish and sea mammals and traveled by dugout canoe. Their houses were large, highly decorated multifamily dwellings made of planks. Tlingit craftsmen carved giant totem poles to commemorate events or achievements, and executed elaborate masks. Their society was marked by social classes and hereditary slavery. The hardy Apaches were notorious raiders, first against Pueblo villages, then against the Spanish. The Navahos also preyed upon the Pueblo Indians, but learned from their victims to weave and till the soil. Spanish missionaries taught the Navahos how to raise sheep, which led to their noted craft—the production of remarkable geometrically designed blankets. Later they added superb silversmithing to their accomplishments.

The Uto-Aztecan, Kiowa-Tanoan, Keresan and Zunian families. Many of these relatively peaceful pueblo dwellers were the most thoroughgoing farmers among the Indians of the United States. Unlike all others in this country, they wore clothes made of cotton. Their principal art consisted of textiles, pottery with striking designs, fine murals and sand paintings. The famous Indian woman Sacajawea, the guide for Lewis and Clark on their expedition into the West, was a member of the Shoshoni, a branch of the Uto-Aztecan tribe.

Tecumseh,
the Shawnee chief

Chief Joseph of the Nez Percé
(see page 86)

Sitting Bull, influential
Sioux medicine man

Geronimo, the Apache chief
(see page 86)

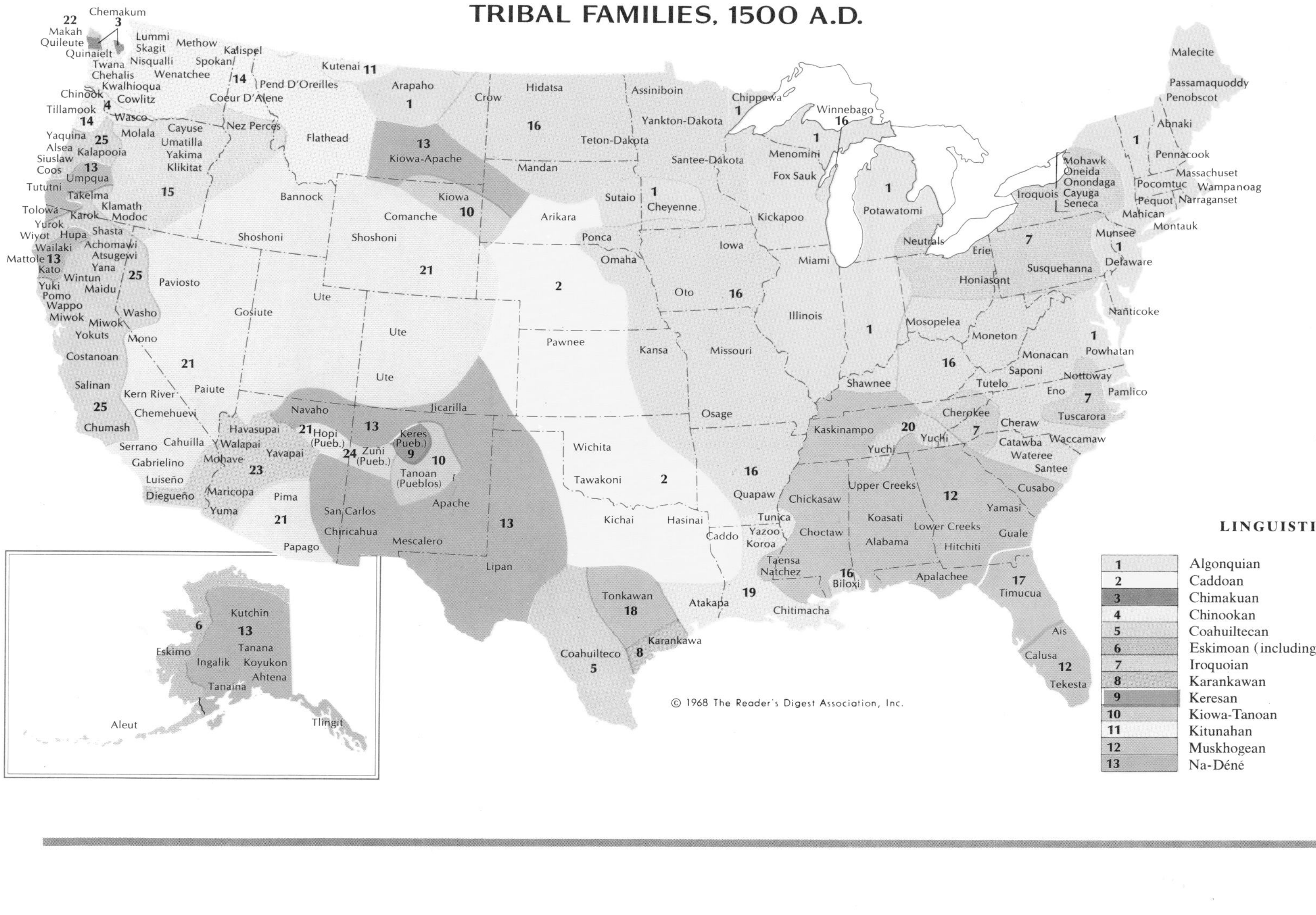

LINGUISTIC STOCKS

1	Algonquian	14	Salishan
2	Caddoan	15	Shapwailutan
3	Chimakuan	16	Siouan
4	Chinookan	17	Timucuan
5	Coahuiltecan	18	Tonkawan
6	Eskimoan (including Aleut)	19	Tunican
7	Iroquoian	20	Uchean
8	Karankawan	21	Uto-Aztecan
9	Keresan	22	Wakashan
10	Kiowa-Tanoan	23	Yuman
11	Kitunahan	24	Zuñian
12	Muskhogean		
13	Na-Déné	25	Small linguistic groups of California and Oregon

THE COLONISTS AND THE INDIANS

The successful founding of the 13 colonies was due, in large part, to the defeat of the Spanish Armada by the English in 1588. The victory left Britain in full command of the North Atlantic, able to furnish her settlements with supplies and with colonists.

There was no lack of people willing to make the grueling six- to eight-week voyage to the New World, even though only three out of four, on the average, survived. Possibly the greatest incentive was the burning desire for freedom of worship, which was denied in the homeland. Also, England in the early 1600's was plagued with unemployment. Much of the land had been taken over for the profitable raising of wool. With the farms turned into pastures for the grazing of sheep, thousands of tenant farmers and their families roamed the countryside, homeless and hungry. To them America was not only a land of opportunity but a God-sent haven.

Some of the early colonists were fleeing political oppression. Others boarded the crowded sailing vessels in the hope of bettering their lot in life by acquiring property in the distant land and thus elevating themselves into the privileged freeman class. Still others were adventurers, seekers of gold and persons fleeing from the law.

A great many emigrants were unable to pay for their passage and became indentured servants, voluntarily mortgaging themselves to work without pay, usually from four to seven years, before being granted freedom from their masters. There were also those who were kidnaped and sent to the colonies by force, to be sold as indentured servants to the highest bidders. Convicts were shipped out by the English government, as well as orphans, vagrants and other public charges. Troublesome Scotch and Irish prisoners of war were disposed of in the same way.

A large segment of the colonial population was made up of Negroes brought by slave traders from the Gold Coast and adjacent regions of West Africa. During the first half of the seventeenth century Negroes were treated the same as white indentured servants, and were freed after a period of years. This was changed in 1661, when the Virginia Assembly ruled that Negroes were to be regarded as "perpetual servants." Other states enacted similar laws resulting in permanent bondage.

Settlers came from many non-English nations, especially from Germany, where unemployment was high. Scotch-Irish emigrants from northern Ireland swelled the list, as did Lowlanders and Highlanders from Scotland and Protestant Huguenots from France. In 1610 just 350 persons were in the English colonies. In 1620, this had increased to 2302; in 1630 to 4646; in 1640 to 26,643; in 1650 to 50,386; and by 1780 almost three million inhabited the 13 colonies.

Government. There were basically three types of English colonies: a corporate colony, organized by a joint-stock company to do business in the New World (a variation of this was the Massachusetts Bay Colony which was a trading corporation run as a religious commonwealth); a proprietary colony, administered by one or more men; and a royal colony with its governor and officials appointed by the king. With the exception of Maryland, Pennsylvania and Delaware, which remained proprietary colonies, and Rhode Island and Connecticut, which evolved into self-governing ones, all the others ended up as royal colonies.

Separated from the mother country by the broad Atlantic, the various settlements soon developed forms of self-government, beginning with Virginia's representative House of Burgesses. The right of voting was given only to the property owners; women, slaves, indentured servants and tenant farmers were excluded.

Early Conflicts. The English settlers, under constant menace of Indian attack, soon adopted the militia system, which required every able-bodied man to bear arms in home defense. This proved effective in combating isolated Indian raids as well as widespread hostilities such as the Pequot War of 1636–37, when Indians of that tribe attempted to wipe out the New England colonies.

The settlers were faced with another and bloodier Indian uprising in 1673. Called King Philip's War after the name of the Indian chieftain, the conflict required the combined efforts of militia units from the colonies of Massachusetts Bay, Connecticut and Plymouth to contain the rampaging natives. Forty of the 90 New England towns were attacked, 12 of them were burned, and the lives of almost 1000 colonists out of a total New England population of 50,000 persons were lost.

From 1689 to 1755 the people of the English colonies were engaged in a series of skirmishes and battles with the French—echoes of thunderous clashes overseas between the two great European powers, France and England. Indians, frequently led by Frenchmen, raided towns in New England. Schenectady was put to the torch in 1690 and Deerfield, Massachusetts, endured a gruesome massacre in 1704. Troops from Massachusetts, New Hampshire and Connecticut captured the French stronghold of Fort Louisbourg on Cape Breton Island, Nova Scotia, in 1745. It was returned, but the British gained territory in eastern Canada, and an even greater struggle loomed.

FRENCH AND INDIAN WAR, 1755-63

(Numbers indicate positions on map at lower right)

In 1749 the French began to build a chain of forts across Pennsylvania to block English colonial traders and settlers. In answer the British dispatched General Edward Braddock to capture the key French defense post Fort Duquesne, erected in 1753 on the site of the present city of Pittsburgh. While Braddock was en route, British forces captured Fort Beauséjour (**1**) in Nova Scotia from the French, June 16, 1755.

Less than a month later, on July 9, 1755, Braddock's army of 2000 had advanced to within seven miles of Fort Duquesne (**2**) where it was ambushed by a small French force of less than 1000 men, predominantly Indian. Braddock himself was killed, and two thirds of his army wiped out. A young colonel of the Virginia militia named George Washington and other members of Braddock's colonial detachment, all trained in frontier fighting, covered the retreat of the survivors.

The effect of Braddock's defeat was heightened when the French, under the leadership of the brilliant Marquis de Montcalm, swept down from Montreal to overrun the British fort of Oswego (**3**) on Lake Ontario on August 14, 1756. In June of the next year Montcalm began another successful offensive from Ticonderoga on Fort William Henry (**4**). Already in control of western New York, the French now had mastery over the entire Lake Champlain territory as well.

Despite this superiority, the fortunes of war began to turn. On July 26, 1758, British sea and land units under Lord Jeffrey Amherst were dispatched to Nova Scotia and captured Louisbourg (**5**). This was followed by the conquest of Fort Frontenac (**6**) on Lake Ontario in August 1758, by an army of British and colonial troops from Albany. On November 25, 1758, an English force took Fort Duquesne (**7**), which Braddock had failed to do three years earlier. Still another victory fell to the British with the seizure of Fort Niagara (**8**) in July.

The most significant engagement of the entire war was about to begin. British General James Wolfe had been laying siege to the French city of Quebec for most of the summer. On September 13, 1759, he launched a surprise attack on the garrison, commanded by Montcalm (**9**). Wolfe was killed in the ensuing struggle, as was Montcalm, but victory went to the British. The following year, 1760, Montreal (**10**) surrendered. And, in 1763, when the war officially ended, Britain possessed practically all of the French territory in North America.

It was a staggering conclusion to the war, one in which the American militiaman had played a vital part. Yet his greatest battles were to come, for within 16 years the colonist-soldier was facing up to a new conflict, his most important one—the Revolution.

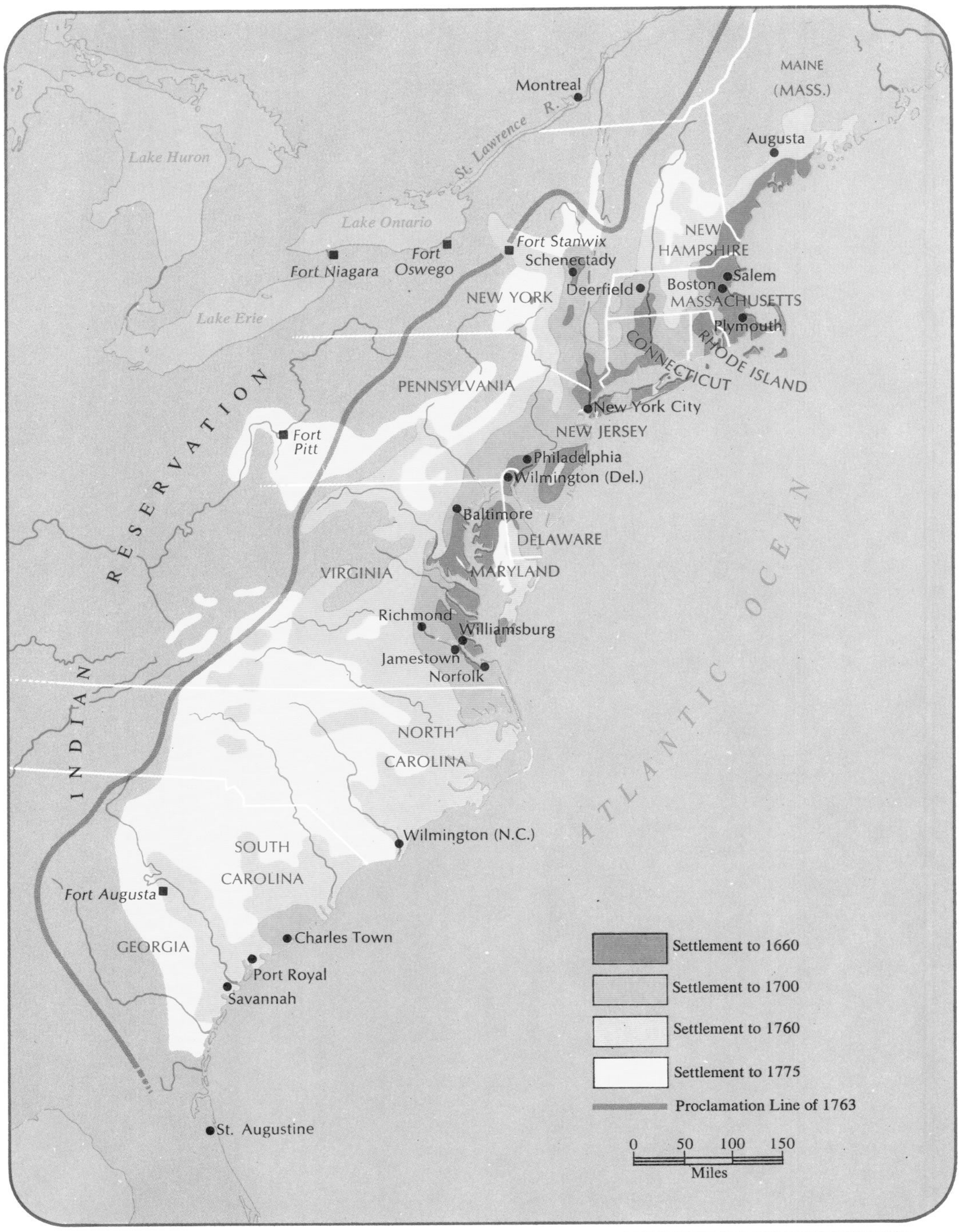

POPULATION DISTRIBUTION, 1790

	Total Population	English	Scotch	Scotch-Irish and Irish	German	Dutch	French	Swedish	Negro	Other
Maine (Mass.)	96,540	59.6%	4.5%	11.6%	1.3%	0.1%	1.3%	0.0%	0.6%	21.0%
New Hampshire	141,885	60.5	6.2	7.5	0.4	0.1	0.7	0.0	0.6	24.0
Vermont	85,425	75.7	5.1	5.1	0.2	0.6	0.4	0.0	0.3	12.6
Massachusetts	378,787	80.9	4.3	3.8	0.3	0.2	0.8	0.0	1.4	8.3
Rhode Island	68,825	66.5	5.4	2.6	0.5	0.4	0.7	0.1	6.4	17.4
Connecticut	237,946	65.5	2.1	2.8	0.3	0.3	0.9	0.0	2.3	25.8
New York	340,120	47.9	6.5	7.5	7.6	16.2	3.5	0.5	7.6	2.7
New Jersey	184,139	43.4	7.1	8.8	8.5	15.3	2.2	3.6	7.7	3.4
Pennsylvania	434,373	34.3	8.4	14.2	32.5	1.8	1.8	0.8	2.4	3.8
Delaware	59,096	39.0	6.3	9.2	0.9	3.4	1.3	7.0	21.6	11.3
Maryland	319,728	42.2	5.0	8.0	7.6	0.3	0.8	0.3	34.7	1.1
Virginia and West Virginia	747,610	40.7	6.0	6.9	3.7	0.2	0.7	0.4	40.9	0.5
North Carolina	393,751	48.4	10.8	8.1	3.4	0.2	1.2	0.1	26.9	0.9
South Carolina	249,073	33.9	8.5	7.8	2.8	0.2	2.2	0.1	43.7	0.8
Georgia	82,548	36.7	9.9	9.8	4.8	0.1	1.5	0.4	35.9	0.7
Kentucky and Tennessee	109.368	49.3	8.5	10.4	11.9	1.1	1.9	0.4	14.9	1.6
Total Population	3,929,214	49.2%	6.7%	7.8%	7.0%	2.7%	1.4%	0.6%	19.3%	5.3%

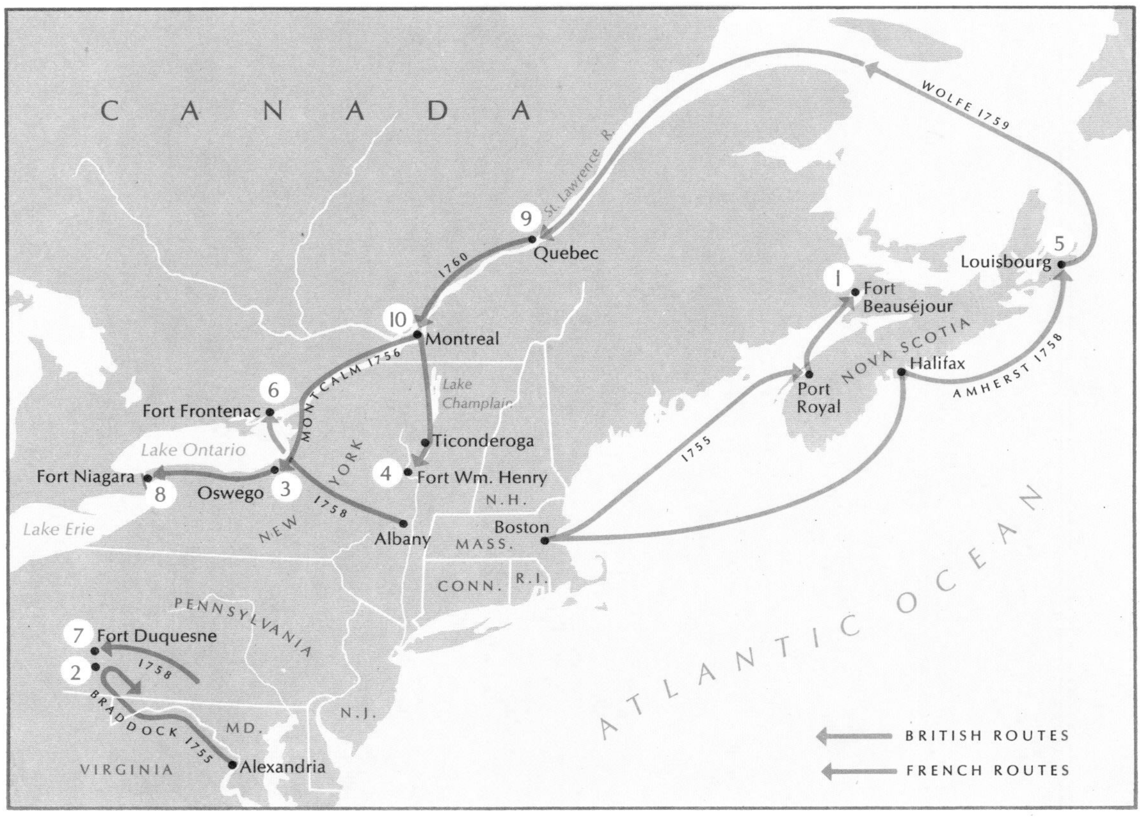

THE AMERICAN REVOLUTION

In Boston, "the cradle of liberty," the fuse to the War of Independence was lit. It was the scene of the "massacre" of 1770 when British soldiers fired into a crowd of hostile civilians, killing five; the place where in 1773 a shipload of English tea was dumped into the harbor at the famous "tea party" protest against the import tax. And it was from Boston that Lieutenant General Thomas Gage sent out a force of some 800 British soldiers on the night of April 18, 1775, to seize rebel military supplies at Concord, Massachusetts.

1775

The following morning, April 19, members of the local militia, forewarned by patriot Paul Revere, clashed with the British at Lexington (**1**, see map). "Here once the embattled farmers stood," wrote the poet Ralph Waldo Emerson, "And fired the shot heard round the world." Eight minutemen were killed in the brief engagement. The British column continued on to Concord (**2**), where arms and ammunition were seized and destroyed. When the British began their return march to Boston, they ran into a hornet's nest of opposition from the aroused colonists along the countryside. The rebels had inflicted heavy casualties on the British before the remnant of the force could finally gain the safety of Boston.

Soon angry patriots from all the New England colonies headed for Boston. An army of 16,000, mostly untrained and undisciplined, took up positions around the city.

While the siege of Boston continued, the second major incident of the war took place. Colonel Benedict Arnold and Colonel Ethan Allen with a small group of Green Mountain Boys attacked and overran Fort Ticonderoga (**3**), the strategic British stronghold on Lake Champlain, on May 10. There the rebels captured military supplies and more than 100 cannons. Two days later the patriots occupied Crown Point (**4**), which the British had evacuated.

The rebellion was now rapidly spreading throughout the country as royal local governments were overthrown, one after another. The Second Continental Congress, which met in Philadelphia, voted on June 14, to recruit ten companies of riflemen for the defense of the colonies. The following day the legislators appointed forty-three-year-old George Washington commander in chief of "all the Continental forces, raised or to be raised."

General Washington's task was prodigious and immediate. In a plan to tighten the siege of Boston, Washington had his men occupy and fortify Breed's Hill and Bunker Hill, which overlooked the city. On June 17, 2500 British army regulars commanded by General Howe left Boston under orders to clear the Americans from their position (**5**). It required three massive assaults by the redcoats to dislodge the 1200 fighting Americans, but only after the enemy had suffered the crippling loss of over 1000 dead and wounded. The British, shaken and dismayed, fell back to their Boston base and the siege continued.

In the autumn of 1775, American forces initiated an audacious offensive against the British fortifications in Canada. One army of more than 1000 men under the command of Colonel Arnold advanced through the northern wilderness toward Quebec City (**6**), Britain's key Canadian base. A second army of 2000 under General Richard Montgomery struck up through Lake Champlain to conquer Montreal (**7**) on November 13, then moved on to make contact with Arnold's army close to Quebec. The united American forces launched an all-out attack on the Canadian city which lasted for two days, December 30–31, 1775. In a desperate battle, the British garrison of 1800 repulsed the Americans who suffered heavy losses. General Montgomery was killed and Colonel Arnold severely wounded. The American army withdrew and put Quebec under siege for the remainder of the winter.

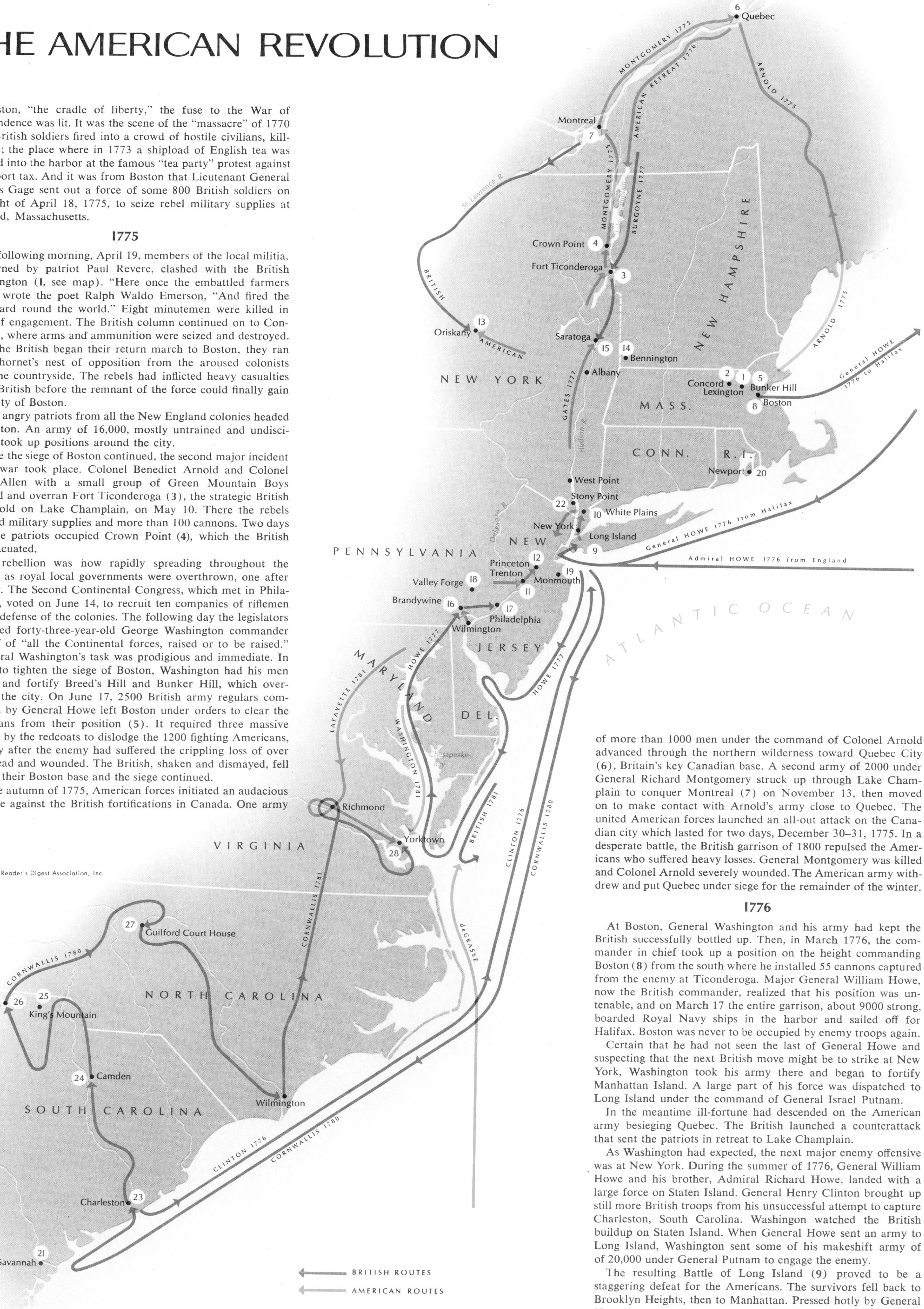

1776

At Boston, General Washington and his army had kept the British successfully bottled up. Then, in March 1776, the commander in chief took up a position on the height commanding Boston (**8**) from the south where he installed 55 cannons captured from the enemy at Ticonderoga. Major General William Howe, now the British commander, realized that his position was untenable, and on March 17 the entire garrison, about 9000 strong, boarded Royal Navy ships in the harbor and sailed off for Halifax. Boston was never to be occupied by enemy troops again.

Certain that he had not seen the last of General Howe and suspecting that the next British move might be to strike at New York, Washington took his army there and began to fortify Manhattan Island. A large part of his force was dispatched to Long Island under the command of General Israel Putnam.

In the meantime ill-fortune had descended on the American army besieging Quebec. The British launched a counterattack that sent the patriots in retreat to Lake Champlain.

As Washington had expected, the next major enemy offensive was at New York. During the summer of 1776, General William Howe and his brother, Admiral Richard Howe, landed with a large force on Staten Island. General Henry Clinton brought up still more British troops from his unsuccessful attempt to capture Charleston, South Carolina. Washington watched the British buildup on Staten Island. When General Howe sent an army to Long Island, Washington sent some of his makeshift army of 20,000 under General Putnam to engage the enemy.

The resulting Battle of Long Island (**9**) proved to be a staggering defeat for the Americans. The survivors fell back to Brooklyn Heights, then to Manhattan. Pressed hotly by General Howe's troops, the Americans, with Washington in charge, retreated to White Plains. After a hard-fought engagement there (**10**), Washington led his decimated army across the Hudson River into New Jersey. To add to the American commander in chief's troubles, 5000 British reinforcements led by Major General Charles Cornwallis had landed near Fort Lee, New Jersey. Washington and his men finally slipped into Pennsylvania, where the coming of winter stopped pursuit.

The American leader now had about 8000 poorly clothed and underfed Continental regulars. The morale of the country was extremely low. Even Washington himself was so pessimistic that on December 20, 1776, he wrote the Congress that the Army would cease to exist in ten more days. Then, on Christmas night, 1776, the American leader made a desperate effort to raise the hopes of the people by giving them a victory. Washington crossed the ice-clogged Delaware River with his slim force and attacked the British garrison at Trenton, New Jersey (**11**). The enemy was taken completely by surprise, and the Americans captured over 1500 prisoners. The success was followed by another at Princeton (**12**) one week later. The triumphs thrilled the country and restored its fighting spirit.

1777–79

To the north a victory of major proportions for the American cause was in the making. Lieutenant General John Burgoyne, in command of a British army in Canada, advanced southward through the Lake Champlain district to overrun Ticonderoga on June 27, 1777. As the British continued in the direction of Albany, American resistance was gathering strength. Washington dispatched troops he could not afford to spare in order to bolster the forces of Major General Horatio Gates, the new commander of the northern army. After a series of fierce battles and skirmishes, notably at Oriskany, New York (**13**) and at Bennington (**14**), the British force was soundly defeated in the Battle of Saratoga (**15**) on October 17, 1777. General Burgoyne surrendered his army of 5000 men and all of their equipment and supplies.

The success put new life into the discouraged patriots and brought about the entry of France into the war on the side of the Americans. Yet ultimate victory was still far away. General Washington's attempt at Brandywine (**16**) to block General Howe's advance on Philadelphia (**17**) failed, and that city was occupied by the British. Again American morale dipped, and the winter of 1777–78, which Washington and his army spent at Valley Forge (**18**), was one of extreme privation and hardship. Nor did the coming of spring bring a change for the better. An attack by an American force on the British army which was then evacuating Philadelphia was repulsed at the Battle of Monmouth (**19**) on June 28, 1778, and a combined American and French assault on British-held Newport, Rhode Island (**20**), in mid-August turned into a fiasco. The enemy ended the year with another triumph, the capture of Savannah, Georgia (**21**), on December 29, 1778.

The American fortunes of war at last began to swing the other way. Lieutenant Colonel George Rogers Clark climaxed his campaign against British-held posts in the Northwest by the capture of Fort Vincennes, February 25, 1779. And the enemy seizure of Stony Point (**22**) on the Hudson River, May 31, 1779, was nullified when General "Mad Anthony" Wayne at the head of a group of patriots retook the fort in a wild bayonet charge.

The country was further electrified by the sensational naval victory of Captain John Paul Jones, who had been harassing the British Navy unmercifully. On September 23, 1779, aboard his ship, the *Bonhomme Richard,* Captain Jones defeated the enemy man-of-war, H.M.S. *Serapis* off the coast of England.

1780–81

The main theater of war in America now shifted to the South. There British troops seized Charleston, South Carolina (**23**), on May 12, 1780, and routed General Gates's army at Camden, South Carolina (**24**), August 16, 1780. (In the North, only the fortunate interception of the British spy Major John André prevented the traitorous Benedict Arnold from delivering the New York stronghold of West Point to the enemy in the fall of 1780.) American guerrilla bands of riflemen turned the tide in the South by fighting a successful delaying action at King's Mountain, South Carolina (**25**), on October 7, 1780. General Nathanael Greene, the officer Washington had put in command of the southern armies, began a concerted drive against the forces of Cornwallis. The British were defeated at Cowpens, South Carolina (**26**), January 17, 1781, and at Guilford Court House, North Carolina (**27**), March 15, 1781.

Events now brought the war to a swift climax. Cornwallis withdrew to Wilmington, North Carolina, then north into Virginia. Near Richmond he parried an attack by an army commanded by Lafayette and proceeded to Yorktown (**28**) on Chesapeake Bay. The help he hoped to get from the British Navy was cut off by the arrival of a superior French naval fleet under the command of Admiral François de Grasse in Chesapeake Bay. Cornered by a concentration of more than 17,000 American and French troops under Washington, the situation soon proved hopeless for Cornwallis and his 8000 men, and, on October 19, 1781, the British general surrendered.

The long struggle was finally over. After six and a half years the 13 colonies had become the free and independent United States of America.

Two years later, on November 2, 1783, Congress ordered the Continental Army disbanded. In 1784, because of trouble with the Indians, the Government authorized the raising of 700 untrained militia to garrison the western posts. In 1794 when farmers in Pennsylvania revolted against a Federal tax on whiskey, 13,000 militiamen were called into service. The "Whiskey Rebellion" was quickly put down.

Federal troops were called out again in 1799 to quell another emergency in Pennsylvania—this one over a tax on property. Despite these disturbances, the enrollment in the Regular Army remained at less than 7000 men until the War of 1812.

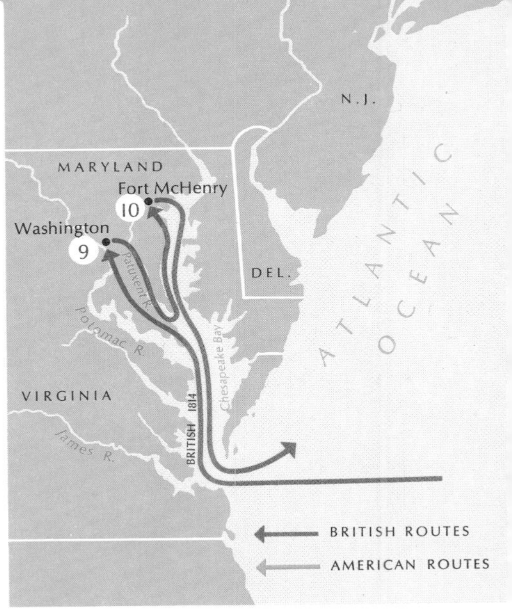

WAR OF 1812

This conflict has been called "The Second War for American Independence." There were a number of reasons for its outbreak—the seizure of American ships and cargoes by the British; the impressment of American sailors to serve on British ships; the rivalry between the British and Americans in the Northwest Territory and the prevailing desire of many Americans to annex Canada.

It was generally believed that the fall of Canada could be accomplished with ease. The first attempt was launched from the frontier post of Fort Detroit. On July 5, 1812, an army of 1800 poorly led and poorly prepared Americans, advanced across the Detroit River into Canada. When confronted by a numerically smaller British force, they retreated to Fort Detroit (**1**, see map above), which was then surrendered to the pursuing enemy.

Still another penetration failed when American forces were stopped by British detachments at Queenston (**2**) on the Niagara River, October 13, 1812. The following year in April an American army crossed Lake Ontario from Sackett's Harbor to York, now Toronto (**3**), the capital city of Upper Canada. After capturing York, the troops burned the public buildings. The British-held posts of Fort George (**4**) and Queenston were taken the next month, then lost again. So went the seesaw war across the border.

Suddenly the course of events was reversed by Commodore Oliver Hazard Perry. On September 10, 1813, with a small fleet of ships which had been built on the shores of Lake Erie, Perry met and defeated a British fleet at Put-in-Bay (**5**). His message, "We have met the enemy, and they are ours," became immortal words in American history.

Brigadier General William H. Harrison, later President of the Republic, reoccupied Fort Detroit in the fall of 1813. At the Battle of the Thames (**6**), northeast of Detroit in Canada, General Harrison won an important victory. Not only was the British army defeated but the powerful Indian chief and British ally, Tecumseh, was killed. A new Indian confederacy, formed to dominate the Ohio Valley ended.

In July 1814, after capturing Fort Erie (**7**), an American army of over 3000 men fought a vicious battle at Lundy's Lane (**8**) with an evenly matched British army. Both sides claimed victory. The withdrawal of the American force marked the last attempt by the United States to invade Canada.

Action opened up on another front when a British naval force sailed into Chesapeake Bay in August 1814. An army of 4000 landed on the shore of the Patuxent River and marched on the city of Washington (**9**). Most of the public buildings were set afire, including the White House and the Capitol. Returning to the fleet, the British sailed north and attacked Fort McHenry (**10**). Francis Scott Key immortalized the fort's stubborn resistance in "The Star-Spangled Banner." Finally the British gave up the siege.

In the meantime, a second naval victory was won by the United States on September 11, 1814, on Lake Champlain (**11**). A British naval force supporting an impending invasion of New York State was destroyed, and the invasion was stopped before it had begun.

The end of the war was in sight. While peace negotiations were being held at Ghent in the Netherlands, a British expeditionary force of 14,000 men landed at the Mississippi Delta for an attack on New Orleans (**12**, below). Under the leadership of General Andrew Jackson, an American army of 5000 met the enemy in a bloody battle on January 8, 1815, with the defenders mowing down the British force to win the conflict. None of the combatants knew that the Treaty of Ghent had brought the War of 1812 officially to a close 15 days before.

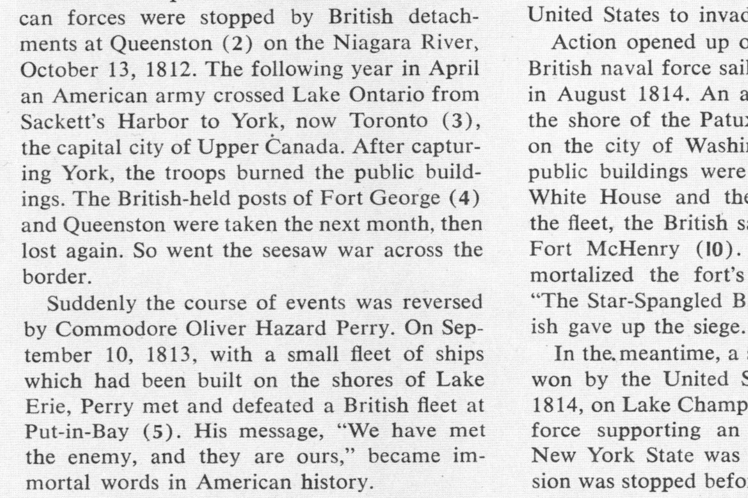

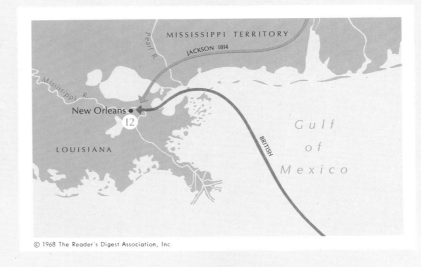

WESTWARD EXPANSION

LEGEND

- ■ Forts ◻ Gold Mining Towns
- Passes
- Canals
- Railroad Lines
- Pony Express
- Kittanning Path
- El Camino Real
- Braddock's Road
- Forbes Road
- National (Cumberland) Road
- Wilderness Road
- Butterfield Southern Route
- Central Overland Route
- Natchez Trace
- California Trail
- Chisholm Cattle Trail
- Mormon Trail
- Old Spanish Trail
- Oregon Trail
- Santa Fe Trail

WESTERN LAND CLAIMS 1781

DISPUTED WESTERN LAND CLAIMS

- Claimed by Virginia
- Claimed by New York
- Claimed by Massachusetts and New York
- Claimed by Connecticut and Pennsylvania
- Claimed by North Carolina
- Claimed by South Carolina
- Claimed by Georgia
- Claimed by South Carolina and Georgia

SETTLEMENTS

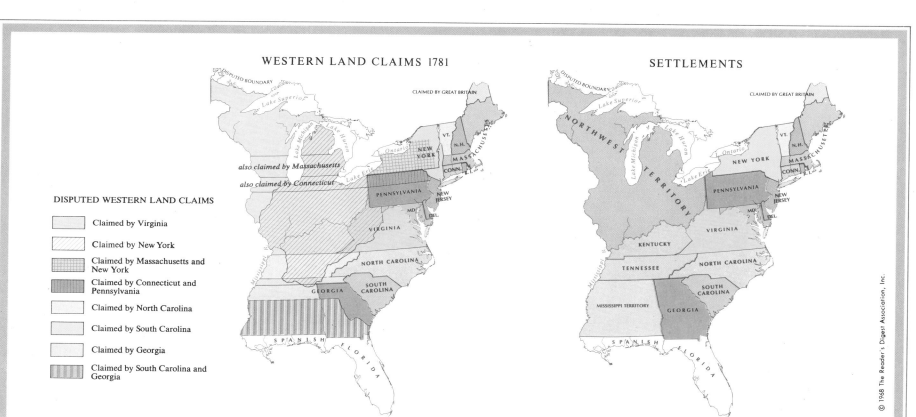

LAND CLAIMS OF THE 13 ORIGINAL STATES

After the defeat of the French and their withdrawal from the North American continent under the terms of the Treaty of Paris (1763), the western lands between the Appalachian Mountains and the Mississippi River became attractive to the people of the British colonies. Following the Revolution, seven of the 13 – Massachusetts, Connecticut, New York, Virginia, North Carolina, South Carolina and Georgia—made conflicting claims to sections of this territory. With the exception of New York, the new states based their cases on early sea-to-sea grants. The wording of these documents was frequently vague. The 1628 Massachusetts charter, for instance, granted land extending from "the Atlantick to the south sea." New York rested its case on the terms of a treaty with the Iroquois Indians.

Virginia sought ownership of what is now Kentucky in addition to parts of Illinois, Indiana, Ohio, Michigan and Wisconsin; Georgia sought to extend her border all the way to the Mississippi, as did North Carolina and South Carolina; while Connecticut, Massachusetts and New York staked out immense western tracts as their own.

The six states which made no property claims beyond their recognized borders—Pennsylvania, Maryland, Delaware, New Jersey, New Hampshire and Rhode Island—were bitterly opposed to the others. They took the position that the western territory belonged to all and should be controlled and administered by the central government.

In 1781 Congress was endeavoring to have each state ratify a charter for the United States. The Articles of Confederation, as the document was called, had been adopted by Congress in 1777, but the required unanimous approval of the 13 states had not been obtained.

Led by Maryland, the states that made no claims to western lands balked at ratifying the Articles until the others had relinquished their territorial demands. After much arguing and discussion, the claimant states finally yielded when Congress pledged that the immense new territory would be used for the "common good." Money from the sale of lands was to be used to support an army to protect new settlers. The Articles of Confederation were signed in 1781 by all 13 states, and the issue that had threatened the very Union itself now became a force to strengthen and preserve it.

The first settlers who moved west after the Revolutionary War undoubtedly followed trails used by Indians and pioneer hunters and trappers. In the South, such a trail passed through Cumberland Gap (1, see map above). After buying territory in Kentucky and Tennessee from the Cherokee in 1775, the Transylvania Land Company hired Daniel Boone and a party of 30 men who opened the Wilderness Road (2) to attract settlers. Until 1796, when the track was widened to permit passage of wagons, migrants trudged on foot or rode horseback through the narrow gap between steep 500-foot walls. By 1800 more than 200,000 persons had used this route to new farmlands and to the Ohio River.

Beyond the Appalachians. Farther north, westward travel before 1800 was possible only by jolting, lumbering wagons on two trails to Pittsburgh, Braddock's Road (3) and Forbes Road (4), both pre-Revolutionary military routes. The former followed the Potomac River to Cumberland, Maryland, and then passed northwestward, while the latter, with a postwar extension to Philadelphia, ran across southern Pennsylvania. A third trail to the same destination, the Kittanning Path (5) along the Susquehanna and Juniata valleys, is today the roadbed of the Pennsylvania Railroad. When the pioneers, wagon-weary and footsore, reached the Ohio, they built rafts or arks, loaded livestock and vehicles aboard and floated down with the current, braving rapids and eddies. When they reached sites for new homes, their crude vessels furnished the lumber for houses.

Steamboats appeared on the Ohio and Mississippi rivers in 1818, not only making travel more comfortable but also enabling passengers and cargo to move upstream as well as down. In New York, the Mohawk Valley and the plain south of Lake Ontario offered a level route to Lake Erie, another waterway to the West. The magnet which attracted these settlers was land along the waterways—vast tracts of fertile soil, unbroken by the plow and superior to the fields which had been depleted by unrotated crops. Owned by the Federal government, it was usually sold at auction. The minimum price was $1 an acre in 1795, $2 in 1800 and $1.25 from 1820 until the Civil War.

When migration resumed after the War of 1812, it was for a time speeded by the completion in 1818 of the National (or Cumberland) Road (6) from Cumberland to Wheeling. This highway was magnificent for its day—more than 60 feet wide, except in mountain country, with such innovations as drainage ditches on each side and bridges of masonry instead of logs. Because of it, the Wilderness Road through Cumberland Gap was abandoned. The first great westward movement was soon, however, slowed to a stop with the panic of 1819, by which time nine new states had been added to the original 13.

Canals and Trails. Completion of the Erie Canal (7) in 1825 from Lake Erie to the Hudson River greatly increased travel to the old Northwest Territory. Built by the state of New York, it was longer than all of England's canals put together. It was also profitable; some of the early railroads which paralleled its route were forbidden to carry freight, or had to pay the same tolls to the state that were charged for canal traffic. Extension of the National Road westward across Ohio was also started in 1825, until it finally reached Vandalia, then the capital of Illinois. During this period, as more and more settlers arrived, the land between the rivers was populated. The success of the Erie Canal touched off a canal-building boom to carry the produce of this area to market; Lake Erie was connected with the Ohio (8) and the Wabash (9) rivers, Lake Michigan with the Mississippi (10). Pioneers crossed the latter river and pushed up its western tributaries. Thousands of American colonists moved overland into Texas, still part of Mexico. Large-scale immigration from Europe began, and many of the newcomers headed west. By the time another financial crisis in 1837 checked the westward flow, five more states had joined the Union.

Even earlier, the Great Plains west of the Mississippi had been described as combining "within its frightful and extensive limits, the steppes of Tartary and the moving sands of the African desert." Explorers and travelers spread this same myth. Consequently, the next wave of migrants crossed the treeless expanse as rapidly as possible and established the new frontier on the Pacific. As in the East, they followed river valleys and Indian trails explored by hunters and trappers. Up to the 1850's almost all the traffic to the Far West was funneled through South Pass (11) in what is now Wyoming. This 7750-foot-high passage across the Continental Divide was reached by following the river valleys from Independence, Missouri—the Kansas, Little Blue, North Platte and Sweetwater. On the other side of the Rockies settlers headed out along the Snake and Columbia rivers for the rich farmlands of the Willamette Valley in the Oregon Territory. The first wagon train crossed this Oregon Trail (12) in 1841. The Mormons, pulling their handcarts to the Promised Land, branched off after South Pass to Salt Lake City on what later became a shortcut for the California Trail. The latter (13) originally started at Soda Springs on the Oregon Trail, led down the Humboldt, across the Nevada desert, up the valley of the Truckee to Donner Pass in the Sierra Nevadas and down the American River to the Sacramento Valley.

The Frontier Moves West. Donner Pass (14) was named for the leader of an ill-fated party trapped there by blizzards during the winter of 1846. Only 47 of 87 people survived, and the confirmed rumors of cannibalism horrified the world. However, this was the gateway to California for an estimated 40,000 persons during the 1849 California Gold Rush, and millions have used it since then. Later the first transcontinental railroad would cross the Sierra through this pass, a route it now shares with U.S. 40, which constitutes part of the coast-to-coast Lincoln Highway.

Other fortune hunters used southern routes opened up

by the cession of Mexican territory in 1848. Gold and silver were found in Nevada and Colorado. The gold fever was so virulent that visitors to mining towns in the early 1860's would not have known a war was in progress in the East. The period of migration and settlement which ended in 1861 brought the number of states to 34.

The final phase of westward expansion began after the Civil War, filling up the Great Plains. Now government land cost nothing. Under the Homestead Act of 1862 settlers received 160 acres of free land after cultivating it for five years. (The United States still owns 464,000,000 acres of public lands, primarily in the West and Alaska. Most of it is too dry, rough or otherwise unsuitable for cultivation.) The population movement was accelerated in the 1880's by the construction of more railroads from the Mississippi to the West Coast. The railroads and transatlantic steamship lines used superlatives to describe the rich harvests of the prairies. One poster began: "The attention of the industrious is directed to the Garden Spot of the West. There is no portion of the world where all the conditions of climate and soil so admirably combine." Land buyers poured in from the East and from Europe. The peak year for immigration before the turn of the century was 1882, and large numbers of those who came from the Old World settled on the plains. An era was coming to an end. The frontier was officially considered that area where there were fewer than six but more than two persons per square mile. In its report on the 1890 census, the government announced: "The unsettled area has been so broken into by isolated bodies of settlement that there can hardly be said to be a frontier line." By that time ten new states had brought the total to 44. Except in spirit, the American Frontier had vanished.

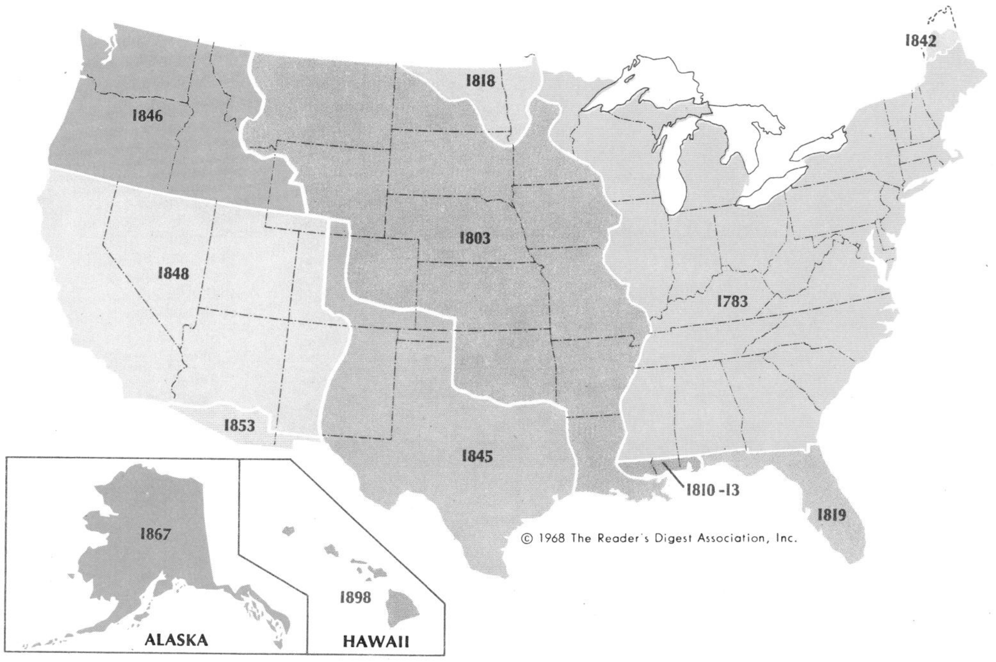

LAND ACQUISITIONS

- **1783**—Original 13 colonies and territory acquired from Great Britain as a result of the Revolutionary War.
- **1803**—Louisiana Territory was purchased from France for $14,500,000. The undefined boundaries were settled by treaties with Britain (1818) and Spain (1819).
- **1810-13**—West Florida from the Mississippi east to the Perdido River, Florida's present boundary, was annexed from Spain by Presidential proclamation on October 27, 1810, but the entire area did not come under United States jurisdiction until. American troops occupied Mobile in April 1813.
- **1818**—A treaty with Britain established the 49th parallel as the northern boundary of the Louisiana Territory from Lake of the Woods to the Rocky Mountains.
- **1819**—Florida was acquired from Spain in exchange for assumption by the United States of $5,000,000 in claims by American citizens against the Spanish government.
- **1842**—A treaty with Britain settled a controversy over the Maine frontier, the United States obtaining 7000 of the disputed 12,000 square miles.
- **1845**—The Republic of Texas was annexed.
- **1846**—A treaty with Britain divided the disputed Oregon country by continuing the 49th-parallel boundary from the Rocky Mountains to Vancouver Island.
- **1848**—After the Mexican War, Mexico ceded territory south of the Oregon country under the Treaty of Guadalupe Hidalgo for $15,000,000.
- **1853**—In the Gadsden Purchase, a strip of territory was bought from Mexico for $10,000,000 to permit construction of a southern transcontinental railroad.
- **1867**—Alaska was purchased from Russia for $7,200,000.
- **1898**—The Republic of Hawaii was annexed.

For historical dates of outlying possessions and administrative areas, see pp. 71-72.

INDIAN WARS OF THE WEST

Explorers, fur trappers and traders in the days before settlement presented no threat to Indian hunting grounds, or to the deer and buffalo which provided food and clothing. But the farmers who followed the trails of the pioneers cleared the land and destroyed the cover for game. No sooner had the Indians been guaranteed by treaty a peaceful possession of regions beyond the frontier than successive waves of white migration swept across the agreed boundaries, compressing the tribes into territory that gradually grew smaller and smaller.

For nearly a hundred years the United States obtained land from the Indians under treaties. Between 1784, when the Iroquois surrendered their claims to western lands in the Treaty of Fort Stanwix, and 1871, when Congress ended the system, more than 370 treaties had been concluded. These were negotiated on the assumption that the tribes were sovereign nations, that their chieftains were empowered to represent them and that they held title to the land on which they lived and hunted. The tribes were anything but sovereign nations; many refused to be bound by the signatures of chiefs (some of whom were government-appointed) in ceding territory. Private ownership of property was not the Indian way of life. The forests and prairies were community property for the general welfare. Impatient white men violated the treaties by pushing into country reserved for various tribes. Hunters slaughtered buffalo indiscriminately. Miners stampeded into any area where gold and silver had been found. The Indians protested these violations in vain; they were neither taxpayers nor voters. War was the inevitable result, and hostilities continued for a century until the last organized resistance ended during the 1890's.

East of the Mississippi. In the Northwest Territory the first campaign which began disastrously with Shawnee victories in Ohio in 1790 and 1791, ended with General "Mad Anthony" Wayne's victory at Fallen Timbers in 1794. The resulting Treaty of Greenville opened most of Ohio and part of Indiana to settlement. The Shawnee were soon on the warpath again, but General William Henry Harrison's victories at Tippecanoe in 1811 and at the Thames River in Canada in 1813, where the Indians and their British allies were routed, extended the pacified area to Lake Michigan. The defeat of the Sauk and Fox under Chief Black Hawk after a series of skirmishes in Illinois and Wisconsin finally cleared the rest of the Northwest Territory.

In the South, General Andrew Jackson took the field against hostile Indians encouraged by early British victories during the War of 1812. He routed the Creeks at Alabama's Horseshoe Bend in 1814 and forced them to surrender 22,000,000 acres of land. They were one of the so-called Five Civilized Tribes whose territories whetted the appetites of land-hungry immigrants moving west from the southern coastal states.

Pressure was brought on Congress to pass the Indian Removal Act of 1830. Under its terms the five tribes were moved west of the Mississippi. Many Seminoles, however, refused to leave, and took refuge in the Florida Everglades. Military action to oust them began in 1835, and although Osceola, their chief, was captured by treachery two years later, this Seminole War did not end until 1842. By that time few Indians remained east of the Mississippi.

Years of Strife. The Great Plains area in the heart of the United States was set aside by Congress as a reservation "forever." When settlers began encroaching, tribal raids and retaliatory bloody massacres opened a period of almost continuous warfare. It has been estimated that between 1865 and 1898 the United States Army conducted 12 campaigns in the plains and the Southwest and took part in more than 900 engagements with Indians, ranging from skirmishes to battles. The Comanches and the Apaches kept Texas and parts of adjacent areas in an uproar until the 1870's. It was not until 1886 that the last Apaches, some led by Geronimo, surrendered. The Navahos were subdued by Colonel Kit Carson in Arizona in 1864.

In the North the Sioux battled tenaciously in the unequal struggle. First came the Minnesota uprising in 1862 under Chief Little Crow. Two years later the destruction of an Indian village in Colorado and the massacre of many of its inhabitants set off a war of revenge by the Sioux, Cheyenne and Arapahos. Chief Red Cloud attacked garrisons in the north and closed the Bozeman Trail in Montana. Another Sioux uprising took place in 1876 when their reservation was invaded by miners seeking gold in the Black Hills of South Dakota. One episode in this war was General George Custer's famous "Last Stand" on the Little Big Horn in Montana; the Indian leaders were Sitting Bull, Crazy Horse and Red Cloud. Sitting Bull was killed in 1890, and the last of his tribe surrendered the following year. An unforgettable incident took place in Idaho in 1877 when the Nez Percé tribe ably led by Chief Joseph was defeated. Chief Joseph's impassioned lament at his failure to save his people constitutes one of the finest pieces of rhetoric in Indian history.

Settlements in the Hunting Grounds. By this time most Indians realized the futility of further resistance. Their hunting grounds had vanished; the West was dotted with Army posts; settlements made a nomadic life impossible; disease introduced by the white man had taken a higher toll than warfare. As a consequence the Indian population in the United States dropped steadily over the years until in 1887 it had reached its lowest ebb – 200,000 people. Then, shortly after the turn of the century, the Indian birthrate began to rise. By 1965 it was almost double that of the national average, and in that year 580,000 Indians inhabited the United States, including Alaska. Far from vanishing they have now become the fastest-growing people in the land.

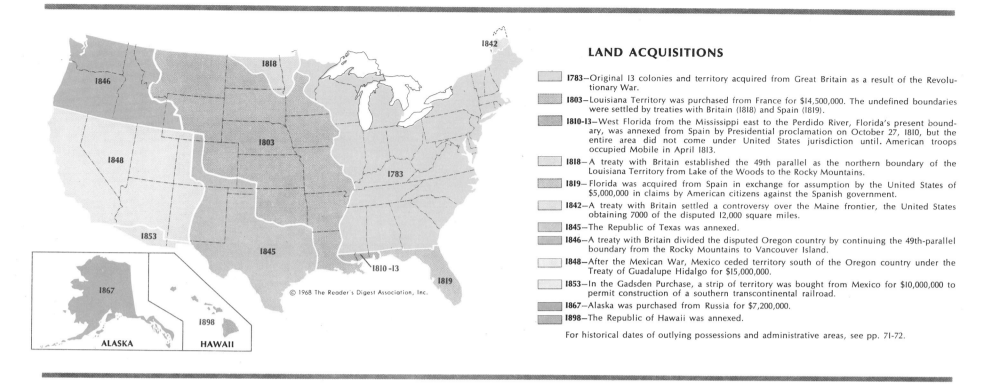

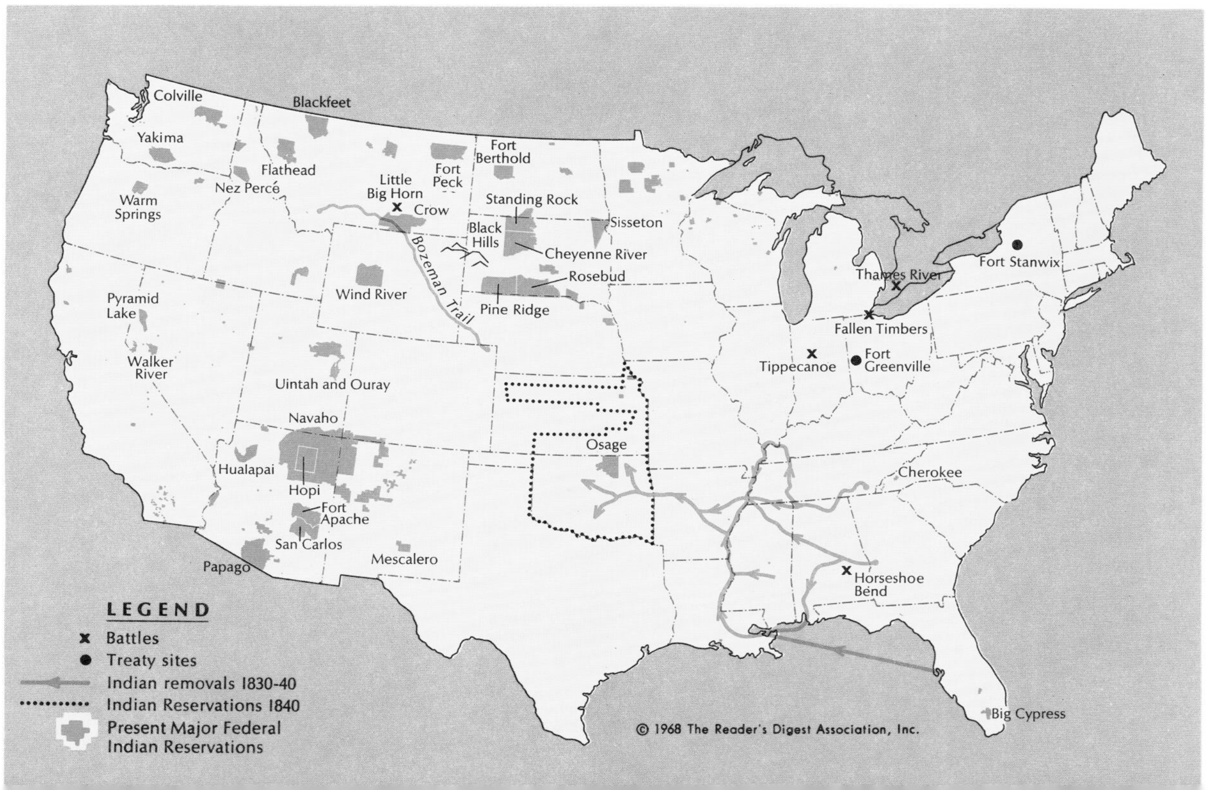

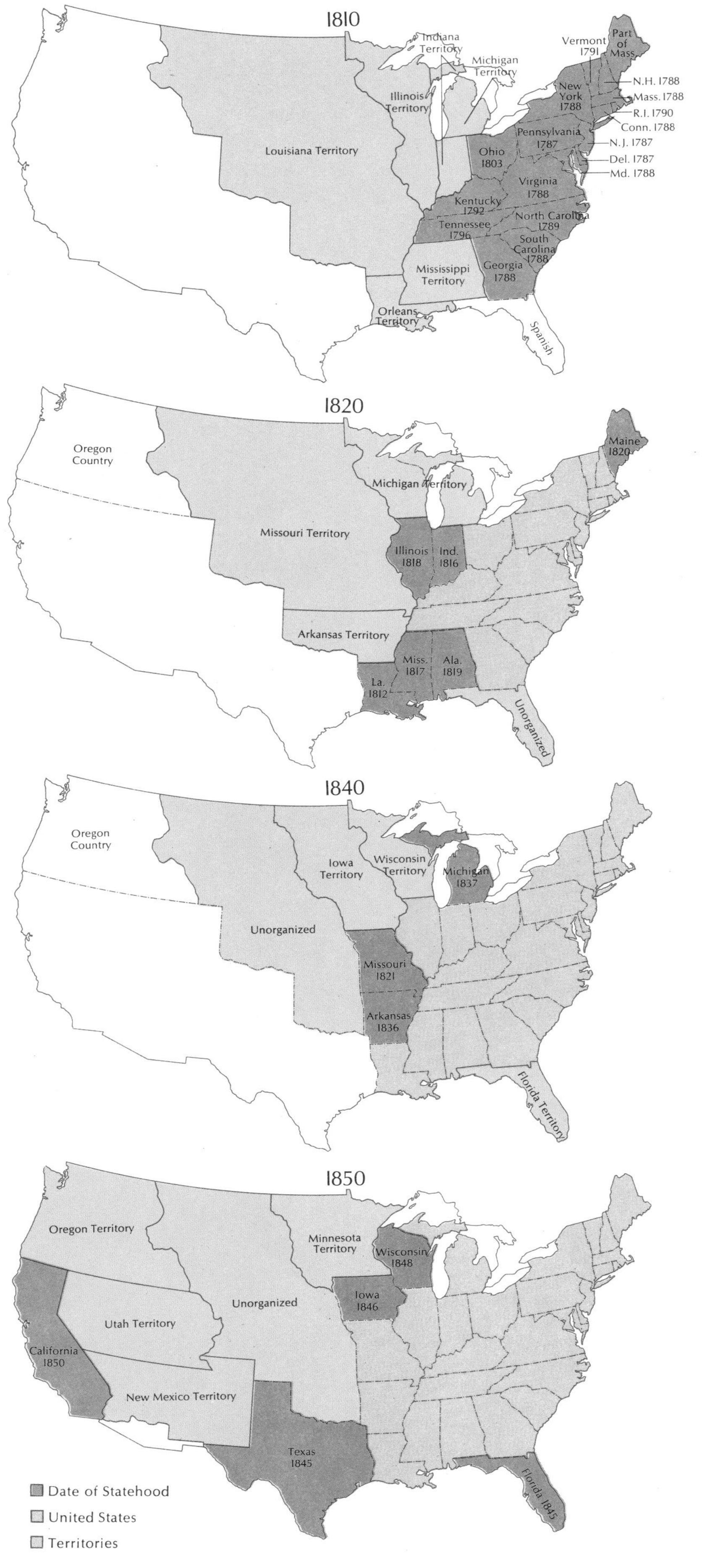

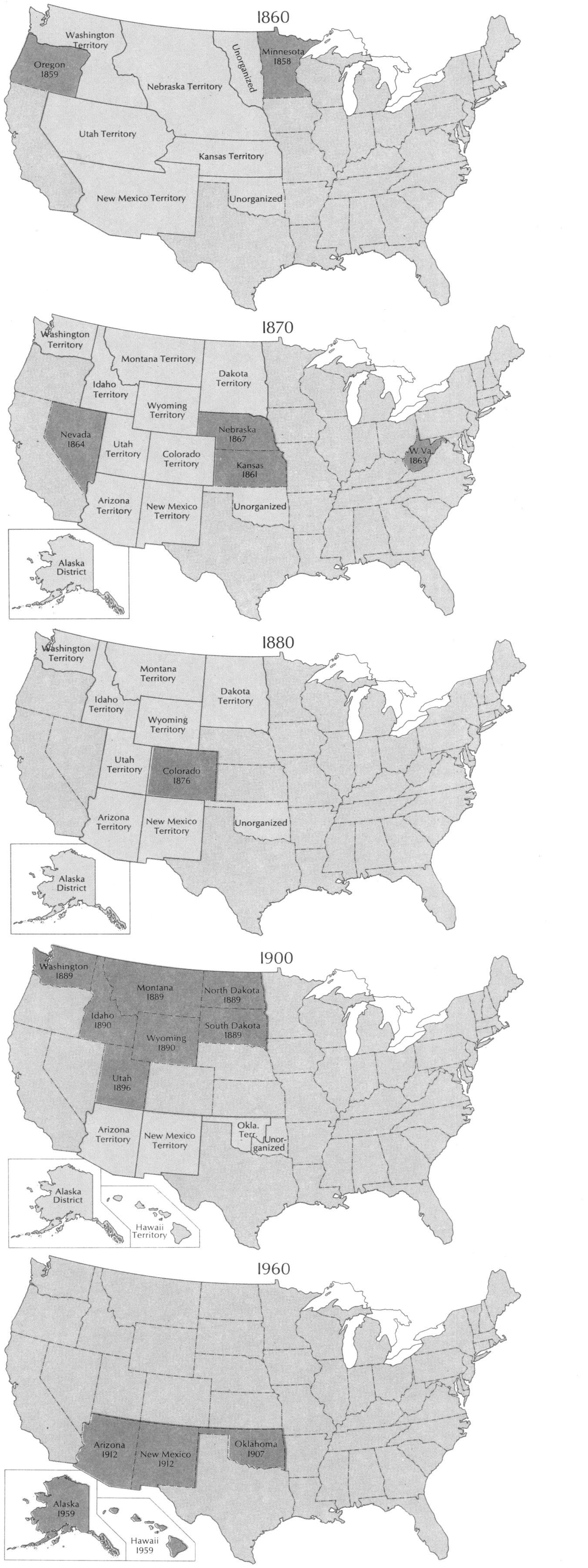

FROM TERRITORIES TO STATES

Americans who had fought a war for self-government wanted to keep their hard-won political rights when they left the original 13 states and moved out to settle the wilderness beyond the Appalachians. In taking these western lands, the national government promised to form from them new states which would have the same rights and powers as those already in the Union. The Northwest Ordinance of 1787, one of the most important enacted under the Articles of Confederation, set up a three-stage procedure under which not more than five states were to be created in the land north of the Ohio River. This ordinance established a general pattern that was followed in governing new territories during the next century and a half.

In the first stage a governor, a secretary and three judges named by Congress administered the Territory. When the adult male population exceeded 5000, the Territory was entitled to elect its own legislature, which shared power with a council selected by Congress. The legislature named a delegate to the House of Representatives in Washington, who was allowed to speak before that body but not to vote. (Delegates of later territories were elected by popular vote.) Finally, when the population reached 60,000, the Territory could frame a constitution and ask Congress for admission to the Union as a full-fledged state.

Although most territories had the same names as present-day states, they frequently extended over a much greater area. They were divided and subdivided again and again as the population increased, and as states were formed from sections of them. When the original Northwest Territory was divided in 1800, for instance, the western portion was organized as the Indiana Territory. By 1803 it included what are now the states of Michigan, Illinois and Wisconsin and part of Minnesota, as well as Indiana. Michigan was split off as a separate territory in 1805 and, when Indiana was reduced to its present size four years later, the Illinois Territory was created from what was left. With the admission of Illinois to the Union in 1818, the remaining area was annexed to the Michigan Territory. In 1836, just before Michigan became a state, the rest of the Michigan Territory was incorporated in a vast Wisconsin Territory, which extended as far as today's Montana. The Wisconsin Territory, in turn, was divided until Wisconsin attained its present shape and statehood in 1848.

Six states have been admitted without going through the preliminary territorial phases: Vermont had established an independent government in 1777 before the Constitutional Convention; Kentucky was part of the state of Virginia, and Maine part of Massachusetts; Texas was first an independent nation; California inaugurated its own state government before its admission in 1850 because Congressional action was delayed by the slavery argument; and West Virginia broke away from Virginia during the Civil War in order to remain in the Union.

MEXICAN WAR

Soon after Mexico had won her freedom from Spain in 1821, Americans began to settle in the Texas portion of the state of Coahuila. In 1836, the Texans demanded their independence and, following the heroic action at the Alamo mission in San Antonio, declared it. Nine years later, in 1845, the new Republic of Texas was annexed by the United States to become the twenty-eighth state.

Mexico refused to recognize either the independence or the annexation and was further provoked when the United States claimed that the southern boundary of Texas was defined, not by the Nueces River, but by the Rio Grande, 60 miles farther south. On April 25, 1846, a Mexican military force of 1600 clashed in the disputed territory with a reconnoitering party of 60 United States cavalrymen. In the skirmish all of the Americans were either killed or captured. An aroused Congress passed a resolution that a state of war existed between the United States and Mexico.

1846

(Numbers indicate positions on map at right)

The first battle of the war took place on May 8, 1846, at Palo Alto (**1**). Brigadier General Zachary Taylor and 2300 American troops defeated a Mexican army of more than 4000 men that had advanced beyond the Rio Grande into Texas. The next day retreating Mexicans made a stand at a place called Resaca de la Palma (2) near Fort Brown (now Brownsville), but were again routed. They were pursued across the Rio Grande, and nine days later the Mexican town of Matamaros (3) was occupied. Taylor planned to head 130 miles upriver to attack the fortified city of Monterrey, the capital of Nuevo León, but was obliged to wait weeks for the necessary steamboats and wagons.

Finally supplied with transportation, General Taylor moved upriver to assault Monter-

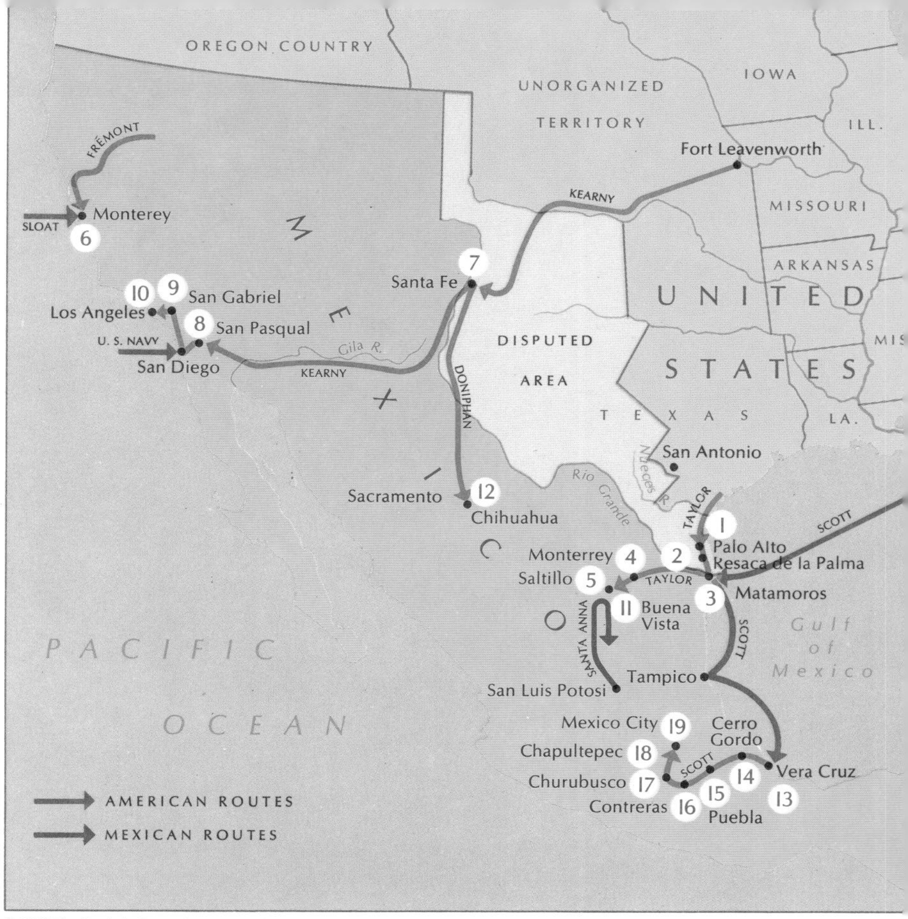

CIVIL WAR

Many causes have been given for the Civil War but the main issue that divided the Northern and Southern states was that of slavery. Offended by the election of Abraham Lincoln to the Presidency in November 1860, South Carolina seceded from the Union on December 20. Mississippi, Georgia, Alabama, Louisiana, Florida and Texas soon followed. Delegates from these secessionist states met at Montgomery, Alabama, in February 1861, and formed a government of the Confederate States of America. Jefferson Davis, who had been a U.S. Senator from Mississippi, was elected provisional president.

On April 17, 1861, Virginia joined the Confederacy, and within two months Arkansas, North Carolina and Tennessee had also become members. The four remaining slave states – Missouri, Kentucky, Maryland and Delaware – stayed in the Union.

1861–62

(Numbers indicate positions on Maps 1 and 2)

The war broke out in the early morning of April 12, 1861, when Confederate forces under the command of General Pierre G. T. Beauregard shelled Fort Sumter (**1**) in Charleston Harbor, South Carolina. After a 34-hour continuous bombardment, the 90-man Federal garrison was forced to surrender.

Because of its vast superiority in manpower and resources, the North expected a relatively easy invasion of the South and a quick end to the war by the capture of the Confederate capital of Richmond, Virginia. These hopes were eclipsed by the first major engagement of the war. On July 21, 1861, an army of 35,000 Union troops attacked a Confederate force of 20,000 at Bull Run (**2**), a stream near Manassas Junction, a rail and road center 30 miles south of Washington, D.C. The stubborn refusal to retreat by the Southern General Thomas "Stonewall" Jackson and his brigade, earned him his nickname and was responsible in large part for the ultimate routing of the Federals and the Confederate victory.

Minor successes came to the North on August 28-29 with the capture by a Federal navy force of the Confederate Fort Hatteras (**3**) and Fort Clark (**4**) built on Hatteras Inlet, North Carolina. These triumphs were followed on November 7 by an amphibious assault by Union forces on the deep-water base of Port Royal (**5**), close to Charleston, South Carolina. There were no further important military actions in the year 1861.

A determined effort was made in February 1862 by the North to capture the Southern fortifications that controlled vital water traffic on the Tennessee and Cumberland rivers in the Mississippi Valley. On February 6, Fort Henry (**6**) surrendered, and Fort Donelson (**7**) fell six days later. Brigadier General Ulysses S. Grant, commander of the Federal attackers, won the nickname Unconditional Surrender Grant by denying the request of Fort Donelson's defenders for more lenient terms.

The North still hoped to capture Richmond, and Union General George B. McClellan proposed to move his army from Washington down the Potomac to Fort Monroe, then overland via the peninsula between the York and James rivers. For this plan to be successful, the North had to continue its naval superiority. This was challenged in the famous battle at Hampton Roads (**8**), March 9, 1862, between the ironclad gunboat *Monitor,* of the Federal navy, and the Confederate armored ship *Merrimac.* The battle ended with no decisive victory, but the *Merrimac* continued to be a threat to Federal ships using the James River.

The second great battle of the war was taking shape in the west. On April 6, a Confederate army of some 40,000 men attacked a Federal force of 38,000 under the command of General Grant at Pittsburg Landing, Tennessee. In the Battle of Shiloh (**9**), which was named after a nearby church, the Southern forces finally retreated in good order. Casualties ran high on both sides.

The emphasis now was focused on another area. Captain David G. Farragut, in command of a Union fleet of 23 ships, daringly sailed past Fort St. Philip and Fort Jackson in the mouth of the Mississippi to capture the city of New Orleans (**10**) on April 25, 1862.

The commander of what was now called the Army of the Potomac, Union General McClellan, moved his force of over 100,000 men from Alexandria, Virginia, near Washington, sailed down to Fort Monroe and began advancing up the peninsula toward Richmond. To drain off some of the Federal attacking force, General Stonewall Jackson with more than 15,000 Confederate troops kept up a diversionary campaign along the Shenandoah Valley. In a number of well-executed feints and advances west of Washington (see map 2, **11**), from May 15, to June 9, 1862, Jackson defeated numerically superior Federal armies in a

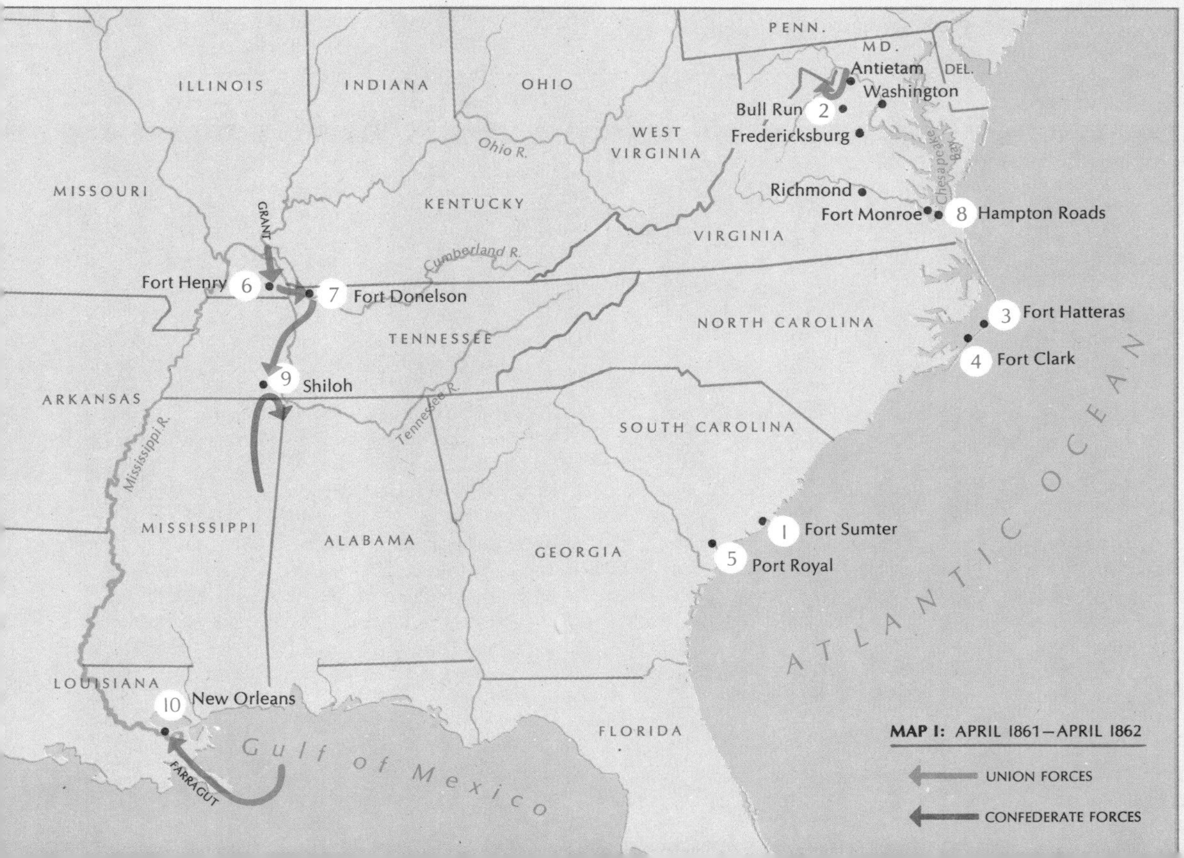

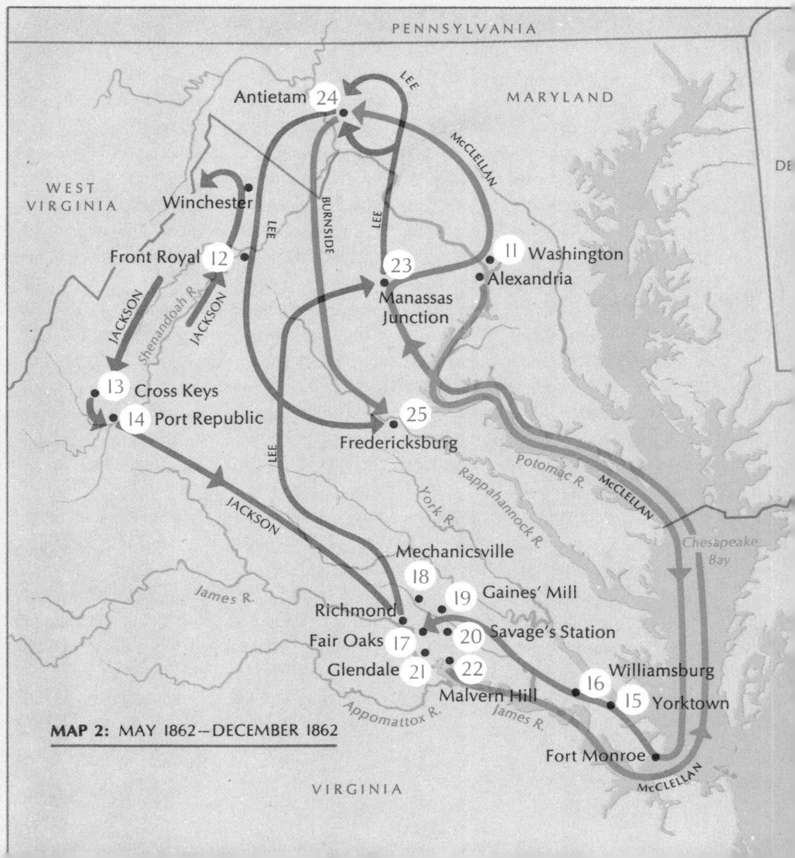

rey (4) on September 21. After a three-day battle, the garrison of 9000 Mexican troops surrendered. The Americans continued their offensive and on November 16 occupied Saltillo (5), the capital city of the state of Coahuila.

Another phase of American war strategy was the wresting of the west from Mexican control. To this end a U.S. naval unit under Commodore J. D. Sloat was put ashore near the California capital of Monterey (6). There, after uniting with Captain John C. Frémont and a group of volunteers, Sloat entered Monterey unopposed on July 7, 1846. Meanwhile, a detachment of 1600 men under Colonel Stephen W. Kearny had left Fort Leavenworth in mid-June, bound for Santa Fe, in Mexican territory. After a 900-mile march, Kearny and his troops took possession of Santa Fe (7) on August 18 and proclaimed the annexation of New Mexico to the United States.

In September, Colonel Kearny continued his march to the coast. The Americans were met by a large enemy force at the Indian village of San Pasqual (8), where a hard-fought battle ensued December 6. Although defeated in the engagement, Kearny and his men reached San Diego December 12, and joined a U.S. Navy land detachment.

1847

The combined American force ushered in the new year by defeating an enemy unit at San Gabriel (9) on January 8, 1847. They then marched on Los Angeles (10) and occupied the city January 10. California had, for all practical purposes, passed from Mexican to American control.

A plan had been evolved in Washington to crush all enemy resistance by sending an expeditionary force to attack and capture the capital, Mexico City. This necessitated transferring 8000 of General Taylor's troops from Saltillo to two nearby Gulf of Mexico ports where they waited to board sea transports coming from New Orleans. The move left Taylor with less than 5000 men.

General Santa Anna, president of Mexico and one of her ablest military leaders, had gathered together his country's main army of 20,000 at San Luis Potosí to block an expected southward drive by General Taylor. Learning of the weakening of Taylor's army, the Mexican commander decided to attack. A savage battle developed at Buena Vista (11) near Saltillo on February 22. The next day, Taylor's outnumbered army fought brilliantly, defeating the Mexicans and forcing them to retreat.

Mexico suffered another defeat a short time later when, on February 28, Colonel Alexander W. Doniphan and 900 American volunteers who had set out from Santa Fe attacked and routed a Mexican army of 2500 at the Battle of Sacramento, north of the city of Chihuahua (12). The Mexicans lost heavily in the engagement.

The final phase of the war was rapidly approaching. Major General Winfield Scott, Commanding General of the U.S. Army since 1841, was put in direct charge of the crucial advance on Mexico City. Scott's troop transports, convoyed by a naval force from New Orleans, picked up the units of Taylor's army waiting near Matamoros and at Tampico. On March 9, the American force of more than 13,000 men made a landing near Vera Cruz (13) and placed the city under siege. The Mexican garrison of 4000 held out for almost three weeks before capitulating.

General Scott began his march to Mexico City 250 miles away and on April 18 defeated a Mexican army of 12,000 men, commanded by General Santa Anna, at a place named Cerro Gordo (14). Puebla (15) was taken by the Americans May 15; Contreras (16), August 18-20; and Churubusco (17), August 20.

On September 13, General Scott's men conquered the massive stone fortress of Chapultepec (18) which was built into a hill a mile outside Mexico City. This was followed by the successful storming of the Belen *garita* and Cosme *garita*—the twin gates to the capital city. Mexican resistance was at an end. Mexico City (19) itself capitulated the next day, with General Santa Anna abdicating the presidency.

1848

Mexico had been completely defeated, her armies crushed, her land occupied. She had lost every battle of the war with the exception of San Pasqual. By the terms of the Treaty of Guadalupe Hidalgo, which was signed on February 2, 1848, the Rio Grande was established as the international border, and Mexico ceded to the United States the provinces of New Mexico, Utah, Nevada and sections of Wyoming and Colorado. Also ceded by Mexico was Upper California, the present state of California.

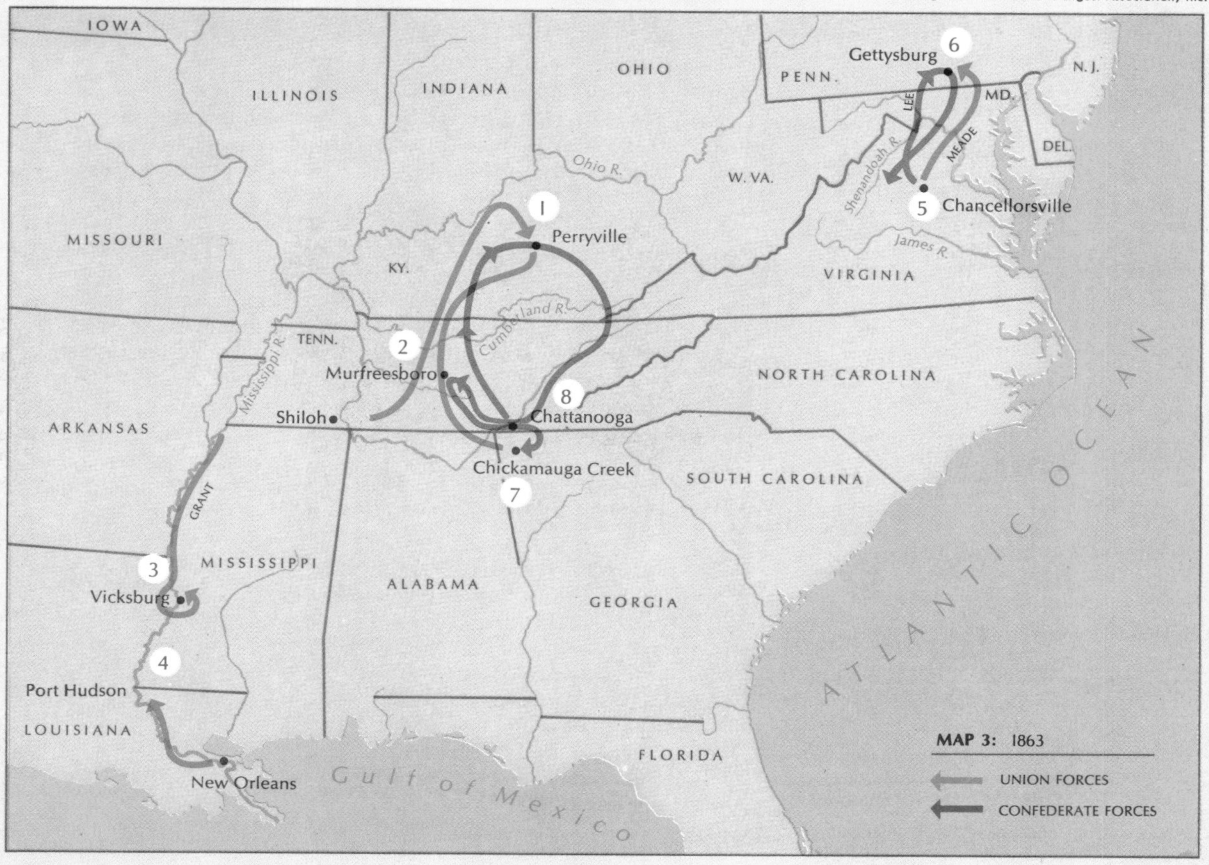

series of engagements at Front Royal (12), Cross Keys (13) and Port Republic (14).

While Jackson's brilliant maneuvering was in progress, the Army of the Potomac besieged and occupied Yorktown (15), then continued on toward Richmond. On May 5, 1862, General McClellan's advance was momentarily halted at Williamsburg (16) with a Confederate rearguard action. Resuming the offensive, Union troops crossed the Chickahominy River and clashed with Southern forces near Fair Oaks (17), where the Confederates were defeated. The Southern commanding general Joseph E. Johnston was wounded and was replaced by General Robert E. Lee. The Confederates retreated to Richmond.

Reinforced by General Jackson's troops from Port Republic, General Lee launched an offensive against the Federal forces. Following the savage Seven Days' Battle at Mechanicsville (18), June 26; Gaines' Mill (19), June 27; Savage's Station (20), June 29; Glendale (21), June 30; and finally at Malvern Hill (22) on July 7, Union troops retreated, and the threat to Richmond was removed.

When General Lee advanced a section of his army northward toward Washington, General McClellan dispatched a large Federal force to counter the move. The two armies of 54,000 Confederates and 63,000 Federals met on August 29-30 at Manassas Junction (23), close to where the Battle of Bull Run had been fought the previous year. General Lee routed the Union force.

One of the bloodiest battles of the war was fought the following month at the village of Sharpsburg on the Antietam (24), a small stream in western Maryland. McClellan's army of 85,000 Union troops faced Lee's 50,000 Confederates on September 17. Both sides sustained heavy casualties—more than 10,000 dead each. There was no definite winner, but Lee retired into Virginia, thus lifting the danger of a Confederate invasion of the North. It was after Antietam that President Lincoln announced the Emancipation Proclamation.

The North made another major effort to capture Richmond when 115,000 troops commanded by General Ambrose E. Burnside began a march from Antietam to the Confederate capital. Attempting to cross the Rappahannock River at Fredericksburg, Virginia (25), the Federal troops were confronted by Lee's army of close to 80,000 entrenched on the other side on December 13. The Union troops were thrown back with casualties of over 12,000 while the Confederate loss was 5000. The battle was a serious blow to the North and caused General Burnside to be relieved of his command.

1863

(Numbers indicate positions on Map 3)

In the spring of the previous year, following the Battle of Shiloh in Tennessee on April 6, 1862, the Confederates advanced into Kentucky, only to be forced back to Tennessee once more on October 8, 1862, after defeat in a costly battle at Perryville, Kentucky (1). Confederate forces moved to the south and at Murfreesboro (2), or Stone's River, Tennessee, the Southern army of 35,000 met 45,000 Federal troops. The battle began on the last day of 1862 and ended on January 2, 1863. The result was a draw, with the Confederate force ultimately retiring and the Federals taking possession of Murfreesboro. Again casualties were high: the Confederates lost 10,000 men; the Union 13,000.

Repeated Federal attempts had been made to take Vicksburg, Mississippi (3). On March 29, Grant launched another offensive and by May 19, he had Vicksburg with its 30,000 Confederate defenders surrounded. A 47-day siege followed before the Southern commander finally capitulated on July 4. Less than a week later, Port Hudson (4) was captured by a Union force which had moved north from New Orleans. This put the entire Mississippi River under Union control.

Meanwhile a series of battles between the Army of the Potomac and General Lee's Confederate army were fought from May 2 to May 4, 1863, at the small Spotsylvania County village of Chancellorsville (5). The result was the victory of Lee's 60,000 over the Union army of 134,000. Casualties were extremely heavy on both sides—the Union suffering the loss of 18,000 men; the Confederates some 13,000. Lee's defeat of the Federal army was overshadowed by the accidental fatal wounding of the Southern general Stonewall Jackson by one of his own men.

Spurred on by this thorough victory, General Lee began an invasion of the North. During the first part of June, the Confederates progressed up the Shenandoah Valley into Pennsylvania. A large Union force under Major General George G. Meade, who had recently been named commander of the Army of the Potomac, followed Lee's forces northward and met the Southerners at Gettysburg (6). The battle that was to become the most famous of the Civil War took place on the first three days of July. On the final day a valiant effort was made by 15,000 Confederate troops under the command of Major General George E. Pickett to break the Union line. The heroic charge failed and the Confederates retreated southward to Virginia. The turning point of the war had taken place. The South had lost over 20,000 dead and wounded; the Union about 18,000.

Union efforts were now concentrated on capturing the vital communications center of Chattanooga in Tennessee. As a Northern army of 65,000 advanced, the defending Southerners withdrew south of the city to Chickamauga Creek (7). In the resulting battles, on September 19–20, the attacking Federals were repulsed.

The Confederates took positions on Lookout Mountain and Missionary Ridge, south of Chattanooga, which had been occupied by Federal troops. Using their artillery, the Southerners were able to prevent supplies from reaching the Union army. A large Federal force was dispatched under the overall command of General Grant, who had been made the commander of the Division of the Mississippi. On November 23–25, the Battle of Chattanooga (8) was joined. Federal troops stormed and took nearby Lookout Mountain, and Missionary Ridge fell to the

North after a wild bayonet charge. The victory at Chattanooga, one of the Confederacy's most strategic points, proved to be a staggering blow to Southern hopes. The way was now open for a Federal sweep into Georgia and the rest of the South. It was the last major engagement in the year 1863.

1864

(Numbers indicate positions on Map 4)

Early in the spring of 1864 President Lincoln made General Grant commander of all the Union forces. He had a clear, strategic plan for winning the war and soon put it into effect. On May 4, strong Union forces of 100,000 men under General Grant crossed the Rapidan in a desolate section of northern Virginia overgrown with almost impenetrable thickets. The next day, General Lee's Confederate army launched an attack in what has been called the Battle of the Wilderness (1). In this engagement, with troops of both sides confused by the heavily wooded area and by the numerous fires that swept through the underbrush, the Union advance was stopped, and Grant's attempt to envelop Lee's forces failed.

The bitter fighting moved a few miles to the village of Spotsylvania, Virginia (2), where for five days Lee's men withstood two concentrated onslaughts by Union troops. Again there were staggering losses on both sides.

General Lee, under extreme pressure from the enemy, withdrew to Cold Harbor (3), about 10 miles from Richmond, where strong earthwork defenses had been built. On June 3, Union forces released a massive frontal assault.

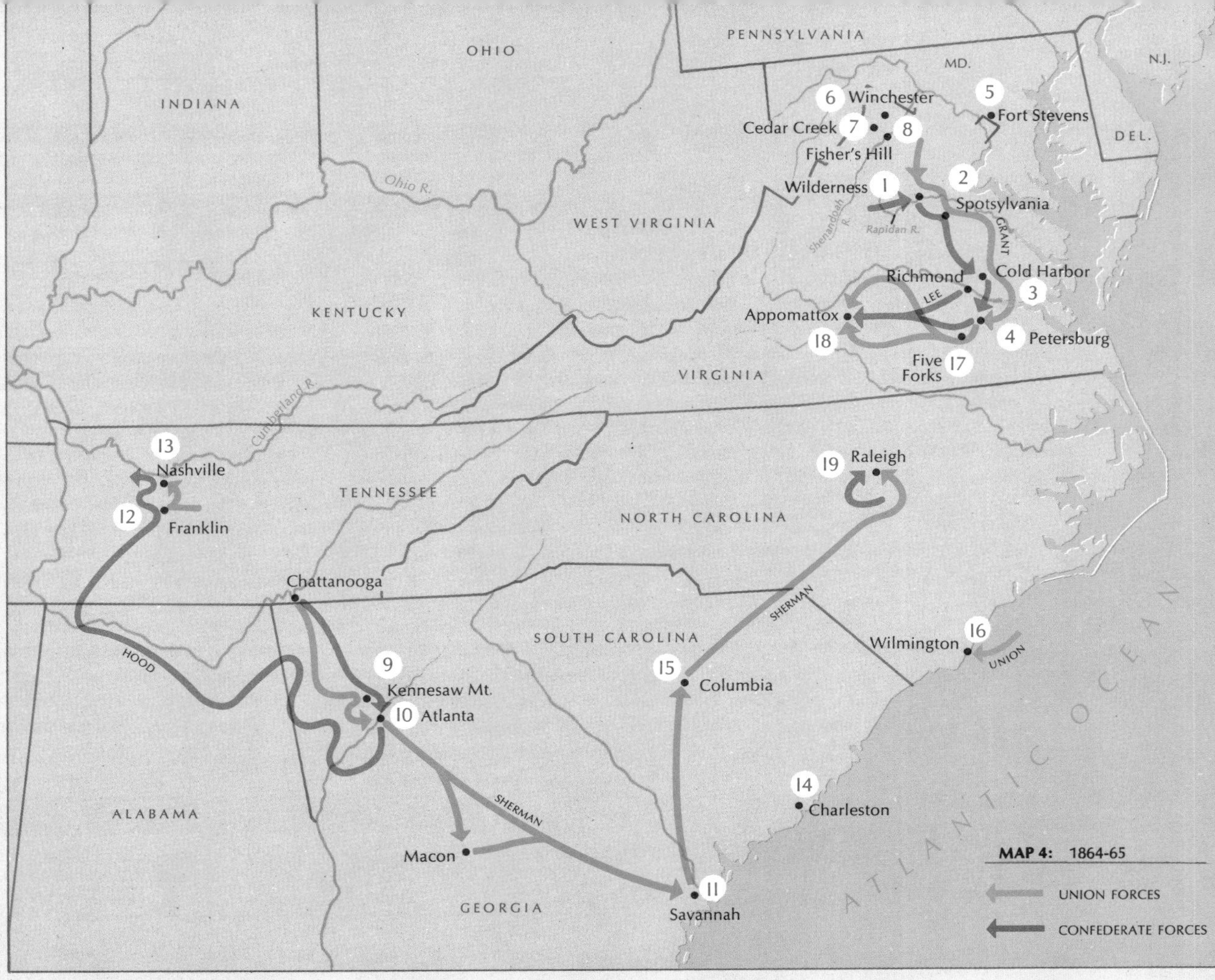

GLOBAL COMMITMENTS

Victory in the Spanish-American War in 1898 established the United States as a major power with new territory and expanding interest in both hemispheres. America became involved in the opening up of China to free trade and in building the Panama Canal, but remained off the stage of Old World politics.

The outbreak of World War I did not appear at once to affect either the security or the traditional isolation of the United States. Then the growing specter of a German Empire in control of Europe brought full-scale American support that contributed decisively to Allied victory (1918) and to the postwar establishment of the League of Nations.

After this wartime interlude, American statesmen sought a return to "normalcy," demobilizing and spurning membership in the League of Nations. World War II reversed the trend. This time America shared the decisive roles with Britain and the Soviet Union. Postwar Soviet-American confrontations in many areas greatly increased American activity abroad. Support of the United Nations, massive foreign-aid programs, military alliances, military intervention in Korea and Southeast Asia—all indicated the vast range of America's involvement in world affairs.

SPANISH-AMERICAN WAR, 1898

As a result of the sinking of the U.S. battleship *Maine* on February 15, 1898, in the harbor of Havana (1), the United States declared war against Spain in April 1898. The first blow was struck, not in Cuba, but in the Philippines. Steaming in from the China coast on May 1, Commodore George Dewey of the U.S. Navy shattered Spanish gunboats in Manila harbor (2) and blockaded the city until American troops arrived to seize Spain's colony.

On June 1, 1898, another American fleet sailed from the United States and blockaded Santiago de Cuba (3), where Spain's Atlantic fleet had taken refuge. The Spanish ships were destroyed on July 3 attempting to escape from the harbor (4). American land forces pressed the siege of Santiago which surrendered in mid-July. Another expedition attacked the Spanish colony of Puerto Rico (5). Spain sued for peace on August 14, 1898.

The peace treaty ceded to the United States Puerto Rico in the West Indies, Guam and the Philippines in the Pacific, and guaranteed Cuban independence with the United States temporarily in control. A semiautonomous government was created for Cuba (1902), and full independence recognized (1934), with the United States retaining a naval base at Guantánamo. The United States paid Spain $20,000,000 for the Philippines, and granted independence to the Republic of the Philippines in 1946.

(Note: For other American acquisitions, see "Possessions and Administrative Areas," pages 71, 72.)

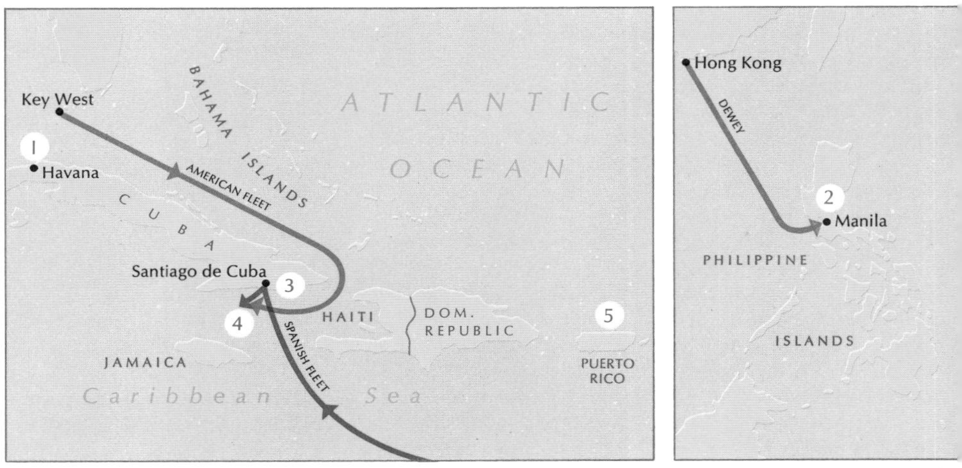

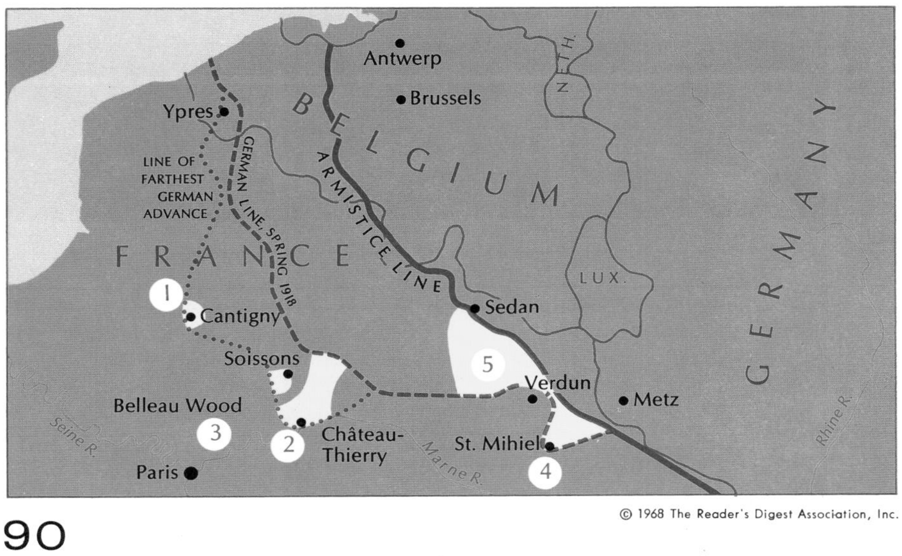

WORLD WAR I, 1917-18

MAJOR UNITED STATES OPERATIONS. When the Germans began their final attack in the spring of 1918, American troops had arrived at frontline battle sectors. Cantigny (1) was the scene of the first offensive American action in the war. There on May 28, U.S. troops, interspersed with gravely depleted Allied forces, reduced a salient and held it during three days of fierce German counterattacks. Between June 1 and June 4, only 40 miles from Paris, an untested division of American soldiers defended the Marne River crossings at Château-Thierry (2). Another American division held the Château-Thierry–Paris road, and on June 6 mounted a successful attack called the Battle of Belleau Wood (3). In mid-July Americans again stood firm at the Marne crossings. Then the initiative passed to the Allies.

British and French offensives in July and August 1918 were vigorous; American units and their staffs improved rapidly with combat experience. General John J. Pershing now got his own command along a specific fighting front stretching northwestward from the Swiss border to meet the French lines. Reduction of the key German salient at St. Mihiel (4), part of the Allied Meuse-Argonne offensive, was the first major independent American operation. The main thrust (5), involving over one million American troops, lasted 47 days (September 26–November 11). This battle severed German railway lines feeding the western front; the Germans signed an armistice on November 11, 1918.

This was driven back with a loss of 6000 Northern troops.

Hoping to surprise his opponent, General Grant made a sudden advance against Petersburg (4), a rail and road center south of Richmond, on June 14. A subsequent attack on the city on June 18 was repulsed by the Confederates, as were succeeding Northern drives. Secretly, Union forces dug a tunnel under Petersburg's defenses and exploded a powerful mine, which caused the death of many Southern troops. But Union attacks were again stopped. Grant finally put the city under siege until April 1 of the following year, 1865. In the Wilderness campaign, the North lost 55,000 men and the South 39,000.

During Petersburg's stubborn defense, Lee dispatched a raiding expedition through the Shenandoah Valley much like that of Stonewall Jackson's in the spring of 1862. The Confederates now reached the outskirts of Washington and attacked Fort Stevens (5). Pursued by Union troops, the raiders were finally defeated in battles at Winchester (6), Cedar Creek (7) and nearby Fisher's Hill (8).

While Grant was hammering away at the forces of General Lee, action was taking place on other battlefronts. On August 5, David G. Farragut, now an admiral, successfully sailed his naval squadron into the mined harbor at Mobile in Alabama (not shown on Map 4). Here he made his stirring battle cry, "Damn the torpedoes! Full steam ahead!"

Union General William T. Sherman had also been on the move. Leaving Chattanooga with an army of 100,000, he headed for Atlanta. There were a number of running fights with Confederates, culminating in Sherman's assault on Southern positions at Kennesaw Mountain (9), where he was repulsed. Continuing his dogged advance, Sherman occupied Atlanta (10) on September 1–2, after forcing General John B. Hood to evacuate the city. Shortly thereafter General Sherman left Atlanta on his famous march across Georgia to Savannah on the sea. On the way he laid in ruin everything in his path—property, crops, railways, stores. He entered Savannah (11) on December 21.

After retreating from Atlanta on August 31, 1864, General Hood led his Confederate army northwest into Tennessee in an effort to cut General Sherman's line of communication and supply. Anticipating Hood's intention, Sherman dispatched 30,000 men to reinforce the Union army at Nashville, Tennessee. The two combatants met on November 30, at Franklin, Tennessee (12), with the Confederates obliged to retire. The Union army advanced to Nashville, reinforcing the Federals already there. A major encounter took place on December 15, when Union forces attacked Hood's Confederates close to Nashville (13). The battle lasted two days and saw the end of Hood's army as a fighting force. Confederate losses were approximately 4500 men. The North lost between 2000 and 3000.

1865

In January 1865 General Sherman's army left Savannah and headed north through the Carolinas. Confederate resistance was weakening. Charleston (14) fell after being isolated by Sherman's troops. Columbia (15), the capital of South Carolina, was captured. Wilmington, North Carolina (16), was taken by a Federal land-sea force.

The situation was worsening by the hour for General Lee and his Army of Northern Virginia. The Confederates had maintained their fortified positions at Petersburg and Richmond, but their resistance was weakening. Lee now made a last desperate bid for victory. Faced by some 125,000 Union troops, the Confederate general's force of 57,000 was small indeed. A segment of Lee's army attacked and captured one of Grant's fortifications. It was soon retaken after a strong counterattack. On March 29, Grant began the last maneuver by attempting to encircle the Confederate position. After a number of engagements, notably at Five Forks (17), the Confederate line was broken, and Lee was forced to withdraw his troops from Petersburg and Richmond. Endeavoring to rendezvous with a Confederate army to the South, Lee hurriedly retreated along the Appomattox River with Grant in pursuit. A running fight ensued for four days until finally Lee's course was blocked at Appomattox Court House (18) by a Union force that had circled ahead.

On April 9, 1865, General Robert E. Lee met General U. S. Grant at Appomattox and surrendered. General Johnston capitulated to General Sherman near Raleigh (19) on April 26. The war was at last over.

The terrible holocaust had taken more American lives than any other war. In the grim accounting afterward, the North had a total of 365,000 dead, while the unofficial figure on Confederate deaths was estimated at 133,000.

WORLD WAR II, 1941-45

U.S. ACTION IN THE PACIFIC. After the attack on America's Pacific islands (1) in December 1941, the Japanese, in a series of well-executed campaigns, gained all the territory they had planned to occupy. By the end of summer 1942, Americans were ready to take the offensive and stop further Japanese expansion or consolidation. Two American naval victories, in the Coral Sea (2), May 7–8, 1942 and at Midway (3), June 3–6, 1942, were the turning points in the war. The U.S. land offensive began with the invasion of Guadalcanal (4) in the Solomon Islands, August 7, 1942; in six months of fighting, the Japanese lost heavily in the battle of attrition. The United States secured the rest of the Solomons in the fall of 1942 and rapidly advanced along the northern shore of New Guinea (5), thus largely completing the southern Pacific campaign by the end of 1943.

In the northern Pacific, Americans recaptured the Aleutians (6) during 1943. The main U.S. advance, the central Pacific campaign, began in November 1943 through the Gilbert, Marshall and Mariana islands (7). The American island-hopping tactics allowed U.S. troops to bypass and isolate without hope of rescue more than 100,000 Japanese. At this point, it was decided to recapture the Philippines and head north to the Japanese home islands. The decisive American naval victory at Leyte Gulf (8), October 23–25, 1944, assured success in the Philippines, and while that campaign progressed, Marines won the fanatically defended island of Iwo Jima (9) in March of 1945. After the largest Pacific amphibious assault, Okinawa (10) was conquered in nearly three months of battle, April 1–June 21. By May, America and her allies defeated Japanese forces in Burma (11). As U.S. forces prepared to invade the Japanese home islands a superfortress dropped an atomic bomb on Hiroshima (12). August 6, 1945; three days later Nagasaki (13) was the target of a second bomb. Japan's surrender was formally accepted in Tokyo Bay on September 2, 1945.

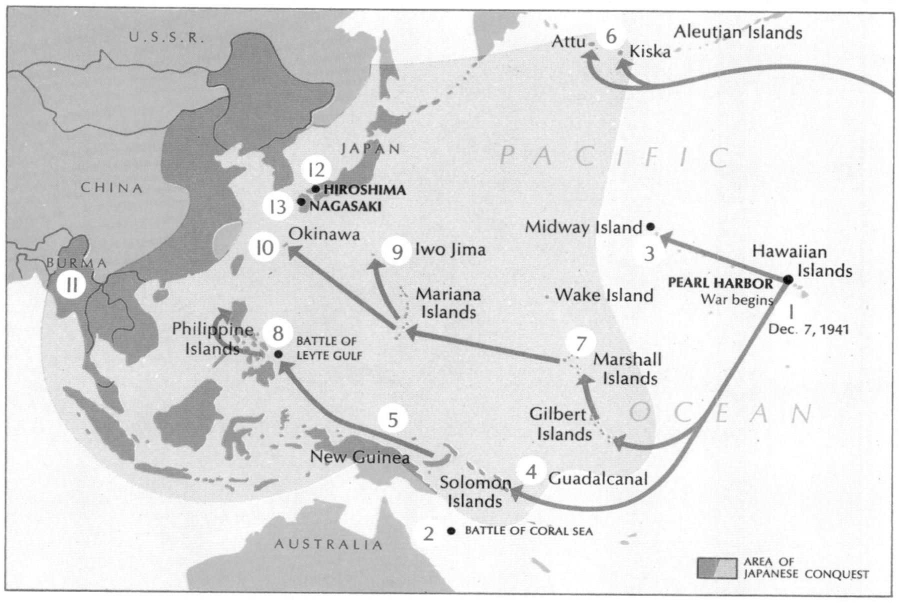

ALLIED CAMPAIGNS IN NORTH AFRICA AND EUROPE. Although America entered World War II in December 1941, nearly a year passed before American and British troops under U.S. command invaded North Africa. A vast war fleet landed troops at Casablanca (1), Oran (2) and Algiers (3) in November 1942, to form the western front of a two-pronged attack on the German desert army. The British army had already engaged the Germans in the east, and the two-front action forced the surrender of 250,000 Axis troops at Tunis (4), in May 1943. During July of 1943 an American-British force invaded Sicily (5). By September the British crossed to the toe of Italy, and the Americans landed at Salerno (6), south of Naples. In January 1944, the Allies landed at Anzio (7), south of Rome. Slow, rugged fighting followed; the Allies pinned down nearly 20 German divisions—which would have served either on the eastern front where the Soviets were taking the offensive, or on the Atlantic coast which the Allies were preparing to invade.

Now added to England's air bases, the air bases in southern Italy put the Allies within range of enemy industrial targets. By 1944, Germany was being squeezed in a gigantic vise.

Allied invasion forces struck through Normandy (8) in June 1944 and southern France (9) in August. During December 1944, the Soviet army captured Warsaw and Budapest. Allied armies on both fronts pressed relentlessly toward the German heartland.

A totally surprising last-ditch German push, known as the Battle of the Bulge, was received mainly by American forces in the Ardennes (10) in December 1944–January 1945. Despite deep German penetration into Belgium and heavy Allied casualties, it failed to produce significant results for the Germans, and four months later Germany surrendered on May 7–8, 1945.

Austria and Germany were divided into U.S., British, French and Soviet occupation sectors. The capital cities of Vienna and Berlin were likewise divided; they lay inside the Soviet sectors and were connected with the other zones by corridors. The attempt of the U.S.S.R. to close the Berlin corridor caused the dramatic Berlin airlift episode in 1948–49. The city was supplied by the United States entirely by air. By 1955 all foreign troops were withdrawn from Austria, and full sovereignty was restored to the Federal Republic of West Germany (the U.S., British and French sectors). American troops remained in Berlin and West Germany, to bear the chief responsibility for resistance to any possible Soviet advance into Western Europe.

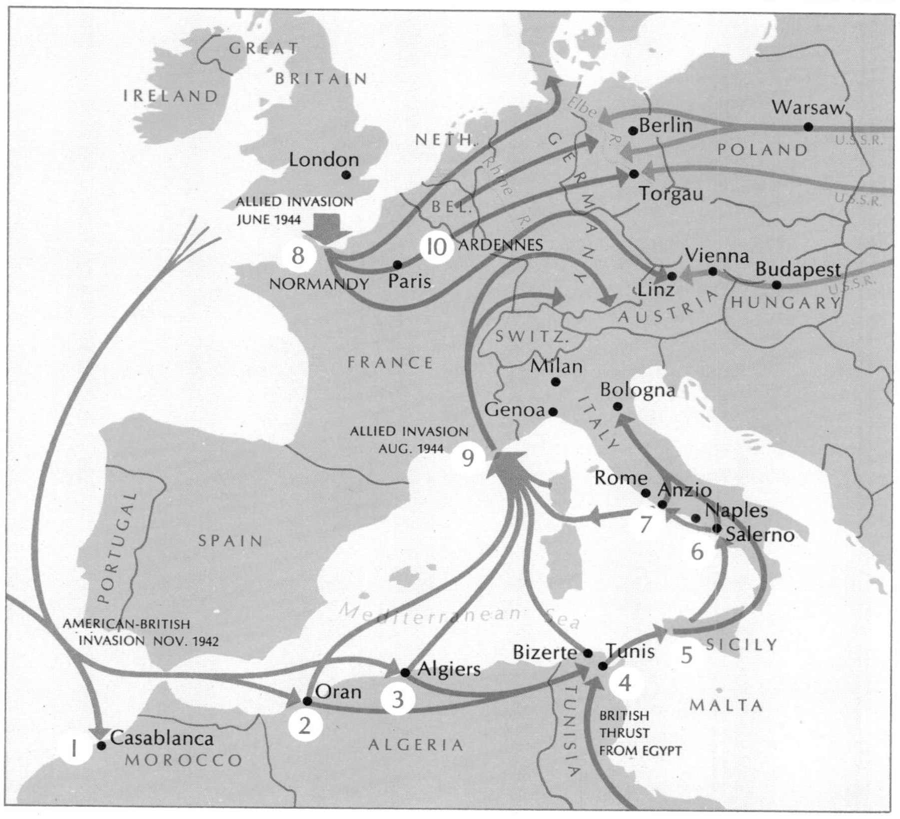

THE KOREAN WAR, 1950-53

In 1945 Korea was taken from Japan and divided along the 38th Parallel. Soviet forces occupied the north; American forces, the south. The Soviet Union and the United States became deadlocked on procedures for the unification and independence of Korea, and the United States turned to the United Nations for a solution. The General Assembly established a Korean Commission to conduct free elections in that country, but the Soviet Union refused the U.N. Commission entrance to the northern zone. The 38th Parallel division became permanent. An election in South Korea, supervised by the United Nations, established an independent anti-Communist government. In 1949 the United States withdrew its troops from the Republic of Korea, leaving the defense of the country to a small, ill-equipped Korean army. The Soviets established a Communist government in the north, with a large Soviet-trained and equipped army of Koreans at its command.

In June 1950, Communist North Korean troops, without warning, crossed the 38th Parallel and attacked South Korea (1). The U.N. Security Council (with the Soviet Union absent) recommended that U.N. member nations aid South Korea in repelling the aggressors. American troops were rushed in but were forced back all the way to a perimeter around Pusan (2), their one port. There they held until an amphibious attack at Inchon (3) crippled the North Korean army. This allowed U.S. troops, reinforced by U.N. contingents from other countries, to mount an offensive (4) from Pusan, link up with troops advancing from the Inchon operation and push deep into North Korea (5).

The entry into the war of Communist China with a strong surprise invasion (6) smashed the American Eighth Army's drive to the Yalu River border of China and necessitated a massive sea evacuation of U.N. troops and refugees at Hungnam (7).

Over Soviet-bloc opposition, the U.N. Assembly voted to condemn the Communist Chinese and to impose an embargo on war matériel shipments to them.

United Nations forces managed to establish themselves generally along the 38th Parallel (8), responding to Chinese offensives with counterattacks. Months of bloody hill-fighting preceded a cease-fire in July 1953.

Since U.N. troops fought under the concept of limited warfare in order to restore the status quo, operations were confined to the area up to the south bank of the Yalu River, the boundary between North Korea and Chinese Manchuria. Never had Americans fought a more frustrating war, yet for the first time aggression was discouraged and defeated by prompt collective military action under the United Nations flag.

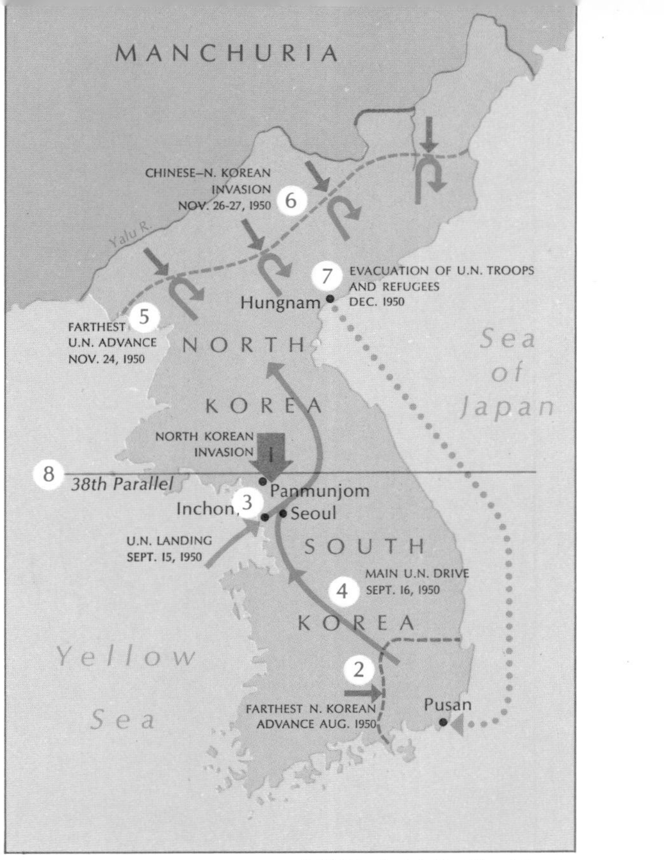

WAR IN VIETNAM

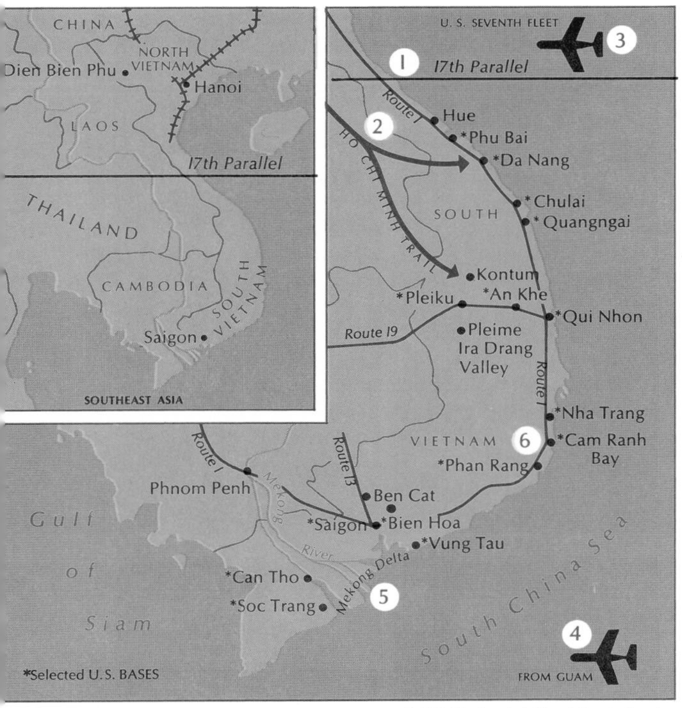

In the mid-nineteenth century, France conquered what is now North and South Vietnam, together with other sections of French Indochina. After World War II, during which the Japanese occupied Vietnam, France tried to regain control. The Viet Minh, a mixed force of nationalists and Communists led by Ho Chi Minh, fought almost eight years, finally defeating French forces in 1954 at Dien Bien Phu (see inset map).

In 1954 the Geneva Conference of nine nations, including France, Great Britain, the United States, the U.S.S.R., China and neighboring nations agreed to partition the new nation temporarily along the 17th Parallel (1) and called for free elections within two years to unify the country. The Communist regime in the North was headed by Ho Chi Minh, and an anti-Communist government was established in the South.

From 1956 to 1959, after elections were canceled, guerrilla rebels—the Viet Cong—supplied from the North via the Ho Chi Minh Trail (2), spread sporadic terror and subversion. These rebels were steadily winning control of large areas of South Vietnam. United States involvement in the early stages was limited to economic aid and military training and supply missions. In 1960 the North Vietnamese sent fighters southward, initiating full-scale guerrilla warfare. Alarmed, the United States in 1961 responded by dispatching combat support units, limited to advisory roles. In 1963 these units totaled more than 16,000 men. In November 1963, South Vietnam's President Diem was ousted and assassinated, and, until General Nguyen Cao Ky assumed power in 1965, political instability permitted a surge of Viet Cong activity.

By 1964 U.S. strength had increased to 23,000 men. Their military role changed from an advisory one to that of active combat. In that year air strikes from the U.S. Seventh Fleet (3) and from Guam (4) were made against North Vietnamese installations and Viet Cong bases in the South. Soviet advisory personnel have been stationed in North Vietnam, with Soviet-made planes and antiaircraft equipment. The Chinese maintain two rail supply lines to Hanoi, the capital of North Vietnam.

The American commitment had increased dramatically to more than 450,000 troops by mid-1967, and U.S. combat operations began in the heavily populated Mekong Delta (5). Airfields and shipping facilities were built on rice paddies and sand dunes. The port at Cam Ranh Bay (6) became one of the largest deepwater ports in Southeast Asia, capable of bearing a heavy share of support for the war effort in Vietnam. Highway routes 1, 13 and 19 have served as principal U.S. supply routes while the railway parallel to Route 1 has been subjected to unremitting guerrilla sabotage. In 1967 the Viet Cong still controlled many parts of the South.

FOREIGN AID AND INTERNATIONAL COÖPERATION

From 1945 through 1965, the United States extended over $100 billion in economic and military aid to 100 nations. Some 70 percent of this was in the form of grants and outright gifts, and the remaining 30 percent in repayable loans. The total involved was more than any other nation has ever spent on foreign aid in peacetime and the fact that about two thirds of the aid was for economic purposes makes it even more impressive.

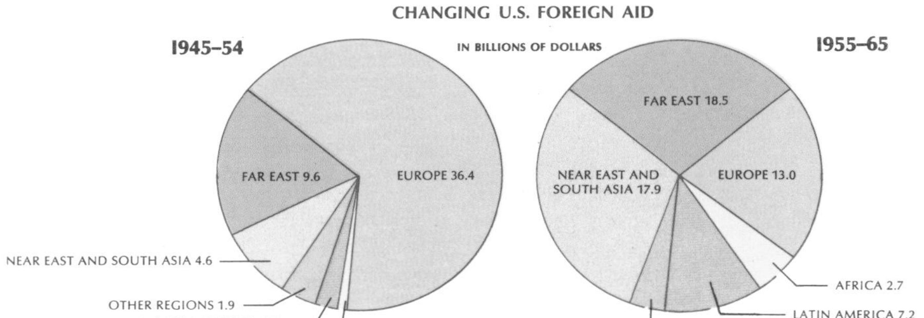

European Recovery. World War II left European nations disorganized and in ruin. The United States recognized the threat that Communist power posed for the perilously weak Western nations and proposed aid and recovery plans to support them against direct and indirect aggression. The first countries to benefit were Greece and Turkey. After Axis occupation during World War II, Greece fell into chaos, and soon Communist guerrillas were gaining ground in taking over the country. American aid bolstered the economy, and military assistance enabled the Greek government to assert its authority throughout the land. With American help, Turkey regained enough armed strength to withstand pressing Soviet demands for control of the vital Dardanelles, the eastern entrance to the Mediterranean Sea.

This was only a prelude to the vast American measures undertaken to revive Europe. Under the Marshall Plan (1948–52), $13 billion in American aid was extended to 16 coöperating European nations. The project brought dramatic recovery, and with it the unity and general political stability of the West. After the Marshall Plan, some smaller programs were continued; then in 1963 U.S. economic assistance to Europe ceased altogether.

In 1949, with the enactment of the Mutual Defense Assistance Act, military aid to foreign nations became part of U.S. foreign policy and played an important role in European defense in the 1950's. By the mid-1960's, military support to Europe was greatly reduced. Since 1961 an arm of the State Department—the Agency for International Development (AID)—has coördinated both economic and military aid programs.

Programs for Developing Countries. The Point Four Program, initiated in 1949, has provided large-scale technical assistance to developing nations. Highly skilled experts advise and train local citizens. Under AID, more than 5000 technicians were at work by 1965 in the underdeveloped countries.

Over the years U.S. foreign aid has undergone a notable shift. The Korean War served as a reminder that industrial rehabilitation in Europe would not prevent the cold war from becoming hot in other parts of the world. America redirected her aid program, first to the Far East and southern Asia, then to Latin America and Africa.

Founded in 1961, the Alliance for Progress was the first attempt since the Marshall Plan to introduce regional organization into U.S. aid. The Alliance employs multilateral action by South and Central American countries to solve their economic and social problems.

On much of the African continent, European nations still carry the main responsibility for assistance to their former colonies. Recently the United States has augmented Belgian, French and British assistance with technical coöperation in national development programs in Africa.

The Peace Corps, founded in 1961, employs volunteers to work in developing nations. Volunteers fill the gap between the relatively unskilled local labor and the highly skilled technical advisers of the Point Four Program. They usually serve under host-country supervision in a wide variety of jobs—as teachers, agricultural extension workers, surveyors, medical technicians, nurses, youth-group organizers and community-development workers. In 1965 nearly 11,000 volunteers were working in some 46 countries overseas, in Latin America, Africa, the Near East, South Asia and the Far East.

Community of Nations. In addition to its system of mutual-defense treaties the United States has hundreds of formal treaties and agreements with the world community about such areas as Outer Space, the High Seas and Antarctica.

Through the United Nations, the United States has made considerable contributions in maintaining some semblance of order in the postwar world. America annually contributes a substantial portion of the budget of the U.N. Development Fund, which has supported modest economic programs in developing nations. The U.N. has undertaken peacekeeping operations in such diverse places as Indonesia, Greece, Palestine, Kashmir, Trieste, Suez, Lebanon, Laos, the Congo, West New Guinea (now West Irian), Yemen and Cyprus. American troops have fought with U.N. forces against aggressors in Korea.

The aim of the United States among developing countries has been to create, through concerted foreign assistance, a community of independent and self-supporting nations which can live in peace.

DEFENSIVE MILITARY ALLIANCES

The United States has military alliances with more than 40 nations on five continents to supply effective counteraction against aggression. Alliance arrangements provide a threatened country—for example, Korea—with the will to deter or check aggression by guaranteeing that it will not have to stand alone. The charter of the United Nations (Articles 51 and 52) foresaw the need for independent regional alliances to maintain peace and security. Such free agreements are the only means of collective security where the processes of the U.N. are blocked or its action rendered ineffective. The regional system is not an alternative to the U.N. but complementary to it.

NATO. The North Atlantic Treaty Organization, formed in the cold-war atmosphere of 1949, rose out of the need to align the defenses of the United States and Western Europe. The expansionist policy of the U.S.S.R. was demonstrated by the *coup d'état* which took over the Czechoslovakian government and by the Berlin Blockade, a Soviet attempt to take over Berlin. NATO maintains that an armed attack on one member is an attack on them all. A system of unified political coöperation and military planning is continuously maintained. Originally composed of 12 nations, NATO admitted the eastern Mediterranean countries of Greece and Turkey in 1952 and West Germany in 1955. During 1966 President de Gaulle withdrew French forces from the integrated military system of NATO, posing major problems for future strategy. Since 1963 the United States has committed to NATO's European command in Belgium a number of Polaris submarines equipped with nuclear missiles, and has retained operational control of them. Members have committed to NATO important elements of their armies, navies and air forces and maintain 220 standard NATO airfields. A number of the aircraft and weapons in use by national troops have been jointly developed or produced by NATO allies.

ANZUS Pact. The ANZUS Treaty of Australia, New Zealand and the United States was signed in 1951. Still in force, its operation was a step toward formation of the more inclusive Southeast Asia Treaty Organization.

SEATO. The Southeast Asia Treaty Organization, formed in 1954, comprises the United States, Great Britain, Australia, New Zealand, France, Thailand, Pakistan and the Philippine Republic. It is committed to build up collective economic and military strength for joint defensive action in the event of direct or indirect Communist agression against a member state or against the "protocol" states of Laos, Cambodia and South Vietnam. SEATO lacks a central command structure (each member's armed forces remain under national control) and it has not acted collectively in the Vietnamese war. Although five member nations—the United States, Australia, New Zealand, Thailand and the Philippines—have sent troops to South Vietnam, they have done so through bilateral arrangements with the South Vietnamese government. In 1965 France hinted that she might resign from SEATO in protest against U.S. Vietnam policy. Thus little military and economic integration has been achieved, and SEATO has become chiefly an expression of anti-Communism. Rounding out America's Far Eastern military alliances are bilateral mutual-defense treaties with the Philippines (1951), the Republic of China (Taiwan) (1954), South Korea (1954) and Japan (1960).

CENTO. Eager to promote peace and stability in the Middle East and desirous of a geographic link between NATO and SEATO, the United States was instrumental in forming the Middle East Treaty Organization (METO). This alliance, including Iran, Iraq, Pakistan, Turkey and the United Kingdom, was signed in 1955. In 1959 Iraq withdrew from METO; the four remaining members chose a new name, the Central Treaty Organization (CENTO). Though a nonmember, the United States is represented in CENTO on its scientific council and on the military, economic and countersubversion committees. The United States is also an observer on the CENTO Ministers Council. While there is no unified armed-forces command for CENTO, the defense position of Turkey, Iran and Pakistan has been bolstered by U.S. military assistance.

OAS. In 1947 the United States and the 21 Latin-American republics entered into the Rio Treaty, which provided for the common defense of the Western Hemisphere in accordance with United Nations Charter provisions permitting regional defensive action. The next year members formed the Organization of American States, and added other nonmilitary agreements to the treaty. Its member nations have worked very well through the OAS to settle hemispheric problems. At an OAS conference in 1962, Communist Cuban subversion was challenged, and Cuba was removed from the hemispheric military defense planning agency and from all OAS functions. OAS forces intervened to keep peace during the outbreak of civil war in the Dominican Republic in the summer of 1965.
(U.S. alliances are shown in color on the map below.)

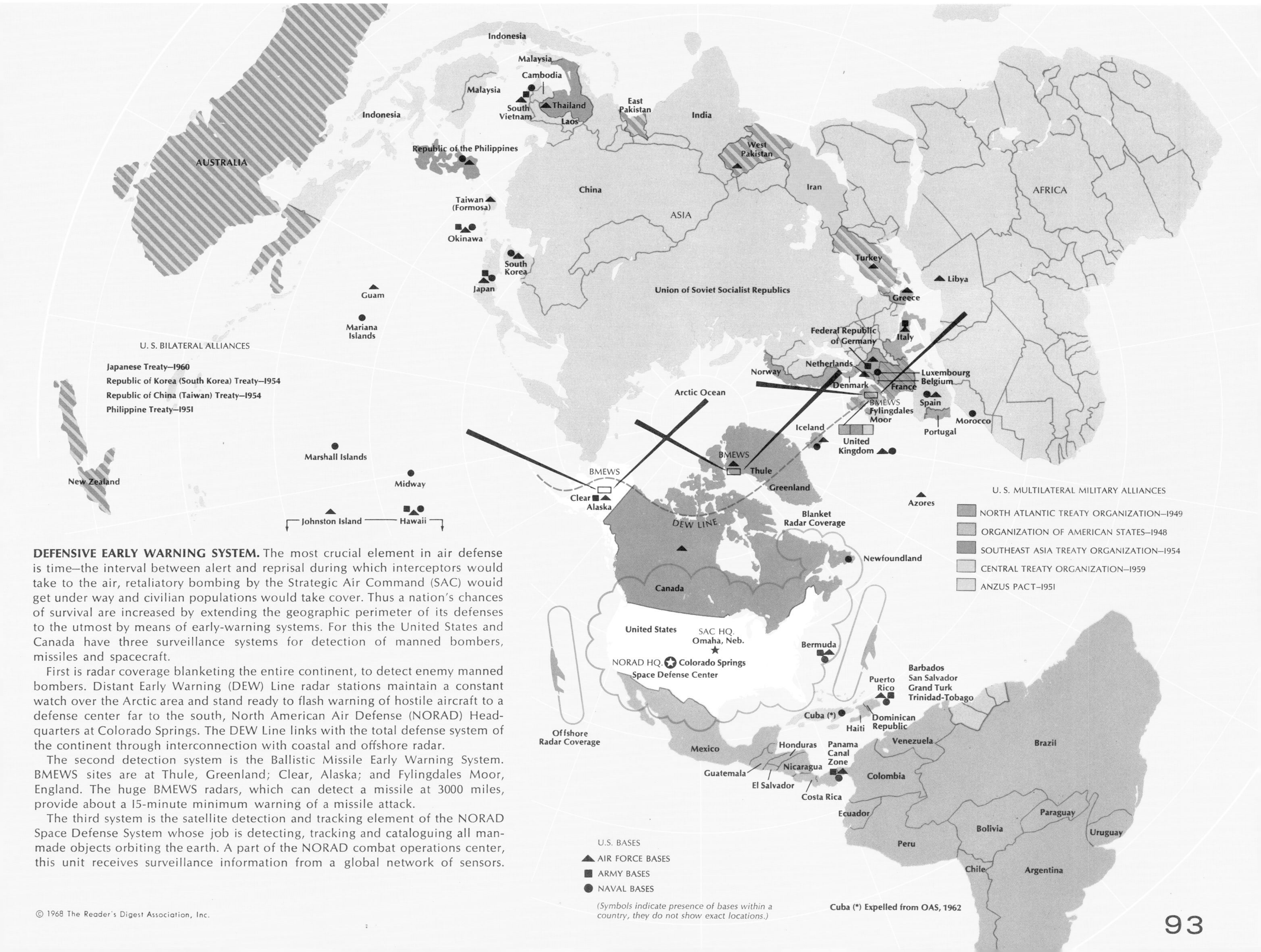

DEFENSIVE EARLY WARNING SYSTEM. The most crucial element in air defense is time—the interval between alert and reprisal during which interceptors would take to the air, retaliatory bombing by the Strategic Air Command (SAC) would get under way and civilian populations would take cover. Thus a nation's chances of survival are increased by extending the geographic perimeter of its defenses to the utmost by means of early-warning systems. For this the United States and Canada have three surveillance systems for detection of manned bombers, missiles and spacecraft.

First is radar coverage blanketing the entire continent, to detect enemy manned bombers. Distant Early Warning (DEW) Line radar stations maintain a constant watch over the Arctic area and stand ready to flash warning of hostile aircraft to a defense center far to the south, North American Air Defense (NORAD) Headquarters at Colorado Springs. The DEW Line links with the total defense system of the continent through interconnection with coastal and offshore radar.

The second detection system is the Ballistic Missile Early Warning System. BMEWS sites are at Thule, Greenland; Clear, Alaska; and Fylingdales Moor, England. The huge BMEWS radars, which can detect a missile at 3000 miles, provide about a 15-minute minimum warning of a missile attack.

The third system is the satellite detection and tracking element of the NORAD Space Defense System whose job is detecting, tracking and cataloguing all man-made objects orbiting the earth. A part of the NORAD combat operations center, this unit receives surveillance information from a global network of sensors.

THE MOLDING OF AMERICAN DEMOCRACY

1789, 1792

"Long Live the President!"

A button worn at the time of Washington's election celebrated the fact that the country was headed by an elected president rather than a hereditary king.

Washington unanimous choice of electors in both contests

These states either did not cast electoral ballots or were not in the Union in 1789

1796

"Stand with Washington."

Federalists under Adams used this slogan to rally support for their programs in the name of George Washington.

Adams Jefferson

1800

"Lord! How the
Federalists will stare
At Jefferson
in Adams' chair!"

The last two lines of a Democratic-Republican campaign song taunted the Federalists with their impending downfall.

Adams Jefferson

1804

"Our farmers on the sea coast:
May their cornfields be
defended against
Gun Boat Number Three."

Federalists offered this humorous toast to deride the failures of Jefferson's naval gunboats, one of which had been washed ashore in a storm. But Jefferson won the election.

Jefferson Pinckney

The political system of the United States did not spring full-blown from the American Revolution but grew slowly from ideas of representative government brought over from England long before that great struggle. Colonial experience with representative government, and then the war itself, produced changes which made the American system rather different from its English model. But once the central authority of the British Crown was removed, strong leadership was needed to draw together the 13 new states. Bound only by the loose Articles of Confederation, adopted in 1781, they contributed funds to Congress as they wished or not at all, failed to maintain a common army and had no judicial system to settle disputes across their borders. Finally, in 1787, 55 delegates meeting in Philadelphia managed to frame a new, stronger Federal Constitution.

Elections of 1789 and 1792. When George Washington took the oath of office as first President on April 30, 1789, only 11 of the 13 states had ratified the Constitution. North Carolina and Rhode Island did so only when they realized they could not prosper separately outside the Federal Union. Washington, admired by everyone, received the full 69 first-choice votes of the electors. John Adams got 34 second-choice votes and the remaining 35 were split among others. Adams thus became the Vice President.

All of the candidates were Federalists in the sense that all supported the new Constitution. The votes for Vice President were cast on personal, local or sectional lines. There were, however, economic conflicts to be reconciled. Washington, who was essentially a conservative landholder, appointed a Northerner concerned with business and finance, Alexander Hamilton, as his Secretary of the Treasury, while at the same time naming the Virginia plantation owner Thomas Jefferson as his Secretary of State. Hamilton favored a strong national government and a diversified economy. Jefferson, fearing the power of the central government, championed the rights of the states and hoped that the country would remain chiefly agricultural. Washington, reelected without opposition in 1792, did his best to keep these rivals working together until the country could grow strong enough to stand the strain of open division.

Election of 1796. With Washington declining to run for a third term, the two factions which had been struggling to gain the upper hand during his Presidency now developed into full-fledged political parties: the Federalists, led by Alexander Hamilton, and the Democratic-Republicans, led by Jefferson and his Virginia friend, James Madison. The Federalists carried the day in 1796, electing John Adams President, but the Democratic-Republicans gained strength steadily. Aside from the economic issues of the times, the two parties clashed over foreign policy. The French Revolution of 1789 had delighted Jefferson's followers, but, especially after the execution of King Louis XVI, the "excesses" of the revolutionaries alarmed the Federalists.

Fearing that French radicalism would invade the United States and that an actual war between America and France was then likely, they passed the Sedition Act of 1798, which provided that anyone who criticized government officials might be imprisoned, and the Alien Act, which authorized the deportation of "dangerous" foreigners. The Federalists viewed these acts as a wall of protection against a revolution of the bloody French type in America. But the Democratic-Republicans considered them unconstitutional violations of the rights of American citizens. When the French, turning in a conservative direction, made peaceful overtures, the war scare evaporated. A reaction against the Alien and Sedition Acts followed which added immeasurably to the strength of the Jeffersonians.

Elections of 1800–20. The election of 1800 reflected this reaction. Thomas Jefferson became President. Four years later the voters reelected him by an even greater majority. This election of 1804 consolidated the hold of Democratic-Republicans on the apparatus of government while at the same time indicating a westward shift of voting power in the country. The Federalists were becoming chiefly a northeastern party. In 1808 they had little success elsewhere in a campaign against James Madison, Jefferson's handpicked successor. Then, in 1812, they supported a fusion group opposed to "Mr. Madison's" War of 1812 against Great Britain, but to no avail. In the era of intense nationalism following the war, the doom of the Federalist Party was sealed. In 1816 their candidate, Rufus King, was swamped by James Monroe. They had resisted too long the democratic spirit of the times, and their best ideas, such as the Bank of the United States and the protective tariff, had been taken over by the Democratic-Republicans. In the election of 1820 the Democratic-Republicans, led by Monroe, captured all but one of the electoral votes in a one-sided contest with a small splinter group called the Independent Republicans.

Elections of 1824–32. The political power of Western and Southern farmers and frontiersmen, together with that of small tradesmen and mechanics in the towns, was gradually increasing, but it had not yet been brought into focus. In the contest of 1824 all the candidates considered themselves heirs of Jefferson. The votes of the country were split between four favorite sons from different sections: the New Englander John Quincy Adams; General Andrew Jackson, hero of the Battle of New Orleans; William H. Crawford of Georgia; and Henry Clay of Kentucky. No candidate got a majority of the electoral votes, though Jackson led with 99. The election was thrown into the House of Representatives where Clay's influence gave second-runner Adams the Presidency. In 1828 the electorate united under two banners: Jackson's Democratic Party and Adams' National Republicans. John C. Calhoun of South Carolina, who had been elected Vice President in 1824, ran for that office again on the Jackson ticket. This alliance of the South and the West won a substantial victory.

As President, Jackson continued the Jeffersonian tradition of limiting Federal authority and encouraging popular democracy. He also added innovations of his own, and greatly extended the not-so-laudable "spoils system" under which public appointments were used to pay off political debts. During his time in office Jackson welded together a national political machine whose later breakup was to be partly responsible for sectionalism that brought on the Civil War. At the polls in 1832, he repeated his success, this time against Clay. A tiny minority party, the Anti-Masons, ran a candidate named William Wirt in the same election. Influential, though insignificant as a party, the Anti-Masons created the concept of a national party convention at which the Presidential candidate is selected. This method was quickly adopted by the major parties. Previously, legislative or congressional party members in each state had determined the candidate.

Elections of 1836–52. In these elections the candidates of the Whig Party, a new coalition of lesser parties, opposed the Jacksonian Democrats. The Whigs' most prominent leader was Henry Clay, under whom various dissident elements had gathered. In 1836 there were three segments of the Whig Party, and each nominated a Presidential candidate. Democrat Martin Van Buren easily defeated them. The chief element that joined all Whigs in support of William H. Harrison in 1840 was the shared dislike of Jackson and his policies. The Whigs so disagreed on other issues that they never produced a party platform.

In a twist of clever campaign tactics, the Whigs created an image of Harrison as a poor, rugged frontiersman, though he was comfortably wealthy. Ironically, Van Buren, who had been born poor, was attacked for his supposed snobbishness and high living in the White House. The aged Harrison won, died within a month, and John Tyler became President. Tyler, a states'-rights advocate from Virginia, opposed everything that the other Whig leaders, Daniel Webster and Henry Clay, stood for, except dislike of Jackson and Van Buren. The party was divided once more. The Whigs lost the election of 1844 to Democrat James K. Polk, then, behind the popular Mexican War general, Zachary Taylor, won again in 1848. During the course of these campaigns both parties tried to avoid the growing

PRESIDENTIAL ELECTIONS: 1796–1964

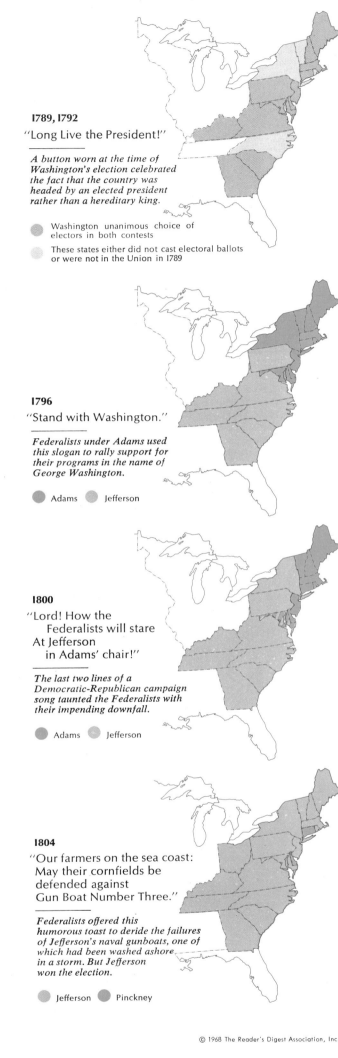

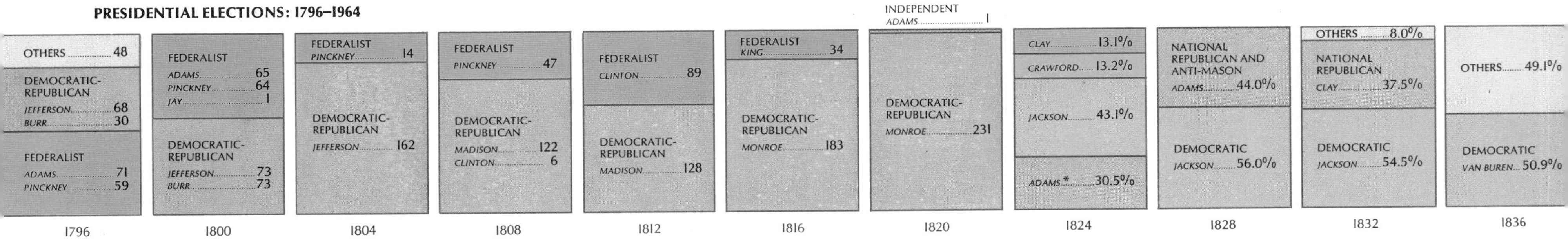

NOTE: In the elections of 1789 to 1800, each elector cast two votes for separate Presidential candidates. The candidate with the most votes became President, the next became Vice President. After 1800, the Twelfth Amendment provided that the Presidential and Vice Presidential candidates be of the same party. Electors were, and still are today, appointed in a manner designated by the legislature of each state.

Records of the popular vote before 1824 are almost nonexistent. For these years the electoral vote is given. For elections of 1824 to 1964 percentages of the popular vote are given. Candidates who received less than 10 percent of the popular vote are listed as "others" rather than by name.

**Indicates winner. In 1824, Adams received a smaller percentage of both the popular and electoral vote than did Jackson, but was chosen President by vote in the House of Representatives. In two other elections—1876 and 1888—the winner received a greater percentage of the electoral vote even though he had a smaller percentage of the popular vote.*

slavery question, which threatened to split their northern and southern wings. Four years after Taylor's success the Whigs finally became entangled in bitter debates over the problem, and Franklin Pierce, backed by the still-united Democrats, was thus elected by a huge majority of the electoral vote.

Elections of 1856 and 1860. The slavery dispute was now out in the open among the Whigs, and some of the party's northern wing joined with like-minded Democrats to form the Republican Party, which was dedicated to preventing the expansion of slavery into any new territory. In 1856 its candidate, John C. Frémont, carried the Northeast and most of the central states, but Democrat James Buchanan won the election. Two years later in the Illinois senatorial election the Republicans found a new standard-bearer, Abraham Lincoln. The little-known lawyer and politician who was running against the nationally prominent Democrat Stephen A. Douglas, engaged his opponent in a series of debates. Douglas argued that Lincoln and the Republicans were pursuing policies that would destroy the Union. He was elected senator, but clever questions by Lincoln had so forced him to compromise his position on slavery in the territories that his southern support faded and with it his dreams of being elected President in the next campaign.

With the South regularly frustrated as new states were joining the Union, it was evident that an open clash could not long be postponed. Under the Compromise of 1850, for example, California had been admitted to the Union as a free state. The best the South could gain was a promise that New Mexico and Utah would, on their admission, be allowed to decide the status of slavery in their territories. In the election of 1860 the Republicans came out four-square against any extension of slavery to new areas. In addition they appealed to farmers of the West by calling for a transcontinental railroad and a law giving land in the West free to homesteaders. Unfortunately for the Democratic Party, it split into northern and southern wings. The Southerners nominated John Breckinridge, who wanted slavery extended to new territories. The Northerners chose Stephen A. Douglas, who argued for local self-determination of the slavery issue. A fourth element in the election was John Bell's Constitutional Union Party, a moderate faction centered in the border states. The Republicans won with Lincoln, and within a few months 11 Southern states had seceded, forming the Confederate States of America. This action drew off much of the Democratic voting strength in Congress, leaving the Republicans in control of the House until 1871 and of the Senate until 1879.

Election of 1864. In the 1864 wartime election there was, of course, no direct Southern opposition. The Democrats of the North and West were led by General George McClellan. Some of McClellan's followers, called Copperheads, advocated an immediate end to the war and the recognition of Southern independence. Many in the North were heartily tired of the terrifying casualty lists and discouraging course of the war. A series of victories by the Union armies brought fresh strength to the Republicans. Lincoln was elected to a second term, receiving more than half of the popular vote and most of the electoral. The Republicans were now committed to the abolition of slavery, their radicals favoring strong measures to reshape the South completely once the war was won.

With the Union preserved and the slaves freed, Lincoln, a man of charitable nature, favored a quick reconciliation with the South. But after his assassination, radical Republicans sought, by the strong use of Federal authority, to force the South to give the Negro political and social equality with whites. In 1867 these Republicans in Congress took over Reconstruction, overriding the objections of Lincoln's successor, Andrew Johnson. Some say Reconstruction failed because it was not carried far enough; others insist corruption and white Southern resistance to Negro equality doomed it from the start. Whatever the answer, Reconstruction's failure recoiled upon the unfortunate Negroes when Southern whites again assumed full power. In addition, Southern bitterness generated by loss

1824

"John Quincy Adams,
who can write
And Andrew Jackson,
who can fight."

A pro-Jackson jingle contrasted Jackson's military victories with his opponent's lofty words.

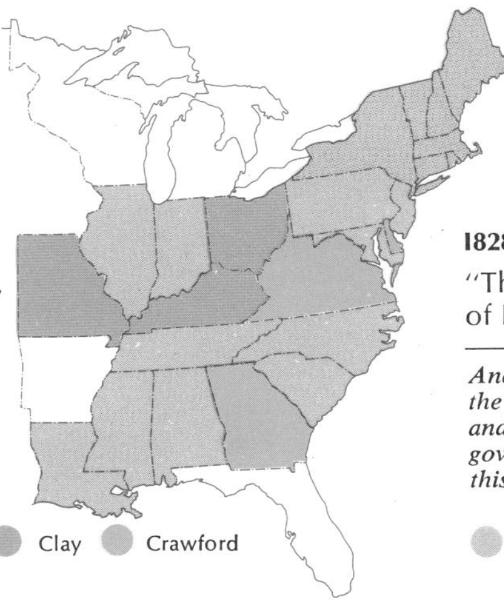

1828

"The Democracy of Numbers"

Andrew Jackson attacked the aristocratic few and boosted popular government with this catchy phrase.

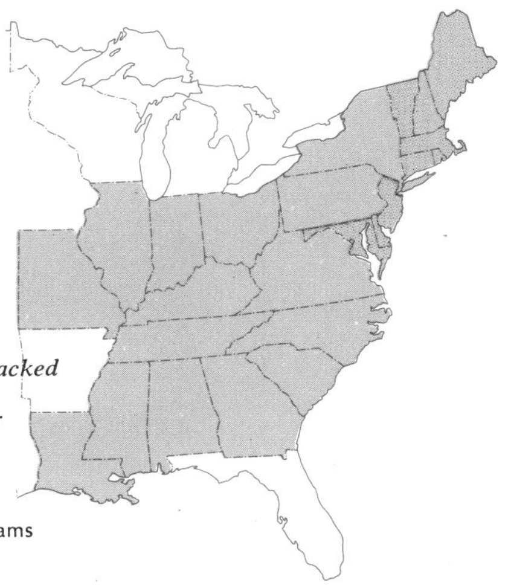

The county election maps for 1860 and 1864 reveal the division within the country. Had the South participated in the 1864 election, Lincoln would probably have been defeated.

1860

"Justice and Fairness to All"

Lincoln used this phrase to indicate his position on a number of important issues.

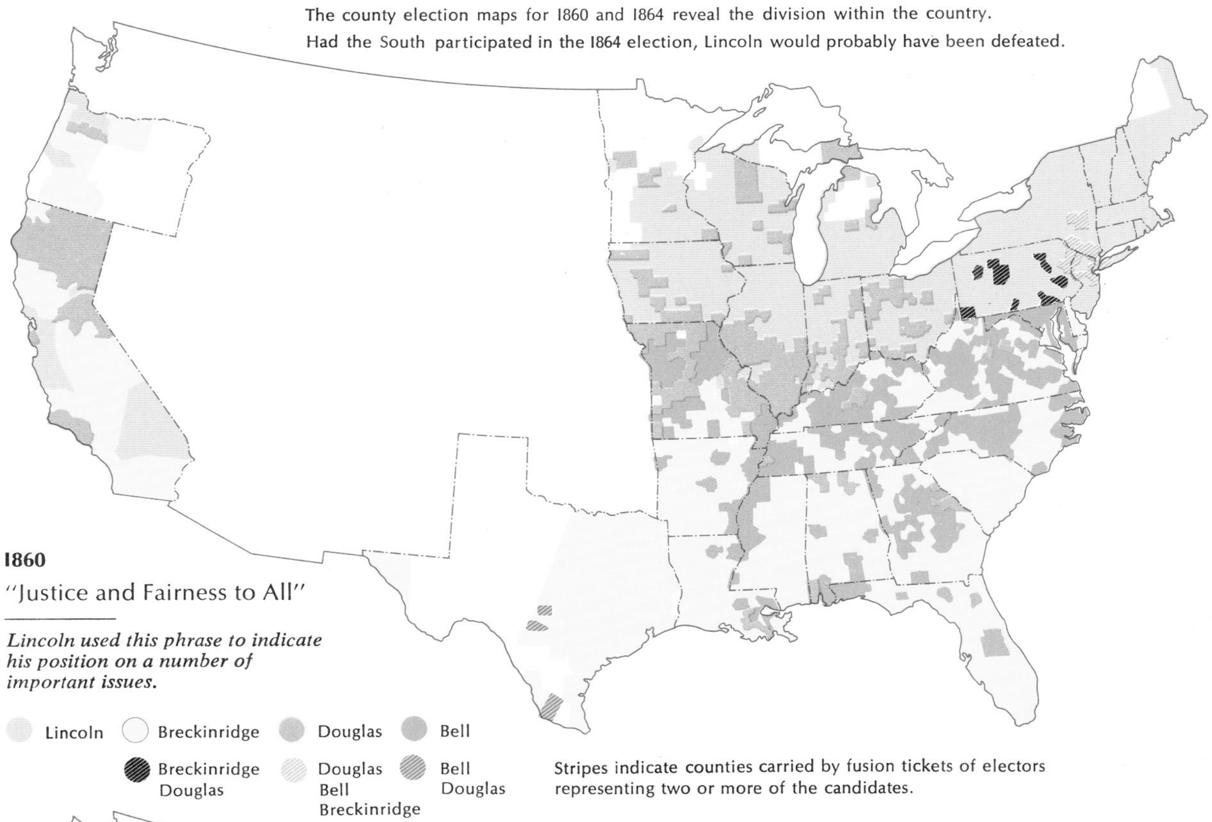

Stripes indicate counties carried by fusion tickets of electors representing two or more of the candidates.

1864

"Don't swap horses
in the middle of the stream."

To warn against changing leaders in the middle of a war, Republicans used this line from a Lincoln story about an old Dutch farmer.

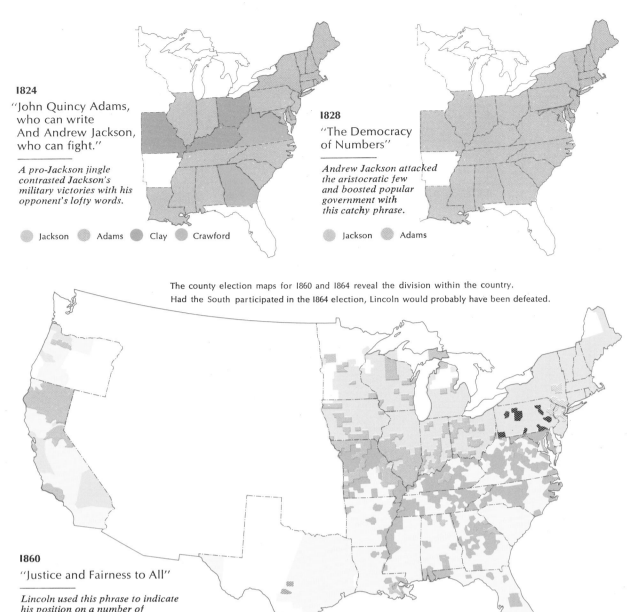

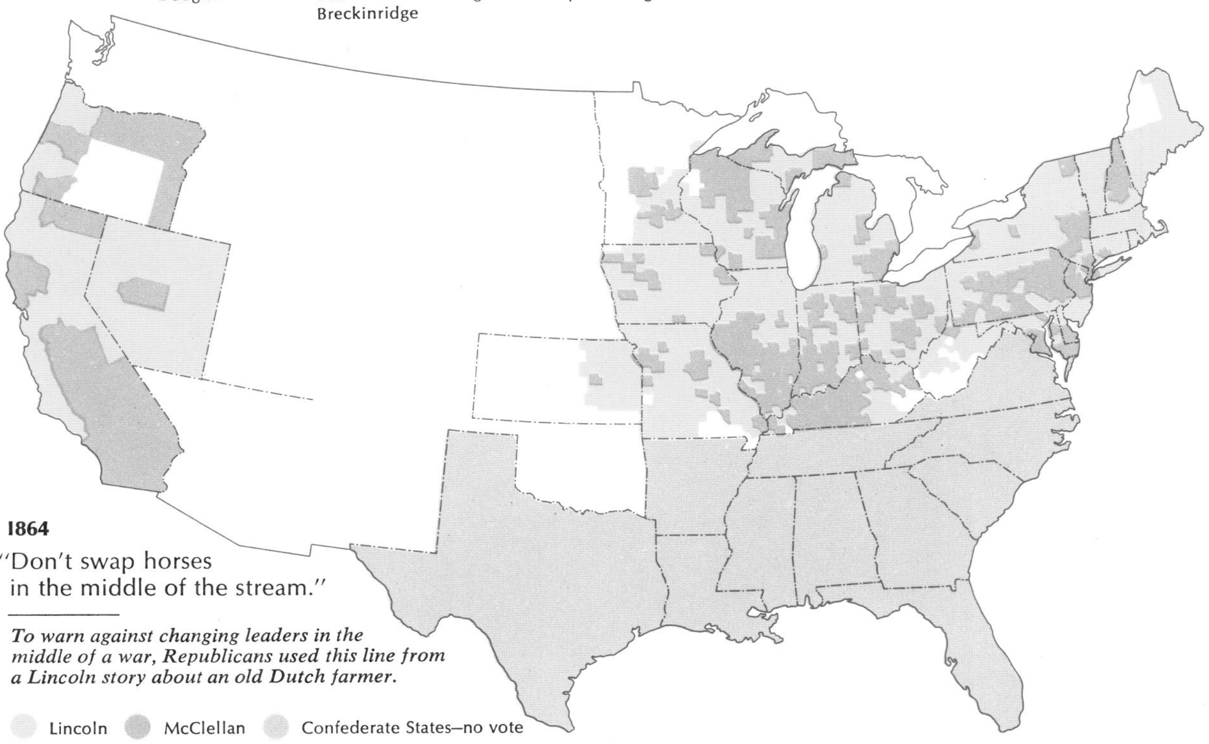

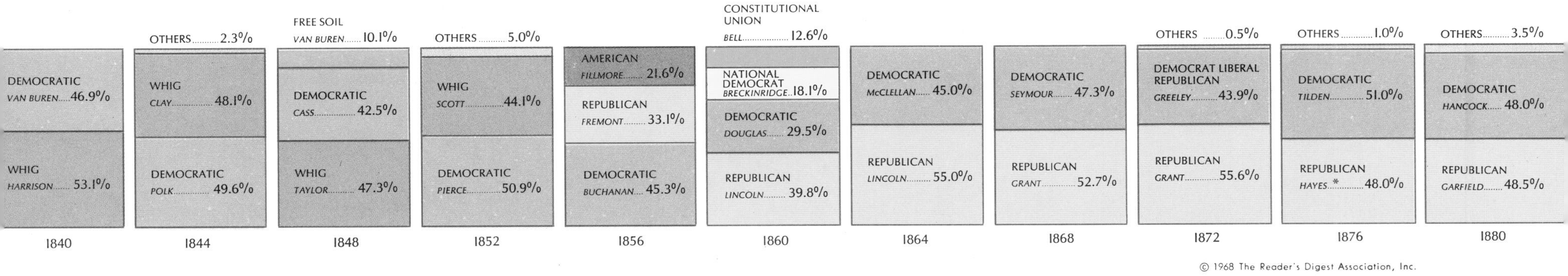

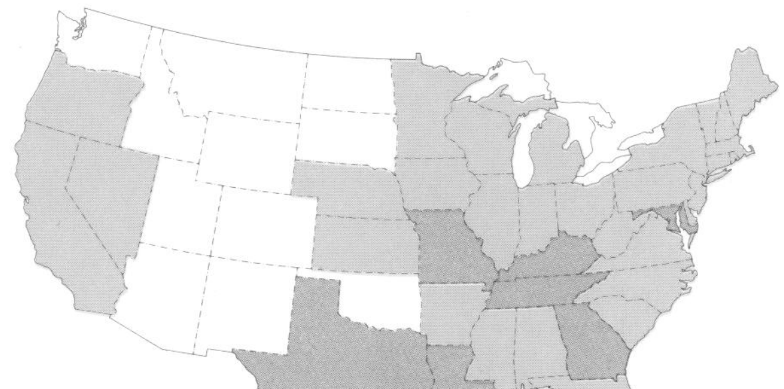

1872

"Turn the rascals out!"

In a bitter campaign Horace Greeley coined this phrase to vilify the scandals in the first administration of Ulysses S. Grant.

Grant Greeley and Democratic-Liberal Opposition

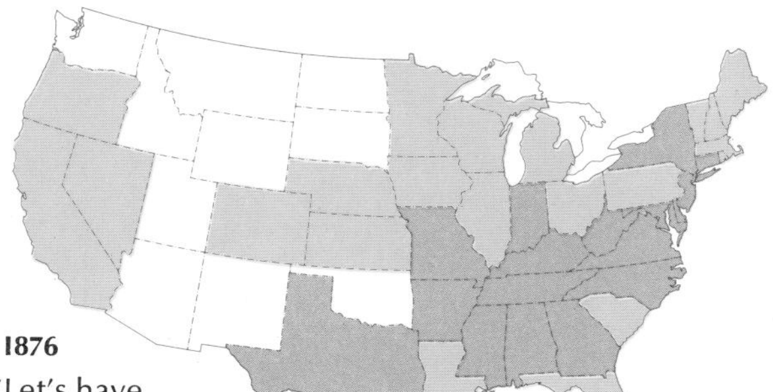

1876

"Let's have a clean sweep."

The Democrats again accused the Grant Republicans of devious practices in the famous slogan calling for a new administration in Washington.

Hayes Tilden

of the war and dislike of Republican control during Reconstruction helped create a solid bloc of Democratic votes upon which the party could count, regardless of its programs, for more than a hundred years.

Elections of 1868–76. General Ulysses S. Grant won the elections of 1868 and 1872 at the head of the Republican ticket, in both instances with massive help from Negro voters. However, a different alignment of political forces was beginning to take shape. Grant's administrations were fouled by corrupt officials and by partisan practices which disturbed even many Republicans. Rutherford B. Hayes, the Republican candidate of 1876, ran on a platform of reform, sound money and Federal assistance for the South. This proved hardly enough, for Hayes actually trailed his Democratic opponent, Samuel Tilden, by almost a quarter of a million popular votes. Hayes won by a majority of one in the electoral vote because a Republican-controlled commission awarded him 20 disputed ballots, at least some of which he was probably not entitled to. Confusion, even another civil war, might have resulted if Tilden had not conceded without dispute. In return for this, Hayes agreed to withdraw the few remaining Federal soldiers from the South, thus formally ending Reconstruction.

Election of 1880. From the election of 1880, when Republican James Garfield defeated Democrat Winfield Scott Hancock (with an almost even division in the popular vote), through that of 1904, the United States continued to undergo radical changes which molded the future course of American politics and the development of American democracy. As the country moved into the full flood of the industrial revolution, the nature of farming altered. Heavy machinery required large capital outlays. This forced farmers to rely even more heavily on industry for equipment and on banks for loans to finance its purchase. As food prices dropped, farmers demanded "cheap" money (paper greenbacks and other devaluation that would make it easier to pay debts). Many important banking and industrial interests, foreseeing ruination in such inflationary practices, naturally opposed them. Economic change was creating a new situation in American political life, one which would exercise a profound effect on national elections.

Elections of 1884 and 1888. During the period when farmers were developing as a political bloc, eastern and midwestern industry was growing by mighty leaps. Cities like Cleveland, Chicago and Pittsburgh were emerging as industrial centers and railroads were reaching across the nation. Huge monopolistic corporations were formed by strong-willed men. Their activities led to excesses and corruption that aroused much public resentment. But the campaign of 1884 essentially ignored economic issues and concentrated on personalities. Chester A. Arthur had become President when Garfield was assassinated, but James G. Blaine took the Republican nomination away from him. Blaine's Democratic opponent was Grover Cleveland of New York. A group of reform-minded easterners in the Republican Party, known as Mugwumps, bolted to support Cleveland. He won and gave the country four years of honest, if somewhat conservative and unimaginative, leadership. In 1888 he made lowering the tariff the main issue of the election. Cleveland obtained a majority of the popular vote, but as in 1876, the Republicans won a majority of the electoral votes and Benjamin Harrison became the next President.

Elections of 1892–1900. In 1892 western farmers, debtors and those interested in plentiful silver coinage formed the Populist Party, running James B. Weaver against the Democrat Cleveland and the Republican Harrison. The Populists secured 10 percent of the popular vote and 22 electoral votes, but Cleveland was elected President by carrying both the Solid South and a number of key industrial states in the North. The great depression of 1893–96 hurt the Democrats badly, however. Industrial workers and other city dwellers flocked to the Republicans. In 1896 and in 1900, William Jennings Bryan of Nebraska, running as Fusion Democrat and Populist candidate, raised the issue of cheap silver money again in his ringing "cross of gold" speech. He was decisively defeated by Republican William McKinley both then and in 1900. For a full generation thereafter, the Republicans were the majority party of the country.

Election of 1904. The frontier, which had always attracted those who wished to better their lot, had now almost disappeared. More and more industrial workers were joining unions to fight for improvement of their conditions. The bulk of the middle class distrusted labor unions, but the excesses of some business leaders led many voters to turn to politicians who criticized big corporations. Theodore Roosevelt became President in 1901 after Republican William McKinley was assassinated. Roosevelt could hardly be called a radical, but when he ran for office in 1904, his reputation as a "trust-buster" led wage earners, farmers, small businessmen and many other groups to support him eagerly. With his bluff, rugged style, Roosevelt won the election, receiving 7,623,468 popular votes, losing only in the South. His aggressive foreign policy was also popular. He had arrived on the scene when the country was gaining awareness of its importance in world affairs. First winning national fame as colonel of the "Rough Riders" in the Spanish-American War, he roused America with his expansionist policies, such as the acquisition of territory in Panama to build an interoceanic canal.

Election of 1908. Roosevelt's handpicked successor, William H. Taft, though rather colorless, defeated Bryan in the campaign of 1908. Despite his intelligence and good intentions, Taft alienated the liberal wing of his party by tariffs which kept domestic prices high and by policies which damaged conservation. Roosevelt broke with him and became the leader of these dissident Republicans. Eventually he organized his following as the Progressive or "Bull Moose" Party. Its platform was reformist in nature, its life short.

Election of 1912. The Democratic candidate Woodrow Wilson, who campaigned against what he claimed was the domination of government by a small clique of great wealth, won because the Republicans split their votes between Taft and Roosevelt. This college-president-turned-politician at first raised the banner against strong central government. Influenced by the old Jeffersonian distrust of the regulatory state, he called for a "New Freedom" where monopoly would be checked by free competition and the small businessman would come again into his own. Once in office, however, he modified his views and adopted many of the ideas that Roosevelt and other believers in strict government control of the economy had advocated.

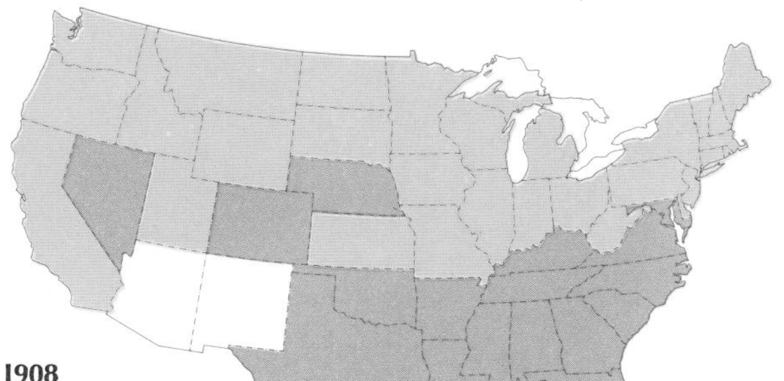

1908

"A Square Deal"

William Howard Taft, Teddy Roosevelt's personal choice as a successor, benefited from Roosevelt's slogan, and promised to continue attacks on trusts and monopolies.

Taft Bryan

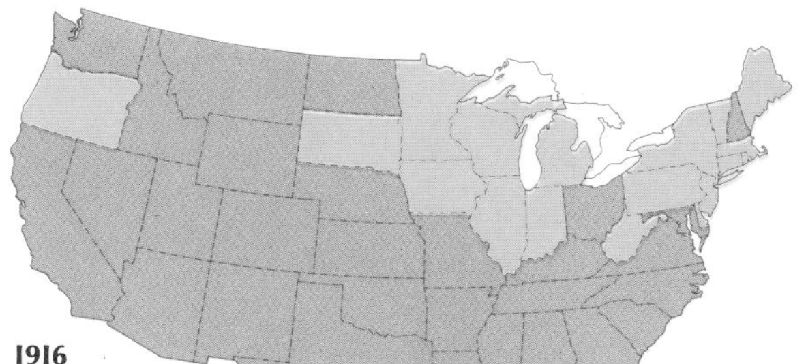

1916

"He kept us out of war."

For two years Wilson held America neutral during World War I; Democrats seized upon this appeal to help him win again.

Wilson Hughes

1912

"I feel as strong as a bull moose."

Roosevelt's new "Bull Moose" Party got its name from his statement made at a convention.

Wilson Roosevelt Taft

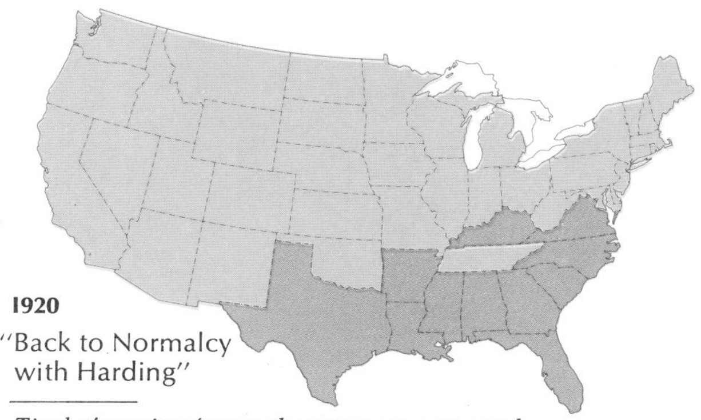

1920

"Back to Normalcy with Harding"

Tired of wartime frenzy, the voters were attracted by the visions of peace engendered when Harding used the word "normalcy" in a speech.

Harding Cox

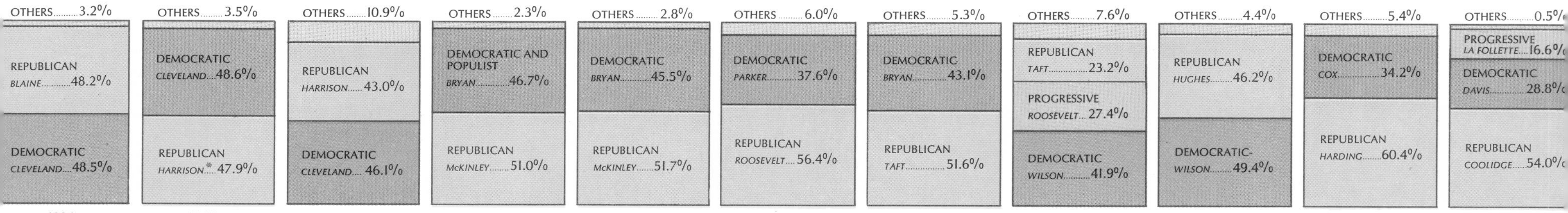

**Indicates winner. In 1824, Adams received a smaller percentage of both the popular and electoral vote than did Jackson, but was chosen President by vote in the House of Representatives. In two other elections—1876 and 1888—the winner received a greater percentage of the electoral vote even though he had a smaller percentage of the popular vote.*

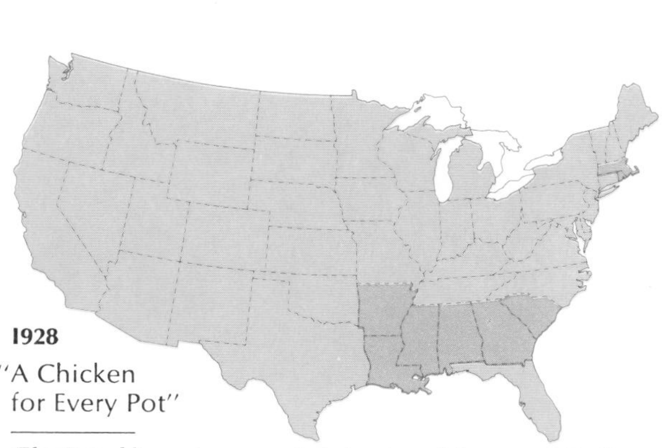

1928
"A Chicken for Every Pot"

This Republican slogan reminded voters of the prosperity they were enjoying under a GOP administration.

Hoover Smith

1932
"The New Deal"

Depression stalked the land as Franklin D. Roosevelt campaigned on this rewrite of Teddy Roosevelt's slogan of 1904.

Roosevelt (F.D.) Hoover

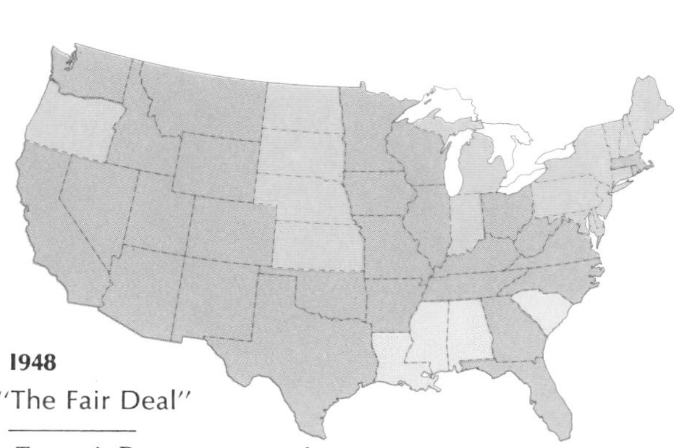

1948
"The Fair Deal"

Truman's Democrats enticed voters with another variation of the successful "Deal" catchword.

Truman Dewey Thurmond

Election of 1916. Wilson's first administration was highly successful in pacifying both the low-tariff farm bloc and the foes of industrial monopoly. After war broke out in Europe in 1914, domestic reform seemed less important. In 1916 Wilson won reelection as the man who had kept the country out of this terrible war, despite the strength of Republican Charles Evans Hughes in many of the northeastern and north-central states where business interests were opposed to Wilson's progressive ideas. Only a few months later, after German attacks against defenseless merchant ships, Wilson became convinced that world peace could be restored only through American intervention. Wilson asked the Congress to declare war.

Election of 1920. By 1920 other political forces were becoming major influences in elections. Women now had the right to vote and though they did not act as a bloc, there is little doubt that the handsome Warren G. Harding had strong appeal for them. The main factor in 1920 was a general reaction against Wilsonian idealism and the war, which had cost so much and produced so few benefits. Harding rolled up an enormous majority over his Democratic rival, James M. Cox. Harding proved a weak President, and his administration was riddled by corruption. He died in the middle of his term and was succeeded by Vice President Calvin Coolidge of Massachusetts.

Elections of 1924 and 1928. The Republicans held the Presidency through these elections with honest, plainspoken Coolidge winning in 1924 and engineer-economist Herbert Hoover in 1928. Hoover's victory was notable because he carried some of the normally Democratic Southern states against his Roman Catholic opponent, Alfred E. Smith.

Elections of 1932–44. The country had been in a boom since the end of the war, but by 1929 severe weaknesses had developed in the economy. Agricultural prices, on a downward slide since 1921, slumped disastrously, and many farmers were thrown into bankruptcy. Some stayed on the land as tenants; others, fleeing worn-out land and drought, began to head west for California. Shutdowns of failing industries threw millions of factory hands out of work. International trade losses aggravated the situation. The economy staggered, faltered, stopped, and the Democrats elected Franklin D. Roosevelt over Hoover in a massive political victory of the discontented.

The new President had some of the same qualities which had made his cousin Theodore so attractive to voters. Possessed of an aristocratic mien, he was also blessed with the common touch. His New Deal program strongly appealed to the desperate country. Roosevelt sought to pull America from the Depression by positive Federal action. By increasing the amount of money in circulation and spending freely, he caused prices to rise and industrial activity to pick up. Unemployment declined. As a result, he built a popular political coalition of farmers, organized labor and the Southern bloc, a combination never before seen in the United States. To mossback conservatives he seemed a dangerous radical, but to millions who benefited from the bounty he dispensed he was a savior. Roosevelt went on to defeat Alfred Landon in 1936, and ran successfully for a third term against Wendell L. Willkie four years later, the New Deal coalition holding firm.

Roosevelt's program had boosted the economy by alleviating immediate need, but the Depression's problems were solved only by the business boom that followed the outbreak of World War II in 1939. On December 7, 1941, when the Japanese attacked Pearl Harbor, most partisan politics were put aside in favor of patriotic unity. Roosevelt won a fourth term in 1944, defeating Thomas E. Dewey. Five months later, exhausted by wartime duties, he collapsed and died.

Election of 1948. Harry S. Truman became President on April 12, 1945. A relatively unknown senator from Missouri, Truman surprised many by providing strong leadership during the difficult years of struggle between the non-Communist Western world and the Communist East, led by the U.S.S.R. To the shock of pollsters, he was elected in 1948 over Dewey despite the defection of four Deep South states to the Dixiecrat candidate Strom Thurmond, and further splintering of the vote by Henry Wallace's Progressives. The Southern defection, the first important one in almost a century, was a protest against Truman's antisegregation policies as well as his Fair Deal program of domestic reform.

Elections of 1952 and 1956. In the election campaign of 1952 the increased centralization of government during the 20 Democratic years was one of the major issues. The Korean War and the desire to see it end was the other. Republican Dwight D. Eisenhower hardly needed issues to win. The beloved "Ike," commander of the Allied armies in World War II, inspired confidence in old and young. He swamped his intellectual opponent, Adlai E. Stevenson. Eisenhower's policies favored business, and his approach to human rights was basically liberal. In 1956 he again defeated Stevenson, this time by an even larger majority.

Election of 1960. The campaign of 1960 produced a different set of candidates. Under a constitutional amendment Eisenhower and all future Presidents were limited to two terms. Vice President Richard M. Nixon ran against Senator John F. Kennedy, a young Democrat from a wealthy Boston family of Irish descent. Kennedy faced difficulties in parts of the country because of his Roman Catholicism but gained strength from the first face-to-face television debates between rival Presidential candidates. Though he won the popular vote by only a shade, his electoral vote, carefully collected by campaigning in key states, was larger.

Many of the policies of Kennedy's "New Frontier" brought bitter criticism from the Republicans, but even his most severe critics hailed his masterful handling of Soviet threats during the Cuban missile crisis. The nation was shocked and saddened by his assassination on November 22, 1963, in Dallas, Texas.

Senator Lyndon B. Johnson, who had battled Kennedy down to the wire during the Democratic convention but then had accepted the Vice Presidential spot, now became President. He had been active in politics since the early days of Franklin Roosevelt's New Deal, and his know-how, gleaned from years of experience, stood him in good stead. Massive batches of stalled legislation were put through Congress without a hitch.

Election of 1964. Johnson was a clear favorite to win the 1964 election. He did so in the most overwhelming landslide since 1820 as millions of moderate Republicans broke ranks in fright over the policies of his conservative opponent, Republican Barry Goldwater. Johnson announced a "Great Society" program aimed at improving the lot of the poor and expanding the opportunities of all citizens. Critics complained that this would require a still greater increase in Federal power and would be too costly. War in Vietnam, civil-rights struggles and poor management of some of the huge Federal programs plague his administration. So the ever-growing, ever-changing story of American politics continues.

1952
"I shall go to Korea."

Eisenhower promised to try to settle the Korean War by going to the battle zone himself.

Eisenhower Stevenson

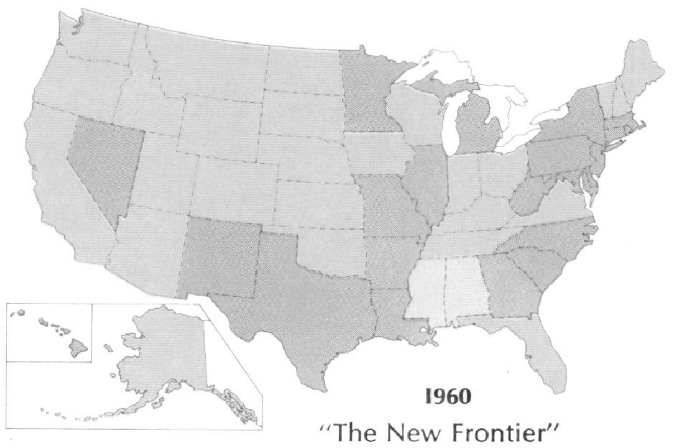

1960
"The New Frontier"

John F. Kennedy's talk of goals such as the "reach the moon" program launched new as well as traditional aspirations in this slogan.

Kennedy Nixon Byrd

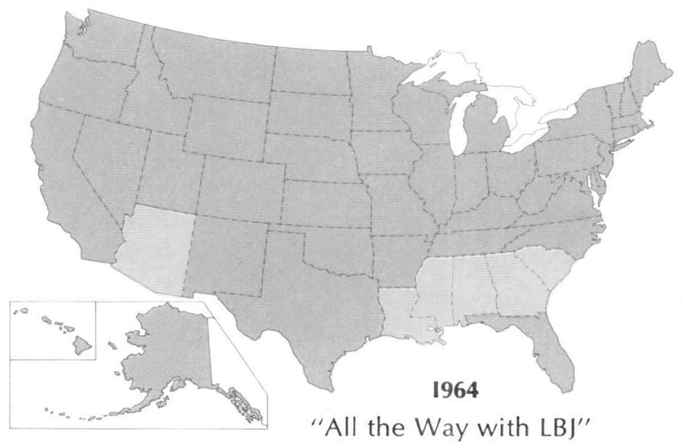

1964
"All the Way with LBJ"

The Democratic cry was later supplanted by the Johnson phrase "the Great Society," which promised a broad variety of social advances.

Johnson Goldwater

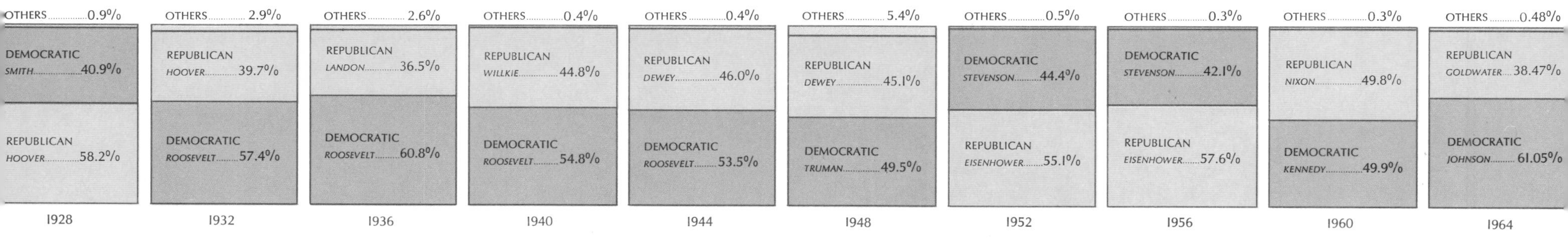

OUR LIVING CONSTITUTION

What should the Federal government be empowered to do—and what powers should be kept by the states—in the people's interest? In 1787, delegates of all 13 original states, except Rhode Island, met in Philadelphia to resolve this issue. Through a summer of debate and compromise they created a brief, concise document that brought into being an effective central government, ending the difficult times following the War for Independence (see pages 82-83) when the states were unable to act together for the good of all.

Today, 181 years later, that document—the Constitution of the United States—still serves the will of the people as the supreme law of the land. It has been amended only 24 times, and most of these amendments have represented additions to its substance, not changes. Yet our government itself has changed enormously, in scope and in complexity, from those earliest days of our Republic. What are the major characteristics of this vital work, the provisions which, broadly interpreted, have permitted a vast range of governmental action?

GOVERNMENTAL POWERS

The Federal Constitution (1) grants and limits the powers of the national and state governments; (2) expresses the liberties of the people and (3) establishes a three-branch system of Federal government—legislative, executive and judicial. Represented below are the main powers and restraints of the Federal and state governments today.

★ ★ ★ DISTRIBUTION OF POWER ★ ★ ★

STATES MAY	FEDERAL GOVERNMENT MAY	BOTH MAY	STATES MAY NOT	THE FEDERAL GOVERNMENT MAY NOT	BOTH MAY NOT
Control elections, local governments, public health, safety and morals, within their boundaries. (This includes such matters as commerce within the state, marriage, divorce, education and general voting qualifications.)	Regulate commerce over state lines, i.e., between two or more states, and with foreign nations. Ratify treaties and conduct foreign relations. Establish rules of bankruptcy. Maintain post offices and post roads. Grant patents and copyrights. Coin money and regulate its value. Declare war. Raise, support and make rules for regulation of an army and navy.	Levy taxes. Build roads. Borrow money. Spend money for the general welfare.	Interfere with the major functions of the Federal government, such as making war, writing treaties with foreign nations, maintaining armies or navies, or printing their own currency; or interfere with obligations under contracts.	Favor one state at the expense of another. Grant titles of nobility. Suspend habeas corpus (right of arrested individual to statement of charges against him and speedy trial) except in cases of rebellion or invasion.	Deprive persons of life or property without due process of law, or pass laws incriminating persons for acts that were not illegal when committed.

RIGHTS OF THE PEOPLE

When the first Congress elected under the new Constitution convened in 1789, it was faced by numerous demands that the document be amended. These demands were answered, for the most part, by the passage of the first ten amendments, "The Bill of Rights." They were designed to protect individual freedom by imposing restraints on the power of the Federal government.

GUARANTEES OF THE BILL OF RIGHTS

THE PEOPLE SHALL HAVE

Freedom of speech, press and religion.

The right to assemble peaceably and to petition the government.

The right, if accused, to counsel, speedy trial and an impartial jury.

The right not to bear witness against oneself.

The right to keep and bear arms.

The right not to be deprived of life, liberty or property without due process of law.

THE GOVERNMENT SHALL NOT

Quarter troops in a private house without the owner's consent.

Make unreasonable search of persons and houses.

Mete out excessive fines, bails or cruel punishment.

Have its courts try an acquitted person twice for the same offense.

THE STATES OR THE PEOPLE SHALL HAVE

All powers not delegated to the Federal government or prohibited to them by the Constitution.

SEPARATION OF FEDERAL POWERS

How could the government be structured so that each part would check, or balance, the power of the other two, so that any one part could not assume more than its proper role in the affairs of the nation? To do this, the builders of the Constitution provided for *separation of powers* among the three branches of the government: the Executive, Legislative and Judicial.

★ ★

CHECKS AND BALANCES OF FEDERAL GOVERNMENT

EXECUTIVE

May check Congress by: Vetoing legislation. ∗ Recommending legislation. ∗ Calling Congress into special session.

May check the Federal Judiciary by: Nominating judges to serve on the Court.

LEGISLATURE

Congress may check the President by: Refusing to pass legislation or appropriate funds. ∗ Overriding his veto by a two-thirds vote of both Houses. ∗ The Senate's disapproving his appointments and not ratifying treaties. ∗ Impeachment charges, brought by the House of Representatives and heard before the Senate.

Congress may check the Judiciary by: Enacting new laws to replace laws held unconstitutional. ∗ Initiating amendments to the Constitution. ∗ Increasing or decreasing the number of judges on the Supreme Court. ∗ Passing laws defining the jurisdiction of the Federal Courts.

Congress itself is checked by: Requirements that both the House and the Senate must pass bills if they are to become laws.

JUDICIARY

The Supreme Court may check the President by: Declaring unconstitutional acts of the Executive branch.

The Supreme Court may check Congress by: Declaring laws unconstitutional.

CONGRESS

In creating the U.S. Congress, the Founding Fathers struck a balance between the states as governmental powers—who insisted on equal representation—and the voting strength of the people within each state. In the Senate, each state would have equal voice, with two senators each. In the House of Representatives, each state would have a variable number of representatives based on a certain population ratio. (Currently the ratio is approximately one representative for each 410,000 persons). The strength of each state in the House is as illustrated below.

Alabama	8
Alaska	1
Arizona	3
Arkansas	4
California	38
Colorado	4
Connecticut	6
Delaware	1
Florida	12
Georgia	10
Hawaii	2
Idaho	2
Illinois	24
Indiana	11
Iowa	7
Kansas	5
Kentucky	7
Louisiana	8
Maine	2
Maryland	7
Massachusetts	12
Michigan	19
Minnesota	8
Mississippi	5
Missouri	10
Montana	2
Nebraska	3
Nevada	1
New Hampshire	2
New Jersey	15
New Mexico	2
New York	41
North Carolina	11
North Dakota	2
Ohio	23
Oklahoma	6
Oregon	4
Pennsylvania	27
Rhode Island	2
South Carolina	6
South Dakota	2
Tennessee	9
Texas	22
Utah	2
Vermont	1
Virginia	10
Washington	7
West Virginia	5
Wisconsin	10
Wyoming	1

PRESIDENTIAL POWER

Under the Constitution, one man is vested with executive power: the President of the United States. To this end, he is sworn to "preserve, protect and defend" the Constitution. And he is empowered to appoint—with the approval of a majority of the Senate—all officers, judges and ambassadors of our country; to call Congress into special session to declare war, ratify treaties or deal with other critical matters. He is also commander in chief of the Armed Forces.

Despite the checks placed upon him by the Constitution, the President is today regarded as the most powerful elected official in the world. The stature of his office has become so great that—in addition to the impact of his veto—he plays a major role in initiating legislation. (The Constitution says he may "recommend" measures to Congress.) He is the head of one of the two major political parties. Upon his shoulders rests the responsibility for conducting the foreign affairs of the United States; he may, under certain circumstances, commit the Armed Forces to hostilities without a formal declaration of war by Congress. And he presides over an enormous network of agencies and departments for which the framers of the Constitution made no provision, since they could not foresee the changing, growing needs of government 181 years ahead. Following are the titles of the components of this Executive Establishment:

PRESIDENT'S CABINET

Secretary of State
Secretary of the Treasury
Secretary of Defense
Attorney General
Postmaster General
Secretary of the Interior
Secretary of Agriculture
Secretary of Commerce
Secretary of Labor
Secretary of Health, Education and Welfare
Secretary of Housing and Urban Development
Secretary of Transportation

EXECUTIVE OFFICES

The White House Office
Bureau of the Budget
Council of Economic Advisers
National Security Council
Central Intelligence Agency (CIA)
National Aeronautics and Space Council
Office of Economic Opportunity
Office of Emergency Planning
Office of Science and Technology
Office of the Special Representative for Trade Negotiations

INDEPENDENT REGULATORY COMMISSIONS

Federal Aviation Agency
Federal Communications Commission
Federal Maritime Commission
Federal Power Commission
Federal Trade Commission
Interstate Commerce Commission
National Labor Relations Board
Securities and Exchange Commission

OTHER MAJOR AGENCIES

Atomic Energy Commission
Civil Aeronautics Board
Farm Credit Administration
Federal Deposit Insurance Corporation
Federal Mediation and Conciliation Service
Federal Reserve System
General Services Administration
National Aeronautics and Space Administration
Selective Service System
Small Business Administration
Tennessee Valley Authority
United States Information Agency
United States Arms Control and Disarmament Agency
Veterans Administration

THE ADAPTABILITY OF THE CONSTITUTION

As the times have changed, so has the place of America in the world changed—and, accordingly, the role of our government has changed. The foregoing list not only describes the broad scope of tasks carried out by the Executive branch of government, under the direction of the President, it also presents dramatic evidence of the ability of our Constitution to meet the governmental needs of a new day.

Thus, the Constitution contains language that has made far-reaching change lawful. In the past century, important reliance was placed by the Supreme Court upon the clause that gives Congress power "To make all laws which shall be necessary and proper for carrying into execution" all other powers expressed. Much of the flexibility of the Constitution—a document only 7024 words long—springs from that clause. Two other clauses have been crucially important, as Congress, with the continual review and check of the Supreme Court, has interpreted the meaning of the Constitution, and as the President or other officials have established precedents that have come to stand as interpretations of the meanings *implied* in the Constitution.

These clauses concern the congressional powers to "regulate" interstate commerce and to "provide for the general welfare." Commerce, as defined by the workings of our Federal government, applies not only to transportation but to television and radio broadcasting, and any form of telegraphed information and certain other transactions across state lines. The right to appropriate money for the general welfare has enabled the government to launch vast programs of social reform: Social Security, Medicare, aid to education. In such ways the Constitution signed with goose-quill pens is still changing, and still the foundation of government for America in the Space Age.

From the beginning, some groups have contested the growth of government and the extent of constitutional power granted to the Federal government. They have argued that the Constitution stated the *specific* areas of Federal authority. But those who support a broad interpretation of the Constitution contend it is necessary to enable the nation to achieve the Constitution's essential goals as expressed in the Preamble:

We the People of the United States, in Order to Form a more perfect Union, establish Justice, insure domestic Tranquility, provide for the common defence, promote the general Welfare, and secure the Blessings of Liberty to ourselves and our Posterity, do ordain and establish this Constitution for the United States of America.

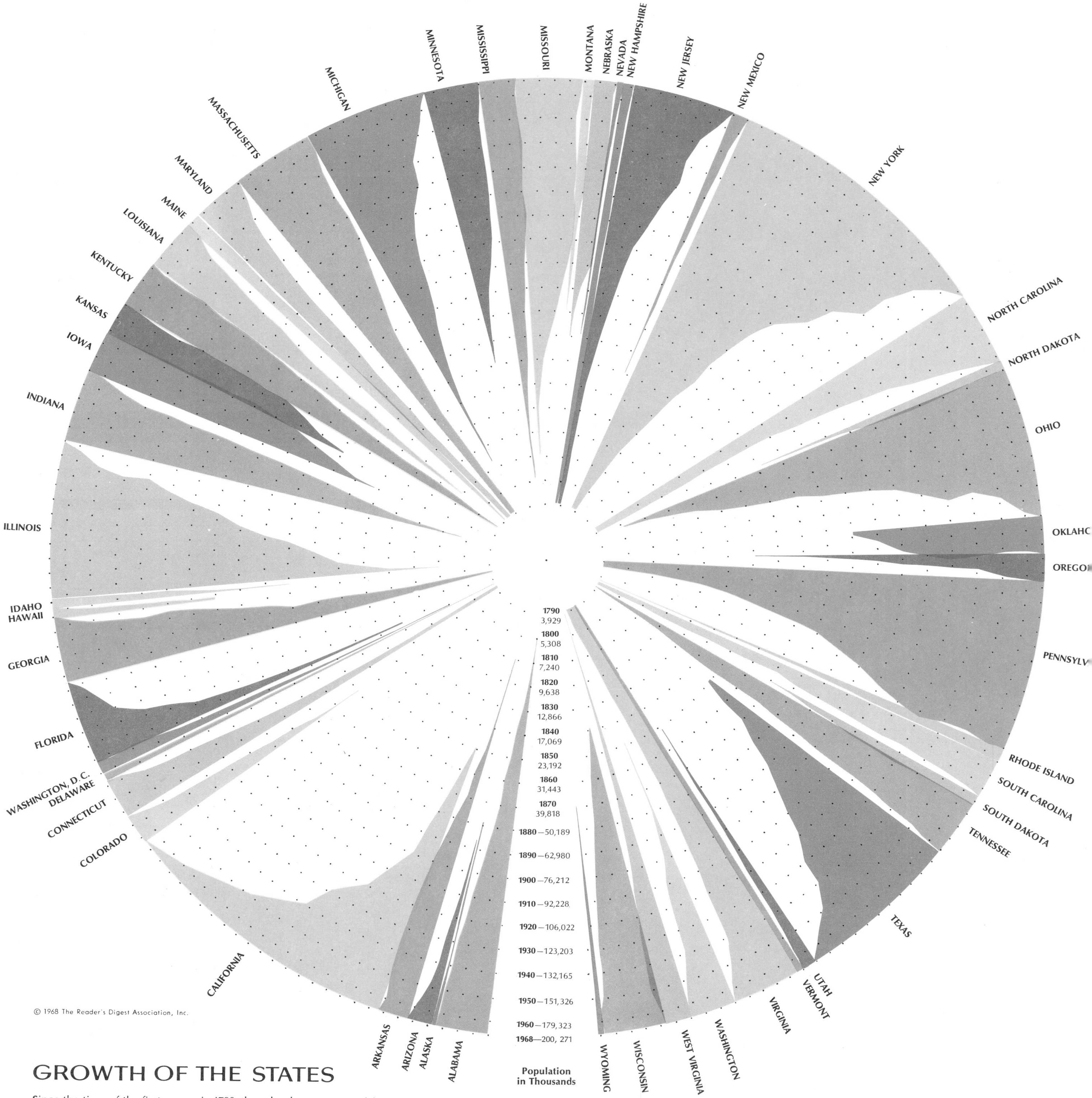

The wheel above shows how each state grew or receded in population from the time of its entry into the union. The circles of dots, as they move outward from the center, represent the census of each decade from the first one starting in 1790. The space between dots around the circles represents one million in population.

GROWTH OF THE STATES

Since the time of the first census in 1790, there has been an ever-rising increase of people each decade in the United States. Colonial women married young and had large families. Children were considered an economic asset, who contributed so many more hands to clear the wilderness and work the land. Birthrates of the time approached the maximum of which the human race is capable. It has been estimated that colonial mothers had an average of eight births by the time they had completed their fertility span. Chevalier Félix de Beaujour, a French consular official in the United States, wrote after he returned to Europe in 1814: "No human consideration there operates as a hindrance to reproduction, and the children swarm on the rich land." In some decades between 1620 and 1830, the United States population, expanded also by a healthy immigration, grew as much as 35 percent. The greatest waves in population occurred between 1900 and 1910, when a robust birthrate coincided with a tide of immigrants from Europe; between 1920 and 1930, a time of unusual prosperity; and after 1946, the decade of the great baby boom. The only important reversal in the population trends came in the Depression decade of 1930–40, when the birthrate sank to an all-time low.

Most of the boom following World War II occurred in Arizona, California, Florida, Illinois, Louisiana, Maryland, Michigan, New Jersey, New York, Ohio and Texas, which received large migrations from other states. California and Florida shared the largest population growth. Between 1950 and 1963 California gained 8.8 million people to supplant New York as the first in the nation. Florida's growth was even more phenomenal, considering its size. It added 3 million people to attain a total of nearly 5 million. Arkansas, Maine, Mississippi, North and South Dakota, Pennsylvania, Wyoming, West Virginia, Vermont and Oklahoma grew little during this period. After California and New York in population come Pennsylvania, Illinois, Texas and Ohio. Alaska, with 272,000 in 1966, is the least populous.

IMMIGRATION

In 1608 eight laborers arrived in Jamestown, Virginia, and within three weeks they had a glass furnace glowing. Among them were Jur Mata, Zbigniew Stefanski, Michal Lowicki, Stanislaw Sadowski, Karol Zranica and Jan Bogdan. These were Poles, others were Germans, but with the English colonists who had preceded them by a year they set a pattern of diversity that American immigration was to follow through the centuries. In the chart at the right may be seen the peak years of immigration from 1820, when the counting of immigrants began.

From the Revolution to 1820, the population rose from 2 million to 9.6 million, but it is uncertain how much of that increase can be attributed to immigration. Most of the increase may have been due to a high birthrate.

After 1820, immigration struck America in two waves. Newcomers arrived at a steady rate through 1840, then came the upward surge of what is known now as the "Old Immigration." This occurred between 1840 and 1860, when 4.5 million people arrived in the United States. Most emigrated from Ireland, Germany, Great Britain and Scandinavia and northwestern Europe, driven out of their countries by poor harvests, unemployment, famines, war or political conflict. Between 1845 and 1851, the years of the Great Famine in Ireland, 860,000 Irish immigrated to the United States.

As the Civil War began, immigration slackened, but after Appomattox it swelled to a torrent. This "New Immigration" made the old one seem a trickle. In 1865, 248,000 persons arrived in American ports, and the rate rose steadily every year thereafter until World War I. In each of six separate years between 1905 and the war, more than a million immigrants arrived in the United States.

THE POPULATION EXPLOSION

No other major country has ever grown so fast in so short a time as has the United States. Some experts feel that, in numbers of people, its present increase may, among the great nations, be exceeded only by India and possibly China. (India's gain of 84 million in the two decades 1938–1958 was about twice that of the United States.) Since the nation was founded less than 200 years ago it has grown over a hundredfold, from 2 million people in the original 13 colonies to more than 200 million in the 50 states. Our present population is the fourth largest, after China (700 million), India (499 million) and the U.S.S.R. (233 million). If the U.S. birthrate continues, we may soon be catching up with the Soviet Union.

We have about 6 percent of the world's people living on about 6 percent of the world's land, averaging 55 people per square mile. That is not very crowded when one considers the Netherlands with more than 800 people per square mile, or Japan with more than 600.

During the great Depression the number of births declined from 2.6 million a year to less than 2.3 million, and many thought the population finally was leveling off. Then, during World War II, births began to climb. They reached 3.4 million in 1946, and went up to 4.3 million annually in the late 1950's. About 30 million people were added to the population between 1953 and 1962, a number equal to the entire increase in the two and a half centuries between the landing of the Pilgrims and the Civil War.

Prewar population experts had not taken into account the romantic appeal of the soldier or the exigencies of war. The rush to the altar began in 1942 with an unprecedented 1.7 million marriages. Then, when the boys began coming home in 1946, marriages hit an all-time high of 2.3 million. Between the years 1946 and 1950, 9 million marriages were performed.

Now the daughters of these marriages are marrying at a good (though not a record) rate themselves—just over 1.5 million a year. About half of them are under twenty, nearly two years younger than their grandmothers and great-grandmothers when they married. However, the girls of today are married at about the same age as those of colonial days.

Divorce in the United States has always been regarded as extremely high. Before World War II about 1 in 7 marriages ended in divorce; after the war, this rose to 1 in 4. This has not, of course, affected the high marriage rate or the number of children in the average family—about 3.4.

Because of the continuous birth surge, we are a nation of young people. About 3.5 million persons annually reach the age of eighteen, and the figure is climbing; our schools and colleges have already felt the severe strain. About 1.7 million persons a year reach sixty-two, the earliest age for Social Security retirement. The declining death rate has also added to the population increase. In 1900 the annual death rate was about 17 in every 1000 Americans; now the figure is 9. It is estimated there are now more than 90 million persons in the United States under the age of twenty-five, 58 million who are twenty-five to fifty, and 45 million who are over fifty.

Life expectancy for a man in 1900 was forty-six, now it is sixty-seven; for a woman it was forty-eight and now it is seventy-three. Thus the excess of females over males has increased, even though there are about 105 boys born to every 100 girls. There are now about 96 men to every 100 women, and experts predict a decline in the proportion of older males in the future. In 1970 there are expected to be about 90 men per 100 females aged fifty-six to sixty-four; in 1985 the ratio probably will drop to about 86 to 100.

Nonwhites (about 95 percent Negro) increased more rapidly than whites from 1960 to 1965—about 13 percent as compared with 8 percent for whites. (About 12 percent of the total population is nonwhite.)

In all these facts and figures, one key point stands out: We appear to be on the threshold of a population boom that could make the last one look like a small firecracker. Our population condition could be likened to a multistage space rocket. The first stage, the baby boom of the 1950's, provided the momentum for the second stage, the babies that are about to be born. Then these babies provide a new momentum...and so on. Many experts predict that the population of the United States will reach over 250 million by 1985. If this happens, the problems of housing, school, transportation, crime, pollution of water and air, and other population-related changes will be incalculable.

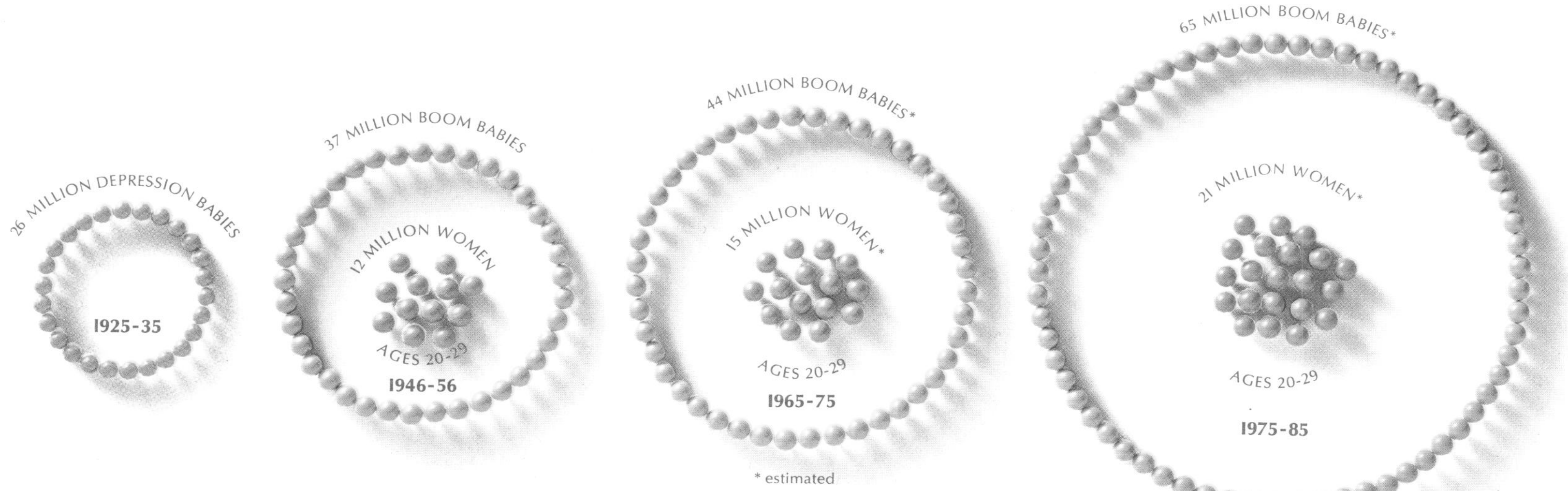

* estimated

BABY BOOMS

Above is a projection showing how many babies may be added to the population of America in the next two decades if the birth pattern of recent years continues. Each outer bead represents a million babies; each center bead a million mothers. In the years 1925 to 1935, including the Depression years when there was a record low birthrate, about 26 million babies were born. By the end of World War II, when the daughters in this small group reached the prime childbearing ages of twenty to twenty-nine, they began having babies at a record rate. They were largely responsible for the so-called baby boom of 1946–56. During this period 12 million young mothers bore almost all of that decade's 37 million babies, at a rate of about 3000 babies per 1000 young women.

Now there is an even greater baby boom in the making. The daughters of these prolific mothers of 1946–56 are coming into childbearing age, and indications are that they will create a baby boom beginning in the late sixties that will make the previous one seem small. These 15 million young women may, and probably will, have 44 million babies in the decade 1965–75, and the childbearing group of the next decade will have between 60 million and 70 million. In a projection based on the childbearing possibilities of one sample group of 000 young women, the Bureau of the Census estimates that the number of births around 1985 could reach almost 7 million a year.

A small ray of hope—the recent decline of birth numbers—has been discounted by the experts. In 1960, 4,258,000 babies were born, and by 1965 the figure had dropped to 3,806,000. But this is misleading: Large numbers of new mothers from the baby boom of 20 years ago have not yet begun to have their babies. By 1970, we may have a different story, and the population problems of the next decade depend upon the fertility of these new mothers.

THE FUTURE

The bar graph at the far right shows what will happen to the population if the present birthrate continues. The blue column represents the population of about 200 million; the yellow is the increase to 1985 and the red represents the number of people in the United States by 2065—one billion! In contrast, the shorter bar shows what would happen if the population were to grow at the Depression rate, the lowest in our history. The yellow segment indicates an increase of only 20 million by 1985, and the red 400 million by 2065.

As it stands, every year we are adding to our population at the rate of a city the size of Chicago.

More than half of the "New Immigration" came from southern and eastern Europe, and those who had been immigrants themselves not long before complained of the crowding, misery and lower standard of living the new people purportedly caused. In 1917 Congress passed a law aimed at the newer arrivals, which required proof that they could read and write in at least one language. Still they came, and in 1921 Congress passed the first quota law limiting immigration to no more than 150,000 a year.

After World War II, the Displaced Persons Act permitted as many as 400,000 a year to enter the country. Then, in 1952, the Immigration and Nationality Act was passed, combining all immigration rules under one Congressional statute. Thereafter the quotas were set at 154,657 people a year, although some quota-free immigrants were admitted under the Refugee Relief Act of 1953.

Peak Year	Country	Total 1820–1964
1851	Ireland	4,699,064
1851	France	703,786
1882	Germany	6,822,807
1882	Sweden	1,257,492
1882	Norway	846,012
1882	China	415,084
1888	Great Britain	3,869,816
1907	Italy	5,030,394
1907	Austria–Hungary	4,282,823
1907	Greece	503,463
1907	Japan	341,861
1913	Russia	3,345,161
1921	Poland	458,107
1924	Canada–Newfoundland	3,784,763

THE CHALLENGE OF THE CITIES

The population of the United States is not only exploding, it is becoming busier and busier. Human activity and exchange, the experts say, increase in direct proportion to numbers of people and their nearness to one another. For example, think of each person in a city as representing a tiny sandpile. As these sandpiles move closer together, they become one large sandpile. The height and width of the large sandpile increase as more small sandpiles are added. In the model viewed at right and below, the height and width of the sandpiles (or cones) represent both the population density and comparative activity in cities.

The curved lines, or numbered rings, show the various levels of activity in and around the cones and in the nation at large. To create the model, experts fed numerous factors—density of population, communications, transportation, land values, and other items—into a computer to get a picture of the comparative density and activity of population in different parts of the country. From all these items an index—0 to 3000—was arrived at to measure population "strength." Thus the highest cone, New York City, is the one which has the greatest density and human exchange—telephone calls, mail, banking, hotel registrations, taxes, business firms and so on.

The outer limits of the New York metropolitan area are calibrated at about 1000, while the very center of the city, the nation's most powerful in terms of population density and activity, hits 2872 at the top of the cone. Other peaks occur in Philadelphia at 1387 and Chicago at 1039.

Cities like Los Angeles and San Francisco, with peaks of 516 and 692 respectively, are powerful too, but their populations are spread over a wider area. Los Angeles, for example, has only 20,000 people in a comparatively small downtown core of 1.65 square miles, while New York has 600,000 in its 9-square-mile core. Los Angeles has 2.5 million people within its city limits of 455 square miles, while New York has 7.7 million within 315 square miles. Metropolitan Los Angeles has 6.7 million within 4800 square miles to New York's 11 million in 2100 square miles.

As the cones grow taller—that is, as more people crowd together—the bases around them also rise and spread. New York and Philadelphia have almost joined at the base. The density in this combined section is 600 persons per square mile—the highest in the nation for a region that size. In fact, as a traveler goes from Boston to Washington (ring 550) through what is popularly known as megalopolis—New Haven, New York, Philadelphia—he sees little but houses, buildings and factories. The farms and estates here are usually owned by people with other income. And it appears that the whole area as far west as Chicago may within 10 years reach an average strength index of 550.

The same is happening in many megalopolis areas—Los Angeles and San Diego, San Francisco and Oakland, Chicago and Milwaukee—as their populations grow and join. But this is not true in the vast remaining sections of the United States. The farms, villages and towns are losing people to the cities, both large and small. Half of the 3134 counties in the nation lost population in the last decade as citizens moved to urban areas for greater economic opportunity. A man parachuting at random west of the Mississippi today would have less chance of landing near a dwelling than in 1900.

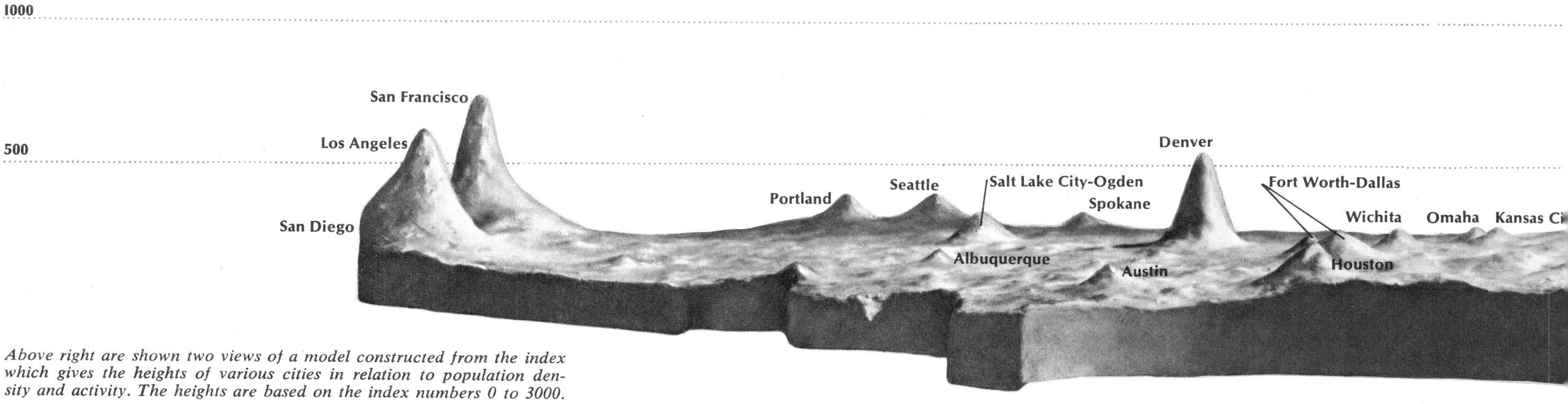

Above right are shown two views of a model constructed from the index which gives the heights of various cities in relation to population density and activity. The heights are based on the index numbers 0 to 3000.

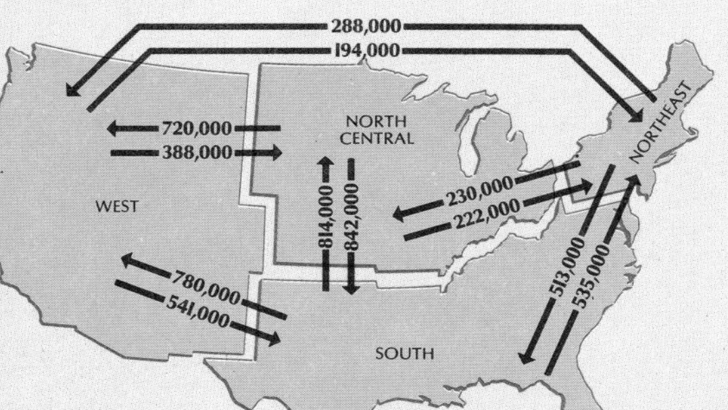

POPULATION SHIFT

The desire for better jobs, working in warmer climes and for the good life generally has caused the growing mass of humanity in America to move about in greater numbers than ever before. The United States Bureau of the Census, in a survey of one 12-month period—from March 1964 to March 1965—found that 6 million people migrated across state borders, and about half of these moved to other regions. Between 1955 and 1965 the greatest migration, from all sections and from all strata of society, was to the Far West (see map above), largely to California and Arizona. Nearly a third of all the people who moved between regions had the West as their destination.

The South saw a great deal of movement, both in and out—although this section lost population overall. Southern Negroes moved en masse to northern cities. Florida was second to California in net in-migration as many persons fleeing the winter cold joined workers seeking employment with expanding industry. From 1960 to 1964 Florida registered 100,000 more incoming than outgoing people, while California gained 314,000.

This migration, however, was only a fraction of the moving that went on in the country. A great in-and-out shifting took place around cities. As rural folk flocked in from the farms and small towns, city people moved to the suburbs. In large numbers, Puerto Ricans moved to mainland cities, mostly to New York and Chicago. In 1965, almost 40 million people, about one fifth of the population, changed their residences.

HOW CITIES GROW AND SUBURBS SCATTER

As our metropolitan areas merge in megalopolis fashion, the smaller cities break through their boundaries to join each other or nearby cities. The United States is undergoing what is called "total urbanization." For example, the small-town complex of Anaheim, Santa Ana and Garden Grove in California boomed to metropolitan status during the past decade. These towns overlapped, increasing almost 10 percent in population between 1960 and 1964. This aggregate of more than a million people had the highest rate of urban growth in America.

No Longer Small Cities. The same thing has happened to the San Bernardino–Riverside–Ontario section of California, which increased 5 percent to 994,000 people. Tampa–St. Petersburg in Florida and Paterson–Clifton–Passaic in New Jersey are other complexes no longer considered small, separate cities. Meanwhile, the larger cities continue to grow and spread. Every one of the 38 principal metropolitan areas in the United States gained in population in the 1960–64 period except Pittsburgh, which declined less than 1 percent. The urbanization of the United States is creating great change in our lives, and intensifying the problems that already exist in many cities.

While some small towns have grown into metropolises and prospered, many have experienced economic extinction. This is especially true in the outlying areas of the South, Midwest and West, which were deserted by citizens seeking better opportunities in the big cities.

Cities on the Move. A boon to urbanization, and at the same time a bane, was the proliferation of expressways across the nation. Small towns died as they were bypassed by the superhighways. Such towns were trading centers for the farmers and places of enjoyment for the entire family on a Saturday. When expressways were built, the farmer drove his family to the big city.

Expressways were not a complete boon even to the metropolis. They cost millions to build and maintain, and the city had to pay its share, thus adding to its financial woes. Superhighways also contributed to the deterioration of the downtown areas: those who could afford it moved

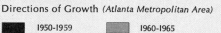

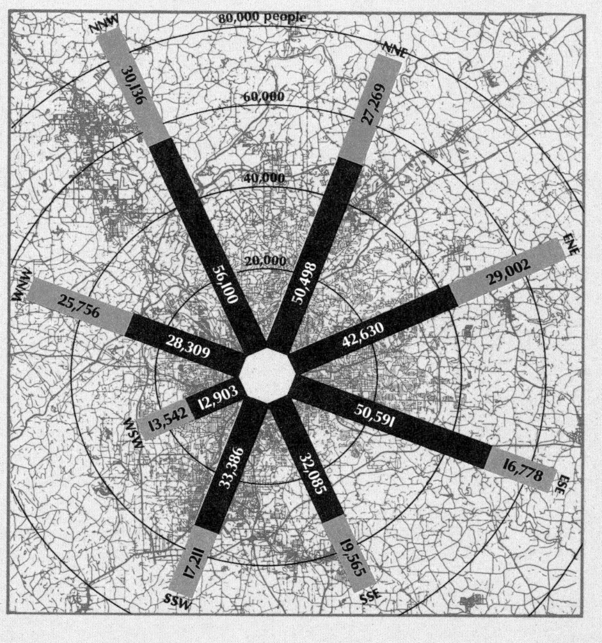

ATLANTA EXPANSION

Directions of Growth *(Atlanta Metropolitan Area)*

■ 1950-1959 ■ 1960-1965

The recent pattern of growth of the Atlanta metropolitan area, shown on the map (left) in eight directions, is typical of that of many of the older big cities of the United States. Its population had a net increase of more than 60 percent—from 727,000 to 1,175,000—between 1950 and 1965. About 38,000 people, most of the upper-income white families, moved from the old 37-square-mile central city (roughly represented by the octagon in the center) to greener suburbs and outlying districts. A further significant change took place during these 15 years. Within the present city limits of 128 square miles, the white population declined, while the population of the lower-income Negroes, mostly migrants, increased to 43.5 percent of the total. Experts say this has occurred in New York, Chicago, Los Angeles and other older large cities in the North and West as well as in the South. Higher-income white families move outward to pleasanter areas; lower-income nonwhites move in from rural areas and cannot afford to stave off the deterioration of whole sections into slums.

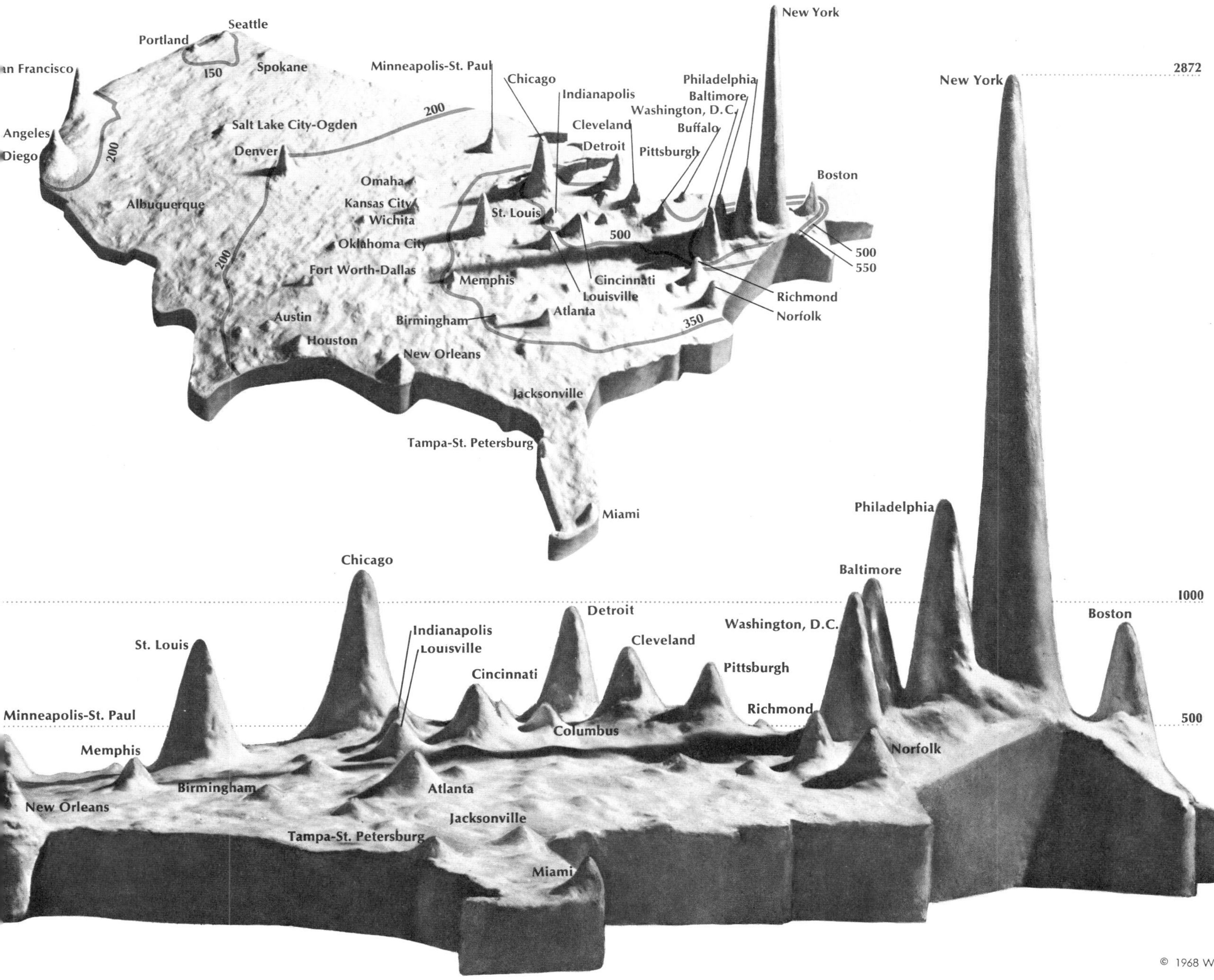

POPULATION DENSITY AND ACTIVITY

Albuquerque	205
Atlanta	492
Austin	256
Baltimore	1082
Birmingham	404
Boston	940
Buffalo	548
Chicago	1039
Cincinnati	655
Cleveland	788
Columbus	600
Dayton	598
Denver	455
Detroit	893
Fort Worth-Dallas	382
Houston	338
Indianapolis	593
Jacksonville	317
Kansas City	420
Los Angeles	516
Louisville	555
Memphis	416
Miami	266
Minneapolis-St. Paul	500
New Orleans	454
New York	2872
Norfolk	582
Oklahoma City	324
Omaha	364
Philadelphia	1387
Pittsburgh	737
Portland	257
Richmond	621
Salt Lake City-Ogden	219
San Diego	252
San Francisco	692
Seattle	222
Spokane	162
St. Louis	872
Tampa-St. Petersburg	323
Washington, D. C.	1023
Wichita	308

to the suburbs—seeking open spaces, green lawns and better schools—and drove to the city to work. Low-income groups, mostly Negroes from the South, moved into city houses and apartments formerly belonging to upper-income groups. These dwellings had been divided into smaller sizes, often one-room units. Slums appeared, and the slums bred crime. Commerce and industry moved away. Transportation became a nightmare as thousands of cars—many with suburbanites—clogged the streets and expressways. Transit and commuter lines often became rundown and antiquated.

Urban Planning. Some cities have been making gigantic efforts to meet these problems, especially in slum clearance or renewal. Boston has replaced slum areas in the center of town with a huge government center; Washington has turned a slum near the Capitol into imaginative, modern housing; Chicago has rebuilt hundreds of city blocks; Los Angeles has scores of renewal projects under way; and St. Louis has rebuilt its waterfront. In 1966 there were more than 1500 Federally assisted urban-renewal projects working or being studied in more than 800 urban areas. An aid to this renewal process was the Federal Demonstration Cities Bill passed in 1966 providing $1.3 billion for a three-year period. Each city would concentrate on trying new techniques of rehabilitation in one blighted neighborhood.

In transportation the cities have been trying to revitalize commuter lines. With city subsidy, the Pennsylvania Railroad has reduced fares, speeded up schedules, built new facilities in Philadelphia and renovated a huge station in New York City. In Chicago commuters have been wooed back to the Chicago and North Western Railway with improved service, and in the San Francisco Bay area citizens of three counties have voted for a radically new rapid-transit system that will cost a billion dollars.

On the outskirts of cities, communities are being built to handle population overflow. Some are designed to take care of every human need, from garbage service to a place to work. An example is the Fairless Hills community of 2000 homes constructed near the Fairless Steel Works in eastern Pennsylvania by New York realtor John Galbreath. One survey reports that there were more than 300 of these communities either in operation or abuilding in 1966, at least 100 of them in California.

Yet with all this planning the question remains: Will we be ready for the greatest population surge in our history when it comes in the next decade?

PHILADELPHIA RENEWAL

One of the best ways for a city to upgrade its deteriorating center is to use historical and traditional sites as focal points for renewal. For years Philadelphia's Independence Hall had languished in an atmosphere of slums and old warehouses. Then, in a $350 million project, the city restored the Independence Hall section and an adjacent residential area called Society Hill, for a total of 30 blocks.

To begin with, in 1953 the city cleared and planted a three-block park immediately fronting the Hall. (*Below left,* the park before, and *below right,* after renewal.) Beneath the park, it constructed a 600-car garage to provide parking for visitors and office workers. To keep the area on the same dignified level as the Hall and nearby historic buildings, the city permitted the building of only the most prestigious and important edifices for its Independence Mall, such as the U.S. Mint, the U.S. Federal Courthouse, banks, museums and churches.

The Mall renewal project was part of Philadelphia's Comprehensive Plan, a $3.2 billion long-range program that touched every major facet of the city's life—housing, transportation, industry, commerce, recreation and water and sewage.

The housing plan provided for the renewal of some 61,000 homes and apartments, more than 10 percent of the city's total. In many instances, improvements were to be "seeded" through a slum area and made with paintbrush and trowel rather than with steam shovel and earthmover. The transportation plan called for an expressway system around the city in a rectangular pattern, crossing its center and providing access from eight directions. The transit system was to be rehabilitated and a new commuter depot was planned for under the city's center.

To accommodate its industries, the city is converting 18,000 acres, 25 percent of the city's land, to factory use. In the commercial area, one huge shopping complex covering three center-city blocks was built, another was under way nearby. Recreational facilities will consist of 300 parks and playgrounds. And some $400 million was earmarked for refurbishing the city's water and sewage system. Philadelphia hopes to present this new face to the world by 1985.

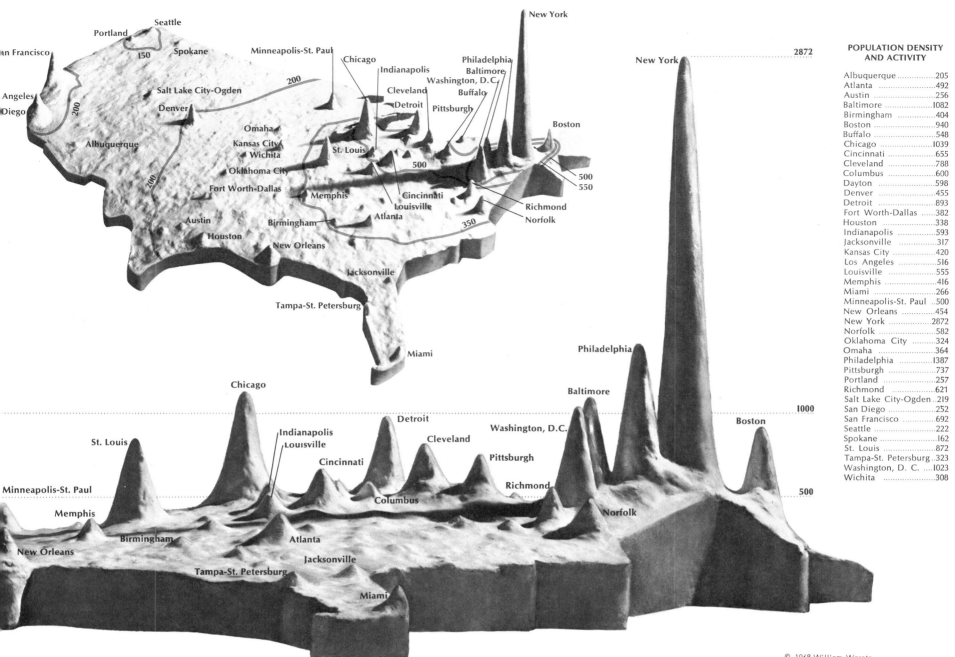

EDUCATION IN SURGING NUMBERS

COLONIAL COLLEGES

Harvard University was founded in 1636—just 16 years after the landing of the Pilgrims. It is the oldest institution of higher education in the United States, although there were earlier unsuccessful attempts to establish colleges in the New World. William and Mary, the second-oldest school in the United States, had its beginnings in Henricopolis University, which was founded by the Virginia settlers in 1619 only to be forced to discontinue because of the Indian wars.

The Massachusetts Bay Colony assembly in 1634 voted about $2000 for a "schoale or colledge" to be called Newtowne College at Newtowne near the Charles River. Two years later the school was named Harvard after John Harvard, a Puritan clergyman who left his library and half his fortune to the college. At the same time, the town was renamed Cambridge, after the university in England.

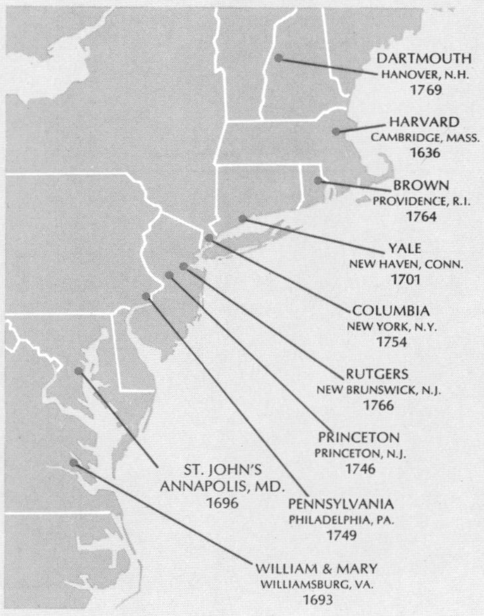

As in the lower schools in colonial days, religion was dominant in the early colleges. King's College (later Columbia) and William and Mary were operated by Anglicans; the Congregationalists founded Yale and Dartmouth; Princeton was Presbyterian; Brown, Baptist; and Rutgers, Dutch Reformed. Only Ben Franklin's College of Philadelphia (later the University of Pennsylvania), which he founded as an academy in 1749, was not under religious control.

Classes were often held in the home of the president, who might be the lone faculty member, teaching all subjects. The curriculum consisted usually of Greek, Latin, mathematics—in some cases little more than today's elementary school arithmetic—and religion. Yet these colonial colleges produced the intellectual and political leaders of our early history: Alexander Hamilton; Presidents Thomas Jefferson, John Adams and James Madison; and the first Chief Justice of the Supreme Court, John Jay. George Washington was not considered a college graduate although he received his surveyor's certificate from William and Mary in 1749.

By 1800 there were 25 colleges in the United States, but their enrollments were small. During its first 65 years Harvard graduated an average of nine men a year. In 1838 Harvard had an enrollment of 216, and as late as 1870 the enrollment of Columbia in New York was a mere 122.

The private religious academies and colleges continued to flourish throughout the nineteenth century. Between 1800 and the Civil War, 166 Protestant and 14 Roman Catholic colleges were founded—all remain in operation to this day.

LAND-GRANT COLLEGES

The passage of the Morrill Act in 1862, after five years of controversy in the Congress, was a triumph for the ideal of higher education and all who might desire it. The new law set aside allotments, in units of 30,000 acres, according to the number of senators and representatives in each state. The land, or proceeds from it, was to support colleges instructing in "agriculture and the mechanical arts without excluding other scientific and classic studies, including military tactics." If a state contained no public land, and most Atlantic Coast states did not, it could select its acreage anywhere from national holdings. The total land granted under the act eventually came to 11,596,082 acres.

The red circles on the map at right indicate the 18 schools which were in existence when the Morrill Act was passed and which received land grants under its provisions; in black are those established afterward.

Morrill Act. When the land-grant bill was first introduced in 1857 by Representative Justin Morrill of Vermont, it was opposed by Westerners who did not want their land sold to outsiders, and by Southerners who saw it as an invasion of states' rights, a dominant issue of the day because of slavery. The bill finally passed both Houses in 1859, but it was vetoed by President Buchanan, who was fearful of further aggravating sectional hostility. Morrill's second and successful attempt came in 1862. The nation was split by Civil War, the Southerners were not in Congress, and President Lincoln signed the bill into law.

Although the states rushed to share in the land-grant bounty, it was not always handled well. Many states were unable to sell all the lands they were granted and what they did sell went at ridiculously low prices. Maryland, for example, received 210,000 acres of property scattered through four Western states and territories. Impatient at the prospect of any prolonged negotiations, the state let most of the tracts go to an

WONDROUS DIVERSITY

Our 2300 colleges and universities range from those with only a few dozen students to immense state mega-universities that spread over several campuses and enroll 50,000 students or more. Some of our colleges take a few hundred students of top ability; others take all comers and give courses in everything from knitting to nuclear physics.

In the late 1960's there were 840 junior colleges and more than 1500 four-year institutions. Of the latter, 472 offered work through the master's degree level only and 227 granted the doctorate as well. Among them were 12 under Federal control—such as military and government-service schools—424 under state control and 354 under local government. Nonreligious private colleges numbered 524, Protestant 484, Roman Catholic 381, and other denominations 28. Some 518 were exclusively for men, or for women, but a few were starting to admit members of the opposite sex.

Private colleges and universities are supported by endowments, tuition fees and grants. Public colleges—state, municipal and community institutions—are largely supported by tax funds. Tuition in these schools either does not exist or is very low for residents of the state or community. The public institutions enroll the vast majority of students—nearly 100 percent more than private schools—and, as the college-age population continues to expand in the 1960's, these have assumed the burden of the rise in enrollment.

The great increase in college enrollment reflects the growing desire for higher education but not the ability to pursue it. As college enrollments have risen, so too has the number of college dropouts. In 1961, 780,510 students entered four-year college and 245,577 entered two-year college; four years later, 492,984 graduated from four-year college (some of this number were transfers from junior college).

The Popularity of Education. World War II brought about vast changes in higher education. As the war gathered momentum, thousands of students entered military service and hundreds of college professors went to work in war agencies. About one third of the nation's colleges started service programs to train men in scientific fields and in the skills needed in modern warfare. After V-J Day, servicemen swarmed to the campuses to take advantage of the GI Bill of Rights, which offered free tuition. A seriousness of purpose had been kindled in many young people. The total enrollment in 1950, nearly double that of 1940, was 2,659,000; in 1960 it reached 3,300,000. Then, in the mid-1960's, the children of the postwar baby boom began entering college, and freshman enrollment was on the way to doubling again. The colleges will not be filled by students born during 1947–51 until the oldest are seniors in 1969. By 1970, educators predict college enrollment may reach 7.3 million.

The Trend to Science. In 1957 the launching of the world's first space satellite, the Soviet sputnik, added fuel to the education explosion. Federal government officials suddenly realized that the U.S.S.R. was a formidable rival and that future world leadership depended on the classroom. Colleges, burdened with debt by postwar expansion, were the immediate beneficiaries. The National Defense Education Act was passed in 1958 to provide billions of dollars "to improve the national welfare and space exploration through education." Thousands of students applied for NDEA graduate fellowships. By the mid-sixties, NDEA was paying out $162 million annually in fellowships and loans to more than 400,000 students. The National Science Foundation and the National Aeronautics and Space Administration joined in the crusade, contributing $70 million a year in science fellowships. Private industry participated by setting up the National Merit Program whereby large corporations provide scholarships to deserving high school students.

Under the impact of this growing concern for education, teaching methods and curriculums were upgraded and tightened considerably. Some schools started year-round programs, enabling students to take A.B. degrees in less than three years. Many high schools gave college-level courses so that the more advanced students could be better prepared for the university program. Colleges eliminated many specialized "snap" subjects. The University of Southern California cut the number of courses offered in its catalogue by half. More emphasis was put on subjects such as nuclear energy and electronics. A number of educators decried this trend, contending that the pendulum had swung too far from the humanities and general culture. Nonetheless most college students, for whatever reason, seemed far more learned than ever before.

High School to College. *This bar chart shows how the desire for a college education has increased among high school graduates. In 1940, 35 percent of the graduates went on to college; in 1965, 55 percent. When one considers that the high school graduating classes in the early 1940's were less than half those in the 1960's, three times as many high school students are going on to college. Almost five times as many students are entering graduate school now.*

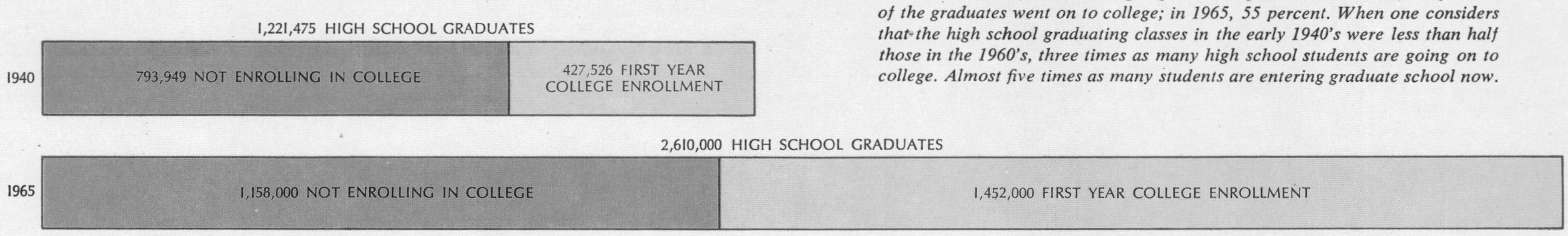

Ohio speculator for as little as 53 cents an acre, realizing a total of only $112,504.

The land-grant bill was nevertheless the giant step that led eventually to today's great state universities. Later acts and amendments were passed which added continuous funds to the original endowment. In 1887 the Hatch Act set up a system of agricultural experiment stations as an adjunct to land-grant schools. In 1890 the second Morrill Act was passed to supplement regular land-grant income with direct appropriations from the Federal government. And in 1914 the Smith-Lever Act established extension services to bring to adults the most recent developments in agriculture.

Not even Morrill himself could have envisioned the role that the 68 land-grant colleges have played in our nation's history. Some educational historians conjecture that the Morrill Act has meant as much to America as any law Congress has ever passed.

JUNIOR COLLEGES-HIGHER EDUCATION FOR ALL

The greatest phenomenon of the education explosion of the past two decades has been the proliferation of junior colleges across the land (see maps below). In 1950 there were 244,000 junior college students on some 450 campuses; in 1966 there were more than 1,500,000 on 840 campuses. While the number of four-year institutions remained relatively static, about 20 new two-year colleges were being established every year during the postwar decades. Fifty opened in 1965, and fifty also in 1966. Nearly 200 new junior colleges were being planned in the nation for the four years ending in 1970, when the American Association of Junior Colleges expects 1000 to be in operation.

Community Colleges. About a third of all two-year colleges are privately operated, but most of them are the older institutions which have only 5 percent of the total enrollment. The majority are a new breed in higher-education institutions—the two-year community colleges. These have no dormitories; the local students commute by car and bus. The colleges are financed by local county and state taxes and operate much as a local high school, but on a larger scale. Most are controlled by state governments, as in Alabama. Others, such as the Florida Keys Junior College, which is part of the Monroe County school system, are operated as though they were school districts with a local board and chief administrator.

The community colleges stemmed in part from the crowded public colleges of the 1950's. During that decade, the public universities set up branches in other parts of their states to accommodate first- and second-year students. If these students maintained a sufficient grade level, they moved to the main campuses. But, as the demand increased, many communities asked that the central state university create more extensions. When these were not forthcoming, they started their own two-year colleges, which granted the same privileges and accreditation as the university extensions. Then vocational courses, such as nursing, salesmanship, electronics, dental hygiene, were added as a public service—and the new concept in higher education took hold.

Typical of this evolution was the community college movement in Pennsylvania. In the early 1960's Pennsylvania, the nation's third largest state, had 111 four-year colleges; all but a handful were small private schools, and there was one large, centrally located public university—Pennsylvania State. Only two fifths of the state's high school graduates entered college, and Pennsylvania ranked forty-eighth in money spent per capita for higher education. One educator contended that Pennsylvania was wedded to the tradition that "only the economically and academically able are entitled to higher education." In 1963, as Pennsylvania State and its extensions overflowed, Governor William Scranton repudiated this tradition by signing into law the Community College Act, which created a new state office to set up a network of colleges. Four of the new colleges were built and put in operation within two years, and ground-breaking for three more was approved. Other states by this time were well along in the community college movement.

New College Pattern. Today the steady growth of two-year community colleges continues, and some educators predict that most secondary school students soon will be entering these colleges as a matter of course, much as they now go to high school. In general, the new schools probably will follow the pattern of Cleveland's Cuyahoga Community College, which opened in 1963 as the first community college in Ohio. It registered 3000 students within a week; within two years the enrollment was 10,000. Among the students were some who planned to go on to four-year degree colleges, vocational students earning associate degrees in special skills, housewives studying home economics and older people attending evening classes to develop new interests.

California, with 80 junior colleges, ranks first among the states (13 more are planned for 1970). New York is next with 67, and Texas third with 47 (see maps below). California also has the largest enrollment of the two-year institutions—24,185 in Long Beach City College. Only Nevada among the states, with its small population, has no junior colleges. By 1970, the U.S. Office of Education predicts nearly one third of the students entering into higher education will be enrolling in community colleges.

450 ESTABLISHED BEFORE 1950

390 BUILT IN 15 YEARS, 1951-66*

200 TO BE BUILT IN 4 YEARS, 1967-70

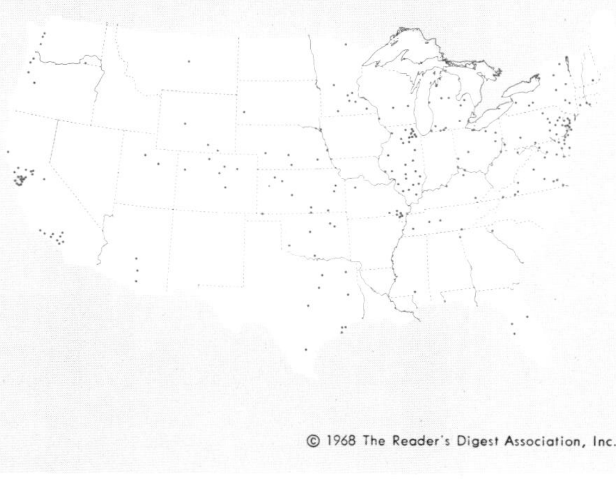

**State-approved and accredited junior colleges in existence in 1966*

THE AMERICAN TREND

Over the past century, despite all its problems and growing pains, American education has proved the most broadly effective in the world. In this period the United States has taken into its classrooms more children of school age than any other nation and has kept them there for more years of study. American education has reached the smallest hamlets, so that now nearly every citizen has attended, or is attending, some kind of school. In all, 2,500,000 teachers are instructing 55,900,000 Americans of every age past toddling. There is little doubt that the all-pervasiveness of schooling has been a factor in making the United States the powerful nation it is today.

Colonial Education. In the beginning, the schools were the product of the social patterns and mores brought from Europe by the first settlers. The early Puritans extended their religious beliefs through their schools as well as through their pulpits. Calvinism decreed that each person was responsible for knowing God's will, and this he could accomplish only by knowing how to read the Bible. Under the pressure of this religious belief, the Massachusetts legislature in 1642 passed the first compulsory school law in the colonies, requiring that every child be taught to read. Five years later another law was passed ordering all towns of 50 or more families to provide a teacher for reading and writing, and all towns of more than 100 families to establish Latin schools, which were roughly equivalent to our present-day high schools.

Although these latter schools were public in that they were open to all the people, they were influenced greatly by the clergy, and usually operated on some sort of tuition basis. Learning for poorer people ended after they had absorbed the rudiments of reading and writing. Mostly the sons of the wealthy went to Latin school and then on to the only college, Harvard. There they studied for the ministry, government or the practice of law. Only a minority of the students considered careers in commerce. Despite its limitations, however, Massachusetts schooling was successful in the broad sense. Historians estimate that about 95 percent of Massachusetts men could read and write in 1700, when illiteracy was widespread among the other colonies. In the largest cities, private masters taught more secular subjects not available in the religious academies: mathematics, bookkeeping, penmanship, science and basic industrial technologies. But only gradually did the early schools include these subjects in their curriculums.

Free and Universal Education. Private religious influence in the education of the nation was slow in passing. The citizenry was not aware of the democratic advantage of "free" or public schools. Our Constitution did not mention universal education although an ordinance was passed to set aside land for public schools in the Northwest Territory. Not until well into the 1800's, and only after bitter controversy, were tax-supported free school programs adopted in a few states. Massachusetts authorized the first general public school taxes in 1827.

PUBLIC SCHOOLS

American education perhaps would not be the mighty structure it is today were it not for two doughty New Englanders who fought for public school improvement in the 1800's. In the early part of the century, "free schools," as they were called, existed in just a few localities, and received halfhearted attention. Then in the 1830's Horace Mann and Henry Barnard launched their separate crusades.

The Fathers of Modern Schooling. In 1837 Mann gave up a profitable law practice to become Massachusetts' first Board of Education secretary. A graduate of Brown University, he was determined to make educational opportunity available to the many. During his 12 years in office, he succeeded in doubling the local tax appropriations for schools. He exhorted towns and cities to hire better teachers and provide better texts and he roused local communities to build 50 new public high schools.

In two neighboring states, Henry Barnard occupied a place similar to Mann's. As head of the Board of Education in Connecticut and then Rhode Island, he published a periodical, the *American School Journal*. In 1867 he became the first U.S. Commissioner of Education.

Aside from these two innovators, other forces, of course, worked to improve the public schools. Following the Civil War, organized labor insisted that workers' children receive more education, and many persons strove for betterment at the grass-roots level. The rapidly expanding economy by itself created a demand for better education on a broader base.

In the late 1800's and early 1900's the "ladder" type of progression through the school system began taking form. Pupils were graded according to proficiency and grouped into classes. Higher grades were added and attendance at high schools became general about the time of World War I. After World War I, immigrants poured into this nation, especially from eastern Europe, and one of the great accomplishments of the public school system was the efficiency with which it helped advance their children.

The Postwar Crisis. After weathering the Great Depression of the 1930's, public schools were hit by possibly the greatest crisis of their existence. Following World War II the birthrate soared, and the resulting crowding of the grade schools caught district boards and the public off guard. Very little building had been added to the public school system since the WPA days of the Depression. School boards tried to handle the overflow by curtailing classes, splitting the school day into two sessions and increasing the pupil-teacher ratio to as much as 60 to 1. Church basements and empty storerooms were commandeered for extra classes, an almost frantic hiring of new teachers took place and construction of new facilities began.

The public school population increased by more than a third to 36,000,000 in the decade of the 1950's. Costs tripled, rising to $15 billion by 1960, and forecasters saw no end in sight. By 1975, the annual bill may be nearly $36 billion, the number of students 46,500,000.

Dropouts. Without a high school education, a young citizen has little chance of finding his best opportunity in the competitive American economic system. Of 3,156,000 pupils entering high school in 1961, only 2,362,000 graduated in 1965. Industrial schools, which also teach the rudiments of general learning as they prepare teen-agers for jobs, may be the answer for many. There were 1,088,000 students in Federally aided trade and industrial programs in the nation in 1965.

Teacher Shortage. The crowding of schools also seemed to aggravate other long-standing problems. Almost every school district in the 1950's had a teacher shortage. As more and more classrooms were built, fewer and fewer teachers were available to staff them. Greater economic rewards in other fields enticed many who might otherwise have trained for teaching. And rising living costs forced many already in the profession to leave for greener fields. The raising of the national average salary of teachers by more than half to $6500 between 1955 and 1965 seemed to have little effect. Some teachers skipped from state to state—$4190 was the average in Mississippi, $8150 the average in California. Merely by crossing a state line a teacher might go from $6350 (in Ohio) to $7050 (in Indiana). (See chart below.)

Desegregation. Another problem involved segregation. The U.S. Supreme Court decision of 1954 ordering all schools to integrate with "deliberate speed" caused bitter disputes in many school districts. In the South, the depth of feeling was such that violence erupted. Nonetheless, integration continued. By 1965, a decade after the decision, 3250 of the 5000 school districts in 17 Southern states had been integrated. These included complete integration in Dallas, Atlanta and Louisville.

In the North, Negroes protested *de facto* segregation, in which public schools in the big cities had become completely Negro because they were in solidly Negro neighborhoods. Integration here posed a problem almost as difficult to solve as that in the South. Some cities tried to distribute white and Negro students by bus in an effort to equalize enrollment on a racial basis. Progress in this direction was slow, and many felt that elimination of *de facto* segregation would be a long time coming. There were not enough white children in central city areas to go around, and many all-white schools were too far from colored districts to make busing practicable.

Church and State. The issue of the separation of church and state also plagued the school boards. In several decisions, the U.S. Supreme Court declared prayer or any other religious exercise in the public schools unconstitutional. Some members of Congress, with the backing of religious groups, tried several times with no success to authorize voluntary prayer exercise in the schools.

The tradition of separation of church and state posed a problem with the Roman Catholic Church. When a bill to grant Federal aid to public schools was first introduced in the early 1960's, Catholic Church officials asked that parochial schools be included. President Kennedy, a Catholic himself, dissented, contending that such aid was con-

ELEMENTARY AND SECONDARY SCHOOL FACTS AND FIGURES 1966	California	New York	Texas	Ohio	Pennsylvania	Illinois	Michigan	New Jersey	Florida	North Carolina	Indiana	Georgia	Massachusetts	Virginia	Missouri	Tennessee	Wisconsin	Alabama	Minnesota	Louisiana	Maryland	Washington	Kentucky	South Carolina	Iowa	Mississippi
Student Enrollment (in millions)	4.348	3.260	2.564	2.320	2.237	2.132	2.017	1.312	1.247	1.202	1.146	1.075	1.041	1.008	.982	.890	.878	.849	.824	.818	.779	.739	.677	.651	.637	.59
Number of Teachers (in thousands)	167.0	152.5	105.6	91.9	92.9	93.6	76.1	61.7	50.0	46.8	47.1	39.6	47.0	41.2	38.7	32.7	40.2	30.9	36.1	32.8	32.5	31.2	27.1	25.2	30.3	21.
Additional Schoolrooms Needed (in thousands)	33.5	22.9	13.3	15.1	16.9	13.5	14.7	6.5	10.0	8.1	7.3	9.6	5.0	7.8	4.9	6.7	4.9	7.1	3.8	5.6	6.6	4.3	4.4	5.7	3.5	5.
Average Annual Teacher's Salary (in dollars)	8150	7700	5950	6350	6410	7123	6850	6968	6435	5337	7050	5350	7100	5650	5857	5100	6425	5150	6641	6039	6878	6825	4930	4675	6050	419
Total Average Expenditures per Pupil (in dollars)	746	1040	542	610	613	699	678	795	592	442	595	438	583	503	576	422	708	401	721	555	734	688	431	401	662	36
Federal Aid Spent by Elementary and Secondary Schools, not including maintenance (in millions of dollars)	157.453	126.647	105.290	56.999	68.344	59.619	47.601	41.191	49.733	63.373	24.596	53.669	28.630	52.891	34.118	39.103	20.624	44.321	24.661	31.564	35.891	27.279	38.308	32.494	19.187	25.

trary to Constitutional provisions on the separation of church and state. Previous court cases had established that a state may provide transportation, books, lunches and medical care to parochial students, although many states do not support these services in church schools.

As often happens, the troubled and critical years following World War II brought with them many changes for the better. New methods of teaching, revisions in the curriculum and technical innovation emerged. These included the use of closed-circuit television, tape recorders, movies, teaching machines and teacher assistants. The so-called New Math, with its use of symbolic logic and deductive thinking, and new ways of learning foreign languages were introduced in both grade and high schools. But these innovations were only a part of the revolution going on in our schools from day to day in the 1960's—the products of invention fostered by necessity.

WHY SUBURBAN SCHOOLS ARE BETTER

The map at right shows strikingly why suburban schools generally are better than city schools—suburbanites are willing to pay more for their support. Property owners in the five counties in the New York City School District paid only $14.56 in 1965 school taxes for every $1000 of real estate value, while in the commuter counties surrounding New York the amount was as much as $20.52. And more money was spent per child. All the surrounding counties exceeded New York City's appropriation of $937 per pupil. Suffolk and Rockland were low with $945 and $963 respectively, but each of the others spent over $1000, with Westchester spending the highest at $1059. Yet New York City has more valuable taxable property to support education than these suburban counties: the city's property value amounts to $43,456 per pupil; the lowest suburban rank is Suffolk's $23,166 and the highest is Westchester's $41,637.

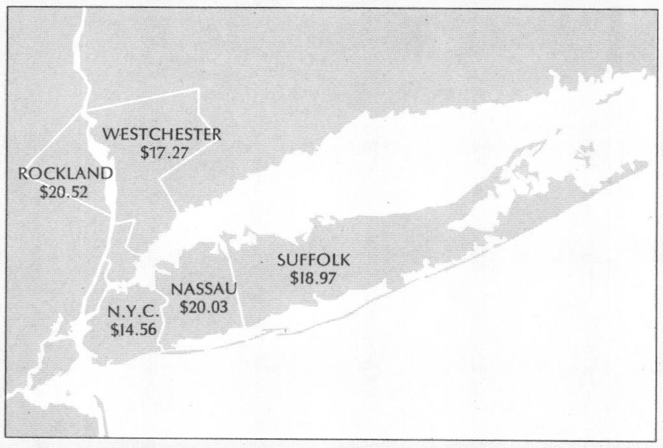

SCHOOL DISTRICTS

Our school districts come in all sizes and shapes. Alaska's School District One, geographically the nation's largest, contains all the schools of the forty-ninth state except those of 20 towns and villages. Hawaii is actually one large statewide district. And there are many countywide and citywide districts. But most school districts are town and township units, controlled by an elected board of education. Up to 1965, the property owners of these 26,983 individual districts bore the major share of the public school costs in direct local taxes.

Because of economic differences, the levels of education offered by school districts around the nation are understandably varied. Some simply cannot afford the necessary facilities and faculty. Many suburban and rural districts, under pressure from the population boom and too small to provide efficient programs, consolidated with nearby systems in the late 1950's and early 1960's. A number of them, unfortunately, could not, because they were too remote geographically. And others refused to do so. Half of the nation's school districts in the late 1960's had fewer than ten teachers, and in the early 1960's there were more than 9000 elementary schools with only one teacher. Many districts of moderate size—under 750 students—had difficulty in supporting a modern building program and in providing enough range in subjects for adequate training.

Big-City Decline. The school districts in the cities, which educate half the nation's pupils, were considered the aristocrats of public education before World War II. New York City especially, with more than a million students, was noted for the superior quality of its teachers and high schools. In the last two decades there has been a change.

The influx of low-income migrants, mostly Negroes from the South and Puerto Ricans, along with the exodus of higher-income families to the suburbs, was responsible for the decline of many big-city schools. Language difficulties, impoverished home life and weak motivation contributed to lowered standards, delinquency and dropouts. Many of the best teachers, lured by better pay and living conditions, departed for the suburbs.

Suburban schools have become the elite in public education. The best schools in the nation are now found in such affluent suburbs as New York's Scarsdale, Cleveland's Shaker Heights and California's Palo Alto. While many city schools, run-down and dilapidated, are staffed with about 35 professionals—teachers, administrators, librarians—for every 1000 students, suburban schools, often modern and spacious, may be staffed by as many as 70 professionals for every 1000 students.

Exceptional Schools. The exception to this is the specialized public high school—such as New York's Bronx High School of Science. Bronx, and several like it in the city, enroll gifted students from the schools of the five boroughs. A few institutions of this kind also flourish in Boston and Philadelphia. Generally, however, the standard suburban high school is superior to that of the large city.

Schools in smaller cities of 10,000 to 60,000 population are also considered more than satisfactory. Here businessmen, labor leaders and the citizenry have a strong interest in their schools. The one or two high schools in town may be popular social and cultural gathering places. Local industries and labor unions set up apprentice programs so that youths may go right to work in the plants after graduation. And the basketball and football teams are a particular source of local pride. In these cities, increases in the school budget and bond issues for improvements are usually accepted with little opposition.

Federal Support. Between 1960 and 1965, the ratio of payment to the public schools from government sources changed little, hovering at about 56 percent from the local school districts, 40 percent from the state and only 4 percent from the Federal government. But in the decade prior to 1965 the support from property taxes for the local school districts rose nearly two and a half times, and the Congress recently has begun to show signs of recognizing the plight of the school districts and local property owners. More than $5 billion in Federal funds was authorized for public schools for 1966 and 1967, mostly for needy districts.

CALIFORNIA – THE SCHOOL MUSHROOM

California has the largest, most comprehensive and most expensive public education system of any state in the nation. It adds more students every year than any other state, and its educational problems are magnified versions of those in the country at large.

With a high birthrate and heavy migration from the rest of the country, California has acquired the greatest population of all the states. Elementary and secondary school enrollment in 1965 increased by more than 400 pupils each school day. Nearly 3 million attended the grade schools, 1.5 million the high schools. To handle the crowds, California in 1965 had to build 221 elementary schools and 44 new high schools as well as additions to existing schools—7500 new classrooms in all. Every Monday morning, five new schools opened their doors in the state.

Rising Costs. As the school-age population continued to rise in the late 1960's, it posed a financing problem of gigantic proportions for Californians. Despite expenditures of $3.5 billion in 1965–66, construction and facilities fell short of what was needed. Tax resources have been strained to the limit. The state could look forward to only one certain new source of funds for its lower grades. In 1966, some $181 million in Federal aid was authorized for elementary and secondary education. This was only a trickle compared to the amount needed.

A good part of California's tremendous school expenditure went to public higher education—some $608 million in 1966. Yet the state's high school students were not taking full advantage of it. Less than half of the 1965 graduating class went on to state colleges.

In all, California has more than 780,000 in its public institutions of higher education. The University of California with its nine campuses has the largest enrollment of any university complex of its kind in the world—86,000.

	Oklahoma	Connecticut	Kansas	Colorado	Arkansas	Oregon	West Virginia	Arizona	Nebraska	Utah	New Mexico	Maine	Idaho	Montana	South Dakota	Hawaii	Rhode Island	North Dakota	District of Columbia	New Hampshire	Delaware	Nevada	Wyoming	Vermont	Alaska
Student Enrollment 43,004,000	595	.587	.515	.497	.460	.457	.438	.380	.326	.293	.272	.226	.179	.170	.170	.166	.159	.153	.148	.130	.111	.108	.088	.085	.061
Number of Teachers 1,793,000	25.5	26.1	27.9	22.9	17.9	21.9	17.0	16.5	16.1	11.3	11.5	9.6	7.6	8.0	8.8	5.7	6.9	7.6	5.8	5.7	5.0	4.5	4.4	4.0	2.8
Additional Schoolrooms Needed 286,000	3.1	2.0	2.7	3.6	2.6	2.2	4.0	2.6	1.5	2.3	1.6	1.1	1.1	0.9	0.6	1.2	1.1	0.8	1.1	0.7	0.5	0.6	0.4	0.3	0.2
Average Annual Teacher's Salary $6500	5650	7200	5785	6391	4740	6650	4990	7025	5225	6250	6356	5550	5685	5800	4650	6929	6325	5120	7500	5650	7150	7025	6119	5640	8240
Total Average Expenditures per Pupil $641	551	718	592	653	463	742	396	582	519	643	681	483	465	660	570	621	695	583	711	646	828	574	650	554	852
Federal Aid Spent by Elementary and Secondary Schools $1,620,447,000	9.662	11.840	19.571	22.756	24.158	12.576	18.850	21.306	11.658	10.193	22.654	7.338	6.411	8.502	9.238	14.590	7.201	7.112	11.164	4.773	4.197	5.670	3.490	2.537	13.747

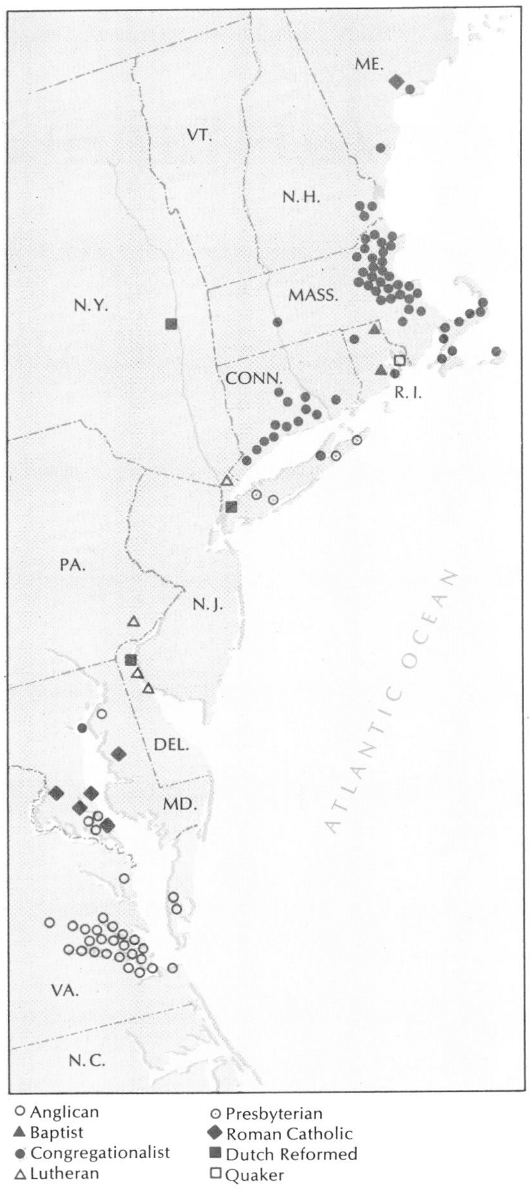

CHURCHES IN 1650

By this date, 113 congregations had built churches in the British colonies. All these were members of a few dominant sects. The Anglicans centered in Virginia, the Baptists in Rhode Island; Congregationalists were paramount through New England while Lutherans had gathered in New York, lower Pennsylvania and Delaware. Long Island was Presbyterian; there were Quakers in Rhode Island; Roman Catholics prevailed in Maryland; and New York City and Albany, New York, contained most of the Dutch Reformed in the New World.

RELIGION IN AMERICA

Colonial Churches. America was discovered just about the time that religious reforms were beginning to sweep Europe. These reformations produced dissenters who were hounded and persecuted for their beliefs. As a natural result, whole groups of them sought a haven in the vast territories across the sea. The majority of the refugees settled in areas claimed by England, largely because France and Spain kept a tight rein on religious practice in lands they controlled.

So it was that in the original British colonies a generous measure of religious freedom became the established way of life from the very start. Colonial leaders in Maryland, Rhode Island and Pennsylvania supported tolerance because they themselves cherished a belief that people had a right to their own forms of worship, provided these did not interfere with the rights of others.

The American Revolution caused changes in every sect in the 13 colonies. All were induced by circumstances to set up American-based organizations. Most sects soon brought pressure for complete independence of decision and operation. Some religious groups took advantage of newly won political freedom to press firmly for inclusion of religious liberty and the separation of church and state in the legal codes of the country.

Frontier Religion. After the Revolution the westward migration drew a number of American churches into the wilderness to serve and convert families there. Two of the most active were the Methodists, whose circuit-riding ministers and lay preachers attracted thousands, and the Baptists, whose farmer-preachers migrated with entire communities. The Presbyterians and Congregationalists, joining their efforts under a Plan of Union, were also successful in gaining members, though many of the churches established under this plan later became completely Presbyterian. The rough and democratic frontier life soon produced new modes of religious expression generally known as revivalism. The formal sermons and prayers of the eastern churches were replaced with emotional exhortations by ministers and demonstrative responses from congregations. These satisfied the needs of frontier people who lived in isolation. And those sects that made full use of revivalism —Methodists, Baptists and to some degree Presbyterians— increased their membership in the West much faster than those, such as the Lutherans and Episcopalians, who held to the older forms of services.

Revivalist practices proved a mixed blessing. Methodists, Baptists and Presbyterians suffered serious schisms, and in time dissenters (often revivalists) established entirely different sects. Other new denominations developed around strong leaders. The Church of Jesus Christ of Latter Day Saints (Mormons) and the Seventh-Day Adventists are two of these, both founded in upper New York State.

Slavery and Immigrants. The divisive question of the morality of slavery had for years been a growing problem for many U.S. sects. Eventually it created rifts which cut almost all the great Protestant groups into two segments— one North, the other South. Some of these would not reunite until many years after the Civil War and some have not yet done so. In mid-century a potato blight in Ireland and a revolution in Germany were among the factors that brought a wave of immigrants to America, many of them Roman Catholics. By 1860 more than 5 million Catholics had settled in the northeastern and central states.

Another influx of immigrants, Jews from central and eastern Europe, further diversified the picture. U.S. Jewry had, up to then, begun to show signs of drawing together. Under the impact of the ideas of the new arrivals, however, it divided into distinct Orthodox, Reformed and Conservative organizations.

The Later Revivalists. After the Civil War, families made wealthy by growing industries donated large sums to established denominations. Less fortunate members felt ill at ease in the elaborate churches built by the rich. Even the old revivalist camp-meeting grounds, such as that at Lake Chautauqua, New York, had become summer resorts with musical entertainment, lectures and educational services. Turning away from such activities, many left the prosperous sects and sought comfort in Pentecostal and Holiness bodies such as Assemblies of God and the Church of the Nazarene. These espoused a return to fundamentalism, a belief based on stricter adherence to the words of the Bible.

Twentieth-Century Diversification. By 1900 the Russian Orthodox Church, which had taken root in Alaska and on the West Coast some decades earlier, and the Greek Orthodox Church began to increase their memberships by the thousands through fresh immigration from Europe. At the same time an influx of Japanese and Chinese laborers in Hawaii created a large Buddhist population in the territory.

PATTERNS OF RELIGION

The chart below shows when various denominations first appeared in America, the period during which some of them divided, creating new churches and, later, when mergers began to take place. At present, a number of other churches are also undertaking or considering unification.

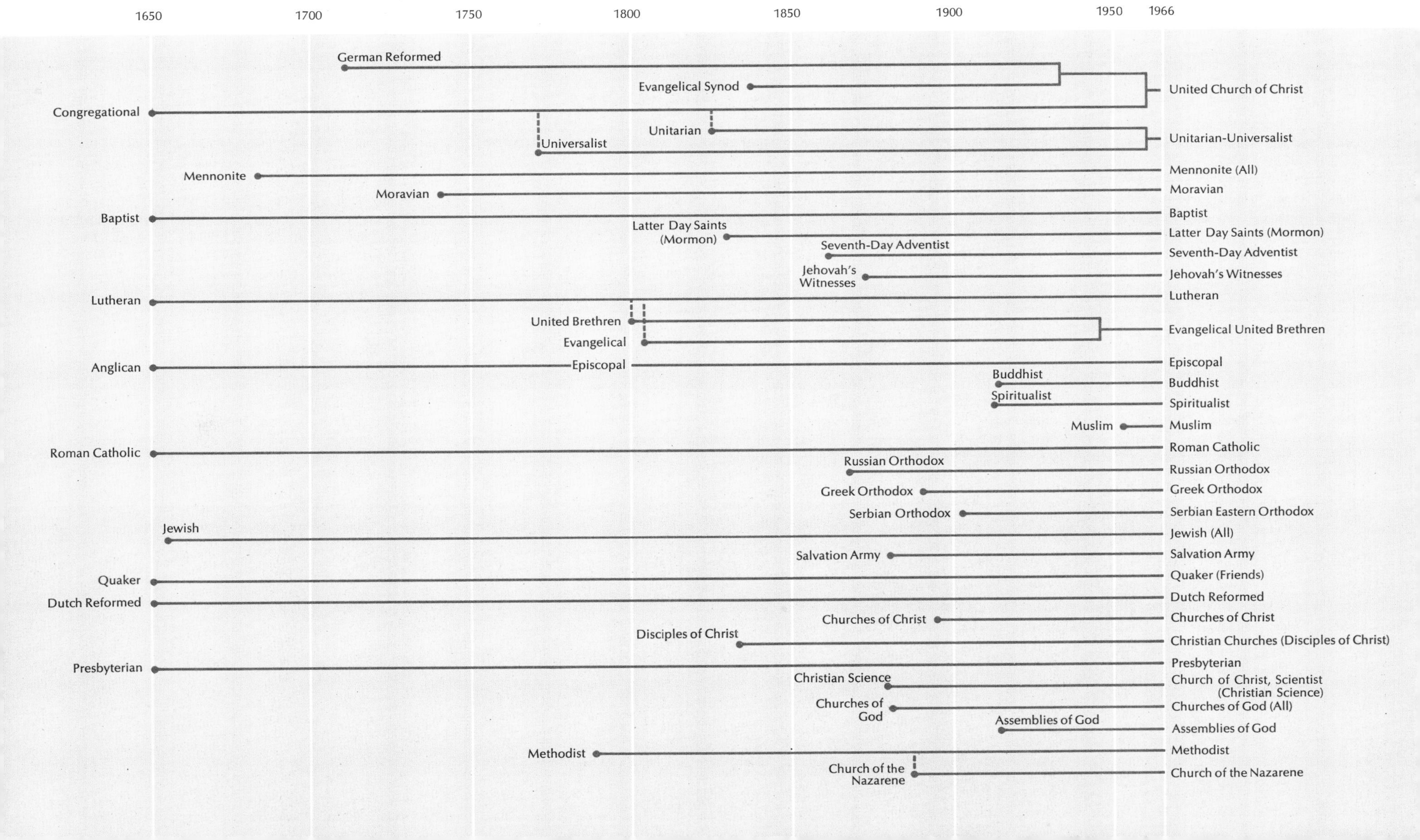

Pacifism and Social Welfare. World War I brought forth the same crusading religious fervor that had arisen during America's other wars. But, reacting to the horror and brutality of the struggle, a great number of churchmen turned to causes devoted to pacifism and the abolition of war. This active group attracted many who were not pacifist Quakers and Mennonites. Representing both clergy and laity, they not only strongly supported the League of Nations, but pledged never to tolerate armed force again.

In the grim years of the Depression of the 1930's, churches wholeheartedly distributed their shrinking resources to those in want. So great was the need that even the most conservative denominations abandoned their tradition of remaining aloof from political activity. They actively sought government help for those whom the churches could not relieve.

The attack on Pearl Harbor caused many a religious pacifist to modify his ideas, and members of all faiths joined in the task of winning the war. Symbolic of this spirit of self-sacrifice was that of four chaplains—a Catholic priest, two Protestant ministers and a Jewish rabbi—in giving up their life jackets to men aboard the sinking transport *Dorchester*.

Ecumenism and Confederation. American churches responded to the challenge of war relief. Secular agencies and such groups as Church World Service and the Catholic Relief Services donated millions of dollars and gave countless hours of physical and spiritual assistance. Some churches worked urgently for changes in U.S. immigration laws which would allow religious refugees of all sects to enter this country.

Out of the wartime and postwar relief effort grew a spirit of unity among U.S. and international church bodies. A number of Protestant groups have merged (see chart below on opposite page). The first Assembly of the World Council of Churches met in Amsterdam in 1948 and issued an unprecedented declaration on religious liberty. In 1962–63 the Ecumenical Council of the Roman Catholic Church turned in the direction of greater coöperation with other denominations.

Modern Mass Communications. New evangelistic trends have appeared, strongly resembling earlier movements but interdenominational in character. The Reverend Billy Graham, for example, born a Presbyterian but now a Baptist, seeks converts to Christ and Christian principle, not to a particular sect. Graham, Bishop Fulton J. Sheen and others spread the gospel not only in traditional mass public meetings but through television and radio. Famous preachers such as Dr. Norman Vincent Peale and Rabbi Joshua Loth Liebman have helped millions of people find rededication through widely circulated books and publications.

Social Problems. Since the Supreme Court school desegregation decision of 1954, priests, ministers and rabbis have been foremost among those pressing for the legal means to guarantee all citizens their just rights and for changing the hearts of those they feel are blocking the movement toward equality. Most American religious groups have thrown themselves into the struggle against the illiteracy, poverty and despair that afflict segments of the U.S. population.

Traditional church-state separation was a relatively simple matter in earlier years. The Constitution and the law were clear. However, the burst of population and the drive for better education have increased the strain on church-school systems. Some groups have roused public controversy by seeking public support for their parochial schools (see "Church and State," page 106). Another religious issue arose from the Supreme Court decision against prayer in the public schools.

Birth control (also a question made critical by the population explosion) might have caused conflict among American church sects, except that open discussion has allayed the severity of the controversy between them. The Roman Catholic position has been undergoing reexamination.

All American religious bodies have been highly concerned with the search for peace in the world. Both individual and multichurch organizations have helped in arranging truces, have acted as mediators and have adopted public positions for lessening tensions between nations. The Vietnamese war has produced dissent among churchmen.

The Modern Churchman. Clergy today not only serve their congregations but have taken the lead in solving local social questions. They act as committee members in community activities, organize nonsectarian as well as religious youth groups and take part in many other religious and community functions.

American churches today are thus experiencing what some Protestants call "a new Reformation." Peace and ecumenism are not the only causes that stir religious thought. Traditional religious beliefs are receiving a new examination and interpretation; laymen are being invited into central church operation, where their leadership and knowledge can make a vital contribution; and national organizations are encouraging greater local responsibility. In part the historic role of the churches of America remains the same but at the same time that role and the structural organization are changing.

UNITED CHURCH OF CHRIST
Membership: 2,070,413

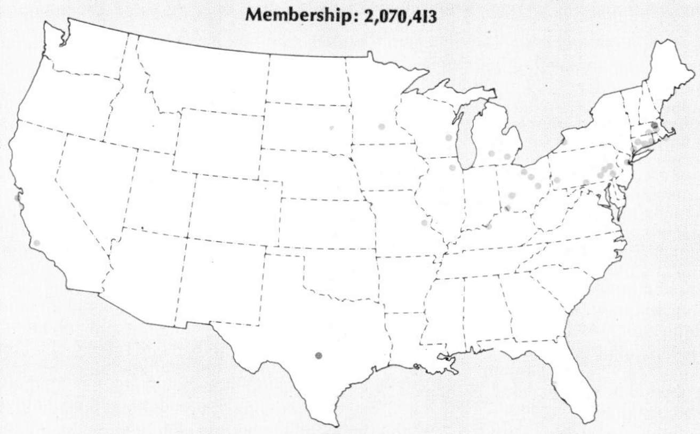

BAPTIST
Membership: 23,812,119 (estimate)

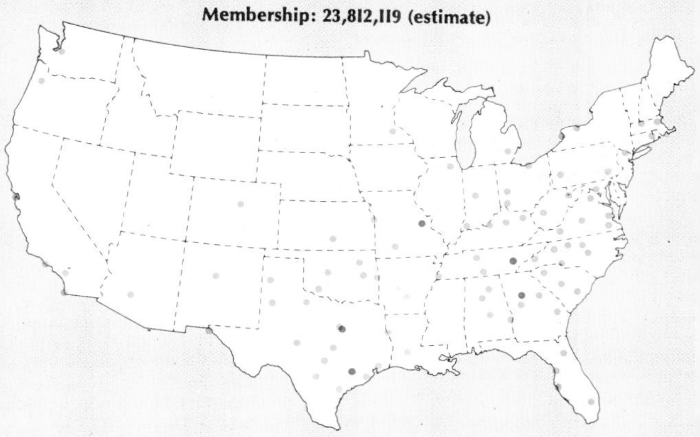

LUTHERAN
Membership: 8,794,106 (estimate)

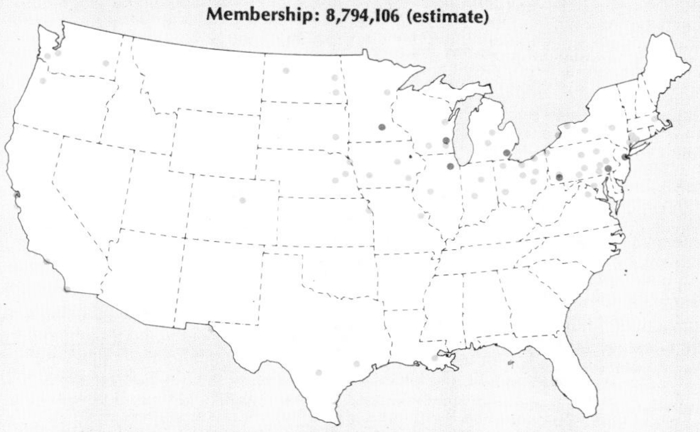

EPISCOPAL
Membership: 3,410,657

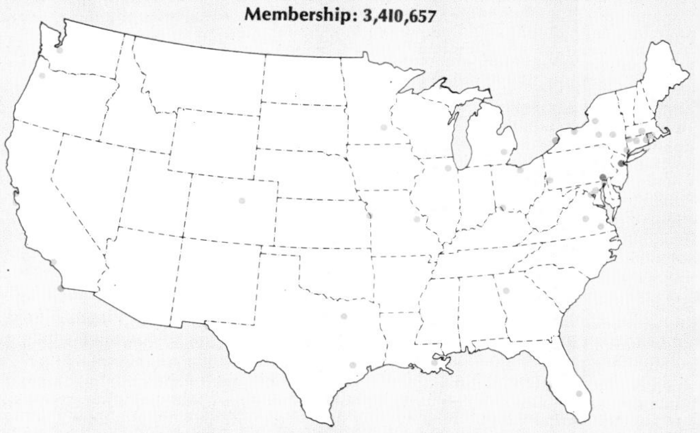

ROMAN CATHOLIC
Membership: 46,246,175

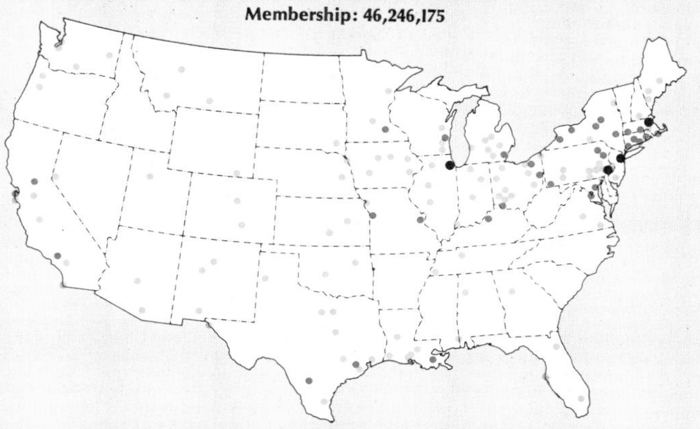

JEWISH
Membership: 5,600,000 (estimate)

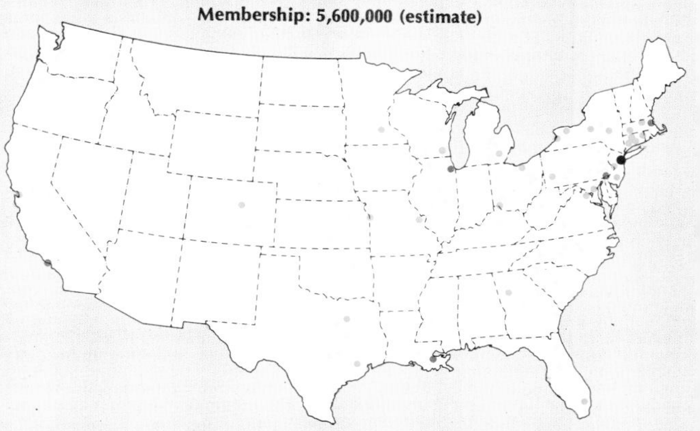

PRESBYTERIAN
Membership: 4,420,556

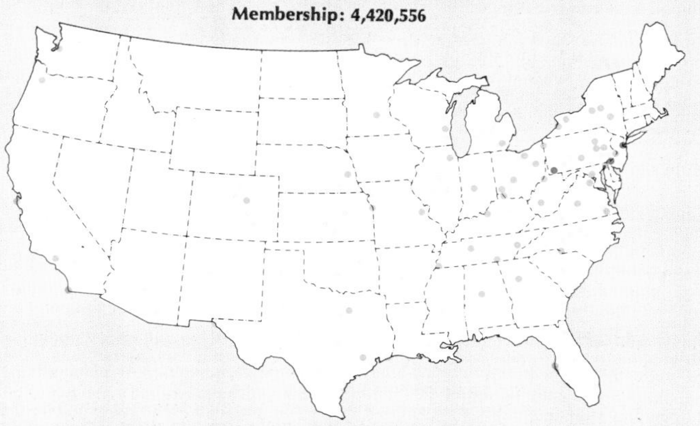

METHODIST
Membership: 13,287,081

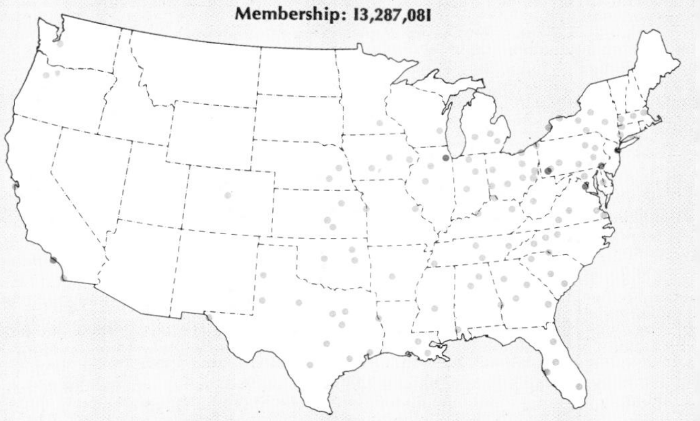

500 to 10,000 · 10,000 to 100,000 · 100,000 to 1 million · over 1 million

CHURCH MEMBERSHIP DISTRIBUTION

These maps show the approximate distribution of membership by metropolitan areas of eight major religious groups in the United States. They are based on a 1952 study by the National Council of Churches, the most recent available. Though most religious authorities agree that the pattern of distribution of churches has remained largely the same, to some degree there have been changes through the expanding and shifting population which have not been reported in terms of religion.

Above the maps, total membership figures for 1966 are given. Even here there are differing methods of counting membership; Roman Catholics include young children in their total, others do not. Sects, not shown, whose membership distribution is sizable are: the 1,936,008 members of the Church of Jesus Christ of Latter Day Saints (Mormons), heavily concentrated in Utah, Idaho and the Los Angeles and San Francisco areas; the 1,927,380 Disciples of Christ located mostly in midwestern, southern and central plains states; 725,723 members of the Evangelical United Brethren centered in Illinois, Indiana, Ohio and Pennsylvania; the 572,123 members of Assemblies of God scattered throughout the country; the 530,630 membership of the Churches of God with heavy concentrations in the Midwest and South; the Seventh-Day Adventists with 364,000 members scattered more or less evenly across the United States; the 175,500 Mennonites located largely in Pennsylvania, Ohio and Indiana; the 166,000 Unitarian-Universalists centered mostly in New England and some midwestern cities; and the 127,500 Quakers (Friends) in the Philadelphia area and in Indiana and North Carolina.

HEALTH, A REVOLUTION

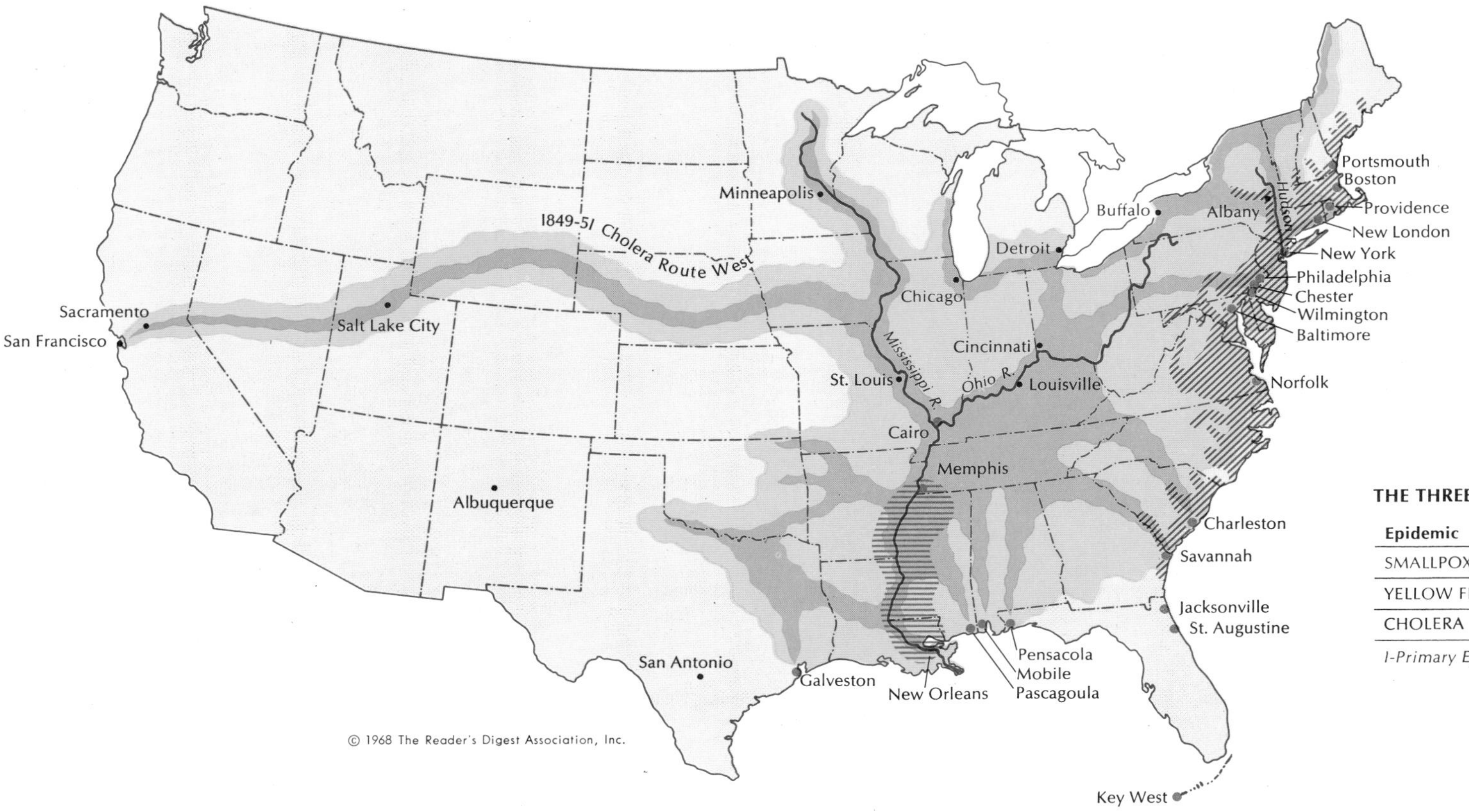

THE THREE MAJOR EPIDEMIC DISEASES IN THE U.S.

Epidemic	Area	Recurrences
SMALLPOX	(diagonal hatching)	1633 through 1799
YELLOW FEVER	(horizontal lines) ●	1699 through 1900
CHOLERA	1 2	1832-34, 1849-51, 1866, 1873

1-Primary Epidemic Route 2-Other Areas Affected

AMERICA'S BATTLE AGAINST THE GREAT EPIDEMICS

The epidemic diseases that afflicted Americans from colonial days up through the nineteenth century were brought to the New World by early colonists from Europe, by slaves from Africa and the West Indies, and later by some travelers and settlers from all over the globe. Outstanding epidemics visited upon America were smallpox during the seventeenth and eighteenth centuries, yellow fever in the eighteenth and nineteenth centuries and cholera in the first half of the nineteenth. The deadly influenza, which blazed across the world, struck America in 1918–19. It afflicted 20 million people, killing half a million in seven months, and was unique for its intense savagery. Except for isolated outbreaks of bubonic plague—the earliest and most severe at San Francisco's Chinatown in 1900 to 1902—the United States has been spared the disease that had so ravaged Europe.

The American Indians were periodically devastated by onslaughts of epidemic diseases brought by Europeans and for which they had no natural immunity. Smallpox epidemics in the seventeenth century accounted for dreadful losses among Indians and whites alike. In 1633 epidemics raged in the New England area and among Dutch settlements. For the century following, smallpox outbreaks occurred in New England, around Charleston, South Carolina, and in other settled colonies, especially New York and New Jersey. In the Boston epidemic of 1721 one out of seven died, and a thousand people fled the city. Only after widespread application of Dr. Edward Jenner's vaccine (discovered in 1800), did smallpox diminish as a major killer.

Yellow fever first hit America in 1699 at Charleston and Philadelphia. Until effective control measures were applied in the early 1900's as a result of the pioneering research of Dr. Walter Reed and his colleagues, the dread "Yellow Jack" struck repeatedly at the eastern seaboard with particular virulence in the larger ports. It moved inland as well, with most devastating effect in 1878–79. Thousands died. Many of the interior towns of the Mississippi Valley were ravaged; and more than 20,000 people perished in the area between New Orleans and Memphis.

Cholera was transported to the United States from Europe in 1832, killing 5000 New Yorkers in that year alone. The disease surged overland on the waves of westward migration and by ships pushing up the Mississippi and its tributaries. Four distinct epidemics — 1832–34, 1849–51, 1866 and 1873—killed thousands, although some preventive measures lowered the toll of life in the final two epidemics. Generally cholera raged over the most settled areas—intensely in the Mississippi and Ohio valleys—and the course of the disease was extended to the West Coast in 1848–50 with the trek of the Forty-niners to California. During the Civil War the many lessons learned about quarantine control, sanitation and public health were put to good and lasting use.

For the most part in our history there were few effective safeguards and remedies during peak epidemic periods. Yet, whatever their ravages over some 200 years, and with however much dread these killer diseases once filled Americans, today they have become virtually extinct in the United States.

INCREASE IN LIFE-SPAN

A person born in the mid-sixties in the United States can expect to live on the average for 70.2 years, matching the Biblical "three score years and ten." At any given age, five or eighty-five, a person's life expectancy is greater than it was in 1900 at the corresponding age. Life expectancy for the total population is nearly 23 years higher than it was in 1900, when individuals could look forward to a life-span of 47.3 years. Women live longer than men: males average 66.6 years and females almost six years longer. The trend for both continues upward. At present estimates for 1975, the life-span for men will average 69.5 years and for women 75.8.

Today, the number of people aged sixty-five and over has increased sixfold—from about 3 million in 1900 to more than 18 million in the mid-1960's. Those who are ill and who are not entirely self-supporting have created new health problems for the nation. The Social Security amendments of 1965 (Medicare) provide a variety of medical and health services for them.

CAUSES OF DEATH BY AGE GROUPS

The accident—at home, on the highways, at work and at play—has increasingly become fatal in America. Active, mobile living, linked with carelessness, makes accidental deaths high in all age groups. For adults in their early twenties, accidents cause more than half of all deaths, two thirds of them by motor vehicles.

For those aged fifteen to twenty-four, cancer ranks second. Suicide is third and takes fourth place from ages twenty-five to forty-four. Homicide ranks fourth as a cause of death for those fifteen to twenty-four, and is also major in the mid-twenties to mid-thirties.

Despite medical progress, influenza and pneumonia remain primary killer diseases from birth through age fourteen and then disappear as leading causes of death until age sixty-five and over. Heart disease, stroke and cancer cause most deaths in the fifth, sixth and seventh decades of life. For these, new techniques and treatments are becoming more readily available as regional health centers are being established across the country.

INFANT AND MATERNAL HEALTH

A steady decrease in infant mortality took place from 1919 to 1949, followed by a more gradual decline after World War II, but recent national surveys indicate that during the past decade the nonwhite (mostly Negro) infant death rate has been nearly twice that of the white.

The number of mothers who died during childbirth or immediately following has declined markedly since 1900. In the 1920's, for every 10,000 childbirths, 68 women died. By 1963, there were only 4 deaths per 10,000 women.

For the decade 1953–63, maternal deaths among nonwhites (largely Negro) remained fairly constant—a rate four times higher than for whites.

Reduction in infant and maternal mortality has resulted from greater knowledge of the complications of pregnancy, better prenatal and obstetrical care, antibiotics and improved sanitation and techniques in hospitals. Mortality is higher in rural areas, where not all babies are born in hospitals, and often mothers are still not attended by physicians or do not receive high-quality care.

FIVE LEADING CAUSES OF DEATH BY AGE GROUP

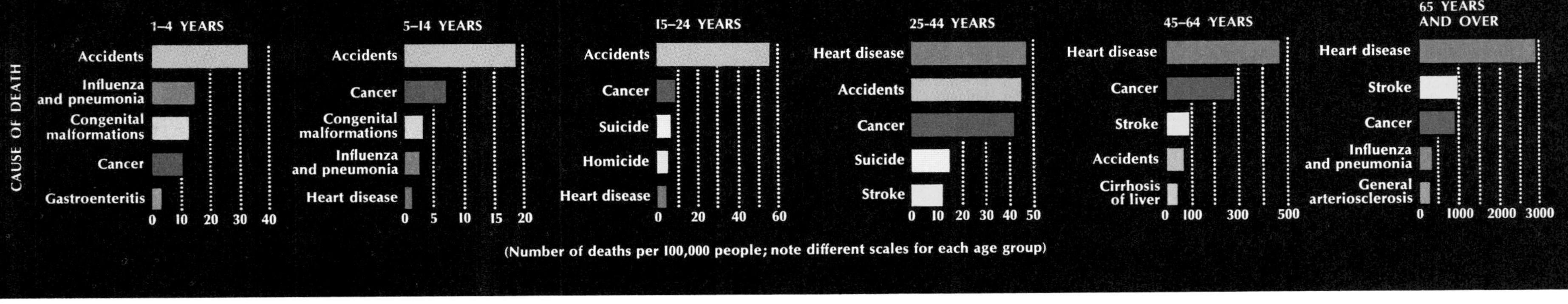

(Number of deaths per 100,000 people; note different scales for each age group)

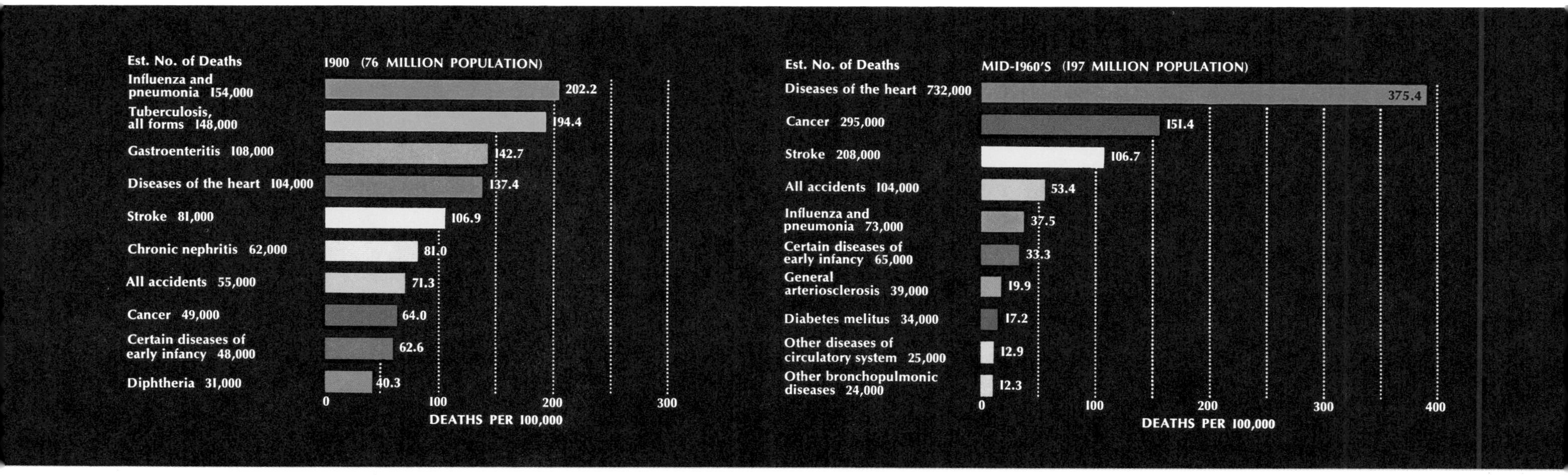

CHANGING CAUSES OF DEATH

The three major "killer diseases" today are those of cancer, of the heart and stroke. High blood pressure and arteriosclerosis are the underlying causes of most fatalities from the latter two. However, things were different 50 and more years ago. Heart disease, cancer and stroke were killers then, too, but for many thousands, other diseases struck before these could become fatal.

At the turn of the century, when the attending physician filled out a death certificate, the "cause of death" in most instances was a communicable disease: influenza, pneumonia, tuberculosis or stomach and intestinal upsets (grouped statistically as gastroenteritis). These were the major killers of 1900 and in their train came diphtheria, smallpox, typhoid fever and measles.

The remarkable change in the kinds of fatalities is undoubtedly proof of progress in preventing the communicable ills. Deaths from poliomyelitis, diphtheria, whooping cough and pneumonia have been reduced to low levels. Smallpox has been virtually eliminated. Improved standards of sanitation, better housing, widespread immunization and better methods of detecting and diagnosing disease provide protection for a greater number of Americans. In addition to better living, school health programs and public health clinics have played an important part in bringing this about.

Another change is attributed partly to the decrease in fatalities caused by infectious diseases. As a result, accidental death has jumped in relative importance from seventh place in 1900 to fourth place among all age groups, behind the chronic diseases which have risen to top rank. Cirrhosis of the liver, however, has ranked tenth in the recent past, and a current development has been the rapid increase in bronchopulmonic diseases as a cause of death.

DISABILITY FROM ACUTE CONDITIONS

In recent years it has been obvious that the common cold is still the acute illness most likely to keep people away from school, work or play. Respiratory ailments comprise about one half the total number causing temporary disability. Others are dental disorders, sprains, fractures, dislocations and acute bacterial infections, such as streptococcal sore throat and meningitis.

On the average, a person in the civilian population can expect to experience in one year about 2.1 acute illnesses or injuries that require medical attention or reduce his regular activity—usually for about 8.3 days per year, of which 3.5 days are spent in bed. (See Disability Chart for the national totals.)

Injury continues to cause a surprising amount of disability, estimated at 56.4 million cases annually. As many as 30 out of 100 persons sustain significant injuries in a given year.

Children are more subject to infective and parasitic diseases than adults are. As people grow older, the number of acute illnesses to which they are susceptible decreases. Among the elderly, however, infections are significant, particularly respiratory diseases.

Children six to sixteen miss an average of 4.6 days from school every year, for which infective, parasitic and respiratory diseases are to blame. For the employed population seventeen years and over, 1.6 bouts with some acute illness occur on the average each year, causing the loss of 3.4 days from work. (See Disability Chart for the national totals.)

Even though acute conditions do not cause the number of fatalities today that they once exacted, short-term illness is costly and widespread, an indication that preventive medicine has not yet solved all the problems of communicable and infective diseases.

For purposes of distinguishing between acute and chronic conditions, it is usually assumed that those which are acute last for less than a three-month period. Chronic conditions are of far greater concern. They may interfere not only with an individual's ability to work, but limit many of his other activities as well.

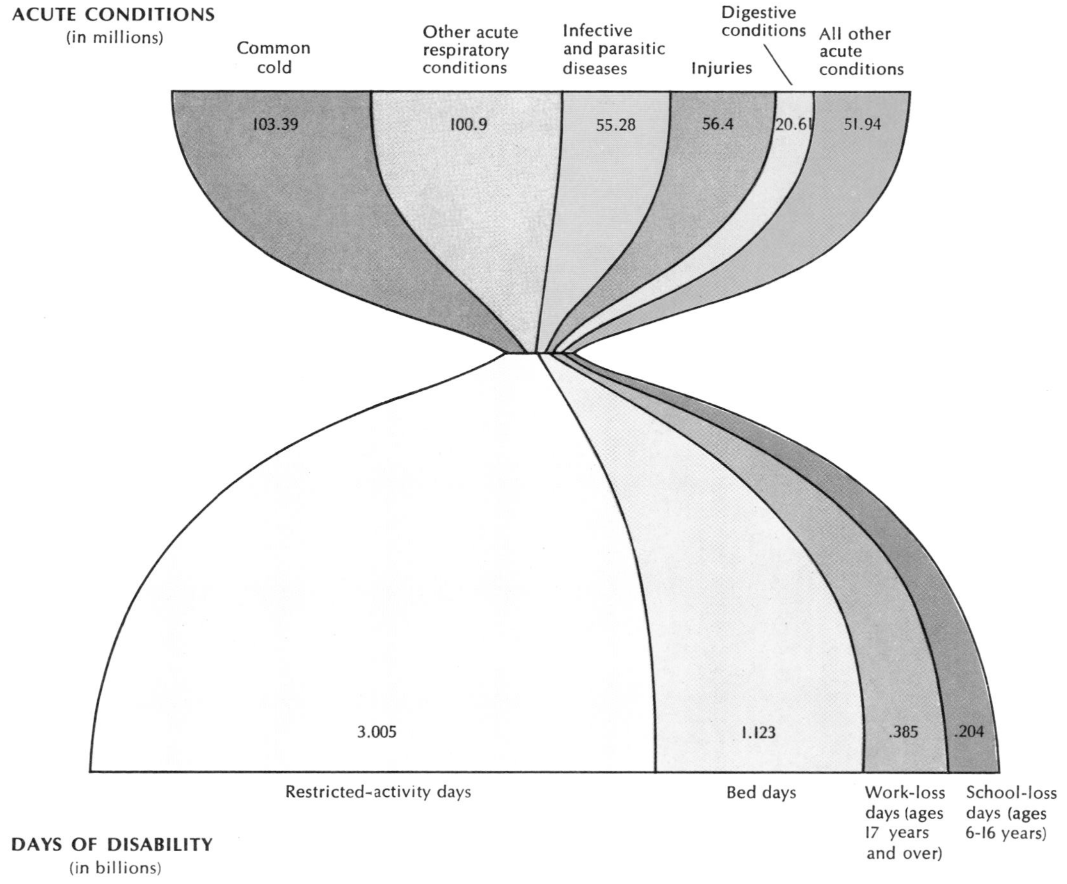

NOTE: Estimated annual averages based on 1963–64 interviews for the civilian, noninstitutional population. The frequencies for acute conditions include only cases for which a doctor was consulted or which caused the person to restrict his normal daily activities for at least one day. The figures for days of disability are not mutually exclusive. A day lost from work or school may also be a day in bed. Work-loss days, school-loss days and bed days are included in restricted-activity days.

DISABILITY FROM CHRONIC CONDITIONS

Over a two-year period, the National Health Survey found that 74 million persons in the United States have one or more chronic conditions, such as heart disease, arthritis or impairment of the back or spine. This accounts for over one third of the population of the country. Almost 20 million of these are limited in what they can do. Four million persons are so completely disabled that they cannot carry on their major activity.

Faced with an increasing number of older people in the population whose mobility and enjoyment of life are decreased by chronic disease, health research is being pressed to speed up its control and relief.

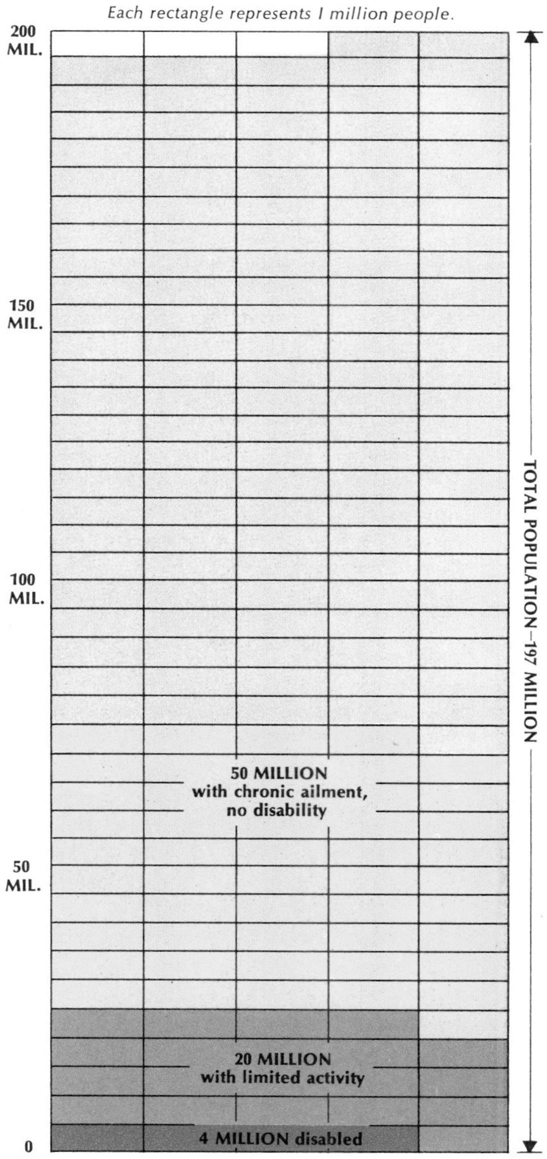

HEALTH MANPOWER

In the twentieth century, the doctor—traditionally the arbiter of all things medical—found that he could not become proficient in all facets of knowledge burgeoning in his profession. In a relatively short time, scientists have progressed from Pasteur's discovery of the relationship of bacteria to disease, to the breaking of the genetic code that governs animal life. This impact is almost unbelievable.

Faced with such overwhelming developments, the number of medical services in many fields has increased enormously—technical, therapeutic, psychological and dozens of other medical disciplines.

The traditional professions in relation to other health personnel have changed greatly during the past 65 years. In 1900, for every 100 physicians, there were 60 health professionals in other fields, including 24 dentists, 1 registered nurse, 35 pharmacists and others. By 1965, for every 100 physicians there were 371 other professionally trained health personnel.

Shortages in the Medical Field. One thing is certain: personnel in all categories is in short supply. Even though training facilities are increasing annually, any estimate of the number of future graduates indicates that the training of health personnel will fall behind the needs. Fortunately, American medicine has developed research, treatment and training to a high degree. And there is a sizable reservoir of generally educated manpower with which to expand and innovate.

Between 1900 and 1960 the number of professional health personnel increased nearly sixfold. At the turn of the century there were fewer than 200,000 of these professionally trained; in 1960 they exceeded 1.1 million. But by the 1960's, medical needs had greatly changed and it has become much more difficult to estimate shortages. The health profession is unevenly distributed among the population. There is wasteful duplication of services, and many skilled persons work only part-time in the medical professions.

Reliable information on the distribution and use of health manpower for the nation as a whole is not available. The situation can only be sketchily illustrated.

Future Needs. At the end of 1965 the United States had 292,000 M.D.'s and 13,000 D.O.'s (Doctors of Osteopathy), or 153 M.D.'s and D.O.'s for every 100,000 persons. To maintain this ratio, 352,000 physicians will be needed in 1975, at our present population growth. This means that the number of students graduating from medical schools each year (most of which annually graduate fewer than 100 students) must increase by approximately 25 percent, or from 7800 to 10,000. Aggravating the shortage is the fact that there are proportionately fewer physicians in patient-care practice. The total number has declined from 109 per 100,000 civilians in 1950 to 97 in the mid-sixties.

The ratio of active dentists for every 100,000 civilians declined from 49.9 in 1950 to 44.9 in the mid-sixties. There were 550,000 professional nurses practicing in 1962; of these 117,000 were working only part-time. The Surgeon General has estimated that 850,000 will be needed by 1975. This would require the graduating of 100,000 nurses annually by 1969. In 1965 only 33,200 graduated. The current national supply of physical therapists is 10,000 and the estimated need is for 15,000. We have 34,000 active registered medical technologists and will need 40,000 by 1975; the present rate of those entering this field is half the need—only 3900 each year. The same kind of disparity exists for all types of public health and environmental health personnel. Such shortages can be partly relieved by stretching further the skills of the physician and using his health-care associates more effectively.

With more than 3 million people in all the interrelated occupations, health is one of the nation's largest and fastest growing industries. Health services involve not only the prevention, control and rehabilitative treatment of personal illness but also environmental work—such as inspection of food, restaurants, water—designed to protect the population from common health hazards.

Regional Health Services. Currently, an important problem of equitable distribution of health services lies in the difficulty of bringing together the geographic, political and financial responsibilities of various overlapping "health communities." By tradition, hospitals have been organized and operated independently, except for those publicly funded to care for low-income groups. Medical services have not usually been organized to cope with all modern health problems.

A health community to control air pollution, for example, includes an area bounded by wind conditions—not by town limits or state lines. A health community concerned with water covers the watershed of an entire river system. In disease control, if an influenza epidemic strikes a region located at the crossroads of three states, it becomes the joint responsibility of health officials in all three.

Billions of dollars annually are allotted by Federal, state and local governments to support health services. All types of community programs are financed through a combination of public and private funding agreements. With the increase of both public and private health insurance programs, the individual today can obtain and pay for a wider range of health care, no matter where he may reside and travel.

NUMBER OF PHYSICIANS, DENTISTS, NURSES AND HOSPITAL BEDS BY STATE

Civilian Physicians			Civilian Dentists			Active Professional Nurses			Acceptable General Hospital Beds			Acceptable Mental Hospital Beds			Acceptable Long-term Care Beds		
(per 100,000 Civilians: 1965)						(per 100,000 Civilians: 1962)			(per 1000 Civilians: 1965)								
Rank	State	No.	Rank	State	No.	Rank	State	No.	Rank	State	No.	Rank	State	No.	Rank	State	No.
1.	N. Y.	214	1.	N. Y.	66	1.	MASS.	502	1.	MINN.	4.85	1.	R. I.	4.15	1.	WASH.	5.32
2.	MASS.	199	2.	OREG.	66	2.	N. H.	491	2.	N. DAK.	4.51	2.	N. Y.	3.73	2.	MINN.	5.04
3.	CONN.	179	3.	HAWAII	65	3.	VT.	445	3.	WIS.	4.43	3.	MD.	3.68	3.	OKLA.	5.00
4.	CALIF.	177	4.	WASH.	63	4.	CONN.	440	4.	W. VA.	4.41	4.	WIS.	3.22	4.	R. I.	4.17
5.	VT.	170	5.	MASS.	58	5.	R. I.	396	5.	KANS.	4.30	5.	MO.	3.14	5.	NEBR.	3.61
6.	COLO.	169	6.	MINN.	57	6.	DEL.	391	6.	NEBR.	4.16	6.	NEBR.	3.10	6.	ARK.	3.48
7.	MD.	166	7.	UTAH	57	7.	N. Y.	388	7.	OKLA.	4.06	7.	CALIF.	3.07	7.	OREG.	3.34
8.	R. I.	150	8.	CONN.	56	8.	MINN.	384	8.	N. Y.	4.01	8.	N. J.	3.07	8.	N. DAK.	3.20
9.	MINN.	149	9.	N. J.	53	9.	MAINE	371	9.	S. DAK.	3.98	9.	OKLA.	3.00	9.	TEX.	3.16
10.	WASH.	146	10.	COLO.	51	10.	PA.	371	10.	MONT.	3.95	10.	VA.	3.00	10.	MONT.	3.02
11.	PA.	144	11.	NEBR.	51	11.	COLO.	370	11.	ILL.	3.92	11.	N. DAK.	2.89	11.	COLO.	2.96
12.	FLA.	141	12.	PA.	51	12.	MONT.	349	12.	DEL.	3.90	12.	MICH.	2.82	12.	IDAHO	2.88
13.	OREG.	141	13.	ILL.	50	13.	N. J.	348	13.	PA.	3.88	13.	LA.	2.78	13.	S. DAK.	2.71
14.	HAWAII	139	14.	WIS.	50	14.	OREG.	348	14.	VT.	3.80	14.	GA.	2.76	14.	IOWA	2.69
15.	ILL.	135	15.	CALIF.	49	15.	N. DAK.	340	15.	ARK.	3.75	15.	MISS.	2.75	15.	CALIF.	2.56
16.	N. J.	135	16.	IOWA	48	16.	WASH.	337	16.	LA.	3.74	16.	PA.	2.64	16.	WIS.	2.53
17.	UTAH	132	17.	MONT.	48	17.	ARIZ.	335	17.	IOWA	3.73	17.	OREG.	2.63	17.	LA.	2.44
18.	DEL.	131	18.	R. I.	48	18.	WIS.	332	18.	ALA.	3.72	18.	MINN.	2.59	18.	CONN.	2.33
19.	N. H.	131	19.	MICH.	47	19.	WYO.	325	19.	FLA.	3.71	19.	W. VA.	2.54	19.	N. J.	2.33
20.	OHIO	130	20.	IDAHO	45	20.	CALIF.	324	20.	MASS.	3.71	20.	CONN.	2.50	20.	FLA.	2.28
21.	MO.	124	21.	MO.	43	21.	IOWA	320	21.	MO.	3.65	21.	N. H.	2.42	21.	HAWAII	2.24
22.	MICH.	123	22.	WYO.	42	22.	NEBR.	320	22.	TENN.	3.62	22.	N. C.	2.39	22.	ILL.	2.10
23.	ARIZ.	122	23.	OHIO	41	23.	FLA.	302	23.	ARIZ.	3.57	23.	MONT.	2.38	23.	DEL.	2.09
24.	WIS.	116	24.	FLA.	40	24.	OHIO	295	24.	R. I.	3.53	24.	KANS.	2.34	24.	MO.	2.05
25.	LA.	113	25.	KANS.	40	25.	ILL.	291	25.	N. J.	3.49	25.	S. DAK.	2.34	25.	PA.	2.02
26.	NEBR.	113	26.	IND.	39	26.	HAWAII	288	26.	GA.	3.43	26.	ILL.	2.32	26.	N. Y.	1.91
27.	VA.	113	27.	N. H.	39	27.	ALASKA	287	27.	NEV.	3.40	27.	OHIO	2.32	27.	VA.	1.91
28.	TENN.	112	28.	MAINE	38	28.	KANS.	284	28.	OHIO	3.40	28.	MAINE	2.22	28.	MD.	1.87
29.	KANS.	111	29.	VT.	38	29.	IDAHO	276	29.	WYO.	3.39	29.	MASS.	2.13	29.	TENN.	1.83
30.	TEX.	108	30.	S. DAK.	37	30.	S. DAK.	270	30.	N. C.	3.38	30.	DEL.	2.01	30.	MASS.	1.79
31.	IOWA	104	31.	TENN.	37	31.	MICH.	266	31.	COLO.	3.37	31.	FLA.	1.94	31.	ALASKA	1.78
32.	N. C.	103	32.	N. DAK.	36	32.	NEV.	262	32.	TEX.	3.33	32.	IND.	1.90	32.	NEV.	1.67
33.	MAINE	102	33.	MD.	35	33.	IND.	248	33.	MAINE	3.32	33.	ARK.	1.87	33.	UTAH	1.63
34.	IND.	101	34.	OKLA.	34	34.	W. VA.	248	34.	OREG.	3.32	34.	COLO.	1.87	34.	W. VA.	1.57
35.	GA.	100	35.	ARIZ.	33	35.	MD.	246	35.	MICH.	3.28	35.	VT.	1.87	35.	KANS.	1.53
36.	OKLA.	98	36.	VA.	33	36.	VA.	235	36.	MISS.	3.26	36.	NEV.	1.81	36.	IND.	1.49
37.	KY.	97	37.	W. VA.	33	37.	UTAH	234	37.	VA.	3.26	37.	HAWAII	1.80	37.	ALA.	1.41
38.	MONT.	96	38.	DEL.	32	38.	N. C.	231	38.	KY.	3.20	38.	WYO.	1.74	38.	MICH.	1.41
39.	W. VA.	96	39.	KY.	32	39.	MO.	220	39.	N. H.	3.13	39.	TENN.	1.71	39.	GA.	1.34
40.	NEV.	95	40.	LA.	31	40.	S. C.	214	40.	S. C.	3.12	40.	KY.	1.64	40.	ARIZ.	1.32
41.	IDAHO	90	41.	TEX.	31	41.	N. MEX.	213	41.	HAWAII	3.10	41.	WASH.	1.64	41.	WYO.	1.31
42.	WYO.	90	42.	NEV.	30	42.	LA.	198	42.	ALASKA	3.05	42.	ALA.	1.55	42.	N. MEX.	1.24
43.	N. MEX.	89	43.	ALA.	28	43.	GA.	194	43.	CONN.	3.03	43.	IOWA	1.52	43.	KY.	1.21
44.	N. DAK.	88	44.	ALASKA	27	44.	TENN.	177	44.	IND.	3.03	44.	TEX.	1.43	44.	OHIO	1.17
45.	ARK.	87	45.	ARK.	27	45.	KY.	175	45.	WASH.	2.81	45.	ARIZ.	1.05	45.	S. C.	1.06
46.	S. C.	80	46.	N. C.	27	46.	TEX.	172	46.	MD.	2.72	46.	ALASKA	1.02	46.	N. C.	.76
47.	ALA.	79	47.	N. MEX.	26	47.	OKLA.	163	47.	N. MEX.	2.55	47.	S. C.	.98	47.	VT.	.66
48.	S. DAK.	77	48.	GA.	25	48.	ALA.	157	48.	UTAH	2.43	48.	N. MEX.	.46	48.	N. H.	.61
49.	MISS.	74	49.	MISS.	25	49.	MISS.	142	49.	IDAHO	2.38	49.	IDAHO	.21	49.	MAINE	.47
50	ALASKA	70	50.	S. C.	20	50.	ARK.	120	50.	CALIF.	2.12	50.	UTAH	.17	50.	MISS.	.39

OUR HOSPITALS

For almost a century, the general hospital was the place where comparatively few people went when they were acutely ill or in need of surgery. In the past few decades, its services have become so diversified and extended in many communities that the hospital has become the major focal point for community health care.

The modern general hospital is a medical center. Its emergency department is called upon to aid people who have no family physician, who need help when their general medical practitioner is not available or who require highly urgent treatment that the emergency department offers the seriously injured or critically ill person. Its outpatient clinic is, in many cases, the only doctor's office some patients know. Many doctors admit patients for diagnostic tests and evaluations to a hospital that has the necessary equipment and skilled staff required to operate it. Open heart surgery and other specialized treatment can be provided only at selected medical centers.

Use of Hospital Beds. Many hospital beds continue to be occupied for short periods of time by patients with acute illnesses, for surgery and for childbirth. In addition, in 1966 more than 1000 hospitals were providing short-term treatment to psychiatric patients. Rehabilitation services for those disabled by injury or by chronic conditions are still another dimension of a modern hospital's functions.

There is now a great variation among the states in the number of available hospital beds ranked as "acceptable" in terms of fire, health or safety regulations. In the mid-sixties, the number of general hospital beds ranged from 2.12 for every 1000 persons in California to 4.85 in Minnesota, with an average for the entire nation of 3.48. The picture, nationally, is improving. Construction funds have been granted mostly for rural areas since 1946 under the Hill-Burton Act. In 1948, only 59 percent of the total need for general hospital beds was being met, but by the mid-sixties, about 85 percent were in existence. Many hospitals operate home-care services for recuperating patients, which free hospital beds for those who need them most.

Facilities for Chronic and Aged Patients. The situation is far worse for persons who need custodial or hospital care over a long period. The bed shortage for them is more than three times that of general hospital patients. Traditionally, chronic-disease hospitals and nursing homes are the two types of facilities that meet the needs of such patients as well as those of old age who require skilled nursing care around the clock.

In hospitals that treat chronic conditions the number of long-term-care beds available per 1000 population varies: from 0.39 in Mississippi to 5.32 in the state of Washington. In hospitals or nursing homes, long-term care beds for persons sixty-five years of age and over range from the rate of 4.1 per 1000 in Maine to 55.6 per 1000 in Alaska.

A decade ago, long term care beds met about 20 percent of the need. Currently almost half of the need is being met, but many elderly patients who are able to walk and are not bedridden must rely on inadequate custodial care in hospitals because they have no place else to go. Thousands of elderly patients in this category are now resident in remote state mental hospitals. Through modern medical and psychiatric therapy, many could be returned to their home communities. Local home-care and housing arrangements are now in the planning stage.

MENTAL ILLNESS

Today an estimated 19 million people in the United States (approximately one in ten) suffer from mental or emotional disturbance and could benefit from some form of treatment. Slightly more than half of the hospital beds in the United States are occupied by mental patients. This situation exists even though there is a trend away from treatment in mental hospitals. Tranquilizers and other drugs, including the psychic energizers, have ushered in a striking change in the treatment of mental illnesses. They permit outpatient care and have practically eliminated the nightmare of the violent ward.

In 10 years, the number of patients in mental hospitals has been reduced 15 percent (from 558,922 in 1955 to 475,761 in 1965), even though 136,443 more patients were admitted to mental hospitals in 1965 than had been admitted in 1955. The number of patients released each year rose 126 percent—from 126,000 in 1955 to 287,000 in 1965. Nevertheless, only about 50 percent of the psychiatric beds needed are being provided. There is a wide variation among states in this matter. The range is from 0.17 beds per 1000 population in Utah to 4.15 in Rhode Island. Although in 1965 the number of psychiatrists and parapsychiatric trained personnel totaled about 65,000 compared with 23,000 in 1950, it is now estimated that we need an additional 10,000 psychiatrists to fill present and projected positions.

More people are now being treated for psychiatric disorders outside of public mental hospitals. In 1965, of the estimated total of 3,921,000 Americans treated, 1,300,000 received private office care; 950,000 received treatment in outpatient clinics; 600,000 in general hospitals; 110,000 in private mental hospitals; 14,000 in psychiatric day-care or night-care units for patients who spend part of every 24 hours at home; and 140,000 in Veterans Administration hospitals. There were 188,332 hospitalized in institutions for the mentally retarded. However, among the mentally ill not being treated were 4 million children under the age of fourteen; and of these as many as one quarter were seriously disturbed.

The cost in human misery cannot be estimated, but the probable overall financial cost of mental illness in the United States today is approximately $5 billion per year.

By 1963, public demand for improved treatment for the mentally ill and mentally retarded, who number about 5.5 million, had set off a chain reaction of legislation. The Community Mental Health Centers Act (administered by the National Institute of Mental Health), adopted in 1963 and amended in 1965, provides Federal funds to aid states and local communities in constructing the centers and helping to pay costs of the staff. The trend is away from large hospitals and toward smaller units in the community so that the mentally ill and retarded can be near families and possible jobs. The goal established by Congress is 500 centers by 1970 and 2000 by 1975.

AIR POLLUTION IN SELECTED CITIES

Pollutants were graded 1 through 5 according to degree of concentration, 5 being the highest. Carbon monoxide, chiefly from motor vehicle exhaust, was not recorded. This survey is based on Public Health Service information.

◆ **Total Suspended Particles**—Smoke, soot and dust particles having their sources in fuel combustion and various industrial processes. Hydrocarbon particles are emitted during the incomplete combustion of almost all fuels, auto exhaust being the major source.

■ **Sulfur Dioxide**—A by-product of burning all fossil fuels, whether for heating buildings, generating electric power or for various industrial processes. This pollutant is widespread and especially prevalent in cities.

● **Nitrogen Dioxide**—A yellow-brown gas produced during high temperature combustion of coal, oil or gasoline in power plants and internal combustion engines. Along with hydrocarbon, it is an important component of photochemical smog.

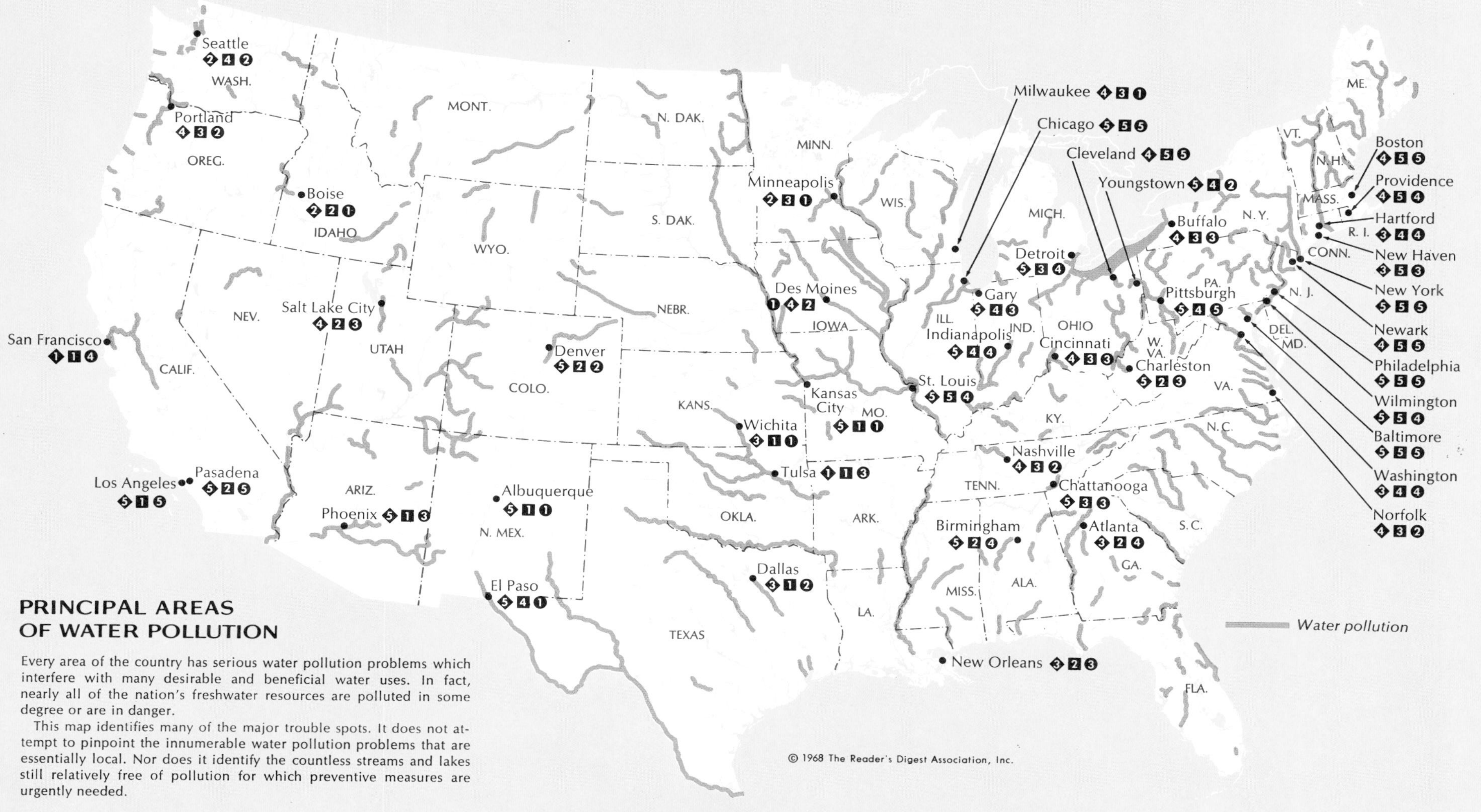

PRINCIPAL AREAS OF WATER POLLUTION

Every area of the country has serious water pollution problems which interfere with many desirable and beneficial water uses. In fact, nearly all of the nation's freshwater resources are polluted in some degree or are in danger.

This map identifies many of the major trouble spots. It does not attempt to pinpoint the innumerable water pollution problems that are essentially local. Nor does it identify the countless streams and lakes still relatively free of pollution for which preventive measures are urgently needed.

AIR AND WATER POLLUTION

Two lakes—Tahoe in California and Erie in New York—offer prime warnings for America to "stop, look and listen." Lake Erie is already polluted from surface wave to bottom mud. Tahoe, the Indian's "Lake of the Sky," may soon cease to reflect its namesake.

For air pollution, a tale of two cities—Los Angeles and New York City—is exemplary. Los Angeles was faced some 30 years ago with air problems evident to the tear ducts of every resident, and acted to improve its air cap. New York City has only begun to effect changes—such as compulsory incinerator controls and use of low sulfur-content fuels.

In the entire United States, the vital concern over control of the pollution of breathable air and drinkable and recreational water is a Johnny-come-lately. Efforts to conserve and protect air and water resources did not become an issue until the 1930's. Some say it is already too late for many city atmospheres and certain bodies of water.

The Case for Clean Air. The first major metropolitan drive to clean the air over a city occurred in Pittsburgh. When the smoke and grime of the famous steel industry penetrated every house, the citizens finally rebelled. The cost of cleaning smoke particles from the stacks proved not to be prohibitive.

Where once the nuisance of smoke was the major reason for initiating air-pollution control, the situation today is much more complex. The principal pollutants now are gases, such as carbon monoxide, sulfur dioxides, nitrogen dioxides—as well as particles of all kinds, from dust to the hydrocarbons of smoke. Mixtures of gases and particles—for which the automobile is largely responsible—are manufactured by sunlight into photochemical smog. The most dangerous of all are radioactive air pollutants which add strontium 90 to milk.

The Case for Clean Water. In the past, the danger signals of foul water came from diseases such as typhoid fever traced to wells, sparkling brooks and rivers and lakes that had been turned into sewers. Later the problem of water supply for expanding cities proved to be a major issue.

The Izaak Walton League of America was the first citizens' group to become concerned about water pollution and to campaign for legislation. Not until 1948 did Congress pass the first Federal Water Pollution Control Act, which was never backed by adequate funds. Then in 1956, 1961 and 1965, Federal legislation moved further, always preserving states' rights in the matter of water control. The Federal Water Quality Act of 1965 established June 30, 1967, as the deadline for all states to institute basic standards, and provided for Federal enforcement of such standards for interstate waters.

Since the national supply of water is relatively constant and its use and reuse is increasing with the expanding urban population, the problems of controlling water pollution are complex. Time to meet those problems is running out. Urgent discussions began to take place in the mid-sixties among a wide variety of public and private officials—in industrial, metropolitan, regional, state and Federal groups. They were faced with devising means to pay for the abatement of industrial contamination, providing adequate municipal sewerage and enforcing water standards in entire river basins. In the 1960's the race is between clean-up programs and the increasing pollution of twentieth-century living.

SPORTS AND RECREATION

The age of leisure for the American people reached a peak in the 1950's and 1960's with the shortened work week, higher income and almost universally generous vacation time. In recent years the annual purchase of sporting goods alone exceeded $3 billion.

It is impossible to tell how many families or individuals enjoy the pleasures of driving, sightseeing, walking, dancing, swimming and picnicking. However, the more formal sports and recreations—both participant and spectator—have been recorded, and the figures are given in the boxes to the right.

Bicycling, the great craze of the 1880's, is the current top participant sport (59 million). Even so, it is outranked by the 68 million people who attend horse racing, the spectator activity that heads the list. The popularity of the sport of kings is far from new in America, dating back to colonial times when races were held in New York and Virginia.

The leading indoor participant sport is bowling. Introduced into this country by the Dutch as "ninepins," it was probably America's first game. Basketball, invented in 1891 by a YMCA instructor who used fruit baskets for hoops, is the leading indoor spectator sport with 15 million more watchers than its nearest rival.

The sites and areas listed here have been carefully chosen by experts as representative of the thousands of outstanding sport and recreation centers in the nation.

PARTICIPANTS IN GAMES AND RECREATION—1966

1. Cycling	59,000,000	11. Shooting sports	20,000,000
2. Boating	40,370,000	12. Table tennis	20,000,000
3. Volleyball	40,000,000	13. Golf	10,025,000
4. Bowling (ten pin)	39,000,000	14. Shuffleboard	10,000,000
5. Camping	37,000,000	15. Tennis	9,100,000
6. Fishing	36,200,000	16. Water-skiing	9,100,000
7. Ice-skating	30,000,000	17. Horseshoes	9,005,000
8. Softball (12-inch)	25,800,000	18. Archery (target)	8,000,000
9. Roller-skating	25,000,000	19. Handball	6,250,000
10. Billiards	23,000,000	20. Skiing	4,625,000

A SELECTION OF SPECIAL SITES

Automobile Racing (ar) · Baseball (bb) · Basketball (bk) · Fishing (fi) · Football (fb) · Horse Racing (hr) · Ice-hockey (ih) · Mountain Climbing (mc) · Skiing (sk) · Surfing (su) · Trails · Sports Complex

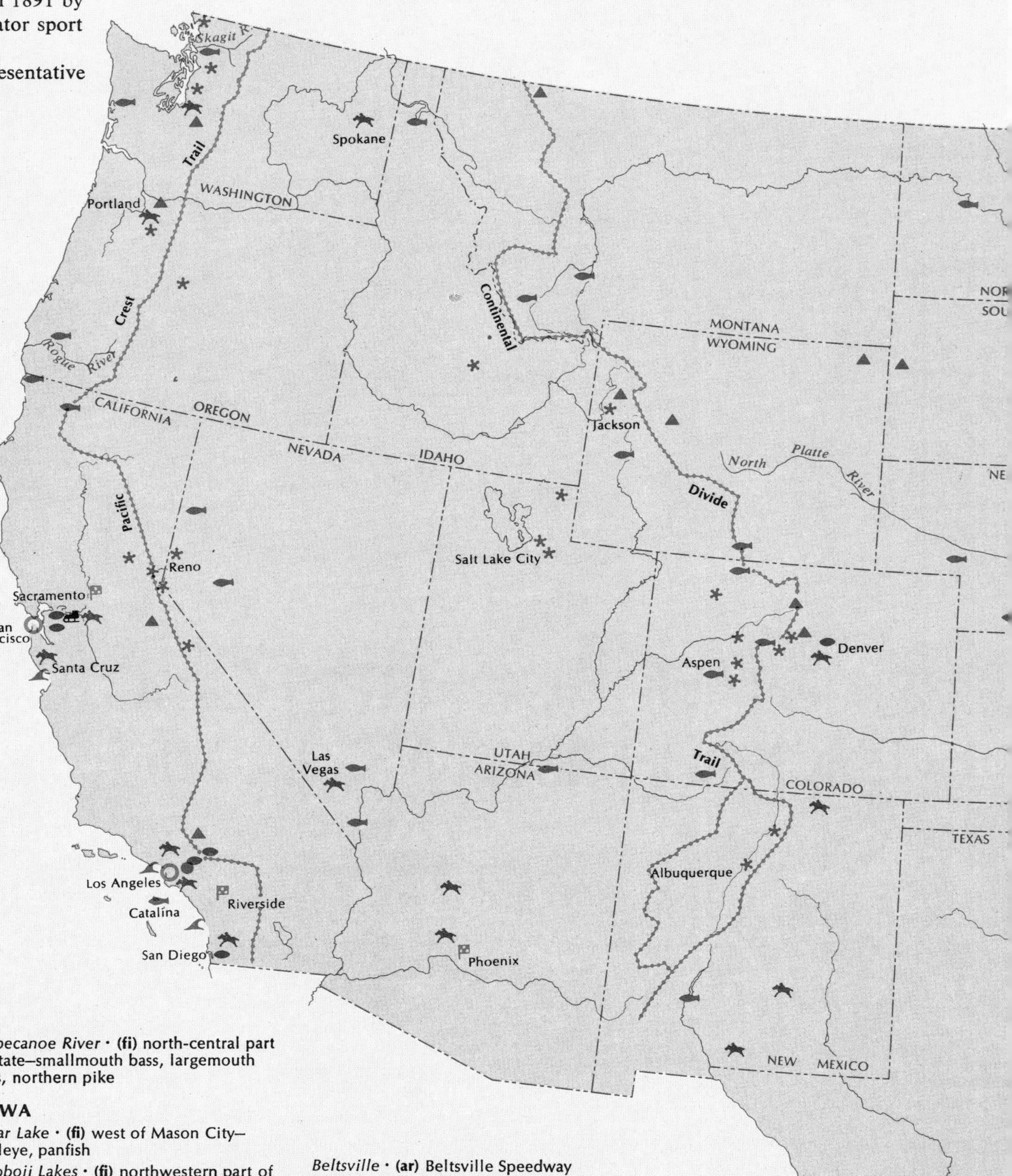

ALABAMA
Lake Lewis Smith · (fi) near Cullman—spotted bass
Tennessee River · (fi) at Florence—smallmouth bass

ALASKA *(not shown)*
Arctic · (fi) king salmon, silver salmon, grayling, northern pike, rainbow trout, lake trout, sheefish, Dolly Varden, chum salmon, pink salmon
South Central · (fi) king salmon, silver salmon, sockeye salmon, pink salmon, steelhead, Dolly Varden, rainbow trout, lake trout, grayling, Arctic char
Southeast · (fi) king salmon, silver salmon, halibut, sea-run cutthroat, Dolly Varden, pink salmon, steelhead, eastern brook trout, rainbow trout, grayling

ARIZONA
Lake Mohave · (fi) Nevada border—largemouth bass, rainbow trout
Lake Powell · (fi) Utah border—rainbow trout, largemouth bass
Phoenix · (ar) International Raceway; (hr) Turf Paradise
Prescott · (hr) Prescott Downs

ARKANSAS
Buffalo River · (fi) northwestern part of state—smallmouth bass
Greers Ferry Reservoir · (fi) near Little Rock—largemouth bass
Hot Springs · (hr) Oaklawn Park

CALIFORNIA
Albany · (hr) Golden Gate Fields
Anaheim · (bb) Anaheim Stadium
Arcadia · (hr) Santa Anita Park
Berkeley · (fb) Memorial Stadium
Catalina Island · (fi) south of Los Angeles—general saltwater fishing
Del Mar · (hr)
Huntington Beach · (su)
Inglewood · (hr) Hollywood Park
Klamath River · (fi) south of Crescent City—steelhead
Los Angeles · (bb) Dodger Stadium; (bk) Memorial Sports Arena; (fb) Memorial Coliseum; (ih) The Forum
Malibu · (su)
Mammoth Lakes · (sk) Mammoth Mountain
Norden · (sk) Sugar Bowl
Oakland · (fb) County Stadium; (ih) Oakland Coliseum
Pasadena · (fb) Rose Bowl
Riverside · (ar) International Speedway
Sacramento · (ar) State Fairgrounds
San Diego · (fb) Balboa Stadium
San Francisco · (bb) Candlestick Park; (bk) Civic Auditorium; (fb) Kezar Stadium
San Mateo · (hr) Bay Meadows
Santa Cruz · (su) Steamer Lane
Smith River · (fi) north of Crescent City—Chinook salmon
Stateline · (sk) Heavenly Valley
Tahoe City · (sk) Alpine Meadows, Squaw Valley
Taquitz Rock · (mc) near Los Angeles
Yosemite National Park · (mc)

COLORADO
Aspen · (sk)
Crested Butte · (sk)
Denver · (fb) Bear Stadium
Dillon · (sk) Arapahoe Basin
Dillon Reservoir · (fi) rainbow trout, brown trout
Eldorado Springs · (mc) near Boulder
Estes Park · (mc) near Boulder
Lake John · (fi) near Walden—rainbow trout, brown trout
Littleton · (hr) Centennial Park
Navajo Reservoir · (fi) southwest of Pagosa Springs—rainbow trout, brown trout
Roaring Fork River · (fi) west-central part of state—rainbow trout, brown trout
Steamboat Springs · (sk) Mount Werner
Vail · (sk)
Winter Park · (sk)

CONNECTICUT
Enfield Dam · (fi) at Windsor Locks—shad
Middlefield · (sk) Powder Hill
New Haven · (fb) Yale University Bowl

DELAWARE
Stanton · (hr) Delaware Park

FLORIDA
Big Pine Key · (fi) Florida Keys—tarpon
Boca Grande · (fi) near Fort Myers—tarpon
Cocoa Beach · (su)
Daytona Beach · (ar) International Speedway
Hallandale · (hr) Gulfstream Park
Hialeah · (hr) Hialeah Park
Islamorada · (fi) Florida Keys—general saltwater fishing
Lake Kissimmee · (fi) in Osceola County—largemouth bass
Miami · (fb) Orange Bowl; (hr) Tropical Park
Oldsmar · (hr) Florida Downs
Palm Beach · (fi) sailfish

GEORGIA
Atlanta · (ar) International Raceway; (bb) (fb) Atlanta Stadium
Flint River · (fi) Atlanta headwaters—bass

HAWAII *(not shown)*
Hawaii · (fi) Keahole Light, Kona Coast and South Point—marlin, tuna, mahimahi, ono
Kauai · (fi) North Shore—marlin, tuna, mahimahi, ono, bonito, bonefish
Maui · (fi) off coast of Lanai and Kahoolawe—marlin, tuna, mahimahi, ono
Oahu · (su) Makaha; (fi) Penguin Banks, Barber's Point and Waianae Coast—marlin, tuna, mahimahi, ono

IDAHO
Lake Pend Oreille · (fi) near Sandpoint—rainbow trout
Sun Valley · (sk)

ILLINOIS
Arlington Heights · (hr) Arlington Park
Chicago · (bb) Comiskey Park; (bb) (fb) Wrigley Field; (bk) International Amphitheater; (fb) Soldier Field; (hr) Hawthorne Park, Sportsman's Park; (ih) Chicago Stadium
DuQuoin · (ar) (hr) State Fairgrounds
Homewood · (hr) Washington Park
Mississippi River · (fi) from East Dubuque to Hamilton—walleye, blue catfish, flathead catfish
Springfield · (ar) State Fairgrounds
Urbana · (fb) Memorial Stadium

INDIANA
Clermont · (ar) Indianapolis Raceway Park
Indianapolis · (ar) State Fairgrounds; (bk) Butler Field House
Kankakee River · (fi) northwestern part of state—smallmouth bass, northern pike, walleye
Notre Dame · (fb) Notre Dame Stadium
Speedway City · (ar) Indianapolis Motor Speedway
Tippecanoe River · (fi) north-central part of state—smallmouth bass, largemouth bass, northern pike

IOWA
Clear Lake · (fi) west of Mason City—walleye, panfish
Okoboji Lakes · (fi) northwestern part of state—largemouth bass
Spirit Lake · (fi) Minnesota border—largemouth bass, panfish

KANSAS
Neosho River · (fi) southeastern part of state—channel catfish, flathead catfish
Tuttle Creek Reservoir · (fi) near Manhattan—largemouth bass, channel catfish

KENTUCKY
Barren River Reservoir · (fi) near Glasgow—bass, muskellunge
Florence · (hr) Latonia Race Course
Kentucky Lake · (fi) southeast of Paducah—largemouth bass, white bass, sauger
Lexington · (hr) Keeneland Race Course
Louisville · (hr) Churchill Downs
Nolin Reservoir · (fi) near Mammoth Cave National Park—bass, muskellunge

LOUISIANA
D'Arbonne Lake · (fi) northwest of Monroe—largemouth bass
Lafayette · (hr) Evangeline Downs
Lake Nantaches · (fi) southeast of Natchitoches—bass
Lake Vernon · (fi) northwest of Leesville—bass
New Orleans · (fb) Sugar Bowl, Tulane University Stadium; (hr) Fairgrounds

MAINE
Kingfield · (sk) Sugarloaf
West Grand Lake · (fi) near Grand Lake Stream—smallmouth bass

MARYLAND
Baltimore · (bb) (fb) Memorial Stadium; (bk) Civic Center; (hr) Pimlico Race Course
Beltsville · (ar) Beltsville Speedway
Bowie · (hr) Bowie Race Course
Laurel · (hr) Laurel Race Course
Ocean City · (fi) eastern shore—marlin
Tilghman Island · (fi) Chesapeake Bay opposite Easton—striped bass

MASSACHUSETTS
Boston · (bb) (fb) Fenway Park; (bk) (ih) Boston Garden
East Boston · (hr) Suffolk Downs
Hancock · (sk) Jiminy Peak
New Ashford · (sk) Brodie Mountain
Pittsfield · (sk) Bousquet
Quabbin Reservoir · (fi) west of Worcester—trout, bass

MICHIGAN
Ann Arbor · (fb) Michigan University Stadium
Big Huron River · (fi) near Marquette—coho salmon
Boyne Falls · (sk) Boyne Mountain
Detroit · (bb) (fb) Tiger Stadium; (bk) Cobo Arena; (ih) Olympia
Iron Mountain · (sk) Pine Mountain
Livonia · (hr) Detroit Race Course
Manistee River · (fi) near Manistee—coho salmon

MINNESOTA
Bear Track Lake · (fi) in St. Louis County—Ohrid trout
Bloomington · (bb) (fb) Metropolitan Stadium
Chester Lake · (fi) Cook County—Ohrid trout
Minneapolis · (fb) University of Minnesota Stadium; (ih) Metropolitan Sports Center
Steep Lake · (fi) St. Louis County—Ohrid trout

MISSISSIPPI
Ross Barnett Reservoir · (fi) northeast of Jackson—largemouth bass

MISSOURI
Kansas City · (bb) (fb) Municipal Stadium
Lake Taneycomo · (fi) between Table Rock and Bull Shoals—rainbow trout, kokanee salmon
St. Louis · (bb) (fb) Busch Stadium; (bk) Kiel Auditorium; (ih) St. Louis Arena
Table Rock Lake · (fi) Arkansas border—largemouth bass, spotted bass

MONTANA
Glacier National Park · (mc)
Hap Hawkins Reservoir · (fi) near Dillon—rainbow trout
Madison River · (fi) southwest part of state—trout

NEBRASKA
Lake McConaughy · (fi) near Ogallala—smallmouth bass, walleye, rainbow trout
Omaha · (hr) Ak-Sar-Ben
Red Willow Reservoir · (fi) west of McCook—largemouth bass

NEVADA
Lake Mead · (fi) Arizona border—largemouth bass
Las Vegas · (hr) Las Vegas Downs
Pyramid Lake · (fi) near Reno—rainbow trout

SPECTATORS OF SPORTS—1966

Sport	Spectators
Horse Racing	**68,495,454**
Thoroughbreds	40,913,694
Trotting	27,581,760
Automobile Racing*	**39,390,000**
Baseball	**35,193,461**
Major Leagues (20 clubs)	25,132,209
Minor Leagues (19 circuits)	10,061,252
Football	**34,537,742**
Collegiate (616 schools)	25,275,899
National Football League	5,337,038
American Football League	2,160,369
Continental Football League	640,000
Post-Season Bowl Games (Colleges and Pros)	1,124,436
Basketball	**19,694,048**
1060 colleges	17,107,663
National Basketball Association	2,586,385
Greyhound Racing	**11,120,293**
Wrestling*	**4,630,000**
National Hockey League	**2,941,164**
Track and Field*	**2,900,000**
Soccer*	**2,500,000**
Boxing*	**1,883,000**

**Estimated, exact figures not available.*

Reno · **(sk)** Slide Mountain
Walker Lake · **(fi)** north of Hawthorne—cutthroat trout

NEW HAMPSHIRE

Androscoggin River · **(fi)** above Berlin—rainbow trout, landlocked salmon
Connecticut River · **(fi)** near Colebrook—rainbow trout, brown trout
Franconia · **(sk)** Cannon Mountain
Mount Washington · **(mc)**
Newbury · **(sk)** Mount Sunapee
North Conway · **(sk)** Cranmore Mountain
Pinkham Notch · **(sk)** Wildcat
Salem · **(hr)** Rockingham Park
Waterville · **(sk)** Waterville Valley

NEW JERSEY

Atlantic City · **(hr)** Atlantic City Race Track
Camden · **(hr)** Garden State Park
Oceanport · **(hr)** Monmouth Park
Seaside Heights · **(su)**
Trenton · **(ar)** New Jersey Fairgrounds

NEW MEXICO

Albuquerque · **(sk)** Sandia Peak
Elephant Butte Lake · **(fi)** near Truth or Consequences—largemouth bass
Raton · **(hr)** La Mesa Park
Ruidoso · **(hr)** Ruidoso Downs
Sunland · **(hr)** Sunland Park
Taos · **(sk)** Taos Ski Valley

NEW YORK

Buffalo · **(fb)** War Memorial Stadium
Canandaigua Lake · **(fi)** at Canandaigua—rainbow trout, lake trout, walleye
Cayuga · **(fi)** near Ithaca—California Chinook salmon
Elmont · **(hr)** Belmont Park
Hunter · **(sk)** Hunter Mountain
Islip · **(ar)** Islip Speedway
Little Green Pond · **(fi)** near Saranac—kokanee
Montauk · **(fi)** eastern end of Long Island—general saltwater fishing
New York · **(bb) (fb)** Shea Stadium, Yankee Stadium; **(bk) (ih)** Madison Square Garden
Niagara River · **(fi)** near Grand Island—smallmouth bass, muskellunge
North Creek · **(sk)** Gore Mountain
Ozone Park · **(hr)** Aqueduct Race Track
Pine Hill · **(sk)** Belleayre Mountain
St. Lawrence River · **(fi)** between Clayton and Ogdensburg—smallmouth bass, muskellunge
Saratoga Springs · **(hr)** Saratoga Raceway
Shawangunk Mountains · **(mc)**
Westbury · **(hr)** Roosevelt Raceway
Wilmington · **(sk)** Whiteface Mountain
Windham · **(sk)**
Yonkers · **(hr)** Yonkers Raceway

NORTH CAROLINA

Charlotte · **(ar)** Charlotte Speedway
Currituck Sound · **(fi)** north of Kitty Hawk—largemouth bass
Hatteras · **(fi)** red drum (in surf), blue marlin (offshore)
Hickory · **(ar)** Hickory Speedway
North Wilkesboro · **(ar)**
Rockingham · **(ar)**
Winston-Salem · **(ar)** Winston-Salem Speedway

NORTH DAKOTA

Garrison Reservoir · **(fi)** northwest of Bismarck—sauger, walleye, northern pike

OHIO

Akron · **(hr)** Ascot Park
Cincinnati · **(bb)** Crosley Field; **(bk)** Cincinnati Gardens; **(hr)** River Downs
Clendening Reservoir · **(fi)** in Harrison County—catfish, muskellunge
Cleveland · **(bb) (fb)** Municipal Stadium
Columbus · **(fb)** Ohio State University Stadium; **(hr)** Beulah Park
Leesville Reservoir · **(fi)** Carroll County—catfish, muskellunge
North Randall · **(hr)** Cranwood Park, Randall Park
Ohio River · **(fi)** above and below Cincinnati—smallmouth bass, spotted bass, largemouth bass, sauger, channel catfish, crappie, white bass, rainbow trout

OKLAHOMA

Eufaula Reservoir · **(fi)** near Oklahoma City—largemouth bass, channel catfish
Keystone Lake · **(fi)** near Tulsa—white bass, largemouth bass, channel catfish
Lake Hudson · **(fi)** near Pryor—crappie, white bass
Grand Lake O' the Cherokees · **(fi)** northeast corner of state—largemouth bass, white bass, crappie
Norman · **(fb)** Owen Field
Thunderbird Lake · **(fi)** east of Norman—channel catfish, blue catfish

OREGON

Bend · **(sk)** Mount Bachelor
Government Camp · **(sk)** Timberline
Mount Hood · **(mc)**
Portland · **(hr)** Portland Meadows
Rogue River · **(fi)** steelhead

PENNSYLVANIA

Big Fishing Creek · **(fi)** in Clinton County—rainbow trout, brown trout
Langhorn · **(ar)** International Speedway
Philadelphia · **(bb)** Connie Mack Stadium; **(bk)** Convention Hall; **(fb)** Franklin Field, Kennedy Stadium; **(ih)** Spectrum
Pittsburgh · **(bb)** Forbes Field; **(fb)** Pitt Stadium; **(ih)** Civic Center
Pymatuning Reservoir · **(fi)** Crawford County—largemouth bass, walleye
Susquehanna River · **(fi)** at Falmouth below Harrisburg—muskellunge
Tannersville · **(sk)** Camelback
Uniondale · **(sk)** Elk Mountain

RHODE ISLAND

Lincoln · **(hr)** Lincoln Downs
Narragansett Bay · **(fi)** general saltwater fishing
Pawtucket · **(hr)** Narragansett Park

SOUTH CAROLINA

Columbia · **(ar)** Columbia Speedway
Darlington · **(ar)** Darlington Speedway
Santee-Cooper · **(fi)** north of Charleston—landlocked striped bass

SOUTH DAKOTA

Black Hills · **(mc)**
Fort Randall Reservoir · **(fi)** south-central part of state—sauger, walleye, northern pike

TENNESSEE

Bristol · **(ar)** International Speedway
Gatlinburg · **(sk)** Gatlinburg Ski Resort
Lake Barkley · **(fi)** Kentucky border—largemouth bass
Nashville · **(ar)** Fairgrounds Speedway

TEXAS

Austin · **(fb)** Texas Memorial Stadium
Dallas · **(fb)** Cotton Bowl
Houston · **(bb)** Astrodome; **(fb)** Rice University Stadium
Lake o' the Pines · **(fi)** west of Jefferson—largemouth bass
Sam Rayburn Reservoir · **(fi)** southwest of Nacogdoches—largemouth bass

UTAH

Big Cottonwood Canyon · **(sk)** Solitude
Park City · **(sk)** Snow Park
Salt Lake City · **(sk)** Alta

VERMONT

Fayston · **(sk)** Glen Ellen
Jeffersonville · **(sk)** Madonna Mountain
Lamoille · **(fi)** northeast of Burlington—rainbow trout
Londonderry · **(sk)** Magic Mountain
Manchester · **(sk)** Bromley
North Troy · **(sk)** Jay Peak
Rutland · **(sk)** Pico Peak
Sherburne · **(sk)** Killington
Stowe · **(sk)** Mount Mansfield—Spruce Peak
Stratton Mountain · **(sk)**
Waitsfield · **(sk)** Mad River Glen
Warren · **(sk)** Sugarbush
West Dover · **(sk)** Mount Snow
White River · **(fi)** east-central part of state—rainbow trout, brown trout
Wilmington · **(sk)** Haystack Mountain

VIRGINIA

John H. Kerr Reservoir · **(fi)** near Danville—striped bass
Manassas · **(ar)** Old Dominion Speedway
Rappahannock River · **(fi)** between Remington and Fredericksburg—smallmouth bass
Richmond · **(ar)** Virginia State Fairgrounds
Smith Mountain Reservoir · **(fi)** near Roanoke—smallmouth bass
Virginia Beach · **(su)**

WASHINGTON, D.C.

(bb) (fb) District of Columbia Stadium

WASHINGTON (State)

Bellingham · **(sk)** Mount Baker
Enumclaw · **(sk)** Crystal Mountain
Leavenworth · **(sk)** Stevens Pass
Mount Rainier National Park · **(mc)**
Renton · **(hr)** Longacres
Skagit River · **(fi)** near Seattle—steelhead
Spokane · **(hr)** Playfair Race Course
Westport · **(fi)** Chinook salmon, coho salmon

WEST VIRGINIA

Charles Town · **(hr)** Charles Town Race Course, Shenandoah Downs
Chester · **(hr)** Waterford Park
Seneca Rock · **(mc)**
Summersville Reservoir · **(fi)** east of Charleston—largemouth bass, walleye

WISCONSIN

Cable · **(sk)** Mount Telemark
Chippewa Flowage · **(fi)** near Chippewa Falls—muskellunge
Devil's Lake · **(mc)**
Eagle River Region · **(fi)** Michigan border—muskellunge
Green Bay · **(fb)** Lambeau Field
Hayward Region · **(fi)** southeast of Superior—muskellunge
Milwaukee · **(ar)** State Fairgrounds; **(fb)** Milwaukee Stadium

WYOMING

Devil's Tower · **(mc)**
Encampment River · **(fi)** above Encampment—rainbow trout, brown trout
Grand Tetons · **(mc)**
Green River · **(fi)** north of Pinedale—rainbow trout
Jackson · **(sk)** Jackson Hole
Wind River · **(mc)**

GREAT CHARACTERS OF FOLKLORE

It's a rare person who can sort the real from the mythical in America's colorful gallery of folklore figures. Which man was flesh and blood and which was dreamed up—the one who killed 4861 buffalo in a season, or the one who alone shocked a whole stand of wheat in a single day? Live or legendary, such characters are the indispensable subjects of tall stories and songs. News was scarce in pioneering times; resourceful yarn-spinners gave charm and fascination to the hours around the cracker barrel or the campfire. Folk tales are still at the heart of this nation's celebrated humor.

1. Johnny Appleseed *(John or Jonathan Chapman).* This native of Springfield, Massachusetts—famed in ballads and poems—sowed apple orchards in remote places over hundreds of frontier miles in Ohio and Indiana. His seeds were gathered from cider presses in western Pennsylvania. Settlers transplanted Johnny's seedling trees to start their own orchards. He died in 1845 in Allen County, Indiana, at age seventy-one.

2. P. T. *(Phineas Taylor)* **Barnum.** A Connecticut showman, his motto was "There's a sucker born every minute." He opened Barnum's American Museum in New York where he exhibited the famous dwarf Tom Thumb. In 1871, Barnum introduced his circus—"The Greatest Show on Earth." Jumbo, his and America's first elephant, stands stuffed at Tufts University in Medford, Massachusetts.

3. Sam Bass. Desperado, train robber, cattle thief, Sam was supposed to have buried gold in caves in central and northern Texas. One of his men betrayed him to the Texas Rangers and he was killed in 1878. The search for his treasure goes on to this day, and folk ballads about him are still sung.

4. Judge Roy Bean. A Kentucky native, Judge Bean was appointed justice of the peace of Langtry, Texas, in 1882. His Jersey Lily Saloon was his impromptu hall of justice: "Hear ye, hear ye," Judge Bean declared, "this honorable court is now in session, and if any galoot wants a snort before we start, step up to the bar and name your poison."

5. Big Frank *(mythical).* Big Frank worked from Texas to the Dakotas and specialized in harvesting wheat. He once bet big money that he could shock a whole field single-handed before sundown, and he won.

6. Billy the Kid *(Henry McCarty, born in New York in 1859).* Taken west by his family as a child, Billy is said to have killed 21 men during his 21 years of life. He was shot down near Fort Sumner, New Mexico, by Sheriff Pat Garrett who mourned that Billy was a fine lad but "circumstances favored the worser angle and the Kid fell."

7. Black Caesar, an escaped slave, captured small ships off the coast of Florida, killing captains who picked him up in their boats, thinking he had been shipwrecked. Later he left his prisoners to starve on one of the smaller Florida Keys and joined the notorious pirate Blackbeard. During the 1718 sea battle in which Blackbeard was killed, Black Caesar tried in vain to blow up his ship, but was captured and executed. According to legend, he had a harem of more than 100 women.

8. The Bloomer Girl. Mrs. Amelia Bloomer founded *The Lily,* a feminist temperance magazine, at Seneca Falls, New York, in 1849. She urged less cumbersome clothing for women and advocated the costume of Turkish ladies, with trousers and an overskirt. "Bloomers" came into use for feminine gym classes and for swimming.

9. The Blue Lady *(mythical).* A beautiful girl, dressed all in blue, she visited Indian tribes of the Southwest to tell them about the Christian God before the arrival of any Christian missionaries in the region. Indians spoke of her to some of the first Spanish explorers who arrived in New Mexico, Arizona and Texas. From time to time her appearance is still reported.

10. Nellie Bly *(pen name).* Elizabeth Cochrane Seaman, a reporter for the New York *World,* set out from New York in November 1889 to break the fictional record of Phileas Fogg in *Around the World in Eighty Days* by Jules Verne. She made the trip in 72 days, 6 hours and 11 minutes.

11. Daniel Boone. A hunter at the age of twelve, he blazed the trail for pioneers through the Cumberland Gap into Kentucky in 1775; built a fort at Boonesborough; left for frontier Missouri at the age of sixty-five, saying, "I want more elbow room."

12. Bowleg Bill, the Seagoing Cowboy *(mythical).* Reputed to be eight feet, four inches tall, Bill was an incorrigible cowboy from Laramie, Wyoming. Shanghaied in San Francisco, he always referred to the ship as a "roundup wagon" and never knew enough to spit to leeward.

13. Jim Bridger. Fur trader, guide and probably the first white man to see the Great Salt Lake in Utah, he built Fort Bridger on the Oregon Trail (1843) and discovered Bridger Pass through the Rocky Mountains (1856). Bridger told fanciful tales of Yellowstone and the Grand Canyon (one of which he concluded by saying an Indian killed him).

14. Buffalo Bill *(William H. Cody).* Celebrated Indian scout and hunter, Buffalo Bill earned his nickname at twenty-six by supplying buffalo meat to the Kansas Pacific railway construction crews. He claimed a kill of 4861 buffalo in one season. In 1883, at Omaha, Nebraska, he opened his "Wild West, Rocky Mountain and Prairie Exhibition." "Wild Bill" Hickok, Annie Oakley and Sitting Bull (see numbers 27, 36 and 46) were three of his stars. He was one of the founders of Cody, Wyoming, a town named in his honor.

15. John Brown. During the night of October 16, 1859, John Brown and 18 men crossed the bridge from Maryland to Harper's Ferry, Virginia, and seized the government arsenal. It was intended to be a first step in what he hoped would be a general uprising against slaveholders. Thirty important hostages were held. Captured, John Brown was convicted of treason at Charles Town and hanged there on December 2, 1859.

16. Paul Bunyan *(mythical),* the giant lumberjack of the North Woods, combed his curly beard with a pine tree, loved to eat popcorn by the wagonload and dug the Grand Canyon. He was usually accompanied by Babe, his big blue ox.

17. Kit Carson. Famed desert and mountain scout, he accompanied one of the first overland expeditions to California in 1829–31 and in 1842 became the guide for Frémont's exploring trips. He played a major role in taking California during the Mexican War, and served as an officer in the Civil War.

18. Calamity Jane. Martha Jane Canary grew up as a riding, shouting tomboy in a Montana mining community. She dressed like a man, and later became a rider for the Pony Express. Jane got her nickname because she jauntily asserted that anyone who offended her was courting calamity. She lived in Deadwood, South Dakota, and was buried near her friend "Wild Bill" Hickok. Calamity Jane was the heroine of a series of popular dime novels in the mid-1880's.

19. Davy Crockett. Known as the Coonskin Congressman from Tennessee, this backwoodsman possessed a silver tongue. He died at the Alamo in San Antonio in 1836, defending that Texas mission fortress against the Mexicans.

20. Jim Crow. The term "Jim Crow" was first brought into public use in 1828, in Louisville, Kentucky, by T. D. Rice, a vaudeville performer. Rice had heard an old Negro groom singing as he shuffle-danced around a horse: "Wheel about, turn about/Do jis so/An' ebery time I wheel about/I jump Jim Crow." When he first introduced the song, Rice also imitated the little limping figure he had seen, who soon became a stock vaudeville character. "Jim Crow" is used today to describe segregationist policies in the South.

21. The Dutchman *(Jacob Walz or Wolz).* A prospector of the 1870's, he surprised three Mexicans at their gold mine in the Superstition Mountains in Arizona, killed them and took over the lode. He kept its location secret, murdering at least eight men who tried to follow him. Since his death in 1891, thousands have tried in vain to find the Lost Dutchman Mine. Some have never returned, and as a result many people believe the mine is cursed.

22. Febold Feboldson *(mythical).* This resourceful Swedish pioneer in Nebraska sold sands from Death Valley, California, to gold prospectors at $50 a bushel. His sales pitch: "The sands of the desert never grow cold."

23. Mike Fink. All the ports on the Ohio and Mississippi rivers were stopping-places for this indomitable Indian scout who became a flatboat or keelboat pilot, and was known as King of the Keelboatmen and The Snapping Turtle of the Ohio. He prospered until steamboats began plying the rivers.

24. Barbara Frietchie. The poet John Greenleaf Whittier combined two real ladies to tell the legend of Barbara Frietchie ("Shoot, if you must, this old gray head"). Mary S. Quantrell raised her Union flag as "Stonewall" Jackson's troops marched through Frederick, Maryland; and Barbara Frietchie, 96 years old, waved hers at General Ambrose E. Burnside six days later in the same town.

25. Hank, the Free Wheeler *(mythical).* As a boy back on the farm, he speeded up chores by teaching the cows to ride bicycles from the pasture to the barn at milking time. Anything on wheels delighted Hank, so he gravitated to Detroit and its auto factories.

26. John Henry. According to legend, he weighed 44 pounds at birth and when, as a baby, he cried, the force of his breath blew out lamps. In the Big Bend Tunnel of the Chesapeake and Ohio Railroad at Hinton, West Virginia, he was the only steel driver (making holes for dynamite charges) who could work 20-pound hammers in each hand, simultaneously. He died after winning a heroic contest with a steam drill.

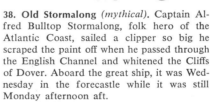

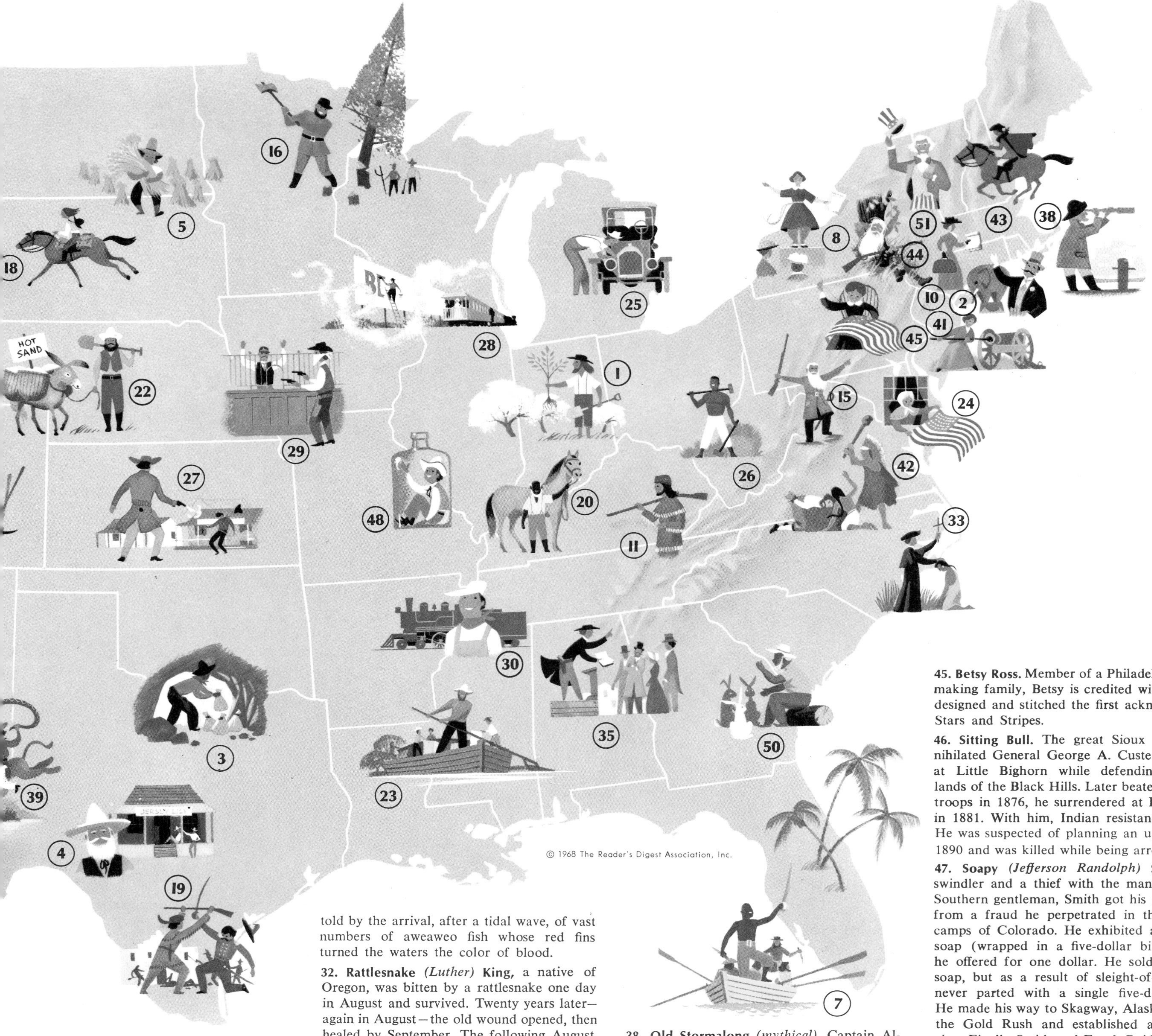

27. "Wild Bill" *(James B.)* **Hickok.** The famed Indian scout became a marksman by shooting at a dime at 50 paces. He served as a Union Army soldier, a peace officer in Abilene, Kansas, and he escorted freight supplies out of Wichita, Kansas. While prospecting for gold in Deadwood, he was fatally shot during a poker game in a saloon, in 1876.

28. Slappy Hooper *(mythical).* No surface was too much of a challenge for Slappy, the world's greatest sign painter. He once produced a sign that stretched from one end of a railroad line to the other, and the only way to read it was to catch a through train.

29. Jesse James. Folk songs celebrate this American Robin Hood—"he stole from the rich and he gave to the poor." He once gave a widow whom he had met casually $1400 to pay off a mortgage. In 1882, while living under the assumed name of Thomas Howard, he was killed by twenty-year-old Robert Ford, whom he had trusted. A ballad mourns: "But the dirty little coward, he shot Mr. Howard and he laid poor Jesse in his grave."

30. Casey Jones *(John Luther Jones was born near Cayce, Kentucky, in 1863—hence his nickname "Casey").* When this famous engineer blew his whistle in his own inimitable way, residents all along the tracks would say, "There goes Casey Jones." On his last trip when Casey was approaching Vaughan, Mississippi, several boxcars appeared unexpectedly crossing the main line. Casey was found dead in the wreckage, with one hand on the whistle, the other on the air-brake lever. His story is one of our great folk-song classics.

31. Kamehameha. The greatest of the Hawaiian chiefs, Kamehameha was the first king of all the islands. It was believed that he was born during a torrential thunderstorm and taken from his mother, a noblewoman, lest he be killed as a potential rival of the local king. After the forces of an opponent were almost wiped out by a volcanic eruption, natives maintained that Pele, the fire goddess (see no. 40), had acted in his favor. According to folklore, his death in May 1819 was foretold by the arrival, after a tidal wave, of vast numbers of aweaweo fish whose red fins turned the waters the color of blood.

32. Rattlesnake *(Luther)* **King,** a native of Oregon, was bitten by a rattlesnake one day in August and survived. Twenty years later—again in August—the old wound opened, then healed by September. The following August, the same phenomenon occurred and continued until Rattlesnake King, famous for his mysterious affliction, finally succumbed after the twelfth year.

33. Manteo. This North Carolina Indian went to England in 1584 with the first explorers to land on the Carolina coast, Philip Amadas and Arthur Barlow. Later he helped establish friendly relations between the English and the Indians when the group known in history as the Lost Colony settled on Roanoke Island in 1587. Manteo was the first person in North America known to be baptized in English and was created Lord of Roanoke by Sir Walter Raleigh. When Governor John White returned from England in 1591 after a trip for supplies, the colonists—and Manteo—had disappeared.

34. Dan McGrew *(mythical),* a card-playing Alaskan, met his end in the Malamute saloon. He was killed by a piano-playing "miner from the creeks," whom McGrew mortally wounded before he himself expired. The cause of the famous barroom duel: "the lady that's known as Lou." The story was immortalized in Robert W. Service's poem, "The Shooting of Dan McGrew."

35. John Murrell. A Southern outlaw of the early 1800's, Murrell headed a gang that specialized in holding camp revival meetings. While a self-styled "reverend"—sometimes said to be Murrell himself—preached to the crowd, the rest of the gang stole horses and enticed away slaves who had accompanied families to the gatherings to care for the children.

36. Annie Oakley. A phenomenal markswoman, Annie could hit targets from the back of a galloping pony. Star of Buffalo Bill's Wild West Show, she once shot a cigarette out of the Kaiser's mouth. (Complimentary theater tickets are called "Annie Oakleys" because they have holes punched in them.)

37. Old Jim *(mythical).* Champion grower of Idaho potatoes, Old Jim wouldn't sell customers a mere hundred pounds, because it was against his policy to cut a potato in half.

38. Old Stormalong *(mythical).* Captain Alfred Bulltop Stormalong, folk hero of the Atlantic Coast, sailed a clipper so big he scraped the paint off when he passed through the English Channel and whitened the Cliffs of Dover. Aboard the great ship, it was Wednesday in the forecastle while it was still Monday afternoon aft.

39. Pecos Bill *(mythical).* His horse "Widow-Maker" killed everyone who rode him but Bill. He invented the art of roping; dug the Rio Grande; subdued a mountain lion, mounted him and used a long rattlesnake as a whip to make him go faster.

40. Pele *(mythical).* The fire goddess of the Hawaiians lived in the lava lake of the volcanic crater Kilauea, which erupted whenever she became angry. The fear inspired by Pele disappeared after Kapiolani, a convert to Christianity, defied the goddess by tossing rocks into the lava lake and then returning unscathed.

41. Molly Pitcher. Mrs. Mary Hays carried water in a pitcher to the wounded during the Revolutionary War battle in Monmouth, New Jersey. She also relieved her husband at his artillery position.

42. Pocahontas. Legends relate that at Jamestown, Virginia, this Indian maiden saved Captain John Smith when her father, Chief Powhatan, intended to kill him. She married colonist John Rolfe and became a celebrity in England when she returned with him in 1614.

43. Paul Revere. This noted Boston silversmith was immortalized in Longfellow's poem for his midnight ride on horseback from Charlestown to Lexington on April 18, 1775. He warned the Massachusetts patriots that British troops were planning to attack.

44. Rip van Winkle *(mythical)* lived in a small Hudson River village and went hunting in the Catskill Mountains to escape his nagging wife. Meeting some gnomelike men, he was invited to join them at ninepins and to drink their liquor. The mountain brew put him to sleep for 20 years, and he could not understand why nobody recognized him at first when he returned home after his "nap."

45. Betsy Ross. Member of a Philadelphia flag-making family, Betsy is credited with having designed and stitched the first acknowledged Stars and Stripes.

46. Sitting Bull. The great Sioux chief annihilated General George A. Custer's troops at Little Bighorn while defending Indian lands of the Black Hills. Later beaten by U.S. troops in 1876, he surrendered at Fort Peck in 1881. With him, Indian resistance ended. He was suspected of planning an uprising in 1890 and was killed while being arrested.

47. Soapy *(Jefferson Randolph)* **Smith.** A swindler and a thief with the manners of a Southern gentleman, Smith got his nickname from a fraud he perpetrated in the mining camps of Colorado. He exhibited a cake of soap (wrapped in a five-dollar bill) which he offered for one dollar. He sold a lot of soap, but as a result of sleight-of-hand, he never parted with a single five-dollar bill. He made his way to Skagway, Alaska, during the Gold Rush and established a criminal ring. Finally Smith and Frank Reid, a leader of vigilantes, shot each other in a face-to-face confrontation in 1898.

48. Stackalee *(mythical).* Stackalee sold his soul to "Old Scratch," the devil. That was why Stack could walk into a bottle and sit on the bottom, or walk barefoot on hot slag out of a pig-iron furnace. Stack lived on Market Street in St. Louis. He could "whup the blues on a guitar and beat out boogie-woogie music." His girl friend, Stack O'Dollars, smoked cheroots and had diamond fillings in her teeth. Stackalee wound up serving 75 years in the Jefferson County jail for shooting Billy Lyons, who had stolen his "magic" stetson hat.

49. Tommy Knawkers *(mythical).* These gnomelike creatures accompanied the Cornish miners who came to Colorado from Britain to dig for gold and silver. If they were friendly to a miner, they indicated by rapping on the walls where the richest veins of metal could be found, and many a prospector left an open bottle of whiskey for them on New Year's Eve. The Tommy Knawkers also warned when a cave-in was imminent by rattling wooden supports and saved many lives in that manner. They played pranks, such as hiding or upsetting lunch pails and putting stones on the tracks to delay mine cars.

50. Uncle Remus *(mythical)* was the creation—in 1880—of Georgia writer Joel Chandler Harris. The elderly Negro narrated the animal legends of the old plantation to a seven-year-old white boy. The leading, recurring character is the nimble Brer Rabbit who, time after time, outwits Brer Fox. The stories were drawn from interviews with former slaves and from the author's own memories of the tales which he had heard as a child.

51. Uncle Sam *(mythical).* During the War of 1812, Samuel Wilson, known as Uncle Sam, inspected meat for the U.S. Army, at Troy, New York, stamping it "U.S." An anonymous soldier handling shipments decided that "U.S." meant "Uncle Sam," and that he represented the government.

CALENDAR OF FESTIVALS AND SPORTS

Listed below are events representative of the thousands which take place each year.

Sports events are in roman type, *others are in italics.*

JANUARY

The Narcissus Festival, Hawaii (all islands) (also Feb.)
Natl. Football League Playoff Bowl, Miami
Natl. and American Football League Super Bowl Playoff*
College Football Cotton Bowl, Dallas
College Football Orange Bowl, Miami
College Football Rose Bowl, Pasadena, Calif.
College Football Sugar Bowl, New Orleans
Master International Ski Jump, Lake Placid, N. Y.
Natl. Football League All-Star Game, Los Angeles
Natl. Basketball Assn. All-Star Game*
Knights of Columbus Indoor Track Meet, Boston
Invitational Indoor Track Meet, Los Angeles
Wanamaker Millrose Indoor Track Games, New York City
U.S. Figure Skating Championships*
U.S. Natl. Outdoor Speed Skating Championships*
Boston Athletic Assn. Indoor Track Meet, Boston

FEBRUARY

INQUIRER Indoor Track Games, Philadelphia
Knights of Columbus Indoor Track Meet, New York City
Vail Cup Skiing Championships, Vail, Colo.
TIMES Indoor Track Games, Los Angeles
Roch Cup Skiing Championships, Aspen, Colo.
U.S. Ski Assn. Jumping Championships*
Gold Rush Days, Wickenburg, Ariz.
Westminster Kennel Club Dog Show, New York City
U.S. Track and Field Federation Indoor Championships, New York City
N. Y. Athletic Club Indoor Track Games, New York City
American Bowling Congress Tournament* (to early April)
Miami-Lucaya,Bahamas,Yacht Race, Miami
Mardi Gras Festival, New Orleans (week before Ash Wednesday)

MARCH

Cherry Blossom Festival, Hawaii (all islands) (also April)
Southern Conference Basketball Championship Tournament, Charlotte, N. C.
Eastern Intercollegiate Wrestling Assn. Championships*
N.C.A.A. Indoor Track Championships*
E.C.A.C. Hockey Championships, Boston
N.C.A.A. Skiing Championships*
Easter Concerts, Lindsburg, Kans., Holy Week (March or April)
Atlantic Coast Conference Basketball Championship Tournament, Charlotte, N. C.
Natl. Assn. of Intercollegiate Athletics Basketball Championships, Kansas City, Mo.
A.A.U. Indoor Track Championships, Oakland, Calif.
Natl. Invitation Basketball Tournament, New York City
N.C.A.A. College Division Championship Basketball Tournament, Evansville, Ind.
N.C.A.A. Basketball Championships*
Intercollegiate Fencing Assn. Championships*
N.C.A.A. Swimming Championships*
N.C.A.A. Hockey Championships*
Natl. Alpine Skiing Championships*
U.S. Junior Skiing Championships*
A.A.U. Boxing Championships*
N.C.A.A. Wrestling Championships*
N.C.A.A. Fencing Championships*

APRIL

Intl. Kennel Club Dog Show, Chicago
Masters Golf Tournament, Augusta, Ga.
A.A.U. Natl. Wrestling Championships (Freestyle and Greco-Roman)*
U.S. Open Badminton Championships*
Men's A.A.U. Swimming Championships (indoor)*
Fiddlers' Festival, Union Grove, N. C.
Golf Tournament of Champions, Las Vegas, Nev.
Cane Futurity Race, Yonkers Raceway, Yonkers, N. Y.
Intl. Pace, Yonkers Raceway, Yonkers, N. Y.
Spring Fiesta, New Orleans
Women's A.A.U. Swimming Championships (indoor)*
Arts Festival, Tucson, Ariz.
Arts Festival, Birmingham, Ala.
A.A.U. Judo Championships*
Drake Relays, Des Moines, Iowa
Penn Relays, Philadelphia
Natl. Hockey League Stanley Cup Playoffs* (also early May)
May (Music) Festival, Ann Arbor, Mich. (formerly in May)

MAY

Captain Cook Festival, Kona Coast, Hawaii, Hawaii
The Kentucky Derby, Churchill Downs, Ky.
Houston Champions Intl. Golf Tournament, Houston, Tex.
A.A.U. Natl. Volleyball Championships*
Dad Vail Rowing Assn. Regatta for University 8-oared Shells, Philadelphia
A.A.U. Gymnastics Championship*
Norwegian Folk Festival, Petersburg, Alaska
American Music Festival, Washington, D. C. (also early June)
Florida Folk Festival, White Springs, Fla.
Natl. Folk Festival, Denver
American Bowling Congress Masters Tournament*
Eastern Assn. of Rowing Colleges Sprints Championships, Lake Quinsigamond, Worcester, Mass.
Bach Festival, Providence
Bach Choir, Bethlehem, Pa.
Song Festival, Waikiki, Hawaii
Music Festival, Ojai, Calif.
Arts Festival, New Haven, Conn.
Song Festival, Benton, Ky.
Old Fiddlers' Reunion, Athens, Tex.
California Relays, Modesto, Calif.
The Preakness, Pimlico, Baltimore
The Jersey Derby, Garden State Park, Camden, N. J.
The Metropolitan Handicap, Aqueduct, Ozone Park, N. Y.
The Realization Pace, Roosevelt Raceway, Westbury, N. Y.
Memorial Day 500-mile Auto Racing Championships, Indianapolis
600-mile Stock Car Racing Championship, Charlotte, N. C.
400-mile Stock Car Championship, Darlington, S. C.
Three Rivers Art Festival, Pittsburgh (also early June)

JUNE

Buick Open Golf Championship*
The Belmont, Belmont Park, Elmont, N. Y.
Compton Invitational Track and Field Meet, Los Angeles
Strawberry Festival, Haines, Alaska (also July)
Indian Dance Festival, Tanana, Alaska
Music Festival, Robin Hood Dell, Philadelphia (also July)
New York Shakespeare Festival, New York City (also July, Aug.)
American Shakespeare Drama Festival, Stratford, Conn. (also July, Aug., Sept.)
Summer Symphony, Houston, Tex. (also July, early Aug.)
N.C.A.A. Track and Field Championships*
U.S. Track and Field Federation Championships*
N.C.A.A. Tennis Championships*
U.S. Golf Assn. Open Championships*
N.C.A.A. Baseball Championships*
Newport to Bermuda Yacht Race, Newport, R. I.
American Power Boat Assn. President's Cup Regatta, Washington, D. C.
Harvard-Yale College Crew Regatta, Connecticut River, from New London to Derby, Conn.
Midnight Sun Festival, Nome, Alaska
American Folk Music Festival, Olive Hill, Ky.
Music Festival, Virginia Beach, Va.
Shakespeare Drama Festival, San Diego, Calif. (also July, Aug., early Sept.)
Alaska Festival of Music, Anchorage, Alaska
Arts Festival, Annapolis, Md.
West Virginia Folk Festival, Glenville, W. Va.
Music Festival, Milwaukee, Wis. (also July)
Natl. Challenge Cup Soccer Finals*
Summer Opera Festival, Cincinnati (also July)
Chamber Music Festival, New Haven, Conn. (also July, early Aug.)
Summer Music Festival, Stanford, Calif. (also July, early Aug.)
Old-Time Fiddlers' Contest, Weiser, Idaho
State Singing Convention, Benson, N. C.
Music Festival (Opera), Central City, Colo. (also July)
Singing on the Mountains Music Festival, Linville, N. C.
Congregation of the Arts Music Festival, Hanover, N. H. (also July, Aug.)
Music Festival, Interlochen, Mich. (also July, Aug.)
Music Festival, Aspen, Colo. (also July, Aug.)
Music Festival, Redlands, Calif. (also July, Aug.)
Ravinia Music Festival, Highland Park, Ill. (also July, Aug., early Sept.)
Music Festival, Woodstock, N. Y. (also July, Aug.)
Music Festival, Chautauqua, N. Y. (also July, Aug.)
Pawnee Powwow Dance Festival, Pawnee, Okla. (also early July)
A.A.U. Track and Field Championships*
Coaching Club American Oaks Stakes Race, Belmont Park, Elmont, N. Y.
N.C.A.A. Golf Championships*
The Realization Trot, Roosevelt Raceway, Westbury, N. Y.
U.S. Natl. Fencing Championships*
Intercollegiate Rowing Assn. 3-mile Championship, Lake Onondaga, N. Y.
Pikes Peak Stock and Sport Auto Racing Championship, Colorado Springs, Colo.

JULY

Music at the Vineyards Festival, Saratoga, Calif. (also Aug.)
Bon Dances, Hawaii (all islands) (also Aug.)
Pennsylvania Dutch Festival, Kutztown, Pa.
Jacob's Pillow Dance Festival, Lee, Mass. (also Aug.)
Esplanade Concerts, Boston
Hollywood Bowl Music Festival, Hollywood, Calif. (also Aug.)
Forest Hills Music Festival, Forest Hills, N. Y. (also Aug.)
Coaches' All-America Football Game, Atlanta
Suburban Handicap, Aqueduct, Ozone Park, N. Y.
U.S. Golf Assn. Women's Championships*
The Hollywood Derby, Hollywood Park, Inglewood, Calif.
Major League All-Star Baseball Game (American League *versus* National League)*
Gold Cup Power-Boat Racing Regatta (generally held at either Detroit or Seattle)
Indian Powwow Dance Festival, Flagstaff, Ariz.
Jazz Festival, Newport, R. I.
Marlboro Music Festival, Marlboro, Vt. (also Aug.)
Summer Concerts, Yale Music School Festival, Norfolk, Conn.
Powwow Dance Festival, Toppenish, Wash.
Berkshire Music Festival (Tanglewood), Lenox, Mass. (also Aug.)
Opera Festival, Santa Fe, N. Mex. (also Aug.)
Arts Festival, Norfolk, Va.
Music Mountain Music Festival, Falls Village, Conn. (through Labor Day)
400-mile Stock Car Championship, Daytona Beach, Fla.
Music Arts Festival, Jackson Hole, Wyo. (also Aug.)
Gilbert and Sullivan Music Festival, Falmouth, Mass. (also Aug.)
Breyard Music Festival, Brevard, N. C. (also Aug.)
Festival of Music, Hartford, Conn.
Indian Powwow Dance Festival, Okmulgee, Okla.
Asolo Theater Drama Festival, Sarasota, Fla. (also Aug.)
Arts Festival, Laguna Beach, Calif. (also Aug.)
Frontier Days, Cheyenne, Wyo.
Performing Arts Center Festival, Saratoga Springs, N. Y. (also Aug.)
Women's Intl. Bowling Congress Championship Tournament*
Intl. World Championships Trot, Roosevelt Raceway, Westbury, N. Y.
The Monmouth Handicap, Monmouth Park, Oceanport, N. J.
Hopi Indian Dance Festival, Winslow, Ariz.
Shakespearean Drama Festival, Cedar City, Utah
Shakespearean Drama Festival, Ross, Calif. (through Labor Day)
Bach Music Festival, Carmel, Calif.
Repertory Theater Drama Festival, Tampa, Fla.
All-Texas Jazz Festival, Corpus Christi, Tex.
Folk Festival, Newport, R. I.
Golden Days Celebration Folk Festival, Fairbanks, Alaska
Shakespearean Drama Festival, Ashland, Ore. (also Aug., early Sept.)
Lake George Opera Festival, Glens Falls, N. Y. (also Aug.)
N. Y. Philharmonic Music Festivals, New York City parks (also Aug.)
Florida Intl. Music Festival, Daytona Beach, Fla. (also Aug.)
Gospel Singing Convention, Mount Nebo, W. Va.
Indian Ceremonial Powwow Dance Festival, Winnebago, Nebr. (also early Aug.)
Shakespeare Drama Festival, Boulder, Colo. (also early Aug.)
American-National Stakes Pace, Sportsman's Park, Chicago
The Brooklyn Handicap, Aqueduct, Ozone Park, N. Y.
Juvenile Championship for Thoroughbreds, Hollywood Park, Inglewood, Calif.
Yonkers Futurity Trot, Yonkers Raceway, Yonkers, N. Y.
The Delaware Handicap, Delaware Park, Stanton, Del.
Professional Golf Assn. Championship*
South Mountain Concerts, Pittsfield, Mass. (also Aug.)
Natl. Skeet Shooting Assn. Championships*

AUGUST

Mountain Dance Festival, Asheville, N. C.
Opera Festival, Newport, R. I.
Midsummer Serenade, Philharmonic Hall, New York City
Shakespearean Drama Festival, Burlington, Vt.
Gift of the Waters Pageant, Thermopolis, Wyo.
Contemporary Music Festival, Brunswick, Me.
Hula Dance Festival, Waikiki, Hawaii
Western Open Golf Championships*
College Football All-Stars *versus* Natl. Football League Champions, Chicago
Thunderbird Golf Classic*
Open Golf Tournament, Cleveland
Natl. A.A.U. Men's and Women's Swimming Championships*
400-mile Stock Car Championship, Atlanta
Inter-Tribal Ceremonial Dance Festival, Gallup, N. Mex.
Old Fiddlers' Contest, Galax, Va.
Indian Powwow Dance Festival, Tulsa, Okla.
Festival of Nations Folk Festival, Red Lodge, Mont.
Smoki Ceremonials Dance Festival, Prescott, Ariz.
The Travers Stakes, Saratoga Race Track, Saratoga Springs, N. Y.
American Casting Assn. Championships*
Plains Indians Ceremonial Dance Festival, Anadarko, Okla.
American Dance Festival, New London, Conn.
Cabrillo Music Festival, Aptos, Calif.
Chicagoland Music Festival, Chicago
Philadelphia Golf Classic, Philadelphia
The Hambletonian Trot, Du Quoin, Ill.
U.S. Natl. Water Skiing Championships, Miami, Fla.
Grand American Trapshooting Tournament*
Hall of Fame Tennis Tournament (Men), Newport, R. I.

SEPTEMBER

William Tell Pageant, New Glarus, Wis.
The New Hampshire Sweepstakes Classic, Rockingham Park, Salem, N. H.
U.S. Lawn Tennis Assn. Championships, Forest Hills, N. Y.
The Aqueduct, Aqueduct Race Track, Ozone Park, N. Y.
Mallory Cup, North American Men's Yachting Championship, Riverside, Conn.
Pendleton Roundup, Pendleton, Ore.
Sears Cup, North American Junior Yachting Championship, Chicago
500-mile Stock Car Championship, Darlington, S. C.
Jazz Festival, Monterey, Calif.
Piano Festival, San Diego, Calif.
The United Nations Handicap, Atlantic City Race Track, Mays Landing, N. J.
Arlington-Washington Futurity, Arlington Heights, Ill.
Double 500 Sports Car Championship, Bridgehampton, N. Y.
Little Brown Jug Pace, Fairgrounds, Delaware, Ohio

OCTOBER

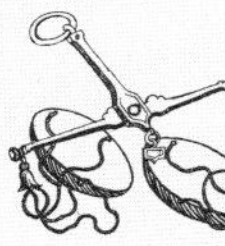

Baseball World Series, American League Champions *versus* National League Champions*
Alaska Day Festival, Sitka, Alaska
Aloha Week, Hawaii (all islands) (also Nov.)
The Woodward, Aqueduct, Ozone Park, N. Y.
Pacific Coast Tennis Championships, Berkeley, Calif.
U.S. Grand Prix Auto Racing (Sports Car) Championship, Watkins Glen, N. Y.
Pennsylvania Natl. Horse Show, Harrisburg Armory, Harrisburg, Pa.
The Champagne Stakes, Belmont Park, Elmont, N. Y.
The United Nations Trot, Yonkers Raceway, Yonkers, N. Y.
500-mile Stock Car Championship, Charlotte, N. C.
Music Festival, Worcester, Mass.
Natl. Horse Show, New York City (also early Nov.)
Intl. Horse Show, Washington, D. C.
Jockey Club Gold Cup, Belmont Park, Elmont, N. Y.
The Messenger Stake Pace, Roosevelt Raceway, Westbury, N. Y.
500-mile Stock Car Championship, Rockingham, N. C.
Ozark Folk Festival, Eureka Springs, Ark.

NOVEMBER

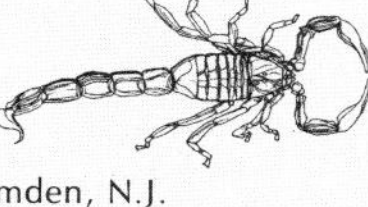

The Garden State Stakes, Garden State Park, Camden, N.J.
The Washington, D. C., International for Thoroughbreds, Laurel Park, Laurel, Md.
Professional Bowlers' Assn. Natl. Championships, New York City
Army-Navy Football Game, Kennedy Stadium, Philadelphia

DECEMBER

N.C.A.A. Soccer Championship*
Natl. Football League Championship*
E.C.A.C. Holiday Hockey Tournament, New York City
E.C.A.C. Boston Holiday College Hockey Tournament, Boston
American Football League Championship*
College Football Gator Bowl, Jacksonville, Fla.
Classic Basketball Tournament, Los Angeles
E.C.A.C. Holiday Basketball Festival, New York City
E.C.A.C. Quaker City Basketball Tournament, Philadelphia
All-College Basketball Tournament, Oklahoma City

*Site determined annually.

Abbreviations: A.A.U.—Amateur Athletic Union of the United States N.C.A.A.—National Collegiate Athletic Association E.C.A.C.—Eastern College Athletic Conference

PART III

The American Land

NATURAL WONDERS

America has always been proud of its man-made wonders: its tallest buildings and longest bridges, its multilane highways, enormous dams and bustling airports. Only in recent times have we become fully aware that nature has bestowed countless wonders on this land: vast canyons, unusual waterfalls, rare trees and other marvels. As we have come to prize these wonders, we have at the same time found them threatened by an expanding civilization. Badly eroded wasteland, with pillars and spires painted in unusual colors by oxidized minerals, was once considered useless; we look upon it now as an awesome possession for all to see and contemplate. A stand of giant sequoias is no longer just lumber, but a forest primeval where peace of mind and refreshment of spirit may be gained. We may still believe that a swamp must be drained, but before we bulldoze the ditches, we pause to recognize it as a valuable wildlife haven. On these pages you will find just a few scenes of the natural heritage that is yours.

1. Minerva Terrace, Mammoth Hot Springs, Yellowstone National Park, Wyo.

2. Devil's Tower, Wyo.

3. Olympic National Park rain forest, Wash.

4. Sequoia National Park, Calif.

5. Seacoast, Acadia National Park, Maine

6. Wizard Island, Crater Lake, Oreg.

7. Angel Arch, Canyonlands National Park, Utah

1. Yellowstone's pools of mineral water, hot geysers like Old Faithful (one of about 3000 in the park), falls and hot springs make it one of the truly great natural-wonder regions. Terraces, created by limestone deposited from hot water, are located at the north gate in the Mammoth Hot Springs section of the park.

2. Rising 865 feet from the surrounding countryside, the Devil's Tower dominates the skyline of this section of northeast Wyoming. The first designated national monument (1906), the tower is a lava plug—all that remains of an eroded volcanic cone that perhaps 50 million years ago was forced up through the earth's crust.

3. The rain forest of Olympic National Park contains moss- and vine-covered spruce, hemlock and fir in great abundance. The lush vegetation and the noble size of the trees are caused by the almost constant moisture in the air. The annual rainfall here is nearly 150 inches. This area is one of the few remaining examples of untouched, primeval wilderness.

4. Located in the High Sierras, massive groves of giant sequoias are protected from destruction by their inclusion in a national park. The trees, numbered among the oldest living things, are certainly also among the largest. Some of them stand almost 300 feet high and are believed to be over 3000 years of age. A trunk 30 feet in diameter is not uncommon.

5. Situated mostly on Mount Desert Island in Maine, Acadia's evergreen-covered acres enclose ponds, lakes and harbors. A rugged, sheer cliff (Otter), 100 feet above the south coast, overlooks the sea. In 1947 a catastrophic forest fire destroyed thousands of acres in the area, but new growth is now replacing the lost beauty.

6. The bowl of Crater Lake was formed when the top of Mount Mazama collapsed 7000 years ago. Today the deep-blue body of water sits thousands of feet above sea level. In its center is Wizard Island, which is a second, smaller volcano. Another formation, the Phantom Ship, rests perpetually "at anchor" near lava cliffs.

7. Angel Arch is in the southeastern section of the recently created Canyonlands National Park, and it towers higher than 200 feet. Other wonders of this area include odd pillars, arches and towers of sandstone. The weird landscape, a harsh country seamed and worn by nature over many eons, is cut by the fresh, winding waters of the Colorado and Green rivers.

8. Lava spurts into the air as an eruption shakes the island of Hawaii. The best known of the remaining active volcanic fissures in the United States are located here. Ancient Hawaiians believed the deity Pele lived in the Kilauea Crater, and they offered human sacrifices to placate the goddess. The last volcanic eruption in Hawaii took place in December 1965.

9. When the fall chill slips south over the New England landscape, touching the maples, birches, oaks and other trees, a superb symphony of color sweeps across the countryside. Few other areas in the world can boast each year of the multitude of tints and tones produced during these few weeks of glory.

10. Manganese and iron oxides in the shale and limestone give

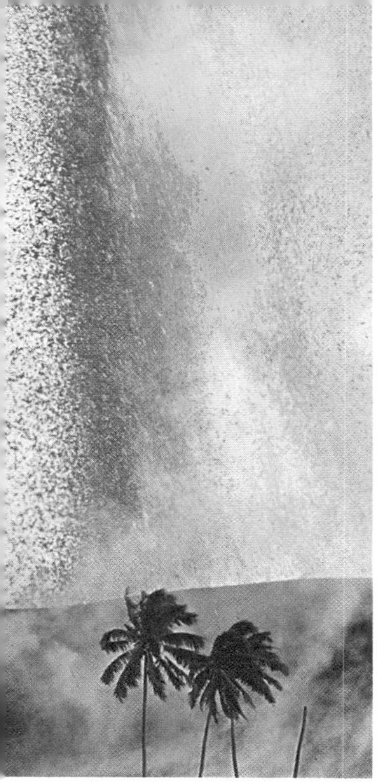

8. Volcano, island of Hawaii

9. Autumn trees, New England

10. Fairyland, Bryce Canyon, Utah

11. Bristlecone pine forest, Calif.

12. Mammoth Cave, Ky.

13. Havasu Falls, Ariz.

14. Colony Glacier, Alaska

15. Old Man of the Mountain, N. H.

16. Sand dunes, Sleeping Bear Point, Mich.

17. Grand Teton National Park, Wyo.

18. Everglades National Park, Fla.

the erosion-produced spires and walls of Bryce Canyon their brilliant, sometimes translucent, coloring. Red and pink predominate with hues of lavender. In one section, called the Queen's Garden, there stands a form resembling Queen Victoria.

11. Bristlecone pines grow high in the mountains in a dry, hostile environment, yet they represent one of the oldest living things on earth. The stumpy, erosion-smoothed tree maintains life by sacrificing most of itself and using the sparse supply of moisture and nutrients in the soil to keep a small segment in growing, cone-producing condition.

12. Mammoth Cave contains many beautiful formations of onyx, limestone and gypsum; high domes and deep pits; and a river that flows some 360 feet below the surface of the earth. Ghostly whitefish, completely blind, swim in the dark waters, and numerous bats make the cave their home. Only about 150 miles of the cave have been explored. Here the slow death of the trapped Floyd Collins roused national sympathy in 1925.

13. Havasu Falls is in a rather remote part of the western section of the Grand Canyon. Near the Havasupai Indian reservation, the area in its lushness is in stark contrast to the rest of the park. The Grand Canyon is a home of the apus, a creature over 100 million years old, which looks like a horseshoe crab.

14. Colony Glacier spreads its way through Alaska's crags. Glacial action is not usually perceptible to a casual onlooker, but some masses of ice, such as Muir Glacier, have been known to "gallop" up to 30 feet in a single day. They are rarely still, always either melting back or advancing.

15. The Old Man of the Mountain, known as such since colonial times, hangs on the edge of a mountain in New Hampshire more than 1000 feet up. The face is made of oddly placed ledges, three in all, which total 48 feet in height. This startling apparition overlooks a clear lake, which is often called the "Wash Bowl" because of its location under the face.

16. The Michigan dunes are located on the eastern coast of Lake Michigan. Known for their "singing sands," because their purity causes them to squeak when stepped upon, these dunes may reach a height of 200 feet. Winds often shift them so much that groves of trees may be covered one year and uncovered the next.

17. The Grand Teton peaks were used by Indians and trappers as landmarks. Towering 7000 feet above the floor and lakes of the valley, they were thrust up in comparatively recent geologic ages, but are numbered among U.S. mountains formed from the oldest rock on earth, during the Archeozoic era of more than 2 billion years ago. Below, the clear waters of Jackson Lake grew from melting glaciers.

18. Swamp areas have been the last primeval wonders to be recognized by man as worthy of preservation. One of the greatest in the world is Everglades National Park, with swamp cypress, mangroves and seas of saw grass supporting thousands of alligators and rare wading birds. A layer of sediment sitting in a water-filled limestone basin, the park also contains many royal palms.

THE CHANGING TERRAIN

600 MILLION YEARS OF SHIFTING EARTH AND SEAS

Geologic history is the history of rock formations. In this record lies the secret of what happened to the earth after it had progressed from a cloud of dust and gas into a whirling, rocky globe about 4.5 billion years ago. And rocks tell of subsequent events—where and when plant and animal life began, how mountains rose up, canyons were carved and lakes created.

Earth's oldest rock formations were molten, or "igneous." These are classified as Archeozoic, the name given to the earliest of five geologic eras. Scientists have found it no easy task to locate these Archeozoic rocks, for they are mostly covered over by later formations. In the United States, patches of them appear in the central Rocky Mountains and in the regions of Minnesota stretching north to Canada.

If Archeozoic outcroppings are plotted on a map they form a triangular-shaped base, nearly 1,800,000 square miles in size, for most of the North American continent. Because of its durable character it is called the Shield and because most of its expanse lies to the north, in Canada, it is known as the Canadian Shield.

The next oldest rock formations belong to the Proterozoic era. They are 1 to 2 billion years old and constitute the foundations of the southern Rockies and the Midwest. Younger belts of Proterozoic rocks can be found in the Adirondacks, in the Piedmont of the Atlantic States and in scattered spots from the Ozarks to Texas. The Archeozoic and Proterozoic eras cover such a vast span of time, almost 4 billion years, that they are often grouped together under the term Precambrian.

FOSSILS

There are distinctive fossils of every stage of geologic time, revealing the age of the rock formation in which they are found. The older rocks contain the simpler types of plants and animals that lived during the early eras of the earth; the younger rocks reveal more highly developed ones.

The Precambrian eras were first thought to have no fossils. Yet a variety of lowly sorts of life have now been found in many places. Generally, they range from mere bacteria and seaweed to primitive segmented animals such as worms. The shape and patterns of the ancestral seaweeds (algae) are preserved in Precambrian limestones. These organic structures may be found in rocks from the Adirondacks to Wyoming. The earliest algal fossils date from about 3 billion years ago.

GEOLOGIC ERAS AND PERIODS

The main divisions in geologic time—shown at the right of the page—are called eras. After the Archeozoic (meaning ancient life) and the Proterozoic (former life) come the Paleozoic (old life), beginning 580 million years ago; the Mesozoic (intermediate life), beginning 225 million years ago; and the Cenozoic (recent life), from 65 million years ago to the present.

Each era is subdivided into periods. The name for each period is usually taken from a geographic feature, such as a state, mountain or river where the particular rocks were first discovered, or from the character of the formation itself.

The first period of the Paleozoic era is the Cambrian. (All over the world any rocks dating earlier than this period are called Precambrian.) The name is taken from Cambria, the Latin word for Wales, which was the site of the oldest fossiliferous rocks ever found in Britain. The terms Ordovician and Silurian come from the names of the ancient British tribes who inhabited regions where particular rocks of this age were located; the Devonian period refers to Devonshire, England; the Carboniferous, sometimes separated into Mississippian and Pennsylvanian, includes the great coal fields. The name for the Permian period comes from Perm, a Russian province; Triassic from a threefold division of rocks in Germany; Jurassic from the Jura Mountains in the Alps. Cretaceous, from the Latin word *creta,* meaning "chalk," applies to a worldwide chalk formation of this period. The Tertiary period refers to "third," as it used to be considered the third era, but the name now applies to the period when mammals became dominant. Quaternary, named from the Latin word for "four," now covers the last 3 million years with its subdivisions of the Pleistocene epoch (the Ice Age) and Holocene epoch (the most recent).

The length of an era or of a period is approximate, and the age of most groups of rocks cannot be precisely determined. However, when rocks contain uranium, scientists are able to determine exact ages.

GEOLOGIC OUTCROPS AND FOSSILS

The various outcrops of ancient rocks found on the surface of the United States today are depicted on the four composite maps below. In the column at the extreme right are illustrations of representative fossils located in the various outcroppings. None is given for the Holocene or Pleistocene epochs, because glaciation during these times moved many rocks far from their places of origin.

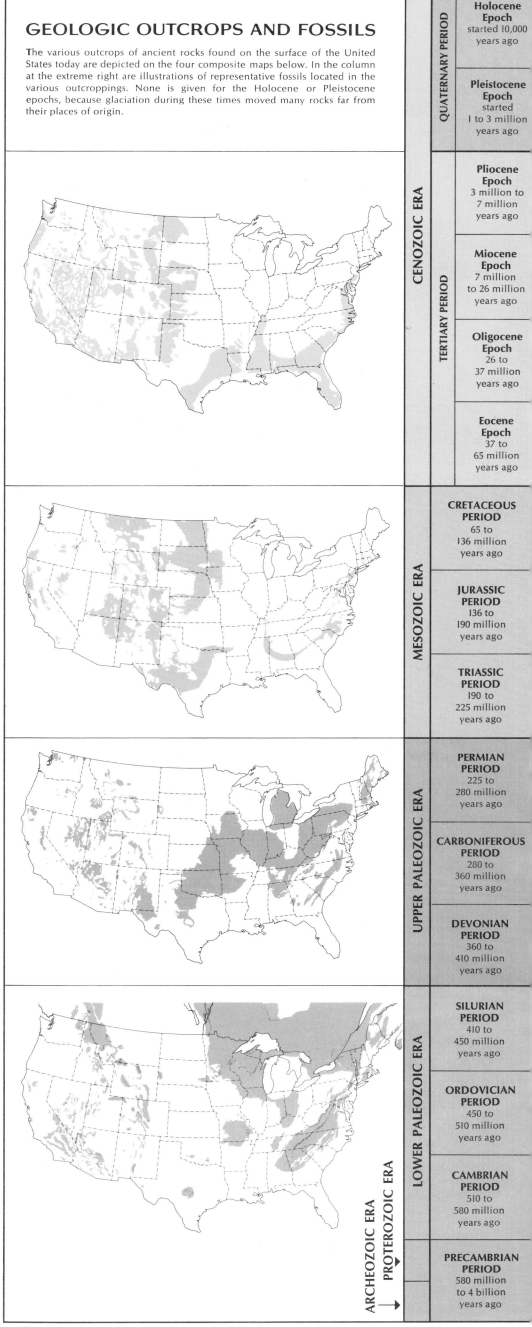

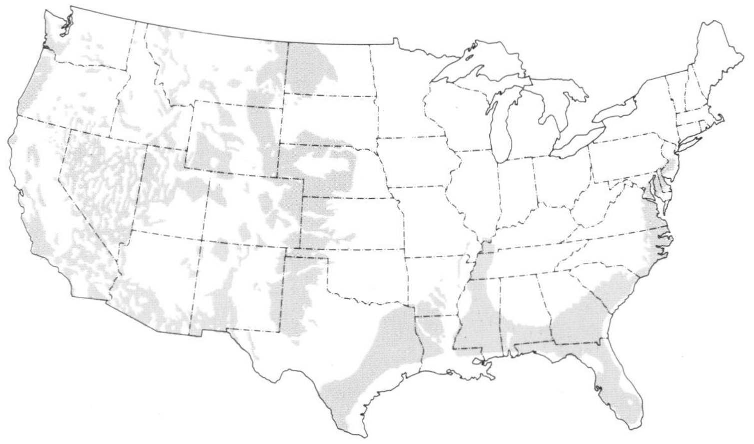

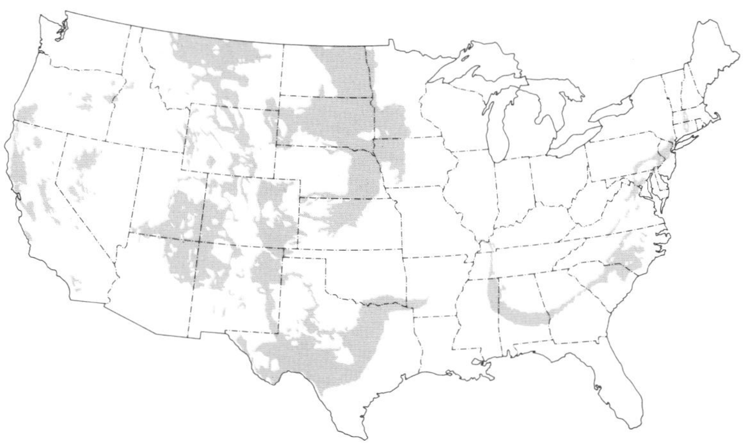

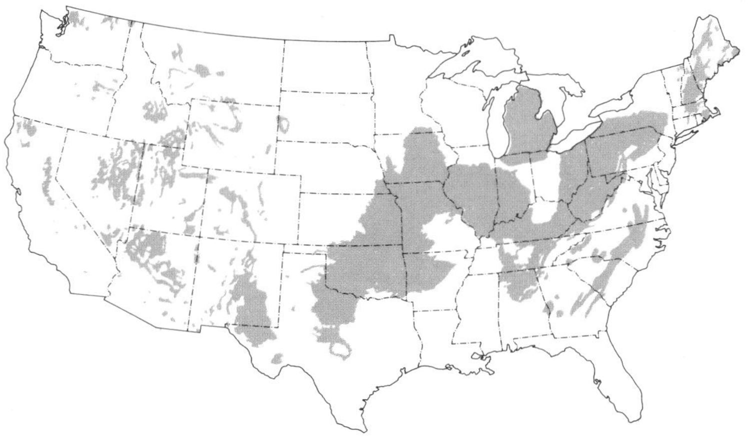

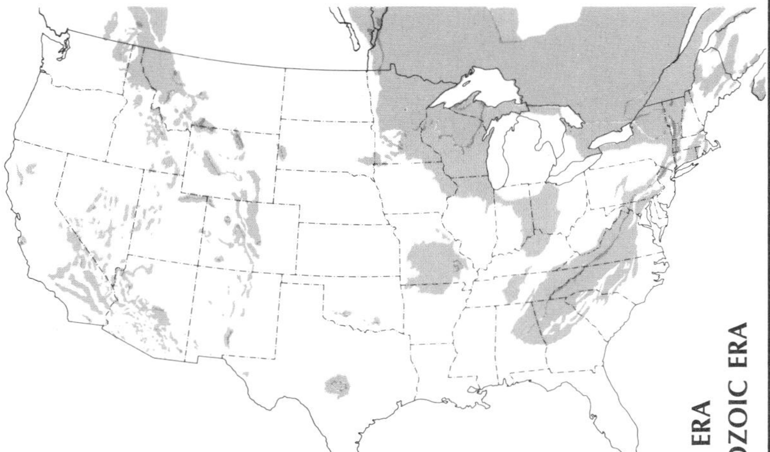

CENOZOIC ERA	QUATERNARY PERIOD	Holocene Epoch started 10,000 years ago
		Pleistocene Epoch started 1 to 3 million years ago
	TERTIARY PERIOD	Pliocene Epoch 3 million to 7 million years ago
		Miocene Epoch 7 million to 26 million years ago
		Oligocene Epoch 26 to 37 million years ago
		Eocene Epoch 37 to 65 million years ago
MESOZOIC ERA	CRETACEOUS PERIOD 65 to 136 million years ago	
	JURASSIC PERIOD 136 to 190 million years ago	
	TRIASSIC PERIOD 190 to 225 million years ago	
UPPER PALEOZOIC ERA	PERMIAN PERIOD 225 to 280 million years ago	
	CARBONIFEROUS PERIOD 280 to 360 million years ago	
	DEVONIAN PERIOD 360 to 410 million years ago	
LOWER PALEOZOIC ERA	SILURIAN PERIOD 410 to 450 million years ago	
	ORDOVICIAN PERIOD 450 to 510 million years ago	
	CAMBRIAN PERIOD 510 to 580 million years ago	
ARCHEOZOIC ERA / PROTEROZOIC ERA	PRECAMBRIAN PERIOD 580 million to 4 billion years ago	

.OCATIONS NOT DEFINED

.OCATIONS NOT DEFINED

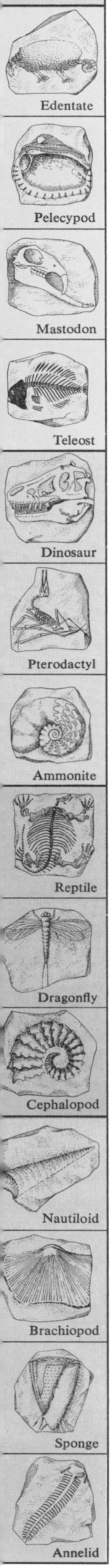

HOW LAND IS FORMED

THE INVADING SEAS

Time and again over the course of many millions of years, shallow seas have invaded the North American continent only to retreat. This give-and-take has been brought about by the endless oscillations of land and sea levels. When ocean water becomes locked up in a mass of glacial ice, the sea level drops. The process is reversed when glaciers melt and release huge quantities of water that sweep across low-lying areas.

At each flooding the invading sea becomes silted with sediments washed from the land. These sink to the bottom and turn into layers of fossil-filled sedimentary rock (Figure 1).

The greatest display of layers of sedimentation can be seen in the Grand Canyon where the Colorado River has cut a gash 10 miles wide, 215 miles long and 1 mile deep (Figure 2). Here the formations have been sliced through like a wedge of layer cake, and the early history of the earth can be read clearly in the many bands of colored rock. Down the sides of the canyon, each formation is older than the one above, until at the bottom the walls are 2 billion years old.

The orderliness of this unusual area, with every layer in level position exactly as it was laid down, does not always happen. A good example of distortion can be found in the Garden of the Gods at Colorado Springs. Here violent uplift caused the sandstone which was originally horizontal to become vertical, so that massive red and white slabs of rock project upright.

Figure I

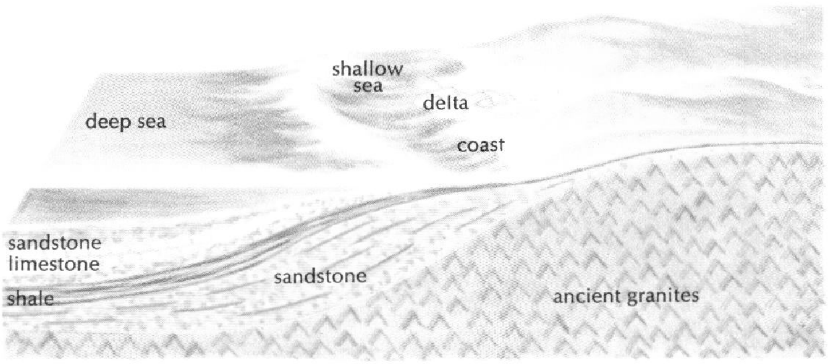

Figure 2

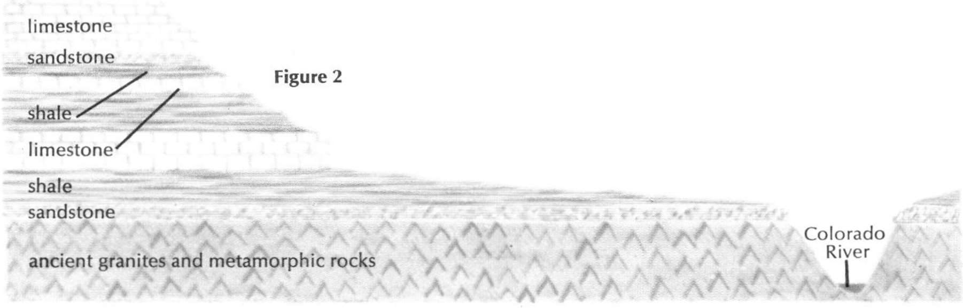

MOUNTAIN BUILDING

The earth's crust is never stable. Internal forces have repeatedly formed great depressions in the surface usually running parallel to the continental coastlines. These broad troughs or geosynclines (as they are called by geologists) are frequently thousands of miles long. It is here that miracles of growth have taken place (Figure 3).

Created in low-lying ground, the troughs fill with water from the sea and layers of sediment are collected at the bottom. Through millions of years the process continues until thousands of feet of material have been deposited. (It has been estimated that more than 500,000 cubic miles of such material was carried into the Appalachian geosyncline.) In time, the accumulation becomes rock and the enormous weight causes weaker parts of the earth's crust to give way, allowing vast quantities of sediment to sink to a depth of five miles or more. Here, because of radioactive elements, temperatures soar to 1500–2000°F. Under this terrific heat the sediments are turned into metamorphic rock (such as marble, quartzite, schist and slate) and are often melted to form magma. Frequently, volcanic action results when the magma erupts as lava (see "Volcanoes," below).

The sinking action of the trough leads to the collapse of the sides. As they are pushed inward toward each other in a squeezing action, the rocks near the surface are crushed and folded together. In the grip of tremendous heat below and gigantic pressures above, the whole complex of the geosyncline becomes convulsed in a slow but violent spasm of upheaval. Constantly folding and fracturing, great masses of the earth's crust are forced up higher and higher until finally after many ages have passed a mountain range is formed (Figure 4).

The new range is immediately subjected to the forces of erosion—rain, wind and frost. Rock particles are washed away and carried by streams and rivers to the sea, where they are deposited, build up pressures—and a whole new cycle of mountain building begins. It is believed that the amount of sediment (as much as 700,000 cubic miles) deposited by the Mississippi River in the Gulf Coast geosyncline in the Gulf of Mexico may well be forming a mountain range that will rise in some future geologic time.

Despite the inroads of erosion, the uplift process is greater than the wearing down so that the mountain range continues to rise higher and higher for some time. Eventually the growth slows and erosion takes over until a majestic mountain range is finally reduced to a comparatively low elevation, such as the present Appalachians, or even to a featureless plain.

Figure 3

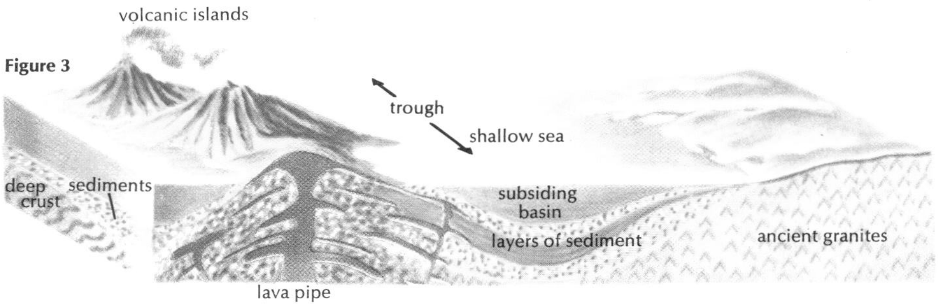

Figure 4

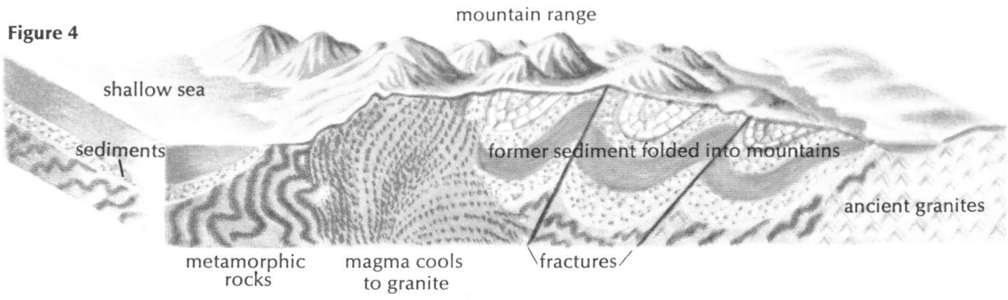

VOLCANOES

Another great land builder is the volcano, with its mighty brew of lava and ash. In fact, mountain building is usually accompanied in part by some volcanic activity. Lava covers almost 200,000 square miles of the western United States (see Volcanic Rocks on map, page 129). Some of these accumulations are many thousands of feet thick.

There are basically two types of volcanoes. One, the "shield" volcano (Figure 5), directs its outflow to the surface through deep cracks or "faults" in rock formation. The upward surge of bubbling molten-rock material meets little resistance and spreads across the land. The second type, the "strato" volcano (Figure 6), forces its way to the surface, bursting into the open with an explosive force sometimes equal to 100 megatons (100 million tons) of TNT, forming enormous craters. There are close to 500 active volcanoes in the world, including several in the Hawaiian Islands and over 30 in Alaska and the Aleutian Islands.

Figure 5 Shield Type Volcano

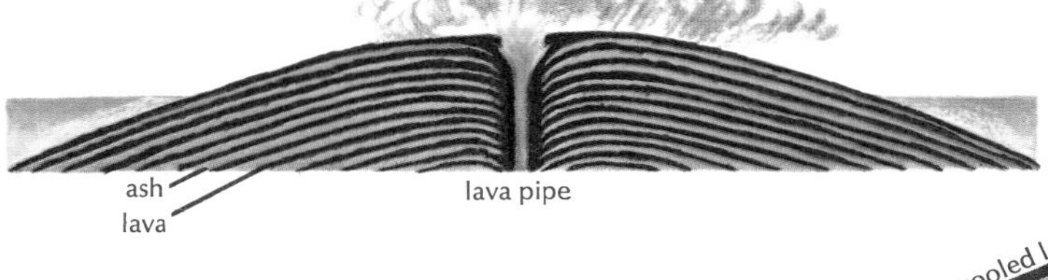

Figure 6 Strato Type Volcano

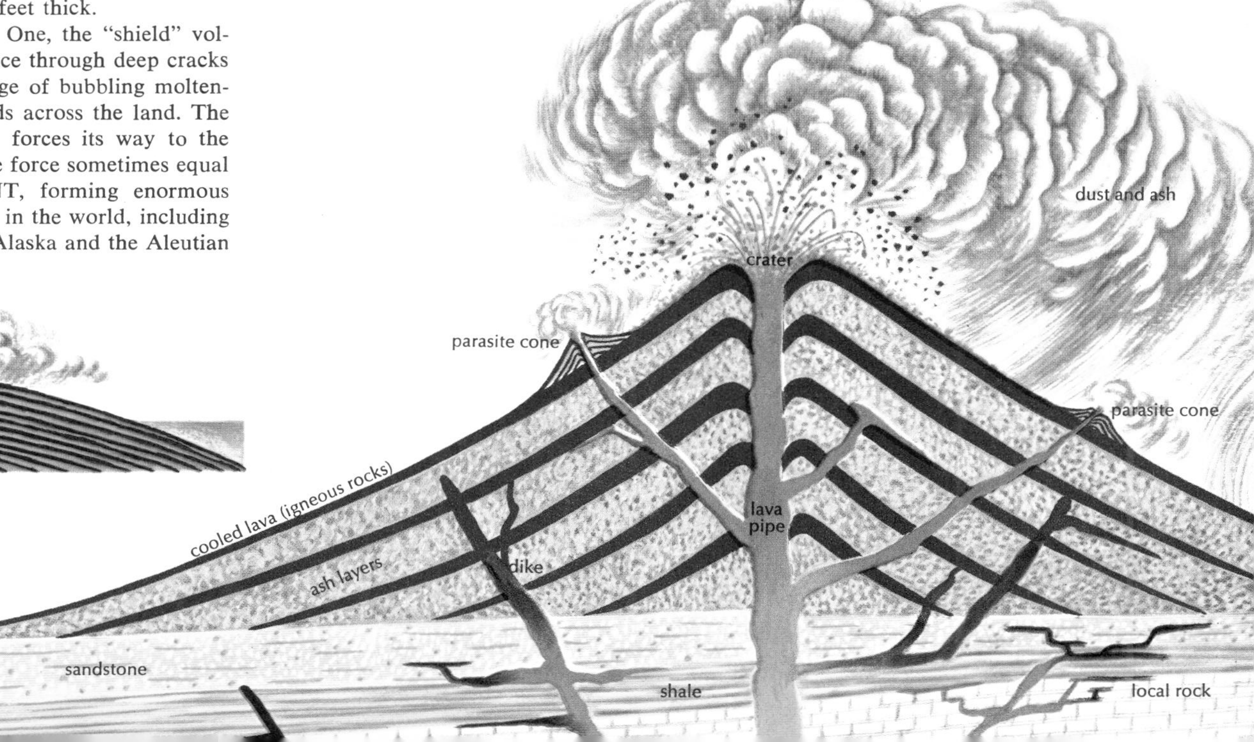

THE PALEOZOIC ERA

Comparatively little is known about the history of the earth during the 3 billion and more years of Precambrian time. Only with the beginning of the Paleozoic era, some 580 million years ago, have geologists been able to decipher in detail (thanks to the discovery of plentiful fossils of ancient living creatures) the records of the landforming that molded the planet. From this information it has been possible to prepare maps showing the earthly scene as it might have looked in those far-off days—a different yet still recognizable world.

The foundations of the North American continent had been firmly established when the Paleozoic era dawned. But it is generally believed among geologists that there was no Atlantic Ocean as we know it at this time. Along the present East Coast, there was probably a belt of land. In the west, much of the Pacific coastal area was deep under ocean water. Throughout this era great changes began to take place. Erosion lowered the land while the level of the ocean rose and washed over the continent again and again. The earth revolved on a different axis; it is believed the North Pole was located somewhere beyond Hawaii, and the equator lay across the United States. A tropical climate prevailed.

The land and sea areas of each geologic period have been pictorially mapped, based on the work of Erwin Raisz.

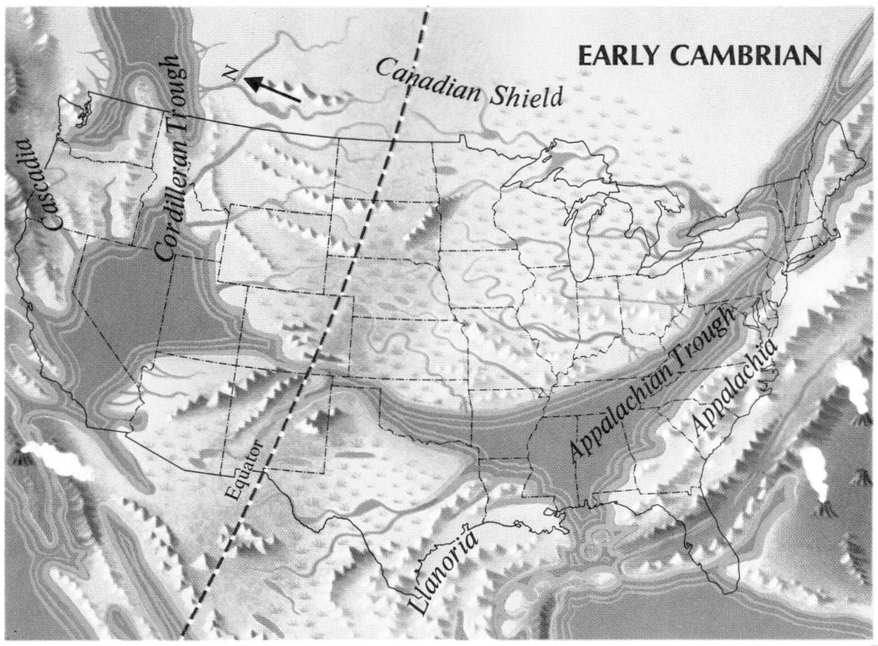

CAMBRIAN

During this period there were four ancient provinces in North America which ranged from large land areas to belts of scattered islands. The most important was the Canadian Shield to the north. A second, called Appalachia by scientists, of unknown extent, was situated east of the present Appalachian Mountains. The third, a land given the name of Llanoria, lay to the south in Louisiana, Texas and Mexico, while still another island belt, Cascadia, paralleled the Pacific Coast.

Along the eastern border of the continent was a depression termed the Appalachian Trough. Through it flowed ocean waters from the Caribbean to Newfoundland. On the west a similar trough, the Cordilleran, extended from Alaska through Nevada and Arizona into Mexico. These troughs were eventually to cause violent mountain-building revolutions, as the invading seas brought in vast quantities of sediment.

Plant life—such as the lime-secreting collenia, which existed only in the sea—had developed through some 2 billion years of Precambrian time. Chemical changes in the seawater around the beginning of the Cambrian period permitted the evolution of major groups of marine animals which could build skeletons and shells of lime. The crablike trilobite was the most important of these. As it changed form in developing over millions of years, its various fossil shapes help identify the different geologic periods in which the trilobite forms are found. Sponges, worms and jellyfish were also important types of the period.

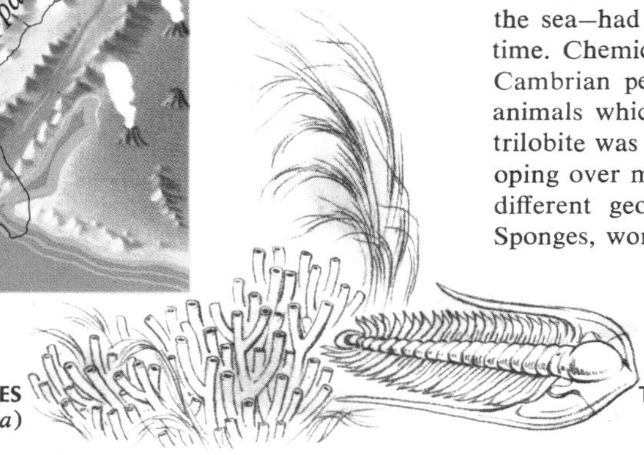

SPONGES (*Porifera*)   **TRILOBITE** (*Paradoxides*)

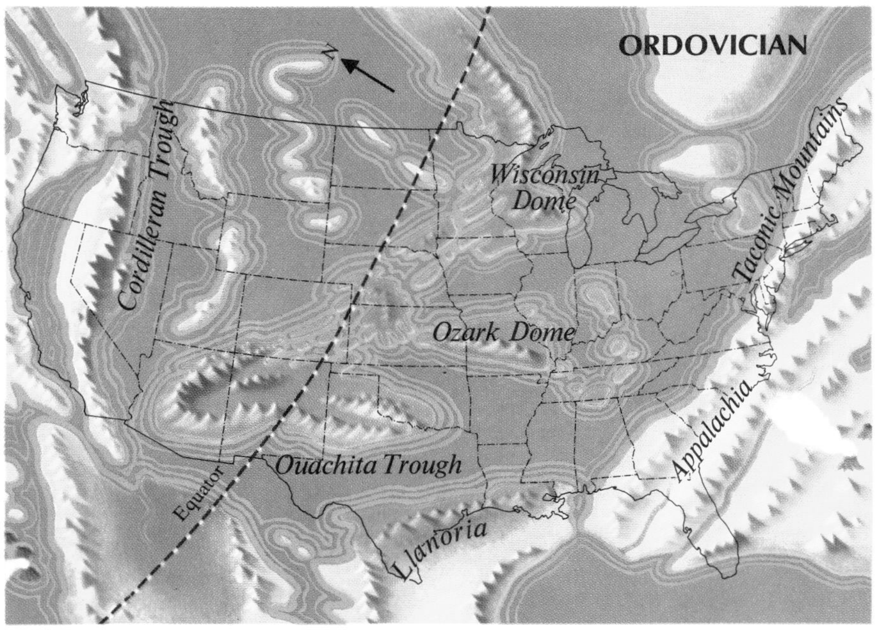

ORDOVICIAN

Beginning 510 million years ago, this period witnessed subtle changes on the North American continent. More of the crust was covered by shallow seas than at any other time. Here and there a number of islands still remained, such as the Wisconsin and Ozark domes (areas of moderate height). A new depression, the Ouachita, cut across the south, joining the Cordilleran with the Appalachian Trough.

The Ordovician saw widespread limestone deposits laid down in the open seas and extraordinary new living creatures came into being. A noteworthy development was the appearance of the first vertebrates (animals with backbones), in the form of bony, armored fish — the ostracoderms.

Toward the close of this period there was renewed uplift along the Appalachian belt, especially in the Taconic Mountains of New England.

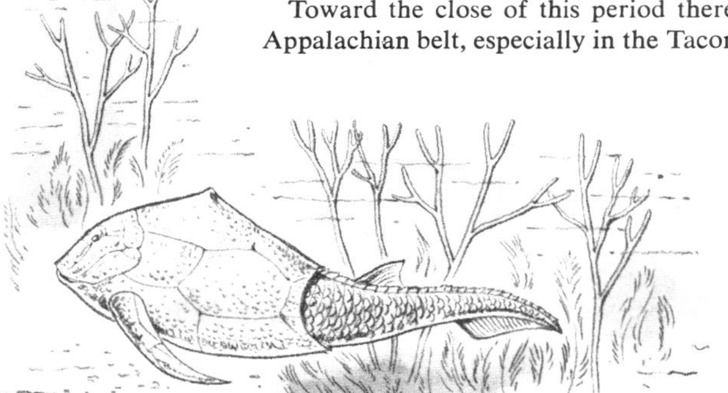

OSTRACODERM (*Pterichthys*)

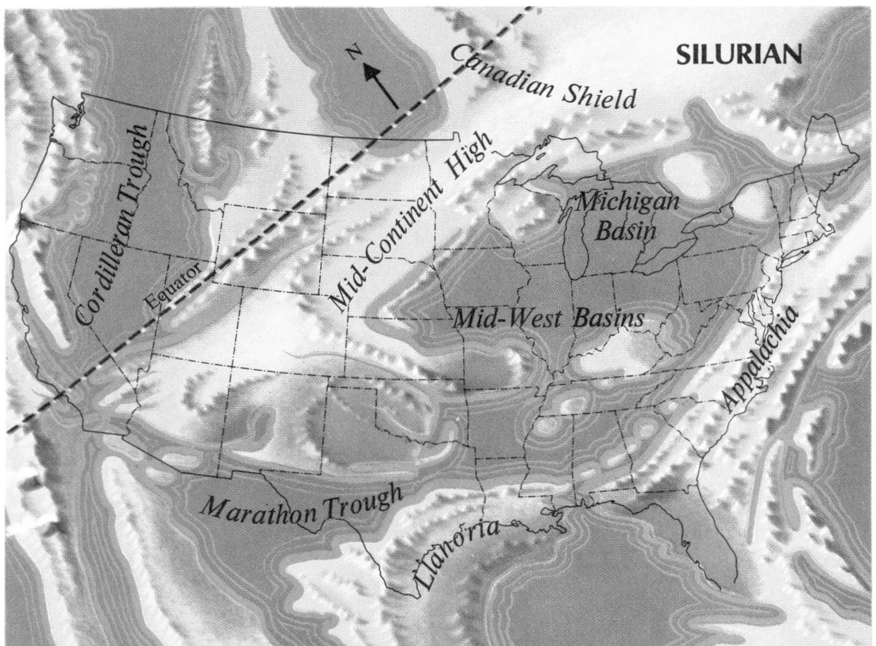

SILURIAN

This was the time of more mountain-building activities along the Appalachian belt. The great shallow seas that had flooded most of the United States receded somewhat and landforms reappeared. Most important was a "Mid-Continent High" that extended into the Southwest from the Canadian Shield. Some of the larger depressions became partly blocked off from the free circulation of the ocean, which turned them into dead, salty seas. This isolation brought about repeated evaporation, building up thick salt deposits, mainly sodium chloride (rock salt) and gypsum. Erosion attacked the new mountains from the east and the west, continuing to pile up thick sediments in the troughs.

No record exists of life on land, but a variety of marine invertebrates were developing, among them huge sea scorpions—the eurypterids, some reaching nine feet in length. Plant life—sea lilies, sponges, seaweeds and others—was becoming more varied in swamps and lakes.

By the end of the Silurian period most of the North American continent was above water.

CRINOIDS—Sea Lilies (*Eucalyptocrinus*)

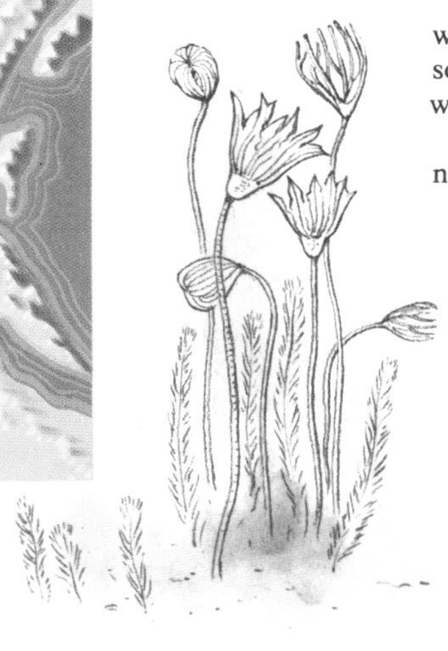

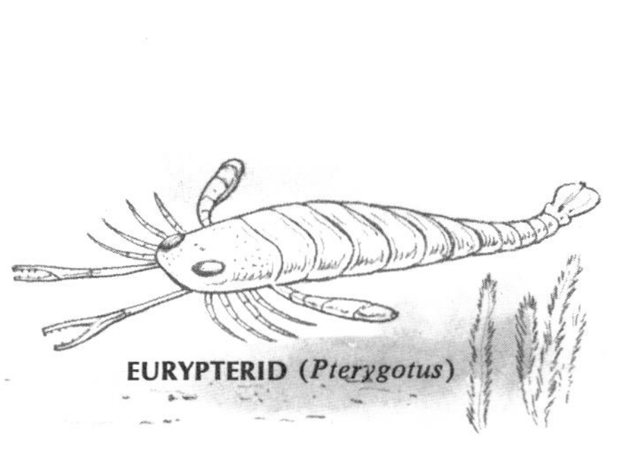

EURYPTERID (*Pterygotus*)

DEVONIAN

Across the broad, shallow basins of the mid-continent, the Devonian seas (to some extent like those of the Silurian) left large deposits of limestone. Coral reefs were widespread. Arches and domes jutted up as islands between the central lowlands. In the Appalachian belt there was renewed folding and uplift. The new mountains were immediately subjected to erosion, and quantities of sediment washed down to form vast deltas at the mouths of the mountain rivers. One of the most famous of these "fossil" deltas is found today in the Catskills of New York State, reaching westward for 100 miles from the Hudson.

Vegetation was developing rapidly on land. Fossils of large horsetails and seed ferns as high as 40 feet are still to be found in the Catskill delta, in Pennsylvania and elsewhere along the Appalachians.

At this time the shellfish (lobsterlike organisms, crabs, clams, mussels, sea snails and many others) had grown hard outer shells but no backbones. In the oceans, fish were evolving with great vigor, and this period is known as the Age of Fish. The placoderms, fish with well-developed jaws and bony head armor, appeared. Primitive sharks reached a length of 20 feet. With spinal columns and external muscle development, the amphibians evolved to the higher branches of vertebrates. Spiders and wingless insects also arrived.

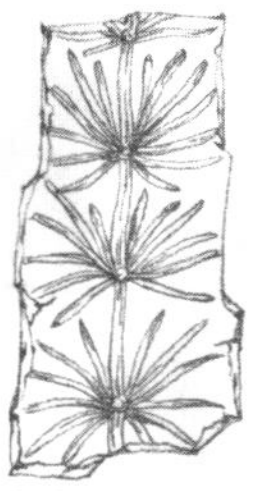

HORSETAIL
(*Annularia*)

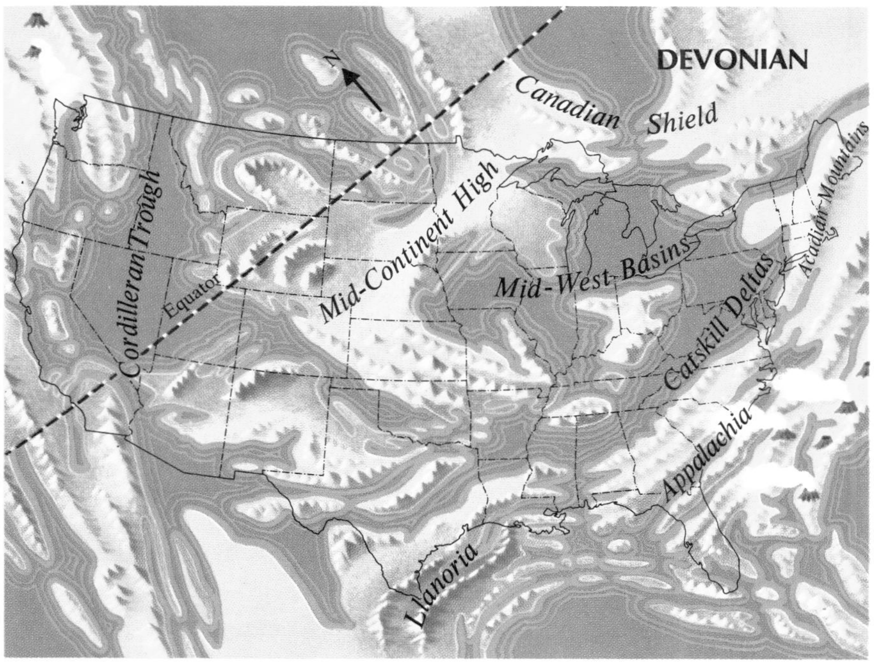

PLACODERM (*Dinichthys*)

CARBONIFEROUS

In North America, the Age of Coal is often divided into two parts—the earlier part, the Mississippian, which was best developed in the Midwest, and the latter half, the Pennsylvanian, found most extensively in the Appalachians.

Many of the vast, swampy basins and troughs that were formed from the Appalachians across the country to Illinois contained fresh water, where tropical ferns, cordaites and conifers 100 feet tall (notably pines) flourished in abundance. Again and again the ocean rose and fell, during the freezing and melting of a great ice age in the Southern Hemisphere. The swamps, repeatedly flooded by invading seas, were buried with sediments of sand, shale and limestone. This "cycle" burial of layers of lush tropical vegetation under heavy layers of sediment produced the future coal seams of Pennsylvania and West Virginia, the source of industrial wealth for the United States during the nineteenth and twentieth centuries.

Giant insects, some with wingspans of two or three feet, evolved in the swamps, as did amphibious beasts varying in size from small salamanders to creatures 15 feet in length. The first reptiles appeared at this time.

Great mountain-building events occurred in the late Carboniferous era, both in the East and in the far West. These are generally known as the Appalachian folding. The old troughs were now filled and uplifted. They became a mighty range of mountains, extending from Newfoundland to the Ouachitas and from Washington to Mexico. Much of the Midwest emerged from its former blanket of shallow seas.

CORDAITE TREE
(*Coniferophyta*)

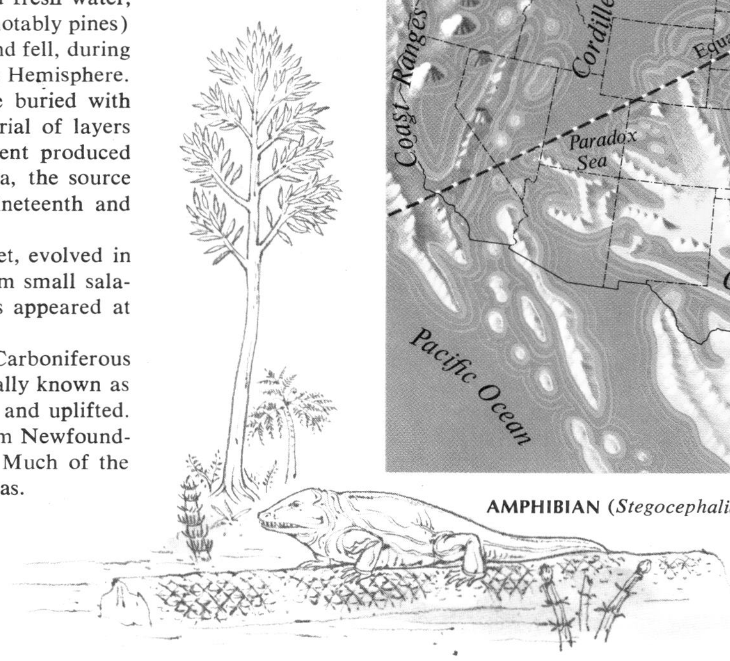

AMPHIBIAN (*Stegocephalian*)

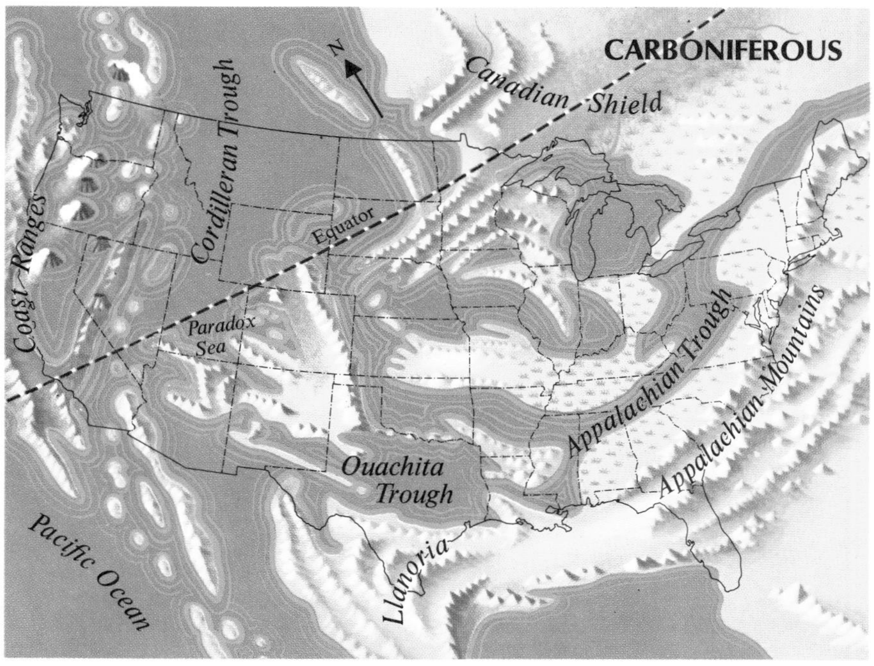

PERMIAN

The rugged Appalachian chain of mountains which extended from the Gulf of Mexico to eastern Canada reached its greatest height during the Permian period, and the east and central part of the country was never again invaded by seas. The period was highlighted by a shift of activity to the Southwest. Vast deposits of salt and gypsum were formed in shallow basins and gulfs of the prairie states. In the region of Oklahoma and western Texas, abundant plant life developed in warm seas, regions which would ultimately become great oil fields. Severe glaciation in the Southern Hemisphere had cooled the whole world, bringing about reduced evaporation from the seas and less rainfall. This resulted in drier interior lands, and sand dunes became common. Cooler seasons led to the development of deciduous trees, which drop their leaves to survive frost.

The fossils from that time are still dominated by the invertebrates, the trilobites and the simpler forms of shelly organisms. Pioneering strains of amphibians and reptiles appeared on the land, and insects multiplied greatly. Then a mysterious blight descended on the face of the earth. By the end of the Permian period more than half of the Paleozoic families, including trilobites, had simply died out, never to reappear.

The cause of such extinctions is still not understood. Many explanations have been advanced, such as climatic extremes, showers of ash or poisonous gases from volcanoes, natural parasites and radiation damage. Modern research suggests it had something to do with cosmic radiation during shifts in the polar axis, but scientists are not yet in agreement on this. This extraordinary change in the world's animal life prompted the early geologists to draw a boundary here—marking the end of the Paleozoic era and the beginning of the Mesozoic. A tree of this era that still survives today is the ginkgo, which has a fernlike leaf marking its transition from earlier forms.

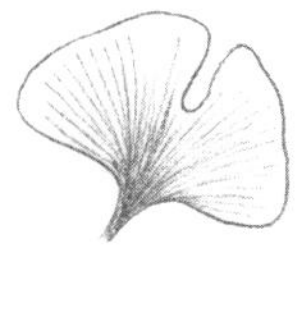

GINKGO LEAF
(*Ginkgo biloba*)

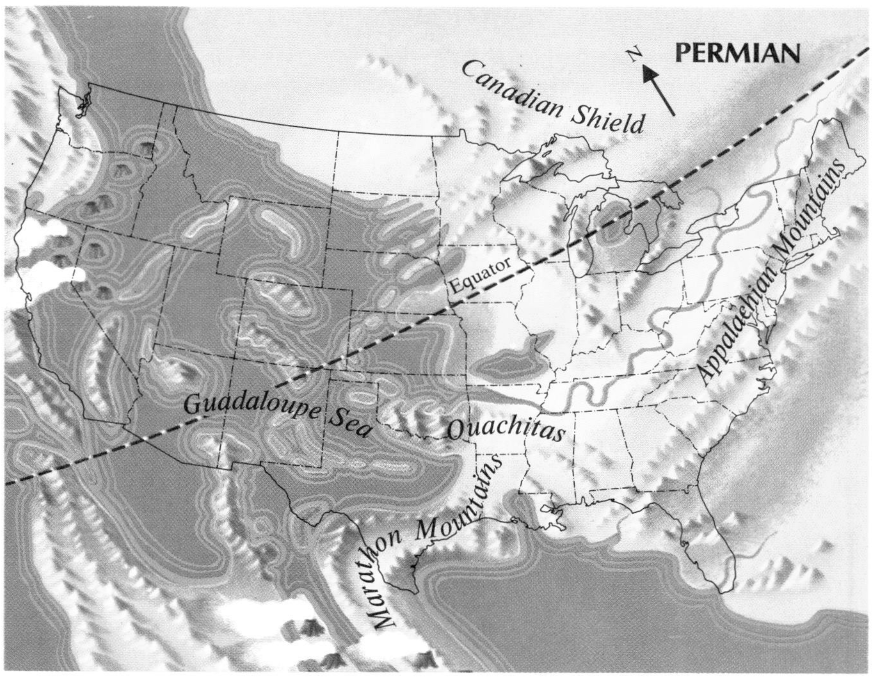

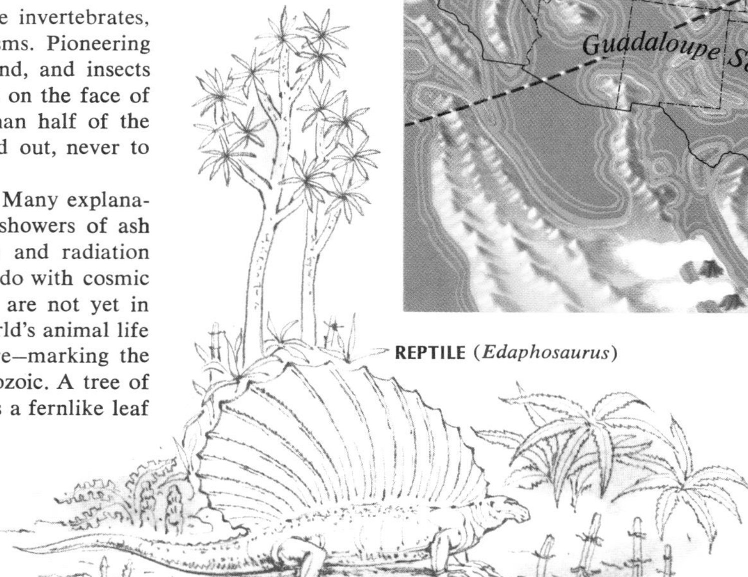

REPTILE (*Edaphosaurus*)

THE MESOZOIC ERA

The Mesozoic era began 225 million years ago. With the common Paleozoic forms of life almost completely gone, vigorous survivors began to build up new strains and the Age of Reptiles dominated the era. These outstanding beasts included the dinosaurs, as well as the incredible flying reptiles.

At this time the evolution of modern forms came about in warm climates: deciduous trees, flowering plants, the arrival of warm-blooded birds and the appearance of mammals.

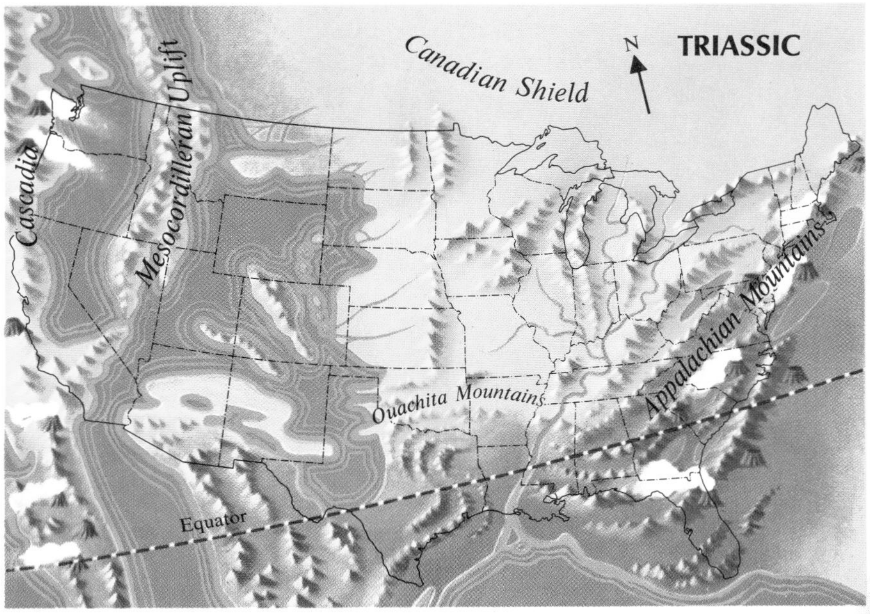

DINOSAUR
(*Coelophysis*)

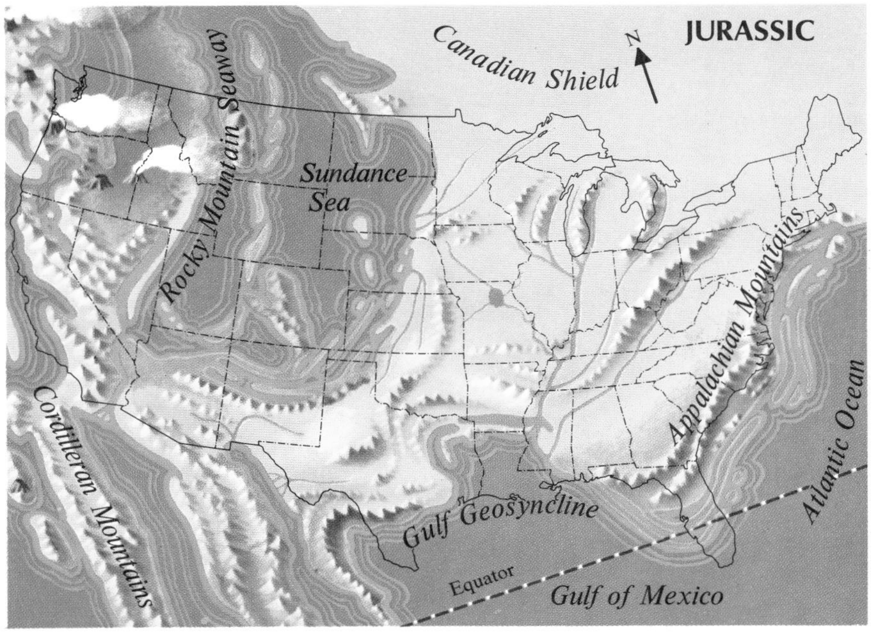

FISH LIZARD
(*Ichthyosaur*)

CYCAD
(*Cycadophyta*)

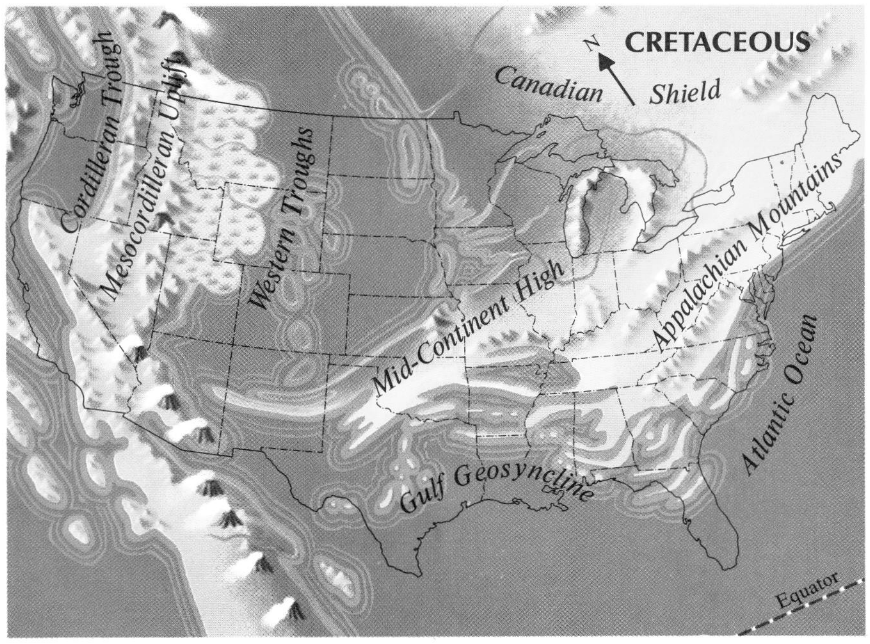

DINOSAUR
(*Triceratops*)

TRIASSIC

Although the Appalachian Mountains had been extensively worn by erosion, there were repeated stirrings in the roots 20 to 50 miles below the surface in the Triassic period. Great fractures occurred from one end of the mountain chain to the other. Some blocks of crustal rock rose, some tilted, while many subsided. Lake basins formed in the depressions. There was an extensive development of volcanoes as lava gushed up through fractures in the crust.

On the deltas and mudbanks roamed dinosaurs and in the waters swam a variety of fish that had changed from earlier periods. The placoderms of the Devonian had become extinct. Bony fishes and lung fishes were plentiful, as well as shark types. The climate was tropical, for the equator still lay across the United States with the North Pole in northeastern Asia. Iron oxides turned the soil rust-colored. Triassic sediments in North America are recognizable by their red color.

The Midwest became largely plains, and farther west, from Montana to Arizona and Texas, many lakes, deltas and swamps dotted the region. Here great thicknesses of red shale and sandstone, known as redbeds, collected. Here, too, existed dinosaurs, devouring the abundant plant life on the marshy shores. Primitive mammals, the earliest warm-blooded creatures, were evolving from the reptiles, but their fossils have not yet been found in the United States. A number of areas in the interior became extremely dry, creating deserts.

Farther west, from British Columbia down to Lower California, a great belt of deep troughs cut into the crust, parallel to the Pacific Ocean. Silts and clays began to fill the troughs. Erupting volcanoes along the mountainous coastline added ash and lava.

Sometime during the middle of the Triassic era, earthshaking stresses affected the entire margin of the Pacific Ocean. A tremendous elevation of land, called the Mesocordilleran uplift, occurred in the western United States. This widespread upward movement merged the scattered islands into a range of mountainous dry land extending from Idaho to California. The result was that the waters of the Pacific which earlier had access to the Midwest and Texas were cut off, and a new phase of the country's geologic history had begun.

JURASSIC

The Jurassic period was a time of worldwide mild conditions and lush vegetation. No ice sheets marked the poles. The equator crossed the southeastern United States and Mexico.

The Appalachians and the Midwest remained stable for a long period, developing big river systems and furnishing sediments to the basins in the West and South. The Jurassic marked the forming of the present Gulf of Mexico. Where there had been shallow, swampy plains and basins there now appeared a brand-new branch of the ocean. A deep trough also appeared around the southern border of the country, called the Gulf Geosyncline. Destined to fill gradually with sediment to a depth of 30,000 to 50,000 feet, it would provide one of the major oil fields in the world, as well as incomparable sources of salt and sulfur.

Another invasion of the sea came from the Arctic in the far Northwest, striking down through Canada to reach Wyoming and Utah. The southern part of this "Rocky Mountain Seaway" is named the Sundance Sea. Broad marshy areas bordered these inland seas, where pines, ferns and the cycads (ancestors of flowering plants) grew profusely. It was an ideal place for dinosaurs and some of the finest fossils of these "terrible lizards" have been discovered here. Flying reptiles ruled the air, and great swimmers, the ichthyosaurs, dominated the seas.

Volcanoes lined the western coast of the country, spewing out lava and ash, while in the interior plateaus severe deformative disturbances took place. This region provides most of the uranium ore that has helped make the Colorado Plateau famous. Today, some of the most colorful Jurassic rocks, deeply eroded, can be seen in Zion Canyon, Utah.

CRETACEOUS

Widespread deposits of white limestone from the shells and skeletons of small sea organisms were laid down during the Age of Chalk. This resulted in such formations as the cliffs of Dover in England, the Austin Chalk of Texas and others.

There were no glacial regions during the Cretaceous, and the oceans were universally warm. The sea level rose higher as the period advanced, so that water swept down from the Arctic to join up with the southern gulf, dividing the continent into two giant islands. The shores of this seaway continued to be the sites of broad deltas and swamps, the habitat of dinosaurs and primitive birdlife.

East of the Appalachians, the Atlantic Ocean overran the present coast, extending around to the mouth of the Mississippi and Texas. Little is known of the Atlantic itself at this time, but it is believed that it may have been much smaller, with land connections to western Europe.

From the end of the Jurassic to the early and middle Cretaceous, deep silting of 50,000 or more feet poured into the western troughs, which paralleled a line of volcanic islands. These troughs gradually sank into the earth's crust and the heat level within the compressed area rose, passing the melting point of over 2000°F. As a result, molten rock material was formed and made part of the core of what was to be the mighty Rocky Mountains. This ultimately cooled to become granite, as exposed today in Idaho, the Sierra Nevada and the ranges running down into Lower California.

Toward the close of the Mesozoic another curious blight descended on living things. The great reptiles and many other families died out, but mammals still remained, small and inconspicuous. Fossils of primitive marsupials, the pouch-bearing mammals, have been found in the United States. The *Hesperornis,* or Western Bird, chiefly a swimmer but also a great diver, and a small land-bird fossil have been discovered in Kansas. Plant life took a great stride forward with the evolution of the seed-bearing trees—the angiosperms—figs, magnolias, poplar and modern hardwoods such as the maple and oak. Fruit-producing forms of the grasses were the ancestors of our modern vegetables.

THE CENOZOIC ERA

The last of the five great eras, the Cenozoic, extends from 65 million years ago to the present time. Called the Age of Mammals, it is marked not only by the evolution of primitive vertebrates but also by the emergence of man, though not in the Western Hemisphere. It also saw the shaping of the Sierras and the Rocky Mountains.

The Cenozoic is divided into two periods, the Tertiary and the Quaternary. The first, the Tertiary, lasting more than 60 million years, has been subdivided into four parts called epochs: Eocene, Oligocene, Miocene and Pliocene. (Sometimes a fifth epoch, Paleocene, is used as an early part of the Eocene.)

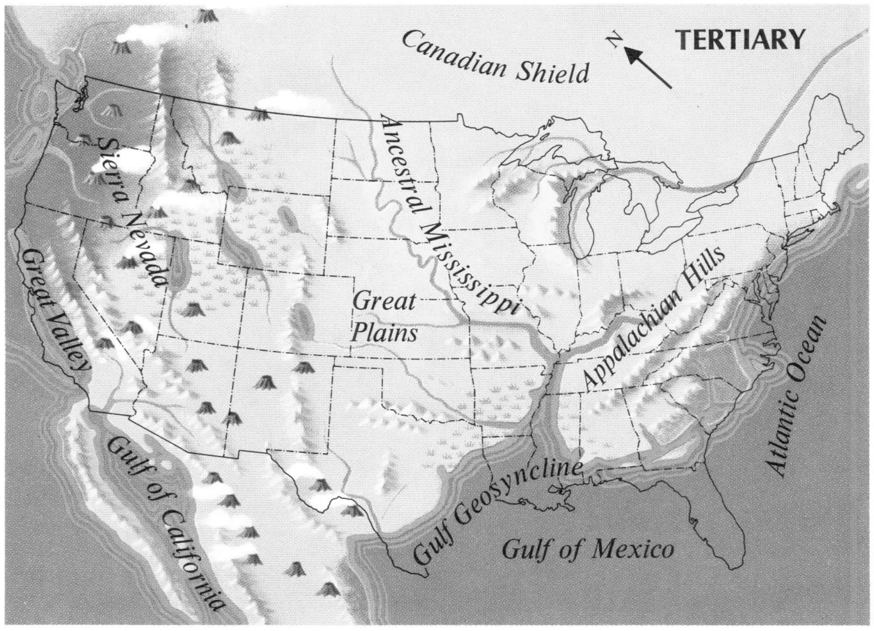

TERTIARY

EOCENE

During this epoch of 29 million years there was continued growth in the Rocky Mountains from Montana to New Mexico. A warm climate persisted in the interior of the United States, allowing tropical species of plants and trees to thrive. Flies, bees, butterflies and beetles were prevalent because of the numerous fruit-bearing plants.

Birdlife increased with the appearance of eagles, bitterns, grouse, cranes, sandpipers and owls, among others. Running flightless birds such as the seven-foot-tall *Diatryma* frequented Wyoming. The four-toed ancestor of the horse also made its home in Wyoming, as did numbers of freshwater fish. Hippopotamus-like mammals inhabited the swamps of the western United States.

The Eocene epoch saw the development of the first bats in the United States, and the first camels, as well as the most primitive primate, the lemur, the ancestor of monkeys and apes. In the adjacent ocean waters swam an early species of the whale.

OLIGOCENE

During the Oligocene epoch, vast amounts of sediment from the newly uplifted Rocky Mountains spread over the Great Plains. Along the Pacific Coast, there were tremendous new trenches from the Sacramento Valley to the Great Valley and on down to the Gulf of California. Much volcanic action took place, particularly in the Yellowstone Park area of Wyoming and in Colorado. On the Atlantic and Gulf coasts the seas partly withdrew from the land.

Fertile grasslands spread across the plains, providing food for such mammals as the three-toed horse *Mesohippus,* an animal that measured 40 inches in length, and the massive Brontops. During this time the early cat, dog and bear evolved, as did the beaver, mouse and rat.

MIOCENE

Many new basins were formed by the crustal stretching and fractures in the Rocky Mountain uplift. Volcanic action continued in the West with violent outpourings of lava in Washington, Idaho and Oregon. In the Columbia Plateau alone, 35,000 cubic miles of lava were poured out.

Around the eastern seaboard, from northern Maine to the Gulf of Mexico, there was repeated overflowing of the borders of the continent by a warm Atlantic Ocean. Subtropical climates prevailed in the United States, with considerable rainfall which stimulated the growth and spread of the maple, oak, poplar and other deciduous trees. The grasslands of the Great Plains flourished.

Mammals increased in number and variety. The shovel-tusked mastodon *Amebelodon* could be found, along with many other relatives of the elephant family. A pig the size of a hippopotamus inhabited the land, as did dogs as large as bears. There was a greater variety of birds in the air—including cormorants, plovers, parrots, kites. Sheep, goats, antelopes and cattle roamed far and wide.

About this time a land bridge formed between Asia and North America which brought about the exchange of animals. South America, however, was cut off from the north by ocean waters.

PLIOCENE

The great Cenozoic mountain building was climaxed in the United States with new upthrusts in the Rockies, the Sierra Nevada and other ranges. This vast folding no doubt had something to do with the climatic change of the Ice Age that followed. Cool weather replaced the humid subtropical climate that had prevailed. Present desert areas began to dry out and grasslands increased in extent. There was an abundance of marine invertebrates such as the pelecypods and gastropods.

Grass, including oats, rice and wheat, was perhaps the most important plant family that developed during the entire Tertiary period. It not only provided grazing for animals, but slowed down erosion and allowed soil to accumulate.

The mammals were now evolving with even greater rapidity, especially the grazing animals such as the horse. Warmth-loving primates disappeared from the North American continent while grass-eating animals became more abundant—antelopes, camels, horses, mastodons—as did the carnivorous mammals—bears, wolves and dogs.

LEMUR
(*Notharctus*)

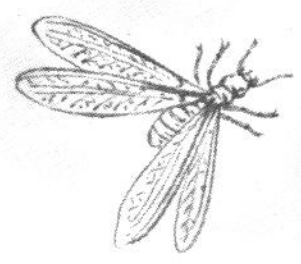

TERMITE
(*Isoptera*)

BRONTOPS
(*Titanothere*)

GIANT PIG
(*Dinohyus*)

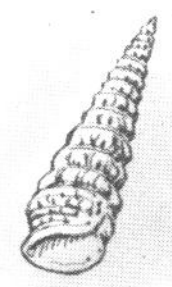

GASTROPOD
(*Cerithium*)

CAMEL
(*Procamelus*)

THE EVOLUTION OF THE HORSE

The evolution of the horse began in North America and Europe 50 million years ago with the appearance of the 12-inch-high dawn-horse or *Hyracotherium*. After 20 or more million years, descendants of *Hyracotherium* became extinct in Europe, while those in North America flourished. Here the *Mesohippus* (middle horse) developed about 30 million years ago. This dog-sized animal was succeeded by a number of strains which grew larger and swifter as they roamed the wide expanses of the great Western Plains, culminating (some 3 to 5 million years ago) in *Pliohippus*, the one-toed forerunner of the modern horse. (Since the days of the four-toed dawn-horse, the foot had undergone a gradual transformation into a single undivided hoof.)

When the Bering land bridge opened (7 to 26 million years ago), followed by the Panama land bridge (3 million years ago), horses migrated to Asia and South America. Then, probably 10,000 to 15,000 years ago, the horse mysteriously vanished from the Western Hemisphere, as other mammals—the mastodon and mammoth, the dire wolf and the saber-toothed tiger—had, at various periods. It has been conjectured that the horse was wiped out by plague, by the glaciation of the Ice Age or by primitive hunters.

Only when the Spanish explorers arrived in the early 1500's were horses reintroduced to North America, where they soon became wild again.

PLIOHIPPUS

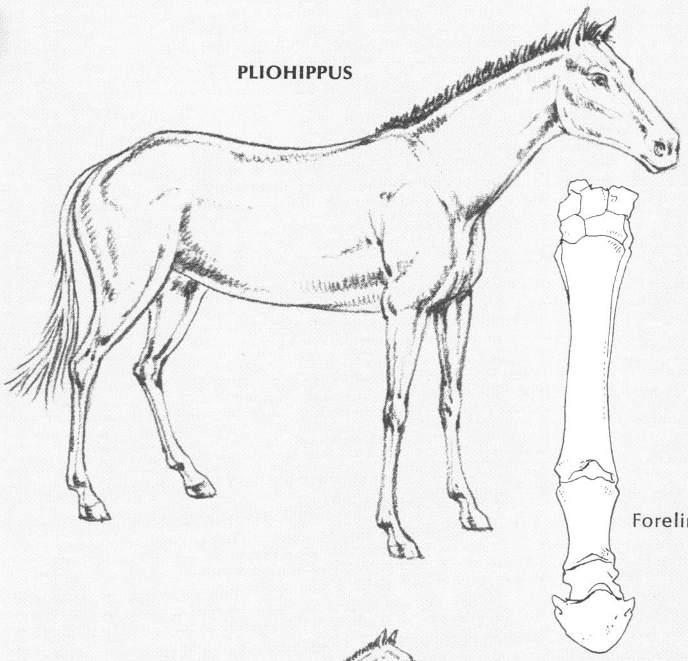

Forelimb

MESOHIPPUS

Forelimb

HYRACOTHERIUM
(*Dawn-horse*)

Forelimb

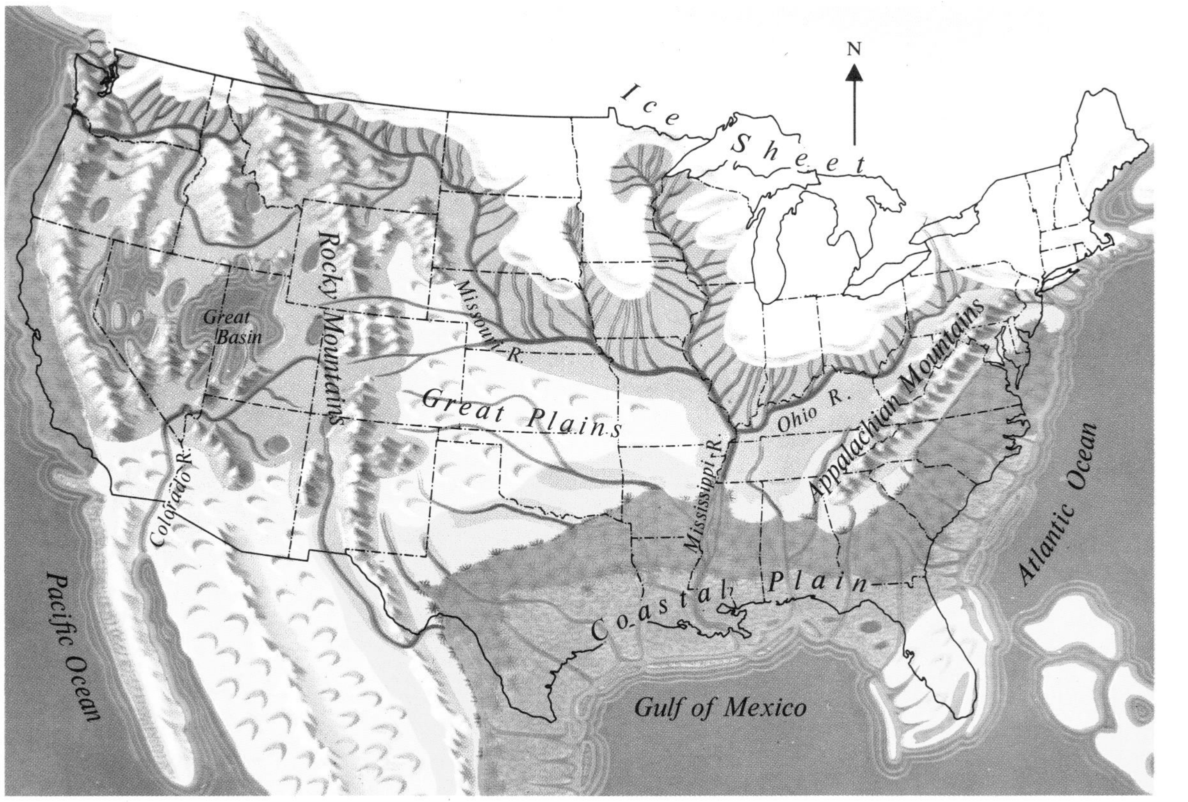

DEVELOPMENT OF THE GREAT LAKES

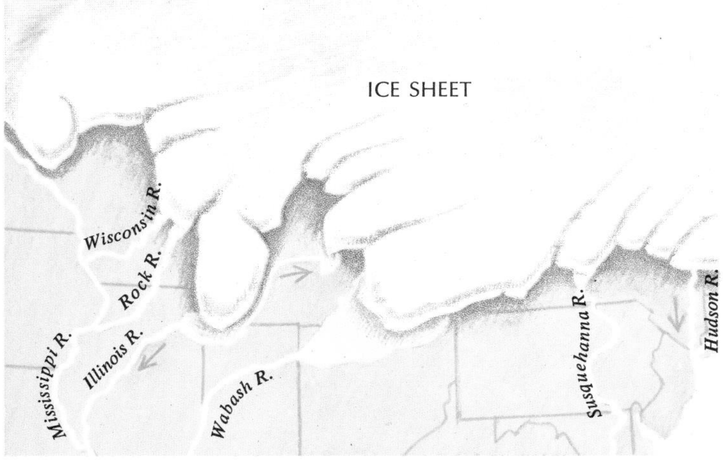

11,000 B.C.: The ice sheet that had covered the land (later to be occupied by the Great Lakes) began to retreat. A network of rivers drained southward.

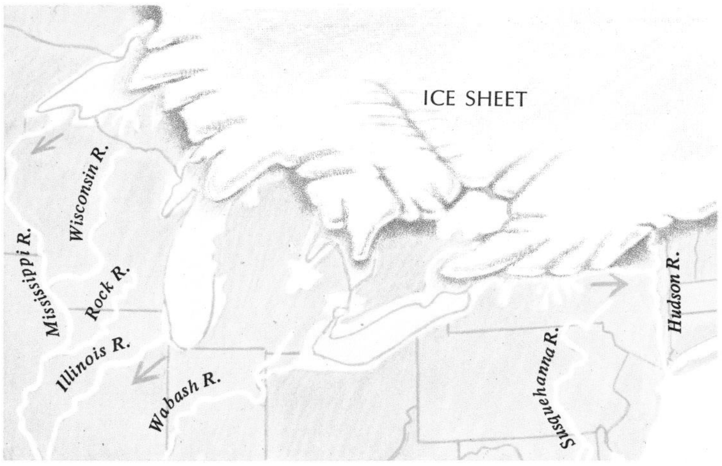

9000 B.C.: The glacial retreat continued, and vast quantities of released water filled the depressions scooped out during the ice advance. At this period, the partially formed lakes had a greater expanse than now.

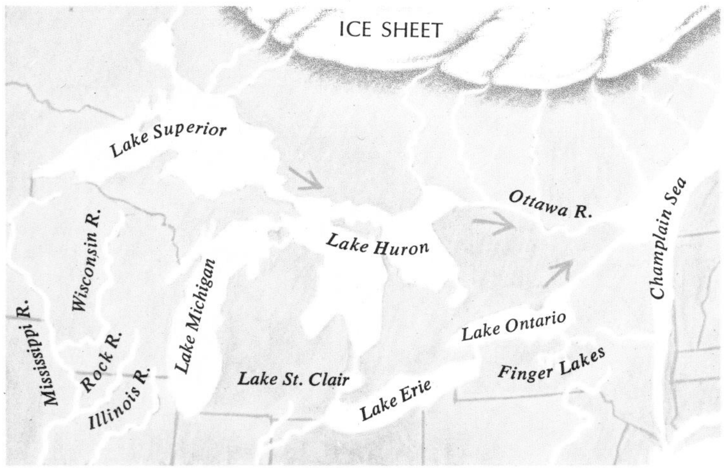

2000 B.C.: With the area completely free of ice, the shape of the lakes and the river system began to take on the form of the present-day Great Lakes.

MAMMOTH
(*Mammuthus*)

SABER-TOOTHED TIGER
(*Smilodon*)

SLOTH
(*Megatherium*)

BISON
(*Bison antiquus*)

QUATERNARY – *THE ICE AGE*

Ice ages seem to have occurred once every 200 million years or so in the geologic past. The latest, the Quaternary Ice Age, is still on hand, as the ice conditions of Greenland and Antarctica will attest.

During the late Tertiary period, there was a shift of the earth's poles from eastern Siberia and the southern Indian Ocean to their present positions. This gave rise to a series of important events. With the South Pole in the great mountainous Antarctic continent, the ordinary rainfall and precipitation turned to snow and then ice. The snowfields built up into glaciers and, growing larger, the ice spread out over the lowlands.

The drop in sea level, because of the freezing of Antarctica, caused all the land areas to become relatively higher and wider. In this way alone, the North American continent gained 2,200,000 square miles.

PLEISTOCENE

In the early part of the Pleistocene epoch of the Quaternary period, the ice in North America was limited to the mountains of Alaska, the Rockies, the Canadian Arctic and Greenland. But, during the last half million years, continental glacier ice came down across the prairies, the last advance reaching to the present position of New York City and a line from Long Island out to Nantucket.

With the advance of ice across the plains two important changes took place. The usual vegetation—prairie, conifer forest, broad-leaved forest, subtropical forest—shifted to the south. The tundra belt with its areas of marshy muskeg was pushed from northern Canada down to the latitudes of St. Louis and Philadelphia. The tropical belt was forced out of the country completely and, instead, a cold, semidesert zone (rather like the Gobi Desert of Mongolia) extended at certain times from Nebraska to Florida.

Until the coming of the continental ice from Canada, the majority of streams and rivers in the northeastern part of the United States flowed northward into the St. Lawrence and Hudson Bay. Streams as far west as Montana and the Dakotas also moved in a northerly direction. The arrival of the ice shut off the northward flow of most of these rivers, such as the Ohio, which was turned southward into the present Ohio-Mississippi system. However, the Red River in Minnesota still flows in a northerly direction, as does the mighty St. Lawrence.

Before the advent of the glaciers, the land present in the Great Lakes area was devoid of any great bodies of water. The force of the moving ice gouged out mammoth scoops from soil and rock. These vast areas were filled with water during the retreat of the ice sheet, thereby forming the Great Lakes system (see diagrams, left). Niagara Falls was created at this time.

The low sea level of the glacial stages turned the Bering Strait into a dry-land connection with Siberia. North American horses strayed across, spread over Asia and finally reached Europe, while African and Eurasian animals like the woolly mammoth, the mastodon and the bison came to North America, together with man (see "The First Americans," pages 74, 75). Eventually, the extreme cold caused the ultimate demise of the North American mastodon and mammoth. Bones, teeth and tusks of these enormous animals are found across the continent in sediments dated as recently as 5000 years ago.

Some animals migrated to South America over the Panama land bridge which opened up during the latter part of the Pleistocene epoch. Among those that traveled into the Southern Hemisphere were the saber-toothed tiger, the camel, dogs, peccaries and the many forms of rodents. Reversing the migration, giant ground sloths left their native habitat and traveled to North America.

Each time the continental ice front withdrew, there was general melting, and floods scoured out deeper valleys than existed before. In the Great Basin of Utah, and numerous other smaller basins in the Rocky Mountains from Nevada to Colorado, the water from the melting ice and snow could not run off but built up into immense numbers of freshwater lakes. These "pluvial lakes" have now dried up completely or have been reduced to the salty brine found in the Great Salt Lake today.

Behind the retreating glacial ice, vast belts of "till" were left. Till consists of the scooped-up soil and scoured rock, pushed and scraped off the land surface as the ice advanced. Much of it became frozen into the ice and many boulders were carried as far as 1000 miles from their source regions. Some boulders in the till on Long Island, for example, are recognized as having come down from eastern Canada. The ridges humped up around the ice front are called moraines.

The last general melting began about 17,000 years ago, slowly at first and with numbers of small advances. Around the borders of the melting ice, bodies of water were formed similar to the Great Lakes. The Mississippi, the Susquehanna, the Hudson and the St. Lawrence were filled with vast torrents of floodwater that at times muddied and clouded half the North Atlantic Ocean.

By 10,000 years ago about half the continental ice was gone and profound warming changes affected the world. Many plants survived the Ice Age by migrating to southern regions, while during mild interglacial stops, some southern flora, such as the cypress, moved northward. Pines and other conifers spread under the cold conditions.

HOLOCENE

The last 10,000 years of the Quaternary are known as the Holocene epoch, or informally as the Recent or postglacial stage. Some 6000 years ago the average mean temperature in the mid-latitudes had risen 5°F. above the present level. Since then it has varied, and is gradually cooling off. A series of "little Ice Ages" occurred about 3000 years ago and also during the Middle Ages. These lasted a few decades before warmer conditions returned. Present indications are that the world is now probably partway toward the next great glacial phase, which is expected in about 10,000 years.

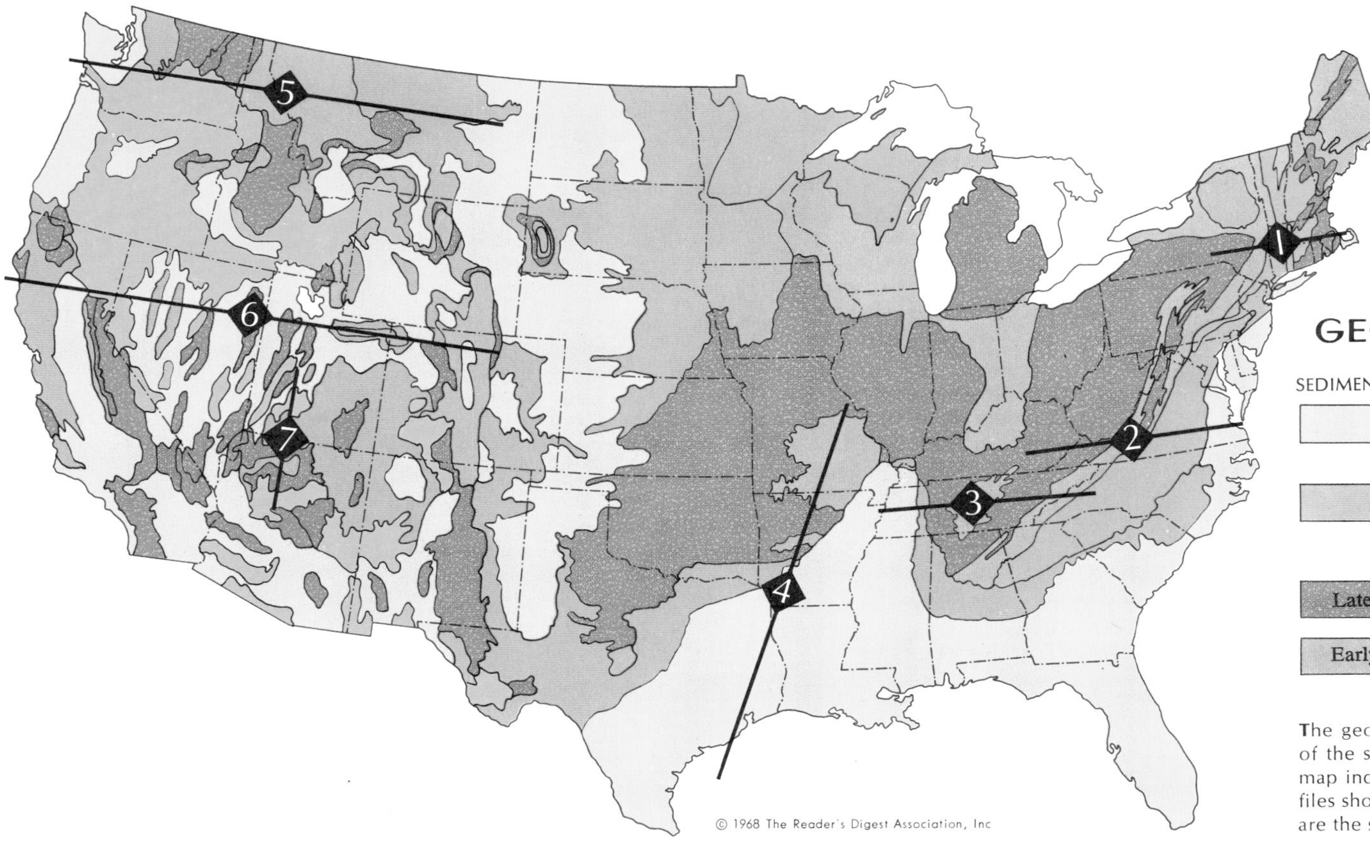

GEOLOGIC FORMATIONS
SEDIMENTARY ROCKS
Cenozoic
Quaternary
Tertiary
Mesozoic
Cretaceous
Jurassic
Triassic
Paleozoic
Late
Permian
Carboniferous
Devonian
Early
Silurian
Ordovician
Cambrian
IGNEOUS (INTRUSIVE & METAMORPHIC) ROCKS
Post Precambrian
Precambrian
VOLCANIC ROCKS
(Mostly Cenozoic)
The geologic map at left gives the locations (by number) of the seven cross sections of land illustrated below. The map indicates the surface outcrops of rock while the profiles show the land formations in depth. Identifying colors are the same in both cases.
© 1968 The Reader's Digest Association, Inc
1 The Catskills eastward to the Atlantic, sculptured during the Ice Age.
WEST
EAST
CATSKILLS
HUDSON RIVER
BERKSHIRES
BOSTON BASIN
Devonian
Ordovician
Paleozoic
Precambrian
Triassic
Precambrian
Paleozoic
Post Precambrian
Carboniferous
2 Appalachians to Chesapeake Bay.
WEST
EAST
APPALACHIAN PLATEAU
VALLEY AND RIDGE
GREAT VALLEY
BLUE RIDGE
PIEDMONT
FALL BELT
COASTAL PLAIN
Paleozoic
Precambrian
Cretaceous
Tertiary
3 Tennessee: from the Mississippi Valley to the folded rocks of the Great Smokies.
WEST
EAST
MISSISSIPPI VALLEY
NASHVILLE DOME
CUMBERLAND PLATEAU
GREAT VALLEY
GREAT SMOKIES
Tertiary
Cretaceous
Paleozoic
Precambrian
4 The Gulf of Mexico in Texas northeast to the Missouri.
SOUTH
NORTH
GULF OF MEXICO
EAST TEXAS PLAIN
RED RIVER
OUACHITA MOUNTAINS
ARKANSAS VALLEY
OZARK PLATEAU
MISSOURI RIVER
Tertiary
Cretaceous
Paleozoic
Paleozoic
Precambrian
5 Pacific Ocean, at Puget Sound, east through Montana.
WEST
EAST
VANCOUVER ISLAND
OLYMPIC RANGE
PUGET SOUND
CASCADE MOUNTAINS
COLUMBIA PLATEAU
NORTHERN ROCKIES
GREAT PLAINS
Post Precambrian
Tertiary
Cenozoic Lava
Post Precambrian
Cretaceous
6 The Pacific Coast north of San Francisco east to the Front Range north of Denver.
WEST
EAST
PACIFIC OCEAN
COAST RANGES
GREAT VALLEY
SIERRA NEVADA
GREAT BASIN
GREAT SALT LAKE
WASATCH MOUNTAINS
COLORADO PLATEAU
ROCKY MOUNTAINS– FRONT RANGE
Mesozoic
Tertiary
Post Precambrian
Paleozoic
Precambrian
Tertiary
Paleozoic
Paleozoic
7 Arizona due north across the Grand Canyon into Utah.
SOUTH
NORTH
GRAND CANYON
COCONINO PLATEAU
ZION CANYON
PINK CLIFFS
VERMILION CLIFFS
LAVA PLATEAU
KAIBAB PLATEAU
BRYCE CANYON
Tertiary
Paleozoic
Precambrian
Mesozoic

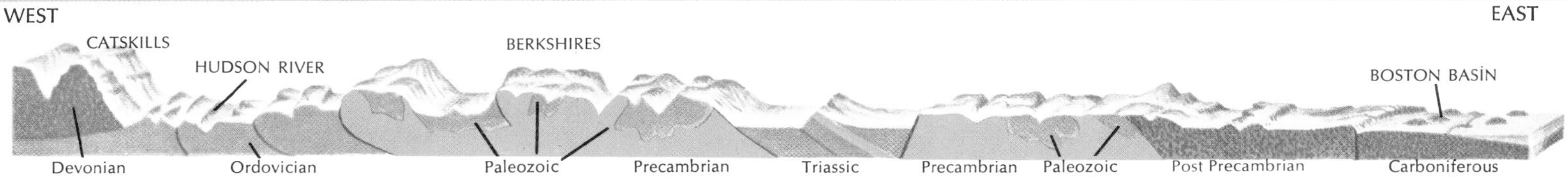

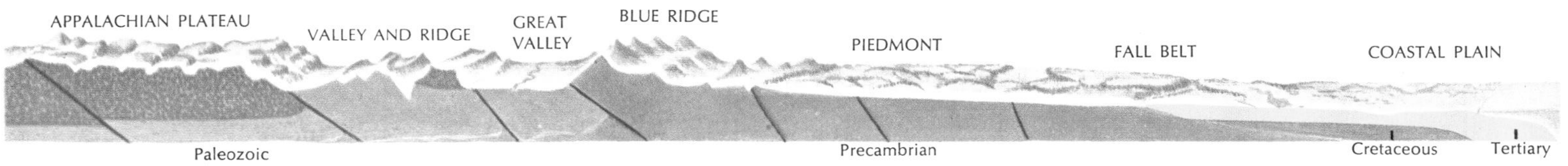

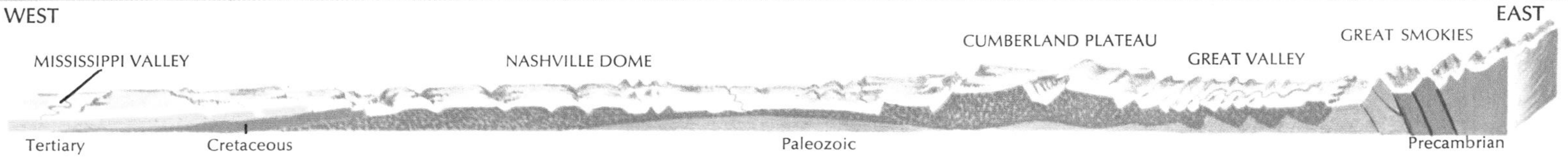

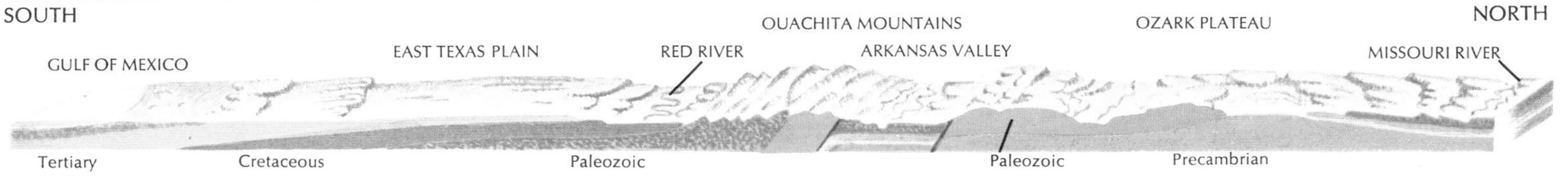

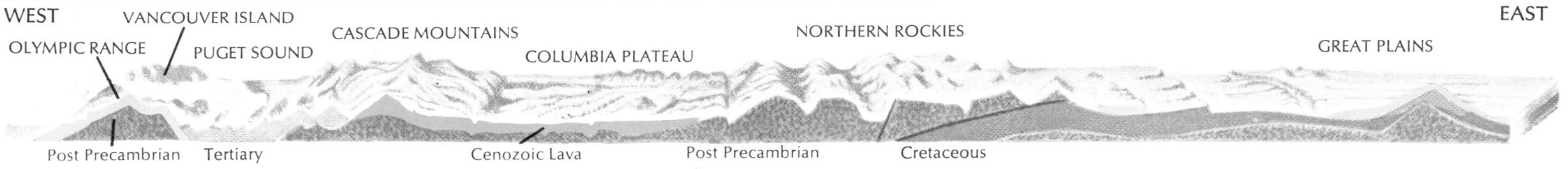

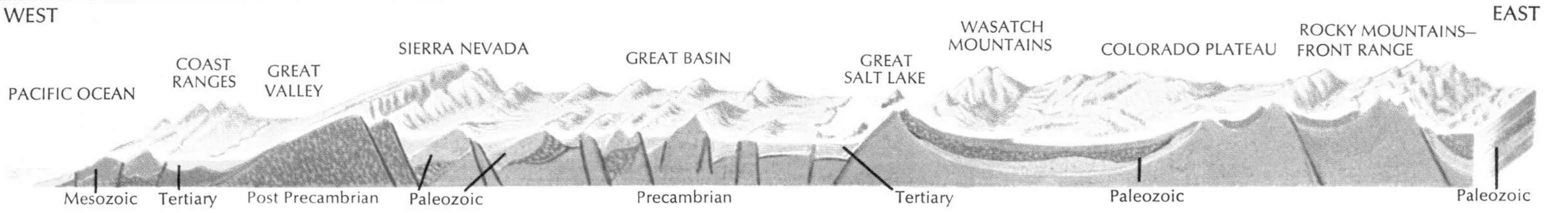

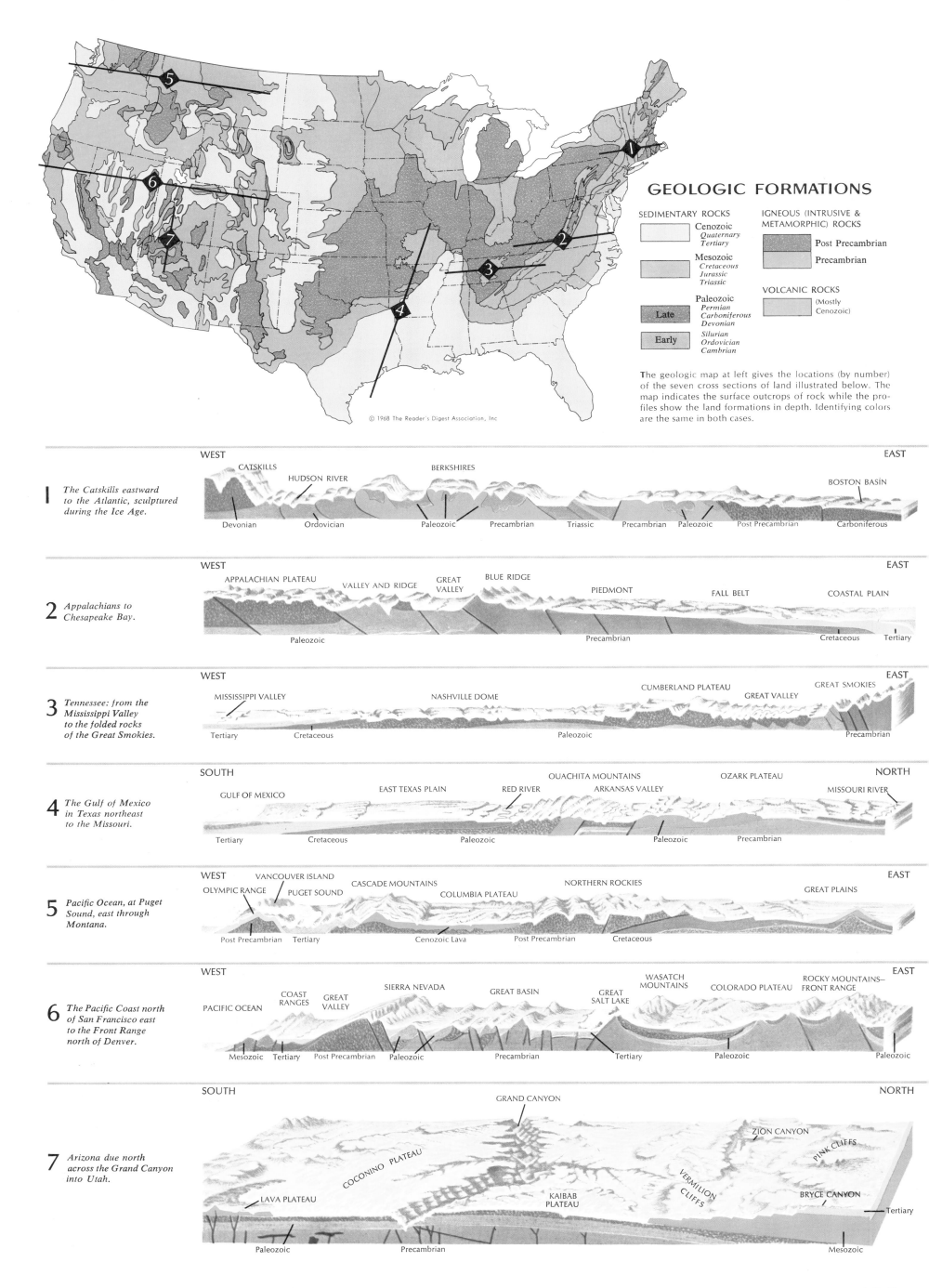

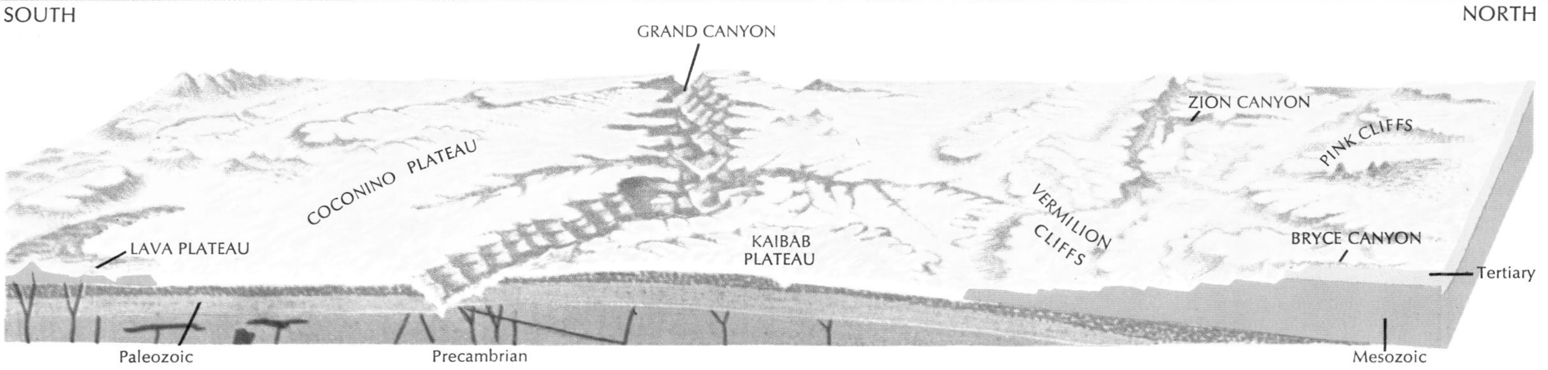

NATIONAL AND STATE PARKS

America's vast wilderness, a challenge to our forefathers, was looked on as a wild beast to be subdued. In the 80 years after 1790, a primeval continent was beaten into submission as 4 million people became 40 million. By 1872 that wilderness was a remnant, but a group of farsighted men banded together in the hope of preserving some still-untouched areas. Their success was the establishment of Yellowstone National Park and it was followed by more than 30 other sections which have been saved by Federal protection and management. The pressures of a population nearing 200 million bring continual threats of encroachment not only on these national treasures but on the protected territory of several hundred state parks. Americans have learned that the remaining wilderness is a friend, not an adversary, and that it must be husbanded if it is to continue to exist for present and future generations.

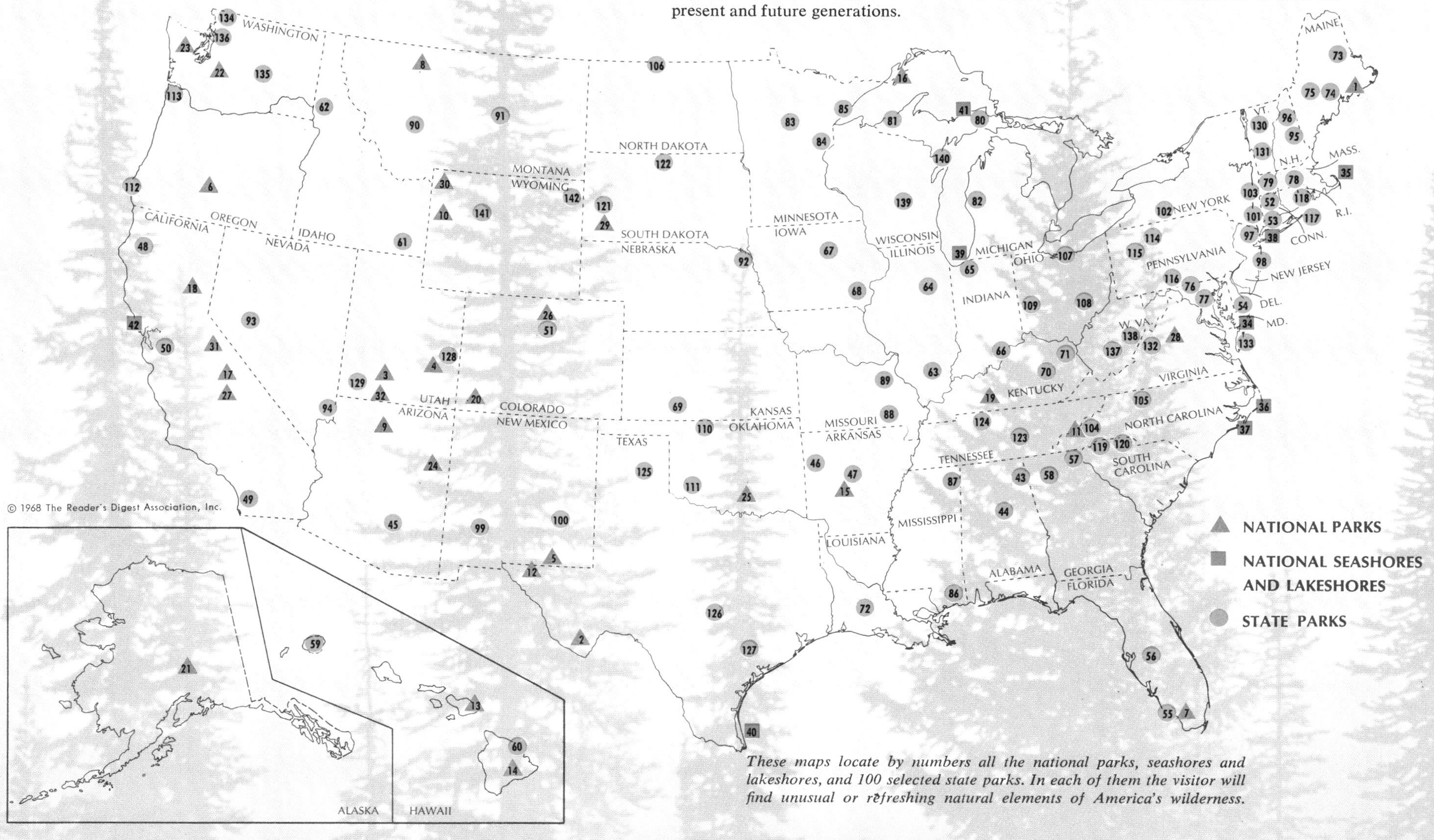

These maps locate by numbers all the national parks, seashores and lakeshores, and 100 selected state parks. In each of them the visitor will find unusual or refreshing natural elements of America's wilderness.

NATIONAL PARKS

1. *Acadia (Maine).* Mount Desert Island, Schoodic Peninsula and half of Isle au Haut with rugged cliffs and shore. Established 1919, named 1929: 41,634 acres.

2. *Big Bend (Tex.).* Desert and mountain scenery, enclosed in a bend of the Rio Grande. Established 1944: 708,221 acres.

3. *Bryce Canyon (Utah).* Contains unusual and unique forms of erosion, highly colored and grotesque. Established 1928: 36,010 acres.

4. *Canyonlands (Utah).* Wild and towering spires, rocks and mesas, some reaching more than 7800 feet. Established 1964: 257,640 acres.

5. *Carlsbad Caverns (N. Mex.).* Caves and underground chambers make up one of the largest subsurface parks. Established 1930: 46,753 acres.

6. *Crater Lake (Oreg.).* A clear, deep lake has formed in the crater of a once active volcano. Established 1902: 160,290 acres.

7. *Everglades (Fla.).* Subtropical, partially swampy wilderness is the habitat of alligators, rare birds and other animals. Established 1947: 1,400,533 acres.

8. *Glacier (Mont.).* Glaciers, lakes and mountain scenery located high in the Rocky Mountain country. Established 1910: 1,013,029 acres.

9. *Grand Canyon (Ariz.).* Extends 105 miles along the Colorado River; width ranges from 4 to 18 miles; one mile deep. Established 1919: 673,575 acres.

10. *Grand Teton (Wyo.).* Rugged 13,000-foot peaks tower over winter feeding grounds of our largest elk herd. Established 1929: 310,350 acres.

11. *Great Smoky Mountains (N.C. and Tenn.).* At least 130 native American tree species cover rolling hills; massive peaks. Established 1934: 512,674 acres.

12. *Guadalupe Mountains (Tex.).* Extensive fossil deposits and limestone reefs, some of the greatest in the world. Authorized 1966: 77,582 acres.

13. *Haleakala (Hawaii).* Contains the 10,023-foot-high dormant volcano of Haleakala and its colorful crater. Established 1961: 26,403 acres.

14. *Hawaii Volcanoes (Hawaii).* Active craters and fissures, superb tropical vegetation with rare species. Established 1961: 220,345 acres.

15. *Hot Springs (Ark.).* Some 47 hot mineral springs —a health as well as a scenic attraction. Established 1921: 1035 acres.

16. *Isle Royale (Mich.).* This island in Lake Superior is the home of a large moose herd that roams the wilderness. Established 1940: 539,347 acres.

17. *Kings Canyon (Calif.).* Mountain wilderness encloses two large canyons of the Kings River. Groves of giant sequoias are within park. Established 1940: 460,331 acres.

18. *Lassen Volcanic (Calif.).* Contains the most recently erupting volcano in the continental United States. Last eruption in 1917. Established 1916: 106,934 acres.

19. *Mammoth Cave (Ky.).* Underground passages, pits and domes and a river 360 feet below the surface. Fully established 1941: 51,354 acres.

20. *Mesa Verde (Colo.).* Well-preserved and valuable cliff houses and relics of high Indian culture (see pages 74, 75). Established 1906: 52,074 acres.

21. *Mount McKinley (Alaska).* Mountains, one of which is the highest in North America, provide a home for bears, wolves, moose and other wildlife. Established 1917: 1,939,493 acres.

22. *Mount Rainier (Wash.).* An ancient volcano which is covered with thick forests and brilliantly flowering meadows. Established 1899: 241,983 acres.

23. *Olympic (Wash.).* A superb rain forest which contains towering trees and large numbers of giant ferns. Established 1938: 896,599 acres.

24. *Petrified Forest (Ariz.).* Includes part of the Painted Desert and large natural exhibits of petrified wood. Established 1962: 94,189 acres.

25. *Platt (Okla.).* Numbers of cold mineral springs and several bromide springs. Established 1906: 912 acres.

26. *Rocky Mountain (Colo.).* Has 107 named peaks which tower over 10,000 feet; numerous glacial lakes. Established 1915: 262,324 acres.

27. *Sequoia (Calif.).* Huge groves of giant sequoia trees up to 4000 years old, probably the world's oldest living objects. Established 1890: 386,863 acres.

28. *Shenandoah (Va.).* Contains a portion of the Skyline Drive, which traverses beautiful timberland. Established 1935: 212,303 acres.

29. *Wind Cave (S. Dak.).* Limestone caverns make up the underground section of this park in the Black Hills. Established 1903: 28,059 acres.

30. *Yellowstone (Wyo., Mont., Idaho).* The first of the national parks, it has 3000 hot springs and geysers. Established 1872: 2,221,773 acres.

31. *Yosemite (Calif.).* Includes gorges, cliffs, three groves of giant sequoias and numerous breathtaking waterfalls. Established 1890: 760,951 acres.

32. *Zion (Utah).* Colorful canyon and mesa country including fabulous, vertical-walled Zion Canyon. Established 1919: 147,035 acres.

33. *Virgin Islands (U.S.V.I.—not shown).* On island of St. John, the forests, once destroyed, have again covered the area. Established 1956: 15,150 acres.

NATIONAL SEASHORES AND LAKESHORES

34. *Assateague Island (Va. and Md.).* Sand beaches and hillocks on which live the Chincoteague ponies, wild descendants of horses which escaped during the early colonial period. Authorized 1965: 30,182 acres.

35. *Cape Cod (Mass.).* Ocean beaches, dunes, freshwater ponds, woods and marshes. Authorized 1961: 44,600 acres.

36. *Cape Hatteras (N. C.).* Beaches which take in Pea Island Wildlife Refuge (5846 acres). Established 1953: 28,500 acres.

37. *Cape Lookout (N. C.).* Land and water which include Core and Shackeford Banks and Portsmouth Island. Authorized 1966: 30,000 acres.

38. *Fire Island (N. Y.).* Dunes and beach sand which provide shelter for part of the south coast of Long Island. Established 1964: 19,311 acres.

39. *Indiana Dunes (Ind.).* Sand dunes along Lake Michigan; partly forested, the dunes have scientific interest and offer scenic vistas. Authorized 1966: 8700 acres.

40. *Padre Island (Tex.).* Extends 80 miles along the Gulf coast, home of many wild birds and marine creatures. Authorized 1962: 133,918 acres.

41. *Pictured Rocks (Mich.).* Reaches along 39 miles of the south shore of Lake Superior in Michigan's Upper Peninsula area. Authorized 1966: 65,000 acres.

42. *Point Reyes (Calif.).* Tall cliffs and long beaches, forests, lagoons on a peninsula north of San Francisco. Authorized 1962: 64,546 acres.

SELECTED STATE PARKS AND NATURAL AREAS

43. DeSoto–Ala.
44. Oak Mountain–Ala.
45. Picacho Peak–Ariz.
46. Devil's Den–Ark.
47. Petit Jean–Ark.
48. Humboldt Redwoods–Calif.
49. Anza-Borrego Desert–Calif.
50. Mount Diablo–Calif.
51. Golden Gate Canyon–Colo.
52. Burr Pond–Conn.
53. Kettletown–Conn.
54. Trap Pond–Del.
55. Collier-Seminole–Fla.
56. Highlands Hammock–Fla.
57. Black Rock Mountain–Ga.
58. Amicalola Falls–Ga.
59. Waimea Canyon–Hawaii
60. Akaka Falls–Hawaii
61. Lava Hot Springs–Idaho
62. Heyburn–Idaho
63. Giant City–Ill.
64. Starved Rock–Ill.
65. Indiana Dunes–Ind.
66. Brown County–Ind.
67. Rock Creek–Iowa
68. Geode–Iowa
69. Meade County–Kans.
70. Natural Bridge–Ky.
71. Carter Caves–Ky.
72. Chicot–La.
73. Baxter–Maine
74. Camden Hills–Maine
75. Mount Blue–Maine
76. Cunningham Falls–Md.
77. Gambrill–Md.
78. Ashland–Mass.
79. John C. Robinson–Mass.
80. Tahquamenon Falls–Mich.
81. Porcupine Mountains–Mich.
82. Ludington–Mich.
83. Itasca–Minn.
84. St. Croix–Minn.
85. Gooseberry Falls–Minn.
86. Magnolia–Miss.
87. Tishomingo–Miss.
88. Big Spring–Mo.
89. Meramec–Mo.
90. Lewis and Clark Caverns–Mont.
91. HellCreek–Mont.
92. Ponca–Nebr.
93. Ichthyosaur–Nev.
94. Valley of Fire–Nev.
95. Echo Lake–N. H.
96. Franconia Notch–N. H.
97. Palisades Interstate Park–N. J., N. Y.
98. Island Beach–N. J.
99. City of Rocks–N. Mex.
100. Bottomless Lakes–N. Mex.
101. Bear Mountain–N. Y.
102. Allegheny–N. Y.
103. Taconic–N. Y.
104. Mount Mitchell–N. C.
105. Hanging Rock–N. C.
106. Lake Metigoshe–N. Dak.
107. Kelley's Island–Ohio
108. Burr Oak–Ohio
109. Huestan Woods–Ohio
110. Alabaster Caverns–Okla.
111. Quartz Mountain–Okla.
112. Humbug Mountain–Oreg.
113. Ecola–Oreg.
114. Black Moshannon–Pa.
115. Cook Forest–Pa.
116. Cowans Gap–Pa.
117. Burlingame–R. I.
118. Beach Pond–R. I.
119. Table Rock–S. C.
120. Kings Mountain–S. C.
121. Custer–S. Dak.
122. Lake Hiddenwood–S. Dak.
123. Fall Creek Falls–Tenn.
124. Cedars of Lebanon–Tenn.
125. Palo Duro Canyon–Tex.
126. Longhorn Caverns–Tex.
127. Palmetto–Tex.
128. Dead Horse Point–Utah
129. Dixie–Utah
130. Mount Mansfield–Vt.
131. Emerald Lake–Vt.
132. Douthat–Va.
133. Seashore–Va.
134. Larabee–Wash.
135. Sun Lakes–Wash.
136. Deception Pass–Wash.
137. Watoga–W. Va.
138. Lost River–W. Va.
139. Devils Lake–Wis.
140. Peninsula–Wis.
141. Hot Springs–Wyo.
142. Keyhole–Wyo.

AMERICAN WILDLIFE

MAMMALS, AMPHIBIANS, REPTILES

The teeming animals of America meant life itself to Indians and early settlers. America's most valuable resource in those days was the beaver, *Castor canadensis.* This glistening creature, descendant of the largest rodent ever to walk the earth—the incredible 700-to-800-pound *Castoroides* of a million years ago—bears the superb pelt which initiated America's first big-business enterprise. On May 2, 1670, the famous Hudson's Bay Company was formed to harvest its fur. By the turn of the nineteenth century a good trapper could earn $18 a day, compared to the 50-cent daily earnings of the average eastern farmer. The invention of the steel trap by Seville Newhouse in 1823 launched a ruthless quest by trappers searching for beaver through countless waterways of the nation.

More dramatic and hardly less important was the multitude of magnificent beasts which grazed and stampeded across the land. In 1800, a traveler estimated a single herd of buffalo to be 4 million in number. Millions of American caribou, deer, elk and pronghorn (popularly called antelope) roamed the ranges, and along numerous watercourses the wing-antlered moose added to the spectacle. On the cliffs and ledges of the Rocky Mountains herds of wild goats and horned sheep could be seen from almost every bend, and they in turn were hunted by predators: lynxes, cougars, timber wolves and the largest carnivores on earth—the grizzly and brown bears.

Then came the extermination—a few decades of slaughter and animals vanished like rain in a desert. By the 1890's, the bison, elk and pronghorn were reduced to scattered remnants. Grizzlies retreated to inaccessible mountains and remote plateaus. The gray wolf disappeared. The wolverine is nearly extinct in the northwestern states. (Now, with Alaska in the Union, we have not only the wolf, wolverine and grizzly but the great Kodiak and polar bears as well.)

Conservation. Early in this century Americans came to their senses. Wildlife laws, hunting regulations and "big game" refuges are protecting and will hopefully lead to the increase of our native mammals. After little more than a half century of conservation, the bison, pronghorn, moose, bobcat and grizzly, once at the brink of extinction, have been saved. The Florida manatee, the red wolf and the prairie dog, however, are still in danger.

Some of the smaller animals have flourished with civilization; chipmunks and cottontail rabbits are more numerous now than when the country was forested. Mice and squirrels are on the increase; the deer and the fox thrive on farms and in suburban fields; raccoons enjoy orchards and grainfields and plunder the family garbage can. The coyote has been transported east by man and has crossed with various breeds of dogs, producing hybrids called "coydogs" or "dogotes."

The continental United States has more than 350 species of mammals, ranging from tiny shrews to the big brown or Kodiak bear which stands eight feet tall and may weigh as much as 1500 pounds. Hawaii, on the other hand, has no native mammals; all of them were introduced by man.

Reptiles. Many of the 330 species of reptiles in the continental United States were once abundant. Alligators and crocodiles of the sloughs of Florida and the Gulf Coast brought wealth to hunters and tanneries. Like the mammals, they were slaughtered for their hides. Crocodiles are virtually extinct there. Alligators have fared poorly but somewhat better; their concentration of population is in Everglades National Park, where they have been protected by law since 1947. It is not only illegal to shoot them, but they may not even be kept as pets. Yet tens of thousands have died in the last five years. Man-made dams and dikes, together with a natural period of drought, lowered the water table and eliminated the fish they feed on. Other reptiles protected in some localities are the horned lizard, box turtle, desert tortoise, Gila monster and green anole (known as the chameleon).

Of the 111 species of snakes in this country, only the coral, the swamp- and water-inhabiting cottonmouth and various copperheads and rattlesnakes are poisonous; our Gila monster is one of two poisonous lizards in the world.

Less spectacular than the reptiles are the amphibians—206 species of salamanders, toads, newts and frogs. The United States has more salamanders than any other country in the world, about 125 species, and more are being discovered. The siren (see next page) and the amphiuma live only in North America. *The ranges of the animals illustrated below are indicated on the accompanying maps.*

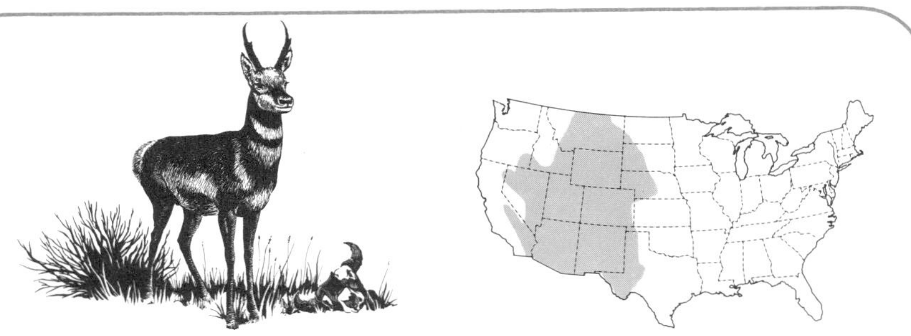

PRONGHORN OR "ANTELOPE" (*Antilocapra americana*)
On the open prairies, deserts and tablelands of the West dwells this unique North American animal that looks like an antelope but is not. It is the only member of its family. One of the fastest mammals, the pronghorn's movement is different from all other runners of its class because its weight is carried on the front feet. When the animal is alarmed, the white hairs on its round rump patch are flashed upward in a signal that is read by other pronghorns.

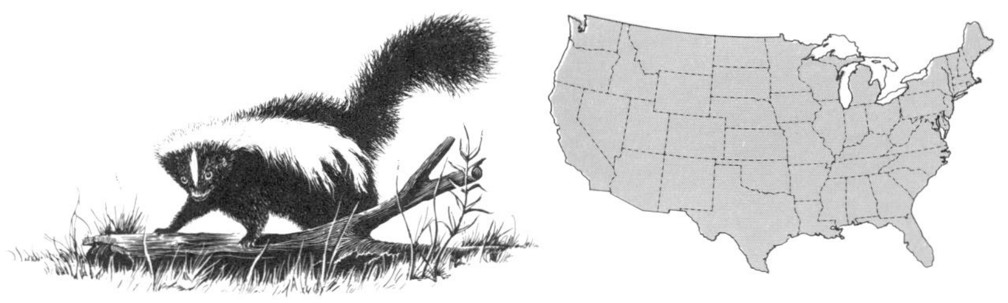

STRIPED SKUNK (*Mephitis mephitis*)
No member of the mustelid family—which includes weasels, minks and ferrets—is so well known. This skunk can throw a spume 15 feet, an accomplishment peculiarly its own. Though armed for several quick shots, the skunk uses its musky ammunition sparingly, probably because it takes three weeks to replace the entire supply.

SEWELLEL OR "MOUNTAIN BEAVER" (*Aplodontia rufa*)
Neither "beaver" nor necessarily a mountain dweller, this appealing little animal is the last survivor of a primitive race of rodents. Found nowhere in the world except along the Pacific Northwest coast, it spends most of its life underground. The name *sewellel* is Chinook Indian for "robe"—the fur is luxuriant and was prized by them. Mammalogists put the unusual mountain beaver in a family by itself.

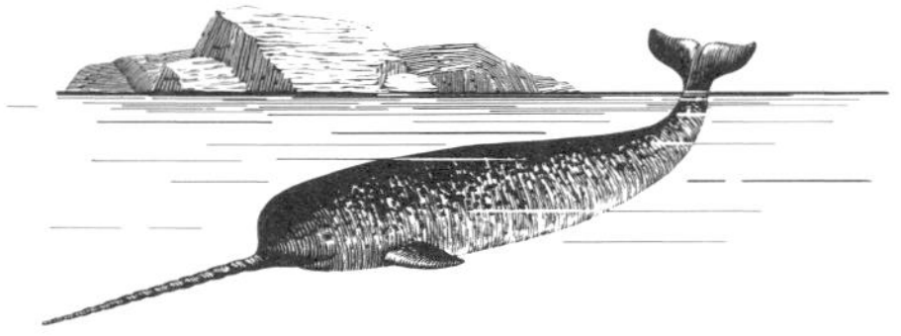

NATIVE OF NORTH ATLANTIC AND ARCTIC WATERS

NARWHAL (*Monodon monoceros*)
This sea mammal, gray on top and white below, started the stories of the unicorn when its strange tooth was found by Scandinavians. The tusk, an upper left canine up to nine feet long, shaped like a horn, evidently is not a weapon and just what purpose it serves is debatable. The narwhal, a small whale, is not in the same family as the large whales.

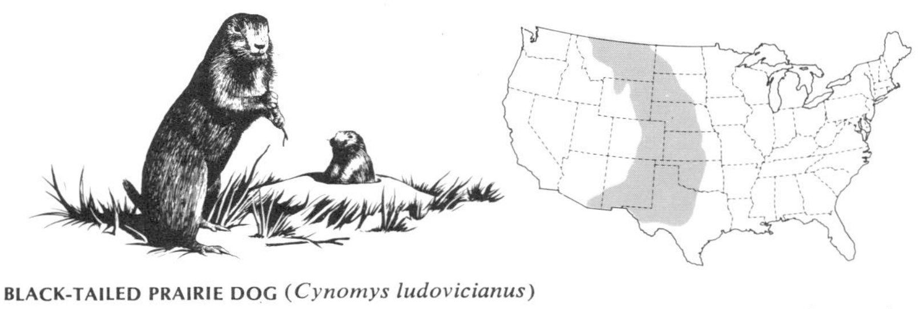

BLACK-TAILED PRAIRIE DOG (*Cynomys ludovicianus*)
An inhabitant of the plains and foothills, this is a perky rodent that has habits and a social life unusual in the ground-squirrel family. Congregating in "towns," these animals dig homes with bedchambers, toilets and guardrooms. When enemies approach, a bark alarm is sounded and all vanish underground. They can contend with hawks, snakes and owls, but man's poisons (to save forage for cattle and sheep) have reduced their numbers from some 400 million in 1830 to mere thousands today.

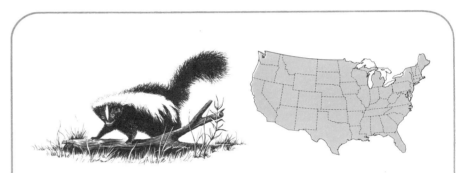

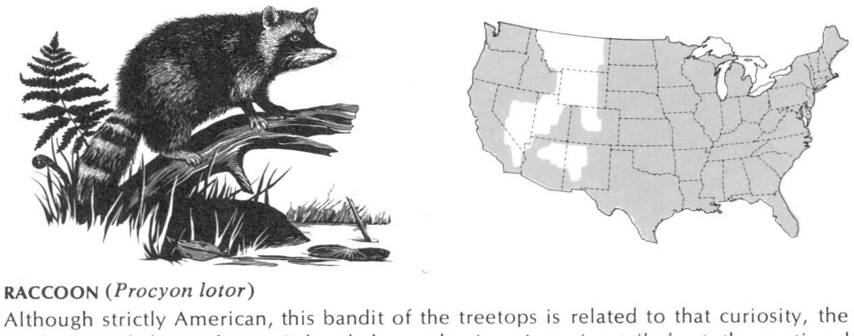

RACCOON (*Procyon lotor*)
Although strictly American, this bandit of the treetops is related to that curiosity, the six-foot panda bear of Asia. Related also to the American ring-tailed cat, the coati and the kinkajou of South America, it walks, like a man, on the soles of its five-toed feet. The highly intelligent raccoon is able to stack blocks, open fastened-down garbage cans and also invent games which it enjoys playing.

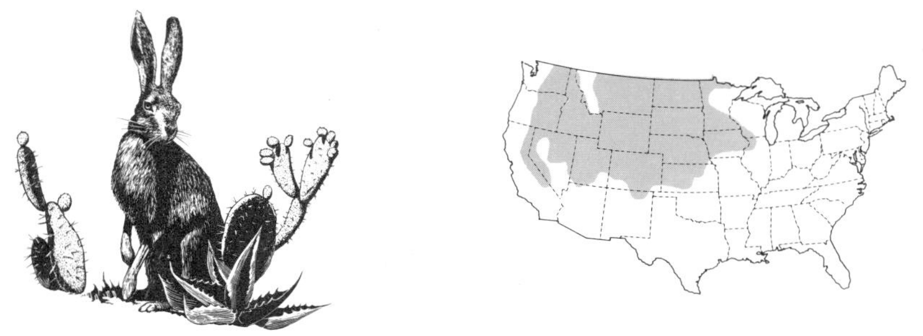

WHITE-TAILED JACKRABBIT (*Lepus townsendii*)
A familiar character of the West, this species has a talent that no other beast can duplicate. When pursued it twists the white fur of its belly up one side and pulls the brown top fur down on the other. Flashing brown and white while it runs, the rabbit warns other jackrabbits of the presence of a predator.

BIG SHORT-TAILED SHREW (*Blarina brevicauda*)
Although shrews are worldwide, this American short-tailed shrew is unique. It is one of the few mammals which carry a poison resembling that of the cobra. A large dose drawn from the salivary glands in the lower jaw can kill a mouse bigger than the shrew itself. Rarely seen by humans, it devours insects and rodents in great quantities, because, with a high metabolism, it must eat constantly to survive.

EASTERN CHIPMUNK (*Tamias striatus*)
This nimble creature likes rocky walls, fences and the gardens of suburbia—and can be easily trained to come for handouts. With five stripes down its back, and a tail that sticks up straight like a flagpole when the chipmunk is running, this darting little animal is instantly recognizable. There are various other chipmunks *(Eutamias)* in the western United States and at least one in Asia.

ARMADILLO (*Dasypus novemcinctus*)
The nine-banded armadillo, wrapped in a heavy coat of mail, curls into a ball when attacked. It is unable to bite and grunts while consuming ants, beetles and scorpions. Though a good swimmer, this armored creature often just walks underwater to cross a shallow stream or pond. The only member of the edentate group (anteaters and sloths) to be found in the United States, the armadillo is gradually extending its range in the South and has become established in Florida.

VIRGINIA OPOSSUM (*Didelphis marsupalis*)
According to the laws of survival, the opossum should have been wiped out long ago by the more aggressive carnivorous mammals which developed later. Only in Australia have marsupials (which carry their young in a pouch) been cut off from the rest of the world, leaving them protected. Toothy, hissy, sluggish, but well-loved, only this one species exists in the United States. Once confined to the South, it lives as far north as Vermont but is not adapted to the cold—its ears and tail become frostbitten.

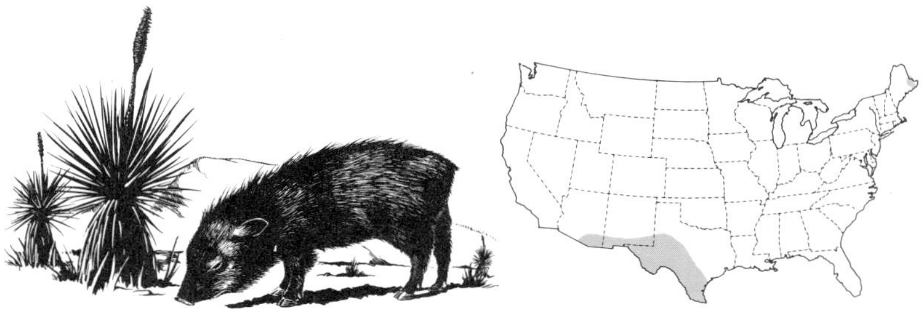

PECCARY (*Pecari angulatus*)
These coarse-coated, piglike animals are not true pigs. Largely concealed tusks grow from their upper jaws, and they have no extra "toe" on the sides of their rear feet, as pigs do. Prickly pear is their favorite food, and they gobble it spines and all. Expert rattlesnake killers, they cut up the reptiles by slashing simultaneously with all four hooves. The peccary belongs to one of America's oldest mammal families, *Tayassuidae*.

COUGAR, PUMA OR MOUNTAIN LION (*Felis concolor*)
This graceful six-foot beast is North America's main contribution to the cat family. A big-game predator, it leaps 20 feet to attack elk, pronghorn or deer and drags its 150-pound victim for 100 yards. Swifter than the jaguar (the only other large New World cat), the cougar seemed to be diminishing in numbers, but has recently been recorded in Michigan and rediscovered in Maine.

GREATER SIREN (*Siren lacertina*)
Dwelling among the roots of the water hyacinths in the South are a family of salamanders, the *Sirenidae* or sirens. They are found nowhere else in the world. Eel-like in appearance, the siren passes through a tadpole stage when it has gills. But in the mature stage it develops only a front pair o legs, not a back pair as other amphibians do.

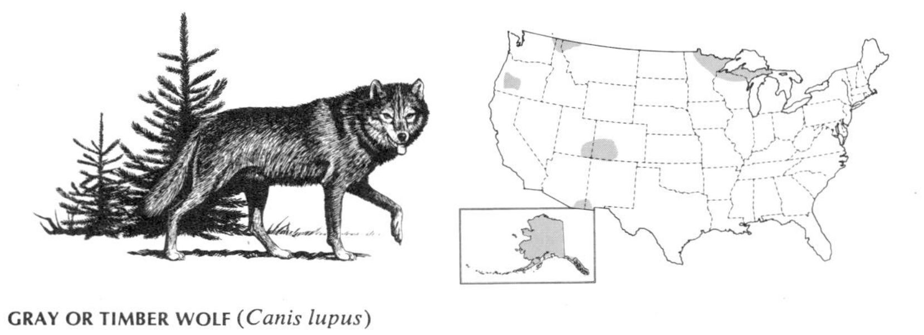

GRAY OR TIMBER WOLF (*Canis lupus*)
This wild dog is the biggest in the world, sometimes reaching well over 100 pounds. The encroachment of civilization has restricted its U.S. range mostly to Alaska, just as its small cousin, the red wolf *(Canis niger)*, is now found only in the Ozark Mountains. Another cousin, the "singing" coyote of the West *(Canis latrans)*, casts an eerie spell through the night with a vibrating howl that can be heard for many miles.

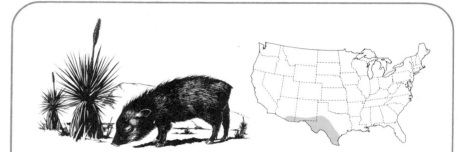

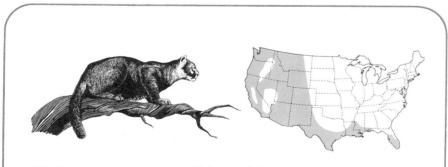

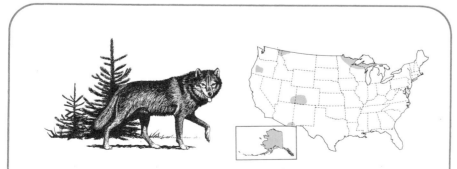

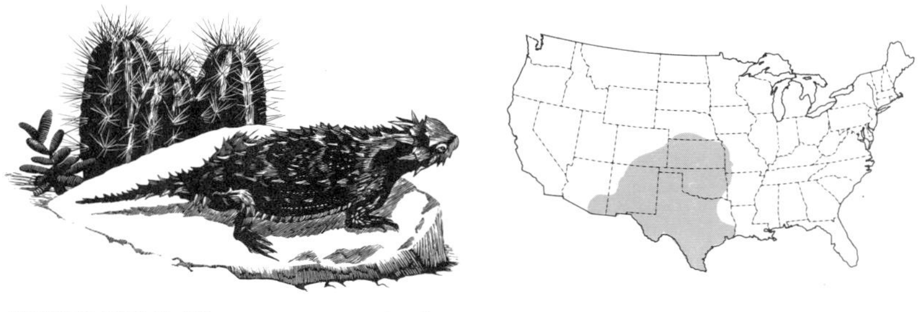

HORNED LIZARD (*Phrynosoma cornutum*)
This bizarre horned lizard, commonly called horned toad, is unique to the United States and Mexico, as are most members of its genus. Members of the reptile class—air-breathing vertebrates that are covered with scales or bony plates—the horned lizards are among the most astonishing creatures in the world. When attacked by a hawk, roadrunner or larger lizard, they shoot blood out of their eyes.

NATIVE FISH

Across the United States some 500 native freshwater fish dwell in our water thoroughfares. Some are magnificent—the streamlined trout; others are odd—the blindfish of the caves; and still others are touching—the male catfish that holds its young in its mouth, tending them gently until they are strong enough to escape enemies.

No matter what their character and habits, each kind tends to live in a certain environment. For freshwater fish, these different worlds have been named according to the types that dominate them: "the trout stream," "the bass stream," "the sturgeon river" (which can be different sections of the same river) and "the lake-trout lake." These names indicate to the expert not only the principal fish inhabiting each, but also the condition of the water: the temperature, rate of flow, amount of dissolved oxygen, as well as other living things—algae, snails, mosses, mussels, crayfish, insects. Each environment is a community. As in all communities, some outsiders or transients appear—the American eel may be found at various times in all of them.

BROOK STICKLEBACK *(Eucalia inconstans)*

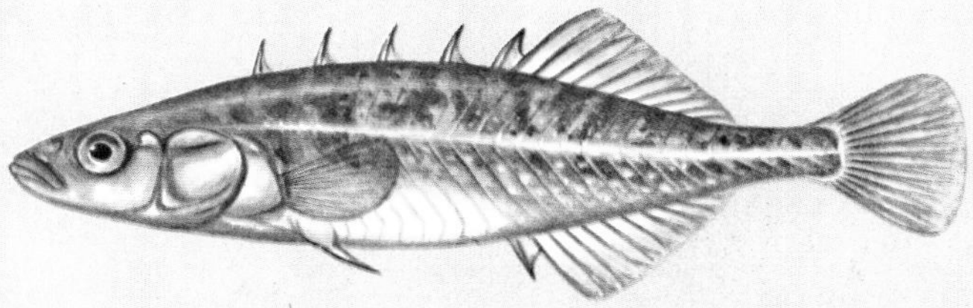

THE TROUT STREAM

To many Americans the trout stream is the most beautiful of all. Remote, usually in forested mountains near the source, the water is swift and clear; the bottom of the stream is stony. The trout stream cascades and tumbles; ferns and wild flowers grow along its course (it is almost completely shaded by trees, for trout water must be cold). Its temperature must not rise above 70°F. for more than a few days in summer, nor can it have less than five parts per million of dissolved oxygen or the trout will die.

Principal fish of the trout community:

1. Brook trout (*Salvelinus fontinalis*)
2. Rainbow trout (*Salmo gairdnerii*)
3. Brook stickleback (*Eucalia inconstans*)
4. Dolly Varden trout (*Salvelinus malma*)
5. Mudminnow (*Umbra pygmaea*)
6. Sand shiner (*Notropis cornutus*)

BLUEGILL *(Lepomis macrochirus)*

THE BASS STREAM

Downhill from the trout community lies "the bass stream." The water is somewhat slower and warmer. Summer temperatures are often far above 70°F. because more than three quarters of the water's surface runs in sunlight. There are also quiet spots—some 30 percent of the surface is made up of calm eddies and pools. Less oxygen is dissolved in this water, and it is richer in animal and plant life. A greater variety of fish have adapted to it.

Principal fish of the bass community:

1. Largemouth bass (*Micropterus salmoides*)
2. Smallmouth bass (*Micropterus dolomieu*)
3. Bluegill (*Lepomis macrochirus*)
4. Yellow perch (see The Lake-Trout Lake, right)
5. Black crappie (*Pomoxis nigromaculatus*)
6. White crappie (*Pomoxis annularis*)
7. Northern pike (see The Lake-Trout Lake)
8. Johnny darter (*Etheostoma nigrum*)
9. Black-nosed dace (*Rhinichthys atronasus*)
10. Creek chub or blunt-nosed minnow (*Hyborhynchus notatus*)
11. Rainbow darter (*Etheostoma caeruleum*)
12. Common sucker (*Catostomus commersonii*)
13. Brown bullhead (*Ictalurus nebulosus*)
14. Creek chub sucker (*Erimyzon oblongus*)
15. Brook stickleback (see The Trout Stream, left)

THE STURGEON RIVER

As the stream becomes a river and widens to meet the sea, it creates yet another environment—a community of fish where the sturgeon and its associates live. The waters are deep and warm and slower than the trout and bass streams. Shade occurs only at the edges; most of the river is in sunlight and the warmth supports much more life than the bass stream. The Mississippi is a classic example of the sturgeon river. However, all rivers near the sea are alike, the same families of fish mixing with each other in the same environment.

Principal fish of the sturgeon river:

1. Atlantic sturgeon (*Acipenser oxyrhynchus*)
2. Channel catfish (*Ictalurus punctatus*)
3. Carp (*Cyprinus carpio*)
4. Rock bass (*Ambloplites rupestris*)
5. Freshwater drum (*Aplodinotus grunniens*)
6. Buffalo fish (*Ictiobus cyprinellus*)
7. American shad (*Alosa sapidissima*)
8. Pacific and Atlantic salmon (family Salmonidae)
9. Alewife (*Alosa pseudoharengus*)
10. Alligator gar (*Lepisosteus spatula*)

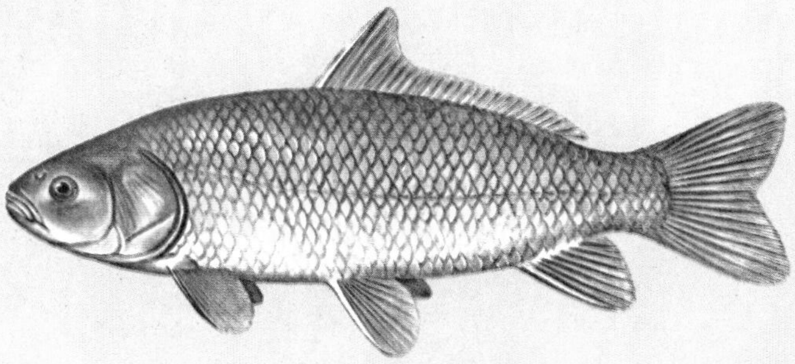

BUFFALO FISH *(Ictiobus cyprinellus)*

THE LAKE-TROUT LAKE

The lakes—those landlocked diadems of water that decorate the northern half of the continent—are dominated by splendid lake trout and whitefish. Older lakes and those farther south feature the perch, bullheads and carp. These fish have adapted to the physical nature of a deep lake, its principal force being the annual "overturn," a displacement of water due to its heating and cooling in spring and fall. This slow roll brings the bottom to the top and vice versa twice a year, and changes the oxygen, mineral and organic content of the lake.

Principal fish of the lake-trout community:

1. Lake trout (*Salvelinus namaycush*)
2. Lake whitefish (*Coregonus clupeaformis*)
3. Pumpkinseed (*Lepomis gibbosus*)
4. Yellow walleye (*Stizostedion vitreum*)
5. White bass (*Roccus chrysons*)
6. Freshwater drum (see The Sturgeon River, above)
7. Common bullhead (*Ameirus nebulosus*)
8. Paddlefish (*Polydon spathula*)
9. Northern pike (*Esox lucius*)
10. Yellow perch (*Perca flavescens*)
11. Bowfin (*Amia calva*)
12. Gizzard shad (*Dorosoma cepedianum chrysochloris*)
13. Chain pickerel (*Esox niger*)

PADDLE FISH *(Polyodon spathula)*

THE OCEAN

Few ocean fish developed in North American waters. Because of varying depths, the ocean is divided into several communities. One of the most general is Inshore fish, those caught either by dropping a line off a pier or casting from the shore. They need the conditions that the tide creates, inshore foods, light and aeration. Bluefish and croakers mark this group. The next category, the Offshore fish, are those beyond the surf that can be reached only in fishing boats. Here swordfish and tuna are prominent. Finally, the Deep-ocean (or pelagic) fish dwell in the abyss beyond the drop of the continental shelf. They are markedly affected by their world. In almost total darkness, the angler fish have grown their own fishing lines from their heads to attract the few fish that pass their way. Here also live the largest fish in the world—the whale shark and ocean sunfish—but they are surface dwellers.

SKATE (family Rajidae)

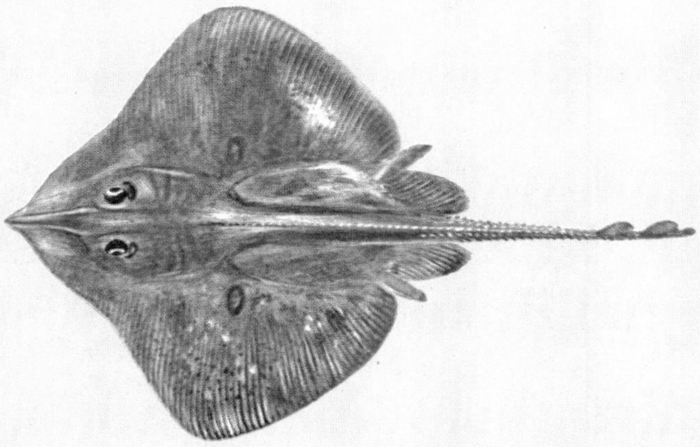

Dominant fish and mollusks of the Inshore community:

1. Bluefish (family Pomatomidae)
2. Grouper, weakfish, Atlantic croaker (family Serranidae)
3. Sea bass (family Serranidae)
4. Flounder (family Pleuronectidae)
5. Silver perch (family Serranidae)
6. Red and black drum (family Sciaenidae)
7. Mullet (family Mugilidae)
8. Porgy (family Sparidae)
9. Hogfish, tautog and cunner (family Labridae)
10. Sand shark (family Carchariidae)
11. Striped bass (family Serranidae)
12. Skate (family Rajidae)
13. Razor clam (family Solenidae) and surf clam (family Mactridae)

FLYING FISH (family Exocoetidae)

Principal fish, mollusks and crustaceans of the Offshore community:

1. Swordfish (family Xiphiidae)
2. Bonito, albacore, bluefin tuna (family Scrombridae)
3. Marlin and sailfish (family Istiophoridae)
4. Tarpon (family Elopidae)
5. Red snapper (family Lutjanidae)
6. Dolphin (family Coryphaenidae)
7. Flying fish (family Exocoetidae)
8. Pilot fish (family Carangidae)
9. Kingfish (family Serranidae)
10. Mackerel shark (family Lamnidae)
11. Atlantic mackerel (family Scombridae)
12. Oyster (family Ostreidae)
13. Shrimp (*Peneus setiferus* and *brasiliensis*) and mud shrimp (*Palaemonetes vulgaris*)

Principal fish of the Deep-ocean community:

1. White shark (family Rhincodontidae)
2. Angler fish (family Lophiidae)
3. Ocean sunfish (family Molidae)

AMERICAN BIRDS

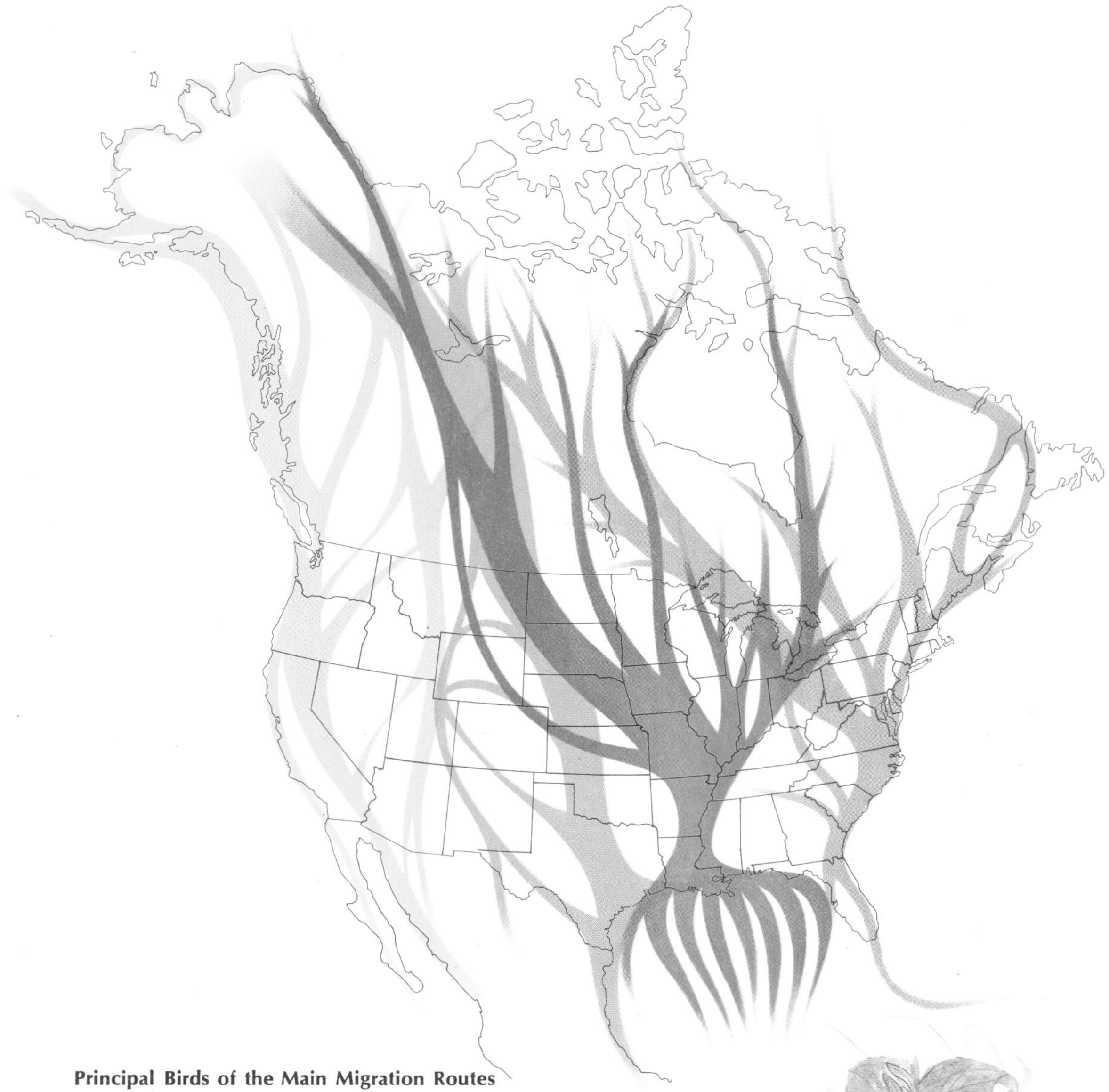

In late August, when the breeding season of the birds is largely over and the young are testing their wings, about 20 billion—645 species—color the trees, deserts and plains of the United States. Less than 6 billion are year-round residents; the remainder are summer dwellers only, each species or family with its own dates of departure in the fall and return in the spring. In season the four migration routes become flowing rivers of life (see map at left). Spring migrations begin in February and continue until June. The fall migrations, to a warmer climate and a more plentiful food supply, last from June to December and for some kinds involve a different route from the one taken in the spring. Many United States birds winter in Central and South America, and many from the Arctic spend the winter here. No South American birds migrate to this country.

Some—like the blue goose with a journey of 1700 miles from James Bay in Canada to the Gulf of Mexico—travel nonstop. Probably the longest of all migrations is that of the Arctic tern, which breeds in the Arctic and winters in the Antarctic, 11,000 miles away. Most North American migrations are from north to south and return, but various species—the evening grosbeak, for one—migrated from west to east and back until they became established in the east. Others, especially those that do most of their traveling on foot (certain grouse and quails), travel only from the mountains to the lower slopes and vice versa.

The 6 billion birds that do not migrate have adapted to snow and cold largely because they are seedeaters and do not depend on an insect

Principal Birds of the Main Migration Routes

Atlantic Coast Route: common loon, black duck, common eider, great blue heron, clapper rail, piping plover, laughing gull, black skimmer, black-throated blue warbler, yellowthroat, rose-breasted grosbeak and song sparrow.

Mississippi Valley Route: many Canada geese, white-fronted goose, mallard, common (green-winged) teal, wood duck, whooping crane, buff-breasted sandpiper, least tern, red-headed woodpecker, veery, bobolink, dickcissel and Le Conte's sparrow.

Great Plains—Rocky Mountain Route: gadwall, American widgeon, turkey vulture, various hawks, golden eagle, sandhill crane, avocet, long-billed curlew, western kingbird, Say's phoebe, rock wren, sage thrasher, mountain bluebird, western meadowlark and Baird's sparrow.

Pacific Coast Route: brant (black-bellied), wandering tattler, surfbird, black turnstone, glaucous-winged gull, pigeon guillemot, several auklets, calliope hummingbird, violet-green swallow, varied thrush, Townsend's warbler and golden-crowned sparrow.

Extensions of main migration routes southward: coot, sora, killdeer, lesser (or American) golden plover, black-bellied plover, common snipe, whimbrel, spotted sandpiper, greater yellowlegs, least sandpiper, black-billed cuckoo, belted kingfisher, yellow-bellied sapsucker, barn swallow, black-polled warbler, bobolink.

Many widely distributed species migrate on a very broad front, hence are not "typical" for any one particular route. Among these are tanagers, orioles, thrushes and various sparrows.

RUFFED GROUSE *(Bonasa umbellus)*
Grouse and ptarmigans are chickenlike birds whose family is an ancient one, dating back some 20 million years. Although capable of flight, they nest and spend most of their time on the ground. The ruffed grouse—a favorite game bird—is confined mostly to the northern states. Its prominent tail bears a black band.

YELLOW WARBLER *(Dendroica petechia)*
A bright-colored member of a beautiful family often called the "butterflies" of the bird world, its habitat is spread over most of the United States. When a cowbird, which lays eggs in other birds' nests, leaves one for the yellow warbler to raise, the warbler may build a new nest level right over the egg. It is one of the earliest songbird migrants to the South.

WILD TURKEY *(Meleagris gallopavo)*
Spanish explorers brought the turkey to Europe from Mexico as early as 1541. Later European colonists in America recognized the larger wild bird they found here in great abundance. Once threatened with extinction, it has again become fairly widespread under state management. The barnyard turkey and the wild bird are the same species, although there are various domesticated strains.

population for food. One exception is the woodpecker with its unusual drill for reaching larvae in trees. The hairy woodpecker and the great horned owl are year-round residents all the way from Alaska to Florida, and the house sparrow and rock dove (domestic pigeon) are at home in all seasons throughout the continental United States except perhaps Alaska.

Most birds, whether migrants or not, have specific ranges. The western and mountain bluebirds live only west of the Rocky Mountains, and the eastern bluebird stays east of them. The snow bunting is confined mostly to the treeless tundra of Alaska and Canada, the spruce grouse to the northwestern evergreen forests, the tufted titmouse to the deciduous forests farther south, the sage grouse to the western plains and the roadrunner to southwestern deserts. The birds with the smallest breeding ranges are Kirtland's warblers, limited to an area of 100 by 60 miles in Michigan, and Hawaii's Laysan ducks and Laysan finches, found nowhere but on the tiny island of Laysan.

The smallest bird is the $2\frac{3}{4}$-inch calliope hummingbird. The largest are the trumpeter swan, whooping crane and California condor; the latter two are battling extinction. The remaining whooping cranes number about 60 and now winter only in Texas, on or near the Aransas National Wildlife Refuge. The 40 or so condors live in California's Los Padres National Forest. The bald eagle may be approaching extinction also—from the pesticide residues in the fish which make up most of its diet. During the last 200 years three birds have completely vanished from the continental United States—the Labrador duck, the heath hen and the passenger pigeon. Hawaii has lost 14 species.

Members of eight major bird families of North America are portrayed below with paintings by John James Audubon.

INSECTS AND LOWER FORMS

Number of identified insect species in the world: 1,000,000
Number of identified species in the United States: 82,394

Most devastating insects and lower forms

European corn borer
Boll weevil *(cotton)*
Cattle grub
Corn earworm
Tobacco hornworm
Grasshopper *(grain)*
Coddling fruit moth
Spruce budworm *(forests)*
Nematodes *(potatoes, soybeans, corn, citrus trees)*
Starfish *(clams, oysters, scallops)*
Japanese beetle *(field and fruit crops, shade trees, lawns)*

Most beneficial insects and lower forms

Honeybee *(pollinates flowers)*
Earthworm *(aerates soil)*

The following creatures prey on damaging insects:

Dragonfly
Damselfly
Aphis lion
Praying mantis
Lady beetle
Spider
Parasitic wasps—ichneumonids, braconids and chalcids
Parasitic flies—tachinids and sacrophagids

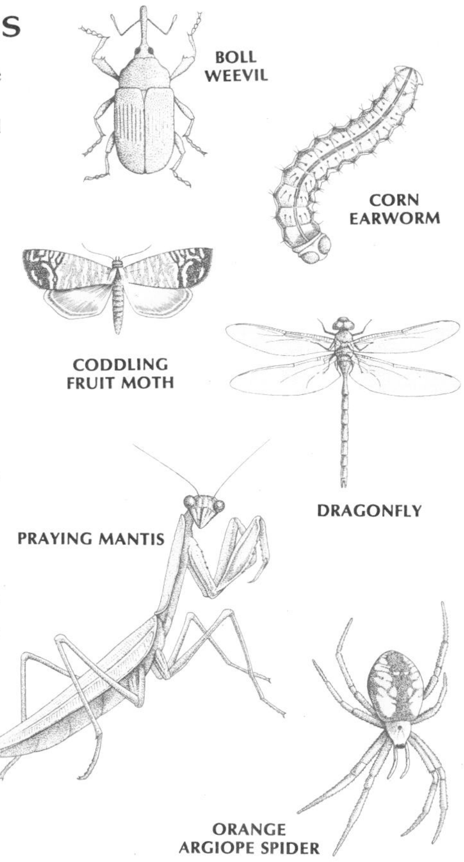

RED-EYED VIREO *(Vireo olivaceus)*
Although some vireos now occur in South America, their place of origin was in North America. There are varied types in addition to the one shown—black-capped, yellow-throated, white-eyed and others. Some wear what appear to be eyeglasses, composed of a light circle of feathers. Great singers, they are second only to mockingbirds in their persistent warbling.

CALIFORNIA CONDOR
(Gymnogyps californianus)
These magnificent birds with a wingspread of 8 to 10 feet are splendid soarers which travel hundreds of miles a day. They seek upward warm thermal currents when the land begins to heat the air. They nest every two years, not often enough to replace annual losses in population. The black and turkey vultures belong to the same family.

MOCKINGBIRD *(Mimus polyglottos)*
The finest singer among North American birds has a repertoire that is staggering, and it sings by day or night, perched or in flight. The mockingbird and its relatives, the catbirds and thrashers, have such powers of mimicry that by listening to only one of these songsters, it is possible to tell what other birds are in the vicinity. Although called mimic thrushes, they are not true thrushes.

LIMPKIN *(Aramus pictus)*
A cranelike bird of Florida, the limpkin is the only species of its family. Feeding on freshwater snails, it seizes one, carries it to shallow water and there, perched on one leg, extracts the animal from its shell. Its harsh cries, heard by day and night, have caused it to be named "The Crying Bird."

HOUSE WREN *(Troglodytes aedon)*
Small, stumpy, with tails cocked in the air, these songsters bathe often and are energetic, restless creatures. In the spring the male runs wild filling holes, often stuffing even socks on a clothesline with twigs. Other species have adapted to marshes, coniferous forests, deserts and cliffs.

NATIVE FLOWERING PLANTS

The flowering plants that evolved in the United States—many of which have been carried throughout the world—are about 20,000 species. Always some are in bloom somewhere throughout the year. They range from Arctic miniatures that blossom in the vast northern reaches on permanently frozen soil to the giant flowers of two tiny pockets of tropical clime in the continental United States—in Texas and Florida. Native wild flowers inhabit seashores, margins of rivers and lakes, bogs and swamps, forests and woodlands, prairies, plains and dry deserts. The only places they cannot be found are on glaciers and in deep water.

When Europeans discovered North America the land supported a rich flora. The great majority of plants were completely unknown to the newcomers. For the first time they saw flowering dogwood, sunflowers, phloxes, trailing arbutus, mayapple, pitcher plants and many others.

In the far north and fingering southward along mountain ranges a few species grew that also occurred in northern Europe and northern Asia, but these represented an infinitesimal proportion of the flowers native to the new

Indian Paintbrush *(Castilleja mineata)*. Semiparasitic, it obtains part of its nourishment by tapping the roots of nearby plants. Showy parts of plant are bracts, not flowers. Habitat: Washington, Saskatchewan, Idaho and Montana.

Firecracker Plant *(Brodiaea idamaia)*. A stagecoach driver called it Ida May, after his daughter, hence the Latin name. Habitat: California.

Common Blue Flag *(Iris versicolor)*. This is the most widely distributed wild member of the iris family. Habitat: eastern Canada to Pennsylvania and Minnesota.

Bee Balm or Oswego Tea *(Monarda didyma)*. Ruby-throated hummingbirds and butterflies are attracted to this plant; Indians and colonists brewed tea from the leaves. Habitat: Quebec to Georgia and Tennessee.

Spring Beauty *(Claytonia acutifolia)*. This Alaskan wild flower, like other varieties of spring beauties, closes its blossoms at night, during cloudy weather or when picked.

Camas *(Camassia quamash)*. One Indian war was caused by white settlers trespassing on camas fields of the Nez Percé tribe, who ate its bulbs. Habitat: British Columbia to California.

Desert Agave *(Agave deserti)*. Buds, rich in sugar, are edible. The cactus woodpecker uses dried stems of the plant as a nesting site. Habitat: California.

American Wayfaring Tree *(Viburnum alnifolium)*. Since the drooping branches often trip woodsmen and hikers, it is also known as hobblebush. Habitat: New Brunswick to North Carolina and Minnesota.

American Cranberry *(Vaccinium macrocarpon)*. The trailing evergreen's tart berries are a traditional part of Thanksgiving dinners. Habitat: Newfoundland to North Carolina and Minnesota.

Common Sunflower *(Helianthus annuus)*. Native only to America, this species was exported and grown in Europe in 1568. Despite popular belief, sunflowers do not always face the sun. Habitat: Minnesota and Saskatchewan to Texas and westward.

Wild Passionflower *(Passiflora incarnata)*. The parts of this flower are similar to those of tropical kinds which symbolized the Crucifixion for early Christian travelers. Habitat: Virginia to Florida and Texas.

Black-Eyed Susan *(Rudbeckia hirta)*. These native Americans traveled to the Old World in bales of hay. Habitat: Ontario to Florida and Texas.

Blue-Eyed Grass *(Sisyrinchium angustifolium)*. This delicate plant fills meadows with blossoms on a bright day. Each flower remains open but a few hours, then closes forever. Habitat: throughout North America.

Mountain Laurel *(Kalmia latifolia)*. Swallowtail butterflies lay eggs on its leaves. Indians used the poisonous foliage to commit suicide. Habitat: New Brunswick to Florida, westward to Ohio and Tennessee.

Forget-Me-Not *(Myosotis alpestris)*. There are many species native to the U.S., some preferring damp ground, others thriving in dry alpine situations. Habitat: Alaska, South Dakota, Colorado.

Avalanche Lily *(Erythronium montanum)*. This cousin of the eastern American dogtooth violet blooms almost before the winter snows have retreated. Habitat: Washington and Oregon.

Texas Bluebonnet *(Lupinus subcarnosus)*. Once this was thought to be a favorite food of buffalo herds. Habitat: Texas.

Mistletoe *(Phoradendron flavescens)*. The American species inherited from Europe the legend that mistletoe once was a symbol of hate; then the god of love became its patron. Later, it became customary at Christmastime for those who stood beneath it to be kissed. Habitat: New Jersey to southern Missouri, south to Florida, Texas and New Mexico.

Indian Pipe *(Monotropa uniflora)*. These ghostly flowers lack chlorophyll, collapse and blacken when exposed to the sun or handled. Habitat: Maine to Washington, south to Florida, California.

Pipsissewa *(Chimaphila umbellata)*. Algonquian Indians named this year-round evergreen beauty, which is a favorite in glass-bowl gardens in the winter. Habitat: Canada southward to Virginia, West Virginia, Colorado and California.

Saguaro *(Carnegiea gigantea)*. Elf owls nest in pockets hollowed out by Gila woodpeckers. The fruit is edible, raw or cooked. Habitat: southeast California, Arizona.

Flowering Dogwood *(Cornus florida)*. Wilderness improvisers use frayed dogwood twigs as toothbrushes; they have a cleansing and whitening property. Habitat: Maine to Florida and Texas.

White Trillium *(Trillium grand florum)*. An early-spring riser, colloquial name is wake-robi Pure-white petals gradually chang to dull rose or pink. Habita Quebec to North Carolina ar Missouri.

Barrel Cactus *(Ferocactus acanthodes)*. The alkaline juice of this speci has been used as a thirst-quench only by desperately thirsty trave ers. Habitat: southern Nevad California.

Bitterroot *(Lewisia rediviva)*. Ca tain Meriwether Lewis noted t plant's ability to revive after lo periods of drought. Habitat: B ish Columbia to and including t Rocky Mountains.

Air Plant *(Tillandsia fasciculata)* relative of the pineapple and Spanish moss, this orchid- beauty perches on trees but ta no nourishment from them. Ha tat: Florida.

continent. All other species in the Arctic and to the south grew nowhere but in North America.

As colonization pushed westward additional flowers became known—the large number of cactuses, the wealth of pentstemons and rare orchids among them. The Pacific Coast presented entirely different but equally exciting revelations. Here were farewell-to-spring, globe tulips, mariposa lilies and the California poppy, to name a few.

Early settlers sent seeds back to the Old World, and European botanists were soon collecting American plants. But the traffic was not one-way. Settlers brought with them, by design and accident, many European and Asian wild flowers. Some were planted in gardens as medicinals, for beauty, or from nostalgia. Others came as weeds with packing materials, agricultural seeds and other shipments. Some found conditions to their liking and multiplied greatly—today wild chicory, oxeye daisy, red clover, celandine, viper's bugloss and butter-and-eggs decorate many parts of North America.

Man has brought such vast changes to the land that in numerous places the environment is completely different from that of earlier times. Certain native wild flowers and all foreign introductions are more plentiful than they were; others, among them the most lovely, are much scarcer. Few, if any, have been altogether eliminated but the threat is very real, even so. The disturbance of our natural environment — forests, rivers, swamps, grasslands — can never be undone.

On this page are selections of some of the most interesting and beautiful American native wild flowers.

agnolia or Bull Bay *(Magnolia andiflora)*. One of the world's ost magnificent evergreen trees. is American native is widely anted in mild regions elsewhere. bitat: Georgia, South Carolina, abama, Louisiana, Texas.

ododendron or Mountain Rose-y *(Rhododendron catawbiense)*. oney made from its nectar is be-ved to be poisonous; animals are ry of eating the leaves. Habitat: ountains, Virginia to Georgia.

ailing Arbutus or Mayflower *igaea repens)*. The Pilgrims dis-vered this flower after their first nter at Plymouth. Habitat: New-undland to Florida and Kentucky.

yberry *(Myrica pensylvanica)*. erican colonists used the aro-tic wax coating of its grayish rries to make candles. Habitat: va Scotia to Florida and Ala-na, shores of Lake Erie.

Turtlehead *(Chelone glabra)*. This blossom resembles a turtle's head. If a bee is busy inside, the "turtle" seems to be chewing. Habitat: Newfoundland to Georgia and west to Minnesota.

Sea Grape *(Coccoloba uvifera)*. Missionaries in Mexico are said to have used the leaves for writing notes; a sharp nib makes white letters on the green surface. Habitat: southern Florida.

Beach Plum *(Prunus maritima)*. This shrub bears edible fruit which is made into jellies and jams. Habitat: New Brunswick to Virginia, along the coast.

Early Saxifrage *(Saxifraga virginiensis)*. The name of this rock-loving plant comes from the Latin *saxum*, "rock," and *frangere*, "to break." Habitat: New Brunswick to Georgia and Tennessee.

Monkey Flower *(Mimulus ringens)*. *Mimulus* means "little ape" and refers to the "face" inside the blossom. Habitat: Nova Scotia to Manitoba to Virginia and Texas.

Pussy Willow *(Salix discolor)*. Like other willows, this species contains salicin (the name is derived from *Salix*). Discovery of this substance and later synthesis produced aspirin. Habitat: Newfoundland to British Columbia, south to Delaware, Kentucky and Missouri.

Beach Morning Glory or Pohuehue *(Ipomoea pes-caprae)*. Hawaiians believed that whipping the sea with the vine produced high waves for surf-riders. Habitat: Hawaii.

Prairie Rose *(Rosa setigera)*. The flowers are used in recipes for rose-petal jam, potpourris and sachets, cosmetics and rosewater. Habitat: Ontario to Florida and Texas.

Cow Parsnip *(Heracleum lanatum)*. Related to the poison hemlock used to kill Socrates, this benign plant provides excellent forage. Habitat: Labrador, Newfoundland, Ontario to Alaska, south to North Carolina, Texas, New Mexico and California.

Dune Primrose *(Oenothera deltoides)*. The yellow-green crab spider, camouflaged in the plant's leaves, hides in them to await its prey. Habitat: California, eastern Oregon, Nevada, Arizona and Utah.

Sea Pink or Rose of Plymouth *(Sabbatia stellaris)*. The blossoms are often picked for church altar bouquets. The Pilgrims are said to have seen it first on a Sabbath. Habitat: Massachusetts to Florida.

Yucca or Adam's Needle *(Yucca filamentosa)*. This plant and a species of moth are completely interdependent. Seed production depends upon fertilization by the moth, whose larvae feed only on yucca seeds. Habitat: North Carolina to Florida and west to Missouri.

Fringed Gentian *(Gentiana crinita)*. This plant is considered by some the most beautiful wild flower. Wind blows its seeds so far that this biennial is frequently not found in the same place a second season. Habitat: Maine to Michigan, northern Minnesota, southward to Pennsylvania.

Bearberry or Kinnikinnick *(Arctostaphylos uva-ursi)*. The springy evergreen has red berries and leaves with medicinal value. Habitat: Labrador to Alaska, south to Virginia, Illinois, New Mexico and California.

Sea Lavender *(Limonium carolinianum)*. Housewives along the coast dry it for winter bouquets; it is supposed to discourage moths. Habitat: southern New York to Mexico, in salt marshes.

Venus's-Flytrap *(Dionaea muscipula)*. Its rattrap-like leaves spring shut and imprison insects alighting upon them. Bodies of prey provide nutrients for the plant. Habitat: North and South Carolina.

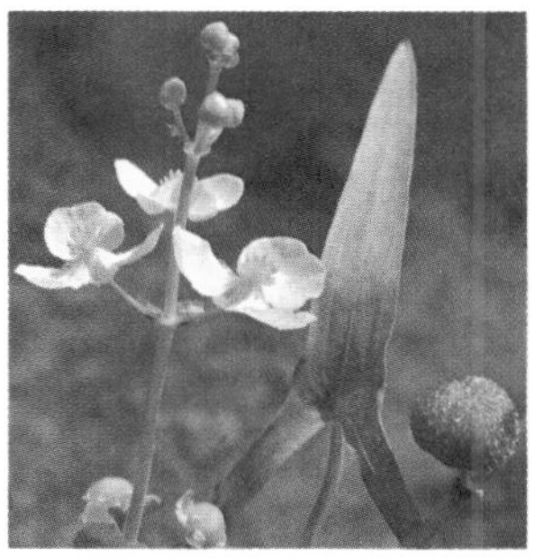

Arrowhead *(Sagittaria latifolia)*. Named for the shape of the leaf. Members of the Lewis and Clark expedition ate the roots boiled or roasted. Habitat: throughout North America.

Goldenrod *(Solidago speciosa)*. Healing properties have been attributed to the genus. More than 125 species of goldenrod are found in the U.S. Habitat: Massachusetts to North Carolina and Arkansas.

Jewelweed or Touch-Me-Not *(Impatiens capensis)*. The seedpod contains a taut spring which explodes violently when touched. The flower resembles a tiny orchid. Habitat: Newfoundland to Saskatchewan, southward to South Carolina, Arkansas and Oklahoma.

Bloodroot *(Sanguinaria canadensis)*. Indians obtained bright red dye from the roots of this plant. Habitat: Nova Scotia to Manitoba, southward to Florida, Alabama and Oklahoma.

NATURAL VEGETATION

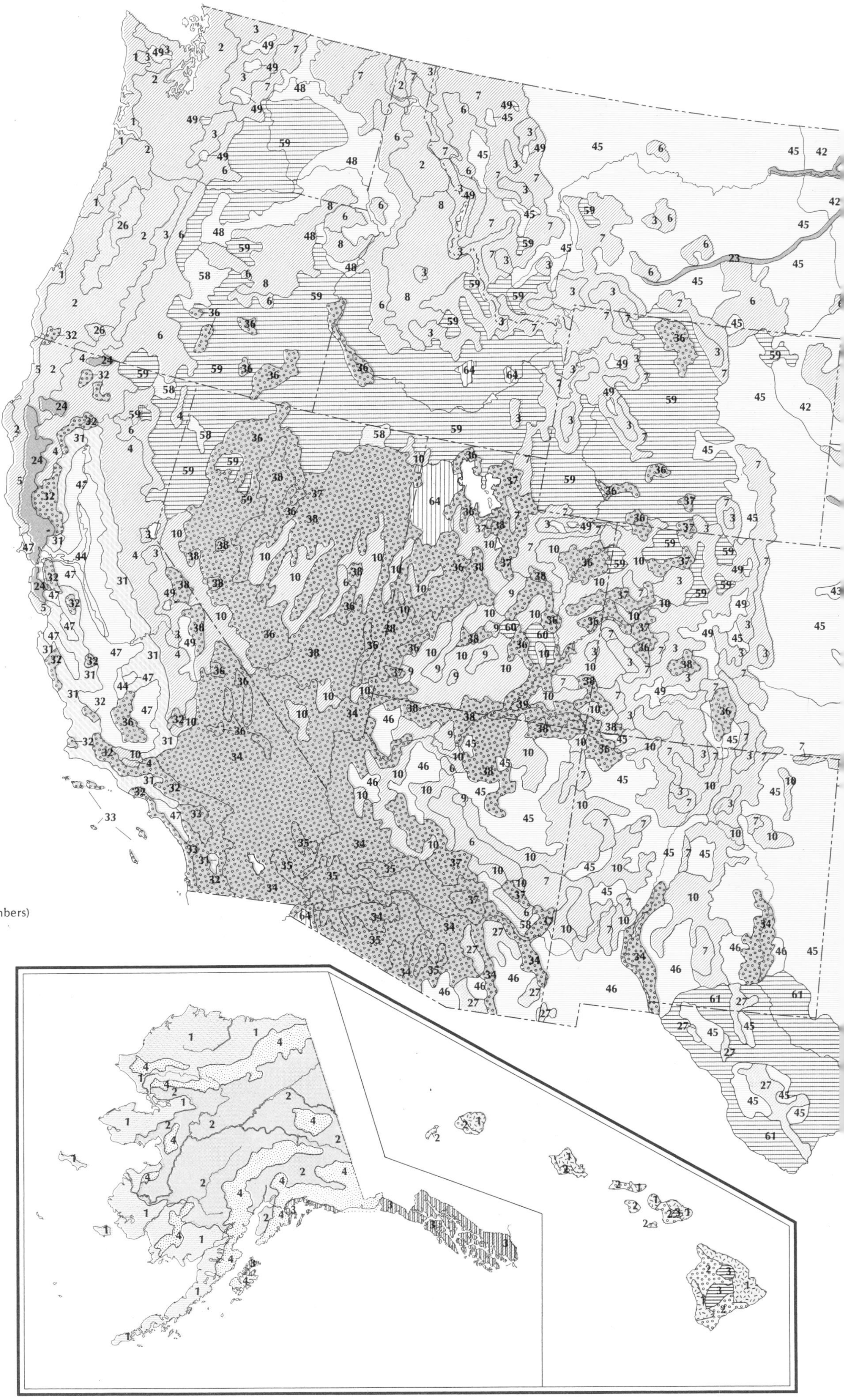

Needleleaf Evergreen Forests:
1 Spruce-cedar–hemlock
2 Cedar–hemlock–Douglas fir
3 Subalpine forest
4 Mixed conifers
5 Redwoods–Douglas fir
6 Pine
7 Pine–Douglas fir
8 Grand fir–Douglas fir
9 Fir–spruce–Douglas fir
10 Juniper–pine
11 Spruce–fir
12 Conifer bog
13 Pond pine (pocosin)
14 Sand pine scrub
15 Subtropical pine

Broadleaf Evergreen Forests:
16 Mangrove

Broadleaf Deciduous Forests:
17 Oak
18 Mixed mesophytic forest
19 Beech–maple
20 Oak–hickory
21 Elm–ash
22 Maple–basswood
23 Cottonwood–willow–elm

Broadleaf and Needleleaf Evergreen Forests:
24 Mixed evergreen forest

Broadleaf and Needleleaf Deciduous Forests:
25 Oak–tupelo–bald cypress

Broadleaf Deciduous and Needleleaf Evergreen Forests:
26 Oak–Douglas fir
27 Oak–juniper
28 Northern hardwoods
29 Oak–pine
30 Southern mixed forest

Broadleaf Deciduous and Evergreen Forests:
31 Oakwoods

Shrub Formations:
32 Chaparral
33 Coastal sagebrush
34 Creosote bush
35 Palo verde–cactus
36 Saltbush–greasewood
37 Mountain mahogany–oak scrub
38 Big sagebrush
39 Blackbrush
40 Cenizo–mesquite

Grasslands:
41 Tall-grass prairie
42 Midgrass prairie
43 Sandhills prairie
44 Marsh grass
45 Short-grass prairie
46 Grama–tobosa
47 Needlegrass
48 Bluebunch wheatgrass
49 Alpine meadow and barren

Grassland–Tree Combinations:
50 Cypress savanna
51 Live oak savanna
52 Mesquite–oak savanna
53 Juniper–oak savanna
54 Oak+bluestem mosaic (cross timbers)
55 Cedar glades
56 Oak–hickory + tall-grass mosaic
57 Oak savanna
58 Juniper–sagebrush savanna

Grassland–Shrub Combinations:
59 Sagebrush–wheatgrass
60 Mormon tea steppe
61 Tarbush–creosote bush savanna
62 Mesquite savanna
63 Palmetto savanna

Desert:
64 Vegetation largely absent

ALASKA

1 Tundra
2 Spruce–birch forest
3 Hemlock–spruce forest
4 Mountain tundra and barren

HAWAII

1 Tropical rain forest
2 Tropical savanna and scrub
3 Lava desert

Many a suburban homeowner expends prodigious amounts of energy and money for seed, fertilizer, weed- and pest-controls and other chemicals in his effort to grow a beautiful lawn. It is not the lack of a green thumb which frequently thwarts his attempts. The natural vegetation of his particular area—the plants that would prevail if man had not cleared them away—was probably not grass at all. Before the first pioneer settler or farmer swung his axe and began to interfere with the natural growth, oak forests (type 17 on the accompanying map) covered the ground on which Boston, New York and Philadelphia have been built, and a mixture of oak and pine (type 29) predominated on the sites of Baltimore and Atlanta. According to an old story, a squirrel in the sixteenth century could travel 1000 miles inland from the Atlantic without touching the ground.

A combination of natural conditions caused these trees to flourish to the virtual exclusion of numerous different types of plant life. Rain and sunshine, temperature and wind, soil and elevation and many other features affect the growth of plants everywhere. Special conditions such as salt spray along the seashore or sand dunes and alkali deposits in the desert impose even more limitations. The natural vegetation faithfully reflects the physical and chemical nature of the sites on which it grows.

In many regions the natural vegetation still exists, but in even more, man has destroyed it, replacing it with his fields, pastures and settlements. If he abandons his fields, the natural vegetation will reestablish itself if given enough time. This is well illustrated by the conditions prevailing in the spruce-fir forests (type 11) of Acadia National Park on Mount Desert Island in Maine. In 1947, a catastrophic fire denuded thousands of acres there. Soon, small wild flowers settled in the burned areas, followed by berry bushes. These, in turn, were succeeded by birches and aspens. Finally, in the shade of these trees, spruce and fir seedlings have become established. Sooner or later, they will grow into a forest of the original type, and the scar will have healed. This last phase in the development of the vegetation is called the "climax" phase; it is the most stable phase and lasts until the natural environment changes or until man destroys it.

The land area of the United States is so large that conditions vary considerably from one region to the next. As a result, we have forests of oaks, maples and other trees in the east, prairies of bluestem, grama and innumerable other grasses in the center, giant Douglas firs in the west, the bleak tundra in Alaska and tropical rain forests in Hawaii. The sagebrush of the Great Basin and the creosote bush of the Mojave Desert are other examples, and many more could be added.

Basically, all vegetation can be divided into three major classes: forests, grasslands and shrub formations. These can then be subdivided into units that are described by their leaves: evergreen or deciduous plants, broadleaf or needleleaf plants or, indeed, plants without any leaves. Such subdivisions can then be broken down still further according to kinds—oaks, pines, magnolias, buffalo grass, mesquite, and so on. The number of kinds is very great and, in the latitude of the United States, the wealth of

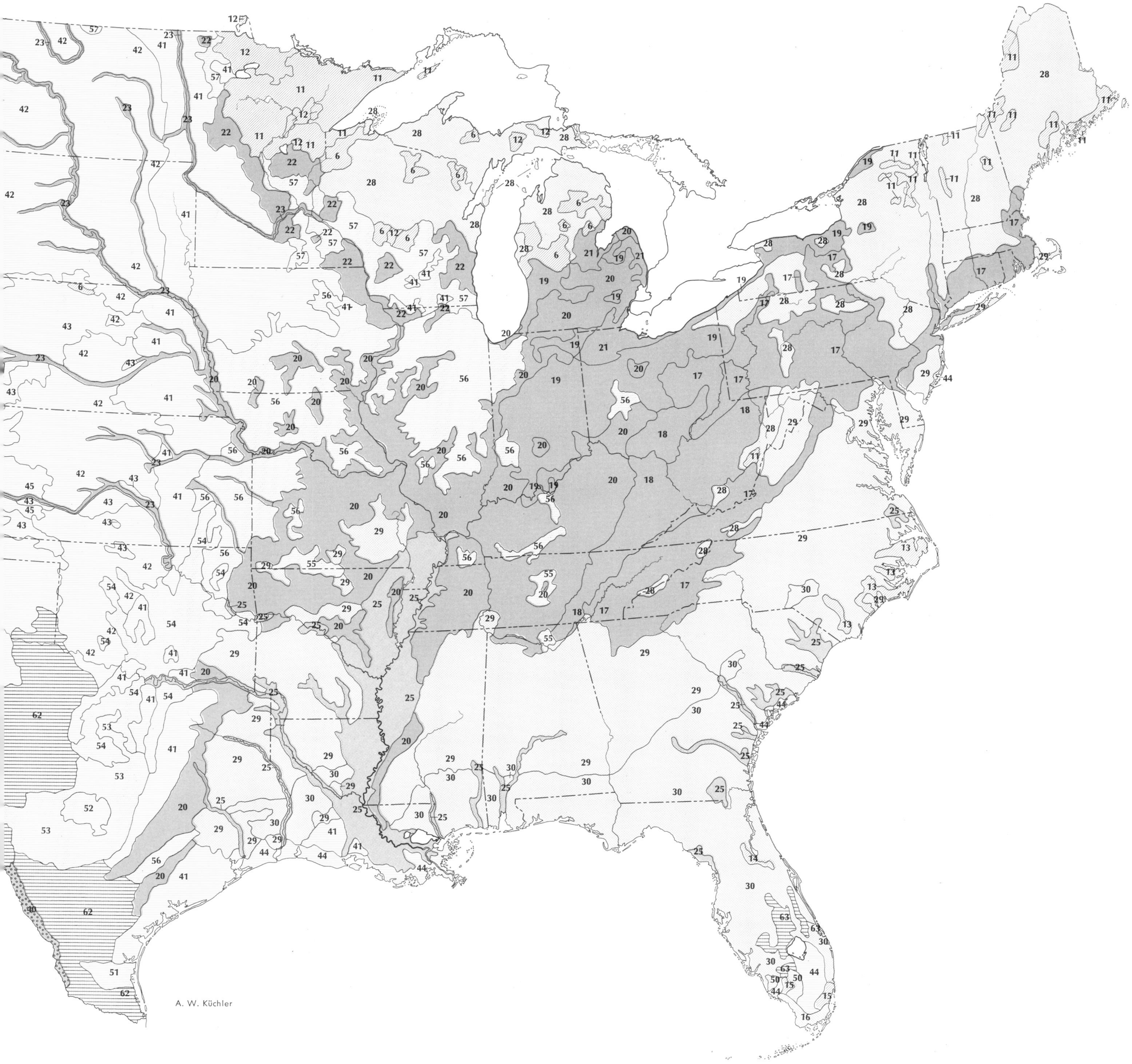

species is matched only by that of China and her Far Eastern neighbors.

Few of the types of vegetation shown on the above map have distinct boundaries. Usually, a type merges gradually with its neighboring types, and the boundary on the map gives only the approximate location of the change. Sometimes, long fingers of one variety may extend far into the territory of another; for instance, the cottonwood-willow-elm combination (type 23) winds its way through the prairies of the Dakotas, Nebraska and Kansas along the banks of the Missouri, Platte and Arkansas rivers. The areas occupied by some types of vegetation are so small that they cannot be shown on a continental map such as the one above. The Monterey cypress is the dominant plant on the Monterey Peninsula in California, and this small area is also the only place in the world where it grows naturally.

The story of natural vegetation is believed to have started about 500 million years ago when algae and fungi from the oceans obtained a foothold on land. It was roughly 150 million years before they had evolved slowly into mosses and ferns, some of which grew to tree size. For instance, in the Catskill Mountains of New York, fossil fern trunks three feet in diameter have been found. In the course of time, some species died out completely, new ones came into being and some have remained practically the same for very long periods. Tree fossils of 75 million and more years ago include deciduous types much like our present figs, magnolias, poplars and plane trees.

The distribution of natural vegetation does not remain static. In many regions, of course, the paramount plant forms have been the same for centuries; in others they have been changing because of altered soil and water conditions. A volcano erupts; a river carves a new course, enlarges a valley or carries off soil; rotting vegetation gradually fills lakes and creates solid ground; plants reclaim tidal mud flats; weathering turns rock into soil. In the heart of the United States, an arid climate transformed the forests of earlier geological periods into vast prairies. Millions of grazing animals as well as fires set by lightning —and later by Indians, too—brought about this change.

During recent centuries, plants have moved into their present environment by various means. The wind carries almost weightless seeds to new habitats, rivers float them downstream.

Man has been particularly effective in transplanting all kinds of species to new habitats, deliberately and accidentally. He has taken his crop plants along on his migrations together with his domestic animals. Seeds of weedy annual grasses traveled in the hairs of Spanish asses to Mexico. From here they spread to California, crowding out the native perennial grasses. The northern Europeans brought along dandelions, plantains and hordes of other weeds. Modern man has profoundly disturbed or, indeed, destroyed much of the natural vegetation. In some places, the environment has been so altered that a new natural vegetation may differ appreciably from the original one. But in most areas, the original vegetation has shown a remarkable power of recuperation. If protected, it will once again establish itself, slowly perhaps but surely.

OUR UNIQUE WEATHER

There is nothing quite like American weather anywhere else in the world. To be sure, its ingredients are the same as those of every country: sunshine and cloud, cold and heat, rain and snow, atmospheric pressures and winds. But in the shuffling of sharply accented weather sequences, bringing sudden changes, American weather attains unrivaled individuality.

The chief causes of this individuality are two: the constant assailing of the skies by vast air masses of widely contrasted qualities, ranging from hot to cold and moist to dry; and the constant modification of these air masses by the terrain.

Most of these air masses originate in one of six areas: the North Pacific, which produces what meteorologists call Pacific polar maritime air; the Central Pacific (Pacific tropical maritime air); the Canadian Far North (polar continental air); the American Southwest and adjacent Mexican plateau (tropical continental air); the North Atlantic (Atlantic polar maritime air); and the Central Atlantic—Caribbean (Atlantic tropical maritime air). On almost any given day, one or more of these air masses will be in evidence over large parts of the nation. The map below presents the characteristics of the six air masses. Of the six, only three, indicated by blue arrows, were influencing the weather on this day (a fairly typical ratio). The others were skirmishing around the continental flanks, forming for a new assault. Their general course is indicated by red arrows.

The American terrain plays almost as large a role in our weather as the air masses. Because the major mountain systems run north-south, the heart of the continent has no defense against periodic invasions of south-moving polar air. In winter, cold "northers" are felt all the way to the Gulf Coast and beyond, and the snow zone (see annual snowfall map, opposite page) swings farther south in the Mississippi Valley than in any other lowland area in the Northern Hemisphere. By way of partial compensation, heat waves reach farther north than in Europe and Asia, and for the same reason: there are no major east-west mountain ranges like the Alps or Himalayas to block a northerly advance of tropical air. Because the western mountain ranges run the entire length of the country—and beyond—they constitute a stiff obstacle to inland penetration by Pacific air masses. Nowhere else do mountains consistently stand in the path of so much clouded air.

In these ways, the north-south "ribbing" of the terrain leaves America open, to a unique extent, to the north-south flow of heat and cold, while restraining the eastward flow of moisture. Thus the mountain ranges contribute greatly to the styles—good, bad and indifferent—of "the varied year" of our weather. But despite its changeableness, certain patterns are evident, as shown in the Calendar of U.S. Weather on pages 142 and 143. To understand these patterns of weather is to understand that, wayward as the course of our weather may be, it has a basic order and follows it from season to season.

HOW TO READ A WEATHER MAP

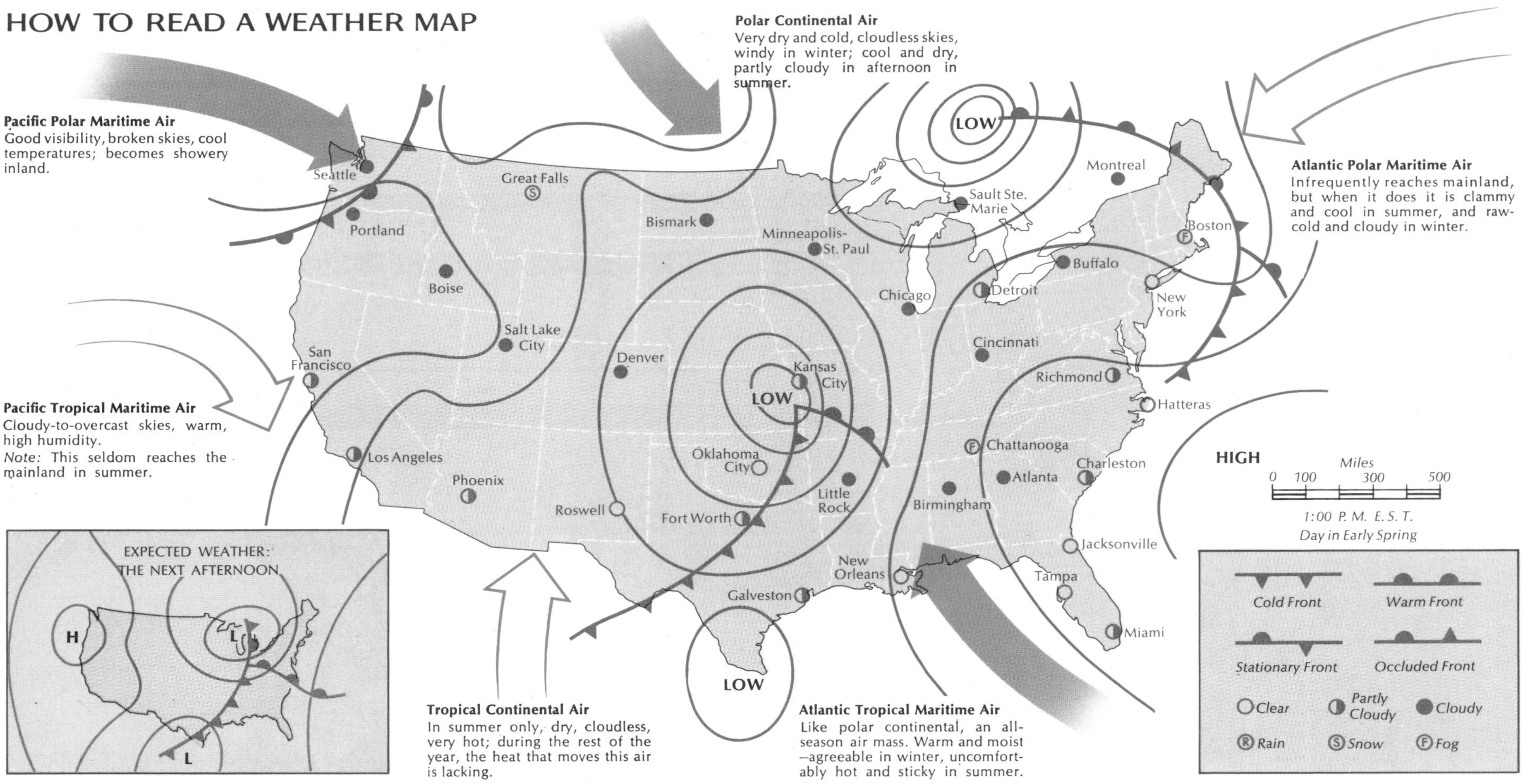

Polar Continental Air
Very dry and cold, cloudless skies, windy in winter; cool and dry, partly cloudy in afternoon in summer.
Pacific Polar Maritime Air
Good visibility, broken skies, cool temperatures; becomes showery inland.
Atlantic Polar Maritime Air
Infrequently reaches mainland, but when it does it is clammy and cool in summer, and raw-cold and cloudy in winter.
Pacific Tropical Maritime Air
Cloudy-to-overcast skies, warm, high humidity.
Note: This seldom reaches the mainland in summer.
Tropical Continental Air
In summer only, dry, cloudless, very hot; during the rest of the year, the heat that moves this air is lacking.
Atlantic Tropical Maritime Air
Like polar continental, an all-season air mass. Warm and moist—agreeable in winter, uncomfortably hot and sticky in summer.
LOW
LOW
LOW
HIGH
Seattle
Portland
Great Falls
Bismark
Minneapolis-St. Paul
Sault Ste. Marie
Montreal
Boston
Buffalo
Detroit
Chicago
New York
Boise
Salt Lake City
San Francisco
Denver
Kansas City
Cincinnati
Richmond
Hatteras
Los Angeles
Phoenix
Oklahoma City
Roswell
Fort Worth
Little Rock
Chattanooga
Atlanta
Birmingham
Charleston
Jacksonville
New Orleans
Galveston
Tampa
Miami
Miles
0 100 300 500
1:00 P.M. E.S.T.
Day in Early Spring
EXPECTED WEATHER: THE NEXT AFTERNOON
H
L
L
Cold Front
Warm Front
Stationary Front
Occluded Front
Clear
Partly Cloudy
Cloudy
Rain
Snow
Fog

EXPECTED WEATHER. The map, center, shows actual weather conditions at 1 p.m. on a day in early spring. The inset map at its lower left-hand corner shows the weather expected on the afternoon of the following day. Usually the pattern of weather is what is shown on these maps: the dominant Highs, Lows and fronts are moving eastward. The rate of this movement is highly variable, but most often ranges between 15 and 25 miles per hour in summer and between 25 and 35 miles per hour in winter.

LOCAL WEATHER. The weather map at best can give only the broad pattern of weather, and the forecasts of the Weather Bureau can deal only with the probable conditions over large areas. Both map and forecasts leave plenty of room for the amateur weatherman to try his hand at local interpretation. For this he will need to take good account of his surroundings. In wooded country he must scale down the predicted wind speed. In a built-up area, the chances are that the temperature will be somewhat higher than that expected generally. In a valley, there will almost certainly be differences in the amount of cloud, precipitation, fog, sunshine and frost between one side and the other, and between the bottom and the top—all at variance with what the weatherman predicted for the region at large. Wind strength and direction in official forecasts will also need to be revised if a person lives in a valley or on an exposed hilltop.

PRESSURES AND WINDS. Most air masses keep on the move. This is because air, like water, is a fluid that cannot rest on a slope, and the earth's atmosphere is full of sloping "surfaces" known as pressure gradients. The weather map shows the location of pressure areas by isobars, which are lines indicating equal barometric pressure. ("Pressure" refers to the weight, or density, of air and is measured by the barometer in terms of the height of a column of mercury it will support in a tube.)

A crowding of the isobars, which occurs in the Low near the center of the map above, indicates that the pressure gradient is steep, causing strong winds. A wide spacing of the isobars, characteristic of a High, indicates that the pressure gradient is gentle—a sign of light winds. The greater the difference in pressure between two adjacent areas, the stronger is the movement of air from the higher to the lower pressure area.

Wind speed tends to increase toward the center of a Low, and to decrease toward the center of a High. Although differences in atmospheric pressure set wind in motion, the path of the wind from high- toward low-pressure areas is not direct. The eastward-spinning earth drags the atmosphere with it, because the rough terrain acts as a deflecting force upon the wind. In the Northern Hemisphere, the wind is turned toward the right of its straightest, "downhill" path from a high- to a low-pressure area. Therefore it moves clockwise in relation to the center of a High but counterclockwise in relation to the center of a Low.

FRONTAL WEATHER. The contact zone between two masses of air is known as a front. When the two have widely contrasting temperatures and densities, the warm air takes the form of an inclined plane (see "Warm Front" illustration at bottom of page). Frequently the plane develops waves, at the crest of which low pressure areas appear. A full-fledged Low of this kind, formed along the front between a polar continental air mass and an Atlantic tropical maritime air mass, is shown on the weather map above, in the vicinity of Kansas City. Many Lows move eastward or northeastward, leaving the country via the Great Lakes, the St. Lawrence Valley or the New England coast.

The Warm Front. The leading edge of a warm air mass is known as the warm front. Ahead of it, warmer and lighter air gets pushed up the inclined "wedge-shape" of colder and heavier air. As the warmer air rises, it cools. If this air is compelled to rise high enough, the moisture in it condenses into cloud particles. The first frontal clouds likely to be seen by a viewer on the ground are the high, thin, veil-like cirrus. Behind them, the clouds become progressively lower and thicker (such as cirrostratus, altostratus and nimbostratus). Well in advance of the surface front, such clouds are usually "heavy" enough to yield rain or snow: a 200-mile-wide belt of precipitation is not uncommon. As the warm front passes a given location, the rain or snow ends; the temperature rises and the clouds lift and break.

The Cold Front. The leading edge of a cold air mass is called a cold front. Here the fast-moving colder air (cold air moves up to 20 percent faster than warm air) undercuts the warmer air ahead of it, forcing the warm air aloft and triggering vigorous cumulonimbus cloud development, usually setting off thundershowers and possibly wind squalls as it does so. The wind shifts its direction, and the temperature drops as the front passes.

Occluded Fronts: Warm and Cold. When a cold front finally overtakes a warm front, the warm air is lifted off the ground. The front is then said to be occluded. A warm occlusion is one in which the air the cold front encounters, after driving the warm air mass aloft, is colder than the air of the cold front. If, after lifting the warm air off the ground, the cold front chances to encounter warmer air than its own, the occlusion is then termed a cold occlusion. When occlusion does take place, the weather in the low-pressure system is usually at its worst, and may be characterized by strong wind, heavy rain and poor visibility. However, all signs of the system are likely to disappear within a period of 48 hours.

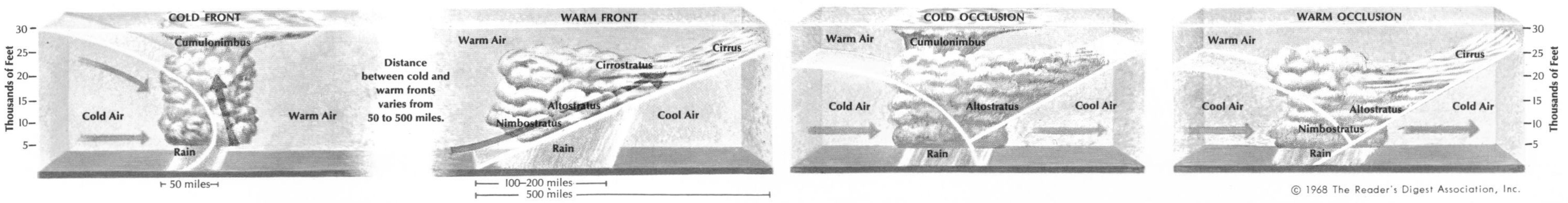

COLD FRONT
Cumulonimbus
Cold Air
Warm Air
Rain
50 miles
Thousands of Feet
30
25
20
15
10
5
Distance between cold and warm fronts varies from 50 to 500 miles.
WARM FRONT
Warm Air
Cirrus
Cirrostratus
Altostratus
Nimbostratus
Cool Air
Rain
100–200 miles
500 miles
COLD OCCLUSION
Warm Air
Cumulonimbus
Cold Air
Altostratus
Cool Air
Rain
WARM OCCLUSION
Warm Air
Cirrus
Cool Air
Altostratus
Nimbostratus
Cold Air
Rain

THE WEATHER YEAR: ITS ELEMENTAL INGREDIENTS

Different parts of the United States vary greatly in the basic ingredients of their weather and in the amount of each that is received. The weather map on the opposite page illustrates the kind of variation that occurs in the most basic of weather ingredients—pressure and the air movement to which it gives rise. The geographical distribution of some of the other ingredients is shown in simplified form on the maps below—except for that of Alaska and Hawaii. The main characteristics of these two states are presented separately.

The story of U.S. weather, month by month, begins on the following page.

AVERAGE NUMBER OF HOURS OF ANNUAL SUNSHINE

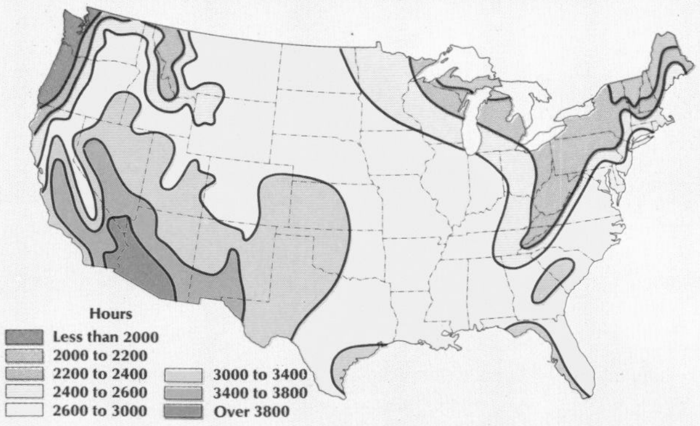

PERCENTAGE OF DAYLIGHT HOURS OF CLOUD COVER

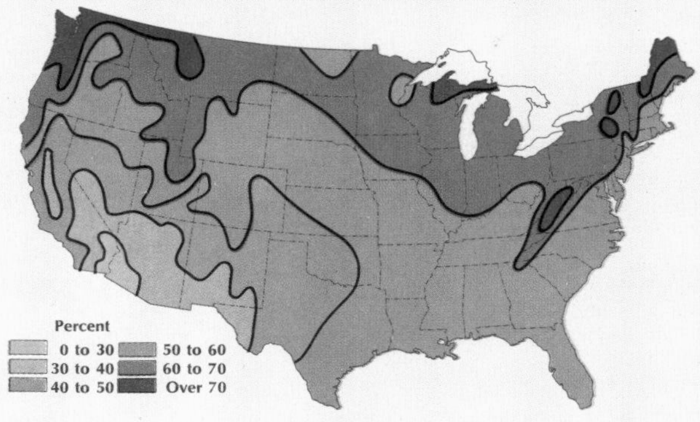

AVERAGE DAILY MINIMUM TEMPERATURE—JANUARY

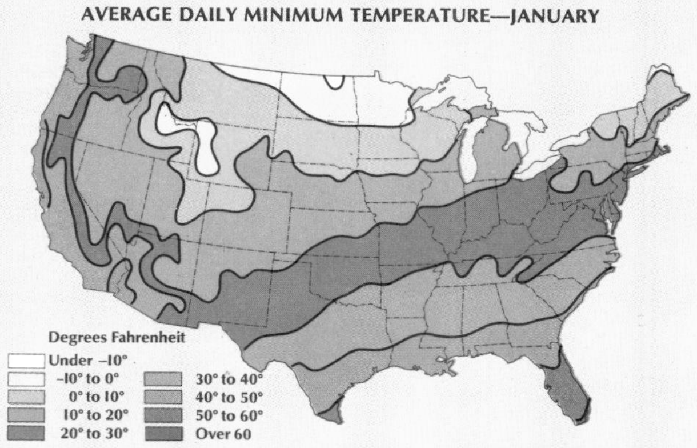

AVERAGE DAILY MAXIMUM TEMPERATURE—JULY

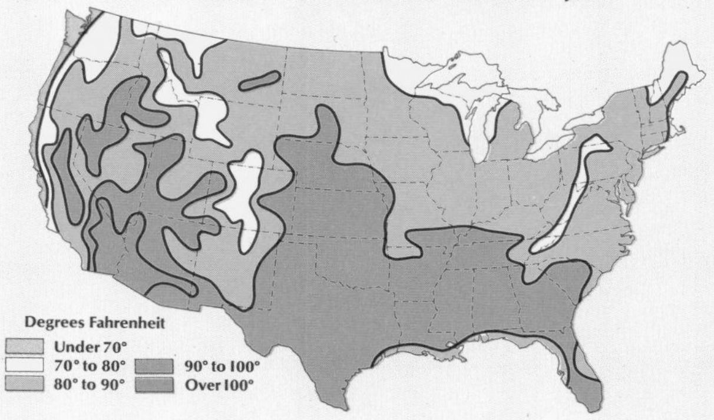

AVERAGE ANNUAL TOTAL PRECIPITATION (excluding snowfall)

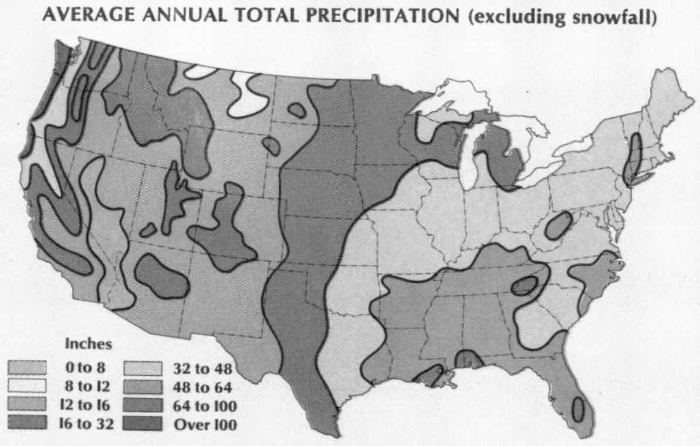

AVERAGE ANNUAL SNOWFALL

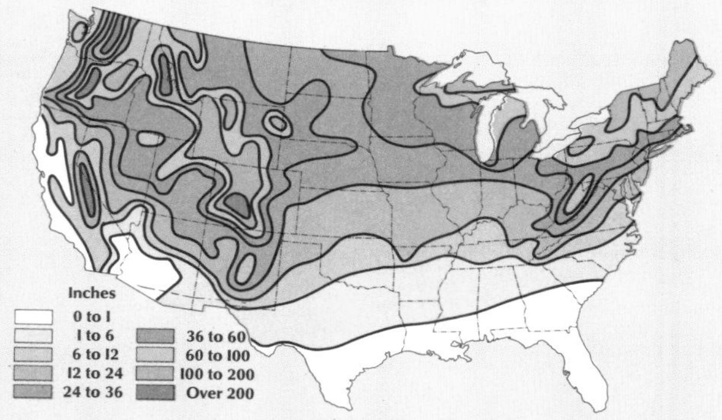

ALASKA

The weather of Alaska is the most varied of any state in the United States. The maps show the extreme variation, from region to region, of its temperature (summer and winter) and its precipitation (rainfall and snowfall). From the tip of its Panhandle—the region that stretches south along the Canadian border—to Point Barrow at its distant north, Alaska spans more than 1300 miles, a succession of high ice- and snow-covered mountains, deep valleys and broad unsheltered plains and plateaus unmatched by any other state. The three main climatic regions, described below, cannot do more than suggest the real diversity of Alaska's weather.

AVERAGE ANNUAL PRECIPITATION (including snowfall)

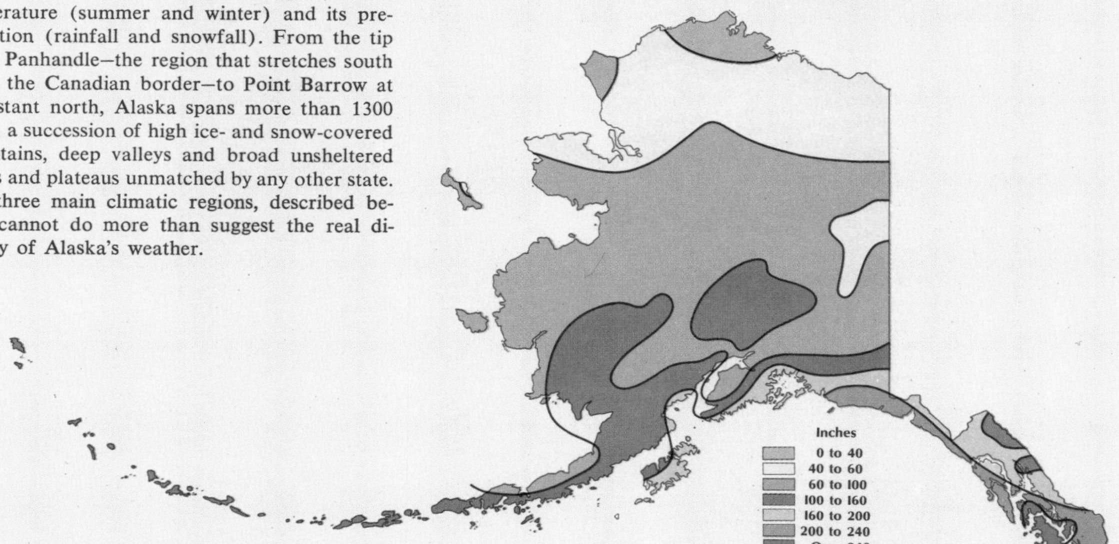

AVERAGE DAILY MINIMUM TEMPERATURE—JANUARY

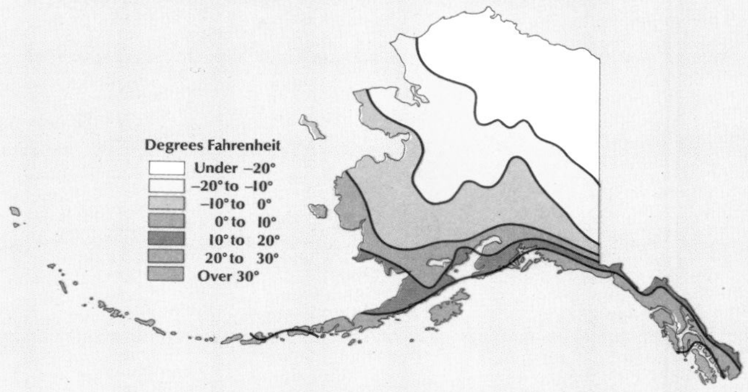

AVERAGE DAILY MAXIMUM TEMPERATURE—JULY

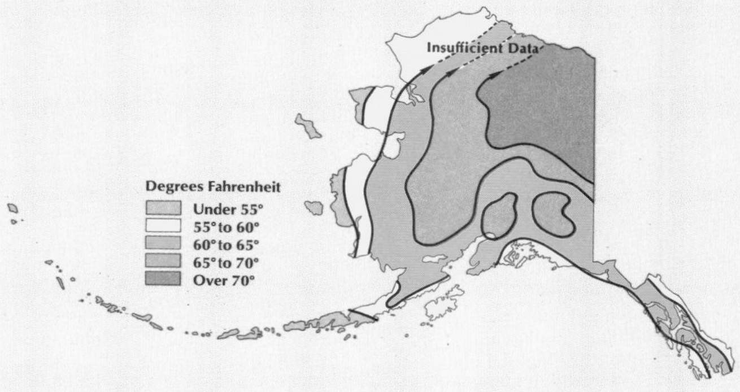

THE PACIFIC COAST. A mild-weather area, by comparison with the rest of Alaska, winter temperatures average between 20° F. and 35° F. Summer temperatures are usually in the 50's with high daily readings from time to time in the 70's—especially in the Panhandle. Much of the region is warmed by winds that have traveled far across comparatively warm Pacific water. In some parts of the Aleutians the thermometer has never fallen below zero. Rain or snow is likely two days out of three, so skies are often overcast—few places have more than 40 clear days a year. Fog occurs 20 to 30 days annually, and high winds are frequent—especially in the Aleutians.

THE INTERIOR VALLEYS. Winter temperatures in some parts may average well below zero. Daily minimums are −40°F. and −50°F. In the summer, temperatures are somewhat higher than on the Pacific Coast. Precipitation is light the year around because mountains wall off the valleys from moisture-bearing winds. Winds are generally light, except for those that get "funneled" down the mountain valleys. In winter fog occurs frequently.

THE ARCTIC COAST. Cold, short days and wind characterize the winter in this region. Temperatures maintain an average daily low of −25° F.; −50° F. is frequently reached. Such temperatures, combined with almost constant winds, create the severest "wind chill"—the maximum body-cooling rate—known anywhere in North America. Winter is a long twilight here. (At Barrow the sun is not seen between late November and late January.) Summer, at the opposite extreme, is one long day, but the air is still uncomfortably cool: temperatures are generally in the 40's, and snow may occur at almost any time.

HAWAII

For pleasant tropical weather few places can rival Hawaii. The facts speak for themselves:

Average sea-level temperatures vary from 70° F. during the coolest month to 77° F. during the warmest. Even in the hottest and most humid weather there is usually a cooling breeze—the trade wind—off the Pacific. The daily range of temperature is around 10°. Frost occurs only above the 2500-foot level, and the only snow is that which falls atop the volcanic mountains Mauna Loa and Mauna Kea. Thunderstorms, gales, hailstorms—such misbehavior of the weather is uncommon in these favored islands, where the sun shines almost every day of the year. Smog? There is none.

Rainfall is another story, as the map shows. It is heavy, but varies greatly over short distances. In one place rainfall can reach more than 90 inches annually, and five miles away the yearly total may be a mere 25 inches. Wind direction and mountains are key determining factors. The central part of the Koolau Range on Oahu receives on the average more than 300 inches; the windward slopes of Mt. Waialeale on Kauai get the world-record amount of more than 450 inches of rainfall annually, but the leeward slopes of these same mountains receive less than 20 inches. There are also wide variations in the monthly and seasonal distribution of rainfall. Some places with as much as 100 inches of rain have at least one month during which less than an inch of rain falls. Some of the driest spots, on the other hand, get more rain in one month than in all the rest of the year.

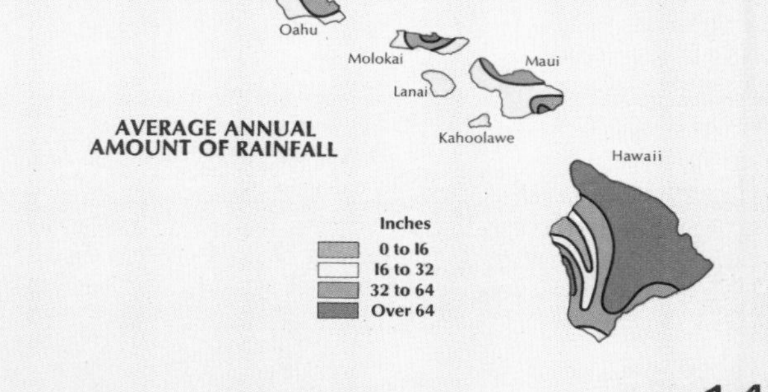

A CALENDAR OF UNITED STATES WEATHER

The timing of the beginning and end of the four seasons across the country is as different as the weather that goes into their making. Many of us have seen autumn leaves in one place, only to travel some distance to the south and discover summer and all its greenery. What, then, of the precise three-month intervals of the seasons that are designated on our calendars? For purposes of understanding the weather, they are almost meaningless. Spring begins, the calendar says, on March 20 (or March 21, depending on the year). At the right, a table shows what thermometers have read—averaged over the years—on that date.

Despite the tricks the weather plays with the months and the seasons, certain kinds, or styles, of weather have become associated with each month of the year in the minds of most of us. The following calendar sketches some of the monthly styles of our American weather.

	Degrees F.
SOUTHERN FLORIDA	69
NEW JERSEY	43
MAINE	30
UPPER MICHIGAN	29
IOWA	41
SOUTHERN LOUISIANA	64
WESTERN TEXAS	60
KANSAS	48
MONTANA	36
COLORADO	40
NORTHERN CALIFORNIA	51
SOUTHERN CALIFORNIA	58

JANUARY

The Coldest Month

The interval between the shortest day and coldest day varies considerably, but the chances are that most of the country will experience its coldest spell of weather in January. (The coldest *day* may fall in early November or late April in some places, though in most states it occurs usually in early February.)

The severest of weather news in winter is the ice storm. It disrupts traffic and communications more than almost any other atmospheric phenomenon.

The main ingredient of an ice storm is either supercooled rain with a temperature just below freezing, which falls onto a surface with about the same temperature, or ordinary rain falling onto a surface below freezing. The first kind is unlikely to cause great inconvenience or damage, because it becomes a powder of ice particles on the ground. But the second falls as rain and freezes on contact with already frozen surfaces. In this case, every exposed object becomes coated with a layer of ice or glaze, which can weigh 20 times as much as, say, the tree limb or transmission line it covers.

The favorite haunt of the ice storm is an L-shaped belt extending from central Texas northward to Kansas, then eastward across the Ohio Valley and the lower Great Lakes to New England and the Middle Atlantic States. Throughout this area there is at least a 1-in-3 chance of a serious ice storm every winter.

FEBRUARY

Month of the Snowflake

With two or three days less than other months, February is still the month of greatest snow in many states and second only to January in most others. It is the skier's month, because the snow accumulation is at or near its seasonal maximum. Heavy rainfalls, which can destroy a skier's paradise, are least likely to occur during February. And though the sun is gathering power, prolonged spring thaws are usually a month or more away.

Even a small snow crystal represents the combining of a million or so ice particles. Each particle originates from a nucleus which may consist of a frozen cloud droplet (see *June*) or a solid particle such as a speck of dust. After nucleation—a process about which little is known—the ice crystals continue to grow by the spreading (diffusing) of water vapor upon their growing surfaces.

On the trip to earth, the crystals acquire different weights because they collide with each other, attaining different velocities of descent. In dense clouds, collisions are sometimes so frequent that the snowflakes grow to be as much as an inch or so in diameter and assume shapes of astonishing loveliness. Scientists have yet to tell us what causes the infinite variety of forms to be found in snow crystals. Wilson Bentley of Vermont spent 50 years photographing them and examining their patterns under a microscope without ever finding two exactly alike!

MARCH

The Windy Month

March tops all other months for wind velocity, with April running a close second. During these months the Canadian Arctic has scarcely begun to see the sun, so that its temperatures are still hovering around the winter minimum, and high pressure prevails over most of the area. In the southern United States, the midday sun is already high in the heavens, the earth is warming up rapidly and pressures are generally low. This means that, on the average, there is a fairly steep temperature gradient from north to south. Such a state of affairs promotes the movement of air, active fronts and their attendant storm centers.

APRIL

Showers and Storms

In spite of its deserved reputation for showers, April is not noticeably a very wet time (see Rain Table, *July*). In no state is it the wettest month; in most of New England, it is the driest. Why? Spring and winter showers are not nearly so heavy as summer rains.

The overturning of the atmosphere that brings April showers, as mobile Arctic air masses pick up moisture over every water body on their journey into warmer southern regions, is responsible for most of the month's thunder. Cool-season thunder (for heat thunderstorms, see *July*) is often heard in mountain country. The upward motion imparted to cold air—already made unstable by its passage above the relatively warm water—as it meets a mountain broadside is frequently just enough to touch off thunder. Away from the mountains, thunder can be triggered when polar maritime air overtakes warmer air—as sometimes happens at a cold front—or, alternatively, walls up (occludes) against it.

MAY

Now Gentle, Now Wild

May can caress with one hand and buffet with the other. Before the month is half gone, it can have played all the lovely songs of spring and still have pulled from its repertoire a tornado and a shower or two of walnut-sized hail.

The cause of tornadoes is obscure. However, they most often seem to take place when two highly contrasted air masses—usually tropical maritime (warm) and polar maritime (cold)—come together like two fast-flowing converging rivers. A vortex or "whirlpool" of air can be formed, similar to the whirlpools that occur when water currents meet. When the whirling motion becomes intense enough, the vortex descends from the cloud to the earth in a writhing "rope" that often ranges from 200 to 600 feet in diameter. A partial vacuum—very low pressure—exists at the center of the vortex. This is why buildings lying in the path of a tornado frequently "explode"; the air inside them, at normal pressure, pushes windows and doors and walls outward.

Though tornadoes happen most often in May, they strike in every month, and in many states, as shown in the map and table below:

NUMBER OF TORNADOES (14-year national average)

Jan.	Feb.	Mar.	Apr.	May	June	July	Aug.	Sept.	Oct.	Nov.	Dec.
10	20	42	94	148	120	70	43	29	17	22	10

AVERAGE ANNUAL FREQUENCY OF TORNADOES

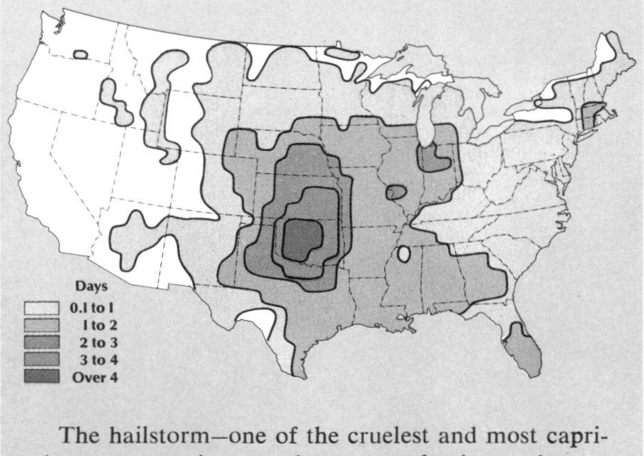

The hailstorm—one of the cruelest and most capricious weapons in nature's armory, for it can destroy a farmer's standing crops while leaving his neighbor's untouched—also occurs most frequently in May, as this table shows:

REPORTS OF MAXIMUM HAIL OCCURRENCE
(from 200 weather stations)

Jan.	Feb.	Mar.	Apr.	May	June	July	Aug.	Sept.	Oct.	Nov.	Dec.
4	2	24	56	72	36	11	1	1	5	1	0

The table reveals, too, that at least three quarters of the reported hailstorms occur when the sun is making its northward springtime journey. Most of these storms seem, in fact, to "follow the sun," as the hail belt shifts from Texas in March to the northern plains states in June. Thereafter, the belt retreats southward, disintegrating and disappearing as it goes.

It takes nothing less than a thunderstorm to produce large, damaging hailstones. Presumably a thunderstorm has sufficiently turbulent rising air currents to bring about the collision of water drops, the stuff of which hailstones are made, and then to carry the merged drops aloft to levels where the cold air will "quick-freeze" them.

Sooner or later, the lifting power of the thunderstorm's air currents ceases to be strong enough to keep the hailstones suspended, and they begin their journey earthward, partially melting and losing weight as they leave the freezing air. Frequently, it appears, the melting stones become "re-elevated" into the freezing zone, where they acquire a new coating of ice. This may happen repeatedly, in a "shuttlecock" sequence. Hailstones have been found with as many as 24 layers of ice.

AVERAGE ANNUAL NUMBER OF DAYS WITH HAIL

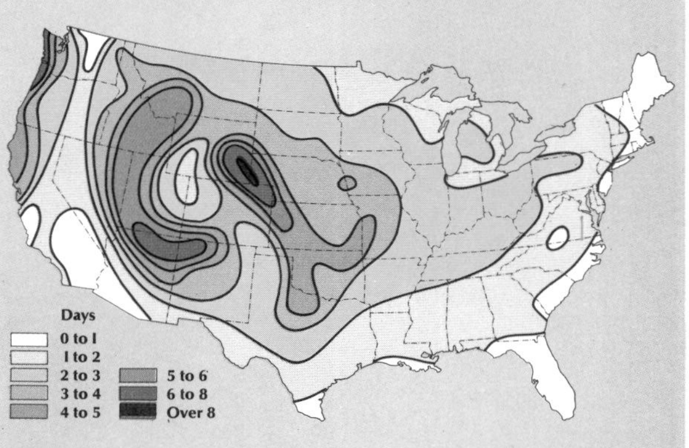

JUNE

The White-Cloud Month

Of all the months of the year, none has been so widely sung or greatly loved as June. Almost everywhere it is a balmy month. Frontal clouds—bringers of storms—are short-lived now, and in their place are commonly seen "cotton wool," cumulus-flecked skies.

What makes these lovely clouds—or *any* cloud, for that matter—is a process of moisture gathering, lifting, cooling and condensing, which, in June, is intensified by warm weather. Warm air can absorb far more water vapor than cold air. For example, air at 80°F. can hold just over five times as much water vapor in the invisible state as air at freezing point. (This explains why you see your breath, as a kind of cloud, in winter but not in summer.)

Moisture gets into the air primarily through evaporation. Fanned by the wind, the surface film of water and water particles given off by trees and plants turns to vapor. Millions of tons of moisture are daily converted to water vapor in the atmosphere of the United States. To lift this enormous weight, Nature's chief device is convection—the vertical movement of air that is warmer, and so, lighter, than the air around it. Clouds are held aloft by the upward lift of wind deflected from mountainsides and by frontal as well as convective forces.

But something more than an air "elevator" is required to make the visible water drops that constitute clouds: namely, millions of nuclei to which particles of invisible water vapor become attached. In the atmosphere, these nuclei are made up of pollen, plant spores, smoke, salt from sea spray, volcanic ash, cosmic dust and other pollutants.

JULY

Time of Heat and Thunder

With July's heat (see July Temperature Map, page 141) comes the master storm-maker, the thundercloud. For thunderstorms, lightning and rain, July—the time when most states experience their hottest weeks of the year—leads all others.

The essential conditions for the development of a heat thunderstorm are: a large surface area over and around which there is an almost unlimited supply of moist air; little or no wind; and the sun's heating of the surface of the ground which, in turn, heats the underside of the air mass above the surface by contact and by radiation. This causes the underside layer of air to expand, which, apparently, it can do only by breaking into "cells" through the center of which the heated air rises. As it rises it cools. Cooling leads to condensation. Condensation liberates heat—often enough to allow convection to continue to a height of five miles or more.

More thunderstorms happen in July than in any other month, and more during June, July and August than in the rest of the year.

REPORTS OF MAXIMUM THUNDERSTORM ACTIVITY
(from 218 weather stations)

Jan.	Feb.	Mar.	Apr.	May	June	July	Aug.	Sept.	Oct.	Nov.	Dec.
2	3	2	1	10	51	129	14	5	0	0	1

A thundercloud is a kind of wind-driven dynamo, generating electricity much as power stations do. But exactly how the thunderclouds do this, nobody knows. What is known is that the mechanism inside a thundercloud causes a piling up of negative electrical charges in one part and of positive charges in another. These mutually attracted charges are in some way prevented from meeting. Finally, the accumulated energy in each of them becomes so great that a dart of electrons is shot from one charge to the other, joining the positive and the negative. A rush of current generates light, heat and sound and also sends out radio waves, which are heard on radios as static. A single flash of lightning has been estimated to develop a million times the voltage used in ordinary house wiring.

Heavy summer rain is mostly convectional; it is produced by the local heating of moist, unstable air masses. It is more likely to come in the form of passing showers, often accompanied by thunder, rather than steady, day-long downpours. The concentration of heavy rains in the summer months (for all states except Alaska and Hawaii) is brought out strikingly in the table below.

REPORTS OF HEAVIEST 24-HOUR RAINFALL
(from 48 weather stations, for ten years or more)

Jan.	Feb.	Mar.	Apr.	May	June	July	Aug.	Sept.	Oct.	Nov.	Dec.
4	1	3	0	2	8	9	6	8	4	2	1

AUGUST

"It's not the humidity, it's the heat."

Not a summer passes that Americans living east of the Mississippi do not complain about "the humidity"—the moisture that clogs the air during the hot months. But, contrary to popular belief, it is summer's heat that causes the humidity.

The story of June weather, opposite page, told how moisture gets into the air through evaporation. The effectiveness of this process varies with the dryness of the air: the drier the air to start with, the greater the evaporation. On a good "drying" day in summer the surface level of a pond or lake may be lowered ½ to ¾ of an inch as a result of evaporation, and an almost equivalent loss of water may be sustained by plant-covered soils. The loss in a single summer month may be as much as 20 to 22 inches. It is because most of this moisture stays in the air that we complain about the humidity. (The wintertime rate of evaporation is generally less than half that of summer.)

The close, often cloying atmosphere of August causes many persons to think of a trip to the mountains. Even modest mountains like the Adirondacks and Ozarks have a very different climate from the valleys around them. Invariably they have more wind. And they are cooler—especially by day. By night they can be warmer. A hill only 200 feet high frequently enjoys a pleasant evening breeze while the valley becomes chilly and damp.

SEPTEMBER

Prime Vacation Month?

September has many virtues and few vices. It can be very hot, but seldom is it as hot or as humid as August or July. It can be very wet, but the chances are it will be drier than they. And it generally has far fewer thunderstorms than June.

Even in sunshine, September compares favorably with its more popular—or perhaps better advertised—competitors for Best Vacation Month.

MEAN AMOUNT OF SUNSHINE (percent of total possible)

	June	July	Aug.	Sept.
NEW ENGLAND COAST (Portland, Me.)	61	64	63	61
MIDDLE ATLANTIC COAST (Norfolk, Va.)	62	65	64	63
GREAT LAKES (Chicago)	70	73	69	64
SOUTHERN CALIFORNIA (San Diego)	62	68	72	73
FLORIDA COAST (Miami)	62	67	69	65

This splendid month is not without its special menace: although hurricanes may occur from May to December, they are most likely to arrive in September.

	June–July	Aug.	Sept.	Oct.	Nov.–May
NO. OF HURRICANES (W. Indian-Atlantic region) 1901–63	32	73	112	57	16

In their actions, hurricanes resemble tornadoes, but they are very much larger, and they last longer. The exceptional tornado may leave a 100-mile long, 600-foot-wide trail of ruin, and last for several hours. The typical full-grown hurricane spreads over a more or less circular area 300 to 500 miles in diameter, and lasts for days, during which it may cover an area of between 250,000 and 500,000 square miles.

The cause of hurricanes is not yet fully understood. Their early disintegration after passing from sea to land suggests that they depend greatly upon water vapor for their energy. Convection also seems to play a part, since most of them originate over the tropical Atlantic in the unstable air of the heat equator—the zone of maximum sea temperature. But hurricanes are seasonal, while convection is perennial at the heat equator, so the mystery of their origin persists.

OCTOBER

Warmer Than Springtime

Take the monthly temperature averages of almost any weather station in North America and you will find that the three autumn months of September, October and November are warmer than the spring months of March, April and May. Why? The sea holds the answer. The land experiences its greatest heat in July (or August at the latest), but the sea does not reach its peak of warmth until late August or early September. Similarly with the minimum temperatures: over land these occur usually in January, or, at the latest, February; over the sea, not much before the middle or end of February.

The dominant air masses—polar and tropical—are another important factor. In the spring, tropical air masses are seldom able to penetrate very far into the heart of the continent before being stopped by cold waves. In the fall, the northern half of the continent is still enjoying the afterglow of its long summer day: its rivers and lakes are still for the most part unfrozen, and although there may be snow on the ground before November, at least the air masses are not at all as cold as those coming at winter's end when the land is still numb from its exposure to the long Arctic night. And because many of these tropical air masses originate over the still warm air of the Caribbean and the Gulf of Mexico, their arrival is more likely to produce a spell of belated summery weather than the arrival of a cold wave is to produce premature winter weather.

The weather year is full of such oddities—unexpected changes, sharp reverses and days quite out of tune with the month. There are even, so we are sometimes tempted to think, misplaced seasons. Indian summer is such a one and most agreeably so. It comes usually in the second half of October or the first half of November, after the first chill winds of autumn have been felt.

NOVEMBER

Fog and Fading Light

By late autumn the sun has lost much of its strength and is less able to "burn off" the early morning shroud of moisture and set the air in turbulent—or convective—motion than it was during summer. The nights get longer as the sun "goes south," so that stagnating air has more chance of cooling and turning to dew.

Weak sunlight and nights of cool air: if these were the only factors, it would seem that winter would be the time of greatest fog. In fact, autumn is, with November the leading month.

Several additional factors make it so. Winds are generally lighter in the autumn. Maritime air masses—the most powerful fog-breeders—have a somewhat higher water content in autumn than in winter when the sea is colder. The temperature of the sea is higher in autumn, in relation to the temperature of the land than in any other season, with the result that the air coming off the sea stands more chance of cooling, and so condensing. (More fog is produced along the seacoasts of New England and central California—where the winds are prevailingly onshore—than anywhere else in the United States. See map below.)

AVERAGE NUMBER OF DAYS OF DENSE FOG PER YEAR

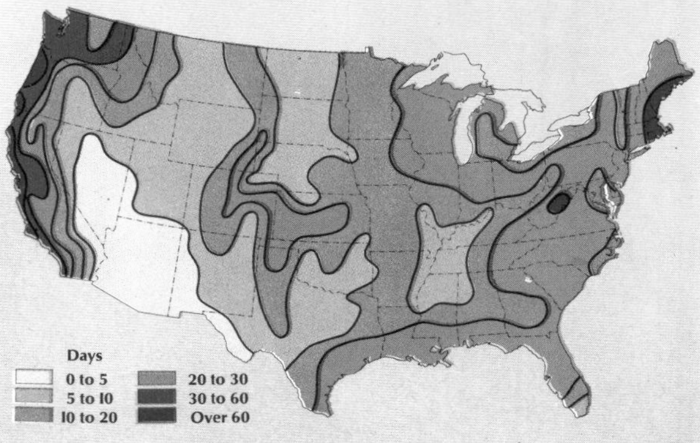

Mountaintops and hilltops are prolific breeders of fog. Whereas the cooling of horizontally moving air proceeds slowly under normal circumstances (usually about 1° to 2°F. per 100 miles), the cooling of vertically rising air occurs at a rate of 1° to 2° per 500 feet.

Before a fog can form, the lower layers of the atmosphere must be so chilled that the temperature increases, not decreases, with height. When this happens, the vertical displacement of air is sharply curtailed, or stopped entirely. The resulting inversion acts as a ceiling that prevents the escape of surface air to higher levels. When smoke and other pollutants are present, they combine with fog to produce smog.

DECEMBER

When Winter Comes

December is considered the first month of winter. But winter's arrival, like that of all the seasons, varies greatly across the country. If the year is divisible into four equal seasons (a highly erroneous assumption for most areas), winter is obviously the coldest of the four. Equally obvious, then, the date of the onset of the coldest three-month period is the beginning of winter.

This "start" of winter, as shown below, varies from November 25 to December 10. If we think of winter as arriving when the temperature falls below the freezing point of 32°F., the variation is even greater: November 10 to December 15, with some parts of the country experiencing no such "winter" at all!

START OF THREE COLDEST MONTHS

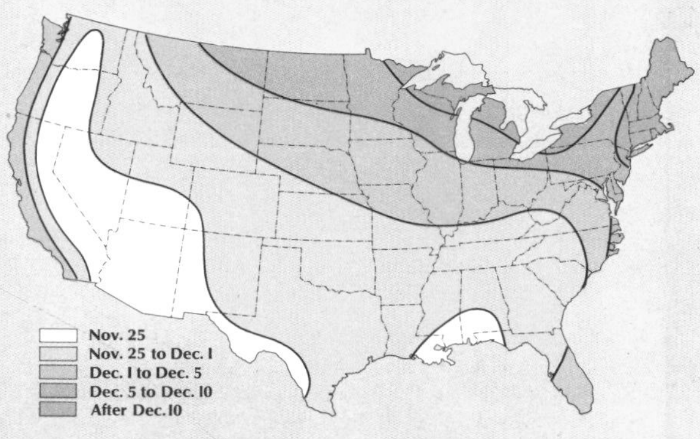

So, this makes nonsense of the astronomically based idea that winter starts with the shortest day of the year, the winter solstice (December 21 or 22). Nor is the shortest day the coldest day. On the average, the coldest day of winter occurs later in the season, for three good reasons: 1) the surface of the earth goes on losing more heat than it gains from the sun long after the winter solstice; 2) the cold of the far north—brought to the United States by winter winds—goes on getting more severe all the while the sun stays below the horizon; 3) the great continental snowfields expand as winter progresses, leading to a lowering of surface temperature and making even colder the winds that blow over them. But, for a white Christmas, the chances are, in more than three quarters of the United States—it won't happen. In most parts of the country, there is a greater likelihood of enjoying sunshine than snow.

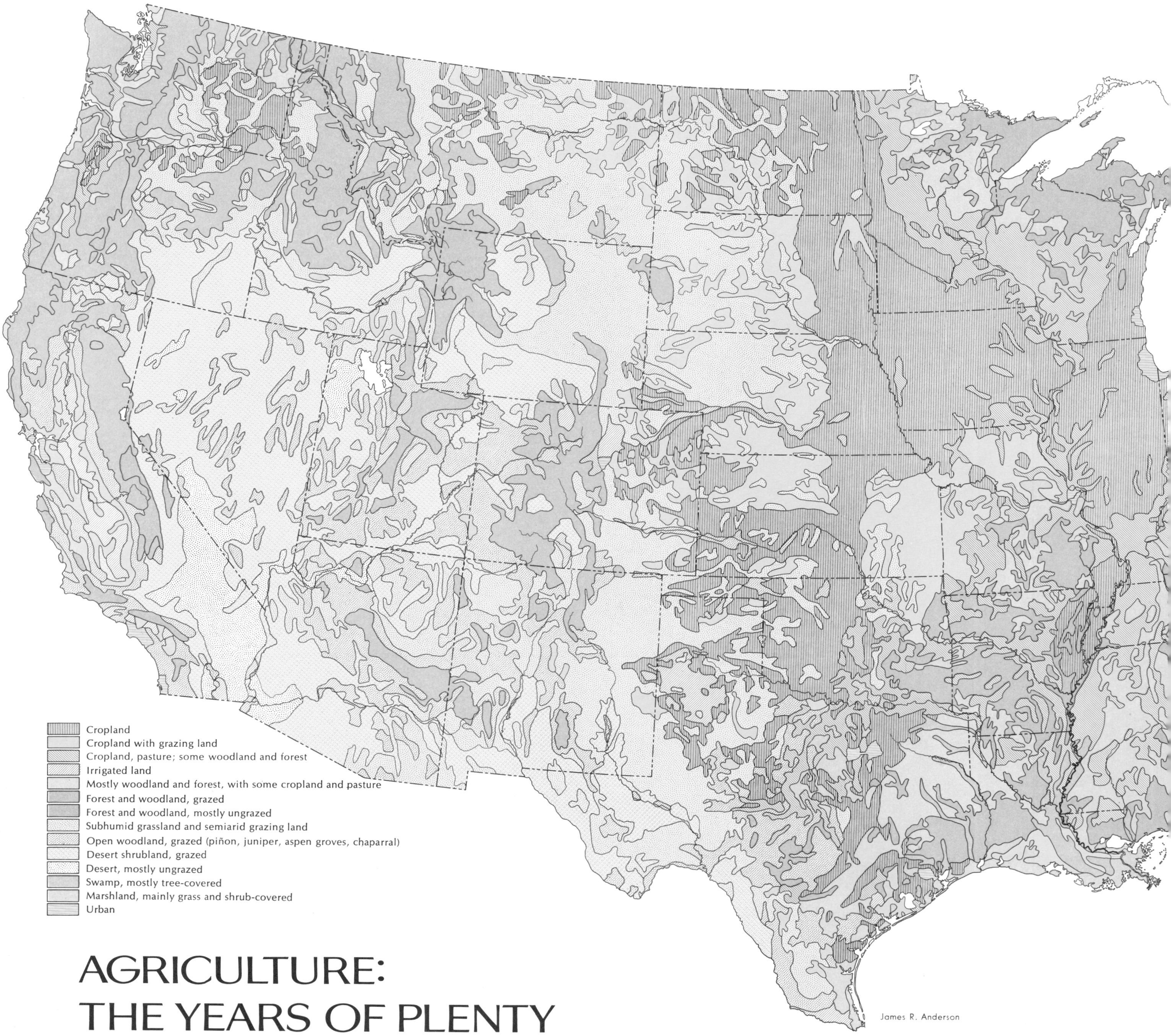

AGRICULTURE: THE YEARS OF PLENTY

THE USE OF THE LAND

Compared to other countries of the world, America has soil of great variety, much of it rich in quality.

The United States, except for Hawaii and Alaska, occupies only 6 percent of the earth's land surface, yet contains 18 percent of its cropland—with soil capable of yielding fruits, grains and vegetables. Few nations have more than our amount of such arable land per capita—3 acres. Canada, with its small population, has 6.7 acres per capita, but France has only 1.2, Norway 0.6, India 0.9 and the Soviet Union about 2.8.

Part of the American West, from the Pacific to the Rocky Mountains, is largely irrigated for farming where water is available, and given over to grazing and forest where crops cannot be grown.

The Plains area, extending from the Rockies through the westernmost central states, is transitional, primarily subhumid or semiarid. Grazing and irrigated agriculture in the western Plains give way to extensive cultivation of major crops in the eastern section—wheat, corn, cotton, barley, hay and sorghums. Some of the world's most fertile soils are located in the Plains, but because of limited and erratic rainfall, it is a land of both bumper harvests and occasional disastrous crop failures.

The greatest variety in land use is found east of the Plains. The Corn Belt is the heartland of American agriculture, the "breadbasket of the nation." Fertile soil, favorable rainfall and gently rolling topography combine to produce corn, soybeans, alfalfa and oats in abundance, as well as other feed for thousands of head of livestock. The Dairy Belt stretches from Iowa and Minnesota to New England. The Cotton Belt is rich in tobacco, peanuts and rice. Southward, in Florida and the Gulf states, vegetables grow in fall, winter and spring for northern markets.

Of the 1.9 billion acres in the 48 contiguous states, some 435 million are cropland, including 58 million devoted to pasture. An additional 640 million acres are used for the grazing of animals.

The most rapid expansion of cropland occurred after 1880, when farming reached the far boundaries of the Pacific Northwest. In the next 40 years the acreage of harvested cropland jumped from 178 million acres, mostly in the East, to 362 million acres across the country. But the native grasslands and forests were reduced by 400 million acres as cities and railroads were built and homesteading farmers began to plow vast stretches of the Plains states and the West.

Since the 1920's the amount of cropland has dropped from about 480 million to some 435 million acres, decreasing as production per acre increased, and as acreage allotment, soil banks and other Federal programs were put into effect. Some cropland also has been taken over by expanding cities, highways, airports and other facilities. The U.S. Department of Agriculture has estimated that agriculture must be extended as the population grows. Most of this acreage will be made available by diverting more grazing land to crops, stepping up irrigation in the West, draining swampland and further clearing. Agronomists will continue to expand yields per acre through scientific advances; the nation will not be heavily dependent upon new areas for agriculture to keep up with the rapidly rising population. The limit of arable land that could be used for cultivation, according to the U.S. Soil Conservation Service, is approximately 600 million acres.

About 140 million acres are occupied by urban areas, military installations, parks, highways and the like. As more land is used in this way, the amount available for crop production is, of course, reduced. At present only the areas around cities are most affected.

Forests once covered more than half of the United States. Now 300 million acres are in woodland. In the western states, virgin timber is being harvested faster than new growth can replace it. The use and value of lumber continue to rise, but tree farms are multiplying; the area and quality of woodland are on the increase.

Seventy million acres are desert, open marsh, sand dunes and rocky land. Some of this land is used for recreation, some is valuable as a habitat for wildlife.

The statehood of Alaska and Hawaii brought the total U.S. land surface to 2.2 billion acres. Of Alaska's 365 million acres, only 24,000 are cropland, with 3 million in pasture and grazing land. Hawaii's 4 million acres contain 500,000 of cropland and less than a million for pasture and grazing.

CONSERVATION AND RECLAMATION

Not so long ago—about a hundred years—much of the United States was still virgin territory. West of the Mississippi River, as far as the eye could see from the hills and high mountains, there were fertile valleys, unexplored forests, rolling prairies and grassy plains. Within 50 years after farmers began settling the Dakotas and other states of the dry plains west of the Corn Belt, millions of acres had been scarred by careless, wasteful use. An estimated 700 million acres of these western plains alone were depleted or damaged by the overgrazing of livestock and the breaking of sod. Stripped of its natural vegetation, some land could no longer retain water effectively and became badly eroded or crumbled to dust. The rich surface soil was washed into the rivers. In the 1930's the

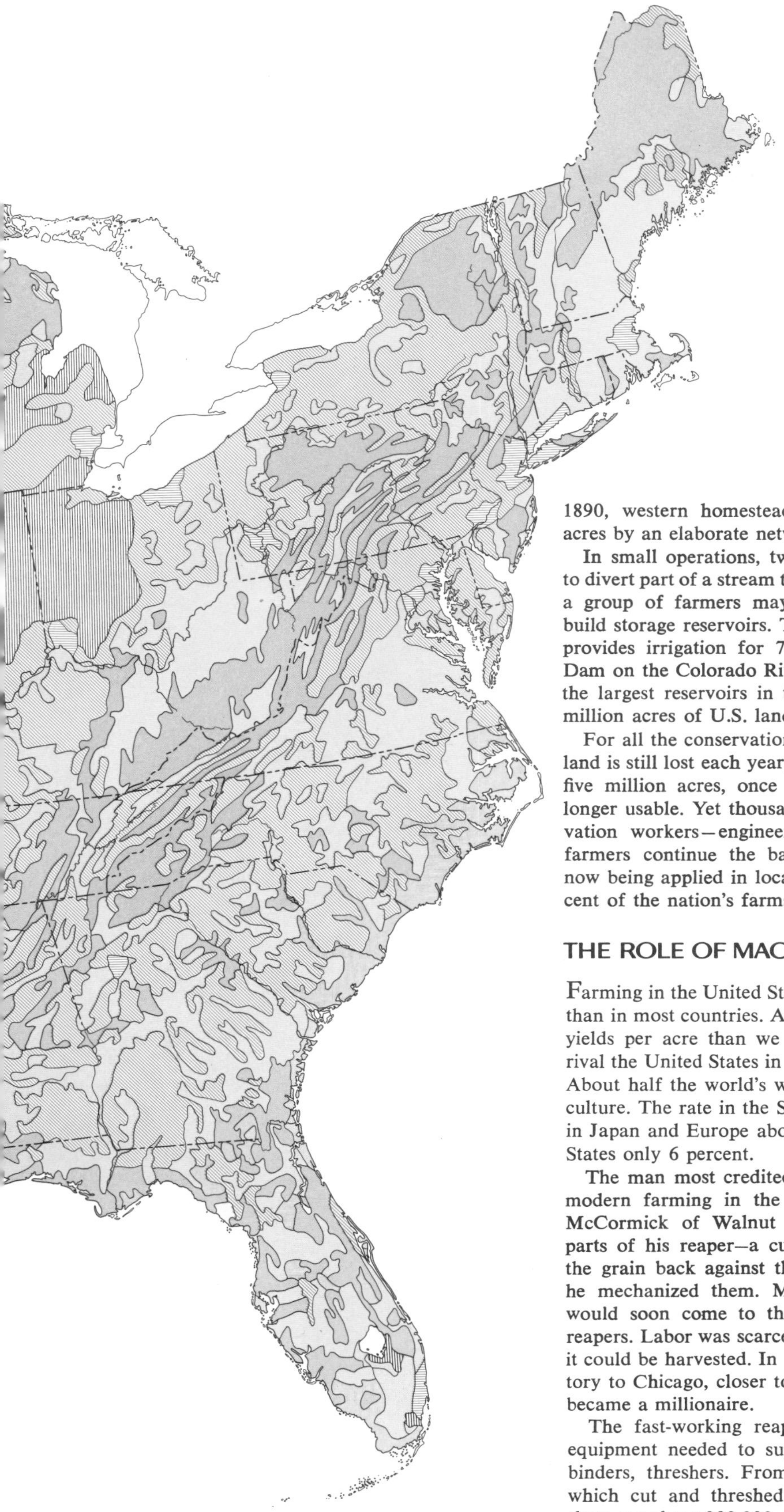

farmers of the dry western plains especially were reaping the harvest of misuse. When they plowed without irrigating and rainfall was slight, the soil turned to dust. Dust storms blew vast clouds of soil as far east as Chicago.

Poor management of soil occurred not only in the West; it had been the same in the East and South in earlier periods. Few had given any thought to conserving the abundance or balance of water, land and forest. Before the Civil War in the South, cotton and tobacco were the crops that made plantation owners wealthy. These were planted in long downhill rows and clean-tilled to keep out weeds. Runoff water from heavy rains carried this soil down gulleys by the ton. When a field was depleted, another was cleared and the process started all over.

By 1929 widespread concern about this kind of waste caused Congress to authorize eight experimental stations in different parts of the country to study erosion. In 1933, when dust storms were at their fiercest, a soil conservation agency was created as an emergency measure and made permanent two years later. The same legislation set up local conservation districts, and through these the campaign to conserve soil finally got under way.

Each district, governed by a board of local citizens, usually farmers, decided on a plan of action. After public meetings and consultation with soil specialists, work proceeded with Federal funds. "Contour" plowing and many other practices were introduced to control erosion, and soil was enriched by growing—and plowing under—suitable grasses on millions of acres in the West.

Probably the earliest form of land improvement practiced in the United States was irrigation. The Hohokam Indians built canals to water their crops in Arizona's Salt River Valley as early as 600 A.D. Later, Spanish settlers brought irrigation processes from their homeland to California. By 1890, western homesteaders were watering 3.6 million acres by an elaborate network of ditches.

In small operations, two or three farmers usually join to divert part of a stream to their lands. For larger projects, a group of farmers may organize a water district and build storage reservoirs. The U.S. Bureau of Reclamation provides irrigation for 7 million acres. It built Hoover Dam on the Colorado River to create Lake Mead, one of the largest reservoirs in the world. Today more than 37 million acres of U.S. land are irrigated.

For all the conservation and reclamation activity, cropland is still lost each year, mostly through erosion. Thirty-five million acres, once suitable for cultivation, are no longer usable. Yet thousands of Federal and state conservation workers—engineers, agronomists, biologists—and farmers continue the battle. Conservation methods are now being applied in local districts which include 96 percent of the nation's farms and ranches.

THE ROLE OF MACHINES AND SCIENCE

Farming in the United States is more advanced technically than in most countries. Although many obtain higher crop yields per acre than we do, only Canada and Australia rival the United States in output per man-hour in farming. About half the world's working force is engaged in agriculture. The rate in the Soviet Union is about 33 percent; in Japan and Europe about 25 percent; but in the United States only 6 percent.

The man most credited with speeding the evolution of modern farming in the United States was Cyrus Hall McCormick of Walnut Grove, Virginia. The principal parts of his reaper—a cutter bar and a reel which bent the grain back against the bar—were well known before he mechanized them. McCormick saw that agriculture would soon come to the prairies, the ideal terrain for reapers. Labor was scarce; grain rotted in the fields before it could be harvested. In 1845 McCormick moved his factory to Chicago, closer to his market, and in a short time became a millionaire.

The fast-working reaper generated a boom in other equipment needed to supplement it—seeders, cultivators, binders, threshers. From the reaper grew the combine, which cut and threshed grain in one operation. Today there are about 900,000 combines in the United States.

The second great stride forward was the development of the tractor to pull farm implements. First came the old steam-powered traction engine, used mostly in the Great Plains. Then the gasoline engine replaced the steam engine, and the present-day tractor evolved. Power equipment revolutionized the nation's agriculture: in 1910 a farmer had to work 135 hours to produce 100 bushels of corn; by the 1960's he needed only 23 hours to harvest the same amount.

Electricity, a much later arrival, also provided impetus to production. In 1935 a little over 10 percent of American farms had electricity from a central station. The next year, Congress passed the Rural Electrification Act, and electricity was brought within reach of nearly every farmer. The act authorized loans to rural organizations to construct power stations, lines and other facilities.

Chemical Innovations. The use of chemicals, also a comparatively recent development, may well be the most significant of any in agriculture. Scientists say that the application of chemicals as insecticides, for weed-killing and for the regulation and stimulation of plant growth will perhaps be the best means of feeding an ever-expanding world population.

As fertilizer, chemicals have been part of farming for centuries. Bone meal had been used in Europe. Scientists discovered in the mid-1800's that rock phosphate became an excellent fertilizer when treated with sulfuric acid. Today the foremost user and manufacturer of fertilizer is the United States, where hundreds of companies turn out a wide variety of such products. The American farmer and home gardener buy 31 million tons a year, at a cost of more than a billion dollars.

Chemicals may be used to stimulate plant life, retard it or kill it. Chemical regulation of plants was developed in the 1920's. Since then, more than a thousand compounds have made plants behave in different ways: Some plants hold water longer, enabling them to grow in drought areas; others resist low temperatures and frost; still others which grew on land now grow in water. Dozens of weed killers followed the discovery of 2,4–D in 1944, and tons of these herbicides are now spread on croplands, range and pasture.

The chemical war against insects is similar to that on weeds in that it seems never-ending. DDT, like 2,4–D, was developed during World War II. When first introduced, it produced astonishing results, but certain insects soon became so immune to it that they could survive in a screen cage solidly coated with DDT. This compound and other insecticides, however, continue to be used widely and successfully. Some are also toxic to man, birds and animals. Rachel Carson, the biologist, harshly criticized the use of farm chemical killers in her book *Silent Spring*.

One of the most effective ways of battling destructive insects is by using other insects. *Laricobius erichsoni*, a beetle similar to the ladybug, was shipped from Europe to attack the balsam woolly aphid, which destroys fir trees in the United States. *Bathyplectes curculionis*, a black wasp, was brought from Italy to fight the alfalfa weevil.

Another method of combating harmful insects is with sterilization. Thousands of males of a species are sterilized by exposure to radiation, then released over vast infested areas to mate with females. Reproduction is thus drastically reduced. The Department of Agriculture is still experimenting with insect-against-insect control.

SOCIAL AND ECONOMIC CHANGE

Farming is the nation's largest industry. It employs nearly 6 million workers, more than the public utilities, steel and automotive industries combined. Another 10 million people have jobs storing, transporting, processing and merchandising farm products. Agriculture's total assets in 1967 were $270 billion, about two thirds the value of all corporation assets in United States at that time.

Despite the extent and importance of agriculture, its work force has been shrinking. A hundred years ago farm communities and villages were self-sufficient. Almost everyone in the nation either farmed or was in some way or another connected with farming. By the latter 1960's, less than 6 percent of the population—about 11.6 million—lived on farms, and that number was decreasing.

This sociological change in farm life has resulted from the economic upheaval occurring in American agriculture since World War II. Great advances in mechanization and chemistry, and a rapidly expanding world population have brought about greater and greater food production. The demand has led to larger and larger commercial farms, often owned by corporations, which produce more at lower cost. Less than a third of the nation's 3,252,000 farms—those with yearly sales of $10,000 or more—did 85 percent of the farm business in 1966. Thus new technologies and market demands brought unprecedented prosperity for some; others, faced with a steadily declining income, sold out and moved to urban areas to find work.

Depression and Recovery. Until the recent upsurge of population, hard times had been almost a chronic condition for U.S. farmers. Overproduction had plagued them since World War I, when a boom-bust cycle started. To boost wartime production, farmers mortgaged their farms to buy more land. Then, as European nations recovered, prices started down and mortgage payments could not be met. By the Depression year of 1932, gross farm income had dropped to $6 billion. (In 1919 it had been $18 billion.)

The farmer's plight became so desperate that the government finally stepped in with a form of subsidy. The Commodity Credit Corporation was set up by Congress to grant the farmer price-support loans. If prices went above the loan level, he sold his crops and repaid the C.C.C. When prices fell below the loan level, he turned his crops over to the C.C.C. as repayment. Gradually the C.C.C. took in crops by the thousands of tons, and the surplus piled up wherever the government could lease storage space—cribs, barns, even idle ships. The government also paid farmers not to plant some of their acreage.

Another development that helped the farmer was the coöperative movement, which had begun as early as 1810. By the 1950's nearly every farmer doing any kind of business belonged to one coöperative or another. There were almost 10,000 coöperatives in the marketing sector of agriculture, and about 15,000 dealing in such services as insurance, utilities, credit and banking.

While farm income had been moving downward during the 1920's and 1930's, other factors had been at work to reverse the trend. Improved transportation, mass purchasers, such as the supermarkets, and food processors, including the frozen-food companies, were coming ever closer to the farmer's door. Meanwhile, foreign countries bought much of the surplus piled high by the Commodity Credit Corporation, thus bolstering domestic prices. Despite the plight of the small farmer, net income for farms as a whole in 1966 was at its highest level since 1947—$16.42 billion.

LIVESTOCK

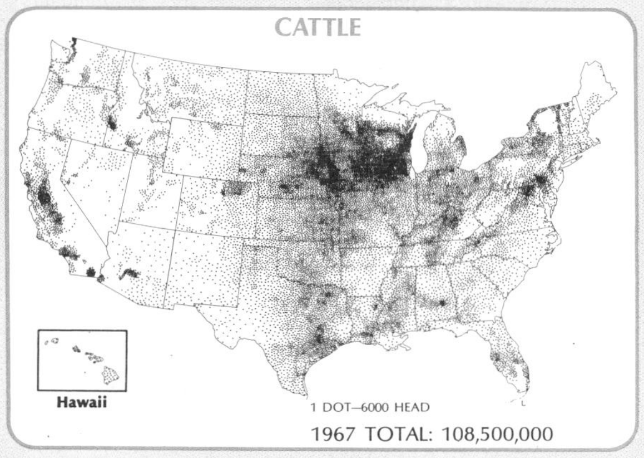

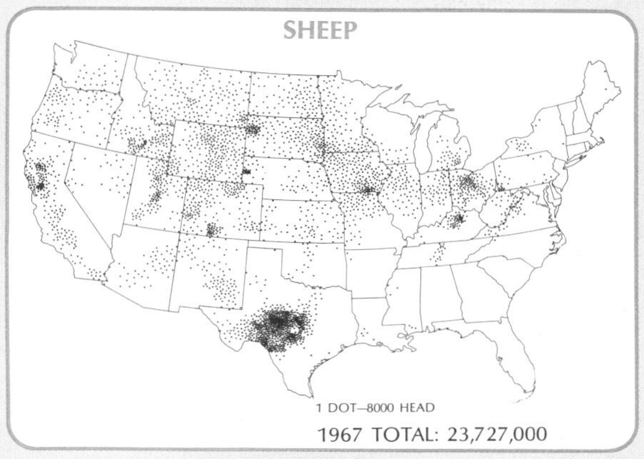

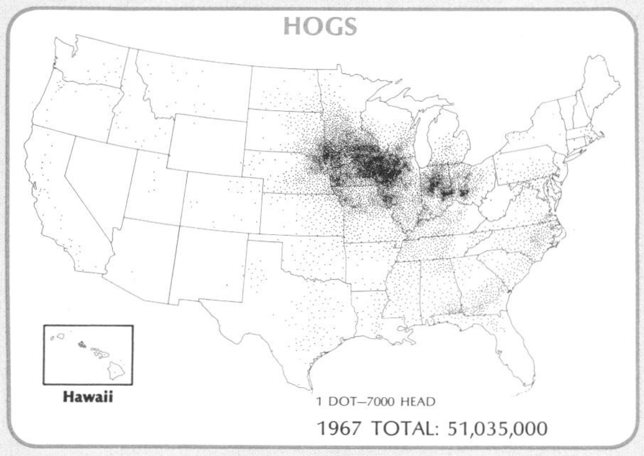

In many states, cattle are the most valuable farm commodity—for meat, milk and hides. There are 108.5 million cattle on our farms and ranches, the sale of which brings in over $10 billion annually.

The cattle population has risen by more than 30 percent since World War II, mainly because of greater demand for meat. Since 1950, beef consumption in the nation has increased from 63 pounds per person a year to 104 pounds.

Texas was the leading cattle state in 1967 with 10.8 million head on its ranches. Iowa had 7.5 million and Nebraska 6.4 million. Both Iowa and Nebraska abound in feeder lots, while Texas both breeds and feeds. The Midwest, because of its feeder lots, is far ahead of other areas in cattle population (as may be seen from the map, above). California, Kansas, Minnesota, Missouri, Oklahoma, South Dakota and Wisconsin all have 4 million or more head each.

Cattle may be divided roughly into three kinds—beef, dairy and those which provide both meat and milk. The five principal breeds of beef cattle in the United States are Shorthorn, Hereford, Aberdeen-Angus, Santa Gertrudis and Brahman.

Whiteface Herefords are the most popular breed because they forage well and are resistant to disease. They graze on western ranchlands until mature and ready for market, or are shipped to Midwest feed lots for fattening on grain. Shorthorns gain weight rapidly and need not be grain-fed for market. The Aberdeen-Angus is noted for its finely marbled and tasty meat. Brahman cattle are popular in southern states. They were bred especially for hot, humid weather. The Santa Gertrudis is a cross between the Shorthorn and Brahman, developed to provide a little more meat and at the same time resist heat.

Sheep have a double value for farmers, providing both meat and wool. They may be bred primarily for their wool, for their meat or for both. Eastern states were once more important in producing sheep, but now, on the dry rangelands of the West, where land is abundant, sheep graze over wide areas. Dual-purpose sheep are bred in both areas.

Sheep were raised by man long before he began to write history. Today there are almost a billion sheep in 80 countries. Australia leads with more than 170 million. The United States ranks eighth, behind the Soviet Union, China and others. Of the states, Texas is the first with 4.8 million sheep, Wyoming next with 1.9 million and California third with 1.6 million.

Sheep-raising has been declining in the United States for two main reasons: the increased use of synthetic fibers has cut into the wool market; and Americans are eating less domestic mutton and lamb but more beef. Although the production of meat from sheep went up from 597 million pounds in 1950 to 650 million pounds in 1966, it was not enough of an increase to reflect the tremendous rise in population during that time. But per capita consumption of lamb and mutton, because of increased imports, remained at about the same level (4 pounds). Our use of wool per capita declined by more than half in that period, from 4.2 pounds annually to 2 pounds.

The patriarch of nearly all domestic sheep is the Spanish Merino. In Spain, so prized did these animals become that the government forbade their export. Some were smuggled out, however, and crossbred with sheep in Europe and America in the early 1800's. Today American Merino sheep are considered the best in the world.

Two post-World War II developments have caused the hog population of the United States to decrease considerably. Before the war, pork fat which was sold for lard accounted for a substantial part of a hog farmer's income. Lard was widely used for cooking and other purposes. But in the 1950's commercial shortenings made from vegetable oils began replacing lard, and, as its price fell, farmers started to cut down on fatty hogs in their herds, concentrating more on bacon and meat types. Then, about the same time, Americans became more and more a nation of beef eaters. The 69 pounds of pork consumed per capita in 1950 dwindled to 58 pounds in 1966 as beef consumption increased (see "Cattle," left). By the late 1960's there were 51 million hogs, 15 percent fewer than in 1950.

Not that the hog is not still an important farm animal. In addition to producing a variety of meats and hide, the animal furnishes such specialties as hair for bristles and glands for insulin and ACTH. Hog fat is still turned into a base for soap, candles, shaving cream, salves and lubricating oils.

Since corn is the prime hog food, hog-raising is concentrated in the midwestern Corn Belt on thousands of so-called corn-hog farms. The Corn Belt states (see map, above) raise 60 percent of the nation's hogs. The leading states in 1967 were Iowa with 13.1 million, Illinois with 6.7 million and Indiana with 4.1 million.

There are about a dozen principal breeds of hogs in the United States: among them are the Berkshire, a black-and-white meat type; the Chester White, Tamworth and Yorkshire, which are raised mainly for the bacon they produce; the Duroc; the black-and-white Hampshire; the Ohio Imported Chester and the Poland China.

CROPS

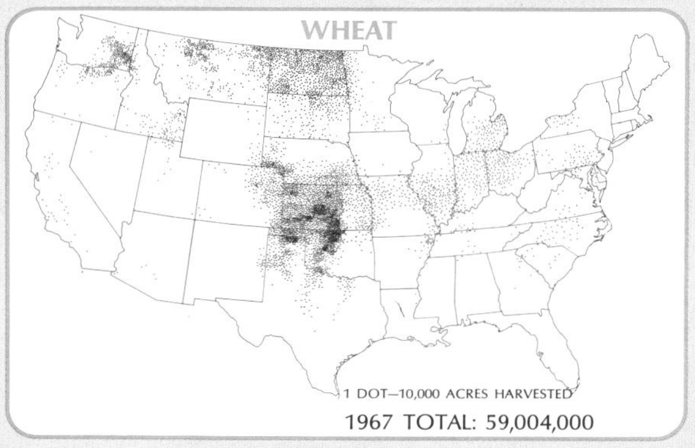

Wheat is man's principal food, grown in more places than any other food crop. The world's farmers grow about 9 billion bushels of wheat a year, of which the United States raises 1.3 billion. The United States is second only to the Soviet Union, which produced approximately 2.2 billion bushels. Kansas (see map, above) is the leading wheat-growing state with 227 million bushels. From 1950 to 1967, the average yield per acre had increased through modern methods from 16.5 to 25.8 bushels.

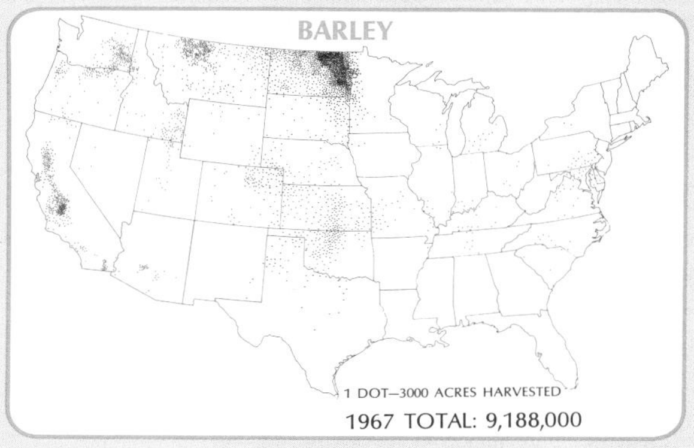

Barley is one of the oldest cereals known to man. Grains found by scientists in Egypt are believed to be 5000 years old. About 4.7 billion bushels of barley are produced in the world annually, with the Soviet Union growing about one fifth. The United States is second with more than 370 million bushels. Of the states, North Dakota led in 1967 with 85 million bushels and California was second with 75 million. Sixty-five percent of the crop is used as animal feed.

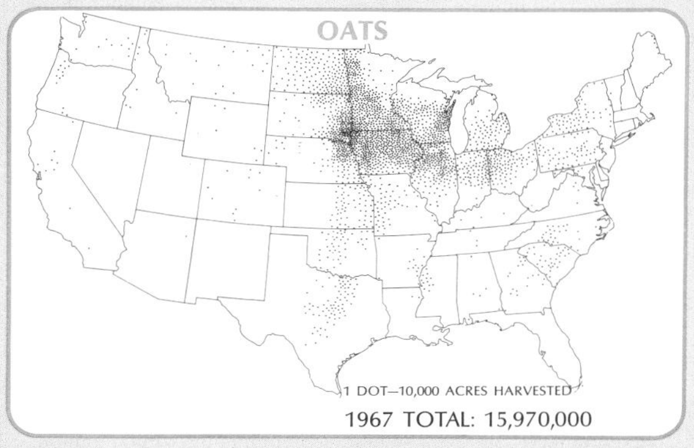

Oats are found in nearly every state, but they flourish best in a cool, moist climate. About 3 billion bushels are grown throughout the world, a third of which is U.S. production. Some 441 million bushels were raised in Canada and 427 million in the U.S.S.R. in 1965. Among the states, Minnesota harvested 157 million bushels in 1967, South Dakota 110 million and Wisconsin 107 million. Although oats are used mostly as feed for livestock, they are also a favorite breakfast cereal.

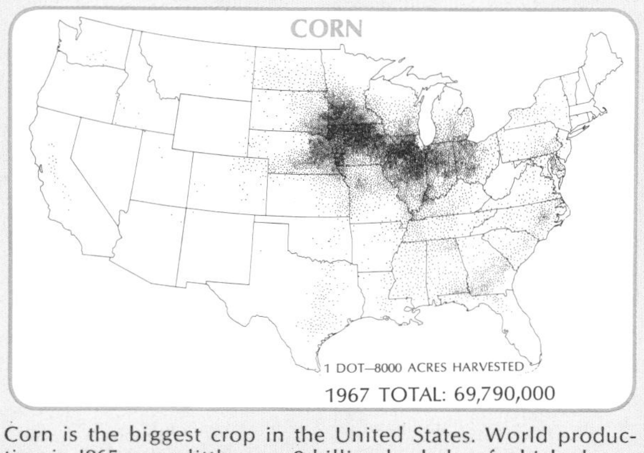

Corn is the biggest crop in the United States. World production in 1965 was a little over 9 billion bushels, of which almost 4.2 billion (excluding sweet corn, classed as a vegetable) were grown in the United States. Three fourths of American corn is raised in Iowa, Illinois, Minnesota, Indiana, Nebraska, Ohio, Missouri and South Dakota. Illinois led in the production of corn in 1967, turning out 1.1 billion bushels. Iowa was next with 930 million and Indiana third with 448 million.

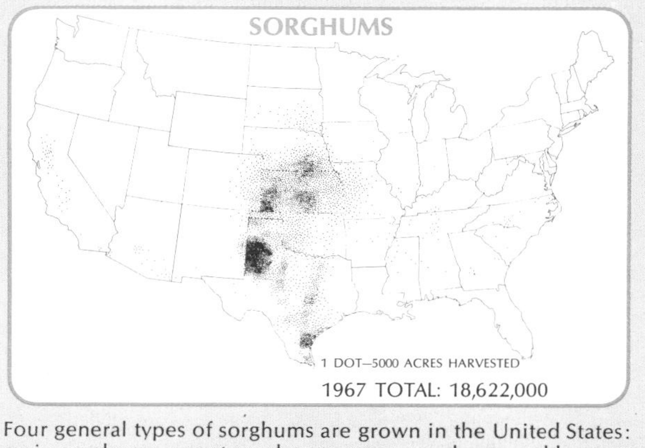

Four general types of sorghums are grown in the United States: grain sorghums, sweet sorghums, grassy sorghums and broomcorn. Grain sorghums, a substitute for corn in feeding livestock, are the most important, and three states are far ahead of the others in its production. Texas delivered almost 344 million bushels in 1967, Kansas 149 million and Nebraska 131 million. Sweet sorghums grow juicy stems that are used for syrup. Grassy sorghums make excellent summer pasturage.

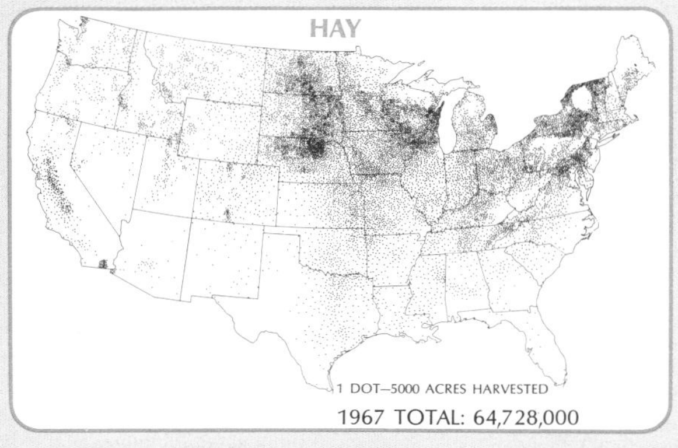

Hay includes bluegrass, timothy, brome, orchard grass and other grasses, as well as barley, rye and oats. Legumes include alfalfa, lespedeza and clovers. About 126 million tons of hay worth $2.9 billion are harvested annually. Hay is grown in every state, on 65 million acres; Wisconsin was first in production in 1967, with 10.3 million tons. Next were Minnesota and California, each with about 7.6 million tons. California farmers harvest as many as nine crops a year.

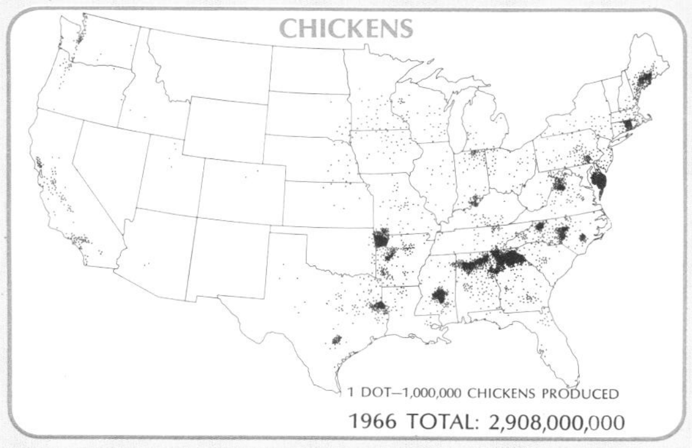

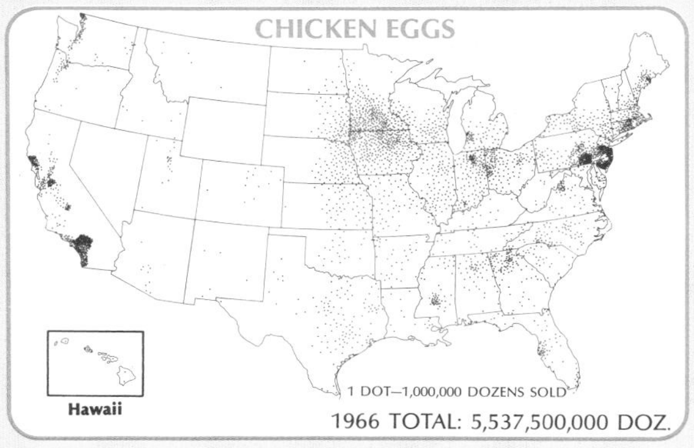

POULTRY AND EGGS

Poultry-raising on a large scale is a comparatively recent farming development. It used to be that farmers kept chickens, ducks and turkeys as a lesser part of their total operation. The small flocks generally were cared for and fed by the women and children, and the proceeds from their labor was called "egg money," to be used for clothing and incidentals. About 1925, scientists discovered that chickens given enough Vitamin D—the "sunshine vitamin" —in their feed could be kept indoors. Chickens were confined in long factory-like buildings where efficient methods could be applied to their feeding and management, and poultry-raising became a million-dollar industry.

Poultry-raising includes birds other than chickens, but the latter are by far the major product. Over 10 billion pounds of chicken were produced in 1966, compared to 2 billion pounds of turkey, the chicken's nearest rival. One reason for the difference is that the sale of turkeys is largely seasonal, most of them being consumed during the Thanksgiving and Christmas holidays. Another factor is that while male turkeys weigh up to 36 pounds and hens as much as 16, the average family cannot very easily use a bird of more than 15 pounds. So farmers are now producing smaller birds. Turkey consumption in the United States has increased in the last decade or so. Today we eat about 8 pounds per person every year.

About 40 percent of all U.S. farms reported poultry of one kind or another in the last Census of Agriculture. Those who specialize in poultry buy baby chicks by the hundreds from a hatchery. Hatcheries are an industry in themselves, using large incubators heated by electricity to keep the eggs at a constant temperature during the incubation period.

American farmers produce more than 2.8 billion meat chickens a year, about 90 percent of which are broilers and fryers. These are young chickens 6 to 13 weeks old, which may weigh as much as 4 pounds because of scientific feeding. Some farmers turn out as many as five broods of broilers and fryers a year.

The tremendous production and resulting low prices in the poultry industry in recent years have made chickens one of our most popular foods. Per-capita consumption of broilers more than tripled from 1950 to 1966, from about 9 pounds to more than 30. Among the states, Georgia leads in raising broilers (see map, left) with 456 million. Arkansas is second with 362 million and Alabama third with 324 million.

Egg farmers buy their laying hens from a hatchery in early spring and keep them in brooder houses until they are about seven weeks old. They are turned loose in the fields until fall, then put in egg-laying houses. A hen today lays about 200 eggs a year. After about 12 months of laying eggs, the hen's production declines and it is sold for meat. Some 300 million hens on farms today produce about 66 billion eggs annually. The leading egg-selling states in 1966 (see map, left) were California with 7.6 billion, Georgia with 4.5 billion, and Iowa with 3.5 billion.

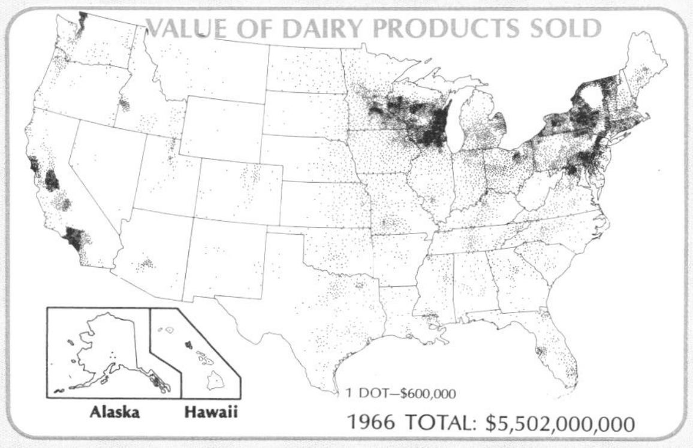

DAIRY PRODUCTS

Milk is considered nature's most nearly perfect food, containing more basic nutrients than any other. Dairy farming includes not only the raising of cows, but also the marketing of milk and its by-products—largely butter and cream. The Dairy Belt stretches west from New England through New York State, Wisconsin, Iowa and Minnesota, but such farming is carried on everywhere in the country, especially near metropolitan areas which have large markets for these products.

Many U.S. farmers raise at least a few cows. Some dairy farms have herds of milk cows ranging from 100 to 1000 or more, but the average per farm was 13. The Dairy Belt benefits from its nearness to large urban centers and a climate well suited to the production of hay and pasture—primary fodder for dairy cattle.

Despite the upsurge in the popularity of margarine, which displaced butter on many tables after World War II, the dairy industry as a whole has remained a healthy one. Although butter production fell from 140 million pounds to 16 million between 1956 and 1966, farm income from dairy products rose from $4.5 billion to $5.5 billion in those years. The number of cows dropped from 20.5 million to 14.1 million, and production of milk declined from 125 billion to 120 billion pounds. Milk production per cow, however, increased by nearly 40 percent in that period. The leading states in the sale of dairy products in 1966 (see map, left) were Wisconsin, $742 million; New York, $477 million; and California, $373 million.

The Holstein produces the most milk, although its percentage of butterfat is lower than that of other breeds. Butterfat gives milk the richness needed for butter, cream, ice cream and other products. The Guernsey and Jersey breeds produce a high degree of butterfat—both give 5 percent to the Holstein's 3.7 percent.

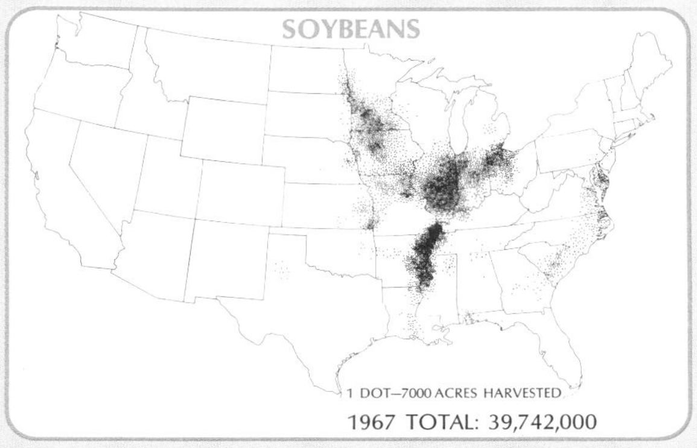

Soybeans supply food for humans and animals and raw materials for industry. The Chinese have used them for centuries as food and even for medicine. This bean contains more calcium than milk, more protein than beef; it is rich in vitamins, minerals and acids. Some 973 million bushels of soybeans, worth $2.5 billion, were produced in the United States in 1967. Illinois led all the states with 184 million bushels. Iowa was next with 146 million and Arkansas third with 92 million.

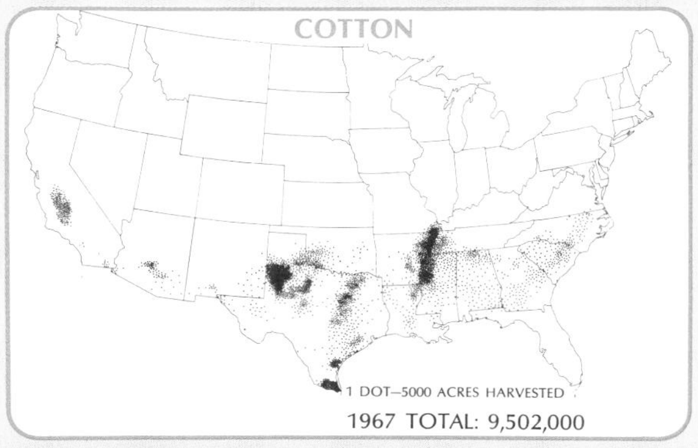

Cotton is the most widely used fiber for clothing. Almost everyone at any given moment is wearing an article made of cotton—from socks to sarongs. The United States leads in cotton production, growing about one third of the total harvest. Of this country's output—7.6 million bales in 1967—Texas produced 2.8 million bales, Mississippi 1.1 million and California 1 million. Cottonseed provides oil for many foods and the linters (fuzz on the seeds) are used in paints and adhesives.

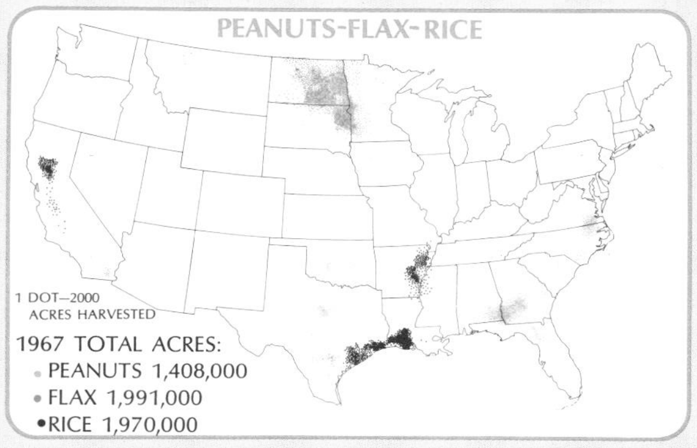

Of the 2 billion pounds of peanuts harvested in the United States in 1967, Georgia gathered the major share, 975 million pounds. North Carolina was second with 363 million and Texas third with 349 million. North Dakota led in flax with about 9 million bushels, South Dakota was second with 6.6 million and Minnesota third with 3.8 million. Texas produced the most rice with an annual harvest of 1.3 million tons, followed by Arkansas and Louisiana with about 1.1 million tons each.

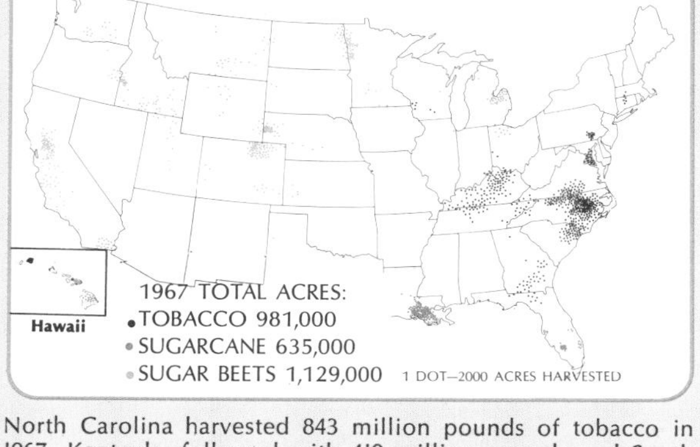

North Carolina harvested 843 million pounds of tobacco in 1967. Kentucky followed with 419 million pounds and South Carolina was third with 165 million pounds. Hawaii grows almost as much sugarcane as the two top producing states on the mainland put together—11 million tons. Louisiana harvests 8 million tons and Florida 6.1 million. California grew about 4.1 million tons of sugar beets in 1967, Idaho 2.9 million and Colorado 2.1 million.

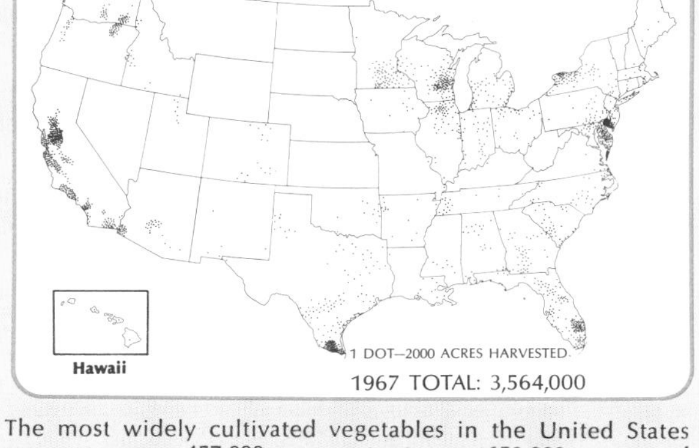

The most widely cultivated vegetables in the United States are green peas, 457,000 acres; sweet corn, 658,000 acres; and tomatoes, 474,000 acres. Tomatoes were the most valuable crop in 1966, worth $416 million; lettuce was next at $212 million and sweet corn third at $115 million. California, besides leading in the production of tomatoes and lettuce, also grows the largest vegetable crop, raising 586 million dollars' worth in 1967.

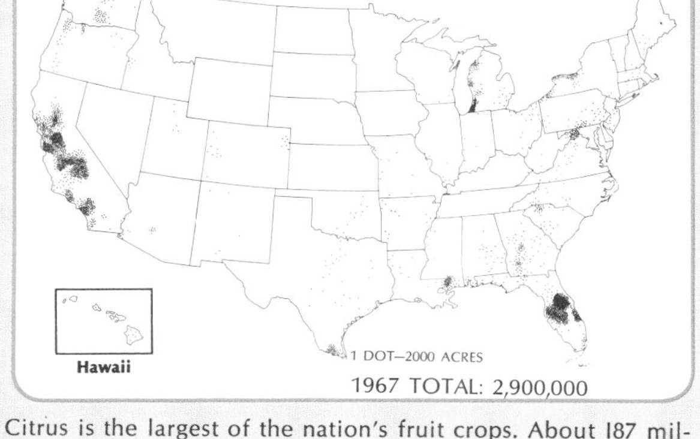

Citrus is the largest of the nation's fruit crops. About 187 million boxes of oranges, grapefruit and lemons were harvested in 1967 by citrus growers, mostly in Florida and California. Other fruits grown in the United States include: apples, 5.5 billion pounds; grapes, 3 million tons; and peaches, 2.7 billion pounds. The principal nut crops are pecans, almonds and walnuts. About 207 million pounds of pecans were grown in 1967, 79,000 tons of almonds and 77,000 tons of walnuts.

THE MIGHT OF INDUSTRY

THE VALUE OF MANUFACTURING BY STATES
(in billions of dollars)

The states are ranked here according to the real value of their manufacturing activities. The worth in dollars of the manufacturing process is called "value added." To calculate this, the cost of raw materials, fuel and other elements is subtracted from the dollar value of the finished product (before shipping). The result gives the value added of the manufacturing process.

State	Value
OVER $10 BILLION	
New York	19.51
California	17.16
Ohio	15.44
Illinois	14.56
Pennsylvania	13.97
Michigan	13.00
$5 TO $10 BILLION	
New Jersey	9.98
Indiana	7.69
Texas	7.05
Massachusetts	6.37
Wisconsin	5.34
$3 TO $5 BILLION	
North Carolina	4.62
Connecticut	4.48
Missouri	4.42
Tennessee	3.34
Georgia	3.24
Virginia	3.06
$2 TO $3 BILLION	
Maryland	2.98
Washington	2.87
Minnesota	2.83
Kentucky	2.46
Alabama	2.34
Florida	2.33
Iowa	2.28
South Carolina	2.12
$1 TO $2 BILLION	
Louisiana	1.92
West Virginia	1.83
Oregon	1.57
Kansas	1.44
Colorado	1.20
Mississippi	1.02
$0.5 TO $1 BILLION	
Oklahoma	.965
Arkansas	.959
Rhode Island	.950
Maine	.779
Nebraska	.743
Utah	.705
Delaware	.666
New Hampshire	.654
Arizona	.617
UNDER $0.5 BILLION	
Idaho	.366
Vermont	.309
Washington, D.C.	.261
Hawaii	.254
Montana	.235
New Mexico	.170
South Dakota	.142
Nevada	.112
Alaska	.089
Wyoming	.083
North Dakota	.072

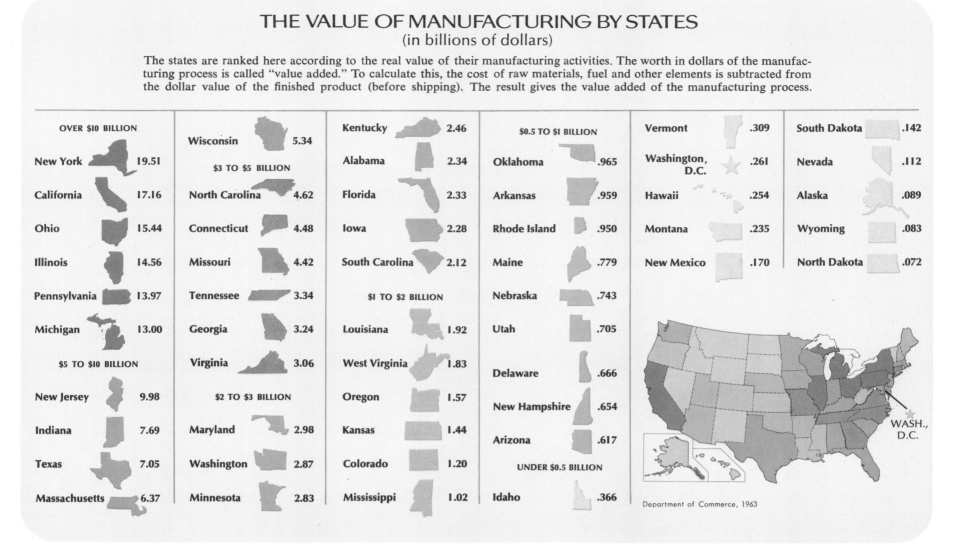

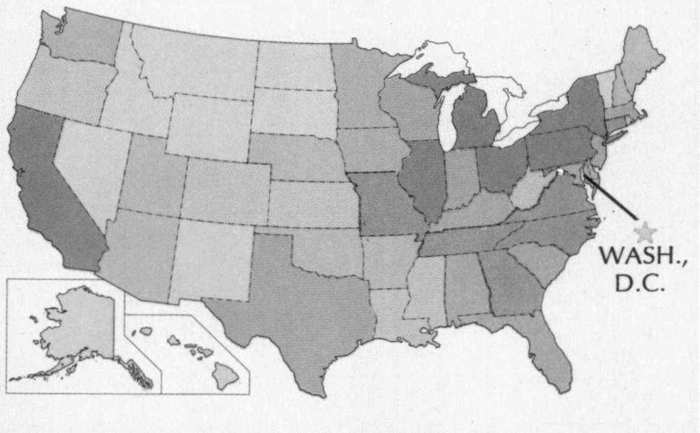

Department of Commerce, 1963

THE EVOLUTION OF AMERICAN INDUSTRY

The growth of the United States as a producer of goods since World War II borders on the fantastic. Between 1947 and 1966 the value added to raw materials by manufacturing more than tripled to $251 billion. This 19-year period saw 10 times more manufacturing than all the years between the Civil War and World War II.

Salaries and wages also tripled in this period, reaching $125 billion. The number of employes in industry rose only 25 percent, however, a commentary on the role of automation in American industry.

The United States turns out more than half the world's manufactured goods. The Soviet Union is believed to be second, although no verifiable figures are available; West Germany was third in 1965 and Great Britain fourth.

The emergence of the United States as a leader in world manufacturing has been comparatively recent. In colonial days, England restricted American manufacturing because it was competitive with her own, and even after the Revolutionary War, America continued to look to England for goods rather than to her own economy. Americans still did not know how to turn out goods cheaply and in quantity. Most American industry was of the small-shop and home variety. Of the 700 families in Lancaster, Pennsylvania, in 1790, for example, 234 were in some kind of manufacturing. Among them were 36 shoemakers, 30 smiths, 28 weavers, 17 saddlers and 14 hatters.

The Machine Age. Textiles and armaments were the first to be mass-produced, and that mechanical genius Eli Whitney had a hand in developing both industries. Because textiles were so important to Britain, she carefully guarded mass-production methods by forbidding plans or drawings of the machinery to leave the country. Then an English textiles mechanic, Samuel Slater, sailed for America secretly. He set up a small English-type cotton-spinning mill in New England, designing and building the machines from memory. At about the same time—1791—Whitney invented the cotton gin, which greatly increased the production of raw cotton. With cheap and plentiful raw materials, new mass-production know-how and ready markets, New England soon became the nation's textile center.

In 1798, the U.S. government asked Whitney to manufacture 10,000 muskets, stipulating that it be done within two years. Whitney knew he could not depend on the usual painstaking workmanship of skilled labor to fulfill his contract within that time, so he set about developing machinery to do the job. The machinery alone was two years in the making, and eight years passed before he delivered all the muskets; but Whitney had made two revolutionary contributions to American industry—the manufacturing of intricate products by machine and the assembling of interchangeable parts.

Once started, machine manufacturing grew rapidly. Each new machine created a demand for another one, and often several others; and an industry in itself, machine-tool manufacturing, began to develop.

Machine tools are the devices that turn, grind, bore, mill and plane materials for making other machines and metal parts. In the early 1800's the English mechanic Henry Maudslay installed a slide rest on the lathe, which held the metal firmly to make closer tolerances possible. Then came the shaper, the steam hammer and finally the high-speed machine tools which increased cutting power.

The spread of mechanization hastened the development of the iron and steel industries. In the mid-1800's Henry Bessemer in England and William Kelly in the United States, within a year of each other, hit upon the idea of blowing a blast of air through molten iron to remove excess carbon. Then they added a mixture of carbon and manganese and had steel. As the century drew to a close, technological developments and the new metal created an intense industrial activity. Construction of railroads, bridges and buildings doubled and redoubled. U.S. production soared from 200,000 tons of steel in 1870 to 12 million tons only 30 years later.

From Waterwheel to Atomic Energy. Additional power sources now became an important factor. The steam engine had been in operation since the early 1800's but American manufacturers did not take advantage of it immediately. Water power was good enough and plentiful. As late as 1869 only 50 percent of industrial power was provided by steam. Then Thomas Edison and George Westinghouse brought a cheap and efficient source of power—electricity—to industry's very doorstep. Edison developed electricity as illumination and Westinghouse built a transformer that permitted the transmission of high voltages over long distances. By 1900 electricity and steam were about equal as industry's power sources. Today 90 percent of the nation's industrial energy comes from motors driven by electricity generated from coal, water, fuel oil, natural gas or atomic energy.

Probably no industry better illustrates the rapid growth of American technology in the twentieth century than does automobile manufacturing. The gasoline automobile was first developed in Europe, but it was America that mass-produced it. Henry Ford was the genius who most successfully combined all the mass-production elements—the moving assembly line, the standardization of parts, the speed of handling. Where others had failed because their cars were too expensive, Ford's idea was to produce an immense volume at a price most people could afford. He standardized body and chassis design and made the cars all the same color. "A customer can have any color he wants as long as it is black," he said. He raised $42,000 as a starter in 1904 and never had to borrow additional money. The Ford Motor Company had rivals, but in 1923 it produced 57 percent of the 4 million cars sold. Within 20 years—led by Ford—automobile manufacturing had come from nowhere to become America's chief industry.

LEADING CENTERS

From colonial days the East has been the dominant manufacturing region of the United States (see chart, above). The East took an early lead in manufacturing because it had all the advantages: abundant natural resources such as iron and coal, ample capital and labor supply and a navigable coastline to provide access to markets. By the beginning of the nineteenth century, 70 percent of the nation's manufacturing was done in the East—the Middle Atlantic states and New England. The West was as yet too sparsely settled to compete seriously, and the 11 Southern states were still too preoccupied with their main source of income—King Cotton.

As the population moved across the country, however, the West began to catch up. By 1900, the Eastern states' share of manufacturing had dropped to 55 percent, and the Midwest's portion had risen to 32 percent. The South accounted for 11 percent and the Pacific Coast for 2 percent. Recently, the Midwest has caught up with the East. Of the top 10 industrial states, four were in the East—New York, Pennsylvania, New Jersey, Massachusetts; and four in the Midwest—Ohio, Illinois, Michigan and Indiana. By the mid-1960's, these Midwestern states led the four in the East by $50.7 billion to $49.8 billion in value of manufacturing. California's $17 billion was second only to New York's $19.5 billion.

WAVE OF THE FUTURE

The boom-bust era of the 1920's and 1930's saw comparatively little technological advance in industry. But once the decade of the Depression was over, a phenomenal series of inventions and experimental projects started. Economists chart the beginning of this remarkable period from the inventions of the 1940's and the industrial stimulation created by World War II.

In the 1930's Dr. Wallace Carothers of Du Pont experimented with man-made fibers, and from this research came nylon. When the Japanese attacked Pearl Harbor, hundreds of textile mills were cut off from their source of raw silk. Du Pont put its product on the market and the mills bought all they could get. Nylon stockings went on sale in department stores, and thereafter silk stockings became virtually extinct. Within 20 years fiber manufacturing became a $2.4 billion industry.

During World War II, a whole spate of developments emerged from drawing boards and laboratories. Among them were microwave radar, jet aircraft, the helicopter and atomic energy. After the war came color television, magnetic tape, instantly developed camera film, xerography. Then also came the liquid-fuel rocket, which opened the way to the limitless exploration of space—one of man's most ancient dreams and also one of his newest industries.

The Computer Innovation. No achievement, however, was more symbolic of postwar industrial ingenuity than the computer. So thoroughly did it invade industry that some economists have taken to calling our present industrial dynamism "The Computer Revolution."

The principle on which the computer is based is as old as the abacus. Seventeenth-century mathematicians used analytical machines derived from this ancient counting device. In 1944, Howard Aiken of Harvard University built an advanced mechanical computer, but it wasn't until electronics was introduced to the calculator by J. Prosper Eckert and John Mauchly of the University of Pennsylvania, in 1946, that it really came into its own. Computers began solving problems so fast the mind boggled. Then the transistor, no bigger than a man's fingernail, was developed by Bell Laboratories as a replacement for the vacuum tube. This further miniaturized the computer so that it could be placed in an aircraft cockpit or a space capsule.

Today, computers can regulate anything in industry from an assembly-line machine to a space shot. In Southwestern refineries, they control the flow of oil from one tank to another; in Midwestern chemical plants they decide which chemicals and how much should go into a particular compound. They can deliver solutions to problems in nanoseconds, or billionths of a second. (A nanosecond has the same relationship to a second as a second has to 30 years.) Computers mark the most revolutionary advance in industry since Henry Ford's assembly line. Computer-guided automation has caused productivity per man-hour to soar. Using the 1957–59 period as an index of 100, output per worker has increased from 84 to 122 in the 10 years to 1965. While the manufacturing labor force has remained virtually static in that time, production in terms of value added has risen from $135 billion to $225 billion.

Newest Developments. Such remarkable inventions as the computer, transistor, jet engine and radar, of course, breed more of the same. Today workshops and laboratories are turning out devices only dreamed of in the works of science-fiction writers. These include the laser, which beams light a billion times more intensely than that of the sun's surface. Focused at close range, it can vaporize any substance on earth. And there are new telephones that permit you to see as well as talk to your caller. A household computer will enable a family to plan expenditures for a year ahead, or help Junior with his homework. In the next 15 years we probably will see more new industrial products and developments than in all of our past.

DURABLE GOODS

		VALUE ADDED (in billions of dollars)	EMPLOYES
1.	Transportation Equipment	$27.73	1,732,434
2.	Machinery	$22.82	1,651,462
3.	Electrical Machinery	$20.22	1,604,451
4.	Primary Metals	$18.76	1,242,583
5.	Fabricated Metals	$14.21	1,160,183
6.	Stone, Clay and Glass Products	$7.92	598,809
7.	Instruments and Related Products	$5.05	327,749
8.	Lumber and Wood Products	$4.39	569,657
9.	Miscellaneous	$4.38	410,021
10.	Furniture and Fixtures	$3.62	407,715

Manufacturing may vary from small craft industries (dressmaking shops and homemade food specialties) to vast complexes that absorb most of the labor of individual cities. Economists generally divide manufacturing into durable and nondurable goods. The durable are defined as products that normally will remain in use a long time, such as automobiles, steel and glassware. Those listed as nondurable are considered by economists to be less lasting, although some of them, such as books and items of clothing, may well outlive automobiles. (For a comparison of durable and nondurable goods, see the latter heading on page 151.)

All manufacturing industries are grouped according to the so-called Standard Industrial Classification. To bring some order to the mass of business statistics it had been gathering since 1809, the Bureau of the Census in 1939 began grouping all industries into these S.I.C. categories. They include mining, retail trade, construction and other divisions, but manufacturing is by far the most important, earning about a third of the nation's income and employing a fourth of its workers.

The durable goods classifications listed at the left are ranked according to their value added. In total production value these products more than doubled in 15 years between 1950 and 1965—from about $90 billion to $225 billion. In the last year of that period, durable goods jumped ahead by almost $20 billion.

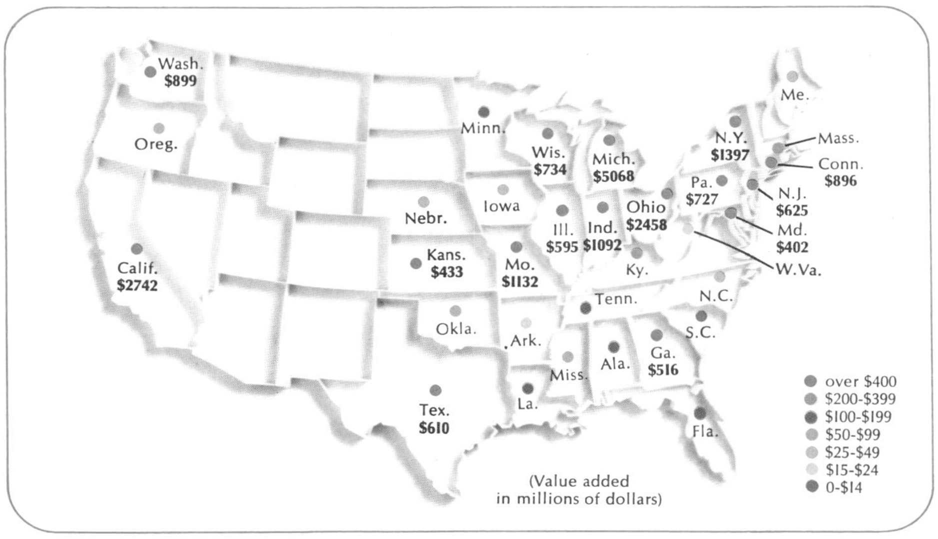

TRANSPORTATION EQUIPMENT

Automobiles, aircraft, ships, railroad cars and locomotives are some of the industries included in transportation equipment. Automobile manufacturing led in this category in 1965, accounting for nearly $16 billion yearly in value added, compared with about $8 billion for aircraft and a little over $1 billion for ships.

Because of its importance as a maker of automobiles, Michigan is the major state in transportation equipment (see map, left). Early in the 1900's automobiles were first made in quantity in Detroit and neither the city nor the state has ever given up its dominance in the field. California is next in transportation because it leads in aircraft production. Its aircraft-manufacturing output, however, is only about half that of Michigan's for automobiles.

Despite an occasional dip in automobile sales at the start of 1967, the industry was expected to maintain the general upward trend in production it has enjoyed nearly every year since World War II. The output of 8.7 million cars during 1966 was second only to the record 9.3 million of 1965. Additional safety items—impact-absorbing steering columns, recessed instruments, door safety latches, improved anchorage of seats—added to the cost of manufacturing.

Aircraft production increased as the 1960's drew to a close, although there was some chance that the critical demands of the military in Vietnam would slow civilian manufacturing. In the five years from 1962 to 1967, aircraft production rose 140 percent, from 10,000 planes to 24,000.

MACHINERY

Machinery is the basis for all industrial manufacturing. The automobile, for example, has some 30,000 parts. Only because each is machined accurately to size can the semiskilled mechanic assemble them and produce an engine that will operate.

Under the machinery classification are construction, industrial, metalworking and farm machinery. Metalworking machinery, largely machine tools, is the most important subindustry, with $4 billion in manufacturing value in 1965. Industrial machinery—elevators, furnaces, pumps, compressors—is next with $3.6 billion and construction machinery is third with $3.5 billion. One of the fastest-growing classifications was air-conditioning, whose shipments rose from $1.5 billion in 1961 to $2.7 billion in 1965. The machine industry centers in the Midwest, especially around Chicago. Among the states, Illinois, Ohio and Michigan are the main producers.

Despite some obstacles in the mid-1960's, the machine-tool industry managed to keep production high. There was a labor shortage in 1965 because the industry was rated nonessential and lost men to the draft or to industries which were considered essential. And in 1966 the government stopped its 7 percent tax credit for new equipment for a time, causing some manufacturers to cancel orders. Nonetheless, orders in 1966 were 15 percent ahead of 1965. Many of the new machines were highly automated, with computer controls and new chemical machining techniques.

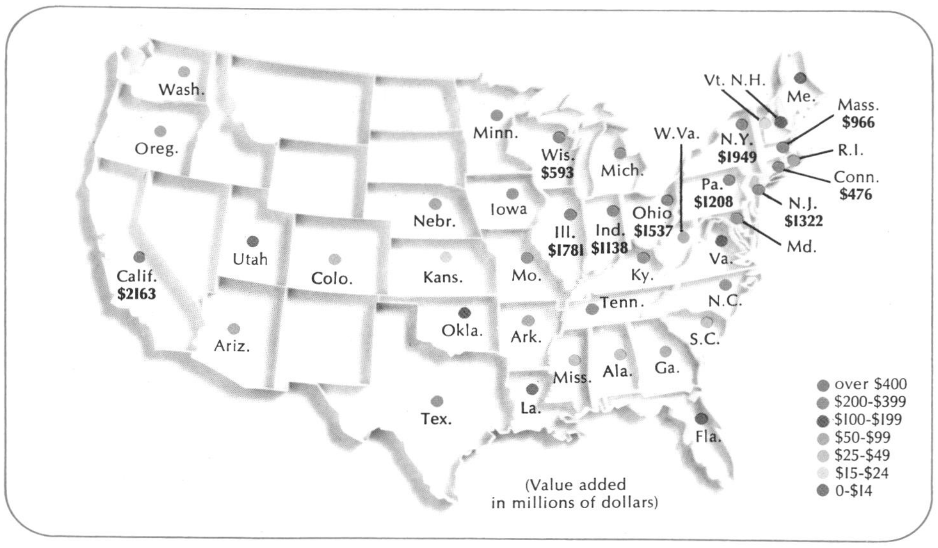

ELECTRICAL MACHINERY

Communications equipment, which includes telephone, telegraph, radio and TV equipment, is the largest industry in this classification, having turned out more than $5.7 billion a year in manufacturing value in 1965. Electronic components are next with $3.3 billion. The leading electrical machinery states are California, New York and Illinois.

The early 1960's were prosperous years for the industry. In the five years to 1965, the output of electrical industrial equipment increased at an annual rate of 5 percent. Transmission of electrical energy underwent major technological changes also. The industry constructed larger and larger generating and transmission units, thus enabling long-distance lines to carry greater voltage.

Growing color-television and defense needs pushed the manufacture of electronics equipment to new records. In 1966, electronics industry sales were well over the $20 billion mark—18 percent above 1965. And for the first time, the industry's employment passed 1 million.

The manufacture of telephone and telegraph equipment rose steadily in the 1960's. Several factors were responsible: the increasing number of households, conversion of central telephone offices to electronic switching and the intensified demand for equipment by the military services.

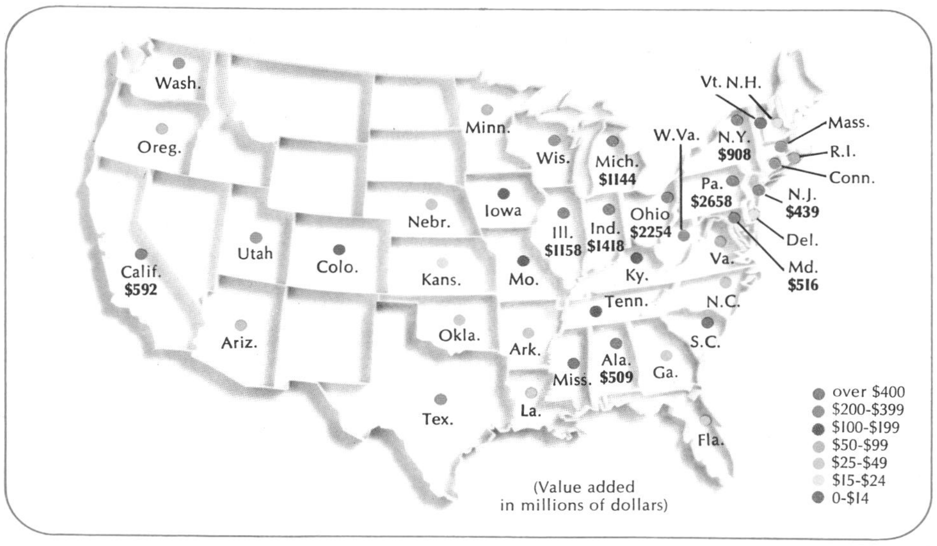

PRIMARY METALS

Steel rolling and finishing, with $10 billion value added in 1965, makes up more than half of this category. Rolling and drawing mills for nonferrous metals such as copper and aluminum were virtually tied for second place. Iron and steel foundries stood at about $2.5 billion each. The leaders among the states in this classification were Pennsylvania, with its great iron and steel complex around Pittsburgh; Ohio, with many plants along the Ohio River Valley and in Cleveland; and Indiana, with steel manufacturing centers at Gary and Hammond.

Modernization and automation brought new efficiency to the steel industry as fewer men were required to produce more steel. In 1955, 117 million tons of steel were produced by 625,000 employes. In 1965, only 584,000 workers were needed to turn out 131 million tons. Thus, in 10 years, output had increased by 12.4 percent while employment declined by 6.5 percent.

Aluminum's principal uses are in construction and transportation vehicles—automobiles, trailers, aircraft, railroad cars—23 percent going to each of the two industries in 1965. The rest went into machinery, containers and other products.

The United States is the free world's leading producer and consumer of copper, producing 38 percent of the world's supply while using about 46 percent in 1965. The switch to copper "sandwich" coins by the Federal government in 1966 assured the metal a good market for years to come.

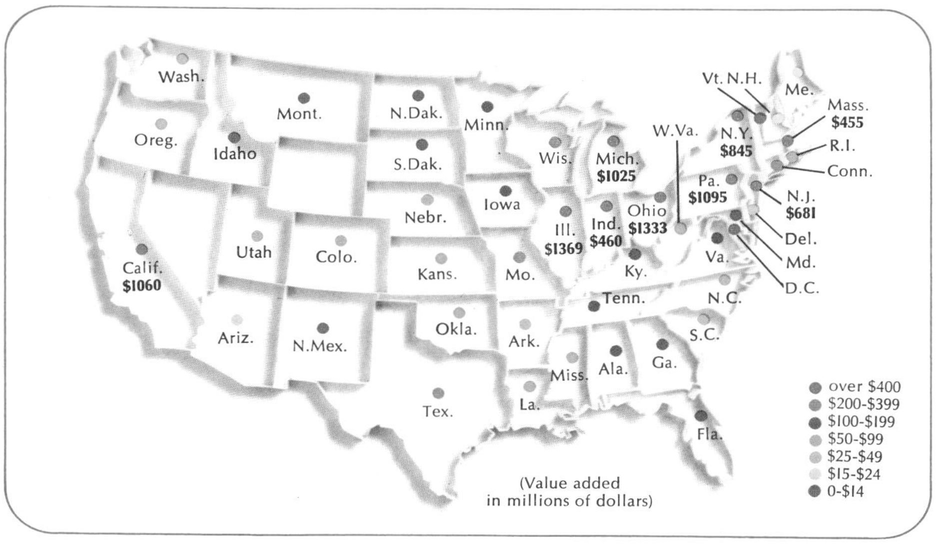

FABRICATED METALS

Large structural-metal products—sheet steel and beams, metal doors, boilers—led this category in 1965 with $3.9 billion in annual manufacturing value. Second, with $2.1 billion, was a grouping of medium-sized products—barrels, drums, pails, safes, vaults. And third, with a little over $2 billion, were such smaller-sized items as hardware, hand tools and cutlery. Other products in the fabricated metals mélange: metal cans, plumbing fixtures, metal stampings, bolts, nuts, valves, pipes and steel springs. Manufacturing centers in the Midwestern states of Illinois and Ohio.

The lag in residential building caused 1966 sales to drop for some of these metals, notably builders' hardware and plumbing materials. But the decrease was more than offset by others, such as structural steel for the busy heavy-construction field—commercial buildings, highways and public projects. This caused an overall product gain of 10 percent for fabricated metals in 1966 over 1965.

About 75 percent of all steel drums manufactured in 1966 went to oil and chemical companies, and about 40 percent of pail production was sold to chemical and paint firms. So the prosperity enjoyed by these customers was handed on to the drum and pail industries.

Good times for food canners, breweries and soft-drink makers in the 1960's also resulted in gains for the 100 companies that make metal cans. The four largest of these 100 firms accounted for 75 percent of the $989 million in manufacturing value recorded in 1966. The can industry utilizes 6 percent of all steel production.

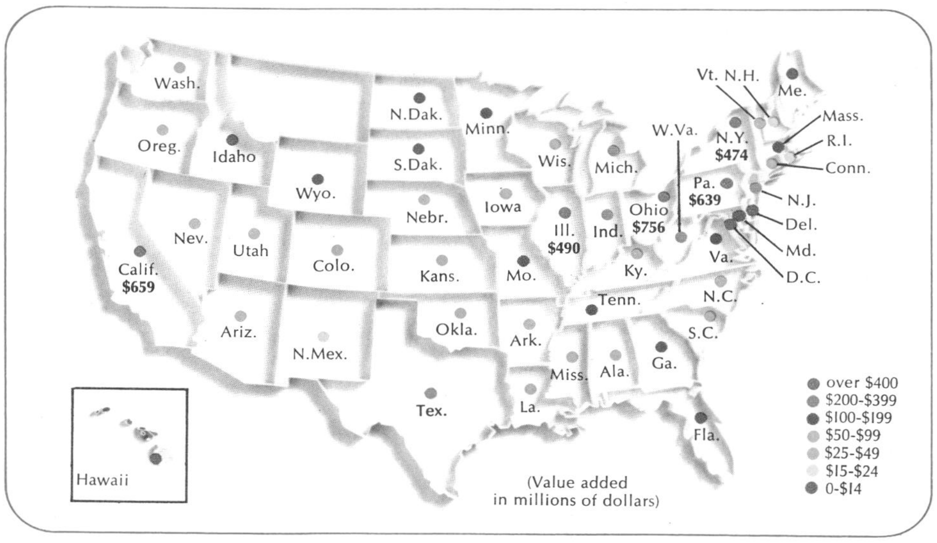

STONE, CLAY AND GLASS

Brick, tile, concrete, asbestos and all kinds of glassware—from flower vases to plate-glass windows—are found in this classification. Most of these products go into building, thus their manufacture is spread through the more populous states such as Ohio, California, Pennsylvania, Illinois and New York. The leading subindustries in this category in 1965 were concrete and plaster with $2.2 billion in value added; asbestos, abrasives and similar products, $1.5 billion; and glassware, $1.2 billion. Cement was much in demand for heavy construction, and producers expanded, modernizing old plants and building new ones.

Despite competition from metal and plastics industries, glass containers remained popular with food and soft-drink manufacturers. Shipments of one variety—nonreturnable bottles—increased 92 percent in 1966 over 1965.

The glass container industry is made up of 41 companies operating 106 plants in 25 states. Four large companies account for 55 percent of total shipments. In 1965, about 29 billion bottles were produced in the United States, with almost a third going to the Middle Atlantic states. The food industry used most of the glass containers, more than 11 billion a year, or nearly 40 percent of all production.

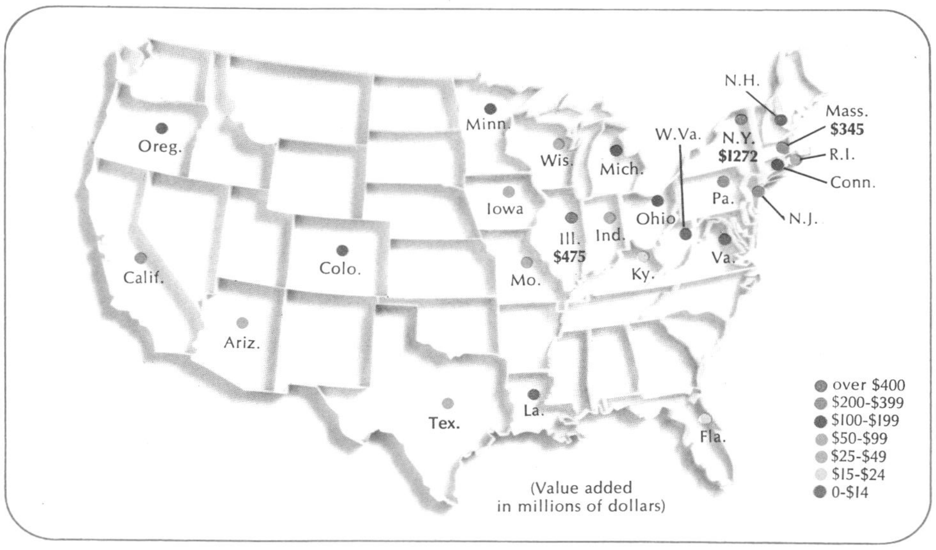

INSTRUMENTS AND RELATED PRODUCTS

Photographic equipment was the leading item in this division in 1965 with added value of $1.7 billion. Mechanical measuring devices, such as temperature or mixing controls, were next with $1.3 billion; medical instruments and supplies were third with $718 million. New York leads the nation in instrument manufacturing with $1.2 billion in value added. Each of the next two states, Illinois and Massachusetts, turns out less than half that amount yearly.

The instrument industry has changed considerably since World War II. In 1947, there were approximately 950 plants; in 1966 there were more than 2200. Many were small firms of less than 50 employes each, founded to produce for the new, expanding science and space industries. However, the larger firms, which constitute 20 percent of the industry, made 90 percent of all the instruments sold in 1966.

In the 15 years to 1965, production of instruments increased by about 50 percent. Today's instruments are far more sophisticated and costly than those of 1950.

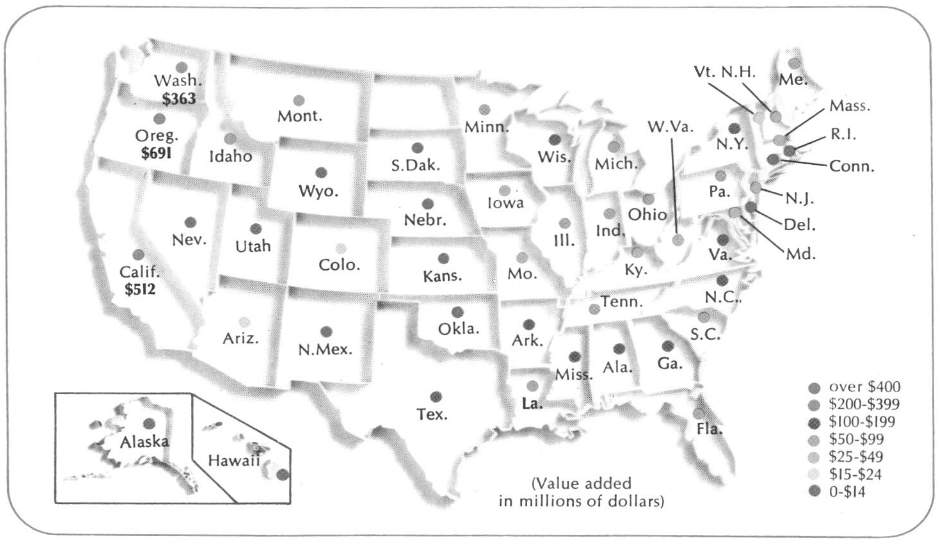

LUMBER AND WOOD

The Pacific Northwest is the center of lumber and wood manufacturing because forests in that area are still large and productive (see page 154). Oregon is the top state in this field, followed by California and Washington. Sawmills and planing mills turned out the most lumber products—flooring and other boards—with $1.6 billion value added. Millwork—plywood and prefabricated woods—was next with $1.3 billion; miscellaneous products, which include particleboard, were third with $600 million. Particleboard, a comparatively new product, is made of chips, shavings, lumber trims and other waste wood processed with resin. The result is a material with the properties of wood. Lumber manufacturers now look to particleboard as a way to increase production by utilizing waste materials. In 1966 there were some 55 particleboard mills in the nation.

The trend in the lumber industry in the 1960's was toward fewer but more modern and efficient mills. In the eight years before 1966 the number of sawmills declined slightly from an estimated 31,600 because of increased automation and the merging of some lumber companies with others producing related goods, such as pulp and paper.

The war in Vietnam created a demand for plywood, and prices rose in response. In 1966 some 12 new plywood plants joined the 179 already in existence.

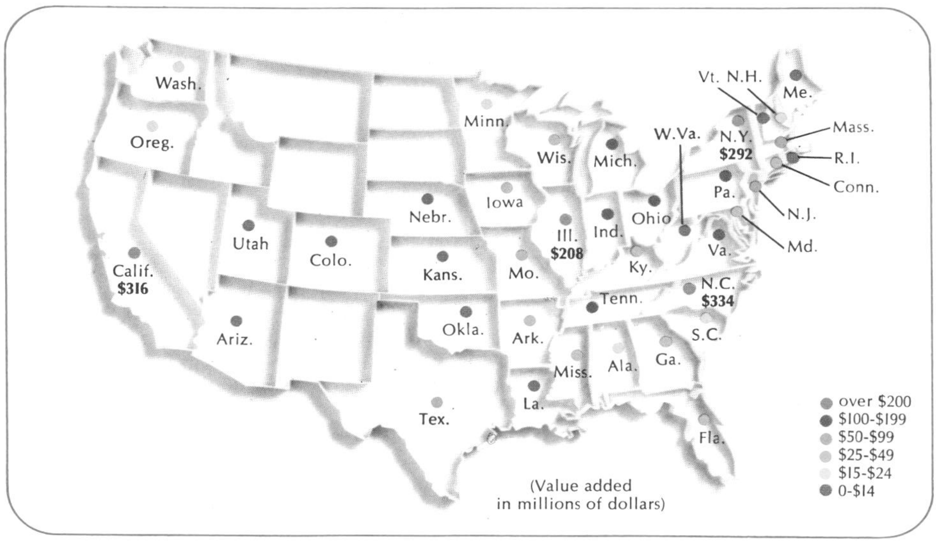

FURNITURE AND FIXTURES

Household furniture is by far the leading industry in this category, producing more than $2 billion value added in 1965. Fixtures and partitions amounted to $500 million and office furniture about $285 million. North Carolina is the leading furniture manufacturing state, although California is running a close second.

Household furniture shipments soared to an all-time high of $4 billion in 1966, 7 percent over the previous year. Reasons for the continued upsurge were the steady rise in personal income and the increase in the marrying and family-forming age group of 20 to 34. The household furniture industry is made up mainly of small companies. About 64 percent of the industry's 5300 firms employ fewer than 20 workers. The large companies—those with more than 250 employes—turn out better than 90 percent of production. In 1966, employment in the entire furniture industry totaled approximately 290,000, a rise of about 7 percent over 1965.

A critical problem in the late 1960's was a shortage of fine hardwoods such as walnut, cherry and maple. Foreign manufacturers with lower labor and transportation costs were outbidding U.S. producers for high-quality logs grown in this country. American manufacturers were turning to plastics to take the place of these woods in some items.

NONDURABLE GOODS

	VALUE ADDED (in billions of dollars)	EMPLOYES
1. Food and Kindred Products	$23.38	1,635,029
2. Chemicals	$19.72	776,217
3. Textiles and Apparel	$15.88	2,203,277
4. Printing and Publishing	$11.88	962,843
5. Paper	$8.40	605,645
6. Rubber and Plastics	$5.65	461,261
7. Petroleum and Coal	$4.15	143,528
8. Leather Products	$2.32	332,554

This division consists of products that will be used up quickly, such as food, paper, petroleum or clothing. In recent years, durable goods have contributed far more to the economy than the nondurable products. In the Depression year of 1933, for example, the total income of durable goods was about $3 billion, while nondurable goods took in nearly $5 billion. In 1947, just after World War II, durable goods moved ahead of nondurables. The great expansion continued, with durables leading nondurables by $86 billion to $57 billion in 1963.

The food and kindred products class—the processing of meat, canned and frozen foods and grain—with $23.38 billion in annual manufacturing value is by far the leader among nondurable goods industries (left). In fact, it is also ahead of every durable goods industry except transportation equipment, which includes the giant automobile industry. However, durable goods industries overall were the acknowledged leaders in the unprecedented economic prosperity of the 1960's.

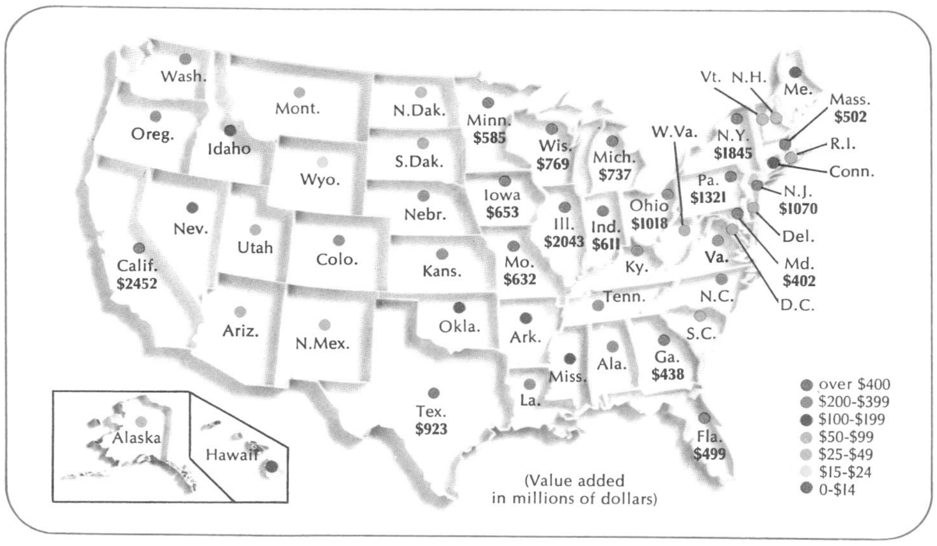

FOOD AND KINDRED PRODUCTS

The manufacturing and processing of foods—from grinding coffee to slaughtering beef cattle—make up this classification. The leading subindustry in the group was beverages, both alcoholic and soft drinks, which produced $4 billion in manufacturing value in 1965. Dairy products were next with $3.3 billion and canned and frozen foods third with $3.1 billion.

As the population rises, so does food consumption. Total sales for the industry in 1966 were nearly 5 percent over 1965. The location of food processing plants also follows closely the concentrations of population. Three of the most populous states—California, Illinois and New York—led in food production.

New techniques as well as population expansion helped the beverage industry. Tab-top cans, twist-off and snap-off caps, and easily tapped kegs were innovations in the beer and ale field. The per-capita consumption of malt liquors was 17.5 gallons in 1966, more than half a gallon per capita over 1965.

Since 1960, per-capita consumption of soft drinks has increased at an average annual rate of 6 percent, largely because of the rise in the youth population.

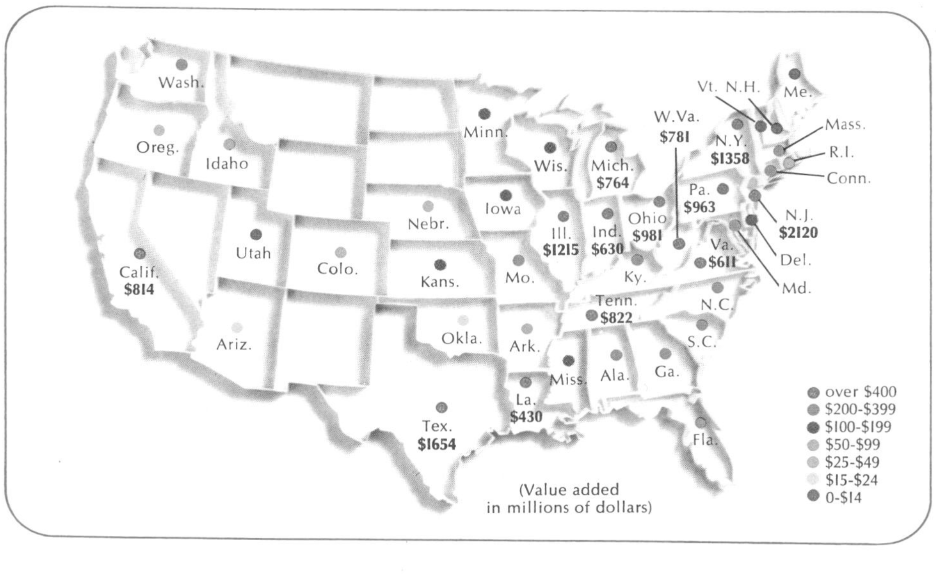

CHEMICALS

Chemicals in some form are used in every industry. In the decade before 1965, they contributed more than 5 percent to the total economy in terms of value added. Shipments in 1966 totaled $38.7 billion, an increase of 7.4 percent over 1965. Despite progress in automation, employment rose in nearly all segments.

Research plays an important role in chemicals. Products that did not exist 20 years ago are now commonplace. New substances—synthetic fibers and leathers, agricultural chemicals and antibiotics—are constantly being introduced.

The most important segment of the industry comprises basic chemicals used to make such products as drugs, explosives and plastics. The materials—coal tar, alkalies, chlorine, industrial gases—accounted for about $1.5 billion in value added in 1965. Basic plastics, fibers and synthetic rubber amount to nearly $690 million and drugs almost $590 million. Much of the industry is in the East. New Jersey and New York together produce more than $3.4 billion annually.

One of the principal basic chemicals is chlorine, which goes into pulp and paper manufacturing, the production of organic chemicals and the treatment of water. Chlorine plants have been operating at or near capacity since 1960. Expansion and the building of new plants was expected to increase chlorine manufacturing capacity to 8 million tons by late 1967—or 23 percent more than in 1966.

TEXTILES AND APPAREL

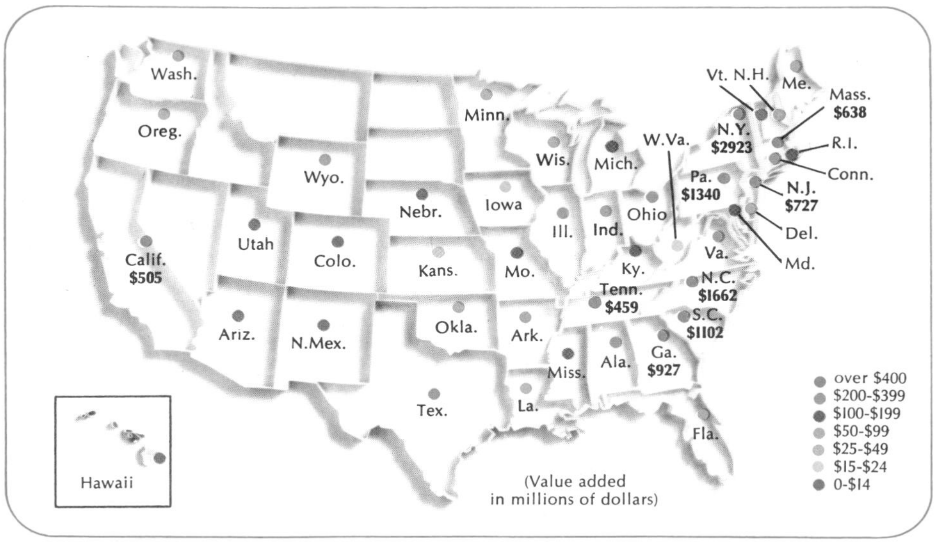

The textile and apparel industries are closely related, totaling $15.8 billion. Most textile plants are in the South, while apparel manufacturing is largely in the North, with more than 40 percent concentrated in New York, Pennsylvania and New Jersey, in that order. The largest segment of the apparel group is women's and misses' wear, which accounted for $2.5 billion in value added in 1965. Men's and boys' furnishings were second with $1.8 billion, and fabricated textiles—curtains, drapes and cloth housefurnishings—were third with $1.2 billion.

More than half of the textile factories are in North Carolina, South Carolina and Georgia. Production rose steadily in the late 1950's and early 1960's with shipments reaching a total of $18.3 billion in 1965—a gain of 7 percent over 1964 and nearly 50 percent over 1938. In terms of manufacturing value, the top classifications in 1965 were knitting mills with $1.64 billion, cotton-weaving mills with $1.62 billion, and yarn and thread mills with $864 million.

Despite steady production increases in both industries, profit margins have remained small. In apparel, profits after taxes rose from 1 percent of sales in 1958 to 2.3 percent in 1965, well below the comparable figures for manufacturing as a whole of 4.2 and 5.6 percent, respectively, for those years. In textiles, profits rose from 1.7 percent in 1958 to 3.8 percent in 1965.

PRINTING AND PUBLISHING

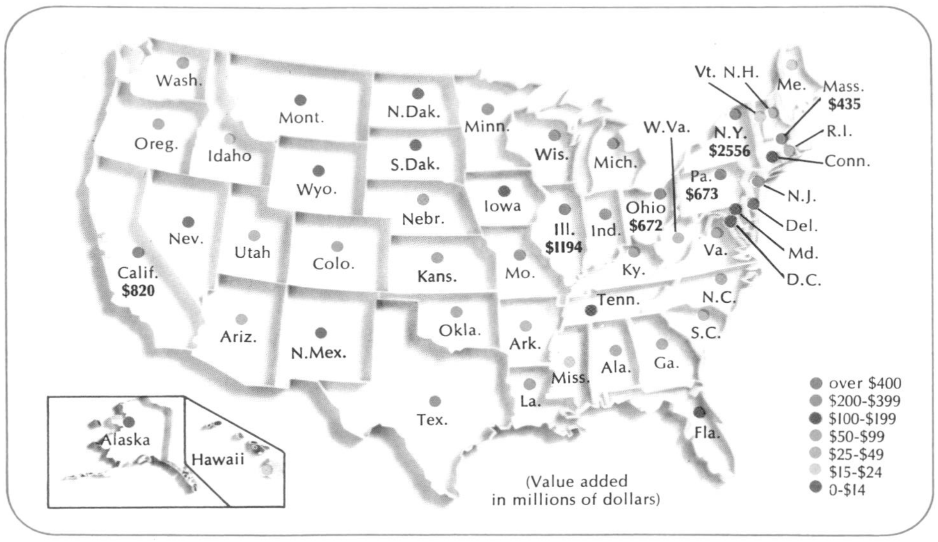

Newspapers, the leading industry in this group, made phenomenal gains in the decade to 1965, more than tripling their manufacturing value to $3.6 billion. Second in the group in 1965 was commercial printing with $3.3 billion; and third, periodicals with $1.56 billion. The book industry tripled its value between 1955 and 1965, growing from $552 million to $1.51 billion. Most printing and publishing is located in New York State, and especially New York City. New York State turns out twice as much printing and publishing as its nearest competitor, Illinois.

In the eight years before 1967, daily newspaper circulation rose by 5.2 percent, although only three new newspapers were founded, bringing the total to 1754. The circulation of all newspapers—daily, Sunday and weekly—increased by almost 10 percent in that time. Meanwhile, newspapers recorded gains in employment, advertising revenue and profits. In 1966 sales hit an all-time high of $5 billion.

Advertising accounts for about 65 percent of all revenues in periodical publishing. Gains in advertising by consumer magazines, farm publications and business papers were responsible for high revenue in the industry in the early 1960's. Profits were $2.5 billion in 1966. Publishing employment has been rising since 1963.

PAPER AND ALLIED PRODUCTS

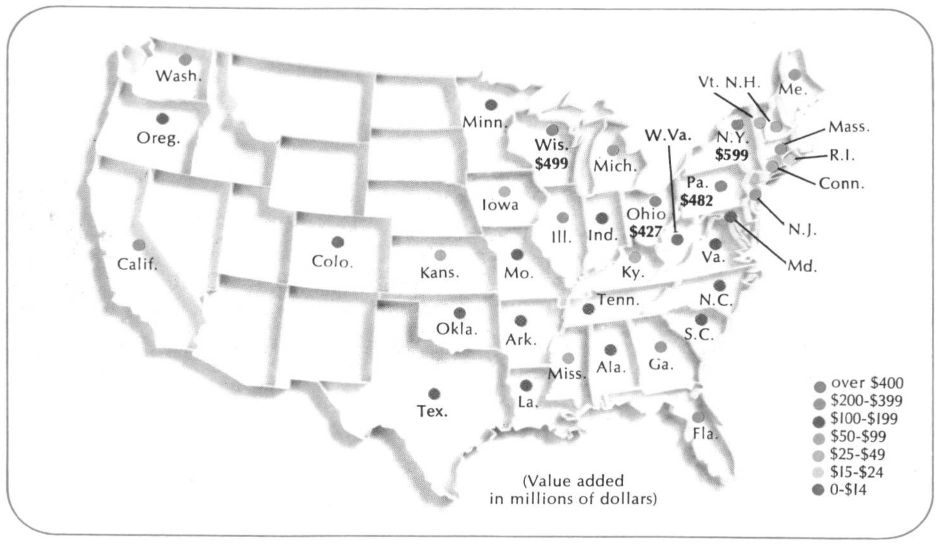

Paperboard container manufacturing is the biggest industry in this group with $612 million in manufacturing value added in 1965. Other leaders are finished paper and paperboard—wallpaper, cartons, newsprint—with $585 million value, and paper mill products—rough primary paper rolls—with $454 million. The leading states are New York, Wisconsin and Pennsylvania, although the South is far ahead from a regional standpoint. The South generally accounted for 43 percent of the national output of paper products in 1964. With their large forestry resources, the South and the West, which produced 13 percent, may be expected to increase their share of the national volume in the future.

Wood pulp and waste paper are the raw materials which are converted into the thousands of paper products used in home and industry. From 1958 to 1967, shipments of paper products rose from $5 billion to $8 billion. In expectation of increased use, the paper industry has been improving its production facilities. Spending for new plants and equipment rose faster in the early 1960's than in any other manufacturing industry; production capacity doubled between 1963 and 1966.

RUBBER AND PLASTICS

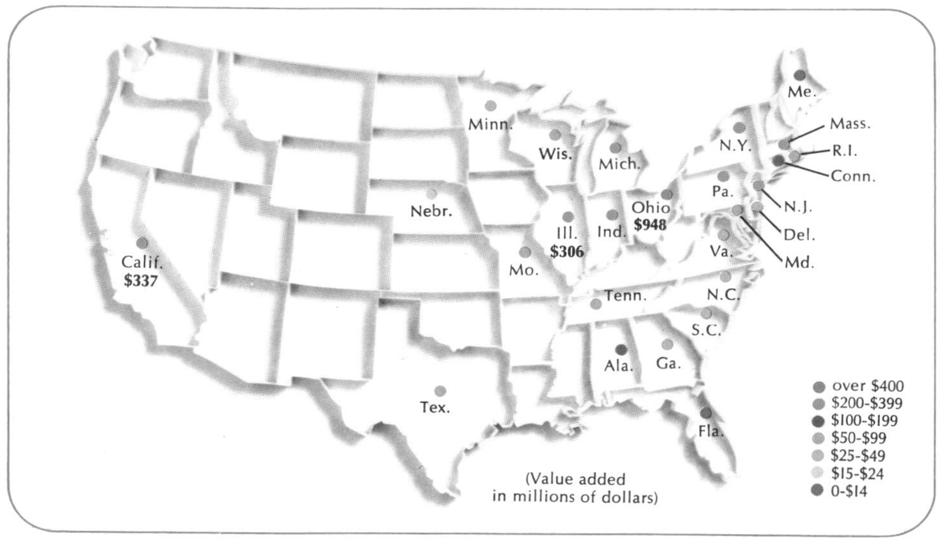

Plastics is a comparatively new and fast-growing industry, and polyethylene, a waxlike compound used in bottles, dishes, insulation and shower curtains, is its liveliest single product. In the seven years to 1967, polyethylene production increased about 20 percent annually. Other common plastics are vinyl, used in phonograph records, raincoats and automobile upholstery, and styrene, an important ingredient in synthetic rubber. The unique qualities of plastic—lightness, good insulating properties, resistance to chemicals and ease of fabrication—make it a tough modern-day competitor of metals, wood, paper and glass.

About 90,000 persons were employed in the plastics industry in 1965. It consisted of some 630 establishments and was growing at the rate of about 30 new companies a year. With more than $2 billion in manufacturing value in 1965, it was fast catching up with rubber products. Tires and tubes had $1.6 billion and rubber products—hoses, gloves, toys—were third with $1.5 billion. The leading rubber and plastics states are California, Illinois and Ohio—the latter state is three times ahead of its nearest rivals.

The rubber-tire industry enjoyed a slight boom in the decade to 1966, when sales reached an all-time high of $3.5 billion. This healthy growth reflected the increase of vehicle registrations from 64 million in 1956 to 90 million 10 years later.

PETROLEUM AND COAL

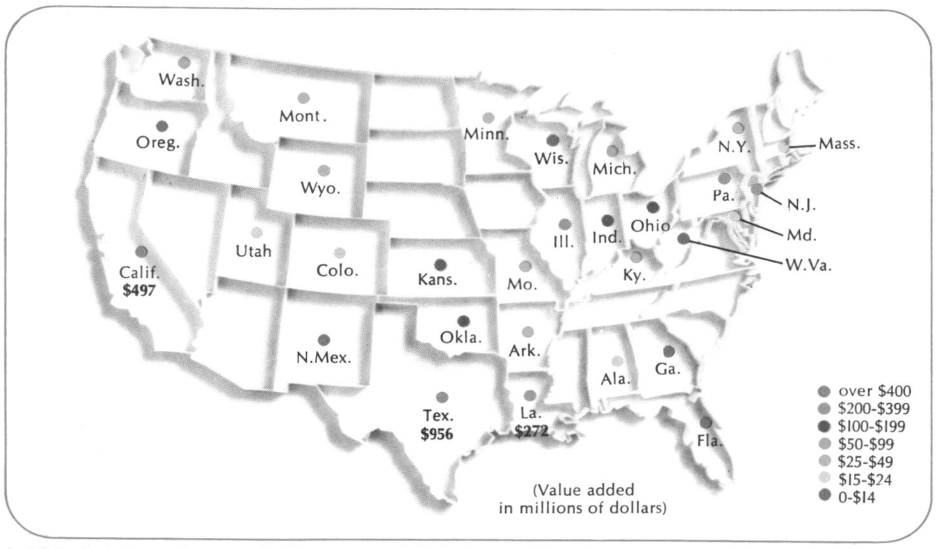

The petroleum refining industry, whose 42,000 companies extend their activities throughout the world, has enjoyed unprecedented prosperity in recent years. Earnings of the leading firms rose about 12 percent in 1966. Net income increased for the eighth consecutive year. Demand for oil products was up 4 percent in the United States in 1966 and 9 percent elsewhere in the free world. Jet fuel production rose about 22 percent in 1966 over 1965. The leading petroleum producing states are Texas, California and Louisiana; the chief coal-mining sections are West Virginia, Kentucky and Pennsylvania.

Thus primary petroleum refining was the most important industry in this category with $3.5 billion in manufacturing value in 1965. Others are coal, paving and roofing materials, and lubricating oils and greases, which all together turned out less than half the production value of petroleum refining—$1.6 billion.

After years of fighting a losing battle against oil and gas competition, coal was on the upswing in the 1960's. Production of bituminous coal rose to 530 million tons in 1966, a gain of about 3 percent over 1965. It was the fifth consecutive year of production increase, although far below the peak year of 1947 with 631 million tons. More than half the coal used in the United States in 1966 was bought by electric power companies, and despite the potential competition from nuclear power, industry leaders believed this rate of consumption would continue through 1975.

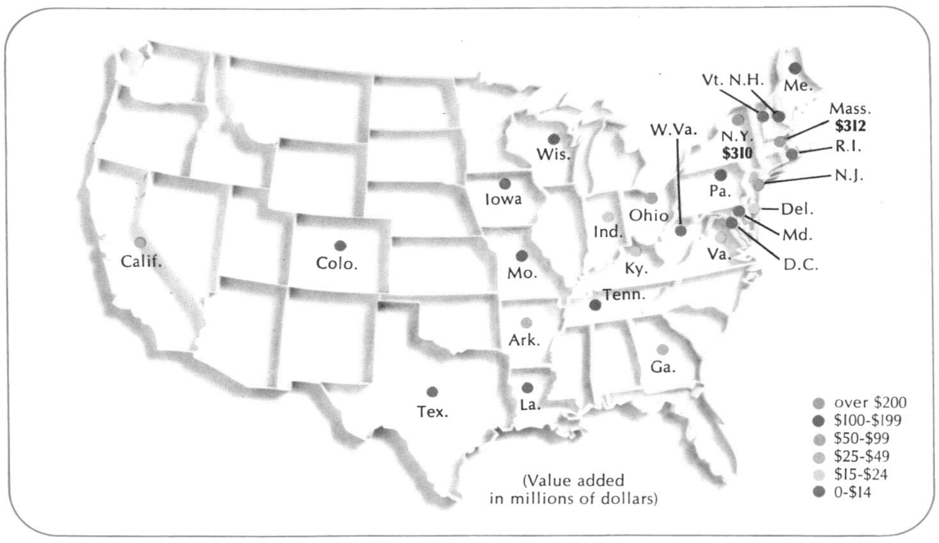

LEATHER PRODUCTS

The biggest industry in the leather classification is footwear, which accounted for $1.4 billion in value added in 1965. Other products included industrial belting, gloves, purses and luggage. Most leather plants are located in the East, where New York and Massachusetts both passed $300 million in value added by manufacturing in 1965. The United States is by far the leading leathermaker in the world, turning about $1.8 billion value added, more than three times as much as its nearest rival, India.

Although all animal skins can be tanned, cattle hides are favored by American tanners, and the shoe industry buys about 80 percent of all U.S. hide production. Since World War II, output of shoes has climbed steadily from 522 million pairs in 1950 to 657 million in 1966.

Understandably, shoe production rises with population. However, style innovations also helped increase the sales. It became fashionable for women to wear leather boots, for example, not only in winter but in other seasons as well. Handsewn moccasins achieved popularity with both men and women. The Vietnam war also put pressure on shoe-production facilities. Military footwear purchases were 163 percent higher in 1966 than in 1965. One innovation that was expected to lessen the use of leather in footwear was the introduction of synthetic materials in shoe manufacture in the 1960's.

INDUSTRIAL GROWTH OF THE CITIES 1947-63

In the great manufacturing surge following World War II, some cities came from virtually nowhere to become industrial giants. At right may be seen the 33 cities and areas in the United States which produced $1 billion or more in value added by manufacturing by 1963. Some of the names on the list are surprising: The Anaheim–Santa Ana, California, metropolitan area, for example, grew from a mere $31 million in value added in 1947 to more than $1 billion in 1963—a 300 percent increase in 16 years. A look at the list shows almost the same story for Flint, Michigan; Paterson–Clifton, New Jersey; San Jose, California; and Seattle, Washington. On the other hand, cities which had been considered manufacturing citadels in prewar days, such as Detroit and Chicago, merely doubled their output, a commentary in itself on the growth of manufacturing in the postwar era.

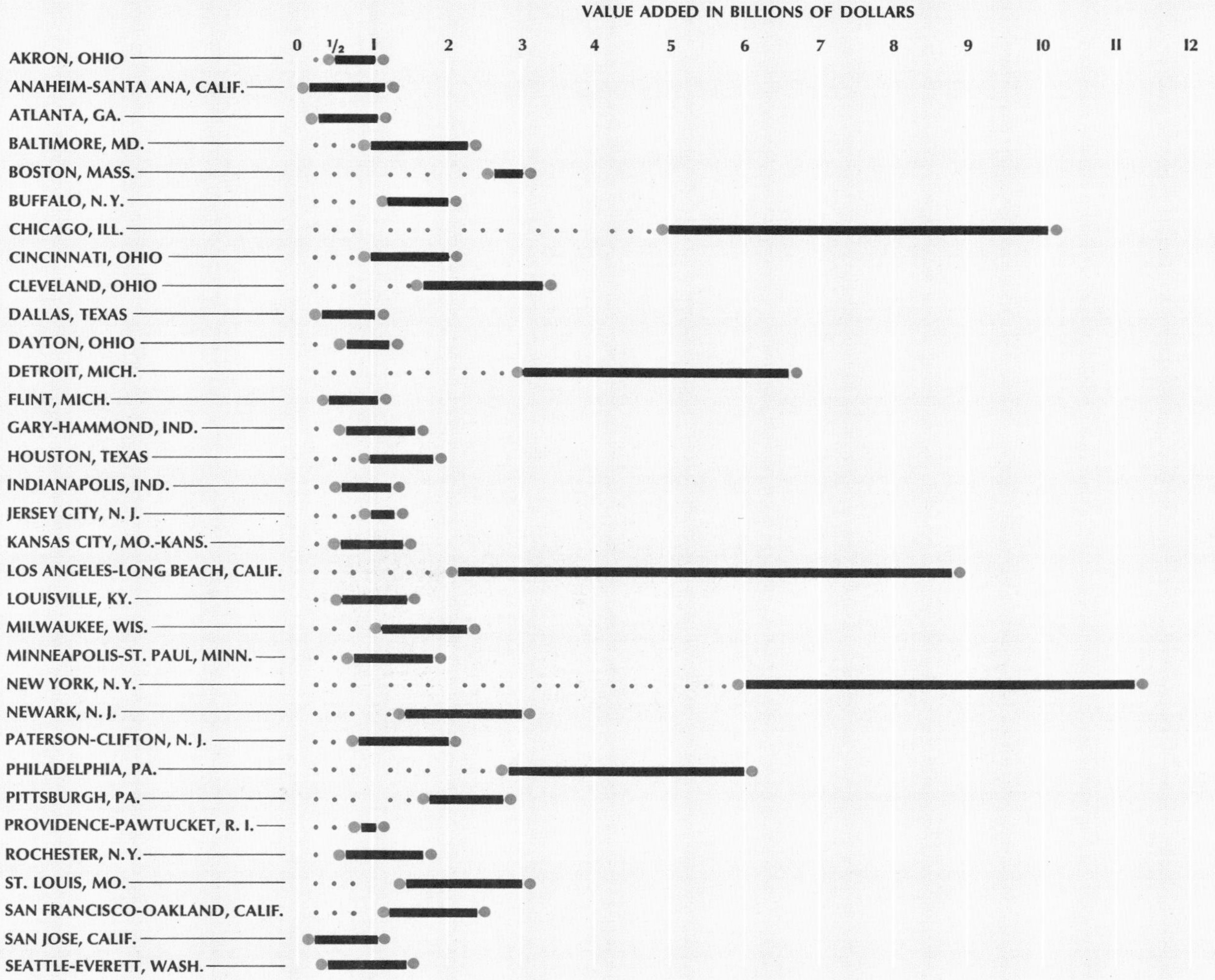

● VALUE IN 1947
▬ GROWTH
● VALUE IN 1963

WHERE THE WORKERS ARE

As new manufacturing enterprises began and old ones expanded in the industrial boom of the 1950's and 1960's, workers moved about the country following job opportunities. Regionally speaking, the South had the largest surge in labor, with Florida, alone, increasing 70 percent during the 1955–65 decade. Other Southern states showed gains up to 50 percent, and most had more than 25 percent. Arizona was ahead of all the states with a 97.6 increase in employes engaged in manufacturing.

The East lost a good deal of its labor force, and the Middle West took the lead in industry (see page 148). New York declined 8.5 percent in manufacturing employes in the 1955–65 decade; Rhode Island was next, losing 8.4 percent. A factor to remember, however, is that percentages never tell the whole story. For example, Arizona's work force doubled, but it started from a very low base—32,000 workers. New York's loss of 8.5 percent, on the other hand, is comparatively minuscule when its huge work force of nearly 2 million is considered. In terms of actual gain in manufacturing employes, California was the leader, adding 287,000 in the 10-year span.

NUMBER OF WORKERS *(in thousands)*

Each bar represents 10,000 workers

Alabama	275.8	Kentucky	206.2	North Dakota	8.5
Alaska	6.2	Louisiana	156.8	Ohio	1317.1
Arizona	64.6	Maine	107.5	Oklahoma	103.0
Arkansas	132.7	Maryland	264.0	Oregon	156.9
Calif.	1408.3	Mass.	666.8	Pennsylvania	1485.9
Colorado	89.0	Michigan	1094.3	Rhode Island	120.7
Connecticut	437.3	Minnesota	258.4	South Carolina	293.1
Delaware	66.8	Mississippi	151.6	South Dakota	13.4
Dist. of Columbia	20.5	Missouri	414.3	Tennessee	387.3
Florida	250.5	Montana	22.1	Texas	571.5
Georgia	400.3	Nebraska	68.6	Utah	49.2
Hawaii	24.5	Nevada	7.0	Vermont	38.6
Idaho	32.5	New Hampshire	89.4	Virginia	321.9
Illinois	1300.7	New Jersey	832.2	Washington	225.6
Indiana	670.5	New Mexico	16.9	West Virginia	128.6
Iowa	190.8	New York	1836.9	Wisconsin	490.0
Kansas	121.3	North Carolina	587.0	Wyoming	7.0

FORESTS AND WOOD

The National Forest System, organized in 1891, came none too soon. The development of conservation and its methods has helped keep a narrow balance between the supply and demand for timber. The United States produced 5.8 billion cubic feet of lumber in 1966, imported approximately 0.9 billion, and exported around 0.2 billion, which means we consumed more than 6.5 billion cubic feet, or about 31 cubic feet for every person in the country. Actually, however, although consumption of wood for commercial purposes increased a full third in the last 40 years, substitution of other fuels in the home brought a sharp drop in firewood use. This kept our overall harvest somewhat stable.

Of the 800 species of trees in the United States, only a limited number are widely used for commercial timber. (See the map on pages 138–39 for the ranges of individual kinds of trees.)

The future of this great natural resource is, in the broadest sense, not very bright. By 1980 we may begin to cut more than is grown. In the year 2000, projections by experts indicate that, after imports, we will still need to cut 21.6 billion cubic feet of timber from the face of the land for lumber and all other uses. Supplies of 18 billion cubic feet, based on present conservation and replanting practices, will thus fall 3.6 billion cubic feet short of keeping a balance with the increasing demand.

However, it is in the area of quality rather than gross quantity that our lumber resource appears primarily threatened. As virgin forests disappear we have to fall back on second-growth trees. Douglas fir, for example, one of the two most important lumber species (the other is southern pine) is lighter in weight and has a lower strength in the newer trees. Slow-growing hardwood trees—oak, maple, hickory and elm—are not being replaced, either because the land on which they are grown has been diverted to other uses or because disease, carelessly imported into this country, is destroying the species. The chestnut blight, introduced by accident in 1904, has wiped out the equivalent of 9 million acres of forest stands of this valuable tree, leaving us principally dead specimens. The western white pine, a softwood of great utility, is under vicious attack by a blister-rust fungus that kills enough yearly to supply lumber for 2 million five-room houses.

Finally, some loggers still ignore basic conservation. The redwood forests of California have been reduced in a little more than 100 years to one eighth their original stand by overactive lumbering; the pressing demand for this superb virgin-growth wood now threatens most of the rest of the redwoods, which conservationists are still trying to save.

Some relief is in sight. An increase in imports could give our forests time to replenish themselves to a certain degree. There appears to be a trend in this direction. Total lumber imports have doubled since 1953 and veneer for plywood (one of the most important forms of lumber today) has shown a tenfold increase in imports in the same period. As people become more aware of the need for timber conservation, especially for the preservation of virgin areas, they have organized groups to protect these for the benefit of future generations and for wildlife. Lumbermen increasingly practice intensive reforestation and selective cutting so that reserves may restock the forest, which, if stripped, may be ruined forever by erosion. New techniques of cutting allow little waste, and even sawdust is turned into useful products.

Science is finding wood replacements in plastics and other chemical materials. New medicines are used to fight diseases which afflict a number of the species, and disease-resistant types are being developed.

Although America may no longer have the forest resources it once had, and while much of that which remains is a poorer quality of timber, it is moving to conserve and rebuild this great natural resource.

10 MOST IMPORTANT AMERICAN TREES

The ranges numbered below are found on the Natural Vegetation map, pages 138–39. In the background of each tree is a photograph of its grain.

1. American beech *(Fagus grandifolia)*
A densely foliaged, pyramid-shaped tree, it often reaches 90 feet in height. The first frost turns its leaves brown and gold. On the surface of a plain-sawed board the pinkish-brown wood is lined with a pleasing hyphenated grain. Beech is both heavy and strong and is processed into such things as furniture veneer, railroad ties and flooring. It is a good wood for boxes and baskets to hold food as it imparts no odor. (Range 19)

2. White oak *(Quercus alba)*
This majestic tree has a long trunk when forest-grown, but given room, the trunk will be short and quite thick, the branches gnarled and twisted. Such a tree gives the impression of massive strength. The dome of leaves becomes purplish-red at the touch of cold weather. Oak wood is almost impervious to water, a quality that makes it an excellent choice for kegs, barrels and for ship- and boat-building. (Ranges 17, 20, others)

3. Sugar maple *(Acer saccharum)*
Maple is one of the most valuable hardwood trees in the United States. It can grow to 120 feet, and the broad branches and wide leaves create a wonderfully cool carpet of shade from the hot summer sun. The boiled sap produces a delicious brownish sugar and pancake syrup. The maple's strong, resilient wood, tough and straight-grained, finds extensive use in flooring for bowling alleys and dance pavilions, and distilled, it produces alcohol and acetic acid. (Ranges 19, 22)

4. Black tupelo *(Nyssa sylvatica)*
The oval, teardrop-shaped leaves change from lustrous green to bright scarlet, as winter nears and brushes this 70-foot tree. But before that happens, little white-green flowers decorate the branchlets and its small fruits provide food for birds. Black tupelo wood, although not exceptionally strong nor heavy, is cut for railroad ties. Large amounts are pulped into paper for books and quality magazines. (Range 25)

5. Redwood *(Sequoia sempervirens)*
From the time the cone seed first takes root the redwood is a rapidly growing forest specimen, sometimes extending 50 feet or more in 20 years. For all this, it is long-lived, with ages of 2000 years not uncommon. A soft, beautiful red-brown bark gives the tree its name. The wood has great decay resistance and is almost termite-proof. Too many of these giants (older trees reach 300 feet) have been cut for house framing, trestles. (Range 5)

6. Shortleaf pine *(Pinus echinata)*
An acre of abandoned field next to a stand of these pines will be swallowed up by a forest of them in several decades. *Pinus echinata* can sprout after fire or excessive cutting, and this ability to replenish quickly makes it one of the most valuable and important commercial trees in the country. Straight of trunk, narrow-crowned and aromatic, the tree provides wood that is light, a major building material and a pulp and turpentine source. (Ranges 6, 30, others)

7. Douglas fir *(Pseudotsuga menziesii)*
Massive stands of these huge (200-foot) trees were first identified by the Scottish botanical collector David Douglas in 1827. This tree seeds prolifically and grows rapidly in the heavy mineral soil of its range. Relatively free of knots, it is a major source of plywood veneer. The lumber is used in railroad car construction, doors, boxes, prefabricated house panels; even sawmill residue is valuable when processed as pulp. (Ranges 2, 5, 7, others)

8. Sitka spruce *(Picea sitchensis)*
Larger than the hemlock, the Sitka thrives close to the Pacific on deep, moist loams. It can live 800 years and attain a height of almost 200 feet. The wood of these evergreen giants is straight-grained, without many defects, and resists warping. Large quantities are pulped or turned into furniture, doors and crates. During World War II, much was cut for aircraft parts. (Range 1)

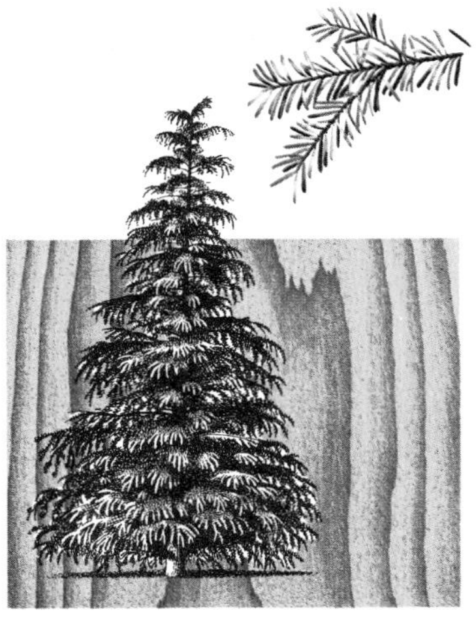

9. Western hemlock *(Tsuga heterophylla)*
Intermingling with the Sitka spruce in northwest coastal areas of Washington, this hemlock has become an economically important tree in recent years, as other types have been depleted. Its bark, reddish brown and deeply furrowed, is a source of tannic acid (tannin) for leather tanning, and the wood itself is widely used for pulp and lumber for flooring. (Ranges 1, 2, Alaska 3)

10. Ponderosa pine *(Pinus ponderosa)*
A towering resident of rather dry regions of the country, this pine tenaciously survives and thrives where others fail. Handsome, ornamental, a young ponderosa's almost-black bark has caused it to be nicknamed blackjack pine. As many as 10,000 young ones can congest a single acre, though the years bring attrition and thinning out. The roots extend deep in arid soil, seeking moisture. Valued for mine timber and paneling. (Ranges 6, 7, others)

Two American Trees That Have Been Badly Depleted by Disease

A. American elm *(Ulmus americana)*
The elm has been greatly reduced in recent years by a fungus carried on the small European elm bark beetle which was accidentally brought into the United States several decades ago. Injections, sprays and the possible development of resistant species offer some hope for a comeback. A tree that lives its full 200-year span can spread branches 150 feet at a 60-foot height. Its wood is used for furniture, fruit crates and boxes. (Range 21)

B. American chestnut *(Castanea dentata)*
The chestnut used to exist in great numbers but during the last 50 years a fungus from Asia, one of the most destructive forest diseases known, has virtually destroyed its stands. It was widely planted as a shade tree, under whose spreading branches our forefathers found relief from summer heat. The bark was a major source of tannic acid and the nuts were wildlife food. Now only scattered trees remain.

MINERAL WEALTH OF AMERICA

Although there are more than 2000 types of minerals on this planet, only a small number have played a major role in the development of civilization. Gold, iron, uranium, coal and petroleum (the latter two, technically not minerals, are usually classed as such) have at different times been among the most important. Deposits of these in the United States have helped this country become a towering giant among present-day nations. The lure of gold brought many of the Spanish and other colonists from Europe to the New World. Although explorers' tales of golden cities were imaginative, the precious metal did exist in large quantities in some areas of North America.

Importance of Iron and Coal. Iron ore was found in America as early as 1584, although it was not until 1646, when a furnace and forge were completed near Hammersmith, Massachusetts, that deposits began to be exploited. Production was relatively low until the mid-1800's. Then the rich lodes of the Lake Superior region—the Vermilion, Menominee and Mesabi ranges—were opened. The latter is a 100-mile-long ridge of ore which is still being worked. The mineral was shipped from the vast open pits in greater and greater quantities, to be smelted with the coal from the massive Appalachian and midwestern fields. In half a century, these mines produced the riches that built many of the cities of America's heartland.

About one third of our iron ore has, in recent years, been imported because the foreign product is richer and therefore less expensive to process. However, improved technology is bringing low-grade ore into a competitive position. Our iron demands may add up to 4 billion long tons by the year 2000, but reserves can more than match this.

At the same time, the United States has a superabundance of coal, but only half is recoverable and much of it at costs exceeding present ones. At the turn of the century, coal was used almost universally to provide heat and energy for homes and industry. Since that time, fuel oil and natural gas have taken over a large part of these markets. Coal, however, in the form of coke is still essential in the production of steel because of its carbon content, and 60 percent of today's electricity is still generated by utilities using coal, although that share is expected to decline (see chart below). Production in 1966 amounted to about half a billion tons. Reserves are estimated at 1.7 trillion tons.

Vital Role of Oil and Gas. Since 1859, when the first successful well was dug in Titusville, Pennsylvania, petroleum has become an increasingly important part of our energy supply. Today the gigantic oil fields of Texas, Oklahoma, Kansas, Louisiana and other states make the United States the world's major producer, with nearly 3 billion barrels pumped annually. Natural gas, a formerly wasted by-product of petroleum wells, is now being used for heating and for providing industrial power. Production is approaching 17 trillion cubic feet yearly, about four tenths of it from Texas wells. Without the huge national reserves of fossil fuels, America most certainly would not be a land where central heating is the rule. Refined oil products power our autos, trucks, trains and planes as well as run electric generators for lighting and operation of industrial plants.

About 20 percent of U.S. oil needs are supplied by foreign petroleum, because its price is lower. Government controls keep the imports from rising further. No one knows how much oil is left in the ground, or how much of what is believed to exist can be economically recovered. New and advanced equipment will be needed to accomplish this. Perhaps as little as 150 billion barrels, perhaps as much as 300, lie in deposits 10,000 feet or more deep or under high seas offshore. Such resources are not likely to be equal to the burgeoning demand as the century nears its end. But tar sands are starting to yield their treasure, and oil shale may soon do so.

Nuclear Minerals. Uranium and thorium—the minerals of nuclear energy—rocketed into prominence after the first atomic bomb was exploded. The implications of nuclear fission and its by-products, both beneficial and destructive, have shaken established concepts in fields as varied as medicine and religion. Medical treatments once limited to expensive radium are, for example, accomplished at less cost with radioactive materials from nuclear research.

Uranium mined in the United States powered the first nuclear-fueled electric generator, submarine and surface ship. This ore is also imported from Canada and Africa. There is now concern that U.S. ore reserves may not be sufficient to meet rapidly rising needs, but scientists believe that renewed exploration will turn up additional sources.

Other Minerals. Copper has been used in America since the days of the Indians who found it in its pure state and molded the soft "red metal" into primitive tools. Today it is an important factor in the electric and electronics industries because it can conduct electricity.

A modern automobile would not be able to function efficiently without lead. More than a third of the total supply consumed each year in the United States is used

LOCATION OF KEY MINERALS

Symbols indicate major producing areas

COAL AND URANIUM

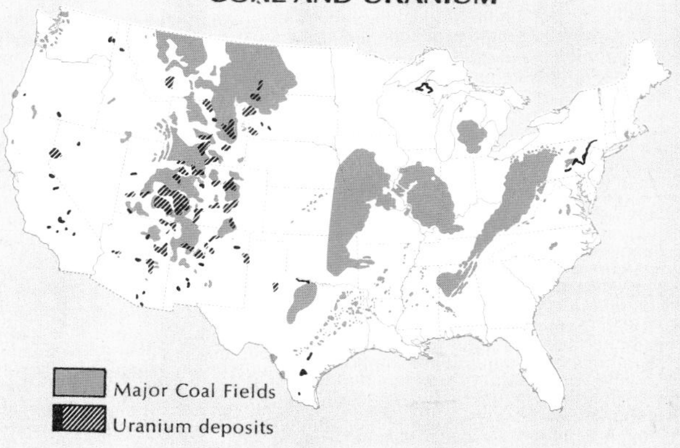

MOLYBDENUM AND VANADIUM

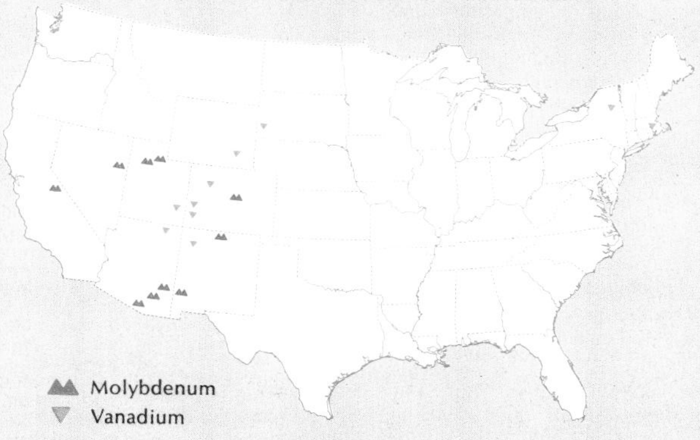

IRON, LEAD, COPPER AND ZINC

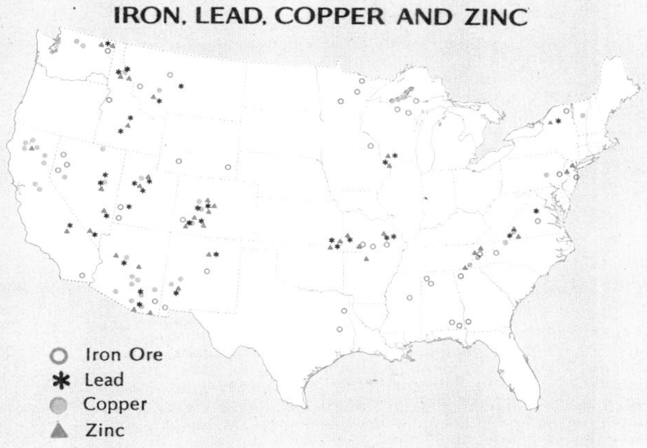

NATURAL GAS

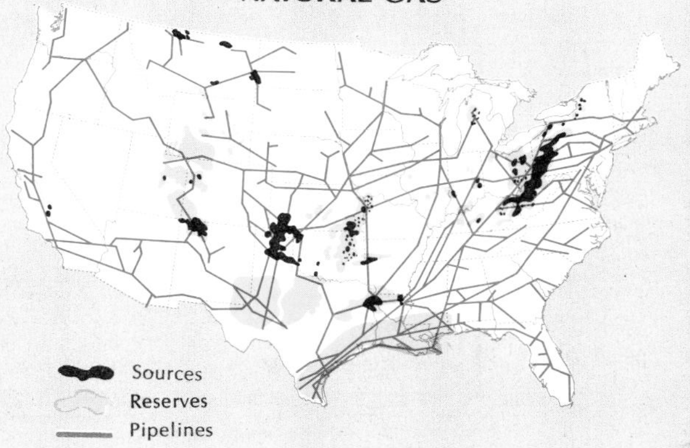

SILVER AND GOLD

POTASH, SULFUR AND PHOSPHATES

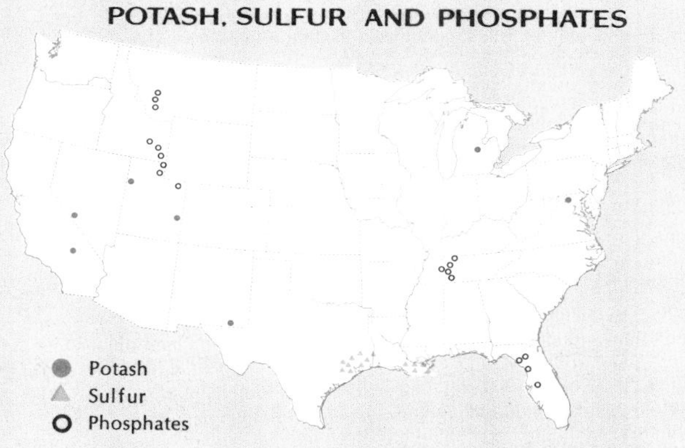

PETROLEUM

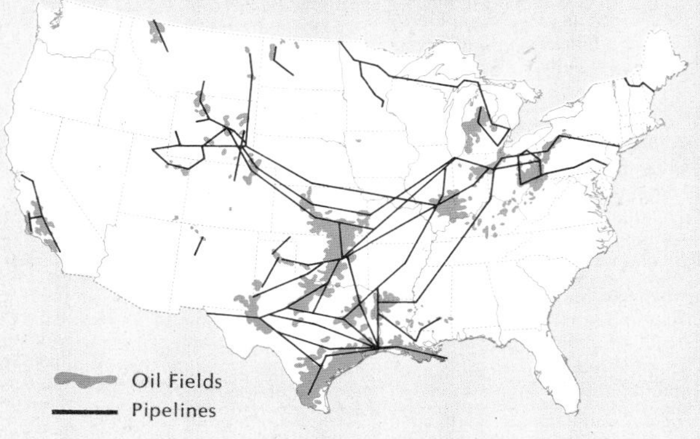

SOURCES OF ELECTRIC POWER, 1960-2000

A little more than 30 years ago waterpower systems (dams) provided about 40 percent of America's electricity. Despite new construction, today they supply less than 18 percent. Experts predict that by the year 2000, water-produced electricity will drop to 10 percent even if every water source in the country is developed. Presently "soft" coal and natural gas rank highest as sources of electric energy. It is believed that by the year 2000, nuclear energy may be used to generate nearly 50 percent of the electricity that will be produced and used in the United States.

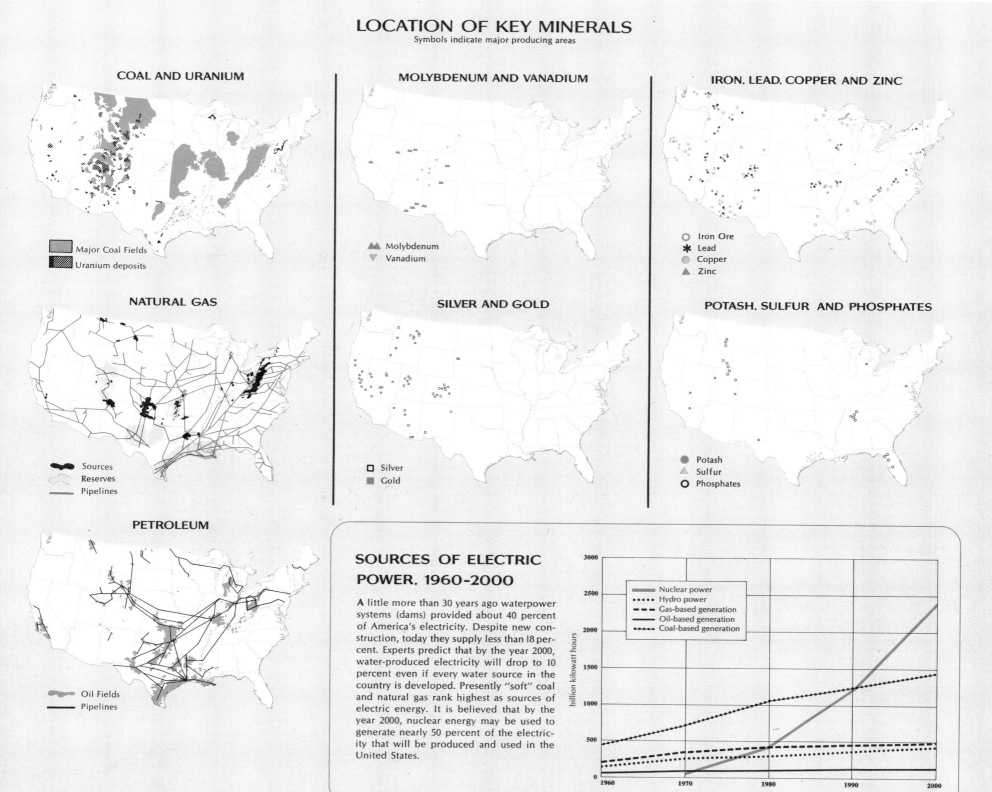

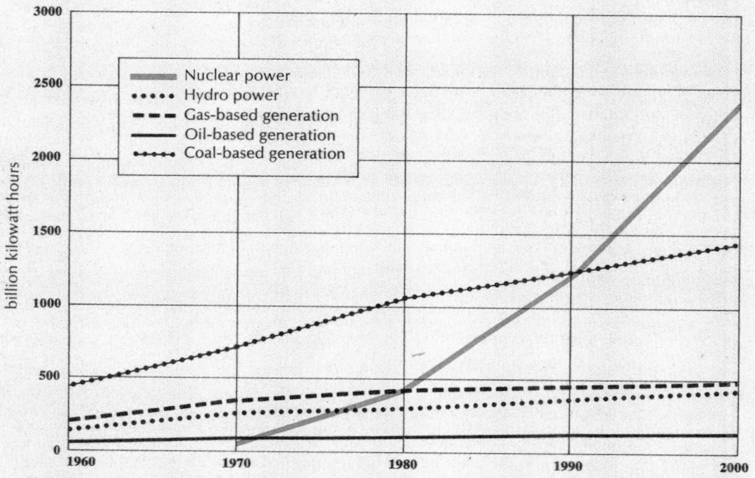

in making storage batteries, and 15 percent goes into gasoline additives: tetraethyl and tetramethyl lead. The most recent application of lead is as a shield against radiation; it is also used as a cable covering because it resists corrosion.

The principal use of zinc is as a coating for iron and steel to protect these metals from the corrosive effects of moisture or gases in the atmosphere. The process by which this coating is applied is called galvanizing, after Luigi Galvani, who discovered the principle on which it is based. Other important uses of this metal are in die castings and as zinc oxide in the manufacture of paints and cosmetics and in the vulcanization of rubber.

Mining is generally assumed to mean the extraction of ore by actual digging. The main sources of sulfur in the United States are exploited, however, by forcing superheated water into them and then pumping out the liquified mineral. Sulfur is also obtained as a by-product of natural gas and petroleum refining. Most sulfur is converted into sulfuric acid. This has a wide variety of uses, principally in the manufacture of fertilizers, steel, rayon, chemicals, paper and pigments.

Molybdenum and vanadium are used almost exclusively in making alloy steels which are harder, stronger and more heat resistant. Most of these steels are consumed by the transportation industry, particularly in automobiles and aircraft, and in manufacturing high-speed tools and parts, propeller shafts, armor-piercing shells and springs and, more recently, in connection with nuclear fission. Vanadium is found in association with many other minerals, but has been produced commercially principally as a by-product of uranium.

Two nonmetallic minerals of which the United States has a large supply are marketed primarily as fertilizers: potash, a potassium oxide, and phosphate, a phosphorous oxide. Phosphates are also used in the chemical industry and potash in glassmaking.

Of the precious metals, gold is used primarily as a standard of value for money and kept in reserve by the government as backing for paper currency, although the latter is not convertible into gold. Jewelry is the second most important market, followed by gold leaf for ornamentation purposes. Silver is used for monetary purposes, but when its price reached a point where it was more profitable to melt coins into bullion than use them for currency, the United States began minting "sandwich" coins with a layer of baser metals between the silver. The jewelry, tableware and photographic industries also consume quantities of this metal.

	1966 Production from Domestic Ore	Domestic Reserves (Conservative estimate)
	(In tons unless otherwise indicated)	
Copper	1,400,000	32,000,000
Zinc	600,000	13,000,000
Lead	300,000	5,000,000
Molybdenum	44,500	1,500,000
Vanadium	6000	600,000
Sulfur	9,000,000	100,000,000
Potash	4,000,000	400,000,000
Phosphate	9,000,000	1,500,000,000
Silver	42,000,000 troy ounces	600,000,000 troy ounces

Deficiencies. The United States does lack adequate supplies of some minerals vital to modern industry. Manganese ore, essential in steelmaking, is one of these. Domestic ores of tungsten, used in making high-grade steel, are poor and costly to work. This country depends heavily on foreign sources for its nickel, although most of it comes from neighboring Canada. Cobalt, important in missiles, glassmaking and motors, is also of short supply. Copper, while plentiful, is locked in ores which are uneconomical to process, and large amounts are purchased from foreign suppliers. The same is true of bauxite, the ore of aluminum. Finally, the United States has but the sparsest deposits of tin and is forced to rely on ores from such countries as Bolivia and Malaysia.

Despite America's deficiencies, the constantly shifting picture of demand and use may, in a few short years, alter the situation for the better. Advancing technology is changing prospects for poor deposits, and new metals which are in good supply have not been fully exploited. Substitute materials are rapidly increasing. Plastics are replacing metals in dozens of ways. Food cans, formerly made of a combination of steel and tin, are now produced with aluminum. Many minerals such as mica, quartz and diamonds are now synthesized.

EARTH TREASURES

Almost every mineral found on earth exists in the United States. As elsewhere, only a few are found in a relatively pure state: gold flakes, silver and diamonds among them. The remainder are usually joined with different elements. Some are oxides, being united with oxygen: hematite (iron oxide) and cuprite (copper oxide). Other metals are fused with sulfur. Cinnabar is a sulfide of mercury, stibnite of antimony, pyrite of iron. Still others, in a multitude of combinations producing wondrously colored pieces, are a joy to the "rock hound" collector though a bitter problem to mineralogists who seek an economical method of separating them easily.

The most glamorous of minerals are the precious and semiprecious gemstones. Of the semiprecious, nearly all, from amethysts to zircons, are found in various amounts in the United States. However the treasure of America's gems does not diminish the true esthetic beauty of more common mineral crystals. Ordinary silica quartz, with its transparent glitter, and malachite, marked by gnarled green swirls, are among the most ornamental stones.

The science of mineralogy may be at some midpoint of discovery in this latter half of the twentieth century. No one can be sure what unknown materials or minerals lie hidden under the oceans or deep in the earth. Exploration and drilling of sea bottoms may reveal startling new discoveries in the next decades. Nor can man be sure that thousands of other strange minerals do not soar in the sky, millions of miles away on the moon or soon-to-be-visited planets.

Listed with the illustrations are the states in which the largest deposits of each specimen are located.

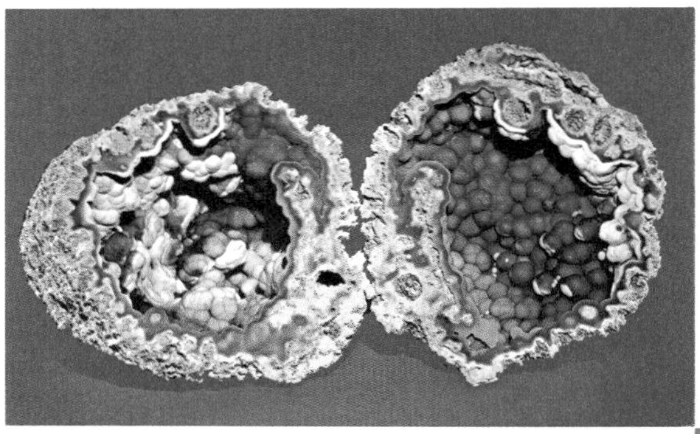

← **Chalcedony.** Named for an Asia Minor city of ancient days (Chalcedon), this quartz or silicon oxide group includes sard, jasper, agate, onyx and other types. The specimen shown here was formed in the hollow of a coral reef. Oregon, Wyoming, California

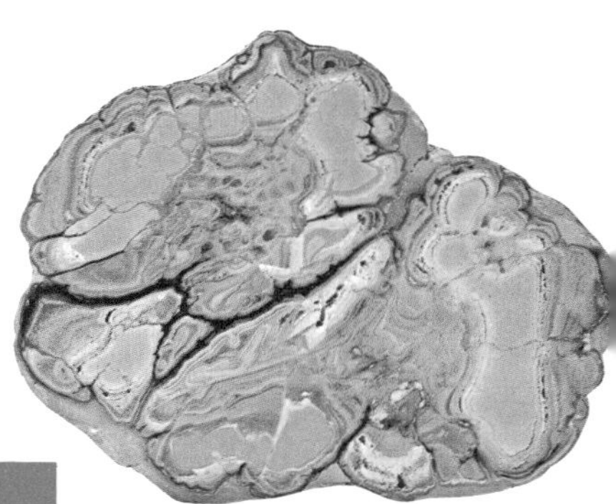

↑ **Variscite.** It looks much like turquoise, but this hydrous aluminum phosphate is lighter and softer. The stone is almost unique to the United States and is very popular as an inexpensive turquoise substitute. Utah, Nevada

→ **Garnet.** These are complex double silicates uniting two metals. The one shown is almandine (aluminum-iron silicate). When such stones are cut in cabochon (rounded) form they are called carbuncles. Georgia, Pennsylvania, Idaho

Turquoise. American Indians value turquoise and have used it for centuries in jewelry in various imaginative silver settings. The name comes from Turkey, through which the first stones reached Europe. New Mexico, Nevada, Colorado, Arizona ↑

→ **Cuprite.** On occasion ancient bronze artifacts will exhibit cuprite which has crystallized on them during years of burial. The copper-oxide ore is often known as ruby or plush copper because of its rich, lush appearance. Arizona.

→ **Muscovite.** An abundant hydrous silicate of aluminum and potassium, this mica can be split into thin sheets called "isinglass." It is used for electric insulation and as a fireproof window glass for stoves and lanterns. New Hampshire

↑ **Azurite.** The deep blue color of azurite, a copper hydroxyl carbonate, not only makes it an attractive gemstone but led to its use as a basis for paint pigments by Renaissance artists. Arizona

← **Beryl.** A common variety of the beryllium aluminum silicate mineral family, beryl is a near cousin of the emerald and aquamarine gemstones. It can occur in very large segments weighing 30 tons or more. North Carolina, Maine

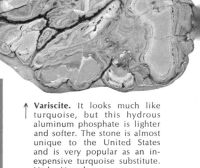

→ **Native Sulfur.** The mineral was known to the ancients as "brimstone." Soft, yellow and present in every active volcano, sulfur burns with a blue flame. Its crystals crackle when held in the hand close to the ear. Louisiana, Texas

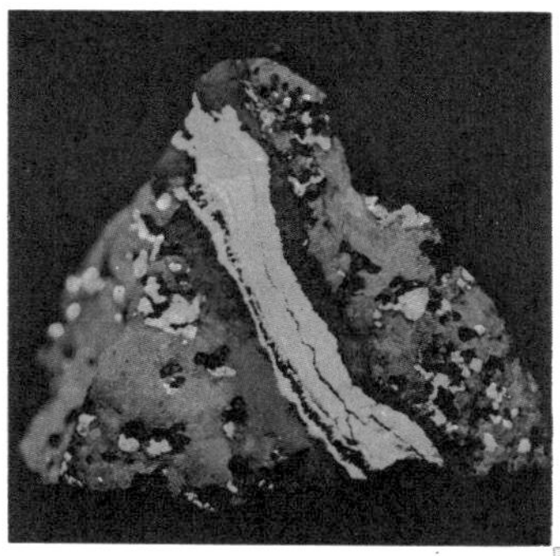

Willemite. The green ore is an important source of zinc. The red stone is calcite. When exposed to ultra-violet rays, as in this picture, the ore glows with fluorescence. New Jersey

Fluorite. Fluorspar, another name for calcium fluoride, melts easily and is added to iron ore to help it "flux" in steel-making. The crystals can exhibit almost any color of the rainbow from red to violet. Illinois, Kentucky

Halite. Better known to the layman as rock salt, sodium chloride is a necessity for the sustenance of life. When broken, a rock salt crystal will divide into smaller and smaller pieces, always in cube form. Texas, Louisiana, New York

"Landscape" Jasper. Impurities which crystallize in chalcedonic quartz, an oxide of silicon, can create landscapes or tree forms. Moss agate, another quartz mineral of the same family, exhibits similar effects. California, Colorado, New Mexico, Arizona

Amethyst. Ancient Greeks thought this silicon dioxide gemstone prevented intoxication. Among the most valuable of all the quartz types, it is prized for its purplish-violet color. The nontransparent varieties were once cut into large ornaments. North Carolina, Arizona, Virginia, New Hampshire

Prehnite. Looking like a bunch of yellow grapes or under ripe brussels sprouts, the mineral is a calcium aluminum hydroxy silicate. It was named for a Dutchman, Colonel Prehn, an eighteenth-century governor of the Cape Colony in South Africa. New Jersey

Huebnerite. Tungsten is widely employed as a filament material in light bulbs and in the manufacture of steel alloys. It is sometimes extracted from this tungstate of manganese and iron. Colorado.

Malachite. This beautiful stone, a copper hydroxy carbonate, ranks as semiprecious. Often cut and polished by modern man, it was also prized by American Indians along with a number of other gemstones. Arizona

Opal. The hydrated form of silicon dioxide is valuable when it exhibits internal sparkle called fire. The fire or opalescence is believed caused by tiny cracks in the stone which interfere with the passage of light. Some people believe the stone brings bad luck. Nevada

Barite. Known in some instances as desert rose because of its unusual form, sulfate of barium, when crushed, is important in drilling oil wells. Barite means "heavy," and, because of its weight, is added to a mud which circulates in the casing of a drill. When the latter hits small pockets of oil and gas under pressure, barite keeps them from blowing to the surface. Arkansas, Missouri, Georgia, Tennessee

Pyromorphite. The name is derived from the Greek words for "fire" and "form," since molten globules of this rather rare chlorophosphate of lead tend to shape into crystals when cooled. Ore has no commercial value. Idaho, Arizona

Aquamarine. These blue to sea-green varieties of beryl retain their shade and color under both natural and artificial light. Very pale types have been used as lenses for spectacles. Heat can intensify color in some examples. Colorado, Connecticut

Alabaster. When gypsum, a hydrous calcium sulfate, occurs in compact, solid masses, it is called alabaster. This translucent mineral, mentioned in the Bible, has been sculpted into ornamental and useful forms for thousands of years. Michigan

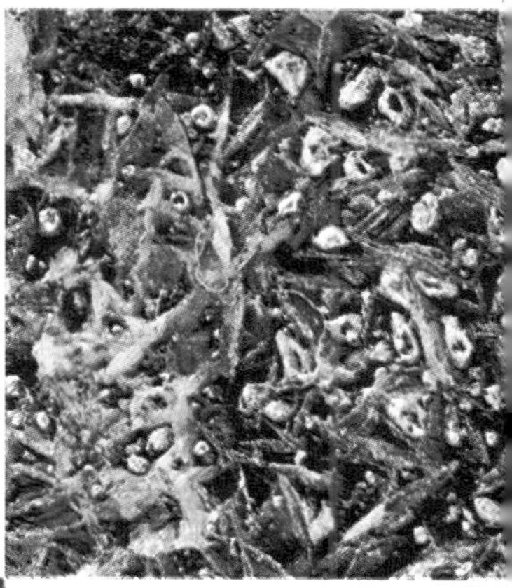

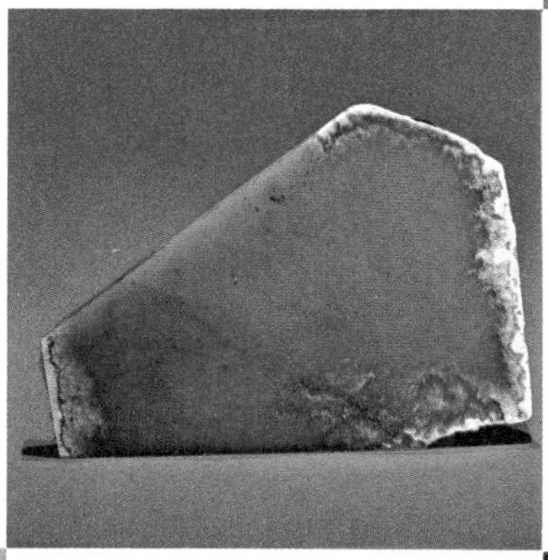

Nephrite. Ranging in color from black to green, this calcium magnesium iron silicate is a form of jade—not as valuable as the Chinese variety. Centuries ago the stone was thought to be a cure for colic, and the name "jade" derives from a Spanish word signifying "colic stone." Wyoming, California, Alaska

Brazilian Emerald. This gemstone is actually a green tourmaline, a complex boron aluminum silicate. When rubbed with cloth, it attracts tiny bits of paper by static electricity. It is not an emerald though often mistaken for one. California

Cinnabar. Globules of mercury can be seen in this specimen of ore from which the metal is extracted. "Quicksilver" has many uses, in scientific instruments, detonators and in the metal, chemical and electrical industries. California, Nevada

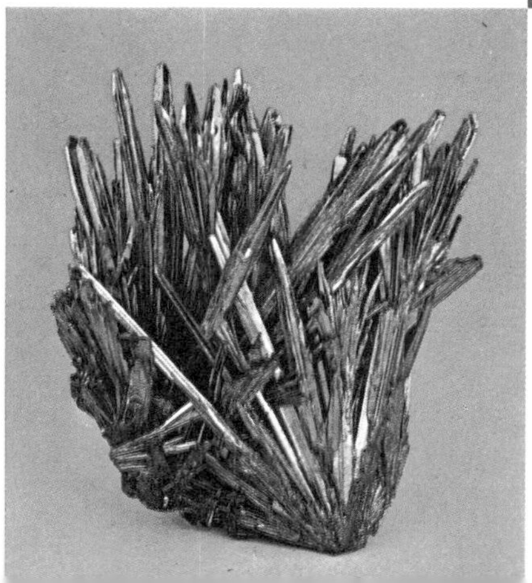

Stibnite. An easily melted antimony sulfide, this is an important source of the metal which is used in pewter and type metal. Ancient peoples used it as a cosmetic to darken their eyebrows. Nevada

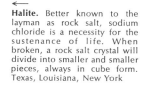

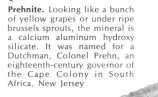

Petrified Wood. Actually this is not wood turned to stone but wood which has been replaced, cell for cell, most frequently by silica. Gemstone woods can be agate, opal, jasper, sard or others of the chalcedony group. Arizona, Utah, Wyoming

THE NATIONAL ECONOMY

Since World War I, the United States has experienced some extremely wide fluctuations in business activity. In 1922 almost a decade of postwar prosperity began after a precipitous drop into a fairly brief but sharp depression. The storied twenties brought a great demand for investment to build new electric power plants and factories, especially for automobiles and all their related parts. Ten billion dollars—a huge sum for that period—was spent on new roads alone. Radios and other electric appliances appeared for the first time in many homes of the nation. The sense of euphoria caused by these boom years resulted in overoptimism and excessive speculation that made all the more severe the abrupt reversal of the Great Depression, beginning with the stock market crash of 1929. Between 1929 and 1933, the Gross National Product (GNP), the total value of annual national output of goods and services, dropped from $103 billion to $56.6 billion. In these years, unemployment rose from 1.6 million to 12.8 million, about 25 percent of the entire civilian labor force. Investment in new factories, machinery and housing dropped from $16.2 billion to $1.4 billion.

Despite heavy government spending (to "prime the pump," as President Franklin Roosevelt expressed it), full recovery did not come until World War II. The massive demands for the goods and munitions of the globe's greatest conflict brought an upward surge of economic vigor. Government spending rose from $14 billion in 1940 to $96.5 billion in 1944. At the same time, the American economy was so fabulously productive that consumers were scarcely deprived of the "good life": private citizens' spending rose from almost $72 billion to $127.7 billion in those years.

After World War II, the American economy took off on a great new wave of peacetime growth. The United States made a major contribution to the reconstruction of war-torn countries in Europe. Consumer spending at home increased by $23.7 billion in the single fiscal year of 1945–46, with full employment and rising prices. Later, the war in Korea also increased production. Although a slowdown in the rate of growth occurred from 1957 to 1961, the following years brought an economic prosperity to the United States that continued upward for the longest unbroken period in peacetime history.

By the mid-sixties, many complex problems were affecting the economy. The expanding labor force (see chart below), the war in Vietnam, Federal and local revenues and expenditures (see next page), continuously expanding productivity, international trade barriers and the "balance of payments" (see "Foreign Trade With Major World Areas," page 160): these are a few.

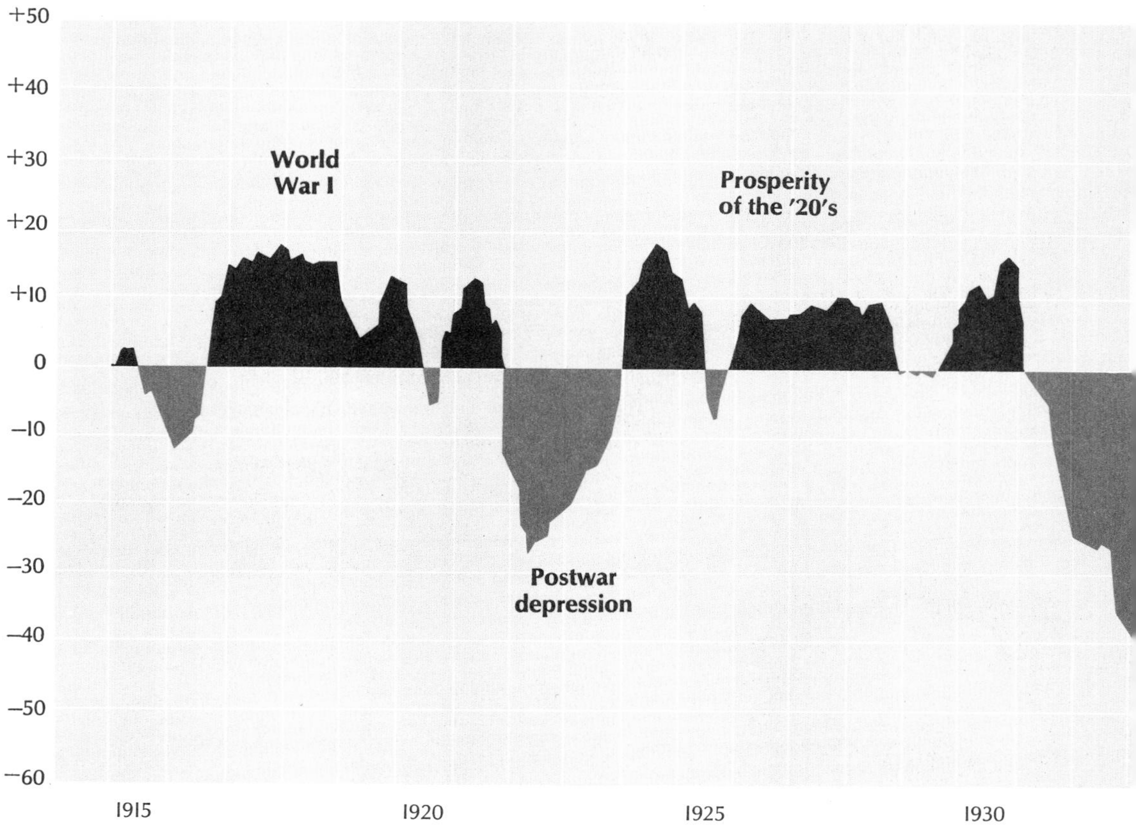

LABOR FORCE

OCCUPATION	(TOTAL IN MILLIONS) 1900	1967
White-Collar Workers	**5.12**	**34.23**
Professional and technical	1.23	9.87
Managers, officials and proprietors	1.70	7.49
Clerical workers	.88	12.33
Sales workers	1.31	4.53
Blue-Collar Workers	**10.40**	**27.26**
Craftsmen, foremen	3.06	9.85
Operatives	3.72	13.88
Nonfarm laborers	3.62	3.53
Service Workers	**2.63**	**9.33**
Private household workers	1.58	1.77
Service workers, excluding private household	1.05	7.56
Farm Workers	**10.88**	**3.55**
Farm owners and managers	5.76	1.97
Farm laborers and foremen	5.12	1.58
Total	**29.03**	**74.37**

The change in the size and composition of the labor force shows the remarkable metamorphosis of our economy since the turn of the century.

The present labor force grew by 10 million in the past decade. It will expand by 15 million in the next decade; so there will be 50 percent more people (mostly the young) looking for jobs. Meanwhile, automation of work goes on —over the past 10 years the output for each hour of labor increased 45 percent.

In 1900, blue-collar workers outnumbered white-collar workers two to one; the latter group forged ahead, shortly after 1955, and is now nearly seven times larger than in 1900. Clerical workers had the biggest gain, from 877,000 to over 12 million. Service workers (except those in private households) increased sevenfold. The number of farm workers dropped sharply, yet agricultural productivity remains at its highest level.

In 1900, only about one out of six workers was a woman. Today, women represent more than one third—about 27 million—of the working force.

UNEMPLOYMENT

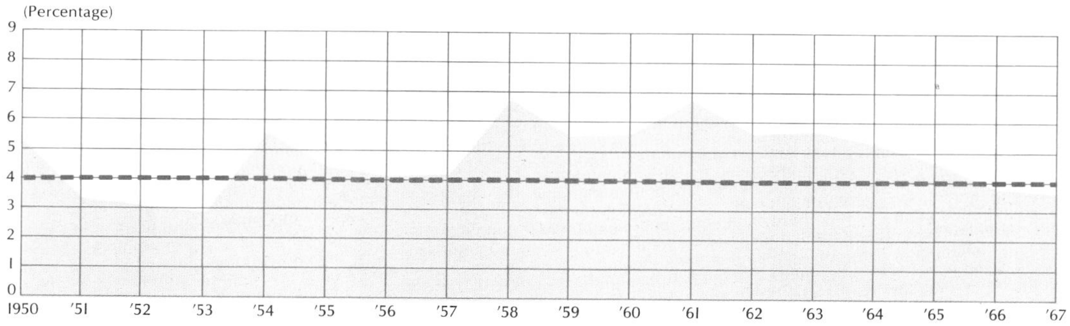

From 1950 to 1966 the percentage of the labor force that was unemployed varied from less than 3 percent to almost 7. Four percent is considered normal unemployment, including those people between jobs. But there are inequities among various groups—with greater need for more jobs among nonwhites and the young. The 1966 unemployment figure was 3.1 percent for whites, but 7.3 percent for Negroes.

With the upper-teen-age population entering the labor force at a maximum rate in 1970 (a result of the baby boom which began in 1946), the employment problems of youth, both Negro and white, will be difficult to solve. By 1975, at least 10 million people, or 1 out of every 20, will probably be without work unless the rate of growth in our economy is even greater in the future than it has been in the past.

NATIONAL INCOME AND WHO EARNS IT

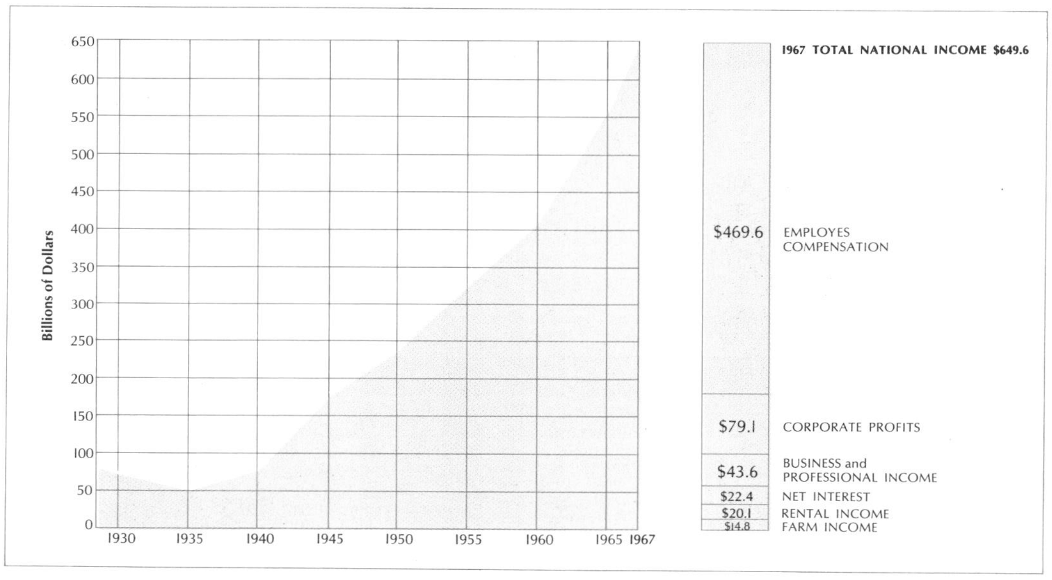

The wealth of the nation—everything from spaceships to a bar of laundry soap to the intercontinental cables under the oceans—added up by one imaginative economist, totals $2 thousand billion (or $2 trillion). This sum does not seem so incomprehensible when one compares $2 thousand billion with the Gross National Product—$740 billion in one year, or more than one third of our total wealth.

Our national income ($649.6 billion in 1967) is actually the GNP minus depreciation and certain taxes. More than 71 percent of it was earned by employes. The profits of corporations amounted to 13 percent of the total. The rest was earned by proprietors—one-man businesses, farmers or partnerships—or as rents and interest on savings and investments.

Individual proprietors—11 million (which include farmers and professional people in business for themselves)—far outnumber partnerships and corporations. Partnerships amount to less than 1 million, corporations slightly over a million. The latter include the big companies, which do five times as much business as all the others combined.

FAMILY AND INDIVIDUAL INCOME

The average family income in 1966 was $7400. It has more than doubled in 20 years ($3033 in 1947). Families with incomes of $10,000 or more rose from 8 percent of the total to 30 percent (these figures have been adjusted to account for inflation). In 1950, the average income per person nationally was $1496; it was $2963 in 1966. Connecticut ranks highest with $3690 per person per year, and Mississippi is lowest with $1777. These averages clearly reflect the relative wealth of the United States, in light of the figure of $100 per year, which is the average income per person in Latin America and Asia.

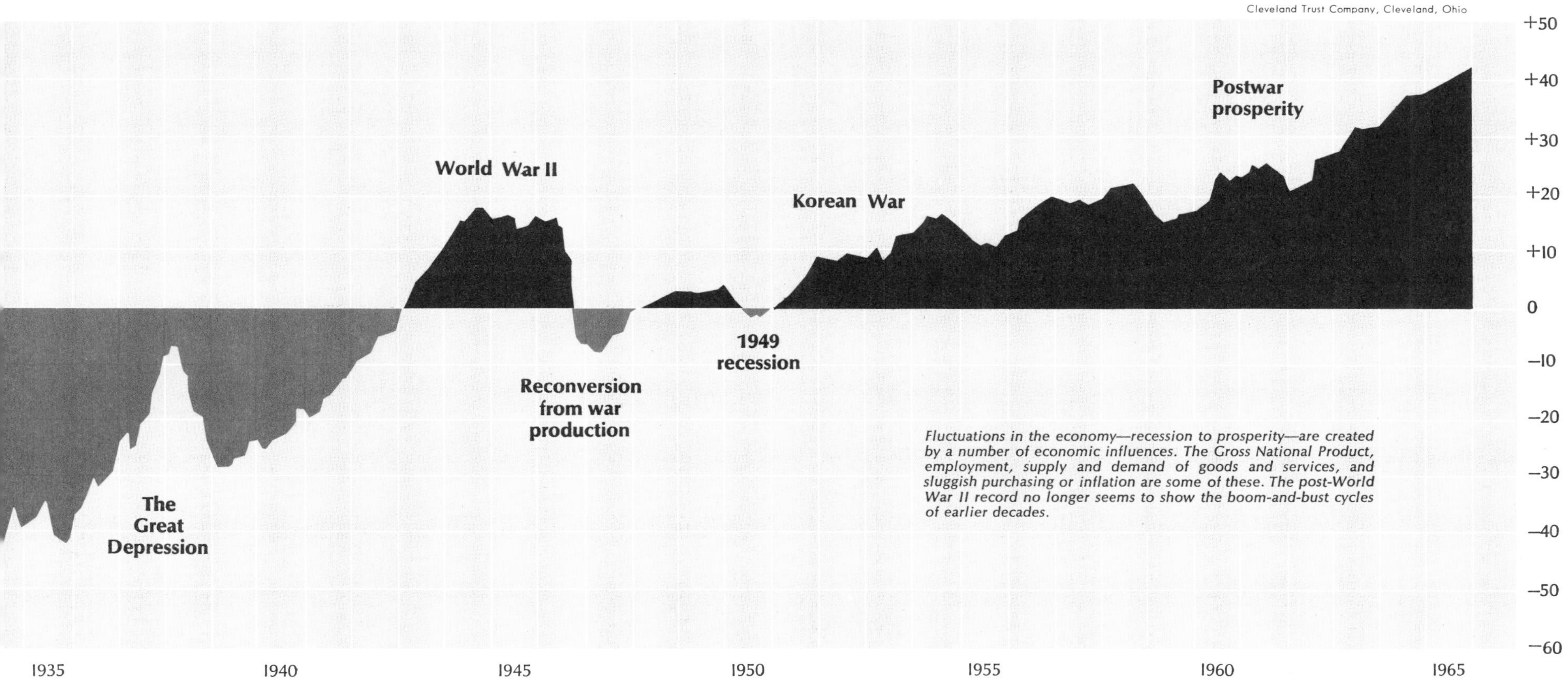

Fluctuations in the economy—recession to prosperity—are created by a number of economic influences. The Gross National Product, employment, supply and demand of goods and services, and sluggish purchasing or inflation are some of these. The post-World War II record no longer seems to show the boom-and-bust cycles of earlier decades.

CITIES WITH BILLION-DOLLAR INCOMES

(total of individual incomes after Federal tax deductions—1965)

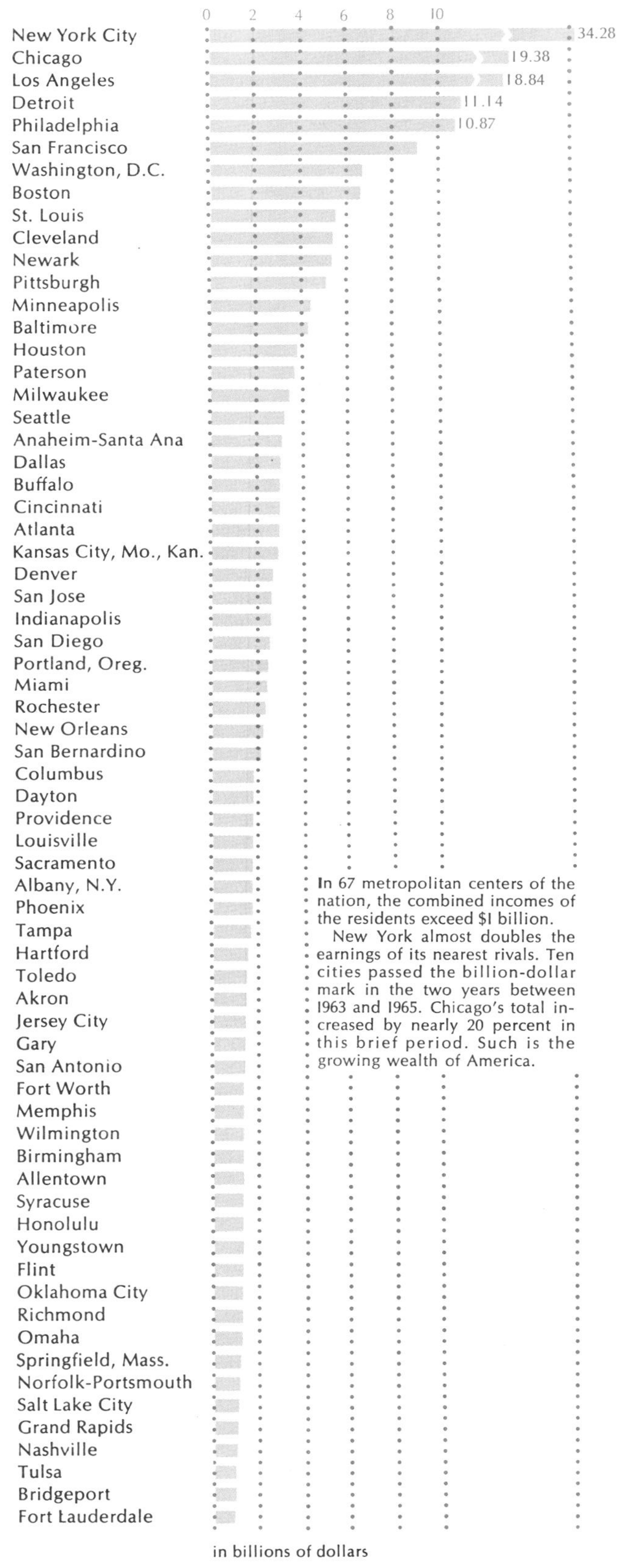

In 67 metropolitan centers of the nation, the combined incomes of the residents exceed $1 billion.

New York almost doubles the earnings of its nearest rivals. Ten cities passed the billion-dollar mark in the two years between 1963 and 1965. Chicago's total increased by nearly 20 percent in this brief period. Such is the growing wealth of America.

DOLLARS FOR GOVERNMENT

About a fifth of all the goods and services produced in the United States are currently absorbed by government—Federal, state and local. Payment for them reached the awesome total of $197 billion in 1966—about two thirds of this spent by the Federal government. The ways in which the Federal government plans to spend its share, some $186 billion in 1969 are given in the Federal budget chart below. This includes for the first time continuing trust funds such as those for Social Security and Highways.

Federal Income. In 1940—some of us nostalgically remember that period—the income tax of all citizens averaged $40.56 for the year. By 1950, this had jumped more than six times—to $257.44. Ten years later, this tax had again doubled—to $511.78. And by 1966, it rose to $658.03.

Total Federal taxes on corporations also soared in these years, jumping ten times over between 1940 and 1950, doubling in the next ten years, and rising 50 percent in the following six years. Of course, the number of businesses grew in these years also.

Federal taxes paid by individuals and corporations in the various states form an arresting pattern: New York, with less population than California in 1966, paid more than twice the amount of taxes ($21.5 billion as against a little more than $9.5 billion). Close on California's heels were Illinois ($8.48 billion), Michigan ($7.77 billion), Ohio ($7.27 billion), Pennsylvania ($6.72 billion). Others ranged from $3.87 billion for Texas to $78.3 million for Alaska.

Federal Spending. By 1969, expenditures of the Federal government may reach $186 billion (compared with $178.1 billion in income). The difference must be borrowed, adding to the national debt each year. This debt is over $340 billion (see next page). The interest paid on it appears in the pie chart below.

FEDERAL BUDGET

(Estimated 1969, in billions of dollars)

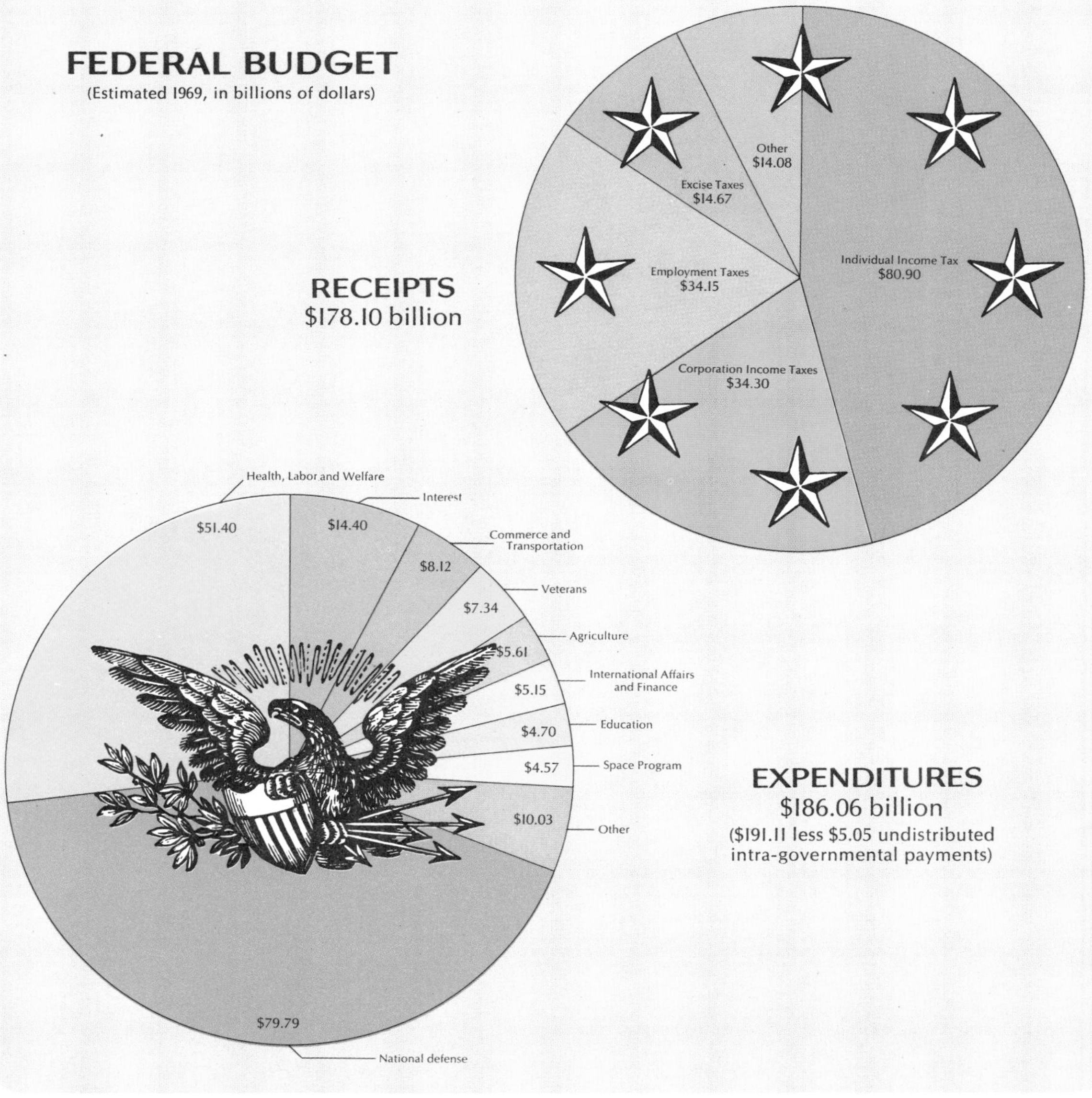

NATIONAL DEBT

Since the 1930's the Federal government has increasingly borrowed money to make up the difference between its expenditures and the amount it acquires through revenues. (In the Federal budget chart on page 159, the section marked "Interest" is chiefly the amount paid on the national debt.) Understandably, the enormous jump in public debt occurred between 1941, when the sum was $55 billion, and 1946, when it was $270 billion. This increase was needed to help pay for World War II, only part of which was financed by taxes. The national debt has exceeded $341 billion, or $1705 for every person in the nation (including children).

But these figures need to be related to other factors. Actually, the government debt since 1946 has been growing more slowly than the national income. Since World War II, the number of taxpayers has also been greatly increasing, as well as the average income of each. So the amount of the "burden" of debt as it falls on each individual has been considerably decreasing.

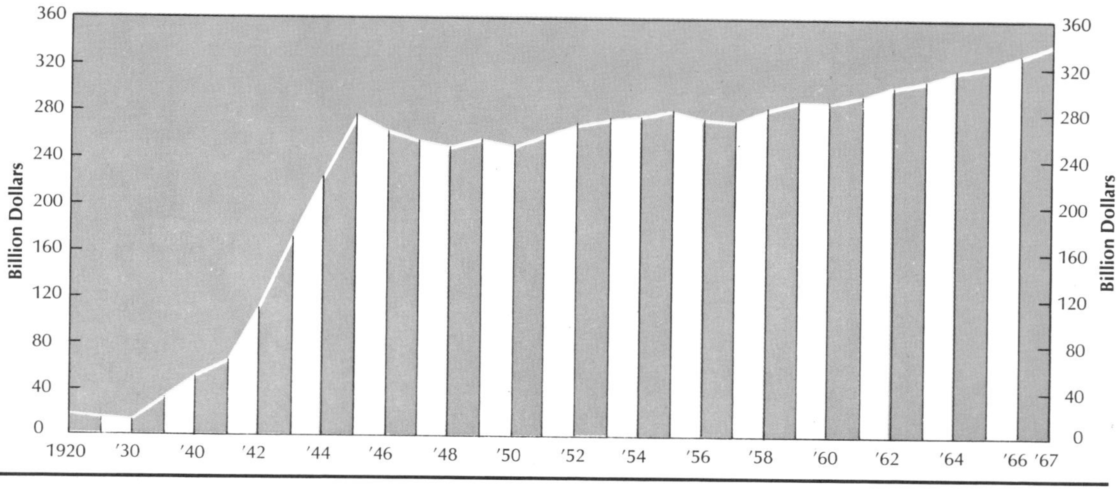

PERSONAL SPENDING

The lion's share of the country's goods and services is bought by the individual consumers—just as most of the national income is earned by individual employes. In 1966, they bought about two thirds of what was produced: $160 billion in services such as medical care, education and rent; $186 billion in non-durable goods such as food, clothing and gasoline; $71 billion in durables such as autos and refrigerators. The government and business firms bought most of the rest. Foreign trade (exports minus imports) accounted for a small part—see below.

Spending power has risen dramatically since 1933 and so has earning power. Average personal spending (called disposable income, excluding taxes but including savings, and adjusted for changes in prices) stood at $893 for each of the 125 million people in 1933 and rose to $2294 per person for each of the 195.8 million people in the mid-1960's.

THE AMERICAN STOCKHOLDER

The number of individuals now owning shares in publicly held corporations of all sizes stands at more than 24 million. This marks an increase of about 40 percent over that of the early 1960's, and nearly a fourfold increase since the early 1950's. One out of every twenty-five Americans owned stock then, compared with one out of eight now. Two thirds of the individual shareholders are in the $5000 to $15,000 income range, although they own considerably less than two thirds of the total shares outstanding. Women represent slightly more than half of the adult total.

AMERICAN BUSINESS FIRMS

American businesses have been getting bigger. Few firms had assets of more than a million dollars a hundred years ago. Of the many multibillion-dollar corporate giants today, 31 have assets over $4 billion and 97 make annual sales of over a billion dollars. This does not signal the end of small businesses. The number of small firms (fewer than 100 employes) is increasing more rapidly than those of medium and big businesses.

10 TOP BILLION-DOLLAR MARKETS

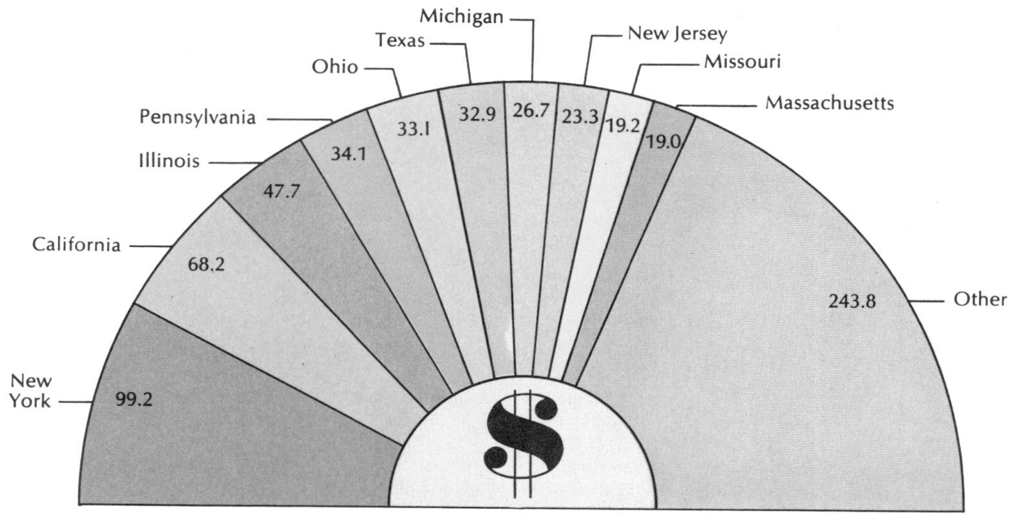

These states were the major purchasers of finished goods and services for the most recent year recorded. The huge sums total all sales and receipts, and so duplicate wholesale and retail transactions.

UNITED STATES INVESTMENTS ABROAD $54.3 Billion

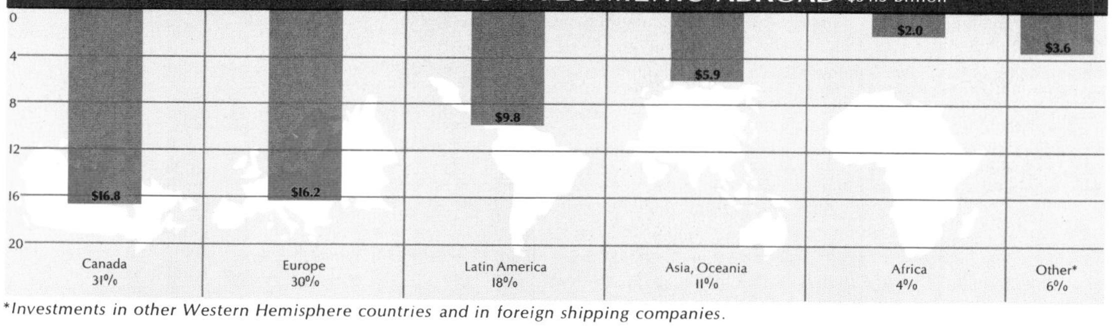

Investments in other Western Hemisphere countries and in foreign shipping companies.

American private investors now have about $55 billion invested on a long-term basis in a variety of economic enterprises outside the U.S. borders. At the end of World War II the amount was $8 billion; the rate of increase has steadily advanced, averaging over 6 percent annually for the 1960's. In the mid-1960's about one third was invested in Canada, one third in Western Europe, one fifth in Latin America, and the balance elsewhere in the world.

In the past, the bulk of our foreign investment was in the extractive industries—petroleum and ores. In this decade, foreign manufacturing ventures have become the most dynamic sector for investment. Simultaneously there has been an unprecedented growth of multinational corporations—firms with subsidiaries in a number of foreign nations. Most are American investments, but European and Japanese companies also have international networks.

FOREIGN TRADE WITH MAJOR WORLD AREAS

The bulk of America's foreign trade is carried on with six major world areas, as shown in the chart at right. Currently U.S. exports amount to $29 billion and imports to $25 billion. More is exported to Western Europe than any other area.

Exports to Asia are higher than those to Latin America—a reflection of our substantial aid programs to Asian nations rather than a normal outflow. Japan is the only Far Eastern nation to attain a high degree of industrialization, and we export more basic materials to her than to any nation or area except Western Europe.

Exports to Africa have barely doubled since the onset of World War II while those to other regions increased fourfold. About three fourths of U.S. exports are finished and semi-manufactured goods—such as electronic parts and automobiles—nearly half of which go to Canada and Latin America.

Agricultural products are also important American exports, with an annual total of $5 billion. Between 10 and 15 percent of American farm employes are engaged in production for export. Japan is the heaviest national purchaser, followed by Canada, the Netherlands, India, West Germany and the United Kingdom. Agricultural products worth $1.6 billion were given by the U.S. government in foreign aid to those nations needing food for their hungry people, especially India.

Slightly less than one half of all U.S. imports originate in the Western hemisphere. Western Europe and Japan are sources of most of the rest. Canada supplies more basic materials (wood pulp, ores, scrap metal) than any other trading area. These have increased in relative importance as the United States has been consuming more minerals than it produces. The United States purchases about $3 billion of petroleum and iron ore, although it ranks first and second in the world production of these essentials. Latin America ships more fuels and more foodstuffs (coffee, fruit and sugar) to us than does any other trading area.

In the twentieth century, a recognition has grown among governments and economists that barriers to trade by tariffs—taxes on goods passing from nation to nation—hurt the economies of all.

Western European economy has been considerably improved by the formation of the European Common Market (or European Economic Community) by six European nations which have dropped trade barriers among them. In 1962, the Trade Expansion Act was passed to grant the President of the United States powers for reducing tariffs within five years. Under this act, agreement was finally reached in 1967 by some 50 nations which generate 80 percent of the world's international commerce to reduce tariffs an average of 35 percent over a period of five years. The reductions would affect products constituting less than one third of America's $54 billion foreign trade.

American "balance of trade" has been advantageous in that during most years exports have exceeded imports. But the "balance of payments" has been the opposite. Largely because of American military payments for foreign bases, investments abroad by American businesses and grants and loans to foreign governments, the United States has paid out more than it has received. It has consequently suffered a persistent loss of gold reserves, which have passed primarily to European countries selling to the United States.

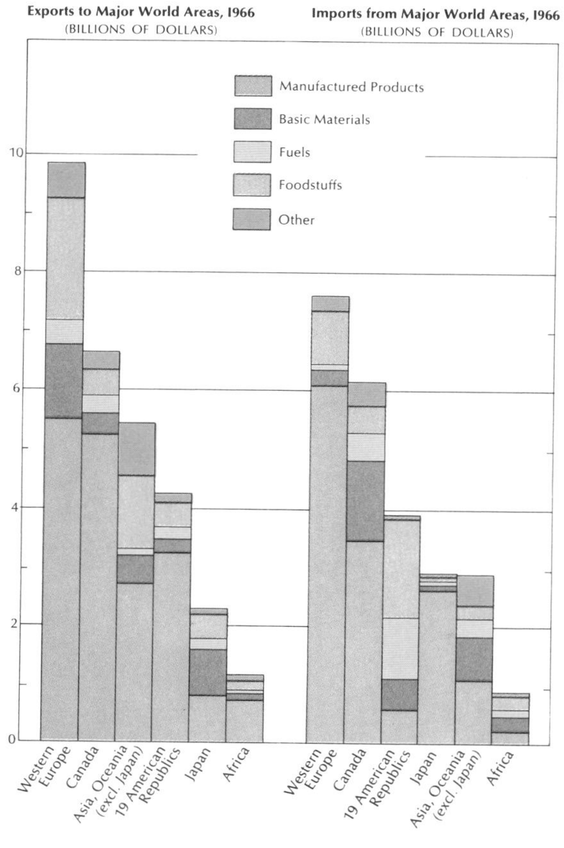

LINES OF COMMUNICATION

One measure of a democracy is the speed, efficiency and accuracy of its means of communication, and, ever since colonial days, Americans have worked hard to improve them. Not until 29 days after the adoption of the Declaration of Independence in Philadelphia did the news of this event reach Charleston, South Carolina. A combination of the Pony Express and the telegraph rushed the news of Abraham Lincoln's election in 1860 to California in six days. One year later the spark of the telegraph key transmitted information instantaneously from coast to coast. The first radio address of a President was made by Warren G. Harding in June 1923. Harry Truman was the first President to be seen and heard throughout the nation on television.

Industry sources estimate that 9 out of 10 adults read a daily newspaper, 98 percent of all American homes are equipped with radios and 94 percent with television sets.

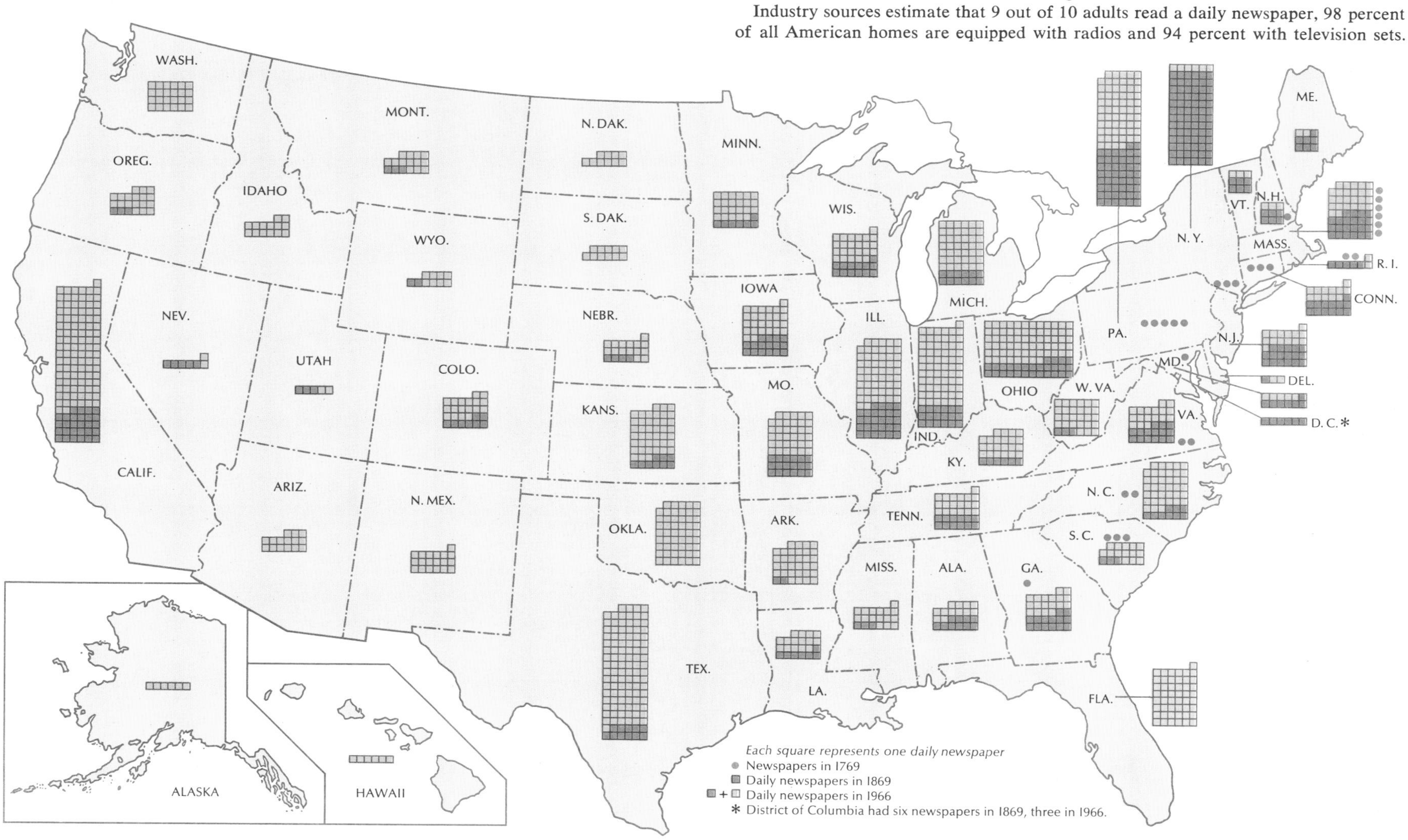

NEWSPAPERS

The first newspaper in the 13 British colonies—*Publick Occurrences Both Forreign* (sic) *and Domestic*—was suppressed four days after its publication in Boston on September 25, 1690, because its contents displeased the governor and his council. The first victory for freedom of the press was soon to come: Peter Zenger, printer of the *New York Weekly Journal,* was acquitted in 1735 of a charge of seditious libel on the grounds that the statements he made were true.

When the Revolutionary War started, there were about 35 newspapers, representing both patriot and loyalist-Tory points of view. Most were small four-page sheets published weekly. The first American daily, the two-page *Pennsylvania Evening Post,* made its appearance in 1783. By 1800 nearly 500 papers had been started. Circulation of most journals was limited by the relatively high price of 6 cents, until the advent of the penny press in the 1830's made newspapers available to lower-income groups.

As the nation grew, so did the newspaper industry. Two other factors were responsible for its expansion: the increase in the country's literacy and technical improvements in the machines. Expanded school systems after the Civil War produced a large literate population by the 1890's. Manufacturers of consumer goods began to distribute products through the newly formed department stores, which in turn supported daily newspapers with full-page advertisements. Newspapers strove to obtain and hold readers by appealing to popular attitudes and interests: the first comic strip—The Yellow Kid—appeared in 1901. The formation in 1848 of the New York Associated Press, a coöperative newsgathering organization, led to the creation of national and world-wide news services which reported domestic and foreign events over telegraph and cable lines. Press associations now supply most of the foreign and national news printed in U.S. papers. Individual newspapers often station correspondents in Washington and foreign capitals.

A new type of newspaper, the tabloid, half the size of standard publications, appeared in the 1920's. It relied heavily on large headlines and extensive use of pictures.

While circulation of daily newspapers has continued a steady growth through the years to more than 61 million, consolidation has reduced the number of publications. It has dropped from a peak of 2400 in 1916 to about 1750 in 1967. Advertising revenue was nearly $5 billion in 1966. Modern presses can turn out between 40,000 and 60,000 copies an hour, and publishers like to boast that the American public is the best informed in the world.

MAGAZINES

Magazines probably cover the widest range of subjects in the field of communications. There are periodicals, both scholarly and popular, which are directed to special-interest groups—from anthropologists and cross-word-puzzle fans to philatelists and zoologists. Trade magazines draw subscribers from specialized business areas—advertising, construction, plumbing or window display. Other publications are edited primarily for men or women, or for children of specific ages. General-interest magazines, because of their wide appeal, achieve circulations running into millions. These periodicals, as the name implies, are published either weekly, monthly, quarterly or at other intervals.

In the 13 colonies and the newly independent nation, the mortality rate for magazines was high. Of the first two published, both in Philadelphia and in January of 1741, one lasted three months, the other six. By 1825 there were about 100, and a quarter of a century later the number had grown to nearly 600. In the days before photo-engraving, *Harper's Weekly* was famous for its woodcut illustrations of the Civil War. Edgar Allan Poe, Bret Harte, William Cullen Bryant, Henry Ward Beecher, James Russell Lowell and William Dean Howells were among the famous magazine editors of this period. The decade after the turn of the century was known as the muckraking period, when, in *McClure's, Collier's, American Magazine* and others, such writers as Lincoln Steffens, Ray Stannard Baker and Ida Tarbell exposed corruption and vice.

America's emergence as a world power after World War I resulted in an increased interest in international affairs. Two new types of periodicals appeared during the 1920's—the pocket-sized digest (*Reader's Digest,* 1922) and the newsmagazine (*Time,* 1923). A third newcomer was the news-picture magazine (*Life,* 1936). Although some publications of long standing disappeared over the years, the industry as a whole continued to grow. By 1966 there were 9000 magazines of all types with a combined average circulation of more than 430 million copies per issue. Advertising revenues were estimated at $1.3 billion.

POST OFFICE

Postal service in colonial days left much to be desired. When roads were not blocked by winter snows or spring floods, horseback riders averaged four miles an hour; it was unusual to cover 50 miles in one day. The cost of sending letters was high because the British expected the post office to be profitable. A second drawback was the possibility that letters might be opened to see if the writer was disloyal to the king.

The first mails between Boston and New York were carried over the Boston Post Road in 1672 on a monthly basis. The postal route was eventually extended as far as Georgia, but in the early eighteenth century it still took four weeks for a letter to reach Williamsburg, Virginia, from Boston. Benjamin Franklin greatly improved the colonial postal system and in 1775 was appointed Postmaster General by the Continental Congress.

In 1789, the United States had about 75 post offices, most of them along the coast, and 2000 miles of post roads. By 1800 the mileage had increased to 20,000, and by 1850 there were more than 40,000 post offices. Postage stamps were introduced in 1847, only a few years after their creation in England. East of the Mississippi, the railroad had largely taken over from the stagecoach the job of transporting the mails. But the frontier area west of that river depended principally on horses until the decade after the Civil War. (See map, pages 84–85.)

As transportation improved, additional services were offered by the Post Office Department. The first deliveries to homes and businesses started in 1863. Rural free delivery began in West Virginia in 1896. May 15, 1918, marked the inauguration of regular airmail service; airplanes and trucks now cover many routes formerly served by trains.

While the Post Office business has increased tremendously since the turn of the century, the number of post offices has dropped from 77,000 to 34,000. With more and better roads and universal use of automobiles, not every small hamlet requires its own post office. The volume of mail has zoomed from 7 billion pieces in 1900 to 80 billion and is likely to continue to grow.

TELEGRAPH

The United States government might be in the telegraph business today had it not decided in 1847 that sending messages by wire would never be profitable. Congress appropriated $30,000 to build a line from Washington to Baltimore, which Samuel F. B. Morse inaugurated on May 24, 1844 with the words, "What hath God wrought!" He and his associates devised a code of dots and dashes —short and long signals—which represented the letters of the alphabet, numbers and punctuation marks. For several months thereafter, few took advantage of the offer to transmit free messages, and finally the line was turned over to a private firm. Then railway companies discovered that the telegraph was an almost indispensable method for sending information about train movements up and down the line. Public messages were easily and cheaply sent on the same wires. By 1851, 50 telegraph companies had been organized. Transmission of messages to Europe over the first successful transatlantic cable began in 1866.

Eventually, smaller businesses were taken over by two nationwide systems which merged in 1943. The old Morse "key" for sending dots and dashes gave way to teleprinters with keyboards resembling those of typewriters. Wires and equipment were developed which could transmit up to 300 messages simultaneously on different frequencies. Many large business firms now lease their own telegraph systems which not only handle typed communications but also transmit facsimile sketches, blueprints and maps. In addition, these systems can relay data for processing by computers. Other lines serve "ticker" machines which print stock, bond and produce prices. The number of miles of telegraph channels in the United States for sending public messages has increased from 933,000 in 1900 to 92 million in 1967.

TELEPHONE

One May morning in 1877, Bostonians found something new offered in the advertising columns of their newspapers: the telephone. With this instrument, the advertisement claimed, "conversation can be easily carried on after slight practice and with the occasional repetition of a word or sentence." The annual rental for phones for "social purposes" was $20—for business houses, $40.

New Haven boasted the first directory, with 21 listings. The use of telephone numbers originated in Lowell, Massachusetts. In the early days, operators knew all their customers by name, but legend has it that a Lowell physician feared a measles epidemic might afflict the regular operators. Substitutes were hastily trained who could connect numbers without knowing the subscribers.

Scientific research developed new equipment and improved service. The first dial phones, installed in Milwaukee in 1896, enabled customers to call other numbers without going through the "central" switchboard operator. Gradually, long-distance lines connected city exchanges; the first transcontinental link, between New York and San Francisco, was opened on January 25, 1915. Twelve years later the Atlantic Ocean was bridged with the inauguration of radio-telephone service between New York and London. By 1930, commercial ship-to-shore communication was available. Englewood, New Jersey, became the first city—in 1951—where telephone subscribers could dial directly almost any city in the country. Modern all-electronic switching equipment can "remember" the dialed number and the dialer's number, and after a call has been completed, computers print bills using the number information stored on magnetic tape.

Sometime in the middle of 1966, the world's 200-millionth telephone was installed. The United States has nearly half the total; Bhutan has none, and the Cayman Islands have 32. Among the cities, New York has nearly 5.5 million, while Jamestown on the island of St. Helena —Napoleon's place of exile—has 65.

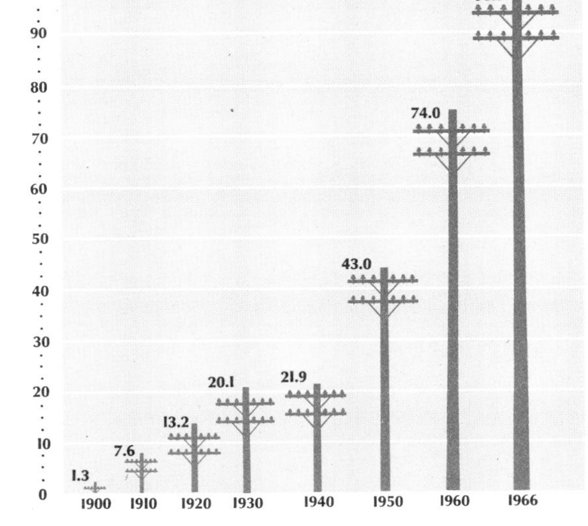

RADIO

On August 28, 1922, a New York real-estate firm paid for the first sponsored radio broadcast, over WEAF. That ten minutes—5 to 5:10 p.m.—cost $100. Forty-five years later, on the successor station WNBC, the price had increased to $250. Despite the competition of television stations which began after World War II, total revenue from advertising in the radio industry has shown an increase—except for two years—ever since 1945, rising from $310 million that year to nearly $1 billion in 1966. By then, there were 250 million radios, 4093 AM (amplitude modulation) and 1564 FM (frequency modulation) stations in the country—an average of 113 for each state in the Union. But these are not evenly distributed. In sparsely populated areas there is not enough advertising revenue to support a dense network of radio stations. In more populated areas the stations are as close together as possible. FM stations are located in these areas, where the demand for radio stations cannot be met by using the AM channels that are available.

Experimental radio broadcasts were made in the United States as early as 1906, with the help of Lee DeForest's invention of the triode vacuum tube. Also in that year radio stations began to broadcast on different wavelengths instead of all on one frequency. The first regularly scheduled programs began in 1920, and listeners heard them by means of crystal detector sets equipped with earphones. The first improvements were the development of the loudspeaker and of the battery-operated tube set. Radio stations began to proliferate. There are only 107 channels in the AM band between 540 and 1600 kilocycles, and it was not long before these channels were too crowded to permit good reception of some programs. Acting on the theory that airwaves were a natural resource belonging to the nation and should be regulated for the common good, Congress in 1927 set up the Federal Radio Commission, with powers to license stations and assign frequencies. In 1934, it was superseded by the Federal Communications Commission.

For more than two decades—until the development of television—it was radio that brought music, drama, news, soap opera and sports events into the home. When the stars of the entertainment world moved over to television, many radio stations expanded their news broadcasts, introduced the "disk jockey" and made more time available for the views and interests of minority groups. The broadcasting of sports events remains an important part of radio programming. A new feature was authorized by the F.C.C. in 1949—the broadcasting of editorials —but not until 1957 did a radio station present them on a daily basis. Public opinion broadcasts in which listeners phone in their opinions are becoming an important forum for discussion. Public service broadcasts are not as common as they would be if more people and groups realized that radio and TV stations are obliged by the F.C.C. to give free time for public service announcements and programs. It is estimated that half of the nation's stations now present editorial comment in addition to straight news reporting.

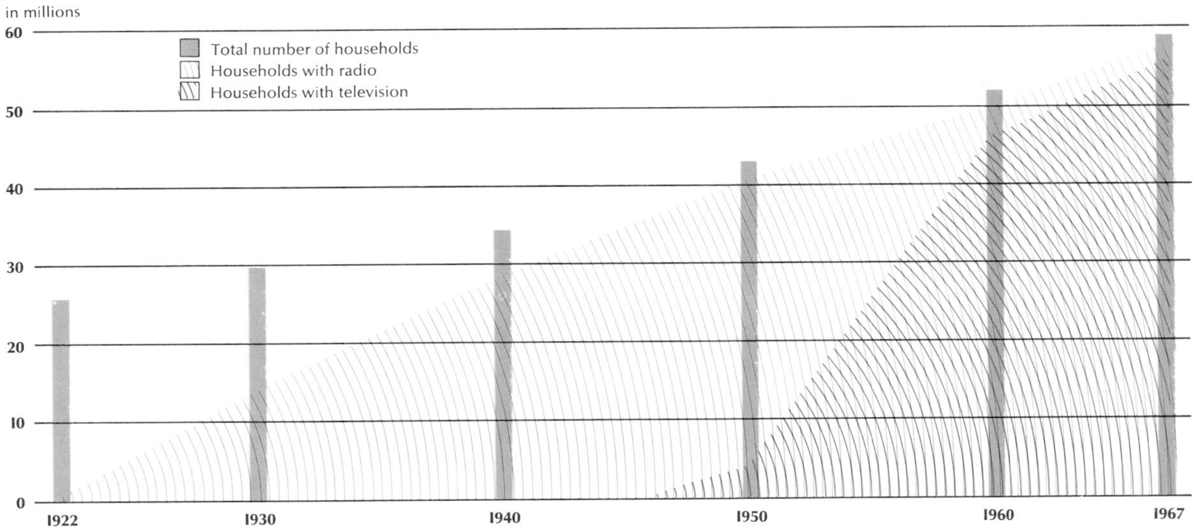

TELEVISION

The explosive growth of the television industry has taken place since the end of World War II. Test programs were broadcast as early as 1928; 17 experimental stations were in operation by 1937, and two years later the first commercial programs were seen in New York. The war stopped production of TV sets, although four stations continued to broadcast. In 1948, there were 29 commercially operated stations; manufacturers turned out 1 million sets, most of them with screens 12 inches in diagonal measurement; and advertising revenues were estimated at $8.7 million. By 1966, the F.C.C. had licensed 617 commercial and 156 noncommercial educational stations; annual production of TV sets had passed the 10 million mark; screens measured 23 and even 27 inches; programs were broadcast in color as well as black-and-white; and advertising income was approaching the $2 billion mark.

There are only 12 channels available for ordinary or very high frequency (VHF) broadcasting, and 70 which use smaller wavelengths, or ultra-high frequency (UHF) channels. (Not all TV sets are equipped to receive the UHF signals.) Because of the small number of VHF bands and the allocation of stations on channels 2—13 to nearby states, the eighth most populous state, New Jersey, has no ordinary TV station. Any New Jersey transmission on these bands would interfere with the programs on established stations. The state does have stations operating on UHF channels.

The medium has had an important impact on politics, bringing the candidates before the voters as if they were in person. Much of the fare offered on commercial television is classed as entertainment, and some programs are as popular abroad as they are in the United States; these are exported to 62 foreign countries on film and the dialogue in the local language is dubbed in. The use of space satellites has made possible the transmission of pictures to and from Europe and Asia (see diagram at right). Closed-circuit TV (carried by cables to specific receivers instead of on public airwaves) enables teachers to instruct many classes at a time. Even more promising for future educational programs is an experiment which demonstrated that a plane circling at 25,000 feet could broadcast to 13,000 schools and colleges within a radius of 200 miles.

SATELLITE

Television signals (waves) travel in a straight line and therefore usually can be received only as far as the horizon visible from the transmitting tower before going off into space as the earth curves. Yet the development of space science has made it possible to send television programs from one continent to another. A satellite placed in an eastward orbit at the equator at 22,300 miles circles the earth every 24 hours and therefore appears to be stationary in relation to the globe. The straight-line television signals are directed toward the satellite at an angle so that they "bounce" off and can be received thousands of miles from the transmitter. Programs are relayed to Hawaii and the Far East by a satellite over the Pacific, to Europe by another over the Atlantic Ocean.

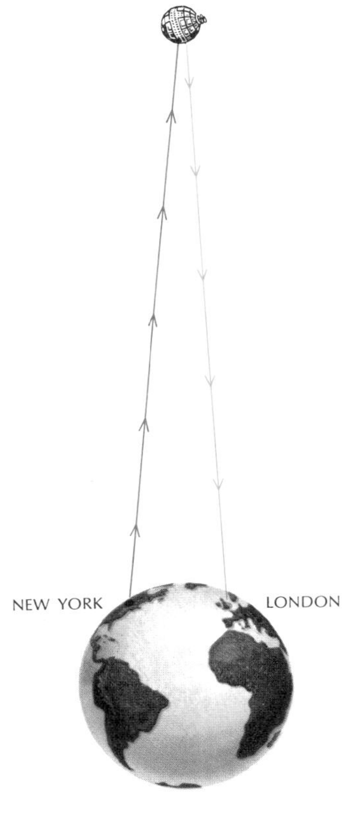

Transportation

A NATION ON WHEELS

The United States is the most mobile, most motorized nation in the world. Americans drive to work, to school and to vacation resorts. They make bank transactions at drive-up windows, see motion pictures at drive-ins and even attend religious services without ever leaving their cars. Some 5 million persons live in vehicles—house trailers, called mobile homes—and travel from one section of the country to another with the change of seasons, a change of employment or as the spirit moves them.

This automotive mobility has been made possible by a vast network of nearly 4 million miles of roads and streets of which about 1 million miles are unsurfaced. Federal, state and local governments spend more than $15 billion a year for the construction and maintenance of new and existing highways. The major portion of this is borne by those who use the roads, as nearly 80 percent is raised by taxes on fuels, parts, vehicles and by other fees.

Time Savers. During the past two decades, much of the money for new construction has been spent for highways which have drastically cut the time required for interurban travel: divided-lane highways, limited-access parkways, turnpikes, freeways or throughways and circumferential or bypass routes. The former have no grade crossings, intersections or traffic lights, and speed limits are usually 60 or 70 miles an hour. Recognizing that slow-moving traffic on this kind of highway can be as great a hazard as excessive speed, authorities also post minimum speeds, such as 45 miles an hour. A number of these are toll roads, but motorists apparently are willing to pay a premium to reach their destinations quickly and without traffic jams.

The circumferential and bypass routes skirt urban areas and eliminate the stop-and-go, bumper-to-bumper driving for through traffic; they also offer a choice of radial avenues for reaching different sections of large cities. One of the best-known is Route 128 around Boston. The interurban traveler may avoid entering the busy Boston area to reach cities to the south, west and north. For those whose destination is Boston, it gives access to principal arteries into the city, all along the perimeter.

Interstate Highway System. By 1972, limited-access roads will connect all the major cities in the country, from coast to coast and from border to border, with the completion of the 41,000-mile National System of Interstate and Defense Highways. Although this network will constitute little more than 1 percent of the nation's total mileage, it is expected to carry a quarter of the traffic estimated for 1975. While a fifth of this vast project will utilize existing rights-of-way, the rest will involve acquisition of 1.5 million acres of land, an area larger than the state of Delaware. States pay 10 percent of the cost, the Federal government the remainder from a Highway Trust Fund into which go most of the taxes for highway use that are imposed by the United States.

While all this construction benefits the interurban or interstate traveler, it does nothing to relieve the plight of cities choked with traffic. City streets constitute only 13 percent of the nation's roads, yet they carry about half the motor vehicle traffic. Many are frequently as impassable in the 1960's as they were decades ago, but now it is traffic, not mud, that impedes the traveler.

Commuting Problem. As wider freeways, bridges and tunnels make a metropolis more accessible, greater numbers of cars pour into the city. In 1965, 82 percent of all working commuters used their cars to get to work. When more people take to their cars, fewer use passenger rail service, and the latter becomes uneconomical. Yet trains are the most efficient means of transporation in metropolitan areas; they can move between 40,000 and 60,000 persons per hour, whereas the peak capacity of the average freeway is about 1500 cars per lane per hour, and cars still have to be parked after they reach the city. San Francisco even voted against constructing two proposed freeways and abandoned construction of a third which was half finished.

Many proposals, ranging from the practical to the idealistic, have been advanced to solve the problem of city traffic: elevated highways, subterranean parking areas, parking lots on the perimeter of a city with frequent rapid transit to the central business district, widening of streets by locating sidewalks in building arcades, special lanes for buses only, reversible lanes for peak morning and evening traffic and a "Motopia" city with buildings all the same height so that roads could run along the tops, with garages on the upper floors.

Little Money for Early Roads. After achieving independence, the United States had enough economic problems on its hands without trying to find money for road building, so states began chartering private companies to build highways financed by tolls. One of the first of these was the Lancaster Turnpike, a stone-surfaced road from Philadelphia to Lancaster, Pennsylvania, which was built between 1792 and 1795. Not until 1806 did Congress authorize a Federal highway, the National (or Cumberland) Road from Cumberland, Maryland, to Wheeling, West Virginia, with later extensions as far as Vandalia, Illinois. But Congress had appropriated money only for construction, not for maintenance. When railroads captured the public's imagination and approval in the 1830's, a sharp decline in road improvement followed. Existing highways deteriorated through neglect and apathy, and by mid-century the "dark ages" for roads had set in.

Strangely enough, it was the bicycle craze of the 1880's and 1890's that revived the demand for better highways. Then the introduction of rural free delivery by the Post Office Department in 1896 provided a further stimulus to road improvements. As the new century began, a rapidly growing army of motorists added its voice to the demand for something better than the mud-clogged, dust-choked rural highways. States, counties and townships built and maintained the roads, and many a farmer exercised his option to work on them instead of paying road taxes.

Federal Aid. Congress did not pass a Federal Road-Aid Act until 1916, and the funds appropriated up to 1941 were restricted to a limited, connected system of primary roads. As passenger-car sales zoomed from 1 million in 1916 to over 4 million in 1929, most of the money for highways came from non-Federal sources. But during the Depression, the government pumped sizable amounts into public works, much of it for road construction. In 1941, Federal aid was extended to many types of highways other than the primary network.

The figures for today's highway use are staggering. More than 100 million licensed operators use 80 billion gallons of fuel annually to drive 970 billion miles in 98 million cars, trucks and buses. Government officials estimate that by 1975 there will be 125 million operators driving 118 million vehicles, with mileage and fuel consumption rising proportionately. This future growth will probably exacerbate such problems as air pollution (insofar as motor vehicles contribute to it), highway safety (9000 persons are now injured daily) and the density of city traffic unless government, regional or private organizations can find solutions.

1936		1967
24,182,662	Number of cars	81,051,000
4,261,611	Number of trucks	16,136,000
62,618	Number of buses	340,000
18.1	Gallons of motor fuel consumed (in billions)	77.8
252	Miles traveled by vehicles (in billions)	967
3,006,000	Miles of roads	3,700,000
$177	Federal fuel taxes (in millions of dollars)	$2970
$687	State fuel taxes (in millions of dollars)	$4975
36,369	Traffic fatalities	53,000

(1967 figures are preliminary)

Interstate Highway Numbering System of Maps on the Following Pages. *Completed sections of the Interstate Highway System are shown in red with black borders. Numbers have been assigned to the different routes under the following system:*

Odd-numbered highways run north and south, starting on the west coast with 5 and ranging up to 95 on the east coast.

Even-numbered highways run east and west, starting with 10, the southernmost route, from Southern California to Florida, while 94 parallels part of the Canadian frontier.

Three-digit figures that begin with an even number designate connecting bypass routes around or in urban areas. Traffic of Highway 94 is carried around Chicago on 294; motorists using 95 skirt Washington, D.C., on 495.

Three-digit figures beginning with an odd number indicate spur or feeder highways to main routes. Highway 580 provides access to 80 from points east of Oakland in California. Traffic from Fall River, Massachusetts, is routed by 195 to the junction with 95 in Providence, Rhode Island.

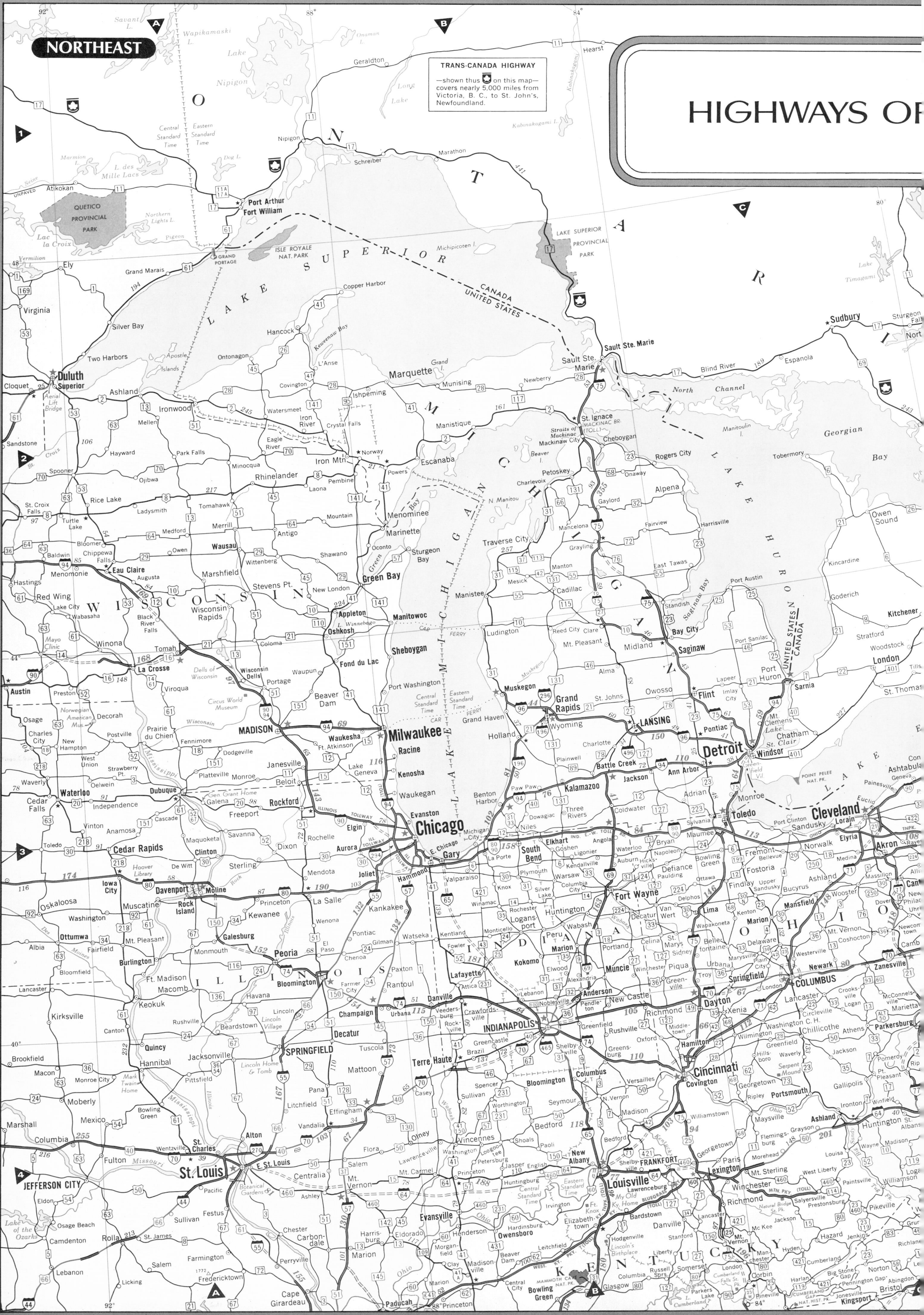

NORTHEAST
HIGHWAYS OF
TRANS-CANADA HIGHWAY
—shown thus on this map—covers nearly 5,000 miles from Victoria, B. C., to St. John's, Newfoundland.
ONTARIO
LAKE SUPERIOR
CANADA
UNITED STATES
Central Standard Time
Eastern Standard Time
QUETICO PROVINCIAL PARK
ISLE ROYALE NAT. PARK
LAKE SUPERIOR PROVINCIAL PARK
MICHIGAN
LAKE MICHIGAN
LAKE HURON
Georgian Bay
North Channel
Straits of Mackinac
WISCONSIN
ILLINOIS
INDIANA
OHIO
KENTUCKY
LAKE ERIE
Port Arthur
Fort William
Duluth
Superior
Sault Ste. Marie
Sudbury
Marquette
Green Bay
Milwaukee
MADISON
Chicago
Gary
Rockford
Peoria
Davenport
Cedar Rapids
SPRINGFIELD
St. Louis
JEFFERSON CITY
Grand Rapids
LANSING
Detroit
Windsor
London
Flint
Saginaw
Toledo
Cleveland
Akron
COLUMBUS
Dayton
Cincinnati
INDIANAPOLIS
Fort Wayne
South Bend
Terre Haute
Evansville
Louisville
FRANKFORT
Lexington
Paducah

THE UNITED STATES

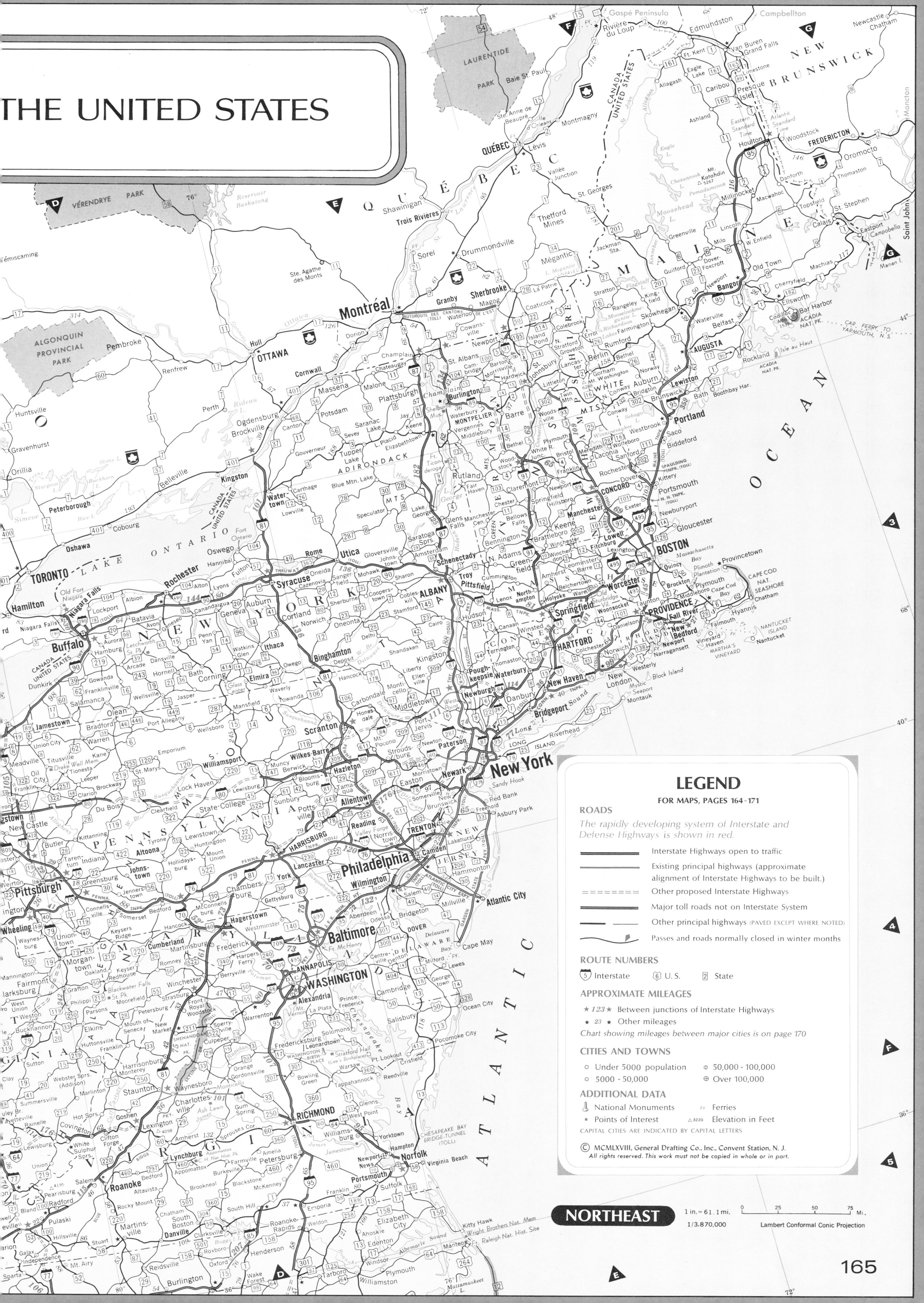

LEGEND

FOR MAPS, PAGES 164-171

ROADS

The rapidly developing system of Interstate and Defense Highways is shown in red.

- Interstate Highways open to traffic
- Existing principal highways (approximate alignment of Interstate Highways to be built.)
- Other proposed Interstate Highways
- Major toll roads not on Interstate System
- Other principal highways (PAVED EXCEPT WHERE NOTED)
- Passes and roads normally closed in winter months

ROUTE NUMBERS

5 Interstate 6 U.S. 2 State

APPROXIMATE MILEAGES

★ *123* ★ Between junctions of Interstate Highways

★ *23* ★ Other mileages

Chart showing mileages between major cities is on page 170

CITIES AND TOWNS

- Under 5000 population
- 5000 - 50,000
- 50,000 - 100,000
- Over 100,000

ADDITIONAL DATA

- National Monuments
- Points of Interest
- FY Ferries
- △3220 Elevation in Feet

CAPITAL CITIES ARE INDICATED BY CAPITAL LETTERS

NORTHEAST

1 in. = 61.1 mi. 1/3,870,000

0 25 50 75 Mi.

Lambert Conformal Conic Projection

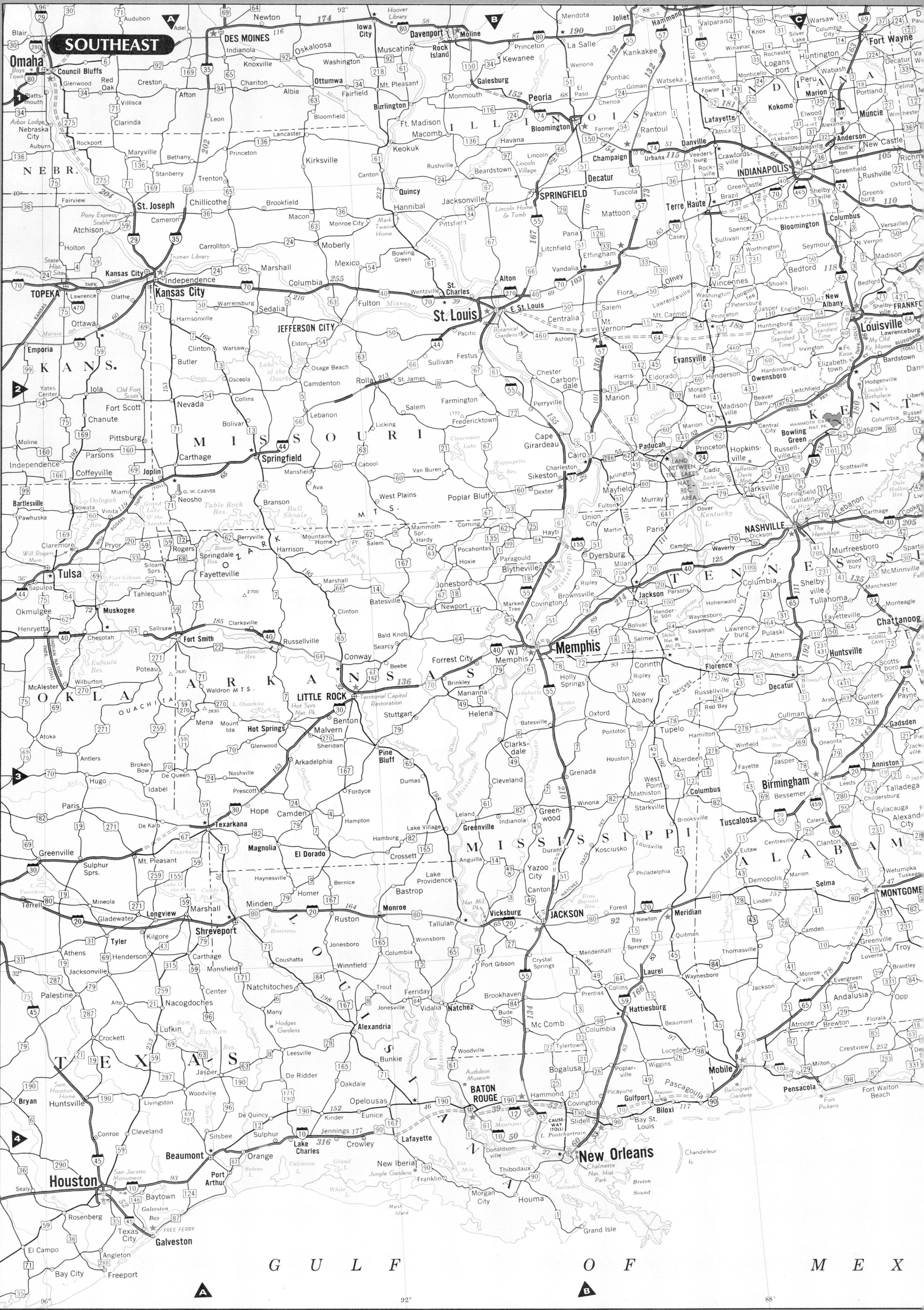

SOUTHEAST
Omaha
Council Bluffs
DES MOINES
Iowa City
Davenport
Moline
Rock Island
Joliet
Hammond
Valparaiso
Fort Wayne
NEBR.
I L L I N O I S
I N D I A N A
Peoria
Bloomington
Champaign
Danville
Lafayette
Kokomo
Muncie
Anderson
INDIANAPOLIS
SPRINGFIELD
Decatur
Terre Haute
St. Joseph
Kansas City
TOPEKA
Independence
Columbia
JEFFERSON CITY
St. Louis
E. St. Louis
Evansville
Louisville
FRANKFORT
K A N S.
M I S S O U R I
Springfield
Joplin
Emporia
Paducah
Owensboro
Bowling Green
K E N T
NASHVILLE
Tulsa
Muskogee
Fort Smith
O K L A.
A R K A N S A S
LITTLE ROCK
Hot Springs
Pine Bluff
Texarkana
Memphis
Jackson
T E N N E S S E E
Chattanooga
Huntsville
Florence
Decatur
Birmingham
Tuscaloosa
Gadsden
Anniston
A L A B A M A
MONTGOMERY
Corinth
Tupelo
Columbus
M I S S I S S I P P I
Greenville
Vicksburg
JACKSON
Meridian
Hattiesburg
Laurel
Mobile
Pensacola
Gulfport
Biloxi
Shreveport
Monroe
Alexandria
L O U I S I A N A
BATON ROUGE
New Orleans
Lafayette
Lake Charles
Beaumont
Port Arthur
Houston
Galveston
Tyler
Longview
Lufkin
Nacogdoches
T E X A S
G U L F O F M E X

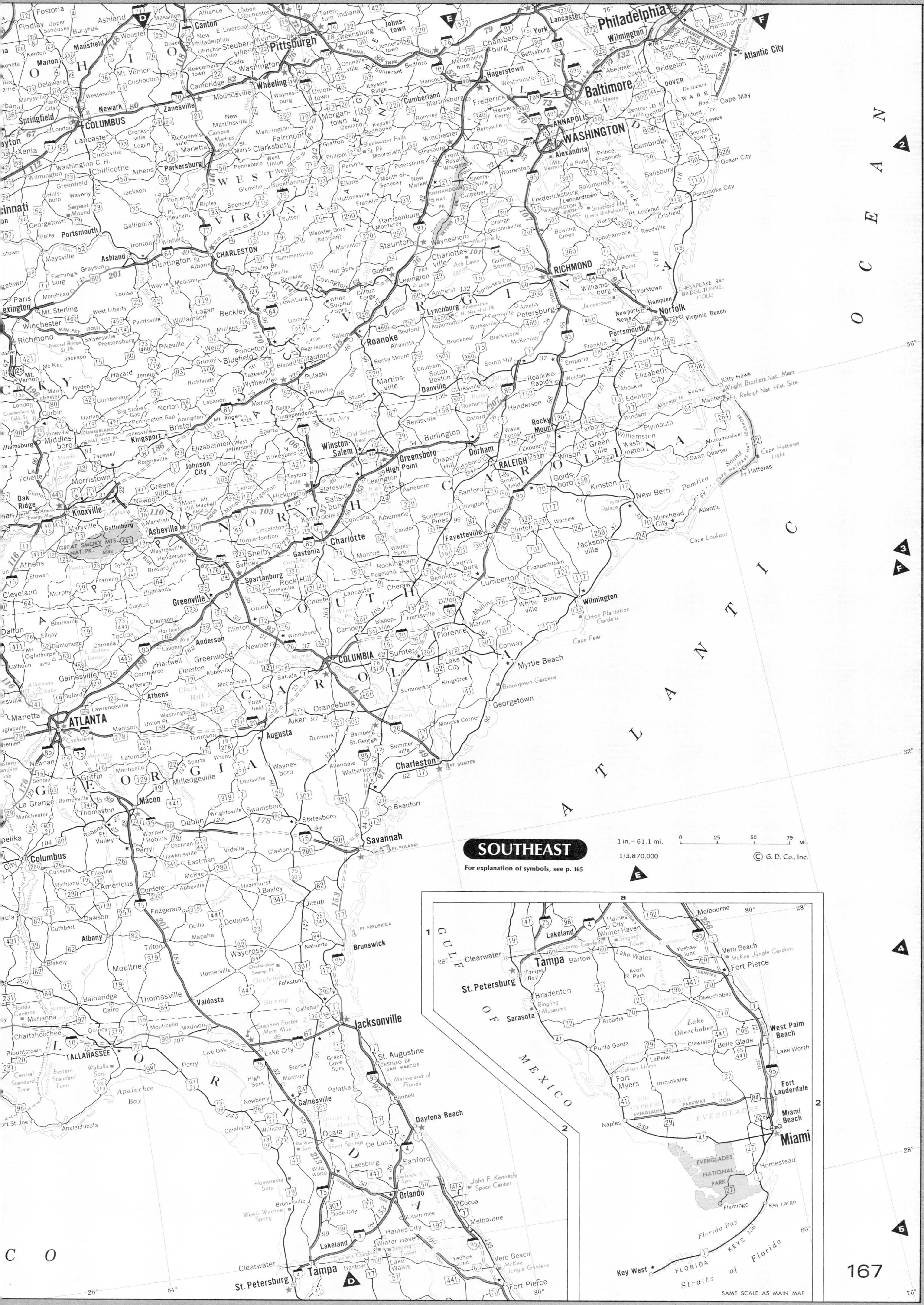
SOUTHEAST
For explanation of symbols, see p. 165
1 in. = 61.1 mi.
1/3,870,000
0 25 50 75 Mi.
© G. D. Co., Inc.
SAME SCALE AS MAIN MAP
ATLANTIC OCEAN
GULF OF MEXICO
OHIO
WEST VIRGINIA
VIRGINIA
MARYLAND
DELAWARE
NORTH CAROLINA
SOUTH CAROLINA
GEORGIA
FLORIDA
KENTUCKY
Philadelphia
Pittsburgh
Baltimore
WASHINGTON
RICHMOND
CHARLESTON
COLUMBUS
Norfolk
Raleigh
Charlotte
Greensboro
Winston-Salem
Durham
Roanoke
Knoxville
Asheville
COLUMBIA
ATLANTA
Augusta
Macon
Columbus
Savannah
Charleston
Wilmington
Jacksonville
TALLAHASSEE
Gainesville
Orlando
Daytona Beach
Tampa
St. Petersburg
Miami
West Palm Beach
Fort Lauderdale
Key West
EVERGLADES NATIONAL PARK
GREAT SMOKY MTS. NAT. PK.
SHENANDOAH NAT. PK.
CHESAPEAKE BAY BRIDGE-TUNNEL (TOLL)
Cape Hatteras
Cape Lookout
Cape Fear
Lake Okeechobee
Apalachee Bay
Florida Bay
Straits of Florida
FLORIDA KEYS
Central Standard Time
Eastern Standard Time

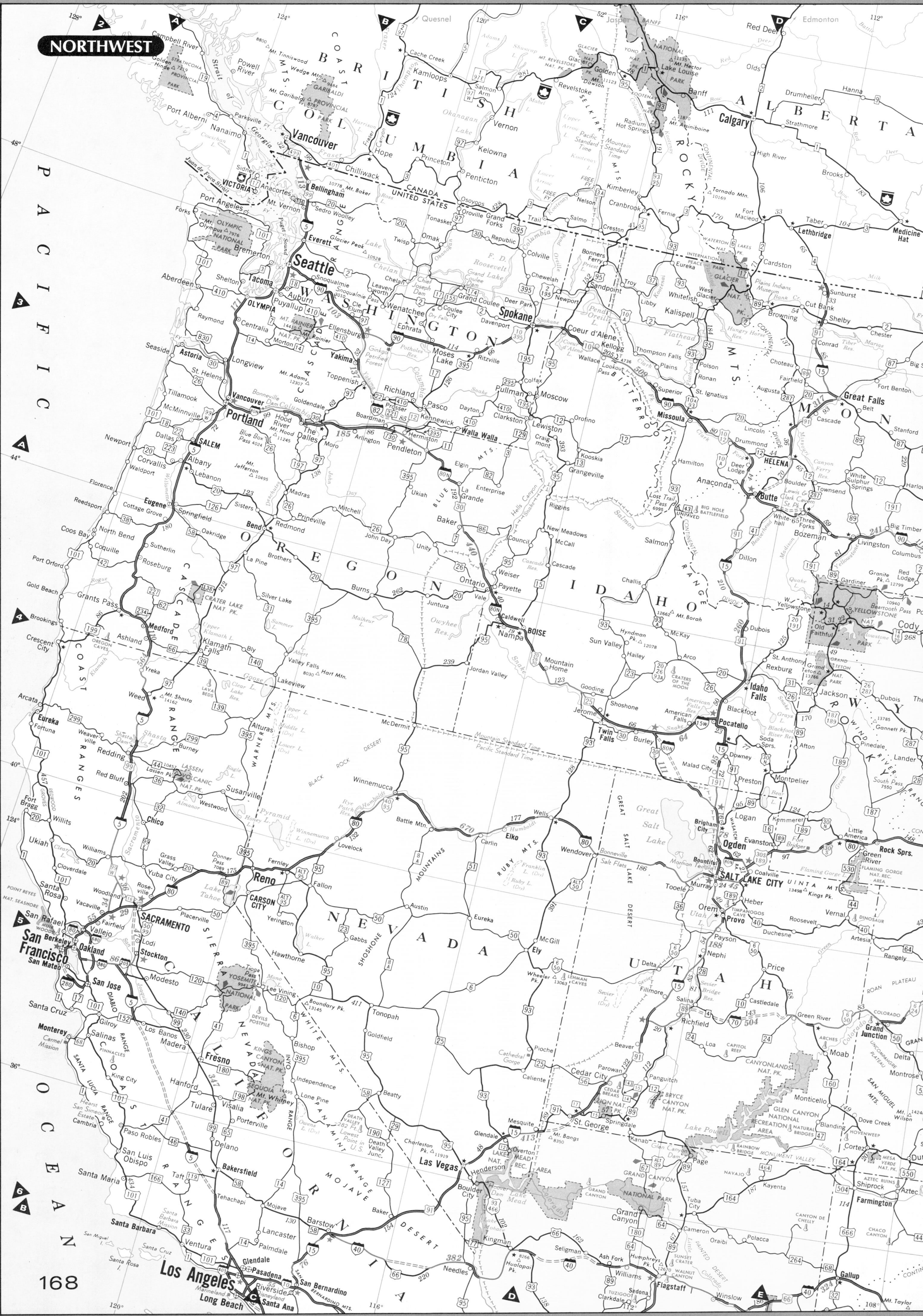

NORTHWEST
BRITISH COLUMBIA
ALBERTA
WASHINGTON
OREGON
IDAHO
MONTANA
WYOMING
NEVADA
UTAH
CALIFORNIA
PACIFIC OCEAN
CANADA
UNITED STATES
Seattle
Portland
Vancouver
Spokane
Boise
Reno
SACRAMENTO
San Francisco
Oakland
San Jose
Fresno
Los Angeles
Long Beach
Las Vegas
SALT LAKE CITY
Ogden
Provo
Calgary
Edmonton
Great Falls
HELENA
Missoula
Butte
Billings
Eugene
SALEM
OLYMPIA
VICTORIA
Tacoma
Yakima
Pocatello
Idaho Falls
Flagstaff
Bakersfield
Stockton
Kamloops
OLYMPIC NATIONAL PARK
MT. RAINIER NAT. PK.
CRATER LAKE NAT. PK.
LASSEN VOLCANIC NAT. PK.
YOSEMITE NATIONAL PARK
KINGS CANYON NAT. PK.
SEQUOIA NAT. PK.
GLACIER NAT. PK.
YELLOWSTONE NAT. PARK
GRAND TETON NAT. PARK
GRAND CANYON NATIONAL PARK
BRYCE CANYON NAT. PK.
ZION NAT. PK.
CANYONLANDS NAT. PK.
ARCHES
Great Salt Lake
GREAT SALT LAKE DESERT
MOJAVE DESERT
CASCADE RANGE
SIERRA NEVADA
COAST RANGES
ROCKY MTS.
BITTERROOT RANGE
BLUE MTS.
RUBY MTS.
WIND RIVER RANGE
Mountain Standard Time
Pacific Standard Time

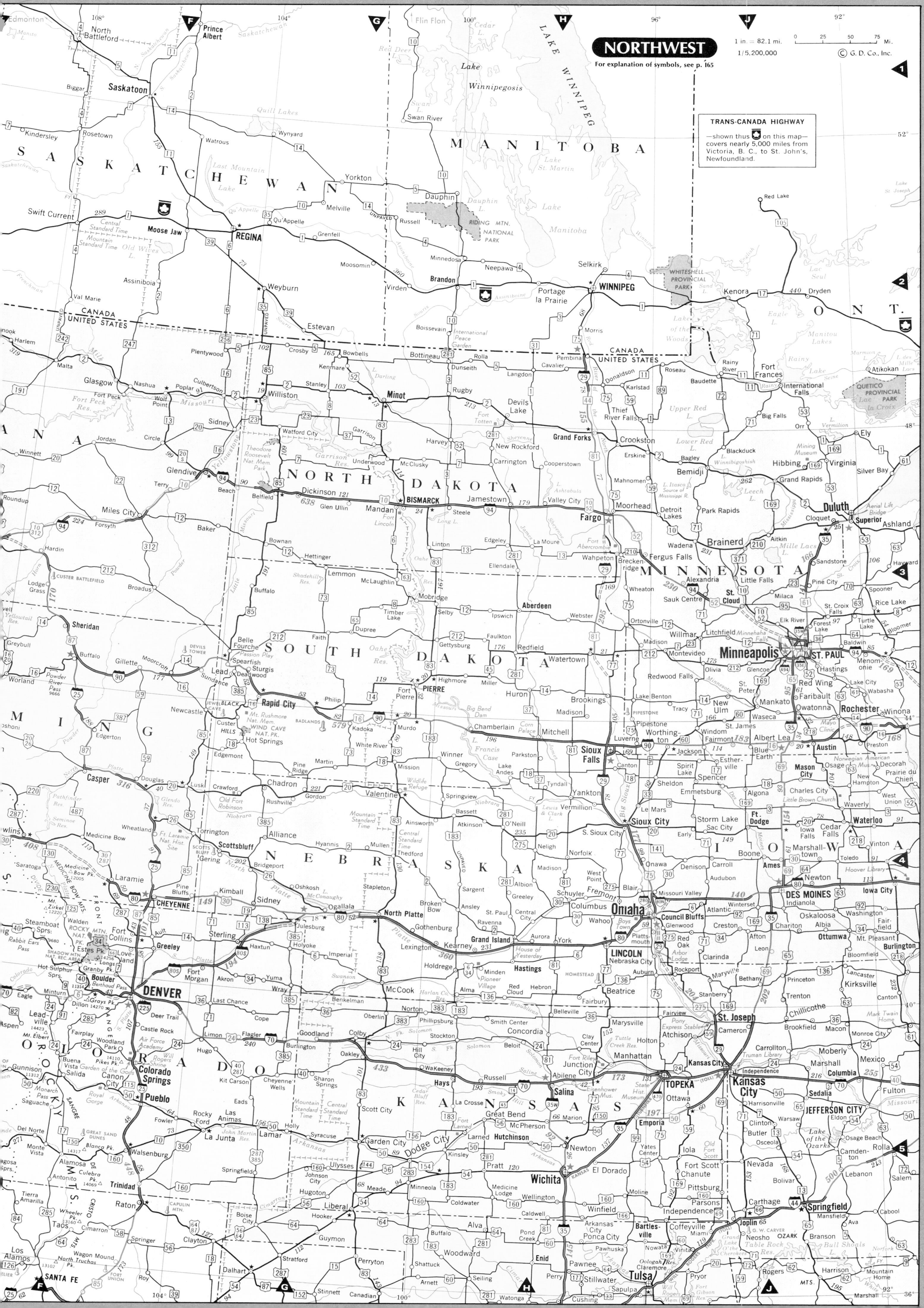
NORTHWEST
For explanation of symbols, see p. 165
1 in. = 82.1 mi.
1/5,200,000
© G. D. Co., Inc.
TRANS-CANADA HIGHWAY
—shown thus on this map—covers nearly 5,000 miles from Victoria, B. C., to St. John's, Newfoundland.
SASKATCHEWAN
MANITOBA
ONT.
CANADA
UNITED STATES
NORTH DAKOTA
SOUTH DAKOTA
NEBRASKA
KANSAS
MINNESOTA
IOWA
COLORADO
Lake Winnipeg
Lake Winnipegosis
Lake Manitoba
Saskatoon
REGINA
Moose Jaw
Swift Current
Yorkton
Brandon
WINNIPEG
Minot
BISMARCK
Fargo
Grand Forks
Duluth
Minneapolis
ST. PAUL
Rapid City
PIERRE
Sioux Falls
Sioux City
Omaha
LINCOLN
CHEYENNE
DENVER
Colorado Springs
Pueblo
DES MOINES
TOPEKA
Kansas City
Wichita
Tulsa
St. Joseph
JEFFERSON CITY
Springfield
SANTA FE

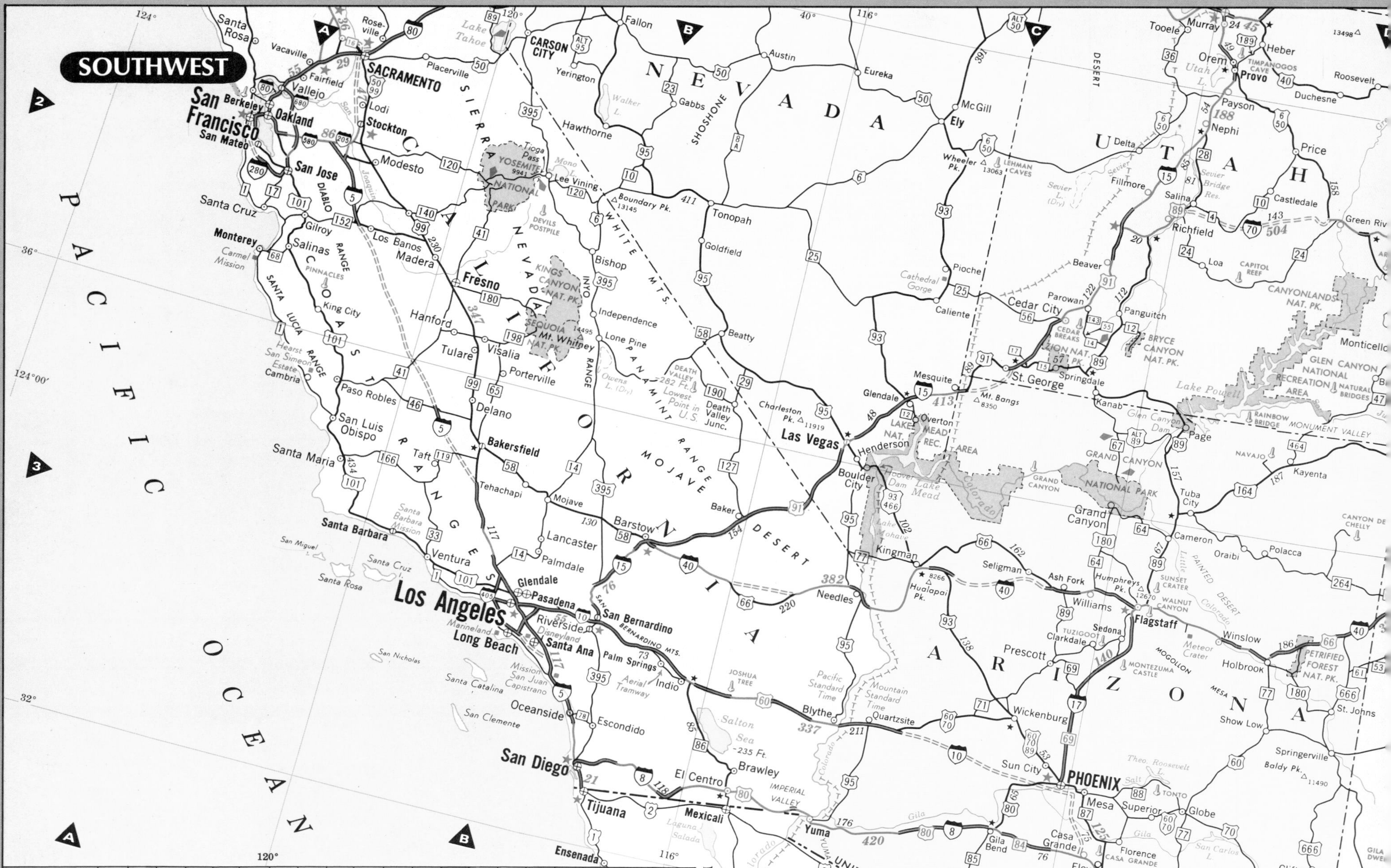

APPROXIMATE MILEAGES	Atlanta	Boston	Chicago	Cleveland	Dallas	Denver	Detroit	Houston	Los Angeles	Miami	Minneapolis	New Orleans	New York	Philadelphia	Portland, Me.	St. Louis	Salt Lake City	San Francisco	Santa Fe	Seattle	Washington, D. C.
Albany, N. Y.	1040	160	810	465	1675	1830	530	1815	2920	1500	1050	1500	160	250	240	1010	2255	3020	2070	2760	390
Atlanta		1100	725	700	820	1440	730	840	2260	665	1155	510	880	790	1175	590	1950	2595	1445	2660	650
Baltimore	670	400	690	355	1435	1640	515	1465	2720	1140	1105	1150	185	100	505	805	2105	2870	1910	2840	40
Birmingham	155	1195	680	740	665	1315	745	675	2085	780	1065	355	985	890	1300	495	1820	2425	1260	2705	755
Bismarck	1555	1840	850	1195	1145	700	1125	1390	1670	2215	440	1610	1695	1620	1885	985	965	1615	1085	1225	1555
Boston	1100		990	650	1805	2000	700	1895	3085	1565	1230	1550	210	300	105	1160	2425	3190	2235	2950	435
Buffalo	955	455	530	185	1395	1550	250	1505	2640	1485	770	1245	360	350	520	730	1975	2740	1790	2480	380
Charleston, S. C.	300	945	910	760	1105	1745	850	1085	2510	605	1325	740	735	645	1050	840	2260	2875	1765	2930	505
Charleston, W. Va.	500	765	470	270	1085	1405	355	1180	2360	1040	880	935	550	485	870	530	1845	2610	1600	2575	350
Chicago	725	990		345	960	1020	275	1100	2120	1400	410	945	845	770	1035	285	1410	2195	1315	2020	705
Cleveland	700	630	345		1210	1360	175	1330	2415	1335	765	1075	475	430	700	535	1785	2550	1600	2485	365
Dallas	820	1805	960	1210		780	1180	245	1425	1370	995	505	1625	1510	1910	650	1265	1785	640	2185	1400
Denver	1440	1990	1020	1360	780		1315	1035	1170	2135	845	1295	1795	1715	2060	875	515	1270	370	1385	1645
Detroit	730	700	275	175	1180	1315		1300	2400	1380	525	1070	650	575	765	515	1710	2475	1555	2230	525
El Paso	1455	2410	1530	1780	625	700	1720	755	805	2005	1420	1115	2205	2060	2515	1230	875	1210	305	1795	2045
Grand Canyon N. P.	1885	2610	1740	2025	1060	805	1950	1245	505	2435	1635	1565	2450	2335	2715	1485	520	835	465	1420	2365
Houston	840	1895	1100	1330	245	1035	1300		1545	1220	1255	360	1655	1565	1975	805	1450	1950	860	2365	1430
Indianapolis	550	915	190	305	900	1070	280	1020	2150	1220	615	825	720	635	985	240	1560	2325	1295	2325	565
Kansas City	815	1420	510	790	495	600	750	740	1610	1530	465	830	1205	1130	1490	255	1135	1890	780	1925	1050
Las Vegas	2025	2790	1790	2170	1240	795	2065	1425	285	2555	1640	1745	2580	2510	2895	1635	440	580	650	1205	2440
Little Rock	565	1470	655	870	335	955	845	435	1700	1170	835	420	1275	1175	1575	360	1465	2040	890	2385	1045
Los Angeles	2260	3085	2120	2415	1425	1170	2400	1545		2820	2010	1920	2875	2795	3115	1895	725	400	860	1180	2725
Louisville	410	960	305	350	840	1125	360	980	2175	1080	730	710	755	675	1065	270	1660	2430	1325	2465	600
Memphis	420	1335	545	730	470	1085	715	575	1835	1030	865	395	1130	1040	1440	285	1600	2175	1025	2400	905
Miami	665	1565	1400	1335	1370	2135	1380	1220	2820		1820	875	1340	1250	1655	1265	2615	3160	2010	3425	1115
Milwaukee	805	1060	90	435	1050	1015	355	1160	2175	1460	355	1000	935	850	1105	360	1435	2190	1225	2020	785
Minneapolis	1155	1230	410	765	995	845	525	1255	2010	1820		1265	1270	1195	1465	550	1285	2040	1210	1680	1130
Nashville	250	1115	460	530	680	1180	540	820	2025	930	885	530	910	820	1220	295	1685	2400	1250	2505	685
New Orleans	510	1550	945	1075	505	1295	1070	360	1920	875	1265		1340	1225	1620	710	1775	2295	1140	2695	1115
New York	880	210	845	475	1625	1795	650	1655	2875	1340	1270	1340		90	315	960	2255	3020	2035	2985	230
Oklahoma City	905	1655	840	1100	210	615	1015	450	1350	1555	835	680	1525	1380	1725	545	1120	1690	540	2035	1375
Omaha	1015	1455	465	825	680	530	745	910	1690	1735	355	1040	1290	1255	1525	450	955	1715	835	1680	1145
Philadelphia	790	300	770	430	1510	1715	575	1565	2795	1250	1195	1225	90		405	880	2175	2940	1945	2905	135
Phoenix	1875	2655	1785	2110	1020	840	2015	1160	385	2410	1680	1520	2500	2380	2760	1535	725	790	515	1595	2340
Pittsburgh	710	575	470	130	1255	1430	290	1375	2510	1240	895	1080	365	285	645	585	1880	2645	1660	2610	230
Portland, Me.	1175	105	1035	700	1910	2060	765	1975	3115	1655	1465	1620	315	405		1245	2485	3250	2295	3185	540
Portland, Oreg.	2740	3175	2225	2545	2090	1335	2500	2290	990	3450	1770	2595	3045	2910	3245	2185	830	655	1475	170	2900
Raleigh	395	700	855	590	1215	1755	700	1250	2625	845	1280	905	495	400	805	865	2215	2955	1805	2985	260
Reno	2475	2960	1940	2317	1690	1050	2240	1875	475	3000	1735	2195	2785	2705	3015	1915	530	220	1100	750	2640
Richmond	540	545	780	445	1310	1715	600	1355	2660	990	1190	1045	330	240	650	845	2155	2910	1905	2855	105
St. Louis	590	1160	285	535	650	875	515	805	1895	1265	550	710	960	880	1245		1385	2140	1060	2175	805
Salt Lake City	1950	2425	1410	1785	1265	515	1710	1450	725	2615	1285	1775	2255	2175	2485	1385		755	615	910	2110
San Antonio	1025	2035	1235	1255	265	935	1415	195	1375	1475	1270	560	1860	1775	2140	940	1335	1780	715	2255	1640
San Francisco	2595	3190	2195	2550	1785	1270	2475	1950	400	3160	2040	2295	3020	2940	3250	2140	755		1200	825	2875
Santa Fe	1445	2235	1315	1600	640	370	1555	860	860	2010	1210	1140	2035	1945	2305	1060	615	1200		1520	1870
Seattle	2660	2950	2020	2485	2185	1385	2230	2365	1180	3425	1680	2695	2985	2905	3085	2175	910	825	1520		2845
Spokane	2365	2900	1910	2255	1855	1070	2185	2100	1245	3065	1340	2330	2755	2680	2945	1750	735	915	1377	285	2615
Washington, D. C.	650	435	705	365	1400	1645	525	1430	2725	1115	1130	1115	230	135	540	805	2110	2875	1870	2845	
Yellowstone N. P.	1895	2410	1475	1780	1355	575	1650	1645	1105	2560	1120	1860	2210	2130	2480	1380	340	985	915	785	2065

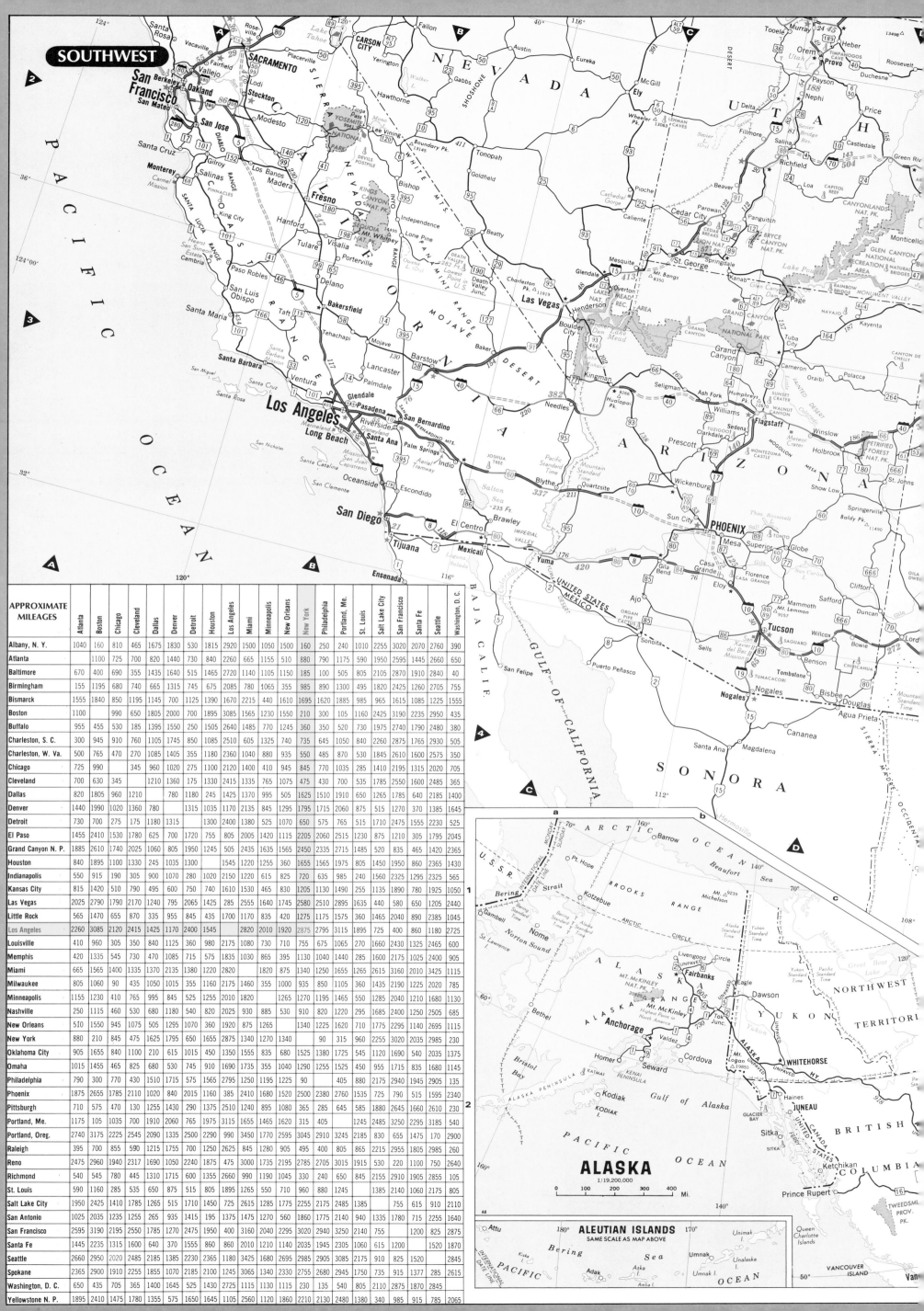

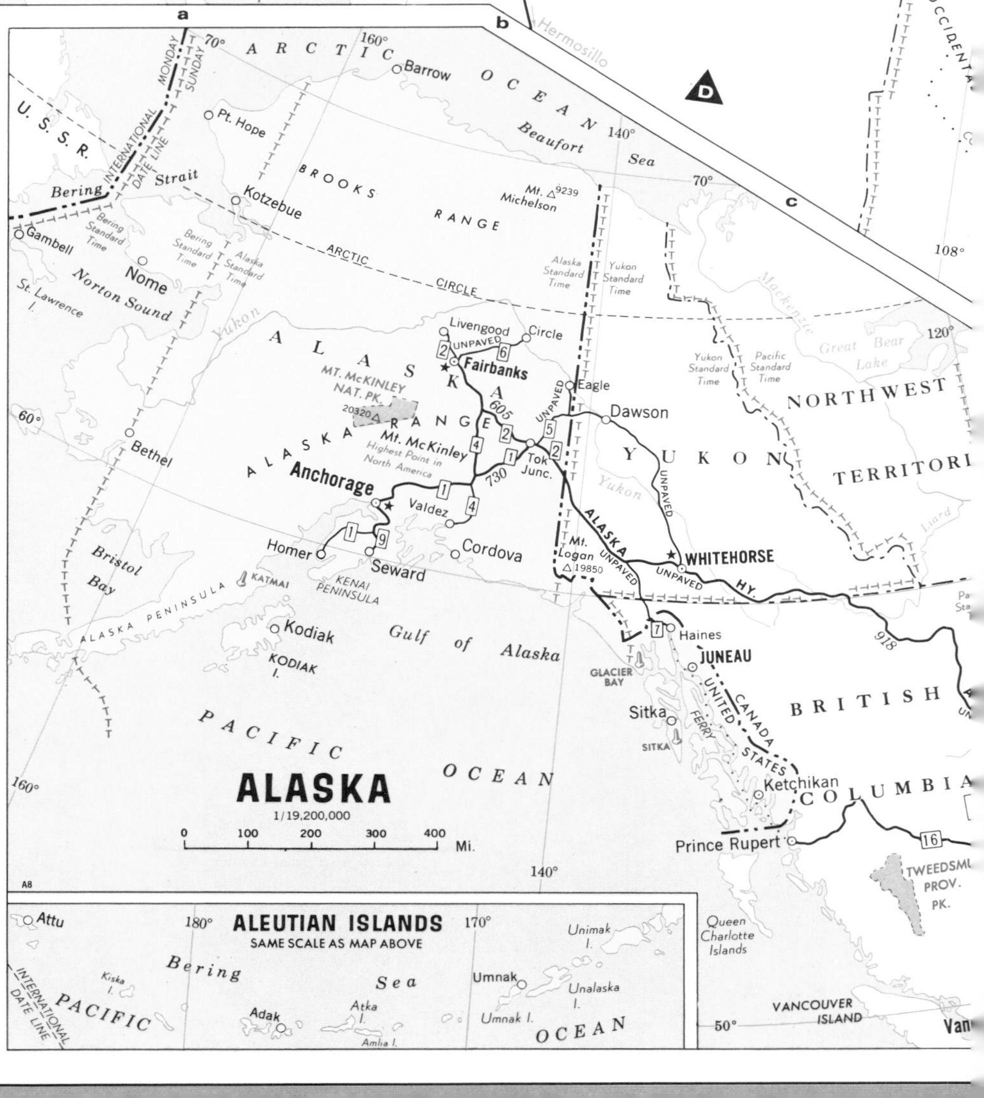

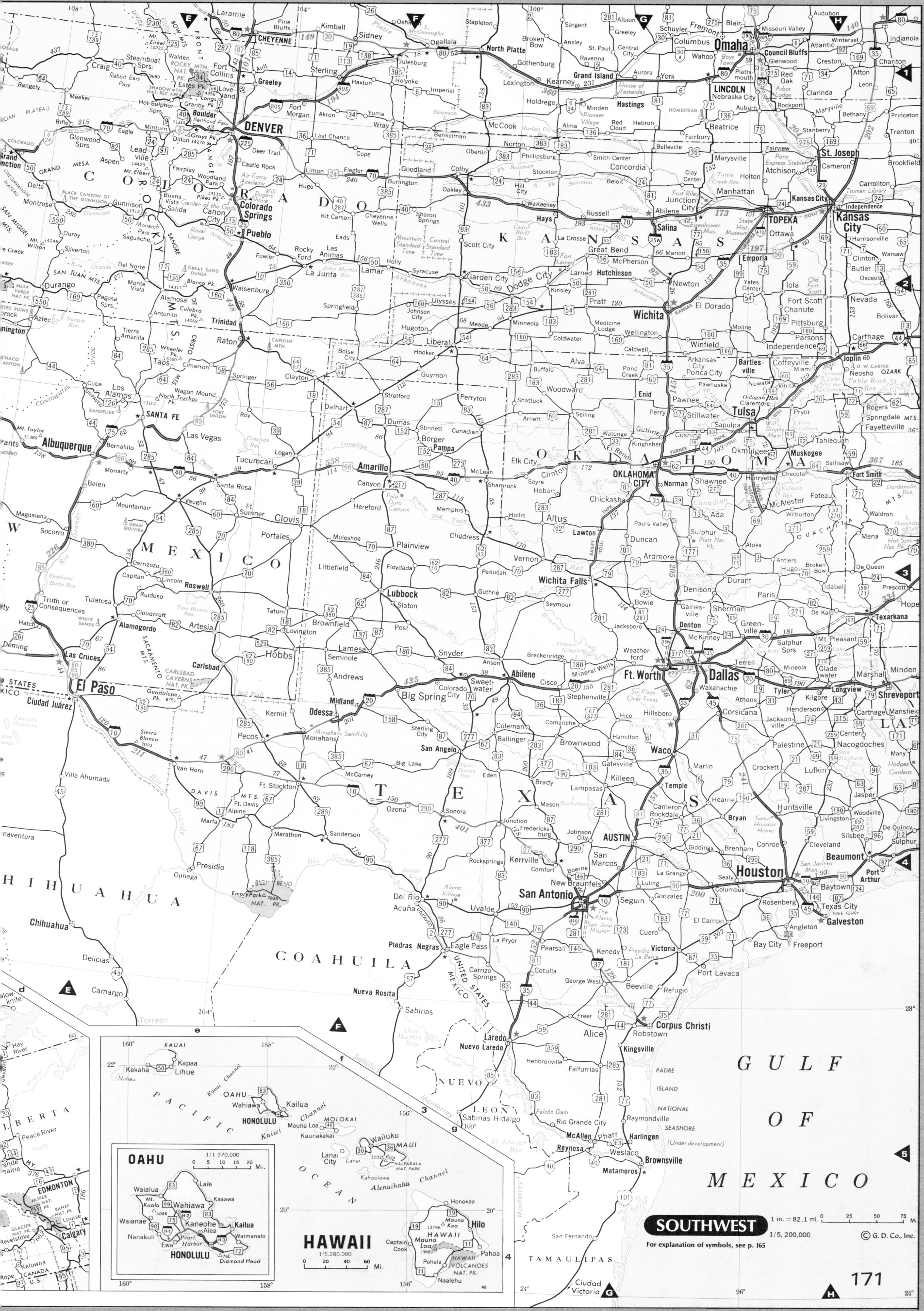
SOUTHWEST
1 in. = 82.1 mi.
1/5,200,000
For explanation of symbols, see p. 165
© G. D. Co., Inc.
COLORADO
KANSAS
OKLAHOMA
TEXAS
NEW MEXICO
CHIHUAHUA
COAHUILA
NUEVO LEON
TAMAULIPAS
GULF OF MEXICO
HAWAII
1/5,280,000
OAHU
1/1,970,000
PACIFIC OCEAN
Denver
Colorado Springs
Pueblo
Cheyenne
Omaha
Lincoln
Kansas City
Topeka
Wichita
Tulsa
Oklahoma City
Amarillo
Lubbock
Albuquerque
Santa Fe
El Paso
Ciudad Juárez
Dallas
Ft. Worth
Waco
Austin
San Antonio
Houston
Galveston
Corpus Christi
Brownsville
Matamoros
Laredo
Nuevo Laredo
Shreveport
Texarkana
Honolulu
Hilo
Calgary
Edmonton

SPACE EXPLORATION

On February 1, 1958, the United States successfully dispatched its first satellite, Explorer 1. A total of 530 American spacecraft have since been launched (as of January 1968) with 268 vehicles still in orbit. The Soviet Union has launched 267 with 66 still in orbit.

The missions of these satellites—a selected number of which appear on the chart to the right—have a wide variety of purpose. *Survey* craft collect information by instruments which measure radiation belts and magnetic fields, determine the planets' atmospheres and photograph the terrain of the earth, the moon and other celestial bodies. *Manned* missions test the effect on humans of many hazards, such as weightlessness and radiation, in order to prepare astronauts for moon landings in the 1970's.

Hurricane and storm areas are tracked by cameras aboard *weather* satellites which provide information that could not be obtained from the surface of the earth. Orbiting *communications* vehicles have already established the beginning of what will be a vast network of global television. (See "Satellite," page 162.) Although their missions are secret, *defense* satellites carry out photo-intelligence duties, and are on the alert to detect the firing of intercontinental ballistic missiles and to monitor nuclear explosions. Among the proposed probes of the future are flights to the asteroid belt, meetings with comets, and journeys to the unknown and mysterious depths of space.

Principal U.S. launch bases are maintained at the John F. Kennedy Space Center, Merritt Island, Florida; Cape Kennedy, Florida; Lompoc, California; White Sands, New Mexico; and Wallops Station, Virginia.

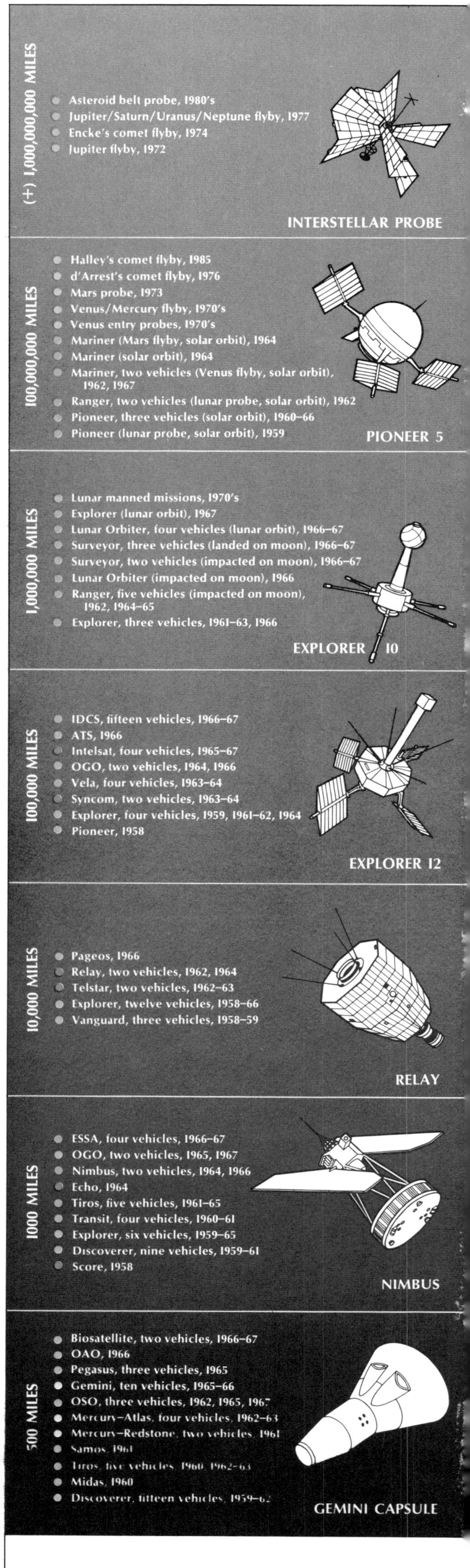

NATURE OF MISSION

- Manned
- Communications
- Defense
- Survey
- Weather
- Proposed

ATS: *Application Technology Satellite*
ESSA: *Environmental Survey Satellite*
IDCS: *Initial Defense Communication Satellite*
OAO: *Orbiting Astronomical Observatory*
OGO: *Orbiting Geophysical Observatory*
OSO: *Orbiting Solar Observatory*

Maximum distances given in chart above.

AIR TRAFFIC: THE SATURATION POINT

One of the great problems of our times is how to accommodate all the aircraft that want to use the nation's airports and the skies above them. In the latter 1960's, aircraft—private planes, helicopters, huge jet airliners—were making close to a million takeoffs and landings a year at the three large airports serving the New York metropolitan area. The world's single busiest airport, Chicago's O'Hare International (see map, below), had 563,000 such operations a year. And more than 20 other airports in the United States, including Honolulu International, were each handling more than 150,000 takeoffs and landings annually.

A tremendous upsurge in airline business in the 1960's accounted for most of this traffic. Almost without warning, air transportation came into its own as a factor in American social and commercial life. Tourist and business flying, and airfreight transport, became commonplace. In the two years from 1964 to 1966, all-cargo freight hauling doubled to 100,000 tons. From a mere 6 percent increase in 1963, domestic air passenger miles jumped by 18, 15 and 22 percent in each of the next three years. The number of passengers riding U.S. airlines rose from 95 million to 114 million in 1965–66, and by 1977 the number is expected to reach 352 million. Air travel was credited with more passenger miles between major cities in 1966 than railroads and bus lines combined, by a 3 to 2 margin. And there is the private and business air fleet to consider. These planes numbered 95,000 in 1966, and are expected to double to 180,000 in 10 years. The nation's airliners, 2500 at present, will increase to 3500 in the same decade.

With all this expansion imminent, air and ground facilities even in 1967 were just about saturated. The situation was not yet critical; actual collision, considering the number of daily flights—200,000—was rare. There were only 25 in 1966. But coping with future expansion calls for heroic efforts. The best hopes of government and civil air officials appear to be vastly improved computerization and radar, and larger, better equipped and more widely dispersed airfields. The Federal Aviation Administration in 1967 was on the verge of completing a nationwide computer system that would give airport controllers greater accuracy in locating and directing the traffic above them. John F. Kennedy International was to receive the first installation. Major airlines were working with manufacturers to produce an on-board computer that would permit planes to land automatically in almost any weather. A new three-dimensional radar system, which would give altitude as well as distance and direction, was being tested. And cities like New York, Kansas City, Boston, Houston and Dallas–Fort Worth were spending billions of dollars on new airports and on improving present facilities.

This quickening of activity was hastened no little by the approach of giant superjets. Boeing's 490-passenger 747 jumbo jet was scheduled for airline service in 1969. A government-sponsored 350-passenger supersonic plane was due in 1975. And Lockheed was considering an 825-passenger subsonic craft called the L-5000. By the time they are flying in any numbers, it is hoped, the major airports will be equipped for them.

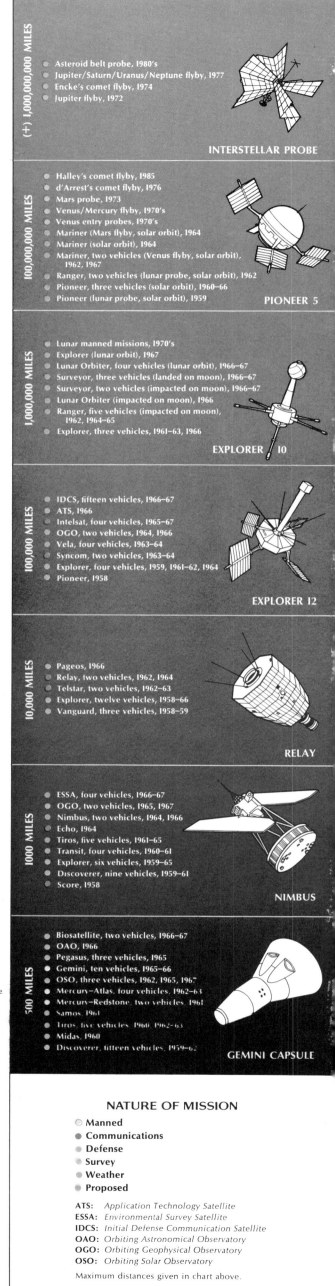

1880 93,267 miles — 1890 163,597 miles — 1900 193,346 miles — 1910 240,439 miles — 1916 254,037 miles

RAILROADS

1916 climaxed the golden era of American railroads with more miles of main-line track than ever before or since. By that time, there was no point in the United States which was not—so it was claimed—within sound of the locomotive whistle. Abraham Lincoln estimated that it would be at least 100 years before railroads would traverse the continent from all important points, but within 50 years, owing to the passionate interest of the American public, they were extended from a mere 35,000 miles in the East in 1865 to the 1916 peak.

Beginning in 1862, the Federal government, responding to public clamor to extend the rails to the Pacific, made direct grants of vast areas of land to the railroad companies. In a checkerboard pattern, from 20 to 40 square miles of land were given for each mile of railroad completed. In all, title to 13,350,534 acres was granted, a land area greater than the old Northwest Territory. Ninety percent of this was in some 20 western states. The grants amounted to sizable proportions of the entire states, as much as 23 percent of North Dakota. Through land sales amounting to $500 million, 18,738 miles of track were built. The speedy construction led to the settling of the West decades earlier than it otherwise might have been, and rates for shipping government goods were reduced 50 percent in return for the grants.

Public mania for railroads had caused the huge effort, but in the 1880's and 90's a new and difficult period developed. The very farmers who were settled in these regions, and the public in general, turned against the railroads because of the rampant struggle for control, stock manipulation by the railroad owners and the cut-rate wars among rival railroad companies. Mergers and receiverships for bankrupt railroads prevailed throughout the last decades of the century. By 1906, two thirds of the railroads of the country had passed into the hands of seven groups. The farmers and commercial shippers sought fair freight rates and demanded legal control by the government over railroad management. Grover Cleveland and Theodore Roosevelt both fought for regulation of the companies, with basic legislation enacted in 1887, 1903 and 1906.

Railroading led to all sorts of innovation in the life of America. Four major time zones replaced the many local time sections of rural America. Rail freight ended the brief era of the cattle drives of the West. Refrigeration of perishable food, luxurious passenger service with sleeping cars and fine food, and 24-hour mail delivery between New York and Chicago were effected by the 1870's. Train wrecks, collapsed bridges and robberies entered into the literature of America, immortalizing Casey Jones and Jesse James (see "Great Characters of Folklore," pages 116–17).

Freight traffic expansion was incredible—stealing almost all business from rivers and canals except on the Great Lakes. The 10 million ton-miles (one-mile movement of one ton) of 1865 were almost doubled by 1890 and expanded 36.6 times by 1916. Passenger business was not quite so spectacular—the 5 billion passenger-miles of 1870 were only 7 times greater by 1916. Railroad investment increased roughly 10 times—from $2.5 billion in 1870 to $21 billion in 1916. Gross revenues rose from $400 million in 1870 to $3.5 billion in 1916. The importance of railroads in the American economy is shown by the fact that more than one person in every 25 of the population, before World War I, was a rail employe. Today approximately one in 300 is a rail worker. In that golden railroad year 1916, the first modern Federal highway construction act was passed by Congress and a new day—no longer dominated by the railroads—dawned.

Both World Wars greatly increased the volume of passengers and freight, and competing facilities appeared. The population took to its own individual wheels in the family car. Highways were built by the national government and airports were financed by cities out of taxes which the railroads were helping to pay. Trucking took the freight business at first because it could manage smaller loads, such as furniture and fresh foods, at short distances. Then enormous long-haul trucks took more. Pipelines absorbed the oil-carrying business to supply the new automobile age. After World War II, passengers swarmed to the airlines.

The Transportation Act of 1958 gave the railroads the freedom to set realistic freight rates. And new technology brought greater speed, cost-saving improvements and electronic control systems. The "piggy back" method involved truck trailers that could combine short-haul service with rail freight by transferring the trailers to flat cars for the longer part of the freight run. The more efficient diesel locomotives replaced steam, and those engines were relegated to the museums. But despite the modern look, rail freight has less than doubled since 1916. And by the 1970's a new competitor will appear in strength: freight by airliner (which has already stolen the lion's share of passenger traffic). Many railroads eliminated passenger service entirely, and commuter lines closed as many as half of their passenger stations. Long-distance passenger lines dropped one half to two thirds of their trains. Passenger service deficits were a half to a third of a billion dollars annually by the 1960's. The new U.S. Department of Transportation may aid more and more lines to achieve high speed and railroads may receive general tax relief. After 50 years of incredible growth, American railroad fortunes have fluctuated for 40 years. What will happen in the next decade, when freight will double to 2.6 trillion ton-miles? Will the railroad, still the most economical method of land transportation, make its comeback?

GROWTH: 1830 23 miles — 1840 2808 miles — 1850 9021 miles — 1860 30,626 miles — 1870 52,922 miles

DECLINE: 1916 254,037 miles — 1920 252,845 miles — 1930 249,052 miles — 1940 233,670 miles — 1950 223,799 miles — 1959 217,565 miles

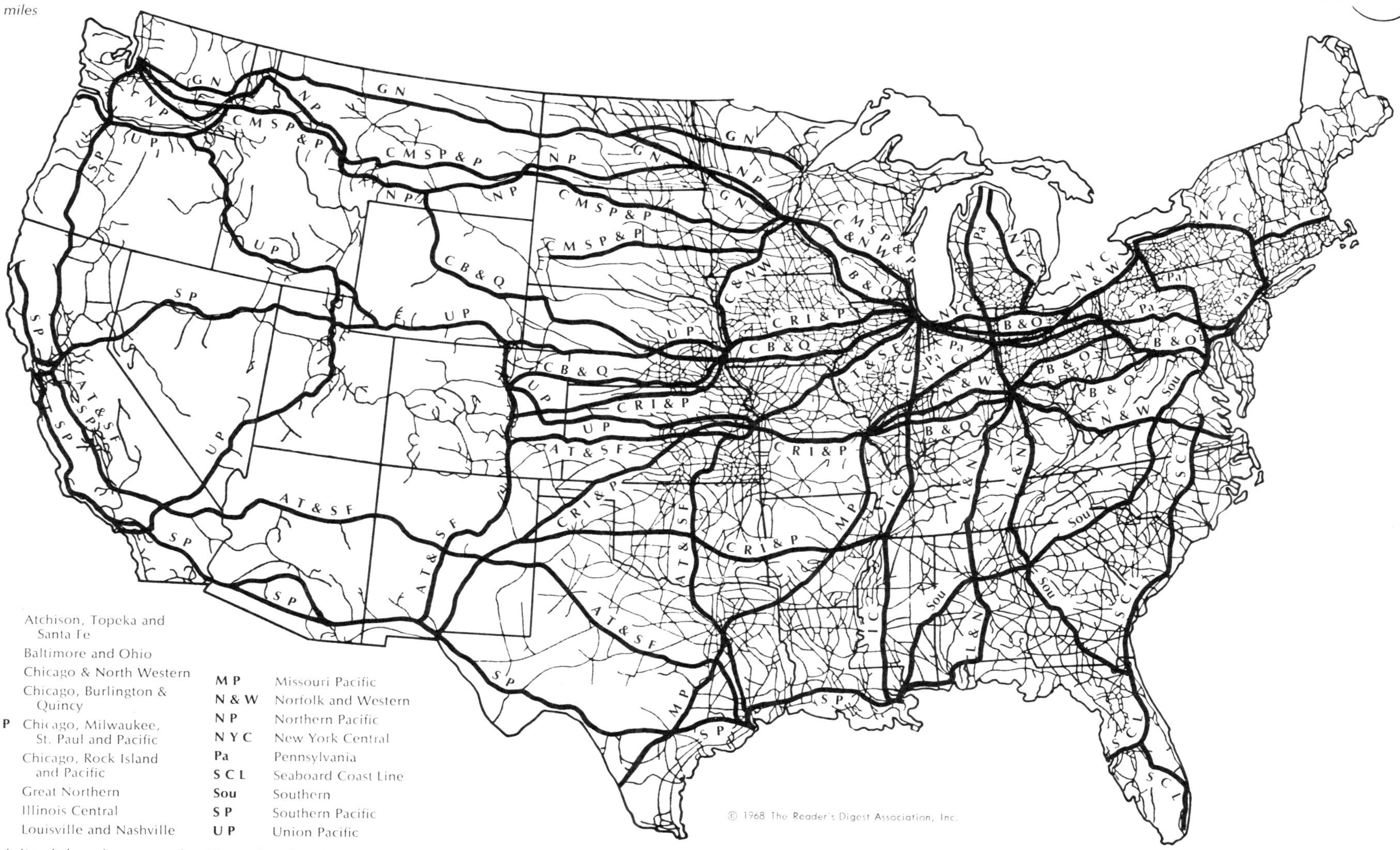

AT&SF	Atchison, Topeka and Santa Fe
B&O	Baltimore and Ohio
C&NW	Chicago & North Western
CB&Q	Chicago, Burlington & Quincy
CMSP&P	Chicago, Milwaukee, St. Paul and Pacific
CRI&P	Chicago, Rock Island and Pacific
GN	Great Northern
IC	Illinois Central
L&N	Louisville and Nashville
MP	Missouri Pacific
N&W	Norfolk and Western
NP	Northern Pacific
NYC	New York Central
Pa	Pennsylvania
SCL	Seaboard Coast Line
Sou	Southern
SP	Southern Pacific
UP	Union Pacific

The railroads listed above have more than 5000 miles of track.

MERCHANT MARINE

In 1900, foreign ships were carrying more than 90 percent of the import-export trade of the United States. When World War I prompted withdrawal of foreign vessels, the government set up a vast shipbuilding program. Between 1918 and 1922 the United States constructed the world's largest merchant fleet, but most ships were delivered after the war was over, and many were ill-suited for peacetime use. Maritime supremacy was short-lived; among the six top maritime nations in 1936, America had dropped to fourth place in cargo-carrying capacity (total deadweight tonnage). In that year, Congress passed a Merchant Marine Act to subsidize a strong, safe merchant marine, capable of acting as a wartime auxiliary fleet.

World War II again spurred shipbuilding, and when peace came, many of the 5592 merchant vessels launched under the government's wartime building program were put up for sale. Between 1947 and 1951 the best were purchased by operators under American ownership, and more than 1000 sold to operators registered under foreign flags. Surplus ships were laid up in reserve "mothball" fleets, but presented operating difficulties because of their age when reactivated for the Korean War and the war in Vietnam. From 1946 through the Korean War period, private American operators were generally heavily engaged in carrying relief supplies to various parts of the world. The privately owned U.S. fleet reached a peak in 1951, with 1262 ships, but the trend since has been generally downward. Only 7 percent of our vast ocean-borne foreign trade in 1966 was carried in American vessels.

The total American merchant marine, both private and government-owned (2292 ships of 1000 gross tons and over), is the world's second largest. But about 1200 of these are government-owned, including many inactive, in the National Defense Reserve Fleet. Liberia has held first place among the world's maritime nations for several years, yet she did not enter the field until 1949. The lure of registry under her "flag of convenience"—permitting cheap labor and minimum safety regulations—has attracted ships from many nations, including more than 150 of America's. In all, about 450 ships owned by foreign affiliates of U.S. companies sail under foreign flags such as the Liberian.

Both American and foreign ships have lost passengers to the airlines. Government-subsidized vessels of the American merchant marine, which operate only on essential trade routes, and a small tramp and tanker fleet which carries foreign aid and other government-financed cargoes, fare quite well in freight operations. But in the field of bulk cargo, which constitutes the major portion of U.S. foreign trade, American shipping is at a disadvantage because of lower labor costs on foreign-flag lines. In 1958 the Maritime Administration planned for a total of 300 new ships over a period of 20 years to replace obsolete vessels in the merchant fleet. To date 150 have been delivered. This program, small though it is, has given us some of the world's fastest and most modern general cargo ships.

Recently, faster service and lower freight rates have been achieved by the container ship, which carries its cargo in large, prepacked containers that can easily be hoisted aboard. In 1967 the United States held the lead in operating such revolutionary vessels.

MAJOR INLAND WATERWAYS

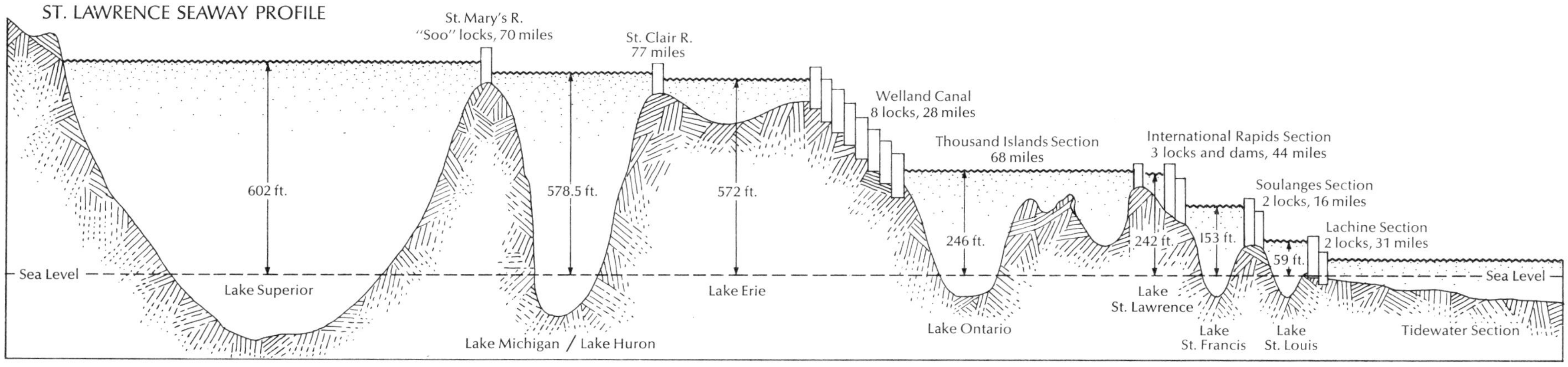

The St. Lawrence Seaway *(illustrated above)* is one of the most notable transportation developments of this century. A joint navigation-power project of Canada and the United States, completed in 1959, it has opened the continent's heartland to large oceangoing vessels.

Winter weather and ice conditions do not permit year-round operation on the Seaway. Although the lakes remain open, the passageway between Montreal and Lake Ontario is generally navigable only between mid-April and early December.

River and Canal Traffic *(Illustrated right).* Most of the nation's navigable waterways and harbors are the responsibility of the Corps of Engineers, U.S. Army, which has built hundreds of locks and dams for purposes of navigation. A few dams also generate hydroelectric power.

Excluding the Great Lakes, more than 25,000 miles of inland waterways are commercially navigable (see mileages on chart). Until the early 1950's, most of the domestic water freight was on the lakes. The picture had changed drastically by the mid-sixties. With new industries established on inland waterways and use of modern diesel towboats, river and canal freight traffic boomed and now amounts to more than six times that of 1940. Gulf Coast river traffic alone increased nearly 40 times. Even with the growing impact of St. Lawrence Seaway operations on lake traffic, canals and rivers account for more than one and a half times the ton-miles of freight on the Great Lakes. In 1966, 115 billion ton-miles (estimate) of freight moved on the latter. Barges, drawn by powerful tows and tugboats, account for most traffic on canals and rivers—an estimated 158 billion ton-miles of freight in 1966.

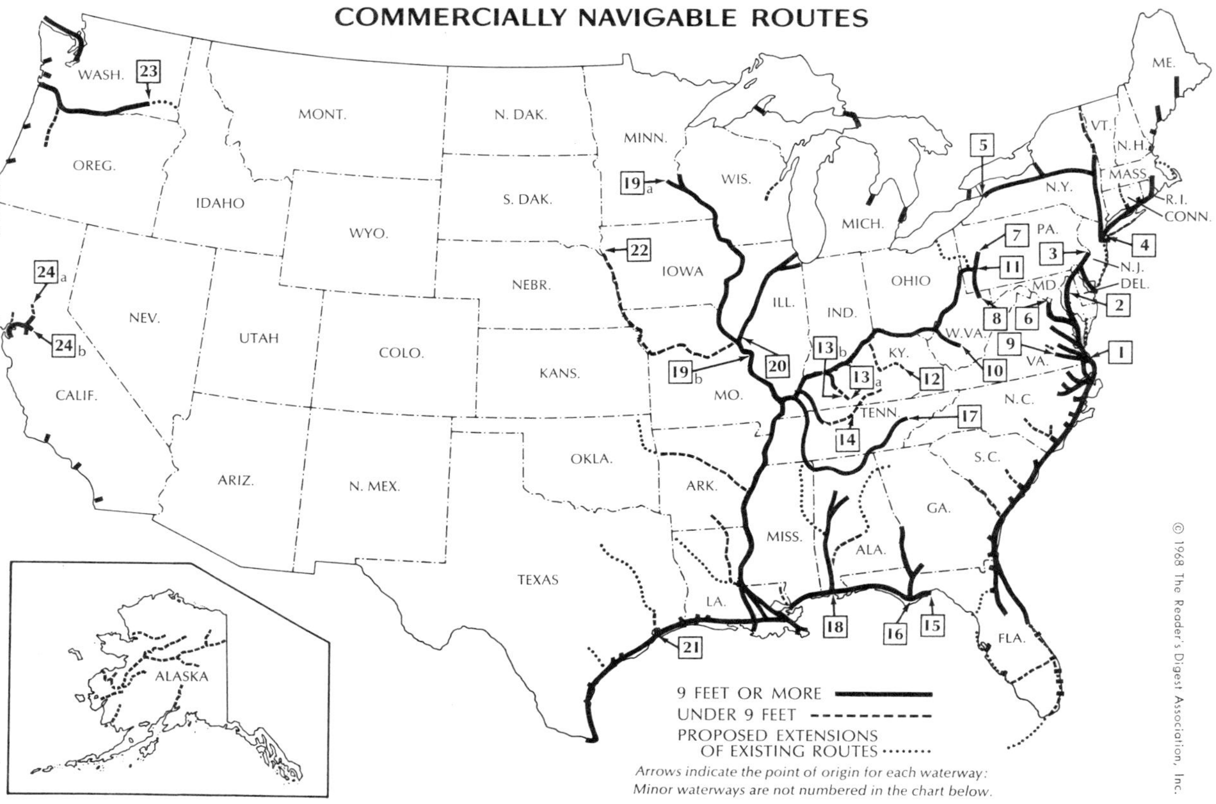

	Name	Section (Miles)	From	To	No. of Locks	Navigation Season
1	**Atlantic Intracoastal Waterway and extensions**	1129	Norfolk, Va.	Miami, Fla.	2	All year
2	**Chesapeake Bay**	200	Baltimore, Md.	Capes of Va.	0	All year
3	**Delaware River**	129	Trenton, N. J.	Delaware Bay	0	All year
4	**Hudson River**	155	Upper Bay, N. Y. (Near N. Y. C.)	Waterford, N. Y., junction with N. Y. S. Barge Canal	0	All year except 8-month season in north
5	**New York State Barge Canal**	522	Niagara River at Tonowanda, N. Y.	Champlain Inlet at Whitehall, N. Y.	58	April-Nov.
6	**Potomac River**	113	Key Bridge, Wash, D. C.	Chesapeake Bay, 80 miles from the Atlantic	0	All year
7	**Allegheny River**	72	East Brady, Pa.	Ohio River	9	All year
8	**Monongahela River**	129	Fairmont, W. Va.	Pittsburgh, Pa.	10	All year
9	**James River**	89	Richmond, Va.	Hampton Roads at Newport News, Va.	0	All year
10	**Kanawha River**	91	Deepwater, W. Va.	Ohio River near Point Pleasant, W. Va.	3	All year
11	**Ohio River**	981	Pittsburgh, Pa.	Mississippi River at Cairo, Ill.	19	All year
12	**Kentucky River**	259	Beattyville, Ky.	Ohio River near Carrollton, Ky.	14	All year
13a	**Green River**	150	Woodburn, Ky.	Ohio River near Evansville, Ind.	4	All year
13b	**Barren River**	30	Bowling Green, Ky.	Green River at Woodburn, Ky.	1	All year

	Name	Section (Miles)	From	To	No. of Locks	Navigation Season
14	**Cumberland River**	317	Carthage, Tenn.	Ohio River at Smithland, Ky.	4	All year
15	**Gulf Intracoastal Waterway**	1113	Apalachee Bay (St. Marks, Fla.)	Brownsville, Tex.	9	All year
16	**Apalachicola-Chattahoochee and Flint River System**	297	Apalachicola Bay	Columbus and Bainbridge, Ga.	3	All year
17	**Tennessee River**	652	Knoxville, Tenn.	Ohio River at Paducah, Ky.	10	All year
18	**Black Warrior-Tombigbee Waterway**	466	Mobile, Ala.	Birmingham Port, Ala.	6	All year
19a	**Mississippi River: Upper**	663	Minneapolis, Minn.	Mouth of Missouri River near St. Louis	30	March-Dec.
19b	**Mississippi River: Lower**	1174	Mouth of Missouri River near St. Louis	Gulf of Mexico	0	All year
20	**Illinois Waterway** *(including Calumet-Sag Channel and the Chicago Sanitary and Ship Canal)*	354	Grafton, Ill.	Turning basin at Calumet River in Chicago area	0	All year
21	**Houston Ship Canal**	50	Galveston Harbor, Tex.	Houston, Tex.	0	All year
22	**Missouri River**	732	Sioux City, Iowa	Mississippi River	0	April-mid-Nov.
23	**Columbia River**	317	Mouth of Snake River, east of Pasco, Wash.	Pacific Ocean	4	All year
24a	**Sacramento River**	145	Colusa, Calif.	Suisun Bay, 48 miles NE of San Francisco	1	All year
24b	**San Joaquin River**	127	Stockton, Calif.	Suisun Bay, 48 miles NE of San Francisco	0	All year

PART IV

Indexes

These pages list the subjects, names and other references that are found in the state descriptions of Part I and in the general articles of Parts II and III.

HOW TO USE THE INDEX TO THE MAPS OF THE UNITED STATES

Physical Features

1. All names of lakes, mountains and other physical features are set in *italic* (slanting) type.
2. If the kind of physical feature cannot readily be recognized by its name, the name is followed by an abbreviation indicating its general category: *Allegheny, r.* (For list of abbreviations, see below.)
3. The physical features are indexed according to the main part of the name: *Mexico, Gulf of; Michigan, L.* This does not apply, however, to a name with several words: *Lake of the Woods.*
4. Names of lesser river tributaries, such as North Fork or South Branch, are generally not listed.

Political Names

Names of cities, counties and other such areas are listed under the complete name, even though physical features may be part of the name: Blue Island (town); Cape Girardeau (county).

Identical Names

When names of two or more places are the same, they are indexed in the alphabetical order of the states in which they appear.

Parts of Names

1. When abbreviations are normally used in names (St.), they are alphabetized as if they were spelled out (Saint).
2. If a name is preceded by "The" or some other word that is an integral part of the name, such a word is alphabetized (The Dalles; La Plata).
3. Names beginning with "Mc" or "Mac" are all alphabetized as "Mac."

References, Numbers and Letters

1. The page number is shown in **bold** type at the end of each entry: Elk City, Idaho **24** B3.
2. A place-name is indexed (except for metropolitan inset maps) only to the page where the city is most prominent: Springfield, Ill. **25** C4.
3. Map references having small letters refer to special inset maps of metropolitan areas: Inglewood, Calif. **16** e11.
4. Where a single letter follows the page entry, it refers to a special map bearing the letter: Puerto Rico **72** n.
5. Latest available figures or official population estimates are given. Figures followed by an asterisk (*) represent official estimates; those followed by the letter "(T)" are township populations.

ABBREVIATIONS USED IN MAPS AND INDEXES

A

A. .... Arroyo
Admin. .... Administration
Ala. .... Alabama
Alta. .... Alberta
Amer. .... American
Arch. .... Archipelago
Ariz. .... Arizona
Ark. .... Arkansas
Atl. Oc. .... Atlantic Ocean
Austl. .... Australia

B

B. .... Bahia, Bay
Bch. .... Beach
Bk. .... Brook
Bor. .... Borough
Br. .... Branch, British
Br. Col. .... British Columbia
Btfld. .... Battlefield

C

C. .... Cape
Calif. .... California
Can. .... Canada, Canal
Cap. .... Capital
Cem. .... Cemetery
Cen. .... Center
Cent. .... Central
C.H. .... Courthouse
Chan. .... Channel
Chih. .... Chihuahua
cm. .... centimeters
Co. .... Cerro
co. .... county
Colo. .... Colorado
Conn. .... Connecticut
Cor., -s .... Corner, -s
Cr. .... Creek
C.Z. .... Canal Zone

D

D. C. .... District of Columbia
Del. .... Delaware
Dep. .... Depot
Dept. .... Department
Des. .... Desert
Dist. .... District
Div. .... Division

E

E. .... East, Eastern
el. .... elevation
Entr. .... Entrance

F

Fk. .... Fork
Fla. .... Florida
For. .... Forest
Fr. .... France, French
ft. .... feet
Ft. .... Fort
Fy. .... Ferry

G

G. .... Gulf
Ga. .... Georgia
Gl. .... Glacier
Gr. .... Grove
Gt. .... Great

H

Hbr. .... Harbor, Harbour
Hd. .... Head
High. .... Highlands
Hist. .... Historical
Hts. .... Heights

I

I., i. .... Island, island
Ill. .... Illinois
in. .... inches
Ind. .... Indiana
Int. .... International
Is. .... Islands

J

Junc. .... Junction

K

Kans. .... Kansas
Kep. .... Island (Indonesian)
km. .... kilometers
Ky. .... Kentucky

L

L. .... Lac, Lago, Lake
La. .... Louisiana
Lag. .... Laguna
lat. .... latitude
Ldg. .... Landing
L.H. .... Lighthouse
Lit. .... Little
long. .... longitude

M

m. .... meters
Mar. Is. .... Mariana Islands
Marsh. Is. .... Marshall Islands
Mass. .... Massachusetts
max. .... maximum
Md. .... Maryland
Me. .... Maine
Mem. .... Memorial
mi. .... miles
Mich. .... Michigan
Mil. .... Military
min. .... minimum
Minn. .... Minnesota
Miss. .... Mississippi
Mo. .... Missouri
Mon. .... Monument
Mont. .... Montana
Mt. .... Mount
Mtn., mtn. .... Mountain, mountain
Mts. .... Mountains
Mun. .... Municipal

N

N. .... North, Northern
N.Amer. .... North America
Nat. .... National
Naut. .... Nautical
N.C. .... North Carolina
N.Dak. .... North Dakota
N.E. .... New England, Northeast, Northeastern
Nebr. .... Nebraska
Nev. .... Nevada
N.H. .... New Hampshire
N.J. .... New Jersey
N.Mex. .... New Mexico
No. .... Number
N.W. .... Northwest, Northwestern
N.Y. .... New York
N.Z. .... New Zealand

O

Okla. .... Oklahoma
Ont. .... Ontario
Oreg. .... Oregon

P

P. .... Punta, Punto
Pa. .... Pennsylvania
Pac. Oc. .... Pacific Ocean
Par. .... Parish
Pd., -s .... Pond, -s
Pen. .... Peninsula
Pk. .... Park, Peak
Pl. .... Place
Plat. .... Plateau
P.O. .... Post Office
Pop. .... Population
P.R. .... Puerto Rico
Pt. .... Point

Q

Qué. .... Québec

R

R., r. .... River, river
Ra. .... Range
Rav. .... Ravine
Rec. .... Recreation
Res. .... Reservoir
R.I. .... Rhode Island

S

S. .... South, Southern
Sa. .... Sierra
Sask. .... Saskatchewan
S.C. .... South Carolina
Sd. .... Sound
S.Dak. .... South Dakota
S.E. .... Southeast, Southeastern
Shls. .... Shoals
Sol. Is. .... Solomon Islands
Sp. .... Spain, Spanish
Spr., -s. .... Spring, -s
Sq. .... Square
st. .... state
St. .... Saint, State
Sta. .... Santa, Station
Ste. .... Sainte
Sto. .... Santo
Str. .... Strait, Stream
S.W. .... Southwest, Southwestern

T

(T) .... Township
Tenn. .... Tennessee
Terr. .... Territory
Tex. .... Texas
Tr. Terr. .... Trust Territory
Twp. .... Township

U

U.K. .... United Kingdom
Univ. .... University
U.S. .... United States

V

V. .... Volcano
Va. .... Virginia
Val. .... Valley
Vil. .... Village
V.I. .... Virgin Islands
Vol. .... Volcano
Vt. .... Vermont

W

W. .... West, Western
Wash. .... Washington
W.I. .... West Indies
Wis. .... Wisconsin
W.Va. .... West Virginia
Wyo. .... Wyoming

A

Aasu, Tutuila 71 c
Abajo Pk., Utah 64 C3
Abarr, Colo. 18 D2
Abbaye, Pt., Mich. 36 C2
Abbeville, Ala., 2,524 11 D4
Abbeville, Ga., 872 22 C3
Abbeville, La., 10,414 31 B4
Abbeville, Miss. 39 C1
Abbeville, co., S.C., 21,417 59 B2
Abbeville, S.C., 5,436 59 B2
Abbotsford, Wis., 1,171 69 C3
Abbott, Miss. 39 D2
Abbott, N. Mex. 46 C1
Abbott, Tex., 289 62 F4
Abbott Butte, Oreg. 55 L3
Abbottsburg, N.C. 50 G3
Abbottsford, Mich. 37 J5
Abbottstown, Pa., 561 56 G6
Abbot Village, Me. 32 B3
Abbyville, Kans., 118 29 D3
Aberdeen, Idaho, 1,484 24 C4
Aberdeen, Ind. 27 C4
Aberdeen, Md., 9,679 33 D1
Aberdeen, Miss., 6,450 39 D2
Aberdeen, N.C., 1,531 50 F2
Aberdeen, Ohio, 774 53 B4
Aberdeen, S. Dak., 23,073 61 C1
Aberdeen, Wash., 18,741 66 B2
Abernant, Ala. 11 B2
Abernathy, Tex., 2,491 62 D3
Abert, L., Oreg. 55 M3
Abie, Nebr., 117 42 H2
Abilene, Kans., 6,746 29 E2
Abilene, Tex., 90,368 62 E3
Abingdon, Ill., 3,469 25 B3
Abingdon, Md. 33 D1
Abingdon, Va., 4,758 66 H4
Abington (part of Pomfret), Conn. 19 G2
Abington, Mass., 10,607(T) 35 L4
Abington, Pa., 8,000* 57 f11
Abiquiu, N. Mex. 46 B1
Abita Springs, La., 655 31 D3
Abo, N. Mex. 46 B2
Aboite, Ind. 27 C1
Abraham, Utah 64 A2
Abraham Lincoln Nat. Hist. Site, Ky. 30 E3
Abraham, Mt., Me. 32 A4
Abraham, Mt., Vt. 65 B2
Abrams, Wis. 69 E3
Absarokee, Mont. 41 D3
Absecon, N.J., 4,320 45 B5
Academy, S. Dak. 61 C2
Acadia, parish, La., 49,931 31 B3
Acadia Nat. Pk., Me. 32 C4
Accident, Md., 237 33 A1
Accomac, Va., 414 67 O3
Accomack, co., Va., 30,635 67 O3
Accord (part of Norwell and Hingham), Mass. 35 L4
Accotink, Va. 67 M2
Acequia, Idaho, 107 24 C4
Achille, Okla., 294 55 G4
Achilles, Kans. 29 B1
Achilles, Va. 67 N3
Ackerly, Tex. 62 D3
Ackerman, Miss., 1,382 39 C2
Ackerville, Wis. 69 a6
Ackia Battleground Nat. Mon., Miss. 39 D1
Ackley, Iowa, 1,731 28 D2
Acme, La. 31 C2
Acme, Mich. 36 F4
Acme, Okla. 54 E3
Acme, Wash. 66 B1
Acme, W.Va. 68 B3
Acoaxet (part of Westport), Mass. 35 K6
Acomita, N. Mex. 46 B2
Acosta, Pa. 56 C5
Acra, N.Y. 49 M6
Acree, Ga. 22 C4
Acres, Kans. 29 C3
Acton, Ala. 11 c7
Acton, Calif. 16 e10
Acton, Me. 32 A5
Acton, Mass., 7,238(T) 35 J3
Acton, Tex. 63 d12
Acushnet, Mass., 5,755(T) 35 L6
Acushnet, r., Mass. 35 L6
Acworth, Ga., 2,359 22 B1
Acworth, N.H. 44 A5
Ada, co., Idaho, 93,460 24 A4
Ada, Kans. 29 E1
Ada, Mich. 36 F6
Ada, Minn. 38 A2
Ada, Ohio 53 B2
Ada, Okla. 54 G3
Adacao, Guam 71 a
Adair, Ill. 25 B3
Adair, co., Iowa, 10,893 28 C3
Adair, Iowa, 742 28 C3
Adair, co., Ky., 14,699 30 E3
Adair, Mich. 37 J6
Adair, co., Mo., 20,105 40 D1
Adair, co., Okla., 13,112 55 J2
Adair, Okla., 434 55 H1
Adairsville, Ga., 1,026 22 B1
Adairville, Ky., 848 30 D4
Adak, Alaska 13 f8
Adak I., Alaska 13 f8
Adamana, Ariz. 14 C2
Adams, co., Colo., 120,296 18 C2
Adams, co., Idaho, 2,978 24 A3
Adams, co., Ill., 68,467 25 A3
Adams, Ill. 25 A4
Adams, co., Ind., 24,643 27 D2
Adams, co., Iowa, 7,468 28 C3
Adams, Kans. 29 E3
Adams, Mass., 11,949;12,391(T) 34 B2
Adams, Minn. 38 C4
Adams, co., Miss., 37,730 39 A4
Adams, co., Nebr., 28,944 42 F3
Adams, Nebr., 387 42 H3
Adams, N.Y., 1,914 49 H3
Adams, co., N. Dak., 4,449 51 L2
Adams, N. Dak., 360 51 N1
Adams, co., Ohio, 19,982 53 B4
Adams, Okla. 54 B1
Adams, Oreg., 192 55 N2
Adams, co., Pa., 51,906 56 G6
Adams, Tenn. 61 H1
Adams, co., Wash., 9,929 66 D2
Adams, co., Wis., 7,566 69 D3
Adams, Wis., 1,301 69 D4
Adams, Mt., N.H. 44 C3
Adams, Mt., Wash. 66 C2
Adams Beach, Fla. 21 G2
Adamsburg, S.C. 59 C2
Adams Center, N.Y. 49 H3
Adams City, Colo. 18 b5
Adams Head, pk., Utah 64 A3
Adams Mtn., Mass. 34 C2
Adams Nat. Hist. Site, Mass. 35 K3
Adams Run, S.C. 59 D4
Adams Station, N.J. 47 a4
Adamston, N.J. 47 c5
Adamstown, Pa., 1,190 57 J5
Adamsville, Ala., 2,095 11 B2
Adamsville, Fla. 21 d11
Adamsville, Mich. 36 E7
Adamsville, Ohio, 167 53 D2
Adamsville, Pa. 56 A2
Adamsville (part of Little Compton), R.I. 58 D2
Adamsville, Tenn., 1,046 61 G2
Adamsville, Tex. 62 E4
Addie, N.C. 50 B2
Addieville, Ill., 231 25 C5
Addington, Okla., 144 54 F3
Addis, La., 590 31 C3
Addison, Ala., 343 11 B1
Addison (part of Glastonbury), Conn. 19 E3
Addison, Ill., 16,997 26 b3
Addison, Me. 32 D4
Addison, Mich., 575 37 G6
Addison, N.Y., 2,185 48 F6
Addison, Ohio 53 C4
Addison, Pa., 222 56 C6
Addison, Tex., 308 63 f11
Addison, co., Vt., 20,076 65 A2
Addison, Vt. 65 A2
Addor, N.C., 118 50 F2
Addy, Wash. 66 E1
Addyston, Ohio, 1,376 52 g10
Adel, Ga., 4,321 22 C4
Adel, Iowa, 2,295 28 C3
Adel, Oreg. 55 N3
Adelanto, Calif. 17 E4
Adell, Wis., 398 69 F4
Adelphi, Ohio, 441 53 C3
Adelphia, N.J. 47 b5
Aden, Ill. 25 D5
Adena, Ohio, 1,317 53 E2
Adger, Ala. 11 B2
Adin, Calif. 17 C1
Adirondack Mts., N.Y. 49 K3
Adjuntas, P.R., 5,318 72 n b1
Admiralty Inlet, Wash. 67 a4
Admiralty I., Alaska 13 K4
Admire, Kans., 149 29 F2
Adobe, Ariz. 14 B3
Adobe Cr. Res., Colo. 18 D2
Adobes, Tex. 62 B5
Adolphus, Ky. 30 D4
Adona, Ark., 154 15 C2
Adrian, Ga., 568 22 D3
Adrian, Ill. 25 A3
Adrian, Mich., 20,347 37 G7
Adrian, Minn., 1,215 38 B4
Adrian, Mo., 1,082 40 B3
Adrian, N.Y. 48 E6
Adrian, N. Dak. 51 N2
Adrian, Oreg. 55 O3
Adrian, Tex., 258 62 C2
Adrian, W.Va. 68 C3
Advance, Mich. 36 F3
Advance, Mo., 692 40 G4
Advance, N.C., 197 50 E2
Aeneas, Wash. 66 D1
Aetna, Ill. 25 D4
Aetna, Kans. 29 D3
Aetna, Tenn. 61 H2
Affton, Mo. 40 F3
Afognak, Alaska, 190 13 E4
Afognak I., Alaska 13 F4
Afono, Tutuila 71 c
Afono Bay, Tutuila 71 c
Afton, Calif. 17 E4
Afton, Iowa, 773 28 C4
Afton, Mich. 37 G3
Afton, Minn., 158 38 d6
Afton, N.Y., 956 49 J6
Afton, Okla., 1,111 55 H1
Afton, Tenn. 61 N1
Afton, Va. 67 L2
Afton, Wis. 69 D5
Afton, Wyo., 1,337 70 A2
Agana, Guam, 1,642 72 a
Agana Bay, Guam 72 a
Agar, S. Dak., 139 61 B1
Agat, Guam, 2,596 72 a
Agat Bay, Guam 72 a
Agate, Colo. 18 D2
Agate, Nebr. 42 A1
Agate Beach, Oreg. 55 K2
Agattu I., Alaska 13 d8
Agattu Str., Alaska 13 d8
Agawam, Mass., 15,718(T) 34 D4
Agawam, r., Mass. 35 M5
Agency, Iowa, 702 28 E4
Agency, Mo., 240 40 B2
Agency L., Oreg. 55 M3
Agency Pk., Colo. 18 B2
Agency Valley Res., Oreg. 55 N3
Agenda, Kans., 124 29 E1
Agfayan Pt., Guam 71 a
Agidyen, i., Jaluit 71 c
Agingan Pt., Saipan 72 f
Agnes, Tex. 63 d11
Agness, Oreg. 55 K3
Agnew, Calif. 16 c8
Agnew, Wash. 66 B1
Agoura, Calif. 16 d10
Agra, Kans., 277 29 C1
Agra, Okla., 265 54 G2
Agricola, Kans. 29 G2
Agricola, Miss. 39 D5
Agrihan, i., Mar. Is. 71 B2
Agua Caliente, Ariz. 14 B3
Agua Caliente Springs, Calif. 17 E5
Aguada, P.R., 3,759 72 n a1
Aguadilla, P.R., 15,943 72 n a1
Aguadilla, B.de, P.R. 72 n a1
Agua Dulce, Tex., 867 62 F6
Agua Fria, N. Mex. 46 C1
Agua Fria, r., Ariz. 14 B3
Agua Nueva, Tex. 62 E6
Aguas Buenas, P.R., 2,470 72 n c1
Aguijan, i., Mar. Is. 72 f
Aguila, Ariz. 14 B3
Aguilar, Colo., 777 18 C3
Aguilares, Tex. 62 E6
Agujereada, P., P.R. 72 n a1
Ahmeek, Mich. 36 C1
Ahoskie, N.C., 4,583 51 J1
Ahtanum, Wash. 66 C2
Ahua Pt., Hawaii 23 e10
Ai, i., Jaluit 72 m
Aibonito, P.R., 5,477 72 n c1
Aid, Ohio 53 C4
Aiea, Hawaii, 11,826 23 J2
Aiken, co., S.C., 81,038 59 C3
Aiken, S.C., 11,243 59 C3
Aiken Summit, Va. 67 K4
Ailey, Ga., 469 22 D3
Ailuk, atoll, Marsh. Is. 176 22
Aina Haina, Hawaii 23 f10
Aineman, i., Jaluit 72 m
Ainsworth, Ind. 26 e4
Ainsworth, Iowa, 371 28 F3
Ainsworth, Nebr., 1,982 42 D1
Air, Tex. 62 E4
Airai, Palau 72 e
Airway Heights, Wash., 708 66 E2
Aitkin, co., Minn., 12,162 38 C2
Aitkin, Minn., 1,829 38 C2
Aitsu, i., Eniwetok 72 k
Aiwokako Passage, Palau 72 e
Aix, Ind. 27 A1
Ajax Mtn., Idaho-Mont. 41 B3
Ajayan Pt., Guam 71 a
Ajo, Ariz., 7,049 14 B3
Ajo Range, Ariz. 14 B3
Akakoa Pt., Hawaii 23 L3
Akaska, S. Dak., 90 61 B1
Akela, N. Mex. 46 B3
Akeley, Minn., 434 38 B2
Akeley, Pa. 56 C2
Akhiok, Alaska, 84 13 E4
Akiachak, Alaska, 229 12 C3
Akiak, Alaska, 187 12 C3
Akin, Ill. 25 D6
Akron, Ala., 604 11 B3
Akron, Colo., 1,890 18 D1
Akron, Ind., 958 27 C1
Akron, Iowa, 1,351 28 A2
Akron, Kans. 29 F3
Akron, Mich., 503 37 H5
Akron, N.Y., 2,786 48 C4
Akron, Ohio, 290,351 53 D1
Akron, Pa., 2,167 57 J5
Akulurak, Alaska 12 C3
Akun I., Alaska 12 B5
Akutan, Alaska, 107 12 B5
Akutan I., Alaska 12 B5
Alabama, st., 3,540,000* 11
Alabama, N.Y. 48 D4
Alabama, r., Ala. 11 B4
Alabama Port, Ala. 11 A5
Alabaster, Ala., 1,623 11 C2
Alabaster, Mich. 37 H4
Alachua, co., Fla., 74,074 21 H2
Alachua, Fla., 1,974 21 H2
Aladdin, Pa. 56 d7
Alafia, r., Fla. 21 d11
Alakai Swamp, Hawaii 22 G1
Alakanuk, Alaska, 278 12 B3
Alalakeiki Chan., Hawaii 23 K3
Alamagan, i., Mar. Is. 71 B2
Alamance, co., N.C., 85,674 50 F2
Alamance, N.C. 50 F1
Alameda, co., Calif., 908,209 17 C3
Alameda, Calif., 63,855 16 b7
Alameda, Idaho, 10,660 24 C4
Alameda (part of Albuquerque), N. Mex. 46 B2
Alameda Cr., Calif. 16 b7
Alamillo, N. Mex. 46 B2
Alamito Cr., Tex. 62 B5
Alamo, Ariz. 14 B2
Alamo, Calif., 1,791 16 b7
Alamo, Ga., 822 22 D3
Alamo, Ind., 144 27 A3
Alamo, Mich. 36 F6
Alamo, Nev. 43 C3
Alamo, N. Dak., 182 51 L1
Alamo, Tenn., 1,665 60 B2
Alamo, Tex., 4,121 62 E6
Alamo, r., Calif. 17 F5
Alamogordo, N. Mex., 21,723 46 B3
Alamogordo Res., N. Mex. 46 C2
Alamo Heights, Tex., 7,552 62 b9
Alamosa, co., Colo., 10,000 18 C3
Alamosa, Colo., 6,205 18 B3
Alamosa, r., N. Mex. 46 B3
Alamosa Cr., Colo. 18 B3
Alamota, Kans. 29 B2
Alanelimo, i., Truk 72 q
Alanreed, Tex. 62 D2
Alanson, Mich., 290 37 H3
Alao, Tutuila 71 c
Alapaha, Ga., 631 22 C4
Alapaha, r., Ga. 22 C5
Alarka, N.C. 50 B2
Alaska, st., 273,000* 12-13
Alaska, Gulf of, Alaska 13 G4
Alaska Pen., Alaska 12 D4
Alaska Range, Alaska 13 E3
Alatna, Alaska 13 E2
Alatna, r., Alaska 13 E2
Alava, C., Wash. 66 A1
Alba, Mich. 37 G4
Alba, Mo., 336 40 B4
Alba, Pa., 192 56 H2
Alba, Tex., 472 63 G3
Albany, Calif., 14,804 16 b7
Albany, Ga., 55,890 22 B4
Albany, Ill., 637 25 B2
Albany, Ind., 2,132 27 C2
Albany, Ky., 1,887 30 E4
Albany, Minn., 1,375 38 B3
Albany, Mo., 1,662 40 B1
Albany, co., N.Y., 272,926 49 M5
Albany, N.Y., 129,726 49 N5
Albany, Ohio, 629 53 C3
Albany, Okla. 55 G4
Albany, Oreg., 12,926 55 L2
Albany, Tex., 2,174 62 E3
Albany, Vt., 169 65 C1
Albany, Wis., 892 69 D5
Albany, co., Wyo., 21,290 70 D3
Albemarle, N.C., 12,261 50 E2
Albemarle, co., Va., 30,969 67 L2
Albemarle Sd., N.C. 51 J1
Alberene, Va. 67 L3
Albert, Kans., 221 29 C2
Albert, Okla. 54 E2
Albert, Tex. 62 E4
Albert, W.Va. 68 D2
Albert, L., S. Dak. 61 D1
Alberta, Ala. 11 B3
Alberta, Va., 430 67 M4
Albert City, Iowa, 722 28 C2
Albert Lea, Minn., 18,454 38 C4
Alberton, Mont., 356 41 A2
Albertville, Ala., 8,250 11 C1
Albia, Iowa, 4,582 28 E3
Albin, Wyo., 172 70 D2
Albion, Calif. 17 B2
Albion, Idaho, 415 24 C4
Albion, Ill., 2,025 25 D5
Albion, Ind., 1,325 27 C1
Albion, Iowa, 588 28 E2
Albion, Me. 32 B4
Albion, Mich., 12,749 37 G6
Albion, Mont. 41 F3
Albion, Nebr., 1,982 42 F2
Albion, N.Y., 5,182 48 D4
Albion, Okla., 161 55 H3
Albion, Pa., 1,630 56 A2
Albion (part of Lincoln), R.I. 58 C1
Albion, Wash., 291 66 E2
Albion, Wis. 69 D5
Albright, W.Va., 304 68 D2
Albuquerque, N. Mex., 201,189 46 B2
Alburg, Vt., 426 65 A1
Alburnett, Iowa, 341 28 F2
Alburtis, Pa., 1,086 57 K4
Alcalde, N. Mex. 46 B1
Alcester, S. Dak., 479 61 D2
Alco, Ark. 15 C2
Alco, La. 31 A2
Alcoa, Tenn., 6,395 61 M2
Alcolu, S.C. 59 D3
Alcona, co., Mich., 6,352 37 H4
Alcona, Mich. 37 H4
Alcorn, co., Miss., 25,282 39 D1
Alcorn College, Miss. 39 A4
Alcova, Wyo. 70 C2
Alcove, N.Y. 49 d14
Alcove Res., N.Y. 49 d14
Alcovy, r., Ga. 22 C2
Alden, Ill. 25 D1
Alden, Iowa, 838 28 D2
Alden, Kans., 239 29 D2
Alden, Mich. 36 F4
Alden, N.Y., 2,694 48 C5
Alden, Okla. 54 E3
Alden, Pa. 57 m17
Aldenville (part of Chicopee), Mass. 34 D4
Alderson, Pa. 57 J3
Alderson, W.Va., 1,225 68 C4
Aldie, Va. 67 M2
Aldora, Ga., 535 22 B2
Aldrich, Mo., 181 40 C4
Aldridge, Ala. 11 A6
Aldridge, Colo. 18 A3
Aledo, Ill., 3,080 25 B2
Aledo, Tex. 63 d11
Alegros Mtn., N. Mex. 46 A2
Aleknagik, Alaska 12 D4
Aleknagik Mission, Alaska, 50 12 D4
Alenuihaha Chan., Hawaii 23 K3
Aleutian Is., Alaska 12 A4
Aleutian Range, Alaska 13 E4
Alewa Heights, Hawaii 23 e9
Alex, Okla., 545 54 F3
Alexander, Alaska 13 F3
Alexander, Ark., 177 15 C3
Alexander, Ga. 22 D2
Alexander, co., Ill., 16,061 25 C6
Alexander, Iowa, 294 28 D2
Alexander, Kans., 153 29 C2
Alexander, Me. 32 D3
Alexander, N.Y., 414 48 D5
Alexander, co., N.C., 15,625 50 D2
Alexander, N.C. 50 C2
Alexander, N. Dak., 269 51 L2
Alexander, W.Va. 68 C3
Alexander Arch., Alaska 13 J4
Alexander City, Ala., 13,140 11 C3
Alexander Mills, N.C., 947 50 C2
Alexandria, Ind., 5,582 27 C2
Alexandria, Ky., 1,318 30 F2
Alexandria, La., 40,279 31 B2
Alexandria, Minn., 6,713 38 B3
Alexandria, Mo., 452 40 E1
Alexandria, Nebr., 257 42 G3
Alexandria, N.H. 44 B4
Alexandria, Ohio, 452 53 C2
Alexandria, Pa., 381 56 E4
Alexandria, S. Dak., 614 61 D2
Alexandria, Tenn., 599 61 J1
Alexandria, Va., 91,023 67 M2
Alexandria Bay, N.Y., 1,583 49 J2
Alexis, Ill., 878 25 B2
Alfalfa, co., Okla., 8,445 54 E1
Alfalfa, Okla. 54 E2
Alford, Fla., 380 21 E1
Alford, Ind. 27 A4
Alford, Mass., 256(T) 34 E4
Alfordsville, Ind., 121 27 A4
Alfred, Me. 32 A5
Alfred, N.Y., 3,383 48 E6
Alfred, N.Dak. 51 N2
Alfred Station, N.Y. 48 E6
Alger, co., Mich., 9,250 36 E2
Alger, Mich. 37 G4
Alger, Ohio, 1,068 53 B2
Algoa, Tex. 63 j15
Algodones, N. Mex. 46 B2
Algoma, Miss. 39 C1
Algoma, Wis., 3,855 69 F3
Algona, Iowa, 5,977 28 C1
Algona, Wash., 1,311 67 b6
Algonac, Mich., 3,190 37 J6
Algonquin, Ill., 2,692 25 D1
Algood, Tenn., 886 61 K1
Alhambra, Calif., 54,807 16 e10
Alhambra, Ill., 537 25 C5
Alia Pt., Hawaii 23 L4
Alice, N. Dak., 124 51 O2
Alice, Tex., 20,861 62 E6
Alicel, Oreg. 55 O2
Aliceville, Ala., 3,194 11 A2
Alicia, Ark., 236 15 D2
Alida, Ind. 26 g4
Alida, Kans. 29 F1
Alikchi, Okla. 55 H3
Aline, Okla., 314 54 E1
Aliquippa, Pa., 26,369 56 A4
Alisal, Calif., 16,473 16 c9
Alkabo, N. Dak. 51 L1
Alkali Flats, Nev. 43 B1
Alkali L., Nev. 43 A1
Alkaline L., N. Dak. 51 N2
Alkol, W.Va. 68 B3
Allaben, N.Y. 49 M6
Allagash, Me. 32 C1
Allagash, r., Me. 32 B2
Allagash Falls, Me. 32 B2
Allagash L., Me. 32 B2
Allaire, N.J. 47 c5
Allakaket, Alaska 13 E2
Allamakee, co., Iowa, 15,982 28 F1
All American Can., Calif. 17 F5
Allamoore, Tex. 62 B4
Allamuchy, N.J. 45 B2
Allardt, Tenn. 61 L1
Allatoona L., Ga. 22 B1
Alleene, Ark. 15 A4
Allegan, co., Mich., 57,729 36 F6
Allegan, Mich., 4,822 36 F6
Allegany, co., Md., 84,169 33 B1
Allegany, co., N.Y., 43,978 48 D6
Allegany, N.Y., 2,064 48 C6
Allegany, Oreg. 55 L3
Alleghany, co., N.C., 7,734 50 D1
Alleghany, co., Va., 12,128 67 J3
Alleghany, Va. 67 J2
Allegheny, co., Pa., 1,628,587 56 A4
Allegheny, r., N.Y.-Pa. 56 B3
Allegheny Mts. 8a
Allegre, Ky. 30 C4
Allemands, La., 1,167 31 D4
Allemands, L. des, La. 31 D4
Allen, co., Ind., 232,196 27 C2
Allen, co., Kans., 16,369 29 G3
Allen, Kans., 205 29 F2
Allen, co., Ky., 12,269 30 D4
Allen, Ky., 370 30 H3
Allen, parish, La., 19,867 31 B3
Allen, Mich., 325 67 G7
Allen, Nebr., 350 42 H1
Allen, co., Ohio, 103,691 53 A2
Allen, Okla., 1,005 55 G3
Allen, S. Dak. 61 B2
Allen, Tex., 659 63 f10
Allendale, Ill., 465 25 E5
Allendale, Ky. 30 E3
Allendale, Mich. 36 E6
Allendale, Mo., 136 40 B1
Allendale, N.J., 4,092 47 c1
Allendale, co., S.C., 11,362 59 C4
Allendale, S.C., 3,114 59 C3
Allenhurst, Ga. 22 E4
Allenhurst, N.J., 795 47 d5
Allen Park, Mich., 37,052 37 c11
Allens, N.J. 47 a5
Allens Hill, N.Y. 48 j18
Allenspark, Colo. 18 a4
Allen Springs, Ky. 30 D4
Allensville, Ky., 286 30 C4
Allensville, Pa. 56 F4
Allenton, Mich. 37 J6
Allenton, R.I. 58 C2
Allenton, Wis. 69 E4
Allentown, Ga., 450 22 C3
Allentown, N.J., 1,393 45 B3
Allentown, N.Y. 48 D6
Allentown, Pa., 108,347 57 K4
Allenville, Ill., 191 25 D4
Allenville, Mich. 37 G3
Allenwood, N.J. 47 c5
Allenwood, Pa. 56 H3
Allerton, Ill., 282 25 E4
Allerton, Iowa, 692 28 D4
Allerton (part of Hull), Mass. 35 L3
Allerton, Pt., Mass. 35 L3
Alliance, Ala. 11 b6
Alliance, Fla. 21 E1
Alliance, Nebr., 7,845 42 A1
Alliance, N.C. 51 J2
Alliance, Ohio, 28,362 53 D2
Alligator, Miss., 227 39 B1
Alligator, r., N.C. 51 J2
Alligator L., Me. 32 C4
Allingtown (part of West Haven), Conn. 19 D4
Allison, Iowa, 952 28 E2
Allison, Kans. 29 B1
Allison, Tex. 62 D2
Allison Park, Pa., 5,100* 56 c7
Allons, Tenn. 61 K1
Alloway, N.J. 45 A4
Alloway Cr., N.J. 45 A4
Allred, Tex. 62 C3
Allsboro, Ala. 11 A1
Alluwe, Okla. 55 H1
Allyn, Wash. 66 B2
Alma, Ark., 1,370 15 A2
Alma, Colo., 107 18 B2
Alma, Ga., 3,515 22 D4
Alma, Ill., 358 25 D5
Alma, Kans., 838 29 F1
Alma, Mich., 8,978 37 G5
Alma, Nebr., 1,342 42 E3
Alma, N. Mex. 46 A3
Alma, N.Y. 48 D6
Alma, Ohio 53 C3
Alma, Okla. 54 F3
Alma, Tex. 63 f12
Alma, Wis. 69 B3
Alma Center, Wis., 464 69 C3
Alma Hill, N.Y. 48 E6
Almanor, Calif. 17 C1
Almanor, L., Calif. 17 C1
Almeda, Tex. 63 j14
Almena, Kans., 555 29 C1
Almena, Wis., 398 69 A2
Almeria, Nebr. 42 E2
Almira, Wash., 414 66 D2
Almond, N.Y., 696 48 E6
Almond, N.C. 50 B2
Almond, Wis., 391 69 D3
Almonesson, N.J., 1,600* 57 f12
Almont, Mich., 1,279 37 H6
Almont, N. Dak., 190 51 M2
Almyra, Ark., 240 15 D3
Alna, Me. 32 B4
Alofau, Tutuila 71 c
Aloha, Mich. 37 G3
Aloha, Wash. 66 A2
Alonzo, Ky. 30 D4
Alorton, Ill., 3,282 40 d10
Aloys, Nebr. 42 H2
Alpaugh, Calif. 17 D4
Alpena, Ark., 283 15 B1
Alpena, co., Mich., 28,556 37 H4
Alpena, Mich., 14,682 37 H3
Alpena, S. Dak., 407 61 C1
Alpena, W.Va. 68 D3
Alpha, Ill., 637 25 B2
Alpha, Mich., 317 36 C2
Alpha, N.J., 2,406 45 A2
Alpha, Va. 67 L3
Alpharetta, Ga., 1,349 22 B1
Alpine, Ariz. 14 D3
Alpine, Ark. 15 B3
Alpine, co., Calif., 397 17 D2
Alpine, Calif., 1,044 17 E5
Alpine, Ill. 26 c4
Alpine, N.J., 921 47 d2
Alpine, N.Y. 48 G6
Alpine, Oreg. 55 L2
Alpine, Tenn. 61 K1
Alpine, Tex., 4,740 62 C4
Alpine, Utah, 775 64 c7
Alpine Junction, Wyo. 70 A2
Alps, N.Y. 49 e14
Alsea, Oreg. 55 L2
Alsea, r., Oreg. 55 L2
Alsek, r., Can.-U.S. 13 J3
Alsen, N. Dak., 228 51 N1
Alsey, Ill., 248 25 B4
Alsip, Ill., 6,336 26 d4
Alstead, N.H. 44 A5
Alston, Ga., 154 22 D3
Alston, Mich. 36 C2
Alta, Iowa, 1,393 28 B2
Altadena, Calif., 40,568 16 e10
Al Tahoe, Calif. 17 C2
Altair, Tex. 62 F5
Alta Loma, Calif. 16 f10
Alta Loma, Tex., 1,020 63 j15
Altamaha, r., Ga. 22 D4
Altamahaw, N.C. 50 F1
Altamont, Calif. 16 c7
Altamont, Ill., 1,656 25 D4
Altamont, Kans., 672 29 G3
Altamont, Mo., 201 40 B2
Altamont, N.Y., 1,365 49 M5
Altamont, Oreg., 10,811 55 M3
Altamont, S. Dak., 77 61 D2
Altamont, Tenn., 552 61 K2
Altamont, Utah, 102 64 B1
Altamonte Springs, Fla., 1,212 21 J3
Altar Wash, Ariz. 14 C4
Altaville, Calif. 17 C2
Alta Vista, Iowa, 276 28 E1
Alta Vista, Kans., 400 29 F2
Altavista, Va., 3,299 67 K3
Altha, Fla., 413 21 E1
Altheimer, Ark., 1,013 15 D3
Altmar, N.Y., 277 49 H3
Alto, Ind. 27 B2
Alto, La. 31 C1
Alto, Mich. 36 F6
Alto, Tex., 869 63 G4
Alton, Ill., 43,047 25 B5
Alton, Iowa, 1,048 28 B2
Alton, Kans., 299 29 D1
Alton, Ky. 30 E2
Alton, Mo., 677 40 E5
Alton, N.H. 44 C5
Alton, N.Y. 48 G4
Alton, Ohio 52 a6
Alton, R.I. 58 B3
Alton, Utah, 116 64 A3
Altona, Ill., 505 25 B2
Altona, Mich. 36 F5
Altona, Nebr. 42 H1
Altona, N.Y. 49 N1
Altona, Okla. 54 E2
Alton Bay, N.H. 44 C5
Altoona, Ala., 744 11 C1
Altoona, Fla. 21 J3
Altoona, Iowa, 2,424 28 D3
Altoona, Kans., 490 29 G3
Altoona, Pa., 69,407 56 E5
Altoona, Wash. 66 B2
Altoona, Wis., 2,114 69 B3
Alto Park, Ga., 2,526 22 A1
Alto Pass, Ill., 323 25 C6
Altuda, Tex. 62 C4
Altura, Minn., 320 38 C3
Alturas, Calif., 2,819 17 C1
Altus, Ark., 392 15 B2
Altus, Okla., 21,225 54 D3
Altus, L., Okla. 54 D3
Alum Cr., Ohio 53 C2
Alum Rock, Calif., 18,942 16 c8
Alunite, Nev. 43 C4
Alutom I., Guam 71 a
Alutom Mt., Guam 71 a
Alva, Fla. 21 J5
Alva, Ky. 30 G4
Alva, Okla., 6,258 54 E1
Alvadore, Oreg. 55 L2
Alvarado, Calif. 16 b7
Alvarado, Minn., 282 38 A1
Alvarado, Tex., 1,907 62 F3
Alvaton, Ga., 24 22 a9
Alverda, Pa., 56 D4
Alverno, Mich. 37 G3
Alvin, S.C. 59 E3
Alvin, Tex., 5,643 62 G5
Alvin, Wis. 69 E2
Alviso, Calif., 1,174 16 c8
Alvon, W.Va. 68 C4
Alvord, Iowa, 238 28 A1
Alvord, Tex., 694 62 F3
Alvord L., Oreg. 55 N3
Alvordton, Ohio, 388 53 A1
Alvwood, Minn. 38 B2
Alzada, Mont. 41 F3
Amado, Ariz. 14 C4
Amador, co., Calif., 9,990 17 C2
Amador, Mich. 37 J5
Amagansett, N.Y., 1,095 49 Q9
Amagon, Ark., 234 15 D2
Amalia, N. Mex. 46 C1
Amaluia, Tutuila 71 c
Amana, Iowa 28 F3
Amanave, Tutuila 71 c
Amanave Bay, Tutuila 71 c
Amanda, Ohio, 732 53 C3
Amanda Park, Wash. 66 A2
Amantes Pt., Guam 71 a
Amargosa, r., Calif.-Nev. 17 E4
Amargosa Ra., Calif. 17 E3
Amarillo, Tex., 137,969 62 C2
Amasa, Mich. 36 C2
Amaua, Tutuila 71 c
Amazonia, Mo., 326 40 A2
Amber, N.Y. 49 m21
Amber, Okla. 54 F2
Amber, Wash. 66 E2
Amberg, Wis. 69 E2
Amberley, Ohio, 2,951 52 j9

For abbreviations and explanation of index, see page 176.

Ambia, Ind., 351 27 A2
Amble, Mich. 36 F5
Ambler, Alaska, 70 13 D2
Ambler, Pa., 6,765 57 L5
Ambo Chan., Kwajalein 72 l
Amboy, Calif. 17 F4
Amboy, Ill., 2,067 25 C2
Amboy, Ind., 446 27 C2
Amboy, Minn., 629 38 B4
Amboy, Wash. 66 B3
Ambridge, Pa., 13,865 56 A4
Ambrose, Ga., 244 22 D4
Ambrose, N. Dak., 220 51 L1
Ambrosia Lake, N. Mex. 46 B2
Amchitka I., Alaska 13 e8
Amchitka Pass, Alaska 13 e8
Amelia, Fla. 21 J1
Amelia, La. 31 C4
Amelia, Nebr. 42 E1
Amelia, Ohio, 913 53 A3
Amelia, co., Va., 7,815 67 L3
Amelia, Va. 67 L3
Amelia I., Fla. 21 J1
Amenia, N.Y. 49 O7
Amenia, N. Dak., 117 51 O2
American, r., Calif. 17 C2
American Falls, Idaho, 2,602 24 C4
American Falls Res., Idaho 24 C4
American Fork, Utah, 6,373 64 B1
American Samoa, Pac. Oc., 21,000* 71 E4
Americus, Ga., 13,472 22 B3
Americus, Ind. 27 B2
Americus, Kans., 300 29 F2
Amery, Wis., 1,769 69 A2
Ames, Iowa, 34,826 28 D2
Ames, N.Y., 162 49 L5
Ames, Okla., 211 54 E1
Ames, Tex. 63 k13
Amesbury, Mass., 9,625; 10,787(T) 35 L1
Amesville, Ohio, 255 53 D3
Amherst, Colo. 18 D1
Amherst, Me. 32 C4
Amherst, Mass., 10,306; 13,718(T) 34 E3
Amherst, Nebr., 220 42 E3
Amherst, N.H. 44 B6
Amherst, N.Y. 48 g15
Amherst, Ohio, 6,750 53 C1
Amherst, S. Dak. 61 D1
Amherst, Tex., 883 62 C2
Amherst, co., Va., 22,953 67 K3
Amherst, Va., 1,200 67 K3
Amherst, Wis., 596 69 D3
Amherstdale, W.Va., 1,716 68 B4
Amidon, N. Dak., 84 51 L2
Amissville, Va. 67 L2
Amistad, N. Mex. 46 D2
Amite, La., 3,316 31 D3
Amite, co., Miss., 15,573 39 B4
Amite, r., La. 31 D3
Amity, Ark., 543 15 B3
Amity, Ga. 22 D5
Amity, Mo., 111 40 B2
Amity, Ohio 52 a5
Amity, Oreg., 620 55 L2
Amity, Pa. 56 A5
Amityville, N.Y., 8,890 47 f3
Amlia I., Alaska 13 g8
Amlin, Ohio 52 a5
Amma, W.Va. 68 B3
Ammon, Idaho, 1,882 24 D4
Ammonoosuc, r., N.H. 44 B3
Amnicon L., Wis. 69 A1
Amonate, Va. 66 H3
Amoret, Mo., 261 40 B3
Amorita, Okla., 74 54 E1
Amory, Miss., 6,474 39 D2
Amouli, Tutuila 71 c
Amsterdam, Mo., 118 40 B3
Amsterdam, N.Y., 28,772 49 M5
Amsterdam, Ohio, 931 53 E2
Amston (part of Hebron), Conn. 19 F3
Amukta I., Alaska 12 A5
Amukta Pass, Alaska 12 A5
Amy, Ark. 15 C4
Amy, Kans. 29 B2
Anacacho, Tex. 62 D5
Anacapa I., Calif. 17 D5
Anaconda, Mont., 12,054 41 B2
Anacortes, Wash., 8,414 66 B1
Anacostia, r., D.C.-Md. 33 b5
Anadarko, Okla, 6,299 54 E2
Anae I., Guam 71 a
Anaheim, Calif., 104,184 17 E5
Anaho I., Nev. 43 A2
Anahola, Hawaii 22 G1
Anahuac, Tex., 1,985 63 G5
Anahulu, r., Hawaii 23 d8
Anaktuvuk, r., Alaska 13 F1
Anaktuvuk Pass, Alaska 13 F1
Anamoose, N. Dak., 503 51 M2
Anamosa, Iowa, 4,616 28 F2
Añasco, P.R., 2,068 72 n a1
Añasco, B.de, P.R. 72 n a1
Anatahan, i., Mar. Is. 71 B2
Anawalt, W.Va., 1,062 68 B4
Anbōru, i., Jaluit 72 m
Ancho, N. Mex. 46 C3
Anchor, Ill., 194 25 D3
Anchorage, Alaska, 44,237 13 F3
Anchorage, Ky., 1,369 30 E2
Anchor Bay, Mich. 37 J6
Anchor Bay Gardens, Mich., 1,830 37 e10
Anchor Point, Alaska 13 F4
Anchorville, Mich. 37 J6
Anclote Keys, Fla. 21 c10
Ancon, C.Z., 1,151 72 o
Ancram, N.Y. 49 N6
Ancramdale, N.Y. 49 N6
Andalusia, Ala., 10,263 11 C4
Andalusia, Ill., 769 25 B2
Anderson, Ala. 11 B1
Anderson, Calif., 4,492 17 B1
Anderson, Ind., 49,061 27 C2
Anderson, co., Kans., 9,035 29 G5
Anderson, co., Ky., 8,618 30 E3
Anderson, Mo., 992 40 B5
Anderson, co., S.C., 98,478 59 B2
Anderson, S.C., 41,316 59 B2
Anderson, co., Tenn., 60,032 61 L1
Anderson, co., Tex., 28,162 63 G4
Anderson, Tex. 63 G4
Anderson I., Wash. 67 a6
Anderson Lakes, Minn. 38 b6
Andersonville, Ga., 263 22 B3
Andes, N.Y., 399 49 L6
Andover, Conn., 1,771(T) 19 F3
Andover, Ill., 295 25 B2
Andover, Kans. 29 E3
Andover, Me. 32 A4
Andover, Mass., 15,878(T) 35 K2
Andover, N.H. 44 B5
Andover, N.J., 734 45 B2
Andover, N.Y., 1,247 48 E6
Andover, Ohio, 1,116 53 E1
Andover, S. Dak., 224 61 D1
Andreafsky, r., Alaska 12 C3
Andreanof Is., Alaska 13 g8
Andres, Ill. 25 E2
Andrew, Iowa, 349 28 G2
Andrew, co., Mo., 11,062 40 B2
Andrew Johnson Nat. Mon., Tenn. 61 N1
Andrews, Ind., 1,132 27 C2
Andrews, N.C., 1,404 50 B2
Andrews, Oreg. 55 N3
Andrews, S.C., 2,995 59 E3
Andrews, co., Tex., 13,450 62 C3
Andrews, Tex., 11,135 62 C3
Androscoggin, co., Me., 86,312 32 A4
Androscoggin, r., Me.-N.H. 32 D3
Androscoggin L., Me. 32 A4
Andry, Ind. 26 h4
Aneta, N. Dak., 451 51 O2
Angaur, i., Palau 72 e
Angelica, N.Y., 898 48 E6
Angelica, Wis. 69 E3
Angelina, co., Tex., 39,814 63 G4
Angelina, r., Tex. 63 G4
Angelo, Wis. 69 C4
Angels, Pa. 57 o16
Angels Camp, Calif., 1,121 17 C2
Angelus, Kans. 29 B1
Angelus, S.C. 59 D2
Angie, La., 254 31 E3
Angier, N.C., 1,344 50 G2
Angles Pk., N. Mex. 46 B1
Angleton, Tex., 7,312 63 G5
Angola, Ind., 4,746 27 D1
Angola, N.Y., 2,550 48 B5
Angoon, Alaska, 395 13 K4
Angora, Nebr. 42 A2
Angora, Okla. 54 D2
Angostura Res., S. Dak. 61 A2
Anguilla, Miss., 580 39 B3
Angutikada Pk., Alaska 13 E2
Angwin, Calif. 17 B2
Aniak, Alaska, 308 12 D3
Aniak, r., Alaska 12 D3
Animas, N. Mex. 46 A4
Animas, r., Colo. 18 B3
Animas Pk., N. Mex. 46 A4
Anita, Ariz. 14 B2
Anita, Iowa, 1,233 28 C3
Anita, Pa. 56 C3
Aniwa, Wis., 247 69 D2
Anjean, W.Va. 68 C3
Ankeny, Iowa, 5,910 28 D3
Ankona, Fla. 21 K4
Anmoore, W.Va., 1,050 68 C2
Ann, C., Mass. 35 M2
Anna, Ill., 4,280 25 C6
Anna, Ohio, 701 53 A2
Anna, Tex., 639 62 F3
Anna, N., r., Va. 67 M3
Anna, S., r., Va. 67 M3
Annabella, Utah, 177 64 B2
Annada, Mo., 105 40 F2
Anna Maria, Fla., 690 21 c11
Annandale, Minn., 984 38 B3
Annandale, N.J. 45 B2
Annandale, Va. 67 M2
Annapolis, Ill. 25 E4
Annapolis, Md., 23,385 33 D2
Annapolis, Mo., 334 40 F4
Annapolis, Wash., 1,472 67 a5
Ann Arbor, Mich., 67,340 37 H6
Annawan, Ill., 701 25 B2
Anne Arundel, co., Md., 206,634 33 D1
Anneta, Ky. 30 D3
Anneta, Tex. 63 d11
Annette, Alaska, 337 13 K5
Annisquam (part of Gloucester), Mass. 35 M2
Anniston, Ala., 33,657 11 C2
Anniston, Mo., 307 40 G5
Annona, Tex., 369 63 G3
Annville, Ky. 30 G3
Annville, Pa., 4,264 56 H5
Anoka, co., Minn., 85,916 38 C3
Anoka, Minn., 11,529 38 C3
Anoka, Nebr., 32 42 F1
Año Nuevo, Pt., Calif. 16 b8
Anselmo, Nebr., 269 42 E2
Ansley, La. 31 B1
Ansley, Nebr., 714 42 E2
Anson, Kans. 29 E3
Anson, Me. 32 B4
Anson, co., N.C., 24,962 50 E3
Anson, Tex., 2,890 62 D3
Ansonia, Conn., 19,819 19 C4
Ansonia, Ohio, 1,002 53 A2
Ansonville, N.C., 558 50 E2
Ansted, W. Va., 1,511 68 B3
Ante, Va. 67 M4
Antelope, Calif. 17 j12
Antelope, Mont. 41 F1
Antelope, co., Nebr., 10,176 42 F1
Antelope, Oreg., 46 55 M2
Antelope, Tex. 62 E3
Antelope Hills, Okla. 54 D2
Antelope I., Utah 64 b6
Antelope Pk., Nebr. 42 E1
Antelope Res., Oreg. 55 O3
Antero, Mt., Colo. 18 B2
Antero Res., Colo. 18 C2
Anthon, Iowa, 681 28 A2
Anthon, Okla. 54 E2
Anthony, Fla. 21 H2
Anthony, Kans., 2,744 29 E3
Anthony, N. Mex.-Tex. 46 B3
Anthony (part of Coventry), R.I. 58 B2
Anthony, Tex., 1,082 62 A3
Anthony, W. Va. 68 C4
Antietam Nat. Battlefield Site, Md. 33 C1
Antigo, Wis., 9,691 69 D2
Antimony, Utah, 161 64 B2
Antioch, Calif., 17,305 17 C3
Antioch, Ill., 2,778 25 D1
Antioch, Ind. 27 B2
Antioch, Nebr. 42 B1
Antioch, Ohio, 110 53 E3
Antioch, Okla. 54 F3
Antiquity, Ohio 53 D4
Antler, N. Dak., 210 51 M1
Antlers, Okla., 2,085 55 H3
Antoine, Ark., 163 15 B3
Anton, Colo. 18 D2
Anton, Tex., 1,068 62 C3
Anton Chico, N. Mex. 46 C2
Antonia, Mo. 40 c11
Antonino, Kans. 29 C2
Antonito, Colo., 1,045 18 C3
Antrim, co., Mich., 10,373 36 F3
Antrim, Mich. 36 F4
Antrim, N.H. 44 B5
Antrim, Ohio 53 D2
Antwerp, N.Y., 881 49 J2
Antwerp, Ohio, 1,465 53 A1
Anutt, Mo. 40 E4
Anvik, Alaska, 120 12 C3
Anvik, r., Alaska 12 C3
Aoa, Tutuila 71 c
Aoa Bay, Tutuila 71 c
Aoloau, Tutuila 71 c
Aoloau Bay, Tutuila 71 c
Aomon, i., Eniwetok 72 l
Apache, co., Ariz., 30,438 14 D2
Apache, Ariz. 14 D4
Apache, Okla., 1,455 54 E3
Apache Creek, N. Mex. 46 A3
Apache Cr., N. Mex. 46 A3
Apache Hills, N. Mex. 46 A4
Apache Junction, Ariz. 14 C3
Apache Mtn., N. Mex. 46 A2
Apache Mts., Tex. 62 B4
Apalachee Bay, Fla. 21 F2
Apalachicola, Fla., 3,099 21 E2
Apalachicola, r., Fla. 21 E1
Apalachin, N.Y. 49 H6
Apex, Ky. 30 C3
Apex, N.C., 1,573 50 G2
Apishapa, r., Colo. 18 C3
Aplington, Iowa 28 E2
Apollo, Pa., 2,694 56 B4
Apollo Beach, Fla. 21 d11
Apopka, Fla., 3,578 21 J3
Apopka, L., Fla. 21 J3
Apostle Is., Wis. 69 C1
Appalachia, Va. 66 G4
Appalachian Mts. 9
Appam, N. Dak. 51 L1
Appanoose, co., Iowa, 16,015 28 E4
Apperson, Okla. 54 G1
Apple, r., Ill. 25 B1
Apple, r., Wis. 69 A2
Apple Creek, Ohio, 722 53 D2
Apple Cr., Ill. 25 B4
Applegarth, N.J. 47 b4
Applegate, Mich., 252 37 J5
Applegate, Oreg. 55 L3
Applegate, r., Oreg. 55 L3
Apple River, Ill., 477 25 B1
Appleton, Ark. 15 C2
Appleton, Me. 32 B4
Appleton, Minn., 2,172 38 A3
Appleton, S.C. 59 C3
Appleton, Wis., 48,411 69 E3
Appleton City, Mo., 1,075 40 B3
Apple Valley, Calif. 17 E4
Appleyard, Wash. 66 C2
Appling, co., Ga., 13,246 22 D4
Appling, Ga. 22 D2
Appomattox, co., Va., 9,148 67 L3
Appomattox, Va., 1,184 67 L3
Appomattox, r., Va. 67 L3
Appomattox C.H. Nat. Hist. Pk., Va. 67 L3
Apponagansett (part of Dartmouth), Mass. 35 K6
Apra Hbr., Guam 71 a
Aptakisic, Ill. 26 c2
Aptos, Calif. 16 c9
Apua Pt., Hawaii 23 L4
Apurashokoru, i., Palau 72 e
Aquarius Mts., Ariz. 14 B2
Aquasco, Md. 33 D2
Aquidneck I., R.I. 58 C2
Aquilla, Ohio, 459 53 D1
Aquone, N.C. 50 B2
Arab, Ala., 2,989 11 C1
Arabela, N. Mex. 46 C3
Arabi, Ga., 303 22 C4
Aragon, Ga., 1,023 22 B1
Arambiru, i., Eniwetok 72 k
Aransas, co., Tex., 7,006 62 F5
Aransas Pass, Tex., 6,956 62 F5
Arapaho, Okla., 351 54 D2
Arapahoe, co., Colo., 113,426 18 C2
Arapahoe, Nebr., 1,084 42 E3
Arapahoe, N.C., 274 51 J2
Ararat, Va. 67 J4
Aravaipa, Ariz. 14 C3
Arbonne, Bayou d', La. 31 B1
Arbor Vitae, Wis. 69 D2
Arbuckle, Calif. 17 B2
Arbuckle, L., Fla. 21 J4
Arbutus, Md. 33 c3
Arbutus Beach, Mich. 37 G4
Arbutus L., Wis. 69 C3
Arbyrd, Mo., 667 40 F5
Arcade, Calif. 17 j12
Arcade, N.Y., 1,930 48 D5
Arcadia, Calif., 41,005 16 e10
Arcadia, Fla., 5,889 21 J4
Arcadia, Ind., 1,271 27 B2
Arcadia, Iowa, 437 28 B2
Arcadia, Kans., 507 29 H3
Arcadia, La., 2,547 31 B1
Arcadia, Mich. 36 E4
Arcadia, Mo., 489 40 F4
Arcadia, Nebr., 446 42 E2
Arcadia, Ohio, 610 53 B1
Arcadia, Okla. 54 F2
Arcadia, Pa. 56 D4
Arcadia (part of Richmond and Exeter), R.I. 58 B2
Arcadia, Tex. 63 j15
Arcadia, Wis., 2,084 69 B3
Arcanum, Ohio, 1,678 53 A2
Arcata, Calif., 5,235 17 A1
Arch, N. Mex. 46 D2
Archbald, Pa., 5,471 57 K3
Archbold, Ohio, 2,348 53 A1
Archdale, N.C., 1,520 50 E2
Archer, Fla., 707 21 H2
Archer, Iowa, 209 28 B1
Archer, co., Tex., 6,110 62 E3
Archer City, Tex., 1,974 62 E3
Archers Lodge, N.C. 50 G2
Arches Nat. Mon., Utah 64 C2
Archibald, La. 31 C1
Archie, La. 31 C2
Archie, Mo., 348 40 B3
Archuleta, co., Colo., 2,629 18 B3
Arco, Idaho, 1,562 24 C4
Arcola, Ill., 2,273 25 D4
Arcola, Ind. 27 C1
Arcola, Miss., 366 39 B2
Arcola, Tex. 63 j14
Arctic (part of W. Warwick), R.I. 58 B2
Arctic Ocean 12 A1
Arctic Village, Alaska, 110 13 G1
Arden, Calif. 17 j12
Arden, Del. 20 b4
Arden, Nev. 43 C4
Arden, N.C. 50 C2
Arden Hills, Minn., 4,436 38 c5
Ardmore, Ala., 439 11 C1
Ardmore, Okla., 20,184 54 F3
Ardmore, Pa., 15,175* 57 L6
Ardmore, S. Dak., 73 61 A2
Ardoch, N. Dak., 106 51 O1
Ardsley, N.Y., 4,486 47 d1
Arecibo, P.R., 28,828 72 n b1
Aredale, Iowa, 153 28 E2
Arekalong Pen., Palau 72 e
Arena, Wis., 309 69 D4
Arena, Pt., Calif. 17 B2
Arenac, co., Mich., 9,860 37 H4
Arenas, P., P.R. 72 n d1
Arendtsville, Pa., 588 56 G6
Arenzville, Ill., 417 25 B4
Argenta, Ill. 25 D4
Argo, Ala. 11 d6
Argo, Ill. 25 B1
Argonia, Kans., 553 29 E3
Argonne, Wis. 69 E2
Argos, Ind., 1,339 27 B1
Arguello, Pt., Calif. 17 C4
Argusville, N. Dak., 118 51 O2
Argyle, Fla. 20 D1
Argyle, Ga., 225 22 D4
Argyle, Mich. 37 J5
Argyle, Minn., 789 38 A1
Argyle, Mo., 99 40 D3
Argyle, N.Y. 49 N4
Argyle, Tex. 63 e10
Argyle, Wis., 786 69 D5
Arial, S.C. 59 B2
Arickaree, Colo. 18 D2
Arickaree, r., Colo. 18 D2
Ariel, Wash. 66 B3
Arimo, Idaho, 303 24 C4
Arion, Iowa, 201 28 B3
Aripeka, Fla. 21 H3
Arispe, Iowa, 125 28 C4
Arista, W.Va. 68 B4
Ariton, Ala., 687 11 D4
Arizona, st., 1,635,000* 14
Arizona, La. 31 B1
Arjay, Ky. 30 G4
Arkabutla Res., Miss. 39 B1
Arkadelphia, Ark., 8,069 15 B3
Arkansas, st., 1,969,000* 15
Arkansas, co., Ark., 23,355 15 D3
Arkansas, r. 8b E–H, 3–4
Arkansas, Salt Fk. of, r., Kans.-Okla. 54 D1
Arkansas City, Ark., 783 15 D4
Arkansas City, Kans., 14,262 29 E3
Arkansas Post, Ark. 15 D3
Arkansaw, Wis. 69 A3
Arkdale, Wis. 69 D3
Arkoma, Okla., 1,862 76 J2
Arkport, N.Y., 837 48 E6
Arlee, Mont. 41 B2
Arley, Ala. 11 B1
Arlington, Ala. 11 B3
Arlington, Colo. 18 D2
Arlington, Fla. 21 J1
Arlington, Ga., 1,462 22 B4
Arlington, Ill., 254 25 C2
Arlington, Iowa, 614 28 F2
Arlington, Kans., 466 29 D3
Arlington, Ky., 584 30 B4
Arlington, Mass, 49,953(T) 35 K3
Arlington, Minn., 1,601 38 B3
Arlington, Nebr., 740 42 H2
Arlington, N.C., 590 50 E1
Arlington, N.Y., 8,317 49 N7
Arlington, Ohio, 955 53 B2
Arlington, Okla. 54 G2
Arlington, Oreg., 643 55 M2
Arlington, Pa. 57 o16
Arlington, S. Dak., 996 61 D1
Arlington, Tenn., 620 60 F2
Arlington, Tex., 44,775 63 e11
Arlington, Vt., 1,111 65 A4
Arlington, co., Va. 163,401 67 M2
Arlington, Wash., 2,025 66 B1
Arlington, Wis., 349 69 D4
Arlington Heights, Ill., 40,622 25 D1
Arlington Nat. Cem., Va. 33 a5
Arm, Miss. 39 C4
Arma, Kans., 1,296 29 H3
Armada, Mich., 1,111 37 J6
Armagh, Pa., 192 56 D5
Armijo, N. Mex. 46 B2
Armington, Ill., 327 25 C3
Armona, Calif., 1,302 17 D3
Armonk, N.Y. 47 e1
Armour, S. Dak., 875 61 C2
Armstead, Mont. 41 B3
Armstrong, Ill. 25 E3
Armstrong, Iowa, 958 28 C1
Armstrong, Mo., 387 40 D2
Armstrong, co., Pa., 79,524 56 C4
Armstrong, co., Tex., 1,966 62 D2
Armstrong, Tex. 62 F6
Armstrong Creek, Wis. 69 E2
Arnaudville, La., 1,184 31 C3
Arnegard, N. Dak., 228 51 L2
Arnett, Okla., 547 54 D1
Arnett, W.Va. 68 B4
Arneytown, N.J. 47 a5
Arnheim, Mich. 36 C2
Arno, atoll, Marsh. Is. 71 D3
Arnold, Calif. 17 C2
Arnold, Kans. 29 B2
Arnold, Md. 33 d4
Arnold, Mich. 36 D2
Arnold, Minn. 38 C2
Arnold, Mo. 40 F3
Arnold, Nebr., 844 42 D2
Arnold, Pa., 9,437 56 B4
Arnoldsburg, W.Va. 68 B3
Arnolds Park, Iowa, 953 28 B1
Arnot, Pa. 56 G2
Arnot Pk., Calif. 17 D2
Arock, Oreg. 55 O3
Aroda, Va. 67 L2
Aroma Park, Ill., 744 25 E2
Aromas, Calif. 16 c9
Arona, Pa., 467 56 d8
Aroostook, co., Me., 106,064 32 C2
Aroostook, r., Me. 32 C2
Aroya, Colo. 18 D2
Arp, Tenn. 60 F2
Arp, Tex., 812 63 G3
Arpelar, Okla. 55 G3
Arpin, Wis. 69 D3
Arran, Fla. 21 F1
Arrey, N. Mex. 46 B3
Arriba, Colo., 296 18 D2
Arrington, Kans. 29 G1
Arrington, Tenn. 61 J2
Arriola, Colo. 18 A3
Arrowbear Lake, Calif. 16 g10
Arrowhead, L., Calif. 16 g10
Arrow Rock, Mo., 245 40 C2
Arrowsic, Me. 32 B5
Arrowsmith, Ill., 319 25 D3
Arroyo, P.R., 3,741 72 n c2
Arroyo Grande, Calif., 3,291 17 C4
Arroyo Hondo, N. Mex. 46 B1
Artas, S. Dak., 87 61 C1
Artesia, Ariz. 14 D3
Artesia, Calif., 9,993 16 e11
Artesia, Colo., 318 18 A1
Artesia, Miss., 469 39 D2
Artesia, N. Mex., 12,000 46 C3
Artesian, S. Dak., 330 61 C2
Artesia Wells, Tex. 62 E5
Arthur, Ill., 2,120 25 D4
Arthur, Iowa, 265 28 B2
Arthur, co., Nebr., 680 42 C2
Arthur, Nebr., 165 42 C2
Arthur, Nev. 43 C1
Arthur, N. Dak., 325 51 O2
Arthur, Tenn. 61 M1
Arthur, Wis. 69 C5
Arthur, L., La. 31 B3
Arthur Kill, N.Y. 47 e3
Artie, W.Va. 68 B4
Artois, Calif. 17 B2
Aruboe, i., Jaluit 72 m
Arukoron C., Palau 72 e
Aru Pt., Ponape 72 h
Arus, P.R. 72 b1
Arvada, Colo., 19,242 18 C2
Arvilla, N. Dak. 51 O2
Arvin, Calif., 5,440 17 D4
Arvonia, Kans. 29 G2
Arvonia, Va. 67 L3
Asan, Guam 71 a
Asan Pt., Guam 71 a
Asbury, Mo., 186 40 B4
Asbury, N.J. 45 A2
Asbury Grove, Mass. 35 L2
Asbury Park, N.J., 17,366 45 D3
Ascension, parish, La., 27,927 31 D3
Ascutney, Vt. 65 C4
Ascutney, Mt., Vt. 65 C4
Ash, N.C. 50 G3
Ash, Oreg. 55 L3
Ashaway, R.I., 1,298 58 A3
Ashburn, Ga., 3,291 22 C4
Ashburnham, Mass., 2,758(T) 35 G2
Ashby, Mass., 1,883(T) 35 G2
Ashby, Minn., 426 38 B2
Ashby, Nebr. 42 C1
Ash Cr., Utah 64 A3
Ashdown, Ark., 3,102 15 A4
Ashe, co., N.C., 19,768 50 D1
Asheboro, N.C., 9,449 50 F2
Ashepoo, S.C. 59 D4
Ashepoo, r., S.C. 59 D4
Asher, Okla., 343 54 G3
Asherton, Tex., 1,890 62 D5
Asherville, Kans. 29 D1
Asheville, N.C., 60,192 50 C2
Ashfield, Mass., 1,131(T) 34 C2
Ash Flat, Ark., 192 15 D1
Ashford, Ala., 1,511 11 D4
Ashford, Conn., 1,315(T) 19 G2
Ashford, N.C. 50 D2
Ashford, Wash. 66 C2
Ashford, W.Va. 68 B3
Ashford, Wis. 69 E4
Ashfork, Ariz. 14 B2
Ash Grove, Kans. 29 D1
Ash Grove, Mo., 886 40 C4
Ashkum, Ill., 601 25 D3
Ash Lake, Minn. 38 C1
Ashland, Ala., 1,610 11 D2
Ashland, Ill., 1,064 25 B4
Ashland, Kans., 1,312 29 C3
Ashland, Ky., 31,283 30 H2
Ashland, La. 31 A1
Ashland, Me. 32 C2
Ashland, Mass., 7,779(T) 35 J3
Ashland, Miss., 309 39 C1
Ashland, Mo., 495 40 D3
Ashland, Mont. 41 E3
Ashland, Nebr., 1,989 42 H2
Ashland, N.H., 1,237 44 B4
Ashland, N.Y. 49 M6
Ashland, co., Ohio, 38,771 53 C2
Ashland, Ohio, 17,419 53 C2
Ashland, Okla., 87 55 H3
Ashland, Oreg., 9,119 55 L3
Ashland, Pa., 5,237 56 J4
Ashland, Va., 2,773 67 M3
Ashland, co., Wis., 17,375 69 C1
Ashland, Wis., 10,132 69 C1
Ashland, Mt., Oreg. 55 L3
Ashland City, Tenn., 1,400 61 H1
Ashley, co., Ark., 24,220 15 D4
Ashley, Ill., 662 25 C5
Ashley, Ind., 721 27 C1
Ashley, Mich., 448 37 G5
Ashley, Mo. 40 E2
Ashley, N. Dak., 1,419 51 N2
Ashley, Ohio, 907 53 C2
Ashley, Pa., 4,258 57 K3
Ashley, r., S.C. 59 D4
Ashley Cr., Utah 64 C1
Ashley Falls (part of Sheffield), Mass. 34 A4
Ashmore, Ill., 447 25 D4
Ashokan, N.Y. 49 M7
Ashokan Res., N.Y. 49 M7
Ashridge, Ala. 11 B1
Ashtabula, co., Ohio, 93,067 53 E1
Ashtabula, Ohio, 24,944 53 E1
Ashtabula, L., N. Dak. 51 O2
Ashton, Idaho, 1,242 24 D3
Ashton, Ill., 1,024 25 C2
Ashton, Iowa, 615 28 B1
Ashton, Kans. 29 E3
Ashton, Md. 33 a4
Ashton, Mich. 36 F5
Ashton, Nebr., 320 42 F2
Ashton (part of Cumberland), R.I. 58 C1
Ashton, S. Dak., 182 61 C1
Ashuelot, N.H. 44 A6
Ashuelot, r., N.H. 44 A5
Ashuelot Pd., N.H. 44 A5
Ash Valley, Kans. 29 C2
Ashville, Ala., 973 11 C2
Ashville, Fla. 21 G1
Ashville, Ohio, 1,639 53 C3
Ashville, Pa., 422 56 D4
Ashwood, Oreg. 55 M2
Asiga Pt., Tinian 72 f
Asili, Tutuila 71 c
Askam, Pa. 57 n17
Askewville, N.C., 195 51 J1
Askov, Minn., 331 38 C2
Aslito, Saipan 72 e
Asotin, co., Wash., 12,909 66 E2
Asotin, Wash., 745 66 E2
Aspen, Colo., 1,101 18 B2
Aspen Butte, Oreg. 55 L3
Aspen Hill, Tenn. 61 H2
Aspermont, Tex., 1,286 62 D3
Aspetuck (part of Easton), Conn. 19 B5
Aspinwall, Iowa, 95 28 B3
Aspinwall, Pa., 3,727 56 c8
Assabet, r., Mass. 35 H3
Assaria, Kans., 322 29 E2
Assateague I., Md.-Va. 33 E2
Assawompset Pd., Mass. 35 L5
Assinins, Mich. 36 C2
Assinippi (part of Hanover and Norwell), Mass. 35 L4
Assiscunk Cr., N.J. 45 B3
Assonet, Mass. 35 K5
Assumption, Ill., 1,439 25 D4
Assumption, parish, La., 17,991 31 C4
Assumption, Ohio 53 A1
Assunpink Cr., N.J. 45 B3
Assyria, Mich. 36 F6
Asti, Calif. 17 B2
Astico, Wis. 69 E4
Astor, Fla. 21 J2
Astoria, Ill., 1,206 25 B3
Astoria, Oreg., 11,239 55 L1
Asuncion, i., Mar. Is. 71 B2
Atafu, i., Tokelau Is. 71 E4
Atalissa, Iowa, 212 28 F3
Atanik, Alaska 13 C1
Atascadero, Calif., 5,983 17 C4
Atascosa, co., Tex., 18,828 62 E5
Atascosa, r., Tex. 62 E5
Atchafalaya, r., La. 31 C3
Atchafalaya Bay, La. 31 C4
Atchison, co., Kans., 20,898 29 G1
Atchison, Kans., 12,529 29 G1
Atchison, co., Mo., 9,213 40 A1
Atco, N.J., 2,500* 45 B4
Atglen, Pa., 721 57 K6
Athalia, Ohio, 341 53 C4
Athelstane, Wis. 69 E2
Athena, Fla. 21 G2
Athena, Oreg., 950 55 N2
Athens, Ala., 9,330 11 B1
Athens, Ark., 67 15 B3
Athens, Ga., 31,355 22 C2
Athens, Ill., 1,035 25 C4
Athens, Ind. 27 B1
Athens, La., 406 31 B1
Athens, Me. 32 B4
Athens, Mich., 966 36 F6
Athens, N.Y., 1,754 49 N6
Athens, co., Ohio, 46,998 53 C3
Athens, Ohio, 16,470 53 C3
Athens, Pa., 4,515 56 H2
Athens, Tenn., 12,103 61 L2
Athens, Tex., 7,086 63 G3
Athens, W.Va., 1,086 68 C4
Athens, Wis., 770 69 C2
Athensville, Ill. 25 B4
Atherton, Calif., 7,717 16 b8
Athol, Idaho, 214 24 A2
Athol, Kans., 140 29 D1
Athol, Mass., 10,161;11,637(T) 34 F2
Athol, N.Y. 49 N4
Athol, Pa. 57 e10
Athol, S. Dak. 61 C2
Athol Springs, N.Y. 48 g16
Atholton, Md. 33 b4
Atka, Alaska, 119 13 g8
Atka I., Alaska 13 g8
Atkins, Ark., 1,436 15 C2
Atkins, Iowa, 527 28 F3
Atkins, Va. 66 H4
Atkinson, co., Ga., 6,188 22 D4
Atkinson, Ga. 22 E4
Atkinson, Ill., 944 25 C2
Atkinson, Nebr., 1,324 42 F1
Atkinson, N.C., 290 50 G3
Atlanta, Ga., 487,455 22 B2
Atlanta, Idaho 24 B4
Atlanta, Ill., 1,568 25 C3
Atlanta, Ind., 602 27 B2
Atlanta, Kans., 267 29 F3
Atlanta, La. 31 B2
Atlanta, Mich. 37 G3
Atlanta, Mo., 386 40 D2
Atlanta, Nebr., 107 42 E3
Atlanta, N.Y. 48 F5
Atlanta, Tex., 4,076 63 G3
Atlantic, Iowa, 6,890 28 C3
Atlantic, co., N.J., 160,880 45 B5
Atlantic, N.C. 51 J3
Atlantic, Pa. 56 A2
Atlantic Beach, Fla., 3,125 21 J1
Atlantic Beach, N.Y., 1,082 47 e3
Atlantic Beach, N.C., 76 51 J3
Atlantic Beach, S.C. 59 F3
Atlantic City, N.J., 59,544 45 C5
Atlantic Highlands, N.J., 4,119 45 D3
Atlantic Mine, Mich. 36 C1
Atlantic Ocean 8b L–N, 2–5
Atlantic Pk., Wyo. 70 B2
Atlas, Ill., 25 B4
Atlas, Mich. 37 H6
Atlasburg, Pa. 56 a8
Atmore, Ala., 11 B4

For abbreviations and explanation of index, see page 176.

B

For abbreviations and explanation of index, see page 176.

For abbreviations and explanation of index, see page 176.

Birch Bay INDEX TO MAPS OF THE UNITED STATES Braddock Heights

Birch Bay, Wash. 66 B1
Birch Cr., Alaska 13 G2
Birchdale, Minn. 38 B1
Birches, Alaska 13 E2
Birch L., Minn. 38 D2
Birch L., Wis. 69 E2
Birchleaf, Va. 66 G3
Birch River, W.Va. 68 C3
Birch Run, Mich., 844 37 H5
Birch Str., Me. 32 C3
Birch Tree, Mo., 420 40 E5
Birchwood, Alaska, 534 12 c7
Birchwood, Minn., 598 38 d5
Birchwood, Wis., 433 69 B2
Bird City, Kans., 678 29 A1
Bird Cr., Okla. 55 G1
Bird Island, Minn., 1,384 38 B3
Birds, Ill., 235 25 E5
Birdsboro, Pa., 3,025 57 K5
Bird Settlement, Alaska, 25 12 c7
Birdseye, Ind., 366 27 B4
Birds Landing, Calif. 16 c6
Birkenfeld, Oreg. 55 L2
Birmingham, Ala., 340,887 11 B2
Birmingham, Ill. 25 B3
Birmingham, Iowa, 441 28 F4
Birmingham, Mich., 25,525 37 c10
Birmingham, Mo., 201 40 b7
Birmingham, Pa., 136 56 E4
Birnamwood, Wis., 568 69 D3
Birney, Mont. 41 E3
Biron, Wis., 726 69 D3
Bisbee, Ariz., 9,272 14 D4
Bisbee, N. Dak., 388 51 N1
Biscayne, Key, Fla. 20 b9
Biscayne Bay, Fla. 20 b9
Biscayne Can., Fla. 20 a9
Biscayne Park, Fla., 2,911 20 b9
Biscoe, Ark. 15 D3
Biscoe, N.C., 1,053 50 F2
Bishop, Calif., 2,958 17 D3
Bishop, Ga., 214 22 C2
Bishop, Tex., 3,722 62 F6
Bishop Hill, Ill., 164 25 B2
Bishopville, S.C., 3,586 59 D2
Bismarck, Ark. 15 B3
Bismarck, Ill. 25 E3
Bismarck, Mo., 1,237 40 F4
Bismarck, N. Dak., 30,584 51 M2
Bismarck, W.Va. 68 D2
Bison, Kans., 291 29 C2
Bison, Okla. 54 F1
Bison, S. Dak., 457 61 A1
Bison Mtn., Colo. 18 a6
Bistineau, L., La. 31 A1
Bitely, Mich. 36 F5
Bithlo, Fla., 168 21 J3
Bitter Creek, Wyo. 70 B3
Bitter L., S. Dak. 61 D1
Bitterroot Ra., Idaho-Mont. 24 B2
Bitterwater, Calif. 17 C3
Bivalve, N.J. 45 A5
Biwabik, Minn., 1,836 38 C2
Bixby, Mo. 40 E4
Bixby, Okla., 1,711 55 H2
Blabon, N. Dak. 51 O2
Blachly, Oreg. 55 L2
Black, Ala., 133 11 D4
Black, r., Alaska 13 H2
Black, r., Ariz. 14 D3
Black, r., Ark.-Mo. 166 B2-3
Black, r., La. 31 C2
Black, r., Mich. 36 A2
Black, r., Mich. 37 G3
Black, r., Mich. 37 J5
Black, r., Mo. 40 F4
Black, r., N.Y. 49 J2
Black, r., N.C. 50 G3
Black, r., Ohio 52 c8
Black, r., S.C. 59 E3
Black, r., Vt. 65 B4
Black, r., Vt. 65 C1
Black, r., Wash. 67 a6
Black, r., Wis. 69 C2
Black Bear Cr., Okla. 54 F1
Blackbeard I., Ga. 22 E4
Blackberry, r., Conn. 19 B1
Black Bk., Me. 32 B3
Blackburn, Ark. 15 A2
Blackburn, Mo., 310 40 C2
Blackburn, Okla., 129 54 G1
Blackburn, Mt., Alaska 13 H3
Blackburn Village (part of Ashburnham), Mass. 35 G2
Black Butte, Oreg. 55 L3
Black Canyon City, Ariz. 14 B2
Black Canyon of the Gunnison Nat. Mon., Colo. 18 B2
Black Creek, N.Y. 48 D6
Black Creek, N.C., 310 50 H2
Black Creek, Wis., 707 69 E3
Black Cr., Ariz. 14 D2
Black Cr., Miss. 39 C4
Black Cr., N.Y. 48 j17
Black Cr., S.C. 59 E2
Black Cr., Vt. 65 B1
Black Diablo Mine, Nev. 43 B1
Black Diamond, Wash., 1,026 66 C2
Blackduck, Minn., 765 38 B2
Black Earth, Wis., 784 69 D4
Blackey, Va. 66 G3
Blackfoot, Idaho, 7,378 24 C4
Blackfoot River Res., Idaho 24 D4
Blackford, co., Ind., 14,792 27 C2
Black Forest, Colo. 18 C2
Blackfork, Ohio 53 C4
Black Hall (part of Old Lyme), Conn. 19 F4
Black Hawk, Colo., 171 18 b5
Blackhawk, Ind. 27 C3
Black Hawk, co., Iowa, 122,482 28 E2
Black Hawk, S. Dak. 61 A1
Black Hawk, Wis. 69 C4
Blackhawk Beach, Ind. 26 f4
Black Hills, S. Dak. 61 A1
Blackinton (part of N. Adams), Mass. 34 B2
Black Jack, Mo. 40 d9
Black Lake, N. Mex. 46 C1
Black L., La. 31 A2
Black L., Mich. 37 G3
Black L., N.Y. 49 J2
Black L., Wash. 67 a7
Blackledge, r., Conn. 19 F3
Blacklick, Ohio 52 b5
Black Lick, Pa. 56 C5
Blacklick Cr., Ohio 52 b6
Blacklick Cr., Pa. 56 C5
Blacklog Cr., Pa. 56 F5
Black Mesa, Ariz. 14 C1
Black Mesa, Okla. 54 A1
Black Mountain, N.C., 1,313 50 C2
Black Mtn., Me. 32 A4
Black Mtn., N. Mex. 46 A3
Black Mtn., N.Y. 49 O3
Black Mts., Ariz. 14 A2
Black Mts., Tex. 62 B4
Black Oak, Ind. 26 e4
Black Pk., N. Mex. 46 A3
Black Point, Calif. 16 a6
Black Point (part of E. Lyme), Conn. 19 G4
Black Pd., Me. 32 B2
Black Range., N. Mex. 46 B3
Black River, Mich. 37 H4
Black River, N.Y., 1,237 49 J2
Black River Falls, Wis., 3,195 69 C3
Black River Village, N. Mex. 46 C3
Black Rock, Ark., 554 15 D1
Black Rock, Utah 64 A2
Black Rock Des., Nev. 43 A1
Black Rock Des., Utah 64 A2
Black Rock Ra., Nev. 43 A1
Blacksburg, S.C., 2,174 59 C1
Blacksburg, Va., 7,070 67 J3
Blackshear, Ga., 2,482 22 D4
Blacksher, Ala. 11 B4
Black Springs, Ark. 15 B3
Black Springs, N. Mex. 46 A3
Blackstock, S.C. 59 C2
Blackstone, Mass., 5,130(T) 35 H4
Blackstone, Va., 3,659 67 M3
Blackstone, r., Mass. 35 H4
Black Str., Me. 32 B4
Blacksville, W.Va., 211 68 C2
Black Top Mtn., N. Mex. 46 B3
Blackville, S.C., 1,901 59 C3
Black Walnut, Mo. 40 c9
Black Warrior, r., Ala. 11 B2
Blackwater, Mo., 284 40 D3
Blackwater, Va. 67 A4
Blackwater, r., Fla. 20 D1
Blackwater, r., Mo. 40 C3
Blackwater, r., N.H. 44 B5
Blackwater, r., Va. 67 K3
Blackwater, r., Va. 67 M3
Blackwater Cr., Fla. 21 d11
Blackwell, Okla., 9,588 54 F1
Blackwell, Tex., 314 62 D3
Blackwell Bk., Conn. 19 G2
Blackwood, N.J., 3,100* 45 A4
Bladen, Nebr., 322 42 F3
Bladen, co., N.C., 26,605 50 G3
Bladen, Ohio 53 C4
Bladenboro, N.C., 805 50 G3
Bladensburg, Md., 3,103 33 b4
Bladensburg, Ohio 53 C2
Blades, Del., 729 20 A3
Bladon Springs, Ala. 11 A4
Blain, Pa., 336 56 G5
Blaine, co., Idaho, 4,598 24 B4
Blaine, Ind. 27 C2
Blaine, Kans. 29 F1
Blaine, Ky. 30 H2
Blaine, Me. 32 D2
Blaine, Minn., 15,544 38 C3
Blaine, co., Mont., 8,091 41 D1
Blaine, co., Nebr., 1,016 42 D2
Blaine, co., Okla., 12,077 54 E2
Blaine, Oreg. 55 L2
Blaine, Wash., 1,735 66 B1
Blair, Nebr., 4,931 42 H2
Blair, Okla., 893 54 D3
Blair, co., Pa., 137,270 56 E4
Blair, Wis., 909 69 B3
Blairs, Va. 67 K4
Blairsburg, Iowa, 287 28 D2
Blairsden, Calif. 17 C2
Blairstown, Iowa, 583 28 E3
Blairstown, Mo., 177 40 B3
Blairstown, N.J. 45 B2
Blairsville, Ga., 437 22 B1
Blairsville, Ind. 27 A4
Blairsville, Pa., 4,930 56 C5
Blaisdell, N. Dak. 51 L1
Blakely, Ga., 5,190 22 B4
Blakely, Pa., 6,374 57 n16
Blake Pt., Mich. 36 b8
Blakesburg, Iowa, 401 28 E4
Blalock, Oreg. 55 M2
Blanca, Colo., 233 18 C3
Blanca, Sa., N. Mex. 46 B3
Blanca, Sa., Tex. 62 B4
Blanca Pk., Colo. 18 C3
Blanchard, Iowa, 174 28 B4
Blanchard, La. 31 A1
Blanchard, Me. 32 B3
Blanchard, Mich. 36 F5
Blanchard, Ohio 53 B2
Blanchard, Okla., 1,377 54 F2
Blanchard, Wash. 66 B1
Blanchard, r., Ohio 53 B1
Blanchardville, Wis., 632 69 D5
Blanchester, Ohio, 2,944 53 B3
Blanco, N. Mex. 46 B1
Blanco, Okla. 55 H3
Blanco, co., Tex., 3,657 62 E4
Blanco, Tex., 789 62 E4
Blanco, r., Tex. 62 E4
Blanco, C., Oreg. 55 K3
Blanco Cr., N. Mex.-Tex. 46 D2
Blanco Trading Post., N. Mex. 46 B1
Bland, Mo., 654 40 E3
Bland, co., Va., 5,982 67 H3
Bland, Va. 67 H3
Blandburg, Pa. 56 E4
Blandford, Mass. 34 C4
Blanding, Utah, 1,805 64 C3
Blandinsville, Ill., 853 25 A3
Blandon, Pa., 57 h14
Blaney Park, Mich. 36 F2
Blanket, Tex., 320 62 E4
Blasdell, N.Y., 3,786 48 C5
Blawnox, Pa., 2,085 56 c8
Bleckley, co., Ga., 9,642 22 C3
Bledsoe, co., Tenn., 7,811 61 K2
Bledsoe, Tex. 62 C3
Bleecker, N.Y. 49 M4
Blencoe, Iowa, 286 28 A3
Blenheim, N.J., 57 f12
Blenheim, S.C., 185 59 E2
Blenker, Wis. 69 D3
Blessing, Tex. 62 F5
Blevins, Ark., 198 15 B4
Blewett Falls L., N.C. 50 F2
Bliss, Idaho, 91 24 B4
Bliss, Mich. 37 G3
Bliss, N.Y. 48 D5
Blissfield, Mich., 2,653 37 G7
Blissfield, Ohio 53 D2
Blitchton, Ga. 22 E3
Blocher, Ind. 27 C4
Blocker, Okla. 55 H2
Blockhouse, Wash. 66 C3
Block I., R.I. 58 B4
Block I. Sd., R.I. 58 A4
Blockton, Iowa, 343 28 C4
Blockville, N.Y. 48 A6
Blodgett, Miss. 39 D4
Blodgett, N.H., 1,489 44 C5
Blodgett, Oreg. 55 L2
Blodgett Landing, N.H. 44 A5
Bloodroot Mtn., Vt. 65 B3
Bloods Bk., N.H. 44 A4
Bloom, Kans. 29 C3
Bloomburg, Tex., 383 63 H3
Bloom City, Wis. 69 C4
Bloomdale, Ohio, 669 53 B1
Bloomer, Wis., 2,834 69 B2
Bloomfield, Conn., 13,613(T) 19 D2
Bloomfield, Ill. 25 E4
Bloomfield, Ind., 2,224 27 B3
Bloomfield, Iowa, 2,771 28 E4
Bloomfield, Ky., 916 30 E3
Bloomfield, Mo., 1,330 40 F5
Bloomfield, Nebr., 1,349 42 G1
Bloomfield, N.J., 51,867 45 C2
Bloomfield, N. Mex., 1,292 46 A1
Bloomfield, Ohio 53 D2
Bloomfield, Vt. 65 D1
Bloomfield, Wis. 69 E3
Bloomfield Hills, Mich., 2,378 37 d10
Bloomingburg, N.Y., 303 49 L7
Bloomingburg, Ohio, 719 53 B3
Bloomingdale, Ill., 1,262 26 b3
Bloomingdale, Ind., 455 27 A3
Bloomingdale, Mich., 471 36 E6
Bloomingdale, N.J., 5,293 47 b1
Bloomingdale, N.Y., 490 49 M2
Blooming Glen, Pa. 57 f10
Blooming Grove, Tex., 725 62 F3
Blooming Prairie, Minn., 1,778 38 C4
Bloomington, Idaho, 254 24 D4
Bloomington, Ill., 37,791 25 D3
Bloomington, Ind., 42,058 27 B3
Bloomington, Minn., 66,542 38 b6
Bloomington, Nebr. 42 E3
Bloomington, Tex., 1,756 62 F5
Bloomington, Wis., 735 69 C5
Blooming Valley, Pa., 296 56 A2
Bloomsburg, Pa., 10,655 56 J4
Bloomsbury, N.J., 838 45 A2
Bloomville, N.Y. 49 L6
Bloomville, Ohio, 836 53 B1
Blossburg, Pa., 1,956 56 G2
Blossom, N.Y. 48 h16
Blossom, Tex., 545 63 G3
Blount, co., Ala., 25,449 11 C1
Blount, co., Tenn., 57,525 61 L2
Blountstown, Fla., 2,375 21 E1
Blountsville, Ala., 672 11 C1
Blountsville, Ind., 218 27 C2
Blountville, Tenn. 61 N1
Blowing Rock, N.C., 711 50 D1
Bloxom, Va., 349 67 O3
Blue, Ariz. 14 D3
Blue, Okla. 55 G4
Blue, r., Ariz. 14 D3
Blue, r., Colo. 18 B2
Blue, r., Ind. 27 B4
Blue, r., Mo. 40 a8
Blue, r., Okla. 55 G3
Blue, Mt., Me. 32 A4
Blue, Mt., N.H. 44 B3
Blue Ash, Ohio, 8,341 52 j9
Bluebell, Utah 64 B1
Blue Creek, Utah 64 b4
Blue Creek, W.Va. 68 B3
Blue Cr., Nebr. 42 B2
Blue Cypress L., Fla. 21 K4
Blue Diamond, Nev. 43 C3
Blue Earth, co., Minn., 44,385 38 B3
Blue Earth, Minn., 4,200 38 C4
Blue Earth, r., Minn. 38 B4
Bluefield, Va., 4,235 67 H3
Bluefield, W.Va., 19,256 68 B4
Blue Grass, Iowa, 733 28 G3
Blue Grass, Va. 67 K2
Blue Hill, Me. 32 C4
Blue Hill, Nebr., 723 42 F3
Blue Hill Bay, Me. 32 C4
Blue Hill Falls, Me. 32 C4
Blue Hills (part of Bloomfield), Conn. 19 E2
Blue Island, Ill., 21,986 25 E2
Blue Jacket, Okla., 245 55 H1
Bluejoint L., Oreg. 55 N3
Blue Knob, mtn., Pa. 56 D5
Blue Lake, Calif., 1,234 17 B1
Blue Mesa, Colo. 18 B2
Blue Mound, Ill., 1,038 25 C4
Blue Mound, Tex., 1,253 63 e11
Blue Mounds, Wis., 227 69 D4
Blue Mountain, Ala., 446 11 D2
Blue Mountain, Ark., 94 15 B2
Blue Mountain, Colo. 18 A1
Blue Mountain, Miss., 741 39 D1
Blue Mtn., Ariz. 14 B2
Blue Mtn., Ark. 15 A3
Blue Mtn., Colo. 18 b4
Blue Mtn., N.Y. 49 M3
Blue Mtn., Pa. 56 F5
Blue Mountain Lake, N.Y. 49 M3
Blue Mtn. Pass, Oreg. 55 O3
Blue Mts., Me. 32 A4
Blue Mts., Oreg.-Wash. 55 N2
Blue Nose, mtn., Idaho 24 B3
Blue Point, N.Y. 47 g3
Blue Rapids, Kans., 1,426 29 F1
Blue Ridge, Ga., 1,406 22 B1
Blue Ridge, Va. 67 K3
Blue Ridge, N.Y. 49 L3
Blue Ridge, N.Y. 49 N3
Blue Ridge, mtn. ra. 8a
Blue Ridge L., Ga. 22 E6
Blue Ridge Summit, Pa. 56 G6
Blue River, Oreg. 55 L2
Blue River, Wis., 356 69 C4
Blue Rock, Ohio 53 D3
Blue Springs, Ala., 94 11 D4
Blue Springs, Mo., 2,555 40 B2
Blue Springs, Nebr., 509 42 H3
Bluestone Res., W. Va. 68 B4
Bluewater, N. Mex. 46 A2
Bluff, Ala. 11 B2
Bluff, Alaska 13 b6
Bluff, Okla. 55 H4
Bluff, Utah 64 C3
Bluff City, Ark. 15 B4
Bluff City, Ill. 25 B3
Bluff City, Kans., 152 29 E3
Bluff City, Tenn., 948 61 N1
Bluff Dale, Tex. 63 d12
Bluffdale, Utah 64 b7
Bluff Hall, Ill. 25 A4
Bluff Park, Ala. 11 c7
Bluffs, Ill., 779 25 B4
Bluffside, Ind., 1,372 26 h4
Bluff Siding, Wis. 69 B3
Bluff Springs, Ill. 25 B4
Bluff Springs, Tex. 62 c7
Bluffton, Ark. 15 B3
Bluffton, Ga., 176 22 B4
Bluffton, Ind., 7,052 27 C2
Bluffton, Minn., 211 38 B2
Bluffton, Ohio, 2,591 53 B2
Bluffton, S.C., 356 59 D4
Bluford, Ill., 388 25 D5
Bluit, N. Mex. 46 D3
Blum, Tex., 315 62 F3
Blunt, S. Dak., 532 61 B1
Bly, Oreg. 55 M3
Blyn, Wash. 67 a4
Blythe, Calif., 6,023 17 F5
Blythedale, Mo., 179 40 C1
Blythedale, Pa., 56 c9
Blytheville, Ark., 25,883 15 F2
Blythewood, S.C. 59 D2
Boalsburg, Pa., 56 F4
Boardman, N.C. 50 F3
Boardman, r., Mich. 36 F4
Boaz, Ala., 4,654 11 C1
Boaz, N. Mex. 46 D3
Boaz, Wis., 117 69 C4
Bobs Cr., Pa. 56 D5
Bobtown, Pa., 1,167 56 A6
Boca Chica, Tex. 62 F7
Boca Chica Key, Fla. 21 f14
Boca Grande, Fla. 21 H5
Boca Grande Key, Fla. 21 e14
Boca Raton, Fla., 6,961 21 K5
Bodcau, Bayou, Ark.-La. 15 B4
Bodcaw, Ark. 15 B4
Bode, Iowa, 430 28 C2
Bodega Bay, Calif. 17 B2
Bodfish, Calif. 17 D4
Boelus, Nebr. 42 F2
Boerne, Tex., 2,169 62 E5
Boeuf, r., La. 31 C1
Boeuf, Bayou, La. 31 B2
Bogachiel, r., Wash. 66 A2
Bogallua, i., Eniwetok 72 k
Bogalusa, La., 21,423 31 E3
Bogan, i., Eniwetok 72 k
Bogart, Ohio 53 C1
Bogata, Tex., 1,112 63 G3
Bogen, i., Eniwetok 72 k
Bogenaga, i., Jaluit 72 m
Boger City, N.C., 1,728 50 D2
Boggenatjen, i., Kwajalein 72 l
Boggerik, i., Kwajalein 72 l
Bogia, Fla. 20 C1
Bogombogo, i., Eniwetok 72 k
Bogon, i., Eniwetok 72 k
Bogota, Ill., 25 D5
Bogota, Tenn. 60 F1
Bogue, Kans., 234 29 C1
Bogue, N.C. 51 J3
Bogue Chitto, r., La. 31 D3
Bogue Homa Cr., Miss. 39 C4
Bohemia, N.Y. 47 g2
Bohners L., Wis. 69 a9
Boicourt, Kans. 29 H2
Boiling Springs, N.C., 1,771 50 D2
Boiling Springs, Pa., 1,182 56 G5
Bois Blanc I., Mich. 37 G3
Bois Brule, r., Wis. 69 B1
Bois Bubert I., Me. 32 D4
Bois D'Arc, Mo. 40 C4
Bois de Sioux, r., Minn.-N. Dak. 38 A2
Boise, co., Idaho, 1,646 24 B3
Boise, Idaho, 72,090 24 A4
Boise, r., Idaho 24 B4
Boise City, Okla., 1,978 54 A1
Bokarijiman, i., Jaluit 72 m
Bokchito, Okla., 620 55 G3
Bokeelia, Fla. 21 H5
Bokoshe, Okla., 431 55 J2
Bolanos Mt., Guam 71 a
Bolckow, Mo., 232 40 B1
Bold Spring, Tenn. 61 H2
Boles, Ark. 15 A3
Boley, Okla., 573 55 G2
Boligee, Ala., 134 11 A3
Boling, Tex. 63 F5
Bolinger, La. 31 A1
Bolivar, co., Miss., 54,464 39 B2
Bolivar, Mo., 3,512 40 C4
Bolivar, N.Y., 1,405 48 D6
Bolivar, Ohio, 932 53 D2
Bolivar, Pa., 716 56 C5
Bolivar, Tenn., 3,338 60 F2
Bolivar Pen., Tex. 62 G5
Bolivia, N.C., 201 50 G3
Bolling, Ala. 11 C4
Bollinger, co., Mo., 9,167 40 F4
Bolton, Conn., 2,933(T) 19 F2
Bolton, Ill. 25 C1
Bolton, Kans. 29 G3
Bolton, Mass., 1,264(T) 35 H3
Bolton, Mich. 37 H3
Bolton, Miss., 797 39 B3
Bolton, N.Y. 49 N3
Bolton, N.C., 617 50 G3
Bolton, Vt. 65 B2
Bolton Landing, N.Y. 49 N3
Bolton Mtn., Vt. 65 B2
Bolton Notch (part of Bolton), Conn. 19 F2
Boltonville, Vt. 65 C2
Boltonville, Wis. 69 E4
Boma, Tenn. 61 K1
Bomar, Okla. 54 F4
Bombay, N.Y. 49 L1
Bomoseen, L., Vt. 65 A3
Bona, Mt., Alaska 13 H3
Bon Air, Tenn. 61 K2
Bon Air, Va. 67 M3
Bonanza, Ark., 247 15 A2
Bonanza, Colo. 18 B2
Bonanza, Oreg., 297 55 M3
Bonanza, Utah 64 C2
Bonanza Pk., Wash. 66 C1
Bonaparte, Iowa, 574 28 F4
Bon Aqua, Tenn. 61 H2
Bond, co., Ill., 14,060 25 C5
Bond, Miss. 39 C5
Bond Falls Flowage, Mich. 36 C2
Bondsville (part of Palmer and Belchertown), Mass. 34 E4
Bonduel, Wis., 876 69 E3
Bondurant, Iowa, 389 28 D3
Bondville, Ill. 25 D3
Bondville, Vt. 65 B4
Bone Gap, Ill., 245 25 D5
Bone L., Wis. 69 A2
Bonesteel, S. Dak., 452 61 C2
Bonetraill, N. Dak. 51 L1
Bonfield, Ill., 178 25 D2
Bonham, Tex., 7,357 62 F3
Bon Homme, co., S. Dak., 9,229 61 D2
Bonifay, Fla., 2,222 21 E1
Bonin Is., Pac. Oc. 71 B2
Bonita, Ariz. 14 D3
Bonita, La., 574 31 C1
Bonita Springs, Fla. 21 J5
Bonlee, N.C. 50 F2
Bonneau, S.C., 402 59 E3
Bonner, co., Idaho, 15,587 24 A1
Bonnerdale, Ark. 15 B3
Bonners Ferry, Idaho, 1,921 24 A1
Bonner Springs, Kans., 3,171 29 G1
Bonne Terre, Mo., 3,219 40 F4
Bonneville, co., Idaho, 46,906 24 D4
Bonneville, Oreg. 55 M2
Bonneville Salt Flats, Utah 64 A1
Bonney Lake, Wash., 645 67 b6
Bonnie, Ill., 215 25 D5
Bonnieville, Ky., 376 30 E3
Bonny Res., Colo. 18 D2
Bono, Ark., 339 15 E2
Bono, Ind. 27 A3
Bono, Ohio 53 B1
Bono, Tex. 63 e12
Bonpas Cr., Ill. 25 E5
Boody, Ill. 25 C4
Booker, Tex., 817 62 D1
Booker T. Washington Nat. Mon., Va. 67 K3
Boomer, W. Va., 1,657 68 B3
Boom L., Wis. 69 D2
Boon, Mich. 37 F4
Boone, co., Ark., 16,116 15 B1
Boone, Colo., 548 18 C2
Boone, co., Ill., 20,326 25 D1
Boone, co., Ind., 27,543 27 B2
Boone, co., Iowa, 28,037 28 D3
Boone, Iowa, 12,468 28 D2
Boone, co., Ky., 21,940 30 F2
Boone, Ky. 30 F3
Boone, co., Mo., 55,202 40 D3
Boone, co., Nebr., 9,134 42 F2
Boone, Nebr. 42 F2
Boone, N.C., 3,686 50 D1
Boone, co., W. Va., 28,764 68 B3
Boone, r., Iowa 28 D2
Boone L., Tenn. 61 K1
Boones Mill, Va., 371 67 K3
Booneville, Ark., 2,690 15 A2
Booneville, Ky., 143 30 G3
Booneville, Miss., 3,480 39 D1
Boonsboro, Md., 1,211 33 C1
Boonsville, Tex. 63 d10
Boonton, N.J., 7,981 45 C2
Boonton Res., N.J. 47 b2
Boonville, Calif. 17 B2
Boonville, Ind., 4,801 27 A4
Boonville, Mo., 7,090 40 D3
Boonville, N.Y., 2,403 49 K4
Boonville, N.C., 539 50 E1
Booth, Ala. 11 C3
Booth, Tex. 63 h14
Booth, Utah 64 A1
Boothbay Harbor, Me., 2,252 32 B5
Booth Corner, Pa. 20 b4
Boothton, Ala. 11 B2
Boothville, La. 31 E4
Boqueron, P.R. 72 n d1
Boqueron, B. de, P.R. 72 n a1
Boquillas, Tex. 62 C5
Borah, Mt., Idaho 24 C3
Borculo, Mich. 36 E6
Bordeaux, Tenn. 61 J1
Bordelonville, La. 31 C2
Borden, Ind. 27 C4
Borden, co., Tex., 1,076 62 D3
Borden Mtn., Mass. 34 B2
Borden Springs, Ala. 11 D2
Bordentown, N.J., 4,974 45 B3
Border, Minn. 38 B1
Bordulac, N. Dak. 51 N2
Boreas, r., N.Y. 49 M3
Borger, Tex., 20,911 62 D2
Borgne, L., La. 31 E3
Boring, Oreg. 54 b5
Borland, Mich. 36 F5
Borodino, N.Y. 49 m21
Boron, Calif. 17 E4
Borrego Springs, Calif. 17 E5
Borton, Ill. 25 E4
Borup, Minn., 145 38 A2
Boscawen, N.H. 44 B5
Bosco, La. 31 B1
Boscobel, Wis., 2,608 69 C4
Bosque, Ariz. 14 B3
Bosque, N. Mex. 46 B2
Bosque, co., Tex., 10,809 62 F4
Bosque, r., Tex. 62 F4
Boss, Mo. 40 E4
Bossier, parish, La., 57,622 31 A1
Bossier City, La., 32,776 31 A1
Boston, Ga., 1,357 22 C5
Boston, Ind., 240 27 D3
Boston, Ky. 30 E3
Boston, Mass., 697,197 35 K3
Boston, Ohio 52 e8
Boston, Tex. 63 G3
Boston, Va. 67 L2
Boston Bay, Mass. 35 L3
Boston Harbor, Wash. 67 a6
Boston Heights, Ohio, 831 52 f8
Boston Mts., Ark.-Okla. 8a
Boston Pk., Wash. 66 C1
Bostwick, Ga., 272 22 C2
Boswell, Ind., 957 27 A2
Boswell, Okla., 753 55 H4
Boswell, Pa., 1,508 56 C5
Boswell Bay, Alaska, 32 13 G3
Bosworth, Mo., 465 40 C2
Botetourt, co., Va., 16,715 67 K3
Bothell, Wash., 2,237 66 B2
Bothwell, Utah, 302 64 b4
Botijas, P.R. 72 c1
Botkins, Ohio, 854 52 A2
Botsford (part of Newtown), Conn. 19 B4
Bottineau, co., N. Dak., 11,315 51 M1
Bottineau, N. Dak., 2,613 51 M1
Boudreaux, La. 31 D4
Boulangerville, Okla. 55 G1
Boulder, co., Colo., 74,254 18 C1
Boulder, Colo., 37,718 18 C1
Boulder, Ill. 25 C5
Boulder, Mont., 1,394 41 C2
Boulder, Utah 64 B3
Boulder City, Nev., 4,059 43 C4
Boulder Creek, Calif., 1,306 17 B3
Boulder Cr., Colo. 18 b4
Boulder Dam = Hoover Dam
Boulder Junction, Wis. 69 D2
Boulder Rock Cr., Idaho-Wash. 55 O3
Boundary, Alaska 13 H2
Boundary, co., Idaho, 5,809 24 A1
Boundary, Me. 32 D2
Boundary Mts., Me. 32 A3
Boundary Pk., Calif.-Nev. 43 A3
Bound Brook, N.J., 10,263 45 C2
Bountiful, Utah, 17,039 64 B1
Bouquet, r., N.Y. 49 O2
Bourbeuse, r., Mo. 40 E3
Bourbon, Ind., 1,522 27 B1
Bourbon, co., Kans., 16,090 29 H3
Bourbon, co., Ky., 18,178 30 F2
Bourbon, Mo. 779 40 E3
Bourbonnais, Ill., 3,336 25 D2
Bourg, La. 31 D4
Bourne, Mass., 14,011(T) 35 M6
Bournedale (part of Bourne), Mass. 35 M5
Bourneville, Ohio 53 B3
Bourquim Hill, Nebr. 42 C2
Bouse, Ariz. 14 A3
Bovey, Minn., 1,086 38 C2
Bovill, Idaho, 357 24 A2
Bovina, Tex., 1,029 62 C2
Bovina Center, N.Y. 49 L6
Bowbells, N. Dak., 810 51 L1
Bowdens, N.C., 300 50 G2
Bowdle, S. Dak., 673 61 C1
Bowdoinham, Me. 32 B4
Bowdon, Ga., 1,548 22 A2
Bowdon, N. Dak., 259 51 N2
Bowen, Ill., 559 25 A3
Bowens Corners, N.Y. 49 m19
Bowers, Del., 324 20 B2
Bowerston, Ohio, 463 53 D2
Bowersville, Ohio, 327 53 B3
Bowesmont, N. Dak. 51 O1
Bowie, Ariz. 14 D3
Bowie, Md., 1,072 33 D1
Bowie, co., Tex., 59,971 63 G3
Bowie, Tex., 4,566 62 F3
Bowie Cr., Miss. 39 C4
Bow L., N.H. 44 C5
Bowlder Mtn., Mont. 41 A1
Bowlegs, Okla. 54 G2
Bowler, Wis., 274 69 E3
Bowling Green, Fla., 1,171 21 H4
Bowling Green, Ind., 229 27 B3
Bowling Green, Ky., 28,338 30 D4
Bowling Green, Mo., 2,650 40 E2
Bowling Green, Ohio, 13,574 53 B1
Bowling Green, Va., 528 56 F4
Bowman, Calif. 17 j12
Bowman, Ga., 654 22 D1
Bowman, co., N. Dak., 4,154 51 L2
Bowman, N. Dak., 1,730 51 L2
Bowman, S.C., 1,106 59 D3
Bowman Creek, Pa. 57 n16
Bowman Cr., Pa. 57 J3
Bowmanstown, Pa., 888 57 K4
Bowmansville, N.Y. 48 h16
Bow Mar, Colo., 748 18 b5
Bow Mills, N.H. 44 B5
Bowring, Okla. 55 G1
Box, Okla. 55 H2
Boxboro, Mass. 35 H3
Box Butte, co., Nebr., 11,688 42 A1
Box Butte, Nebr. 42 B1
Box Butte Cr., Nebr. 42 B1
Box Butte Res., Nebr. 42 A1
Box Elder, Mont. 41 D1
Box Elder, S. Dak. 61 A1
Box Elder, co., Utah, 25,061 64 A1
Boxford, Mass., 2,010(T) 35 K2
Boxholm, Iowa, 250 28 C2
Boyce, La., 1,094 31 B2
Boyce, Tex. 63 f12
Boyce, Va., 384 67 L1
Boyceville, Wis., 660 69 A2
Boyd, Fla. 21 G1
Boyd, co., Ky., 52,163 30 H2
Boyd, Minn., 419 38 A3
Boyd, co., Nebr., 4,513 42 F1
Boyd, Okla. 54 C1
Boyd, Oreg. 55 M2
Boyd, Tex., 581 63 d10
Boyd, Wis., 622 69 B3
Boydell, Ark. 15 D4
Boyden, Iowa, 562 28 A1
Boyden L., Me. 32 D3
Boyd Lake, Me. 32 C3
Boyd L., Me. 32 C3
Boydton, Va., 449 67 L4
Boyer, W. Va. 68 D3
Boyer, r., Iowa 28 B3
Boyero, Colo. 18 D2
Boyers, Pa. 56 B3
Boyertown, Pa., 4,067 57 K5
Boyes Hot Springs, Calif. 16 b6
Boyette, Fla. 21 d11
Boykin, Ga., 601 22 B4
Boykin, S.C. 59 D2
Boykins, Va., 710 67 M4
Boyle, co., Ky., 21,257 30 F3
Boyle, Miss., 848 39 B2
Boylston Center, Mass. 35 H3
Boyne City, Mich., 2,797 37 G3
Boyne Falls, Mich., 260 37 G3
Boynton, Okla., 604 55 H2
Boynton Beach, Fla., 10,467 21 K5
Boy River, Minn., 51 38 B2
Boysen Res., Wyo. 70 B2
Boys Town, Nebr., 997 42 H2
Bozeman, Mont., 13,361 41 C3
Brace, Okla. 54 E1
Braceville, Ill., 558 25 D2
Bracey, Va. 67 L4
Bracken, Ind. 27 C2
Bracken, co., Ky., 7,422 30 F2
Bracken, Tex. 62 b8
Brackenridge, Pa., 5,697 56 B4
Brackett, Wis. 69 B3
Brackettville, Tex., 1,662 62 D5
Braddock, N. Dak., 141 51 M2
Braddock, Pa., 12,337 56 B5
Braddock Heights, N.Y. 48 j17

C

Carmel, Ind., 1,442 27 B3
Carmel, Me. 32 B4
Carmel, N.Y., 2,735 49 N8
Carmel, r., Calif. 16 c9
Carmel-by-the-Sea, Calif. 16 c9
Carmel Valley, Calif., 1,143 17 B3
Carmen, Ariz. 14 C4
Carmen, Idaho 24 B3
Carmen, Okla., 533 54 E1
Carmi, Ill., 6,152 25 D5
Carmi, L., Vt. 65 B1
Carmichael, Calif., 20,455 17 C2
Carmichael, Miss. 39 D4
Carmichaels, Pa., 788 56 A6
Carnation, Wash., 490 66 C2
Carnegie, Ga., 113 22 B4
Carnegie, Okla., 1,500 54 E2
Carnegie, Pa., 11,887 56 A5
Carneiro, Kans. 29 E2
Carnes, Miss. 39 C5
Carnesville, Ga., 481 22 C1
Carney, Md. 33 c3
Carney, Mich. 36 D3
Carney, Okla., 227 54 F2
Carneys Point, N.J., 3,600* 45 A4
Carnot, Pa. 56 b7
Caro, Mich., 3,534 37 H5
Caroga Lake, N.Y. 49 M4
Carol Beach, Wis. 26 c1
Carol City, Fla., 21,749 20 a9
Caroleen, N.C., 1,168 50 D2
Carolina, P.R., 3,075 72 n c1
Carolina (part of Charlestown), R.I. 58 B3
Carolina Beach, N.C., 1,192 50 H3
Carolinas Pt., Tinian 72 f
Caroline, co., Md., 19,462 33 E2
Caroline, co., Va., 12,725 67 M3
Caroline, Wis. 69 E3
Caroline, i., Line Is. 71 F4
Caroline Is., Tr. Terr. Pac. Is. 71 B3
Carol Stream, Ill., 2,514 26 b3
Carp, Ind. 27 B3
Carp, Nev. 43 C3
Carp, r., Mich. 37 G2
Carpenter, Iowa, 177 28 E1
Carpenter, Miss. 39 B3
Carpenter, Ohio 53 C3
Carpenter, S. Dak. 61 C1
Carpenter, Wyo. 70 D3
Carpenter Mtn., Oreg. 55 L2
Carpentersville, Ill., 17,424 25 D1
Carpinteria, Calif., 4,998 17 D4
Carpio, N. Dak., 199 51 M1
Carp Lake, Mich. 37 G3
Carp L., Mich. 37 F2
Carp L., Mich. 37 G3
Carr, Colo. 18 C1
Carrabassett, r., Me. 32 A3
Carrabelle, Fla., 1,146 21 F2
Carrboro, N.C., 1,997 50 F2
Carrcroft, Del. 20 b4
Carrier, Okla. 54 E1
Carriere, Miss. 39 C5
Carrier Mills, Ill., 2,006 25 D6
Carrigain, Mt., N.H. 44 C3
Carrington, N. Dak., 2,438 51 N2
Carrington I., Utah 64 A1
Carr Inlet, Wash. 67 a6
Carrizo, Ariz. 14 D1
Carrizo Cr., N. Mex. 46 D1
Carrizo Springs, Tex., 5,699 62 D5
Carrizozo, N. Mex., 1,546 46 C3
Carr Mtn., N.H. 44 B4
Carroll, co., Ark., 11,284 15 B1
Carroll, Ark. 15 C3
Carroll, co., Ga., 36,451 22 A2
Carroll, co., Ill., 19,507 25 C1
Carroll, co., Ind., 16,934 27 B2
Carroll, co., Iowa, 23,431 28 C2
Carroll, Iowa, 8,481 28 B2
Carroll, co., Ky., 7,978 30 E2
Carroll, Me. 32 C3
Carroll, co., Md., 52,785 33 C1
Carroll, co., Miss., 11,177 39 C2
Carroll, co., Mo., 13,847 40 C2
Carroll, Nebr., 220 42 G1
Carroll, co., N.H., 15,829 44 C4
Carroll, N.H. 44 B3
Carroll, co., Ohio, 20,857 53 D2
Carroll, Ohio, 444 53 C3
Carroll, co., Tenn., 23,476 61 G2
Carroll, co., Va., 23,178 67 J4
Carroll Cr., Ill. 25 C1
Carrolls, Wash. 66 B2
Carrollton, Ala., 894 11 B2
Carrollton, Ga., 10,973 22 B2
Carrollton, Ill., 2,558 25 B4
Carrollton, Ky., 3,218 30 E2
Carrollton, Md. 33 C1
Carrollton, Mich., 6,718 37 G5
Carrollton, Miss., 343 39 B2
Carrollton, Mo., 4,554 40 C2
Carrollton, N.Y. 48 C6
Carrollton, Ohio, 2,786 53 D2
Carrollton, Tex., 4,242 63 f11
Carrollton Manor, Md. 33 c4
Carrolltown, Pa., 1,525 56 D4
Carrollville, Wis. 69 b8
Carrothers, Ohio 53 C1
Carrsville, Ky., 166 30 B3
Carrsville, Va. 67 N4
Carrville, Ala., 1,081 11 D3
Carry Falls Res., N.Y. 49 L2
Carry Pond, Me. 32 A3
Carson, Calif., 38,059 16 e11
Carson, Iowa, 583 28 B3
Carson, N. Mex. 46 C1
Carson, N. Dak., 501 51 M2
Carson, Okla. 55 G2
Carson, Oreg. 55 O2
Carson, co., Tex., 7,781 62 D2
Carson, Va. 67 M3
Carson, Wash. 66 C3
Carson, r., Nev. 43 A2
Carson City, Mich., 1,201 37 G5
Carson City, Nev., 5,163 43 A2
Carson L., Nev. 43 A2
Carson Sink, Nev. 43 A2
Carsonville, Mich., 502 37 J5
Cartago, Calif. 17 D3
Carta Valley, Tex. 62 D5
Carter, co., Ky., 20,817 30 G2
Carter, Ky., 122 30 G2
Carter, co., Mo., 3,973 40 E5
Carter, co., Mont., 2,493 41 F3
Carter, Mont. 41 C2
Carter, co., Okla., 39,044 54 F3
Carter, Okla., 364 54 D2
Carter, S. Dak., 18 61 B2
Carter, co., Tenn., 41,578 61 N1
Carter, Tenn. 61 N1
Carter, Wis. 69 E2
Carter Dome, N.H. 44 C3
Carteret, N.J., 20,502 45 C1
Carteret, co., N.C., 30,940 51 J3
Carter Lake, Iowa, 2,287 28 A3
Carter L., Colo. 18 b4
Cartersville, Ga., 8,668 22 B1
Carterville, Ill., 2,643 25 C6
Carterville, Mo., 1,443 40 B4
Carthage, Ark., 528 15 C3
Carthage, Ill., 3,325 25 A3
Carthage, Ind., 1,043 27 C3
Carthage, Miss., 2,442 39 C3
Carthage, Mo., 11,264 40 B4
Carthage, N.Y., 4,216 49 J3
Carthage, N.C., 1,190 50 F2
Carthage, S. Dak., 368 61 D1
Carthage, Tenn., 2,021 61 K1
Carthage, Tex., 5,262 63 G3
Cartwright, Ky. 30 E4
Cartwright, N. Dak. 51 L2
Caruthersville, Mo., 8,643 40 G5
Carver, Mass., 1,949(T) 35 L5
Carver, co., Minn., 21,358 38 C3
Carver L., Minn. 38 d6
Carversville, Pa. 57 f10
Cary, Ill., 3,839 26 a2
Cary, Me. 32 D3
Cary, Miss., 428 39 B3
Cary, N.C., 3,356 50 G2
Caryville, Fla., 730 20 E1
Caryville (part of Bellingham), Mass. 35 J4
Caryville, Tenn. 61 L1
Casa, Ark., 184 15 B2
Casa Grande, Ariz., 8,485 14 C3
Casagrande Nat. Mon., Ariz. 14 C3
Casanova, Va. 67 M2
Casa Piedra, Tex. 62 C5
Casar, N.C. 50 D2
Cascabel, Ariz. 14 C3
Cascade, Colo. 18 c7
Cascade, Idaho, 923 24 B3
Cascade, Iowa, 1,601 28 G2
Cascade, co., Mont., 73,418 41 C2
Cascade, Mont., 604 41 B2
Cascade, Va. 67 L4
Cascade, Wis., 449 69 E4
Cascade Locks, Oreg., 660 55 M2
Cascade Range, Calif.-Oreg.-Wash. 8a
Cascade Res., Idaho 24 B3
Cascade Summit, Oreg. 55 L3
Cascajo, P., P.R. 72 n d1
Cascilla, Miss. 39 B2
Casco, Me. 32 A4
Casco, Wis., 460 69 F3
Casco Bay, Me. 32 A5
Case Inlet, Wash. 67 a6
Caselton, Nev. 43 C3
Caseville, Mich., 659 37 H5
Casey, Ill., 2,890 25 D4
Casey, Iowa, 589 28 C3
Casey, co., Ky., 14,327 30 F3
Casey Fk., r., Ill. 25 D5
Cash, Ark., 141 15 E2
Cash, Tex. 63 g10
Cashie, r., N.C. 51 J1
Cashiers, N.C., 342 50 B2
Cashion, Okla., 221 54 F2
Cashmere, Wash., 1,891 66 C2
Cashton, Wis., 828 69 C4
Casmalia, Calif. 17 C4
Casnovia, Mich., 371 36 F5
Casper, Wyo., 38,930 70 C2
Caspian, Mich., 1,493 36 C2
Caspiana, La. 31 A2
Caspian L., Vt. 65 C1
Cass, Ark. 15 B2
Cass, co., Ill., 14,539 25 B4
Cass, co., Ind., 40,931 27 B2
Cass, co., Iowa, 17,919 28 C3
Cass, co., Mich., 36,932 36 E7
Cass, co., Minn., 16,720 38 B2
Cass, co., Mo., 29,702 40 B3
Cass, co., Nebr., 17,821 42 H3
Cass, co., N. Dak., 66,947 51 O2
Cass, co., Tex., 23,496 63 G3
Cass, W.Va., 327 68 D3
Cass, r., Mich. 37 H5
Cassadaga, N.Y., 820 48 B6
Cassadaga Cr., N.Y. 48 B6
Cass City, Mich., 1,945 37 H5
Casselman, Pa., 103 56 C6
Casselman, r., Pa. 56 C6
Casselton, N. Dak., 1,394 51 O2
Cassia, co., Idaho, 16,121 24 C4
Cassin, Tex. 62 b9
Cassity, W. Va. 68 C3
Cass Lake, Minn., 1,586 38 B2
Cass L., Mich. 37 c10
Cass L., Minn. 38 B2
Cassoday, Kans. 29 F2
Cassopolis, Mich., 2,027 36 E7
Cassville, Mo., 1,451 40 C5
Cassville, N.J. 45 C3
Cassville, N.Y. 49 K5
Cassville, Pa., 208 56 E5
Cassville, Wis., 1,290 69 C5
Castalia, Iowa, 216 28 F1
Castalia, N.C., 267 50 H1
Castalia, Ohio, 954 53 C1
Castana, Iowa, 230 28 B2
Castell, Tex. 62 E4
Castella, Calif. 17 B1
Castile, N.Y., 1,146 48 D5
Castillo de San Marcos Nat. Mon., Fla. 21 J2
Castine, Me. 32 C4
Castine, Ohio, 169 53 A3
Castle, Okla., 149 55 G2
Castleberry, Ala., 669 11 B4
Castle Creek, N.Y. 49 J6
Castle Dale, Utah, 617 64 B2
Castle Danger, Minn. 38 D2
Castle Dome Pk., Ariz. 14 B3
Castleford, Idaho, 274 24 B4
Castle Gate, Utah, 321 64 B2
Castle Hayne, N.C. 50 H3
Castle Hills, Tex., 2,622 62 a8
Castle Mtn., Alaska 13 E1
Castle Pk., Wash. 66 C1
Castle Rock, Colo., 1,152 18 C2
Castle Rock, S. Dak. 61 A1
Castle Rock, Wash., 1,424 66 B2
Castle Rock, mtn., Oreg. 55 N2
Castle Rock Butte, S. Dak. 61 A1
Castle Rock Flowage, Wis. 69 C4
Castle Shannon, Pa., 11,836 56 b8
Castleton, Ill. 25 C2
Castleton, Utah 64 C2
Castleton, Vt. 65 A3
Castleton-on-Hudson, N.Y., 1,837 49 N5
Castlewood, S. Dak., 500 61 D1
Castlewood, Va. 66 G4
Castolon, Tex. 62 C5
Caston, Okla. 55 J3
Castor, La., 142 31 B1
Castor, r., Mo. 40 F4
Castor Bayou, La. 31 B1
Castorland, N.Y., 321 49 J3
Castro, co., Tex., 8,923 62 C2
Castro Valley, Calif., 37,120 16 b7
Castroville, Tex., 1,508 62 E5
Castroville, Calif., 2,838 16 c9
Caswell, co., N.C., 19,912 50 F1
Catahoula, parish, La., 11,421 31 C2
Catahoula L., La. 31 B2
Catalina Pt., Guam 71 a
Catamount Mtn., N.Y. 49 L2
Cataño, P.R., 8,276 72 n c1
Cataract, Wis. 69 C3
Cataract Cr., Ariz. 14 B1
Catarina, Tex., 160 62 E5
Catasauqua, Pa., 5,062 57 K4
Catawba, co., N.C., 73,191 50 D2
Catawba, N.C., 504 50 D2
Catawba, Va. 67 J3
Catawba, Wis., 230 69 C2
Catawba, r., N.C. 50 E2
Catawba L., N.C.-S.C. 50 E2
Catawissa, Pa., 1,824 56 J4
Catawissa Cr., Pa. 56 J4
Cateechee, S.C. 59 B2
Cates, Ind. 27 A2
Catesby, Okla. 54 D1
Catfish Cr., N.Y. 49 m19
Cathance L., Me. 32 D4
Catharine, Kans. 29 C2
Cathay, Calif. 17 D3
Cathay, N. Dak., 110 51 N2
Cathedral Bluffs, Colo. 18 A2
Cathedral City, Calif., 1,855 17 E5
Cathedral Mtn., Tex. 62 B4
Catherine, Ala., 11 B3
Cathlamet, Wash., 615 66 B2
Cathro, Mich. 37 H3
Cat I., Miss. 39 C5
Cat I., Wis. 69 C1
Catlettsburg, Ky., 3,874 30 H2
Catlin, Ill., 1,600 25 E3
Cato, Ind. 27 A4
Cato, N.Y., 476 49 I20
Cato, Wis. 69 F3
Caton, N.Y. 48 F6
Caton Farm, Ill. 26 b4
Catonsville, Md., 37,372 33 D1
Catoosa, co., Ga., 21,101 22 A1
Catoosa, Okla., 638 55 H1
Catron, Mo., 177 40 G5
Catron, co., N. Mex., 2,773 46 A3
Catskill, N.Y., 5,825 49 N6
Catskill Mts., N.Y. 49 L6
Cat Spring, Tex. 62 F5
Cattaraugus, co., N.Y., 80,187 48 C6
Cattaraugus, N.Y., 1,258 48 C6
Cattaraugus Cr., N.Y. 48 C6
Caucomgomoc L., Me. 32 B2
Caufield, Mo. 40 D5
Caughdenoy, N.Y. 49 m19
Cauthron, Ark. 15 A3
Cavalier, co., N. Dak., 10,064 51 N1
Cavalier, N. Dak., 1,404 51 O1
Cavanal Mtn., Okla. 55 J2
Cave City, Ark., 540 15 D2
Cave City, Ky., 1,418 30 E3
Cavecreek, Ariz. 14 C3
Cave in Rock, Ill., 495 25 D6
Cave Junction, Oreg., 248 55 L3
Ca-Vel, N.C. 50 G1
Cavendish, Vt. 65 B4
Caverna, Mo. 40 B5
Cave Spring, Ga., 1,153 22 A1
Cave Springs, Ark., 181 15 A1
Cavett, Ohio 53 A2
Cavour, S. Dak., 140 61 C1
Cavour, Wis. 69 E2
Cawker City, Kans., 686 29 D1
Cawood, Ky. 30 G4
Cayce, S.C., 8,517 59 C3
Cayey, P.R., 19,738 72 n c1
Cayucos, Calif. 17 C4
Cayuga, Ill. 25 D3
Cayuga, Ind., 904 27 A3
Cayuga, co., N.Y., 73,942 48 G4
Cayuga, N.Y., 621 48 G5
Cayuga, N. Dak., 195 51 O2
Cayuga, Tex. 62 F4
Cayuga, Wis. 69 C1
Cayuga Cr., N.Y. 48 g16
Cayuga Heights, N.Y., 3,227 49 H6
Cayuga L., N.Y. 48 G5
Cayuse, Oreg. 55 N2
Cayuta, N.Y. 48 G6
Cayuta Cr., N.Y. 48 G6
Cazenovia, N.Y., 2,676 49 J5
Cazenovia, Wis., 351 69 C4
Cazenovia Cr., N.Y. 48 g16
Cearfoss, Md. 33 C1
Cebolleta, N. Mex. 46 B2
Cebolleta Mts., N. Mex. 46 B2
Cecil, Ga., 279 22 C4
Cecil, co., Md., 48,408 33 E1
Cecil, Ohio, 288 53 A1
Cecil, Oreg. 55 N2
Cecil, Pa. 56 b8
Cecil, Wis., 357 69 E3
Cecilton, Md., 596 33 E1
Cecilville, Calif. 17 B1
Cedar, co., Iowa, 17,791 28 F3
Cedar, Mich. 36 F4
Cedar, co., Mo., 9,185 40 C4
Cedar, co., Nebr., 13,368 42 G1
Cedar, Wis. 69 C1
Cedar, r., Iowa 28 F2
Cedar, r., Mich. 36 D3
Cedar, r., Mich. 37 G4
Cedar, r., Nebr. 42 F2
Cedar, r., N. Dak. 51 L2
Cedar, r., Wash. 67 b6
Cedar Bayou, Tex. 63 k14
Cedar Bayou, r., Tex. 63 k14
Cedar Bluff, Ala., 687 11 D1
Cedar Bluff, Va., 995 66 H3
Cedar Bluff Res., Kans. 29 C5
Cedar Bluffs, Kans. 29 B1
Cedar Bluffs, Nebr., 585 42 H2
Cedar Breaks Nat. Mon., Utah 64 A3
Cedarburg, Wis., 5,191 69 F4
Cedar Bushes (part of Plymouth), Mass. 35 M5
Cedarbutte, S. Dak. 61 B2
Cedar City, Mo. 40 D3
Cedar City, Utah, 7,543 64 A3
Cedar Cove, Colo. 18 b4
Cedar Creek, Ark. 15 B3
Cedarcreek, Mo. 40 D5
Cedar Creek, Tex. 62 F4
Cedar Creek, Utah 64 a4
Cedar Cr., Colo. 18 D1
Cedar Cr., N.J. 45 C4
Cedaredge, Colo., 594 18 B2
Cedar Falls, Iowa, 26,016 28 E2
Cedar Falls, N.C. 50 F2
Cedar Falls, Wash. 66 C2
Cedar Fort, Utah 64 b7
Cedar Grove, Essex Co., N.J., 14,603 47 c2
Cedar Grove, Ocean Co., N.J. 47 c6
Cedar Grove, Wash. 67 b6
Cedar Grove, W.Va., 1,569 68 B3
Cedar Grove, Wis., 1,175 69 F4
Cedar Hill, N.Y. 48 d14
Cedar Hill, Tenn. 61 J1
Cedar Hill, Tex., 1,848 63 e11
Cedar Hills, Oreg. 54 a4
Cedar Hills, N. Dak. 51 L2
Cedarhurst, N.Y., 6,824 47 e3
Cedar Island, N.C. 51 J2
Cedar Key, Fla., 668 21 G2
Cedar Lake, Ind., 7,494 27 A1
Cedar Lake, Mich. 37 G5
Cedar L., Ill. 26 b1
Cedar L., Mich. 37 H4
Cedar L., Minn. 38 b6
Cedar L., Tex. 62 C3
Cedar L., Wis. 69 A2
Cedar Lane, Tex. 63 G5
Cedar Mtn., N. Mex. 46 A3
Cedar Mts., Utah 64 A1
Cedar Pines Park, Calif. 16 g10
Cedar Point, Kans., 87 29 F2
Cedar Rapids, Iowa, 103,545 28 F2
Cedar Rapids, Nebr., 512 42 F2
Cedar Ridge, Ariz. 14 C1
Cedar River, Mich. 36 D3
Cedars, Del. 20 a5
Cedar Springs, Ga. 22 B4
Cedar Springs, Mich., 1,768 36 F5
Cedartown, Ga., 9,340 22 A2
Cedar Vale, Kans., 859 29 F3
Cedarvale, N. Mex. 46 C2
Cedarvale, Tex. 63 g11
Cedar Valley, Tex. 62 b7
Cedarville, Calif. 17 C1
Cedarville, Ill., 570 25 C1
Cedarville (part of Plymouth), Mass. 35 M5
Cedarville, Mich. 37 G2
Cedarville, N.J., 1,095 45 A5
Cedarville, Ohio, 1,702 53 B3
Cedarville, Pa. 57 e11
Ceiba, P.R., 1,644 72 n d1
Celeste, Tex., 588 62 F3
Celestine, Ind. 27 B4
Celina, Ohio, 7,659 53 A2
Celina, Tenn., 1,228 61 K1
Celina, Tex., 1,204 62 F3
Celoron, N.Y., 1,507 48 B6
Cement, Okla., 959 54 E3
Cement City, Mich., 471 37 G6
Cement City, Mo. 40 h7
Cementon, N.Y. 49 M6
Cementon, Pa., 1,900* 57 j18
Centenary, S.C. 59 E2
Centennial Wash, Ariz. 14 B3
Center, Colo., 1,600 18 B3
Center, Mo., 484 40 E2
Center, Nebr., 147 42 G1
Center, N. Dak., 476 51 M2
Center, Tex., 4,510 63 G4
Center Barnstead, N.H. 44 C5
Center Bridge, Pa. 57 f10
Centerbrook (part of Essex), Conn. 19 F4
Center Brunswick, N.Y. 49 e13
Centerburg, Ohio, 963 53 C2
Center City, Minn., 293 38 C3
Center Conway, N.H. 44 C4
Center Cross, Va. 67 N3
Centerdale (part of N. Providence and Johnston), R.I. 58 B1
Centereach, N.Y., 8,524 49 O9
Center Effingham, N.H. 44 D4
Centerfield, Utah, 475 64 B2
Center Groton (part of Groton), Conn. 19 G4
Center Harbor, N.H. 44 C4
Center Hill, Fla., 529 21 J3
Center Hill L., Tenn. 61 K1
Center Line, Mich., 10,164 37 d10
Center Moreland, Pa. 57 n16
Center Moriches, N.Y., 2,521 49 P9
Center Ossipee, N.H. 44 C4
Center Point, Ala. 11 d6
Center Point, Ark., 136 15 A3
Centerpoint, Ind., 268 27 A3
Center Point, Iowa, 1,236 28 F2
Center Point, La. 31 B2
Center Point, Tex. 62 E5
Center Point, W.Va. 68 C2
Center Pd., Mass. 34 B3
Centerport, N.Y., 3,628 47 f2
Centerport, Pa., 208 57 J5
Center Rutland, Vt. 65 A3
Center Sandwich, N.H. 44 B4
Center Square, Pa. 57 f11
Center Strafford, N.H. 44 C5
Centerton, N.J. 45 A4
Centertown, Mo., 190 40 D3
Center Tuftonboro, N.H. 44 C4
Center Valley, Pa. 57 k18
Centerview, Mo., 201 40 C3
Centerville, Conn.=Hamden
Centerville, Del. 20 a4
Centerville, Ind., 2,378 27 C3
Centerville, Iowa, 6,629 28 E4
Centerville, Kans. 29 H2
Centerville, La. 31 C4
Centerville (part of Barnstable), Mass. 35 N6
Centerville (part of Beverly), Mass. 35 L2
Centerville (part of Uxbridge), Mass. 35 H4
Centerville, Mo., 163 40 F4
Centerville, N.J. 57 g10
Centerville, Nev. 43 A2
Centerville, N.C. 50 G1
Centerville, Crawford Co., Pa., 56 B2
Centerville, Washington Co., Pa., 5,088 56 A5
Centerville, S. Dak., 887 61 D2
Centerville, Tenn., 1,678 61 H2
Centerville, Tex., 836 63 G4
Centerville, Utah, 2,361 64 B1
Centerville, Wash. 66 C3
Centerville, Wis. 69 B3
Centrahoma, Okla., 148 55 G3
Central, Alaska 13 G2
Central, Ariz. 14 D3
Central, Ind. 27 B4
Central, N. Mex., 1,075 46 A3
Central, S.C., 1,473 59 B2
Central, Utah, 21 64 A3
Central, Cord., P.R. 72 n b1
Central Aguirre, P.R., 1,689 72 n c2
Central Bridge, N.Y. 49 M5
Central City, Colo., 250 18 C2
Central City, Ill., 1,422 25 C5
Central City, Iowa, 1,087 28 F2
Central City, Ky., 3,694 30 C3
Central City, Nebr., 2,406 42 F2
Central City, Pa., 1,604 56 D5
Central City, S. Dak., 784 61 A1
Central Falls, R.I., 18,677 58 C1
Centralhatchee, Ga., 174 22 A2
Central Heights, Ariz., 2,486 14 C3
Centralia, Ill., 13,904 25 C5
Centralia, Iowa, 85 28 G2
Centralia, Kans., 527 29 F1
Centralia, Mo., 3,200 40 D2
Centralia, Okla., 80 55 H1
Centralia, Pa., 1,435 56 J4
Centralia, Wash., 8,586 66 B2
Centralia, W.Va. 68 C3
Central Islip, N.Y. 49 O9
Central Lake, Mich., 692 36 F3
Central Park, Ill., 2,676 25 E3
Central Point, Oreg., 2,289 55 L3
Central Point, Va. 67 M3
Central Square, N.Y., 935 49 H4
Central Valley, Calif., 2,854 17 B1
Central Village (part of Westport), Mass. 35 K6
Centre, Ala., 2,392 11 D1
Centre, co., Pa., 78,580 56 F4
Centre Hall, Pa., 1,109 56 F4
Centreville, Ala., 1,981 11 B3
Centreville, Ill., 12,769 25 B5
Centreville, Md., 1,863 33 D1
Centreville, Mich., 971 36 F7
Centreville, Miss., 1,229 39 A4
Centropolis, Kans. 29 G2
Centuria, Wis., 551 69 A2
Century, Fla., 2,046 20 C1
Century, W.Va. 68 C2
Ceredo, W.Va., 1,387 68 A3
Ceres, Calif., 4,406 17 C3
Ceres, N.Y. 48 D6
Ceres, Okla. 54 F1
Ceresco, Mich. 37 F6
Ceresco, Nebr., 429 42 H2
Cerro Gordo, Ill., 1,067 25 D4
Cerro Gordo, co., Iowa, 49,894 28 D1
Cerro Gordo, N.C., 306 50 G3
Cerrogordo, Okla. 54 J4
Cerulean, Ky., 206 30 C4
Cestos, Okla. 54 D1
Cetti Bay, Guam 71 a
Ceylon, Minn., 554 38 B4
Chabot, L., Calif. 16 b7
Cha Cha Village, V.I. 72 p
Chaco, r., N. Mex. 46 A1
Chaco Canyon Nat. Mon., N. Mex. 46 A1
Chacon, N. Mex. 46 C1
Chacuaco Cr., Colo. 18 D3
Chadbourn, N.C., 2,323 50 G3
Chadds Ford, Pa. 57 e12
Chadron, Nebr., 5,079 42 B1
Chadwick, Ill., 602 25 C1
Chadwick, N.J. 47 c6
Chadwicks, N.Y. 48 c11
Chafee, N.Y. 48 D5
Chaffee, co., Colo., 8,298 18 B2
Chaffee, Mo., 2,862 40 G4
Chaffee, N. Dak. 51 O2
Chaffinville (part of Holden), Mass. 35 G3
Chagres, r., C.Z. 72 o
Chagrin, r., Ohio 52 f8
Chagrin Falls, Ohio, 3,458 52 f8
Chain Lakes, Me. 32 D4
Chakachamna L., Alaska 13 E3
Chalfont, Pa., 1,410 57 f10
Chalk, Kans. 29 F2
Chalk, Tex. 62 D3
Chalk Draw, r., Tex. 62 C5
Chalkyitsik, Alaska, 57 13 H2
Challis, Idaho, 732 24 B3
Chalmers, Ind., 548 27 A2
Chalmette, La. 31 E4
Chalmette Nat. Hist. Pk., La. 31 E4
Chama, Colo. 18 C3
Chama, N. Mex. 46 B1
Chama, r., N. Mex. 46 B1
Chamberino, N. Mex. 46 B3
Chamberlain, S. Dak., 2,598 61 C2
Chamberlain L., Me. 32 B2
Chamberlin, Tex. 62 C1
Chambers, co., Ala., 37,828 11 D3
Chambers, Ariz. 14 D2
Chambers, Nebr., 396 42 F1
Chambers, co., Tex., 10,379 63 G5
Chambersburg, Ill. 25 B4
Chambersburg, Ind. 27 B4
Chambersburg, Ohio, 205 53 C4
Chambersburg, Pa., 17,670 56 F6
Chambers Cr., Tex. 63 f12
Chambers I., Wis. 69 F2
Chamblee, Ga., 6,635 22 B2
Chamois, Mo., 658 40 E3
Champaign, co., Ill., 132,436 25 D3
Champaign, Ill., 49,583 25 D3
Champaign, co., Ohio, 29,714 53 B2
Champion, Mich. 36 D2
Champlain, N.Y., 1,549 49 N1
Champlain, Va. 67 M2
Champlain, L., N.Y.-Vt. 49 O1
Chana, Ill. 25 C2
Chance, Ala. 11 B4
Chance, Md. 33 D2
Chance, Okla. 55 J1
Chancellor, S. Dak., 214 61 D2
Chancellorsville, Va. 67 M2
Chandalar, Alaska 13 G2
Chandalar, r., Alaska 13 H2
Chandeleur Is., La. 31 E4
Chandeleur Sd., La. 31 E4
Chandler, Ariz., 12,181 14 C3
Chandler, Ind., 1,784 27 A4
Chandler, Okla., 2,524 54 G2
Chandler, Tex. 63 G3
Chandler, r., Alaska 13 E1
Chandler Heights, Ariz. 14 C3
Chandlers Valley, Pa. 56 C2
Chandlerville, Ill., 718 25 B3
Chaneliak, Alaska, 93 12 C3
Chaney, Okla. 54 D1
Chaney L., Mich. 36 B2
Chanhassen, Minn., 563 38 a6
Channahon, Ill. 25 D2
Channel Islands Nat. Mon., Calif. 17 D4
Channel Lake, Ill., 1,969 25 D1
Channing, Mich. 36 C2
Channing, Tex., 351 62 C2
Chantilly, Va. 67 M2
Chanute, Kans., 10,849 29 G3
Chapel Hill, Ga. 22 a7
Chapel Hill, N.C., 12,573 50 G2
Chapel Hill, Tenn., 630 61 J2
Chapin, Ill., 477 25 B4
Chapin, S.C., 358 59 C2
Chapinville (part of Northboro), Mass. 35 H3
Chaplin, Conn., 1,230(T) 19 G2
Chaplinville (part of Rowley), Mass. 35 L2
Chapman, Ala., 617 11 C4
Chapman, Kans., 1,095 29 F2
Chapman, Nebr., 303 42 F2
Chapmanville, W. Va., 1,241 68 A4
Chappaqua, N.Y. 49 N8
Chappaquiddick I., Mass. 35 N7
Chappell, Nebr., 1,280 42 B2
Chappell Hill, Tex. 62 F4
Chappells, S.C., 128 59 C2
Chappel Pd., Mich. 37 G4
Charan Kanoa, Saipan 72 f
Charco, Tex. 62 F5
Chardon, Kans. 29 A1
Chardon, Ohio, 3,154 53 D1
Charenton, La. 31 C4
Chariton, Iowa, 5,042 28 D3
Chariton, co., Mo., 12,720 40 C2
Chariton, r., Iowa-Mo. 28 D4
Chariton, East Fork, r., Mo. 40 D2
Charlemont, Mass. 34 C2
Charleroi, Pa., 8,148 56 B5
Charles, co., Md., 32,572 33 C2
Charles, r., Mass. 35 K3
Charles, C., Va. 67 O3
Charles City, Iowa, 10,419 28 E1
Charles City, co., Va., 5,492 67 M3
Charles City, Va. 67 M3
Charles Mix, co., S. Dak., 11,785 61 C2
Charles Mound, Ill. 25 B1
Charleston, Ark., 1,353 15 A2
Charleston, Ill., 13,611 25 D4
Charleston, Kans. 29 B3
Charleston, Me. 32 B3
Charleston, Miss., 2,528 39 B1
Charleston, Mo., 5,911 40 G5
Charleston, Nev. 43 C1
Charleston, Oreg. 55 K3
Charleston, co., S.C., 216,382 59 D4
Charleston, S.C., 75,940 59 D4
Charleston, Tenn., 764 61 L2
Charleston, W.Va., 85,796 68 B3
Charleston Park, Nev. 43 C3
Charleston Pk., Nev. 43 B3
Charlestown, Ind., 5,571 27 C4
Charlestown, Md., 711 33 D1
Charlestown, N.H., 1,173 44 A5
Charlestown, R.I., 2,586(T) 58 B3
Charles Town, W.Va., 3,329 68 F2
Charlestown Beach (part of Charlestown), R.I. 58 B3
Charlesworth, Mich. 37 G6
Charlevoix, co., Mich., 13,421 36 F3
Charlevoix, Mich., 2,751 36 F3
Charlevoix, L., Mich. 36 F3
Charley, r., Alaska 13 H2
Charlotte, co., Fla., 12,594 21 J5
Charlotte, Iowa, 417 28 G3
Charlotte, Mich., 7,657 37 G6
Charlotte, N.C., 201,564 50 E2
Charlotte, Tenn., 551 61 H1
Charlotte, Tex., 1,465 62 E5
Charlotte, Vt. 65 A2
Charlotte, co., Va., 13,368 67 L3
Charlotte Amalie, V.I., 12,880 72 p
Charlotte Court House, Va., 555 67 L3
Charlotte Cr., N.Y. 49 L6
Charlotte Hbr., Fla. 21 J5
Charlottesville, Va., 29,427 67 L2
Charlson, N. Dak. 51 L1
Charlton, co., Ga., 5,313 22 D5
Charlton, Mass., 3,685(T) 35 G4
Charlton City (part of Charlton), Mass. 35 F4
Charlton Depot (part of Charlton), Mass. 35 G4
Charter Oak, Iowa, 665 28 B2
Chartiers Cr., Pa. 56 A5
Chartley (part of Norton), Mass. 35 K5
Chase, Ala. 11 C1
Chase, Alaska 13 F3
Chase, co., Kans., 3,921 29 F2
Chase, Kans., 922 29 D2
Chase, Mich. 36 F5
Chase, co., Nebr., 4,317 42 C3
Chase, Nebr. 42 C3
Chase, Mt., Me. 32 C2
Chaseburg, Wis., 242 69 B4
Chase City, Va., 3,207 67 L4
Chase L., Me. 32 B2
Chase Mills, N.Y. 49 K1
Chase Pd., Me. 32 B2
Chaska, Minn., 3,268 38 C3
Chasm Falls, N.Y. 49 M1
Chassell, Mich. 36 C1
Chataignier, La. 31 B3
Chatanika, Alaska 13 G2
Chatcolet, Idaho, 101 24 A2
Chateaugay, N.Y., 1,097 49 M1
Chatfield, Ark. 15 E2
Chatfield, Minn., 1,841 38 C4
Chatfield, Ohio, 263 53 C2
Chatfield, Tex. 63 g12
Chatham, co., Ga., 188,299 22 E4
Chatham, Ill., 2,023 25 C4
Chatham, La., 758 31 B1
Chatham, Mass., 3,273(T) 35 P6

For abbreviations and explanation of index, see page 176.

For abbreviations and explanation of index, see page 176.

Dale, co., Ala., 31,066 **11** D4
Dale, Ill. **25** D6
Dale, Ind., 900 **27** A4
Dale, Okla. **54** F2
Dale, Oreg. **55** N2
Dale, S.C. **59** D4
Dale, Tex. **62** c8
Dale, Wis. **69** E3
Dale Hollow Res., Ky.-Tenn. **30** E4
Daleville, Ind., 1,548 **27** C2
Daleville, Miss. **39** D3
Daleville, Pa. **57** n16
Daleyville, Wis. **69** D5
Dalhart, Tex., 5,160 **62** C1
Dall, Alaska **13** F2
Dallam, co., Tex., 6,302 **62** C1
Dallas, co., Ala., 56,667 **11** B3
Dallas, co., Ark., 10,522 **15** C3
Dallas, Ga., 2,065 **22** B2
Dallas, co., Iowa, 24,123 **28** C3
Dallas, Iowa, 392 **28** D3
Dallas, co., Mo., 9,314 **40** C4
Dallas, N.C., 3,591 **50** D2
Dallas, Oreg., 5,072 **55** L2
Dallas, Pa., 2,586 **57** J3
Dallas, S. Dak., 212 **61** C2
Dallas, co., Tex., 951,527 **62** F3
Dallas, Tex., 679,684 **62** F3
Dallas, Wis., 401 **69** B2
Dallas Center, Iowa, 1,083 **28** C3
Dallas City, Ill., 1,276 **25** A3
Dallastown, Pa., 3,615 **56** H6
Dall I., Alaska **13** K5
Dall L., Alaska **12** C3
Dalmatia, Pa. **56** H4
Dalton, Ga., 17,868 **22** A1
Dalton, Kans. **29** E3
Dalton, Mass., 6,436(T) **34** B3
Dalton, Minn., 239 **38** B2
Dalton, Mo., 197 **40** D2
Dalton, Nebr., 503 **42** B2
Dalton, N.H. **44** B3
Dalton, N.Y. **48** E5
Dalton, Ohio, 1,067 **53** D2
Dalton, Pa., 1,227 **57** K2
Dalton, Wis. **69** D4
Dalton City, Ill., 386 **25** D4
Daly City, Calif., 44,791 **17** B3
Damar, Kans., 361 **29** C1
Damariscotta, Me. **32** B4
Damariscotta L., Me. **32** B4
Damariscove I., Me. **32** B5
Damascus, Ark. **15** C2
Damascus, Ga., 297 **22** B4
Damascus, Md. **33** C1
Damascus, Ohio **53** D2
Damascus, Oreg. **54** b5
Damascus, Pa. **57** L2
Damascus, Va., 1,485 **66** H4
Dames Quarter, Md. **33** E2
Damon, Tex. **63** h15
Dan, r., N.C.-Va. **67** K4
Dana, Ill., 240 **25** D3
Dana, Ind., 811 **27** A3
Dana Point, Calif., 1,186 **16** f11
Danboro, Pa. **56** f10
Danbury, Conn., 22,928; 39,382(T) **19** B4
Danbury, Iowa, 510 **28** B2
Danbury, Nebr., 185 **42** D3
Danbury, N.H. **44** B4
Danbury, N.C., 175 **50** E1
Danbury, Tex. **63** j15
Danbury, Wis. **69** A1
Danby, Mo. **40** F3
Danby, Vt. **65** A4
Danby Four Corners, Vt. **65** A4
Danby L., Calif. **17** F4
Dancy, Miss. **39** C2
Dancy, Wis. **69** D3
Dancyville, Tenn. **60** F2
Dandridge, Tenn., 829 **61** M1
Dane, Okla. **54** E1
Dane, co., Wis., 222,095 **69** D5
Dane, Wis., 394 **69** D4
Danforth, Ill., 394 **25** E3
Danforth, Me. **32** D3
Dania, Fla., 7,065 **21** K5
Dania Cut-off Can., Fla. **20** b8
Daniel, Wyo. **70** A2
Daniel, Mt., Wash. **66** C2
Daniels, Md. **33** b3
Daniels, co., Mont., 3,755 **41** F1
Danielson, Conn., 4,642 **19** H2
Danielsville, Ga., 362 **22** F1
Danielsville, Pa. **57** L4
Dannebrog, Nebr., 277 **42** F2
Dannemora, N.Y., 4,835 **49** N1
Dansville, Mich., 453 **37** F6
Dansville, N.Y., 5,460 **48** E5
Dante, S. Dak., 102 **61** C2
Dante, Va., 1,436 **56** A6
Danvers, Ill., 783 **25** C3
Danvers, Mass., 21,926(T) **35** L2
Danville, Ala. **11** B1
Danville, Ark., 955 **15** B2
Danville, Calif., 3,585 **16** c7
Danville, Ga., 264 **22** C3
Danville, Ill., 41,856 **25** E3
Danville, Ind., 3,287 **27** B3
Danville, Iowa, 579 **28** F4
Danville, Ky., 9,010 **30** F3
Danville, La. **31** B1
Danville, N.H. **44** C6
Danville, Highland Co., Ohio **53** B3
Danville, Knox Co., Ohio, 926 **53** C2
Danville, Pa., 6,889 **56** H4
Danville, Vt. **65** C2
Danville, Va., 46,577 **67** K4
Danville, Wash. **66** D1
Danville, W.Va., 507 **68** B3
Danzig, N. Dak. **51** N2
Daphne, Ala., 1,527 **11** A5
d'Arbonne, Bayou, La. **31** B1
Darby, Fla. **21** H3
Darby, Mont., 398 **41** A2
Darby, Pa., 14,059 **57** L6
Darby Cr., Pa. **57** f11
Darbyville, Ohio, 213 **53** B3
Dardanelle, Ark., 2,098 **15** B2
Darden, N.C. **51** J2
Dare, co., N.C., 5,935 **51** K2
Darien, Conn., 18,437(T) **19** B5
Darien, Ga., 1,569 **22** E4
Darien, Mo. **40** E4
Darien, Wis., 805 **69** E5
Darien Center, N.Y. **48** D5
Darke, co., Ohio, 45,612 **53** A2
Dark Harbor, Me. **32** C4
Darling, L., N. Dak. **51** M1
Darlington, Fla. **20** E1
Darlington, Ind., 668 **27** B2
Darlington, La. **31** D3
Darlington, Md. **33** D1
Darlington, Mo., 169 **40** B1
Darlington, Pa., 306 **56** A4
Darlington, co., S.C., 52,928 **59** E2
Darlington, S.C., 6,710 **59** D2
Darlington, Wis., 2,349 **69** C5
Darlington Heights, Va. **67** L3
Darr, Nebr., 11 **42** E3
Darragh, Pa. **56** d8
Darrington, Wash., 1,272 **66** C1
Darrouzett, Tex., 375 **62** D1
Dart, Ohio **53** D3
Dartmouth, Mass, 14,607(T) **35** K6
Darwin, Calif. **17** E3
Darwin, Ill. **25** E4
Darwin, Okla. **55** H3
Darwin, Va. **66** G3
Darwin Pk., Wyo. **70** A2
Dash Point, Wash. **67** b6
Dassel, Minn., 863 **38** B3
Dateland, Ariz. **14** B3
Datil, N. Mex. **46** B2
Dauphin, co., Pa., 220,255 **56** H5
Dauphin, Pa., 638 **56** H5
Dauphin I., Ala. **11** A5
Davenport, Calif. **16** b8
Davenport, Fla., 1,209 **21** J3
Davenport, Iowa, 88,981 **28** G3
Davenport, Nebr., 416 **42** G3
Davenport, N.Y. **49** L6
Davenport, Okla., 813 **54** G2
Davenport, Wash., 1,494 **66** D2
Davey, Nebr., 121 **42** H2
Davey Town, Nev. **43** A1
David, Ky. **30** G3
David City, Nebr., 2,304 **42** G2
David Pt., V.I. **72** p
Davidson, co., N.C., 79,493 **50** E2
Davidson, N.C., 2,573 **50** E2
Davidson, Okla., 429 **54** D3
Davidson, co., Tenn., 399,743 **61** J1
Davidson, Tenn. **61** K1
Davidson Mts., Alaska **13** H1
Davidsonville, Md. **33** c5
Davie, Fla. **20** a8
Davie, co., N.C., 16,728 **50** E2
Daviess, co., Ind., 26,636 **27** A4
Daviess, co., Ky., 70,588 **30** C3
Daviess, co., Mo., 9,502 **40** B2
Davis, Calif., 8,910 **17** C2
Davis, Ill., 434 **25** C1
Davis, co., Iowa, 9,199 **28** E4
Davis, Ky. **30** F2
Davis, N.C. **51** J3
Davis, Okla., 2,203 **54** F3
Davis, S. Dak., 124 **61** D2
Davis, co., Utah, 64,760 **64** A1
Davis, W.Va., 898 **68** D2
Davis, Mt., Pa. **56** C6
Davisboro, Ga., 417 **22** D3
Davisburg, Mich. **37** H6
Davis City, Iowa, 346 **28** D4
Davis Creek, Calif. **17** C1
Davis Dam, Ariz. **14** A2
Davis Dam, Ariz.-Nev. **14** A2
Davis Mts., Tex. **62** B4
Davison, Mich., 3,761 **37** H5
Davison, co., S. Dak., 16,681 **61** C2
Davis Park, N.Y. **47** h3
Daviston, Ala., 129 **11** D2
Davisville, Mo. **40** E4
Davisville, N.H. **44** B5
Davisville, R.I. **58** C2
Davy, W.Va., 1,331 **68** B4
Dawes, Ala. **11** A5
Dawes, co., Nebr., 9,536 **42** A1
Dawn, Mo. **40** C2
Dawn, Ohio **53** A2
Dawn, Tex. **62** C2
Dawson, co., Ga., 3,590 **22** B1
Dawson, Ga., 5,062 **22** B4
Dawson, Iowa, 257 **28** C3
Dawson, Minn., 1,766 **38** A3
Dawson, co., Mont., 12,314 **41** F2
Dawson, co., Nebr., 19,405 **42** E3
Dawson, N. Dak., 206 **51** N2
Dawson, Ohio **53** A2
Dawson, Pa., 707 **56** d9
Dawson, co., Tex., 19,185 **62** C3
Dawson, Tex., 911 **62** F4
Dawson Springs, Ky., 3,002 **30** C3
Dawsonville, Ga., 307 **22** B1
Day, Fla. **21** G1
Day, co., S. Dak., 10,516 **61** D1
Daykin, Nebr., 144 **42** G3
Days Creek, Oreg. **55** L3
Daysville, Ill. **25** C2
Daysville, Ky. **30** C4
Dayton, Ala., 99 **11** B3
Dayton, Idaho, 212 **24** C4
Dayton, Ind. **27** B2
Dayton, Iowa, 820 **28** C2
Dayton, Ky., 9,050 **52** h10
Dayton, Md. **33** b4
Dayton, Nev. **43** A2
Dayton, N.J. **45** B3
Dayton, N.Y. **48** C6
Dayton, Ohio, 262,332 **53** A3
Dayton, Oreg., 673 **55** L2
Dayton, Pa., 769 **56** C4
Dayton, Tenn., 3,500 **61** K2
Dayton, Tex., 3,367 **63** G4
Dayton, Va., 930 **67** K2
Dayton, Wash., 2,913 **66** E2
Dayton, Wis. **69** D5
Dayton, Wyo., 333 **70** C1
Daytona Beach, Fla., 37,395 **21** K2
Dayville (part of Killingly), Conn. **19** H2
Dayville (part of Chester), Mass. **34** C3
Dayville, Oreg., 234 **55** N2
Dazey, N. Dak., 226 **51** N2
Dead, r., Me. **32** A3
Dead, N. Br., r., Me. **32** A3
Dead, S. Br., r., Me. **32** A3
Dead Cr., Vt. **65** A2
Dead Diamond, r., N.H. **44** C1
Dead L., Fla. **21** E1
Dead River Storage Basin, Mich. **36** D2
Dead Str., Me. **32** C3
Deadwood, Oreg. **55** L2
Deadwood, S. Dak., 3,045 **61** A1
Deaf Smith, co., Tex., 13,187 **62** C2
Deal, N.J., 1,889 **45** C3
Deale, Md. **33** D2
Deal Island, Md. **33** D2
Deans, N.J. **47** a4
Dearborn, co., Ind., 28,674 **27** C4
Dearborn, Mich., 112,007 **37** H6
Dearborn, Mo., 444 **40** B2
Dearing, Kans., 249 **29** G3
De Armanville, Ala. **11** D2
Deary, Idaho, 349 **24** A2
Dease Inlet, Alaska **13** E1
Death Valley Junction, Calif. **17** E3
Dead Valley Nat. Mon., Calif. **17** E3
Deatsville, Ala. **11** C3
Deaver, Wyo., 121 **70** B1
De Baca, co., N. Mex., 2,991 **46** C2
De Beque, Colo., 172 **18** A2
Deblois, Me. **32** C4
Decatur, Ala., 29,217 **11** C1
Decatur, Ark., 415 **15** A1
Decatur, co., Ga., 25,203 **22** B5
Decatur, Ga., 22,026 **22** B5
Decatur, Ill., 78,004 **25** C4
Decatur, co., Ind., 20,019 **27** C3
Decatur, Ind., 8,327 **27** D2
Decatur, co., Iowa, 10,539 **28** D4
Decatur, Iowa, 203 **28** D4
Decatur, co., Kans., 5,778 **29** B1
Decatur, Mich., 1,827 **36** E6
Decatur, Miss., 1,340 **39** C3
Decatur, Nebr., 786 **42** H2
Decatur, co., Tenn., 8,324 **61** G2
Decatur, Tenn. 681 **61** L2
Decatur, Tex., 3,563 **62** F3
Decatur, L., Ill. **25** D4
Decaturville, Mo. **40** D4
Decaturville, Tenn., 571 **61** G2
Deceit, Pt., Tutuila **71** c
Decherd, Tenn., 1,704 **61** J2
Decker, Ind., 317 **27** A4
Decker, Mich. **37** H5
Decker Prairie, Tex. **63** h13
Deckers, Colo. **18** C2
Deckerville, Ark., 27 **15** E2
Deckerville, Mich., 798 **37** J5
Declo, Idaho, 237 **24** C4
Decorah, Iowa, 6,435 **28** F1
Decota, W.Va. **68** B3
Decoto, Calif. **16** c7
Dededo, Guam, 2,247 **71** a
Dedham, Iowa, 322 **28** C3
Dedham, Me. **32** C4
Dedham, Mass., 23,869(T) **35** K4
Dee, Oreg. **55** M2
Deedsville, Ind. **27** B2
Deep, r., N.C. **50** F2
Deep Creek, Nev. **43** B1
Deep Cr. L., Md. **33** A1
Deep Creek Ra., Utah **64** A2
Deep Gap, N.C. **50** D1
Deephaven, Minn., 3,286 **38** b6
Deep River, Conn., 2,166; 2,968(T) **19** F4
Deep River, Iowa, 329 **28** E3
Deep Run, N.C., 183 **50** H2
Deep Run, r., N.J. **47** a4
Deepstep, Ga., 139 **22** C2
Deepwater, Mo., 712 **40** C3
Deepwater, N.J. **45** A4
Deer, Ark. **15** B2
Deer, r., Me. **32** B4
Deer, r., N.Y. **49** L1
Deerbrook, Wis. **69** D2
Deer Butte, Oreg. **55** O3
Deer Creek, Okla. **54** F1
Deer Cr., Ill. **26** d4
Deer Cr., Ind. **27** B2
Deer Cr., Nebr. **42** G1
Deer Cr., Ohio **53** B3
Deer Cr., Okla. **54** F1
Deer Creek Res., Utah **64** c7
Deerfield, Ill., 17,245 **25** E1
Deerfield, Kans., 442 **29** A2
Deerfield, Mass., 3,338(T) **34** D2
Deerfield, Mich., 866 **37** H7
Deerfield, N.H. **44** C5
Deerfield, N.J. **45** A3
Deerfield, Va. **67** K2
Deerfield, Wis., 795 **69** D4
Deerfield, r., Mass.-Vt. **65** B5
Deerfield Beach, Fla., 9,573 **21** K5
Deer Grove, Ill., 86 **25** C2
Deerhead, Kans. **29** C3
Deering, Alaska, 95 **12** C2
Deering, Mo., 122 **40** G5
Deering, N. Dak., 117 **51** M1
Deering Res., N.H. **44** B5
Deer Island, Oreg. **55** L2
Deer I., Alaska **12** C5
Deer I., Me. **32** B3
Deer Isle, Me. **32** C4
Deer L., Mich. **36** D2
Deer Lodge, co., Mont., 18,640 **41** B2
Deer Lodge, Mont., 4,681 **41** B2
Deer Lodge, Tenn. **61** L1
Deermont, Colo. **18** b5
Deer Mtn., Me. **32** A3
Deer Park, Ala. **11** A4
Deer Park, Fla. **21** J3
Deer Park, Ill., **26** b2
Deer Park, Md., 379 **33** A1
Deer Park, Mich. **36** F2
Deer Park, N.Y., 16,726 **47** f2
Deer Park, Ohio, 8,423 **52** j9
Deer Park, Tex., 4,865 **63** j14
Deer Park, Wash., 1,333 **66** E2
Deer Park, Wis., 221 **69** A2
Deer Pk., Colo. **18** C2
Deer River, Minn., 992 **38** C2
Deer River, N.Y. **49** J3
Deers Ears Butte, S. Dak. **61** A1
Deerton, Mich. **36** D2
Deer Trail, Colo., 764 **18** D2
Deerwood, Minn., 527 **38** C2
Deeth, Nev. **43** C1
Deferiet, N.Y., 470 **49** J2
Defiance, Iowa, 386 **28** B3
Defiance, co., Ohio, 31,508 **53** A1
Defiance, Ohio, 14,553 **53** A1
Deford, Mich. **37** H5
De Forest, Wis., 1,223 **69** D4
Defreestville, N.Y. **49** e14
De Funiak Springs, Fla., 5,282 **20** D1
DeGraff, Ohio, 996 **53** B2
Degrasse, N.Y. **49** K2
De Grey, S. Dak. **61** C1
De Kalb, co., Ala., 41,417 **11** D1
De Kalb, co., Ga., 256,782 **22** B2
De Kalb, co., Ill., 51,714 **25** D2
De Kalb, Ill., 18,486 **25** D2
De Kalb, co., Ind., 28,271 **27** C1
De Kalb, Miss., 880 **39** D3
De Kalb, co., Mo., 7,226 **40** B2
De Kalb, Mo., 304 **40** B2
De Kalb, S.C. **59** D2
De Kalb, co., Tenn., 10,774 **61** K1
De Kalb, Tex., 2,042 **63** D5
De Kalb Junction, N.Y. **49** K1
De Koven, Ky. **30** B3
Delacroix, La. **31** E4
Delafield, Ill. **25** D5
Delafield, Wis., 2,334 **69** E4
Delair, N.J., 3,075* **45** A4
Delake, Oreg., 803 **55** L2
De Lancey, N.Y. **49** K6
Delanco, N.J., 4,011(T) **57** g11
De Land, Fla., 10,775 **21** J2
De Land, Ill., 422 **25** D3
Delaney, Ark. **15** B2
Delano, Calif., 11,913 **17** D4
Delano, Minn., 1,612 **38** C3
Delano Mines, Nev. **43** C1
Delano Pk., Utah **64** A2
Delanson, N.Y., 398 **49** M5
Delaplaine, Ark., 186 **15** E1
Delavan, Ill., 1,377 **25** C3
Delavan, Wis., 4,846 **69** E5
Delavan L., Wis. **69** E5
Delaware, st., 523,000* **20**
Delaware, Ark. **15** B2
Delaware, co., Ind., 110,938 **27** C2
Delaware, co., Iowa, 18,483 **28** F2
Delaware, Mich. **36** C1
Delaware, Mo. **40** B4
Delaware, N.J. **45** A2
Delaware, co., N.Y., 43,540 **49** K6
Delaware, co., Ohio, 36,107 **53** B2
Delaware, Ohio, 13,282 **53** B2
Delaware, co., Okla., 13,198 **55** J1
Delaware, Okla., 540 **55** H1
Delaware, co., Pa., 553,154 **57** L6
Delaware, r. **165** E3
Delaware Bay, Del.-N.J. **165** E4
Delaware City, Del., 1,658 **20** A1
Delaware Cr., Tex. **62** D4
Delaware Mts., Tex. **62** D4
Delaware Res., Ohio **53** B2
Delaware Water Gap, Pa., 554 **57** L4
Delbarton, W.Va., 1,122 **68** A4
Delcambre, La., 1,857 **31** C4
Del City, Okla., 12,934 **54** F2
Delco, N.C., 466 **50** G3
De Leon, Tex., 2,022 **62** E3
De Leon Springs, Fla. **21** J2
Delevan, N.Y., 777 **48** C6
Delfina, Tex. **62** E6
Delhi, Calif., 1,175 **17** C3
Delhi, Colo. **18** D3
Delhi, Ill. **25** B4
Delhi, Iowa, 464 **28** F2
Delhi, La., 2,514 **31** C1
Delhi, N.Y., 2,664 **49** L6
Delhi, Okla. **54** D2
Delia, Kans., 163 **29** G1
Delight, Ark., **15** B3
Dell (part of Heath), Mass. **34** C2
Dell City, Tex. **62** B4
Delle, Utah **64** A1
Dell Rapids, S. Dak., 1,863 **61** D2
Dellrose, Tenn. **61** J2
Dellroy, Ohio, 391 **53** D2
Dellvale, Kans. **29** C1
Dellwood, Oreg. **55** L3
Dellwood, Wis. **69** D3
Del Mar, Calif., 3,124 **17** k14
Delmar, Del.-Md., 2,225 **20** A3
Delmar, Iowa, 556 **28** G2
Delmar, N.Y. **49** N5
Del Mar Beach, N.C. **51** H3
Delmont, N.J. **45** B5
Delmont, S. Dak., 363 **61** C2
Del Norte, co., Calif., 17,771 **17** B1
Del Norte, Colo., 1,856 **18** B3
Deloit, Iowa, 222 **28** B2
Delong, Ind., **27** B1
De Long Mts., Alaska **12** C1
Del Paso Heights, Calif., 11,495 **17** h12
Delphi, Ind., 2,517 **27** B2
Delphi Falls, N.Y. **49** J5
Delphos, Kans., 619 **29** E1
Delphos, N. Mex. **46** D2
Delphos, Ohio, 6,961 **53** A2
Delray Beach, Fla., 12,230 **21** K5
Delray Gardens, Fla. **20** b8
Del Rey Oaks, Calif., 1,831 **16** c9
Del Rio, Tex., 18,612 **62** D5
Delta, Ala. **11** D2
Delta, co., Colo., 15,602 **18** B2
Delta, Colo., 3,832 **18** A2
Delta, Iowa, 514 **28** E3
Delta, La., 111 **31** C1
Delta, co., Mich., 34,298 **36** E3
Delta, Ohio, 2,376 **53** B1
Delta, Pa., 822 **56** J6
Delta, co., Tex., 5,860 **63** G3
Delta, Utah, 1,576 **64** A2
Delta, Wis. **69** B1
Delta, r., Alaska **13** G3
Delta L., N.Y. **49** K4
Deltaville, Va. **67** M3
Delton, Mich. **36** F6
Del Valle, Tex. **62** c7
Delwin, Mich. **37** G5
Demarcation Pt., Alaska **13** H1
Demarest, N.J., 4,231 **47** d2
Deming, N. Mex., 6,764 **46** B3
Deming, Wash. **66** C1
Democrat, Tex. **62** E4
De Montreville, L., Minn. **38** d5
Demopolis, Ala., 7,377 **11** B3
Demopolis Dam, Ala. **11** B3
Demorest, Ga., 1,029 **22** C1
Demotte, Ind. **27** A1
Dempsey, Okla. **54** D2
Dempster, S. Dak. **61** D1
Denali, Alaska **13** G3
Denay Cr., Nev. **43** B1
Dendron, Va., 403 **67** M3
Denges Passage, Palau **72** e
Denham, Ind. **27** B1
Denham, Minn., 71 **38** C2
Denham Springs, La., 5,991 **31** C3
Denhoff, N. Dak. **51** M2
Denio, Nev. **43** A1
Denison, Iowa, 4,930 **28** B2
Denison, Kans., 184 **29** G1
Denison, Tex., 22,748 **62** F3
Denison, Mt., Alaska **13** E4
Denmark, Ga. **22** E3
Denmark, Kans. **29** D1
Denmark, Me. **32** A5
Denmark, Miss. **39** C1
Denmark, S.C., 3,221 **59** C3
Denmark, Wis., 1,106 **69** F3
Dennard, Ark. **15** C2
Dennis, Kans. **29** G3
Dennis, Mass., 3,727(T) **35** O6
Dennis, Miss. **39** D1
Dennis, Okla. **55** J1
Dennis, Tex. **63** d11
Dennison, Ill. **25** E4
Dennison, Ohio, 4,158 **53** D2
Dennis Port, Mass., 1,271 **35** O6
Dennisville, N.J. **45** B4
Dennysville, Me. **32** D4
Densmore, Kans. **29** C1
Dent, Minn., 176 **38** B2
Dent, co., Mo., 10,445 **40** E4
Dent, Ohio **52** g9
Denton, Ga., 255 **22** D4
Denton, Ky. **30** H2
Denton, Md., 1,938 **33** E2
Denton, Mont., 410 **41** C2
Denton, Nebr., 94 **42** H3
Denton, N.C., 852 **50** E2
Denton, co., Tex., 47,432 **62** F3
Denton, Tex., 26,844 **62** F3
Denton Cr., Tex. **62** F3
Dentsville, S.C. **59** D2
Denver, co., Colo., 493,887 **18** C2
Denver, Colo., 493,887 **18** C2
Denver, Ind., 565 **27** B2
Denver, Iowa, 1,046 **28** E2
Denver, Mo., 116 **40** B1
Denver, N.C., 113 **50** D2
Denver, Pa., 1,875 **57** J5
Denver City, Tex., 4,302 **62** C3
Denville, N.J. **47** b2
Denzer, Wis. **69** D4
Deora, Colo. **18** D3
Depauville, N.Y. **49** H2
De Pere, Wis., 10,045 **69** E3
Depew, N.Y., 18,309 **48** C5
Depew, Okla., 686 **55** G2
Depoe Bay, Oreg. **55** K2
Deport, Tex., 639 **63** G3
Deposit, N.Y., 2,025 **49** J6
Depot L., Me. **32** B2
Depot Mtn., Me. **32** B2
Depue, Ill., 1,920 **25** C2
De Queen, Ark., 3,889 **15** A3
De Quincy, La., 3,928 **31** A3
Derby, Colo., 10,124 **18** C5
Derby, Conn., 12,132 **19** C4
Derby, Ind., **27** B4
Derby, Iowa, 151 **28** D4
Derby, Kans., 6,458 **29** E3
Derby, Me. **32** B3
Derby, Miss. **39** C5
Derby, N.Y. **48** B5
Derby, Ohio **53** B3
Derby, Tex. **62** E5
Derby Center, Vt. **65** C1
Derby Line, Vt., 849 **65** C1
De Ridder, La., 7,188 **31** A3
Dermott, Ark., 3,665 **15** D4
Dermott, Tex. **62** D3
Deronda, Wis. **69** A2
Derrick City, Pa. **56** D2
Derry, N. Mex. **46** B3
Derry, Pa., 3,426 **56** C5
De Ruyter, N.Y., 627 **49** J5
Derwood, Md. **33** a4
Des Arc, Ark., 1,767 **15** D3
Des Arc, Mo., 275 **40** F4
Deschutes, co., Oreg., 23,100 **55** M3
Deschutes, r., Oreg. **55** M2
Deschutes, r., Wash. **67** a6
Desdemona, Tex. **62** E3
Deseret, Utah **64** A2
Deseret Pk., Utah **64** A1
Desert Center, Calif. **17** F5
Desert Hot Springs, Calif., 1,472 **17** E5
Desert Pk., Utah **64** A1
Desert Springs, Calif. **16** f10
Desha, co., Ark., 20,770 **15** D4
Desha, Ark. **15** D2
Deshler, Nebr., 956 **42** G3
Deshler, Ohio, 1,824 **53** A1
Des Lacs, N. Dak., 185 **51** M1
Des Lacs, r., N. Dak. **51** M1
Desloge, Mo., 2,308 **40** F4
De Smet, S. Dak., 1,324 **61** D1
Des Moines, co., Iowa, 44,605 **28** F4
Des Moines, Iowa, 206,739 **28** D3
Des Moines, N. Mex., 207 **46** D1
Des Moines, Wash., 1,987 **67** b6
Des Moines, r., Iowa **28** E3
Desor, L., Mich. **36** a9
Desor, Mt., Mich. **36** a9
De Soto, co., Fla., 11,683 **21** J4
De Soto, Ga., 282 **22** C4
De Soto, Ill., 723 **25** C6
De Soto, Kans., 1,271 **29** G1
De Soto, parish, La., 24,248 **31** A1
De Soto, co., Miss., 23,891 **39** B1
De Soto, Miss. **39** D4
De Soto, Mo., 6,150 **40** F3
De Soto, Tex., 1,969 **63** f11
De Soto, Wis., 357 **69** B4
De Soto City, Fla., Hawaii **21** J4
De Soto Nat. Mem., Fla. **21** H4
Des Plaines, Ill., 50,789 **25** D1
Des Plaines, r., Ill.-Wis. **25** D2
Destin, Fla. **20** D1
Detour, Pt., Mich. **36** E3
Detour Passage, Mich. **37** H3
De Tour Village, Mich., 669 **37** G3
Detrick, Va. **67** L2
Detroit, Ala., 113 **11** A1
Detroit, Ill., 126 **25** B4
Detroit, Mich., 1,670,144 **37** H6
Detroit, Oreg., 206 **55** L2
Detroit, Tex. 576 **63** G3
Detroit, r., U.S. **37** H6
Detroit Beach, Mich., 1,571 **37** H7
Detroit Harbor, Wis. **69** F2
Detroit L., Oreg. **55** L2
Detroit Lakes, Minn., 5,978 **38** B2
Deuel, co., Nebr., 3,125 **42** B2
Deuel, co., S. Dak., 6,782 **61** D1
De Valls Bluff, Ark., 654 **15** D3
Devereaux, Mich. **37** G6
Devereux, Ga. **22** C2
Devers, Tex. **63** k13
Devils, r., Tex. **62** D4
Devils Den, Calif. **17** D4
Devils Head, Colo. **18** b6
Devils Hole Mtn., Colo. **18** A1
Devils Lake, N. Dak., 6,670 **51** N1
Devils L., Mich. **37** G7
Devils L., N. Dak. **51** N1
Devils L., Tex. **62** D5
Devils Postpile Nat. Mon., Calif. **17** D3
Devils Slide, Utah **64** c5
Devils Tower Nat. Mon., Wyo. **70** D1
Devils Track L., Minn. **38** D2
Devine, Tex., 2,522 **62** E5
Devol, Okla., 117 **54** E3
Devon (part of Milford), Conn. **19** C5
Devon, Kans. **29** H3
Devon, Pa., 1,700* **57** f11
Dew, Tex. **62** F4
Dewalt, Tex. **63** h14
Dewar, Okla., 817 **55** H2
Dewatto, Wash. **67** a6
Deweese, Nebr. **42** F3
Dewey, P.R.=Culebra
Dewey, co., Okla., 6,051 **54** D2
Dewey, Okla., 3,994 **55** H1
Dewey, co., S. Dak., 5,257 **61** B1
Dewey, S. Dak. **61** A2
Dewey Corners, N.Y. **48** c11
Dewey Dam, Ky. **30** H3
Deweyville, Tex. **63** m13
De Witt, Ark., 3,900 **15** D3
De Witt, co., Ill., 17,253 **25** D3
De Witt, Ill., 245 **25** D3
De Witt, Iowa, 3,680 **28** G3
De Witt, Mich., 1,238 **37** G6
Dewitt, Mo., 174 **40** C2
De Witt, Nebr., 504 **42** G3
De Witt, N.Y. **49** n20
De Witt, co., Tex., 20,683 **62** F5
De Witt, Va. **67** M3
Dewittville, N.Y. **48** A6
Dewright, Okla. **54** G2
Dewy Rose, Ga. **22** D1
Dexter, Ga., 359 **22** C3
Dexter, Ind. **27** B4
Dexter, Iowa, 670 **28** C3
Dexter, Kans. **29** E3
Dexter, Ky., 250 **30** B4
Dexter, Me., 2,720 **32** B3
Dexter, Mich., 1,702 **37** H6
Dexter, Mo., 5,519 **40** G5
Dexter, N. Mex., 885 **46** C3
Dexter, N.Y., 1,009 **49** H2
Dexter, Ohio **53** C3
Dexter, Oreg. **55** L3
Dexter City, Ohio, 197 **53** D3
Dexterville, Wis. **69** C3
Diablo, Calif., 2,096 **16** c7
Diablo, co., Tex. **62** B4
Diablo, Mt., Calif. **16** c7
Diablo, Sa., Tex. **62** B4
Diablo Heights, C.Z., 1,075 **72** o
Diablo Mtn., Oreg. **55** M3
Diablo Range, Calif. **17** C3
Diagonal, Iowa, 443 **28** C4
Diamond, Mo., 453 **40** B4
Diamond, Oreg. **55** N3
Diamond, Wash. **66** E2
Diamond Bluff, Wis. **69** A3
Diamond Head, Hawaii **23** J2
Diamond Hill, R.I. **58** C1
Diamond Lake, Ill. **26** b2
Diamond L., Ill. **26** b1
Diamond Pk., Colo. **18** A1
Diamond Point, N.Y. **49** N4
Diamondville, Wyo., 398 **70** A3
Diana, W.Va. **68** C3
Dibble, Okla., 127 **54** F2
Diboll, Tex., 2,506 **63** G4
Dibrell, Tenn. **61** K2
Dickens, Iowa, 241 **28** C1
Dickens, Nebr., 25 **42** D3
Dickens, co., Tex., 4,963 **62** D3
Dickens, Tex., 302 **62** D3
Dickenson, co., Va., 20,211 **66** G3
Dickey, Me. **32** B1
Dickey, co., N. Dak., 8,147 **51** N2
Dickey, N. Dak., 143 **51** N2
Dickeyville, Wis., 671 **69** C5
Dickinson, co., Iowa, 12,574 **28** B1
Dickinson, co., Kans., 21,572 **29** E2
Dickinson, co., Mich., 23,917 **36** D2
Dickinson, N.Y. **49** L1
Dickinson, N. Dak., 9,971 **51** L2
Dickinson, Tex., 4,715 **63** G5
Dickson, co., Tenn, 18,839 **61** H1
Dickson, Tenn., 5,028 **61** H1
Dickson City, Pa., 7,738 **57** n16
Diehlstadt, Mo., 141 **40** G5
Dierks, Ark., 1,276 **15** B3
Dieterich, Ill., 591 **25** D4
Dietrich, Idaho, 118 **24** B4
Difficult, Tenn. **61** K1
Diggins, Mo., 101 **40** D4
Dighton, Kans., 1,526 **29** B2
Dighton, Mass., 3,769(T) **35** K5
Dike, Iowa, 630 **28** E2
Dilia, N. Mex. **46** C2
Dilkon, Ariz. **14** C2
Dillard, Oreg. **55** L3
Dill City, Okla., 623 **54** D2
Dilley, Tex., 2,118 **62** E5
Dillingham, Alaska, 424 **12** D4
Dillingham Ranch, Hawaii **23** c8
Dillon, Colo., 814 **18** C2
Dillon, Mont., 3,690 **41** B3
Dillon, co., S.C., 30,584 **59** E2
Dillon, S.C., 6,173 **59** E2
Dillon Res., Ohio **53** C2
Dillonvale, Ohio, 1,232 **53** E2
Dillsboro, Ind., 745 **27** C3
Dillsburg, Pa., 1,322 **56** G5
Dillwyn, Kans. **29** D3
Dillwyn, Va., 515 **67** L3
Dilly, Wis. **69** C4
Dilworth, Minn., 2,102 **38** A2
Dimmit, co., Tex., 10,095 **62** E5
Dimmitt, Tex., 2,935 **62** C2
Dimock, S. Dak. **61** C2
Dimondale, Mich., 866 **37** G6
Dinero, Tex. **62** E5
Ding Dong, Tex. **62** E4
Dingley Dell (part of Brimfield), Mass. **34** F4
Dingmans Ferry, Pa. **57** M3
Dinnebito Wash, Ariz. **14** C1
Dinner Station, Nev. **43** C1
Dinosaur, Colo., 318 **18** A1
Dinosaur Nat. Mon., Colo.-Utah **18** A1
Dinsmore, Fla. **21** J1
Dinuba, Calif., 6,103 **17** D3
Dinwiddie, co., Va., 22,183 **67** M3
Dinwiddie, Va. **67** M3
Dirty Devil, r., Utah **64** B2

For abbreviations and explanation of index, see page 176.

Disappointment — INDEX TO MAPS OF THE UNITED STATES — East Hebron

Disappointment, C., Wash. **66** A2
Disco, Mich. **37** d10
Discovery Bay, Wash. **67** a5
Dishna, r., Alaska **13** D3
Dismal, r., Nebr. **42** D2
Dismal Swamp, N.C.-Va. **67** N4
Dismal Swamp Can., N.C.-Va. **51** J1
Disputanta, Va. **67** M3
Distant, Pa. **56** C4
District Heights, Md., 7,524 **33** b5
District of Columbia, U.S., 802,000* **33** a5
Dittlinger, Tex. **62** b8
Divernon, Ill., 997 **25** C4
Diversey Hbr., Ill. **26** d3
Diversion Chan., r., Mo. **40** G4
Divide, Alaska **13** F3
Divide, Colo. **18** b7
Divide, co., N. Dak., 5,566 **51** L1
Dividend, Utah **64** b8
Dividing Creek, N.J. **45** A5
Division Pk., Nev. **43** A1
Dix, Ill. **25** D5
Dix, Nebr., 420 **42** A2
Dix, r., Ky. **30** F3
Dixboro, Mich. **37** H6
Dixfield, Me., 1,334 **32** A4
Dixie, Ala. **11** C4
Dixie, Ark. **15** D2
Dixie, co., Fla., 4,479 **21** G2
Dixie, Ga., 220 **22** C3
Dixie, Wash. **66** D2
Dixie, W.Va. **68** B3
Dixie Valley, Nev. **43** B2
Dixmont, Me. **32** B4
Dixmoor, Ill., 3,076 **26** d4
Dixon, Calif., 2,970 **17** C2
Dixon, Ill., 19,565 **25** C2
Dixon, Iowa, 280 **28** G3
Dixon, Ky., 541 **30** C3
Dixon, Mo., 1,473 **40** D4
Dixon, co., Nebr., 8,106 **42** H1
Dixon, Nebr., 139 **42** H1
Dixon, N. Mex. **46** C1
Dixon, S. Dak. **61** C2
Dixon, Wyo., 108 **70** C3
Dixon Entr., Can.-U.S. **13** K5
Dixon Springs, Ill. **25** D6
Dixon Springs, Tenn. **61** K1
Dixville Notch, N.H. **44** C1
D'Lo, Miss., 428 **39** C4
Dobbin, Tex. **63** G4
Dobbs Ferry, N.Y., 10,076 **47** d1
Dobson, N.C., 684 **50** E1
Docena, Ala. **11** c6
Dock Junction, Ga., 5,417 **22** E4
Doctors Cr., N.J. **47** a5
Doctors Inlet, Fla. **21** J1
Doddridge, Ark. **15** A4
Doddridge, co., W.Va., 6,970 **68** C2
Doddsville, Miss., **39** B2
Dodge, co., Ga., 16,483 **22** C3
Dodge (part of Charlton), Mass. **35** G4
Dodge, co., Minn., 13,259 **38** C3
Dodge, co., Nebr., 32,471 **42** H2
Dodge, Nebr., 649 **42** H2
Dodge, N. Dak., 226 **51** L2
Dodge, Tex. **63** G4
Dodge, co., Wis., 63,170 **69** E4
Dodge, Wis. **69** B3
Dodge Center, Minn., 1,441 **38** C3
Dodge City, Kans., 13,520 **29** B3
Dodgeville (part of Attleboro), Mass. **35** J5
Dodgeville, Wis., 2,911 **69** C5
Dodson, La., 512 **31** B1
Dodson, Mont., 313 **41** D1
Dodson, Tex., 308 **62** D2
Doebay, Wash. **66** B1
Doe Hill, Va. **67** K2
Doerun, Ga., 1,037 **22** B4
Doe Run, Mo. **40** F4
Doe Run, Pa. **57** e12
Dog, r., Vt. **65** B2
Dog I., Fla. **21** F2
Dogwood, Ind. **27** B4
Doland, S. Dak., 481 **61** C1
Doles, Ga. **22** C4
Dolgeville, N.Y., 3,058 **49** L4
Dolgoi I., Alaska **12** C5
Dollar Bay, Mich. **36** C1
Dollarhide, Tex. **62** C3
Dollarville, Mich. **36** F2
Dolomite, Ala. **11** b7
Dolores, co., Colo., 2,196 **18** A3
Dolores, Colo., 805 **18** A3
Dolores, Tex. **62** E6
Dolores, r., Colo.-Utah **18** A2
Dolph, Oreg. **55** L2
Dolton, Ill., 22,557 **26** d4
Dome, Alaska **13** a6
Dome, Ariz. **14** A3
Dome, The, mtn., Vt. **65** A5
Dome Rock Mts., Ariz. **14** A3
Dome Shaped Mtn., Mont. **41** B2
Domingo, N. Mex. **46** B2
Dona Ana, co., N. Mex., 59,948 **46** B3
Dona Ana, N. Mex. **46** B3
Donahue, Iowa, 133 **28** G3
Doña Juana, Co., P.R. **72** n c1
Donald, Oreg., 201 **55** L2
Donalds, S.C., 416 **59** B2
Donaldson, Ark. **15** C3
Donaldson, Mich. **37** G2
Donaldson, Minn., 64 **38** A1
Donaldsonville, La., 6,082 **31** C3
Donalsonville, Ga., 2,621 **22** B4
Donegal, Pa., 216 **56** C5
Donelson, Tenn., 17,195 **61** K1
Dongola, Ill., 757 **25** C6
Donie, Tex. **62** F4
Doniphan, co., Kans., 9,574 **29** G1
Doniphan, Mo., 1,421 **40** F5
Doniphan, Nebr., 390 **42** F3
Donken, Mich. **36** C2
Donley, co., Tex., 4,449 **62** D2
Donna, Tex., 7,522 **62** E6
Donnellson, Ill., 292 **25** C4
Donnellson, Iowa, 709 **28** F4
Donnelly, Alaska **13** G3
Donnelly, Idaho, 161 **24** B3
Donnelly, Minn., 358 **38** B3
Donner Pass, Calif. **17** C2
Donner und Blitzen, r., Oreg. **55** N3
Donnybrook, N. Dak., 196 **51** M1
Donora, Pa., 11,131 **56** B5
Donovan, Ill., 320 **25** E3
Doole, Tex. **62** E4
Doolittle, Mo., 499 **40** E4
Dooly, co., Ga., 11,474 **22** C3
Doon, Iowa, 436 **28** A1
Doonerak, Mt., Alaska **13** F2
Door, co., Wis., 20,685 **69** F3
Door Village, Ind. **26** g4
Dora, Ala., 1,776 **11** B2
Dora, Mo. **40** D5
Dora, N. Mex. **46** D3
Dorado, P.R., 2,120 **72** n c1
Dora Lake, Minn. **38** C2
Doran, Ill. **25** D4
Doran, Minn., 136 **38** A2
Doraville, Ga., 4,437 **22** B2
Dorcas, Fla. **20** D1
Dorcheat Bayou, Ark.-La. **15** B4
Dorchester, co., Md., 29,666 **33** D2
Dorchester, Nebr., 460 **42** G3
Dorchester, N.H. **44** B4
Dorchester, co., S.C., 24,383 **59** D3
Dorchester, S.C. **59** D3
Dorchester, Wis., 504 **69** C2
Dorena, Oreg. **55** L3
Dormont, Pa., 13,098 **56** b8
Dornsife, Pa. **56** H4
Dorothy, Minn. **38** A2
Dorothy, W.Va. **68** B4
Dorr, Mich. **36** F6
Dorrance, Kans., 331 **29** D2
Dorris, Calif., 973 **17** B1
Dorset, Ohio **53** E1
Dorset, Vt. **65** A4
Dorset Pk., Vt. **65** A4
Dorsey, Ill. **25** C5
Dorsey, Md. **33** c4
Dorseyville, Pa. **56** c7
Dos Bocas, P.R. **72** n b1
Dos Cabezas, Ariz. **14** D3
Dosewallips, r., Wash. **67** a5
Dos Palos, Calif., 2,373 **17** C3
Doss, Tex. **62** E4
Dossville, Miss. **39** C3
Doswell, Va. **67** M3
Dothan, Ala., 31,440 **11** D4
Dot Lake, Alaska **13** H3
Dotsero, Colo. **18** B2
Doty, Wash. **66** B2
Double Bayou, Tex. **63** k14
Double Shoals, N.C. **50** D2
Double Springs, Ala., 811 **11** B1
Double Springs, Tenn. **61** K1
Doubletop Mtn., N.Y. **49** L6
Dougherty, co., Ga., 75,680 **22** B4
Dougherty, Iowa, 398 **28** E2
Dougherty, Okla., 294 **54** F3
Doughton, N.C. **50** E1
Douglas, Alaska, 1,042 **13** K4
Douglas, Ariz., 12,370 **14** D4
Douglas, co., Colo., 4,816 **18** C2
Douglas, co., Ga., 16,741 **22** B2
Douglas, Ga., 8,736 **22** D4
Douglas, co., Ill., 19,281 **25** D4
Douglas, co., Kans., 43,720 **29** G2
Douglas, Mass., 2,559(T) **35** H4
Douglas, Mich., 602 **36** E6
Douglas, co., Minn., 21,313 **38** B3
Douglas, co., Mo., 9,653 **40** D5
Douglas, co., Nebr., 343,490 **42** H2
Douglas, Nebr., 197 **42** H3
Douglas, co., Nev., 3,481 **43** A2
Douglas, N. Dak., 210 **51** M2
Douglas, Okla., 74 **54** F1
Douglas, co., Oreg., 68,458 **55** L3
Douglas, co., S. Dak., 5,113 **61** C2
Douglas, co., Wash., 14,890 **66** D2
Douglas, co., Wis., 45,008 **69** A1
Douglas, Wyo., 2,822 **70** D2
Douglas, Mt., Alaska **13** E4
Douglas, Mt., Mont. **41** C3
Douglas City, Calif. **17** B1
Douglas L., Mich. **37** G3
Douglas L., Tenn. **61** M2
Douglass, Kans., 1,058 **29** F3
Douglass, Tex. **63** G4
Douglassville, Pa. **57** e10
Douglasville, Ga., 4,462 **22** B2
Dousman, Wis., 410 **69** E4
Dove Creek, Colo., 986 **18** A3
Dover, Ark., 525 **15** B2
Dover, Del., 7,250 **20** A2
Dover, Fla. **21** d10
Dover, Ga. **22** E3
Dover, Kans. **29** G2
Dover, Ky., 718 **30** G2
Dover, Mass., 2,846(T) **35** J4
Dover, Mo., 172 **40** C2
Dover, N.H., 19,131 **44** D5
Dover, N.J., 13,034 **45** B2
Dover, N.C., 651 **51** H2
Dover, Ohio, 11,300 **53** D2
Dover, Okla. **54** E2
Dover, Pa., 975 **56** H5
Dover, Tenn., 736 **61** H1
Dover-Foxcroft, Me., 2,481 **32** B3
Dover Plains, N.Y. **49** N7
Dovesville, S.C. **59** D2
Dowagiac, Mich., 7,208 **36** E7
Dowagiac, r., Mich. **36** E7
Dow City, Iowa, 531 **28** B3
Dowdy, Ark. **15** D2
Dowell, Ill., 453 **25** C6
Dowelltown, Tenn., 279 **61** J2
Dowling, Mich. **36** F6
Dowling Park, Fla. **21** G1
Downer, Minn. **38** A2
Downers Grove, Ill., 22,612 **25** D2
Downey, Calif., 82,505 **17** D5
Downey, Idaho, 726 **24** C4
Downieville, Calif. **17** C2
Downing, Mo., 463 **40** D1
Downing, Wis., 241 **69** A2
Downingtown, Pa., 5,598 **57** K5
Downs, Ill., 654 **25** D3
Downs, Kans., 1,206 **29** D1
Downs Mtn., Wyo. **70** B2
Downsville, La. **31** B1
Downsville, N.Y. **49** K6
Downsville, Wis. **69** B3
Downsville Dam, N.Y. **49** L6
Dows, Iowa, 882 **28** D2
Doyle, Calif. **17** C1
Doylestown, Ohio, 1,873 **53** D2
Doylestown, Pa., 5,917 **57** L5
Doylestown, Wis., 249 **69** D4
Doyleville, Colo., **18** B2
Doyline, La., 1,061 **31** A1
Doyon, N. Dak. **51** N1
Dozier, Ala., 335 **11** C4
Dozier, Tex. **62** D2
Dracut, Mass., 13,674(T) **35** J2
Dragerton, Utah, 2,959 **64** B2
Dragon, Utah **64** C2
Dragoon, Ariz. **14** D3
Drain, Oreg., 1,052 **55** L3
Drake, Ariz. **14** B2
Drake, Colo. **18** b4
Drake, N. Dak., 752 **51** M2
Drake, S.C. **59** E2
Drake Pk., Oreg. **55** M3
Drakesboro, Ky., 832 **30** C3
Drakes Branch, Va., 759 **67** L3
Drakesville, Iowa, 197 **28** E4
Dranesville, Ga. **22** B3
Dranesville, Va. **67** M1
Draper, N.C., 3,255 **50** F1
Draper, S. Dak., 215 **61** B2
Draper, Utah **64** B1
Draper, Va., 233 **67** J4
Drasco, Ark. **15** D2
Dravosburg, Pa., 3,458 **56** c8
Draw, Tex. **62** D3
Drayton, N. Dak., 1,278 **51** O1
Drayton Plains, Mich. **37** H6
Drennen, W.Va. **68** C3
Drenthe, Mich. **36** F6
Dresden, Kans., 134 **29** B1
Dresden, N.Y., 437 **48** F5
Dresden, N. Dak. **51** N1
Dresden, Ohio, 1,338 **53** D2
Dresden, Tenn., 1,510 **60** G1
Dresden Station, N.Y. **49** O3
Dresser, Wis., 498 **69** A2
Drew, co., Ark., 15,213 **15** D4
Drew, Miss., 2,143 **39** B2
Drew, Oreg. **55** L3
Drewryville, Va. **67** M4
Drewsey, Oreg., 39 **55** N3
Drews Res., Oreg. **55** M3
Drexel, Mo., 651 **40** B3
Drexel, N.C., 1,146 **50** D2
Drexel Hill, Pa., 39,750* **57** f12
Driftwood, Pa., 203 **56** E3
Driftwood, Tex. **62** b7
Driftwood Branch, Pa. **56** E2
Driggs, Idaho, 824 **24** D4
Drinker, Pa. **57** o16
Dripping Springs, Tex. **62** F4
Driscoll, N. Dak. **51** M2
Driscoll, Tex., 669 **62** F6
Driskill Mtn., La. **31** B1
Driver, Ark., **15** E2
Druid L., Wis. **69** a6
Drum Inlet, N.C. **51** J3
Drummond, Mont., 577 **41** B2
Drummond, Okla., 281 **54** E1
Drummond, Wis. **69** B1
Drummond, L., Va. **67** N4
Drummond Island, Mich. **37** H2
Drummond I., Mich. **37** H2
Drumright, Okla., 4,190 **54** G2
Drums, Pa. **57** K4
Drury (part of Florida), Mass. **34** C2
Dry, r., N.H. **44** C3
Dryad, Wash. **66** B2
Dry Bk. Mass. **34** D2
Dry Creek, La. **31** A3
Dry Cr., Ga. **22** B4
Dry Cr. Butte, Oreg. **55** O3
Dryden, Me. **32** A4
Dryden, Mich., 531 **37** H6
Dryden, N.Y., 1,353 **49** H6
Dryden, Oreg. **55** L3
Dryden, Tex. **62** C4
Dryden, Wash. **66** C2
Dry Falls Dam, Wash. **66** D2
Dry Fork, Va. **56** D6
Dry L., N. Dak. **51** N1
Dry Mills, Me. **32** A5
Dry Prong, La., 360 **31** B2
Dry Ridge, Ky., 802 **30** F2
Dry Run, Pa. **56** F5
Dry Tortugas, is., Fla. **21** k15
Duanesburg, N.Y. **49** M5
Duarte, Calif., 13,962 **16** f10
Dubach, La., 1,013 **31** B1
Dubberly, La., 249 **31** A1
Dublin, Calif. **16** c7
Dublin, Ga., 13,814 **22** C3
Dublin, Ind., 1,021 **27** C3
Dublin, Ky. **30** B4
Dublin, Mich. **36** E4
Dublin, Miss. **39** B1
Dublin, N.H. **44** A6
Dublin, N.C., 347 **50** G3
Dublin, Pa., 517 **57** f10
Dublin, Tex., 2,443 **62** E3
Dublin, Va., 1,427 **56** C5
Dublon, i., Truk **72** g
Dubois, Idaho, 447 **24** C3
Dubois, co., Ind., 27,463 **27** B4
Dubois, Ind. **27** B4
Du Bois, Nebr., 218 **42** H3
Du Bois, Pa., 10,667 **56** D3
Dubois, Wyo., 574 **70** B2
Duboistown, Pa., 1,358 **56** G3
Du Boullie Mtn., Me. **32** C2
Dubre, Ky. **30** E4
Dubuque, co., Iowa, 80,048 **28** G2
Dubuque, Iowa, 56,606 **28** G2
Duchesne, co., Utah, 7,179 **64** B1
Duchesne, Utah, 770 **64** B1
Duchesne, r., Utah **64** B1
Duck, r., Tenn. **61** H2
Duckabush, r., Wash. **67** a5
Duck Cr., Nev. **43** C2
Duck Hill, Miss., 674 **39** C2
Duck L., Me. **32** C4
Duck L., Me. **32** C3
Duck L., Mich. **36** B2
Duck L., Mich. **36** F4
Ducktown, Tenn., 741 **61** L2
Duckwater, Nev. **43** C2
Dudley, Ga., 360 **22** C3
Dudley, Ill. **25** E4
Dudley, Mass., 6,510(T) **35** G4
Dudley, Mo., 287 **40** F5
Dudley, N.C., 158 **50** H2
Dudley, Pa., 295 **56** E5
Dudley, S.C. **59** D2
Duenweg, Mo., 529 **40** B4
Due West, S.C., 1,166 **59** B2
Duffer Pk., Nev. **43** A1
Duffy, Ohio **53** E3
Dufur, Oreg., 488 **55** M2
Dugger, Ind., 1,062 **27** A3
Dugway, Utah **64** A1
Dugway Range, Utah **64** a8
Duke, Okla. **54** D3
Duke Center, Pa. **56** D2
Dukes, co., Mass., 5,829 **35** M7
Dukes, Mich. **36** D2
Dulac, La. **31** D4
Dulce, N. Mex. **46** B1
Duluth, Ga., 1,483 **22** B2
Duluth, Minn., 106,884 **38** D2
Dumas, Ark., 3,540 **15** D4
Dumas, Miss. **39** D1
Dumas, Tex., 8,477 **62** D2
Dumfries, Va., 1,368 **67** M2
Dumont, Colo. **18** a5
Dumont, Iowa, 719 **28** D2
Dumont, Minn., 226 **38** A3
Dumont, N.J., 18,882 **45** C2
Dunbar, Okla. **55** H3
Dunbar, Pa., 1,536 **56** B6
Dunbar, S.C. **59** E2
Dunbar, W.Va., 11,006 **68** B3
Dunbar, Wis. **69** E2
Dunbarton, N.H. **44** B5
Duncan, Ariz., 862 **14** D3
Duncan, Miss., 465 **39** B1
Duncan, Nebr., 294 **42** G2
Duncan, N.C. **40** G2
Duncan, Okla., 20,009 **54** F3
Duncan, S.C., 1,186 **59** B2
Duncan Falls, Ohio **53** D3
Duncannon, Pa., 1,800 **56** H5
Duncansville, Pa., 1,396 **56** E5
Duncanville, Ill. **25** E5
Duncanville, Tex., 3,774 **63** f11
Duncombe, Iowa, 355 **28** C2
Dundalk, Md., 82,428 **33** c3
Dundarrach, N.C., 109 **50** F3
Dundas, Ill. **25** D5
Dundas, Ohio **53** C3
Dundas, Va. **67** L4
Dundee, Fla., 1,554 **21** J3
Dundee, Iowa, 185 **28** F2
Dundee, Kans. **29** D2
Dundee, Ky. **30** D3
Dundee, Mich., 2,377 **37** H7
Dundee, N.Y., 1,468 **48** F5
Dundee, Oreg., 318 **55** L2
Dundee, Wis. **69** E4
Dundy, co., Nebr., 3,570 **42** C3
Dune Acres, Ind., 238 **26** f9
Dunedin, Fla., 8,444 **21** H3
Dunellen, N.J., 6,840 **47** b3
Dunes Park, Ill. **26** c1
Dunfermline, Ill., 284 **25** C3
Dungannon, Va., 444 **66** G4
Dungeness, Wash. **66** B1
Dunkerton, Iowa, 507 **28** E2
Dunkirk, Ind., 3,117 **27** C2
Dunkirk, N.Y., 18,205 **48** B5
Dunkirk, Ohio, 1,006 **53** B2
Dunklin, co., Mo., 39,139 **40** F5
Dunlap, Ill., 564 **25** C3
Dunlap, Ind., 1,935 **27** C1
Dunlap, Iowa, 1,254 **28** B3
Dunlap, Kans., 134 **29** F2
Dunlap, Nebr. **42** B1
Dunlap, N. Mex. **46** C2
Dunlap, Tenn., 1,026 **61** K2
Dunlap, Tex. **62** D2
Dunlevy, Pa., 408 **56** c9
Dunlow, W.Va. **68** A3
Dunmor, Ky. **30** C3
Dunmore, Pa., 18,917 **57** K3
Dunmore, W.Va. **68** D3
Dunmore, L., Vt. **65** A3
Dunn, Ind. **27** A2
Dunn, La. **31** C1
Dunn, N.C., 7,487 **50** G2
Dunn, co., N. Dak., 6,350 **51** L2
Dunn, co., Wis., 26,156 **69** B3
Dunnavant, Ala. **11** e6
Dunn Center, N. Dak., 250 **51** L2
Dunn Corner (part of Westerly), R.I. **58** B3
Dunnell, Minn., 260 **38** B4
Dunnellon, Fla., 1,079 **21** H2
Dunning, Nebr., 212 **42** D2
Dunning Cr., Pa **56** D5
Dunnington, Ind. **27** A2
Dunnsville, Va. **56** G5
Dunnville, Ky. **30** F3
Dunseith, N. Dak., 1,017 **51** M1
Dunsmuir, Calif., 2,873 **17** B1
Dunstable, Mass. **35** J2
Dunton, Colo. **18** A3
Dunwoody, Ga. **22** b6
Du Page, co., Ill., 313,459 **25** D2
Du Page, r., Ill. **25** D2
Duplainville, Wis. **69** a7
Duplin, co., N.C., 40,270 **50** H3
Dupo, Ill., 2,937 **25** B5
Dupont, Colo. **18** c5
Du Pont, Ga., 210 **22** D5
Dupont, Pa., 3,669 **57** n16
Du Pont, Wash., 354 **66** B2
Dupree, S. Dak., 548 **61** B2
Dupuyer, Mont. **41** B1
Duquesne, Pa., 15,019 **56** B5
Du Quoin, Ill., 6,558 **25** C5
Duran, N. Mex. **46** C2
Durand, Ill., 797 **25** C1
Durand, Mich., 3,312 **37** H6
Durand, Wis., 2,039 **69** B3
Durango, Colo., 10,530 **18** B3
Durant, Iowa, 1,266 **28** F3
Durant, Miss., 2,617 **39** C2
Durant, Okla., 10,467 **55** G3
Durants Neck, N.C. **51** J1
Durbin, Fla. **21** J1
Durbin, W. Va., 431 **68** D3
Durham, Calif. **17** C2
Durham, Conn., 3,096(T) **19** E4
Durham, Ind. **26** g4
Durham, Kans., 183 **29** E2
Durham, Me. **32** A5
Durham, N.H., 4,688 **44** D5
Durham, N.Y. **49** M6
Durham, co., N.C., 111,995 **50** G1
Durham, N.C., 78,302 **50** G2
Durham, Okla. **54** D2
Durham, Pa. **57** k18
Durham, Wis. **69** a8
Durham Center (part of Durham), Conn. **19** E4
Durhamville, N.Y. **49** J4
Durkee, Oreg. **55** O2
Duryea, Pa., 5,626 **57** K3
Dushore, Pa., 731 **56** J2
Duson, La., 1,033 **31** B3
Dustin, Okla., 457 **55** H2
Dutchess, co., N.Y., 176,008 **49** N7
Dutch Harbor, Alaska **12** B5
Dutch John, Utah **64** C1
Dutch Mills, Ark. **15** A2
Dutch Mtn., Utah **64** A1
Dutchtown, Mo. **40** G4
Dutton, Mich. **36** F6
Dutton, Mont., 504 **41** C2
Dutton, Okla. **54** E2
Dutton, Va. **67** N3
Dutton, Mt., Utah **64** A2
Duval, co., Fla., 455,411 **21** J1
Duval, co., Tex., 13,398 **62** E6
Duvall, Wash., 345 **66** C2
Duxbury, Mass., 1,069; 4,727(T) **35** M4
Duxbury, Vt. **65** B2
Duxbury Bay, Mass. **35** M4
Dwarf, Ky. **30** G3
Dwight, Ill., 3,086 **25** D2
Dwight (part of Belchertown), Mass. **34** E3
Dwight, Nebr., 209 **42** G2
Dwight, N. Dak., 101 **51** O2
Dwyer, N. Mex. **46** B3
Dyberry Cr., Pa. **57** L2
Dyckesville, Wis. **69** F3
Dyer, Ark., 450 **15** A2
Dyer, Ind., 3,993 **27** A1
Dyer, Ky. **30** D3
Dyer, Nev. **43** A3
Dyer, co., Tenn., 29,537 **60** F1
Dyer, Tenn., 1,909 **60** G1
Dyersburg, Tenn., 12,499 **60** F1
Dyersville, Iowa, 2,818 **28** F2
Dyess, Ark., 409 **15** E2
Dyke, Va. **67** L2
Dysart, Iowa, 1,197 **28** E2
Dysart, Pa. **56** E4

E

Eads, Colo., 929 **18** D2
Eads, Tenn. **60** F2
Eagar, Ariz., 1,172 **14** D2
Eagle, Alaska, 92 **13** H2
Eagle, co., Colo., 4,677 **18** B2
Eagle, Colo., 546 **18** B2
Eagle, Mich., 141 **37** G6
Eagle, Nebr., 302 **42** H3
Eagle, N.Y. **48** D5
Eagle, Pa. **57** K5
Eagle, Wis., 620 **69** E5
Eagle, r., Colo. **18** B2
Eagle Bay, N.Y. **49** L3
Eagle Bend, Minn., 611 **38** B2
Eagle Bridge, N.Y. **49** N5
Eagle Butte, S. Dak., 495 **61** B1
Eagle Cap, mtn., Oreg. **55** O2
Eagle City, Okla. **54** E2
Eagle Cr., Ariz. **14** D3
Eagle Cr., Ky. **30** F2
Eagle Grove, Iowa, 4,381 **28** D2
Eagle Harbor, N.Y. **48** D4
Eagle Hill (part of Ipswich), Mass. **35** L2
Eagle Lake, Fla., 1,364 **21** J4
Eagle Lake, Me. **32** C1
Eagle Lake, Tex., 3,565 **62** F5
Eagle L., Calif. **17** C1
Eagle L., Me. **32** B2
Eagle L., Me. **32** C1
Eagle L., Minn. **38** b5
Eagle L., Wis. **69** a9
Eagle Mills, Ark. **15** C4
Eagle Mills, N.Y. **49** e14
Eagle Mountain, Calif. **17** F5
Eagle Mtn., Minn. **38** D2
Eagle Mtn., Tex. **62** B4
Eagle Mtn. L., Tex. **63** e11
Eagle Nest, N. Mex. **46** C1
Eagle Nest Butte, S. Dak. **61** A1
Eagle Pass, Tex., 12,094 **62** D5
Eagle Pk., N. Mex. **46** A3
Eagle Point, Oreg., 752 **55** L3
Eagle Point L., Minn. **38** d6
Eagleport, Ohio **53** D3
Eagle River, Alaska **12** c7
Eagle River, Mich. **36** C1
Eagle River, Wis., 1,367 **69** D2
Eagle Rock, Va. **67** K3
Eagles Mere, Pa., 138 **56** H3
Eagle Springs, N.C. **50** F2
Eagletown, Okla. **55** J3
Eagleville, Calif. **17** C1
Eagleville (part of Mansfield), Conn. **19** F2
Eagleville, Mo., 341 **40** B1
Eagleville, Pa. **57** f11
Eakly, Okla., 217 **54** E2
Earl, Wis. **69** B2
Earle, Ark., 2,896 **15** E2
Earlham, Iowa, 788 **28** C3
Earlimart, Calif., 2,897 **17** D4
Earling, Iowa, 431 **28** B3
Earlington, Ky., 2,786 **30** C3
Earl Park, Ind., 551 **27** A2
Earlsboro, Okla., 257 **54** G2
Earlton, Kans., 104 **29** G3
Earlville, Ill., 1,420 **25** D2
Earlville, Iowa, 668 **28** F2
Earlville, N.Y., 1,004 **49** K5
Earlville, Pa. **57** e10
Early, co., Ga., 13,151 **22** B4
Early, Iowa, 824 **28** B2
Early, Tex., 819 **62** E4
Early Branch, S.C. **59** D4
Earp, Calif. **17** F4
Earth, Tex., 1,104 **62** C2
Earthquake L., Mont. **41** C3
Easley, S.C., 8,283 **59** B2
Easonville, Ala. **11** C2
East, r., N.Y. **47** d3
East Acton (part of Acton), Mass. **35** J3
East Alburg, Vt. **65** A1
East Alstead, N.H. **44** A5
East Alton, Ill., 7,630 **25** B5
East Amherst, N.Y. **48** h15
East Andover, N.H. **44** B5
East Arcadia, N.C. **50** G3
East Arlington, Vt. **65** A4
East Aspetuck, r., Conn. **19** B6
East Aurora, N.Y. 6,796 **48** C5
East Aux Sable Cr., Ill. **26** a4
East Avon, N.Y. **48** j18
East Baldwin, Me. **32** A5
East Barnard, Vt. **65** B3
East Barnet, Vt. **65** C2
East Barre, Vt. **65** C2
East Barre Res., Vt. **65** C2
East Barrington, N.H. **44** D5
East Baton Rouge, parish, La., 230,058 **31** C3
East Bay, La. **31** D4
East Bay, r., N.Y.-Vt. **65** A3
East Bay, Tex. **63** k15
East Bend, N.C., 446 **50** E1
East Berkshire, Vt. **65** B1
East Berlin, Pa., 1,037 **56** G6
East Bernard, Tex. **63** F5
East Berne, N.Y. **49** M5
East Bernstadt, Ky. **30** F3
East Berwick, Pa., 1,258 **57** J3
East Bethany, N.Y. **48** D5
East Bethel, Vt. **65** B3
East Blackstone (part of Blackstone), Mass. **35** J4
East Bloomfield, N.Y., 488 **48** F5
East Boothbay, Me. **32** B5
East Brady, Pa., 1,282 **56** B4
East Braintree (part of Braintree), Mass. **35** K4
East Braintree, Vt. **65** B3
East Brewster (part of Brewster), Mass. **35** O5
East Brewton, Ala., 2,511 **11** C4
East Bridgewater, Mass. 6,139(T) **35** L4
East Brimfield (part of Brimfield), Mass. **34** F4
Eastbrook, Me. **32** C4
East Brookfield, Mass., 1,150; 1,533(T) **35** F4
East Brookfield, Vt. **65** B2
East Brooklyn, Conn., 1,213 **19** H2
East Brownfield, Me. **32** A5
East Burke, Vt. **65** D1
East Butte, Idaho **24** C4
East Calais, Vt. **65** C2
East Canaan, Conn. **19** B1
East Candia, N.H. **44** C5
East Canon, Colo., 1,101 **18** C2
East Canyon Cr., Utah **64** c6
East C., Fla. **21** g13
East Carondelet, Ill., 463 **40** d10
East Carroll, parish, La., 14,433 **31** C1
East Carver (part of Carver), Mass. **35** M5
East Chan., Eniwetok **72** k
East Charleston, Vt. **65** C1
East Chicago, Ind., 57,669 **27** A1
East Chicago Heights, Ill., 4,715 **26** d4
East Cleveland, Ohio, 37,991 **52** e7
East Columbia, Tex. **63** h15
East Concord, Vt. **65** D2
East Conemaugh, Pa., 3,334 **56** D5
East Corinth, Me. **32** B3
East Corinth, Vt. **65** C2
East Craftsbury, Vt. **65** C1
East Cr., Vt. **65** A3
East Dayton, Mich. **37** H5
East Deerfield (part of Deerfield), Mass. **34** D2
East Dennis (part of Dennis), Mass. **35** O6
East Derry, N.H. **44** C6
East Detroit, Mich., 45,756 **37** e11
East Dorset, Vt. **65** B4
East Douglas, Mass., 1,695 **35** G4
East Dover, Vt. **65** B4
East Dubuque, Ill., 2,312 **25** B1
East Dummerston, Vt. **65** B5
East Dundee, Ill., 2,221 **26** b2
East Ellijay, Ga., 501 **22** B1
East Elmira, N.Y. **48** G6
East Ely, Nev., 1,796 **43** C2
East Entr., Palau **72** e
Eastern, r., Me. **32** B4
Eastern Point (part of Groton), Conn. **19** G4
Eastern Pt., Mass. **35** M2
Eastern Samoa = American Samoa
East Fairfield, Vt. **65** B1
East Fairhaven (part of Fairhaven), Mass. **35** L6
East Falmouth, Mass., 1,655 **35** M6
East Farms (part of Waterbury), Conn. **19** D3
East Feliciana, parish, La., 20,198 **31** C3
East Flat Rock, N.C. **50** C2
East Floyd, N.Y. **48** b10
Eastford, Conn., 746(T) **19** G2
East Foxboro (part of Foxboro), Mass. **35** K4
East Franklin, Vt. **65** B1
East Freetown, Mass. **35** L5
East Fultonham, Ohio **53** C3
East Gary, Ind., 9,309 **27** A1
Eastgate, Nev. **43** A2
Eastgate, Tex. **63** k13
East Georgia, Vt. **65** A1
East Glacier Park, Mont. **41** B1
East Glenville, N.Y. **49** d13
East Gloucester (part of Gloucester), Mass. **35** M2
East Grafton, N.H. **44** B4
East Granby, Conn., 2,434(T) **19** D2
East Grand Forks, Minn., 7,898 **38** A2
East Grand L., Me. **32** D3
East Grand Rapids, Mich., 10,924 **36** F6
East Granville, Vt. **65** B2
East Greenbush, N.Y., 1,325 **49** N5
East Greenfield (part of Greenfield), Mass. **34** D2
East Greenville, Pa., 1,931 **57** f10
East Greenwich, N.Y. **49** O4
East Greenwich, R.I., 8,228(T) **58** B2
East Haddam, Conn., 3,637(T) **19** F4
Eastham, Mass., 1,200(T) **35** O5
East Hampstead, N.H. **44** C6
East Hampton, Conn., 1,574; 5,403(T) **19** E3
Easthampton, Mass., 12,326(T) **34** D3
East Hampton, N.Y., 1,772 **49** Q9
East Hardin, Ill. **25** B4
East Hardwick, Vt. **65** C1
East Hartford, Conn., 43,977(T) **19** E2
East Hartland, Conn. **19** D2
East Harwich (part of Harwich and Chatham), Mass. **35** O6
East Haven, Conn., 21,388(T) **19** D4
East Haven, Vt. **65** D1
East Haverhill, N.H. **44** B3
East Hazel Crest, Ill., 1,457 **26** d4
East Hebron, N.H. **44** B4

For abbreviations and explanation of index, see page 176.

East Helena, Mont., 1,490 **41** C2
East Highgate, Vt. **65** B1
East Hills, N.Y., 8,441 **47** e2
East Hiram, Me. **32** A5
East Holden, Me. **32** C4
East Holliston (part of Holliston), Mass. **35** L4
East Homer, N.Y. **49** H5
East Hope, Idaho, 154 **24** A1
East Islip, N.Y. **47** g3
East Jamaica, Vt. **65** B4
East Jordan, Mich., 1,919 **36** F3
East Kansas City, Mo., 219 **40** b7
East Kent (part of Kent), Conn. **19** B3
East Killingly (part of Dayville), Conn. **19** H2
East Kingsford, Mich., 1,063 **36** D3
East Kingston, N.H. **44** D6
East Knox, Me. **32** B4
Eastlake, Colo. **18** c5
Eastlake, Mich., 436 **36** E4
East Lake, N.C. **51** K2
Eastlake, Ohio, 12,467 **52** e7
East L., Me. **32** B4
Eastland, Tenn. **61** K2
Eastland, co., Tex., 19,526 **62** E3
Eastland, Tex., 3,292 **62** E3
Eastland, Utah **64** C3
East Lansing, Mich., 30,198 **37** G6
East Las Vegas, Nev. **43** C3
East Laurinburg, N.C., 695 **50** F3
East Lee (part of Lee), Mass. **34** B3
East Lempster, N.H. **44** A5
East Leroy, Mich. **36** F6
East Leverett (part of Leverett), Mass **34** E3
East Litchfield (part of Litchfield), Conn. **19** C2
East Liverpool, Ohio, 22,306 **53** E2
East Loch, Hawaii **23** e9
East Longmeadow, Mass., 10,294(T) **34** E4
East Long Pd., Vt. **65** C2
East Los Angeles, Calif. **17** D5
East Lyme = Flanders Village
East Lynn, Ill. **25** E3
East Lynn, W. Va. **68** A3
East Lynne, Mo., 243 **40** B3
East Machias, Me. **32** D4
East Madison, N.H. **44** C4
Eastman, Ga., 5,118 **22** C3
Eastman, Wis., 348 **69** C4
East Mansfield (part of Mansfield), Mass. **35** K4
East Meadow, N.Y., 46,036 **47** e3
East Meredith, N.Y. **49** L6
East Middlebury, Vt. **65** A3
East Millbury (part of Millbury), Mass. **35** H4
East Millinocket, Me., 2,295 **32** C3
East Moline, Ill., 16,732 **25** B2
East Montpelier, Vt. **65** B2
East Nassau, N.Y. **49** e14
East Nicolaus, Calif. **17** h12
East Nishnabotna, r., Iowa **28** B4
East Nodaway, r., Iowa **28** C3
East Northfield (part of Northfield), Mass. **34** E2
East Northport, N.Y., 8,381 **47** f2
East Norton (part of Norton), Mass. **35** K5
East Nueces, r., Tex. **62** D5
East Olympia, Wash. **87** a7
Easton, Calif. **17** D3
Easton, Conn., 3,407(T) **19** B5
Easton, Ill., 361 **25** C3
Easton, Kans., 320 **29** G1
Easton, Me. **32** D2
Easton, Md., 6,337 **33** D2
Easton, Mass., 9,078(T) **35** K4
Easton, Mo., 198 **40** B2
Easton, N.H. **44** B3
Easton, N.Y. **49** N5
Easton, Pa., 31,955 **57** L4
Easton, Wash. **66** C2
Eastondale (part of Easton), Mass. **35** K4
Easton L., Conn. **19** B4
East Orange, N.J., 77,259 **47** c2
East Orleans (part of Orleans), Mass. **35** P5
East Otis (part of Otis), Mass. **34** B4
East Otto, N.Y. **48** C6
Eastover, S.C., 713 **59** D3
East Palatka, Fla., 1,133 **21** J2
East Palestine, Ohio, 5,232 **53** E2
East Pass, Fla. **21** F2
East Passage, R.I. **58** C3
East Patchogue, N.Y. **47** h2
East Paterson, N.J., 19,344 **47** c2
East Pembroke, N.Y. **48** D4
East Penfield, N.Y. **48** k17
East Peoria, Ill., 12,310 **25** C3
East Pepperell (part of Pepperell), Mass. **35** H2
East Peru, Iowa, 173 **28** D3
East Peru, Me. **32** A4
East Petersburg, Pa., 2,053 **56** J5
East Pittsford, Vt. **65** B3
East Plymouth (part of Plymouth), Conn. **19** C3
East Poestenkill, N.Y. **49** e14
Eastpoint, Fla. **21** F2
East Point, Ga., 35,633 **22** B2
East Pt., St. Croix **72** q
East Pt., Mass. **35** L3
Eastport, Idaho **24** B1
Eastport, Me., 2,537 **32** D4
Eastport, Md. **33** d5
Eastport, Mich. **36** F3
Eastport, N.Y. **49** P9
East Portal, Colo. **18** a5
East Poultney, Vt. **65** A3
East Prairie, Mo., 3,449 **40** G5
East Princeton (part of Princeton), Mass. **35** G3
East Prospect, Pa., 623 **56** H6
East Providence, R.I., 44,828 **58** C1
East Putnam (part of Putnam), Conn. **19** H2
East Rainelle, W. Va., 1,244 **68** C4
E. Rainy Butte, N. Dak. **51** L2
East Randolph, N.Y., 594 **48** B6
East Randolph, Vt. **65** B3
East Redmond, Wash., 203 **67** b5
East Rindge, N.H. **44** B6
East River (part of Madison), Conn. **19** E4
East Rochester, N.Y., 8,204 **48** E4
East Rockaway, N.Y., 11,708 **47** e3
East Rupert, Vt. **65** A4
East Ryegate, Vt. **65** C2
East St. Johnsbury, Vt. **65** D2
East St. Louis, Ill., 81,712 **25** B5
East Sandwich (part of Sandwich), Mass. **35** N6
East Sarasota, Fla. **21** d12
East Saugatuck, Mich. **36** E6
East Schodack, N.Y. **49** e14
East Sebago, Me. **32** A5
East Setauket, N.Y., 1,127 **49** O9
Eastside, Miss., 4,318 **39** D5
Eastside, Oreg., 1,380 **55** K3
East Smithfield, Pa. **57** H2
East Sparta, Ohio, 961 **53** D2
East Spring Cr., Colo. **18** D2
East Springfield, Pa., 511 **56** A2
East Stoneham, Me. **32** A4
East Stroudsburg, Pa., 7,674 **57** L3
East Sullivan, N.H. **44** A6
East Surry, Me. **32** C4
East Swanzey, N.H. **44** A6
East Syracuse, N.Y., 4,623 **49** n20
East Tampa, Fla. **21** d11
East Taunton (part of Taunton), Mass. **35** K5
East Tavaputs Plat., Utah **64** C4
East Tawas, Mich., 2,462 **37** H4
East Templeton (part of Templeton), Mass. **35** F2
East Texas, Pa. **57** j18
East Thermopolis, Wyo., 281 **70** C2
East Thetford, Vt. **65** C3
East Thomaston, Ga., 2,237 **22** B3
East Thompson (part of Thompson), Conn. **19** H2
East Tohopekaliga L., Fla. **21** J3
East Topsham, Vt. **65** C2
East Troy, Wis., 1,455 **69** E5
East Trumbull, Ohio **53** D1
East Twin, r., Wis. **69** F3
East Unity, N.H. **44** A5
Eastview, Ky. **30** D3
East Village (part of Webster), Mass. **35** G4
Eastville, Va., 261 **67** N3
East Wakefield, N.H. **44** D4
East Wallingford (part of Wallingford), Conn. **19** D4
East Wallingford, Vt. **65** B4
East Walpole (part of Walpole), Mass. **35** K4
East Wareham (part of Wareham), Mass. **35** M4
East Washington, N.H. **44** B5
East Washington, Pa., 2,483 **56** a9
East Waterboro, Me. **32** A5
East Waterford, Pa. **56** F5
East Weare, N.H. **44** B5
East Wenatchee, Wash., 383 **66** C2
East Westmoreland, N.H. **44** A6
East Weymouth (part of Weymouth), Mass. **35** L4
East Whately (part of Whately), Mass. **34** D3
East Willington (part of Willington), Conn. **19** G2
East Wilson, N.Y. **48** g15
East Wilton, Me. **32** A4
East Windsor (part of Windsor), Mass. **34** B3
East Windsor Hill (part of S. Windsor), Conn. **19** E2
East Winn, Me. **32** C3
East Worcester, N.Y. **49** L5
Eaton, Colo., 1,267 **18** C1
Eaton, Ill. **25** E4
Eaton, Me. **32** D3
Eaton, co., Mich., 49,684 **37** G6
Eaton, N.Y. **49** J5
Eaton, Lorain Co., Ohio **52** c8
Eaton, Preble Co., Ohio, 5,034 **53** A3
Eaton Center, N.H. **44** C4
Eaton Rapids, Mich., 4,052 **37** G6
Eatons Neck, N.Y. **47** f2
Eatonton, Ga., 3,612 **22** C2
Eatontown, N.J., 10,334 **45** C3
Eatonville, Pa. **57** m15
Eatonville, Wash., 896 **66** B2
Eau Claire, Mich., 562 **36** E7
Eau Claire, Pa., 374 **56** B3
Eau Claire, co., Wis., 58,300 **69** B3
Eau Claire, Wis., 37,987 **69** B3
Eau Claire, r., Wis. **69** D2
Eau Claire, L., Wis. **69** B3
Eau Claire Cr., Wis. **69** C3
Eau Galle, Wis. **69** B3
Eau Galle, L., Wis. **69** A3
Eau Gallie, Fla., 12,300 **21** K3
Eauripik, atoll, Car. Is. **71** B3
Ebadon, i., Kwajalein **72** l
Ebeemee L., Me. **32** B3
Ebenezer, Miss. **39** B3
Ebenezer, Florence Co., S.C. **59** E2
Ebenezer, York Co., S.C. **59** C2
Ebensburg, Pa., 4,111 **56** D5
Ebeye, i., Kwajalein **72** l
Ebon, atoll, Marsh. Is. **71** D3
Ebony, Va. **56** E6
Ebro, Fla. **20** E1
Eccles, W. Va., 1,145 **68** B4
Echeconnee Cr., Ga. **22** C3
Echo, Ala. **11** D4
Echo, Minn., 459 **38** B3
Echo, Oreg., 456 **55** N2
Echo Lake Res., N.J. **47** b1
Echols, co., Ga., 1,876 **22** D5
Eckerman, Mich. **37** G2
Eckert, Tex. **62** E4
Eckerty, Ind. **27** B4
Eckford, Mich. **37** G6
Eckley, Colo. **18** D1
Eckley, Pa. **57** K4
Eclectic, Ala., 926 **11** D3
Econfina, r., Fla. **21** G1
Economy, Ind., 280 **27** C3
Ecorse, Mich., 17,328 **37** d12
Ecru, Miss., 442 **39** C1
Ector, co., Tex., 90,995 **62** C4
Edcouch, Tex., 2,814 **62** F6
Eddiceton, Miss. **39** B4
Eddington, Pa., 2,000* **57** g11
Eddy, Ill. **26** c1
Eddy, co., N. Mex., 50,783 **46** C3
Eddy, co., N. Dak., 4,936 **51** N2
Eddystone, Pa., 3,006 **57** f12
Eddyville, Ill., 125 **25** D6
Eddyville, Iowa, 1,014 **28** E3
Eddyville, Ky., 1,858 **30** B3
Eddyville, Nebr., 119 **42** E2
Eden, Ariz. **14** D3
Eden, Ga. **22** E3
Eden, Idaho, 426 **24** B4
Eden, Mich. **37** G6
Eden, Miss., 218 **39** B3
Eden, N.Y., 2,366 **48** C5
Eden, S. Dak., 136 **61** D1
Eden, Tex., 1,486 **62** E4
Eden, Utah **64** c5
Eden, Vt. **65** B1
Eden, Wis., 312 **69** E4
Eden, Wyo. **70** B2
Eden Mills, Vt. **65** B1
Edenton, N.C., 4,458 **51** J1
Eden Valley, Minn., 793 **38** B3
Edenville, Mich. **37** G5
Edgar, co., Ill., 22,550 **25** E4
Edgar, Ill. **25** E4
Edgar, Nebr., 730 **42** G3
Edgar, Wis., 803 **69** D3
Edgard, La. **31** D3
Edgar Hoopes Res., Del. **20** a4
Edgartown, Mass., 1,181; 1,474(T) **35** M7
Edgartown Great Pd., Mass. **35** M7
Edgecliff, Tex., 339 **63** e11
Edgecomb, Me. **32** B5
Edgecombe, co., N.C., 54,226 **50** H2
Edgefield, co., S.C., 15,735 **59** B3
Edgefield, S.C., 2,876 **59** C3
Edgeley, N. Dak., 992 **51** N2
Edgely, Pa. **57** g11
Edgemere, Md. **33** c4
Edgemont, Ark. **15** C2
Edgemont, Colo. **18** b5
Edgemont, S.Dak., 1,772 **61** A2
Edgemoor, Del. **20** a4
Edgemoor, S.C. **59** D2
Edgerton, Minn., 1,019 **38** A4
Edgerton, Mo., 449 **40** B2
Edgerton, Ohio, 1,566 **53** A1
Edgerton, Wis., 4,000 **69** D5
Edgerton, Wyo., 512 **70** C2
Edgeville, Fla. **21** d12
Edgewater, Ala. **11** b6
Edgewater, Colo., 4,314 **18** b5
Edgewater, Fla., 2,051 **21** K3
Edgewater, Md. **33** c5
Edgewater, Wis. **69** B2
Edgewater Gulf Beach, Fla., 70 **20** E1
Edgewater Park, N.J., 2,866(T) **57** g11
Edgewater Park, Ohio **52** b6
Edgewood, Ill., 515 **25** D5
Edgewood, Ind., 2,119 **27** C2
Edgewood, Iowa, 767 **28** F2
Edgewood, Md., 1,670 **33** D1
Edgewood, N. Mex. **46** B2
Edgewood, Tex., 887 **63** g11
Edgeworth, Pa., 2,030 **56** b7
Edgigen, i., Kwajalein **72** l
Edina, Minn., 37,283 **38** b6
Edina, Mo., 1,457 **40** D1
Edinboro, Pa., 1,703 **56** A2
Edinburg, Ill., 1,003 **25** C4
Edinburg, Ind., 3,664 **27** B3
Edinburg, Miss. **39** C3
Edinburg, N. Dak., 330 **51** O1
Edinburg, Tex., 18,706 **62** E6
Edinburg, Va., 517 **56** E4
Edison, Colo. **18** C2
Edison, Ga., 1,232 **22** B4
Edison, Nebr., 249 **42** E3
Edison, N.J., 44,799(T) **47** b3
Edison, Ohio, 559 **53** C2
Edison, Wash. **66** B1
Edison Nat. Hist. Site, N.J. **47** b2
Edisto, r., S.C. **59** D4
Edisto Island, S.C. **59** D4
Edith, Colo. **18** B3
Edith, Ga. **22** D5
Edith, Tex. **62** D4
Edmeston, N.Y. **49** K5
Edmond, Kans., 91 **29** C1
Edmond, Okla., 8,577 **54** F2
Edmonds, Wash., 8,016 **66** B2
Edmondson, Ark., 288 **15** E2
Edmonson, co., Ky., 8,085 **30** D3
Edmonton, Ky., 749 **30** E4
Edmore, Mich., 1,234 **37** G5
Edmore, N. Dak., 405 **51** N1
Edmund, Wis. **69** C5
Edmunds, co., S. Dak., 6,079 **61** C2
Edna, Kans., 442 **29** G3
Edna, Okla. **55** G2
Edna, Tex., 5,038 **62** F5
Edna Bay, Alaska, 135 **13** K4
Edom, Va. **67** L2
Edon, Ohio, 757 **53** A1
Edson, Nebr. **42** C4
Edwall, Wash. **66** E2
Edward, N.C., 212 **51** J2
Edwards, Calif. **17** D4
Edwards, co., Ill., 7,940 **25** D5
Edwards, co., Kans., 5,118 **29** C3
Edwards, Miss., 1,206 **39** B3
Edwards, N.Y., 658 **49** K2
Edwards, co., Tex., 2,317 **62** D5
Edwards, r., Ill. **25** B2
Edwardsburg, Mich., 902 **36** E7
Edwards Plat., Tex. **62** D4
Edwardsport, Ind., 533 **27** A4
Edwardsville, Ill., 9,996 **25** C5
Edwardsville, Pa., 5,711 **57** n16
Eek, Alaska, 200 **12** C3
Eek, r., Alaska **12** C3
Eel, r., Calif. **17** B2
Eel, r., Ind. **27** A3
Eel, r., Ind. **27** C2
Eel Pt., Mass. **35** O7
Effie, Minn., 195 **38** C2
Effigy Mounds Nat. Mon., Iowa **28** F1
Effingham, co., Ga., 10,144 **22** E3
Effingham, co., Ill., 23,107 **25** D4
Effingham, Ill., 8,172 **25** D4
Effingham, Kans., 564 **29** G1
Effingham, S.C. **59** E2
Effingham Falls, N.H. **44** C4
Effner, Ind. **27** A2
Egan, S. Dak., 310 **61** D1
Egan Range, Nev. **43** C2
Egavik, Alaska **12** C2
Egegik, Alaska, 150 **13** D4
Egeland, N. Dak., 190 **51** N1
Eggertsville, N.Y., 44,807 **48** C5
Egg Harbor, Wis. **69** F2
Egg Harbor City, N.J., 4,416 **45** B4
Egg Island Point, N.J. **45** A5
Eggleston, Va. **67** J3
Eglon, Wash. **66** B2
Egmont Key, Fla. **21** c11
Egnar, Colo. **18** A3
Egypt, Miss. **39** D2
Egypt, N.Y. **48** k17
Egypt, Pa., 1,550* **57** j18
Ehren, Fla. **21** d10
Ehrenberg, Ariz. **14** A3
Ehrhardt, S.C., 482 **59** C3
Eightmile, Oreg. **55** N2
Eight Mile Bk., Conn. **19** C4
Eight Mile Bk., Conn. **19** F4
Eightyfour, Pa. **56** b9
Eileen, Ill., 384 **25** D2
Eil Malk, i., Palau **72** e
Eitzen, Minn., 181 **38** D4
Ekalaka, Mont., 738 **41** F3
Eklutna, Alaska, 50 **13** F3
Eklutna L., Alaska **12** c7
Ekron, Ky., 205 **30** D3
Ekuk, Alaska, 40 **12** D4
Ekwak, Alaska **13** D4
Ekwok = Ekwak
Ela, N.C. **50** B2
Elaine, Ark., 898 **15** E3
Elam, Pa. **57** e12
Eland, Wis., 213 **69** D3
Elba, Ala., 4,321 **11** C4
Elba, Colo. **18** D2
Elba, Mich. **37** H5
Elba, Nebr., 184 **42** F2
Elba, N.Y., 739 **48** D4
Elbe, Wash. **66** B2
Elberfeld, Ind., 485 **27** A4
Elberon, Iowa, 211 **28** E2
Elbert, co., Colo., 3,708 **18** C2
Elbert, Colo. **18** C2
Elbert, co., Ga., 17,835 **22** D1
Elbert, Tex. **62** E3
Elbert, Mt., Colo. **18** B2
Elberta, Ala., 384 **11** B5
Elberta, Mich., 552 **36** E4
Elberta, Utah **64** c8
Elberton, Ga., 7,107 **22** C1
Elberton, Wash., 66 **66** E2
Elbing, Kans., 105 **29** E2
Elbon, Pa. **56** D3
Elbow Lake, Minn., 1,521 **38** A3
Elbridge, Ill. **25** E4
Elbridge, N.Y., 870 **49** G4
Elburn, Ill., 960 **25** D2
El Cajon, Calif., 37,618 **17** E5
El Camino del Diablo, mtn., N. Mex. **46** C3
El Campo, Tex., 7,700 **62** F5
El Centro, Calif., 19,414 **17** F5
El Cerrito, Calif., 25,437 **16** b7
Elcho, Wis. **69** D2
Elco, Ill. **25** C6
Elco, Pa., 521 **56** c9
El Cuervo Butte, N. Mex. **46** C2
El Dara, Ill., 98 **25** B4
Eldena, Ill. **25** C2
Elderon, Wis., 177 **69** D3
Eldersburg, Md. **33** b3
Elderton, Pa., 387 **56** C4
El Diente, mt., Colo. **18** A3
Eld Inlet, Wash. **67** a6
Eldon, Iowa, 1,386 **28** E4
Eldon, Mo., 3,158 **40** D3
Eldon, Okla. **55** J2
Eldon, Wash. **66** B2
Eldora, Iowa, 3,225 **28** D2
El Dorado, Ark., 25,292 **15** C4
El Dorado, co., Calif., 43,805 **17** C2
Eldorado, Ill., 3,573 **25** D6
El Dorado, Kans., 12,523 **29** F3
Eldorado, Mich. **37** G4
Eldorado, Nebr. **42** G3
Eldorado, N.C. **50** F2
Eldorado, Ohio, 449 **53** A3
Eldorado, Okla., 708 **54** D3
Eldorado, Tex., 1,815 **62** D4
El Dorado, Wis. **69** E4
Eldorado Pass, Oreg. **55** N2
Eldorado Springs, Colo. **18** b5
El Dorado Springs, Mo., 2,864 **40** B4
Eldred, Fla. **21** K4
Eldred, Ill., 302 **25** B4
Eldred, N.Y. **49** L7
Eldred, Pa., 1,107 **56** E2
Eldridge, Ala. **11** B2
Eldridge, Iowa, 842 **28** G3
Eldridge, Mo. **40** D4
Eldridge, N. Dak. **51** N2
Eleao, pk., Hawaii **23** e9
Electra, Tex., 4,759 **62** E2
Electric City, Wash., 404 **66** D2
Electric Mills, Miss. **39** D3
Electric Pk., Mont. **41** C3
Eleele, Hawaii, 617 **22** G2
Elenore, Mt., Utah **64** A3
Elephant Butte, N. Mex. **46** B3
Elephant Butte Res., N. Mex. **46** B3
Elephant Mtn., Me. **32** A4
Eleroy, Ill. **25** C1
Eleva, Wis., 548 **69** B3
Eleven Mile Canyon Res., Colo. **18** a7
Eleven Point, r., Ark.-Mo. **40** E5
Elfers, Fla. **21** H3
Elfrida, Ariz. **14** D4
Elgin, Ariz. **14** C4
Elgin, Ill., 49,447 **25** D1
Elgin, Iowa, 644 **28** F2
Elgin, Kans., 148 **29** F3
Elgin, Minn., 521 **38** C3
Elgin, Nebr., 881 **42** F2
Elgin, Nev. **43** C3
Elgin, N. Dak., 944 **51** M2
Elgin, Ohio, 80 **53** A2
Elgin, Okla., 540 **54** E3
Elgin, Oreg., 1,315 **55** N2
Elgin, Pa., 218 **56** B2
Elgin, S.C., 329 **59** D2
Elgin, Tex., 3,511 **62** F4
El Granada, Calif. **16** a7
Eli, Nebr. **42** C1
Elida, N. Mex., 534 **46** D3
Elida, Ohio, 1,215 **53** A2
Eli Kanibu, i., Truk **72** g
Elim, Alaska, 145 **12** C2
El Indio, Tex. **62** D5
Elizabeth, Colo., 326 **18** C2
Elizabeth, Ga., 1,620 **22** b6
Elizabeth Ill., 729 **25** B1
Elizabeth, Ind., 214 **27** C4
Elizabeth, La., 1,030 **31** B3
Elizabeth, Minn., 168 **38** A2
Elizabeth, N.J., 107,698 **45** C2
Elizabeth, Pa., 2,597 **56** B5
Elizabeth, W. Va., 727 **68** B2
Elizabeth, L., Wis. **26** b1
Elizabeth City, N.C., 14,062 **51** J1
Elizabeth Is., Jaluit **72** m
Elizabeth Is., Mass. **35** L7
Elizabeth Mtn., Utah **64** B1
Elizabethton, Tenn., 10,896 **61** N1
Elizabethtown, Ill., 524 **25** D6
Elizabethtown, Ind., 417 **27** C3
Elizabethtown, Ky., 9,641 **30** D3
Elizabethtown, N.Y., 779 **49** N2
Elizabethtown, N.C., 1,486 **50** G3
Elizabethtown, Pa., 6,780 **56** H5
Elizabethville, Pa., 1,455 **56** H4
Elizaville, Ind. **27** B2
Elk, Calif. **17** B2
Elk, co., Kans., 5,048 **29** F3
Elk, N. Mex. **46** C3
Elk, co., Pa., 37,328 **56** D3
Elk, Wash. **66** E1
Elk, r., Ala.-Tenn. **61** J2
Elk, r., Colo. **18** B1
Elk, r., Kans. **29** F3
Elk, r., Mich. **37** J5
Elk, r., W. Va. **68** B3
Elkader, Iowa, 1,526 **28** F2
Elkader, Kans. **29** B2
Elk City, Idaho **24** B3
Elk City, Kans., 498 **29** F3
Elk City, Okla., 8,196 **54** D2
Elk Creek, Calif. **17** B2
Elk Creek, Nebr., 170 **42** H3
Elk Creek, Va. **67** H4
Elk Cr., Pa. **56** A1
Elk Cr., S. Dak. **61** A1
Elk Garden, Va. **66** H4
Elk Garden, W. Va., 329 **68** D2
Elk Grove, Calif., 2,205 **17** C2
Elk Grove Village, Ill., 13,155 **26** c2
Elkhart, Ill., 418 **25** C3
Elkhart, co., Ind., 106,790 **27** C1
Elkhart, Ind., 40,274 **27** C1
Elkhart, Kans., 1,780 **29** A3
Elkhart, Tex., 780 **63** G4
Elkhart Lake, Wis., 651 **69** F4
Elk Hill, Pa. **57** K2
Elk Horn, Iowa, 679 **28** B3
Elkhorn, Nebr., 749 **42** H2
Elkhorn, Wis., 3,586 **69** E5
Elkhorn, r., Nebr. **42** G1
Elkhorn City, Ky., 1,085 **30** H3
Elkhorn Cr., Ill. **25** C2
Elkhorn Ranch Site, N. Dak. **51** L2
Elkin, N.C., 2,868 **50** E1
Elkins, N.H. **44** B5
Elkins, N. Mex. **46** C3
Elkins, W. Va., 8,307 **68** D3
Elkins Park, Pa., 12,200* **57** f11
Elkinsville, Ind. **27** B3
Elk L., Mich. **36** F4
Elkland, Pa., 2,189 **56** G1
Elkmont, Ala., 169 **11** C1
Elkmont, Tenn. **61** M2
Elk Mound, Wis., 379 **69** B3
Elk Mountain, Wyo., 190 **70** C3
Elk Mtn., N. Mex. **46** A3
Elk Mtn., Okla. **54** E3
Elk Mtn., Wyo. **70** C3
Elko, Ga., 165 **22** C3
Elko, co., Nev., 12,011 **43** C1
Elko, Nev., 6,298 **43** C1
Elko, S.C., 194 **59** C3
Elk Park, N.C., 460 **50** C1
Elk Point, S. Dak. **61** D2
Elkport, Iowa, 100 **28** F2
Elk Rapids, Mich., 1,015 **36** F4
Elkridge, Md. **33** b4
Elk River, Idaho, 382 **24** A2
Elk River, Minn., 1,763 **38** C3
Elk Run Heights, Iowa, 1,124 **28** E2
Elk Springs, Colo. **18** A1
Elkton, Ill. **25** C5
Elkton, Ky., 1,448 **30** C4
Elkton, Md., 5,989 **33** E1
Elkton, Mich., 1,014 **37** H5
Elkton, Oreg., 146 **55** L3
Elkton, S. Dak., 621 **61** D1
Elkton, Tenn., 199 **61** J2
Elkton, Va., 1,506 **67** L2
Elk Valley, Tenn. **61** L1
Elkville, Ill., 743 **25** C6
Elkwater, W. Va. **68** C3
Ellamar, Alaska **13** G3
Ellaville, Ga., 905 **22** B3
Ellen, Mt., Utah **64** B2
Ellen, Mt., Vt. **65** B2
Ellenboro, N.C., 492 **50** D2
Ellenboro, W. Va., 340 **68** B2
Ellenburg, N.Y. **49** N1
Ellenburg Depot, N.Y. **49** N1
Ellendale, Del., 370 **20** B3
Ellendale, N. Dak., 1,800 **51** N2
Ellensburg, Wash., 8,625 **66** C2
Ellenton, Fla. **21** d10
Ellenton, Ga., 385 **22** C4
Ellenville, N.Y., 5,003 **49** M7
Ellenwood, Ga. **22** b7
Eller, N.C. **50** E2
Eller, i., Kwajalein **72** l
Ellerbe, N.C., 847 **50** F2
Ellerslie, Md. **33** B1
Ellerville, Okla. **55** J1
Ellettsville, Ind., 1,222 **27** B3
Ellicott, Colo. **18** C2
Ellicott City, Md. **33** D1
Ellicott Cr., N.Y. **48** g15
Ellicottville, N.Y., 1,150 **48** C6
Ellijay, Ga., 1,320 **22** B1
Ellington, Conn., 5,580(T) **19** F2
Ellington, Mo., 812 **40** F4
Ellington, N.Y. **48** B6
Ellinwood, Kans., 2,729 **29** D2
Elliot, Ill., 343 **25** D3
Elliot, S.C. **59** D2
Elliot Key, Fla. **21** K6
Elliot Knob, mtn., Va. **67** K2
Elliott (part of Pomfret), Conn. **19** G2
Elliott, Iowa, 459 **28** B3
Elliott, co., Ky., 6,330 **30** G2
Elliott, Miss. **39** C2
Elliott, N. Dak., 62 **51** O2
Elliotville (part of Dayville), Conn. **19** H2
Ellis, Ark. **15** C1
Ellis, Ill. **25** E3
Ellis, co., Kans., 21,270 **29** C2
Ellis, Kans., 2,218 **29** C2
Ellis, co., Okla., 5,457 **54** D1
Ellis, co., Tex., 43,395 **62** F3
Ellis, r., Me. **32** A4
Ellis, r., N.H. **44** C3
Ellisburg, N.Y., 328 **49** H3
Ellisdale, N.J. **47** a5
Ellison, Ind. **27** C1
Ellison Bay, Wis. **69** F2
Ellis Pd., Me. **32** A4
Ellisport, Wash. **67** a6
Elliston, Mont. **41** B2
Elliston, Va. **56** C5
Ellisville (part of Plymouth), Mass. **35** M5
Ellisville, Miss., 4,592 **39** C4
Ellisville, Mo., 2,732 **40** F3
Ellithorpe (part of Stafford), Conn. **19** F2
Elloree, S.C., 1,031 **59** D3
Ellport, Pa., 1,458 **56** A4
Ellsinore, Mo., 311 **40** F5
Ellsworth, Ill., 224 **25** D3
Ellsworth, Iowa, 493 **28** D2
Ellsworth, co., Kans., 7,677 **29** D2
Ellsworth, Kans., 2,361 **29** D2
Ellsworth, Me., 4,444 **32** C4
Ellsworth, Mich., 386 **36** F3
Ellsworth, Minn., 634 **38** B4
Ellsworth, Nebr. **42** B1
Ellsworth, N.H. **44** B4
Ellsworth, Pa., 1,456 **56** c9
Ellsworth, Wis., 1,701 **69** A3
Ellsworth, L., Okla. **54** E3
Ellwood City, Pa., 12,413 **56** A4
Ellzey, Fla. **21** H2
Elm, N.J. **45** B4
Elm, r., S. Dak. **61** C1
Elma, Iowa, 706 **28** E1
Elma, N.Y. **48** h16
Elma, Wash., 1,811 **66** B2
Elm City, N.C., 729 **50** H2
Elm Creek, Nebr., 778 **42** E3
Elm Cr., S. Dak. **61** C1
Elmendorf, Tex. **62** b9
Elmer, Mich. **37** J5
Elmer, Mo., 266 **40** D2
Elmer, N.J., 1,505 **45** A4
Elmer, Okla., 120 **54** D3
Elmer City, Wash., 256 **66** D1
Elmer Hill, N.Y. **48** b10
Elm Grove, Wis., 4,994 **69** a7
Elm Hall, Mich. **37** G5
Elmhurst, Ill., 40,329 **25** E2
Elmhurst, Pa. **57** K3
Elmira, Mich. **37** G3
Elmira, Mo., 123 **40** B2
Elmira, N.Y., 46,517 **48** G6
Elmira, Ohio **53** A1
Elmira, Oreg. **55** L2
El Mirage, Ariz., 3,258 **14** B3
Elmira Heights, N.Y., 5,105 **48** G6
Elm L., S. Dak. **61** C1
Elmo, Mo., 213 **42** A1
Elmo, Mont. **41** A2
Elmo, Utah, 175 **64** B2
Elmo, Wyo., 91 **70** C3
Elmo, L., Minn. **38** d6
Elmodel, Ga. **22** B4
El Modeno, Calif. **16** f11
Elmont, N.Y., 30,138 **47** e3
Elmont, Va. **67** M3
El Monte, Calif., 13,163 **16** e10
Elmora, Pa., 1,057 **56** D4
Elmore, co., Ala., 30,524 **11** C3
Elmore, Ala. **11** C3
Elmore, co., Idaho, 16,719 **24** B4
Elmore, Minn., 1,078 **38** B4
Elmore, Ohio, 1,302 **53** B1
Elmore City, Okla., 982 **54** F3
El Morro, N. Mex. **46** A2
El Morro Nat. Mon., N. Mex. **46** A2
Elmsford, N.Y., 4,031 **47** d1
Elm Springs, S. Dak. **61** A1
Elmwood (part of W. Hartford), Conn. **19** D3
Elmwood, Ill., 1,882 **25** C3
Elmwood (part of E. Bridgewater), Mass. **35** L4
Elmwood, Nebr., 481 **42** H3
Elmwood, Okla. **54** C1
Elmwood, Tenn. **61** K1
Elmwood, Wis., 776 **69** A3
Elmwood Park, Ill., 23,866 **26** c3
Elmwood Park, Wis. **69** b9
Elmwood Place, Ohio, 3,813 **52** h9
El Nido, Calif. **17** C3
Elnora, Ind., 824 **27** A4
Eloise, Mich. **37** c11
Elon College, N.C., 1,284 **50** F1
Elora, Tenn. **61** J2
Eloy, Ariz., 4,899 **14** C3
El Paso, Ark. **15** C2
El Paso, co., Colo., 143,742 **18** C2
El Paso, Ill., 1,964 **25** C3
El Paso, co., Tex., 314,070 **62** A4
El Paso, Tex., 276,687 **62** A4
El Paso Gap, N. Mex. **46** C3
El Portal, Calif. **17** D3
El Portal, Fla., 2,079 **20** b9
El Porvenir, N. Mex. **46** C2
Elrama, Pa. **56** c8
El Rancho, Colo. **18** b5
El Reno, Okla., 11,015 **54** E2
El Rio, Calif., 6,966 **17** D4
El Rito, N. Mex. **46** B1
Elrosa, Minn., 205 **38** B3
Elroy, Wis., 1,505 **69** C4
Elsa, Tex., 3,847 **62** E6
El Saco, P.R. **72** n b1
Elsah, Ill., 218 **25** B5
Elsberry, Mo., 1,491 **40** F2
El Segundo, Calif., 14,219 **16** e11
Elsie, Mich., 933 **37** G5
Elsie, Nebr., 198 **42** C3
Elsie, Oreg. **55** L2
Elsinore, Calif., 2,248 **16** g11
Elsinore, Utah, 483 **64** A2
Elsinore L., Calif. **16** g11
Elsmere, Del., 7,319 **20** A1
Elsmere, Nebr. **42** D1
Elsmere, N.Y. **49** d14
Elsmore, Kans., 128 **29** G3
Elton, La., 1,595 **31** B3
Elton, Wis. **69** E2
El Toro, Calif. **16** f11
El Toro, Tex. **62** F5
El Vado, N. Mex. **46** B1
Elvaston, Ill., 232 **25** A3
Elverson, Pa., 472 **57** K5
Elverta, Calif. **17** j12

For abbreviations and explanation of index, see page 176.

For abbreviations and explanation of index, see page 176.

Gilliam, Mo., 249 40 C2
Gilliam, co., Oreg., 3,069 55 M2
Gillifitz, Yap 72 d
Gillingham, Wis. 69 C4
Gillis, La. 31 A3
Gills Rock, Wis. 69 F2
Gilman, Ill., 1,704 25 DB
Gilman, Iowa, 491 28 E3
Gilman, Vt. 65 D2
Gilman, Wis., 379 69 C2
Gilman City, Mo., 379 40 C1
Gilmanton, N.H. 44 C5
Gilmanton, Wis. 69 B3
Gilmanton Iron Works, N.H. 44 C5
Gilmer, co., Ga., 8,922 22 B1
Gilmer, Ill. 26 b2
Gilmer, Tex., 4,312 63 G3
Gilmer, co., W. Va., 8,050 68 C3
Gilmore, Alaska 13 b6
Gilmore, Ark., 438 15 E2
Gilmore, Ill. 25 D4
Gilmore L., Wis. 69 B1
Gilpin, co., Colo., 685 18 C2
Gilroy, Calif., 7,348 17 C3
Gilson, Ill. 25 B3
Gilsum, N.H. 44 A5
Giltner, Nebr., 293 42 F3
Gings, Ind. 27 C3
Girard, Ga. 22 E2
Girard, Ill., 1,734 25 C4
Girard, Kans., 2,350 29 H3
Girard, Mich. 37 G6
Girard, Ohio, 12,997 53 E1
Girard, Pa., 2,451 56 A1
Girard, Tex. 62 D3
Girardville, Pa., 2,958 56 J4
Girdler, Ky. 30 G4
Girdletree, Md. 33 E2
Girdwood, Alaska, 63 12 c7
Girvin, Tex. 62 C4
Givhans, S.C. 59 D3
Givry, i., Truk 72 g
Glace, W. Va. 68 C4
Glacier, co., Mont., 11,565 41 B1
Glacier, Wash. 66 C1
Glacier Bay, Alaska 13 J4
Glacier Bay Nat. Mon., Alaska 13 J4
Glacier Nat. Pk., Mont. 41 A1
Glacier Pk., Wash. 66 C1
Gladbrook, Iowa, 949 28 E2
Glade, Kans., 133 29 C1
Gladehill, Va. 67 K4
Glade Mills, Pa. 56 c7
Glade Park, Colo. 18 A2
Glades, co., Fla., 2,950 21 J5
Glade Spring, Va., 1,407 66 H4
Gladewater, Tex., 5,742 63 G3
Gladstone, Ill., 356 25 B3
Gladstone, Mich., 5,267 36 D3
Gladstone, Mo., 14,502 40 a7
Gladstone, N. Mex. 46 C1
Gladstone, N. Dak., 185 51 L2
Gladstone, Oreg., 3,854 55 L2
Gladstone, Va. 67 L3
Glad Valley, S. Dak. 61 A1
Gladwin, co., Mich., 10,769 37 G4
Gladwin, Mich., 2,226 37 G5
Glady, W. Va. 68 D3
Gladys, Va. 67 K3
Glamis, Calif. 17 F5
Glandorf, Ohio, 747 53 A1
Glasco, Kans., 812 29 E1
Glasco, N.Y. 49 M6
Glascock, co., Ga., 2,672 22 D2
Glasford, Ill., 1,012 25 C3
Glasgow, Ill., 166 25 B4
Glasgow, Ky., 10,069 30 E3
Glasgow, Mo., 1,200 40 D2
Glasgow, Mont., 6,398 41 E1
Glasgow, Va., 1,091 67 K3
Glasgow, W. Va., 914 68 B3
Glass, Va. 67 N3
Glassboro, N.J., 10,253 45 A4
Glasscock, co., Tex., 1,118 62 D4
Glass Mtn., Calif. 17 C1
Glass Mts., Tex. 62 D4
Glassport, Pa., 8,418 56 B5
Glastenbury Mts., Vt. 65 A5
Glastonbury, Conn., 14,497(T) 19 E3
Glazier, Tex. 62 D1
Gleason, Tenn., 900 61 G1
Gleason, Wis. 69 D2
Gleasondale (part of Stow), Mass. 35 H3
Gleason, L., Minn. 38 b6
Glen, Nebr. 42 A1
Glen, N.H. 44 C3
Glen, Miss. 39 D1
Glen, W. Va. 68 B3
Glenaire, Mo., 341,40 b7
Glenallen, Mo., 113 40 F4
Glen Allen, Va. 67 M3
Glen Alpine, N.C., 734 50 D2
Glen Arbor, Mich. 36 F4
Glenarm, Ill. 25 C4
Glen Aubrey, N.Y. 49 J6
Glenbeulah, Wis., 428 69 F4
Glenbrook (part of Stamford), Conn. 19 A5
Glenbrook, Nev. 43 A2
Glenburn, N. Dak., 363 51 M1
Glenburn, Pa. 57 n15
Glen Burnie, Md. 33 D1
Glen Campbell, Pa., 400 56 D4
Glen Canyon Dam, Ariz. 14 C1
Glen Canyon Nat. Rec. Area, Utah 64 B3
Glen Carbon, Ill., 1,241 25 C5
Glencliff, N.H. 44 B4
Glencoe, Ala., 2,592 11 D2
Glencoe, Ill., 10,472 25 E1
Glencoe, Ky. 30 F2
Glencoe, Minn., 3,216 38 B3
Glencoe, Okla., 284 54 F1
Glen Cove, Me. 32 B4
Glen Cove, N.Y., 23,817 49 N9
Glencross, S. Dak. 61 B1
Glendale, Ariz. 30,760 14 B3
Glendale, Calif., 119,442 17 D4
Glendale, Fla. 20 D1
Glendale, Ind. 29 E2
Glendale, Kans. 29 E2
Glendale (part of Stockbridge), Mass. 34 A3
Glendale, Minn. 38 C1
Glendale, Mo., 7,048 40 c10
Glendale, Nev. 43 C3
Glendale, Ohio, 2,823 52 j9
Glendale, Oreg., 748 55 L3
Glendale, R.I. 58 B1
Glendale, Utah, 223 64 A3
Glendale, Wash. 67 b5
Glendale, W.Va., 1,905 68 C2
Glendale, Wis., 10,432 69 b7
Glendale Hts., Du Page Co., Ill., 7,419 26 b3
Glendale Hts., Pope Co., Ill., 173 25 D6
Glen Dean, Ky. 30 D3
Glendive, Mont., 7,058 41 F2
Glendo, Wyo., 292 70 D2
Glendola, N.J. 47 c5
Glendon, Pa., 555 57 k18
Glendora, Calif., 20,752 16 f10
Glendora, Mich. 36 E7
Glendora, Miss., 147 39 B2
Glendo Res., Wyo. 70 D2
Glen Easton, W. Va. 68 C2
Glen Echo, Md., 310 33 a5
Gleneden Beach, Oreg. 55 K2
Glen Elder, Kans., 444 29 D1
Glenelg, Md. 33 b3
Glen Ellyn, Ill., 18,620 26 b3
Glen Falls, N.Y., 18,580 49 N4
Glenfield, N.Y. 49 K3
Glenfield, Pa., 741 56 b7
Glenfield, N. Dak., 129 51 N2
Glen Flora, Tex. 62 F5
Glen Flora, Wis., 75 69 C2
Glenford, Ohio, 190 53 C3
Glen Gardner, N.J., 787 45 B2
Glengary, W. Va. 68 E2
Glenham, S. Dak., 171 61 B1
Glen Haven, Ga., 4,050 22 c7
Glen Haven, Mich. 36 E4
Glenhaven, Wis. 69 B5
Glenhayes, W. Va. 68 A3
Glen Hope, Pa., 169 56 D4
Glen L., Mich. 36 E4
Glenloch, Pa. 57 e11
Glen Lyon, Pa., 4,173 57 J3
Glen Mills, Pa. 57 e12
Glenmont, N.Y. 49 d14
Glenmont, Ohio, 283 53 C2
Glenmoore, Pa. 57 e11
Glenmora, La., 1,447 31 B3
Glenn, co., Calif., 17,245 17 B2
Glenn, Calif. 17 B2
Glenn, Mich. 36 E6
Glennallen, Alaska, 169 13 G3
Glenn Dale, Md. 33 b5
Glennie, Mich. 37 H4
Glenn Ranch, Calif. 16 g10
Glenns Ferry, Idaho, 1,374 24 B4
Glenn Springs, S.C. 59 C2
Glennville, Calif. 17 D4
Glennville, Ga., 2,791 22 E4
Glenolden, Pa., 7,249 57 f12
Glen Park, N.Y., 561 49 J2
Glenpool, Okla., 353 55 H2
Glen Ridge, Fla., 226 20 b7
Glen Ridge, N.J., 8,322 47 c2
Glenrio, Tex. 62 C2
Glen Rock, N.J., 12,896 47 c2
Glen Rock, Pa., 1,546 56 H6
Glen Rock, R.I. 58 B2
Glenrock, Wyo., 1,584 70 D2
Glen Rose, Tex., 1,422 62 F3
Glen St. Mary, Fla., 329 21 H1
Glenshaw, Pa. 56 c7
Glenside, Pa., 22,600* 57 L5
Glen Summit, Pa. 57 n17
Glentivar, Colo. 18 a6
Glen Ullin, N. Dak., 1,210 51 L2
Glenview, Ill., 23,521 25 E1
Glenville (part of Greenwich), Conn. 19 A5
Glenville, Minn., 643 38 C4
Glenville, N.C. 50 B2
Glenville, W. Va., 1,828 68 C3
Glenwillard, Pa., 1,150* 56 a7
Glenwillow, Ohio, 359 52 f8
Glen Wilton, Va. 67 K3
Glenwood, Ala., 1,145 11 C4
Glenwood, Ark., 840 15 B3
Glenwood, Ga., 682 22 D3
Glenwood, Hawaii 23 L4
Glenwood, Ill., 882 26 d4
Glenwood, Iowa, 4,783 28 B3
Glenwood, Md. 33 a3
Glenwood, Mich. 36 E6
Glenwood, Minn., 2,631 38 B3
Glenwood, Mo., 242 40 D1
Glenwood, N. Mex. 46 A3
Glenwood, N.Y. 48 C5
Glenwood, Oreg. 55 L2
Glenwood, Utah, 277 64 B2
Glenwood, Kitsap Co., Wash. 67 a6
Glenwood, Klickitat Co., Wash. 66 C2
Glenwood, W. Va. 68 A3
Glenwood City, Wis., 835 69 A2
Glenwood Springs, Colo., 3,637 18 B2
Glezen, Ind. 27 A4
Glidden, Iowa, 993 28 C2
Glidden, Wis. 69 C1
Glide, Oreg. 55 L3
Globe, Ariz., 6,299 14 C3
Glorieta, N. Mex. 46 C2
Gloster, Miss., 1,369 39 B4
Gloucester, Mass., 25,789 35 M2
Gloucester, co., N.J., 134,840 45 A4
Gloucester, co., Va., 11,919 67 N3
Gloucester, Va. 67 N3
Gloucester City, N.J., 15,511 57 f12
Gloucester Point, Va. 67 N3
Glouster, Ohio, 2,255 53 C3
Glover, Mo. 40 F4
Glover, Vt., 230 65 C1
Glover Cr., Okla. 55 J3
Glovergap, W. Va. 68 C2
Gloversville, N.Y., 21,741 49 M4
Gluck, S.C. 59 B2
Glyde, Pa. 56 b9
Glyndon, Minn., 489 38 A2
Glynn, co., Ga., 41,954 22 E4
Gnadenhutten, Ohio, 1,257 53 D2
Goat Mtn., N. Mex. 46 B3
Goat Rocks, mtn., Wash. 66 C2
Goback Mtn., N.H. 44 B2
Gobernador, N. Mex. 46 B1
Gobles, Mich., 816 36 F6
Goddard, Kans., 533 29 E3
Godfrey, Ga., 181 22 C2
Godfrey, Ill., 1,231 25 B5
Godley, Tex., 401 63 e12
Godwin, N.C., 149 50 G2
Goehner, Nebr., 106 42 G3
Goerkes Corners, Wis. 69 a7
Goessel, Kans., 327 29 E2
Goetzville, Mich. 37 G2
Gofenu Entr., Yap 72 d
Goff, Kans., 259 29 G1
Goff Cr., Okla. 54 B1
Goffs, Calif. 17 F4
Goffstown, N.H., 1,052 44 B5
Goffton, Tenn. 61 K1
Gogebic, co., Mich., 24,370 36 B2
Gogebic, L., Mich. 36 B2
Gogebic Range, Mich.-Wis. 36 A2
Gogebic Station, Mich. 36 B2
Goikul, Palau 72 e
Golconda, Ill., 864 25 D6
Golconda, Nev. 43 B1
Gold Acres, Nev. 43 B1
Gold Bar, Wash., 315 66 C2
Gold Beach, Oreg., 1,765 55 K3
Gold Creek, Alaska 13 F3
Golddale, Va. 67 M2
Golddust, Tenn. 60 F2
Golden, Colo., 7,118 18 C2
Golden, Idaho 24 B3
Golden, Ill., 491 25 A3
Golden, Okla. 55 J4
Golden Beach, Fla., 413 20 b9
Golden City, Mo., 714 40 B4
Goldendale, Wash., 2,536 66 C3
Golden Eagle, Ill. 25 B5
Golden Gate, Ill., 156 25 D5
Golden Gate, str., Calif. 16 a7
Golden Meadow, La., 3,097 31 D4
Golden Pond, Ky. 30 C4
Golden Spike Nat. Hist. Site, Utah 64 A1
Golden Valley, Minn., 21,428 38 b5
Golden Valley, co., Mont., 1,203 41 D2
Golden Valley, co., N. Dak. 51 L2
Goldenvalley, N. Dak., 286 51 L2
Goldfield, Nev. 43 B3
Gold Hill, Colo. 18 b4
Gold Hill, Nev. 43 A2
Gold Hill, Oreg., 608 55 L3
Gold Hill, Utah 64 A1
Goldman, La. 31 C2
Goldonna, La., 292 31 B1
Gold Point, Nev. 43 B3
Gold Rock, N.C. 50 H1
Gold Run, Calif. 17 C2
Goldsboro, Md., 204 33 E1
Goldsboro, N.C., 28,873 50 G2
Goldsboro, Pa., 542 56 H5
Goldsby, Okla. 54 F2
Goldsmith, Tex., 670 62 C4
Goldston, N.C., 374 50 F2
Goldstream Creek, Alaska 13 a6
Goldthwaite, Tex., 1,383 62 E4
Goldvein, Va. 67 M2
Goleta, Calif. 17 D4
Golf, Ill., 409 26 c2
Golf Manor, Ohio, 4,648 52 h9
Golfview, Fla., 131 20 b7
Goliad, co., Tex., 5,429 62 F5
Goliad, Tex., 1,782 62 F5
Golinda, Tex. 62 F4
Golovin, Alaska 12 C2
Golovnin Bay, Alaska 12 C2
Goltry, Okla., 313 54 E1
Golva, N. Dak., 162 51 L2
Gomez, Fla. 21 K4
Gonvick, Minn., 363 38 B2
Gonzales, Calif., 2,138 17 C3
Gonzales, La., 3,252 31 A3
Gonzales, co., Tex., 17,845 62 F5
Gonzales, Tex., 5,829 62 F5
Goochland, co., Va., 9,206 56 E5
Goochland, Va. 67 M3
Goodell, Iowa, 231 28 D2
Goodells, Mich. 37 J6
Goodfield, Ill., 286 25 C3
Good Hart, Mich. 36 F3
Good Hope, Ill., 394 25 B3
Good Hope, Ohio 53 B3
Goodhope, W. Va. 68 C2
Goodhue, co., Minn., 33,035 38 C3
Goodhue, Minn., 566 38 C3
Gooding, co., Idaho, 9,544 24 B4
Gooding, Idaho, 2,750 24 B4
Goodings Grove, Ill. 26 c4
Goodland, Fla. 21 J6
Goodland, Ind., 1,202 27 A2
Goodland, Kans., 4,459 29 A1
Goodland, Mich. 37 H5
Goodland, Minn. 38 C2
Goodlett, Tex. 62 E2
Goodlettsville, Tenn., 3,163 61 J1
Goodman, Miss., 932 39 C3
Goodman, Mo., 540 40 B5
Goodman, Wis. 69 E2
Goodnews Bay, Alaska 12 C4
Goodnight, Tex. 62 D2
Goodnoe Hills, Wash. 66 C3
Good Pine, La. 31 B2
Goodrich, Colo. 18 C1
Goodrich, Kans. 29 H2
Goodrich, Mich., 701 37 H6
Goodrich, N. Dak., 392 51 M2
Goodrich, Tex. 63 G4
Goodridge, Minn., 134 38 B1
Good Springs, Ala. 11 b6
Goodsprings, Nev. 43 C4
Good Thunder, Minn., 468 38 C3
Goodview, Minn., 1,348 38 D3
Goodwater, Ala., 2,023 11 C2
Goodwater, Okla. 55 J4
Goodwell, Okla., 771 54 B1
Goodwin, S. Dak., 113 61 D1
Goodyear, Ariz., 1,821 14 B3
Goodyear, Conn. 19 H2
Goose, r., N. Dak. 51 O2
Goose Bay, Alaska, 28 12 c7
Goose Creek, S.C., 830 59 D4
Goose Cr., Nebr. 42 D1
Goose Eye Mtn., Me. 32 A4
Gooselake, Iowa, 191 28 G3
Goose L., Calif.-Oreg. 55 M3
Goose L., Minn. 38 d6
Goose Pd., N.H. 44 A4
Gooserock, Ky. 30 G3
Gorda, P., Calif. 17 A1
Gordo, Ala., 1,714 11 B2
Gordon, Ala., 222 11 D4
Gordon, co., Ga., 19,228 22 B1
Gordon, Ga., 1,793 22 C3
Gordon, Kans. 29 F3
Gordon, Nebr., 2,223 42 B1
Gordon, Pa., 888 56 J4
Gordon, Tex., 349 62 E3
Gordon, Wis. 69 B1
Gordon Cr., Nebr. 42 C1
Gordonsburg, Tenn. 61 H2
Gordonsville, Va., 1,109 67 L2
Gore, Okla., 334 55 H2
Gore, Va. 67 L1
Goree, Tex., 543 62 E3
Gore Mtn., Vt. 65 D1
Gore Range, Colo. 18 B2
Goreville, Ill., 625 25 D6
Gorgas, Ala. 11 a6
Gorgorza, Utah 64 c6
Gorham, Ill., 378 25 C6
Gorham, Kans., 429 29 C2
Gorham, Me., 2,322 32 A5
Gorham, N.H., 1,945 44 C3
Gorham, N.Y. 48 F5
Gorin, Mo. 40 E1
Gorman, Calif. 17 D4
Gorman, Tex., 1,142 62 E3
Gormania, W. Va. 68 D2
Gorror, Yap 72 d
Gorst, Wash. 67 a5
Gorum, La. 31 A2
Goshen, Ala., 260 11 C4
Goshen, Calif., 1,061 17 D3
Goshen, Conn., 1,288(T) 19 C2
Goshen, Ind., 13,718 27 C1
Goshen, Mass., 385 34 C3
Goshen, N.H. 44 A5
Goshen, N.Y., 4,175 49 M8
Goshen, Ohio 53 A3
Goshen, Oreg. 55 L3
Goshen, Utah, 426 64 A1
Goshen, Va., 99 67 K3
Goshen, co., Wyo., 11,941 70 D2
Goshen Springs, Miss. 39 C3
Goshute, Utah 64 A2
Goshute L., Nev. 43 C1
Gosper, co., Nebr., 2,489 42 E3
Gosport, Ind., 646 27 B3
Goss, Miss. 39 C4
Goss Heights (part of Huntington), Mass. 34 C3
Gossville, N.H. 44 C5
Gotebo, Okla., 538 54 E2
Gotham, Wis. 69 C4
Gothenburg, Nebr., 3,050 42 D3
Gough, Ga. 22 D2
Gouglersville, Pa. 57 h14
Gould, Ark., 1,552 15 D4
Gould, Colo. 18 B1
Gould, Okla., 241 54 D3
Gould City, Mich. 36 F2
Goulds, Fla., 5,121 21 K6
Gouldsboro, Me. 32 D4
Gouldsboro, Pa. 57 L3
Gouverneur, N.Y., 4,946 49 K2
Govan, S.C., 138 59 C3
Gove, co., Kans., 4,107 29 B2
Gove, Kans., 228 29 B2
Gowanda, N.Y., 3,352 48 B6
Gowen, Mich. 36 F5
Gowrie, Iowa, 1,127 28 C2
Grabill, Ind., 495 27 D1
Grace, Idaho, 725 24 D4
Grace, Mt., Mass. 34 E2
Grace City, N. Dak. 51 N2
Gracemont, Okla., 306 54 E2
Graceton, Minn. 38 B1
Graceville, Fla., 2,307 21 E1
Graceville, Minn., 823 38 A3
Gracey, Ky. 30 C4
Grady, Ala. 11 C3
Grady, Ark., 622 15 D3
Grady, co., Ga., 18,015 22 B5
Grady, N. Mex., 100 46 D2
Grady, co., Okla., 29,590 54 F3
Grady, Okla. 54 F3
Gradyville, Ky. 30 E3
Graettinger, Iowa, 879 28 C1
Graford, Tex., 448 62 E3
Grafton, Ill., 1,084 25 B4
Grafton, Iowa, 273 28 E1
Grafton, Mass., 10,627(T) 35 H4
Grafton, Nebr., 171 42 G3
Grafton, co., N.H., 48,857 44 B4
Grafton, N.H. 44 B4
Grafton, N.Y. 49 O5
Grafton, N. Dak., 7,064 51 O1
Grafton, Ohio, 1,683 53 C1
Grafton, Vt. 65 B4
Grafton, Va. 56 G5
Grafton, W. Va., 5,791 68 D2
Grafton, Wis., 3,748 69 F4
Grafton, Mt., Nev. 43 C2
Grafton Center, N.H. 44 B4
Grafton Pd., N.H. 44 A4
Graham, Ala. 11 D2
Graham, co., Ariz., 14,045 14 D3
Graham, Ga., 130 22 D4
Graham, co., Kans., 5,586 29 C1
Graham, Mo., 215 40 B1
Graham, co., N.C., 6,432 50 B2
Graham, N.C., 7,723 50 F1
Graham, Okla. 54 F3
Graham, Tex., 8,505 62 E3
Graham, Wash. 67 b6
Graham, Mt., Ariz. 14 E2
Graham L., Me. 32 C4
Grahamsville, N.Y. 49 L7
Grahamville, S.C. 59 D4
Grahn, Ky. 30 G2
Grainfield, Kans., 389 29 B1
Grainger, N.C., 188 50 H2
Grainger, co., Tenn., 12,506 61 M1
Grainola, Okla., 67 54 G1
Grainton, Nebr., 35 42 C3
Grain Valley, Mo., 552 40 B3
Grambling, La., 3,144 31 B1
Gramercy, La., 2,094 31 D3
Grampian, Pa., 529 56 D4
Granada, Colo., 593 18 D3
Granada, Minn., 418 38 B4
Granbury, Tex., 2,227 62 E3
Granby, Colo., 503 18 C1
Granby, Conn., 4,968(T) 19 D2
Granby, Mass., 4,221(T) 34 E4
Granby, Mo., 1,808 40 B5
Granby, Vt. 65 D1
Granby, L., Colo. 18 C1
Grand, co., Colo., 3,557 18 B1
Grand, co., Utah, 6,345 64 C2
Grand, r., Mich. 36 E5
Grand, r., Mo. 40 C2
Grand, r., Ohio 53 E1
Grand, r., Okla. 55 H1
Grand, r., S. Dak. 61 B1
Grand Bay, Ala. 11 A5
Grand Blanc, Mich., 1,565 37 H6
Grand Calumet, r., Ill.-Ind. 26 e4
Grand Cane, La., 322 31 A1
Grand Canyon, Ariz. 14 C1
Grand Canyon Nat. Mon., Ariz. 14 B1
Grand Canyon Nat. Pk., Ariz. 14 B1
Grand Chenier, La. 31 B4
Grand Coteau, La., 1,165 31 B3
Grand Coulee, Wash., 1,058 66 D2
Grand Coulee Dam, Wash. 66 D2
Grand Detour, Ill. 25 C2
Grande, Sa., N. Mex. 46 D1
Grande de Anasco, r., P.R. 72 n a1
Grande de Arecibo, r., P.R. 72 n b1
Grande de Loíza, r., P.R. 72 n d1
Grande de Manatí, r., P.R. 72 n c1
Grandeeville, W. Va. 68 B3
Grande Ronde, r., Oreg.-Wash. 66 E3
Grand Falls, Minn. 38 C1
Grandfalls, Tex., 1,012 62 C2
Grand Falls, Ariz. 14 C2
Grand Falls L., Me. 32 D3
Grandfield, Okla., 1,606 54 E3
Grand Forks, co., N. Dak., 38,230 51 O1
Grand Forks, N. Dak., 34,451 51 O2
Grand Haven, Mich., 11,066 36 E5
Grandin, Mo., 259 40 F5
Grandin, N. Dak., 147 51 O2
Grand Island, Nebr., 25,742 42 F3
Grand Island, N.Y. 48 g16
Grand I., Mich. 36 E2
Grand I., N.Y. 48 C5
Grand Isle, La., 2,074 31 E4
Grand Isle, Me. 32 C1
Grand Isle, co., Vt., 2,927 65 A1
Grand Isle, Vt. 65 A1
Grand Isle, Vt. 65 A1
Grand Junction, Colo., 18,694 18 A2
Grand Junction, Iowa, 949 28 C2
Grand Junction, Mich. 36 E6
Grand Junction, Tenn., 446 60 F2
Grand Lake, Colo., 170 18 B1
Grand Lake, La. 31 A3
Grand L., La. 31 B4
Grand L., La. 31 C4
Grand L., Me. 32 C2
Grand L., Me. 32 D2
Grand L., Mich. 37 H3
Grand L., Ohio 53 A2
Grand Lake Stream, Me. 32 D3
Grand Ledge, Mich., 5,165 37 G6
Grand Manan Chan., Me. 32 D4
Grand Marais, Mich. 36 E2
Grand Marais, Minn., 1,301 38 D2
Grand Marsh, Wis. 69 D4
Grand Meadow, Minn., 837 38 C4
Grand Mound, Iowa, 565 28 G3
Grand Mound, Wash. 66 B2
Grand Pass, Mo., 120 40 C2
Grand Portage, Minn. 38 E1
Grand Portage Nat. Mon., Minn. 38 E2
Grand Prairie, Tex., 30,386 63 e11
Grand Rapids, Mich., 202,379 36 F6
Grand Rapids, Minn., 7,265 38 C2
Grand Rapids, N. Dak. 51 N2
Grand Rapids, Ohio, 670 53 B1
Grand Ridge, Fla., 415 21 E1
Grand Ridge, Ill., 659 25 D2
Grand River, Iowa, 284 28 D4
Grand River, Ohio, 477 52 f7
Grand Rivers, Ky., 378 30 B4
Grand Ronde, Oreg. 55 L2
Grand Saline, Tex., 2,006 63 G3
Grand Teton, mtn., Wyo. 70 A2
Grand Teton Nat. Pk., Wyo. 70 A2
Grand Tower, Ill., 847 25 C6
Grand Traverse, co., Mich., 33,490 36 F4
Grand Traverse Bay, Mich. 36 F3
Grand Valley, Colo., 245 18 A2
Grand Valley, Pa. 56 C2
Grand View, Idaho 24 A4
Grand View, Ill. 25 E4
Grandview, Ind., 599 27 A5
Grandview, Iowa, 300 28 F3
Grandview, Mo., 6,027 40 B3
Grand View, N.Y., 349 47 d1
Grandview, Ohio 53 D3
Grandview, Tex., 961 62 F3
Grandview, Wash., 3,366 66 D2
Grandview, Wis. 69 B1
Grand View Beach, N.Y. 48 j17
Grandview Heights, Ohio, 8,270 53 B3
Grandville, Mich., 7,975 36 F6
Grand Wash Cliffs, Ariz. 14 B2
Grandy, N.C. 51 K1
Grange City, Ky. 30 G2
Granger, Ill. 26 b3
Granger, Ind. 27 B1
Granger, Iowa, 468 28 D3
Granger, Mo., 146 40 E1
Granger, Tex., 1,339 62 F4
Granger, Wash., 1,424 66 C2
Granger, Wyo., 159 70 A3
Grangeville, Idaho, 3,642 24 B3
Granite, Md. 33 b4
Granite, co., Mont., 3,014 41 B2
Granite, Okla., 952 54 D3
Granite, Oreg., 3 55 N2
Granite City, Ill., 40,073 25 B5
Granite Falls, Minn., 3,171 38 B3
Granite Falls, N.C., 2,644 50 D2
Granite Falls, Wash., 599 67 b4
Granite Mtn., Utah 64 A2
Granite Pass, Wyo. 70 C1
Granite Pk., Mont. 41 D3
Granite Pk., Utah 64 A1
Granite Quarry, N.C., 1,059 50 E2
Granite Range, Alaska 13 H3
Granite Range, Nev. 43 A1
Granite Springs, Va. 67 M2
Graniteville (part of Westford), Mass. 35 J2
Graniteville, S.C., 1,017 59 C3
Graniteville, Vt. 65 B2
Grannis, Ark., 185 15 A3
Grannys Cap, Me. 32 A3
Gran Quivira, N. Mex. 46 B2
Gran Quivira Nat. Mon., N. Mex. 46 B2
Grant, Ala., 274 11 C1
Grant, co., Ark., 8,294 15 C3
Grant, Colo. 18 C2
Grant, Fla. 21 K4
Grant, co., Ind., 75,741 27 C2
Grant, Iowa, 180 28 C3
Grant, co., Kans., 5,269 29 A3
Grant, co., Ky., 9,489 30 F2
Grant, parish, La., 13,330 31 B2
Grant, La. 31 B3
Grant, Mich., 732 36 F5
Grant, co., Minn., 8,870 38 A3
Grant, co., Nebr., 1,009 42 C2
Grant, Nebr., 1,166 42 C3
Grant, co., N. Mex., 18,700 46 A3
Grant, co., N. Dak., 6,248 51 M2
Grant, Ohio 53 B2
Grant, co., Okla., 8,140 54 F1
Grant, Okla., 286 55 H4
Grant, co., Oreg., 7,726 55 N2
Grant, co., S. Dak., 9,913 61 D1
Grant, co., Wash., 46,477 66 D2
Grant, co., W. Va., 8,304 68 D2
Grant, co., Wis., 44,419 69 C4
Grant Center, Mich. 36 F5
Grant City, Mo., 1,061 40 B1
Grantfork, Ill., 134 25 C5
Grantham, N.H. 44 A5
Grantham, N.C. 50 G2
Granton, Wis., 278 69 C3
Grant Park, Ill., 757 25 E2
Grant Range, Nev. 43 C2
Grants, Me. 32 A3
Grants, N. Mex., 10,274 46 A2
Grantsburg, Ill. 25 D6
Grantsburg, Wis., 900 69 A2
Grantsdale, Mont. 41 B2
Grants Pass, Oreg., 10,118 55 L3
Grantsville, Md., 446 33 A1
Grantsville, Utah, 2,166 64 A1
Grantsville, W. Va., 866 68 B3
Grant Town, W. Va., 1,105 68 C2
Grantville, Ga., 1,158 22 B2
Granville, Ariz. 14 D3
Granville, Ill., 1,048 25 C2
Granville, Mass., 874(T) 34 C4
Granville, N.Y., 2,715 49 O4
Granville, co., N.C., 33,110 50 G1
Granville, N. Dak., 400 51 M1
Granville, Ohio, 2,868 53 C2
Granville, Vt. 65 B3
Granville, W. Va., 806 68 C2
Granville, Wis. 69 a7
Granville Center (part of Granville), Mass. 34 C4
Grapeland, Tex., 1,113 63 G4
Grapeview, Wash. 67 a6
Grapevine, Calif. 17 D4
Grapevine, Tex., 2,821 63 e11
Grapevine Res., Tex. 63 e10
Grasmere, Idaho 24 B4
Grasmere, N.H. 44 B5
Grasonville, Md. 33 D2
Grass, r., N.Y. 49 K1
Grass Creek, Ind. 27 B2
Grass Creek, Wyo. 70 B2
Grassflat, Pa. 56 E3
Grass Lake, Mich., 1,037 37 G6
Grass L., Ill. 26 b1
Grassland, Tex. 62 D3
Grass Pt., St. Croix 72 q
Grassrange, Mont., 222 41 D2
Grass Valley, Calif., 4,876 17 C2
Grass Valley, Oreg., 234 55 M2
Grassy Butte, N. Dak. 51 L2
Grassy Creek, Ky. 30 G3
Grassy Creek, N.C. 50 D1
Grassy Key, Fla. 21 h14
Gratersford, Pa. 57 L5
Gratiot, co., Mich., 37,012 37 G5
Gratiot, Ohio, 222 53 C3
Gratiot, Wis., 294 69 C5
Gratiot L., Mich. 36 C1
Graton, Calif., 1,055 17 B2
Gratz, Ky., 140 30 F2
Gratz, Pa., 704 56 H4
Gravelly, Ark. 15 B3
Graves, co., Ky., 30,021 30 B4
Gravesville, N.Y. 48 c10
Gravette, Ark., 990 15 A1
Gravity, Iowa, 275 28 C4
Gravity, Pa. 57 o16
Grawn, Mich. 36 F4
Gray, Ga., 1,320 22 C2
Gray, Iowa, 152 28 C3
Gray, co., Kans., 4,380 29 B3
Gray, Me. 32 A5
Gray, Okla. 54 C1
Gray, co., Tex., 31,535 62 D2
Grayback Mtn., Oreg. 55 L3
Grayburg, Tex. 63 l13
Gray Court, S.C., 473 59 B2
Grayland, Wash. 66 A2
Grayling, Mich., 2,015 37 G4
Graymont, Ill. 25 D3
Gray Mountain, Ariz. 14 C2
Grays, S.C. 59 C4
Grays Harbor, co., Wash., 54,465 66 B2
Grays Hbr., Wash. 66 A2
Grays Lake, Ill., 4,347 25 D1
Grays L., Idaho 24 D4
Grayson, co., Ky., 15,834 30 D3
Grayson, Ky., 1,692 30 G2
Grayson, La., 428 31 B1
Grayson, co., Tex., 73,043 62 F3
Grayson, co., Va., 17,390 67 H4
Grays River, Wash. 66 B2
Graysville, Ala., 2,870 11 B2
Graysville, Ind. 27 A3
Graysville, Ohio, 127 53 D3
Graysville, Pa. 56 A6
Graysville, Tenn., 838 61 K2
Grayton, Md. 33 C2
Grayton Beach, Fla. 20 D1
Grayville, Ill., 2,280 25 D5
Greasewood, Ariz. 14 D1
Great Averill L., Vt. 65 D1
Great Barrington, Mass., 2,943; 6,624(T) 34 A4
Great Basin, Nev. 43 C1
Great Bay, N.H. 44 D5
Great Bay, N.J. 45 C4
Great Bend, Kans., 16,670 29 D2
Great Bend, N.Y. 49 J2
Great Bend, N. Dak., 164 51 O2
Great Bend, Pa., 777 57 K2
Great Bk., Mass. 34 D4
Great Bk., N.Y. 48 k18
Great Cacapon, W. Va. 68 E2
Great Chazy, r., N.Y. 49 N1
Great Coharie Cr., N.C. 50 G2
Great Divide, Colo. 18 B1
Great East L., Me.-N.H. 32 A5
Great Egg Harbor, r., N.J. 45 B4
Great Egg Harbor, N.J. 45 B5
Great Egg Harbor Inlet, N.J. 45 C5
Greaterville, Ariz. 14 C4
Great Falls, Mont., 55,357 41 C2

H

For abbreviations and explanation of index, see page 176.

Hankamer INDEX TO MAPS OF THE UNITED STATES Hickory

Hankamer, Tex. 63 k14
Hankinson, Miss. 39 A3
Hankinson, N. Dak., 1,285 51 O2
Hanks, N. Dak., 78 51 L1
Hanksville, Utah 64 B2
Hanksville, Vt. 65 A2
Hanlontown, Iowa, 193 28 D1
Hanna, Ind. 27 B1
Hanna, La. 31 A2
Hanna, Okla., 233 55 H2
Hanna, Utah 64 B1
Hanna, Wyo., 625 70 C3
Hanna City, Ill., 1,056 25 C3
Hannaford, N. Dak., 277 51 N2
Hannah, N. Dak., 253 51 N1
Hannawa Falls, N.Y. 49 K1
Hannibal, Mo., 20,028 40 E2
Hannibal, N.Y., 611 49 G4
Hannibal, Ohio 53 E3
Hannibal, Wis. 69 C2
Hannibal Center, N.Y. 49 I19
Hannover, N. Dak. 51 M2
Hanover, Conn. 19 G3
Hanover, Ill., 1,396 25 B1
Hanover, Ind., 1,170 27 C4
Hanover, Kans., 773 29 F1
Hanover, Me. 32 A4
Hanover, Mass., 5,923(T) 35 L4
Hanover, Mich., 449 37 G6
Hanover, N.H., 5,649 44 A4
Hanover, N.J. 47 b2
Hanover, N. Mex. 46 A3
Hanover, Ohio, 267 53 C2
Hanover, Pa., 15,538 56 J3
Hanover, co., Va., 27,550 67 M3
Hanover, Va. 67 M3
Hanover, Wis. 69 D5
Hanover Center, N.H. 44 A4
Hanover Park, Ill., 6,620 26 b3
Hanoverton, Ohio, 442 53 E2
Hansboro, N. Dak., 143 51 N1
Hansels Mts., Utah 64 b4
Hansen, Nebr. 42 F3
Hansford, co., Tex., 6,208 62 D1
Hansford, Tex. 62 D1
Hans Lollik I., V.I. 72 p
Hanson, Ky., 376 30 C3
Hanson, Mass., 4,370(T) 35 L4
Hanson, co., S. Dak., 4,584 61 D2
Hansonville, Va. 66 G4
Hanston, Kans., 279 29 C2
Hansville, Wash. 67 a5
Hapeville, Ga., 10,082 22 b7
Happy, Alaska 12 a6
Happy, Tex., 624 62 C2
Happy Camp, Calif. 17 B1
Happy Jack, Ariz. 14 C2
Harahan, La., 9,275 31 D4
Haralson, co., Ga., 14,543 22 A2
Haralson, Ga., 141 22 B2
Harappu, i., Jaluit 72 m
Harbor, Oreg. 55 K3
Harbor Beach, Mich., 2,282 37 J5
Harbor Creek, Pa. 56 B1
Harbor Springs, Mich., 1,433 37 G3
Harborton, Va. 67 O3
Harbourton, N.J. 57 g10
Harcourt, Iowa, 268 28 C2
Harcuvar Mts., Ariz. 14 B3
Hardee, co., Fla., 12,370 21 J4
Hardee, Miss. 39 B3
Hardeeville, S.C., 700 59 C4
Hardeman, co., Tenn., 21,517 60 F2
Hardeman, co., Tex., 8,275 62 E2
Hardesty, Okla., 187 54 B1
Hardin, co., Ill., 5,879 25 D6
Hardin, Ill., 356 25 B4
Hardin, co., Iowa, 22,533 28 D2
Hardin, co., Ky., 67,789 30 D3
Hardin, Ky., 458 30 B4
Hardin, Mont., 2,789 41 E3
Hardin, co., Ohio, 29,633 53 B2
Hardin, co., Tenn., 17,397 61 G2
Hardin, co., Tex., 24,629 63 G4
Hardin, Tex. 63 k13
Harding (part of Medfield), Mass. 35 J4
Harding, Minn. 38 B2
Harding, co., N. Mex., 1,874 46 D2
Harding, Pa. 57 n16
Harding, co., S. Dak., 2,371 61 A1
Harding, S. Dak. 61 A1
Hardinsburg, Ind., 218 27 B4
Hardinsburg, Ky., 1,377 30 D3
Hardinville, Ill. 25 E5
Hardman, Oreg., 30 55 N2
Hardtner, Kans., 372 29 D3
Hardup, Utah 64 A1
Hardwick, Mass., 2,340(T) 34 F3
Hardwick, Vt., 1,521 65 C2
Hardwood, Mich. 36 D3
Hardwood Mtn., Me 32 A2
Hardy, Ark., 555 15 D1
Hardy, Ky. 30 H3
Hardy, Nebr., 285 42 G3
Hardy, Okla., 6 54 G1
Hardy, co., W. Va., 9,308 68 E3
Hardy Dam Pd., Mich. 36 F5
Hares Corner, Del. 20 a5
Harford, co., Md., 76,722 33 D1
Harford, N.Y. 49 H6
Harford, Pa. 57 K2
Harford Mills, N.Y. 49 H6
Harjo, Okla. 54 G2
Harkers Island, N.C., 1,362 51 J3
Harlan, Ind. 27 D1
Harlan, Iowa, 4,775 28 B3
Harlan, co., Ky., 51,107 30 G4
Harlan, Ky., 4,177 30 G4
Harlan, co., Nebr., 5,081 42 E3
Harlan, Oreg. 55 L2
Harlan County Res., Nebr. 42 E3
Harlem, Ga., 1,423 22 D2
Harlem, Mont., 1,267 41 D1
Harlem, r., N.Y. 47 d2
Harley Dome, Utah 64 C2
Harleysville, Pa. 57 f10
Harleyville, S.C., 561 59 D3
Harlingen, Tex., 41,207 62 F6
Harlow, N. Dak. 51 N1
Harlowton, Mont., 1,734 41 D2
Harman, W. Va., 128 68 D3
Harmersville, N.J. 45 A5
Harmon, Ill., 214 25 C2
Harmon, co., Okla., 5,852 54 D3
Harmon, Okla. 54 D1
Harmony, Ill. 25 D5
Harmony, Ind. 27 A3
Harmony, Me. 32 B4
Harmony, Minn., 1,214 38 C4
Harmony, N.C., 322 50 E2
Harmony, Pa., 1,142 56 A4
Harmony, R.I. 58 B1
Harned, Ky. 30 D3
Harnett, co., N.C., 49,189 50 G2
Harney, co., Oreg., 6,744 55 N3
Harney L., Oreg. 55 N3
Harney Pk., S. Dak. 61 A2
Harold, Fla. 20 D1
Harold, Ky. 30 H3
Haro Str., B.C.-Wash. 66 B1
Harper, Iowa, 177 28 E3
Harper, co., Kans., 9,541 29 D3
Harper, Kans., 1,899 29 D3
Harper, co., Okla., 5,956 54 D1
Harper, Oreg. 55 O3
Harper, Tex. 62 E4
Harper, Wash. 67 b5
Harper, W. Va. 68 B4
Harper, Mt., Alaska 13 G2
Harper L., Calif. 17 E4
Harpers Ferry, Iowa, 211 28 F1
Harpers Ferry, W. Va., 572 68 F2
Harpersfield, N.Y. 49 L6
Harpersville, Ala., 667 22 C2
Harper Woods, Mich., 19,995 37 d11
Harpeth, r., Tenn. 61 J1
Harpster, Ohio, 302 53 B2
Harpswell Center, Me. 32 A5
Harpursville, N.Y. 49 J6
Harrah, Okla., 934 54 F2
Harrah, Wash., 284 66 C2
Harrell, Ark., 267 15 C4
Harrells, N.C., 259 50 G3
Harrellsville, N.C., 171 51 J1
Harriet, L., Minn. 38 b6
Harrietta, Mich., 119 36 F4
Harriman, N.Y., 812 49 M8
Harriman, Tenn., 5,931 61 L2
Harrington, Del., 2,495 20 A3
Harrington, Me. 32 D4
Harrington, S. Dak. 61 B2
Harrington, Wash., 575 66 D2
Harrington L., Me. 32 B3
Harrington Park, N.J. 47 d2
Harris, co., Ga., 11,167 22 B3
Harris, Iowa, 258 28 B1
Harris, Kans., 36 29 G2
Harris, Mich. 36 D3
Harris, Minn., 552 38 C3
Harris, Mo. 40 C1
Harris, Okla. 55 J4
Harris (part of Coventry), R.I. 58 B2
Harris, co., Tex., 1,243,158 63 G5
Harrisburg, Ala. 11 B3
Harrisburg, Ark., 1,907 15 E2
Harrisburg, Ill., 9,171 25 D6
Harrisburg, Ind. 27 C3
Harrisburg, Mo., 124 40 D2
Harrisburg, Nebr. 42 A2
Harrisburg, Ohio, 359 53 B3
Harrisburg, Oreg., 939 55 L2
Harrisburg, Pa., 79,697 56 H5
Harrisburg, S.Dak., 313 61 D2
Harrison, Ark., 7,015 15 B1
Harrison, Ga., 209 22 D3
Harrison, Idaho, 249 24 A2
Harrison, co., Ind., 19,207 27 B4
Harrison, co., Iowa, 17,600 28 B3
Harrison, co., Ky., 13,704 30 F2
Harrison, Me. 32 A4
Harrison, Mich., 1,072 37 G4
Harrison, co., Miss., 119,489 39 C5
Harrison, co., Mo., 11,603 40 B1
Harrison, Mont. 41 C3
Harrison, Nebr., 448 42 A1
Harrison, N.J., 11,743 47 c3
Harrison, N.Y. 47 e2
Harrison, co., Ohio, 17,995 53 D2
Harrison, Ohio, 3,878 53 A3
Harrison, S. Dak. 61 C2
Harrison, co., Tex., 45,594 63 G3
Harrison, co., W. Va., 77,856 68 C2
Harrison, Wis. 69 D2
Harrison Bay, Alaska 13 F1
Harrisonburg, La., 594 31 B2
Harrisonburg, Va., 12,842 67 K2
Harrison City, Pa. 56 d8
Harrison L., Mich. 36 F6
Harrison Valley, Pa. 56 F2
Harrisonville, Md. 33 b3
Harrisonville, Mo., 3,510 40 B3
Harrisonville, Ohio 53 C3
Harriston, Miss. 39 B3
Harrisville, Mich., 487 37 H4
Harrisville, N.H. 44 A6
Harrisville, N.Y., 842 49 k2
Harrisville, Pa., 896 56 B3
Harrisville, R.I., 1,024 58 B1
Harrisville, W. Va., 1,428 68 B2
Harrisville, Wis. 27 C5
Harrodsburg, Ind. 27 B3
Harrodsburg, Ky., 6,061 30 F3
Harrogate, Tenn. 61 M1
Harrold, S. Dak., 255 61 C1
Harrow, Pa. 57 I18
Harry Strunk L., Nebr. 42 D3
Harshaw, Ariz. 14 C4
Harshaw, Wis. 69 D2
Hart, co., Ga., 15,229 22 D1
Hart, co., Ky., 14,119 30 E3
Hart, Mich., 1,990 36 E5
Hart, Tex., 577 62 C2
Hartfield, Va. 67 N3
Hartford, Ala., 1,956 11 D4
Hartford, Ark., 531 15 A2
Hartford, co., Conn., 689,555 19 D3
Hartford, Conn., 162,178 19 E2
Hartford, Ga. 22 C3
Hartford, Ill., 2,355 25 B5
Hartford, Iowa, 271 28 D3
Hartford, Kans., 337 29 G2
Hartford, Ky., 1,618 30 D3
Hartford, Me. 32 A4
Hartford, Mich., 2,305 36 E6
Hartford, N.Y. 49 O4
Hartford, Ohio, 397 53 C2
Hartford, S. Dak., 688 61 D2
Hartford, Tenn. 61 M2
Hartford, Vt. 65 C3
Hartford, W. Va., 376 68 B2
Hartford, Wis., 5,627 69 E4
Hartford City, Ind., 8,053 27 C2
Hartington, Nebr., 1,648 42 G1
Hart L., Oreg. 55 N3
Hartland, Kans. 29 A3
Hartland, Me., 1,016 32 B4
Hartland, Mich. 37 H6
Hartland, Vt. 65 C3
Hartland, Wis., 2,088 69 a7
Hartland Four Corners, Vt. 65 C3
Hartleton, Pa., 234 56 G4
Hartley, Iowa, 1,738 28 B1
Hartley, co., Tex., 2,171 62 C2
Hartley, Tex. 62 C2
Hartline, Wash., 206 66 D2
Hart Lot, N.Y. 49 I20
Hartly, Del., 164 20 A2
Hartman, Ark., 375 15 B2
Hartman, Colo., 164 18 D2
Hart Mtn., Oreg. 55 N3
Harts, W. Va. 68 A3
Hartsburg, Ill., 300 25 C3
Hartsburg, Mo., 158 40 D3
Hartsdale, N.Y. 47 d1
Hartsel, Colo. 18 B2
Hartselle, Ala., 5,000 11 C1
Hartsgrove, Ohio 53 D1
Hartshorne, Okla., 1,903 55 H3
Hartstene I., Wash. 67 a6
Hartstown, Pa. 56 A2
Hartsville, Ind., 399 27 C3
Hartsville (part of New Marlboro), Mass. 34 A4
Hartsville, S.C., 6,392 59 D2
Hartsville, Tenn., 1,712 61 J1
Hartville, Mo., 486 40 D4
Hartville, Ohio, 1,353 53 D2
Hartville, Wyo., 177 70 D2
Hartwell, Ga., 4,599 22 D1
Hartwell Res., Ga.-S.C. 59 A2
Hartwick, Iowa, 126 28 E3
Hartwick, N.Y. 49 K5
Hartwood, Va. 67 M2
Harvard, Idaho 24 A2
Harvard, Ill., 5,019 25 D1
Harvard, Mass., 2,563(T) 35 H2
Harvard, Nebr., 1,261 42 F3
Harvard, N.Y. 49 K6
Harvel, Ill., 285 25 C4
Harvest, Ala. 11 C1
Harvester, Ill., 299 26 c4
Harvey, Ill., 33,230 26 d4
Harvey, co., Kans., 25,865 29 E2
Harvey, Mich. 36 D2
Harvey, N. Dak., 2,365 51 M2
Harvey Cedars, N.J., 134 45 C4
Harveysburg, Ohio, 514 53 B3
Harveys Lake, Pa. 57 J3
Harveyville, Kans., 204 29 F2
Harviell, Mo., 177 40 F5
Harwich, Mass., 3,747(T) 35 O6
Harwich Port (part of Harwich), Mass. 35 O6
Harwick, Pa., 1,520* 56 c7
Harwinton, Conn., 3,344(T) 19 C2
Harwood, Md. 33 c5
Harwood, Tex., 132 62 F5
Harwood Heights, Ill., 8,808 26 c3
Hasbrouck Heights, N.J., 13,046 47 c2
Hash Rock, mtn., Oreg. 55 M2
Haskell, Ark., 215 15 C3
Haskell, co., Kans., 2,990 29 B3
Haskell, N.J. 47 b1
Haskell, co., Okla., 9,121 55 H2
Haskell, Okla., 1,887 55 H2
Haskell, co., Tex., 11,174 62 E3
Haskell, Tex., 4,016 62 E3
Haskell Hill, Mass. 34 B3
Haskells, Ind. 26 g4
Haskins, Ohio, 521 53 B1
Haslet, Tex. 63 e9
Haslett, Mich. 37 G6
Hassayampa, r., Ariz. 14 B2
Hassell, N.C., 147 51 H2
Hastings, Fla., 617 21 J2
Hastings, Iowa, 260 28 B3
Hastings, Mich., 6,375 36 F6
Hastings, Minn., 10,588 38 C3
Hastings, Nebr., 21,412 42 F3
Hastings, N.Y. 49 H4
Hastings, N. Dak. 51 N2
Hastings, Okla., 200 54 E3
Hastings, Pa., 1,751 56 D4
Hastings-on-Hudson, N.Y., 9,777 47 d2
Haswell, Colo., 169 18 D2
Hatboro, Pa., 7,315 57 L5
Hatch, N. Mex., 888 46 B3
Hatch, Utah, 198 64 A3
Hatchie, r., Tenn. 60 F2
Hatchineha, L., Fla. 21 J3
Hatchville (part of Falmouth), Mass. 35 M6
Hat Creek, Calif. 17 C1
Hat Cr., Nebr.-S. Dak. 42 A1
Hatfield, Ark., 337 15 A3
Hatfield, Ind. 27 A5
Hatfield, Mass., 1,330; 2,350(T) 34 D3
Hatfield, Pa., 1,941 57 L5
Hatfield, Wis. 69 C3
Hatillo, P.R., 2,582 72 n b1
Hatley, Wis., 306 69 D3
Hatteras, N.C. 51 K2
Hatteras, C., N.C. 51 K2
Hattertown (part of Newtown), Conn. 19 B4
Hattiesburg, Miss., 34,989 39 C4
Hattieville, Ark. 15 C2
Hatton, Ala. 11 B1
Hatton, Ark. 15 A3
Hatton, N. Dak., 856 51 O2
Hatton, Wash., 65 66 D2
Haubstadt, Ind., 1,029 27 A4
Haugen, Wis., 265 69 L2
Haughton, La., 611 31 A1
Hauppauge, N.Y. 47 g2
Hauser, Oreg. 55 K3
Hauula, Hawaii, 806 23 J2
Havana, Ala. 11 B3
Havana, Ark., 277 15 B2
Havana, Fla., 2,090 21 F1
Havana, Ill., 4,363 25 C3
Havana, Kans., 162 29 G3
Havana, N. Dak., 206 51 O3
Havana, Ohio 53 C1
Havasu L., Ariz.-Calif. 14 A2
Havelock, Iowa, 289 28 C2
Havelock, N.C., 2,433 51 H3
Haven, Kans., 982 29 E3
Haven, Wis. 69 F4
Havensville, Kans., 166 29 G1
Haverford, Pa., 5,400* 57 f11
Haverhill, Fla., 442 20 b7
Haverhill, Mass., 46,346 35 K1
Haverhill, N.H. 44 A3
Haverhill, Ohio 53 C4
Haverstraw, N.Y., 7,293 49 M8
Havertown, Pa., 36,000* 57 f12
Haviland, Kans., 725 29 C3
Havre, Mont., 10,740 41 D1
Havre de Grace, Md., 8,510 33 D1
Haw, r., N.C. 50 F1
Hawaii, st., 741,000* 22-23
Hawaii, co., Hawaii, 61,332 23 K4
Hawaii, i., Hawaii 23 L4
Hawaiian Is., Pac. Oc. 71 E2
Hawaii Volcanoes Nat. Pk., Hawaii 23 L4
Hawarden, Iowa, 2,544 28 A2
Hawesville, Ky., 882 30 D3
Hawi, Hawaii, 985 23 L3
Hawkeye, Iowa, 516 28 F2
Hawkeye, N.Y. 49 N1
Hawkins, co., Tenn., 30,468 61 M1
Hawkins, Tex., 868 63 G3
Hawkins, Wis., 402 69 C2
Hawkins Pk., Utah 64 A3
Hawkinsville, Ga., 3,967 22 C3
Hawk Point, Mo., 270 40 E3
Hawk Run, Pa. 56 E4
Hawks, Mich. 37 H3
Hawk's Nest, mtn., N. Dak. 51 N2
Hawk Springs, Wyo. 70 D3
Hawley, Mass., 251(T) 34 C2
Hawley, Minn., 1,270 38 A2
Hawley, Okla. 54 F1
Hawley, Pa., 1,433 57 L3
Hawley, Tex. 62 E3
Hawleyville (part of Newtown), Conn. 19 B4
Haworth, N.J., 3,215 47 d2
Haworth, Okla., 351 55 J4
Haw River, N.C., 1,410 50 F1
Hawthorn, Pa., 612 56 C3
Hawthorne, Calif., 33,035 16 e11
Hawthorne, Fla., 1,167 21 H2
Hawthorne, Nev., 2,838 43 A2
Hawthorne, N.J., 17,735 47 c2
Hawthorne, N.Y. 47 d1
Hawthorne, Wis. 69 B1
Hawthorne Woods, Ill., 239 26 b2
Haxtun, Colo., 990 18 D1
Hay, Wash. 66 E2
Hay, Mt., Alaska 13 J4
Hay, r., Wis. 69 A2
Hay Canyon Butte, S. Dak. 61 A2
Haycock, Alaska 12 C2
Hayden, Ala., 187 11 C2
Hayden, Ariz., 1,760 14 C3
Hayden, Colo., 764 18 B1
Hayden, Fla., 5,471 21 H4
Hayden, Idaho, 901 24 A2
Hayden Pk., Utah 64 B1
Hayden Row (part of Hopkinton), Mass. 35 J4
Haydenville (part of Williamsburg), Mass. 34 D3
Hayes, La. 31 B3
Hayes, co., Nebr., 1,919 42 C3
Hayes, S. Dak. 61 B1
Hayes, Mt., Alaska 13 G3
Hayes Center, Nebr., 283 42 C3
Hayesville, N.C., 428 50 B2
Hayfield, Minn., 889 38 C4
Hayfield, Va. 67 L1
Hayfork, Calif. 17 B1
Haylow, Ga. 22 D5
Haymarket, Va., 257 67 M2
Hayne, Kans. 29 B3
Haynes, Ark. 15 E3
Haynes, N. Dak., 111 51 L3
Haynesville, La., 3,031 31 A1
Haynesville, Me. 32 C3
Hayneville, Ala. 11 C3
Hays, Kans., 11,947 29 C2
Hays, Mont. 41 D2
Hays, co., Tex., 19,934 62 E4
Haysi, Va., 485 66 G3
Hay Springs, Nebr., 823 42 B1
Haystack Mtn., N. Mex. 46 C3
Haystack Mtn., Vt. 65 B1
Haystack Mtn., Vt. 65 B5
Haystack Pk., Utah 64 A2
Haysville, Ind. 27 A4
Haysville, Kans., 5,836 29 E3
Hayters Gap, Va. 66 G4
Hayti, Mo., 3,737 40 G5
Hayti, S. Dak., 425 61 D1
Hayward, Calif., 72,700 17 C3
Hayward, Okla. 54 F1
Hayward, Wis., 1,540 69 B1
Haywood, Ky. 30 E4
Haywood, co., N.C., 39,711 50 B2
Haywood, N.C., 713 50 F2
Haywood, Okla. 55 H3
Haywood, co., Tenn., 23,393 60 F2
Hazard, Ky., 5,958 30 G3
Hazard, Nebr., 104 42 E2
Hazardville (part of Enfield), Conn. 19 E4
Hazel, Ky., 342 30 B4
Hazel, S. Dak., 128 61 D1
Hazel Crest, Ill., 8,907 26 d4
Hazel Dell, Ill. 25 D4
Hazel Green, Wis., 807 69 C5
Hazel Hurst, Pa. 56 D2
Hazelhurst, Wis. 69 D2
Hazel Park, Mich., 25,631 37 d11
Hazelton, Idaho, 433 24 B4
Hazelton, Kans., 246 29 D3
Hazelton, N. Dak., 451 51 M2
Hazelton, W. Va. 68 D2
Hazelwood, Mo., 6,045 40 c9
Hazelwood, N.C., 1,925 50 B3
Hazen, Ark., 1,456 15 D3
Hazen, Nev. 43 A2
Hazen, N. Dak., 1,222 51 M2
Hazen Bay, Alaska 12 B2
Hazlehurst, Ga., 3,699 22 D4
Hazlehurst, Miss., 3,400 39 B4
Hazlet, N.J. 47 c4
Hazleton, Iowa, 665 28 F2
Hazleton, Pa., 32,056 57 J4
Head Harbor I., Me. 32 D4
Headland, Ala., 2,650 11 D4
Headlee, Ind. 27 B2
Head of the Harbor, N.Y., 714 47 g2
Headquarters, Idaho 24 B2
Headrick, Okla., 152 54 D3
Heafford Junction, Wis. 69 D2
Healdsburg, Calif., 4,816 17 B2
Healdton, Okla., 2,898 54 F3
Healing Springs, Va. 67 J3
Healy, Kans. 29 B2
Healy Fork, Alaska 13 F3
Heard, co., Ga., 5,333 22 A2
Heards, Va. 67 L3
Hearne, Tex., 5,072 62 F4
Heart, r., N. Dak. 51 L2
Heart Butte Dam, N. Dak. 51 M2
Heartwell, Nebr., 113 42 F3
Heartwellville, Vt. 65 A5
Heaters, W. Va. 68 C3
Heath, Mass., 304(T) 34 C2
Heath, Ohio, 6,066 53 C2
Heath, Tex. 63 g11
Heath Springs, S.C., 832 59 D2
Heathsville, Va. 67 N3
Heaton, N.C. 50 C1
Heavener, Okla., 1,891 55 J3
Hebardville, Ga., 2,758 22 D4
Hebbardsville, Ky. 30 C3
Hebbronville, Tex., 3,987 62 E6
Heber, Ariz. 14 C2
Heber, Calif. 17 F5
Heber, Utah, 2,936 64 B1
Heber Springs, Ark., 2,320 15 C2
Hebgen L., Mont. 41 C3
Hebo, Oreg. 55 L2
Hebron, Conn., 1,819(T) 19 F3
Hebron, Ill., 701 25 D1
Hebron, Ind., 1,401 27 A1
Hebron, Me. 32 A4
Hebron, Md., 754 33 E2
Hebron, Nebr., 1,920 42 G3
Hebron, N.H. 44 B4
Hebron, N. Dak., 1,340 51 M2
Hebron, Ohio, 1,260 53 C3
Hebron, Va. 67 M3
Hebron, Wis. 69 E5
Hebronville (part of Attleboro), Mass. 35 J5
Hecker, Ill., 313 25 B5
Hecktown, Pa. 57 k18
Hecla, S. Dak., 444 61 C1
Hector, Ark., 328 15 B2
Hector, Minn., 1,297 38 B3
Hedges, Fla. 21 J1
Hedgesville, W. Va., 342 68 E2
Hedley, Tex., 494 62 D2
Hedrick, Iowa, 762 28 E3
Hedwig, Tex., 1,182 63 h14
Heeia, Hawaii 23 f9
Heel Pt., Wake I. 71 b
Heflin, Ala., 2,400 11 D2
Heflin, La., 289 31 A1
Hegins, Pa. 56 H4
Heiberger, Ala. 11 B3
Heidelberg, Ky. 30 G3
Heidelberg, Miss., 1,049 39 D4
Heidelberg, Pa., 2,118 56 b8
Heil, N. Dak. 51 M2
Heilwood, Pa. 56 C4
Heimdal, N. Dak. 51 N2
Heizer, Kans. 29 D2
Helemano Str., Hawaii 23 d8
Helen, Ga., 227 22 C1
Helen, Mt., Nev. 43 B3
Helena, Ala., 523 11 C2
Helena, Ark., 11,500 15 E3
Helena, Calif. 17 B1
Helena, Ga., 1,290 22 C3
Helena, Ill. 25 E5
Helena, Mont., 20,227 41 B2
Helena, N.Y. 49 L1
Helena, Okla., 580 54 E1
Helenville, Wis. 69 E5
Helix, Oreg., 148 55 N2
Hell, Mich. 37 G6
Hellbranch, r., Ohio 52 a6
Hell Cr., Colo. 18 D2
Hellertown, Pa., 6,716 57 L4
Hellier, Ky., 104 30 H3
Hells Canyon, Idaho-Oreg. 24 A3
Helm, Ill. 25 D5
Helmetta, N.J., 779 45 C3
Helmsburg, Ind. 27 B3
Helmville, Mont. 41 B2
Helotes, Tex. 62 E5
Helper, Utah, 2,459 64 B2
Helton, Ky. 30 G4
Heltonville, Ind. 27 B4
Hemet, Calif., 7,943 17 E5
Hemingford, Nebr., 904 42 A1
Hemingway, S.C., 951 59 E3
Hemlock, Ind. 27 C2
Hemlock, Mich. 37 G5
Hemlock, N.Y. 48 j18
Hemlock L., N.Y. 48 E5
Hemphill, co., Tex., 3,185 62 D2
Hemphill, Tex., 913 63 H4
Hempstead, co., Ark., 19,661 15 B4
Hempstead, N.Y., 37,192 49 N9
Hempstead, Tex., 1,505 62 F4
Hempstead Hbr., N.Y. 47 e2
Henderson, Colo. 18 c5
Henderson, co., Ill., 8,237 25 B3
Henderson, Ill., 212 25 B2
Henderson, Iowa, 191 28 B3
Henderson, co., Ky., 33,519 30 C3
Henderson, Ky., 16,892 30 C3
Henderson, Dickinson Co., Mich. 36 D2
Henderson, Shiawassee Co., Mich. 37 G5
Henderson, Nebr., 730 42 G3
Henderson, Nev., 12,525 43 C3
Henderson, N.Y. 49 H3
Henderson, co., N.C., 36,163 50 C2
Henderson, N.C., 12,740 50 G1
Henderson, co., Tenn., 16,115 61 G2
Henderson, Tenn., 2,691 61 G2
Henderson, co., Tex., 21,786 63 G3
Henderson, Tex., 9,666 63 G3
Henderson, W. Va., 601 68 A3
Henderson Cr., Ill. 25 B2
Hendersonville, N.C., 5,911 50 C2
Hendersonville, Pa. 56 b8
Hendersonville, S.C. 59 D4
Hendersonville, Tenn. 61 J1
Hendley, Nebr., 79 42 E3
Hendricks, co., Ind., 40,896 27 B3
Hendricks, Ky. 30 G2
Hendricks, Minn., 797 38 A3
Hendricks, W. Va., 407 68 D2
Hendrix, Okla. 55 G4
Hendrum, Minn., 305 38 A2
Hendry, co., Fla., 8,119 21 J5
Henefer, Utah, 408 64 c5
Henkel, Ill. 25 C2
Henlawson, W. Va., 1,670 68 B4
Henley, Mo., 73 40 D3
Henlopen, C., Del. 20 B3
Henly, Tex. 62 b7
Hennepin, Ill., 391 25 C2
Hennepin, co., Minn., 842,854 38 C3
Hennepin, Okla. 54 F3
Hennessey, Okla., 1,228 54 F1
Henniker, N.H. 44 B5
Henning, Ill., 271 25 E3
Henning, Minn., 980 38 B2
Henning, Tenn., 466 60 F2
Henrico, co., Va., 117,339 67 M3
Henrietta, Mich. 37 G6
Henrietta, Mo., 497 40 C2
Henrietta, N.Y. 48 E4
Henrietta, Tex., 3,062 62 E3
Henrieville, Utah, 152 64 B3
Henry, co., Ala., 15,286 11 D4
Henry, co., Ga., 17,619 22 B2
Henry, co., Ill., 49,317 25 B2
Henry, Ill., 2,278 25 C2
Henry, co., Ind., 48,899 27 C3
Henry, co., Iowa, 18,187 28 F4
Henry, co., Ky., 10,987 30 E2
Henry, co., Mo., 19,226 40 C3
Henry, Nebr., 138 42 A1
Henry, co., Ohio, 25,392 53 A1
Henry, S. Dak., 276 61 D1
Henry, co., Tenn., 22,275 61 G1
Henry, co., Va., 40,335 67 K4
Henry, Va. 67 K4
Henry, C., Va. 67 O4
Henryetta, Okla., 6,551 55 G2
Henry Lake, Pa. 57 o16
Henry Mts., Utah 64 B2
Henrys Fork, r., Idaho 24 D3
Henryville, Ind. 27 C4
Henshaw, L., Calif. 17 E5
Hensley, Ark. 15 C3
Hensonville, N.Y. 49 M6
Henton, Ill. 25 D4
Hephzibah, Ga., 676 22 D2
Heppner, Oreg., 1,661 55 N2
Herald, Ill. 25 D6
Herbert I., Alaska 12 A5
Herbertsville, N.J. 47 c5
Herbster, Wis. 69 B1
Herculaneum, Mo., 1,767 40 F3
Hercules, Calif., 310 16 b6
Hereford, Md. 33 D1
Hereford, Oreg. 55 O2
Hereford, Tex., 7,652 62 C2
Herendeen Bay, Alaska 12 C5
Herington, Kans., 3,702 29 E2
Herkimer, co., N.Y., 66,370 49 L4
Herkimer, N.Y., 9,396 49 L4
Herlong, Calif. 17 C1
Herman, Mich. 36 C2
Herman, Minn., 764 38 A3
Herman, Nebr., 335 42 H2
Herman, Pa. 56 B4
Hermanas, N. Mex. 46 B4
Hermann, Mo., 2,536 40 E3
Hermansville, Mich. 36 C3
Hermanville, Miss. 39 B4
Herminie, Pa., 1,571 56 B5
Hermiston, Oreg., 4,402 55 N2
Hermitage, Ark., 379 15 C4
Hermitage, Mo., 328 40 C4
Hermleigh, Tex. 62 D3
Hermon, Me. 32 C4
Hermon, N.Y., 612 49 K2
Hermosa, S. Dak., 126 61 A2
Hermosa Beach, Calif., 16,115 16 d11
Hernandez, N. Mex. 46 B1
Hernando, co., Fla., 11,205 21 H3
Hernando, Miss., 1,898 39 C1
Herndon, Kans., 339 29 B1
Herndon, Ky. 30 C4
Herndon, Pa., 622 56 J4
Herndon, Va., 1,960 67 M2
Herndon, W. Va. 68 B4
Herod, Ill. 25 D6
Heron, Mont. 41 A1
Heron Lake, Minn., 852 38 B4
Herreid, S. Dak., 767 61 B1
Herrick, Ill., 440 25 C4
Herrick, S. Dak., 160 61 C2
Herrick Mtn., Vt. 65 A3
Herriman, Utah 64 b7
Herrin, Ill., 9,474 25 C6
Herring, Okla. 54 D2
Herrings, N.Y. 49 J2
Herron, Mich. 37 H3
Herscher, Ill., 658 25 D2
Hersey, Mich., 246 36 F5
Hershey, Nebr., 504 42 D2
Hershey, Pa., 6,851 56 H5
Hersman, Ill. 25 B4
Hertel, Wis. 69 A2
Hertford, co., N.C., 22,718 51 H1
Hertford, N.C., 2,012 51 J1
Hesler, Ky. 30 F2
Hesperia, Calif. 16 g10
Hesperia, Mich., 822 36 F5
Hesperus, Colo. 18 A3
Hess, Okla. 54 D3
Hessel, Mich. 37 G2
Hessmer, La., 433 31 B2
Hesston, Ind. 26 h3
Hesston, Kans., 1,103 29 E2
Hester, Okla., 22 54 D3
Hetherton, Mich. 37 G3
Hetland, S. Dak., 107 61 D1
Hettick, Ill., 253 25 B4
Hettinger, co., N. Dak., 6,317 51 L2
Hettinger, N. Dak., 1,769 51 L2
Heuvelton, N.Y., 810 49 K1
Hewett, W. Va. 68 B4
Hewitt, Wis. 69 C3
Hewlett, Va. 67 M3
Hext, Tex. 62 E4
Heyburn, Idaho, 829 24 C4
Heyburn Res., Okla. 55 G2
Heyworth, Ill., 1,196 25 D3
H-4 Res., Tex. 62 c9
Hialeah, Fla., 66,972 21 K6
Hialeah Gardens, Fla., 172 20 a9
Hiawassee, Ga., 455 22 C1
Hiawatha, Iowa, 1,336 28 F2
Hiawatha, Kans., 3,391 29 G1
Hiawatha, Mich. 36 E2
Hiawatha, Utah, 439 64 B2
Hibbard, Ind. 27 B1
Hibbing, Minn., 17,731 38 C2
Hibernia, N.J. 45 C2
Hickiwan, Ariz. 14 B3
Hickman, co., Ky., 6,747 30 A4
Hickman, Ky., 1,537 30 A4
Hickman, Nebr., 288 42 H3
Hickman, co., Tenn., 11,862 61 H2
Hickok, Kans. 29 A3
Hickory, Ky., 170 30 B4
Hickory, Miss., 539 39 D3
Hickory, co., Mo., 4,516 40 C4
Hickory, N.C., 19,328 50 D2

For abbreviations and explanation of index, see page 176.

For abbreviations and explanation of index, see page 176.

Lakeland INDEX TO MAPS OF THE UNITED STATES Leonore

Lakeland, Fla., 41,350 21 H3
Lakeland, Ga., 2,236 22 D4
Lakeland, Mich. 37 H6
Lakeland, Minn., 598 38 d6
Lakeland, Miss. 39 B3
Lakeland Shores, Minn., 52 38 d6
Lakeland Village, Calif., 3,539 17 E5
Lake Leelanau, Mich. 36 F4
Lake Linden, Mich., 1,314 36 C1
Lakeline, Ohio, 269 52 f7
Lake Lucerne, Ohio 52 f8
Lake Lure, N.C., 233 50 C2
Lake Mead Nat. Rec. Area, 43 C4
Lake Michigan Beach, Mich., 1,092 36 E6
Lake Mills, Iowa, 1,758 28 D1
Lake Mills, Wis., 2,951 69 E4
Lake Minchumina, Alaska 13 E2
Lake Mine, Mich. 36 B2
Lakemont, N.Y. 48 G5
Lakemont, Pa., 1,550* 56 E5
Lakemoor, Ill., 736 26 b1
Lakemore, Ohio, 2,765 53 D1
Lake Mtn., Colo. 18 B2
Lake Mts., Utah 64 c7
Lake Nebagamon, Wis. 69 B1
Lake Odessa, Mich., 1,806 36 F6
Lake O' The Cherokees, Okla. 55 J1
Lake of the Isles, Minn. 38 b6
Lake of the Ozarks, Mo. 40 D3
Lake of the Woods, co., Minn., 4,304 38 B1
Lake of the Woods, Minn. 38 B1
Lake O' The Pines, Tex. 63 G3
Lake Orion, Mich., 2,698 37 H6
Lake Orion Heights, Mich., 1,918 37 H6
Lake Oswego, Oreg., 8,906 55 L2
Lake Owen, Wis. 69 B1
Lake Park, Fla., 3,589 21 K5
Lake Park, Ga., 338 22 C5
Lake Park, Iowa, 952 28 B1
Lake Park, Minn., 730 38 B2
Lake Park, Wash. 67 b6
Lake Parlin, Me. 32 A3
Lake Placid, Fla., 1,007 21 J4
Lake Placid, N.Y., 2,998 49 N2
Lake Pleasant (part of Montague), Mass. 34 E2
Lake Pleasant, N.Y. 49 L4
Lake Pocotopaug, Conn., 1,314 19 F3
Lake Point Junction, Utah 64 b6
Lakeport, Calif., 2,303 17 B2
Lakeport, Fla. 21 J4
Lakeport, Mich. 37 J5
Lakeport, N.H. 44 C4
Lakeport, N.Y. 49 J5
Lake Preston, S. Dak., 955 61 D1
Lake Providence, La., 5,781 31 C1
Lake Range, Nev. 43 A1
Lake Roland, Mich. 36 C2
Lake Ronkonkoma, N.Y., 4,841 47 g2
Lake St. Croix Beach, Minn., 38 d6
Lakeshore, Calif. 17 D3
Lake Shore, Md. 33 d4
Lake Shore, Minn., 264 38 B2
Lakeshore, Miss. 39 C5
Lakeside, Ariz. 14 C2
Lakeside, Calif. 17 E5
Lakeside (part of Morris), Conn. 19 B3
Lakeside, Ind. 27 B2
Lakeside, Iowa, 306 28 B2
Lakeside (part of Westport), Mass. 35 K6
Lakeside, Nebr. 42 B1
Lakeside, N.Y. 48 k17
Lakeside, Ohio 53 C1
Lakeside, Oreg. 55 K3
Lakeside, Utah 64 A1
Lakeside Mts., Utah 64 b6
Lake Stevens, Wash., 1,538 66 C1
Lake Success, N.Y., 3,176 47 d2
Lake Telemark, N.J. 47 a2
Lake Tomahawk, Wis. 69 D2
Laketon, Ind. 27 C2
Laketon, Tex. 62 D2
Laketown, Utah, 211 64 B1
Lake Toxaway, N.C. 50 C2
Lake Valley, N. Mex. 46 B3
Lake Valley, Okla. 54 E2
Lake View, Ark. 15 E2
Lakeview, Calif. 16 g11
Lake View, Iowa, 1,165 28 B2
Lakeview, Montcalm Co., Mich., 1,126 36 F5
Lakeview, Calhoun Co., Mich., 10,384 36 F6
Lake View, N.Y. 48 B5
Lakeview, N.C. 50 F2
Lakeview, Ohio, 1,008 53 A2
Lakeview, Oreg., 3,260 55 M3
Lake View, S.C., 865 59 E2
Lakeview, Dallas Co., Tex. 63 f11
Lakeview, Hall Co., Tex., 219 62 D2
Lakeview, Jefferson Co., Tex., 3,849 63 m14
Lakeview, Utah 64 c7
Lake Villa, Ill., 903 25 D1
Lake Village, Ark., 3,297 15 D4
Lake Village, Ind. 27 A1
Lakeville, Calif. 16 a6
Lakeville (part of Salisbury), Conn. 19 B5
Lakeville, Ind., 757 27 B1
Lakeville, Mass., 3,209(T) 35 L5
Lakeville, Minn., 924 38 C3
Lakeville, N.Y. 48 E5
Lakeville, Ohio, 4,181 53 E1
Lake Waccamaw, N.C., 780 50 G3
Lake Wales, Fla., 8,346 21 J4
Lake Waukomis, Mo., 506 40 a7
Lake Wilson, Minn., 436 38 B3
Lakewood, Calif., 67,126 16 e11
Lakewood, Colo., 19,338 18 C2
Lakewood, Shelby Co., Ill. 25 D4
Lakewood, Du Page Co., Ill. 26 b3
Lakewood, Alpena Co., Mich. 37 H3
Lakewood, Monroe Co., Mich., 1,815 37 H7
Lakewood, N.J., 13,004 45 C3
Lakewood, N. Mex. 46 C3
Lakewood, N.Y., 3,933 48 B6
Lakewood, Ohio, 66,154 53 D1
Lakewood, Tex., 1,882 63 k14
Lakewood, Wash. 67 a6
Lakewood, Wis. 69 E2
Lakewood Club, Mich. 36 E5
Lake Worth, Fla., 20,758 21 K5
Lake Worth Village, Tex., 3,833 63 d11
Lake Zurich, Ill., 3,851 25 E1
Lakin, Kans., 1,432 29 A2
Lakota, Iowa, 459 28 C1
Lakota, N. Dak., 1,658 51 N1
La Lande, N. Mex. 46 C2
La Luz, N. Mex. 46 B3
Lamar, co., Ala., 14,271 11 A2
Lamar, Ark., 514 15 B2
Lamar, Colo., 7,369 18 D2
Lamar, co., Ga., 10,240 22 B2
Lamar, Ind. 27 B4
Lamar, Kans. 29 E1
Lamar, co., Miss., 13,675 39 C4
Lamar, Mo., 3,608 40 B4
Lamar, Nebr., 50 42 C3
Lamar, Okla., 150 55 G2
Lamar, Pa. 56 F3
Lamar, S.C., 1,121 59 D2
Lamar, co., Tex., 34,234 63 G3
La Marque, Tex., 13,969 63 G5
Lamartine, Wis. 69 E4
Lamb, co., Tex., 21,896 62 C2
Lambert, Miss., 1,181 39 B1
Lambert, Mont. 41 F2
Lambert, N.C. 50 E2
Lambert, Okla., 21 54 E1
Lambert Lake, Me. 32 D3
Lambertville, Mich., 1,168 37 H7
Lambertville, N.J., 4,269 45 B3
Lambsburg, Va. 67 J4
Lambs Grove, Iowa, 234 28 D3
Lame Deer, Mont. 41 E3
La Mesa, Calif., 30,441 17 E5
La Mesa, N. Mex. 46 B3
Lamesa, Tex., 12,438 62 C3
Lamine Cr., Mo. 40 D3
Lamison, Ala. 11 B3
Lamlam Mt., Guam 71 a
La Moille, Ill., 655 25 C2
Lamoille, Nev. 43 C1
Lamoille, co., Vt., 11,027 65 B1
Lamoill, r., Vt. 65 C1
La Moine, Calif. 17 B1
La Moine, r., Ill. 25 B3
Lamoni, Iowa, 2,463 28 C4
Lamont, Calif., 6,177 17 D4
Lamont, Iowa, 554 28 F2
Lamont, Kans. 29 G5
Lamont, Mich. 36 F6
Lamont, Okla., 543 54 F1
Lamont, Wash., 111 66 D2
Lamont, Wis. 69 C5
Lamont, Wyo. 70 C2
La Monte, Mo., 801 40 C3
La Motte, Iowa, 323 28 G2
La Motte L., Wis. 69 E3
La Moure, co., N. Dak., 8,705 51 N2
La Moure, N. Dak., 1,068 51 N2
Lampasas, co., Tex., 9,418 62 E4
Lampasas, Tex., 5,061 62 E4
Lampasas, r., Tex. 62 E4
Lamprey, r., N.H. 44 C5
Lamson, N.Y. 49 m20
Lanagan, Mo., 357 40 B5
Lanai, i., Hawaii 23 J3
Lanai City, Hawaii, 2,056 23 J3
Lanaihale, Mt., Hawaii 23 K3
Lanark, Ill., 1,473 25 C1
Lanark, Pa. 57 k18
Lanark Village, Fla. 21 F2
Lancaster, Calif., 26,012 17 D4
Lancaster, Kans., 196 29 G1
Lancaster, Ky., 3,021 30 F3
Lancaster, Mass., 3,958(T) 35 H3
Lancaster, Minn., 462 38 A1
Lancaster, Mo., 740 40 D1
Lancaster, co., Nebr., 155,272 42 H3
Lancaster, N.H., 2,392 44 B3
Lancaster, N.Y., 13,408 48 C5
Lancaster, Ohio, 29,916 53 C3
Lancaster, co., Pa., 278,359 56 J5
Lancaster, Pa., 61,055 56 J5
Lancaster, co., S.C., 39,352 59 D2
Lancaster, S.C., 7,999 59 D2
Lancaster, Tex., 7,501 63 f11
Lancaster, co., Va., 9,174 67 N3
Lancaster, Va. 67 N3
Lancaster, Wash. 66 E2
Lancaster, Wis., 3,703 69 C5
Lance Creek, Wyo. 70 D2
Landa, N. Dak., 110 51 M1
Landaff, N.H. 44 B3
Landenberg, Pa. 57 K6
Lander, co., Nev., 1,566 43 B2
Lander, Wyo., 4,182 70 B2
Landers, Ark. 15 C3
Landes, Ill. 25 E5
Landes, W. Va. 68 D3
Landess, Ind. 27 C2
Landfall, Minn., 731 38 d6
Landgrove, Vt. 65 B4
Landis, N.C., 1,763 50 E2
Landisburg, Pa., 285 56 G5
Landisville, N.J. 45 B4
Lando, S.C. 59 D2
Land O'Lakes, Fla. 21 H3
Land O'Lakes, Wis. 69 D1
Landrum, S.C., 1,930 59 B1
Lane, co., Kans., 3,060 29 B2
Lane, Kans., 282 29 G2
Lane, Okla. 55 G3
Lane, co., Oreg., 162,890 55 L2
Lane, S.C., 497 59 E3
Lane, S. Dak., 99 61 C1
Laneburg, Ark. 15 B4
Lanesboro, Iowa, 258 28 C2
Lanesboro, Mass., 2,933(T) 34 A2
Lanesboro, Minn. 38 D4
Lanesboro, Pa., 502 57 K2
Lanesville (part of New Milford), Conn. 19 B3
Lanesville, Ind., 346 27 B4
Lanesville (part of Gloucester), Mass. 35 M2
Lanett, Ala., 7,674 11 D3
Lanford, S.C. 59 B2
Langar, i., Ponape 72 h
Langdale, Ala., 2,528 11 D3
Langdon, Kans., 97 29 D3
Langdon, N. Dak., 2,151 51 N1
Langford, N.Y. 48 C5
Langford, S. Dak., 397 61 C1
Langhorne, Pa., 1,461 57 g11
Langlade, co., Wis., 19,916 69 D2
Langlade, Wis. 69 E2
Langley, Kans. 29 E2
Langley, Okla., 205 55 H1
Langley, S.C., 1,216 59 C3
Langley, Va. 33 a5
Langley, Wash., 448 66 B1
Langley Park, Md., 11,510 33 a4
Langlois, Oreg. 55 K3
Langsdale, Miss. 39 D4
Langston, Mich. 36 F5
Langston, Okla., 136 54 F2
Langtry, Tex. 62 D5
Lanham, Md. 33 b5
Lanier, co., Ga., 5,097 22 C5
Lanikai, Hawaii, 2,330* 23 f9
Laniloa Pt., Hawaii 23 e8
Lankin, N. Dak., 303 51 N1
Lannon, Wis., 1,084 69 a7
Lansdale, Pa., 12,612 57 L5
Lansdowne, Md. 33 c4
Lansdowne, Pa., 12,601 57 f12
L'Anse, Mich., 2,397 36 C2
L'Anse Bay, Mich. 36 C2
Lansford, N. Dak., 382 51 M1
Lansford, Pa., 5,958 57 K4
Lansing, Ill., 20,926 26 d4
Lansing, Iowa, 1,325 28 F1
Lansing, Kans., 1,264 29 H1
Lansing, Mich., 113,058 37 G6
Lansing, N.Y. 49 m19
Lansing, N.C., 278 50 D1
Lantana, Fla., 5,021 21 K5
Lantry, S. Dak. 61 B1
Laona, N.Y. 48 B6
Laona, Wis. 69 E2
Laotto, Ind. 27 C1
La Palma, Ariz. 14 C3
Lapaz, Ind., 545 27 B1
Lapeer, co., Mich., 41,926 37 H5
Lapeer, Mich., 6,160 37 H5
Lapel, Ind., 1,772 27 C2
Lapine, Ala. 11 C4
Lapine, Oreg. 55 M3
La Place, Ill. 25 D4
Laplace, La., 3,541 31 D3
La Plant, S. Dak. 61 B1
La Plata, co., Colo., 19,225 18 A3
La Plata, Md., 1,214 33 D2
La Plata, Mo., 1,365 40 D1
Laplata, N. Mex. 46 A1
La Plata, r., N. Mex. 46 A1
La Platte, r., Vt. 65 A2
La Plaza, P.R. 72 n c1
La Pointe, Wis. 69 C1
La Porte, co., Ind., 95,111 27 B1
LaPorte, Ind., 21,157 27 B1
Laporte, Minn., 155 38 B2
Laporte, Ohio 52 c8
Laporte, Pa., 195 56 H3
La Porte, Tex., 4,512 63 k14
La Porte City, Iowa, 1,953 28 E2
La Prairie, Ill., 115 25 B3
La Prairie, Minn., 243 38 C2
La Pryor, Tex. 62 D5
La Puente, Calif., 24,723 16 f10
La Push, Wash. 66 A2
Lapwai, Idaho, 500 24 A2
Laramie, co., Wyo., 60,149 70 D3
Laramie, Wyo., 17,520 70 D3
Laramie, r., Colo.-Wyo. 70 D3
Laramie Mts., Wyo. 70 D2
Larchmont, N.Y., 6,860 47 e2
Larchwood, Iowa, 531 28 A1
Laredo, Mo., 370 40 C1
Laredo, Tex., 60,678 62 E6
Lares, P.R., 4,216 72 n b1
Largo, Fla., 5,302 21 c11
Largo, Md. 33 b5
Largo, Key, Fla. 21 K6
Larimer, co., Colo., 53,343 18 C1
Larimer, Pa., 1,525* 56 d8
Larimore, N. Dak., 2,046 51 O2
Lark, Okla. 54 G4
Lark, Tex. 62 D2
Lark, Utah 64 b6
Larkdale, Ill. 26 b1
Larkin, Mich. 37 G5
Larkinsville, Ala. 11 C1
Larkspur, Calif., 5,710 16 a7
Larkspur, Colo. 18 c6
Larksville, Pa., 4,390 57 n16
Larned, Kans., 5,001 29 C2
La Rose, Ill., 192 25 C3
Larose, La., 2,796 31 D4
Larrabee, Iowa, 167 28 B2
Larrabee, Me. 32 D4
Larsen, Wis. 69 E3
Larsen Bay, Alaska, 72 13 E4
Larsmont, Minn. 38 D2
Larson, N. Dak., 62 51 L1
Larto L., La. 31 B2
Larue, co., Ky., 10,346 30 E3
La Rue, Ohio, 842 53 B2
La Russell, Mo., 129 40 B4
Larwill, Ind., 994 27 C1
La Sal, Utah 64 C2
LaSalle, Colo., 1,070 18 C1
La Salle, co., Ill., 110,800 25 D2
La Salle, Ill., 11,897 25 C2
La Salle, parish, La., 13,011 31 B2
La Salle, Mich. 37 H7
La Salle, co., Tex., 5,972 62 E5
La Sal Mts., Utah 64 C2
Las Animas, co., Colo., 19,983 18 C3
Las Animas, Colo., 3,402 18 D2
Las Chavez, N. Mex. 46 B2
Las Cruces, N. Mex., 29,367 46 B3
La Selva Beach, Calif. 16 c9
Las Marías, P.R. 72 n b1
Las Palomas, N. Mex. 46 B3
Las Piedras, P.R., 3,147 72 n d1
Lassen, co., Calif., 17,053 17 C1
Lassen Pk., Calif. 17 C1
Lassen Volcanic Nat. Pk., Calif. 17 C1
Last Chance, Colo. 18 D2
Lastrup, Minn., 138 38 B2
Las Uvas, Sa. de, N. Mex. 46 B3
Las Vegas, Nev., 64,405 43 C3
Las Vegas, N. Mex., 7,790 46 C2
Latah, co., Idaho, 21,170 24 A2
Latah, Wash., 190 66 E2
Latham, Ill., 389 25 C4
Latham, Kans., 203 29 F3
Latham, N.Y. 49 d14
Latham, Ohio 53 B3
Latham, Tenn. 60 G1
Lathrop, Calif., 1,123 17 C3
Lathrop, Mich. 36 D2
Lathrop, Mo., 1,006 40 B2
Lathrop Wells, Nev. 43 B3
Latimer, Iowa, 445 28 D2
Latimer, Kans., 40 29 F2
Latimer, co., Okla., 7,738 55 H3
Latimers Bk., Conn. 19 G4
Latir Pk., N. Mex. 46 C1
Laton, Calif., 1,052 17 D3
La Torrecilla, Lag., P.R. 72 n d1
La Tour, Mo., 68 40 B3
Latrobe, Calif. 17 j12
Latrobe, Pa., 11,932 56 C5
Latta, S.C., 1,901 59 E2
Lattasburg, Ohio 53 C2
Lattingtown, N.Y., 1,631 47 e2
Latty, Ohio, 286 53 A1
Lauderdale, co., Ala., 61,622 11 B1
Lauderdale, Minn., 2,386 38 b6
Lauderdale, co., Miss., 67,119 39 D3
Lauderdale, Miss. 39 D3
Lauderdale, co., Tenn., 21,844 60 F2
Lauderdale by-the-Sea., Fla., 1,327 20 b8
Laughing Fish Pt., Mich. 36 E2
Laughlin Pk., N. Mex. 46 C1
Laughlintown, Pa. 56 C5
Laulau, Saipan 72 f
Laulii, Tutuila 71 c
La Union, N. Mex. 46 B4
Laupahoehoe, Hawaii, 407 23 K4
Laura, Ky. 30 H3
Laura, Ohio, 526 53 A3
Laurel, Del., 2,709 20 A3
Laurel, Fla. 21 H4
Laurel, Ind., 848 27 C3
Laurel, Iowa, 223 28 D3
Laurel, co., Ky., 24,901 30 F3
Laurel, Md., 8,503 33 D1
Laurel, Miss., 27,889 39 C4
Laurel, Mont., 4,601 41 D3
Laurel, Nebr., 922 42 G1
Laureldale, Pa., 4,051 57 h14
Laurel Hill, Fla., 411 20 D1
Laurel Hill, Miss. 39 C3
Laurel Hill, N.C. 50 F3
Laurel Hill, Pa. 56 C5
Laurel Hill Cr., Pa. 56 C6
Laurel Hollow, N.Y., 1,176 47 f2
Laurel Park, N.C., 421 50 C2
Laurel Run, Pa., 855 57 o17
Laurel Springs, N.J., 2,028 57 f12
Laurelton, Pa. 56 G4
Laurelville, Ohio, 539 53 C3
Laurence Harbor, N.J. 47 c4
Laurens, co., Ga., 32,313 22 D3
Laurens, Iowa, 1,799 28 C2
Laurens, N.Y., 291 49 K5
Laurens, co., S.C., 47,609 59 B2
Laurens, S.C., 9,598 59 B2
Laurinburg, N.C., 8,242 50 F3
Laurium, Mich., 3,058 36 C1
Laurys Station, Pa., 57 j18
Lava Beds Nat. Mon., Calif. 17 C1
Lavaca, Ark., 502 15 A2
Lavaca, co., Tex., 20,174 62 F5
Lavaca, r., Tex. 62 F5
Lava Flow, N. Mex. 46 A2
Lava Hot Springs, Idaho, 593 24 D4
Lavalette, W. Va. 68 A3
La Valle, Wis., 417 69 C4
Lavallette, N.J., 832 45 C4
La Ventana, N. Mex. 46 B2
La Verkin, Utah, 365 64 A3
La Verne, Calif., 6,516 16 f10
Laverne, Okla., 1,937 54 D1
La Vernia, Tex. 62 b9
Laverty, Okla. 54 E3
LaVeta, Colo., 632 18 C3
La Villa, Tex., 1,261 62 F6
Lavina, Mont., 212 41 D2
Lavon, Tex. 63 g10
Lavonia, Ga., 2,088 22 C1
Lavon Res., Tex. 63 f10
Lawen, Oreg. 55 N3
Lawler, Iowa, 532 28 E1
Lawn, Tex., 310 62 E3
Lawndale, Calif., 21,740 16 e11
Lawndale, Ill. 25 C3
Lawndale, N.C., 641 50 D2
Lawrence, co., Ark., 17,267 15 D2
Lawrence, co., Ala., 24,501 11 B1
Lawrence, co., Ill., 18,540 25 E5
Lawrence, co., Ind., 36,564 27 B4
Lawrence, Ind., 10,103 27 C3
Lawrence, Kans., 32,858 29 G2
Lawrence, co., Ky., 12,134 30 H2
Lawrence, Mass., 70,933 35 K2
Lawrence, Mich., 773 36 E6
Lawrence, co., Miss., 10,215 39 B4
Lawrence, co., Mo., 23,260 40 C4
Lawrence, Nebr., 338 42 F3
Lawrence, N.Y., 5,907 47 e3
Lawrence, co., Ohio, 55,438 53 C4
Lawrence, Okla. 54 G3
Lawrence, co., Pa., 112,965 56 A3
Lawrence, co., S. Dak., 17,705 61 A1
Lawrence, co., Tenn., 28,049 61 H2
Lawrence, Tex. 63 g11
Lawrence Bk., Mass. 34 F2
Lawrence Bk., N.J. 47 a4
Lawrenceburg, Ind., 5,004 27 C3
Lawrenceburg, Ky., 2,523 30 E2
Lawrenceburg, Tenn., 8,042 61 H2
Lawrenceville, Ga., 3,804 22 C2
Lawrenceville, Ill., 5,492 25 E5
Lawrenceville, N.J., 2,200* 45 B3
Lawrenceville, Pa., 548 56 G2
Lawrenceville, Va., 1,941 67 M4
Laws, Calif. 17 D3
Lawson, Colo. 18 a5
Lawson, Mo., 778 40 B2
Lawsonia, Md. 33 E2
Lawsonville, N.C. 50 E1
Lawton, Ind. 27 B1
Lawton, Iowa, 324 28 A2
Lawton, Kans. 29 H3
Lawton, Mich., 1,402 36 F6
Lawton, N. Dak., 159 51 N1
Lawton, Okla., 61,697 54 E3
Lawton, W. Va. 68 B4
Lax, Ga. 22 C4
Lay L., Ala. 11 C2
Layland, Ohio 53 D2
Layland, W. Va. 68 C4
Layopolis, W. Va., 237 68 C3
Laysan, i., Hawaii 23 a6
Layton, N.J. 47 B1
Layton, Pa. 56 d9
Layton, Utah, 9,027 64 A1
Laytonsville, Md., 196 33 C1
Laytonville, Calif. 17 B2
Lazbuddie, Tex. 62 C2
Lea, co., N. Mex., 53,429 46 D3
Leaburg, Oreg. 55 L2
Leach, Okla. 55 J1
Leachville, Ark., 1,507 15 E2
Lead, S. Dak., 6,211 61 A1
Leadbetter Pt., Wash. 66 A2
Leader, Colo. 28 C2
Lead Hill, Ark., 102 15 C1
Lead Mtn., Me. 32 C4
Leadore, Idaho, 112 24 C3
Leadville, Colo., 4,008 18 B2
Leadwood, Mo., 1,343 40 F4
Leaf, Miss. 39 D4
Leaf, r., Ill. 25 C1
Leaf, r., Miss. 39 C3
Leaf River, Ill., 546 25 C1
League City, Tex., 2,622 63 G5
Leah, Ga. 22 D2
Leake, co., Miss., 18,660 39 C3
Leakesville, Miss., 1,014 39 D4
Leakey, Tex., 587 62 E5
Leaksville, N.C., 6,427 50 F1
Leal, N. Dak., 70 51 N1
Leamington, Utah, 190 64 A2
Learned, Miss., 96 39 B3
Leary, Ga., 848 22 B4
Leasburg, Mo., 176 40 E3
Leasburg, N.C. 50 F1
Leatherwood, Ky., 1,283 30 G3
Leaton, Mich. 37 G5
Leavenworth, Ind., 387 27 B4
Leavenworth, co., Kans., 48,524 29 G1
Leavenworth, Kans., 22,052 29 H1
Leavenworth, Wash., 1,480 66 C2
Leawood, Kans., 7,466 40 a8
Lebam, Wash. 66 B2
Lebanon, Conn., 2,434(T) 19 G3
Lebanon, Ill., 2,863 25 C5
Lebanon, Ind., 9,523 27 B2
Lebanon, Kans., 583 29 D1
Lebanon, Ky., 4,813 30 E3
Lebanon, Mo., 8,220 40 D4
Lebanon, Nebr., 143 42 D3
Lebanon, N.H., 9,299 44 A4
Lebanon, N.J., 880 45 B2
Lebanon, Ohio, 5,993 53 A3
Lebanon, Okla. 54 F4
Lebanon, Oreg., 5,858 55 L2
Lebanon, co., Pa., 90,853 56 J5
Lebanon, Pa., 30,045 56 J5
Lebanon, S. Dak., 198 61 C1
Lebanon, Tenn., 10,512 61 J1
Lebanon, Tex. 63 f10
Lebanon, Va., 2,085 66 G4
Lebanon, Wis. 69 E4
Lebanon Church, Va. 67 L1
Lebanon Junction, Ky., 1,527 30 E3
Lebec, Calif. 17 D4
Lebinao, Yap 72 d
Lebo, Kans., 498 29 G2
Le Center, Minn., 1,597 38 C3
Le Claire, Iowa, 1,546 28 G3
Lecompte, La., 1,485 31 B2
Le Conte, Mt., Tenn. 50 B2
Lecontes Mills, Pa. 56 F3
Lecta, Ohio 53 C4
Ledyard, Conn., 5,395(T) 19 G4
Ledyard, Iowa, 289 28 C1
Lee, co., Ark., 21,001 15 E3
Lee, co., Ala., 49,754 11 D3
Lee, co., Fla., 54,539 21 J5
Lee, Fla., 243 21 G1
Lee, co., Ga., 6,204 22 B4
Lee, co., Ill., 38,749 25 C2
Lee, Ill., 228 25 C2
Lee, Ind. 27 B2
Lee, co., Iowa, 44,207 28 F4
Lee, co., Ky., 7,420 30 G3
Lee, Me. 32 C3
Lee, Mass., 3,078;5,271(T) 34 B3
Lee, co., Miss., 40,589 39 D1
Lee, Nev. 43 C1
Lee, N.H. 44 C5
Lee, N.Y. 48 a10
Lee, co., N.C., 29,197 50 F2
Lee, co., S.C., 21,832 59 D2
Lee, co., Tex., 8,949 62 F4
Lee, co., Va., 25,824 66 F4
Lee Center, N.Y. 49 K4
Leechburg, Pa., 3,545 56 B4
Leech L., Minn. 38 B2
Leechville, N.C. 50 J2
Leedey, Okla., 451 54 D2
Leeds, Ala., 6,162 11 C2
Leeds, Me. 32 A4
Leeds (part of Northampton), Mass. 34 D3
Leeds, N.Y. 49 N6
Leeds, N. Dak., 797 51 N1
Leeds, S.C. 59 C2
Leeds, Utah, 109 64 A3
Leelanau, co., Mich., 9,321 36 F4
Leelanau, L., Mich. 36 F4
Leeper, Pa. 56 C3
Leer, Mich. 37 H3
Leesburg, Fla., 11,172 21 J3
Leesburg, Ga., 774 22 B4
Leesburg, Ind., 427 27 C1
Leesburg, N.J. 45 B5
Leesburg, Ohio, 932 53 B3
Leesburg, Va., 2,869 67 M1
Lees Creek, Ohio 53 B3
Lees Ferry, Ariz. 14 C1
Leesport, Pa., 1,138 57 J5
Lees Summit, Mo., 8,267 40 B3
Lee Store, Tex. 62 D3
Leesville, Ind. 27 B4
Leesville, La., 4,689 31 A2
Leesville, S.C., 1,619 59 C3
Leesville, Tex. 32 c9
Leesville L., Ohio 53 D2
Leetes Island (part of Guilford), Conn. 19 E4
Leeton, Mo., 371 40 C3
Leetonia, Ohio, 2,543 53 E2
Leetsdale, Pa., 2,153 56 b7
Leetsville, Mich. 36 F4
Leeville, La. 31 D4
Lee Vining, Calif. 17 D3
Leffingwell, Conn. 19 G3
Leflore, co., Miss., 47,142 39 B2
Le Flore, co., Okla., 29,106 55 J3
Leflore, Okla. 55 J3
Lefor, N. Dak. 51 L2
Lefors, Tex., 864 62 D2
Legan, i., Kwajalein 72 l
Leggett, Calif. 17 B2
Leggett, Tex. 63 G4
Legion, Tex., 1,691 62 E4
Legion L., Minn. 38 b6
Le Grand, Calif. 17 C3
Lehi, Utah, 4,377 64 B1
Lehigh, Iowa, 846 28 D2
Lehigh, Kans., 178 29 E2
Lehigh, Okla., 296 55 G3
Lehigh, co., Pa., 227,536 57 K4
Lehigh, Pa. 57 o16
Lehigh, r., Pa. 57 K4
Lehigh Acres, Fla. 21 J5
Lehighton, Pa., 6,318 57 K4
Lehman Caves Nat. Mon., Nev. 43 C2
Lehr, N. Dak., 381 51 N2
Lehua I., Hawaii 22 F1
Lehua Landing, Hawaii 22 F1
Leicester, Mass., 1,750;8177(T) 35 G4
Leiscester, N.Y., 365 48 D5
Leicester, Vt. 65 A3
Leicester Junction, Vt. 65 A3
Leigh, Nebr., 502 42 G2
Leighton, Ala., 1,158 11 B1
Leighton, Iowa, 167 28 E3
Leipsic, Del., 281 20 B2
Leipsic, Ohio, 1,802 53 B1
Leipsig, Wis. 69 E4
Leitchfield, Ky., 2,982 30 D3
Leith, N. Dak., 100 51 M2
Leithsville, Pa. 57 k18
Leithton, Ill. 26 c2
Leitner, Ark. 15 C3
Leja Beach, N.Y., 47 h3
Lela, Okla. 54 G1
Lela, Tex. 62 D2
Leland, Ill., 642 25 D2
Leland, Iowa, 209 28 D1
Leland, Mich. 36 F3
Leland, Miss., 6,295 39 B2
Leland, N.C. 50 G3
Leland, Oreg. 55 L3
Leland, Wash. 66 B2
Leland, Wis. 69 C4
Lele, i., Kusaie 72 j
Lele Hbr., Kusaie 72 j
Leleiwi Pt., Hawaii 23 M4
Lelia Lake, Tex. 62 D2
Leloaloa, Tutuila 71 c
Le Mars, Iowa, 7,847 28 A2
Lemasters, Pa. 56 F6
Lemay, Mo. 40 d10
Lemei Rock, mtn., Wash. 66 C2
Lemert, Ohio 53 B2
Lemeta-Johnston, Alaska, 1,227 13 b6
Lemhi, co., Idaho, 5,816 24 B3
Lemhi Ra., Idaho 24 C3
Lemington, Vt. 65 D1
Lemitar, N. Mex. 46 B2
Lemmon, S. Dak., 2,412 61 A1
Lemmon, Mt., Ariz. 14 C3
Lemon Fair, r., Vt. 65 A3
Lemon Grove, Calif., 19,348 17 k15
Lemon Springs, N.C. 50 F2
Lemont, Ill., 4,034 26 c4
Lemont, Pa., 1,153 56 F4
Lemonweir, r., Wis. 69 D4
Lemoore, Calif., 2,561 17 D3
Lemotol Bay, Truk 72 g
Le Moyen, La. 31 B3
Lemoyne, Nebr. 42 C2
Lemoyne, Pa., 4,662 56 H5
Lempster, N.H. 44 A5
Lena, Ill., 1,552 25 C1
Lena, Miss., 307 39 C3
Lena, Nebr. 42 C2
Lena, Ohio 53 A2
Lena, S.C. 59 C4
Lena, Wis., 506 69 E3
Lena, Mt., Utah 64 C1
Lenapah, Okla., 322 55 H1
Lenawee, co., Mich., 77,789 37 G7
Lenexa, Kans., 2,487 40 a8
Lengby, Minn., 181 38 B2
Lenhartsville, Pa., 209 57 K4
Lennon, Mich. 37 G5
Lennox, Calif., 31,224 16 e11
Lennox, S. Dak., 1,353 61 D2
Lennox, Wis. 69 D2
Lenoir, co., N.C., 55,276 50 H2
Lenoir, N.C., 10,257 50 D2
Lenoir City, Tenn., 4,979 61 L2
Lenora, Kans., 512 29 C1
Lenora, Okla. 54 D1
Lenox, Ala. 11 B4
Lenox, Ga., 802 22 C4
Lenox, Iowa, 1,178 28 C4
Lenox, Mass., 1,713;4,253(T) 34 A3
Lenox, Mo. 40 E4
Lenoxdale (part of Lenox), Mass. 34 B3
Lenwood, Calif., 2,407 17 E4
Lenzburg, Ill., 420 25 C5
Leola, Ark., 321 15 C3
Leola, S. Dak., 833 61 C1
Leoma, Tenn. 61 H2
Leominster, Mass., 27,929 35 G
Leon, co., Fla., 74,225 21 F1
Leon, Iowa, 2,004 28 D4
Leon, Kans., 541 29 F3
Leon, N.Y. 48 B6
Leon, Okla., 109 54 F4
Leon, co., Tex., 9,951 63 G4
Leon, W. Va., 236 68 B3
Leon, Wis. 69 C4
Leon, r., Tex. 62 E3
Leona, Kans., 110 29 G1
Leona, Tex. 63 G4
Leona, r., Tex. 62 E5
Leona Mines, Va. 66 F4
Leonard, Mich., 359 37 H6
Leonard, Mo., 142 40 D2
Leonard, N. Dak., 232 51 O2
Leonard, Tex., 1,117 62 F3
Leonardo, N.J. 47 c4
Leonardsville, N.Y. 49 K5
Leonardtown, Md., 1,281 33 D2
Leonardville, Kans., 378 29 F1
Leona Valley, Calif. 17 D4
Leone, Tutuila, 1,192 71 c
Leone Bay, Tutuila 71 c
Leone Pt., Tutuila 71 c
Leoni, Mich. 37 G6
Leonia, Fla. 20 D1
Leonia, N.J., 8,384 47 c2
Leonidas, Mich. 36 F6
Leonore, Ill., 195 25 D2

For abbreviations and explanation of index, see page 176.

Longview, Ill., 270 25 D4
Longview, Miss. 39 D2
Longview, N.C., 3,290 50 D2
Longview, Tex., 40,050 63 G3
Longview, Wash., 23,349 66 B2
Longville, La. 31 A3
Longville, Minn., 159 38 B2
Longwood, Fla., 1,689 21 J3
Longwood, N.C. 50 G3
Longwood, Wis. 69 C3
Lonoke, co., Ark., 24,551 15 D3
Lonoke, Ark., 2,856 15 C3
Lonsdale, Ark., 95 15 C3
Loogootee, Ill. 25 D5
Loogootee, Ind., 2,858 27 A4
Lookeba, Okla., 158 54 E2
Looking Glass, r., Mich. 37 G6
Lookout, Calif. 17 C1
Lookout, Okla. 54 D1
Lookout, W. Va. 68 B3
Lookout, C., N.C. 51 J3
Lookout, Pt., Mich. 37 H4
Lookout Mountain, Tenn., 1,817 61 K3
Lookout Mtn., Ala.-Ga.-Tenn. 11 D1
Lookout Mtn., Alaska 13 D3
Lookout Mtn., N. Dak. 51 N2
Lookout Mtn., N. Mex. 46 A2
Lookout Mtn., Oreg. 55 M2
Lookout Pass, Idaho-Mont. 24 B2
Lookout Pk., Utah 64 B2
Loomis, Calif. 17 j12
Loomis, Mich. 37 G5
Loomis, Nebr., 299 42 E3
Loomis, Wash. 66 D1
Loomis L., Ind. 26 f4
Loon Lake, Ill. 26 b1
Loon Lake, Me. 32 A3
Loon Lake, N.Y. 49 M1
Loon Lake, Wash. 66 E1
Loon L., Me. 32 B2
Loon Lake Mts., N.Y. 49 M1
Lopez, Pa. 56 J3
Lorado, W. Va. 68 B4
Lorain, co., Ohio, 217,500 53 C1
Lorain, Ohio, 68,932 53 C1
Loraine, Ill., 303 25 A3
Loraine, N. Dak., 54 51 M1
Loraine, Tex., 827 62 D3
Loraine, Wis. 69 A2
Loran, Ill. 25 C1
Lorane, Ind. 27 C1
Lorane, Oreg. 55 L3
Loray, Nev. 43 C1
Loray, N.C. 50 D2
Lordsburg, N. Mex., 3,436 46 A3
Lordship (part of Stratford), Conn. 19 C5
Lore City, Ohio, 458 53 D3
Lorentz, W. Va. 68 C2
Lorenzo, Nebr. 42 A2
Lorenzo, Tex., 1,188 62 D3
Loretta, Wis. 69 C2
Loretto, Ky. 30 E3
Loretto, Mich. 36 D3
Loretto, Nebr. 42 F2
Loretto, Pa., 1,338 56 D4
Loretto, Tenn., 929 61 H2
Lorida, Fla. 21 J4
Lorimor, Iowa, 460 28 D3
Loring, Mont. 41 C1
Loris, S.C., 1,702 59 F2
Lorraine, Kans., 157 29 D2
Lorraine, N.Y. 49 J3
Lorton, Nebr., 58 42 J3
Los Alamitos, Calif., 4,312 8,197 16 e11
Los Alamos, Calif. 17 C4
Los Alamos, co., N. Mex., 13,037 46 B2
Los Alamos, N. Mex., 12,584 46 B2
Los Altos, Calif., 19,696 16 b8
Los Altos Hills, Calif., 3,412 16 b8
Los Angeles, co., Calif., 6,038,771 17 D4
Los Angeles, Calif., 2,479,015 17 D4
Los Angeles, r., Calif. 16 d10
Los Banos, Calif., 9,943 17 C3
Los Fresnos, Tex., 1,289 62 F6
Los Gatos, Calif., 9,036 17 C3
Los Lunas, N. Mex., 1,186 46 B2
Los Molinos, Calif. 17 C1
Los Olivos, Calif. 17 C4
Los Osos, Calif. 17 C4
Los Pinos, r., Colo. 18 B3
Los Serranos, Calif. 16 f11
Lost, r., W. Va. 68 E3
Lostant, Ill., 460 25 D2
Lost Cabin, Wyo., 47 70 C2
Lost Chance Cr., Utah 64 B2
Lost City, W. Va. 68 E3
Lost Creek, Ky. 30 G3
Lost Creek, W. Va., 678 68 C2
Lost Cr., Ala. 11 a6
Lost Hills, Calif. 17 D4
Lostine, Oreg., 240 55 O2
Lost L., Minn. 38 B1
Lost Land L., Wis. 69 B1
Lost Nation, Iowa, 567 28 G3
Lost River, Alaska 12 B2
Lost River, Idaho, 58 24 C4
Lost Springs, Wyo., 5 70 D2
Lost Trail Pass, Idaho-Mont 24 B3
Lostwood, N. Dak. 51 L1
Lot, Ponape 72 h
Lothian, Md. 33 c5
Lott, Tex., 924 62 F4
Lottaville, Ind. 26 e4
Lottin, Port, Kusaie 72 j
Lottsburg, Va. 67 N3
Lotts Cr., Ga. 22 E3
Lotus L., Minn. 38 a6
Loudon, N.H. 44 B5
Loudon, Ohio 53 B3
Loudon, co., Tenn., 23,757 61 L2
Loudon, Tenn., 3,812 61 L2
Loudonville, N.Y. 49 d14
Loudonville, Ohio, 2,611 53 C2
Loudoun, co., Va., 24,549 67 M1
Loudville (part of Westhampton and Northampton), Mass 34 D3
Loughman, Fla. 21 J3
Louin, Miss., 389 39 C3
Louis, Okla. 54 D3
Louisa, co., Iowa, 10,290 28 F3
Louisa, Ky., 2,071 30 H2
Louisa, La. 31 C4
Louisa, co., Va., 12,959 67 L3
Louisa, Va., 576 67 L2
Louisburg, Kans., 862 29 H2
Louisburg, Mo. 40 C4
Louisburg, N.C., 2,862 50 G1
Louise, Miss., 481 39 B3
Louise, Tex. 62 F5
Louisiana, st., 3,660,000* 31
Louisiana, Mo., 4,286 40 E2
Louisville, Ala., 890 11 D4
Louisville, Colo., 2,073 18 b5
Louisville, Ga., 2,413 22 D3
Louisville, Ill., 906 25 D5
Louisville, Kans., 204 29 F1
Louisville, Ky., 389,044 30 D2
Louisville, Miss., 5,066 39 D2
Louisville, Nebr., 1,194 42 H2
Louisville, Ohio, 5,116 53 D2
Loup, co., Nebr., 1,097 42 E2
Loup, r., Nebr. 42 G2
Loup City, Nebr., 1,415 42 F2
Louvale, Ga. 22 B3
Louviers, Colo. 18 C2
Love, co., Okla., 5,862 54 F4
Lovedale, Okla. 54 D1
Lovejoy, Ga., 191 22 b3
Lovelace, Tex. 63 e12
Lovelady, Tex., 466 63 G4
Loveland, Colo., 9,734 18 C1
Loveland, Ohio, 5,008 53 A3
Loveland, Okla., 90 54 E3
Lovell, Me. 32 A4
Lovell, Ohio 53 B2
Lovell, Okla., 27 54 F1
Lovell, Wyo., 2,451 70 B1
Lovells, Mich. 37 G4
Lovelock, Nev., 1,948 43 A1
Loves Park, Ill., 10,880 25 C1
Lovettsville, Va., 217 67 M1
Lovewell, Kans. 29 E1
Lovewell Mtn., N.H. 44 A5
Lovewell Pd., Me 32 E4
Lovewell Res., Kans. 29 D1
Lovick, Ala. 11 d6
Lovilia, Iowa, 630 28 D3
Loving, N. Mex., 1,646 46 C3
Loving, co., Tex., 226 62 C4
Lovingston, Va. 67 L3
Lovington, Ill., 1,200 25 D4
Lovington, N. Mex., 9,660 46 D3
Lowden, Iowa, 641 28 F3
Lowe, Kans. 29 B2
Lowell, Ark., 277 15 A1
Lowell, Fla. 21 H2
Lowell, Idaho 24 B2
Lowell, Ind., 2,270 27 A1
Lowell, Me. 32 C3
Lowell, Mass., 92,107 35 J2
Lowell, Mich., 2,545 36 F6
Lowell, Nebr. 42 F3
Lowell, N.Y. 48 b11
Lowell, N.C., 2,784 50 D2
Lowell, Ohio, 783 53 D3
Lowell, Oreg., 503 55 L3
Lowell, Vt. 65 C1
Lowell, Wis., 341 69 E4
Lowell, L., Idaho 24 E4
Lowellville, Ohio, 2,055 53 E1
Lower Bartlett, N.H. 44 C3
Lower Brule, S. Dak. 61 C1
Lower Cabot, Vt. 65 C2
Lower Crab Cr., Wash. 66 D2
Lower Kalskag, Alaska, 122 12 C3
Lower Klamath L., Calif. 17 C1
Lower Lake, Calif. 17 B2
Lower L., Calif. 17 C1
Lower Matecumbe Key, Fla. 21 h14
Lower N.Y. Bay 47 c3
Lower Paia, Hawaii, 925 23 K3
Lower Peach Tree, Ala. 11 B4
Lower Red L., Minn. 38 B1
Lower Rice L., Minn. 38 B2
Lower Sabao L., Me. 32 C3
Lower Sysladobsis L., Me. 32 C3
Lower Village, Hawaii 23 d9
Lowes, Ky. 30 B4
Lowesville, Va. 67 K3
Lowgap, N.C. 50 E1
Lowland, N.C. 50 J2
Lowman, Idaho 24 B3
Lowmansville, Ky. 30 H3
Low Moor, Iowa, 343 28 G3
Lowmoor, Va. 67 K3
Lowndes, co., Ala., 15,417 11 C3
Lowndes, co., Ga., 49,270 22 C5
Lowndes, co., Miss., 46,639 39 D2
Lowndesboro, Ala. 11 C3
Lowndesville, S.C., 274 59 B2
Lowry, S. Dak., 44 61 C1
Lowry City, Mo., 437 40 C3
Lowrys, S.C., 298 59 C2
Lowville, N.Y., 3,616 49 J3
Loxley, Ala., 831 11 B5
Loyal, Okla., 87 54 E2
Loyal, Wis., 1,146 69 C3
Loyalhanna Cr., Pa. 56 C5
Loyall, Ky., 1,260 30 G4
Loyalsock Cr., Pa. 56 H3
Loyalton, Calif., 936 17 C2
Loyalton, S. Dak., 34 61 C1
Loyal Valley, Tex. 62 E4
Loysville, Pa. 56 G5
Luayao, Guam 71 a
Lubbock, co., Tex., 156,271 62 D3
Lubbock, Tex., 128,691 62 D3
Lubec, Me., 1,289 32 D4
Lublin, Wis., 160 69 C2
Lucama, N.C., 498 50 G2
Lucas, co., Iowa, 10,923 28 D4
Lucas, Iowa, 357 28 D3
Lucas, Kans., 559 29 D1
Lucas, Ky. 30 E4
Lucas, Mich. 36 F4
Lucas, co., Ohio, 456,931 53 B1
Lucasville, Ohio, 1,277 53 C4
Luce, co., Mich., 7,827 36 F2
Luce, Nebr. 42 F3
Lucedale, Miss., 1,977 39 D5
Lucerne, Kans. 29 B1
Lucerne, Mo., 157 40 C1
Lucerne, Wash. 66 C1
Lucerne, L., Wis. 69 E2
Lucernes Mines, Pa., 1,524 56 C4
Lucerne Valley, Calif. 17 E4
Lucile, Idaho, 24 A3
Lucin, Utah, 64 C3
Lucinda, Pa. 56 C3
Luck, N.C. 50 C2
Luck, Wis., 853 69 A2
Luckey, Ohio, 946 53 B1
Lucknow, S.C. 59 D2
Ludden, N. Dak., 59 51 N2
Ludell, Kans. 29 B1
Ludington, Mich., 9,421 36 E5
Ludington, Wis. 69 B3
Ludlam, Okla. 54 A1
Ludlam Bay, N.J. 45 B5
Ludlow, Calif. 17 E4
Ludlow, Ill., 460 25 D3
Ludlow, Ky., 6,233 52 h10
Ludlow, Me. 32 C2
Ludlow, Mass. 13,805(T) 34 E4
Ludlow, Miss. 39 C3
Ludlow, Mo., 235 40 C2
Ludlow, Pa. 56 D2
Ludlow, Vt., 1,658 65 B4
Ludlow Center (part of Ludlow), Mass. 34 E4
Ludlowville, N.Y. 49 H5
Ludowici, Ga., 1,578 22 E4
Ludwigs Corner, Pa. 57 e11
Lueders, Tex., 654 62 E3
Luella, Ga. 22 c3
Luera Pk., N. Mex. 46 B3
Lufkin, Tex., 17,641 63 G4
Lugerville, Wis. 69 C2
Lugoff, S.C. 59 D2
Luis Lopez, N. Mex. 46 B2
Luis Peña, Cayo de, P.R. 72 n e1
Lukachukai, Ariz. 14 D1
Luke, Md., 587 33 A1
Lula, Ga., 557 22 C1
Lula, Miss., 484 39 B1
Lula, Okla. 34 E3
Luling, La., 2,122 31 D4
Luling, Tex., 4,412 62 F5
Lulu, Fla. 21 H1
Lulu, Mich. 37 H7
Lum, Mich. 37 H5
Lumber, r., N.C. 50 F3
Lumber Bridge, N.C., 100 50 F3
Lumber City, Ga., 1,360 22 D4
Lumberport, W. Va., 1,031 68 C2
Lumberton, Miss., 2,108 39 C4
Lumberton, N.J. 57 g12
Lumberton, N.C., 15,305 50 F3
Lumberville, Pa. 57 f10
Lumpkin, co., Ga., 7,241 22 B1
Lumpkin, Ga., 1,348 22 B3
Luna, co., N. Mex., 9,839 46 B3
Luna, Catron Co., N. Mex. 46 A3
Luna, Lincoln Co., N. Mex. 46 C3
Lund, Nev. 43 C2
Lund, Utah 64 A2
Lunenburg, Mass., 6,334(T) 35 H2
Lunenburg, Vt. 65 D2
Lunenburg, co., Va., 12,523 67 L3
Lunenburg, Va. 67 L4
Luning, Nev. 43 A2
Lupog, Guam 71 a
Lupton, Ariz. 14 D2
Lupton, Mich. 37 G4
Luquillo, P.R., 2,107 72 n d1
Luquillo, Sa. de, P.R. 72 n d1
Luray, Kans., 328 29 D1
Luray, Mo., 154 40 E1
Luray, S.C., 102 59 C4
Luray, Tenn. 61 G2
Luray, Va., 3,014 67 L2
Lusk, Wyo., 1,890 70 D2
Lustre, Mont. 41 F1
Lutcher, La., 3,274 31 D3
Lutesville, Mo., 658 40 F4
Luther, Ill. 25 C3
Luther, Iowa, 147 28 B3
Luther, Mich., 325 36 F4
Luther, Okla., 517 34 D2
Luthersburg, Pa. 56 D3
Luthersville, Ga., 282 22 B2
Lutherville, Md., 12,265 33 D1
Lutie, Tex. 62 D2
Lutsen, Minn. 38 D2
Luttrell, Tenn. 61 M1
Lutts, Tenn. 61 H2
Lutz, Fla. 21 H3
Luverne, Ala., 2,238 11 C4
Lu Verne, Iowa, 468 28 C2
Luverne, Minn., 4,249 38 A4
Luverne, N. Dak., 109 51 O2
Luxemburg, Mo. 40 c10
Luxemburg, Wis., 730 69 F3
Luxora, Ark., 1,236 15 F2
Luzerne, Mich. 37 G4
Luzerne, N.Y. 49 N4
Luzerne, co., Pa., 346,972 57 J3
Luzerne, Pa., 5,118 57 n16
Lycan, Colo. 18 D3
Lycoming, N.Y. 49 H3
Lycoming, co., Pa., 109,367 56 G3
Lycoming Cr., Pa. 56 G3
Lydia, S.C. 59 D2
Lydick, Ind., 1,217 27 B1
Lyerly, Ga., 409 22 A1
Lyford, Ind. 27 A3
Lyford, Tex., 1,554 62 F6
Lykens, Pa., 2,527 56 H4
Lyle, Kans. 29 B1
Lyle, Wash. 66 C3
Lyles, Tenn. 61 H2
Lyman, Miss. 39 C5
Lyman, Nebr., 626 42 A2
Lyman, N.H. 44 B3
Lyman, Okla. 54 G1
Lyman, S.C., 1,261 59 B2
Lyman, co., S. Dak., 4,428 61 B1
Lyman, S. Dak. 61 C2
Lyman, Wash., 400 66 B1
Lyman, Wyo., 425 70 A3
Lyman L., Wis. 69 A1
Lyme, N.H. 44 A4
Lynbrook, N.Y., 20,784 47 e3
Lynch, Ky., 3,810 30 H4
Lynch, Md. 33 D1
Lynch, Nebr., 409 42 F1
Lynch, Va. 67 K3
Lynchburg, Mo. 40 D4
Lynchburg, Ohio, 1,022 53 B3
Lynchburg, S.C., 544 59 D2
Lynchburg, Tenn., 396 61 J2
Lynchburg, Va., 54,790 67 K3
Lynches, r., S.C. 59 D2
Lynchville, Me. 32 A4
Lynd, Minn., 259 38 B3
Lyndeboro, N.H. 44 B6
Lyndell, Pa. 57 e11
Lynden, Wash., 2,542 66 B1
Lyndhurst, N.J., 21,867 47 c2
Lyndhurst, Ohio, 16,805 53 D1
Lyndon, Ill., 677 25 C2
Lyndon, Kans., 953 29 G2
Lyndon, Vt. 65 C1
Lyndon Center, Vt., 274 65 C1
Lyndon Station, Wis., 335 69 D4
Lyndonville, N.Y., 755 48 D4
Lyndonville, Vt., 1,477 65 D1
Lyndora, Pa., 3,232 56 B4
Lynn, Ala., 532 11 B1
Lynn, Ark., 263 15 D1
Lynn, Fla. 21 J2
Lynn, Ind., 1,260 27 D2
Lynn, Ky. 30 H2
Lynn, Mass., 94,478 35 L3
Lynn, co., Tex., 10,914 62 D3
Lynn, Utah 64 A1
Lynn Crossing, Ala. 11 c6
Lynndyl, Utah, 145 64 A2
Lynnfield, Mass., 8,398(T) 35 K2
Lynnfield Center (part of Lynnfield), Mass. 35 K2
Lynn Gardens, Tenn., 5,261 61 N1
Lynn Grove, Ky. 30 B4
Lynn Haven, Fla., 3,078 21 E1
Lynn Lane, Okla. 55 H1
Lynnville, Ill., 97 25 B4
Lynnville, Ind., 409 27 A4
Lynnville, Iowa, 411 28 E3
Lynnville, Ky. 30 B4
Lynnville, Tenn., 362 61 J2
Lynnwood, Wash., 7,207 66 B2
Lynwood, Calif., 31,614 16 e11
Lynwood, Ill., 255 26 d4
Lynx, Ohio 53 B4
Lynxville, Wis., 183 69 B4
Lyon, co., Iowa, 14,468 28 A1
Lyon, co., Kans., 26,928 29 F2
Lyon, co., Ky., 5,924 30 B3
Lyon, co., Minn., 22,655 38 B3
Lyon, co., Nev., 6,143 43 A2
Lyon Manor, Mich. 37 G4
Lyon Mountain, N.Y. 49 M1
Lyon Mtn., N.Y. 49 N1
Lyons, Colo., 706 18 C1
Lyons, Ga., 3,219 22 D3
Lyons, Ill., 10,891 26 c3
Lyons, Ind., 651 26 c3
Lyons, Kans., 4,592 29 D2
Lyons, Mich., 687 37 G6
Lyons, N.J. 47 a3
Lyons, N.Y., 4,397 48 G4
Lyons, Ohio, 590 53 A1
Lyons, Nebr., 974 42 H2
Lyons, Oreg., 463 55 L2
Lyons, Pa., 571 57 K5
Lyons, Tex. 62 F4
Lyons, Wis. 69 a9
Lyons Falls, N.Y., 887 49 K3
Lyonsville (part of Colrain), Mass. 34 D2
Lyonsville, N.J. 47 b2
Lysander, N.Y. 49 I20
Lytle, Tex., 798 62 E5
Lytle Creek, Calif. 16 q10
Lytton, Iowa, 376 28 C2
Lytton Springs, Tex. 62 c8

M

Maalaea, Hawaii 23 K3
Maalaea Bay, Hawaii 23 K3
Mabana, Wash. 67 b4
Mabank, Tex., 944 62 F3
Maben, Miss., 696 39 C2
Maben, W. Va. 68 B4
Mabie, W. Va. 68 C3
Mable, Oreg. 55 L2
Mableton, Ga., 7,127 22 a6
Mabscott, W. Va., 1,591 68 B4
Mabton, Wash., 958 66 C2
McAdoo, Pa., 3,560 57 J4
McAdoo, Tex. 62 N3
McAfee, N.J. 45 B1
McAlester, Okla., 17,419 55 H3
McAlister, N. Mex. 46 D2
McAlisterville, Pa. 56 G4
McAllaster, Kans. 29 A1
McAllen, Tex., 35,411 62 E6
McAllister, Wis. 69 E2
McAlpin, Fla. 21 H1
McArthur, Calif. 17 C1
McArthur, Ohio, 1,529 53 C3
Macatawa, L., Mich. 36 E6
McBain, Mich., 551 36 F2
McBean, Ga. 22 E2
McBee, S.C., 512 59 D2
McBrides, Mich., 265 37 G5
McCain, N.C. 50 F2
McCall, Idaho, 1,423 24 B3
McCallsburg, Iowa, 272 28 D2
McCamey, Tex., 3,375 62 C2
McCammon, Idaho, 557 24 C4
McCarthy, Alaska 13 H3
McCaskell, Ark., 62 15 B4
McCausland, Iowa, 173 28 G3
McCaysville, Ga., 1,871 22 B1
McClain, co., Okla., 12,740 54 F2
McCleary, Wash., 1,115 66 B2
McClelland, Iowa, 150 28 B3
McClellanville, S.C., 354 59 E3
Macclenny, Fla., 2,671 21 H1
Macclesfield, N.C., 473 50 H2
McCloud, Calif., 2,140 17 B1
McClure, Ill. 25 C6
McClure, Ohio, 651 53 B1
McClure, Pa., 1,001 56 G4
McClure, L., Calif. 17 C3
McClusky, N. Dak., 751 51 M2
McCoin, Tenn. 61 K1
McColl, S.C., 2,479 59 E2
McCollum, Ga. 22 a8
McComas, W. Va. 68 B4
McComb, Miss., 12,020 39 B4
McComb, Ohio, 1,176 53 B1
McCondy, Miss. 39 D2
McCone, co., Mont., 3,321 41 F2
McConnell, Ill. 25 C1
McConnells, S.C., 266 59 C2
McConnellsburg, Pa., 1,245 56 E6
McConnellsville, N.Y. 49 J4
McConnelsville, Ohio, 2,257 53 D3
McConnico, Ariz. 14 B2
McCook, Ill., 441 26 c3
McCook, Nebr., 8,301 42 D3
McCook, co., S. Dak., 8,268 61 D2
McCook, Tex. 62 E6
McCool, Ind. 26 f4
McCool, Miss., 211 39 C2
McCoole, Md. 33 B1
McCool Junction, Nebr., 246 42 G3
McCormick, co., S.C., 8,629 59 B3
McCormick, S.C., 1,998 59 B3
McCoy, Colo. 18 B2
McCoysburg, Ind. 27 B2
McCracken, Kans., 406 29 C2
McCracken, co., Ky., 57,306 30 B3
McCreary, co., Ky., 12,463 30 F4
McCrory, Ark., 1,053 15 D2
McCullom Lake, Ill., 759 26 a1
McCullough, Ala. 11 B4
McCullough, co., Tex., 8,815 62 E4
McCune, Kans., 433 29 G3
McCurtain, co., Okla., 25,851 55 J3
McCurtain, Okla., 528 55 H2
McDade, Tex. 62 F4
McDavid, Fla. 20 C1
McDermitt, Nev. 43 B1
McDermott, Ohio 53 B4
MacDoel, Calif. 17 C1
McDonald, Kans., 323 29 A1
McDonald, co., Mo., 11,798 40 B5
McDonald, N. Mex. 46 D3
McDonald, Ohio, 2,727 53 E1
McDonald, Pa., 3,141 56 A5
McDonald L., Mich. 36 F2
McDonald Pk., Mont. 41 B2
McDonough, Ga., 2,224 22 B2
McDonough, co., Ill., 28,928 25 B3
McDonough, N.Y. 49 J6
McDowell, co., N.C., 26,742 50 C2
McDowell, Va., 127 67 K2
McDowell, co., W. Va., 71,359 68 B4
McDuffie, co., Ga., 12,627 22 D2
Macedon, N.Y., 963 48 F4
Macedon Center, N.Y. 48 k17
Macedonia, Ill., 96 25 D5
Macedonia, Iowa, 290 28 B3
McElmo Cr., Colo. 18 A3
McEwen, Tenn., 979 61 H1
McEwensville, Pa., 795 56 H3
McFadden, Wyo. 70 D3
McFaddin, Tex. 62 F5
McFall, Mo., 206 40 B1
McFarlan, N.C., 161 50 E3
Macfarlan, W. Va. 68 B2
McFarland, Calif., 3,686 17 D4
McFarland, Mich. 36 D2
McFarland, Wis., 1,272 69 D5
McGaffey, N. Mex. 46 A2
McGee, Mo. 40 F4
McGehee, Ark., 4,448 15 D4
McGill, Nev., 2,195 43 C2
McGinnis Slough, Ill. 26 c4
McGrady, N.C. 50 D1
McGrann, Pa. 56 C4
McGrath, Alaska, 241 13 E3
McGrath, Minn., 96 38 C2
McGraw, N.Y., 1,378 49 H5
McGregor, Iowa, 1,040 28 F2
McGregor, Mich. 37 J5
McGregor, Minn., 283 38 C2
McGregor, N. Dak. 51 L1
McGregor, Tex., 4,642 62 F4
McGuffey, Ohio, 647 53 B2
McGuire, Mt., Idaho 24 B3
McHenry, co., Ill., 84,210 25 D1
McHenry, Ill., 3,336 25 D1
McHenry, Ky., 446 30 C3
McHenry, Miss. 39 C5
McHenry, co., N. Dak., 11,099 51 M1
McHenry, N. Dak., 155 51 N2
McHenry Dam, Ill. 26 a1
Machens, Mo. 40 c9
Machias, Me., 1,523 32 D4
Machias, N.Y. 48 C6
Machias, Wash. 67 b5
Machias, r., Aroostook Co., Me. 32 C2
Machias, r., Washington Co., Me. 32 D4
Machias Bay, Me. 32 D4
Machias Lakes, Me. 32 D3
Machiasport, Me. 32 D4
Machipongo, Va. 67 O3
Macho, A. del, N. Mex. 46 C3
McIndoe Falls, Vt. 65 C2
McIntire, Iowa, 270 28 E1
McIntosh, Ala. 11 A4
McIntosh, co., Ga., 6,364 22 E4
McIntosh, Minn., 785 38 A2
McIntosh, N. Mex. 46 C2
McIntosh, co., N. Dak., 6,702 51 N2
McIntosh, co., Okla., 12,371 55 H2
McIntosh, S. Dak., 568 61 B1
McIntyre, Pa. 56 C4
MacIntyre, Mt., N.Y. 49 N2
Mack, Ohio 52 g10
Mackay, Idaho, 652 24 C4
McKay Cr., Oreg. 80 D3
McKean, co., Pa., 54,517 56 D2
McKean, Pa. 56 A2
McKean, atoll, Phoenix Is. 71 E4
McKee, Ky., 234 30 F3
McKee Cr., Ill. 25 B4
McKeesport, Pa., 45,489 56 B5
McKees Rocks, Pa., 13,185 56 A5
McKenna, Wash. 66 B2
McKenney, Va., 519 67 M4
McKenzie, Ala., 558 11 C4
McKenzie, co., N. Dak., 7,296 51 L2
McKenzie, N. Dak. 51 M2
McKenzie, Tenn., 3,780 61 G1
McKenzie, r., Oreg. 55 L2
McKenzie Bridge, Oreg. 55 L2
McKenzie L., Wis. 69 A2
Mackeys, N.C. 51 J2
McKibben, Tex. 62 D1
Mackinac, co., Mich., 10,853 37 G2
Mackinac, Straits of, Mich. 37 G3
Mackinac Island, Mich., 942 37 G3
Mackinac I., Mich. 37 G3
Mackinaw, Ill., 1,163 25 C3
Mackinaw, r., Ill. 25 C3
Mackinaw City, Mich., 934 37 G3
McKinley, Ind. 27 B4
McKinley, Me. 32 C4
McKinley, Mich. 37 H4
McKinley, co., N. Mex., 37,209 46 A2
McKinley, Oreg. 55 L3
McKinley, Mt., Alaska 13 F3
McKinleyville, Calif. 17 A1
McKinney, Tex., 13,763 62 F3
McKinney, L., Kans. 29 A2
McKinney Mtn., Tex. 62 C5
McKinnon, Fla. 20 C1
McKittrick, Calif. 17 D4
McKnight, Okla. 54 D3
McKownville, N.Y. 49 d14
Macksburg, Iowa, 174 28 C3
Macksburg, Ohio, 314 53 D3
Macks Creek, Mo., 123 40 D4
Macksville, Kans., 546 29 D3
Mackville, Ky. 30 E3
McLain, Miss. 39 D4
McLaughlin, S. Dak., 983 61 B1
McLaurin, Miss. 39 C4
McLean, co., Ill., 83,877 25 D3
McLean, Ill., 758 25 C3
McLean, co., Ky., 9,355 30 C3
McLean, N.Y. 49 H5
McLean, co., N. Dak., 14,030 51 M2
McLean, Tex., 1,330 62 D2
McLean, Va. 33 a5
McLeansboro, Ill., 2,951 25 D5
McLennan, co., Tex., 150,091 62 F4
McLeod, co., Minn., 24,401 38 B3
McLeod, Miss. 39 D2
McLeod, N. Dak. 51 O2
McLoud, Okla., 837 54 F2
McLoughlin, Mt., Oreg. 55 L3
McLouth, Kans., 494 29 G1
McMan, Okla. 54 F3
McMechen, W. Va., 2,999 68 C2
McMillan, Mich. 36 F2
McMillan, L., N. Mex. 46 C3
McMinn, co., Tenn., 33,662 61 L2
McMinnville, Oreg., 7,656 55 L2
McMinnville, Tenn., 9,013 61 K2
McMullen, co., Tex., 1,116 62 E5
McMurray, Pa. 56 b8
McNab, Ark., 142 15 B4
McNabb, Ill., 176 25 C2
McNair, Tex., 1,880 63 k14
McNairy, co., Tenn., 18,085 61 G2
McNairy, Tenn. 61 G2
McNary, Ariz., 1,608 14 D2
McNary, Oreg. 55 N2
McNary, Tex. 62 B4
McNaughton, Wis. 69 D2
McNeal, Ariz. 14 D4
McNeil, Ark., 746 15 B4
McNeil, Tex. 62 c5
McNeil I., Wash. 67 a6
McNeill, Miss. 39 C5
Macomb, Ill., 16,094 25 B3
Macomb, co., Mich., 405,804 37 H6
Macomb, Mich. 37 e10
Macomb, Okla., 76 54 F2
Macon, co., Ala., 26,717 11 D3
Macon, co., Ga., 13,170 22 B3
Macon, Ga., 122,876 22 C3
Macon, co., Ill., 118,257 25 D4
Macon, Ill., 1,229 25 C4
Macon, Mich. 37 H6
Macon, Miss., 2,432 39 D2
Macon, co., Mo., 16,473 40 D2
Macon, Mo., 4,547 40 D2
Macon, Nebr. 42 F3
Macon, co., N.C., 14,935 50 B2
Macon, N.C., 187 50 G1
Macon, co., Tenn., 12,197 61 J1
Macopin, N.J. 47 b1
Macoupin, co., Ill., 43,524 25 C4
Macoupin Cr., Ill. 25 C4
McPherson, co., Kans., 24,285 29 E2
McPherson, Kans., 9,996 29 E2
McPherson, co., Nebr., 735 42 C2
McPherson, co., S. Dak., 5,821 61 C1
McQuady, Ky. 30 D3
McQueen, Okla. 54 D3
McQueeney, Tex. 62 b8
McRae, Ark., 578 15 D2
McRae, Ga., 2,738 22 D3
McRoberts, Ky., 1,363 30 H3
McSherrystown, Pa., 2,839 56 G6
Macune, Tex. 63 G4
Macungie, Pa., 1,266 57 K4
McVeigh, Ky. 30 H3
McVeytown, Pa., 488 56 F4
McVille, N. Dak., 712 51 N2
Macwahoc, Me. 32 C3
McWillie, Okla. 54 E1
Macy, Ind., 328 27 B2
Macy, Nebr. 42 H1
Mad, r., Calif. 17 B1
Mad, r., Conn. 19 C3
Mad, r., N.H. 44 B4
Mad, r., Ohio 53 B2
Mad, r., Vt. 65 B2
Madagascal Pd., Me. 32 C3
Madawaska, Me., 4,035 32 C1
Madawaska L., Me. 32 C2
Madbury, N.H. 44 D5
Maddaket (part of Nantucket), Mass. 35 O7
Madden L., C.Z.-Pan. 72 o
Maddock, N. Dak., 740 51 N2
Madeira, Ohio, 6,744 52 j9
Madeira Beach, Fla., 3,943 21 H4
Madelia, Minn., 2,190 38 B3
Madeline, Calif. 17 C1
Madeline I., Wis. 69 C1
Madera, co., Calif., 40,468 17 D3
Madera, Calif., 14,430 17 C3
Madera, Pa. 56 E4
Madge, Okla. 54 C3
Madill, Okla., 3,084 54 G3
Madison, co., Ala., 173,285 11 C1
Madison, Ala., 2,100 11 C1
Madison, co., Ark., 9,068 15 B2
Madison, Calif. 17 B2
Madison, Conn., 1,416;4,567(T) 19 E4
Madison, co., Fla., 14,154 21 G1
Madison, Fla., 3,239 21 G1
Madison, co., Ga., 11,246 22 C1
Madison, Ga., 2,680 22 C2
Madison, co., Idaho, 9,417 24 D4
Madison, co., Ill., 224,689 25 C5
Madison, Ill., 6,861 25 B5
Madison, co., Ind., 125,819 27 C2

For abbreviations and explanation of index, see page 176.

For abbreviations and explanation of index, see page 176.

For abbreviations and explanation of index, see page 176.

N

For abbreviations and explanation of index, see page 176.

O

For abbreviations and explanation of index, see page 176.

For abbreviations and explanation of index, see page 176.

Richfield INDEX TO MAPS OF THE UNITED STATES Rotterdam

Richfield, Wis. 69 a6
Richfield Center, Mich. 37 H5
Richfield Springs, N.Y., 1,630 49 L5
Richford, N.Y. 49 H6
Richford, Vt., 1,663 65 B1
Richford, Wis. 69 D3
Rich Fountain, Mo. 40 E3
Richgrove, Calif. 17 D4
Rich Hill, Mo., 1,699 40 B3
Richland, Ga., 1,472 22 B3
Richland, co., Ill. 16,299 25 D5
Richland, Iowa, 546 28 F3
Richland, parish, La., 23,824 31 C1
Richland, Mich., 511 36 F6
Richland, Mo., 1,662 40 D4
Richland, co., Mont., 10,504 41 F2
Richland, Nebr., 139 42 G2
Richland, N.Y. 49 H3
Richland, co., N. Dak., 18,824 51 O2
Richland, co., Ohio, 117,761 53 C2
Richland, Oreg., 228 55 O2
Richland, Pa., 1,276 56 J5
Richland, co., S.C., 200,102 59 D2
Richland, S.C. 59 A2
Richland, Tex., 287 62 F4
Richland, Wash., 23,548 66 D2
Richland, co., Wis., 17,684 69 C4
Richland Balsam, mtn., N.C. 50 C2
Richland Center, Wis., 4,746 69 C4
Richland Hills, Tex., 7,804 63 e11
Richlands, N.C., 1,079 50 H3
Richlands, Va., 4,963 66 H5
Richland Springs, Tex., 331 62 E4
Richlandtown, Pa., 741 57 L5
Richmond, Calif., 71,854 17 B3
Richmond, co., Ga., 135,601 22 D2
Richmond, Ill., 855 26 a1
Richmond, Ind., 44,149 27 D3
Richmond, Kans., 352 29 G2
Richmond, Ky., 12, 168 30 F3
Richmond, Me., 1,412 32 B4
Richmond, Mass., 890(T) 34 A3
Richmond, Mich., 2,667 37 J6
Richmond, Minn., 751 38 B3
Richmond, Mo., 4,604 40 C2
Richmond, N.H. 44 A6
Richmond, co., N.Y., 221,991 49 M9
Richmond, co., N.C., 39,202 50 F2
Richmond, Ohio, 728 53 E2
Richmond, Okla. 54 D1
Richmond, Tex., 3,668 63 G5
Richmond, Utah, 977 64 c4
Richmond, Vt., 765 65 B2
Richmond, co., Va., 6,375 67 N2
Richmond, Va., 219,958 67 M3
Richmond, Wis. 69 E5
Richmond Beach, Wash. 67 a5
Richmond Dale, Ohio 53 C3
Richmond Furnace (part of Richmond), Mass. 34 A3
Richmond Furnace, Pa. 56 F6
Richmond Heights, Mo., 15,622 40 c10
Richmond Heights, Ohio, 5,068 52 e7
Richmond Highlands, Wash. 67 b5
Richmond Hill, Ga. 22 E4
Richmond I., Me. 32 A5
Richmond Pd., Mass. 34 A3
Richmondville, Mich. 37 J5
Richmondville, N.Y., 743 49 L5
Rich Mtn., Okla. 55 J3
Rich Pond, Ky 30 D4
Rich Square, N.C., 1,134 51 H1
Richton, Miss., 1,089 39 D4
Richvale, Calif. 17 C2
Richville, Mich. 37 H5
Richville, Mo. 40 D5
Richville, N.Y., 292 49 K2
Richwood, N.J. 57 f13
Richwood, Ohio, 2,137 53 B2
Richwood, W. Va., 4,110 68 C3
Richwood, Wis. 69 E4
Richwoods, Mo. 40 E3
Ricketts, Iowa, 133 28 B2
Rickman, Tenn. 61 K1
Rickreall, Oreg. 55 L2
Rico, Colo., 353 18 A3
Riddle, Idaho 24 A4
Riddle, Oreg., 992 55 L3
Riddlesburg, Pa. 56 E5
Ridge, N.Y. 47 h2
Ridgecrest, Calif., 5,099 17 E4
Ridge Farm, Ill., 894 25 E4
Ridgefield, Conn., 2,954;8,165(T) 19 B4
Ridgefield, Wash., 823 66 B3
Ridgefield Park, N.J., 12,701 47 c2
Ridgeland, Miss., 875 39 B3
Ridgeland, Ohio 53 C3
Ridgeland, S.C., 1,192 59 C4
Ridgeland, Wis., 288 69 B2
Ridgeley, W. Va., 1,229 68 E2
Ridgely, Md., 886 33 E2
Ridgely, Tenn., 1,464 60 F1
Ridge Spring, S.C., 649 59 C3
Ridgeview, S. Dak. 61 B1
Ridgeville, Ind., 950 27 D2
Ridgeville, Md. 33 a3
Ridgeville, S.C., 611 59 D3
Ridgeville Corners, Ohio 53 A1
Ridgeway, Iowa, 267 28 F1
Ridgeway, Md. 33 c4
Ridgeway, Mich. 37 H7
Ridgeway, Mo., 470 40 C1
Ridgeway, N.J. 47 b5
Ridgeway, N.C. 50 G1
Ridgeway, S.C., 417 59 D2
Ridgeway, Va., 524 67 K4
Ridgeway, Wis., 455 69 D5
Ridgeway Br., N.J. 47 b5
Ridgewood, Ill. 26 b4
Ridgewood, N.J., 25,391 45 C2
Ridgway, Colo., 254 18 B2
Ridgway, Ill., 1,055 25 D6
Ridgway, Pa., 6,387 56 D3
Ridley Park, Pa., 7,387 57 f12
Ridott, Ill., 221 25 C1
Riegelsville, N.J. 45 A2
Riegelsville, Pa., 953 57 L4
Rieglewood, N.C. 50 G3
Rienzi, Miss., 375 39 D1
Riesel, Tex., 503 62 F4
Rieth, Oreg. 55 N2
Riffe, Wash. 66 B2
Rifle, Colo., 2,135 18 B2
Rifle, r., Mich. 37 G4
Rig, W. Va. 68 D2
Riga, Mich. 37 K7
Rigby, Idaho, 2,281 24 D4
Riggins, Idaho, 588 24 A3
Rigili, i., Eniwetok 72 k
Riley, Ind., 248 27 A4
Riley, co., Kans., 41,914 29 F1
Riley, Kans., 575 29 F1
Riley, N. Mex. 46 B2
Riley, Oreg. 55 N3
Rileyville, Va. 67 L2
Rillito, Ariz. 14 C3
Rillton, Pa. 56 d8
Rimersburg, Pa., 1,323 56 C3
Rimrock, Ariz. 14 C2
Rinard, Ill. 25 D5
Rincón, P.R., 1,094 72 na1
Rincon, Ga., 1,057 22 E3
Rincon, N. Mex. 46 B3
Rincón, B. de, P.R. 72 n c2
Rindge, N.H. 44 B6
Rineyville, Ky. 30 D3
Ringgold, Ga., 1,311 22 A1
Ringgold, co., Iowa, 7,910 28 C4
Ringgold, La., 953 31 A1
Ringgold, Nebr. 42 D2
Ringgold, Tenn. 61 H1
Ringle, Wis. 69 D3
Ringling, Mont. 41 C2
Ringling, Okla., 1,170 54 F3
Ringoes, N.J. 45 B3
Ringold, Okla. 55 H3
Ringsted, Iowa, 559 28 C1
Ringville(part of Worthington), Mass. 34 C3
Ringwood, Ill. 26 a1
Ringwood, N.J., 4,182 45 C1
Ringwood, N.C. 50 H1
Ringwood, Okla., 232 54 E1
Rio, Fla. 21 K4
Rio, Ill., 177 25 B2
Rio, La. 31 E3
Rio, W. Va. 68 E2
Rio, Wis., 788 69 D4
Rio Arriba, co., N. Mex., 24,193 46 B1
Rio Blanco, co., Colo., 5,150 18 A2
Rio Blanco, Colo. 18 A2
Rio Creek, Wis. 69 F3
Rio Dell, Calif., 3,222 17 A1
Río Grande, P.R., 2,763 72 nd1
Rio Grande, co., Colo., 11,160 18 B3
Rio Grande, N.J. 45 B5
Rio Grande, Ohio, 333 53 C4
Rio Grande, r. 8b E–G, 3–5
Rio Grande City, Tex., 5,835 62 E6
Río Grande de Loíza, L., P.R. 72 n d1
Rio Grande Pyramid, pk., Colo. 18 B3
Rio Hondo, Tex., 1,344 62 F6
Rio Linda, Calif., 2,189 17 h12
Rion, S.C. 59 C2
Rio Oso, Calif. 17 h12
Rio Res., N.Y. 57 M2
Rio Tinto, Nev. 43 B1
Rio Vista, Calif., 2,616 16 c6
Rio Vista, Tex., 284 63 e12
Ripley, Ill., 167 25 B3
Ripley, co., Ind., 20,641 27 C3
Ripley, Me. 32 B4
Ripley, Miss., 2,668 39 D1
Ripley, co., Mo., 9,096 40 F5
Ripley, N.Y., 1,247 48 A6
Ripley, Ohio, 2,174 53 B4
Ripley, Okla., 263 54 G1
Ripley, Tenn., 3,782 60 F2
Ripley, W. Va., 2,756 68 B3
Riplinger, Wis. 69 C3
Ripon, Calif., 1,894 17 C3
Ripon, Wis., 6,163 69 E4
Rippey, Iowa, 331 28 C3
Rippon, W. Va. 68 F2
Rippowam, r., Conn.-N.Y. 19 A5
Ripton, Vt. 65 A3
Risco, Mo., 502 40 G5
Risher, Ark. 15 E2
Rising City, Nebr., 308 42 G2
Risingdale (part of Great Barrington), Mass. 34 A4
Rising Star, Tex., 997 62 E3
Rising Sun, Ind., 2,230 27 D4
Rising Sun, Md., 824 33 D1
Risingsun, Ohio, 815 53 B1
Risk, Ill. 25 D3
Risley, N.J. 45 B5
Rison, Ark., 889 15 C4
Rita, La. 31 D4
Rita Blanca Cr., Tex. 62 C2
Ritchey, Mo., 128 40 B5
Ritchie, Md. 33 b5
Ritchie, co., W. Va., 10,877 68 B2
Ritidian Pt., Guam 71 a
Ritter, Oreg. 55 N2
Ritter, Mt., Calif. 17 D3
Rittman, Ohio, 5,410 53 D1
Ritzville, Wash., 2,173 66 D2
Riva, Md. 33 c5
Rivare, Ind. 27 D2
Riverbank, Calif., 2,786 17 C3
Riverdale, Ga., 1,045 22 b7
Riverdale, Ill., 13,761 26 d4
Riverdale, Md., 4,389 33 b5
Riverdale (part of Northbridge), Mass. 35 H4
Riverdale, Mich. 37 G5
Riverdale, Nebr., 144 42 E3
Riverdale, N.J., 2,596 47 b2
Riverdale, N. Dak., 51 M2
Riverdale, Utah, 1,848 64 b5
Riverdale, Va. 67 K4
River Edge, N.J., 13,264 47 c2
River Falls, Ala., 401 11 C4
River Falls, Wis., 4,857 69 A3
River Forest, Ill., 12,695 26 c3
River Grove, Ill., 8,464 26 c3
Riverhead, N.Y., 5,830 49 P9
River Heights, Utah, 880 64 c4
River Hills, Wis., 1,257 69 b7
Riverlea, Ohio, 625 52 a5
River Oaks, Tex., 8,444 63 e11
River Point (part of W. Warwick), R.I. 58 C2
River Rouge, Mich., 18,147 37 d11
Riverside, co., Calif., 306,191 17 E5
Riverside, Calif., 84,332 17 E5
Riverside (part of Greenwich), Conn. 19 A5
Riverside (part of Oxford), Conn. 19 C4
Riverside, Ga., 329 22 C4
Riverside, Ill., 9,750 26 c3
Riverside, Iowa, 656 28 F3
Riverside (part of Gill), Mass. 34 D2
Riverside, Mo., 1,315 40 a7
Riverside, Nev. 43 C3
Riverside, N.J., 8,474(T) 45 A3
Riverside, N.Y., 1,030 48 F6
Riverside, Oreg. 55 N3
Riverside, Pa., 1,580 56 H4
Riverside (part of E. Providence), R.I. 58 C1
Riverside, Tex. 63 G4
Riverside, Utah 64 b4
Riverside, Wash., 201 66 D1
Riverside, Wyo., 87 70 C3
Riverside Res., Colo. 18 C1
Riverton (part of Barkhamsted), Conn. 19 C2
Riverton, Ill., 1,535 25 C4
Riverton, Iowa, 399 28 B4
Riverton, La. 31 B1
Riverton, Nebr., 303 42 F3
Riverton, N.J., 3,324 45 B3
Riverton, Oreg. 55 K3
Riverton, Utah, 1,993 64 A1
Riverton, Vt. 65 B2
Riverton, Va. 67 L2
Riverton, W. Va. 68 D3
Riverton, Wyo., 6,845 70 B2
Riverton Heights, Wash. 67 b6
River View, Ala., 1,171 11 D3
Riverview, Fla. 21 J1
Riverview, Mich., 7,237 37 d12
Riverview, Mo., 3,706 40 d10
Riverview, Nebr. 42 E1
Riverville, Va. 67 L3
Riverwoods, Ill., 1,287 26 c2
Rives Junction, Mich. 37 G6
Rivesville, W. Va., 1,191 68 C2
Riviera, Tex. 62 F6
Riviera Beach, Fla., 13,046 21 K5
Riviera Beach, Md., 4,902 33 D1
Rixford, Pa. 56 D2
Roachdale, Ind., 927 27 B3
Roach Pds., Me. 32 B3
Roan Cr., Colo. 18 A2
Roane, co., Tenn., 39,133 61 L2
Roane, Tex. 63 g12
Roane, co., W. Va., 15,720 68 B3
Roan Mountain, Tenn 61 N1
Roann, Ind., 478 27 C2
Roanoke, Ala., 5,288 11 D2
Roanoke, Ill., 1,821 25 C3
Roanoke, Ind., 935 27 C2
Roanoke, Tex., 585 63 e10
Roanoke, co., Va., 61,693 67 J3
Roanoke, Va. 97,110 67 K3
Roanoke, W. Va. 68 C3
Roanoke, r. 8b L3
Roanoke Rapids, N.C., 13,320 50 H1
Roanoke Rapids L., N.C. 50 H1
Roaring Bk., Conn. 19 E3
Roaring Fk., r., Colo. 18 B2
Roaring River, N.C. 50 D1
Roaring Spring, Pa., 2,937 56 E5
Roaring Springs, Tex., 398 62 D3
Robbins, Calif. 17 h12
Robbins, Ill., 7,511 26 d4
Robbins, N.C., 1,294 50 F2
Robbins, Tenn. 61 L1
Robbinsdale, Minn., 16,381 38 b5
Robbinston, Me. 32 D3
Robbinsville, N.C., 587 50 B2
Robbs, Ill. 25 D6
Robeline, La., 308 31 A2
Roberdel, N.C., 379 50 F3
Robersonville, N.C., 1,684 51 H2
Roberta, Ga., 714 22 B3
Roberta, Okla. 55 G4
Robert Lee, Tex., 990 62 D4
Roberts, Idaho, 422 24 C4
Roberts, Ill., 504 25 D3
Roberts, Mont. 41 D3
Roberts, co., S. Dak., 13,190 61 D1
Roberts, co., Tex., 1,075 62 D2
Roberts, Wis., 308 69 A3
Robertsburg, W. Va. 68 A3
Robertsdale, Ala., 1,474 11 B5
Robertsdale, Pa. 56 E5
Robertson, co., Ky., 2,443 30 F2
Robertson, co., Tenn., 27,335 61 J1
Robertson, co., Tex., 16,157 62 F4
Robertsville, Calif. 16 c8
Robertsville, Ohio 53 D2
Robeson, co., N.C., 89,102 50 F3
Robesonia, Pa., 1,579 57 J5
Robinson, Ill., 7,226 25 E4
Robinson, Kans., 317 29 G1
Robinson, N. Dak., 155 51 N2
Robinson, Tex., 2,111 62 F4
Robinson, L., S.C. 59 D2
Robinsons, Me. 32 D2
Robstown, Tex., 10,266 62 F6
Roby, Mo. 40 D4
Roby, Tex., 913 62 D3
Roca, Nebr., 123 42 H3
Rochdale, Mass., 1,058 35 G4
Rochelle, Ga., 1,235 22 C4
Rochelle, Ill., 7,008 25 C2
Rochelle, Tex. 62 E4
Rochelle, Va. 67 L2
Rocheport, Mo., 375 40 D2
Rochester, Ill., 1,265 25 C4
Rochester, Ind., 4,883 27 B1
Rochester, Mass., 1,559(T) 35 L6
Rochester, Mich., 5,431 37 H6
Rochester, Minn., 47,797 38 C4
Rochester, N.H., 15,927 44 C5
Rochester, N.Y., 305,849 48 E4
Rochester, Pa., 5,952 56 A4
Rochester, Tex., 625 62 E3
Rochester, Vt. 65 B3
Rochester, Wash. 66 B2
Rochester, Wis., 413 69 a9
Rochester Mills, Pa. 56 C4
Rock, Kans. 29 F3
Rock (part of Middleboro), Mass. 35 L5
Rock, Mich. 36 D2
Rock, co., Minn., 11,864 38 A4
Rock, co., Nebr., 2,554 42 E1
Rock, co., Wis., 113,913 69 D5
Rock, r., Ill.-Wis. 25 C2
Rock, r., Iowa-Minn. 28 A1
Rock, r., Vt. 65 A1
Rock, r., Vt. 65 B5
Rockaway, N.J., 5,413 45 C2
Rockaway, Oreg., 771 55 K2
Rockaway, r., N.J. 45 B2
Rockaway Beach, Mo., 177 40 C5
Rockaway Park (part of N.Y.C.), N.Y. 47 d3
Rockaway Pt., N.Y. 47 d3
Rockbridge, Ill., 253 25 B4
Rockbridge, Mo. 40 D5
Rockbridge, co., Va., 24,039 67 K3
Rockbridge Baths, Va. 67 K3
Rockcastle, co., Ky., 12,334 30 F3
Rockcastle, r., Ky. 30 F3
Rock Cave, W. Va. 68 C3
Rock City Falls, N.Y. 49 d12
Rock Creek, Ohio, 673 53 E1
Rock Creek, Baker Co., Oreg. 55 N2
Rock Creek, Gilliam Co., Oreg. 55 M2
Rock Cr., D.C.-Md. 33 a4
Rock Cr., Ill. 25 B2
Rock Cr., Pa. 56 G6
Rock Cr., S. Dak. 61 D2
Rock Cr., Utah 64 B1
Rock Cr., Wash. 66 E2
Rock Cr. Butte, Oreg. 55 N2
Rockdale, co., Ga., 10,572 22 B2
Rockdale, Ill., 1,272 26 b4
Rockdale, Md. 33 c3
Rockdale, N.Y. 49 J6
Rockdale, Tex., 4,481 62 F4
Rockdale, Wis., 191 69 D5
Rock Elm, Wis. 69 A3
Rockerville, S. Dak. 61 A2
Rockfall (part of Middlefield), Conn. 19 E3
Rock Falls, Ill., 10,261 25 C2
Rock Falls, Iowa, 156 28 D1
Rock Falls, Wis. 69 B3
Rockfield, Ky. 30 D4
Rockfield, Wis. 69 a6
Rockfish, Va. 67 L3
Rockford, Ala., 328 11 C3
Rockford, Ill., 132,109 25 D1
Rockford, Iowa, 941 28 D1
Rockford, Mich., 2,074 36 F5
Rockford, Ohio, 1,155 53 A2
Rockford, Tenn. 61 M2
Rockford, Wash., 369 66 E2
Rock Hall, Md., 1,073 33 D1
Rockham, S. Dak., 197 61 C1
Rock Harbor (part of Orleans), Mass. 35 O5
Rock Hbr., Mich. 36 b8
Rock Harbor Lodge, Mich. 36 b8
Rock Hill, Mo., 6,523 40 c10
Rock Hill, N.Y. 49 L7
Rock Hill, S.C., 29,404 59 C2
Rockhill Furnace, Pa. 56 F5
Rockholds, Ky. 30 F4
Rockingham, co., N.H., 99,029 44 C5
Rockingham, Ga. 22 D4
Rockingham, co., N.C., 69,629 50 F1
Rockingham, N.C., 5,512 50 F3
Rockingham, co., Va., 40,485 67 K2
Rock Island, co., Ill., 150,991 25 B2
Rock Island, Ill., 51,863 25 B2
Rock Island, Okla. 55 J2
Rock Island, Wash., 260 66 C2
Rock Lake, N. Dak., 350 51 N1
Rockland (part of Madison), Conn. 19 E4
Rockland, Del. 20 a4
Rockland, Idaho, 258 24 C4
Rockland, Me., 8,769 32 B4
Rockland, Mass., 13,119(T) 35 L4
Rockland, Mich. 36 B2
Rockland, co., N.Y., 192,724* 49 M8
Rockland, N.Y. 49 L7
Rockland, Wis., 257 69 C4
Rockledge, Fla., 3,481 21 K3
Rockledge, Pa., 2,587 57 f11
Rocklin, Calif., 1,495 17 j12
Rocklyn, Wash. 66 D2
Rockmart, Ga., 3,938 22 A1
Rock Point, Ariz. 14 D1
Rock Point, Md. 33 D2
Rockport, Calif. 17 B2
Rockport, Ill. 25 A4
Rockport, Ind., 2,474 27 A5
Rockport, Me. 32 B4
Rockport, Mass., 3,511;4,616(T) 35 M2
Rockport, Miss. 39 B4
Rock Port, Mo., 1,310 40 A1
Rockport, Tex., 2,989 62 F5
Rockport, Wash. 66 C1
Rock Rapids, Iowa, 2,780 28 A1
Rock Rift, N.Y. 49 K6
Rock River, Wyo., 497 70 C3
Rock Run, Ala. 11 D1
Rocksprings, Tex., 1,182 62 D4
Rock Springs, Wis., 463 69 D4
Rock Springs, Wyo., 10,371 70 B3
Rockton, Ill., 1,833 25 C1
Rockton, Pa. 56 D3
Rockton, Wis. 69 C4
Rockvale, Colo., 413 18 C2
Rock Valley, Iowa, 2,072 28 A1
Rockville, Calif. 16 b6
Rockville, Conn., 9,478 19 F2
Rockville, Ind., 2,756 27 A3
Rockville, Md., 26,090 33 C1
Rockville, Mo., 255 40 C3
Rockville, Nebr., 153 42 F2
Rockville (part of Hopkinton), R.I. 58 A2
Rockville, S.C. 59 D4
Rockville, Wis. 69 C5
Rockville Centre, N.Y., 26,413 49 N9
Rockwall, co., Tex., 5,878 62 F3
Rockwall, Tex., 2,166 63 g11
Rockwell, Iowa, 772 28 D2
Rockwell, N.C., 948 50 E2
Rockwell City, Iowa, 2,313 28 C2
Rockwood, Ala. 11 B1
Rockwood, Colo. 18 A3
Rockwood, Ill., 98 25 C6
Rockwood, Me. 32 B3
Rockwood, Mich., 2,026 37 c12
Rockwood, Oreg. 54 a4
Rockwood, Pa., 1,101 56 C6
Rockwood, Tenn., 5,345 36 E6
Rocky, Okla., 343 54 D2
Rocky, r., N.C. 50 E2
Rocky, r., N.C. 50 F2
Rocky, r., Ohio 52 d8
Rocky, r., S.C. 59 B2
Rocky Comfort, Mo., 151 40 B5
Rocky Comfort Cr., Ga. 22 D2
Rocky Ford, Colo., 4,929 18 D2
Rocky Ford, Ga., 241 22 E3
Rocky Fork, r., Ohio 52 b5
Rocky Fork L., Ohio 53 B3
Rocky Gorge Res., Md. 33 b4
Rocky Grove, Pa., 3,168 56 B3
Rocky Hill, Conn., 7,404(T) 19 E3
Rocky Hill, N.J., 528 45 B3
Rocky I., Wis. 69 C1
Rocky L., Me. 32 D4
Rocky Mount, Ga., 83 22 a9
Rocky Mount, N.C., 32,147 50 H2
Rocky Mount, Va., 1,412 67 K3
Rocky Mtn., Me. 32 B1
Rocky Mtn. Nat. Pk., Colo. 18 C1
Rocky Mts. 9
Rocky Point, N.Y., 2,261 49 P9
Rocky Pt., Tutuila 71 c
Rocky Point, N.C. 50 H3
Rocky Ridge, Ala. 11 d7
Rockyridge, Ohio, 441 53 B1
Rocky River, Ohio, 18,097 52 d8
Roda, Va. 66 G4
Rodanthe, N.C. 51 K2
Rodden, Ill. 25 B1
Rodeo, Calif. 16 b6
Rodeo, N. Mex. 46 A4
Rodessa, La. 31 A1
Rodman, Iowa, 144 28 C1
Rodman, N.Y. 49 J3
Rodney, Iowa, 94 28 B2
Rodney, Mich. 36 F5
Rodney, Miss. 39 A4
Roebling, N.J., 3,272 45 B3
Roeland Park, Kans., 8,949 40 a7
Roff, Okla., 638 54 G3
Roger Mills, co., Okla., 5,090 54 D2
Rogers, Ark., 8,284 15 A1
Rogers (part of Killingly), Conn. 19 H2
Rogers, La. 31 B2
Rogers, Nebr., 162 42 H2
Rogers, N. Mex. 46 D2
Rogers, N. Dak., 119 51 N2
Rogers, co., Okla., 20,614 55 H1
Rogers, Tex., 936 62 F4
Rogers, Mt., Va. 66 H4
Rogers City, Mich., 4,722 37 H3
Rogers L., Calif. 17 E4
Rogerson, Idaho 24 B4
Rogersville, Ala., 766 11 B1
Rogersville, Mo., 447 40 D4
Rogersville, Tenn., 3,121 61 M1
Rogue, r., Oreg. 55 K3
Rogue I., Me. 32 D4
Rogue River, Oreg., 520 55 L3
Rohnerville, Calif., 2,268 17 B1
Rohunta, L., Mass. 34 E2
Roi, i., Kwajalein 72 l
Rojo, C., P.R. 72 n a2
Rojoa, i., Eniwetok 72 k
Roland, Iowa, 748 28 D2
Roland, Okla., 100 55 J2
Rolesville, N.C., 358 50 G2
Rolette, co., N. Dak., 10,641 51 N1
Rolette, N. Dak., 524 51 N1
Rolfe, Iowa, 819 28 C2
Rolfe, Pa. 56 D2
Roll, Ariz. 14 A3
Roll, Okla. 54 D2
Rolla, Kans., 464 29 A3
Rolla, Mo., 11,132 40 E4
Rolla, N. Dak., 1,398 51 N1
Rolla, Tex. 62 D2
Rollin, Mich. 37 G7
Rolling Fork, Miss., 1,619 39 B3
Rolling Fk., r., Ky. 30 E3
Rolling Hills, Calif., 1,664 16 e11
Rolling Hills Estates, Calif., 3,941 16 d11
Rolling Meadows, Ill., 13,177 26 c2
Rolling Prairie, Ind. 27 B1
Rollingstone, Minn., 392 38 D3
Rollingwood, Tex. 62 c7
Rollins, Ill. 26 b1
Rollinsford, N.H., 1,210 44 D5
Rollinsville, Colo. 18 a5
Roma-Los Saenz, Tex., 1,496 62 E6
Romanzof, C., Alaska 12 B3
Rombauer, Mo. 40 F5
Rome, Ga., 32,226 22 A1
Rome, Ill., 1,347 25 C3
Rome, Ind. 27 B5
Rome, Me. 32 B4
Rome, Miss., 279 39 B2
Rome, N.Y., 51,646 49 J4
Rome, Ashtabula Co., Ohio 53 E1
Rome, Richland Co., Ohio 53 C2
Rome, Oreg. 55 O3
Rome, Pa., 274 56 J2
Rome, Tenn. 61 J1
Rome, Wis. 69 E5
Rome City, Ind. 27 C1
Romeo, Colo., 339 18 B3
Romeo, Fla. 21 H2
Romeo, Mich., 3,327 37 J6
Romeoville, Ill., 6,358 26 b4
Romero, Tex. 62 C2
Romeroville, N. Mex. 46 C2
Romney, Ind. 27 B2
Romney, W. Va., 2,203 68 E2
Romoland, Calif. 16 g11
Romona, Ind. 27 B3
Romulus, Mich., 1,798 37 c12
Romulus, N.Y. 48 G5
Ronald, Wash. 66 C2
Ronan, Mont., 1,334 41 A2
Roncador Cay, W.I. 72 B3
Ronceverte, W. Va., 1,882 68 C4
Ronda, N.C., 501 50 D1
Rondo, Ark., 219 15 E3
Rondout, Ill. 26 c1
Rondout Res., N.Y. 49 M7
Rongelap, atoll, Marsh. Is. 71 D3
Ronkiti, Ponape 72 h
Ronkonkoma, N.Y., 4,220 47 g2
Roodhouse, Ill., 2,352 25 B4
Rooks, co., Kans., 9,734 29 C1
Roopville, Ga., 203 22 A2
Roosevelt, La. 31 C1
Roosevelt, Minn., 145 38 B1
Roosevelt, co., Mont., 11,731 41 F1
Roosevelt, N.J., 764 45 C3
Roosevelt, co., N. Mex., 16,198 46 D3
Roosevelt, N.Y., 12,883 47 e3
Roosevelt, Okla., 495 54 D3
Roosevelt, Tex. 62 D4
Roosevelt, Utah, 1,812 64 B1
Roosevelt, Wash. 66 C3
Roosevelt Park, Mich., 2,578 36 E5
Root, r., Minn. 38 D4
Root, r., Wis. 69 F5
Roper, Kans. 29 G3
Roper, N.C., 771 51 J2
Ropesville, Tex., 423 62 C3
Rosalia, Kans. 29 F3
Rosalia, Wash., 585 66 E2
Rosalie, Nebr., 182 42 H1
Rosamond, Calif. 17 D4
Rosamond, Ill. 25 C4
Rosamond L., Calif. 17 D4
Rosboro, Ark. 15 B3
Rosburg, Wash. 66 B2
Roscoe, Ill. 25 C1
Roscoe, Mo., 125 40 C4
Roscoe, Nebr. 42 C2
Roscoe, N.Y. 49 L7
Roscoe, Ohio 53 D2
Roscoe, Pa., 1,315 56 c9
Roscoe, S. Dak., 532 61 C1
Roscoe, Tex., 1,490 62 D3
Roscommon, co., Mich., 7,200 37 G4
Roscommon, Mich., 867 37 G4
Rose, Kans. 29 G3
Rose, Nebr. 42 E1
Rose, N.Y. 48 G5
Rose, Okla. 55 H1
Roseau, co., Minn., 12,154 38 B1
Roseau, Minn., 2,146 38 B1
Roseau, r., Minn. 38 A1
Roseboro, N.C., 1,354 50 G3
Rose Bud, Ark. 15 C2
Rosebud, Mo., 288 40 E3
Rosebud, co., Mont., 6,187 41 E2
Rosebud, Mont. 41 E2
Rosebud, S. Dak. 61 B2
Rosebud, Tex., 1,644 62 F4
Roseburg, Mich. 37 J5
Roseburg, Oreg., 11,467 55 L3
Rosebush, Mich. 37 G5
Rose Canyon, Calif. 17 k14
Rose City, Mich., 435 37 G4
Rosecrans, Ill. 26 c1
Rosedale, Colo. 18 b5
Rosedale, Ill. 25 B4
Rosedale, Ind., 726 27 A3
Rosedale, Mich. 37 G2
Rosedale, Miss., 2,339 39 B2
Rosedale, N.J. 57 g10
Rosedale, Ohio, 8,204 53 C2
Rosedale, Okla., 88 54 F3
Rosedale, Wash. 67 a6
Rosedale, W. Va. 68 B3
Roseglen, N. Dak. 51 M2
Rose Hill, Ill., 117 25 D4
Rose Hill, Iowa, 223 28 E3
Rose Hill, Miss. 39 C3
Rose Hill, N.Y. 49 m21
Rose Hill, N.C., 1,292 50 G3
Rose Hill, Tex. 63 f11
Rose Hill, Va. 66 F4
Roseland, La., 1,254 31 D3
Roseland, Nebr., 163 42 F3
Roseland, N.J., 2,804 47 b2
Roseland, Va. 67 L3
Roselawn, Ind. 27 A1
Roselle, Ill., 4,827 25 D2
Roselle, N.J., 21,032 47 c3
Roselle Park, N.J., 12,546 47 c3
Rose Lodge, Oreg. 55 L2
Rosemead, Calif., 15,476 16 e10
Rosemont, Ariz. 14 C4
Rosemont, Cook Co., Ill., 2,283 26 c3
Rosemont, St. Clair Co., Ill. 40 d10
Rosemont, Pa., 3,600* 57 f11
Rosemount, Minn., 1,068 38 C3
Rosenberg, Tex., 9,698 63 G5
Rosendale, Mo., 234 40 B1
Rosendale, N.Y., 1,175 49 M7
Rosendale, Wis., 415 69 E4
Rosenhayn, N.J. 45 A5
Rose Pk., Ariz. 14 D3
Rosepine, La., 414 31 A3
Roseto, Pa., 1,630 57 L4
Rosetta, Ark. 15 B3
Rosette, Utah 64 A1
Roseville, Calif., 13,421 17 C2
Roseville, Ill., 1,065 25 B3
Roseville, Mich., 50,195 37 e10
Roseville, Minn., 29,581 38 c5
Roseville, Ohio, 1,749 53 C3
Roseville, Pa., 162 56 H2
Rosewood, Ind. 27 C4
Rosewood, N.C. 50 G2
Rosewood, Ohio 53 A2
Rosewood Heights, Ill., 4,572 40 d9
Rosharon, Tex. 63 G5
Rosholt, S. Dak., 423 61 D1
Rosholt, Wis., 497 69 D3
Rosiclare, Ill., 1,700 25 D6
Roslyn, N.Y., 2,515 47 e2
Roslyn, Pa., 8,575* 57 f11
Roslyn, S. Dak., 256 61 D1
Roslyn, Wash., 1,283 66 C2
Rosman, N.C., 419 50 C2
Ross, Calif., 2,551 16 a7
Ross, Ind. 26 e4
Ross, Ohio 53 A3
Ross, N. Dak., 167 51 L1
Ross, co., Ohio, 61,215 53 B3
Ross Barnett Res., Miss. 39 C3
Rossburg, Ohio, 295 53 A2
Rosser, Tex. 63 g12
Rossford, Ohio, 4,406 53 B1
Rossie, Iowa, 102 28 B1
Rossie, N.Y. 49 J2
Rossiter, Pa. 56 D4
Ross L., Wash. 66 C1
Rosston, Ark. 15 B4
Rosston, Okla. 54 D1
Rossville, Ga., 4,665 22 A1
Rossville, Ill., 1,470 25 E3
Rossville, Ind., 831 27 B2
Rossville, Kans., 797 29 G1
Rossville, Tex. 62 E5
Roswell, Ga., 2,983 22 B1
Roswell, N. Mex., 39,593 46 C3
Roswell, S. Dak., 39 61 D2
Rota, i., Mar. Is. 71 B3
Rotan, Tex., 2,788 62 D3
Rothbury, Mich. 36 E5
Rothsay, Minn., 457 38 A2
Rothschild, Wis., 2,550 69 D3
Rotterdam, N.Y., 16,871 49 d13

For abbreviations and explanation of index, see page 176.

Rotterdam Junction INDEX TO MAPS OF THE UNITED STATES San Carlos

Rotterdam Junction, N.Y. 49 M5
Rouge, r., Mich. 37 H6
Rougemont, N.C. 50 F1
Rough, r., Ky. 30 D3
Rough Run, W. Va. 68 D3
Roulette, Pa. 56 E2
Round Hill (part of Greenwich), Conn. 19 A5
Round Hill, Va., 430 67 M1
Round Hill Pt., Mass. 35 L6
Round Knob, Ill. 25 D6
Round Lake, Ill., 997 26 b1
Round Lake, N.Y. 49 d13
Round L., Mich. 36 F4
Round L., N. Dak. 51 M1
Round L., Sawyer Co., Wis. 69 B1
Round L., Price Co., Wis. 69 C2
Round Lake Beach, Ill., 5,011 26 b1
Round Lake Park, Ill., 2,921 26 b1
Round Mountain, Calif. 17 C1
Round Mountain, Nev. 43 B2
Round Mountain, Tex. 62 E4
Round Mtn., Me. 32 C2
Round Mtn., N.J. 45 B2
Round Mtn., Vt. 65 D1
Round Mts., Calif. 17 C1
Round Oak, Ga. 22 C2
Round Pd., Me. 32 B2
Round Rock, Tex., 1,878 62 E4
Round Top, Tex., 124 62 F4
Round Top, mtn., Mass. 34 B3
Roundup, Mont., 2,842 41 D2
Rouses Point, N.Y., 2,160 49 O1
Rouseville, Pa., 923 56 B3
Routier, Calif. 17 j12
Routt, co., Colo., 5,900 18 B1
Rouzerville, Pa. 56 G6
Rover, Ga. 22 b9
Rover, Tenn. 61 J2
Rowan, Iowa, 273 28 D2
Rowan, co., Ky., 12,808 30 G2
Rowan, co., N.C., 82,817 50 E2
Rowayton (part of Norwalk), Conn. 19 B5
Rowe, Mass., 231(T) 34 C2
Rowe, N. Mex. 46 C2
Rowena, Colo. 18 b4
Rowena, Tex. 62 D4
Rowesville, S.C., 398 59 D3
Rowland, Nev. 43 C1
Rowland, N.C., 1,408 50 F3
Rowland, Tex. 62 F3
Rowlesburg, W. Va., 970 68 D2
Rowlett, Tex., 1,015 63 f11
Rowlett Cr., Tex. 63 f10
Rowley, Iowa, 234 28 F2
Rowley, Mass., 1,223;2,783(T) 35 L2
Rowley Bay, Wis. 69 F2
Roxana, Ill., 2,090 25 C5
Roxboro, N.C., 5,147 51 F1
Roxboro, Wash. 66 D2
Roxbury, Fairfield Co., Conn. 47 e1
Roxbury, Litchfield Co., Conn., 912(T) 19 B3
Roxbury, Kans. 29 E2
Roxbury, Me. 32 A4
Roxbury, N.Y. 49 L6
Roxbury, Pa. 56 F3
Roxbury, Vt. 65 B2
Roxbury Falls (part of Roxbury), Conn. 19 B3
Roxie, Miss., 585 39 A4
Roxobel, N.C., 452 50 H1
Roxton, Okla. 54 E2
Roxton, Tex. 63 G3
Roy, Mont. 41 D2
Roy, N. Mex., 633 46 C2
Roy, Utah, 9,239 64 A1
Roy, Wash., 246 67 a6
Royal, Ill., 171 25 E3
Royal, Iowa, 475 28 B1
Royal, Nebr., 93 42 F1
Royal, N.C. 51 J2
Royal, r., Me. 32 A5
Royal Center, Ind., 966 27 B2
Royal City, Wash. 66 D2
Royale, I., Mich. 36 b8
Royal Glades Can., Fla. 20 a9
Royal Oak, Md. 33 E2
Royal Oak, Mich., 80,612 37 H6
Royal Palm Beach, Fla. 20 a7
Royalston, Mass., 800(T) 34 F2
Royalton, Ill., 1,225 25 C6
Royalton, Ky. 30 G3
Royalton, Minn., 580 38 B3
Royalton, Ohio 53 C3
Royalton, Vt. 65 B3
Royalton, Wis. 69 E3
Royalty, Tex. 62 C4
Royersford, Pa., 3,969 57 L5
Royerton, Ind. 27 C2
Royse City, Tex., 1,274 63 g11
Royston, Ga., 2,333 22 C1
Rozel, Kans., 207 29 C2
Rozellville, Wis. 69 C3
Rubicon, Wis. 69 E4
Rubidoux, Calif. 16 g10
Rubonia, Fla. 21 H4
Ruby, Alaska, 157 13 E2
Ruby, Ariz. 14 C4
Ruby, Nev. 43 C1
Ruby, S.C., 284 59 D2
Ruby L., Nev. 43 C1
Ruby Mts., Nev. 43 C1
Ruby Range, Mont. 41 B3
Ruby Valley, Nev. 43 C1
Rudd, Iowa, 436 28 E1
Rudolph, Wis. 69 D3
Rudy, Ark., 113 15 A2
Rudyard, Mich. 37 G2
Rudyard, Mont. 41 C1
Rufe, Okla. 55 H3
Ruffin, N.C. 50 F1
Ruffin, S.C. 59 D3
Rufus, Oreg. 55 M2
Rugby, N. Dak., 2,972 51 M1
Ruggles, Pa. 57 m16
Ruggs, Oreg. 55 N2
Ruidosa, Tex. 62 B4
Ruidoso, N. Mex., 1,557 46 C3
Ruidoso Downs, N. Mex., 407 46 C3
Rujiyoru, i., Eniwetok 72 k
Rule, Tex., 1,347 62 E3
Ruleton, Kans. 29 A1
Ruleville, Miss., 1,902 39 B2
Rulo, Nebr., 412 42 J3
Rum, r., Minn. 38 C3
Ruma, Ill., 138 25 B5
Rumford, Me., 7,233 32 A4
Rumford (part of E. Providence), R.I. 58 C1
Rumford, Va. 67 M3
Rumney, N.H. 44 B4
Rumney Depot, N.H. 44 B4
Rump Mtn., Me. 32 A3
Rumson, N.J., 6,405 45 D3
Rumung, i., Yap 72 d
Runge, Tex., 1,036 62 F5
Runnells, Iowa, 322 28 D3
Runnels, co., Tex., 15,016 62 D4
Runnemede, N.J., 8,396 57 f12
Running Springs, Calif. 16 g10
Runu, Yap 72 d
Rupert, Idaho, 4,153 24 C4
Rupert, Vt. 43 A4
Rupert, W. Va., 921 68 C4
Rural, Wis. 69 D3
Rural Hall, N.C., 1,503 50 E1
Rural Hill, Miss. 39 C2
Rural Retreat, Va., 413 67 H4
Rural Ridge, Pa. 56 c7
Rural Valley, Pa., 860 56 C4
Rush, Ark. 15 C4
Rush, Colo. 18 C2
Rush, co., Ind., 20,393 27 C3
Rush, co., Kans., 6,160 29 C2
Rush, N.Y. 48 j18
Rush Center, Kans., 278 29 C2
Rush City, Minn., 1,108 38 C3
Rush Cr., Colo. 18 D2
Rush Cr., Nebr. 42 A2
Rushford, Minn., 1,335 38 D4
Rushford, N.Y. 48 D6
Rushing, Ark. 15 C2
Rush Lake, Wis. 69 E4
Rush L., Minn. 38 B2
Rush L., Wis. 69 E4
Rush Springs, Okla., 1,303 54 F3
Rushsylvania, Ohio, 601 53 B2
Rushville, Ill., 2,819 25 B3
Rushville, Ind., 7,264 27 C3
Rushville, Mo., 253 40 A2
Rushville, Nebr., 1,228 42 B1
Rushville, N.Y., 465 48 F5
Rusk, co., Tex., 36,421 63 G3
Rusk, Tex., 4,900 63 G4
Rusk, co., Wis., 14,794 69 B2
Ruskin, Fla., 1,894 21 H4
Ruskin, Nebr., 203 42 G3
Ruso, N. Dak., 31 51 M2
Russell, co., Ala., 46,351 11 D3
Russell, Ark., 203 15 D2
Russell, Fla. 21 J1
Russell, Ill. 26 c1
Russell, Iowa, 577 28 D4
Russell, co., Kans., 11,348 29 D1
Russell, Kans., 6,113 29 D2
Russell, co., Ky., 11,076 30 E3
Russell, Ky., 1,458 30 F2
Russell, Mass., 1,366(T) 34 C4
Russell, N.Y. 49 K2
Russell, Ohio 52 f8
Russell, Okla. 54 D3
Russell, Pa. 56 C2
Russell, co., Va., 26,290 66 G4
Russell Cave Nat. Mon., Ala. 11 D1
Russell Cr., Ky. 30 E3
Russell Gulch, Colo. 18 a5
Russell Mtn., Me. 32 B2
Russells Point, Ohio, 1,111 53 B2
Russell Springs, Kans., 93 29 A2
Russell Springs, Ky., 1,125 30 E3
Russell Str., Me. 32 B2
Russellton, Pa., 1,613 56 B4
Russellville, Ala., 6,628 11 B1
Russellville, Ark., 10,525 15 B2
Russellville, Ill., 197 25 E5
Russellville, Ind., 372 27 B3
Russellville, Ky., 5,861 30 D4
Russellville (part of Southampton), Mass. 34 C4
Russellville, Mo., 442 40 D5
Russellville, Ohio, 412 53 B4
Russellville, Tenn. 61 M1
Russian, r., Calif. 17 B2
Russian Mission, Alaska, 102 12 C3
Russian Mission, Alaska 12 D3
Russiaville, Ind., 1,064 27 B2
Rustburg, Va. 67 K3
Rustic, Colo. 18 C1
Ruston, La., 13,991 31 B1
Ruston, Wash., 699 67 a6
Ruth, Calif. 17 B1
Ruth, Ky. 30 F3
Ruth, Mich. 37 J5
Ruth, Miss. 39 B4
Ruth, Nev. 43 C2
Ruth, N.C., 529 50 D2
Rutherford, N.J., 20,473 45 C2
Rutherford, co., N.C., 45,091 50 C2
Rutherford, co., Tenn., 52,368 61 J2
Rutherford, Tenn., 983 60 G1
Rutherfordton, N.C., 3,392 50 D2
Ruthton, Minn., 476 38 A3
Ruthven, Iowa, 712 28 B1
Rutland, Ill., 509 25 C3
Rutland, Mass., 1,774; 3,253(T) 35 G3
Rutland, Ohio, 687 53 C3
Rutland, N. Dak., 308 51 O2
Rutland, co., Vt., 46,719 65 A3
Rutland, Vt., 18,325 65 B3
Rutledge, Ala., 276 11 C4
Rutledge, Minn., 146 38 C2
Rutledge, Mo., 158 40 D1
Rutledge, Tenn., 793 61 M3
Ruxton, Md. 33 c3
Ryan, Iowa, 347 28 F2
Ryan, Okla., 978 54 F3
Ryan Pk., Idaho 24 B4
Ryder, N. Dak., 264 51 M2
Ryderwood, Wash. 66 B2
Rye, Ark. 15 D4
Rye, Colo., 179 18 C3
Rye, N.H. 44 D5
Rye, N.Y., 15,332 49 N9
Rye, Tex. 63 G4
Rye Beach, N.H. 44 D6
Ryegate, Mont., 314 41 D2
Ryegate Corner, Vt. 65 C2
Rye L., N.Y. 47 e1
Rye North Beach, N.H. 44 D5
Rye Patch Res., Nev. 43 A1
Ryer I., Calif. 16 b6
Ryus, Kans. 29 A3

S

Sabael, N.Y. 49 M3
Sabana Grande, P.R., 3,318 72 n b1
Sabattus, Me. 32 A4
Sabattus Pd., Me. 32 A4
Sabbatia, L., Mass. 35 K5
Sabetha, Kans., 2,318 29 G1
Sabillasville, Md. 33 C1
Sabin, Minn., 251 38 A2
Sabina, Ill. 25 D3
Sabina, Ohio, 2,313 53 B3
Sabina, r., Tex. 62 E5
Sabinal, Tex., 1,747 62 E5
Sabine, parish, La., 18,564 31 A2
Sabine, co., Tex., 7,302 63 H4
Sabine, Tex. 63 m14
Sabine, r., La.-Tex. 31 A4
Sabine L., La.-Tex. 31 A4
Sabine Pass, Tex. 63 G5
Sabinoso, N. Mex. 46 C2
Sabinsville, Pa. 56 F2
Sable, C., Fla. 21 J6
Sabula, Iowa, 894 28 G2
Sac, co., Iowa, 17,007 28 B2
Sac, r., Mo. 40 C4
Sacajawea Pk., Oreg. 55 O2
Sacandaga, W. Br., r., N.Y. 49 M4
Sacandaga Res., N.Y. 49 M4
Sacaton, Ariz. 14 C3
Sac City, Iowa, 3,354 28 B2
Sachse, Tex., 359 63 f11
Sacketts Harbor, N.Y., 1,279 49 H3
Saco, Me., 10,515 32 A5
Saco, Mont., 490 41 E1
Saco, r., Me.-N.H. 32 A5
Saco, Rocky Br., r., N.H. 44 C3
Sacramento, co., Calif., 502,778 17 C2
Sacramento, Calif., 237,712 17 C2
Sacramento, r., Calif. 17 C2
Sacramento Mts., N. Mex. 46 C3
Sacramento Valley, Calif. 17 B1
Sacred Falls, Hawaii 23 e8
Sacred Heart, Minn., 696 38 B3
Saddle, r., N.J. 45 C1
Saddleback Mtn., Aroostook Co., Me. 32 C2
Saddleback Mtn., Franklin Co., Me. 32 A4
Saddleback Mtn., N.Y. 49 N2
Saddlebunch Keys, Fla. 21 f14
Saddle Buttes, N. Dak. 51 L2
Saddle Buttes, S. Dak. 61 B1
Saddle Mountain, Okla. 54 E3
Saddle Mtn., Colo. 18 C2
Saddle Mtn., Wyo. 70 B1
Saddle River, N.J., 1,776 47 c1
Sadieville, Ky., 276 30 F2
Sadorus, Ill., 384 25 D3
Saegertown, Pa., 1,131 56 A2
Safety Harbor, Fla., 1,787 21 c10
Saffell, Ark. 15 D2
Safford, Ariz., 5,165 14 D3
Sagadahoc, co., Me., 22,793 32 B4
Sagamore (part of Bourne), Mass. 35 M5
Sagamore, Pa. 56 C4
Sagamore Beach (part of Bourne), Mass. 35 M5
Sagamore Hills, Ohio 52 e8
Saganaga L., Minn. 38 D1
Saganashkee Slough, Ill. 26 c4
Saganing, Mich. 37 H5
Sagavanirktok, r., Alaska 13 F1
Sag Bridge, Ill. 26 c4
Sagerton, Tex. 62 E3
Sageville, Iowa, 110 28 G2
Sag Harbor, N.Y., 2,346 49 Q8
Saginaw, co., Mich., 190,752 37 G5
Saginaw, Mich., 98,265 37 H5
Saginaw, Oreg. 55 L3
Saginaw, Tex., 1,001 63 e11
Saginaw, r., Mich. 37 H5
Saginaw Bay, Mich. 37 H5
Sagola, Mich. 36 C2
Saguache, co., Colo., 4,473 18 B2
Saguache, Colo., 722 18 B2
Saguaro Nat. Mon., Ariz. 14 C3
Sahuarita, Ariz. 14 C4
Saidora, Ill. 25 B3
Sailor Springs, Ill., 187 25 D5
St. Agatha, Me. 32 C1
St. Albans, Me. 32 B4
St. Albans, Vt., 8,806 65 A1
St. Albans, W. Va., 15,103 68 B3
St. Albans Bay, Vt. 65 A1
St. Andrews, Ill. 26 b3
St. Ann, Mo., 15,654 40 c10
St. Anne, Ill., 1,378 25 E2
St. Ansgar, Iowa, 1,014 28 E1
St. Anthony, Idaho, 2,700 24 D4
St. Anthony, Iowa, 130 28 D2
St. Anthony, Minn., 7,710 38 b5
St. Anthony, N. Dak. 51 M2
St. Augustine, Fla., 14,734 21 J2
St. Augustine, Ill., 201 25 B3
St. Augustine Beach, Fla., 396 21 J2
St. Bernard, parish, La., 32,186 31 E4
St. Bernard, Ohio, 6,778 52 j10
St. Bernice, Ind. 27 A3
St. Catherine, L., Vt. 65 A4
St. Catherines I., Ga. 22 E4
St. Charles, Ark., 255 15 D3
St. Charles, Idaho, 300 24 D4
St. Charles, Ill., 11,158 25 D2
St. Charles, Iowa, 355 28 D3
St. Charles, Ky., 421 30 C3
St. Charles, parish, La., 21,219 31 D4
St. Charles, Mich., 1,959 37 G5
St. Charles, Minn., 1,882 38 D4
St. Charles, co., Mo., 52,970 40 F3
St. Charles, Mo., 21,189 40 F3
St. Charles, Va., 368 66 F4
St. Charles, r., Colo. 18 C2
St. Clair, co., Ala., 25,388 11 C2
St. Clair, co., Ill., 262,509 25 B5
St. Clair, co., Mich., 107,201 37 J5
St. Clair, Mich., 4,538 37 L6
St. Clair, co., Mo., 8,421 40 C3
St. Clair, Mo., 2,711 40 F3
St. Clair, Pa., 5,159 57 J4
St. Clair, r., Mich.-Ont. 37 J6
St. Clair, L., Mich.-Ont. 37 J6
St. Clair Bottom, Va. 66 H4
St. Clair Shores, Mich., 76,657 37 J6
St. Clairsville, Ohio, 3,865 53 D2
St. Clairsville, Pa., 115 56 E5
St. Cloud, Fla., 4,353 21 J3
St. Cloud, Minn., 37,746 38 C3
St. Cloud, Wis., 530 69 E4
St. Croix, Ind. 27 B4
St. Croix, co., Wis., 29,164 69 A2
St. Croix, i., V.I. 72 q
St. Croix, r., Me.-N.B. 32 D3
St. Croix, r., Minn.-Wis. 38 C3
St. Croix Falls, Wis., 1,249 69 A2
St. Croix Flowage, Wis. 69 A1
St. Croix Str., Me. 32 C2
St. David, Ariz. 14 C4
St. David, Ill., 862 25 B3
St. David, Me. 32 C1
St. Edward, Nebr., 777 42 F2
St. Elias, C., Alaska 13 H4
St. Elias, Mt., Yukon-Alaska 13 H3
St. Elmo, Ill., 1,503 25 D4
St. Francis, co., Ark., 33,303 15 E2
St. Francis, Kans., 1,594 29 A1
St. Francis, Ky. 30 E3
St. Francis, Me. 32 C1
St. Francis, S. Dak., 421 61 B2
St. Francis, Wis., 10,065 69 b8
St. Francis, r., Ark.-Mo. 166 B, 2–3
St. Francis, r., Me. 32 B1
St. Francisville, Ill., 1,040 25 E5
St. Francisville, La., 1,661 31 C3
St. Francisville, Mo. 40 E1
St. Francois, co., Mo., 36,516 40 F4
St. Francois Mts., Mo. 40 F4
St. Froid L., Me. 32 C2
St. Gabriel, La. 31 C3
Ste. Genevieve, co., Mo., 12,116 40 F4
Ste. Genevieve, Mo., 4,443 40 G4
St. George, Alaska 12 A4
St. George, Ga. 22 E5
St. George, Kans., 259 29 F1
St. George, Me. 32 B4
St. George, Mo., 1,323 40 c10
St. George (part of N.Y.C.), N.Y. 47 e3
St. George, S.C., 1,833 59 D3
St. George, Utah, 5,130 64 A3
St. George, W. Va. 68 D2
St. George, C., Fla. 21 F2
St. George, Pt., Calif. 17 A1
St. George I., Alaska 12 A4
St. George I., Fla. 21 F2
St. Georges Island, Md. 33 D2
St. Germain, Wis. 69 D2
St. Hedwig, Tex., 589 62 b9
St. Helen, Mich. 37 G4
St. Helen, L., Mich. 37 G4
St. Helena, Calif., 2,722 17 B2
St. Helena, parish, La., 9,162 31 D3
St. Helena, N.C. 50 G3
St. Helena I., S.C. 59 D4
St. Helens, Oreg., 5,022 55 L2
St. Helens, Mt., Wash. 66 B2
St. Henry, Ohio, 978 53 A2
St. Hilaire, Minn., 270 38 A1
St. Huberts, N.Y. 49 N2
St. Ignace, Mich., 3,334 37 G3
St. Ignatius, Mont., 940 41 A2
St. James, Ill. 25 D5
St. James, parish, La., 18,369 31 D3
St. James, Mich. 36 F3
St. James, Minn., 4,174 38 B4
St. James, Mo., 2,384 40 E3
St. James, N.Y., 3,524 47 g2
St. James City, Fla. 21 H5
St. Jo, Tex., 977 62 F3
St. Joe, Ark. 15 C1
St. Joe, Ind., 499 27 D1
St. Joe, r., Idaho 24 B2
St. John, Ind., 1,128 27 A1
St. John, Kans., 1,753 29 D2
St. John, Mo., 7,342 40 c10
St. John, N. Dak., 420 51 N1
St. John, Utah 64 A1
St. John, Wash., 545 66 E2
St. John, i., V.I. 72 p
St. John, r., Me.-N.B. 32 D1
St. John Pd., Me. 32 B2
St. Johns, Ariz., 1,310 14 D2
St. Johns, co., Fla., 30,034 21 J2
St. Johns, Ill., 206 25 C5
St. Johns, Mich., 5,629 37 G6
St. Johns, r., Fla. 21 J2
St. Johnsburg, N.Y. 48 g15
St. Johnsbury, Vt., 6,809 65 D2
St. Johnsbury Center, Vt. 65 D2
St. Johnsville, N.Y. 49 L4
St. John the Baptist, parish, La., 18,439 31 D3
St. Joseph, Ill., 1,210 25 E3
St. Joseph, co., Ind., 238,614 27 B1
St. Joseph, La., 1,653 31 C2
St. Joseph, co., Mich., 42,332 36 F7
St. Joseph, Mich., 11,755 36 E6
St. Joseph, Minn., 1,487 38 B3
St. Joseph, Mo., 79,673 40 A2
St. Joseph, Tenn., 547 61 H2
St. Joseph, Wis. 69 L4
St. Joseph, r., Ind.-Mich. 36 E7
St. Joseph, r., Ind.-Ohio 53 A1
St. Joseph Pt., Fla. 21 E2
St. Just, P.R. 72 n d1
St. Landry, parish, La., 81,493 31 C3
St. Lawrence, co., N.Y., 111,239 49 K2
St. Lawrence, N.Y. 49 H2
St. Lawrence, Pa., 929 57 h14
St. Lawrence, S. Dak., 290 61 C1
St. Lawrence, r., 165 E–F, 2–3
St. Lawrence I., Alaska 12 A3
St. Leo, Fla., 278 21 H3
St. Leo, Kans. 29
St. Leo, Minn., 129 38 B3
St. Leonard, Md. 33 D2
St. Libory, Ill., 346 25 C5
St. Louis, Mich., 3,808 37 G5
St. Louis, co., Minn., 231,588 38 C2
St. Louis, co., Mo., 703,532 40 F3
St. Louis, Mo., 750,026 40 F3
St. Louis, Okla., 76 54 G2
St. Louis, r., Minn. 38 C2
St. Louis Heights, Hawaii 23 f10
St. Louis Park, Minn., 48,021 38 b6
St. Louisville, Ohio, 349 53 C2
St. Lucie, co., Fla., 39,294 21 K4
St. Lucie, Fla. 21 K4
St. Lucie Can., Fla. 21 K4
St. Maries, Idaho, 2,435 24 A2
St. Marks, Fla. 21 F1
St. Marks, r., Fla. 21 F1
St. Martin, parish, La., 29,063 31 C3
St. Martin, Minn., 215 38 B3
St. Martin, Ohio, 152 53 B3
St. Martin I., Mich. 36 E3
St. Martinville, La., 6,468 31 C3
St. Mary, Ill. 25 A3
St. Mary, Ky. 30 E3
St. Mary, parish, La., 48,833 31 C4
St. Marys, Alaska 12 B3
St. Marys, Ga., 3,272 22 E5
St. Marys, Kans., 1,509 29 G1
St. Marys, co., Md., 38,915 33 D2
St. Marys, Ohio, 7,737 53 A2
St. Marys, Pa., 8,065 56 D3
St. Marys, W. Va., 2,443 68 B2
St. Marys, r., Minn. 37 G2
St. Marys, r., Fla.-Ga. 11 G5
St. Marys, r., Ind.-Ohio 53 A2
St. Marys City, Md. 33 D2
St. Mary's Point, Minn. 38 d6
St. Matthews, Ky., 10,796 30 E2
St. Matthews, S.C., 2,433 59 D3
St. Meinrad, Ind. 27 B4
St. Michael, Alaska, 205 12 C3
St. Michael, Nebr. 42 F2
St. Michael, Pa., 1,292 56 D5
St. Michaels, Ariz. 14 D2
St. Michaels, Md., 1,484 33 D2
St. Nazianz, Wis., 669 69 F3
St. Onge, S. Dak. 61 A1
St. Paris, Ohio, 1,460 53 B2
St. Paul, Ark., 118 15 B2
St. Paul, Ind., 702 27 C3
St. Paul, Kans., 675 29 G3
St. Paul, Minn., 313,411 38 C3
St. Paul, Nebr., 1,714 42 F2
St. Paul, Oreg., 254 55 L2
St. Paul, Va., 1,156 66 G4
St. Paul I., Alaska 12 A4
St. Paul Park, Minn., 5,111 38 c6
St. Pauls, N.C., 2,249 50 G3
St. Paul's Church Nat. Hist. Site, N.Y. 47 d2
St. Peter, Ill., 397 25 D5
St. Peter, Kans. 29 B1
St. Peter, Minn., 8,484 38 B3
St. Peters, Mo., 404 40 F3
St. Peters, Pa. 57 e11
St. Petersburg, Colo. 18 D1
St. Petersburg, Fla., 181,298 21 H4
St. Petersburg, Pa., 417 56 B3
St. Petersburg Beach, Fla., 6,268 21 H4
St. Phillip, Ind. 27 A4
St. Regis, Mont. 41 A2
St. Regis, N.Y. 49 L1
St. Regis, r., N.Y. 49 L1
St. Regis Falls, N.Y. 49 M1
St. Robert, Mo., 860 40 D4
St. Simons, Ga., 3,199 22 E4
St. Simons I., Ga. 22 E4
St. Stephen, S.C., 1,462 59 E3
St. Tammany, parish, La., 38,643 31 D3
St. Thomas, Ind. 27 A4
St. Thomas, N. Dak., 660 51 O1
St. Thomas, Pa. 56 F6
St. Thomas, i., V.I. 72 p
St. Vincent, Minn., 217 38 A1
St. Vincent I., Fla. 21 E2
St. Vrain, N. Mex. 46 D2
St. Vrain, r., Colo. 18 b4
St. Xavier, Mont. 41 D3
Saipan, i., Mar. Is. 71 B2, 72 f
Saipan Channel, Saipan 72 f
Sakonnet (part of Little Compton), R.I. 58 D3
Sakonnet, r., R.I. 58 D2
Sakonnet Pt., R.I. 58 D3
Salado, r., N. Mex. 46 B2
Salamanca, N.Y., 8,480 48 C6
Salamonia, Ind., 142 27 D2
Salamonie, r., Ind. 27 C2
Salat, i., Truk 72 g
Salcha, r., Alaska 13 G2
Sale City, Ga., 275 22 C4
Sale Creek, Tenn. 61 K2
Salem, Ala. 11 D3
Salem, Ark., 713 15 D1
Salem, Conn., 925(T) 19 F4
Salem, Fla. 21 G2
Salem, Ill., 6,165 25 D5
Salem, Ind., 4,546 27 B4
Salem, Iowa, 442 28 F4
Salem, Ky. 30 B3
Salem, Me. 32 A4
Salem, Mass., 39,211 35 L2
Salem, Mich. 37 H6
Salem, Mo., 3,870 40 E4
Salem, Nebr., 261 42 J3
Salem, N.H. 44 C6
Salem, co., N.J., 58,711 45 A4
Salem, N.J., 8,941 45 A4
Salem, N. Mex. 46 B3
Salem, N.Y., 1,076 49 O4
Salem, Ohio, 13,854 53 E2
Salem, Oreg., 49,142 55 L2
Salem, S.C., 206 59 A2
Salem, S. Dak., 1,188 61 D2
Salem, Utah, 920 64 c7
Salem, Va., 16,058 67 J3
Salem, W. Va., 2,366 68 C2
Salem, Wis. 69 a9
Salem, r., N.J. 45 A4
Salemburg, N.C., 569 50 G2
Salem Depot, N.H., 2,523 44 C6
Salem Heights, Oreg., 10,770 55 L2
Salem Maritime Nat. Hist. Site, Mass. 35 L2
Salesville, Tex. 63 d11
Salida, Calif., 1,109 17 C3
Salida, Colo., 4,560 18 C2
Salina, Kans., 43,202 29 E2
Salina, Okla., 972 55 H1
Salina, Utah, 1,618 64 B2
Salinas, P.R., 3,666 72 n c2
Salinas, Calif., 28,957 17 C3
Salinas, r., Calif. 17 C3
Salinas, P., P.R. 72 n c1
Salinas Pk., N. Mex. 46 B3
Saline, co., Ark., 28,956 15 C3
Saline, co., Ill., 26,227 25 D6
Saline, co., Kans., 54,715 29 E2
Saline, La., 329 31 B1
Saline, Mich., 2,334 37 H6
Saline, co., Mo., 25,148 40 C2
Saline, co., Nebr., 12,542 42 G3
Saline, r., Ark. 15 A3
Saline, r., Ark. 15 C3
Saline, r., Ill. 25 D6
Saline, r., Kans. 29 C1
Saline L., La. 31 B2
Salineno, Tex. 62 E6
Salineville, Ohio, 1,898 53 E2
Salisbury, Guam 71 a
Salisbury, Conn., 3,309(T) 19 B2
Salisbury, Md., 16,302 33 E2
Salisbury, Mass., 3,154(T) 35 L1
Salisbury, Mo., 1,787 40 D2
Salisbury, N.H. 44 B5
Salisbury, N.C., 21,297 50 E2
Salisbury, Pa., 862 56 C6
Salisbury, Vt. 65 A3
Salisbury Beach (part of Salisbury), Mass. 35 L1
Salisbury Center, N.Y. 49 L4
Salisbury Heights, N.H. 44 B5
Salix, Iowa, 394 28 A2
Salkehatchie, r., S.C. 59 C3
Salkum, Wash. 66 B2
Salladasburg, Pa., 255 56 G3
Salley, S.C., 403 59 C3
Sallis, Miss., 223 39 C2
Sallisaw, Okla., 3,351 55 J2
Salmo, Wis. 69 C1
Salmon, Idaho, 2,944 24 B3
Salmon, r., Conn. 19 F3
Salmon, r., Idaho 24 B3
Salmon, r., Franklin Co., N.Y. 49 M1
Salmon, r., Clinton Co., N.Y. 49 N1
Salmon Bk., Conn. 19 D2
Salmon Bk., Mass.-N.H. 35 J2
Salmon Cr., Conn. 19 B2
Salmon Falls, r., Me.-N.H. 44 D5
Salmon Falls Cr., Idaho-Nev. 24 B4
Salmon Res., N.Y. 49 J3
Salmon River Mts., Idaho 24 B3
Salol, Minn. 38 B1
Salome, Ariz. 14 B3
Salt, r., Ariz. 14 C3
Salt, r., Ky. 30 E2
Salt, r., Mo. 40 D2
Salt, Mid. Fk., r., Mo. 40 D2
Saltair, Utah 64 b6
Salt Cr., Ill. 25 D3
Salt Cr., Ill. 26 c3
Salt Cr., Ind. 26 f4
Salter Path, N.C. 51 J3
Salters, S.C. 59 E3
Salt Flat, Tex. 62 B4
Salt Fork, Okla. 54 F1
Salt Fk., r., Ill. 25 D3
Saltillo, Ind., 121 27 B4
Saltillo, Miss., 536 39 D1
Saltillo, Ohio 53 C3
Saltillo, Pa., 395 56 E5
Saltillo, Tenn., 397 61 G2
Salt Lake, N. Mex. 46 A2
Salt Lake, co., Utah, 383,035 64 A1
Salt L., Hawaii 23 e9
Salt Lake City, Utah, 189,454 64 A1
Salt Lakes, Tex. 62 B4
Salton Sea, Calif. 17 F5
Salt Rock, W. Va. 68 A3
Saltsburg, Pa., 1,054 56 C4
Saltville, Va., 2,844 66 H4
Salt Wells, Nev. 43 A2
Saluda, N.C., 570 50 C2
Saluda, co., S.C., 14,554 59 C2
Saluda, S.C., 2,089 59 C3
Saluda, Va. 67 N3
Saluda, r., S.C. 59 B2
Salus, Ark. 15 B2
Salvador, L., La. 31 D4
Salvisa, Ky. 30 F3
Salvo, N.C. 51 K2
Salyersville, Ky., 1,173 30 G3
Samburg, Tenn., 451 60 F1
Sammamish, L., Wash. 67 b5
Samos, Va. 67 N3
Samoset, Fla., 4,824 21 H4
Sampson, co., N.C., 48,013 50 G3
Sam Rayburn Res., Tex. 63 G4
Samson, Ala., 1,932 11 C4
Samsonville, N.Y. 49 M7
Samuels, Ky. 30 E3
Sanak I., Alaska 12 C5
San Andreas, Calif., 1,416 17 C2
San Andres Mts., N. Mex. 46 B3
San Andres Pk., N. Mex. 46 B3
San Angelo, Tex., 58,815 62 D4
San Angelo Res., Tex. 62 D4
San Anselmo, Calif., 11,584 16 a7
San Antonio, Fla., 479 21 H3
San Antonio, N. Mex. 46 B3
San Antonio, Tex., 587,718 62 E5
San Antonio, r., Tex. 62 F5
San Antonio Bay, Tex. 62 F5
San Antonio Heights, Calif. 16 f10
San Antonio Mtn., Tex. 62 B4
San Antonio Pk., Calif. 16 f10
San Antonio Pk., N. Mex. 46 B1
San Antonito, N. Mex. 46 B2
San Ardo, Calif. 17 C3
Sanatorium, N.C. 50 F2
Sanatorium, Tex. 62 D4
San Augustine, co., Tex., 7,722 63 G4
San Augustine, Tex., 2,585 63 G4
San Benito, co., Calif., 15,396 17 C3
San Benito, Tex., 16,422 62 F6
San Benito, r., Calif. 17 C3
San Bernard, r., Tex. 62 F5
San Bernardino, co., Calif., 503,591 17 E4
San Bernardino, Calif., 91,922 17 E4
San Blas, C., Fla. 21 E2
Sanborn, Iowa, 1,323 28 B1
Sanborn, Minn., 521 38 B3
Sanborn, N.Y. 48 g15
Sanborn, N. Dak., 263 51 N2
Sanborn, co., S. Dak., 4,641 61 C2
Sanborn, Wis. 69 C1
Sanbornton, N.H. 44 B4
Sanbornville, N.H. 44 C4
San Bruno, Calif., 29,063 16 b7
San Carlos, Ariz. 14 C3
San Carlos, Calif., 21,370 16 b8
San Carlos, r., Ariz. 14 C3

For abbreviations and explanation of index, see page 176.

For abbreviations and explanation of index, see page 176.

For abbreviations and explanation of index, see page 176.

For abbreviations and explanation of index, see page 176.

U

V

W

For abbreviations and explanation of index, see page 176.

X

Y

Z

For abbreviations and explanation of index, see page 176.

HOW TO USE THE GENERAL INDEX

Page numbers in **bold** type indicate the most comprehensive article on a subject. These are often followed by references to additional information on other pages. For example, the listing for Alabama shows that the main text about that state is on page **11**; the entries that follow give the pages concerning its archaeology, early settlements, role in the Civil War, etc.

Entries with *illus.*, *map*, *chart*, or *graph* do not necessarily mean that the subject is treated only by some type of illustration. The page number may also refer to adjacent text. The listings for Acadia National Park, Maine, are "*illus.*, 120; *map*, 130." Both pages also have descriptions of the park.

Plants and animals are usually identified by both their Latin and common, or English, names: *Acipenser oxyrhynchus*, or Atlantic sturgeon, is indexed under both designations.

A

B

C

D

E

F

G

H

I

J

K

L

For explanation of index, see page 228; for abbreviations, see page 176.

M

N

O

P

Q

R

S

T

U

V

W

X

Y

Z

For explanation of index, see page 228; for abbreviations, see page 176.

CREDITS

INTRODUCTION

World map, p. 7, base map, © 1956, Jeppesen & Co., Denver, Colo., all rights reserved; p. 8, North America map, base map, © 1958, Jeppesen & Co., Denver, Colo., all rights reserved; p. 8a, physical map, © Babson Institute, Babson Park, Mass.; p. 8b, political map, © General Drafting Co., Inc., and Western Publishing Co., Inc.

PART I THE 50 STATES

STATE AND OTHER MAPS: pp. 11-72, © General Drafting Co., Inc., and Western Publishing Co., Inc. ALABAMA: p. 11, quotation from *Stars Fell on Alabama,* by Carl Carmer, © 1934, Carl Carmer, pub. by Farrar, Straus & Giroux, Inc. CONNECTICUT: p. 19, quotation from *The Yankees of Connecticut,* by William Storrs Lee, © 1957, William Storrs Lee, pub. by Holt, Rinehart & Winston, Inc. IDAHO: p. 24, quotation from "Idaho," by A. B. Guthrie, Jr., in *American Panorama West of the Mississippi,* a *Holiday* Magazine book, © The Curtis Publishing Co., pub. 1960 by Doubleday & Co., Inc. NORTH DAKOTA: p. 51, quotations from *The Letters of Theodore Roosevelt,* Vol. I, edited by Elting E. Morrison, © 1951, The President and Fellows of Harvard College, pub. by Harvard University Press, and *Autobiography of Theodore Roosevelt,* Centennial Edition, edited by Wayne Andrews, © 1913, Charles Scribner's Sons, renewal © 1941, Edith K. Carow Roosevelt, © 1958, Charles Scribner's Sons, reprinted with the permission of Charles Scribner's Sons. PENNSYLVANIA: p. 57, quotation from *Rudyard Kipling's Verse: Definitive Edition,* © 1910, Rudyard Kipling, reprinted by permission of Mrs. George Bambridge and Doubleday & Co., Inc.

PART II THE PEOPLE OF AMERICA

THE FIRST AMERICANS: p. 74, photo of Cliff Palace, Mesa Verde National Park, Colo., by Harvey Caplin; photo of Anasazi jar, courtesy Museum of the American Indian Heye Foundation; photo of stone pipe, courtesy Field Museum of Natural History, Chicago; Serpent Mound photo, by Tony Linck, courtesy American Heritage Publishing Co., Inc.; p. 75, drawing of Cahokia Mound based on sketch by Nelson A. Reed, St. Louis, Mo. FROM SEA TO SEA: EXPLORATION: p. 76, Vinland map from *The Vinland Map and The Tartar Relation,* by R. A. Skelton, Thomas E. Marston and George D. Painter, © 1965, Yale University, reproduced by permission of Yale University Press. THE STRUGGLE FOR AMERICA: p. 78, Russian map, courtesy the Slavonic Division of the New York Public Library; Spanish map, courtesy the Map Division of the New York Public Library; photos by J. Barnell, Image International; p. 79, French map, courtesy William Clements Library, University of Michigan; British map, courtesy The British Museum, London; Dutch map, courtesy Macpherson Collection, National Maritime Museum, Greenwich, England. THE INDIAN PEOPLES: p. 80, tribal families map based on data from *Atlas of the Historical Geography of the United States,* by Charles O. Paullin, edited by John K. Wright, pub. 1932 jointly by Carnegie Institution and American Geographical Society of New York. THE COLONISTS AND THE INDIANS: p. 81, maps based on data from Paullin, *op. cit.;* population chart data from U.S. Bureau of the Census. THE AMERICAN REVOLUTION: p. 82; WAR OF 1812: p. 83; WESTERN LAND CLAIMS: p. 84; maps based on data from Paullin, *op. cit.* INDIAN WARS OF THE WEST: p. 86, map based on data from U.S. Bureau of Indian Affairs. FROM TERRITORIES TO STATES: p. 87; MEXICAN WAR: p. 88; CIVIL WAR: pp. 88-89; SPANISH-AMERICAN WAR: p. 90, maps based on data from Paullin, *op. cit.* FOREIGN AID: p. 92, charts based on data from U.S. Office of Business Economics. DEFENSIVE EARLY WARNING SYSTEM: p. 93, map based on data from Department of Defense, U.S. Air Force. PRESIDENTIAL ELECTIONS: p. 95, 1860 and 1864 maps based on data from Paullin, *op. cit.* POPULATION EXPLOSION: pp. 100-01, charts, and p. 102, population-shift map, based on data from U.S. Bureau of the Census; Atlanta expansion map from Atlanta Region Metropolitan Planning Commission; pp. 102-03, models of population density and activity, © 1968, Dr. William Warntz; p. 103, photo of Independence Mall before renewal, Lawrence S. Williams, Inc.; photo of Independence Mall after renewal, A. K. Strobl, Philadelphia City Planning Commission. EDUCATION: p. 104, chart based on data from U.S. Office of Education; p. 105, land-grant college map based on data from American Association of Land Grant Colleges; junior college maps based on data from American Association of Junior Colleges; pp. 106-07, school facts and figures chart based on data from U.S. Office of Education; p. 107, New York suburban map based on data from New York Bureau of Statistical Services. RELIGION: p. 108, map based on data from *Historical Atlas of Religion in America,* © 1962, Edwin Scott Gaustad, pub. by Harper & Row; p. 109, maps based on data from National Council of the Churches of Christ in the U.S.A., and from Wilbur Zelinsky. HEALTH: pp. 110-11, charts based on data from *The Facts of Life and Death,* U.S. Public Health Service; p. 112, chart based on data from *Health Resources Statistics,* U.S. Public Health Service; p. 113, base map, © 1958, Jeppesen & Co., Denver, Colo., all rights reserved. Air-pollution data from U.S. Public Health Service, water-pollution data from Federal Water Pollution Control Administration. SPORTS AND RECREATION: p. 114, statistics on participants from The Athletic Institute, Chicago; pp. 114-15, fishing sites map data from "You Should Be There," February 1967, *Field & Stream,* © 1967, and pub. by Holt, Rinehart & Winston, Inc.; p. 115, statistics on spectators from Triangle Publications, Inc. CALENDAR OF FESTIVALS AND SPORTS: p. 118, data from Robert Meyer, Jr. and William Shannon.

PART III THE AMERICAN LAND

NATURAL WONDERS: pp. 120-21, photo credits: 1, Bob and Ira Spring; 2, 5, Ragsdale/F.P.G.; 3, 6, Ray Atkeson; 4, Hallinan/F.P.G.; 7, Hildegard Hamilton; 8, John Lewis Stage/Photo Researchers; 9, Charles C. Johnson; 10, Wendler/F.P.G.; 11, U.S. Forest Service/Leland J. Prater; 12, U.S. Department of the Interior/Sylvania Corp.; 13, Ernest Gay; 14, Steve McCutcheon; 15, Dick Smith; 16, 18, Grant Heilman; 17, Les Blacklock/Shostal. GEOLOGY: pp. 124-28, geologic-era maps based on illustrations by Erwin Raisz in *The Principles of Historical Geology,* by J. Willis Stovall and Harold E. Brown, © 1955, and pub. by Ginn and Co.; p. 129, map based on data from William Lee Stokes, *Essentials of Earth History: An introduction to Historical Geology,* Second Edition, © 1966, by permission of Prentice-Hall, Inc.; cross sections of U.S. based on illustrations by Erwin Raisz, *op. cit.* NATIONAL AND STATE PARKS: p. 130, map based on data from National Park Service and state-park list by James A. Bier. AMERICAN WILDLIFE: pp. 131-32, 13 mammal maps based on data from *The Mammal Guide,* by Ralph S. Palmer, © 1954, Ralph S. Palmer, reprinted by permission of Doubleday & Co., Inc.; p. 132, greater siren and Texas horned lizard maps based on data from *A Field Guide to Reptiles and Amphibians,* by Roger Conant, © 1958, Roger Conant, pub. by Houghton Mifflin Co.; p. 134, map based on data from U.S. Fish and Wildlife Service; pp. 134-35, bird photos courtesy National Audubon Society, Inc. NATIVE FLOWERING PLANTS: pp. 136-37, photo credits—from National Audubon Society, Inc.: spring beauty, Charles J. Ott; Texas bluebonnet, Helen Cruickshank; mistletoe, John H. Gerard; flowering dogwood, William Harlow; bayberry, Charles Mohr; fringed gentian, Louise K. Broman; bearberry, Alvin E. Staffan. Photos of American cranberry, blue-eyed grass, pipsissewa, white trillium, beach plum, pussy willow, sea pink, sea lavender and bloodroot, Gottscho-Schleisner, Inc.; rhododendron and magnolia, Shostal; sea grape and prairie rose, H. W. Rickett; all remaining photos by Charles C. Johnson. NATURAL VEGETATION: pp. 138-39, map by A. W. Küchler. WEATHER: p. 140, "Our Unique Weather," condensed from *Our American Weather,* by George H. T. Kimble, © 1955, George H. T. Kimble, pub. by McGraw-Hill Book Co., Inc.; "How to Read a Weather Map," based on data from *Weather Research Bulletin,* Winter 1957–58, pub. by Stewart, Smith & Co., Inc.; p. 141, maps from U.S. Environmental Science Service Administration; pp. 142-43, weather calendar condensed from Kimble, *op. cit.;* tornado map by H.C.S. Thom, senior research fellow, E.S.S.A.; other maps and charts, U.S. Weather Bureau. AGRICULTURE: pp. 144-45, map by Dr. James Anderson; pp. 146-47, maps based on data from U.S. Department of Agriculture and Dr. James Anderson. INDUSTRY: pp. 148-53, maps and charts based on data from Dr. John Cumberland, except industrial growth of cities, from U.S. Department of Commerce. FORESTS: p. 154, lumber photos from Forest Products Laboratory, U.S. Forest Service. MINERALS: p. 155, maps based on data from U.S. Bureau of Mines; chart based on data from *Resources in America's Future,* by Hans L. Landsberg, Leonard L. Fishman and Joseph L. Fisher, © 1953, The Johns Hopkins Press, pub. for Resources for The Future, Inc., by The Johns Hopkins Press; pp. 156-57, photos by Lee Boltin. NATIONAL ECONOMY: pp. 158-59, business activity chart courtesy Cleveland Trust Co., Cleveland, Ohio; unemployment chart based on data from U.S. Bureau of Labor Statistics; Federal budget charts based on data from *Economic Report of The President, 1967;* labor-force charts based on data from U.S. Department of Commerce and its *Historical Statistics of the United States;* national-income chart based on data from U.S. Office of Business Economics; cities with billion-dollar incomes chart based on data from National Industrial Conference Board; p. 160, national-debt chart based on data from *Economic Report of The President, 1967;* billion-dollar markets chart based on data from U.S. Bureau of the Census; foreign-investment chart based on data from U.S. Office of Business Economics; foreign-trade chart based on data from U.S. Bureau of International Commerce. COMMUNICATIONS: p. 161, newspaper map based on data from 1) *History and Bibliography of American Newspapers 1690–1820,* by Clarence S. Brigham, © 1947, and pub. by The American Antiquarian Society, Worcester, Mass., 2) N. W. Ayer and Son, Inc., and 3) *Editor and Publisher International Yearbook,* © 1967, and pub. by Editor and Publisher Co., Inc.; p. 162, telephone chart based on data from American Telephone and Telegraph Co.; radio and television chart based on data from National Broadcasting Co. TRANSPORTATION: p. 163, statistics 1936–66 from Automobile Manufacturers Association, Inc.; pp. 164-71, road maps, © 1968 General Drafting Co., Inc.; p. 172, map from Federal Aviation Administration; space charts based on data from Goddard Space Flight Center, National Aeronautics and Space Administration; p. 174, St. Lawrence Seaway chart based on data from St. Lawrence Seaway Development Corp.; navigable rivers map and chart based on data from The American Waterways Operators, Inc.